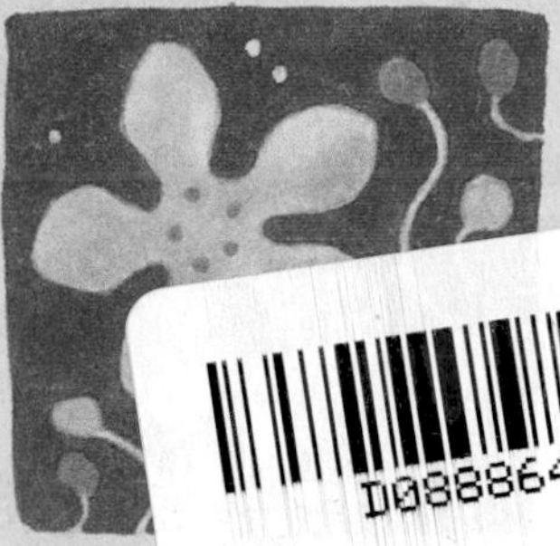

If anyone asked me which season I liked the best, I'd tell them I liked the ... etween the seasons. ... I wasn't allergic to ... I think I'd like it at ... ree times more.

... ubo, 2006

BLEACH is author Tite Kubo's second title. Kubo made his debut with *ZOMBIEPOWDER.*, a four-volume series for *WEEKLY SHONEN JUMP*. To date, *BLEACH* has been translated into numerous languages and has also inspired an animated TV series that began airing in the U.S. in 2006. Beginning its serialization in 2001, *BLEACH* is still a mainstay in the pages of *WEEKLY SHONEN JUMP*. In 2005, *BLEACH* was awarded the prestigious Shogakukan Manga Award in the *shonen* (boys) category.

BLEACH

3-in-1 Edition

SHONEN JUMP Manga Omnibus Edition Volume 8
A compilation of the graphic novel volumes 22–24

STORY AND ART BY
TITE KUBO

English Adaptation/Lance Caselman
Translation/Joe Yamazaki
Touch-up Art & Lettering/Mark McMurray
Design - Manga Edition/Sean Lee
Design - Omnibus Edition/Fawn Lau
Editor - Manga Edition/Pancha Diaz
Editor - Omnibus Edition/Pancha Diaz

Printed in the U.S.A.

Published by VIZ Media, LLC
P.O. Box 77010
San Francisco, CA 94107

10 9 8 7 6 5 4 3 2 1
Omnibus edition first printing, May 2014

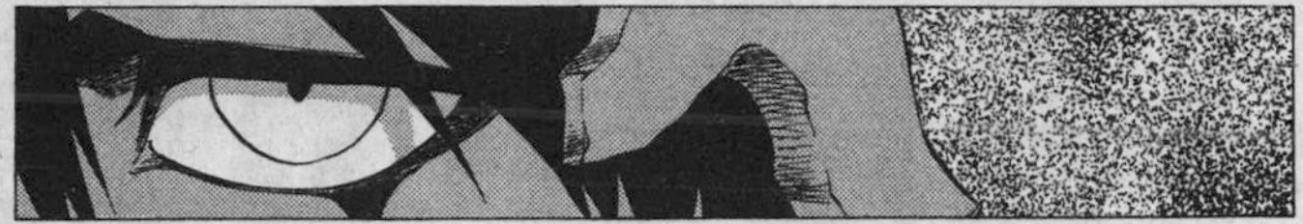

There is no meaning to our world.
There is no meaning to those of us living there.
We meaningless beings ponder the world,
Though the realization of meaninglessness
itself means nothing.

BLEACH 22 CONQUISTADORES

Shonen Jump Manga

STARS AND

Ichigo Kurosaki

黒崎一護

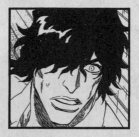

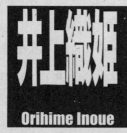

井上織姫

Orihime Inoue

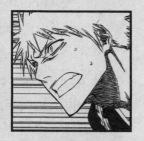

Chad Yasutora

茶渡泰虎

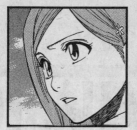

plot

After a fateful encounter with Soul Reaper Rukia Kuchiki, Ichigo becomes a Soul Reaper himself. So, when Rukia is arrested and sentenced to death, Ichigo travels to the Soul Society to rescue her, and in the process uncovers a fiendish plot. But the conspirators escape and Ichigo returns to the world of the living. Now a Deputy Soul Reaper, Ichigo spends his days fighting Hollows. But his life soon gets even more bizarre with the appearance of a new menace, the Arrancar, and the discovery that his own father is a Soul Reaper! And still more disturbing, Ichigo is confronted with the possibility that his own inner demon may be far more terrible than he ever imagined.

BLEACH ALL

Ulquiorra

Yammy

Shinji Hirako

STORIES

BLEACH 22

CONQUISTADORES

Contents

188. CRUSH THE WORLD DOWN

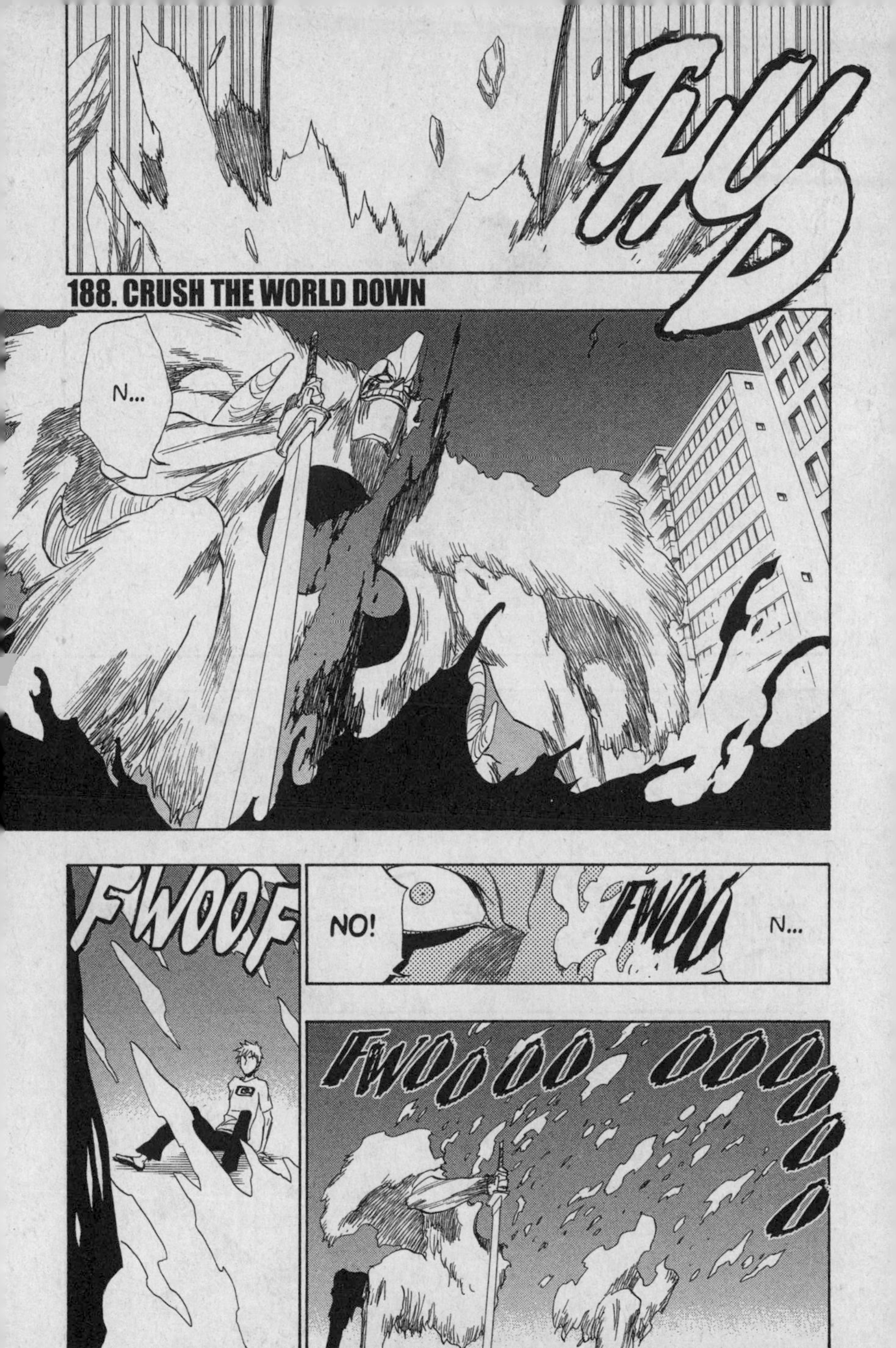
THUD
N...
N...
FWOO
NO!
FWOOOOO OOOOOOO
FWOOF

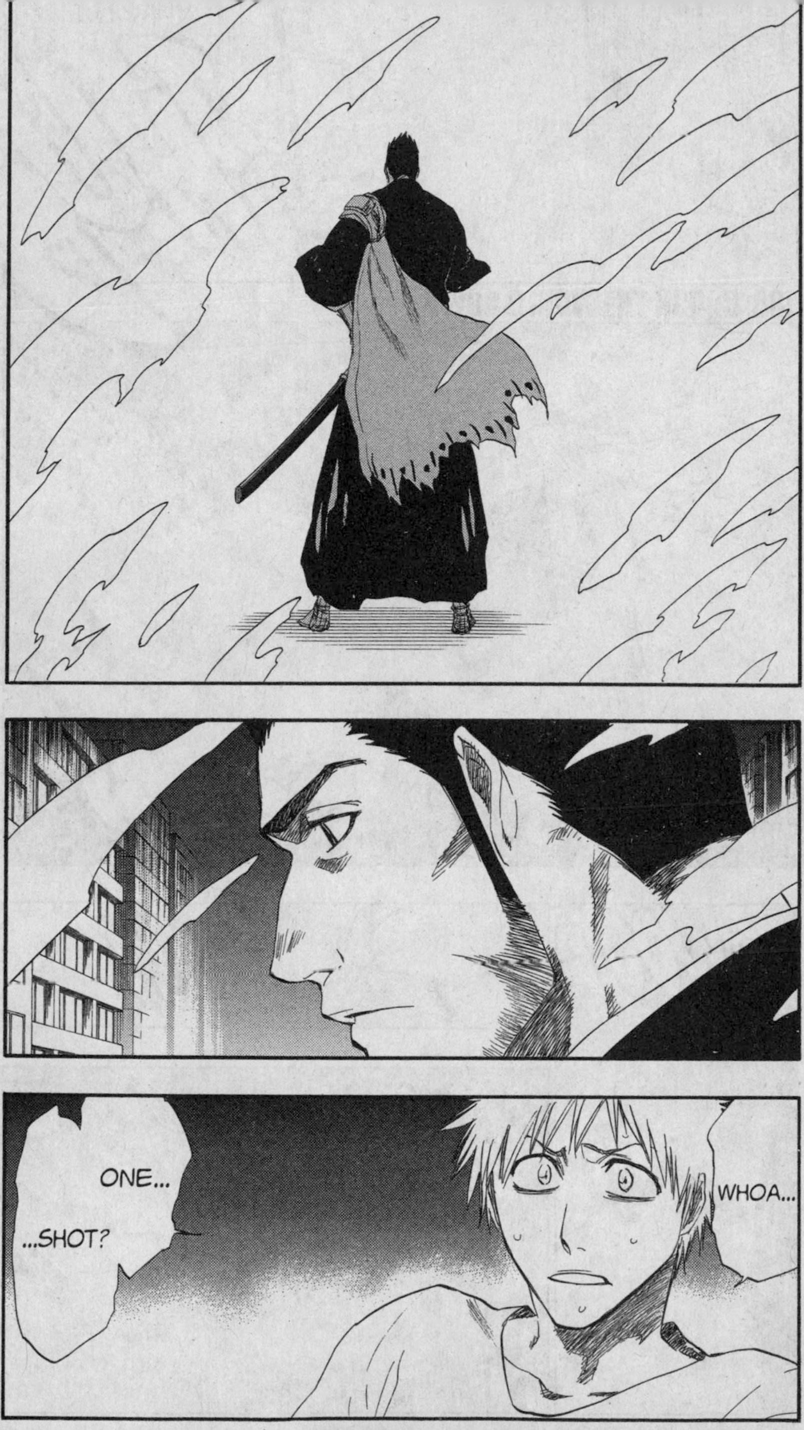
WHOA...
ONE...
...SHOT?

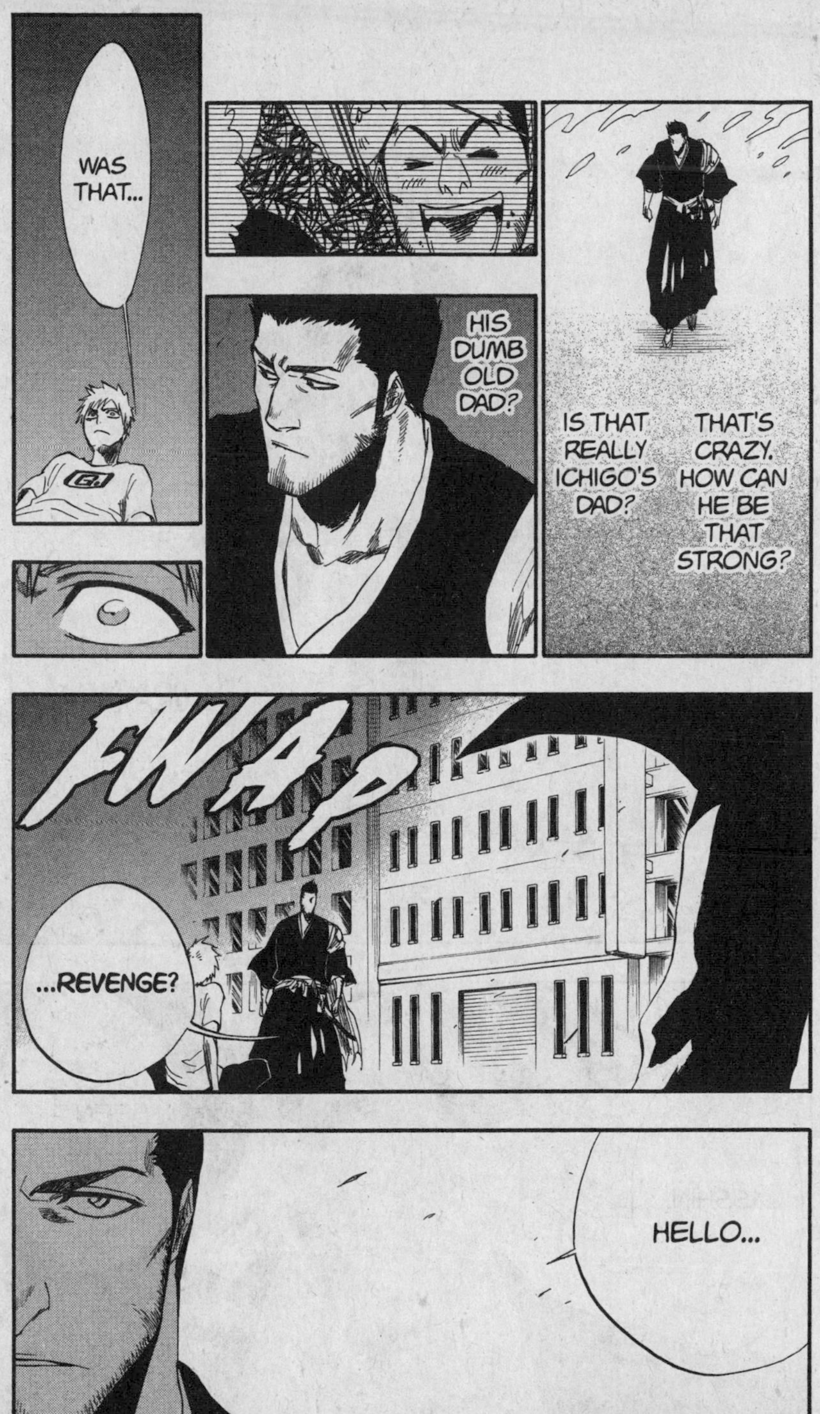
THAT'S CRAZY. HOW CAN HE BE THAT STRONG?
IS THAT REALLY ICHIGO'S DAD?
HIS DUMB OLD DAD?
WAS THAT...
FWAP
...REVENGE?
HELLO...

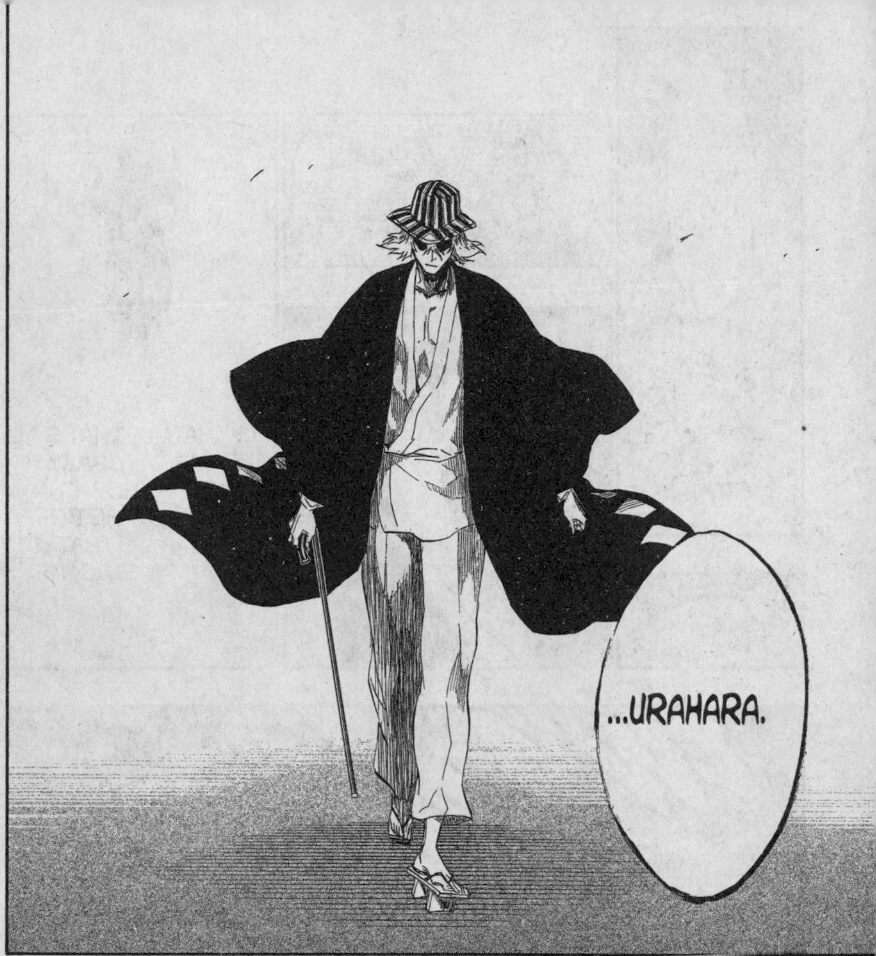
...URAHARA.
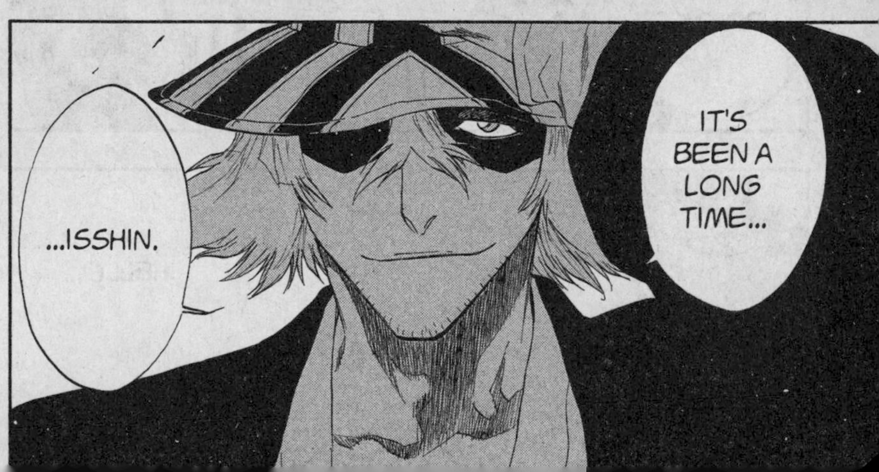
IT'S BEEN A LONG TIME...
...ISSHIN.

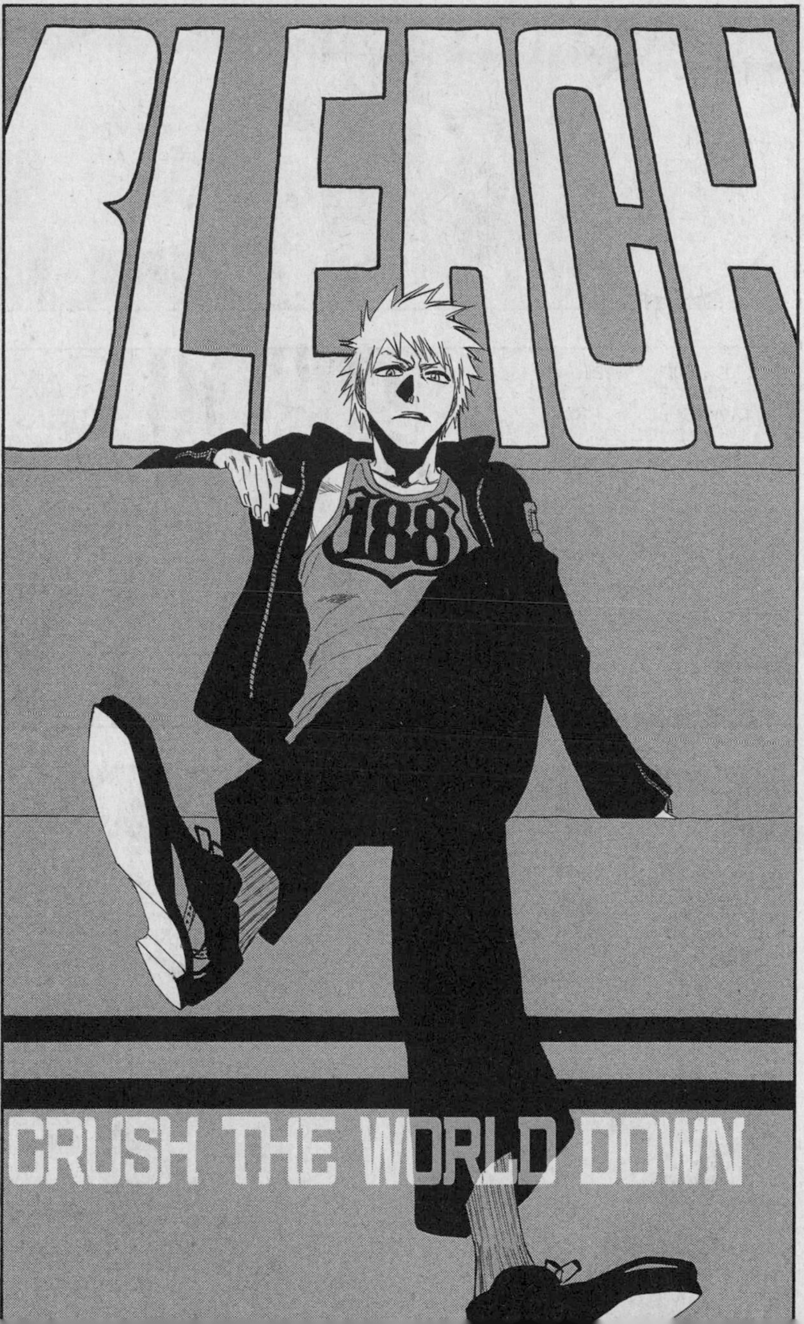
BLEACH
188
CRUSH THE WORLD DOWN

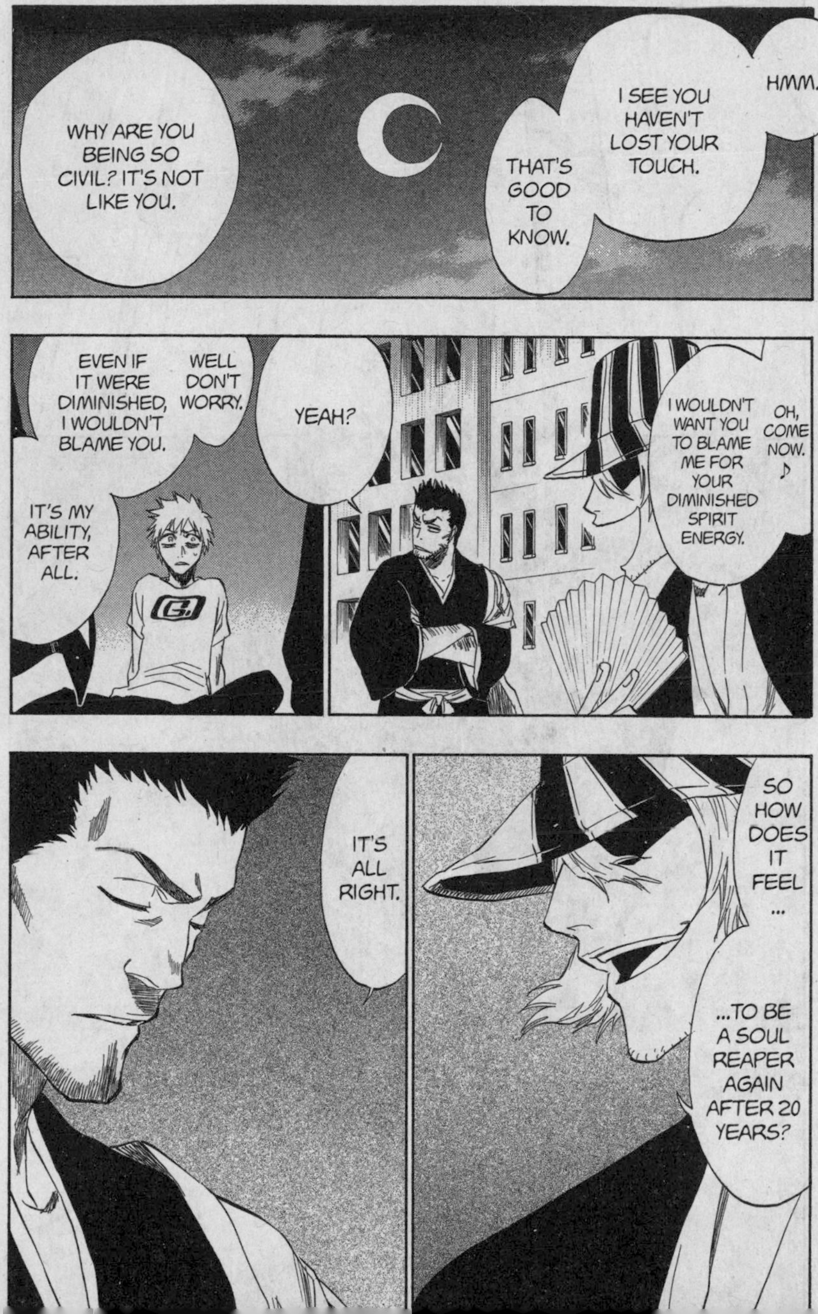
HMM...
I SEE YOU HAVEN'T LOST YOUR TOUCH.
THAT'S GOOD TO KNOW.
WHY ARE YOU BEING SO CIVIL? IT'S NOT LIKE YOU.
OH, COME NOW. ♪
I WOULDN'T WANT YOU TO BLAME ME FOR YOUR DIMINISHED SPIRIT ENERGY.
YEAH?
WELL DON'T WORRY.
EVEN IF IT WERE DIMINISHED, I WOULDN'T BLAME YOU.
IT'S MY ABILITY, AFTER ALL.
SO HOW DOES IT FEEL ...
...TO BE A SOUL REAPER AGAIN AFTER 20 YEARS?
IT'S ALL RIGHT.

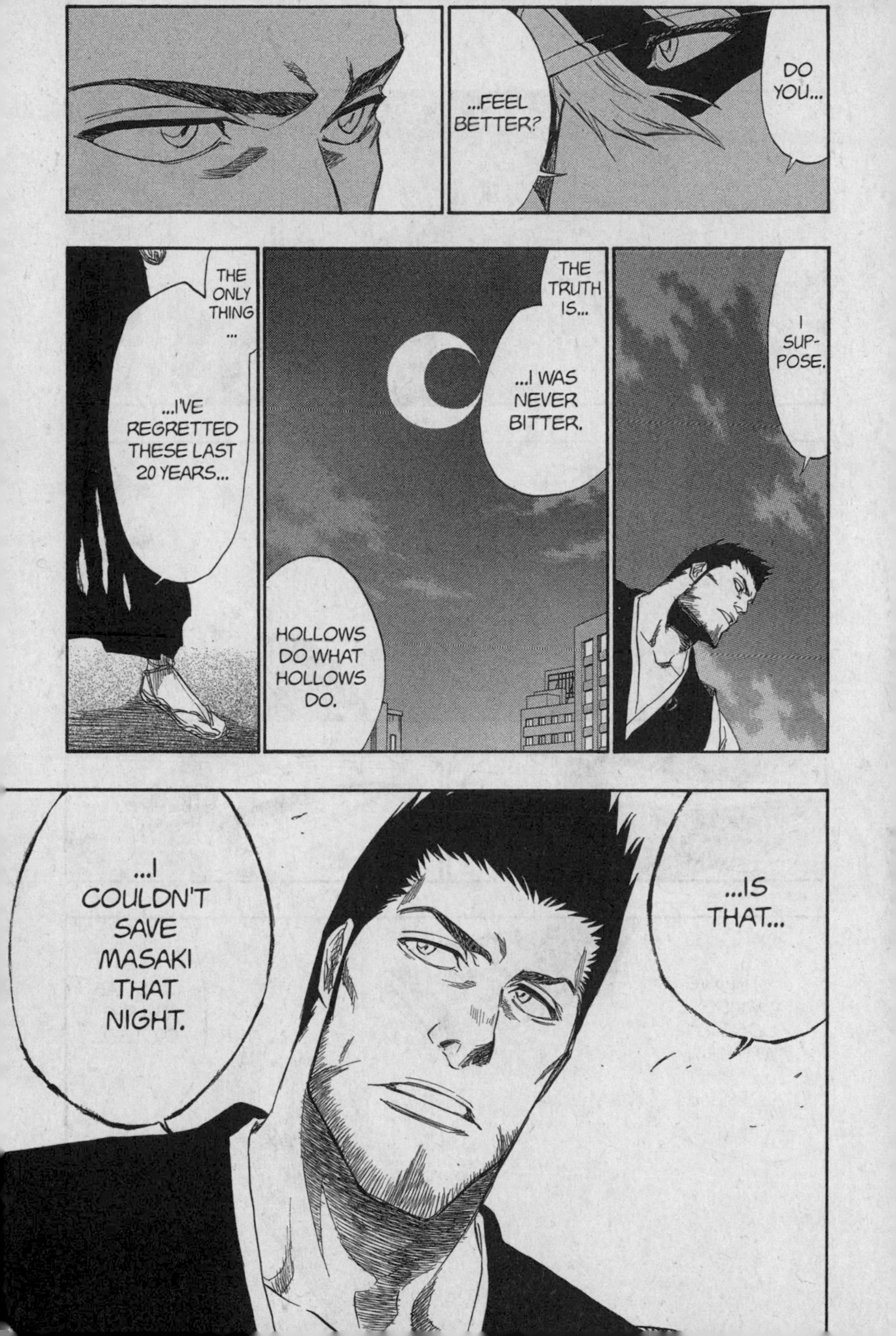
DO YOU...
...FEEL BETTER?
I SUPPOSE.
THE TRUTH IS...
...I WAS NEVER BITTER.
HOLLOWS DO WHAT HOLLOWS DO.
THE ONLY THING...
...I'VE REGRETTED THESE LAST 20 YEARS...
...IS THAT...
...I COULDN'T SAVE MASAKI THAT NIGHT.

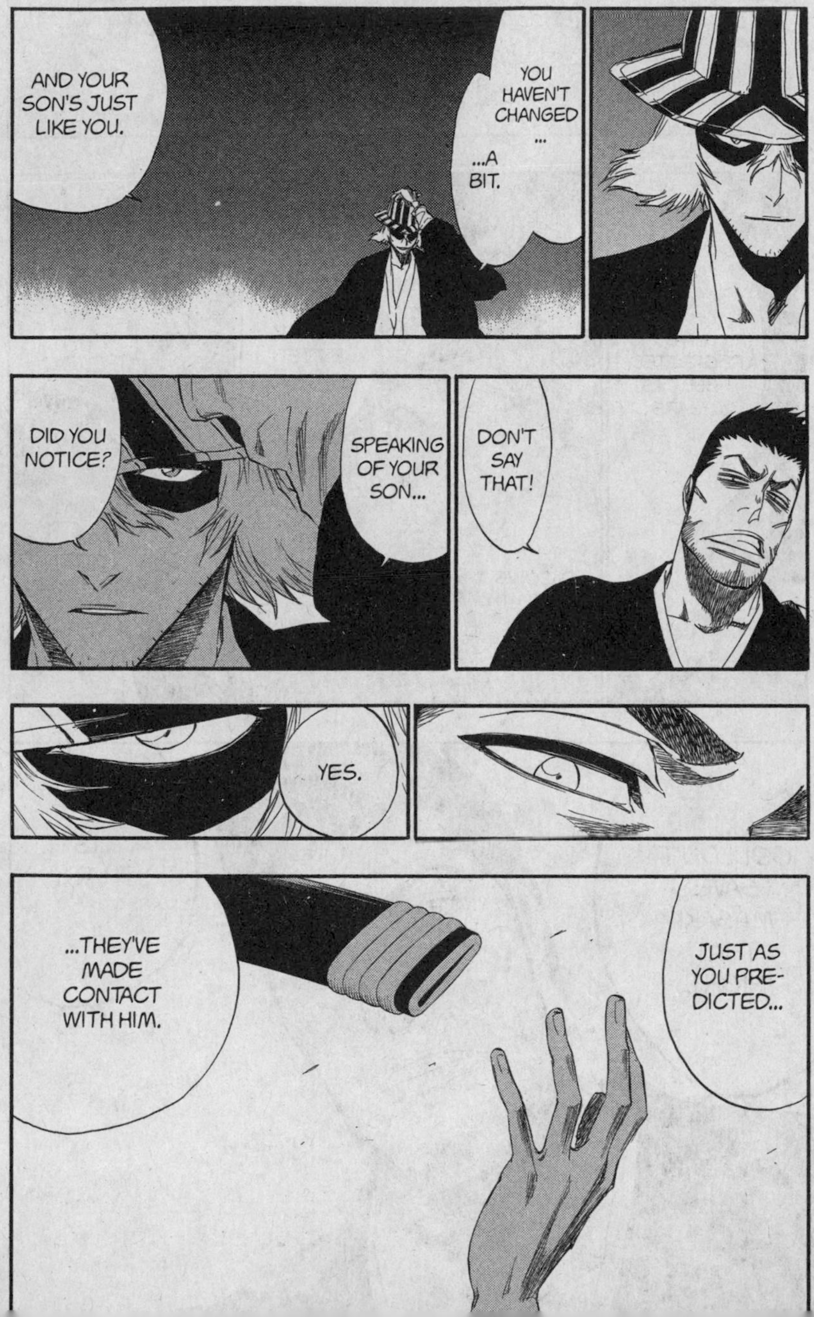
YOU HAVEN'T CHANGED ... ...A BIT.
AND YOUR SON'S JUST LIKE YOU.
DON'T SAY THAT!
SPEAKING OF YOUR SON...
DID YOU NOTICE?
YES.
JUST AS YOU PRE-DICTED...
...THEY'VE MADE CONTACT WITH HIM.

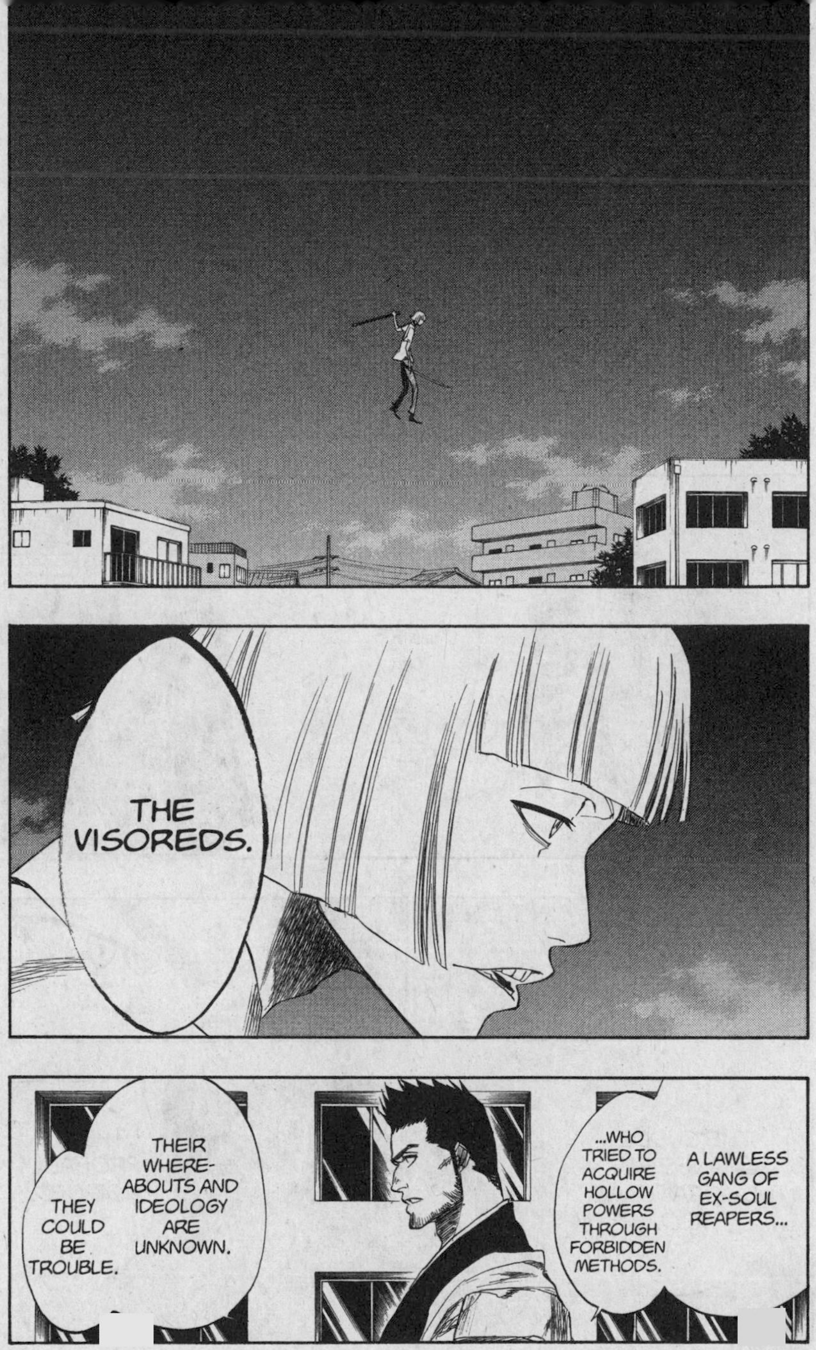
THE VISOREDS.
A LAWLESS GANG OF EX-SOUL REAPERS...
...WHO TRIED TO ACQUIRE HOLLOW POWERS THROUGH FORBIDDEN METHODS.
THEIR WHERE-ABOUTS AND IDEOLOGY ARE UNKNOWN.
THEY COULD BE TROUBLE.

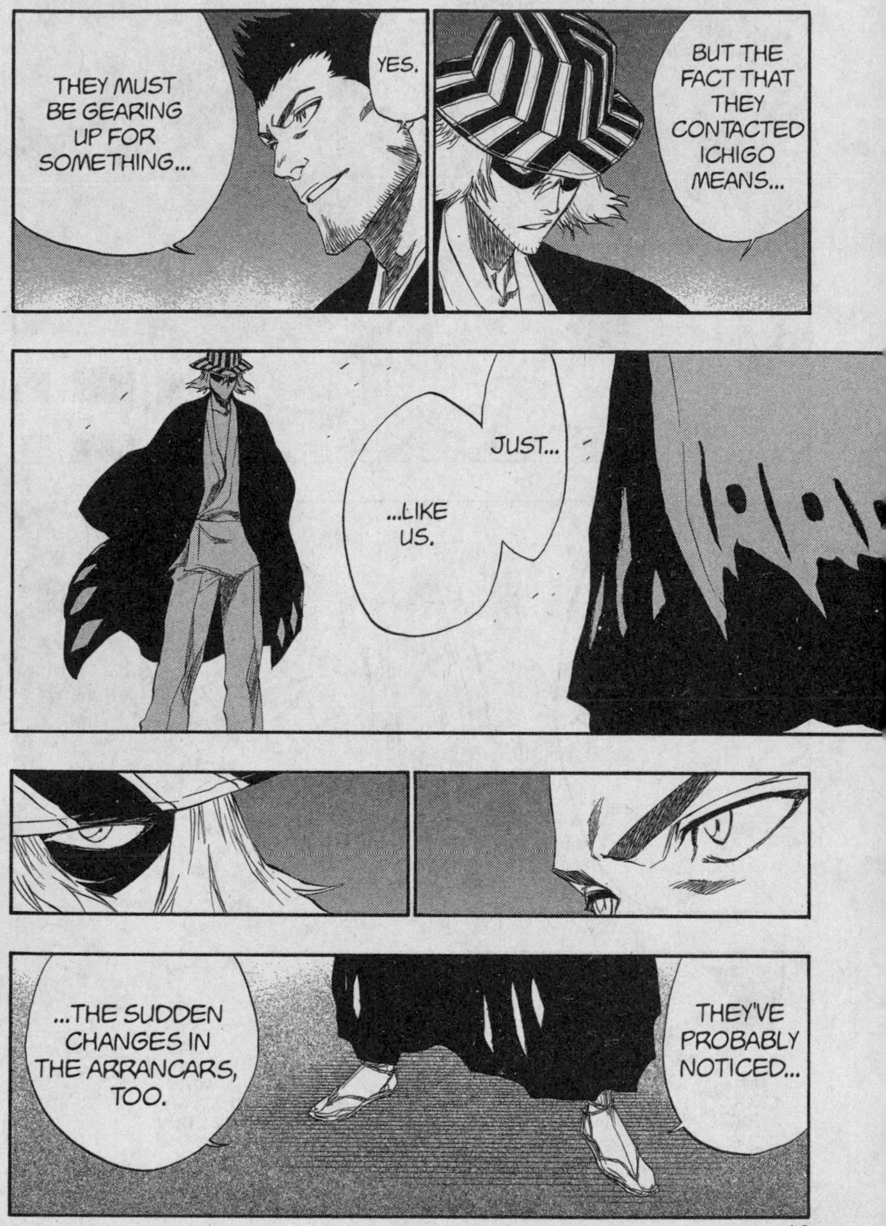
BUT THE FACT THAT THEY CONTACTED ICHIGO MEANS...
YES.
THEY MUST BE GEARING UP FOR SOMETHING...
JUST...
...LIKE US.
THEY'VE PROBABLY NOTICED...
...THE SUDDEN CHANGES IN THE ARRANCARS, TOO.

READ THIS WAY

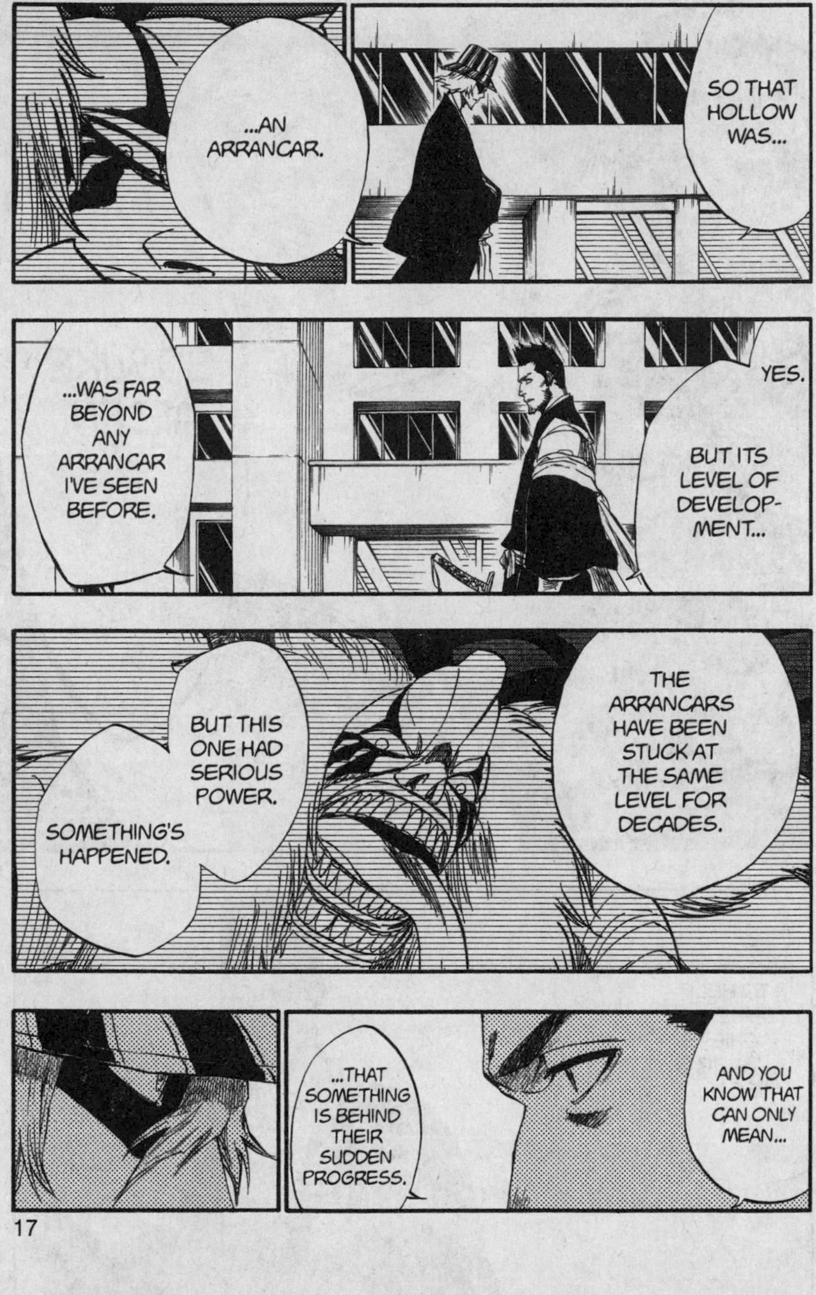
SO THAT HOLLOW WAS...
...AN ARRANCAR.
YES.
BUT ITS LEVEL OF DEVELOPMENT...
...WAS FAR BEYOND ANY ARRANCAR I'VE SEEN BEFORE.
THE ARRANCARS HAVE BEEN STUCK AT THE SAME LEVEL FOR DECADES.
BUT THIS ONE HAD SERIOUS POWER.
SOMETHING'S HAPPENED.
AND YOU KNOW THAT CAN ONLY MEAN...
...THAT SOMETHING IS BEHIND THEIR SUDDEN PROGRESS.

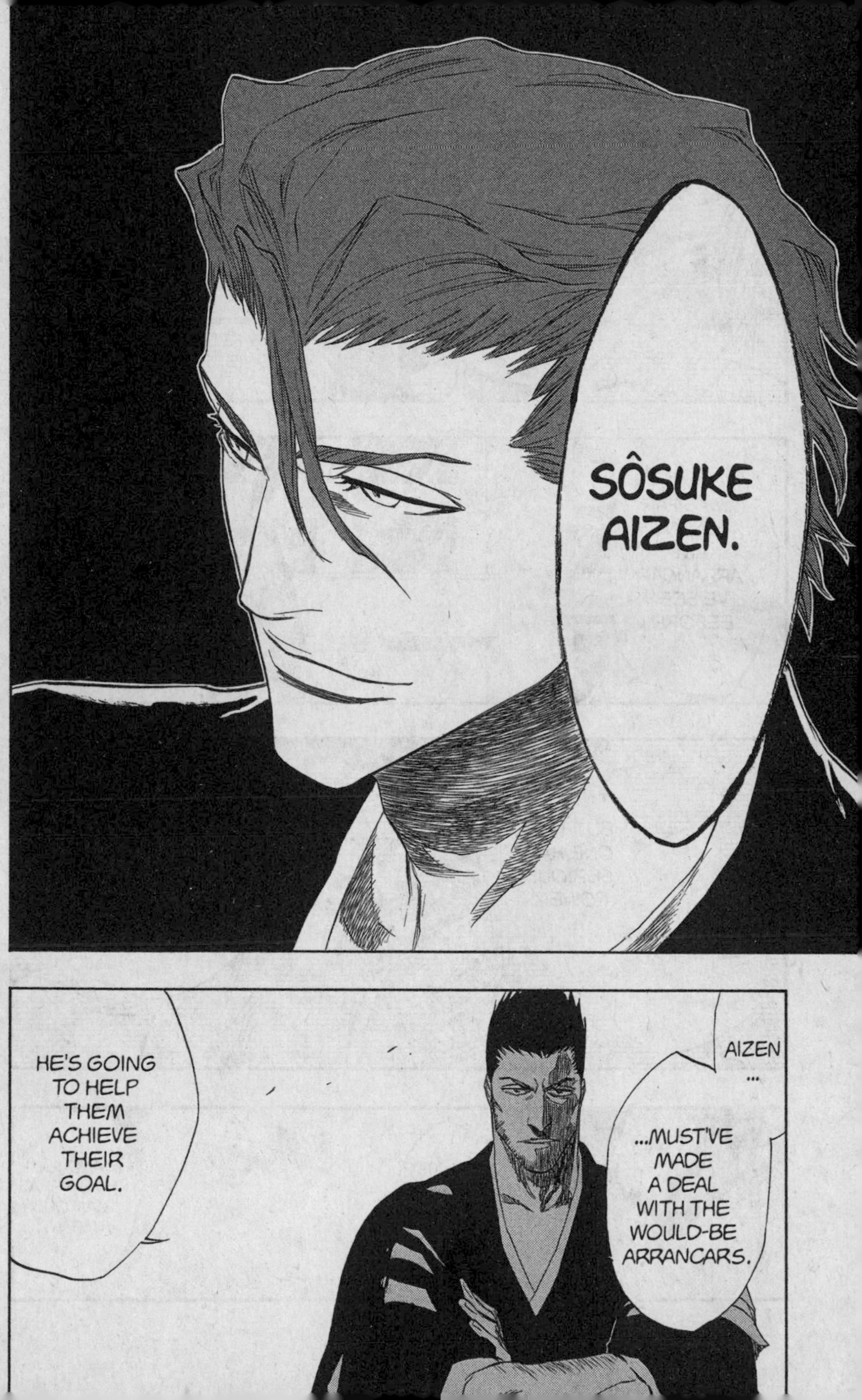
SÔSUKE AIZEN.
AIZEN ...
...MUST'VE MADE A DEAL WITH THE WOULD-BE ARRANCARS.
HE'S GOING TO HELP THEM ACHIEVE THEIR GOAL.

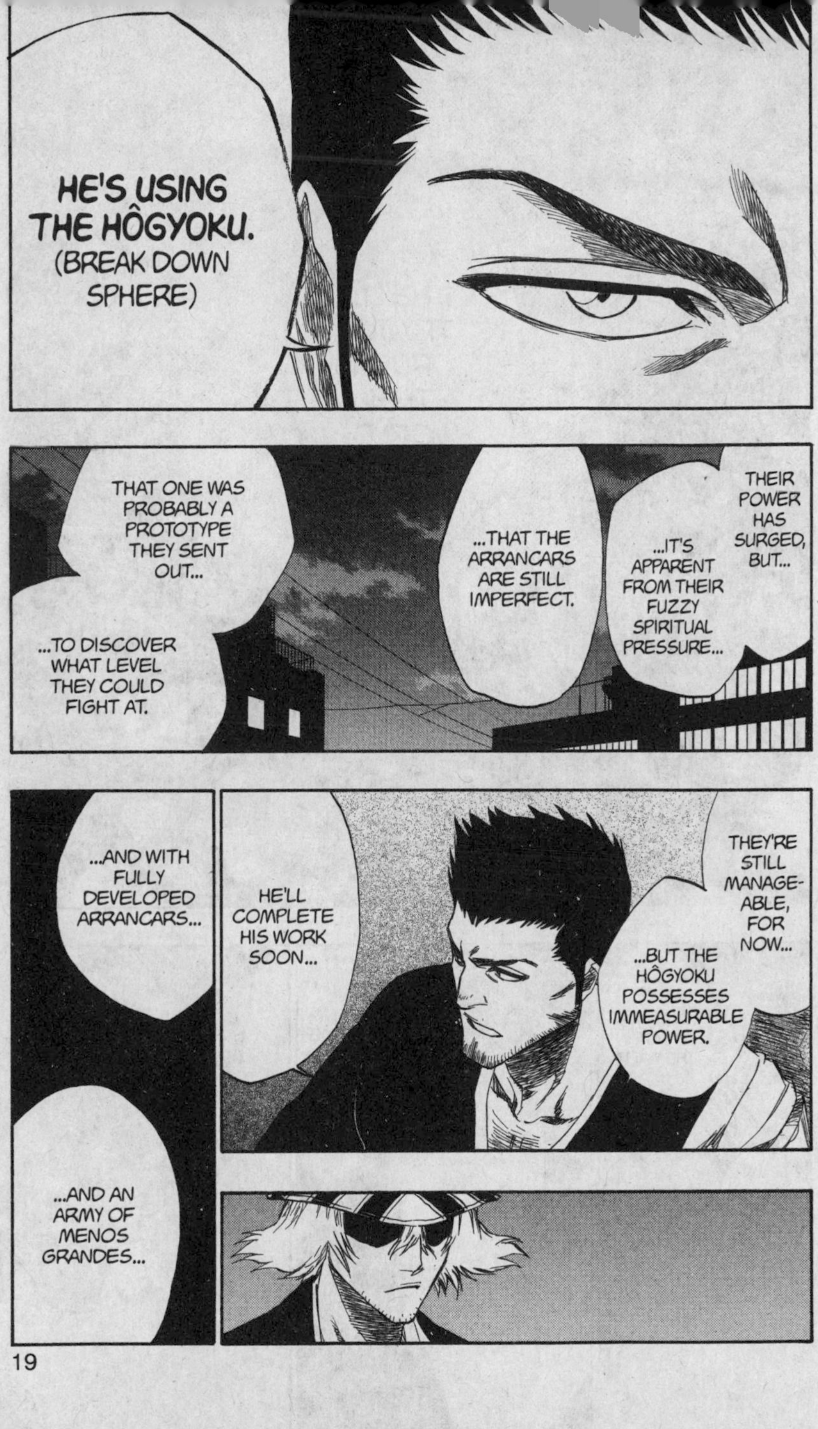
HE'S USING THE HÔGYOKU. (BREAK DOWN SPHERE)
THEIR POWER HAS SURGED, BUT...
...IT'S APPARENT FROM THEIR FUZZY SPIRITUAL PRESSURE...
...THAT THE ARRANCARS ARE STILL IMPERFECT.
THAT ONE WAS PROBABLY A PROTOTYPE THEY SENT OUT...
...TO DISCOVER WHAT LEVEL THEY COULD FIGHT AT.
THEY'RE STILL MANAGEABLE, FOR NOW...
...BUT THE HÔGYOKU POSSESSES IMMEASURABLE POWER.
HE'LL COMPLETE HIS WORK SOON...
...AND WITH FULLY DEVELOPED ARRANCARS...
...AND AN ARMY OF MENOS GRANDES...

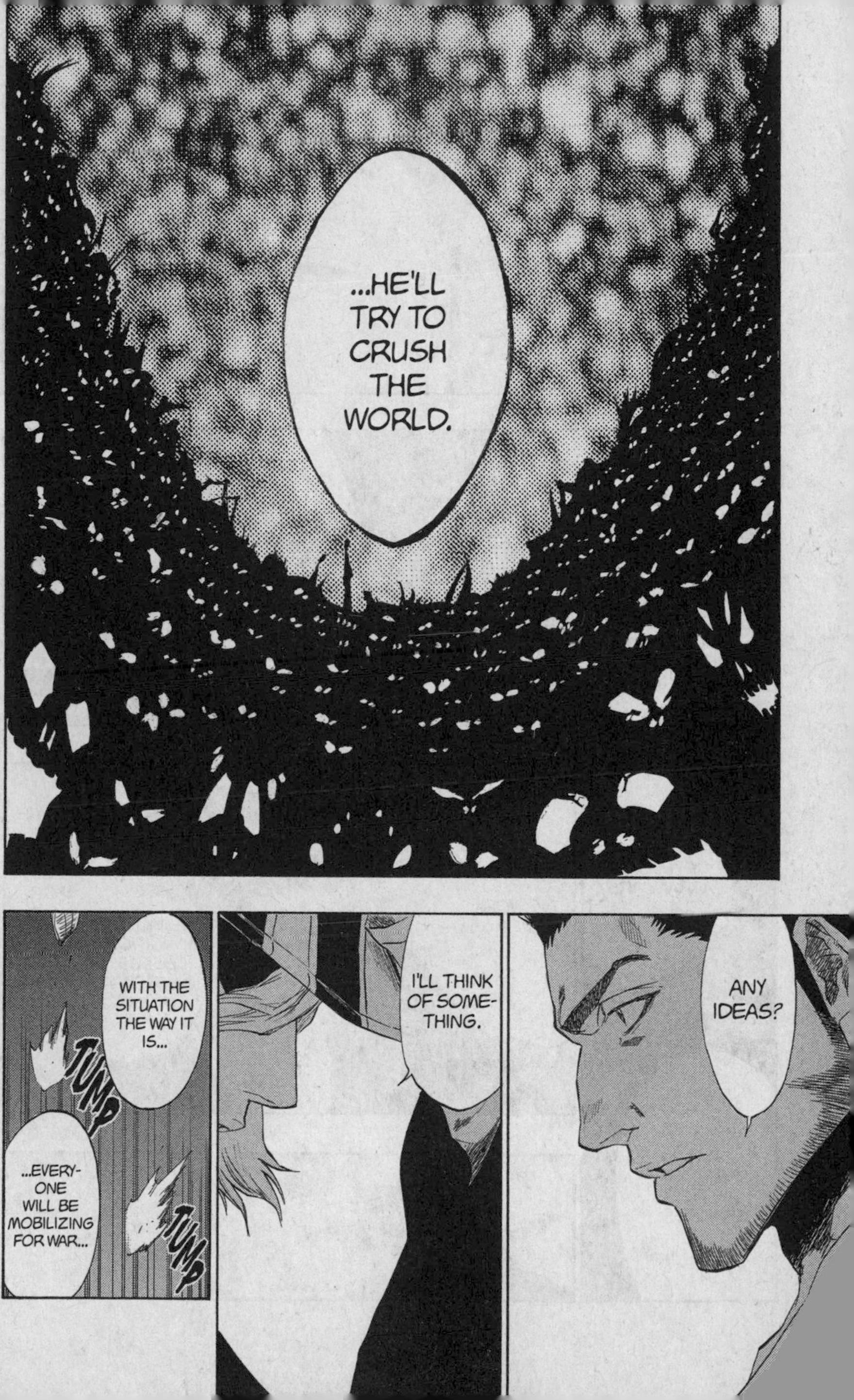
...HE'LL TRY TO CRUSH THE WORLD.
ANY IDEAS?
I'LL THINK OF SOME-THING.
WITH THE SITUATION THE WAY IT IS...
TUMP
...EVERY-ONE WILL BE MOBILIZING FOR WAR...
TUMP

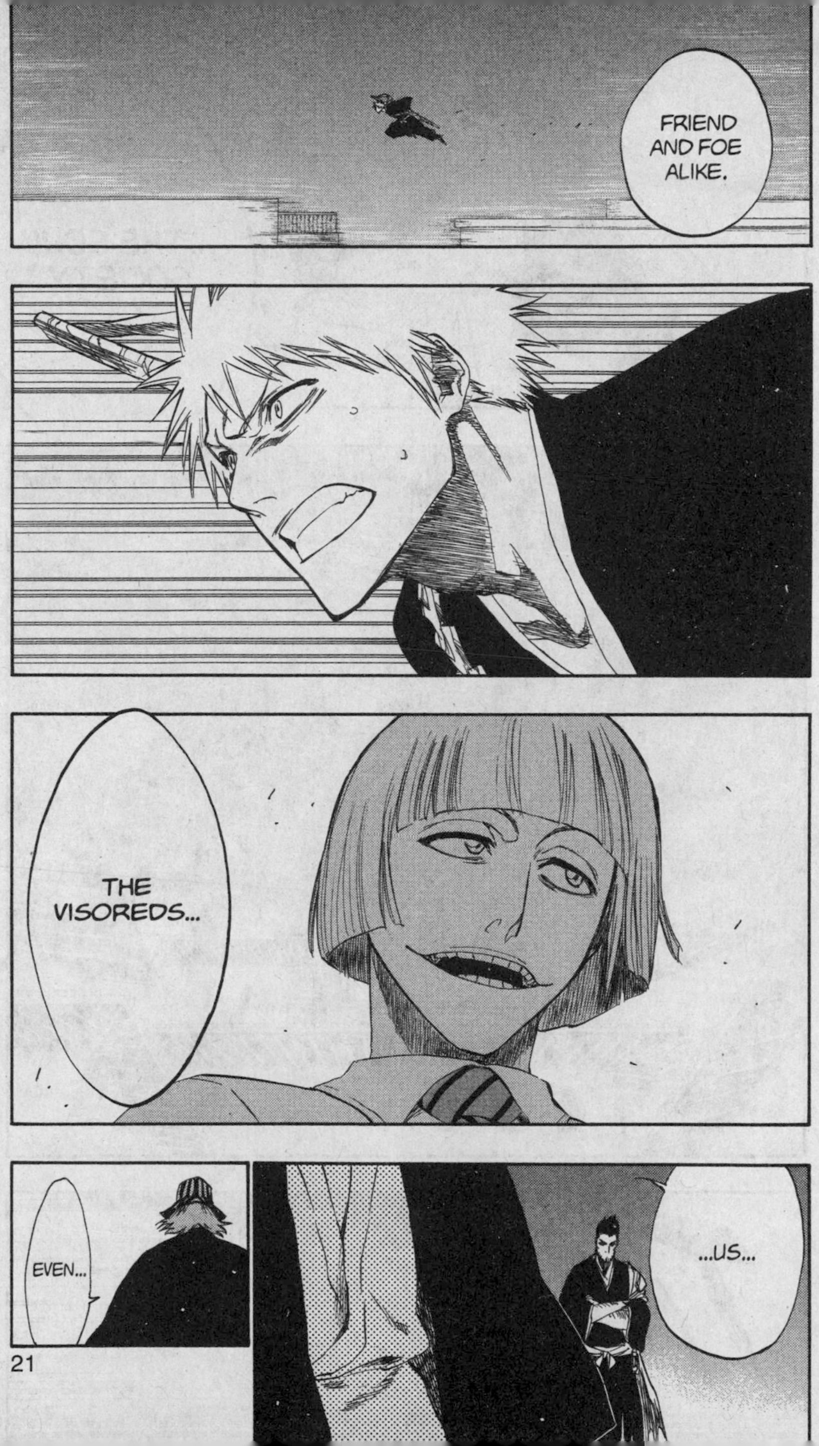
FRIEND AND FOE ALIKE.
THE VISOREDS...
...US...
EVEN...

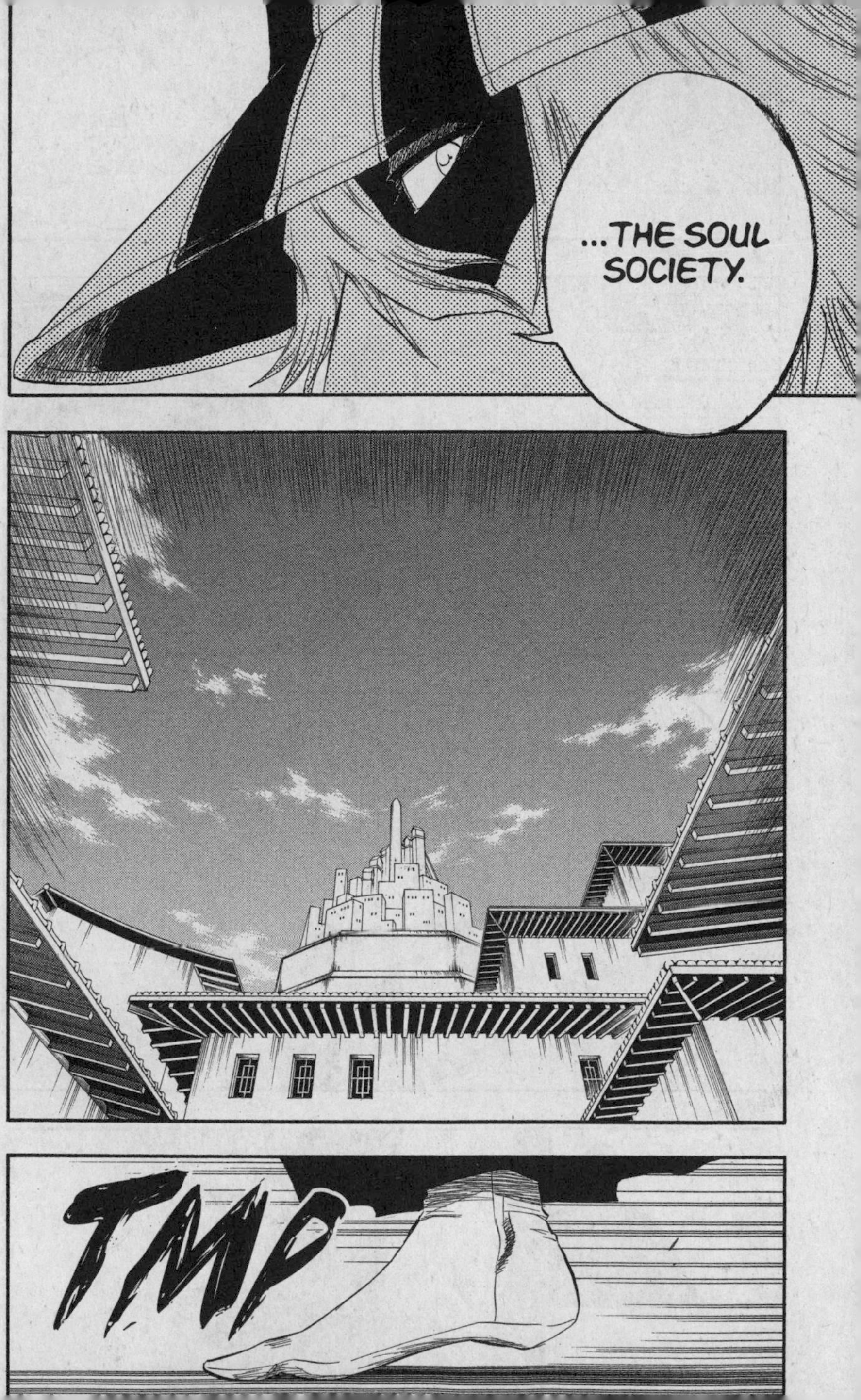
...THE SOUL SOCIETY.
TMP

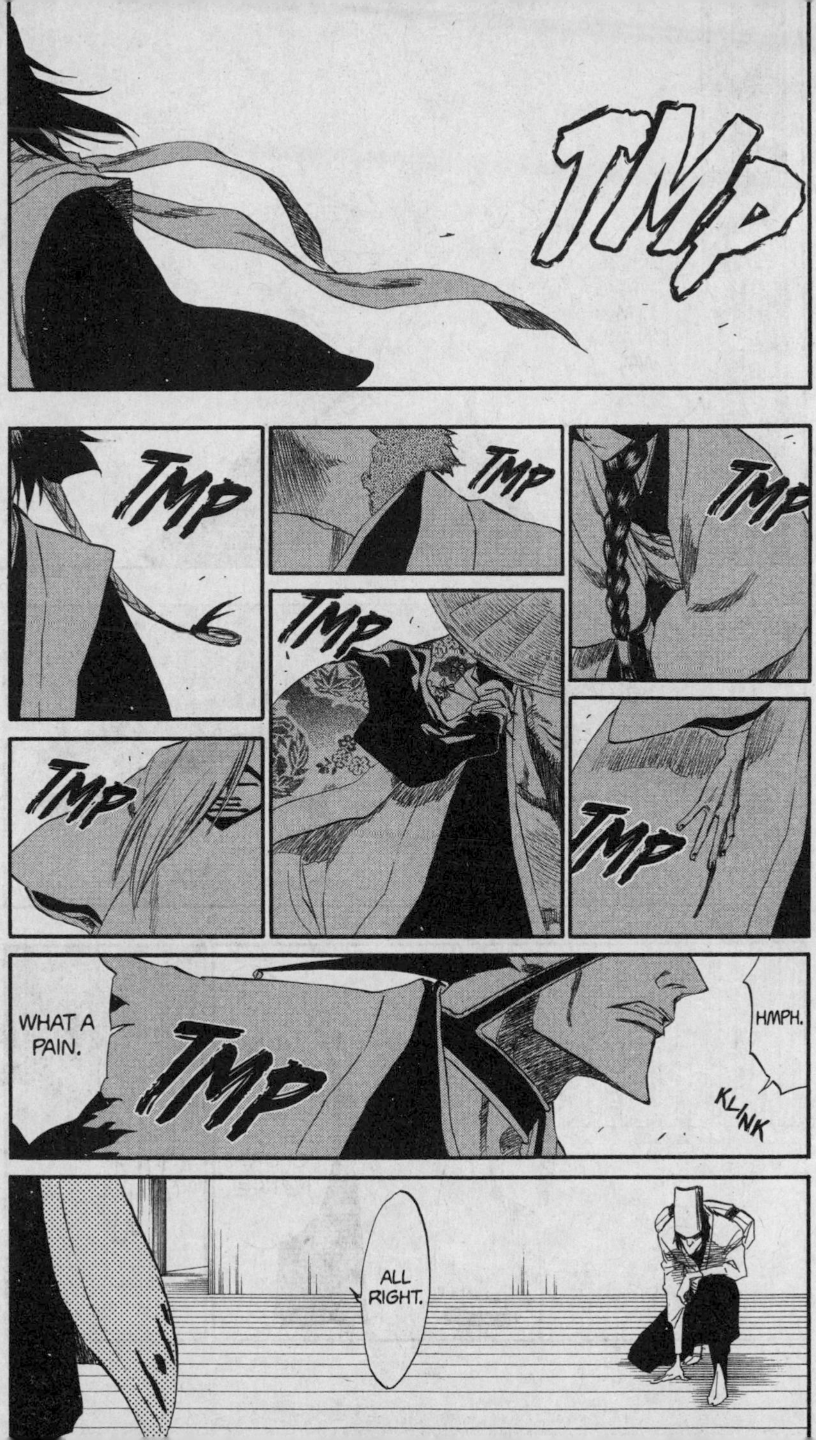
TMP
TMP
TMP
TMP
TMP
TMP
TMP
HMPH.
KLINK
TMP
WHAT A PAIN.
ALL RIGHT.

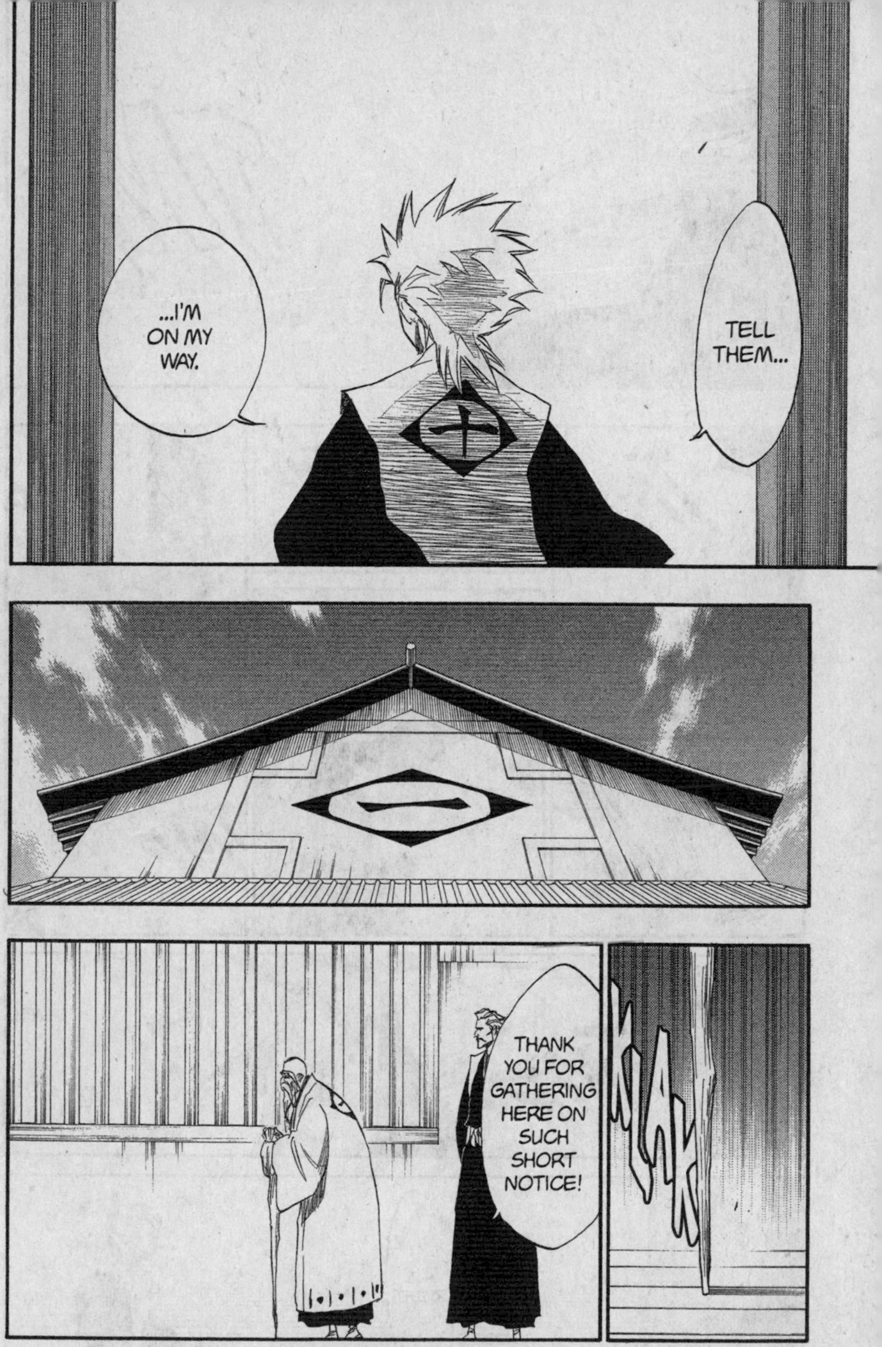
TELL THEM...
...I'M ON MY WAY.
THANK YOU FOR GATHERING HERE ON SUCH SHORT NOTICE!

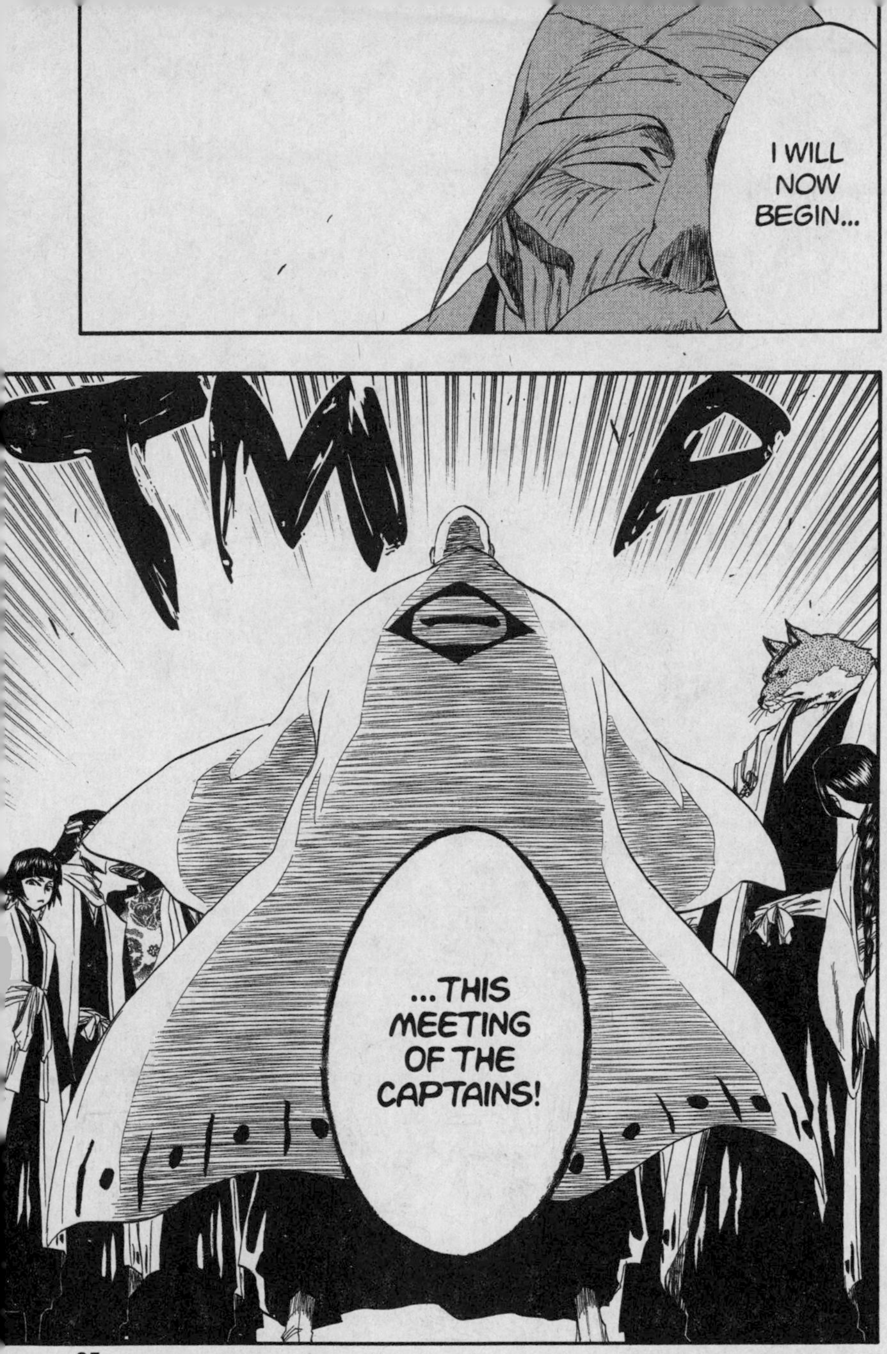
I WILL NOW BEGIN...
TMP
...THIS MEETING OF THE CAPTAINS!

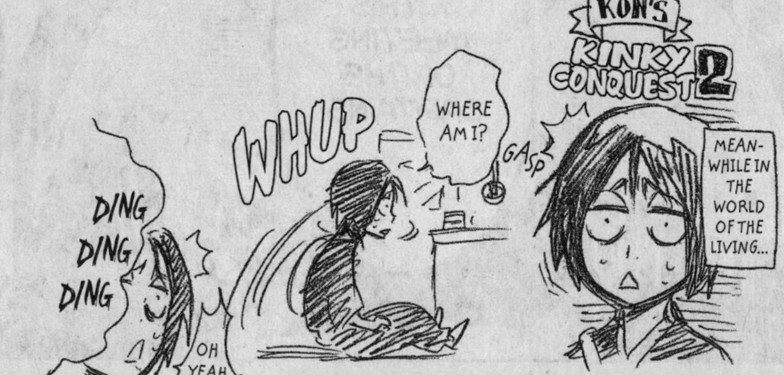
KON'S
KINKY CONQUEST 2
MEAN-WHILE IN THE WORLD OF THE LIVING...
GASP
WHERE AM I?
WHUP
DING DING DING
OH YEAH !!

189. RESOLVE

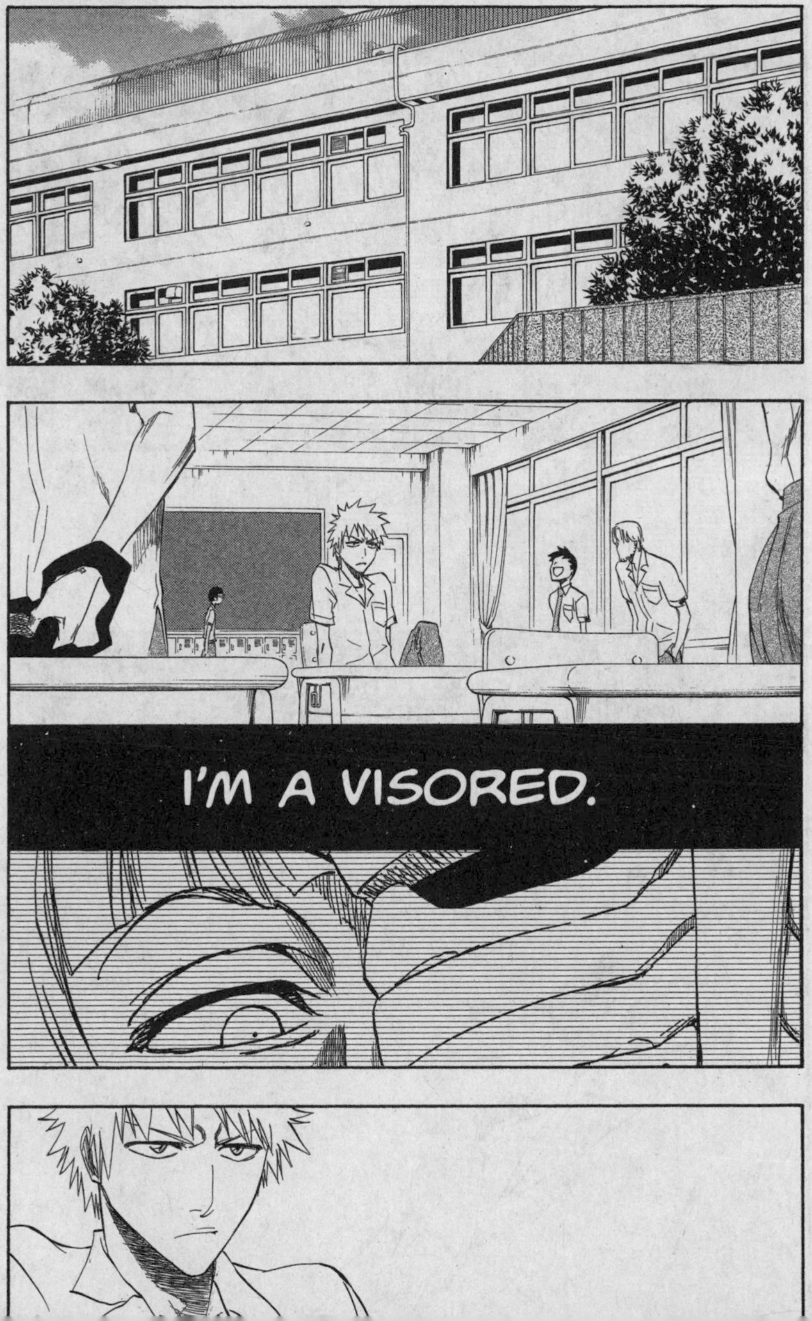
I'M A VISORED.

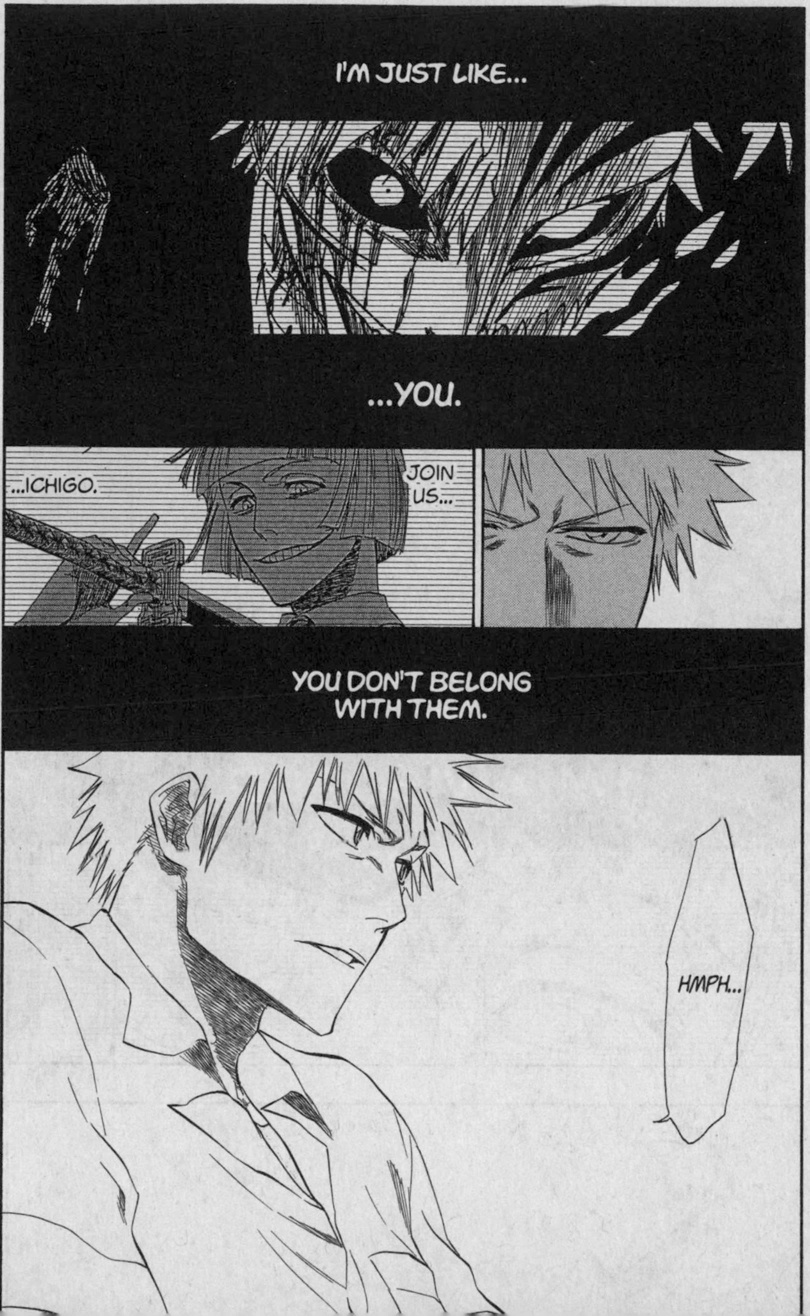
I'M JUST LIKE...
...YOU.
JOIN US...
...ICHIGO.
YOU DON'T BELONG WITH THEM.
HMPH...

READ THIS WAY

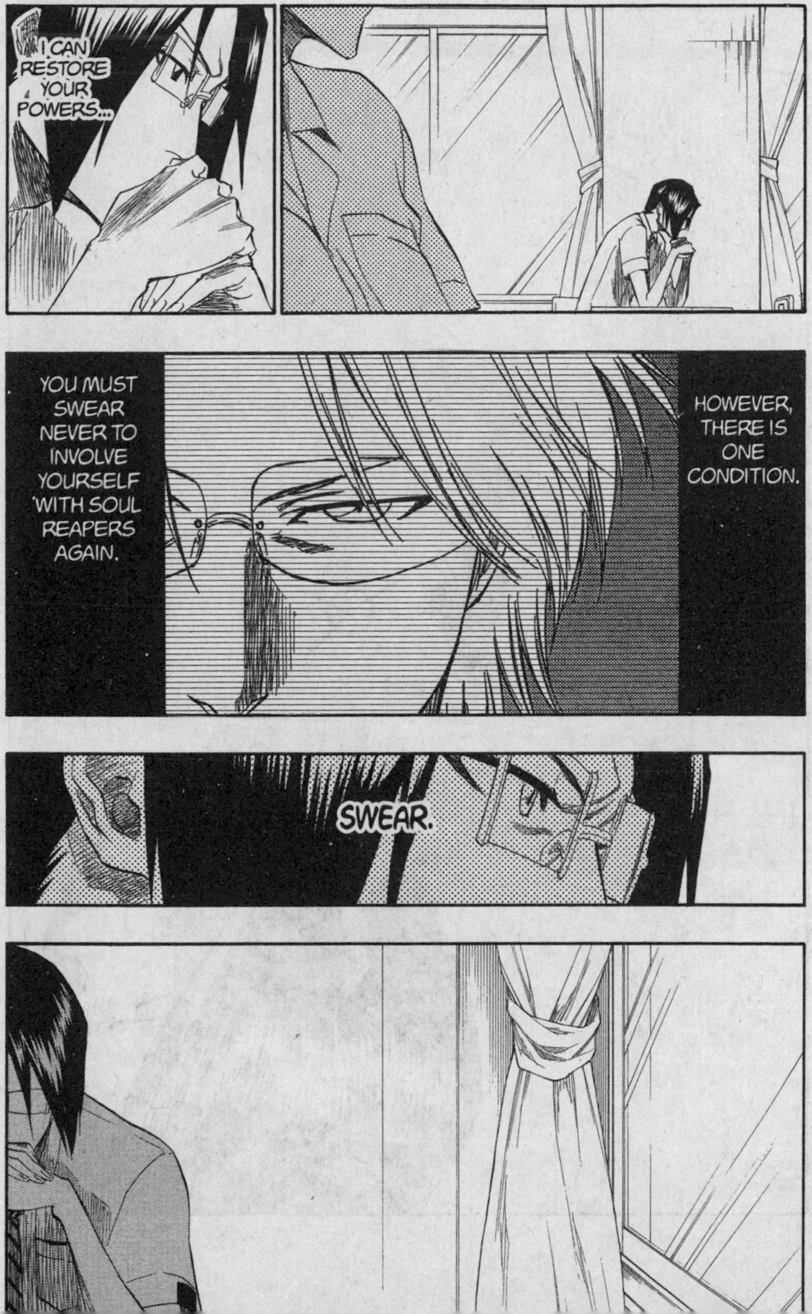
I CAN RESTORE YOUR POWERS...
HOWEVER, THERE IS ONE CONDITION.
YOU MUST SWEAR NEVER TO INVOLVE YOURSELF WITH SOUL REAPERS AGAIN.
SWEAR.

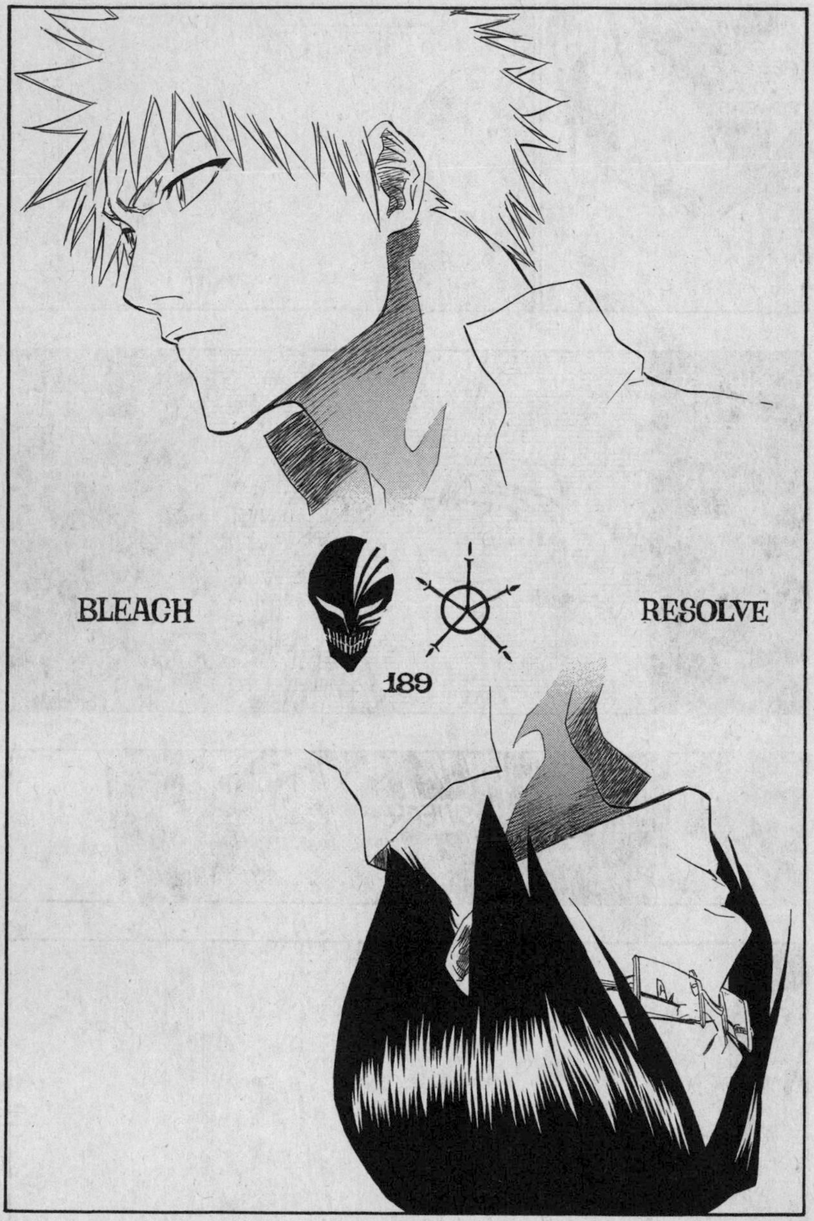
BLEACH
189
RESOLVE

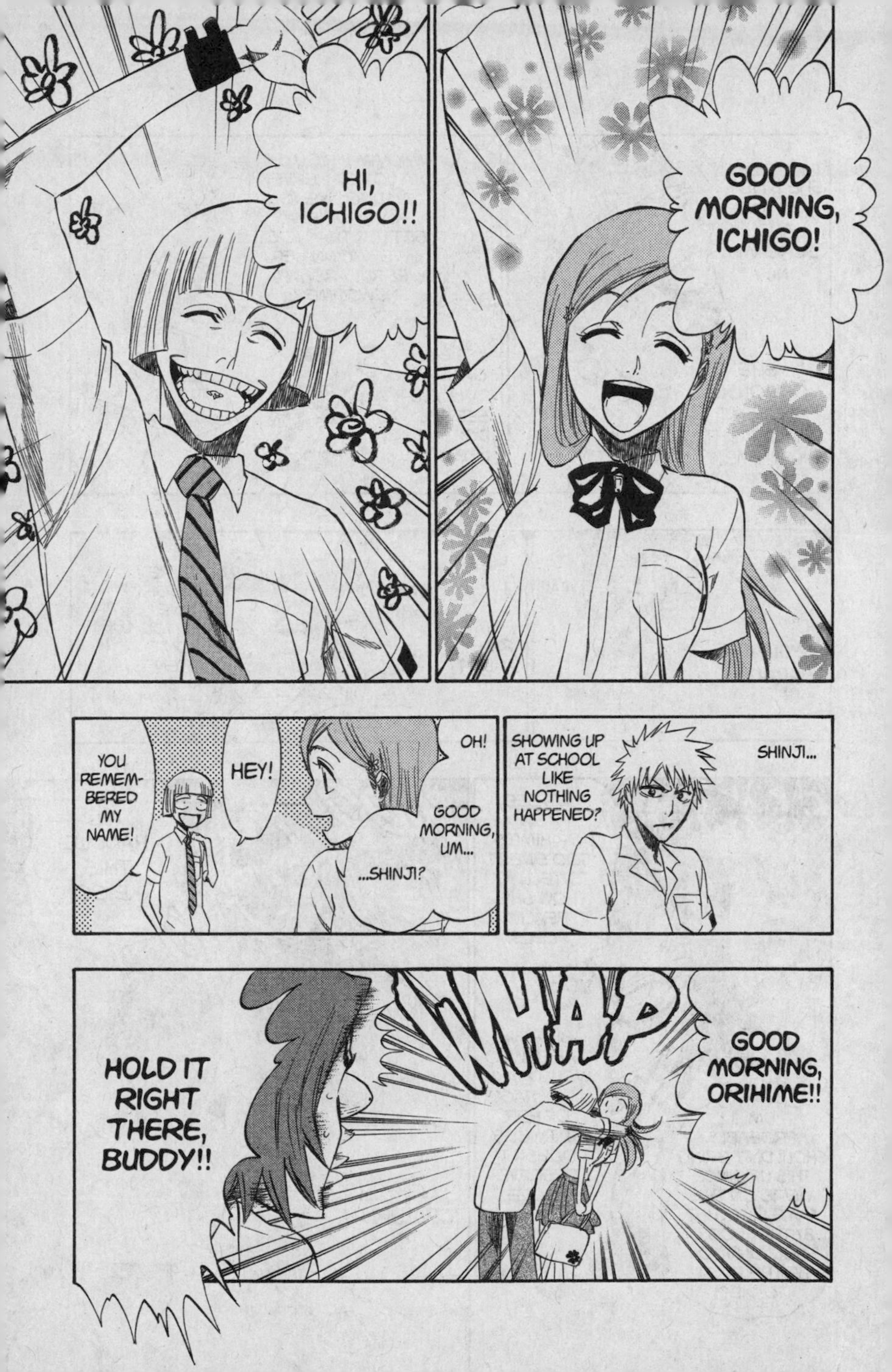
GOOD MORNING, ICHIGO!
HI, ICHIGO!!
SHINJI...
SHOWING UP AT SCHOOL LIKE NOTHING HAPPENED?
OH!
GOOD MORNING, UM...
...SHINJI?
HEY!
YOU REMEMBERED MY NAME!
GOOD MORNING, ORIHIME!!
WHAP
HOLD IT RIGHT THERE, BUDDY!!

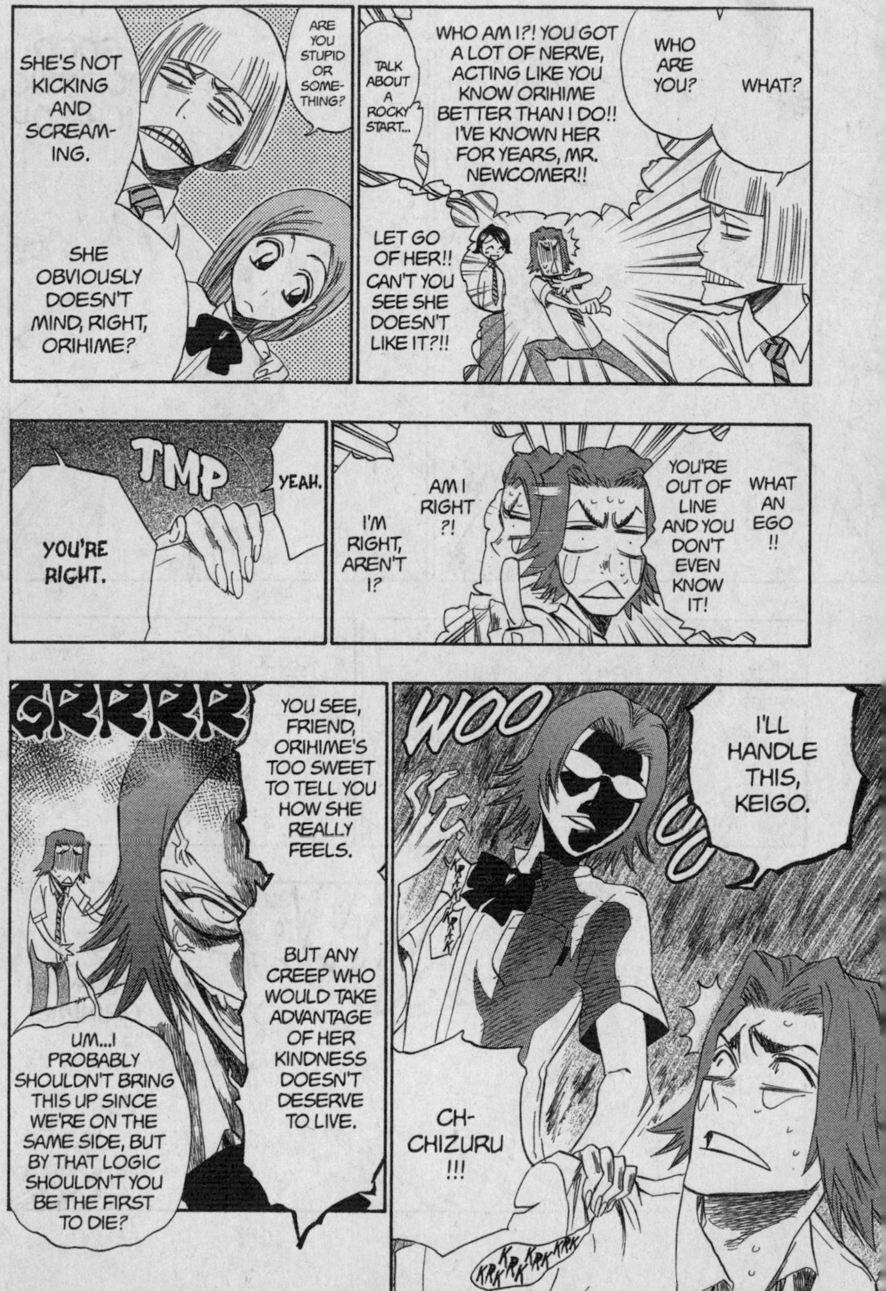
WHAT?
WHO ARE YOU?
WHO AM I?! YOU GOT A LOT OF NERVE, ACTING LIKE YOU KNOW ORIHIME BETTER THAN I DO!! I'VE KNOWN HER FOR YEARS, MR. NEWCOMER!!
TALK ABOUT A ROCKY START...
LET GO OF HER!! CAN'T YOU SEE SHE DOESN'T LIKE IT?!!
ARE YOU STUPID OR SOME-THING?
SHE'S NOT KICKING AND SCREAM-ING.
SHE OBVIOUSLY DOESN'T MIND, RIGHT, ORIHIME?
WHAT AN EGO!!
YOU'RE OUT OF LINE AND YOU DON'T EVEN KNOW IT!
AM I RIGHT?!
I'M RIGHT, AREN'T I?
TMP
YEAH.
YOU'RE RIGHT.
I'LL HANDLE THIS, KEIGO.
WOOOOO
CH-CHIZURU!!!
KRK KRK KRK KRK KRK
YOU SEE, FRIEND, ORIHIME'S TOO SWEET TO TELL YOU HOW SHE REALLY FEELS.
BUT ANY CREEP WHO WOULD TAKE ADVANTAGE OF HER KINDNESS DOESN'T DESERVE TO LIVE.
UM...I PROBABLY SHOULDN'T BRING THIS UP SINCE WE'RE ON THE SAME SIDE, BUT BY THAT LOGIC SHOULDN'T YOU BE THE FIRST TO DIE?

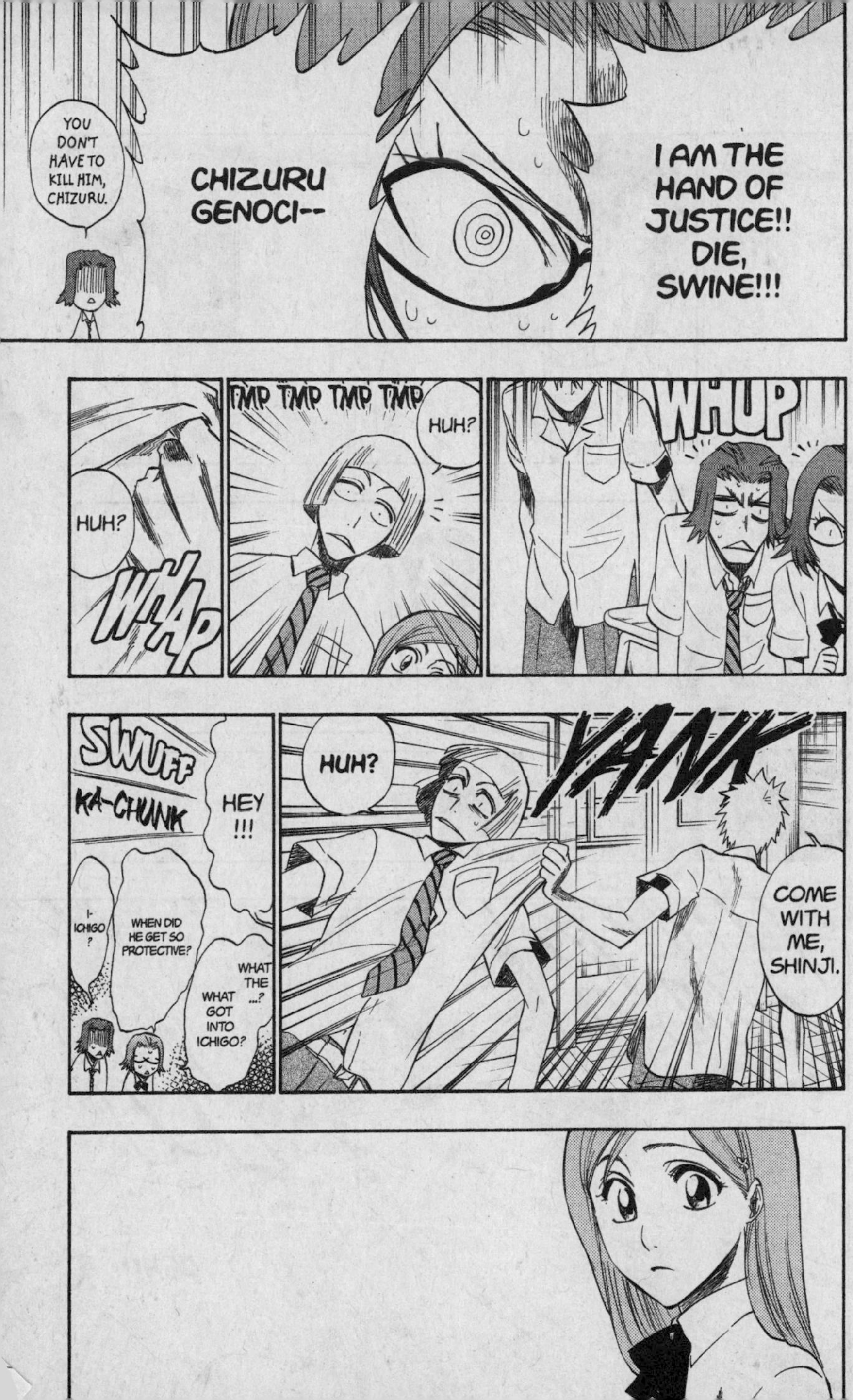
I AM THE HAND OF JUSTICE!! DIE, SWINE!!!
CHIZURU GENOCI--
YOU DON'T HAVE TO KILL HIM, CHIZURU.
WHUP
TMP TMP TMP TMP
HUH?
HUH?
WHAP
YANK
COME WITH ME, SHINJI.
HUH?
SWUFF
KA-CHUNK
HEY !!!
WHAT THE ...?
WHAT GOT INTO ICHIGO?
WHEN DID HE GET SO PROTECTIVE?
I-ICHIGO?

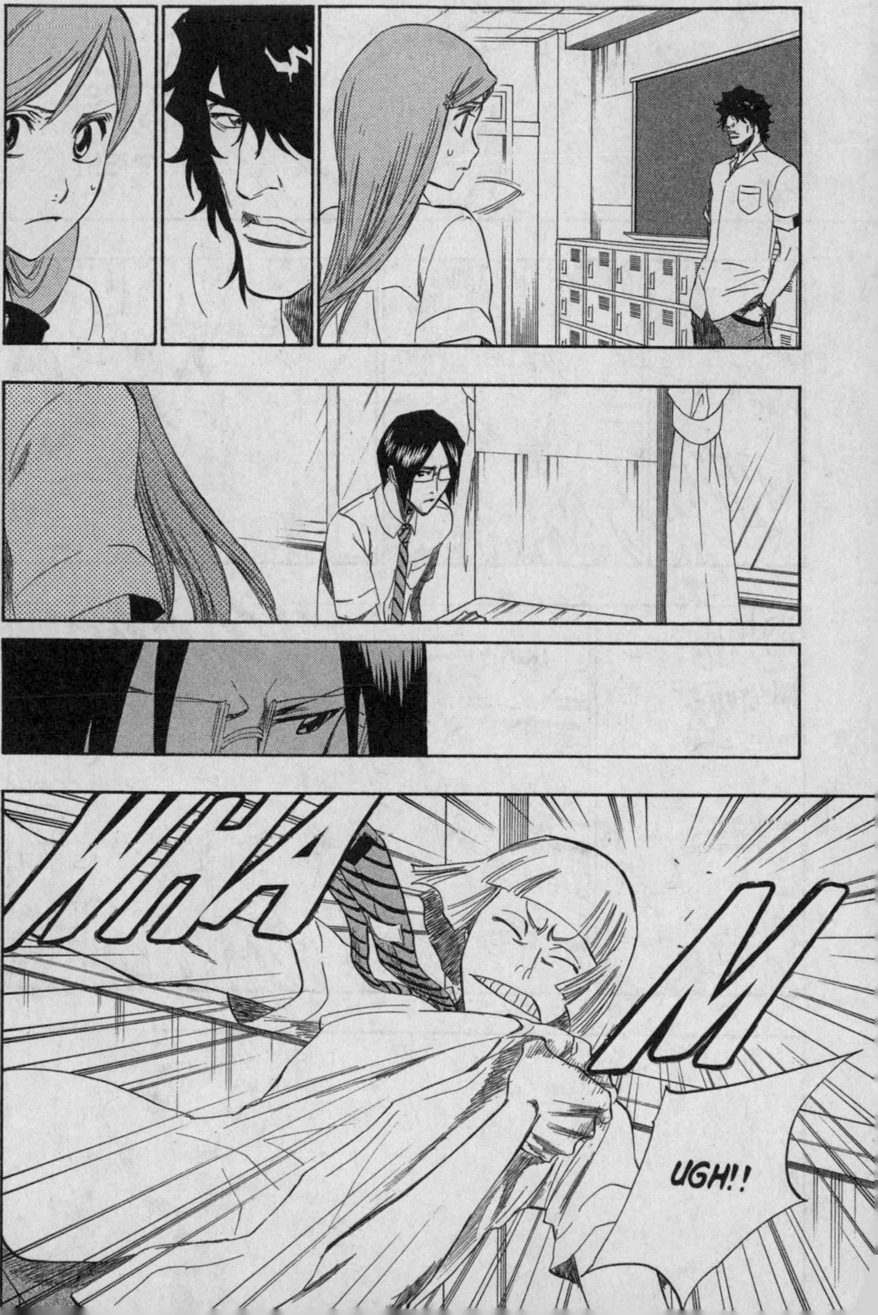
WHAM
UGH!!

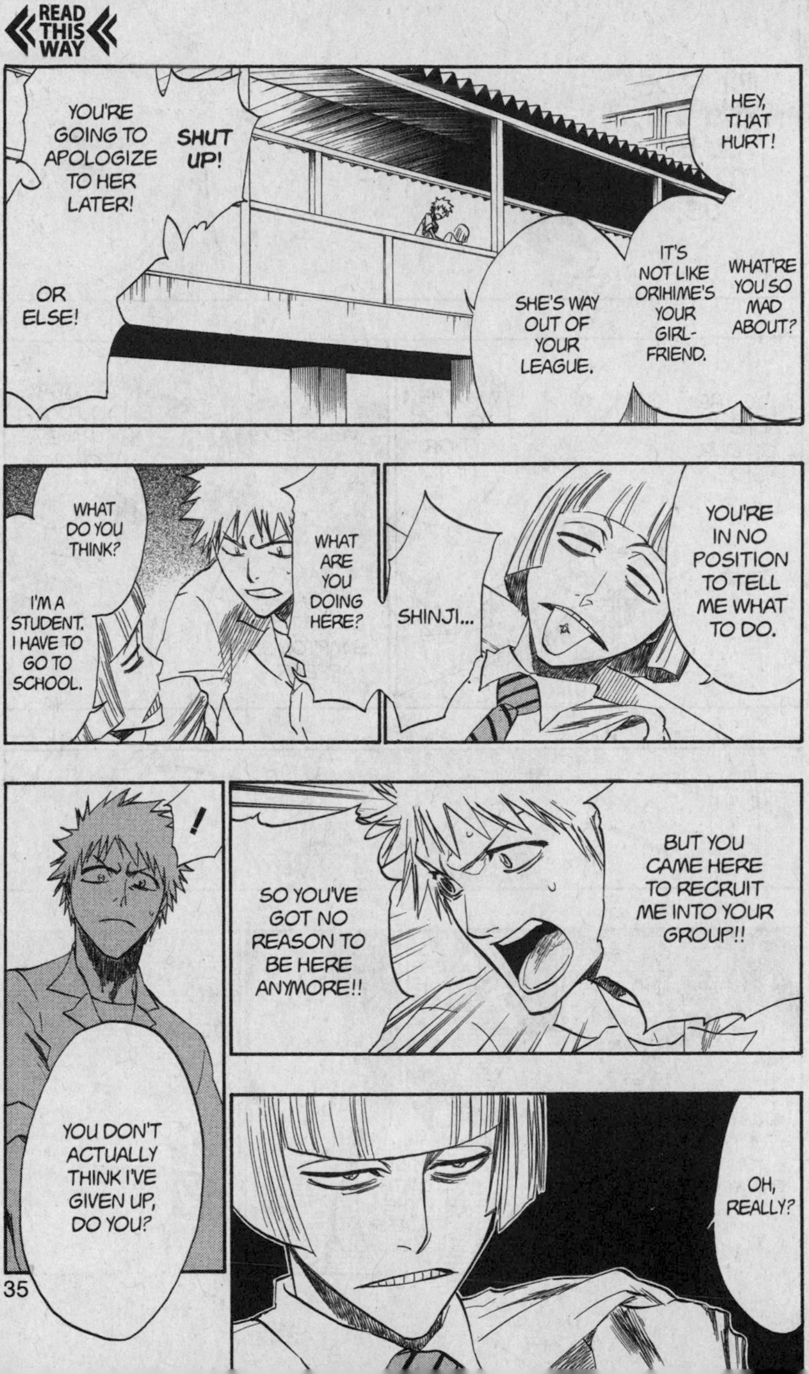
READ THIS WAY
HEY, THAT HURT!
WHAT'RE YOU SO MAD ABOUT?
IT'S NOT LIKE ORIHIME'S YOUR GIRL-FRIEND.
SHE'S WAY OUT OF YOUR LEAGUE.
SHUT UP!
YOU'RE GOING TO APOLOGIZE TO HER LATER!
OR ELSE!
YOU'RE IN NO POSITION TO TELL ME WHAT TO DO.
SHINJI...
WHAT ARE YOU DOING HERE?
WHAT DO YOU THINK?
I'M A STUDENT. I HAVE TO GO TO SCHOOL.
BUT YOU CAME HERE TO RECRUIT ME INTO YOUR GROUP!!
SO YOU'VE GOT NO REASON TO BE HERE ANYMORE!!
OH, REALLY?
!
YOU DON'T ACTUALLY THINK I'VE GIVEN UP, DO YOU?

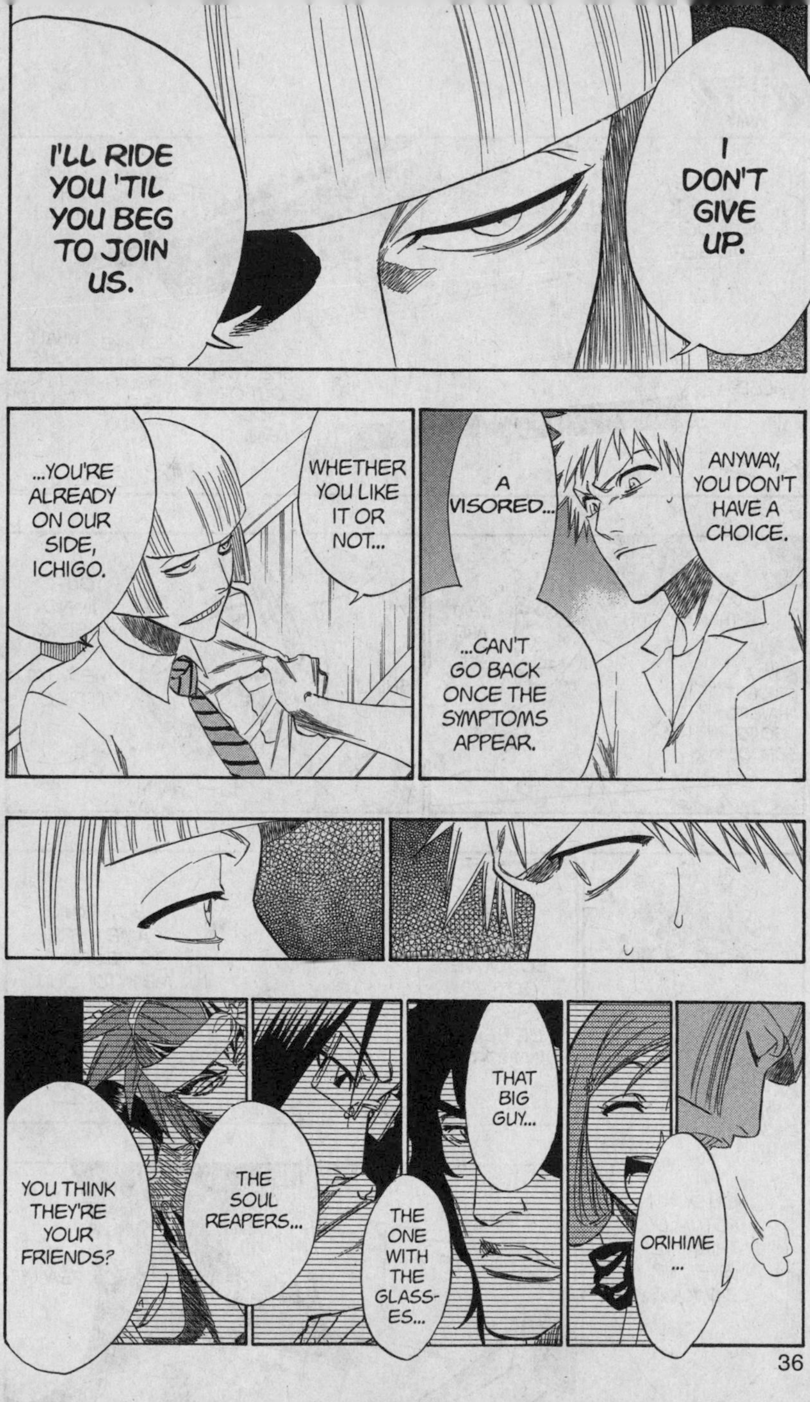
I DON'T GIVE UP.
I'LL RIDE YOU 'TIL YOU BEG TO JOIN US.
ANYWAY, YOU DON'T HAVE A CHOICE.
A VISORED...
...CAN'T GO BACK ONCE THE SYMPTOMS APPEAR.
WHETHER YOU LIKE IT OR NOT...
...YOU'RE ALREADY ON OUR SIDE, ICHIGO.
ORIHIME ...
THAT BIG GUY...
THE ONE WITH THE GLASSES...
THE SOUL REAPERS...
YOU THINK THEY'RE YOUR FRIENDS?

READ THIS WAY

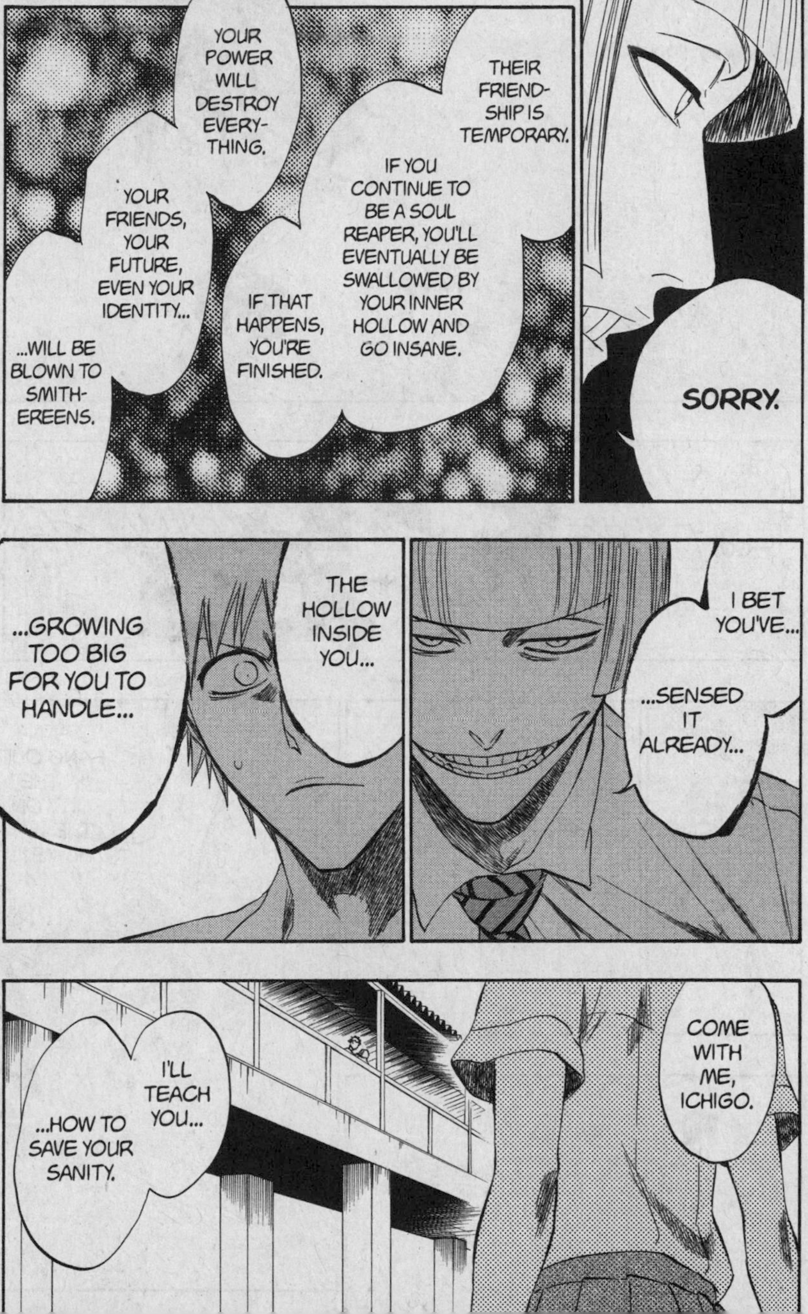
SORRY.
THEIR FRIEND-SHIP IS TEMPORARY.
YOUR POWER WILL DESTROY EVERY-THING.
IF YOU CONTINUE TO BE A SOUL REAPER, YOU'LL EVENTUALLY BE SWALLOWED BY YOUR INNER HOLLOW AND GO INSANE.
IF THAT HAPPENS, YOU'RE FINISHED.
YOUR FRIENDS, YOUR FUTURE, EVEN YOUR IDENTITY...
...WILL BE BLOWN TO SMITH-EREENS.
I BET YOU'VE...
...SENSED IT ALREADY...
THE HOLLOW INSIDE YOU...
...GROWING TOO BIG FOR YOU TO HANDLE...
COME WITH ME, ICHIGO.
I'LL TEACH YOU...
...HOW TO SAVE YOUR SANITY.

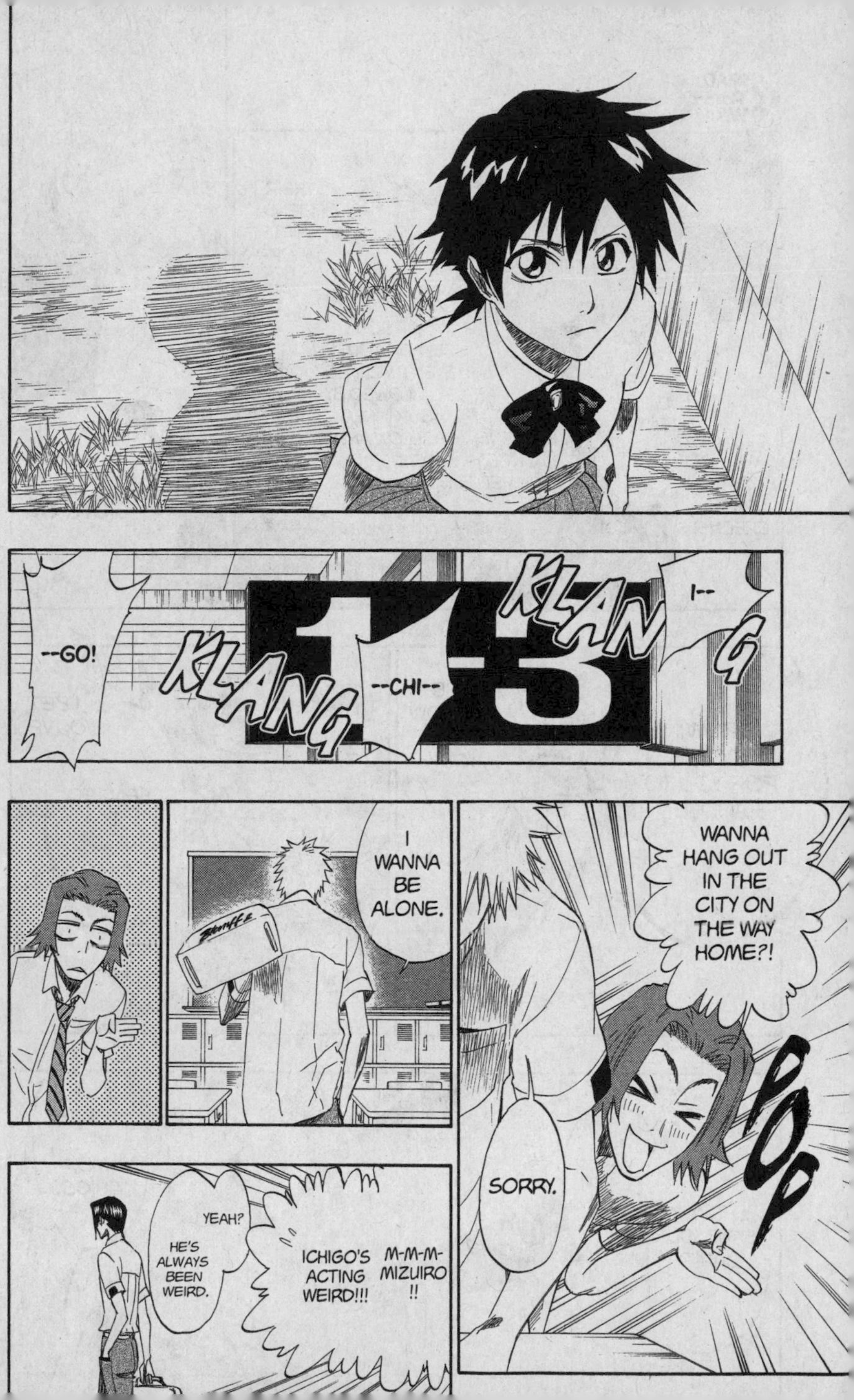
I--
KLANG
--CHI--
KLANG
--GO!
WANNA HANG OUT IN THE CITY ON THE WAY HOME?!
BOOP
SORRY.
I WANNA BE ALONE.
M-M-M-MIZUIRO!!
ICHIGO'S ACTING WEIRD!!!
YEAH?
HE'S ALWAYS BEEN WEIRD.

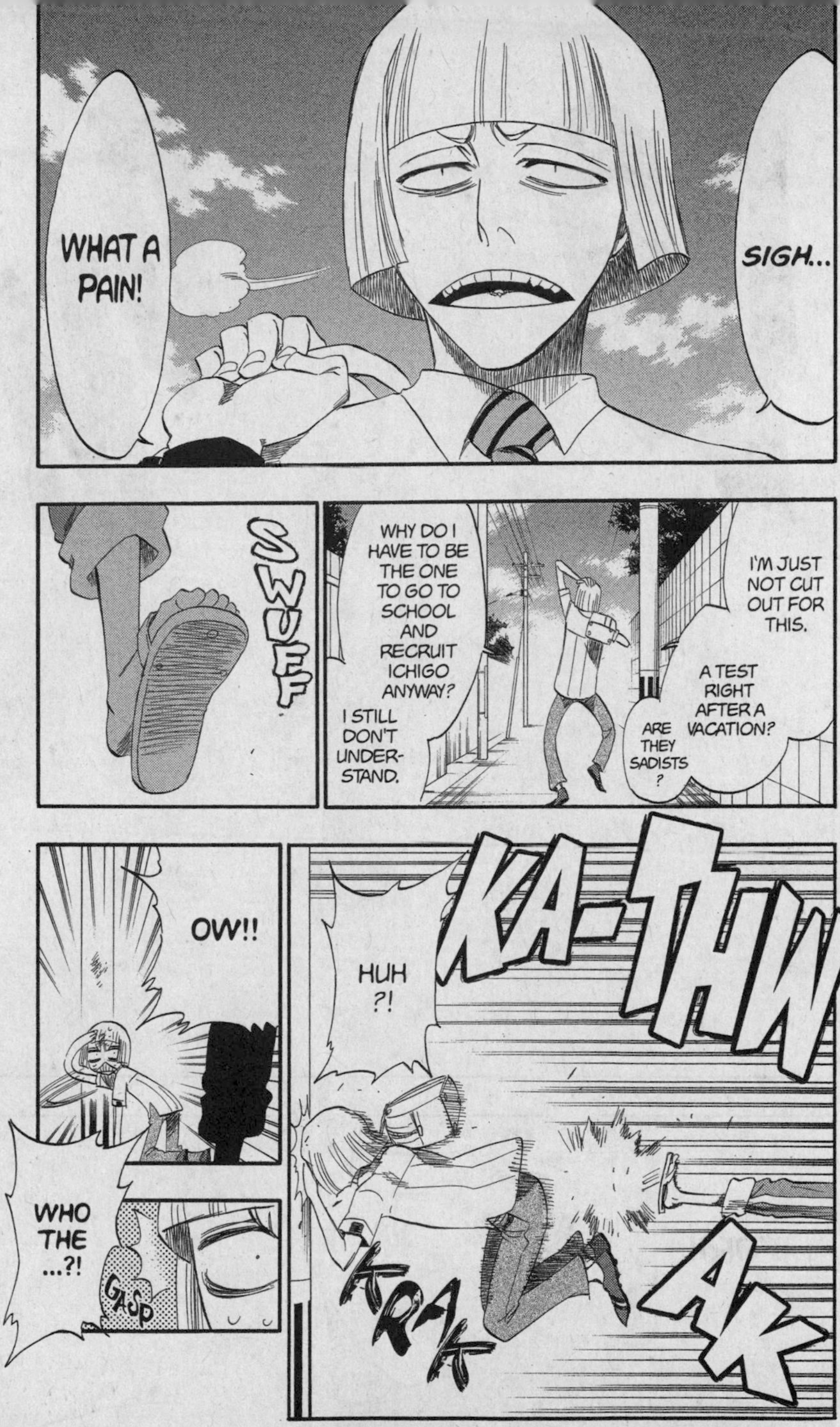
SIGH...
WHAT A PAIN!
I'M JUST NOT CUT OUT FOR THIS.
A TEST RIGHT AFTER A VACATION?
ARE THEY SADISTS?
WHY DO I HAVE TO BE THE ONE TO GO TO SCHOOL AND RECRUIT ICHIGO ANYWAY?
I STILL DON'T UNDER-STAND.
SWUFF
KA-THWAK
HUH ?!
KRAK
OW!!
WHO THE ...?!
GASP

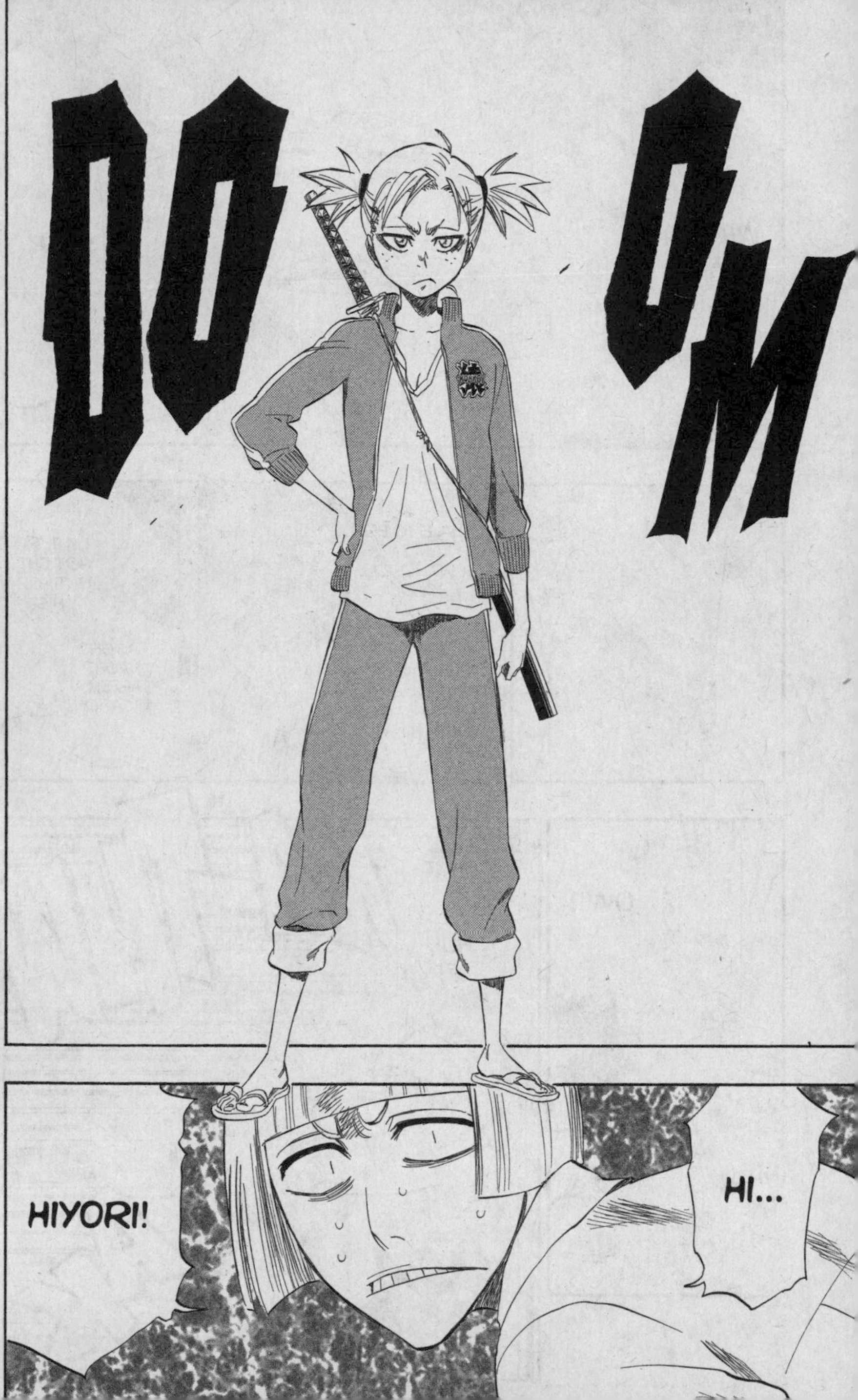
DO
OM
HI...
HIYORI!

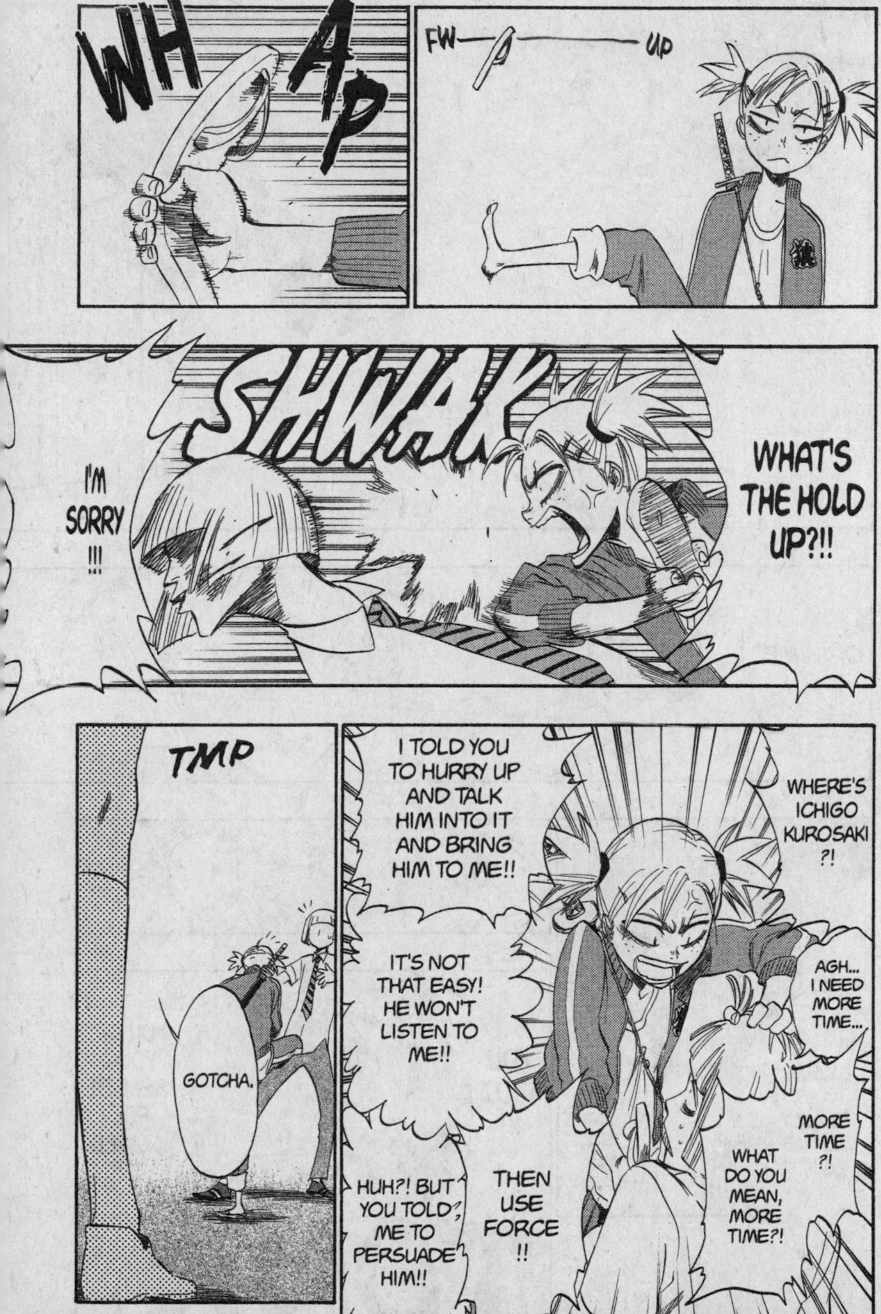
FW—P———UP
WHAP
WHAT'S THE HOLD UP?!!
SHWAK
I'M SORRY!!!
WHERE'S ICHIGO KUROSAKI?!
I TOLD YOU TO HURRY UP AND TALK HIM INTO IT AND BRING HIM TO ME!!
AGH... I NEED MORE TIME...
IT'S NOT THAT EASY! HE WON'T LISTEN TO ME!!
MORE TIME?!
WHAT DO YOU MEAN, MORE TIME?!
THEN USE FORCE!!
HUH?! BUT YOU TOLD ME TO PERSUADE HIM!!
TMP
GOTCHA.

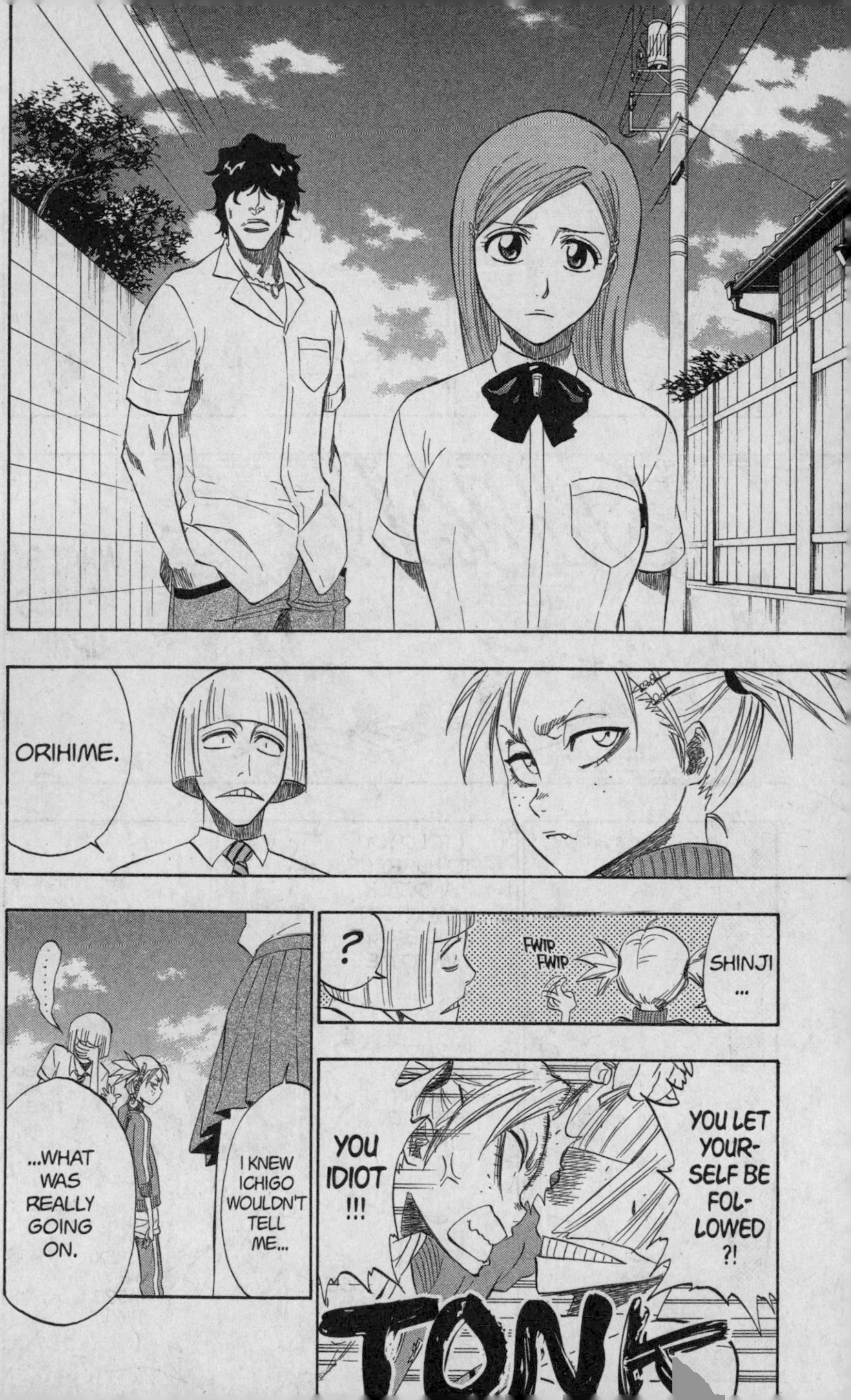
ORIHIME.
SHINJI ...
FWIP FWIP
?
YOU LET YOUR-SELF BE FOL-LOWED ?!
YOU IDIOT !!!
TONK
...
I KNEW ICHIGO WOULDN'T TELL ME...
...WHAT WAS REALLY GOING ON.

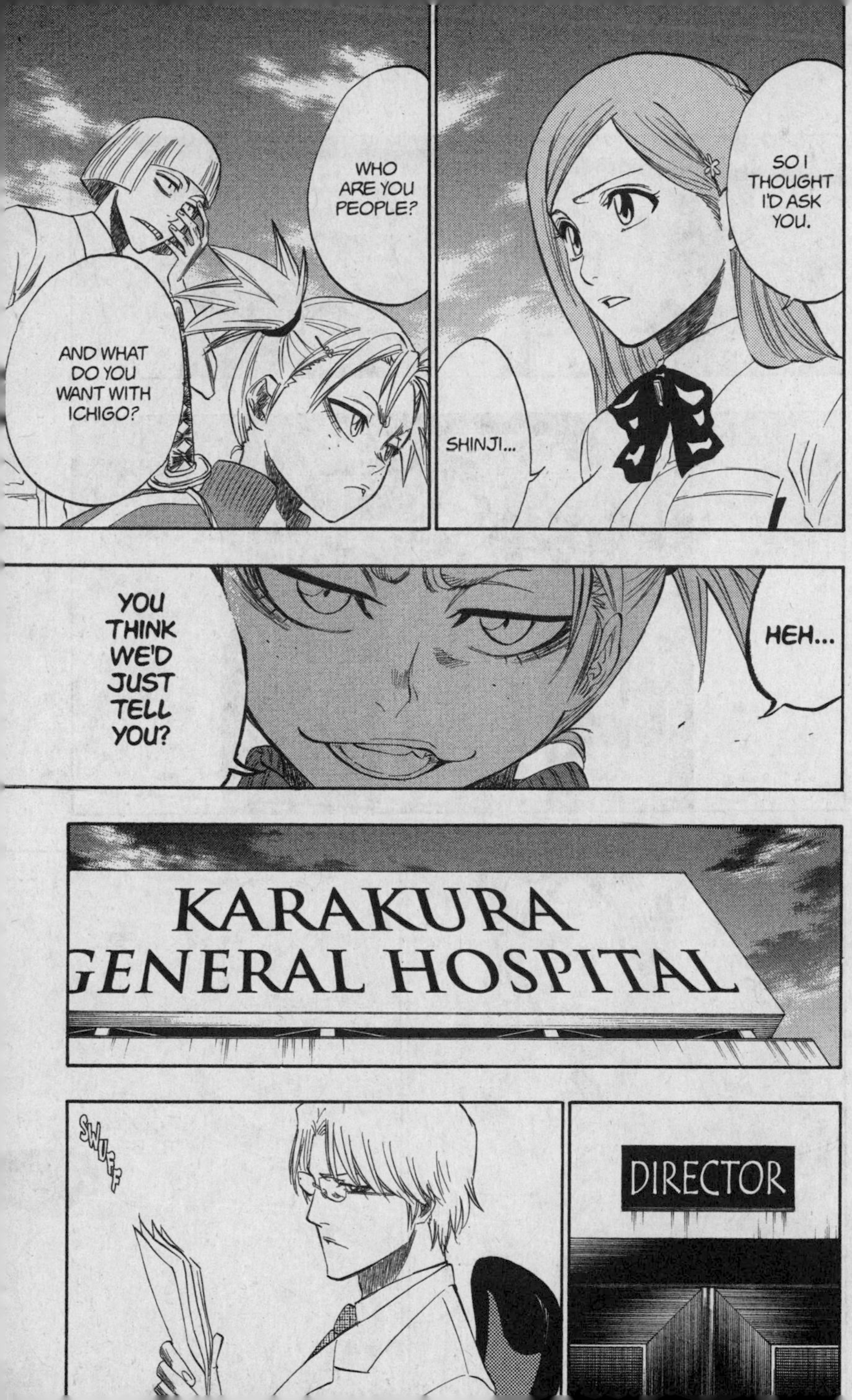
SO I THOUGHT I'D ASK YOU.
SHINJI...
WHO ARE YOU PEOPLE?
AND WHAT DO YOU WANT WITH ICHIGO?
HEH...
YOU THINK WE'D JUST TELL YOU?
KARAKURA GENERAL HOSPITAL
DIRECTOR
SWUFF

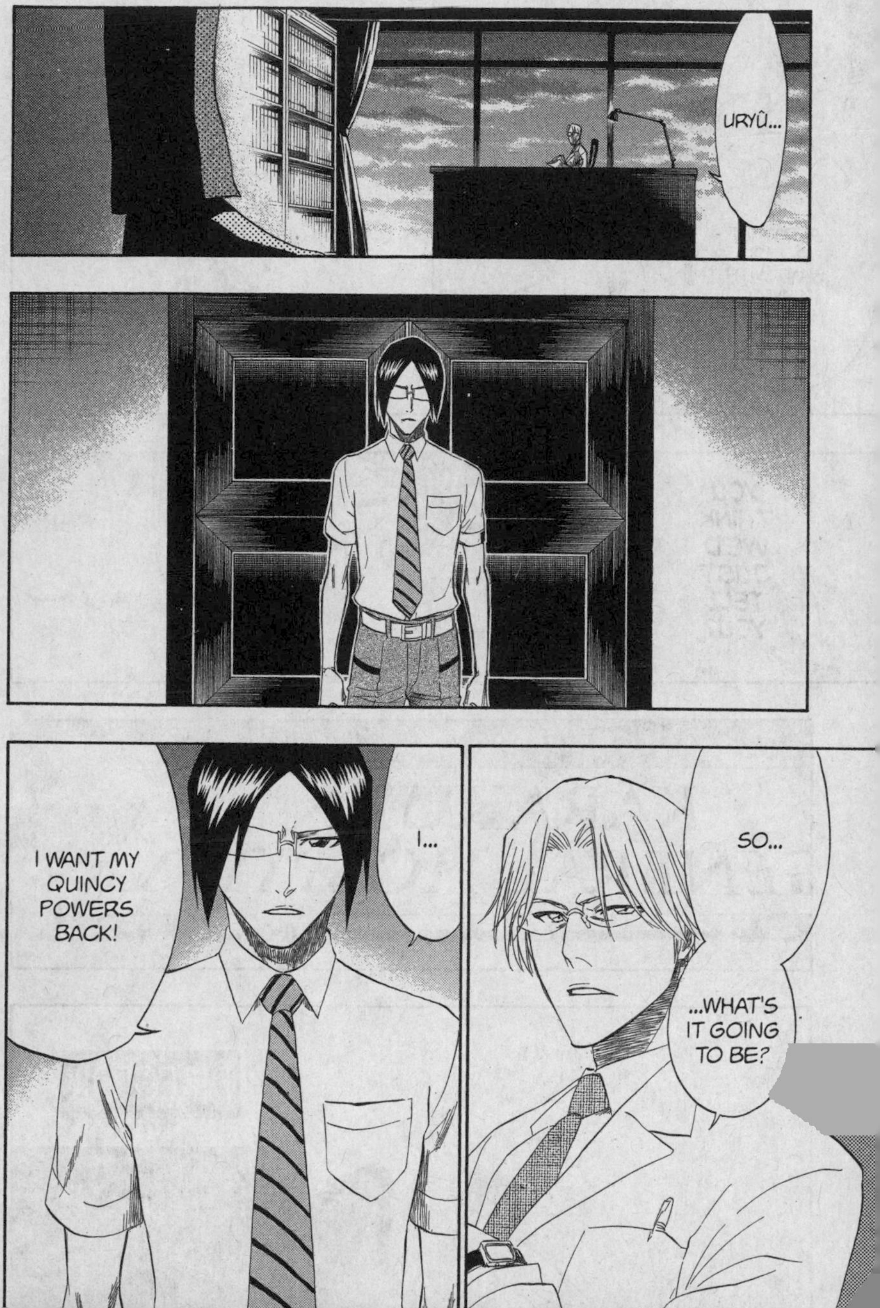
URYÛ...
SO...
...WHAT'S IT GOING TO BE?
I...
I WANT MY QUINCY POWERS BACK!

AND?

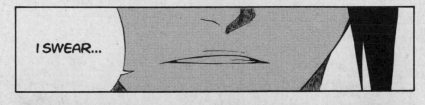

I SWEAR...

...WITH THE SOUL REAPERS AGAIN.

...GET INVOLVED...

...I'LL NEVER...

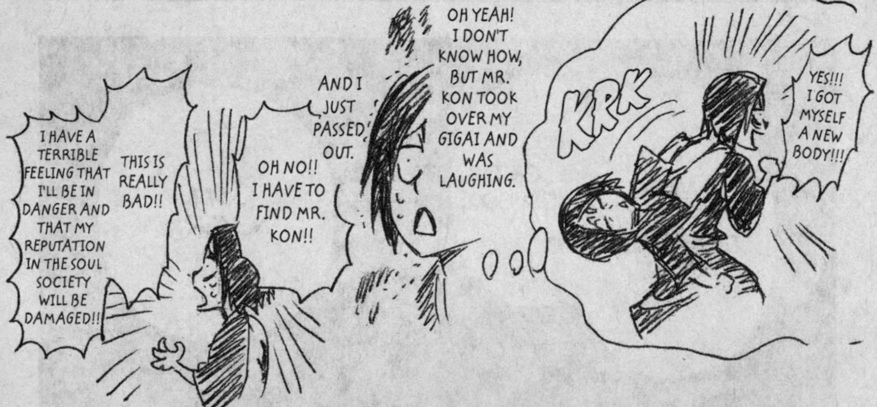
KRK
YES!!! I GOT MYSELF A NEW BODY!!!
OH YEAH! I DON'T KNOW HOW, BUT MR. KON TOOK OVER MY GIGAI AND WAS LAUGHING.
AND I JUST PASSED OUT.
OH NO!! I HAVE TO FIND MR. KON!!
THIS IS REALLY BAD!!
I HAVE A TERRIBLE FEELING THAT I'LL BE IN DANGER AND THAT MY REPUTATION IN THE SOUL SOCIETY WILL BE DAMAGED!!

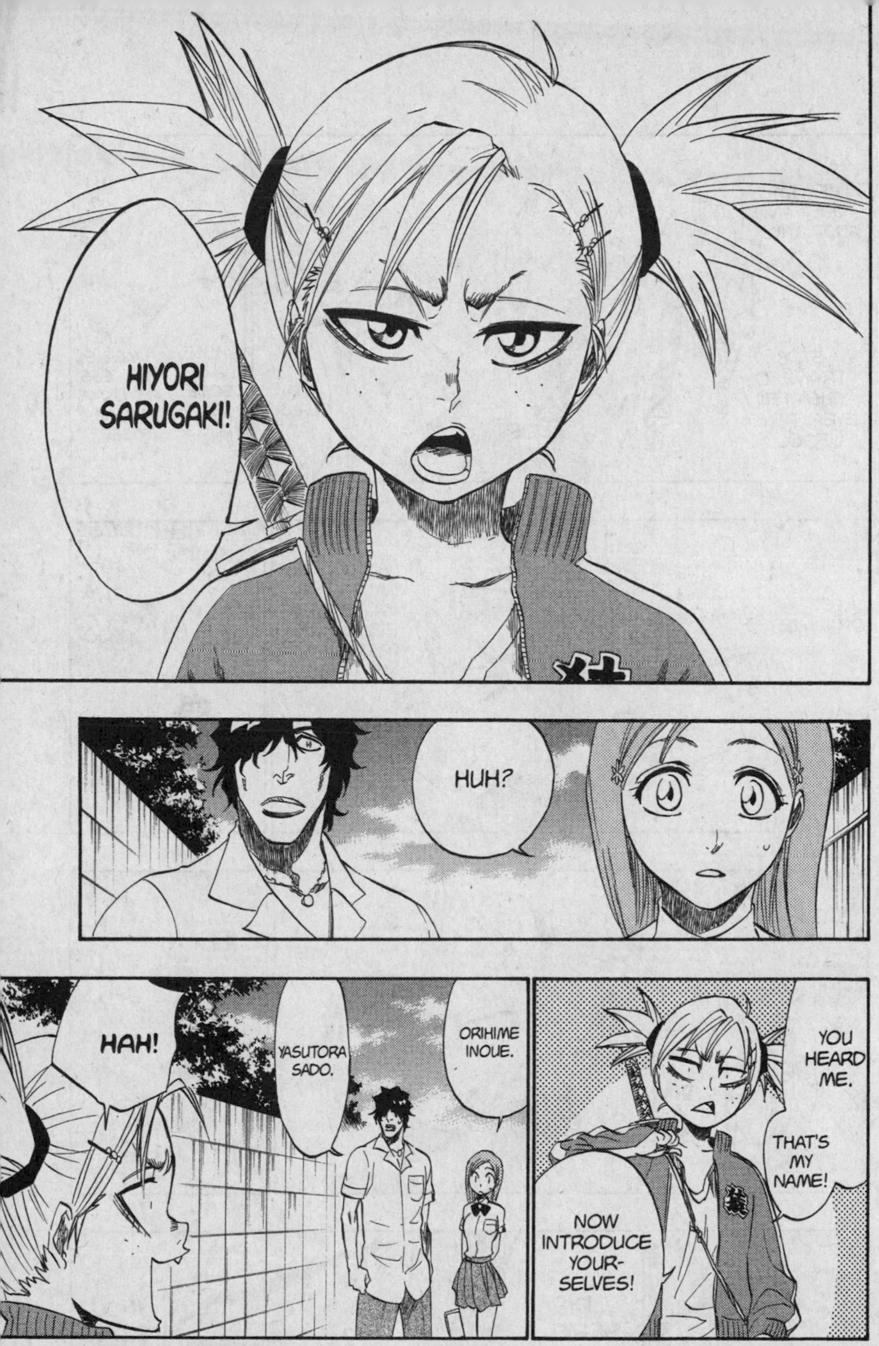
HIYORI SARUGAKI!
HUH?
YOU HEARD ME.
THAT'S MY NAME!
NOW INTRODUCE YOUR-SELVES!
ORIHIME INOUE.
YASUTORA SADO.
HAH!

190. Conquistadores

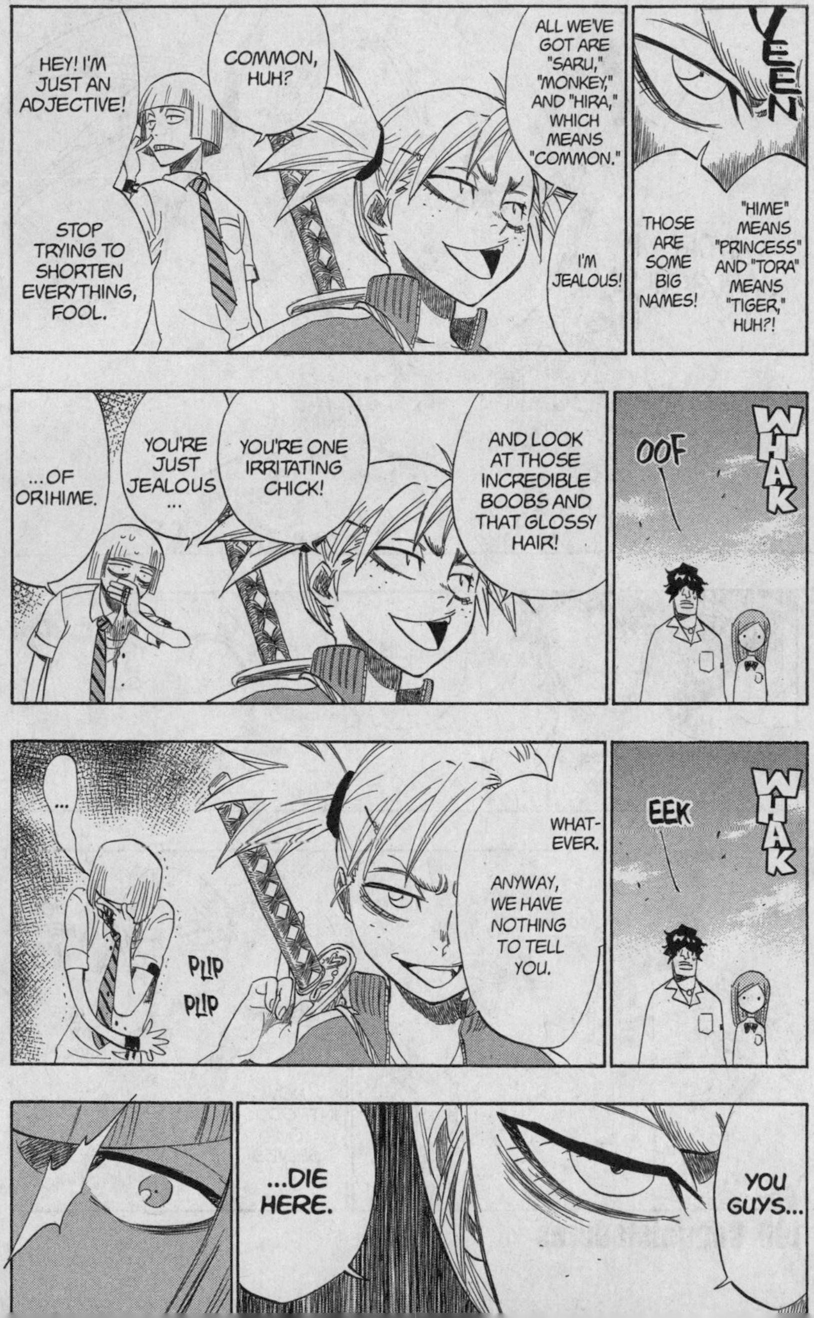
VEEN
"HIME" MEANS "PRINCESS" AND "TORA" MEANS "TIGER," HUH?!
THOSE ARE SOME BIG NAMES!
ALL WE'VE GOT ARE "SARU," "MONKEY," AND "HIRA," WHICH MEANS "COMMON."
I'M JEALOUS!
COMMON, HUH?
HEY! I'M JUST AN ADJECTIVE!
STOP TRYING TO SHORTEN EVERYTHING, FOOL.
WHAK
OOF
AND LOOK AT THOSE INCREDIBLE BOOBS AND THAT GLOSSY HAIR!
YOU'RE ONE IRRITATING CHICK!
YOU'RE JUST JEALOUS...
...OF ORIHIME.
WHAK
EEK
WHAT-EVER.
ANYWAY, WE HAVE NOTHING TO TELL YOU.
...
PLIP PLIP
YOU GUYS...
...DIE HERE.

READ THIS WAY

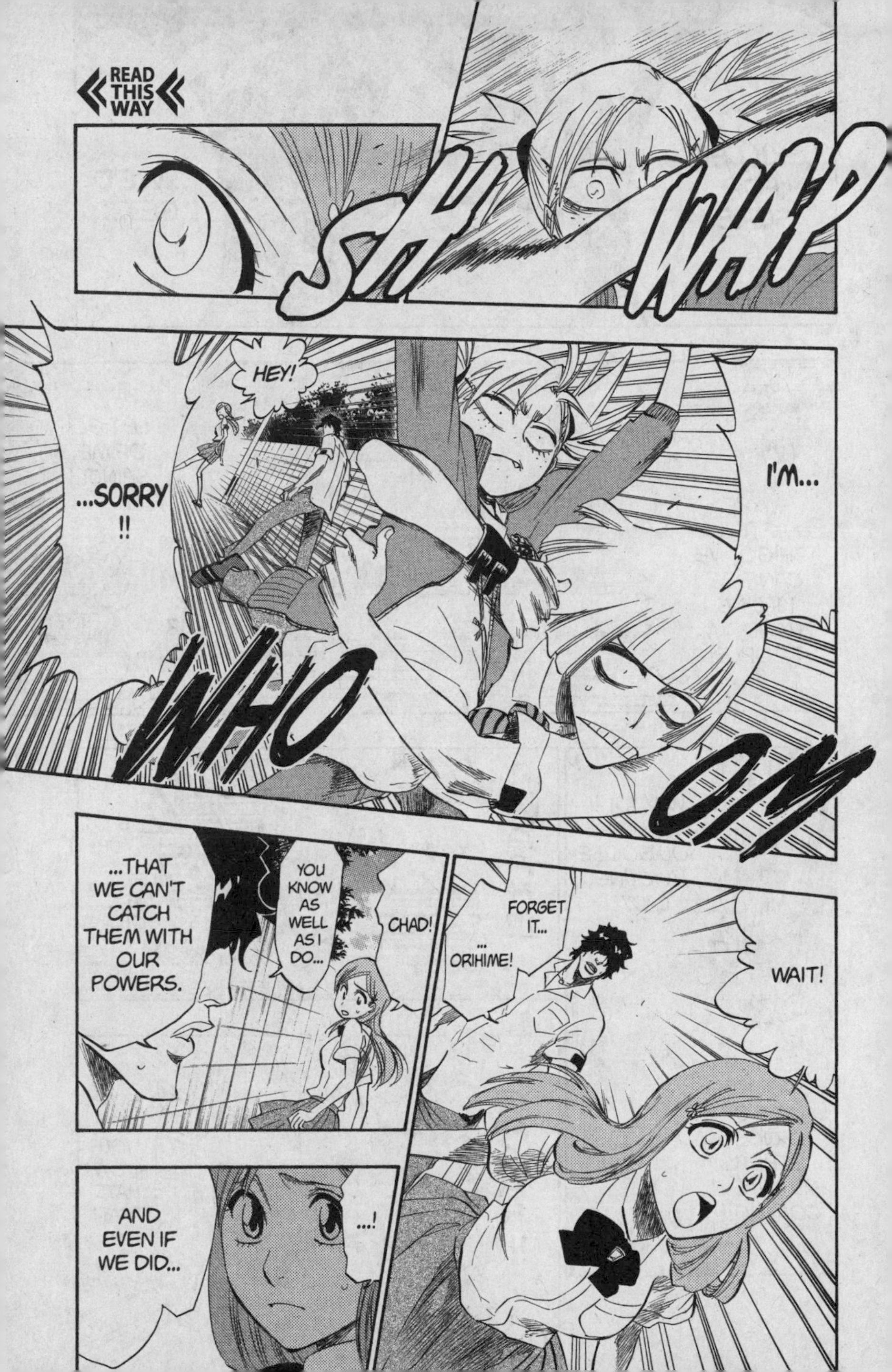
SHWAP
HEY!
I'M...
...SORRY !!
WHOOM
WAIT!
FORGET IT...
...ORIHIME!
CHAD!
YOU KNOW AS WELL AS I DO...
...THAT WE CAN'T CATCH THEM WITH OUR POWERS.
...!
AND EVEN IF WE DID...

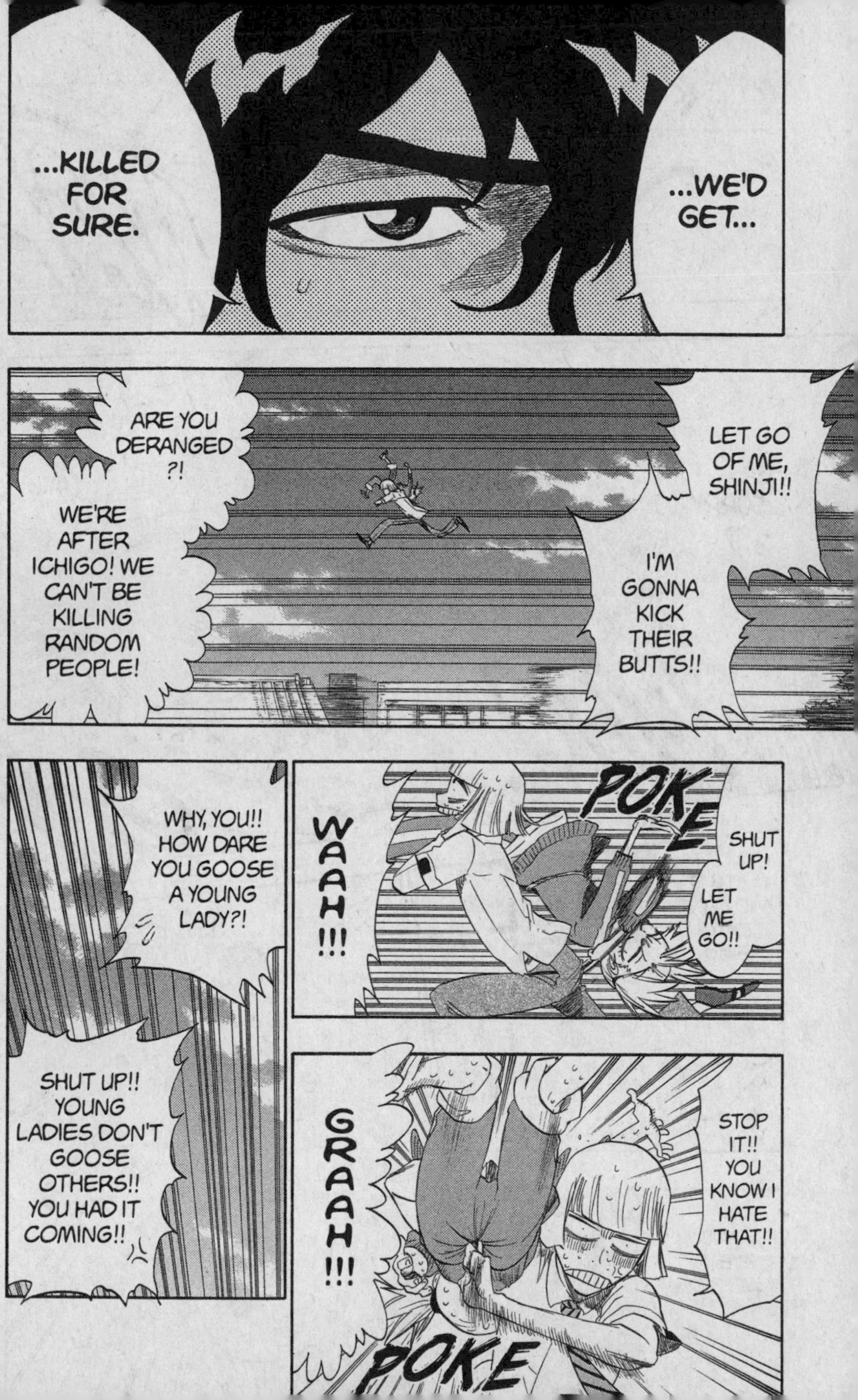
...WE'D GET...
...KILLED FOR SURE.
LET GO OF ME, SHINJI!!
I'M GONNA KICK THEIR BUTTS!!
ARE YOU DERANGED?!
WE'RE AFTER ICHIGO! WE CAN'T BE KILLING RANDOM PEOPLE!
SHUT UP!
LET ME GO!!
POKE
WAAAH!!!
STOP IT!! YOU KNOW I HATE THAT!!
GRAAAH!!!
POKE
WHY, YOU!! HOW DARE YOU GOOSE A YOUNG LADY?!
SHUT UP!! YOUNG LADIES DON'T GOOSE OTHERS!! YOU HAD IT COMING!!

READ THIS WAY

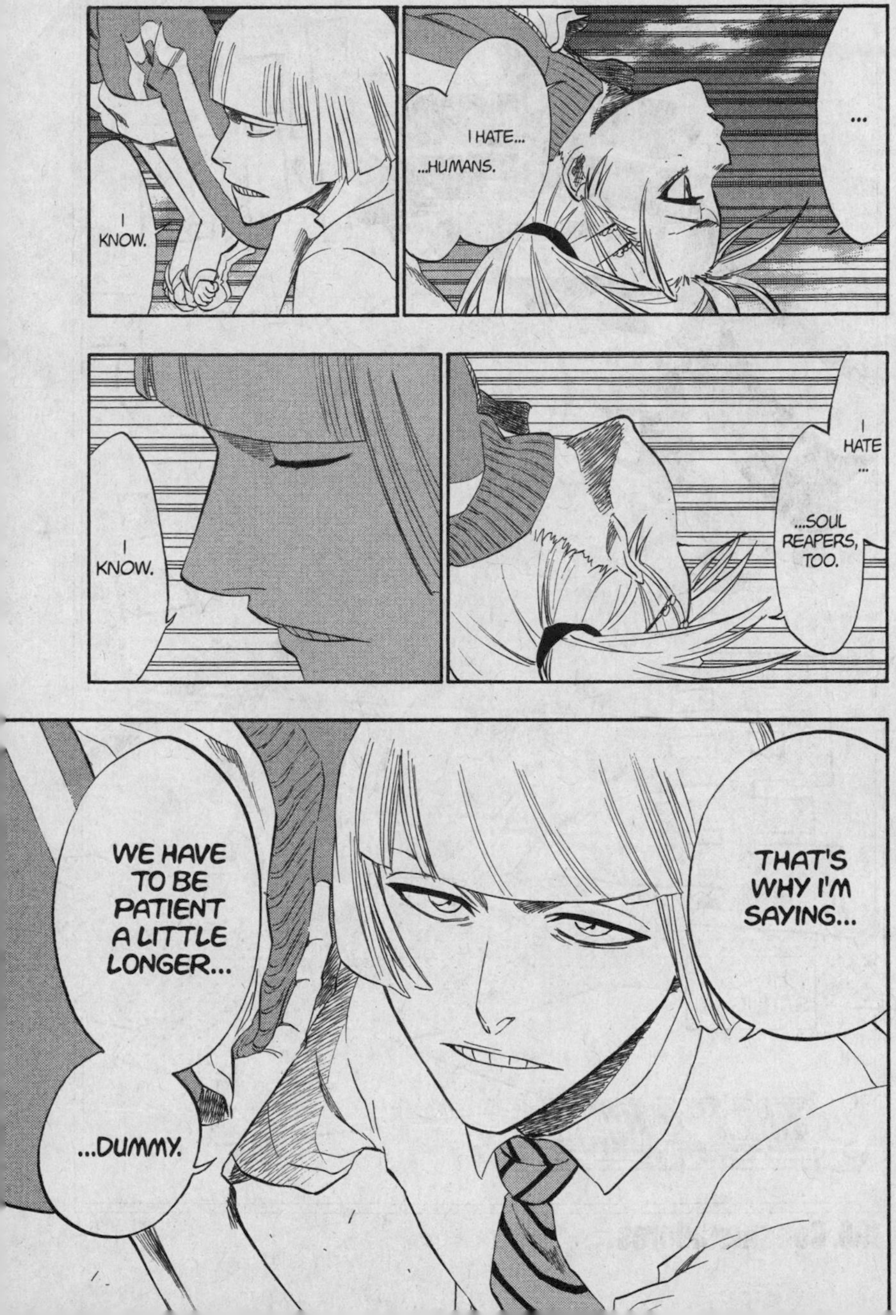
...
I HATE... ...HUMANS.
I KNOW.
I HATE ... ...SOUL REAPERS, TOO.
I KNOW.
THAT'S WHY I'M SAYING...
WE HAVE TO BE PATIENT A LITTLE LONGER...
...DUMMY.

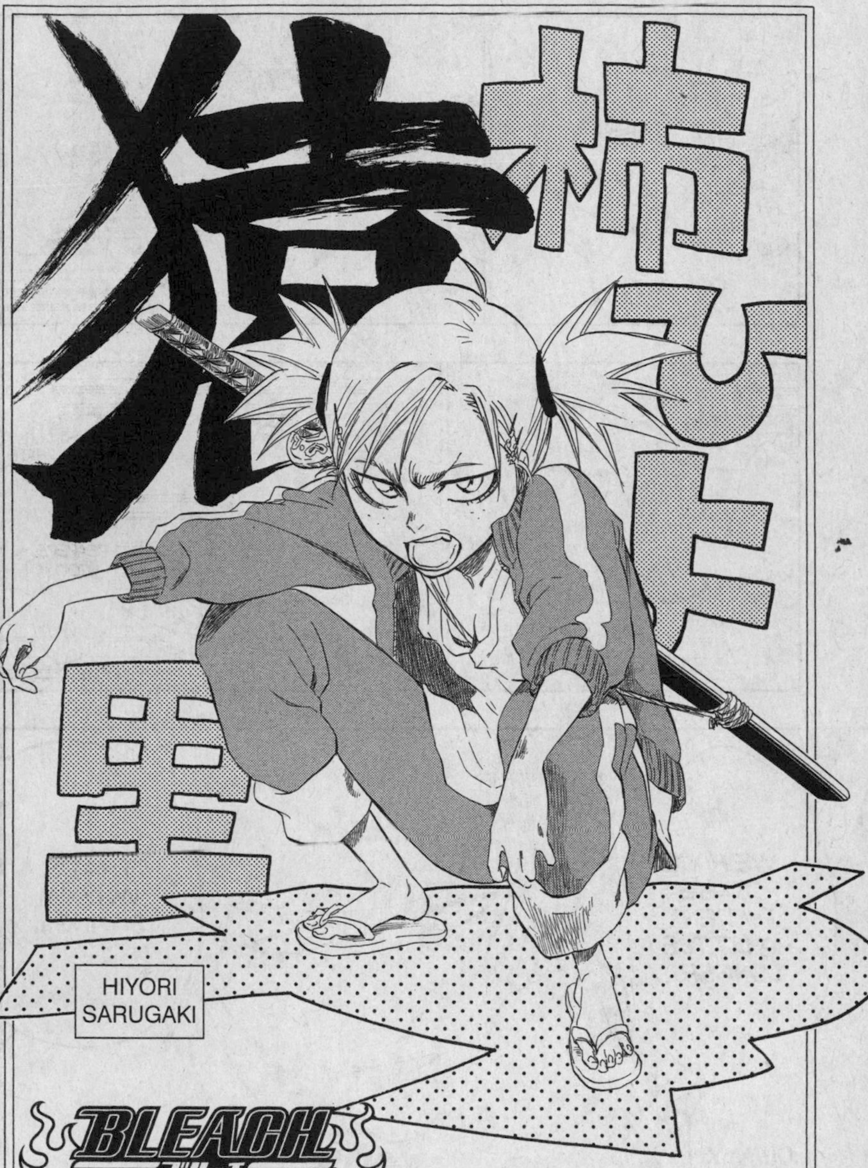
猿柿ひよ里
HIYORI SARUGAKI
BLEACH
ブリーチ

190. Conquistadores

READ THIS WAY

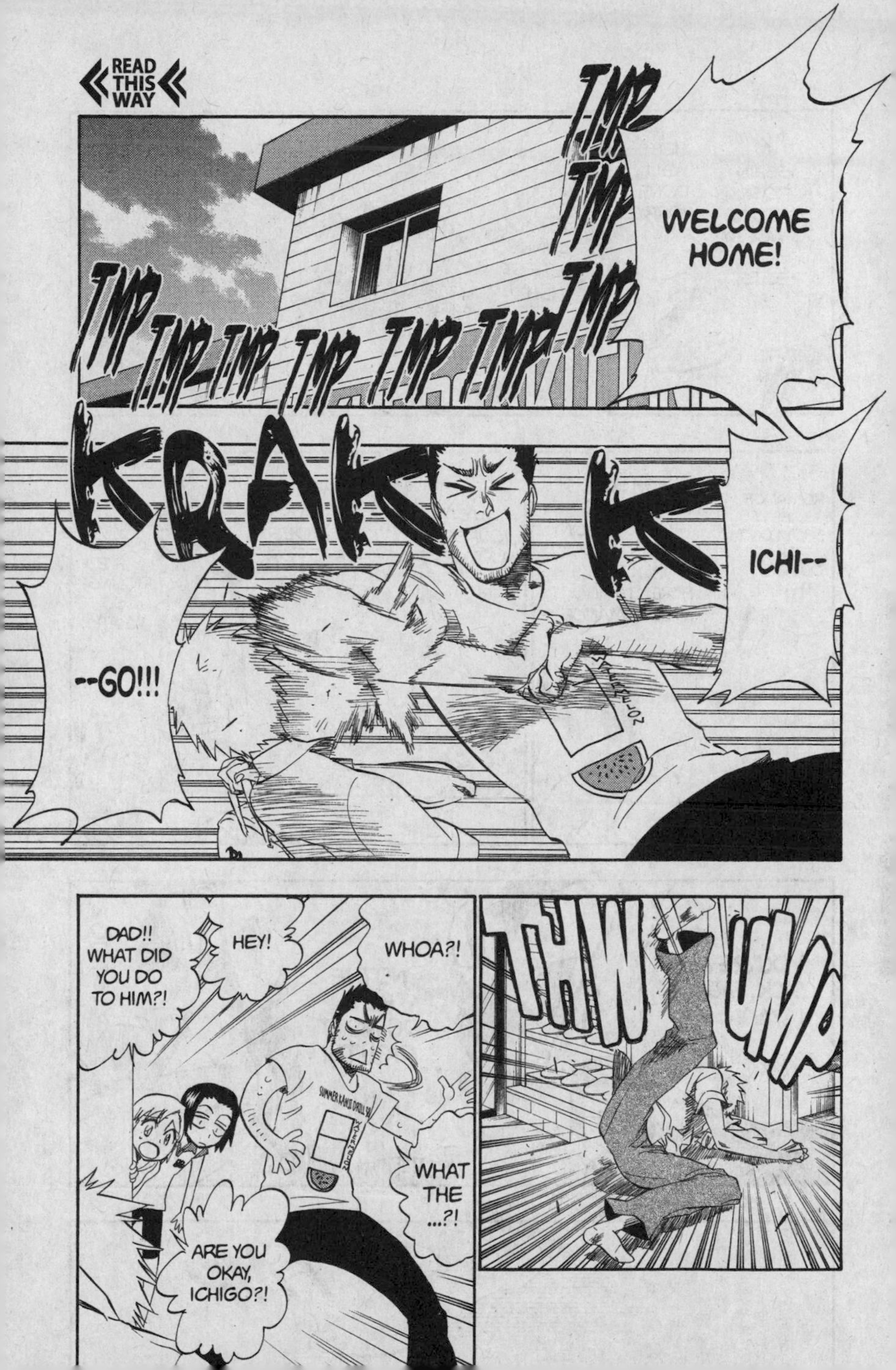

TMP TMP TMP TMP TMP TMP TMP TMP TMP TMP TMP
WELCOME HOME!
KRAKK
ICHI--
--GO!!!
THWUMP
WHOA?!
HEY!
DAD!! WHAT DID YOU DO TO HIM?!
WHAT THE ...?!
ARE YOU OKAY, ICHIGO?!

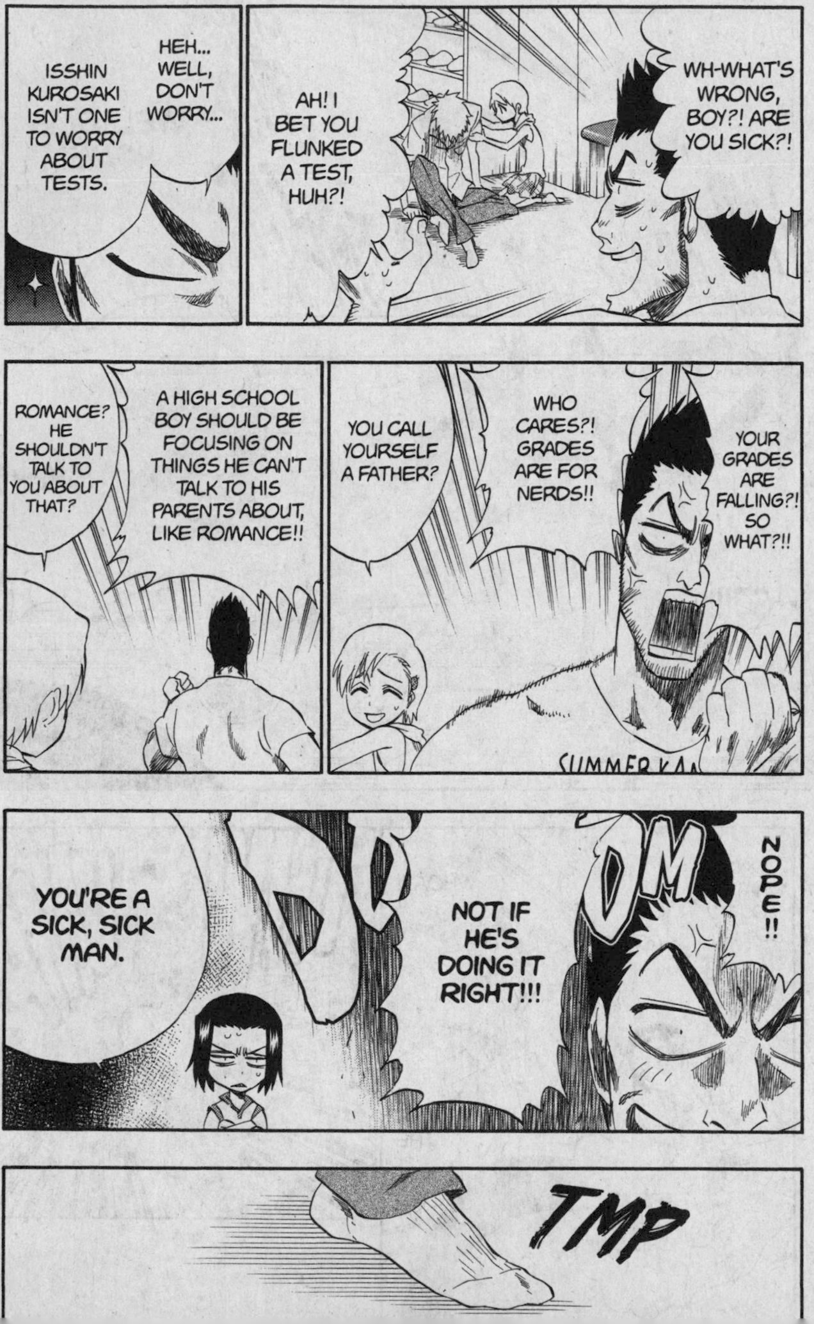
WH-WHAT'S WRONG, BOY?! ARE YOU SICK?!
AH! I BET YOU FLUNKED A TEST, HUH?!
HEH... WELL, DON'T WORRY...
ISSHIN KUROSAKI ISN'T ONE TO WORRY ABOUT TESTS.
YOUR GRADES ARE FALLING?! SO WHAT?!!
WHO CARES?! GRADES ARE FOR NERDS!!
YOU CALL YOURSELF A FATHER?
A HIGH SCHOOL BOY SHOULD BE FOCUSING ON THINGS HE CAN'T TALK TO HIS PARENTS ABOUT, LIKE ROMANCE!!
ROMANCE? HE SHOULDN'T TALK TO YOU ABOUT THAT?
NOPE!!
DOM
NOT IF HE'S DOING IT RIGHT!!!
YOU'RE A SICK, SICK MAN.
TMP

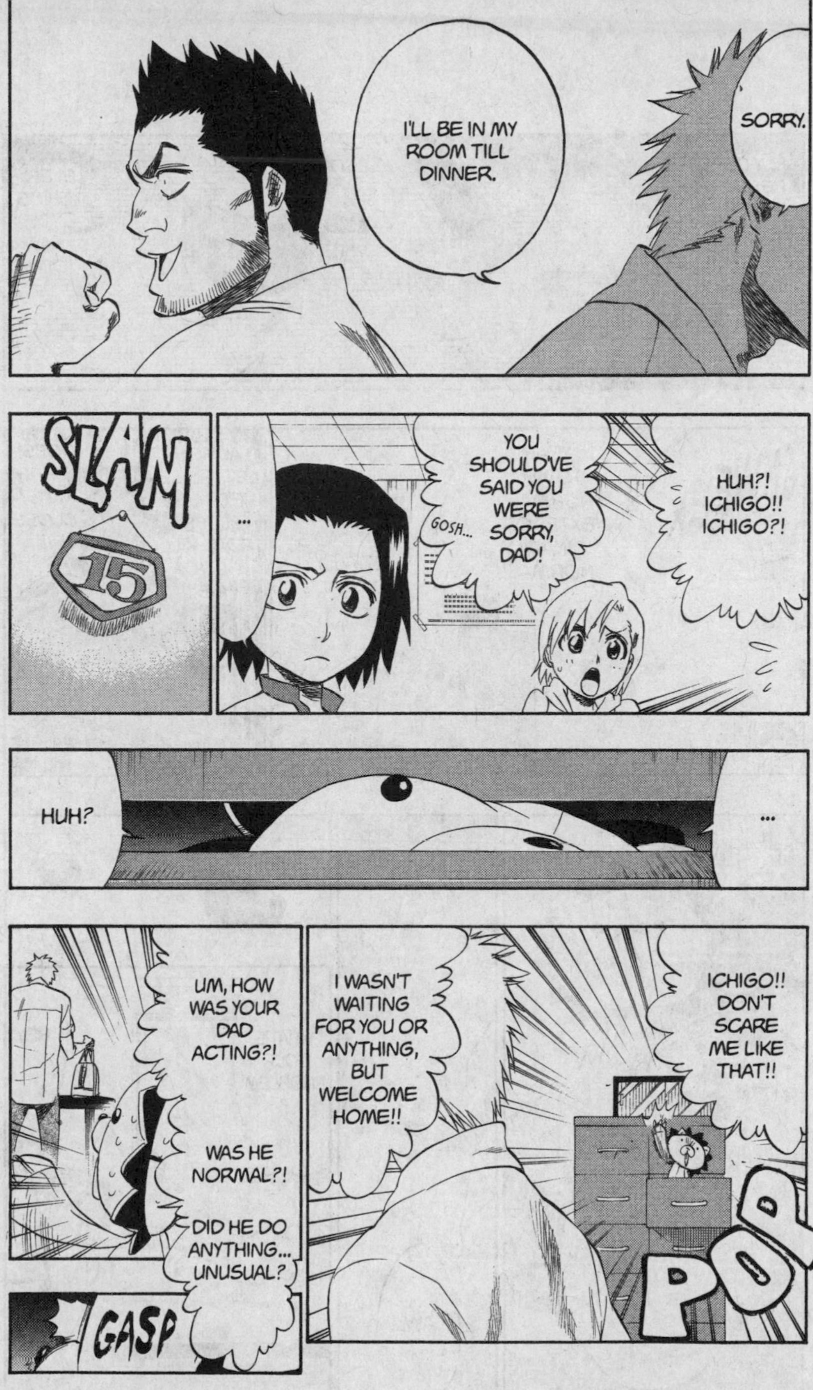
SORRY.
I'LL BE IN MY ROOM TILL DINNER.
HUH?! ICHIGO!! ICHIGO?!
YOU SHOULD'VE SAID YOU WERE SORRY, DAD!
GOSH...
...
SLAM
15
...
HUH?
ICHIGO!! DON'T SCARE ME LIKE THAT!!
POP
I WASN'T WAITING FOR YOU OR ANYTHING, BUT WELCOME HOME!!
UM, HOW WAS YOUR DAD ACTING?!
WAS HE NORMAL?!
DID HE DO ANYTHING... UNUSUAL?
GASP

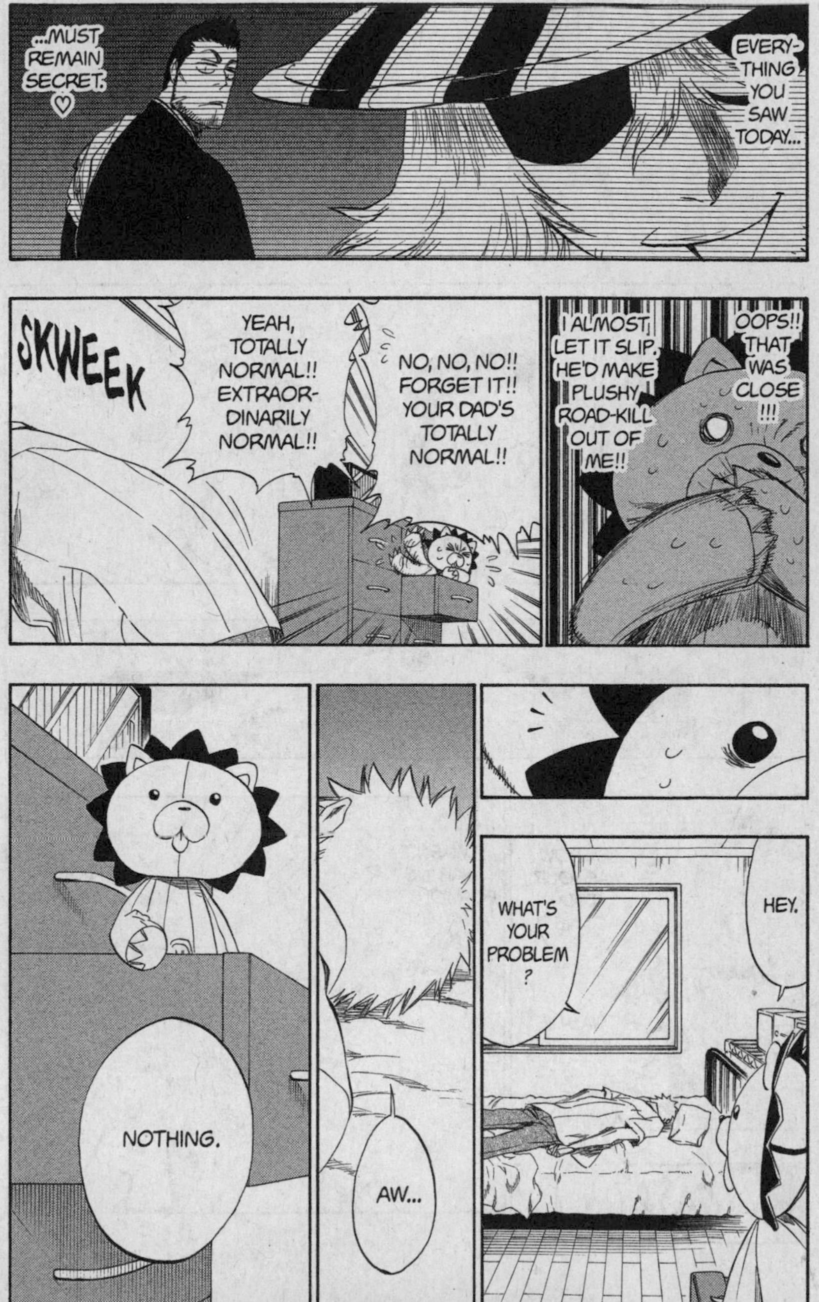
EVERYTHING YOU SAW TODAY...
...MUST REMAIN SECRET. ♡
OOPS!! THAT WAS CLOSE!!!
I ALMOST LET IT SLIP. HE'D MAKE PLUSHY ROAD-KILL OUT OF ME!!
NO, NO, NO!! FORGET IT!! YOUR DAD'S TOTALLY NORMAL!!
YEAH, TOTALLY NORMAL!! EXTRAORDINARILY NORMAL!!
SKWEEK
HEY.
WHAT'S YOUR PROBLEM?
AW...
NOTHING.

READ THIS WAY

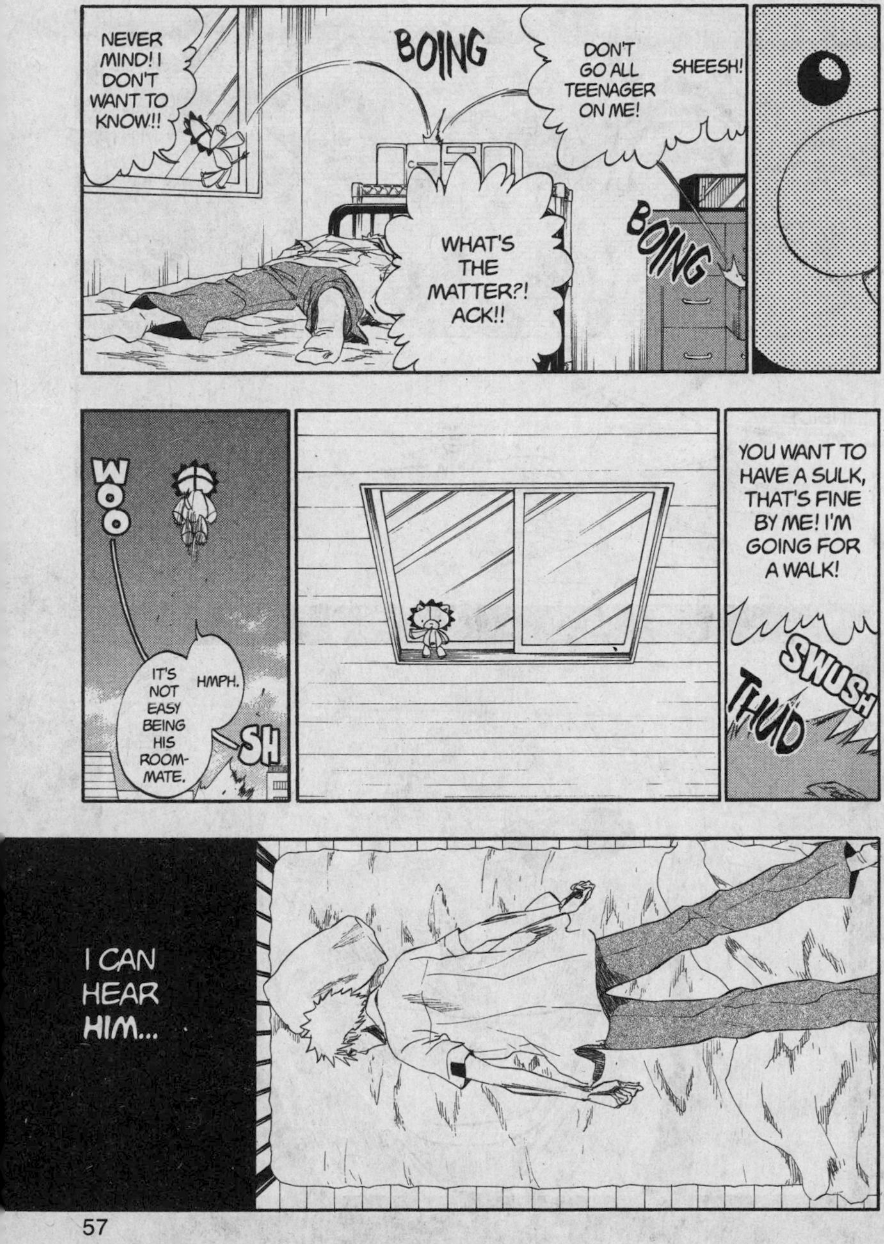
SHEESH!
DON'T GO ALL TEENAGER ON ME!
BOING
NEVER MIND! I DON'T WANT TO KNOW!!
BOING
WHAT'S THE MATTER?! ACK!!
YOU WANT TO HAVE A SULK, THAT'S FINE BY ME! I'M GOING FOR A WALK!
SWUSH
THUD
WOO
HMPH.
IT'S NOT EASY BEING HIS ROOM-MATE.
SH
I CAN HEAR HIM...

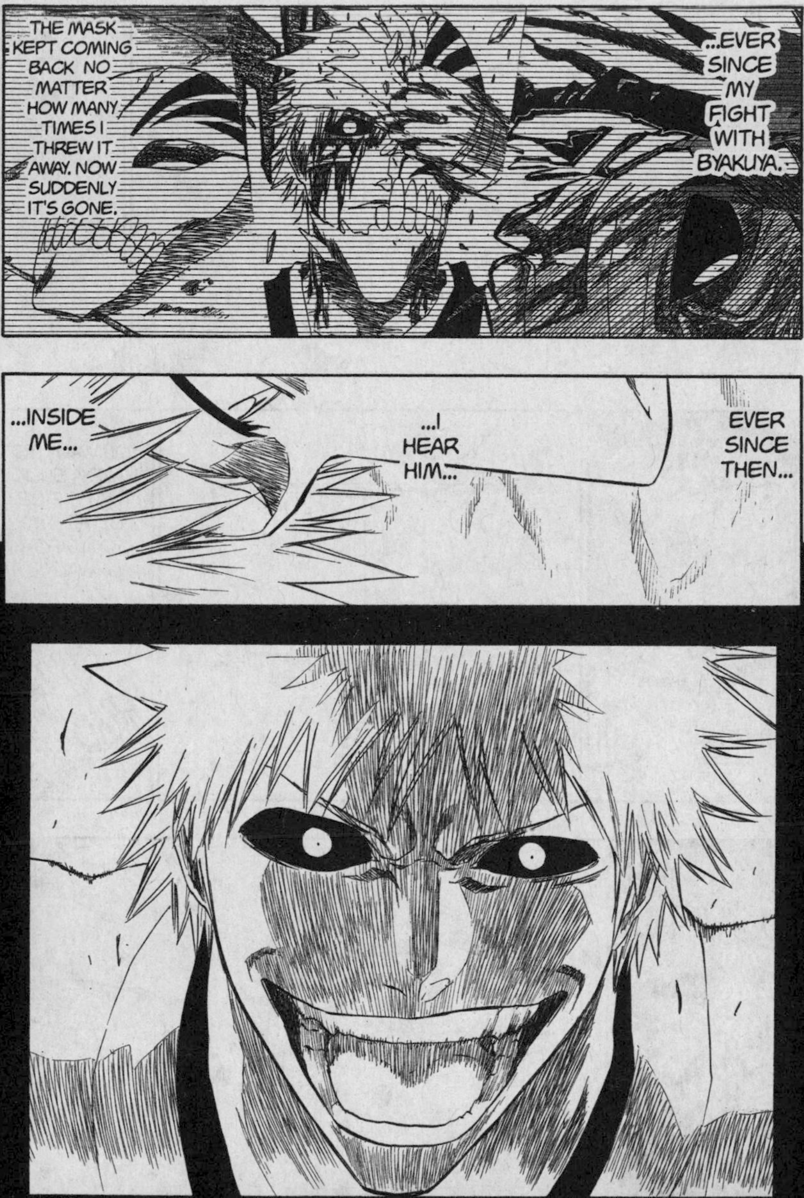

...EVER SINCE MY FIGHT WITH BYAKUYA.
THE MASK KEPT COMING BACK NO MATTER HOW MANY TIMES I THREW IT AWAY. NOW SUDDENLY IT'S GONE.
EVER SINCE THEN...
...I HEAR HIM...
...INSIDE ME...

READ THIS WAY

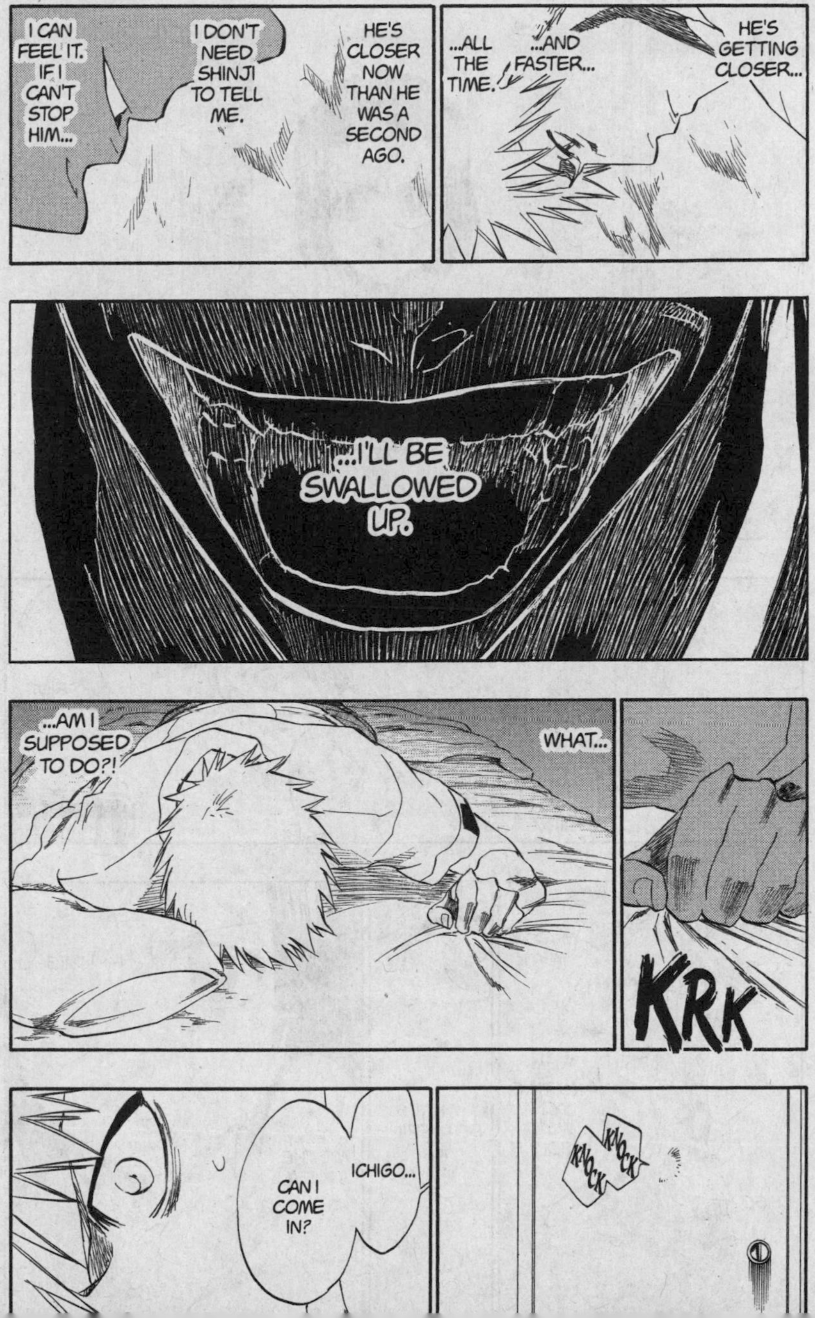
HE'S GETTING CLOSER...
...AND FASTER...
...ALL THE TIME.
HE'S CLOSER NOW THAN HE WAS A SECOND AGO.
I DON'T NEED SHINJI TO TELL ME.
I CAN FEEL IT. IF I CAN'T STOP HIM...
...I'LL BE SWALLOWED UP.
KRK
WHAT...
...AM I SUPPOSED TO DO?!
KNOCK KNOCK
ICHIGO...
CAN I COME IN?

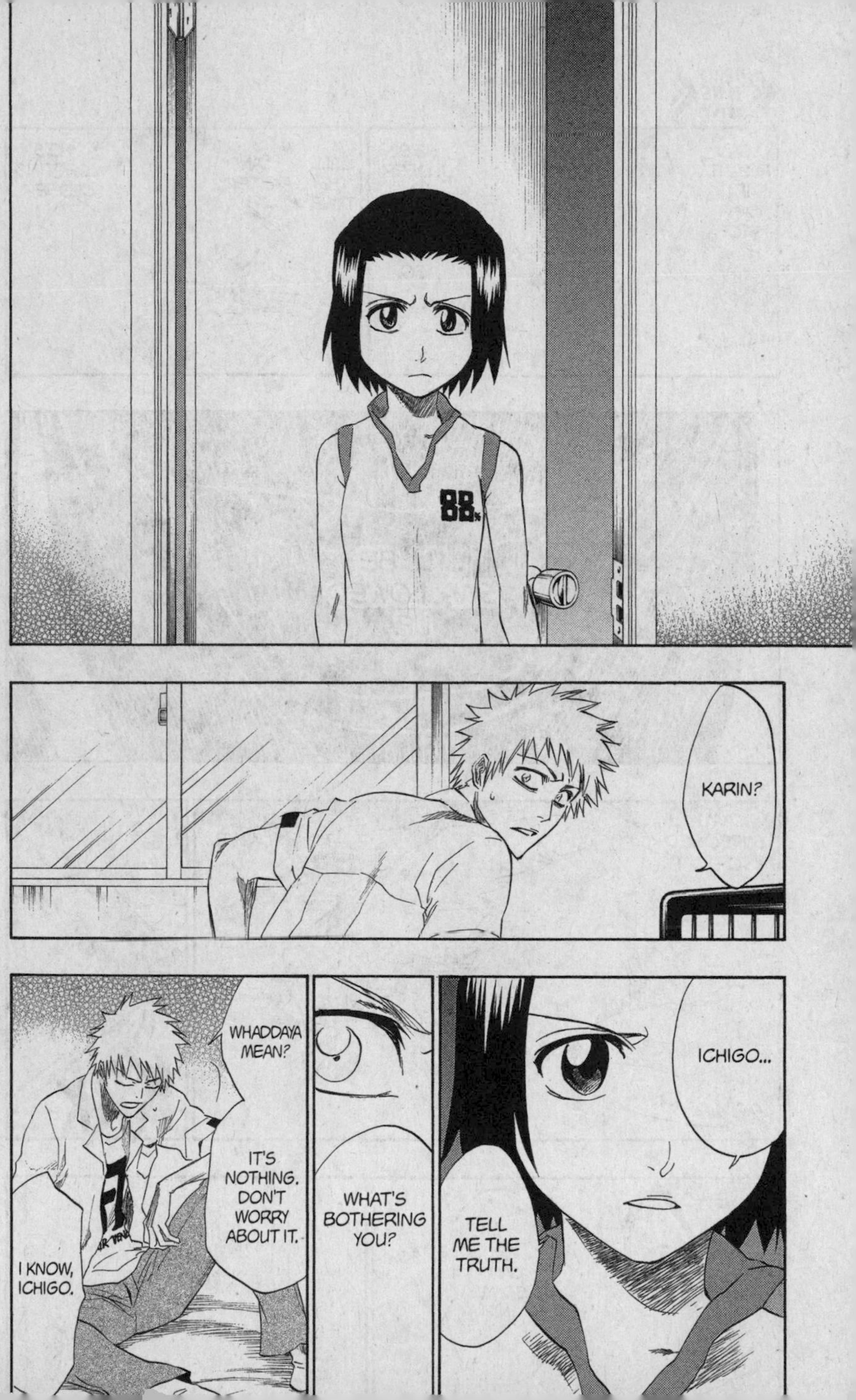
KARIN?
ICHIGO...
TELL ME THE TRUTH.
WHAT'S BOTHERING YOU?
WHADDAYA MEAN?
IT'S NOTHING. DON'T WORRY ABOUT IT.
I KNOW, ICHIGO.

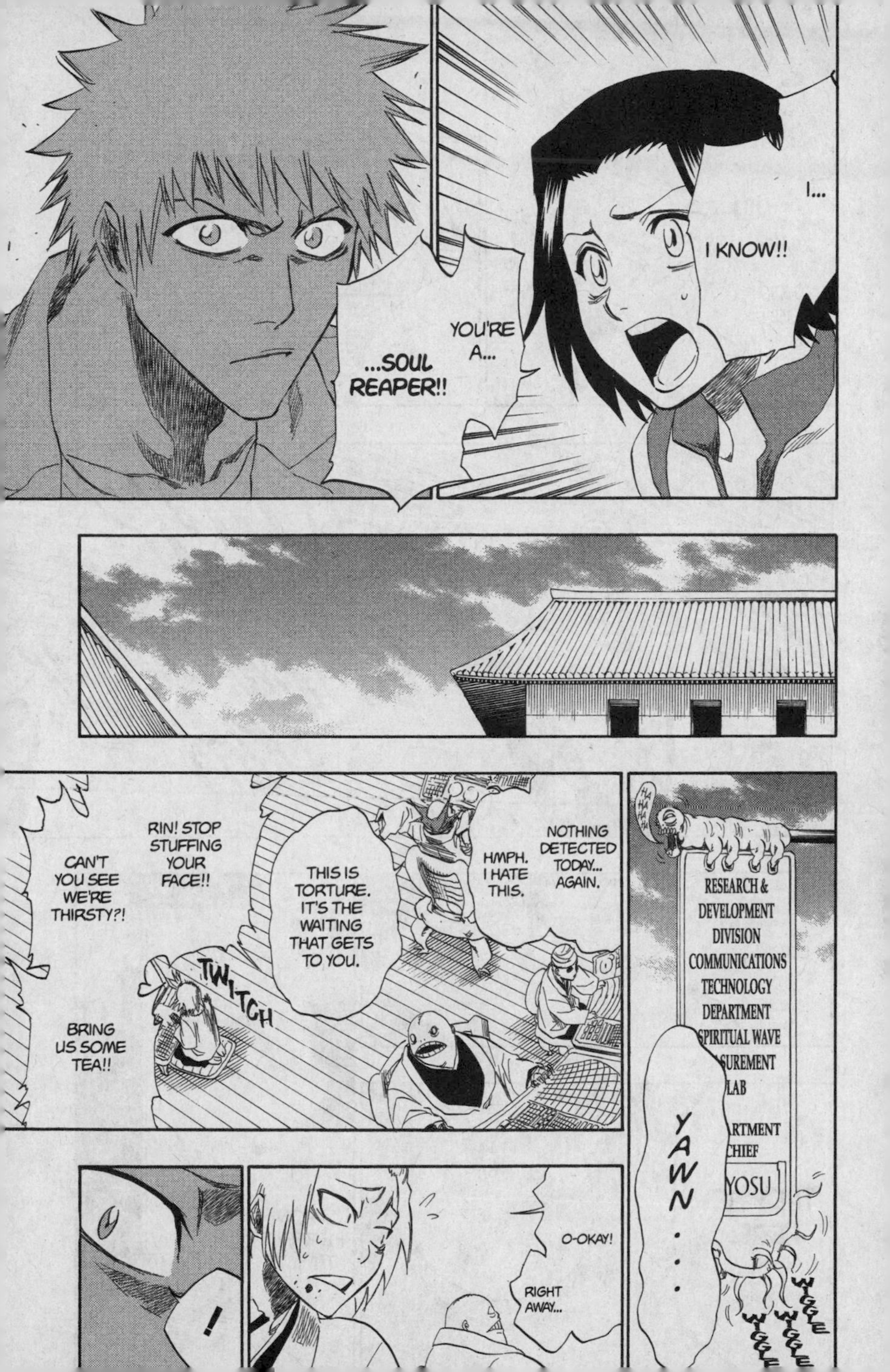

I...
I KNOW!!
YOU'RE A... ...SOUL REAPER!!
HA HA HA HA
RESEARCH & DEVELOPMENT DIVISION COMMUNICATIONS TECHNOLOGY DEPARTMENT SPIRITUAL WAVE SUREMENT LAB ARTMENT CHIEF YOSU
YAWN...
WIGGLE WIGGLE WIGGLE WIGGLE
NOTHING DETECTED TODAY... AGAIN.
HMPH. I HATE THIS.
THIS IS TORTURE. IT'S THE WAITING THAT GETS TO YOU.
RIN! STOP STUFFING YOUR FACE!!
CAN'T YOU SEE WE'RE THIRSTY?!
TWITCH
BRING US SOME TEA!!
O-OKAY!
RIGHT AWAY...
!

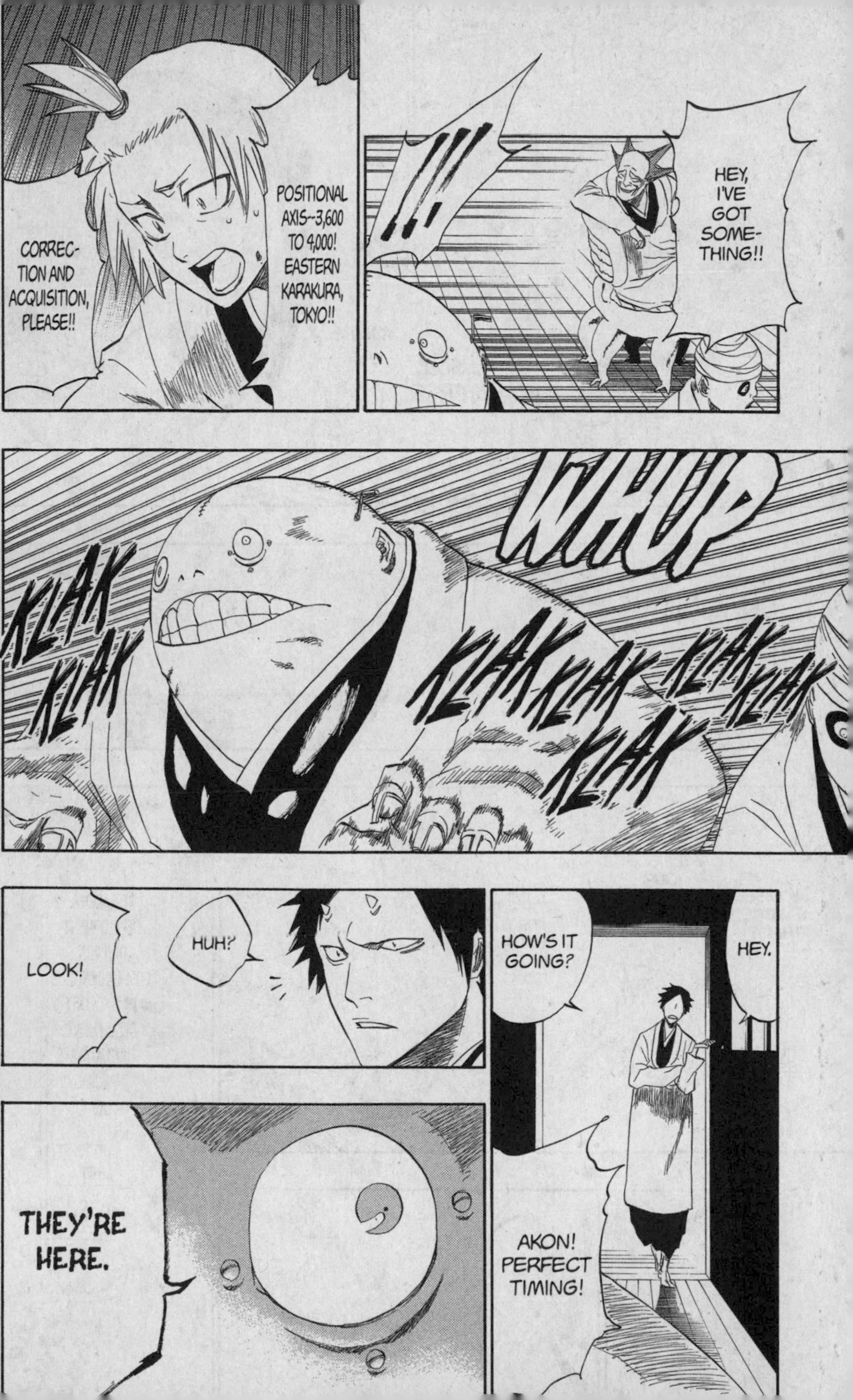

HEY, I'VE GOT SOME-THING!!
!!
POSITIONAL AXIS--3,600 TO 4,000! EASTERN KARAKURA, TOKYO!!
CORREC-TION AND ACQUISITION, PLEASE!!
WHUP
KLAK KLAK KLAK KLAK
KLAK KLAK KLAK KLAK
KLAK KLAK
HEY.
HOW'S IT GOING?
AKON! PERFECT TIMING!
HUH?
LOOK!
THEY'RE HERE.

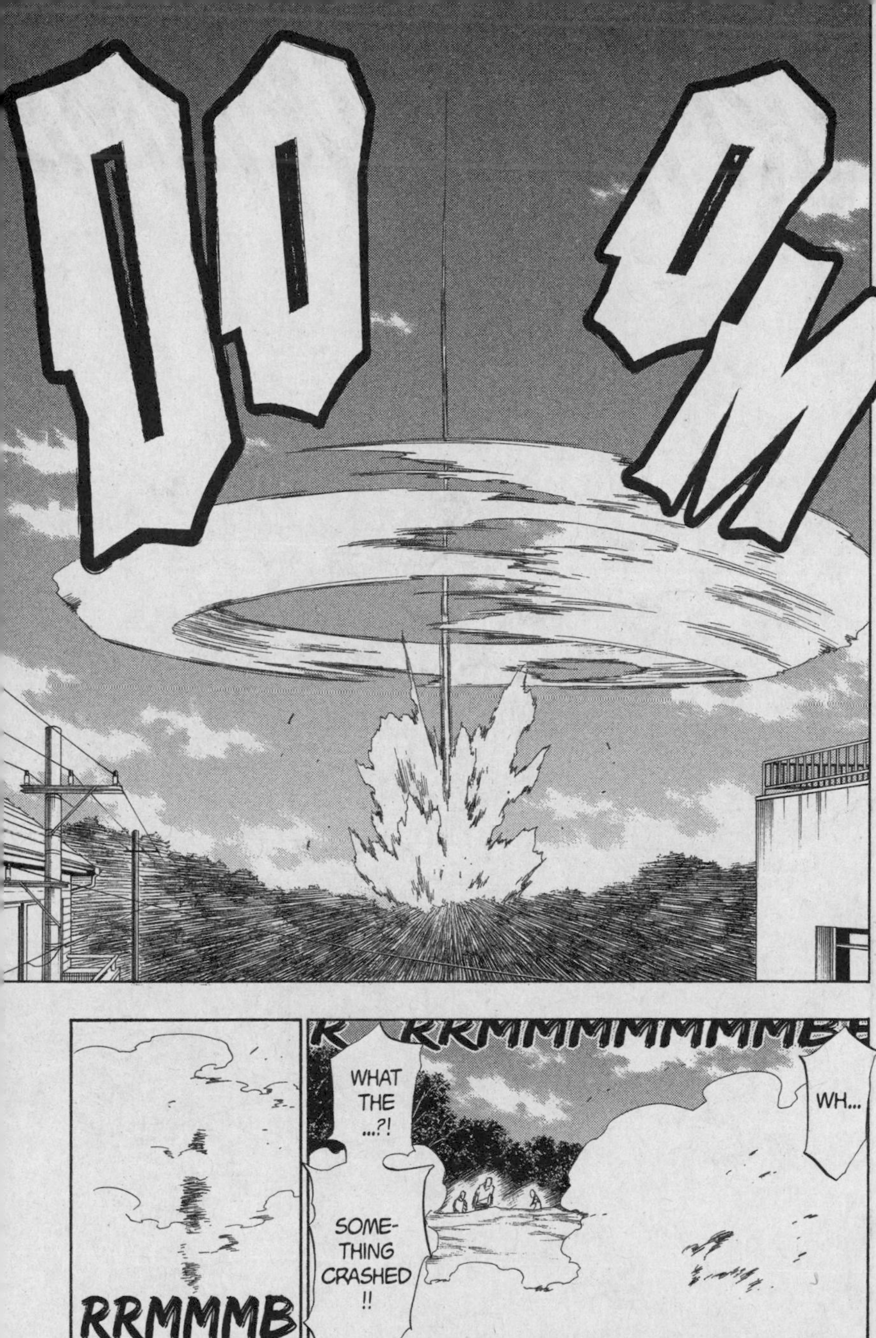
DOOM
R RRMMMMMMMMMB
WH...
WHAT THE ...?!
SOME-THING CRASHED !!
RRMMMB

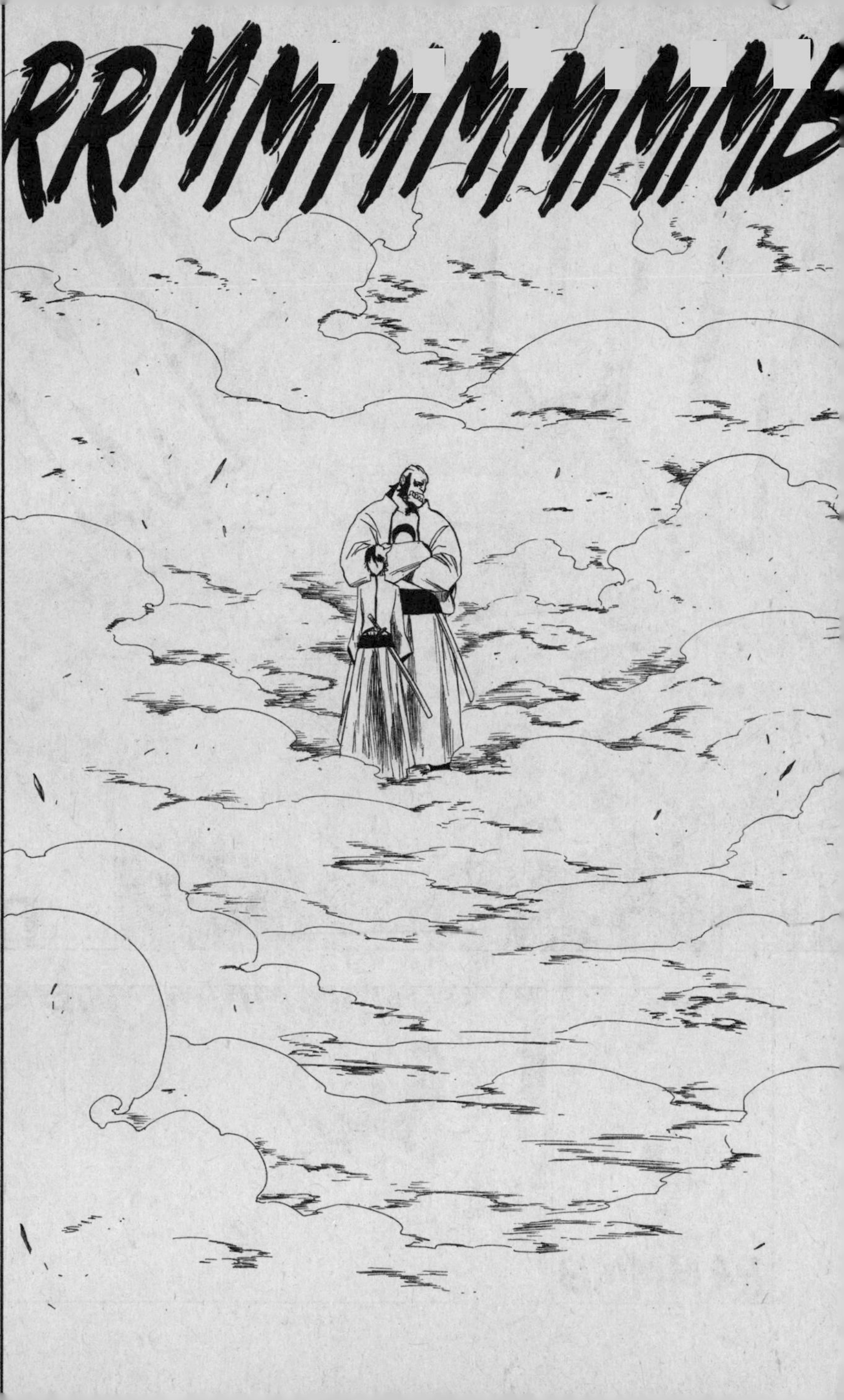
RRMMMMMMMB

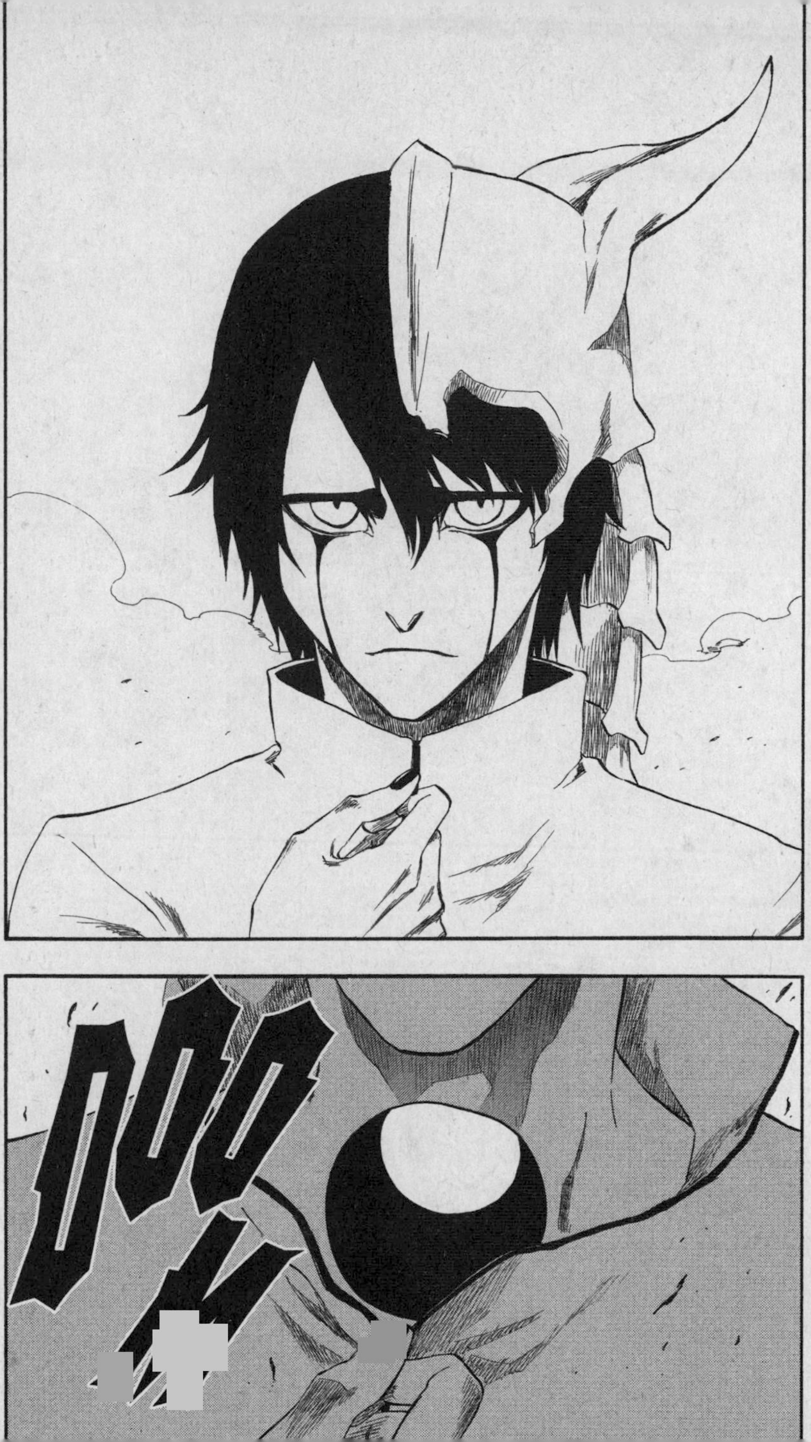

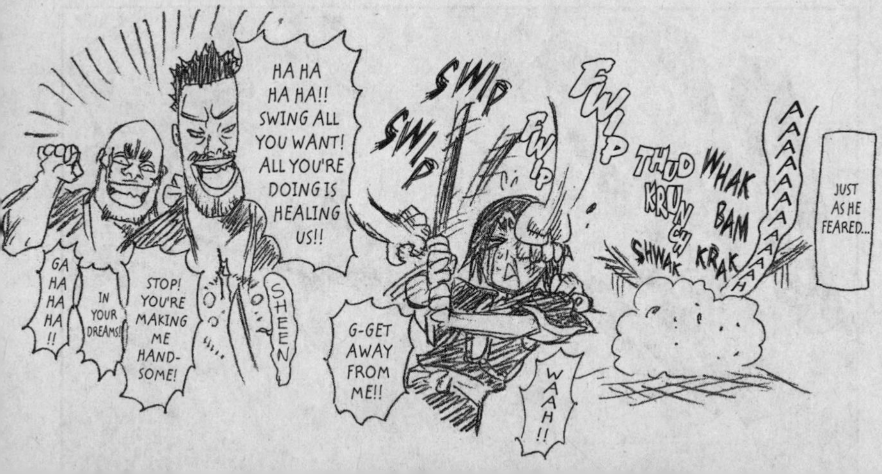
JUST AS HE FEARED...
AAAAAAAAAAAH
WHAK
BAM
KRAK
THUD
KRUNCH
SHWAK
FWIP
FWIP
SWIP
SWIP
WAAH!!
G-GET AWAY FROM ME!!
HA HA HA HA!! SWING ALL YOU WANT! ALL YOU'RE DOING IS HEALING US!!
SHEEN
STOP! YOU'RE MAKING ME HAND-SOME!
IN YOUR DREAMS!
GA HA HA HA!!

191. Conquistadores 2 (Screaming Symphony)

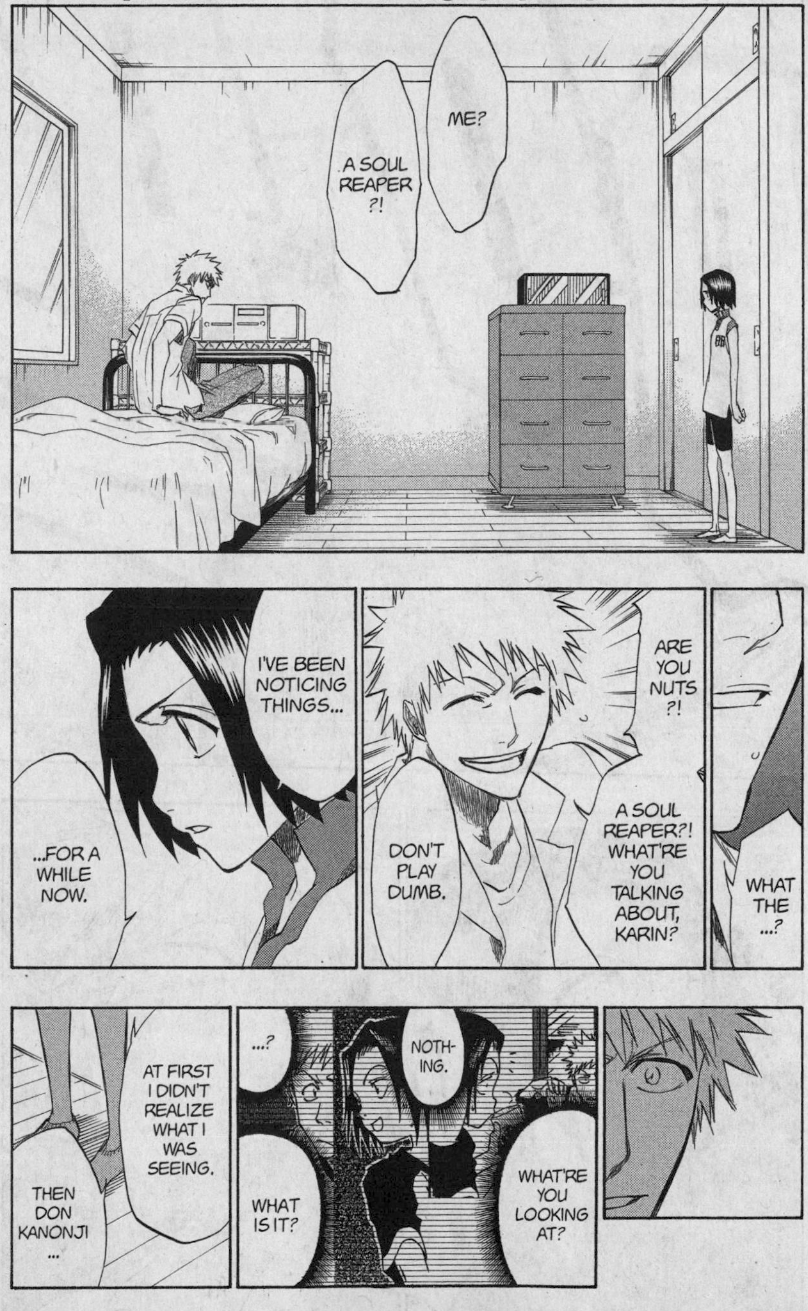
ME?
A SOUL REAPER ?!
WHAT THE ...?
ARE YOU NUTS ?!
A SOUL REAPER?! WHAT'RE YOU TALKING ABOUT, KARIN?
DON'T PLAY DUMB.
I'VE BEEN NOTICING THINGS...
...FOR A WHILE NOW.
NOTH-ING.
...?
WHAT'RE YOU LOOKING AT?
WHAT IS IT?
AT FIRST I DIDN'T REALIZE WHAT I WAS SEEING.
THEN DON KANONJI ...

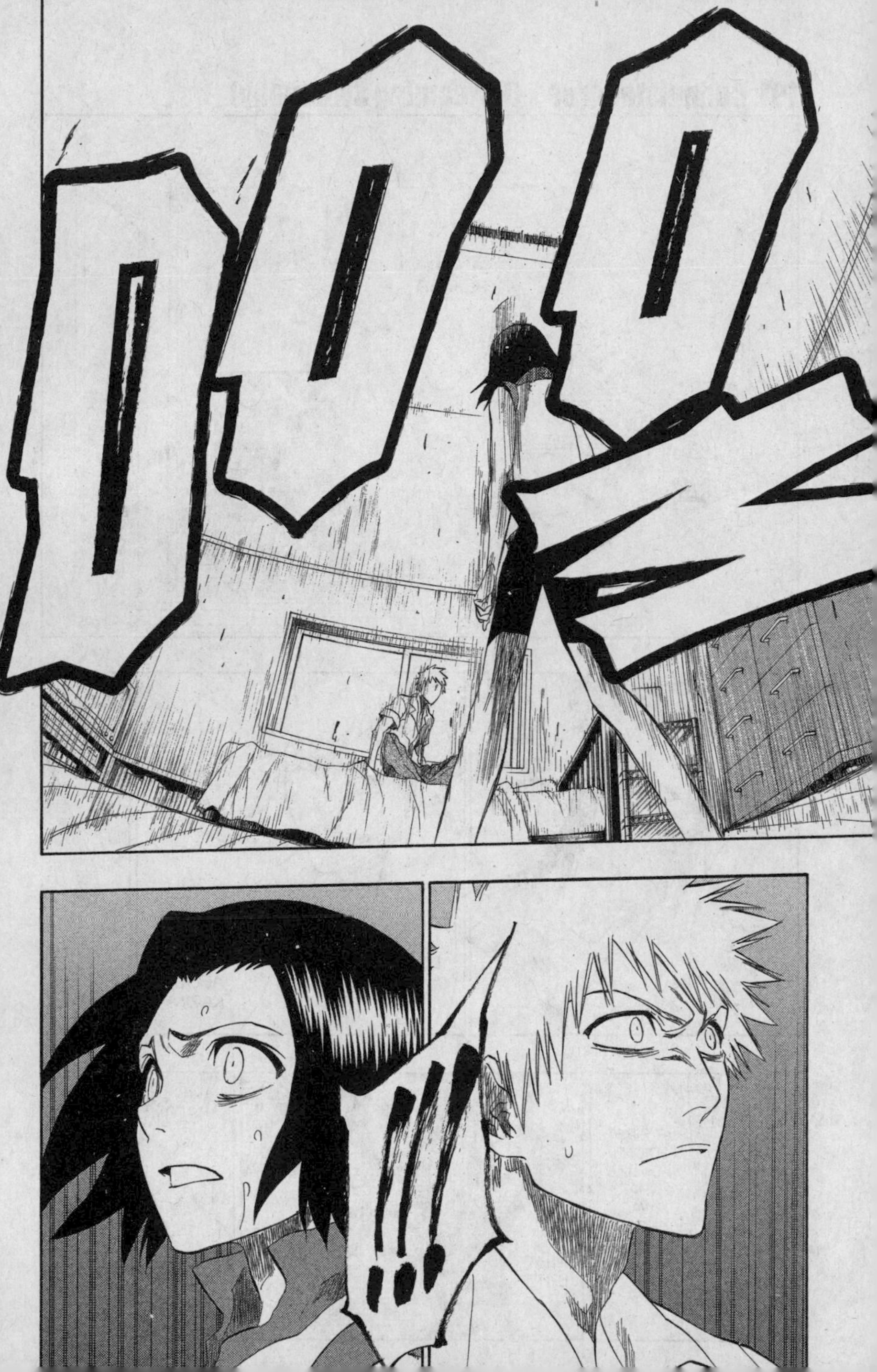
!!!

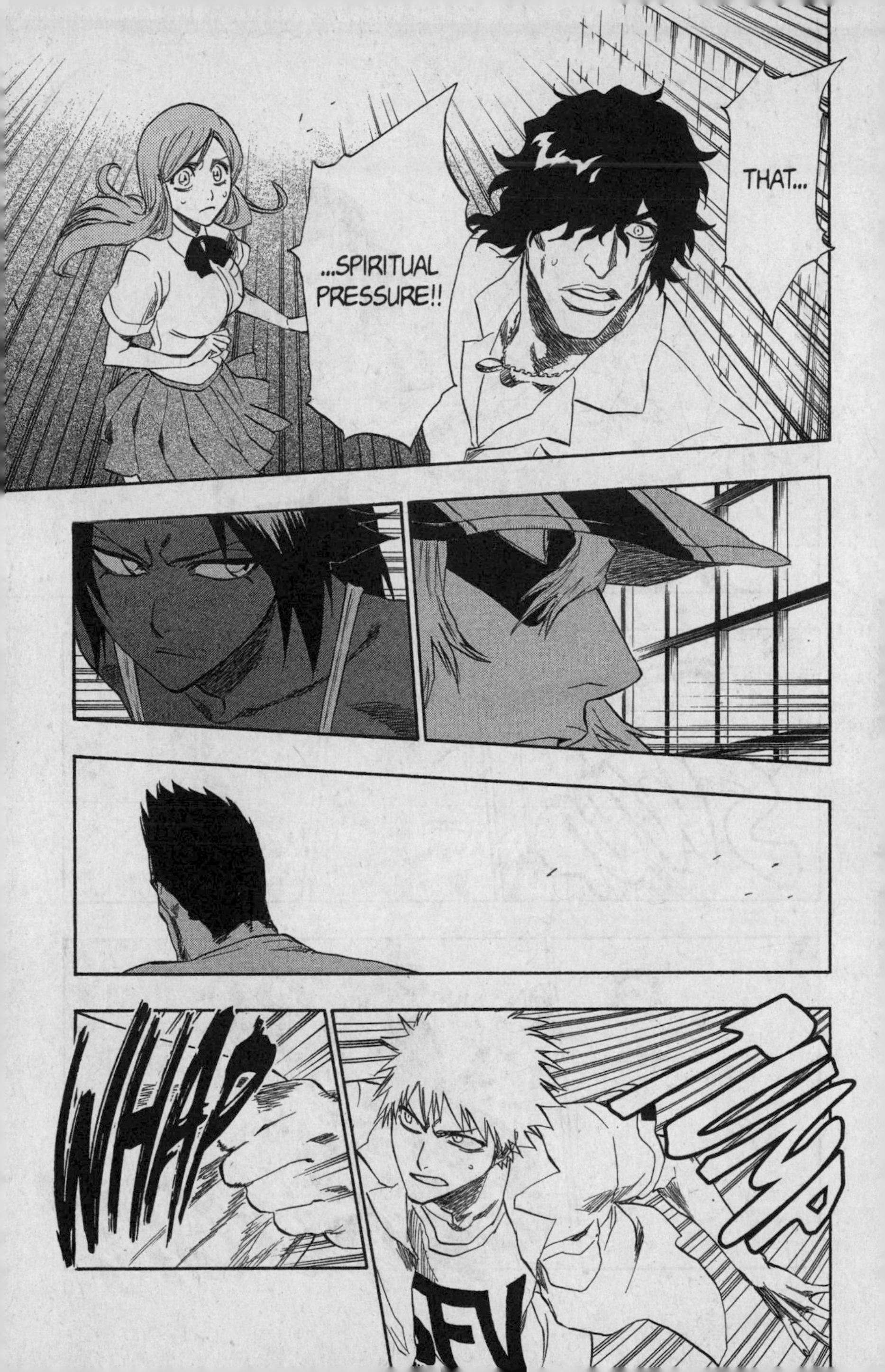
THAT...
...SPIRITUAL PRESSURE!!
WUMP
WHAP

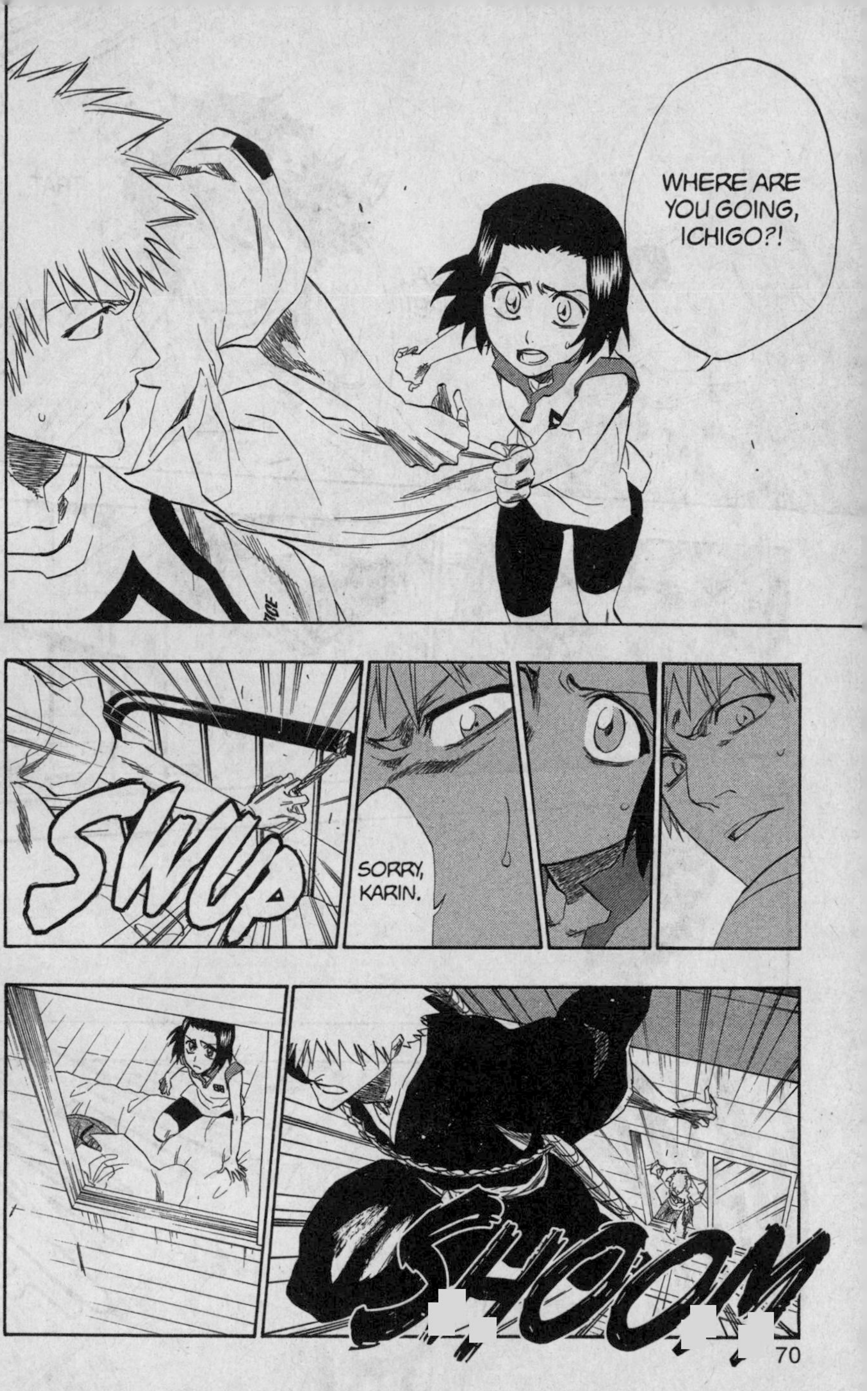
WHERE ARE YOU GOING, ICHIGO?!
SORRY, KARIN.
SWUP
SHOOM

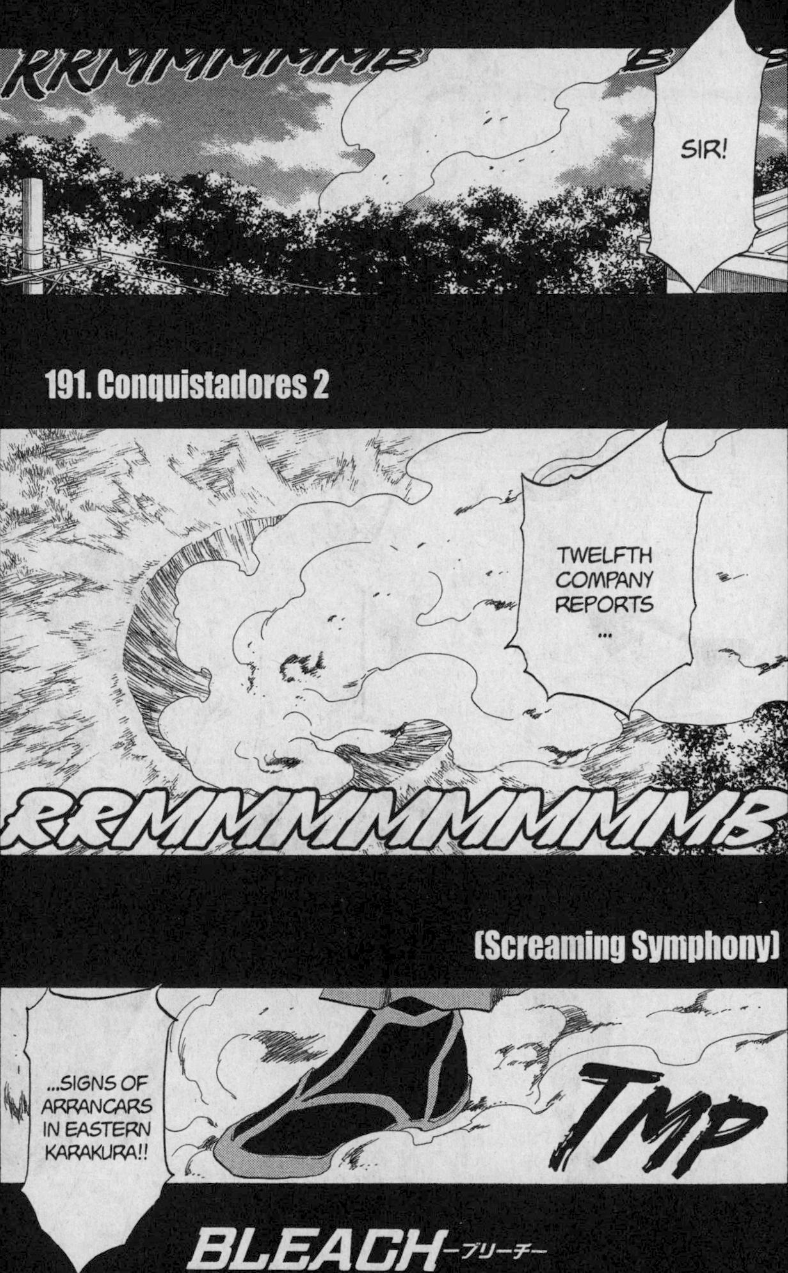
SIR!
RRMMMMMMB
191. Conquistadores 2
TWELFTH COMPANY REPORTS ...
RRMMMMMMMMMMB
(Screaming Symphony)
TMP
...SIGNS OF ARRANCARS IN EASTERN KARAKURA!!
BLEACH ーブリーチー

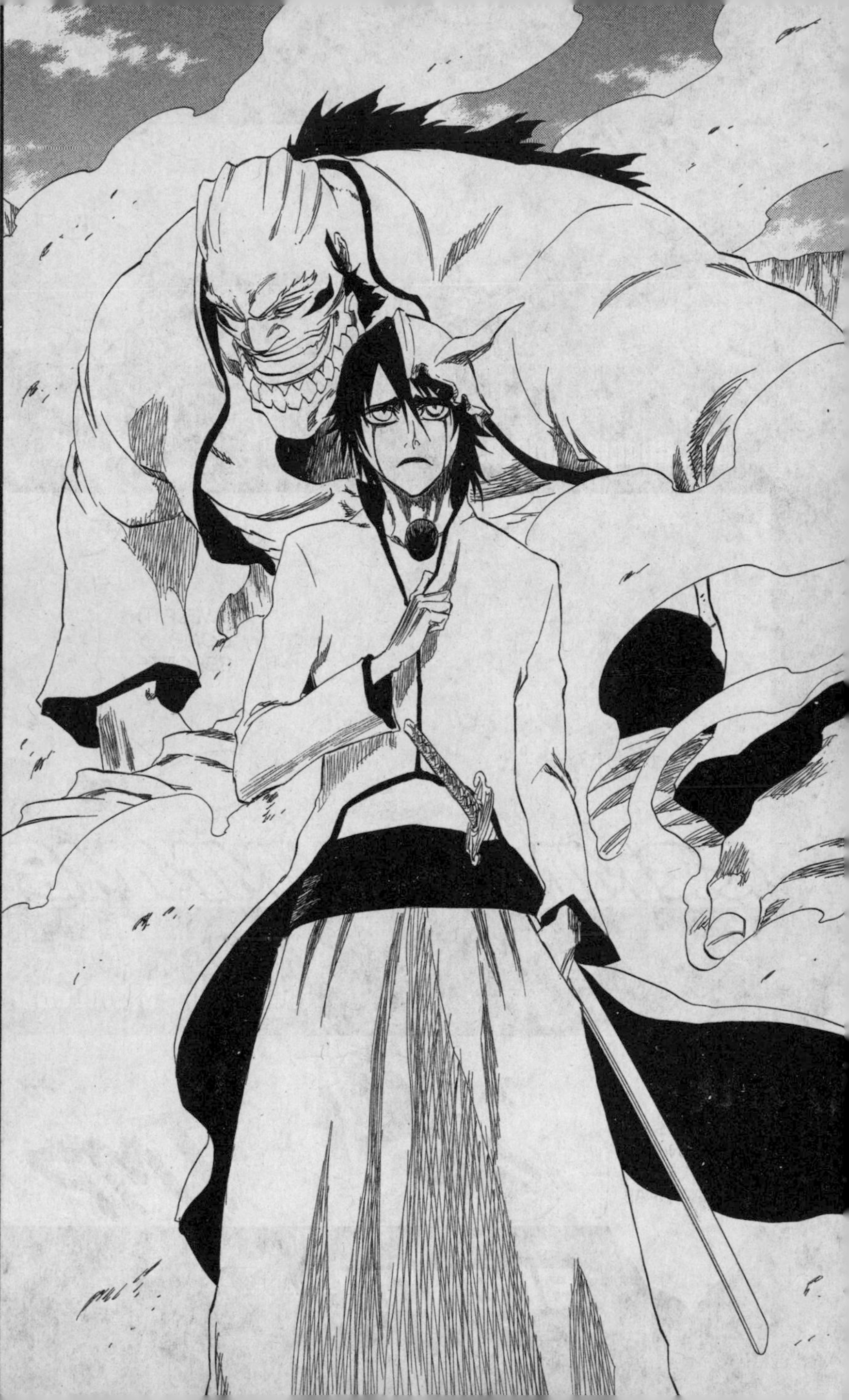

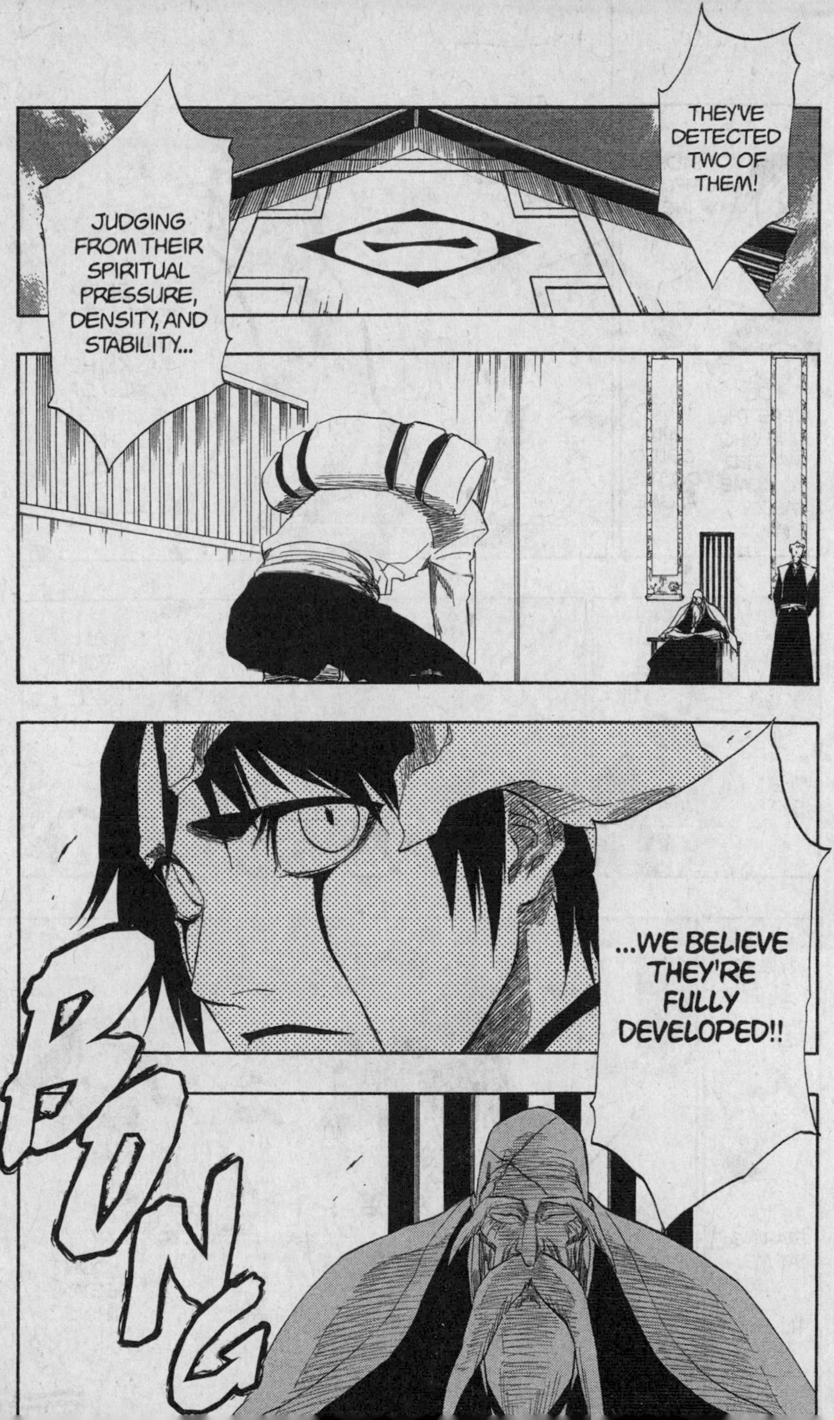
THEY'VE DETECTED TWO OF THEM!
JUDGING FROM THEIR SPIRITUAL PRESSURE, DENSITY, AND STABILITY...
...WE BELIEVE THEY'RE FULLY DEVELOPED!!
BONG

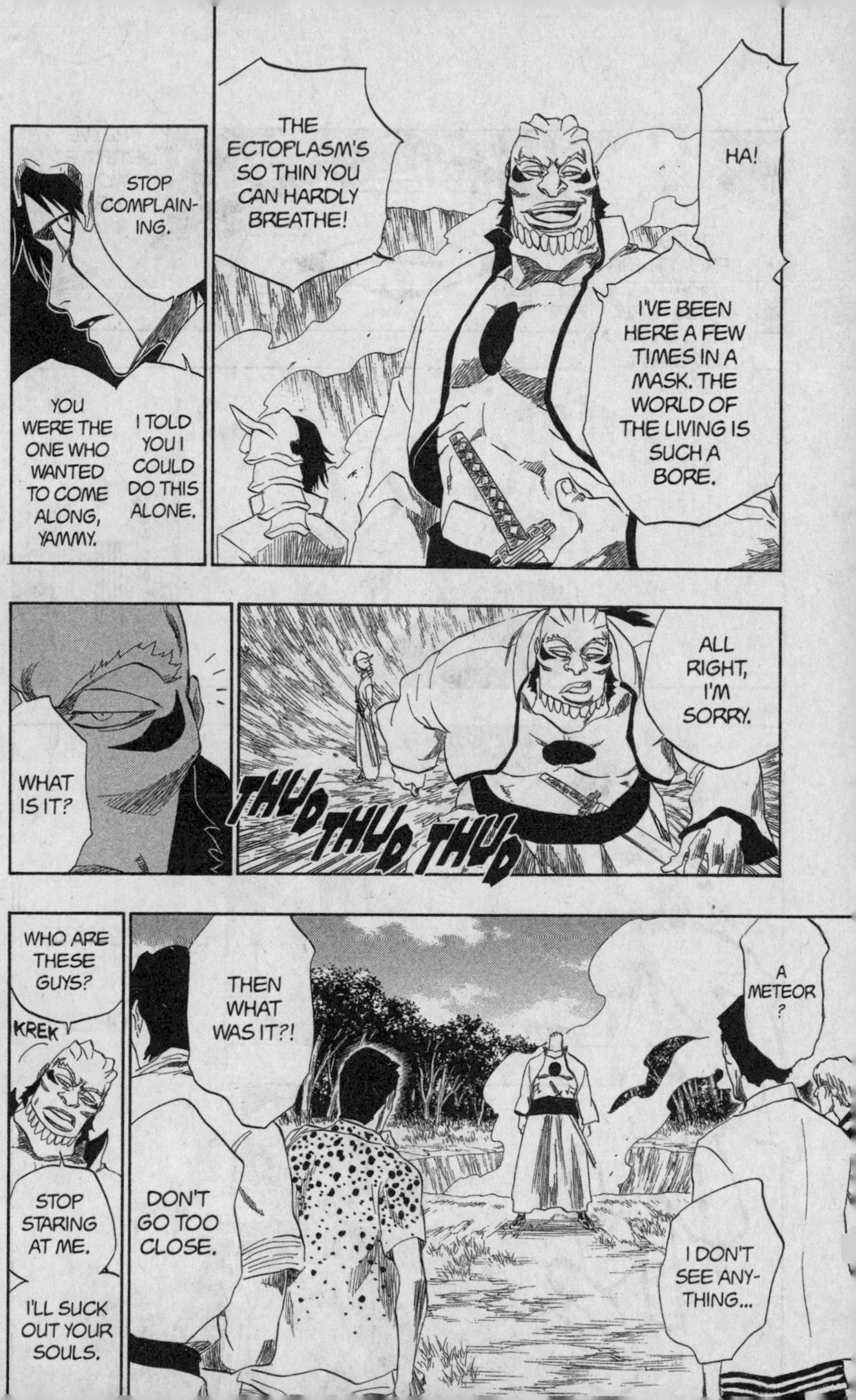
HA!
I'VE BEEN HERE A FEW TIMES IN A MASK. THE WORLD OF THE LIVING IS SUCH A BORE.
THE ECTOPLASM'S SO THIN YOU CAN HARDLY BREATHE!
STOP COMPLAIN-ING.
I TOLD YOU I COULD DO THIS ALONE.
YOU WERE THE ONE WHO WANTED TO COME ALONG, YAMMY.
ALL RIGHT, I'M SORRY.
THUD THUD THUD
WHAT IS IT?
A METEOR?
I DON'T SEE ANY-THING...
THEN WHAT WAS IT?!
DON'T GO TOO CLOSE.
WHO ARE THESE GUYS?
KREK
STOP STARING AT ME.
I'LL SUCK OUT YOUR SOULS.

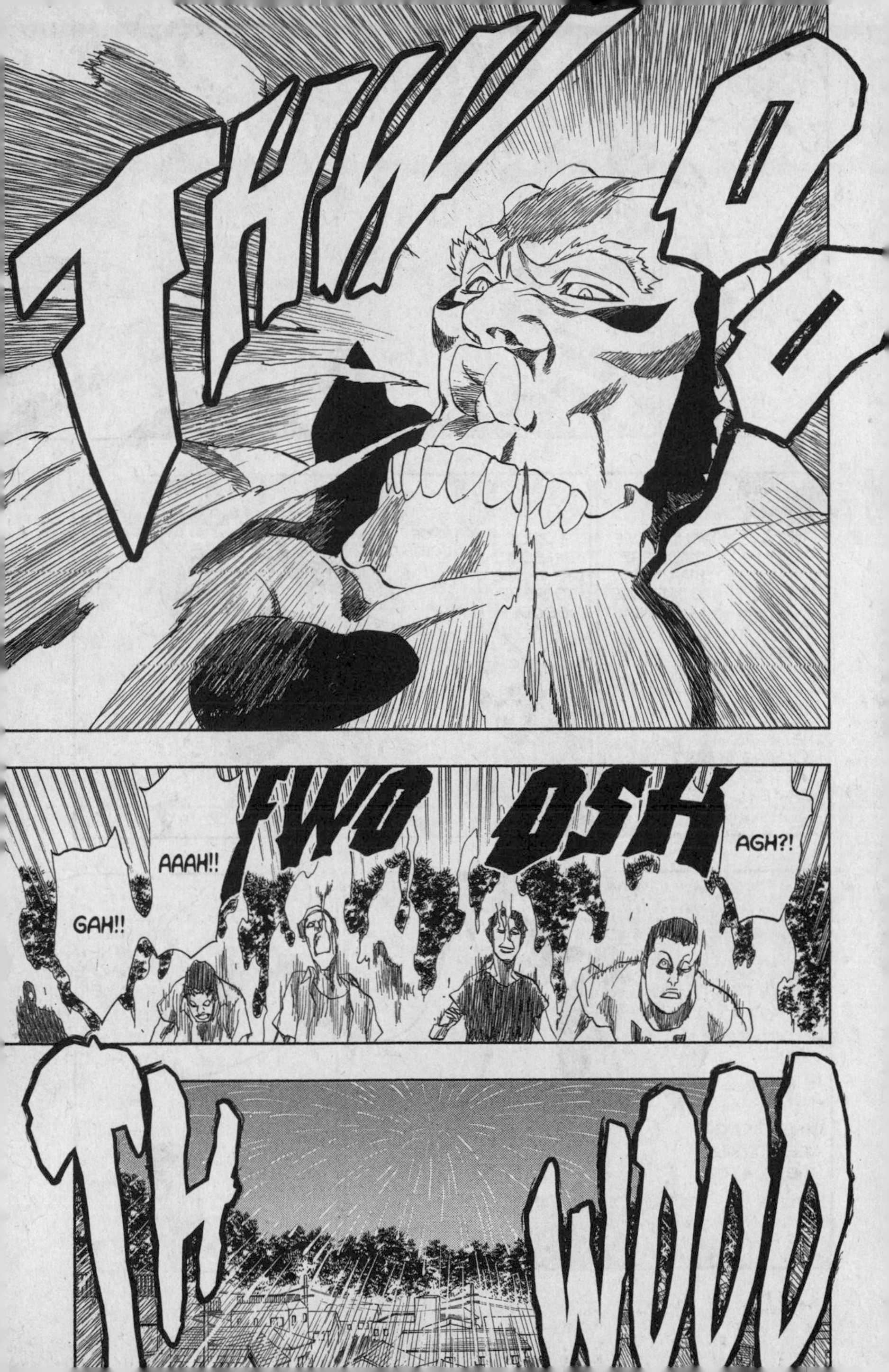
THWOO
FWO OSH
AGH?!
AAAH!!
GAH!!
THWOOD

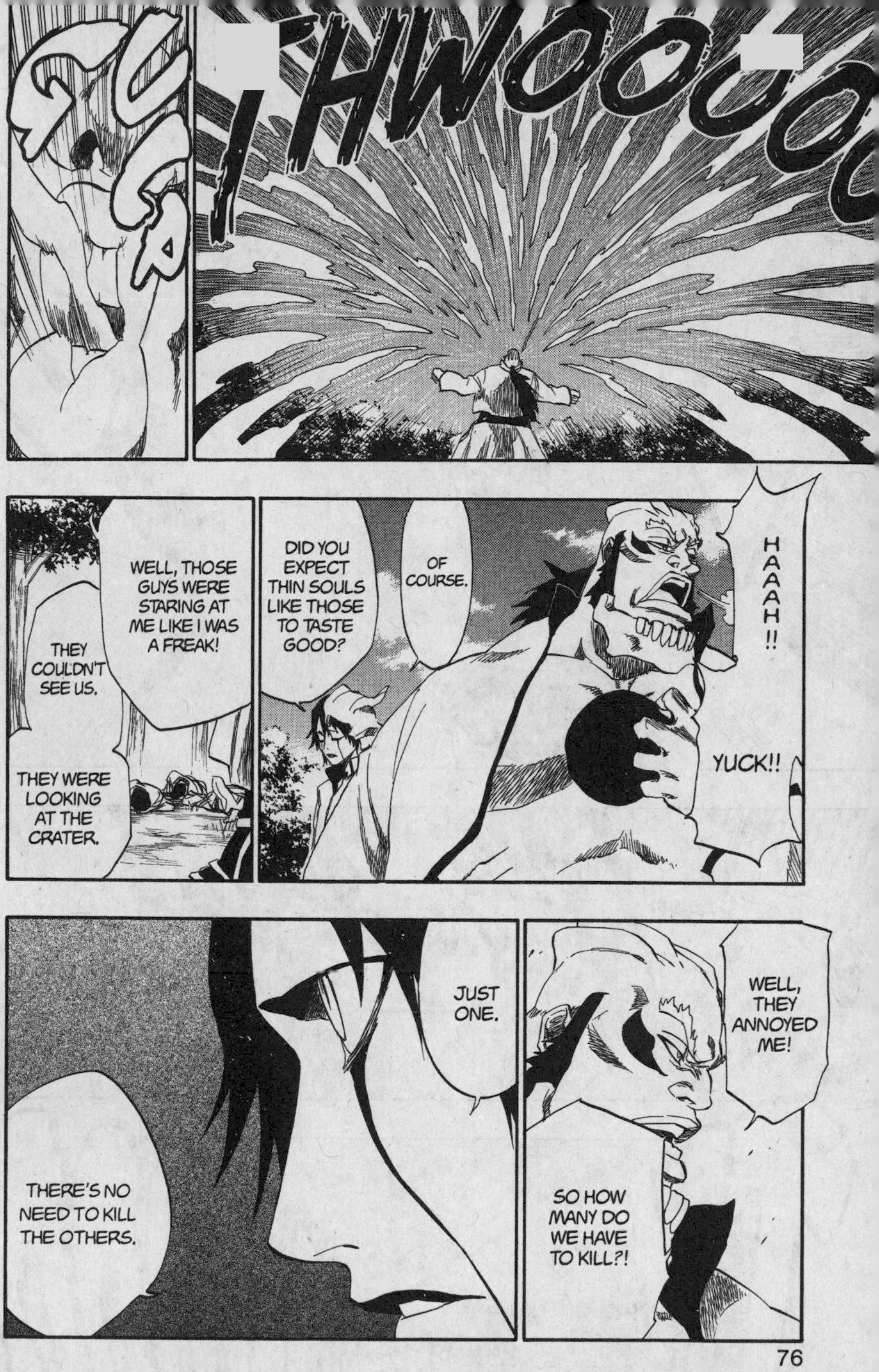
HWOOOO
GULP
HAAAAH!!
YUCK!!
OF COURSE.
DID YOU EXPECT THIN SOULS LIKE THOSE TO TASTE GOOD?
WELL, THOSE GUYS WERE STARING AT ME LIKE I WAS A FREAK!
THEY COULDN'T SEE US.
THEY WERE LOOKING AT THE CRATER.
WELL, THEY ANNOYED ME!
SO HOW MANY DO WE HAVE TO KILL?!
JUST ONE.
THERE'S NO NEED TO KILL THE OTHERS.

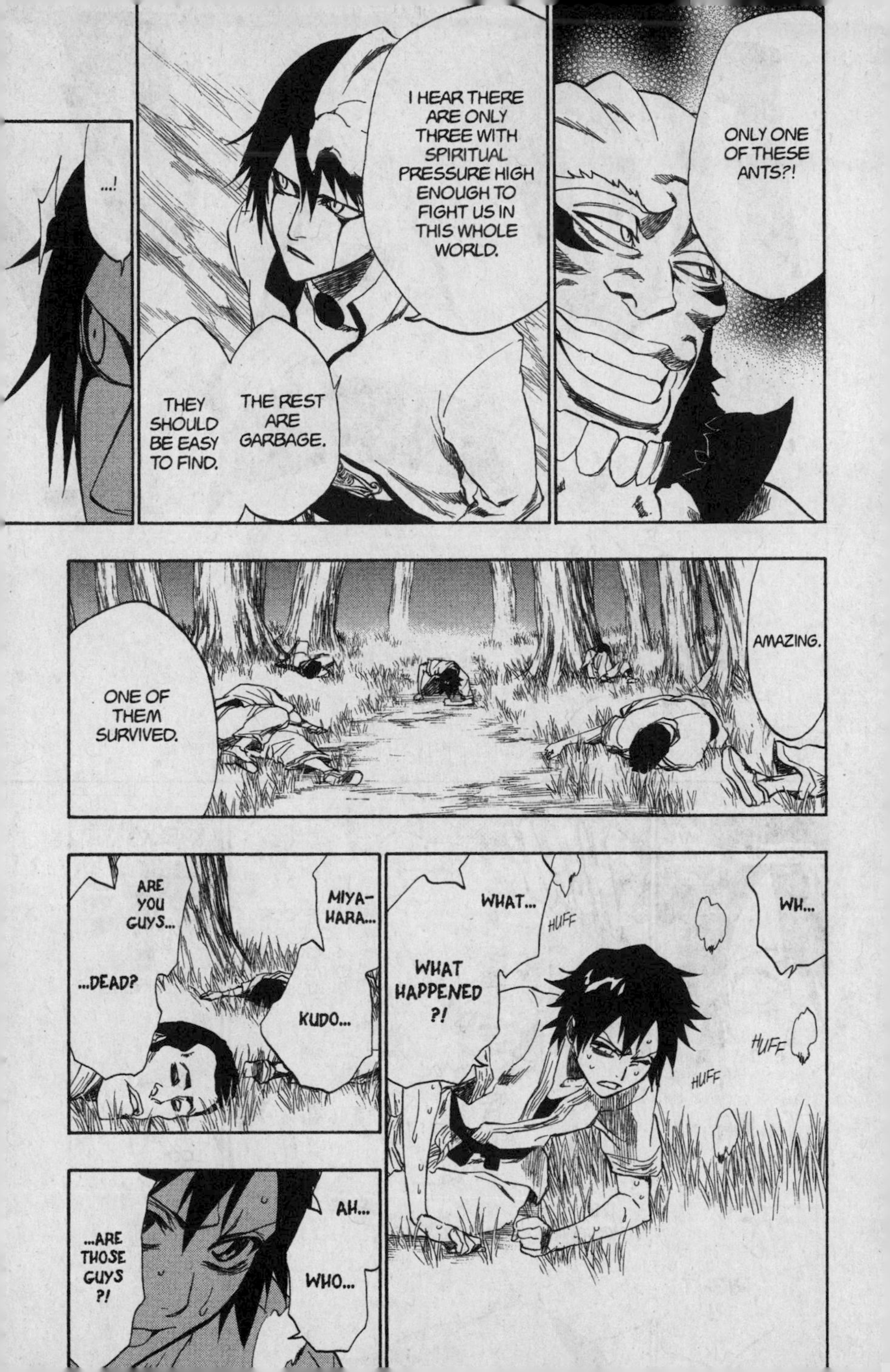
ONLY ONE OF THESE ANTS?!
I HEAR THERE ARE ONLY THREE WITH SPIRITUAL PRESSURE HIGH ENOUGH TO FIGHT US IN THIS WHOLE WORLD.
THE REST ARE GARBAGE.
THEY SHOULD BE EASY TO FIND.
...!
AMAZING.
ONE OF THEM SURVIVED.
WH...
HUFF
HUFF
HUFF
WHAT...
WHAT HAPPENED ?!
MIYA-HARA...
ARE YOU GUYS...
KUDO...
...DEAD?
AH...
WHO...
...ARE THOSE GUYS ?!

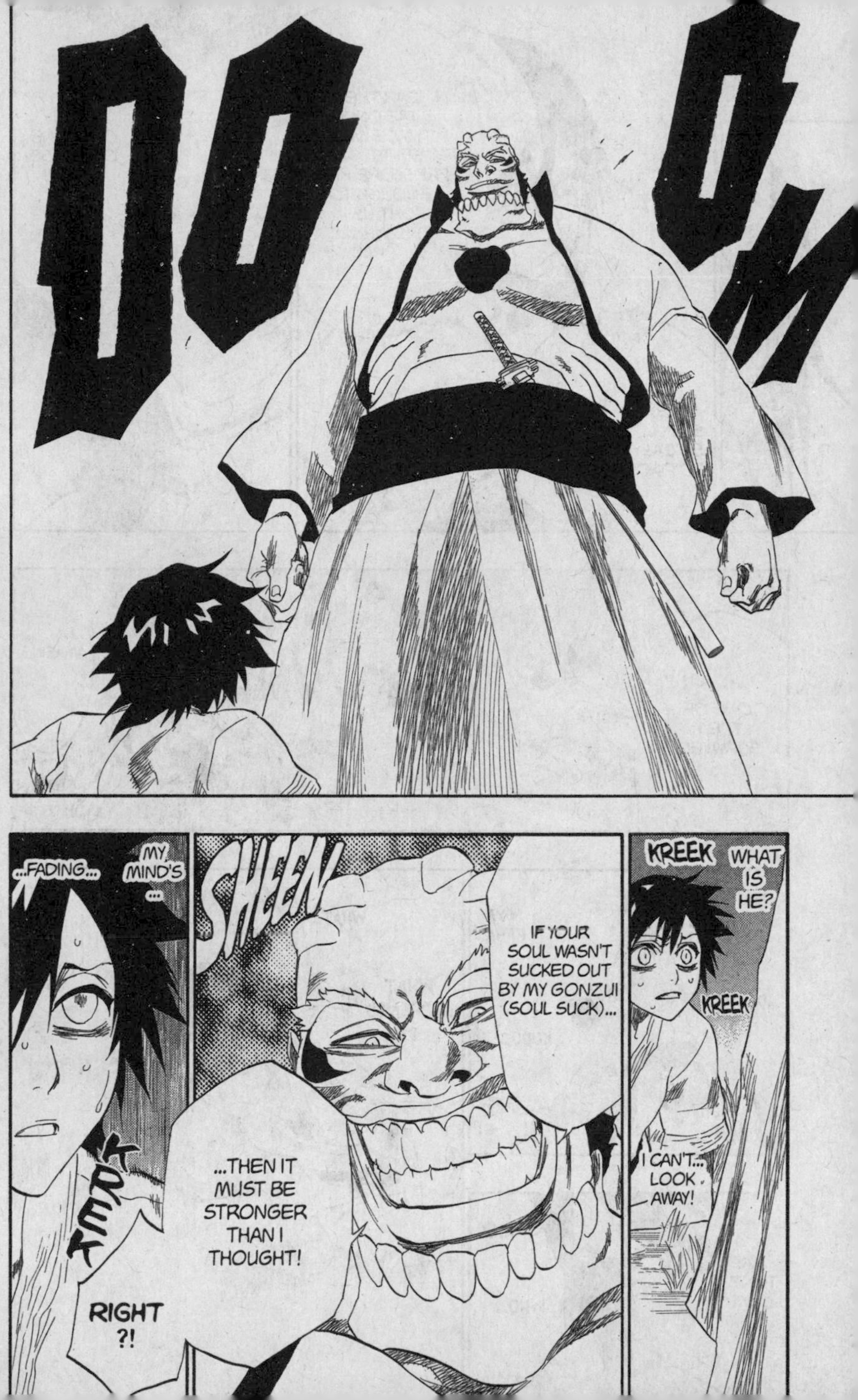
DOOM
KREEK
WHAT IS HE?
KREEK
I CAN'T... LOOK AWAY!
SHEEN
IF YOUR SOUL WASN'T SUCKED OUT BY MY GONZUI (SOUL SUCK)...
...THEN IT MUST BE STRONGER THAN I THOUGHT!
MY MIND'S...
...FADING...
KREEK
RIGHT?!

READ THIS WAY

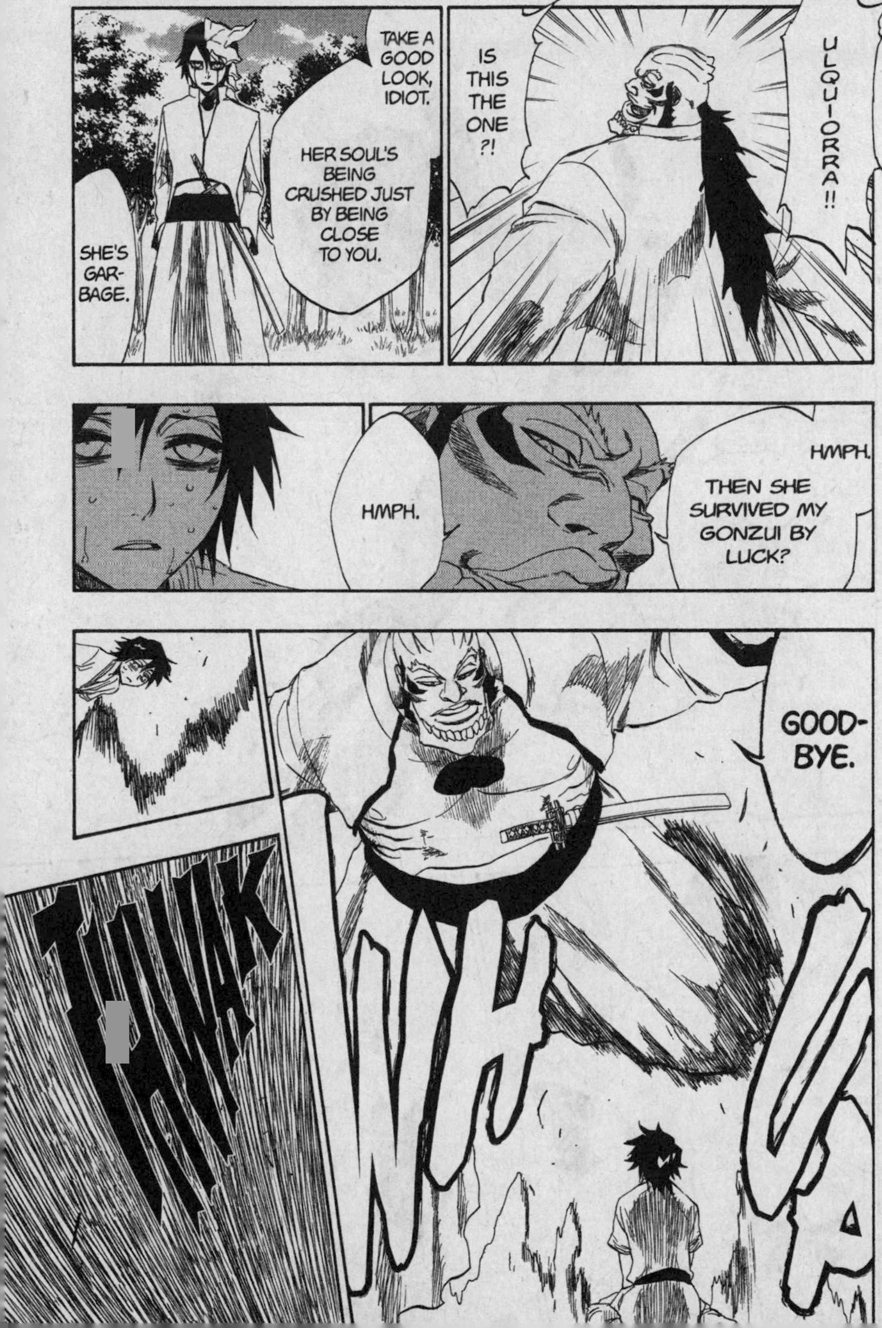
ULQUI-ORRA!!
IS THIS THE ONE?!
TAKE A GOOD LOOK, IDIOT.
HER SOUL'S BEING CRUSHED JUST BY BEING CLOSE TO YOU.
SHE'S GAR-BAGE.
HMPH.
THEN SHE SURVIVED MY GONZUI BY LUCK?
HMPH.
GOOD-BYE.
THWAK

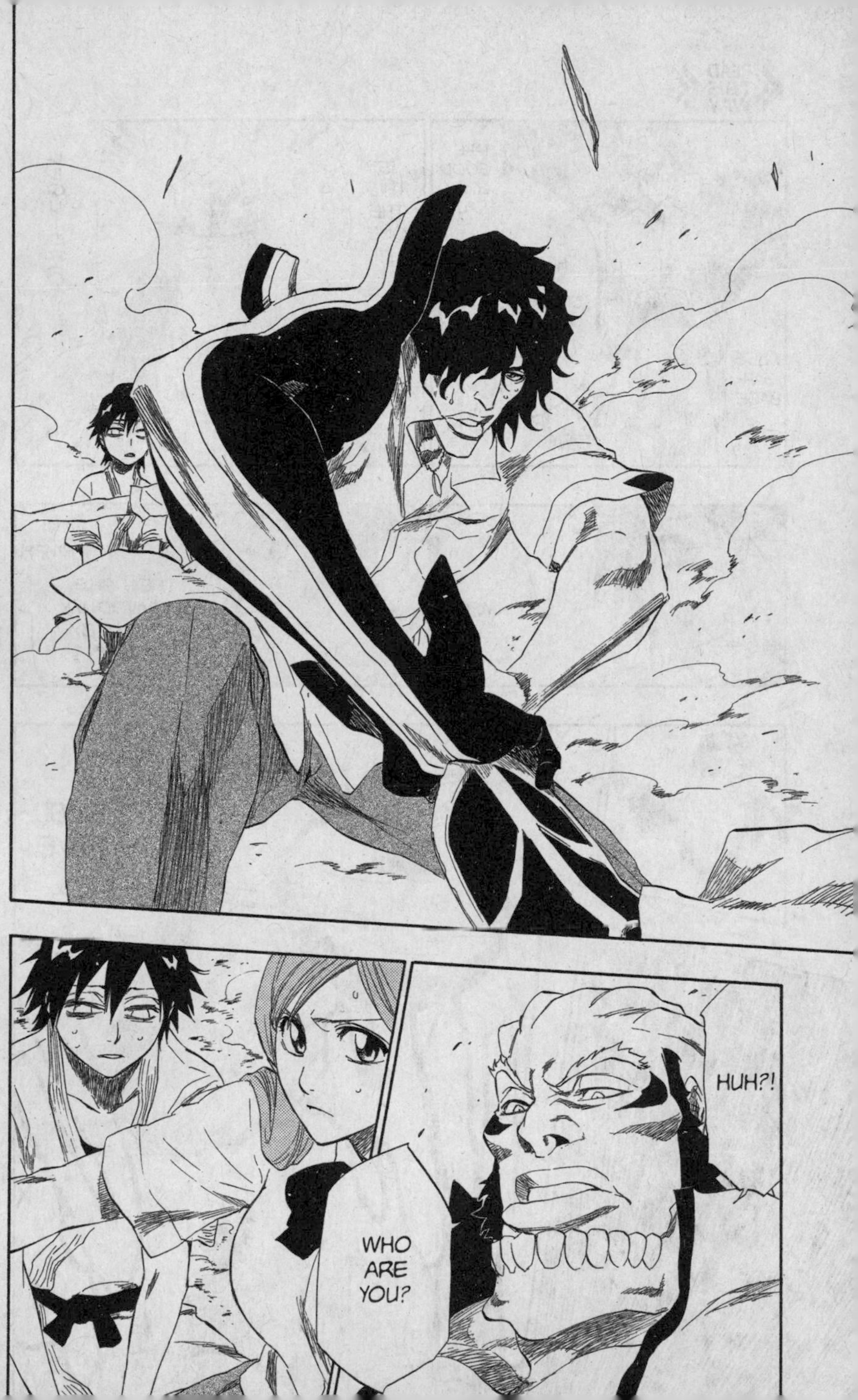
HUH?!
WHO ARE YOU?

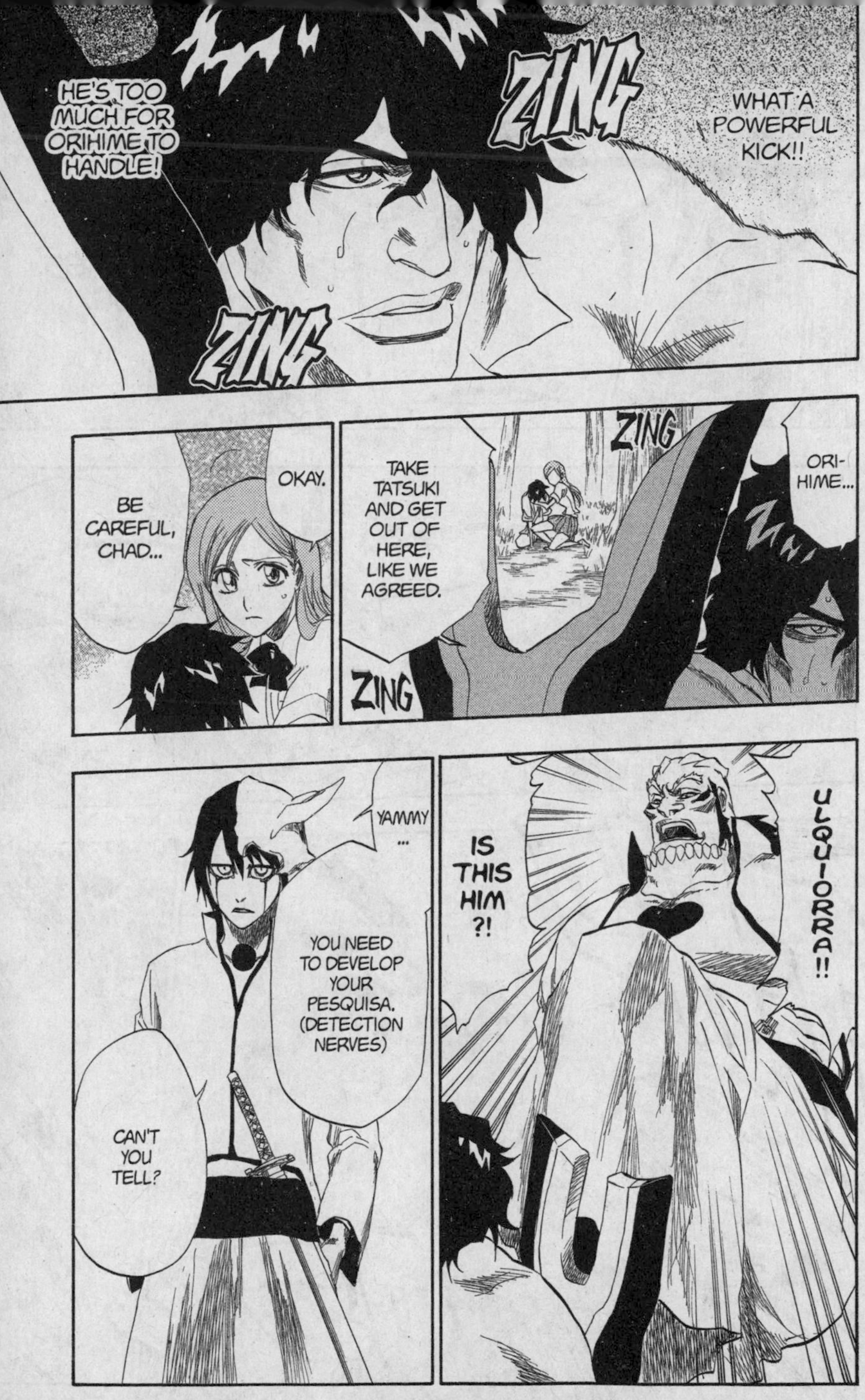
WHAT A POWERFUL KICK!!
ZING
HE'S TOO MUCH FOR ORIHIME TO HANDLE!
ZING
ORI-HIME...
ZING
TAKE TATSUKI AND GET OUT OF HERE, LIKE WE AGREED.
ZING
OKAY.
BE CAREFUL, CHAD...
ULQUIORRA!!
IS THIS HIM?!
YAMMY ...
YOU NEED TO DEVELOP YOUR PESQUISA. (DETECTION NERVES)
CAN'T YOU TELL?

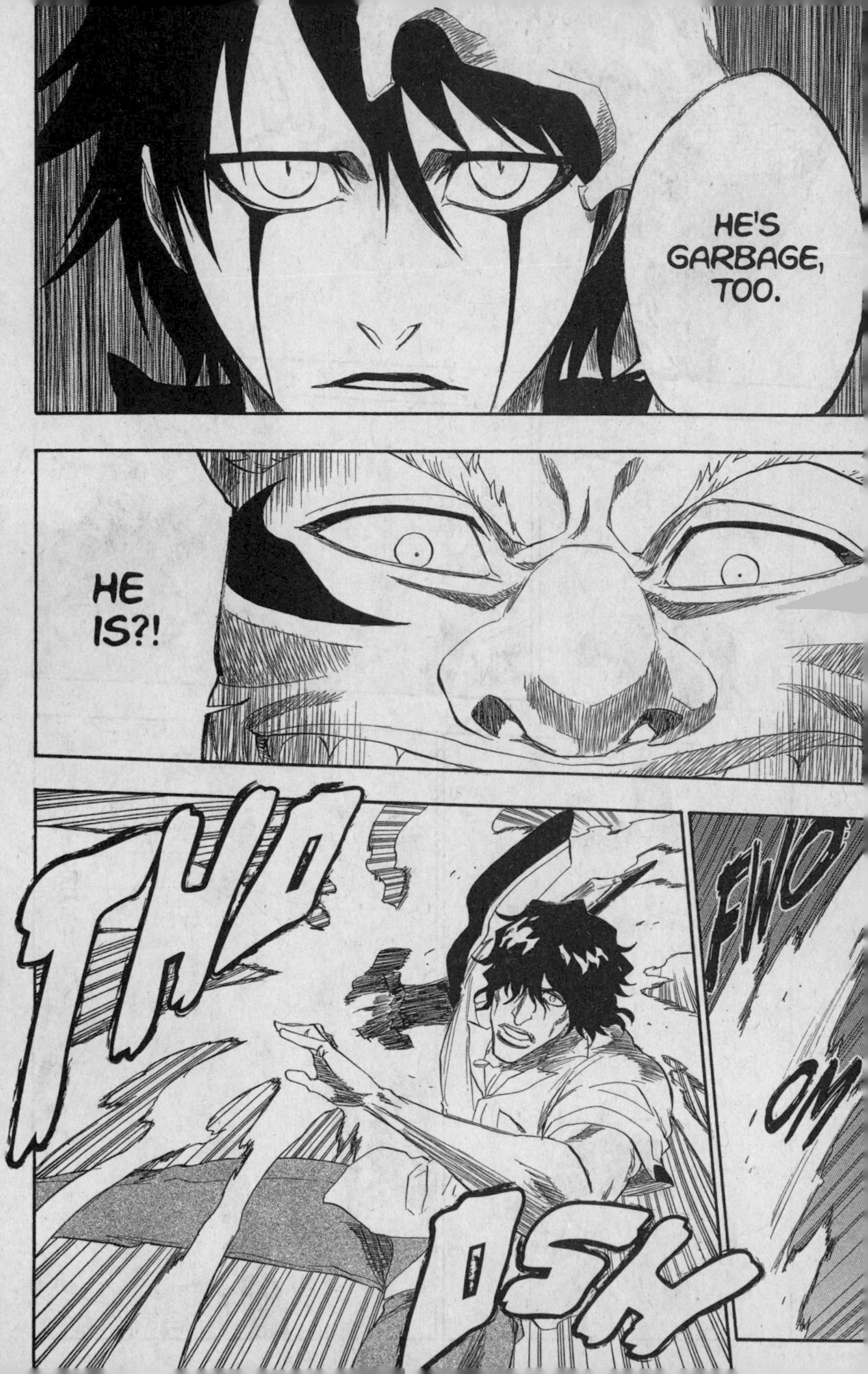
HE'S GARBAGE, TOO.
HE IS?!
FWOOM
THD
DSH

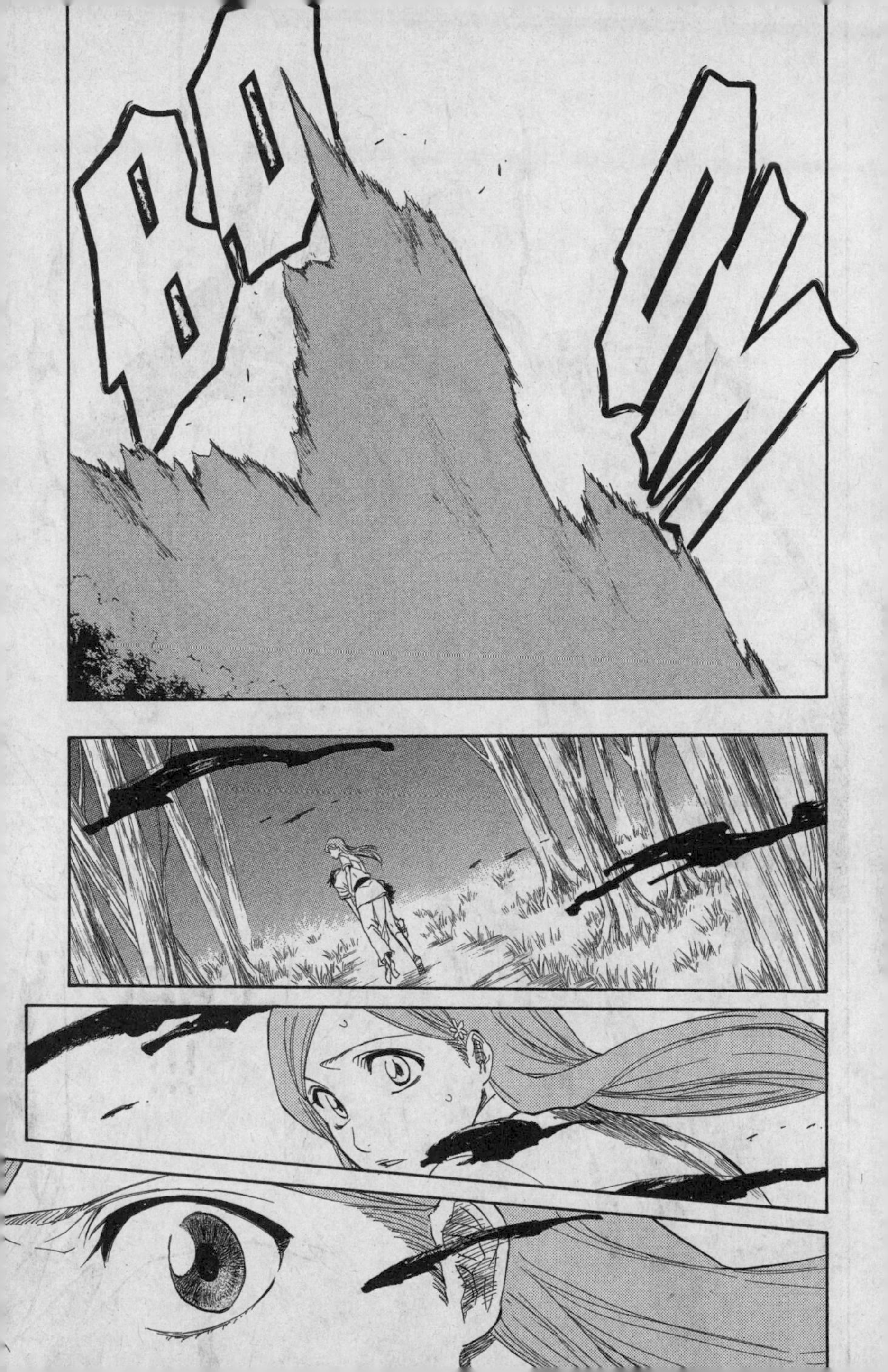
BAOM

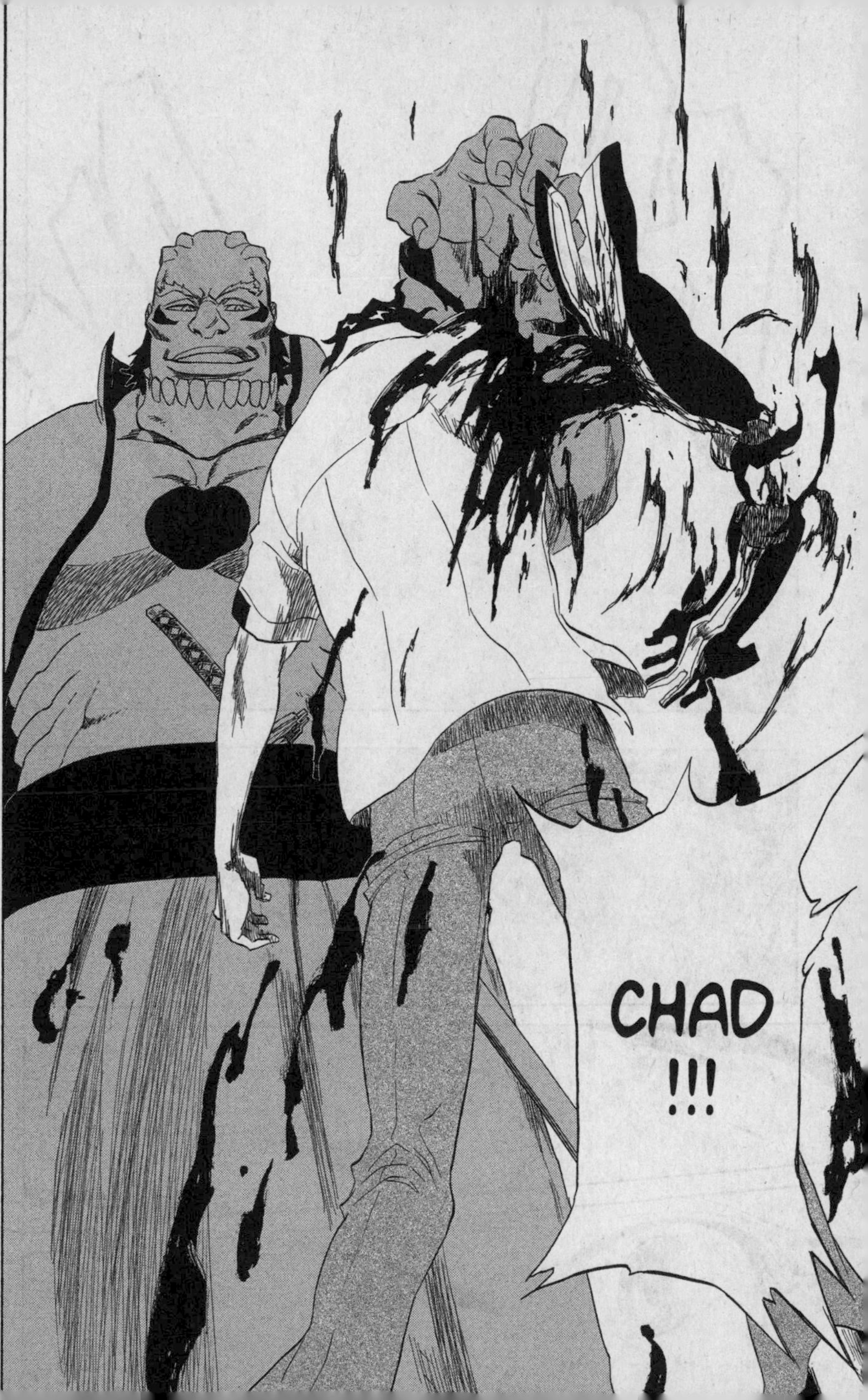
CHAD
!!!

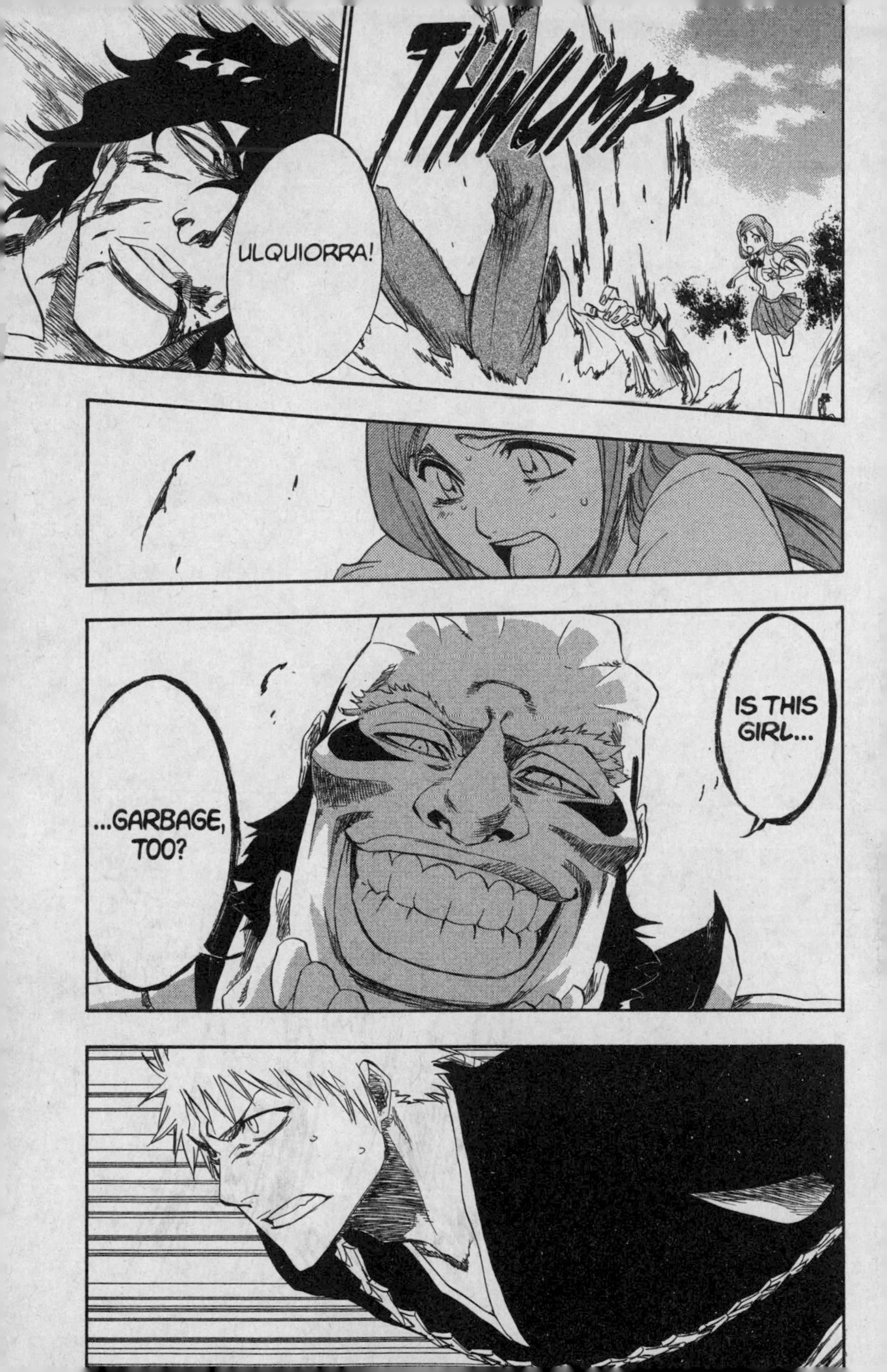
THWUMP
ULQUIORRA!
IS THIS GIRL...
...GARBAGE, TOO?

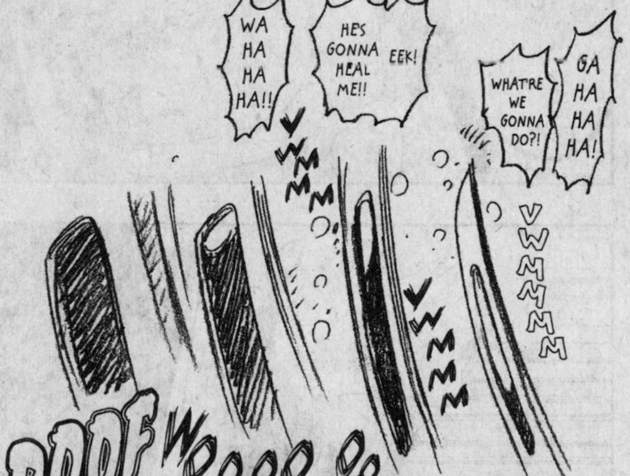
GA HA HA HA!
WHAT'RE WE GONNA DO?!
VWMMMM
VWMMM
EEK!
HE'S GONNA HEAL ME!!
WA HA HA HA!!
VWMMM
POOF
WOOOO OO

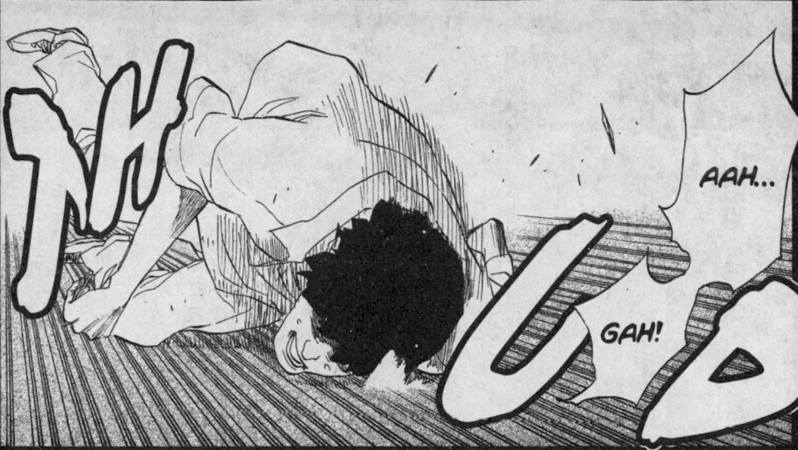
AAH...
THUD
GAH!

192. Conquistadores 3 (Hounded Priestess)

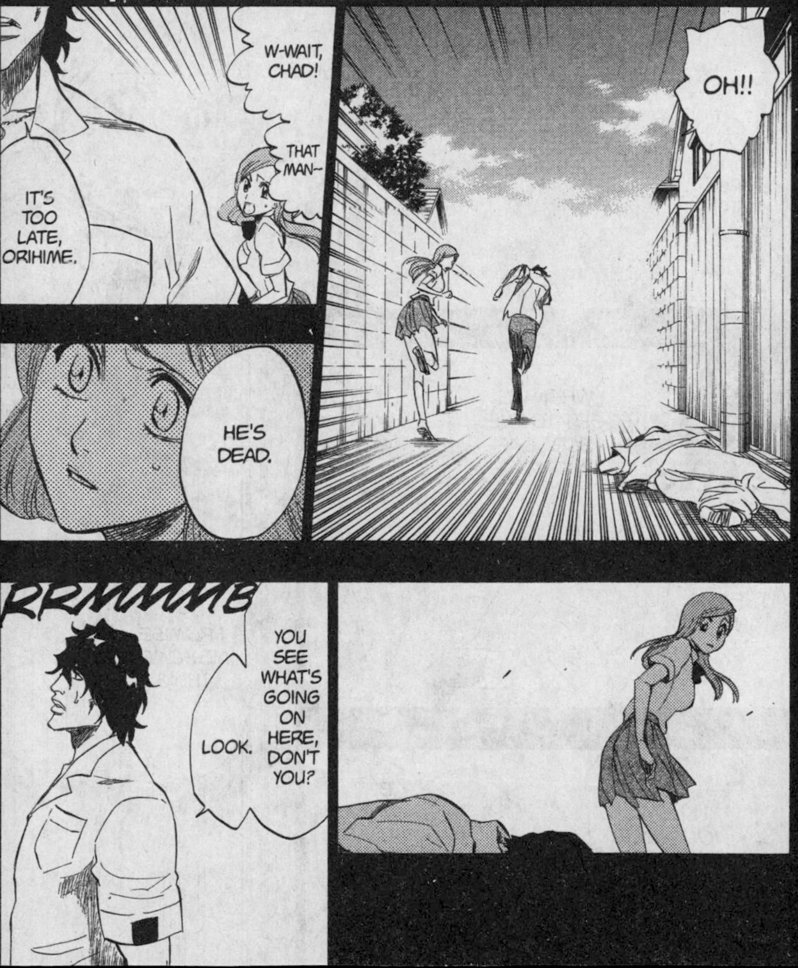
OH!!
W-WAIT, CHAD!
THAT MAN--
IT'S TOO LATE, ORIHIME.
HE'S DEAD.
RRMMMB
YOU SEE WHAT'S GOING ON HERE, DON'T YOU?
LOOK.

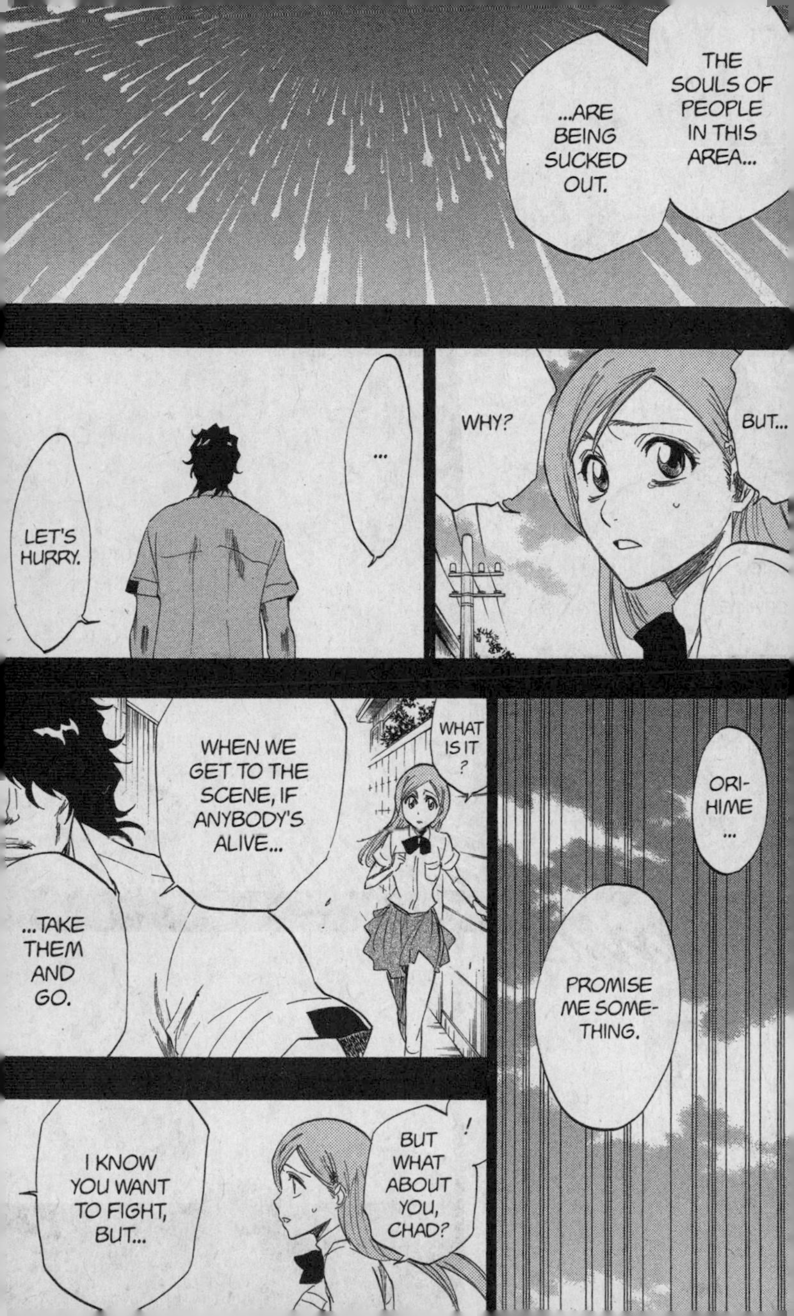
THE SOULS OF PEOPLE IN THIS AREA...
...ARE BEING SUCKED OUT.
BUT...
WHY?
...
LET'S HURRY.
ORI-HIME...
PROMISE ME SOME-THING.
WHAT IS IT?
WHEN WE GET TO THE SCENE, IF ANYBODY'S ALIVE...
...TAKE THEM AND GO.
!
BUT WHAT ABOUT YOU, CHAD?
I KNOW YOU WANT TO FIGHT, BUT...

READ THIS WAY

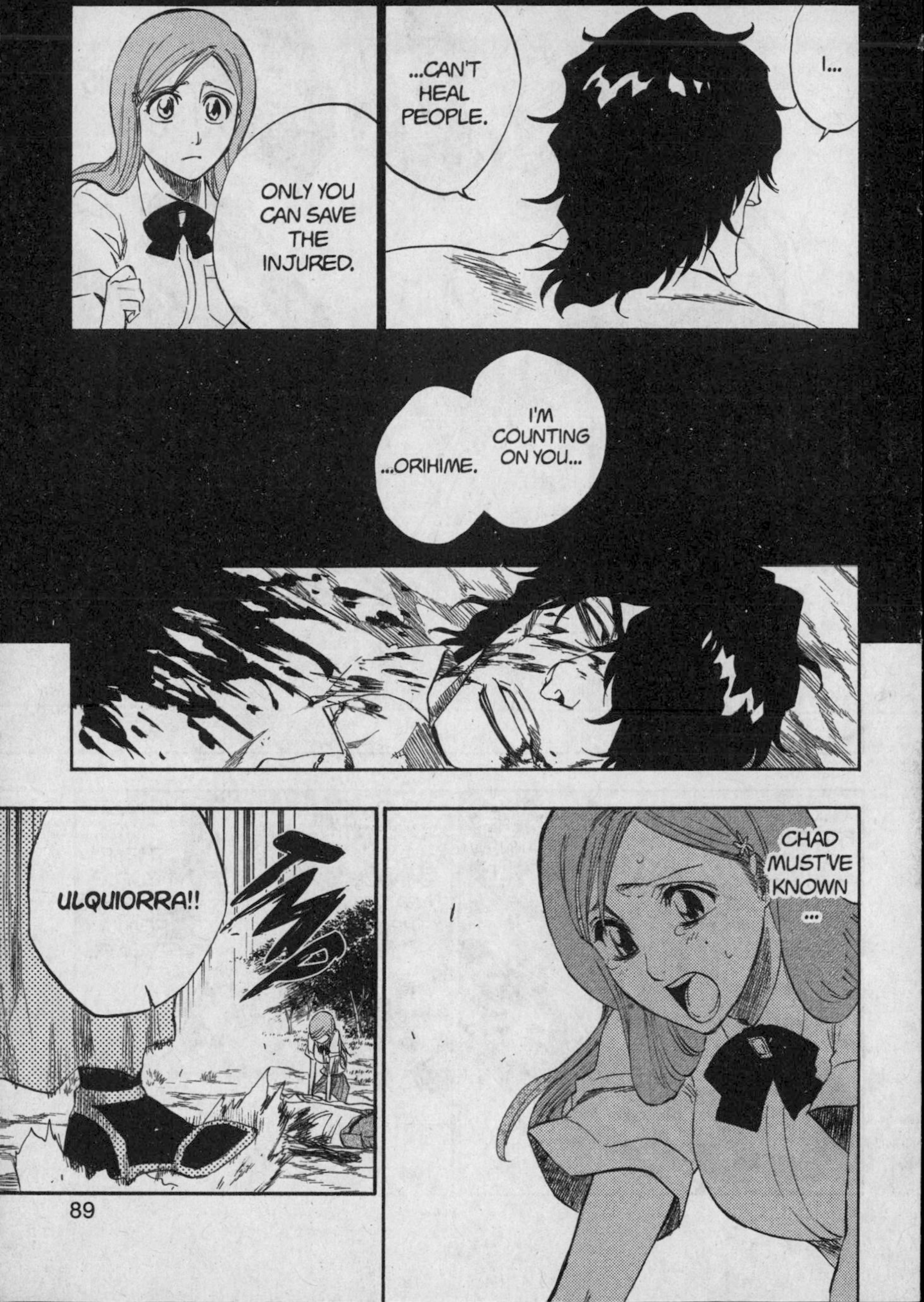

I...
...CAN'T HEAL PEOPLE.
ONLY YOU CAN SAVE THE INJURED.
I'M COUNTING ON YOU...
...ORIHIME.
CHAD MUST'VE KNOWN ...
ULQUIORRA!!

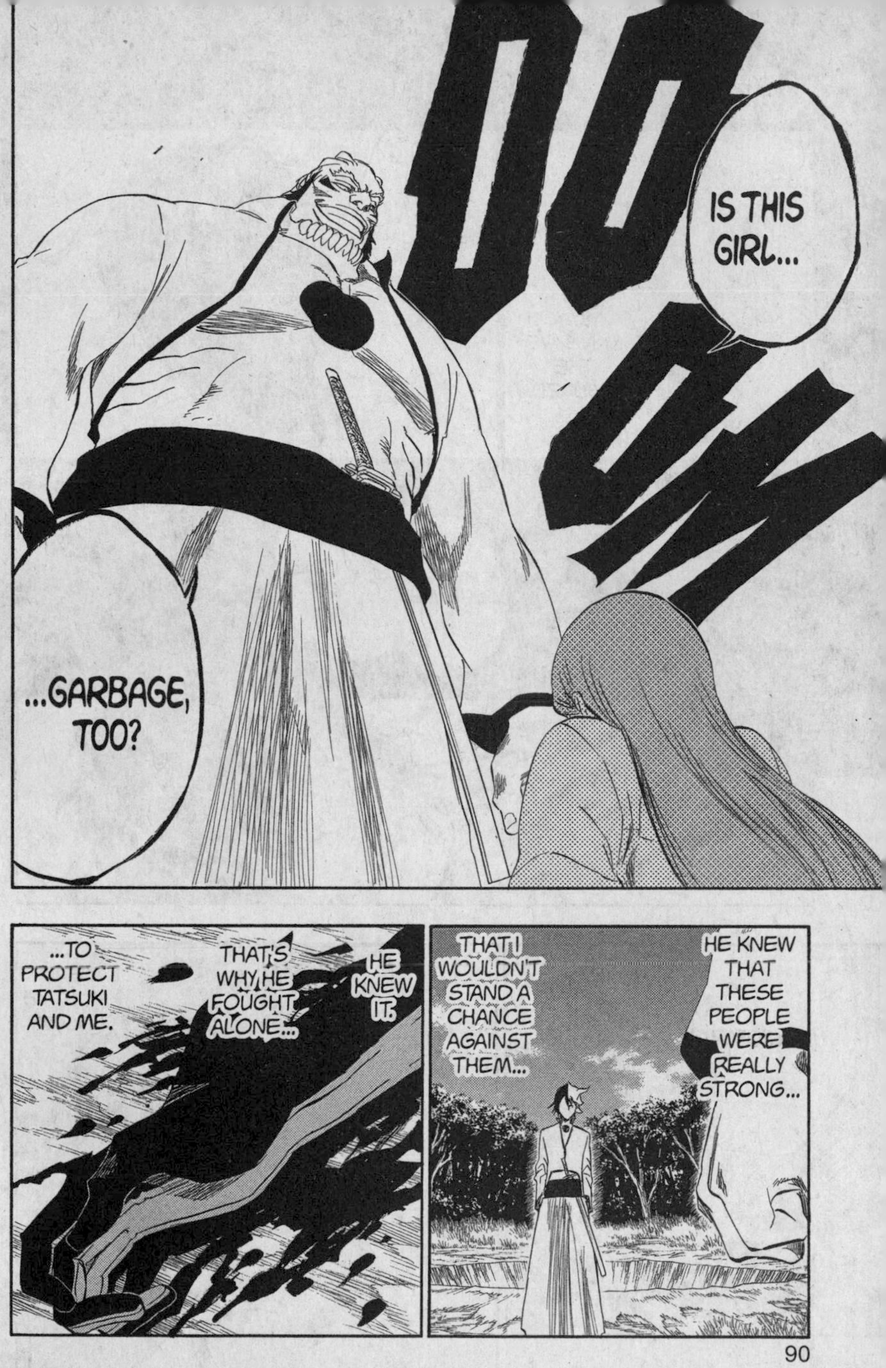
DOOM
IS THIS GIRL...
...GARBAGE, TOO?
HE KNEW THAT THESE PEOPLE WERE REALLY STRONG...
THAT I WOULDN'T STAND A CHANCE AGAINST THEM...
HE KNEW IT.
THAT'S WHY HE FOUGHT ALONE...
...TO PROTECT TATSUKI AND ME.

READ THIS WAY

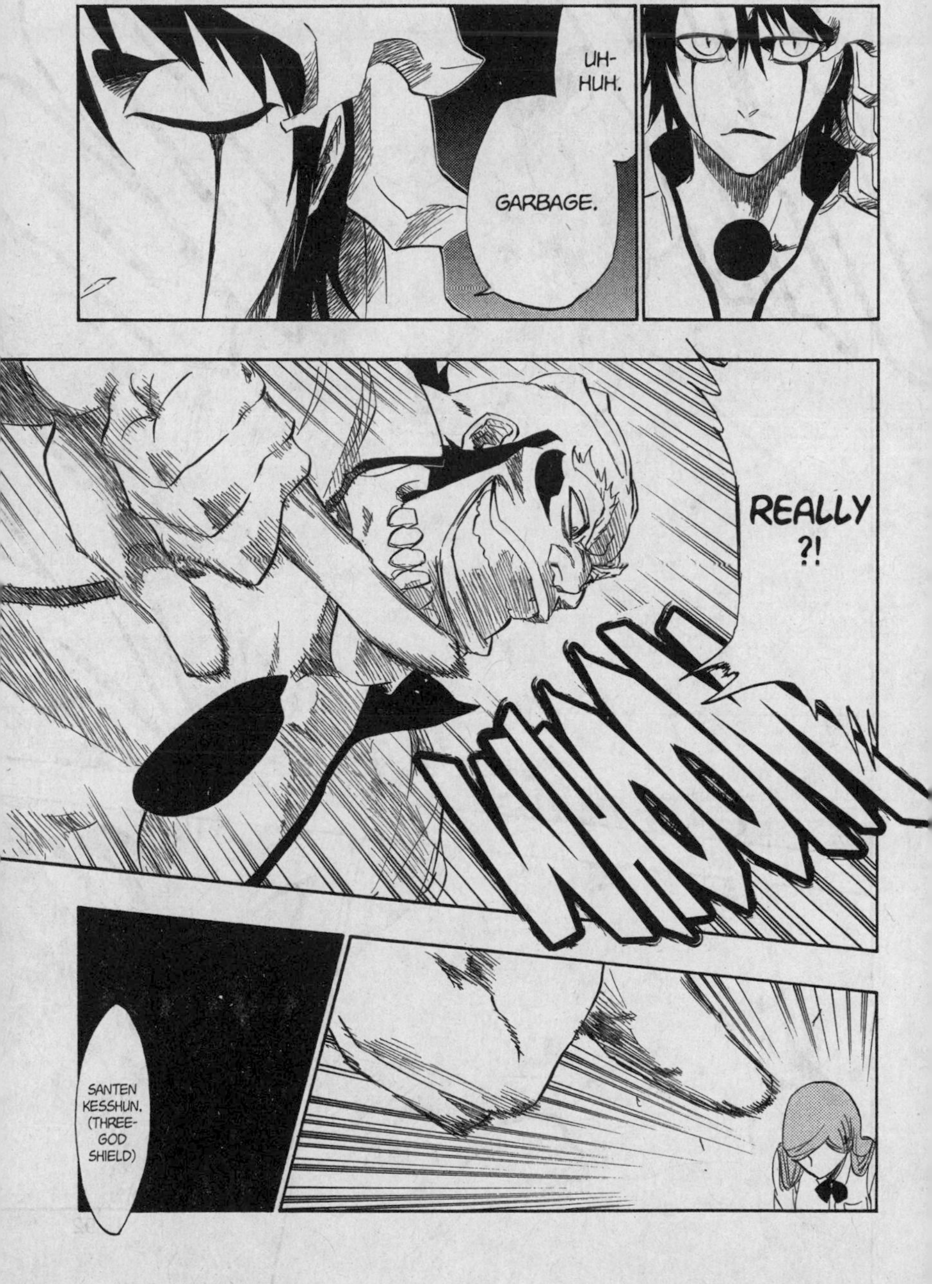
UH-HUH.
GARBAGE.
REALLY?!
SANTEN KESSHUN. (THREE-GOD SHIELD)

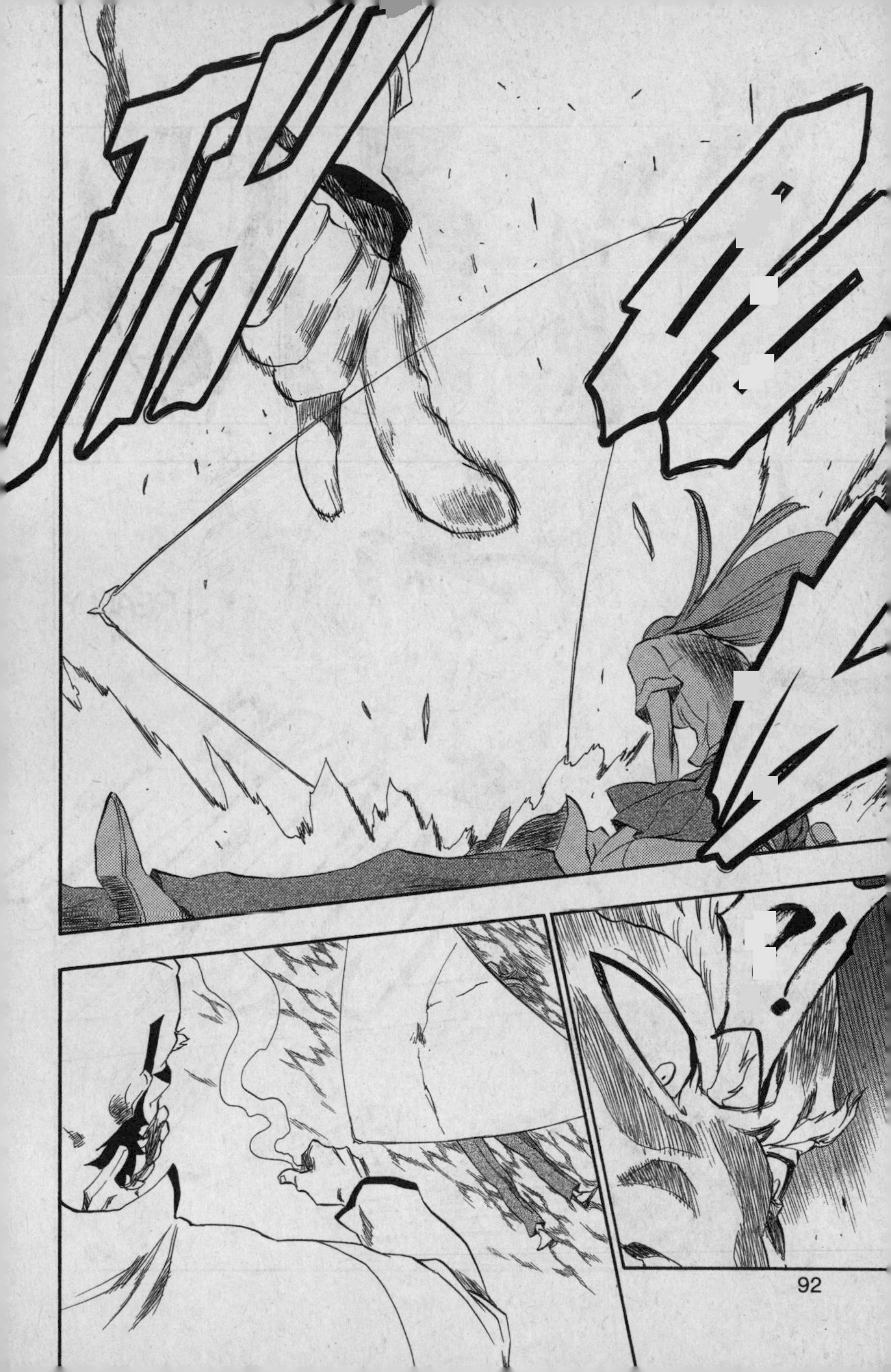
?!

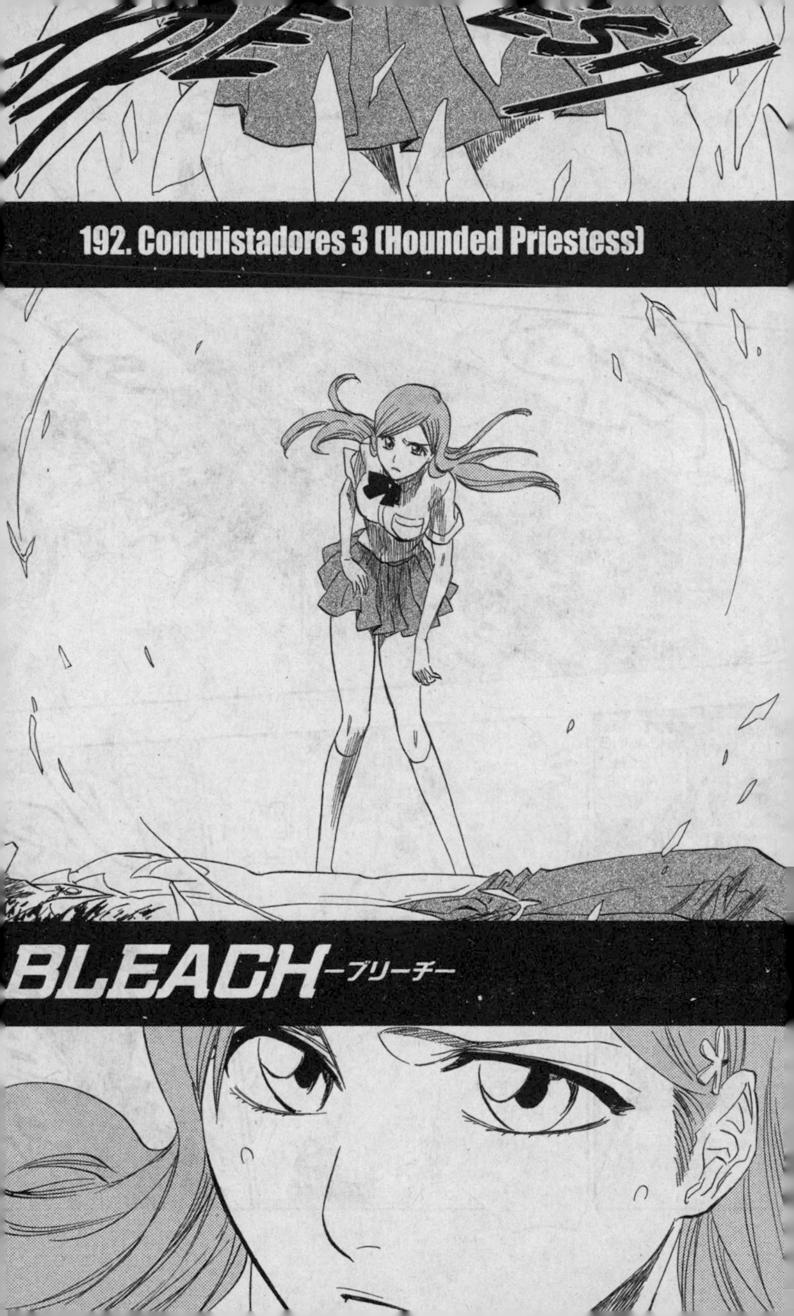
192. Conquistadores 3 (Hounded Priestess)
BLEACH
ーブリーチー

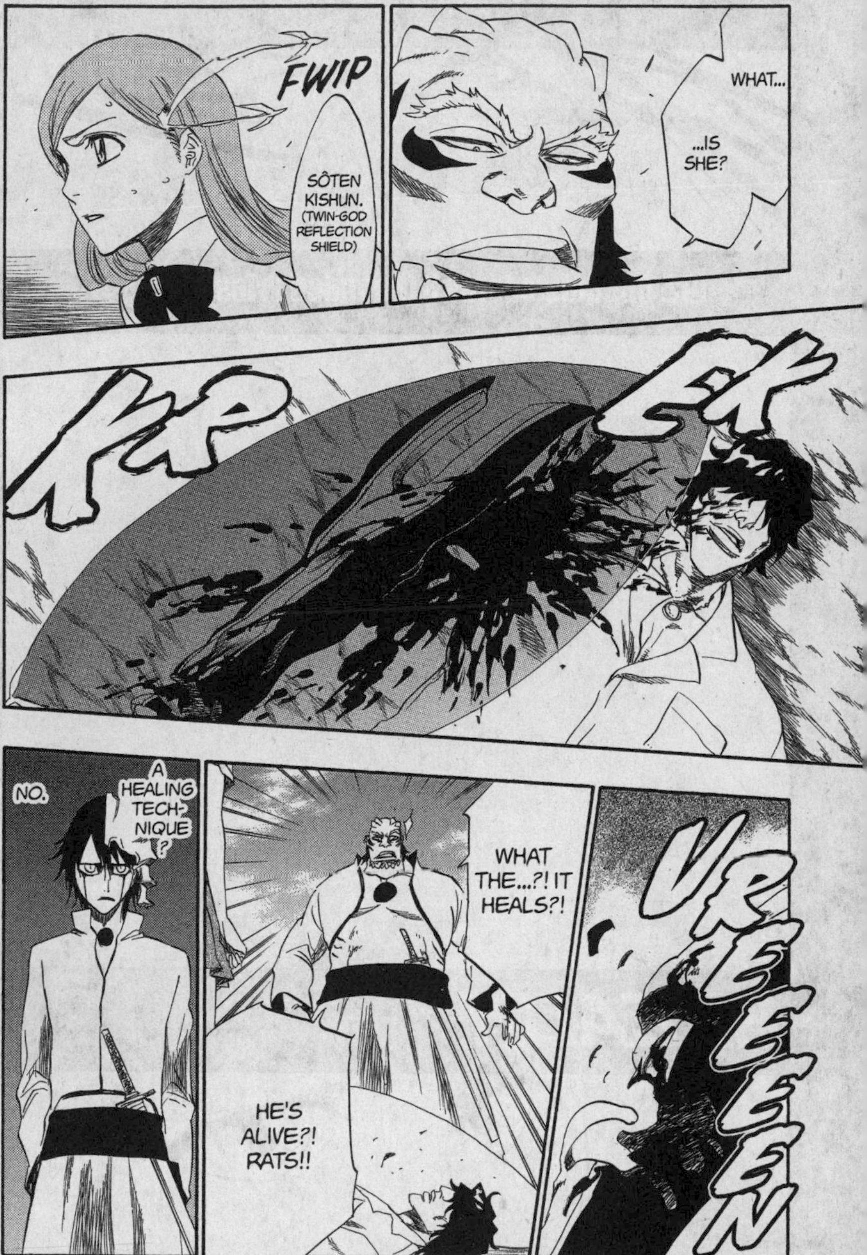
WHAT...
...IS SHE?
FWIP
SÔTEN KISHUN. (TWIN-GOD REFLECTION SHIELD)
WHAT THE...?! IT HEALS?!
HE'S ALIVE?! RATS!!
A HEALING TECH-NIQUE?
NO.

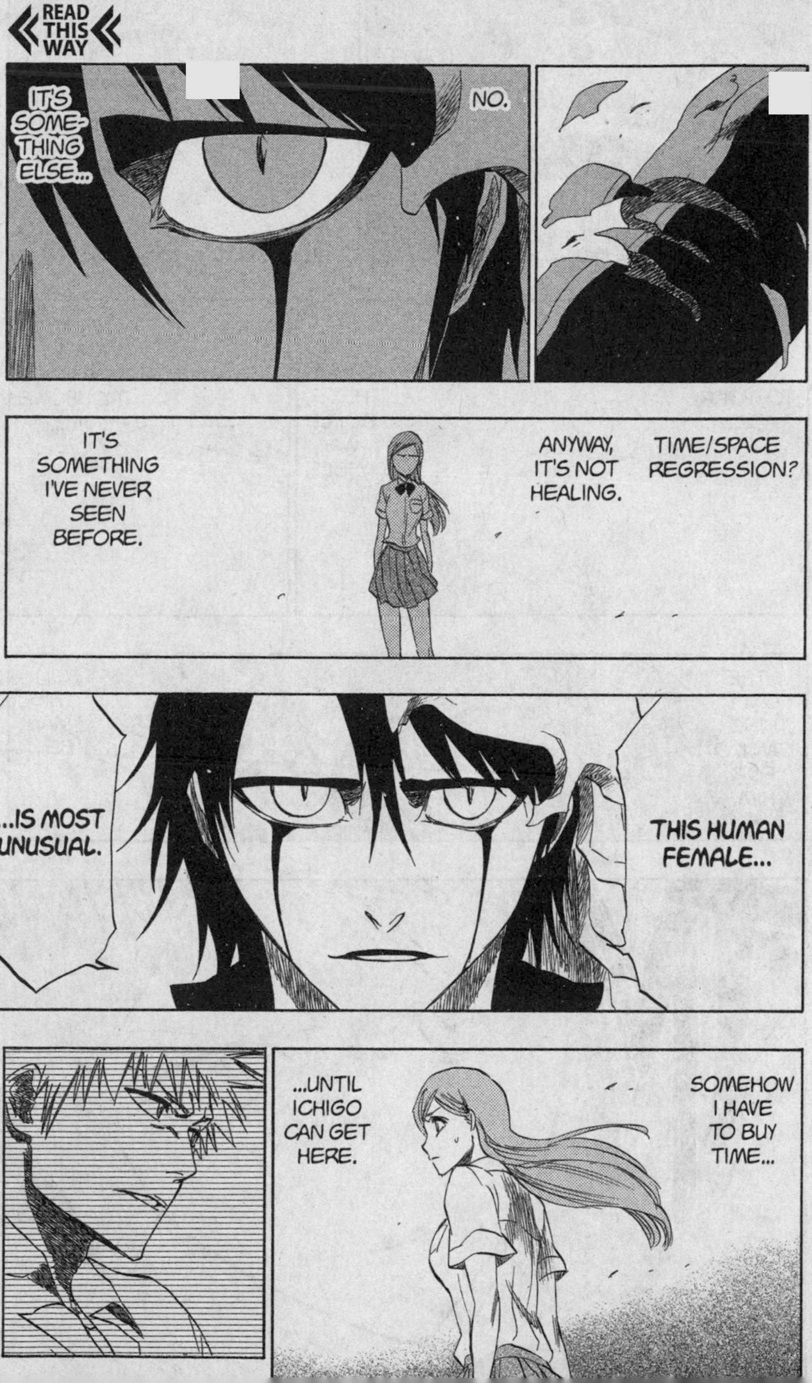
READ THIS WAY
NO.
IT'S SOME-THING ELSE...
TIME/SPACE REGRESSION?
ANYWAY, IT'S NOT HEALING.
IT'S SOMETHING I'VE NEVER SEEN BEFORE.
THIS HUMAN FEMALE...
...IS MOST UNUSUAL.
SOMEHOW I HAVE TO BUY TIME...
...UNTIL ICHIGO CAN GET HERE.

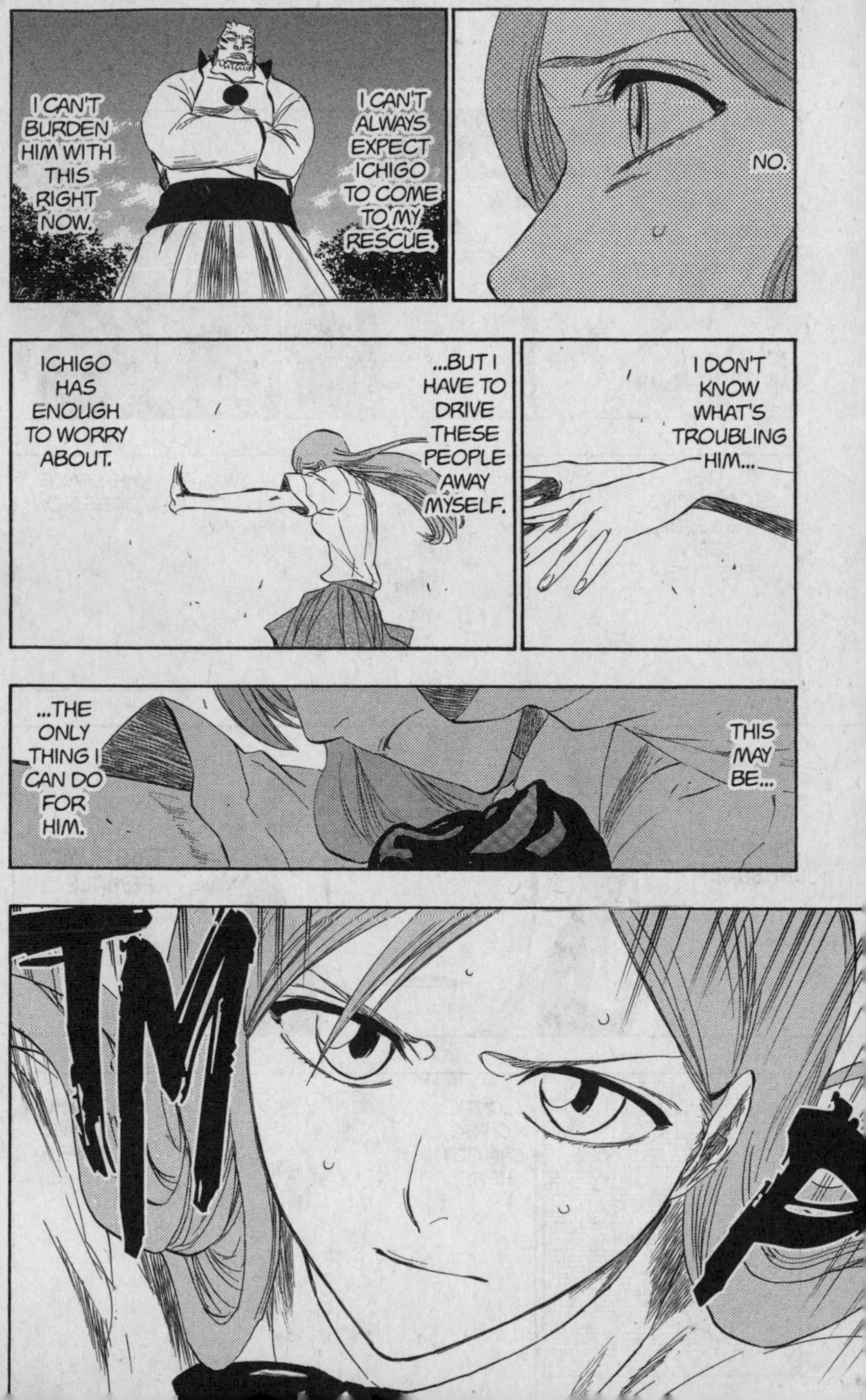
NO.
I CAN'T ALWAYS EXPECT ICHIGO TO COME TO MY RESCUE.
I CAN'T BURDEN HIM WITH THIS RIGHT NOW.
I DON'T KNOW WHAT'S TROUBLING HIM...
...BUT I HAVE TO DRIVE THESE PEOPLE AWAY MYSELF.
ICHIGO HAS ENOUGH TO WORRY ABOUT.
THIS MAY BE...
...THE ONLY THING I CAN DO FOR HIM.
TM

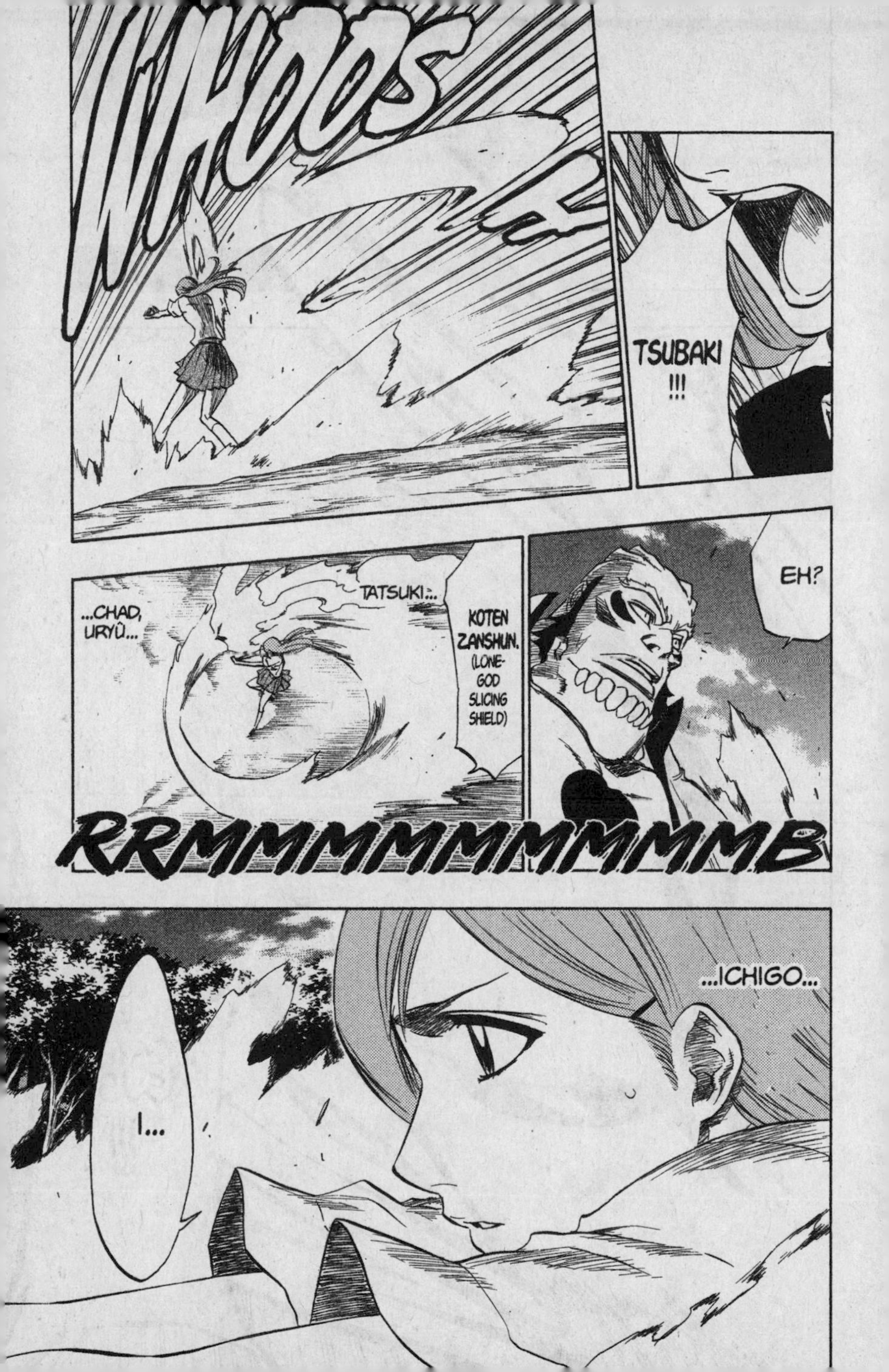

TSUBAKI !!!
WHOOS
EH?
KOTEN ZANSHUN. (LONE-GOD SLICING SHIELD)
TATSUKI...
...CHAD, URYÛ...
RRMMMMMMMMMMMB
...ICHIGO...
I...

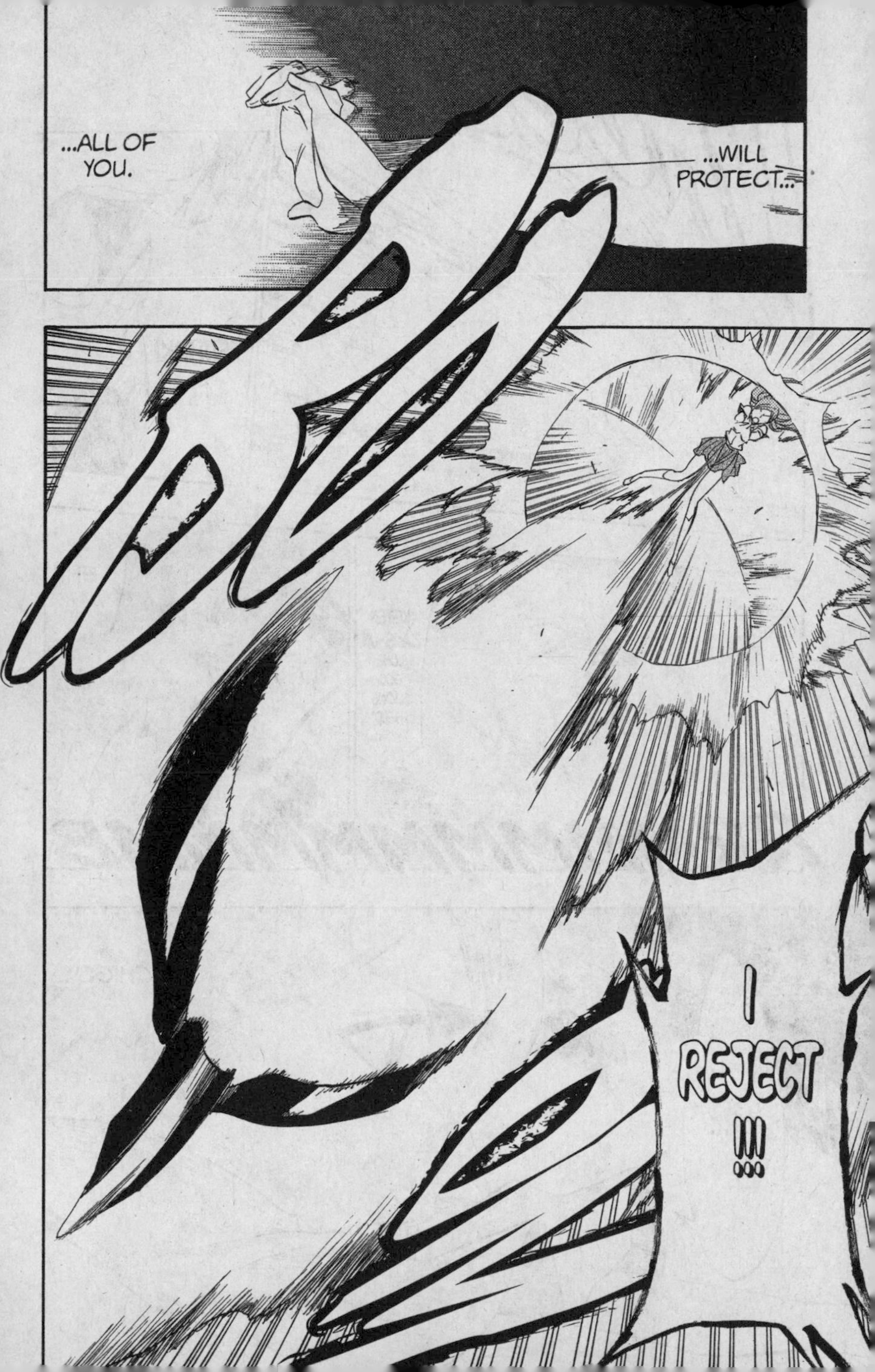
...WILL PROTECT...
...ALL OF YOU.
I REJECT!!!

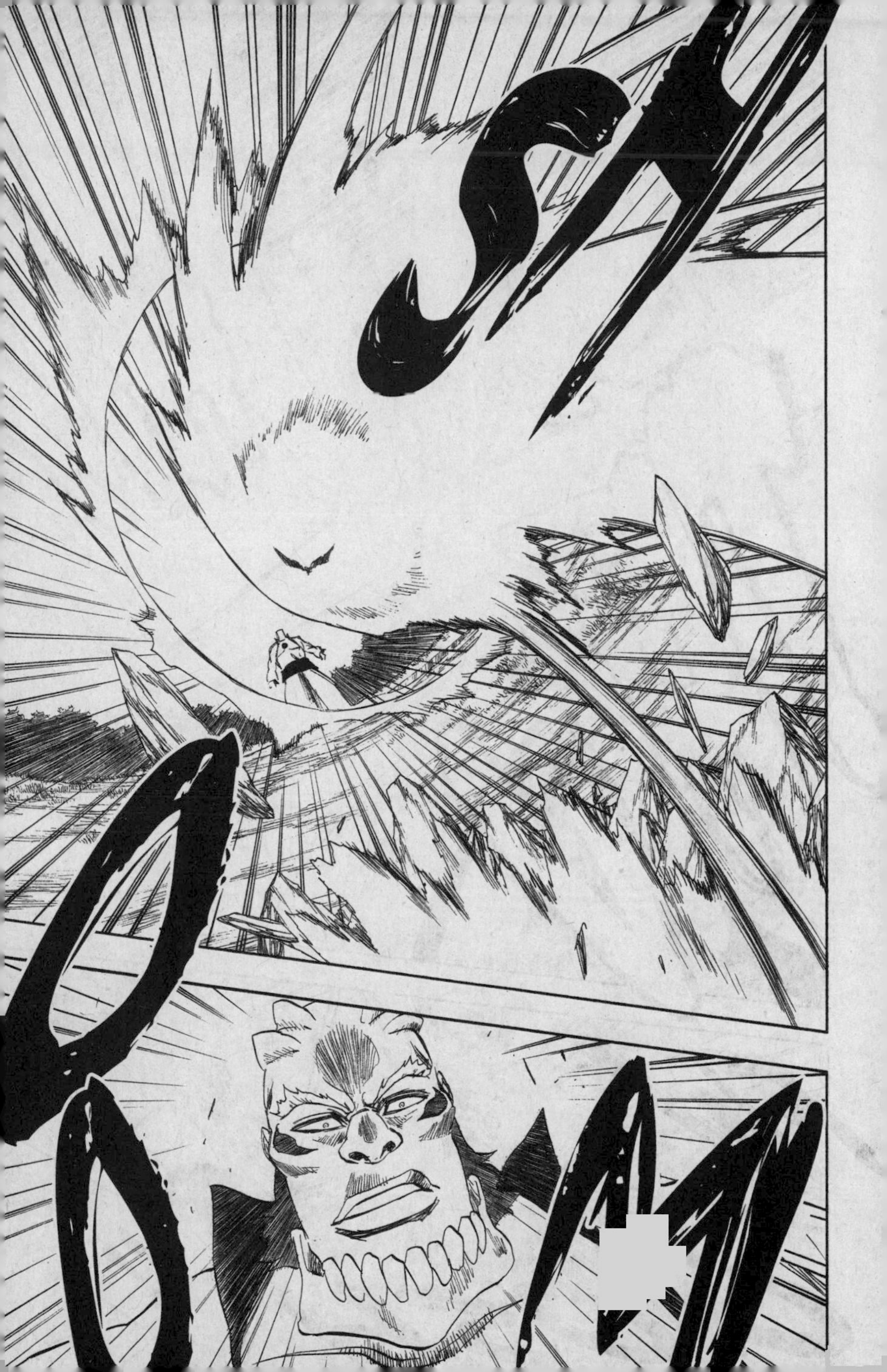
SHOOM

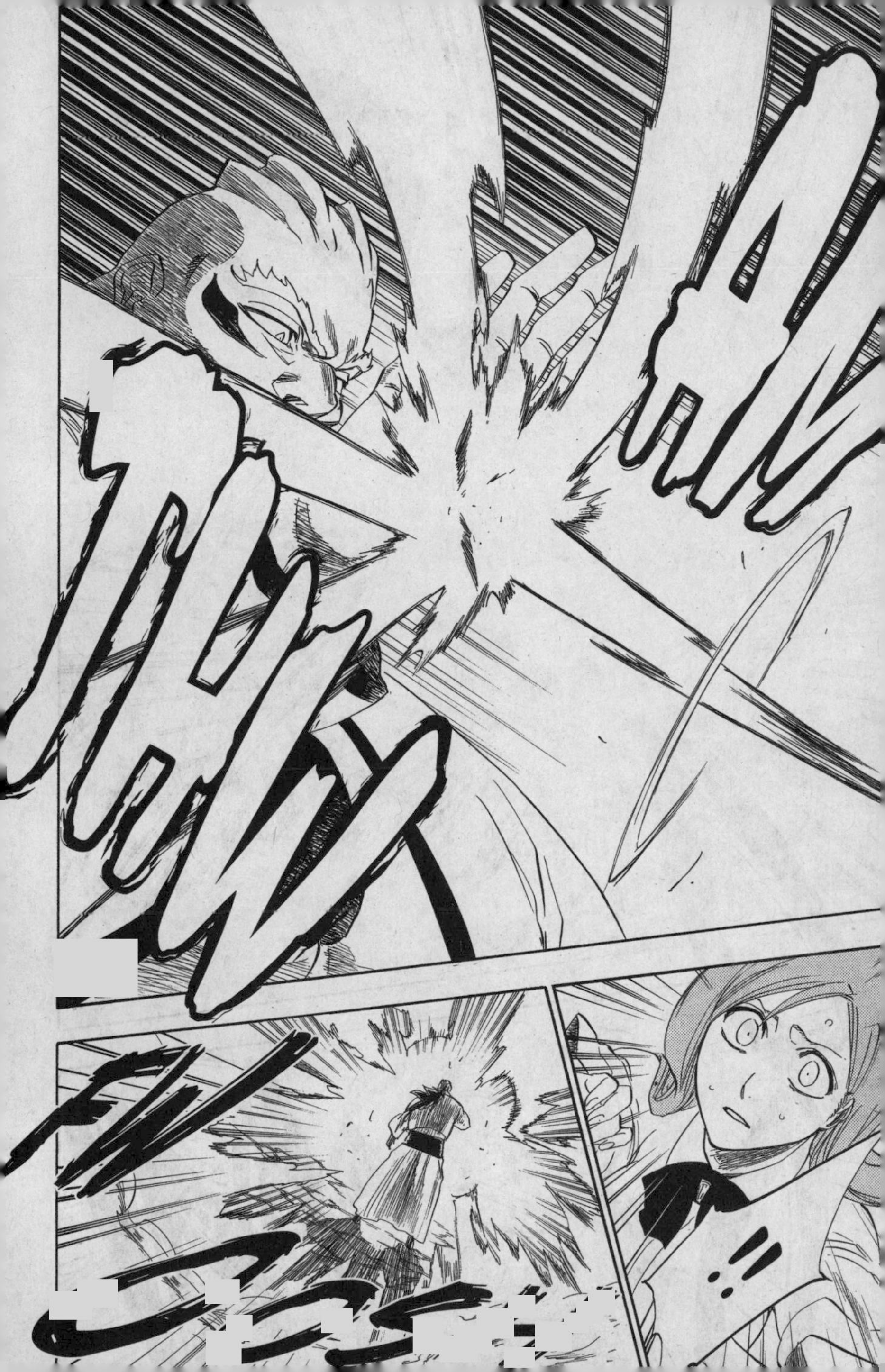
!!

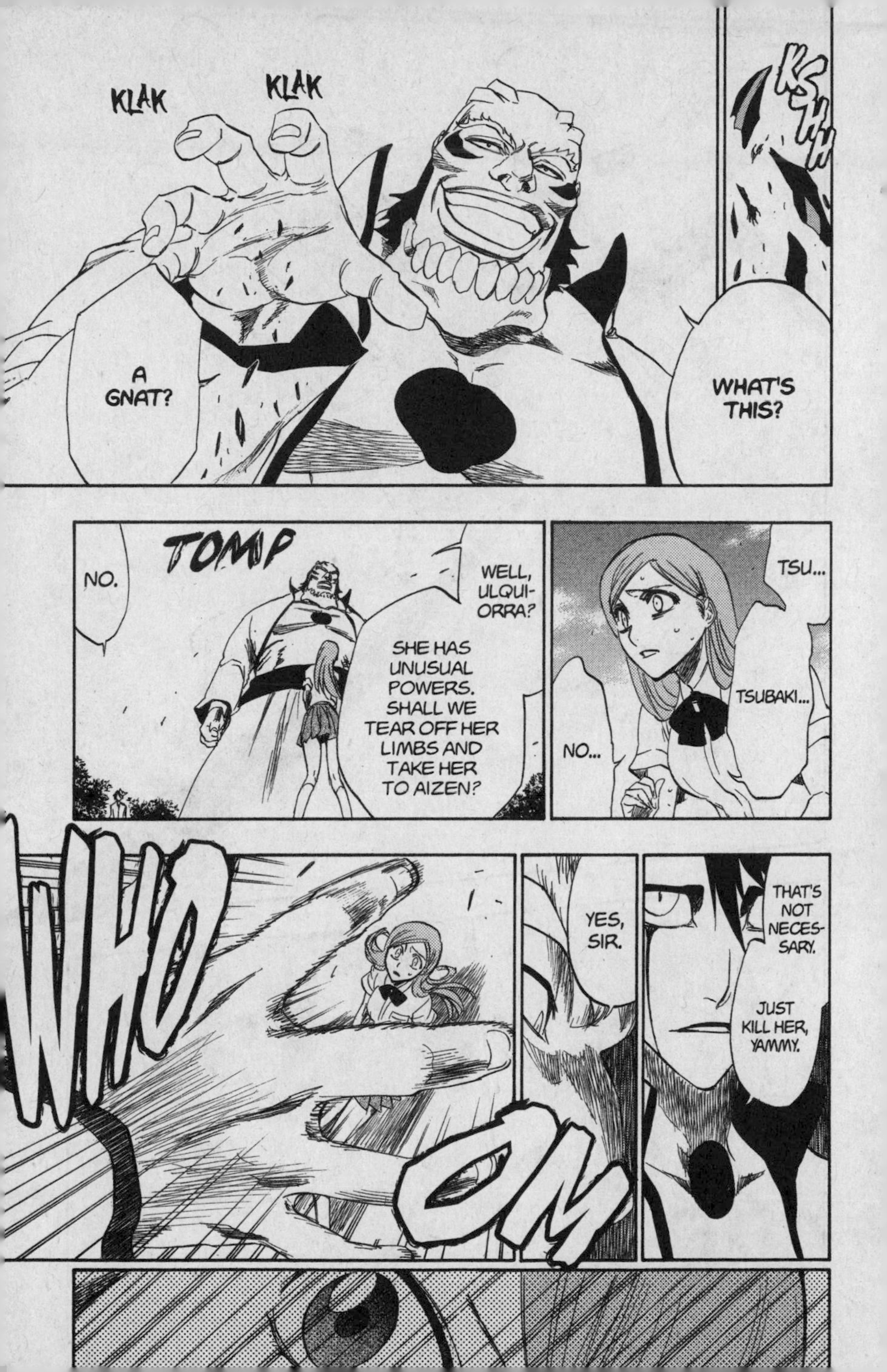
KSHH
KLAK
KLAK
WHAT'S THIS?
A GNAT?
TSU...
TSUBAKI...
NO...
WELL, ULQUI-ORRA?
SHE HAS UNUSUAL POWERS. SHALL WE TEAR OFF HER LIMBS AND TAKE HER TO AIZEN?
TOMP
NO.
THAT'S NOT NECES-SARY.
JUST KILL HER, YAMMY.
YES, SIR.
WHOOM

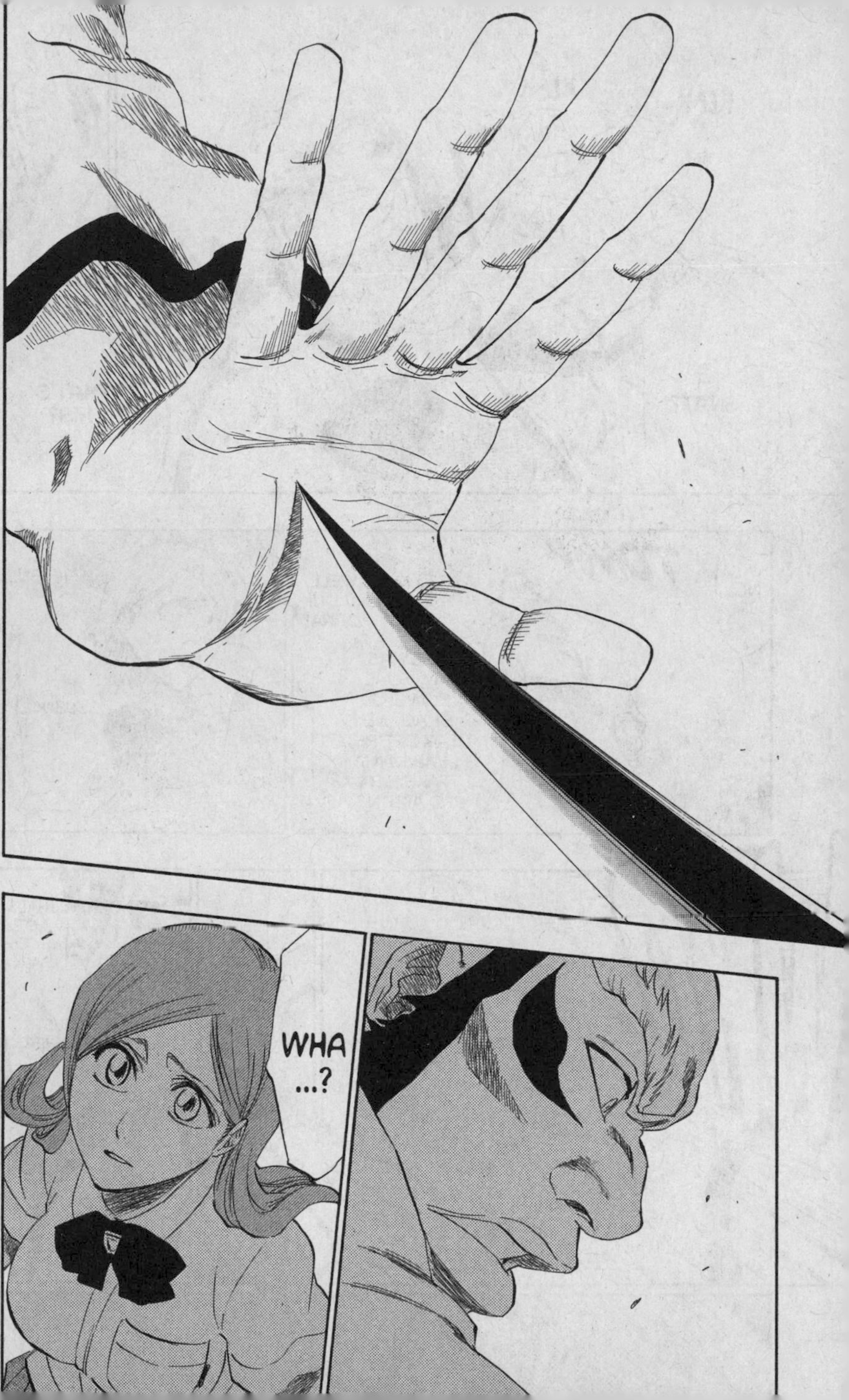
WHA
...?

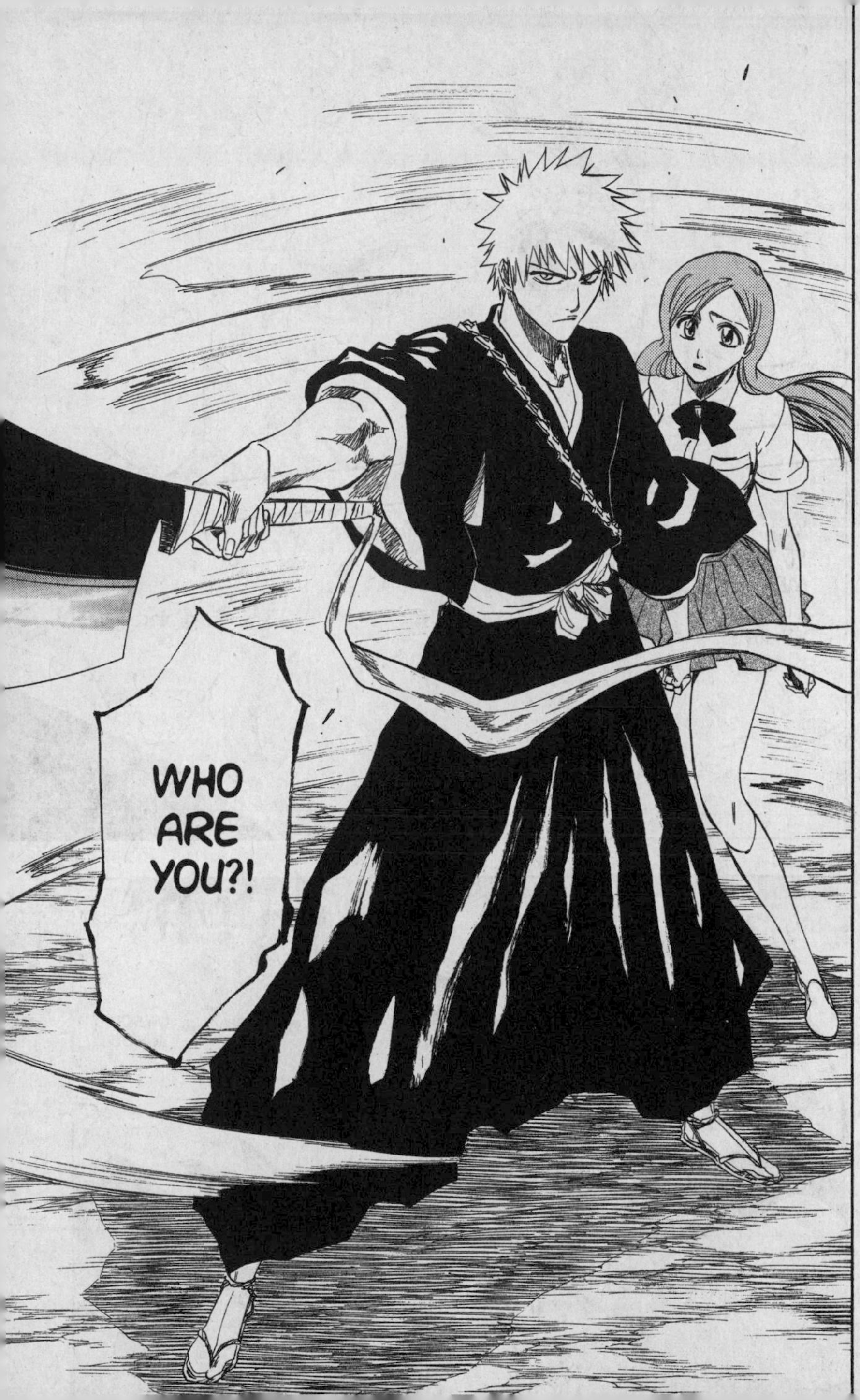
WHO ARE YOU?!

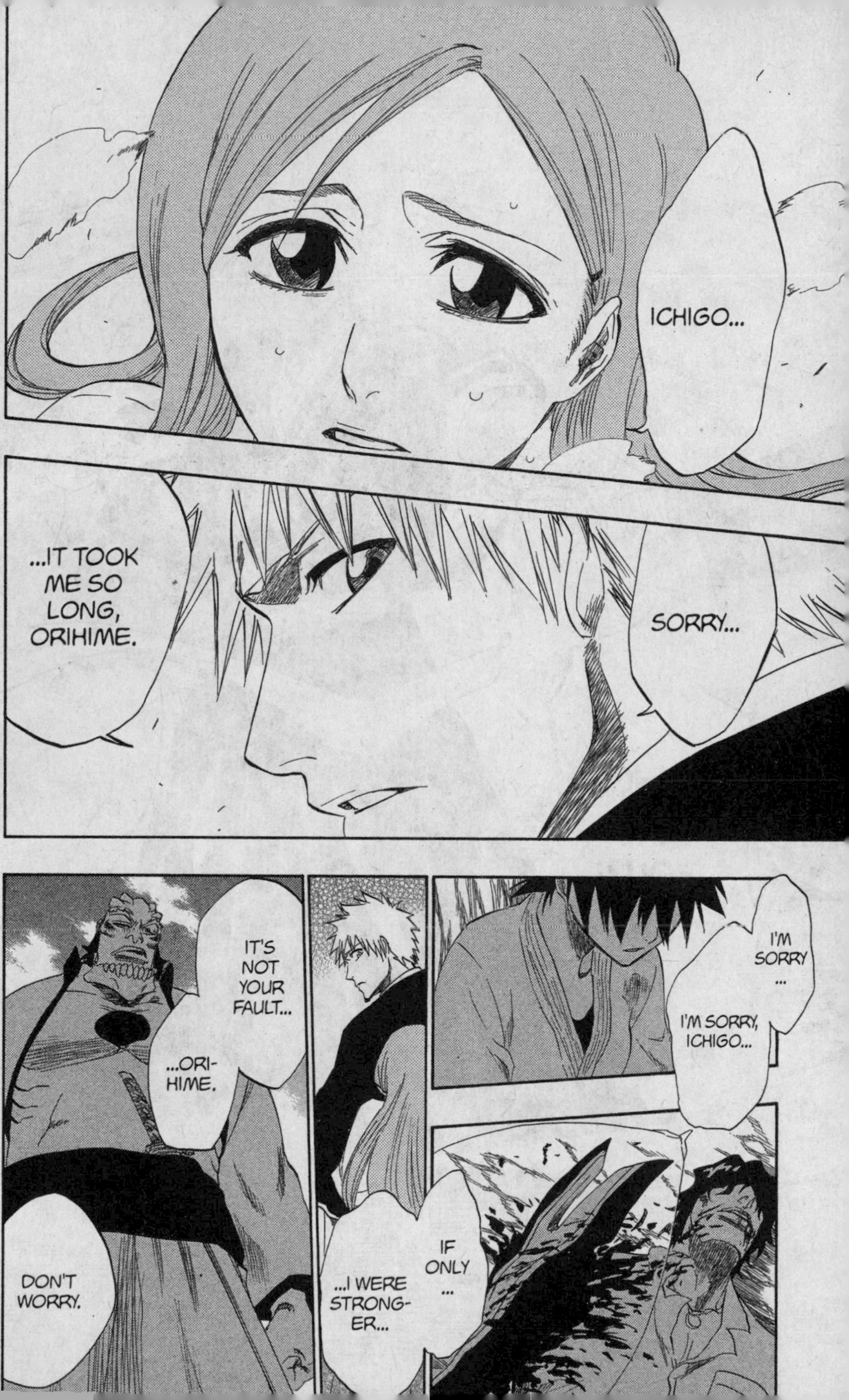
ICHIGO...
SORRY...
...IT TOOK ME SO LONG, ORIHIME.
I'M SORRY...
I'M SORRY, ICHIGO...
IT'S NOT YOUR FAULT...
...ORIHIME.
IF ONLY...
...I WERE STRONGER...
DON'T WORRY.

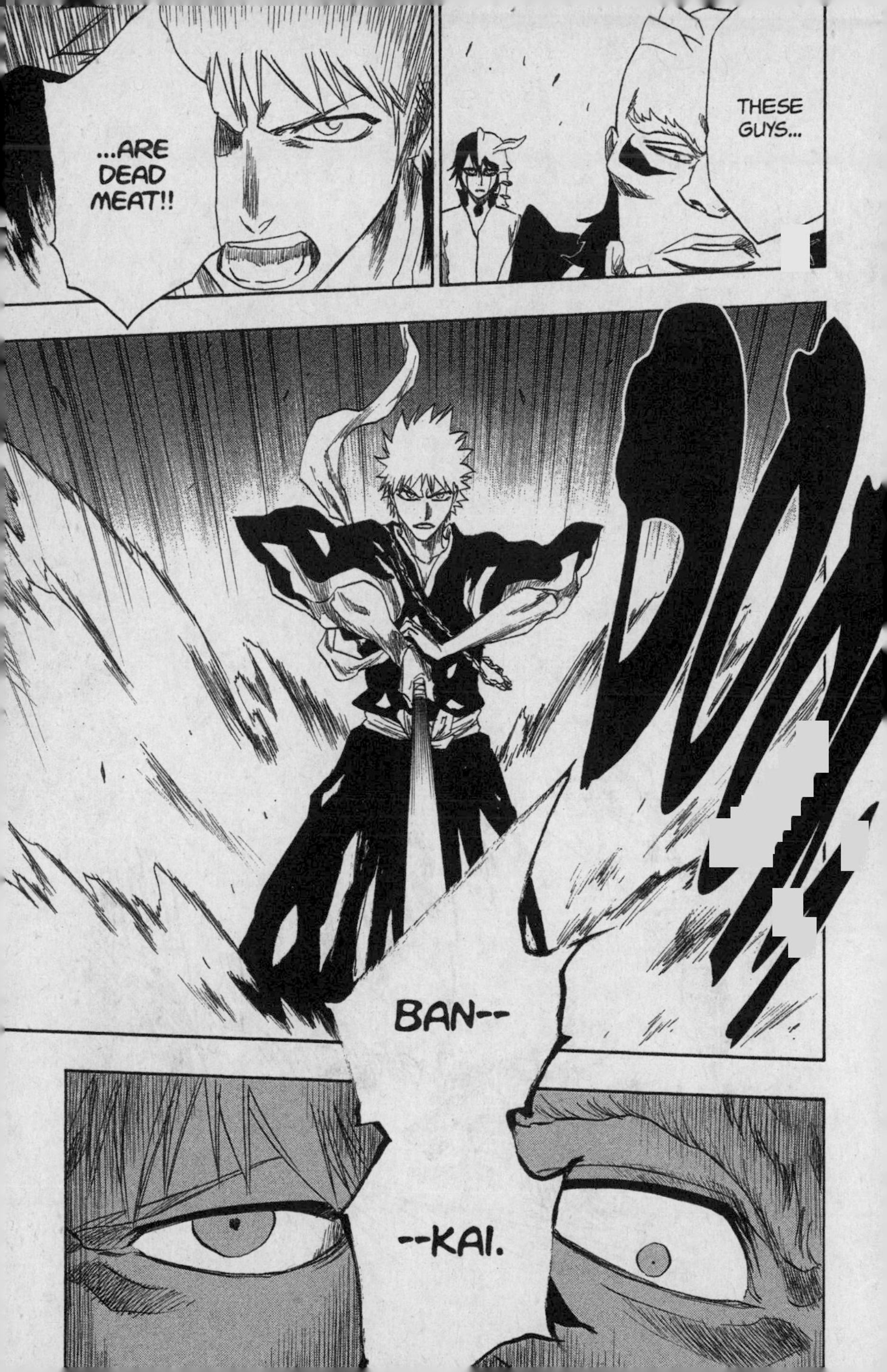
THESE GUYS...
...ARE DEAD MEAT!!
BAN--
--KAI.

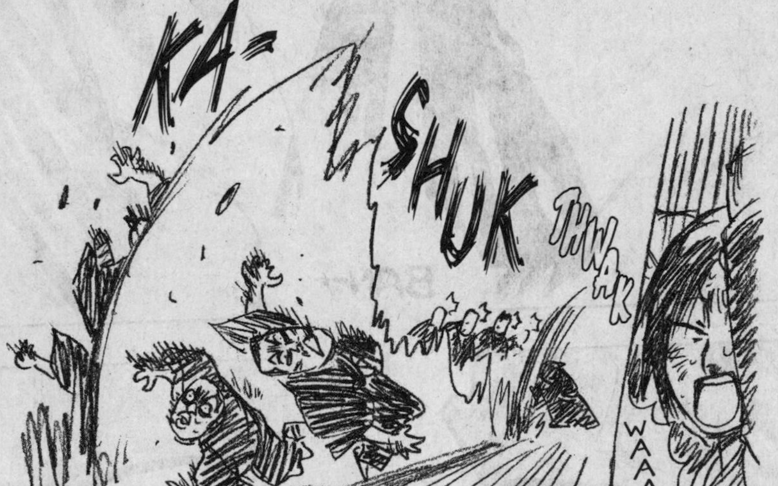
KA-SHUK
THWAK
WAAAAAH!

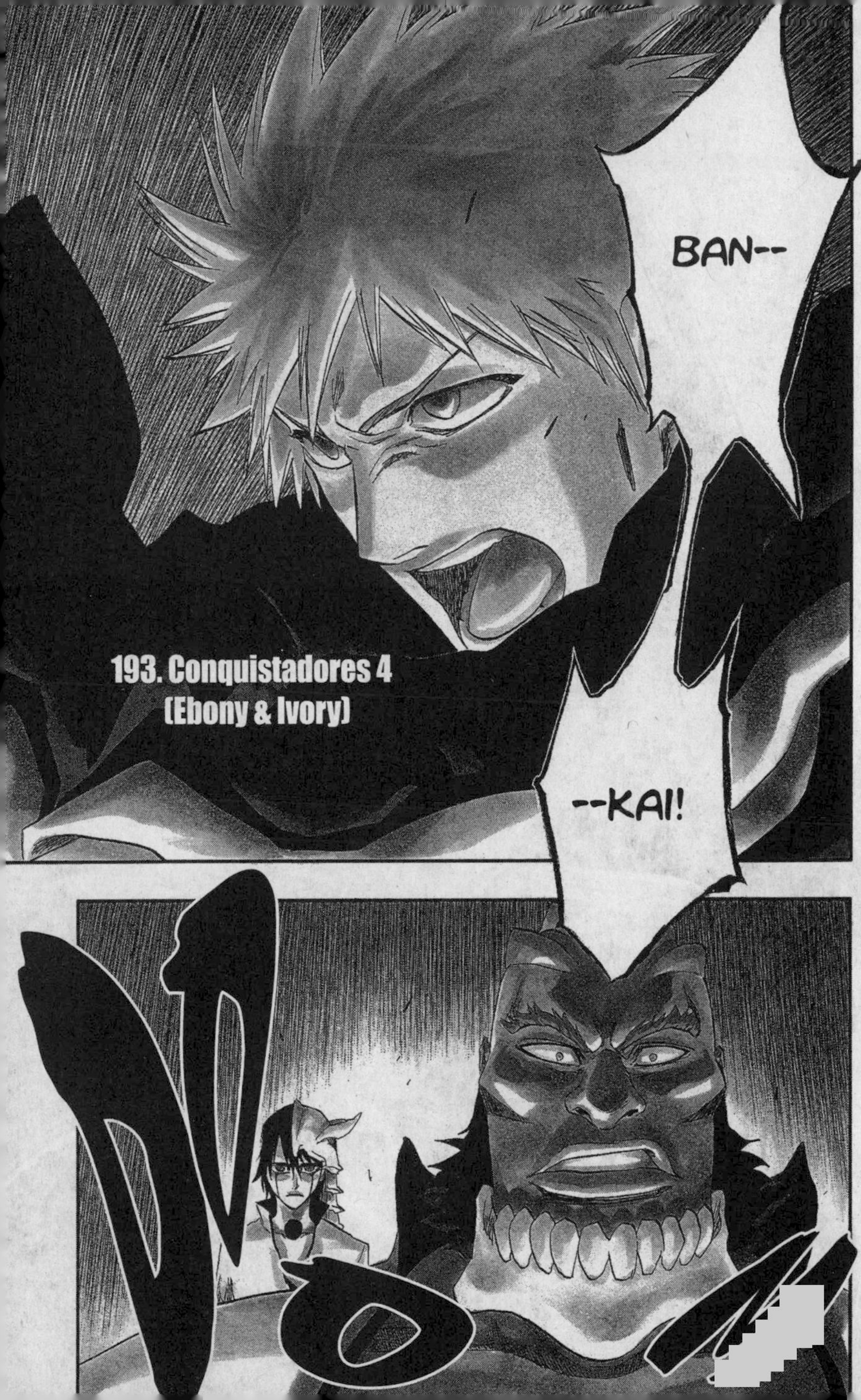
BAN--
--KAI!
193. Conquistadores 4
(Ebony & Ivory)

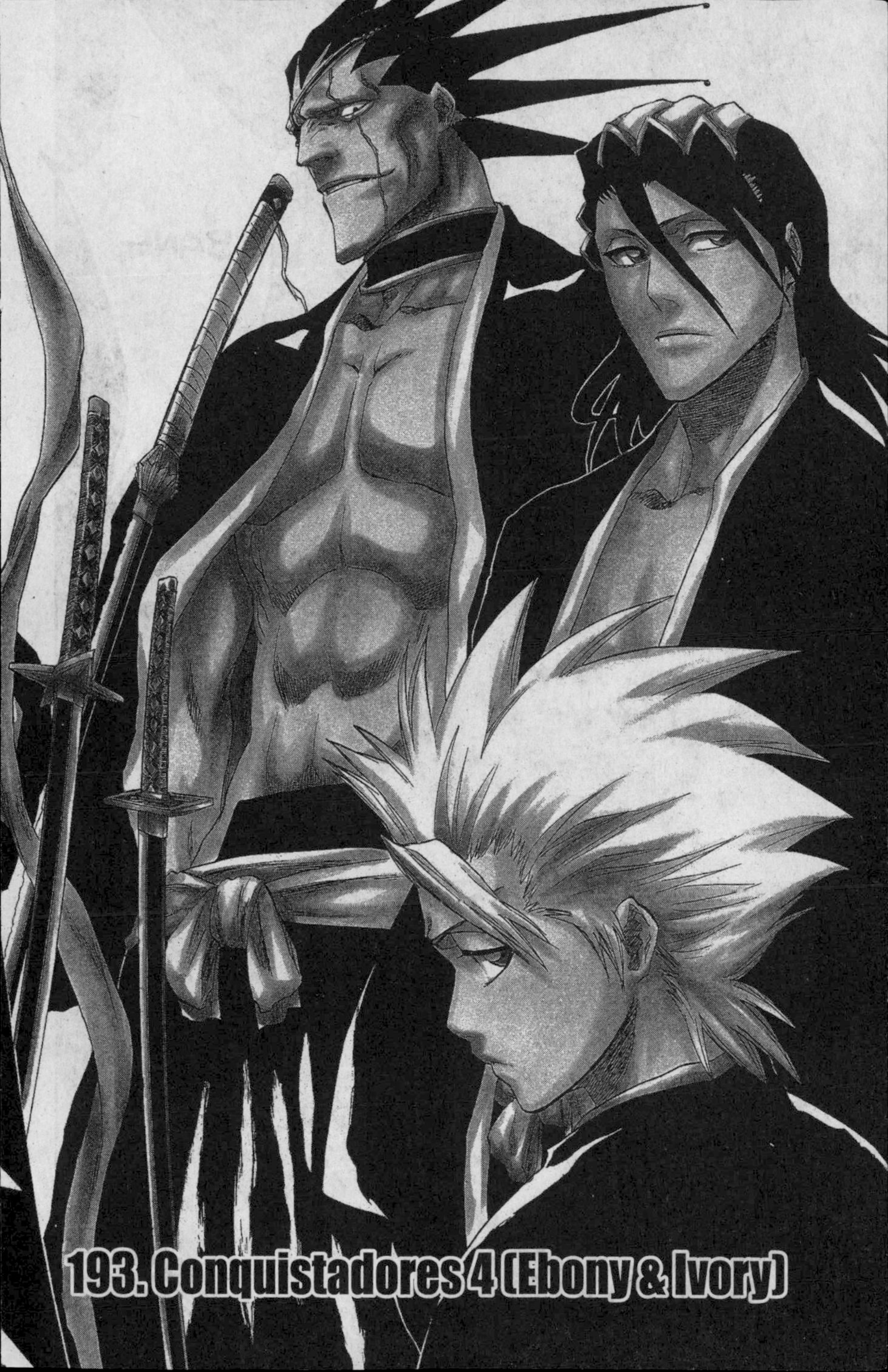

193. Conquistadores 4 (Ebony & Ivory)

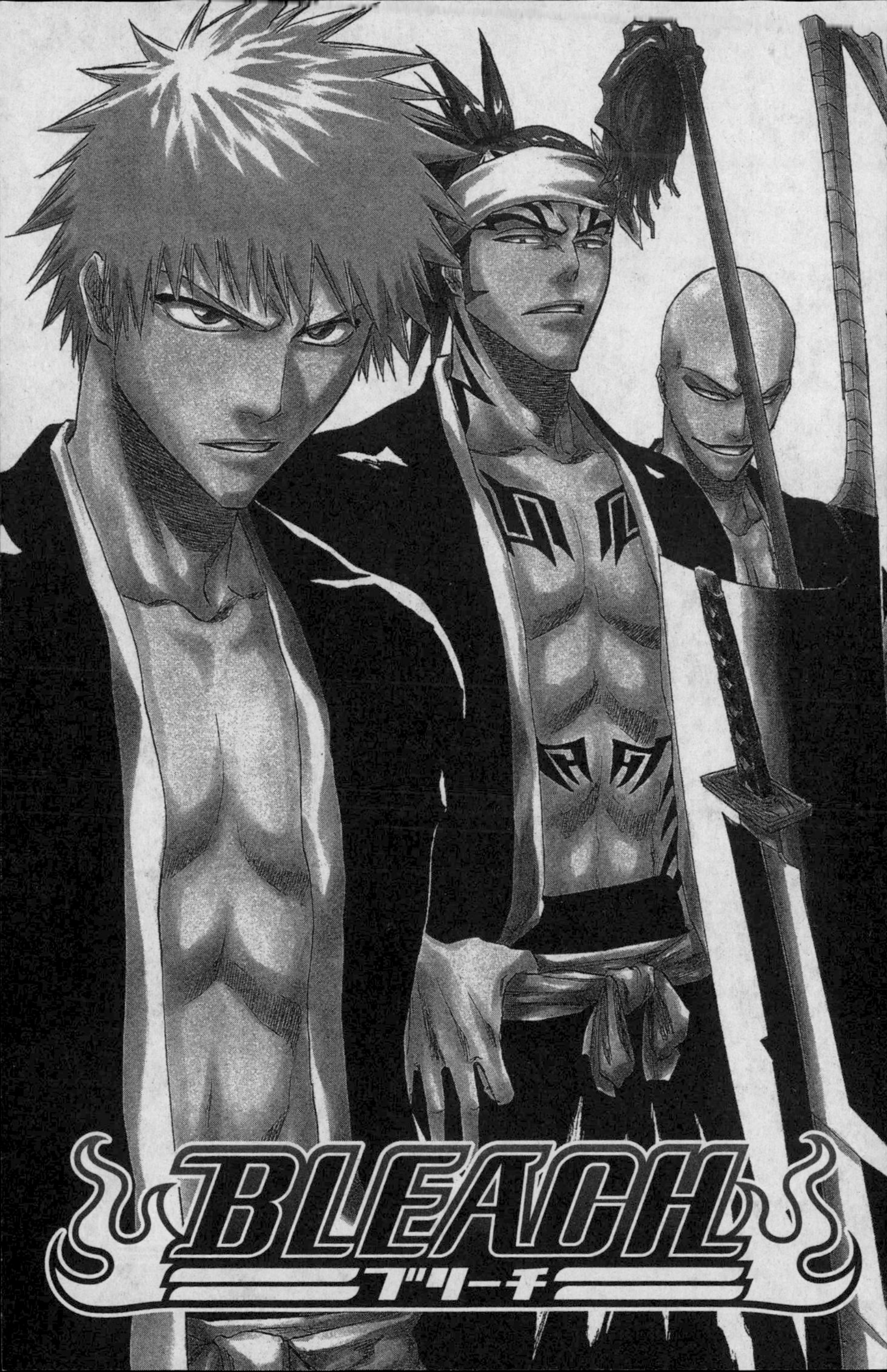
BLEACH
ブリーチ

BLEACH
ブリーチ

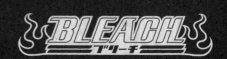

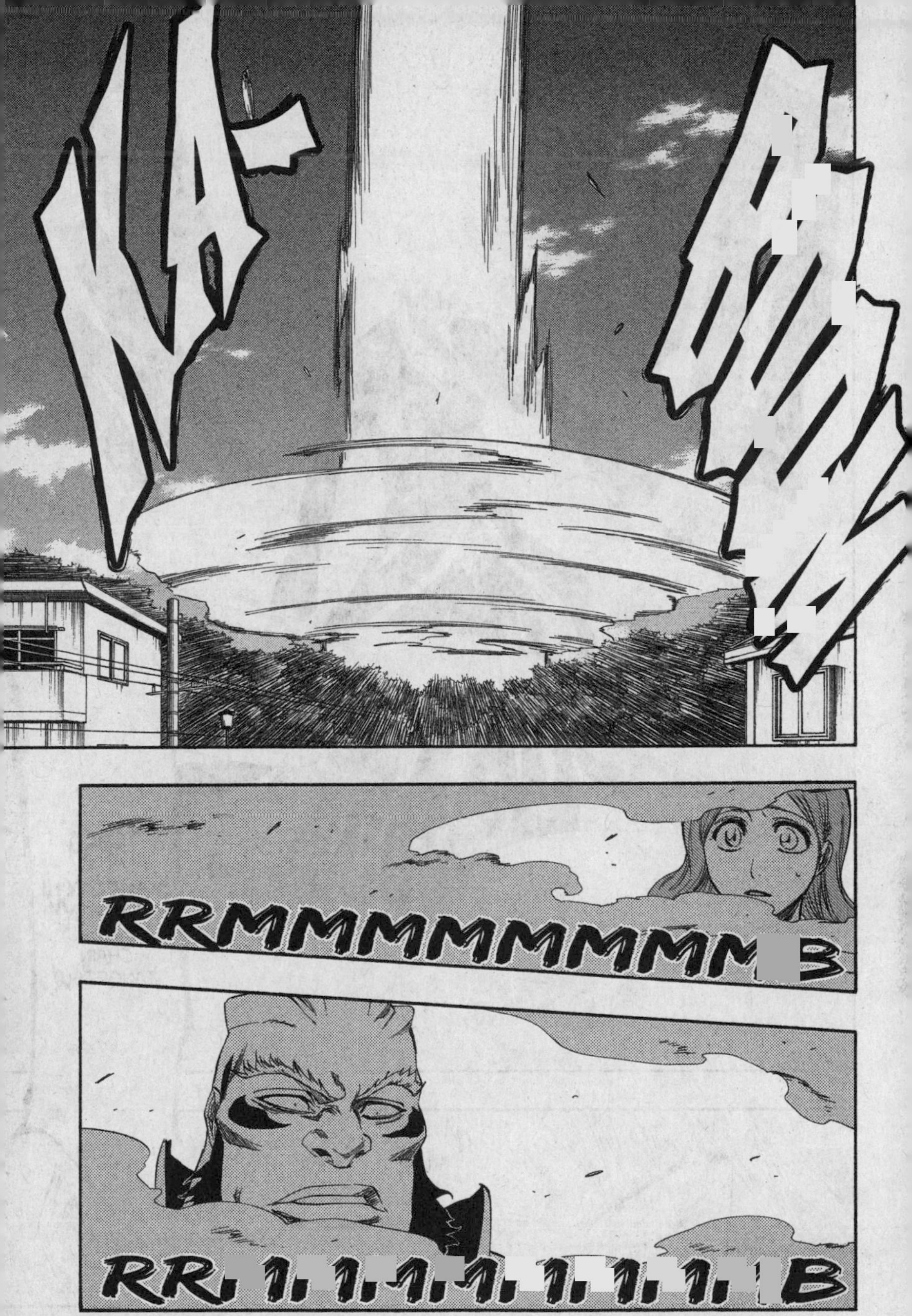
VA-
RRMMMMMMMMMM

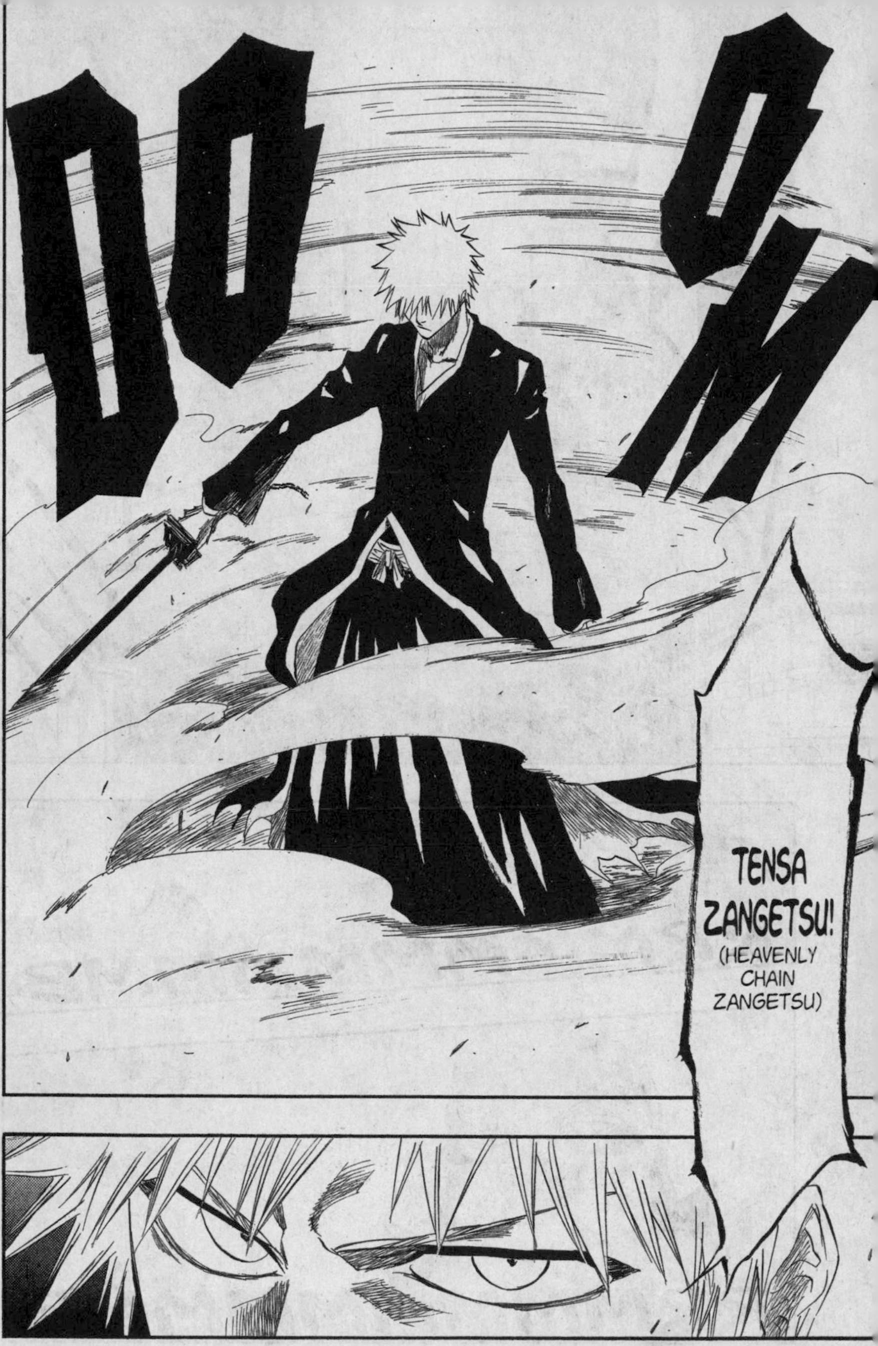
DOOOM
TENSA ZANGETSU! (HEAVENLY CHAIN ZANGETSU)

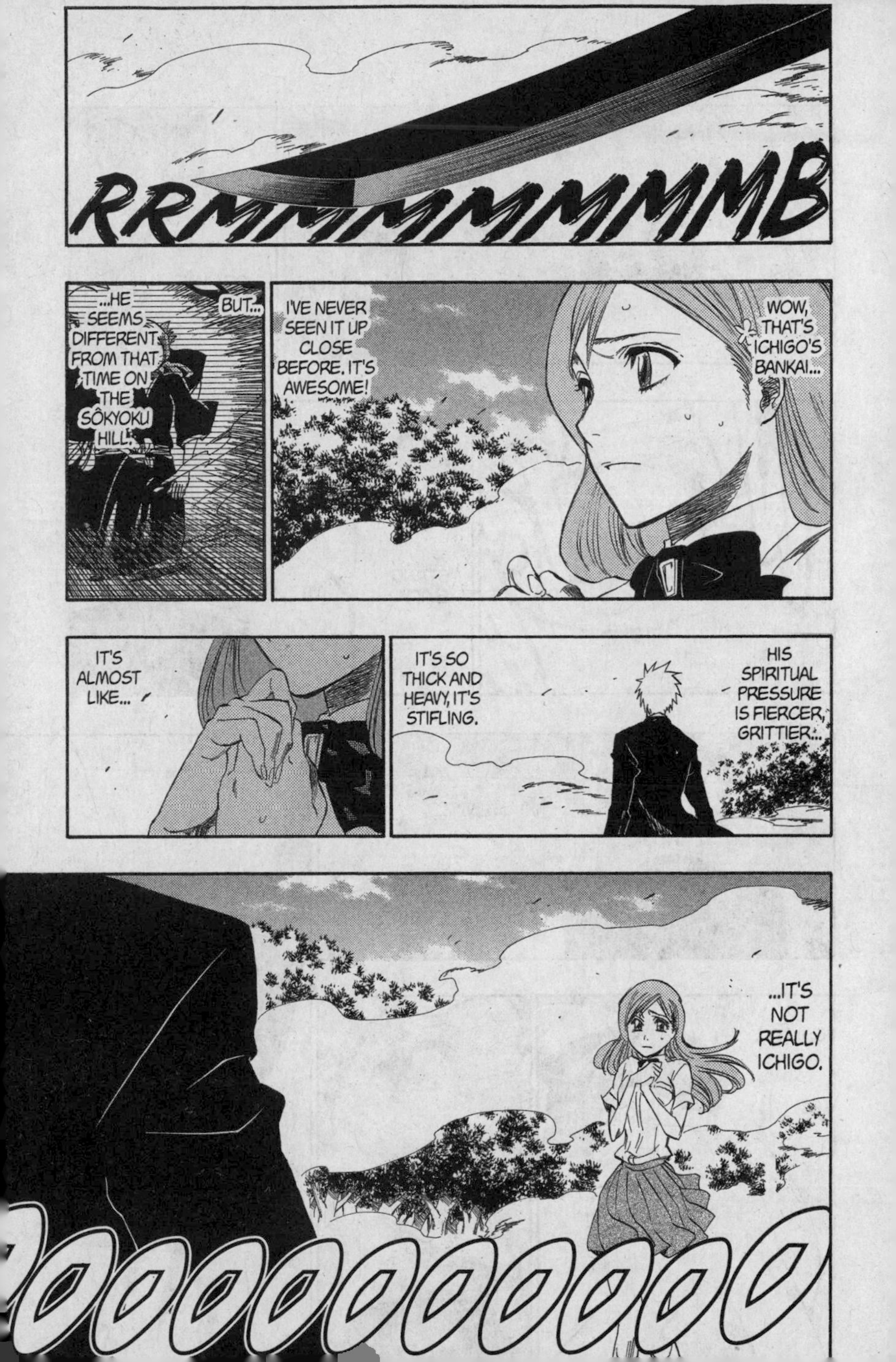
RRMMMMMMMMB
WOW, THAT'S ICHIGO'S BANKAI...
I'VE NEVER SEEN IT UP CLOSE BEFORE. IT'S AWESOME!
BUT...
...HE SEEMS DIFFERENT FROM THAT TIME ON THE SÔKYOKU HILL.
HIS SPIRITUAL PRESSURE IS FIERCER, GRITTIER...
IT'S SO THICK AND HEAVY, IT'S STIFLING.
IT'S ALMOST LIKE...
...IT'S NOT REALLY ICHIGO.

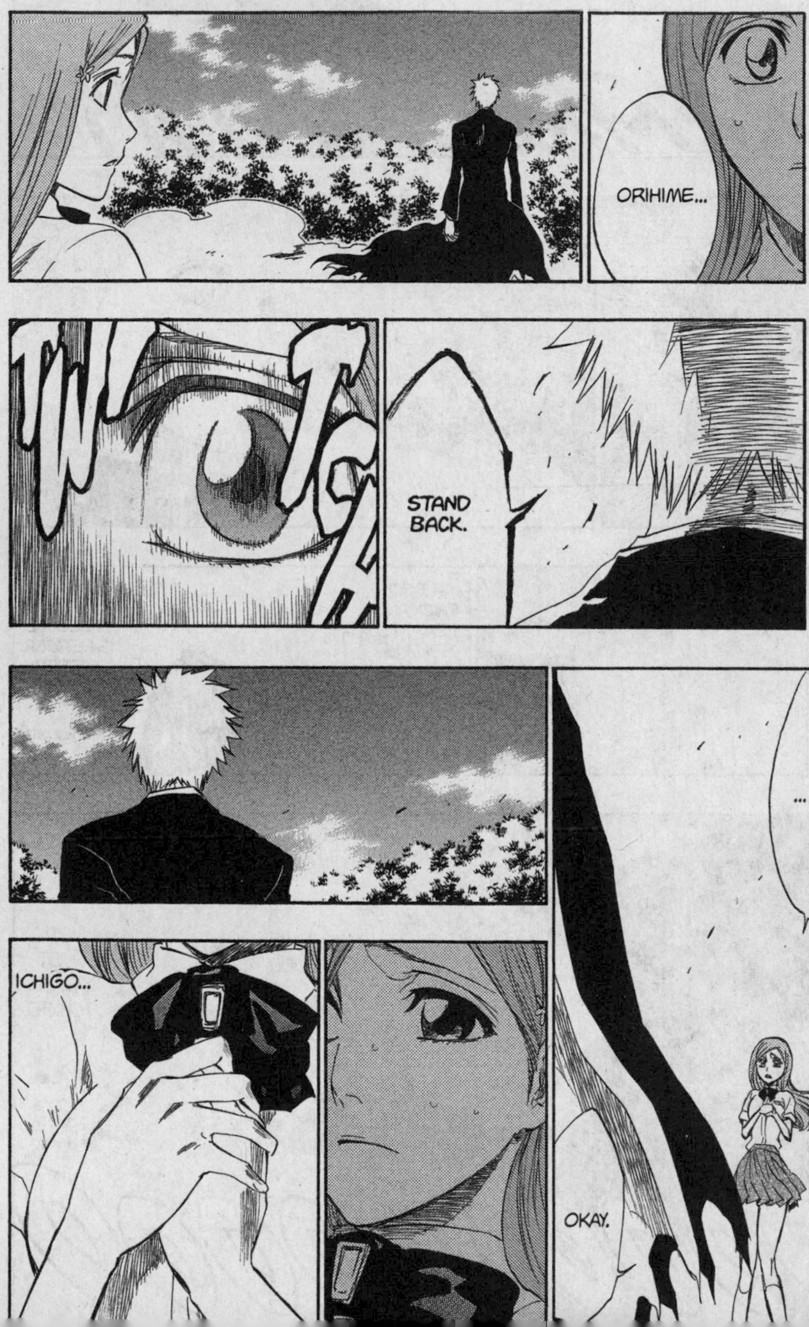
ORIHIME...
STAND BACK.
TWITCH
...
OKAY.
ICHIGO...

READ THIS WAY

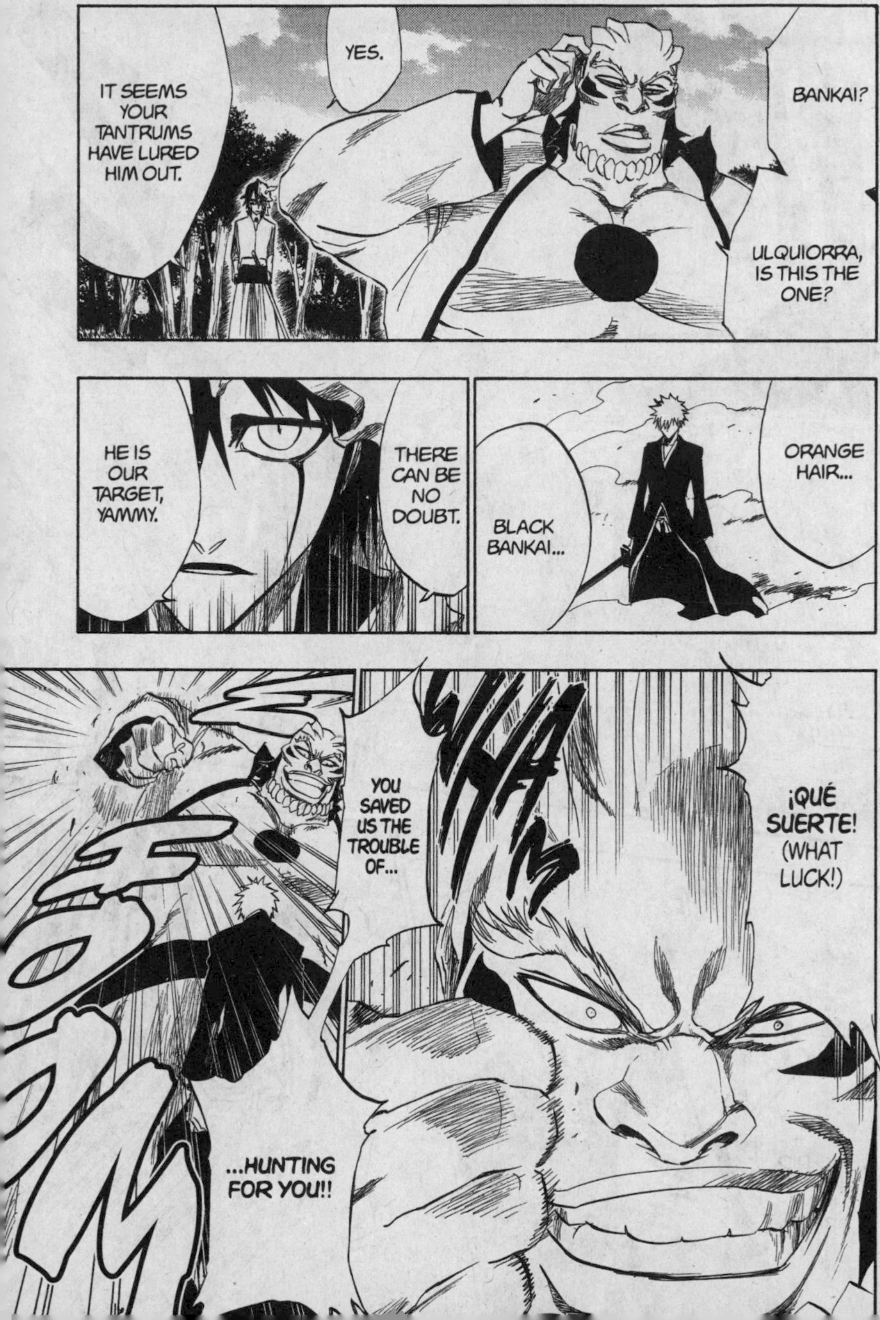
BANKAI?
ULQUIORRA, IS THIS THE ONE?
YES.
IT SEEMS YOUR TANTRUMS HAVE LURED HIM OUT.
ORANGE HAIR...
BLACK BANKAI...
THERE CAN BE NO DOUBT.
HE IS OUR TARGET, YAMMY.
¡QUÉ SUERTE! (WHAT LUCK!)
YOU SAVED US THE TROUBLE OF...
...HUNTING FOR YOU!!

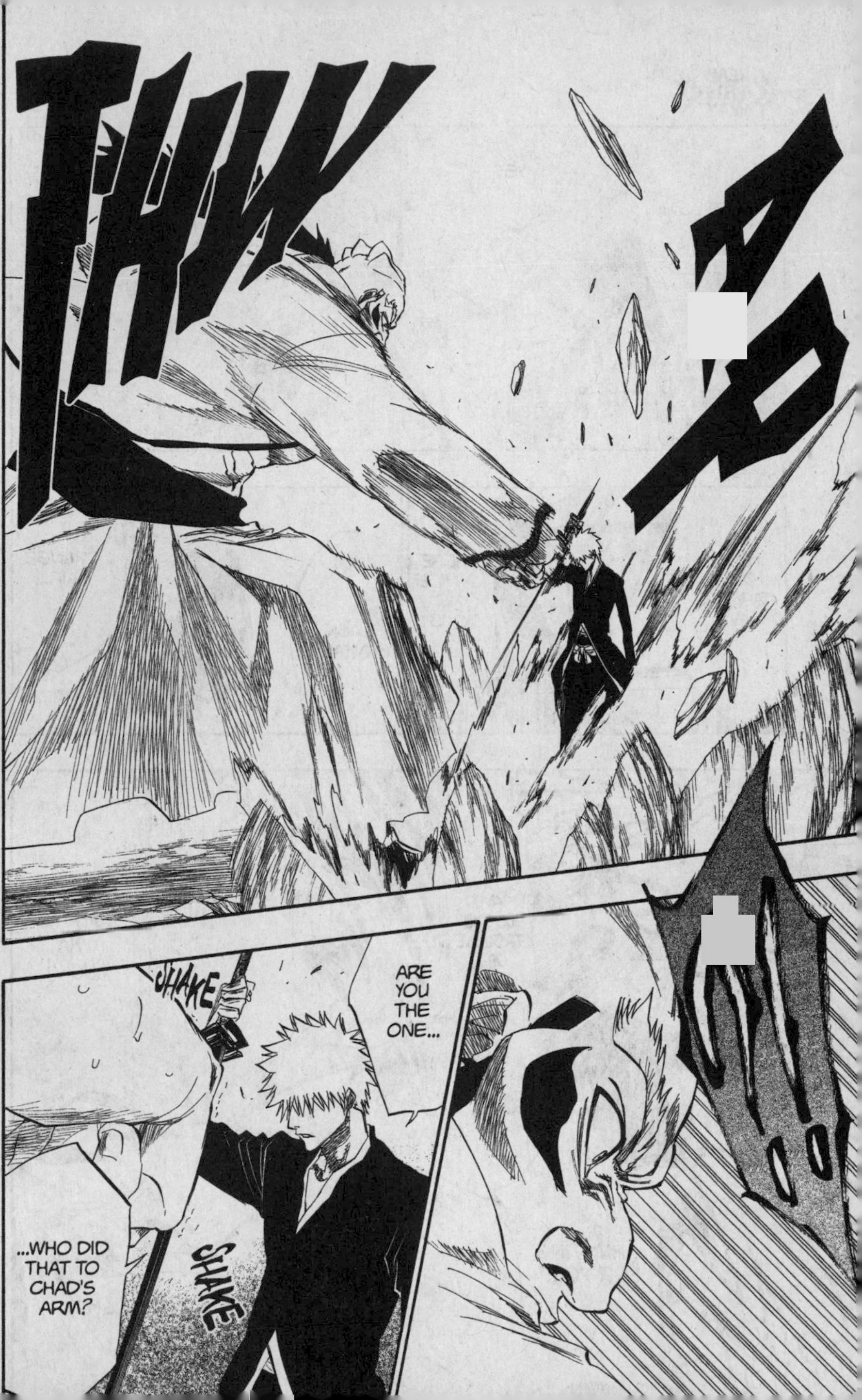
THWK
ARE YOU THE ONE...
SHAKE
...WHO DID THAT TO CHAD'S ARM?
SHAKE

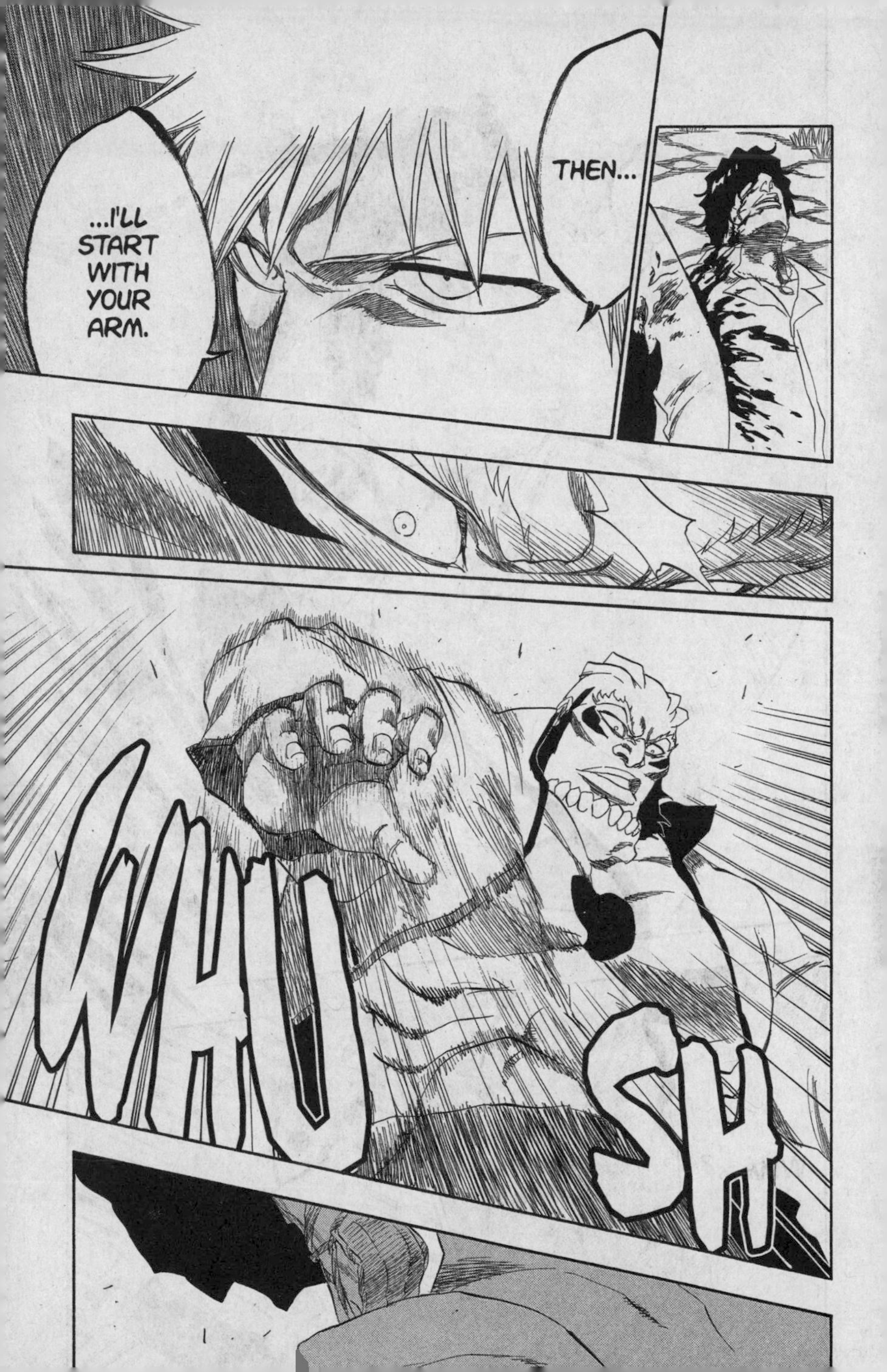
THEN...
...I'LL START WITH YOUR ARM.
WHUSH

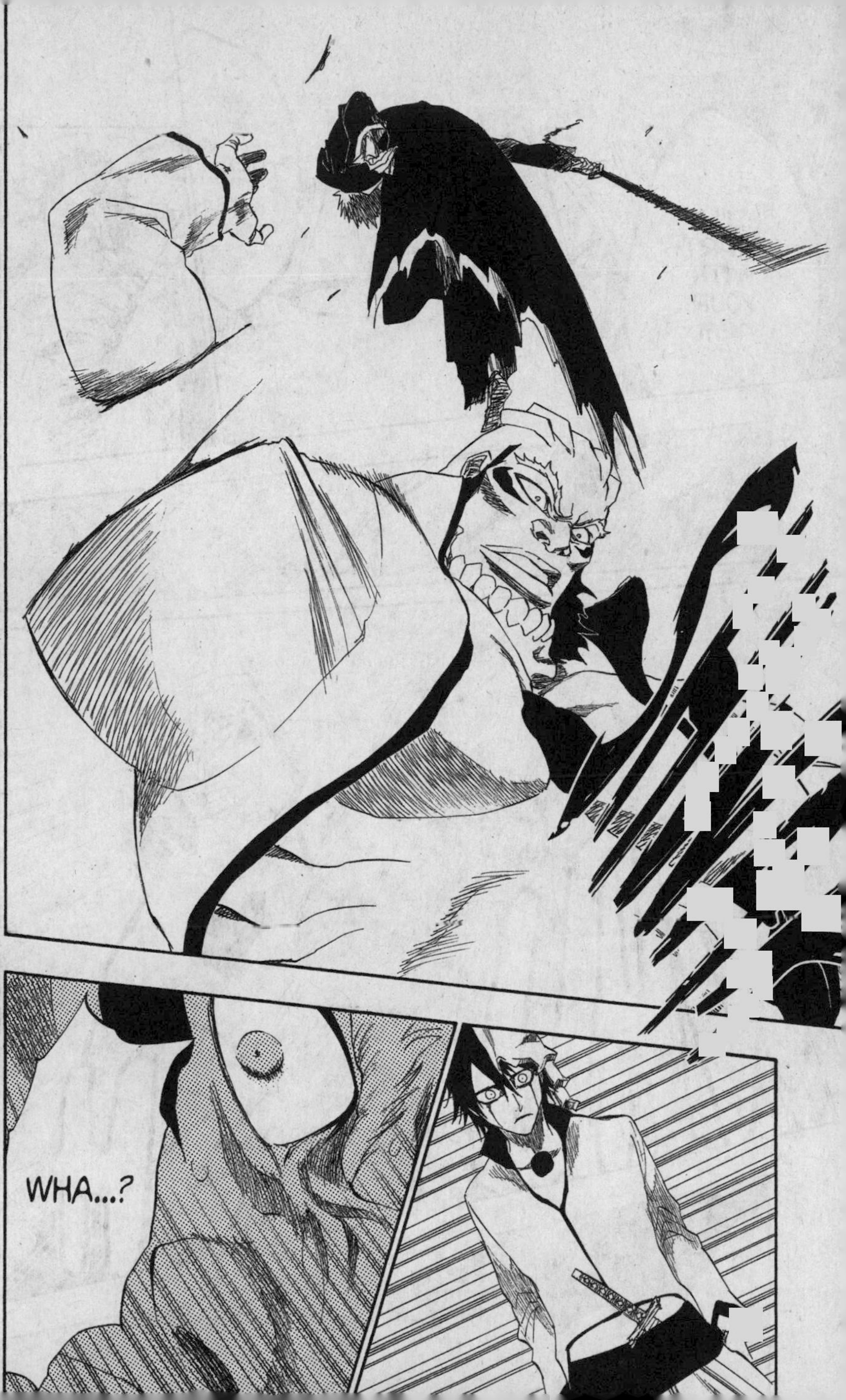
WHA...?

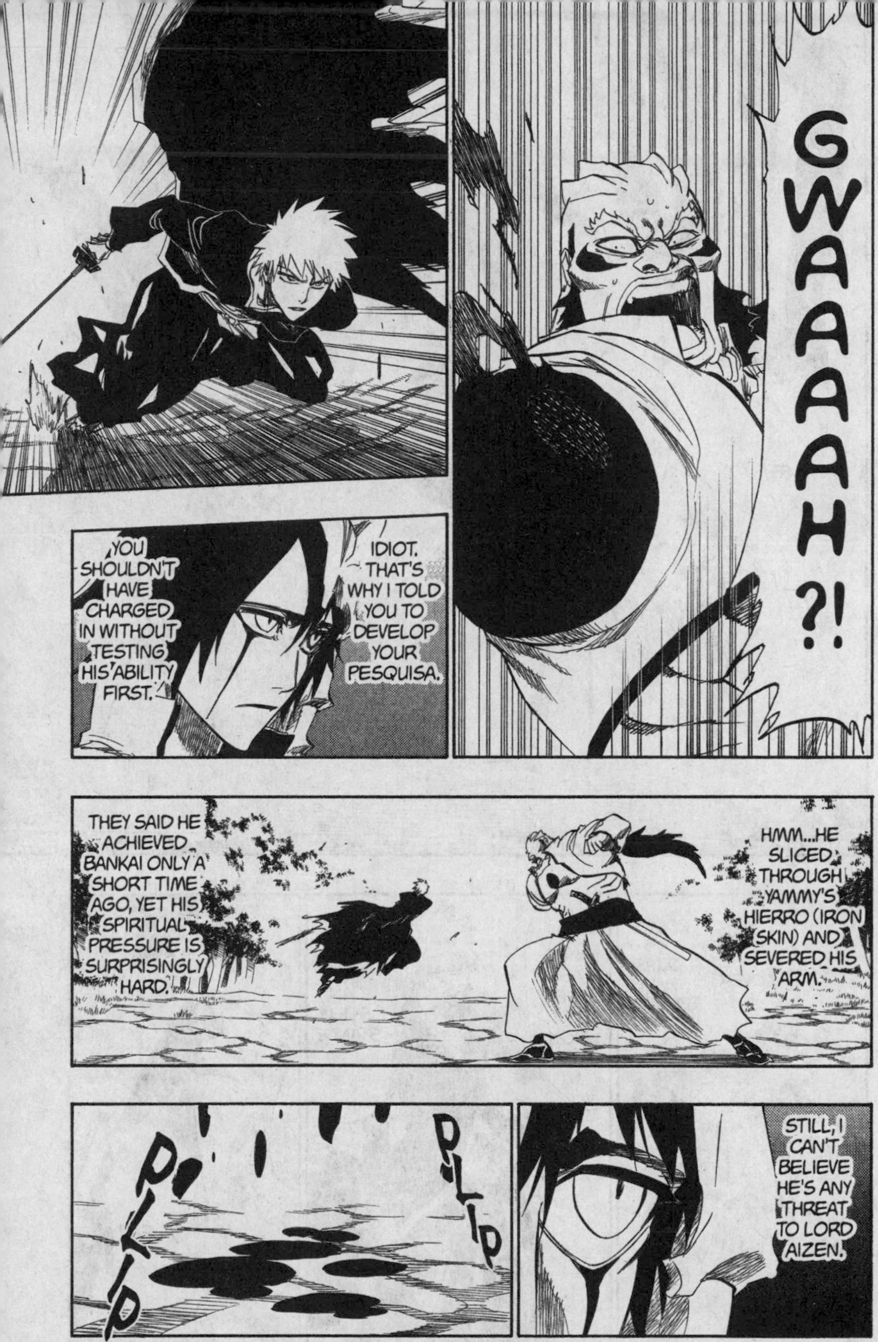
GWAAAAH?!
IDIOT. THAT'S WHY I TOLD YOU TO DEVELOP YOUR PESQUISA.
YOU SHOULDN'T HAVE CHARGED IN WITHOUT TESTING HIS ABILITY FIRST.
HMM...HE SLICED THROUGH YAMMY'S HIERRO (IRON SKIN) AND SEVERED HIS ARM.
THEY SAID HE ACHIEVED BANKAI ONLY A SHORT TIME AGO, YET HIS SPIRITUAL PRESSURE IS SURPRISINGLY HARD.
STILL, I CAN'T BELIEVE HE'S ANY THREAT TO LORD AIZEN.
PLIP
PLIP

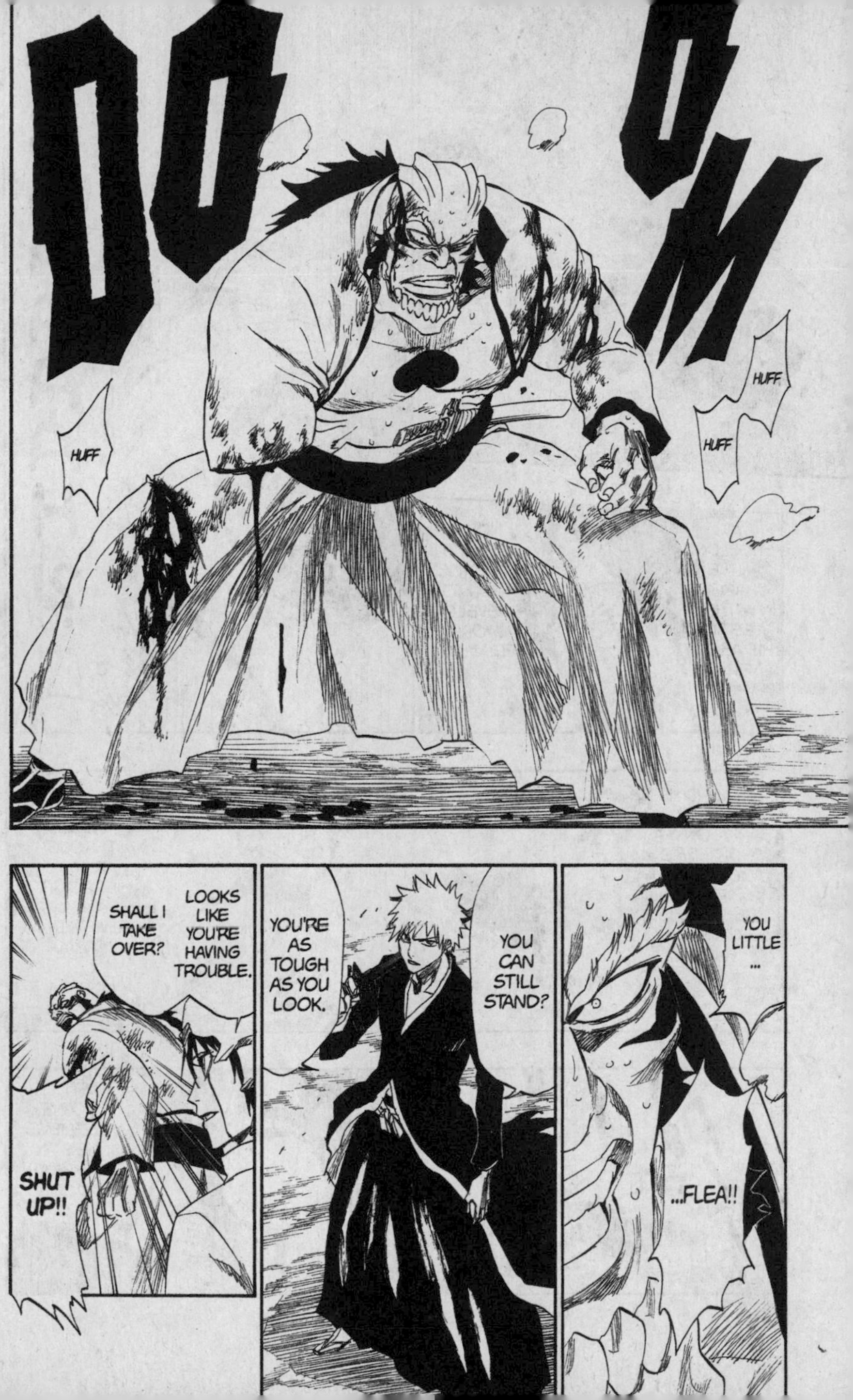
DOOM
HUFF
HUFF
HUFF
YOU LITTLE ...
...FLEA!!
YOU CAN STILL STAND?
YOU'RE AS TOUGH AS YOU LOOK.
LOOKS LIKE YOU'RE HAVING TROUBLE.
SHALL I TAKE OVER?
SHUT UP!!

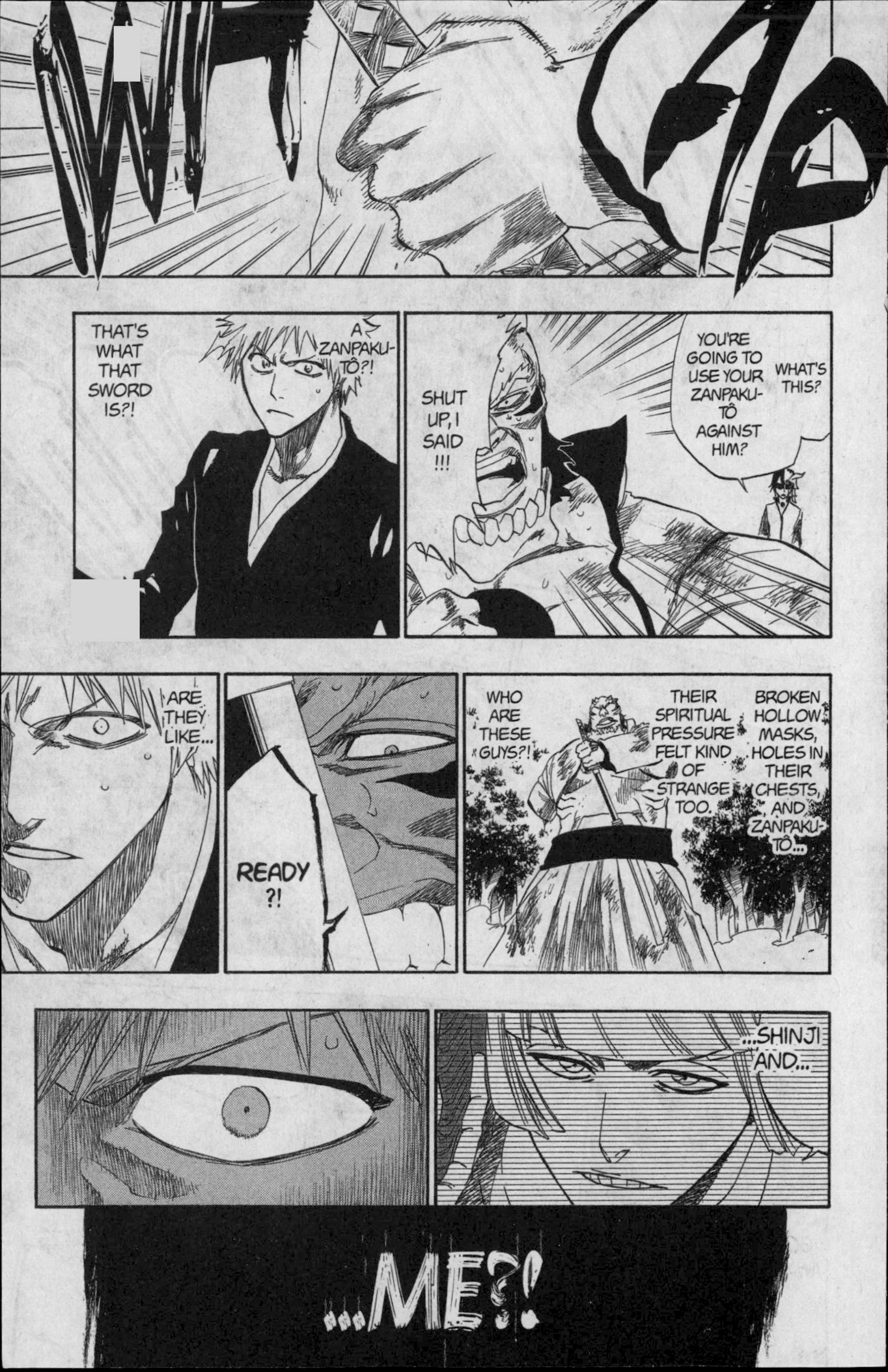
WHAT'S THIS?
YOU'RE GOING TO USE YOUR ZANPAKU-TÔ AGAINST HIM?
SHUT UP, I SAID!!!
A ZANPAKU-TÔ?!
THAT'S WHAT THAT SWORD IS?!
BROKEN HOLLOW MASKS, HOLES IN THEIR CHESTS, AND ZANPAKU-TÔ...
THEIR SPIRITUAL PRESSURE FELT KIND OF STRANGE TOO.
WHO ARE THESE GUYS?!
READY?!
ARE THEY LIKE...
...SHINJI AND...
...ME?!

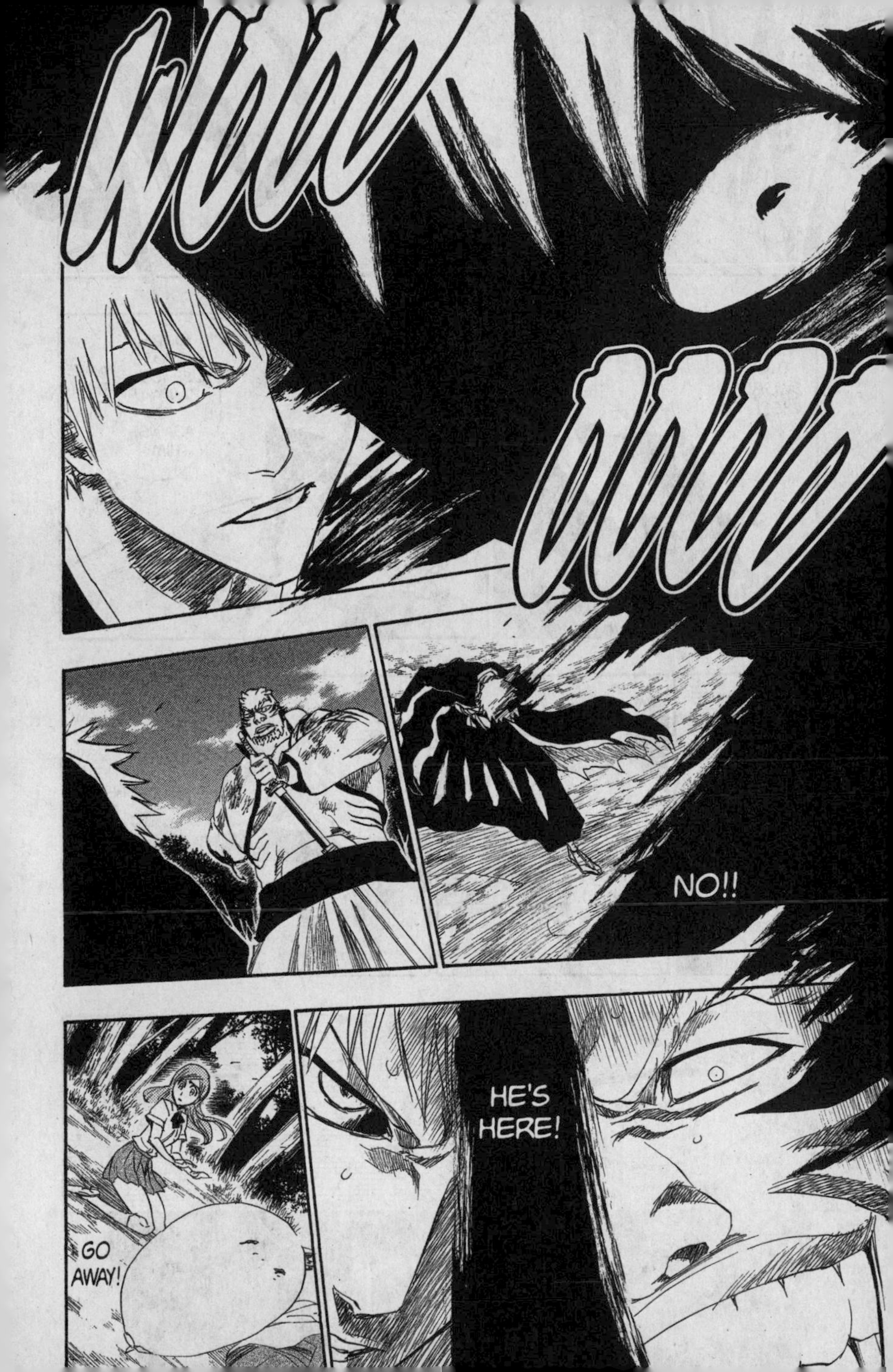
NO!!
HE'S HERE!
GO AWAY!

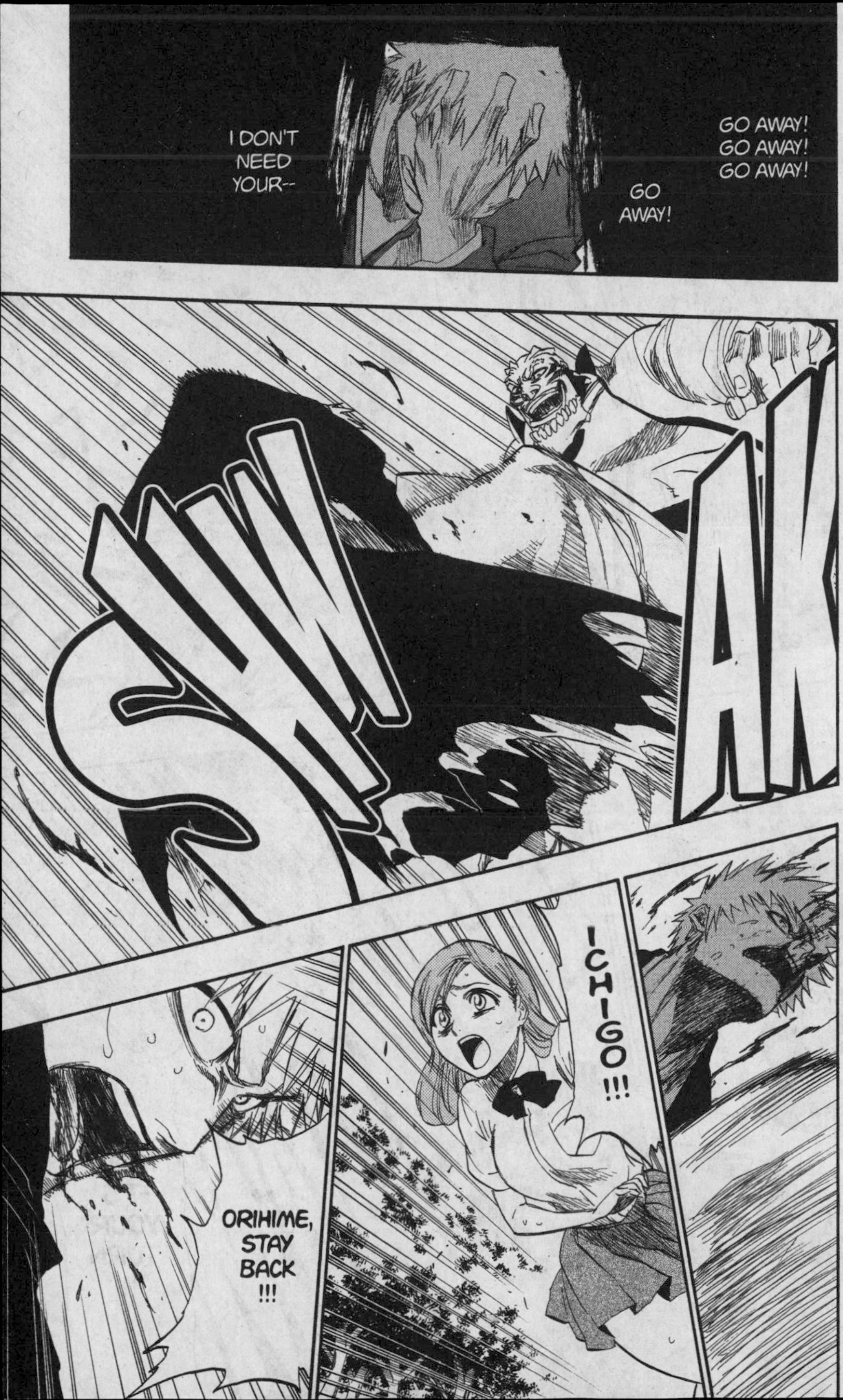
GO AWAY! GO AWAY! GO AWAY!
GO AWAY!
I DON'T NEED YOUR--
SHWAK
ICHIGO!!!
ORIHIME, STAY BACK!!!

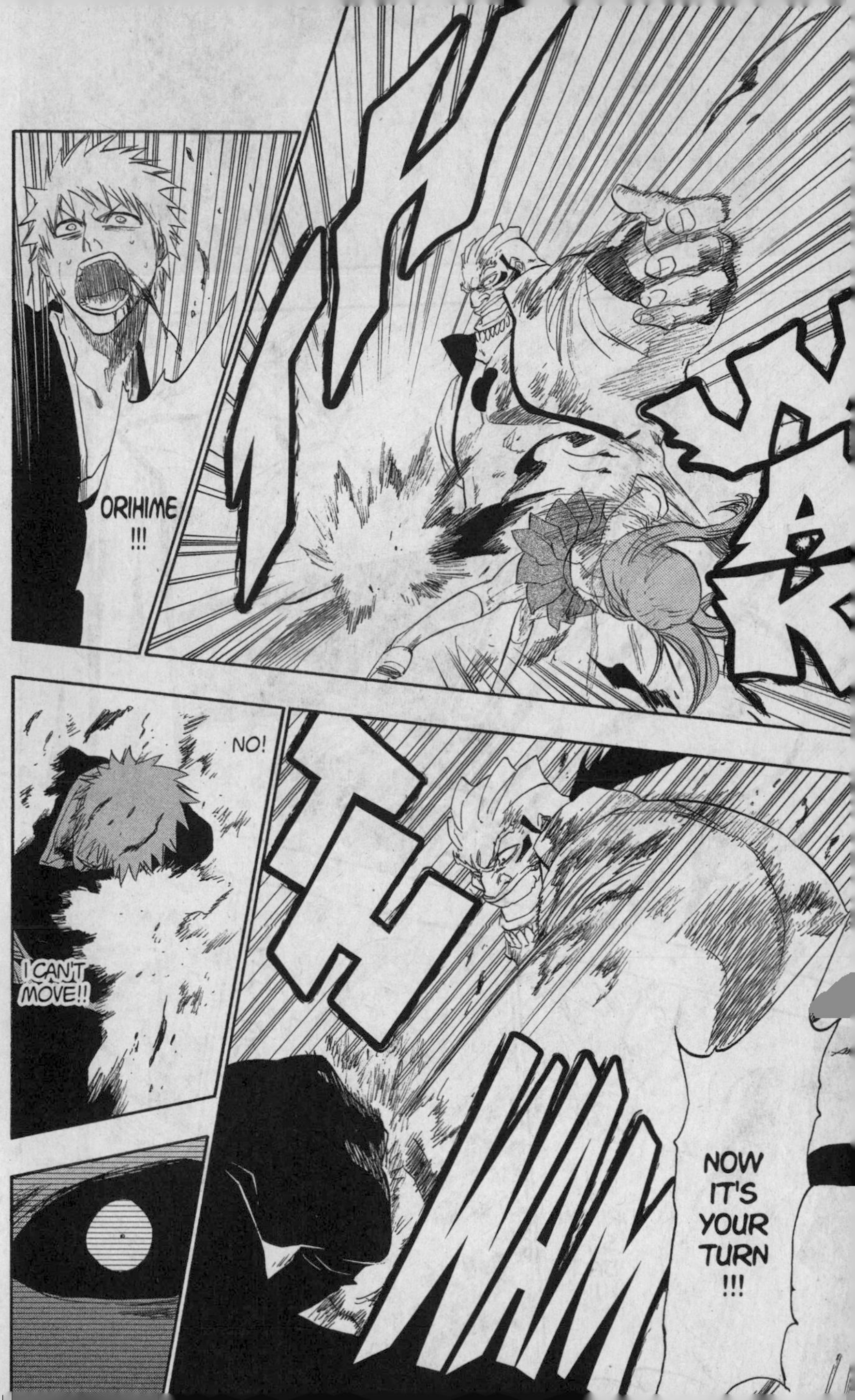
ORIHIME !!!
WHAM
NOW IT'S YOUR TURN !!!
NO!
I CAN'T MOVE!!

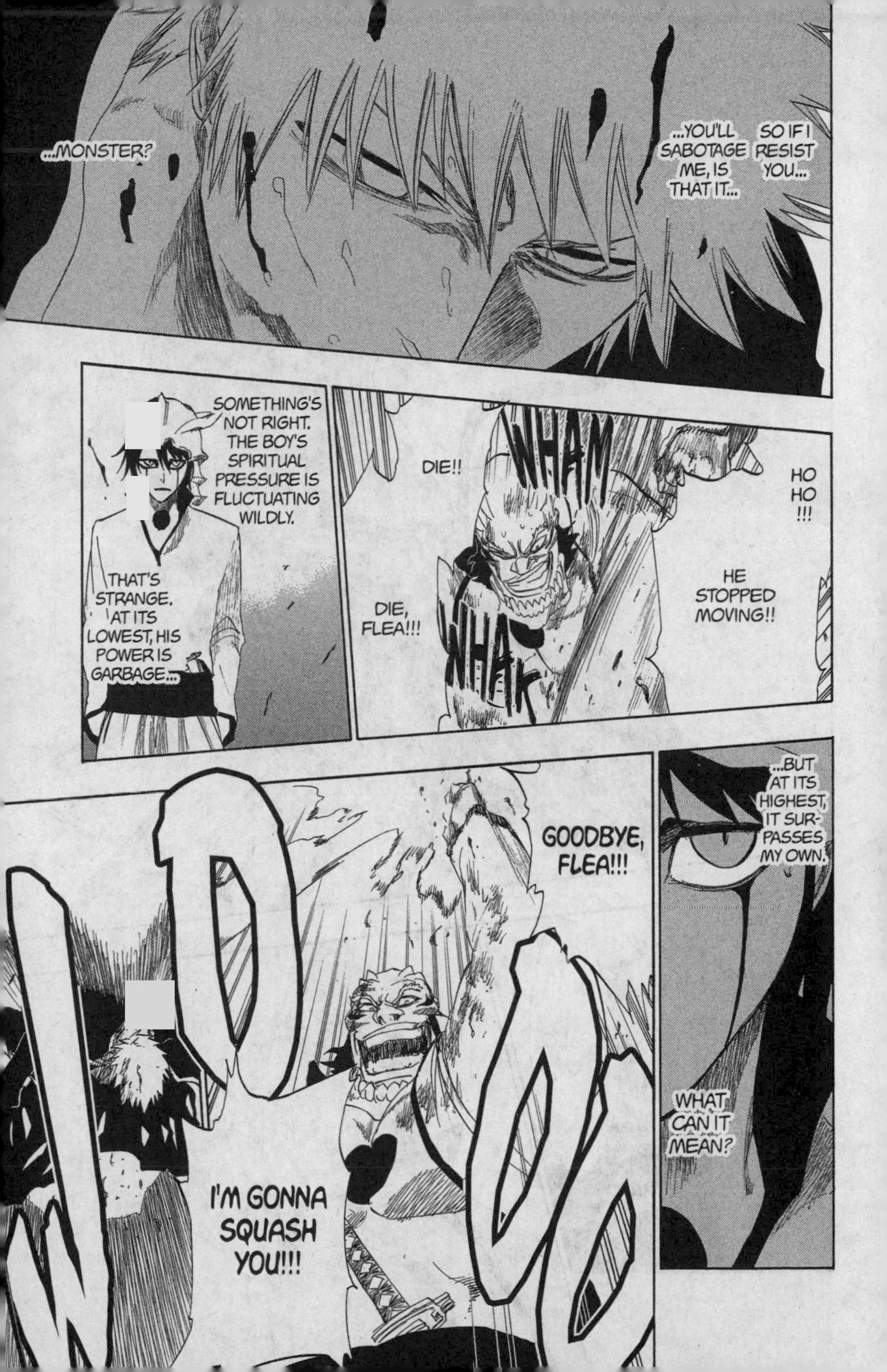
SO IF I RESIST YOU...
...YOU'LL SABOTAGE ME, IS THAT IT...
...MONSTER?
HO HO !!!
HE STOPPED MOVING!!
DIE!!
WHAM
WHAK
DIE, FLEA!!!
SOMETHING'S NOT RIGHT. THE BOY'S SPIRITUAL PRESSURE IS FLUCTUATING WILDLY.
THAT'S STRANGE. AT ITS LOWEST, HIS POWER IS GARBAGE...
...BUT AT ITS HIGHEST, IT SUR-PASSES MY OWN.
WHAT CAN IT MEAN?
GOODBYE, FLEA!!!
I'M GONNA SQUASH YOU!!!

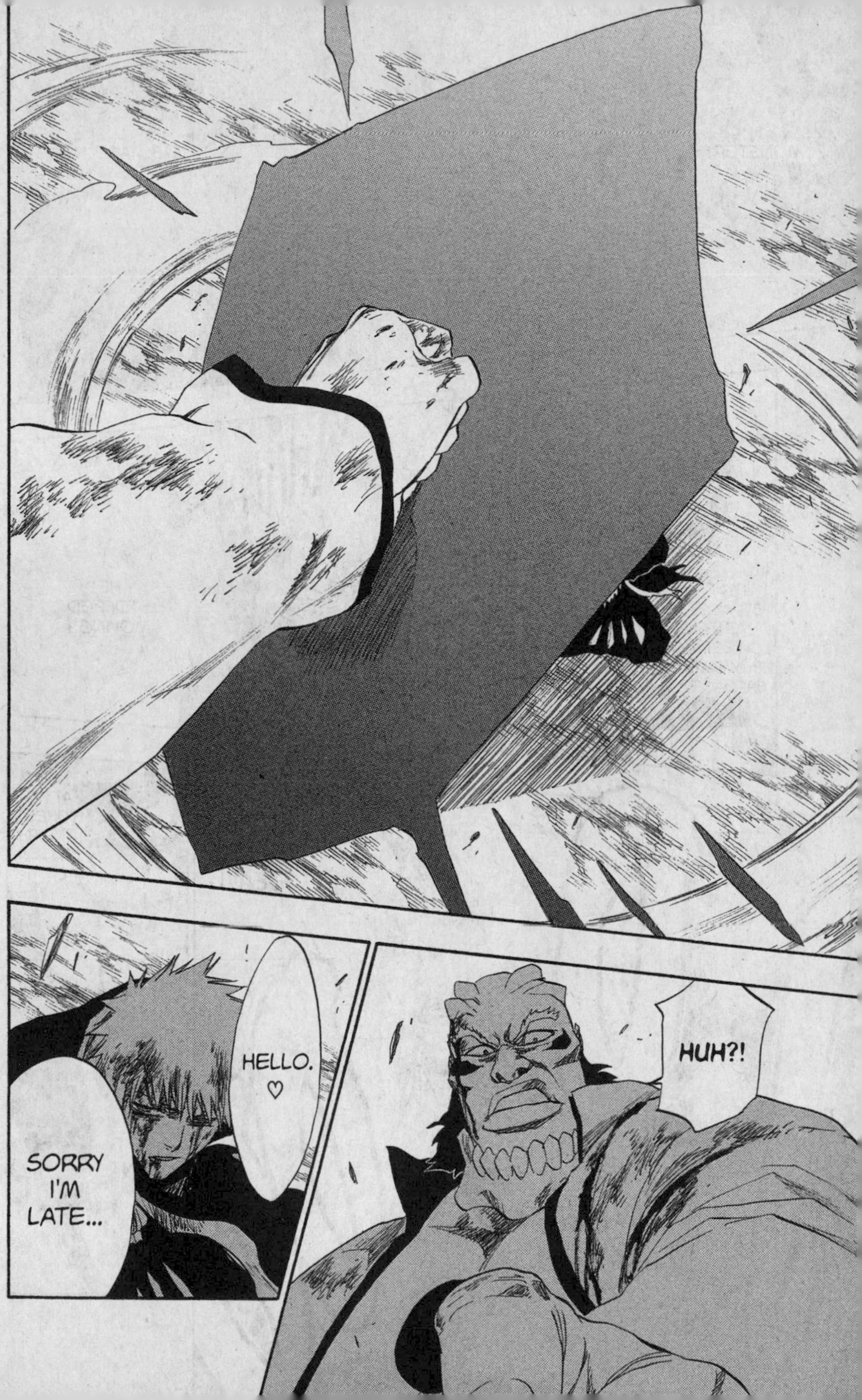
HUH?!
HELLO. ♡
SORRY I'M LATE...

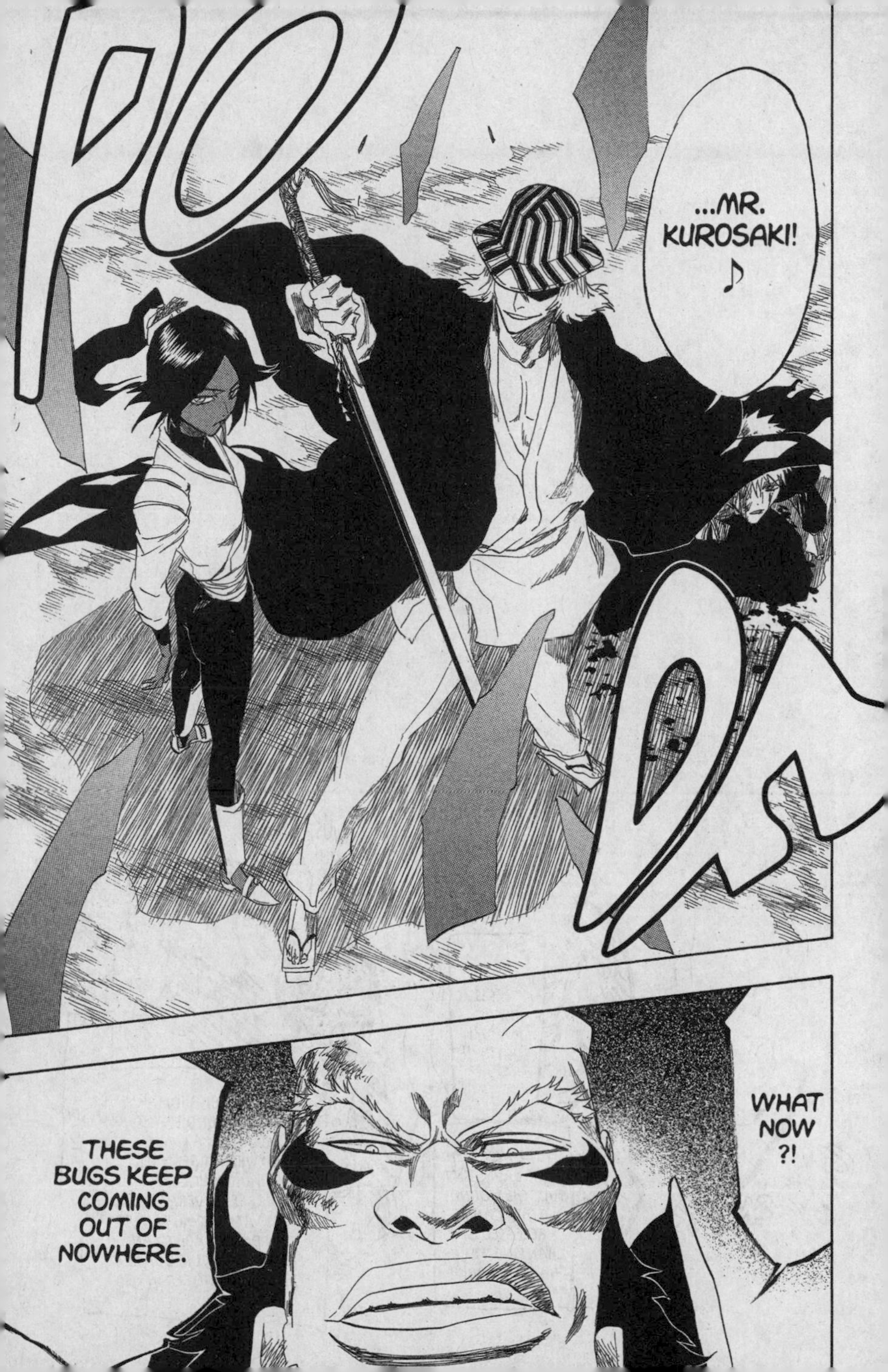
...MR. KUROSAKI! ♪
PO
DA
WHAT NOW ?!
THESE BUGS KEEP COMING OUT OF NOWHERE.

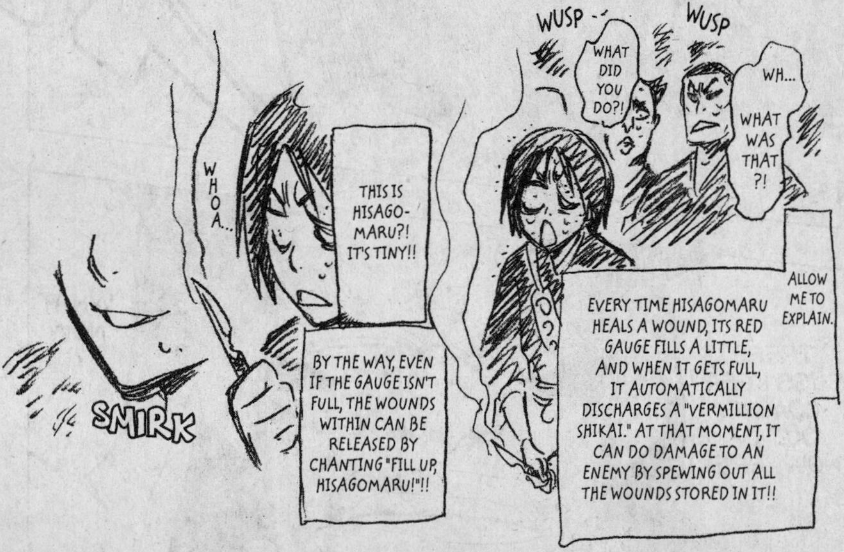
WUSP
WH... WHAT WAS THAT?!
WHAT DID YOU DO?!
WUSP
ALLOW ME TO EXPLAIN.
EVERY TIME HISAGOMARU HEALS A WOUND, ITS RED GAUGE FILLS A LITTLE, AND WHEN IT GETS FULL, IT AUTOMATICALLY DISCHARGES A "VERMILLION SHIKAI." AT THAT MOMENT, IT CAN DO DAMAGE TO AN ENEMY BY SPEWING OUT ALL THE WOUNDS STORED IN IT!!
THIS IS HISAGOMARU?! IT'S TINY!!
WHOA...
BY THE WAY, EVEN IF THE GAUGE ISN'T FULL, THE WOUNDS WITHIN CAN BE RELEASED BY CHANTING "FILL UP, HISAGOMARU!"!!
SMIRK

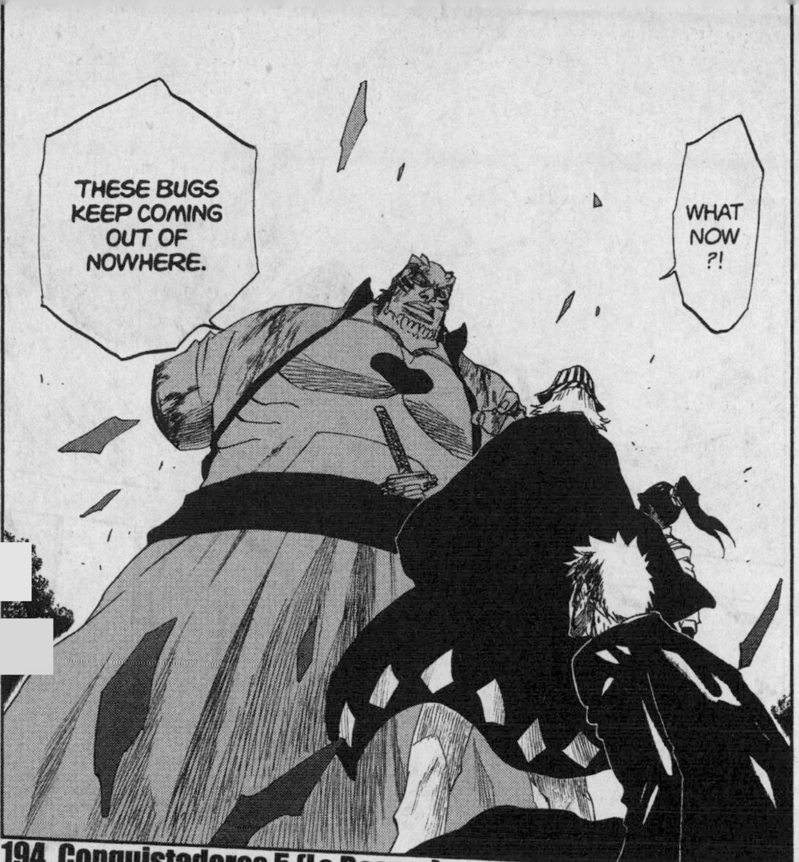
WHAT NOW ?!
THESE BUGS KEEP COMING OUT OF NOWHERE.

194. Conquistadores 5 (La Basura)

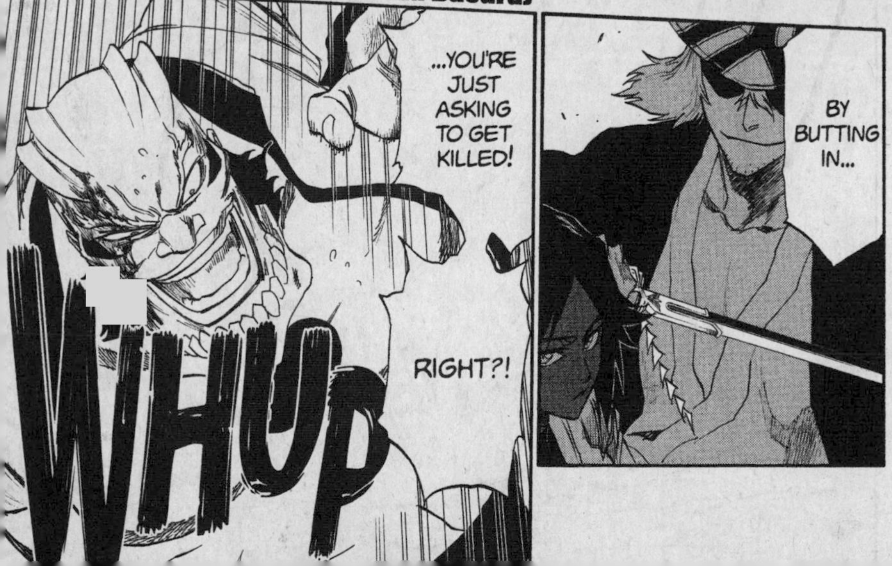
BY BUTTING IN...
...YOU'RE JUST ASKING TO GET KILLED!
RIGHT?!
WHUP

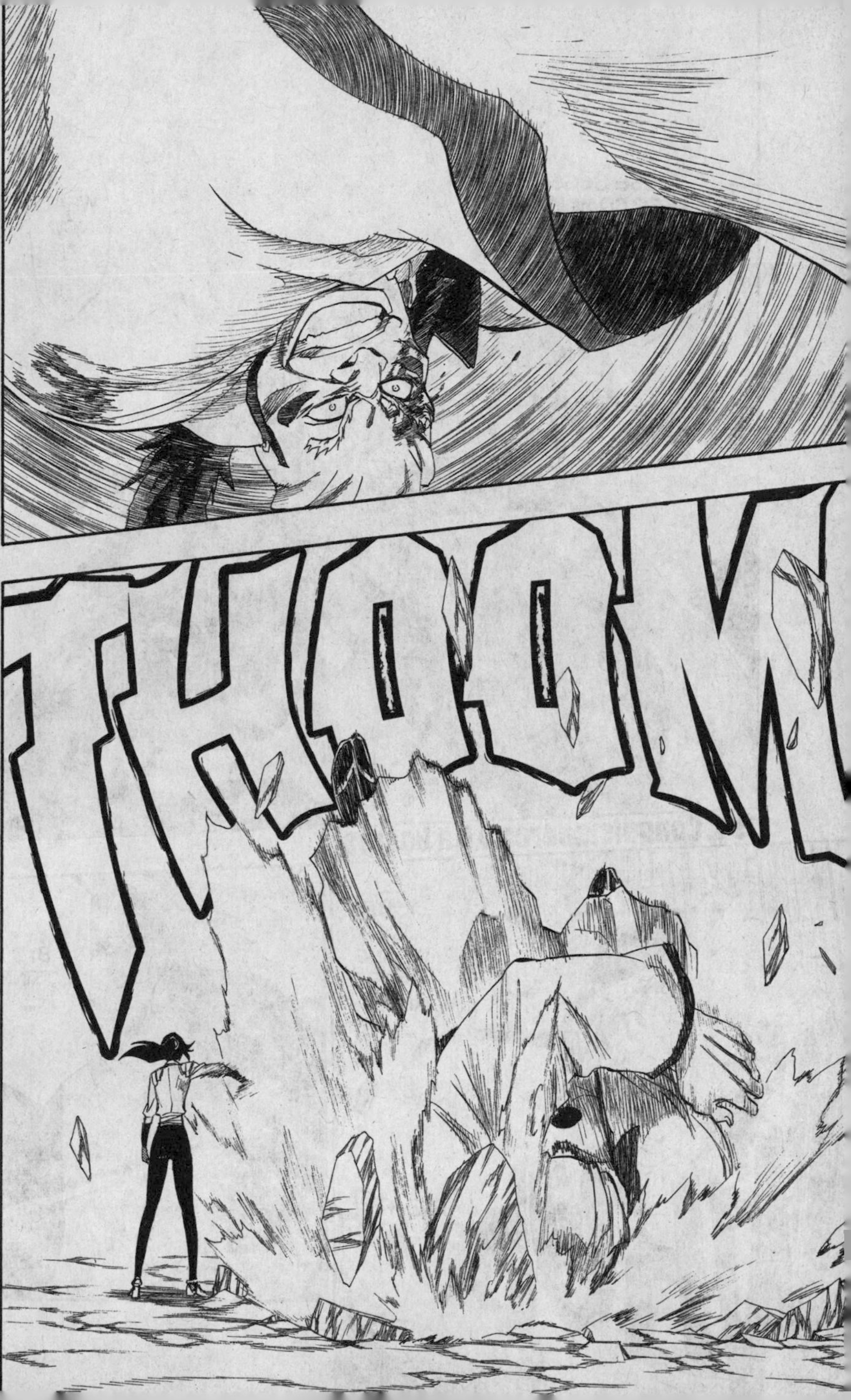
THOOM

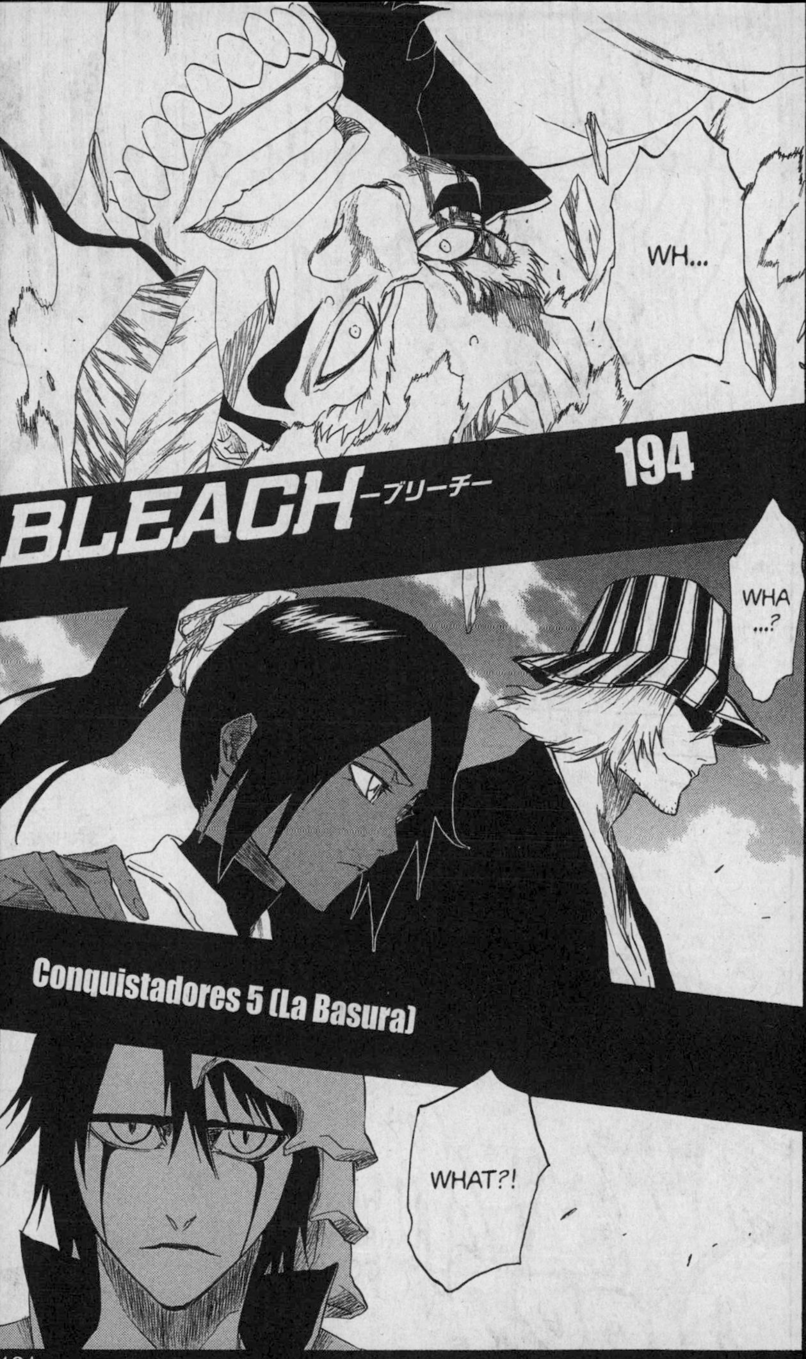
WH...
194
BLEACH -ブリーチ-
WHA ...?
Conquistadores 5 (La Basura)
WHAT?!

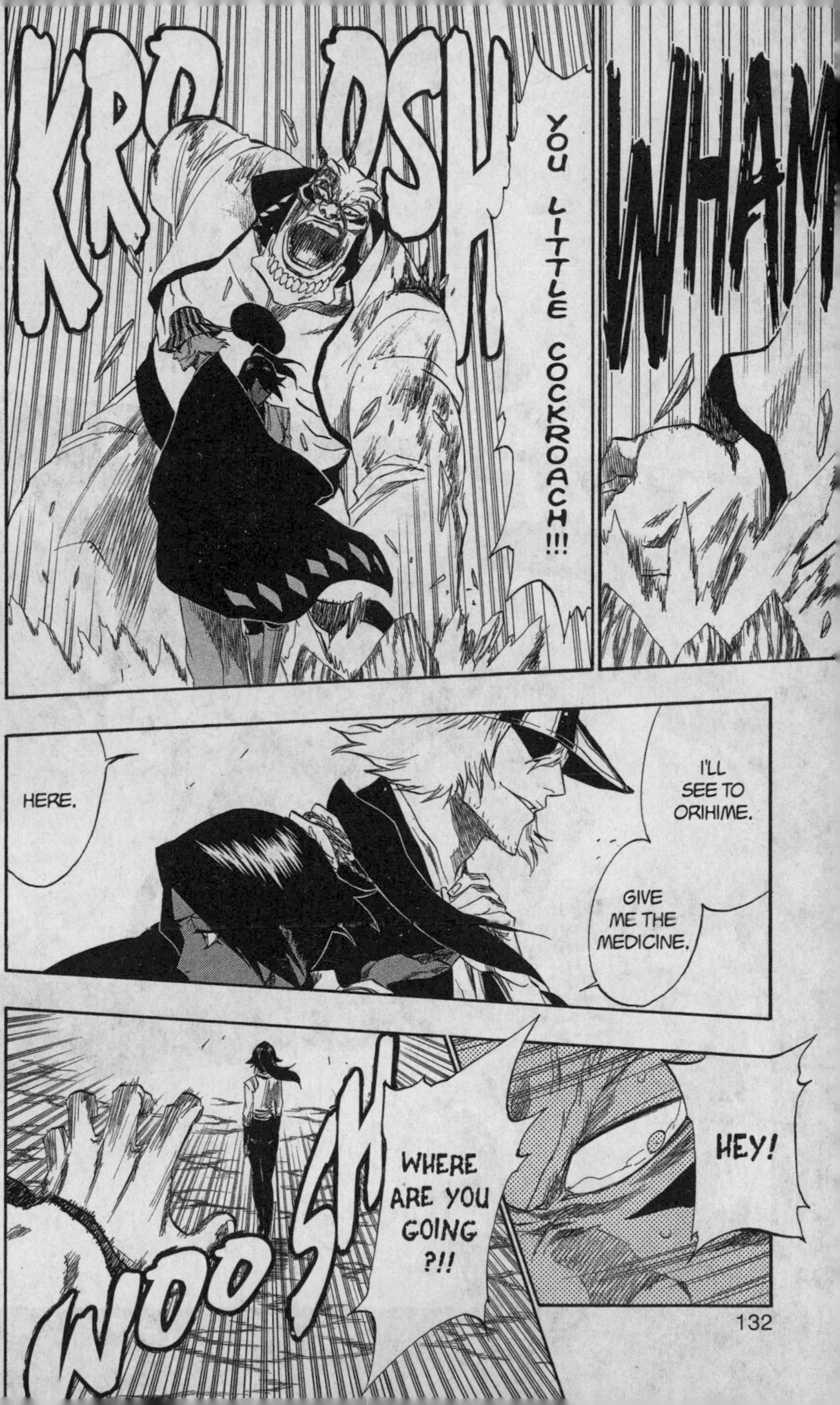
WHAM
KROOSH
YOU LITTLE COCKROACH!!!
I'LL SEE TO ORIHIME.
GIVE ME THE MEDICINE.
HERE.
HEY!
WHERE ARE YOU GOING ?!!
WOOSH

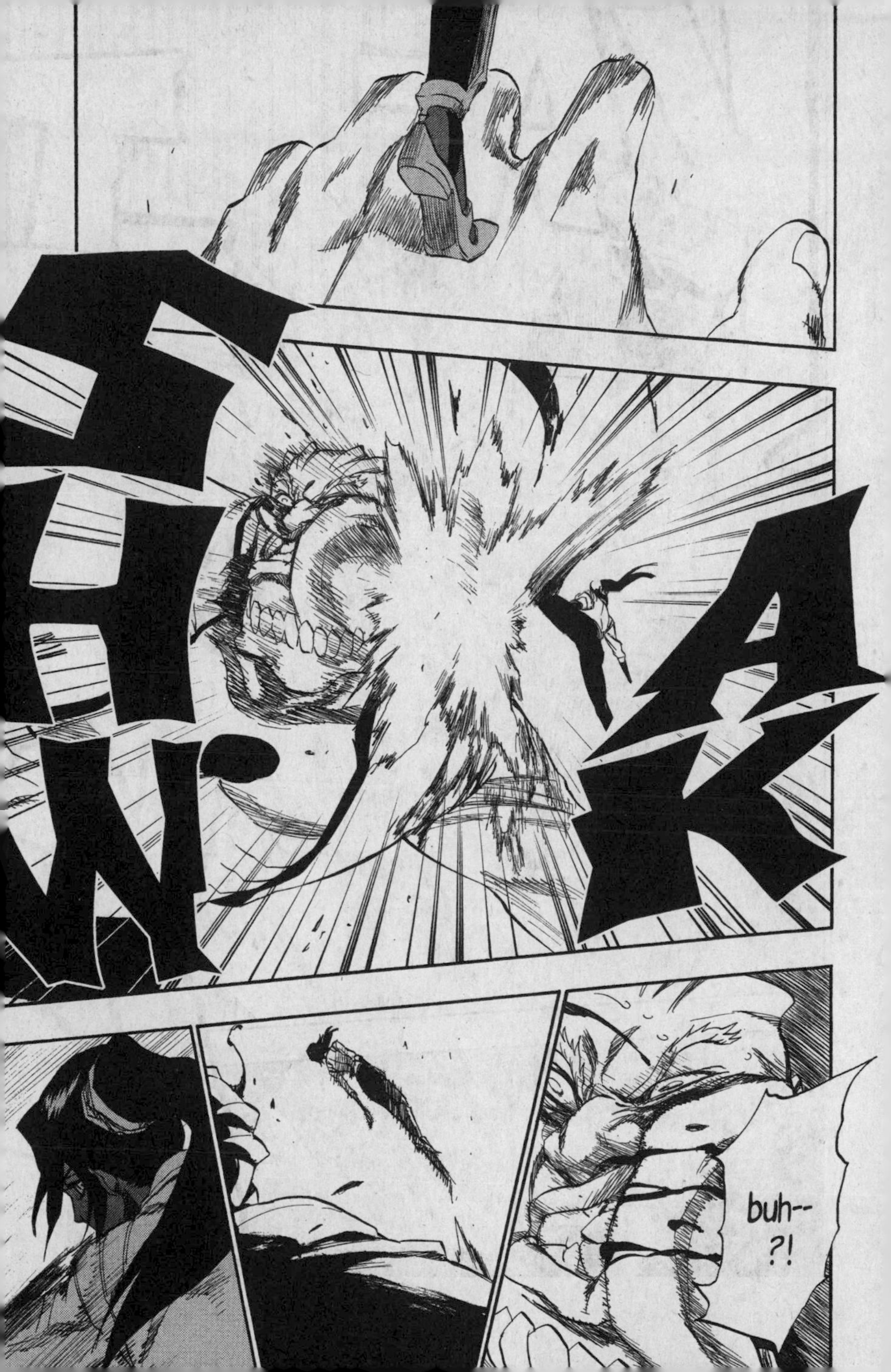
THWAK
buh--
?!

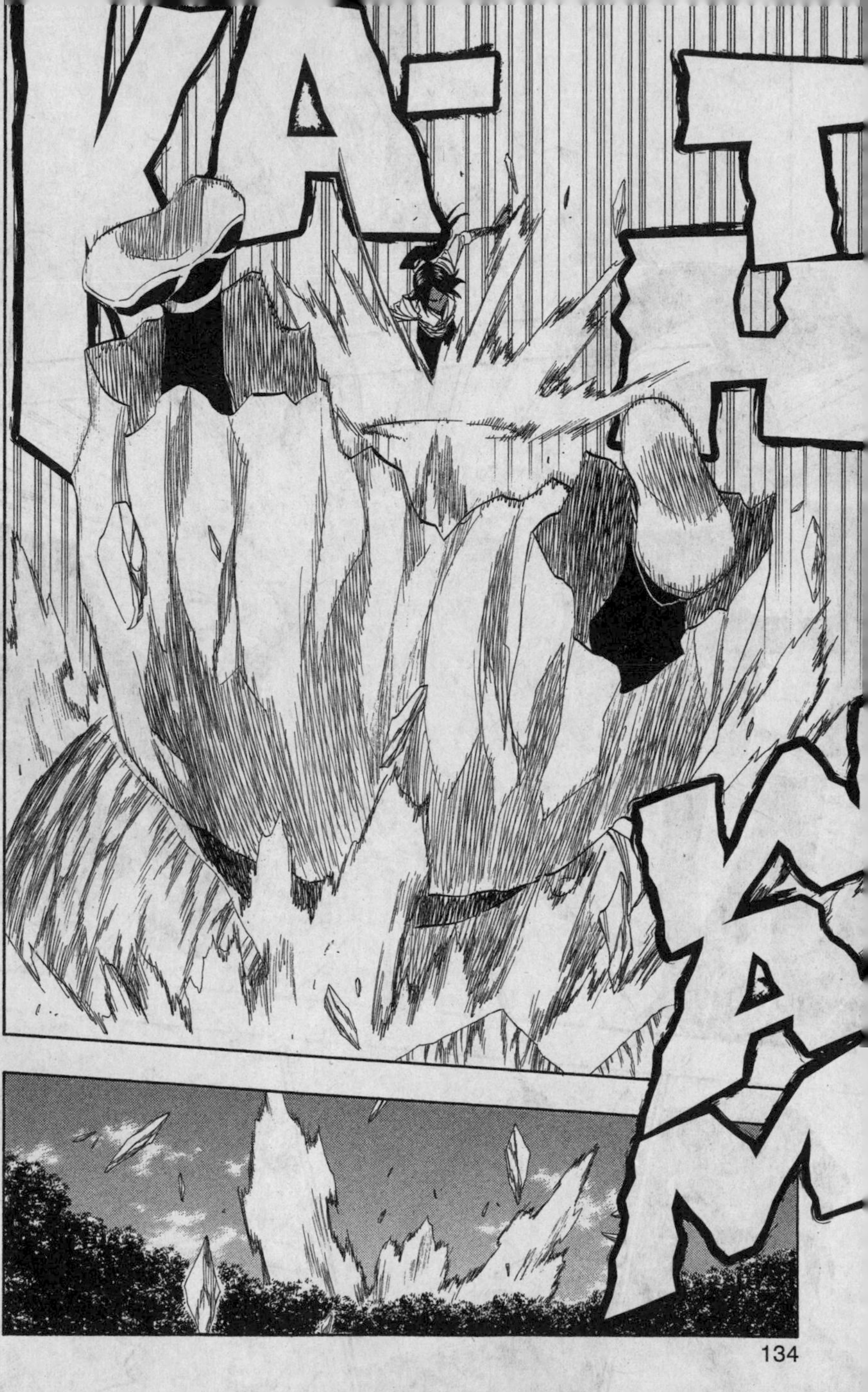
KA-T
KAM

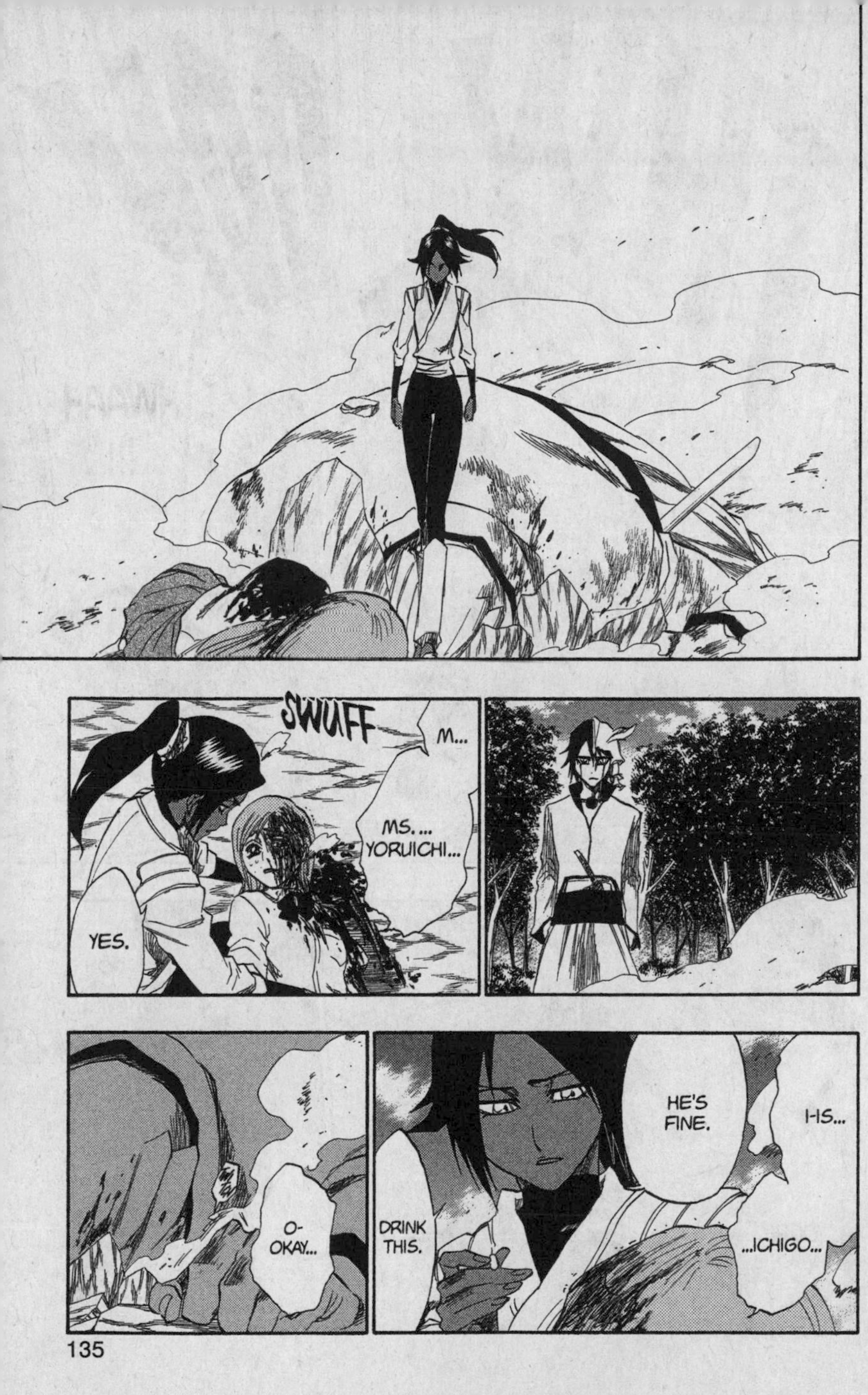
M...
SWUFF
MS. ... YORUICHI...
YES.
I-IS...
...ICHIGO...
HE'S FINE.
DRINK THIS.
O-OKAY...

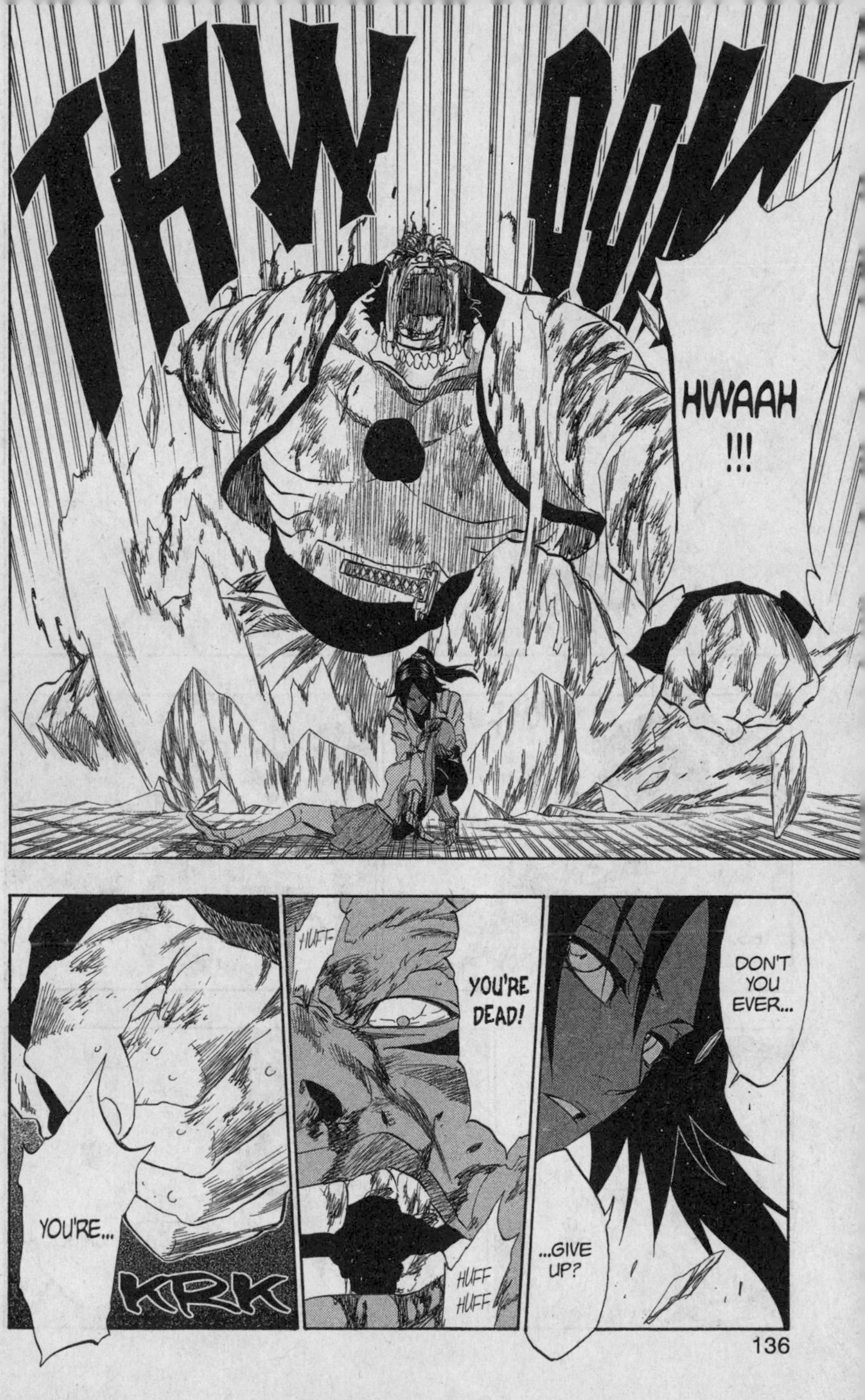
THWOOM
HWAAH!!!
DON'T YOU EVER...
...GIVE UP?
HUFF
YOU'RE DEAD!
HUFF HUFF
YOU'RE...
KRK

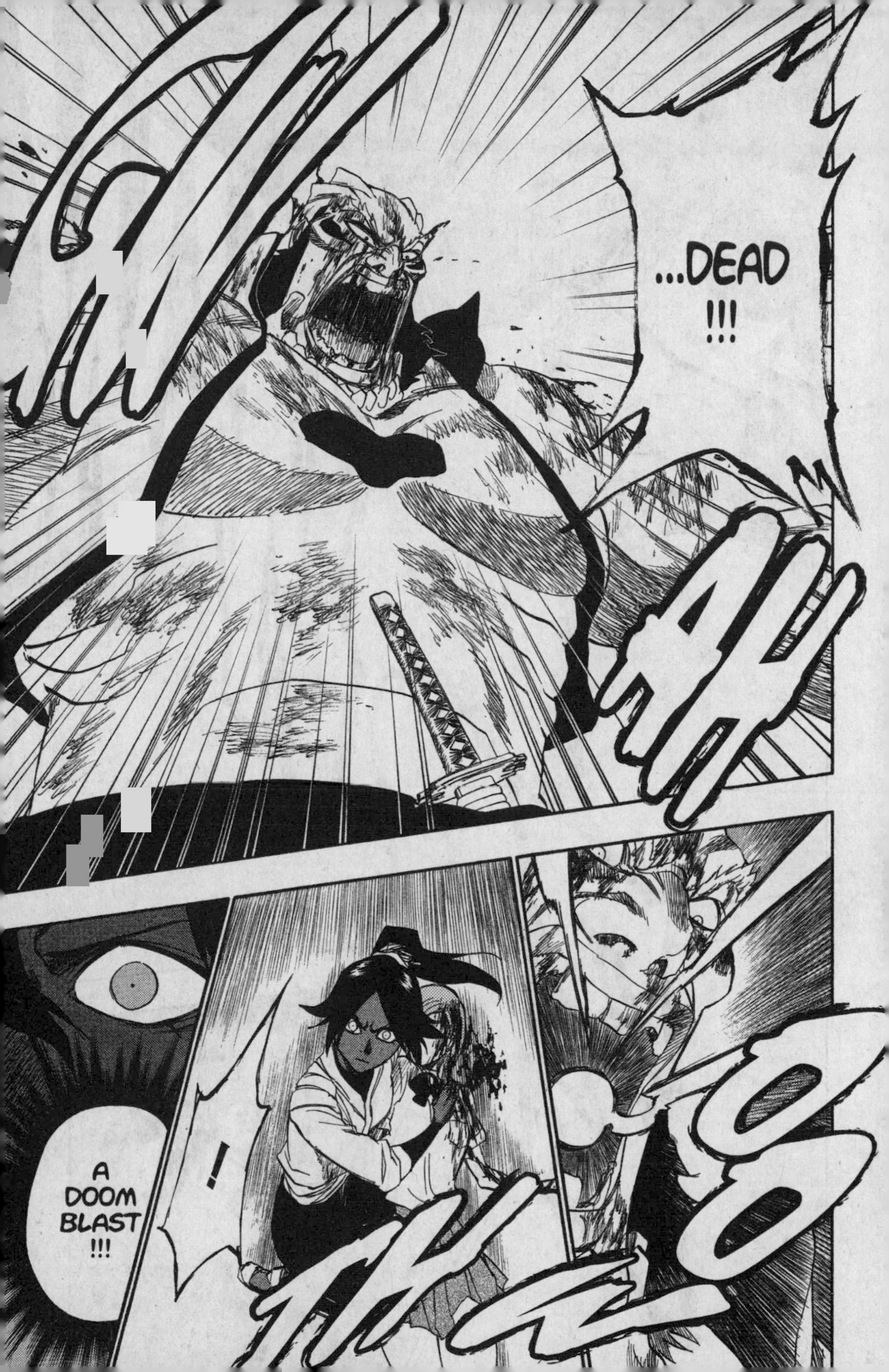
...DEAD !!!
!
A DOOM BLAST !!!

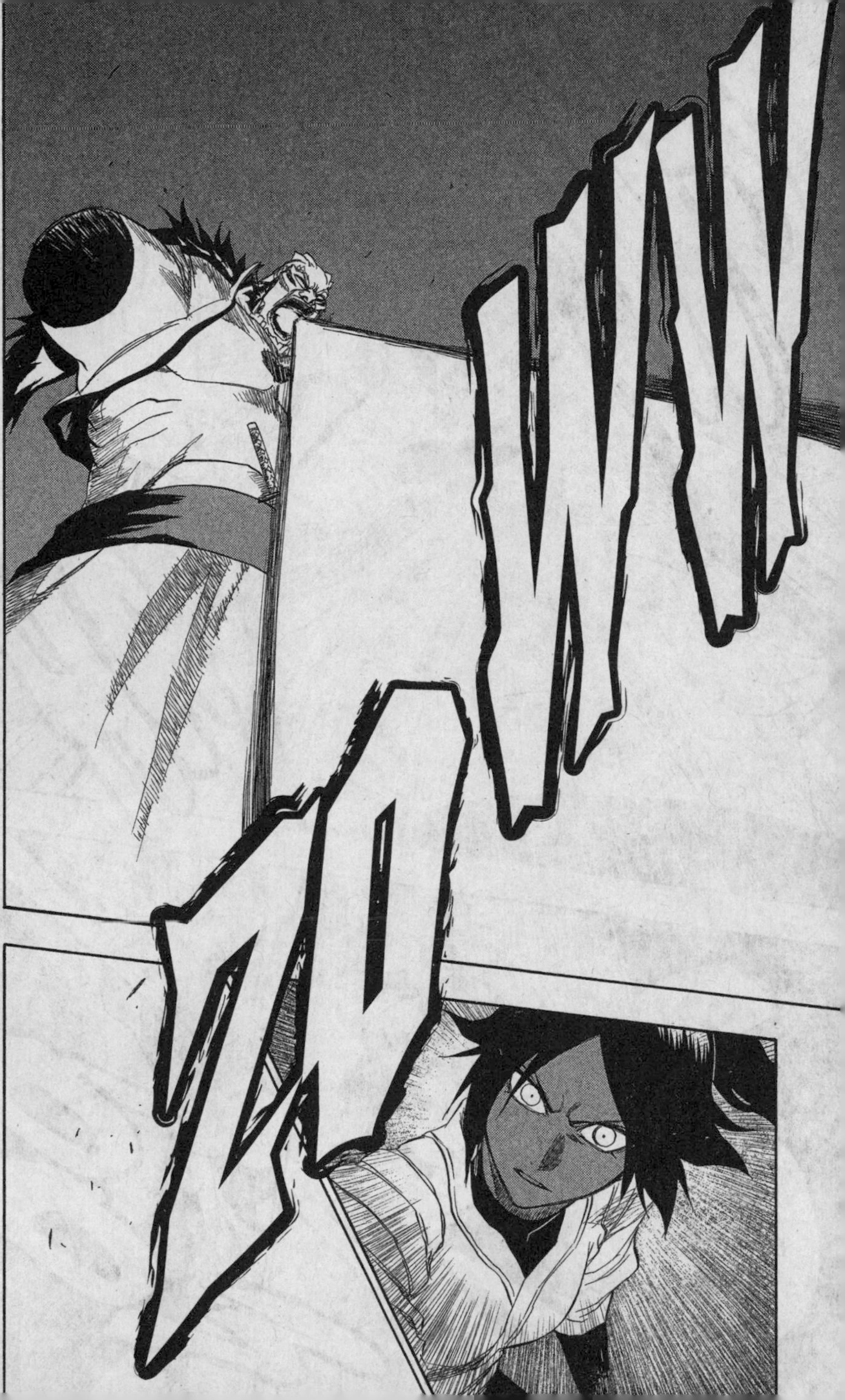
ZOWW

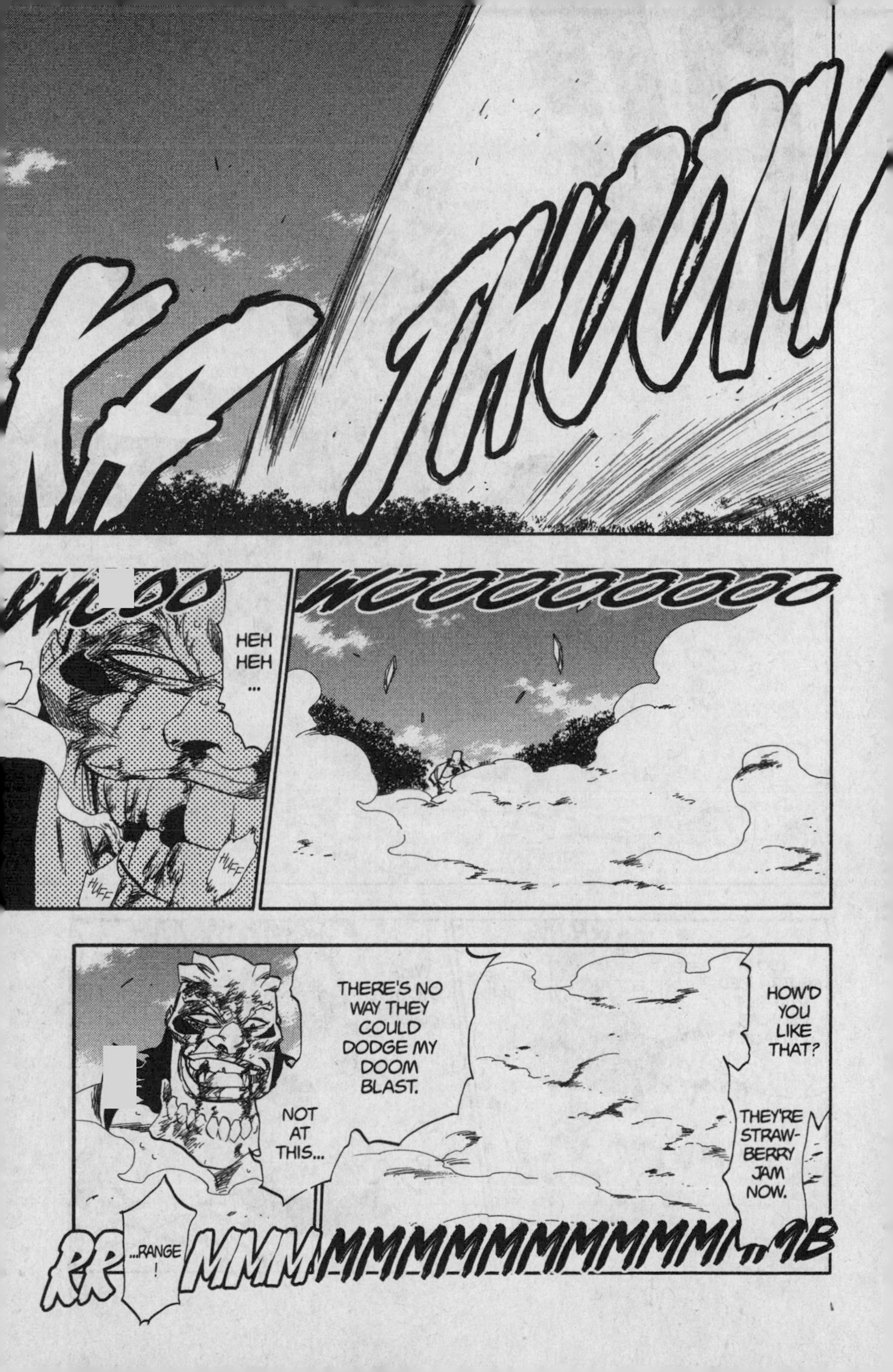

HEH HEH ...
HUFF
HUFF
HOW'D YOU LIKE THAT?
THEY'RE STRAW-BERRY JAM NOW.
THERE'S NO WAY THEY COULD DODGE MY DOOM BLAST.
NOT AT THIS...
...RANGE!

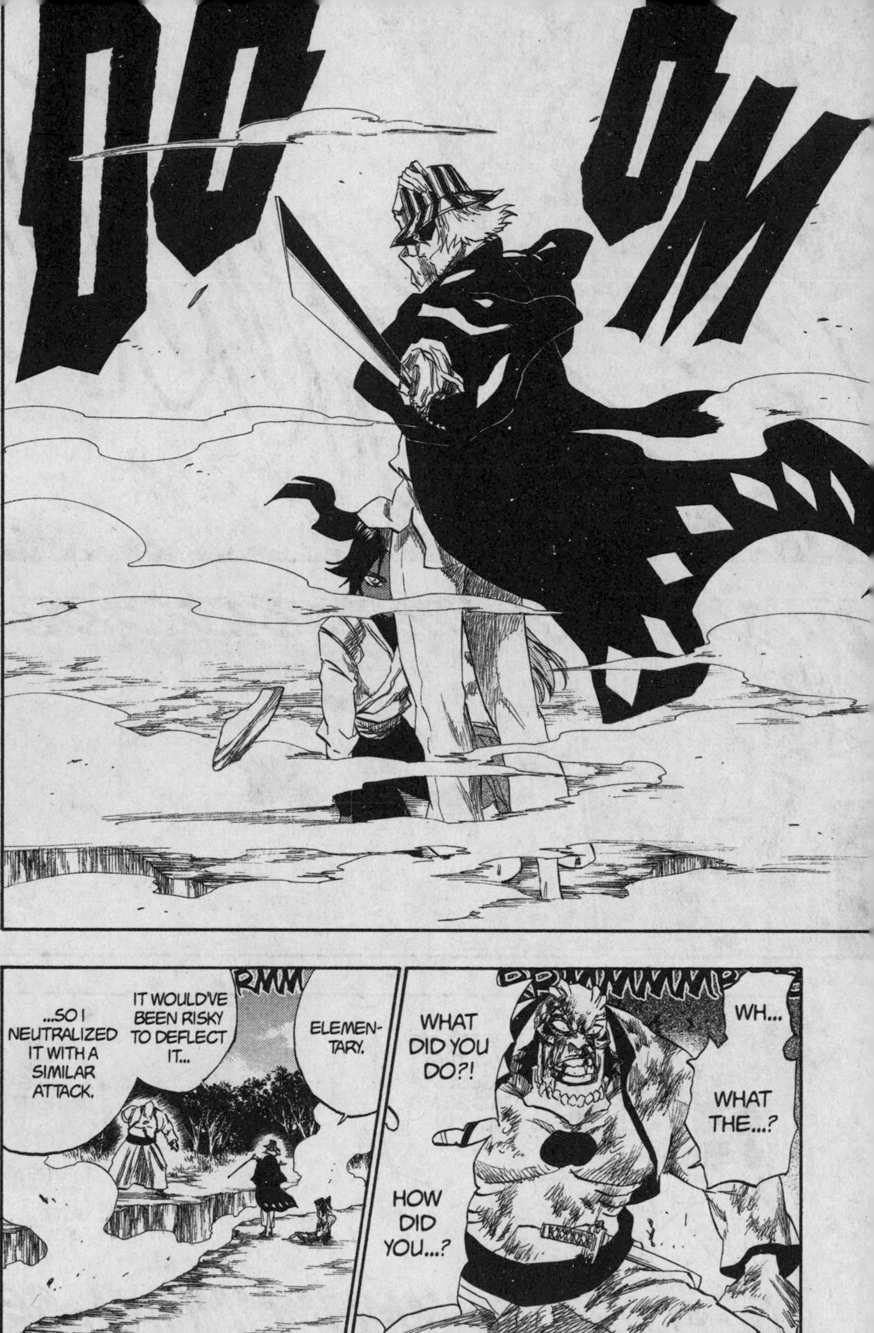
DOOM
WH...
WHAT THE...?
WHAT DID YOU DO?!
HOW DID YOU...?
ELEMENTARY.
IT WOULD'VE BEEN RISKY TO DEFLECT IT...
...SO I NEUTRALIZED IT WITH A SIMILAR ATTACK.

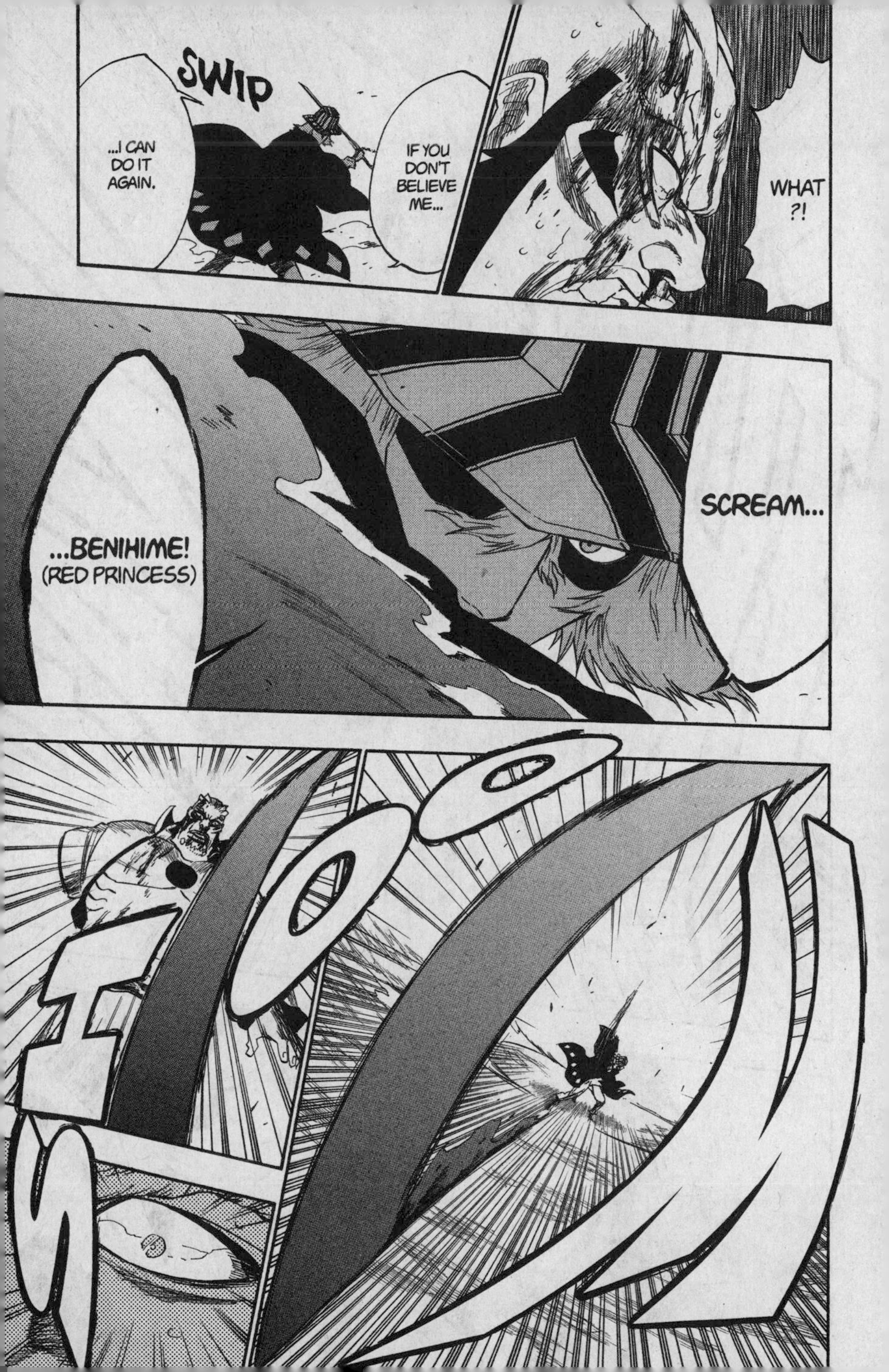
WHAT ?!
IF YOU DON'T BELIEVE ME...
...I CAN DO IT AGAIN.
SWIP
SCREAM...
...BENIHIME!
(RED PRINCESS)
SHOOO

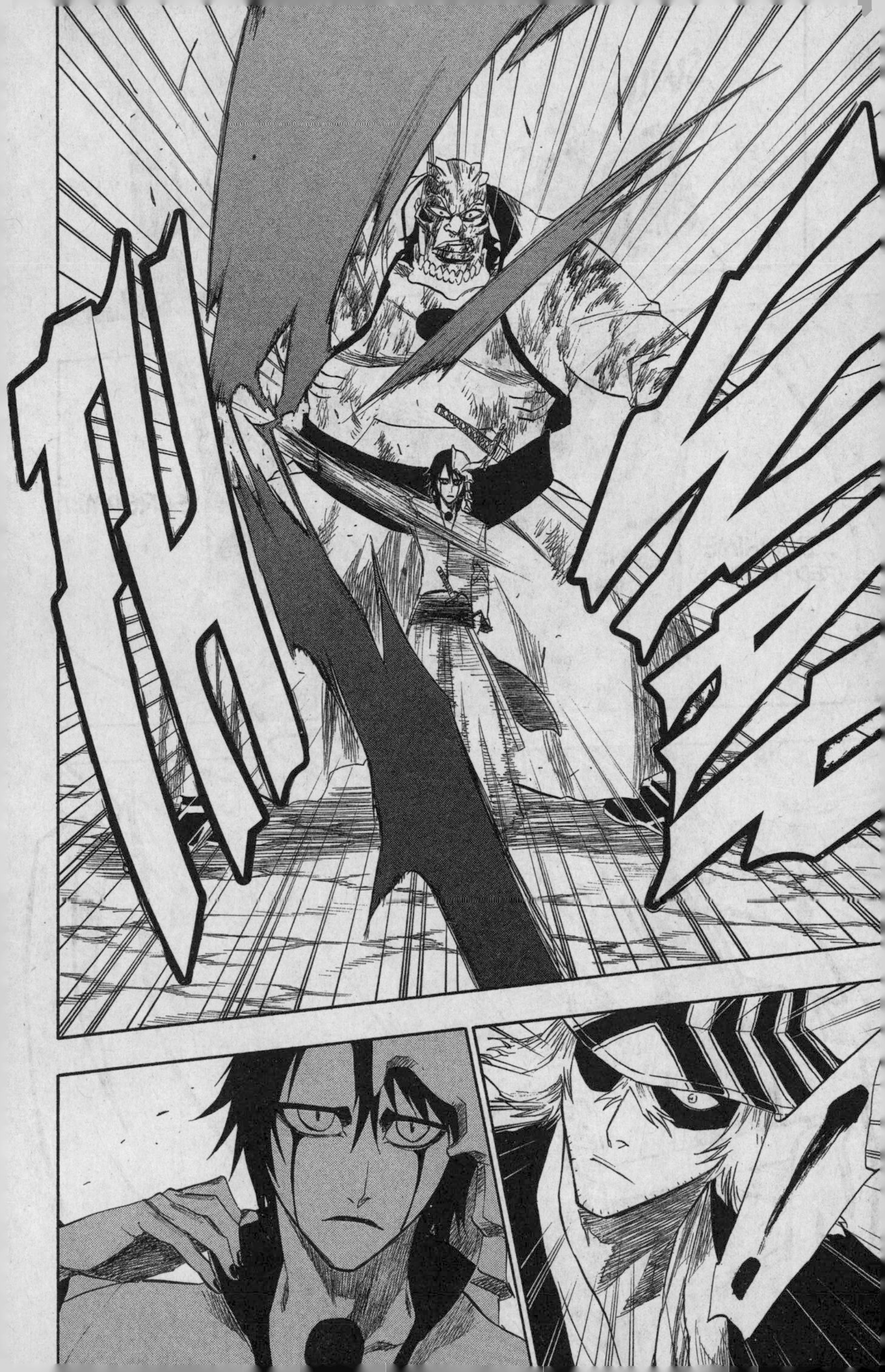

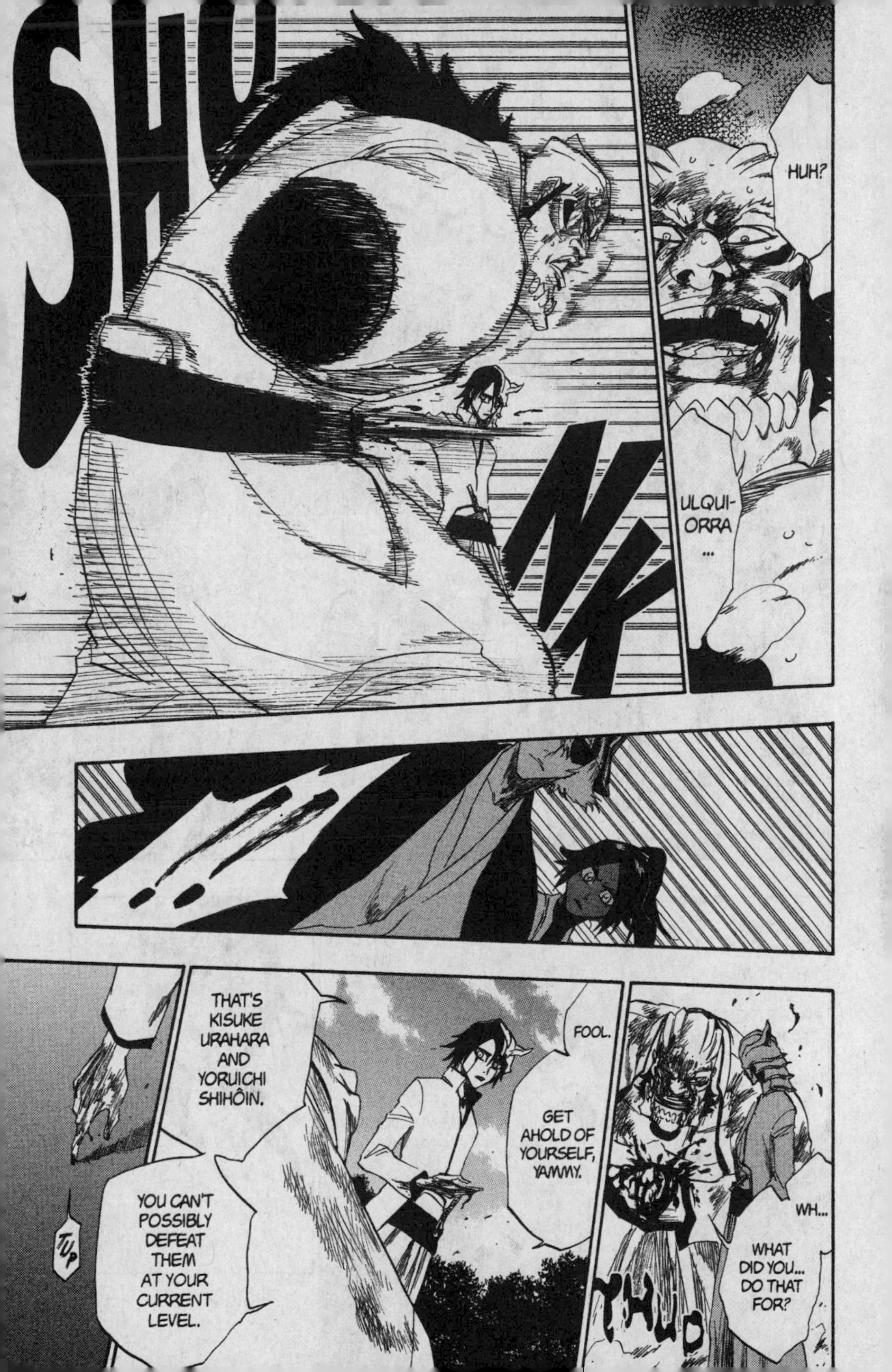
HUH?
ULQUI-ORRA ...
SHU
NK
WH...
WHAT DID YOU... DO THAT FOR?
THUD
FOOL.
GET AHOLD OF YOURSELF, YAMMY.
THAT'S KISUKE URAHARA AND YORUICHI SHIHÔIN.
YOU CAN'T POSSIBLY DEFEAT THEM AT YOUR CURRENT LEVEL.
TUP

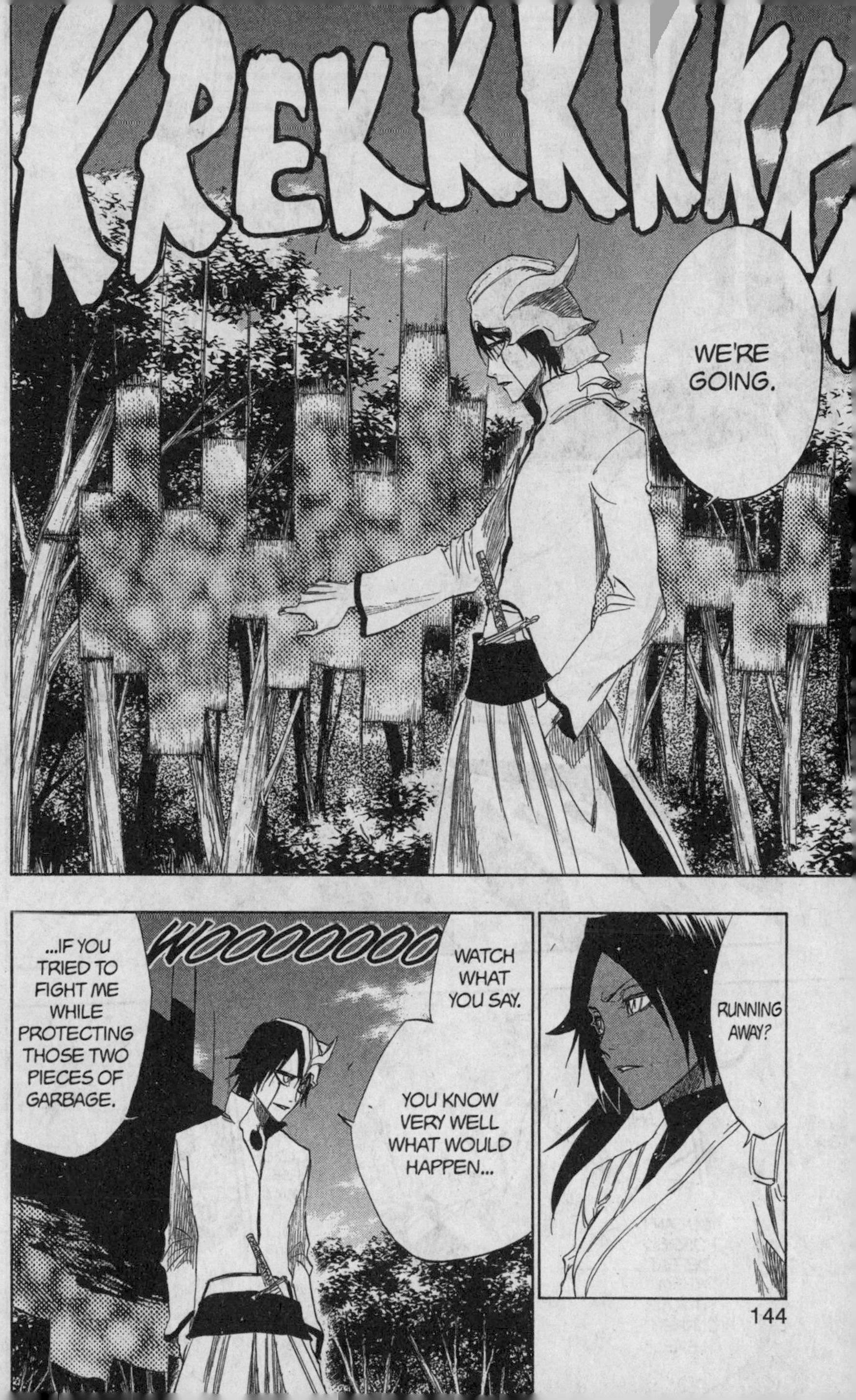
KREKKKKK
WE'RE GOING.
RUNNING AWAY?
WATCH WHAT YOU SAY.
WOOOOOOO
YOU KNOW VERY WELL WHAT WOULD HAPPEN...
...IF YOU TRIED TO FIGHT ME WHILE PROTECTING THOSE TWO PIECES OF GARBAGE.

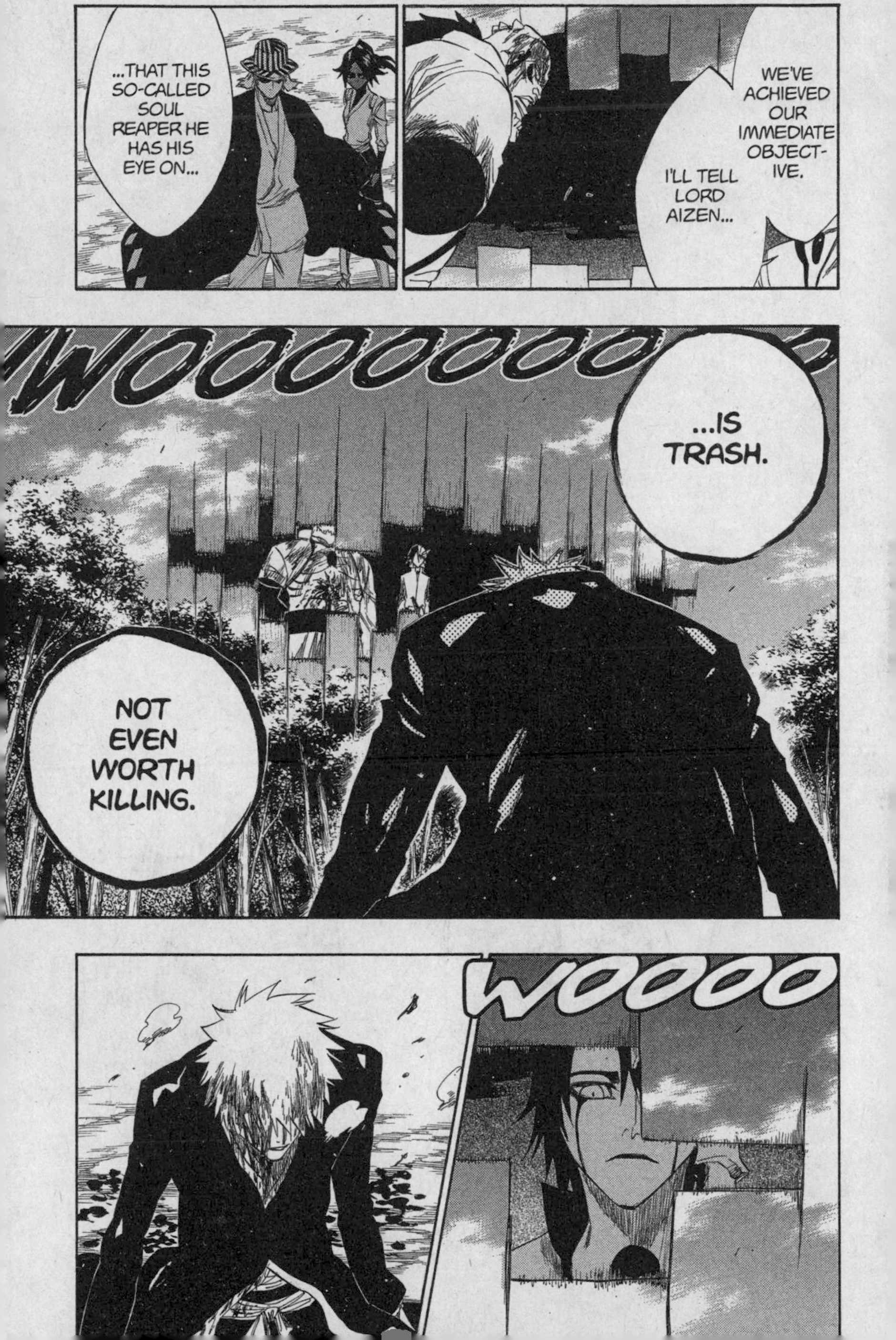
WE'VE ACHIEVED OUR IMMEDIATE OBJECTIVE.
I'LL TELL LORD AIZEN...
...THAT THIS SO-CALLED SOUL REAPER HE HAS HIS EYE ON...
WOOOOOOOO
...IS TRASH.
NOT EVEN WORTH KILLING.
WOOOO

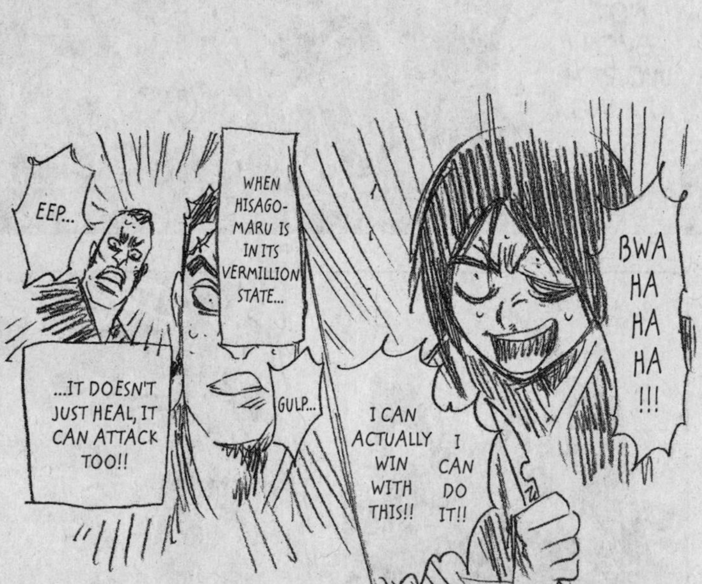
BWA HA HA HA!!!
I CAN DO IT!!
I CAN ACTUALLY WIN WITH THIS!!
WHEN HISAGO-MARU IS IN ITS VERMILLION STATE...
EEP...
GULP...
...IT DOESN'T JUST HEAL, IT CAN ATTACK TOO!!

195. Death & Strawberry (Reprise)

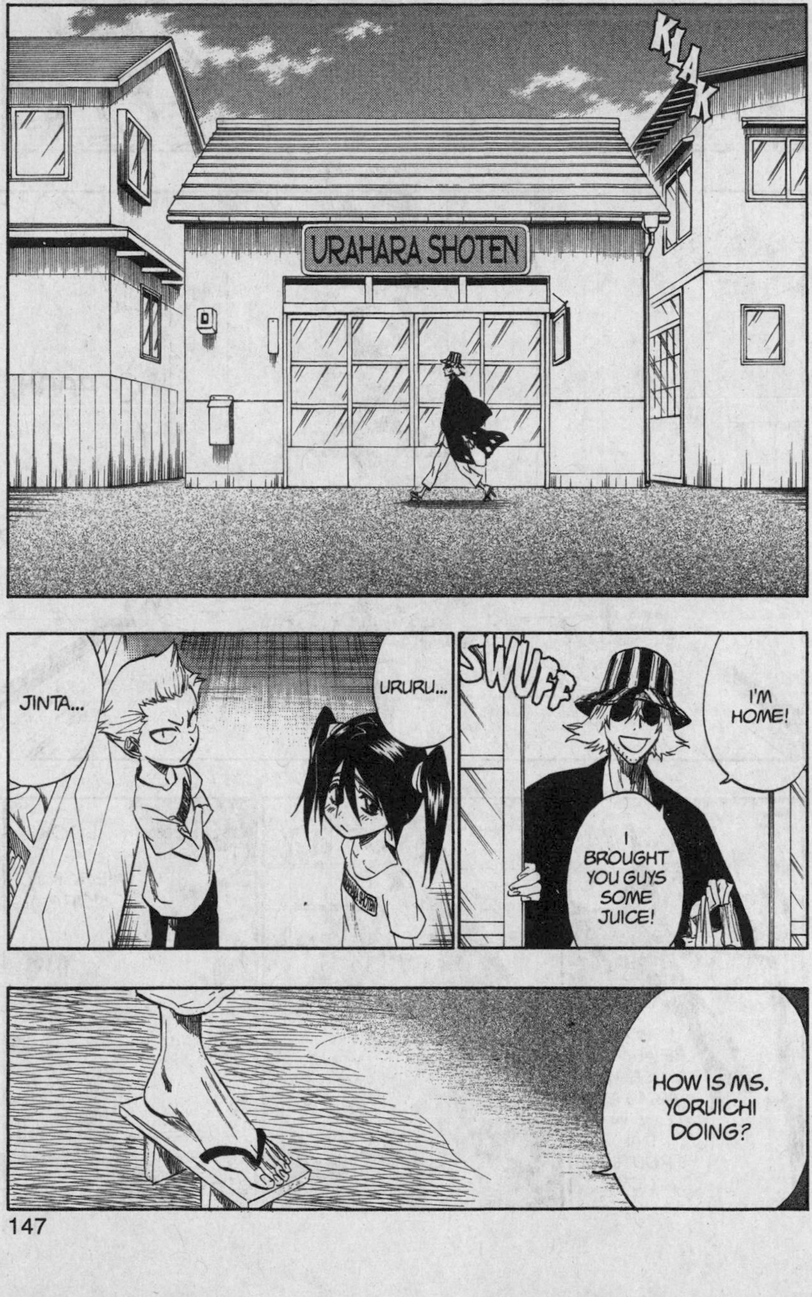

URAHARA SHOTEN
KLAK
SWUFF
I'M HOME!
I BROUGHT YOU GUYS SOME JUICE!
URURU...
JINTA...
HOW IS MS. YORUICHI DOING?

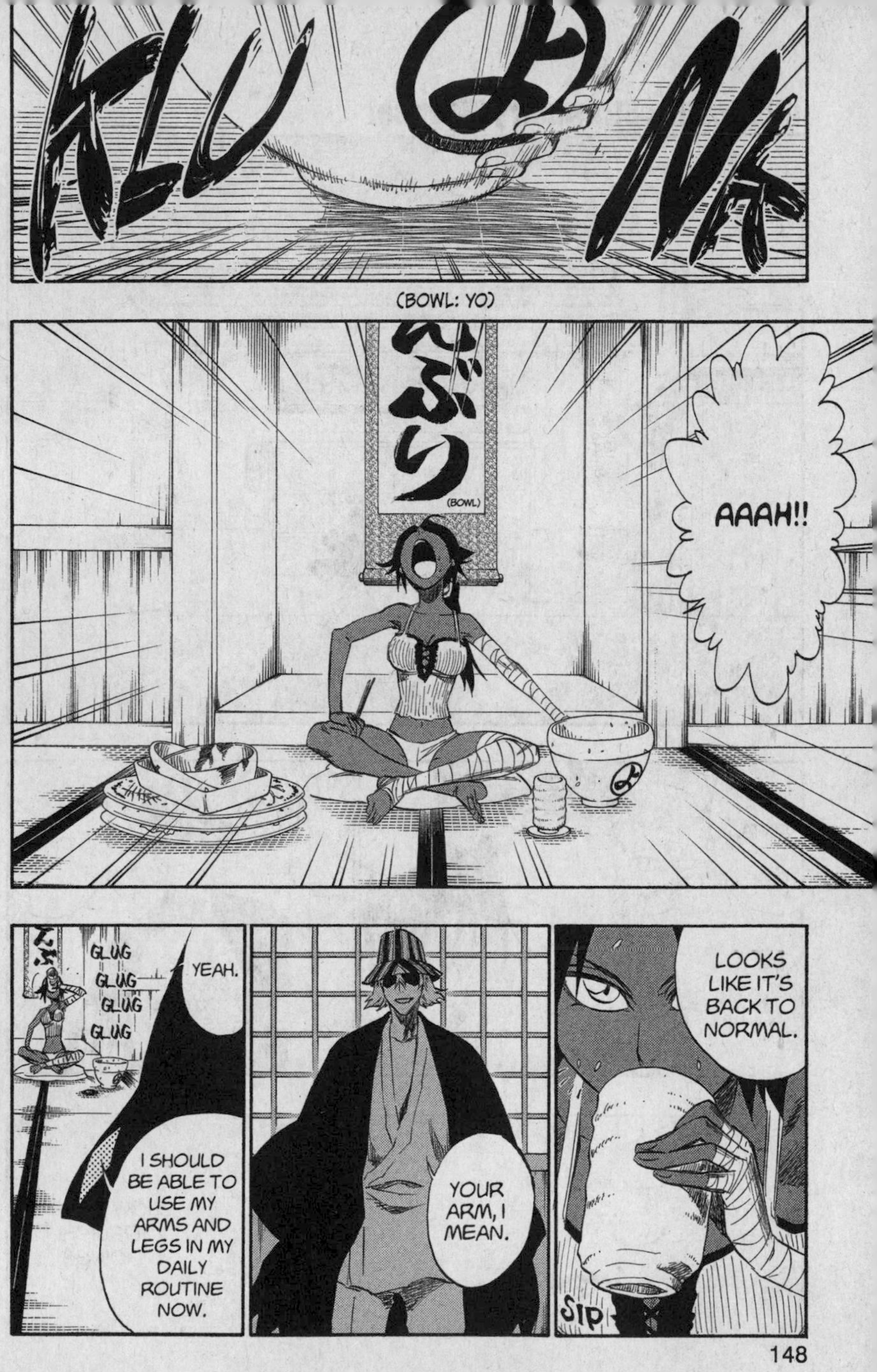
KLU NK
(BOWL: YO)
んぶり
(BOWL)
AAAH!!
LOOKS LIKE IT'S BACK TO NORMAL.
SIP
YOUR ARM, I MEAN.
GLUG GLUG GLUG GLUG
YEAH.
I SHOULD BE ABLE TO USE MY ARMS AND LEGS IN MY DAILY ROUTINE NOW.

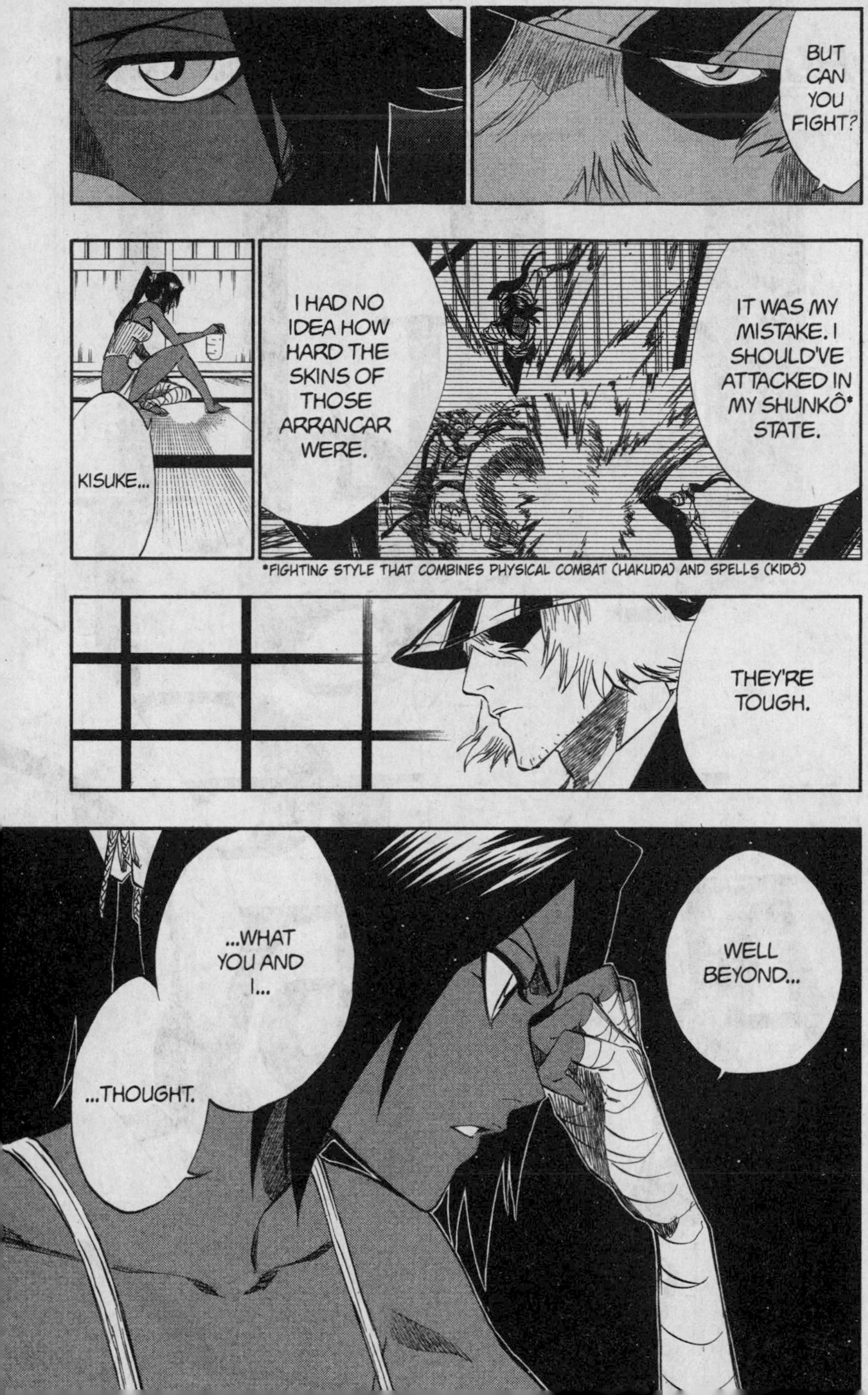
BUT CAN YOU FIGHT?
IT WAS MY MISTAKE. I SHOULD'VE ATTACKED IN MY SHUNKÔ* STATE.
I HAD NO IDEA HOW HARD THE SKINS OF THOSE ARRANCAR WERE.
KISUKE...
*FIGHTING STYLE THAT COMBINES PHYSICAL COMBAT (HAKUDA) AND SPELLS (KIDÔ)
THEY'RE TOUGH.
WELL BEYOND...
...WHAT YOU AND I...
...THOUGHT.

BLEACH

195. Death & Strawberry (Reprise)

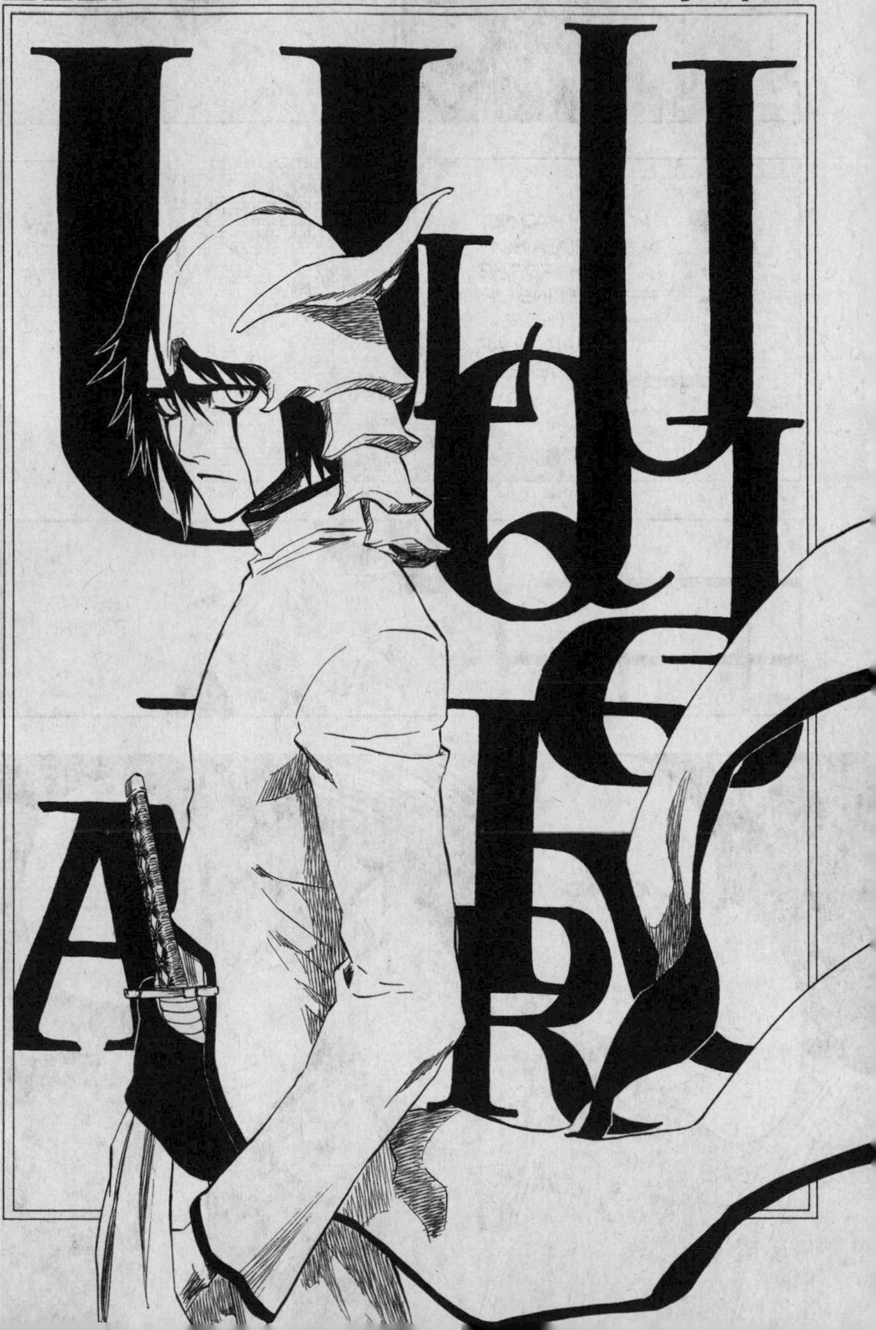

READ THIS WAY

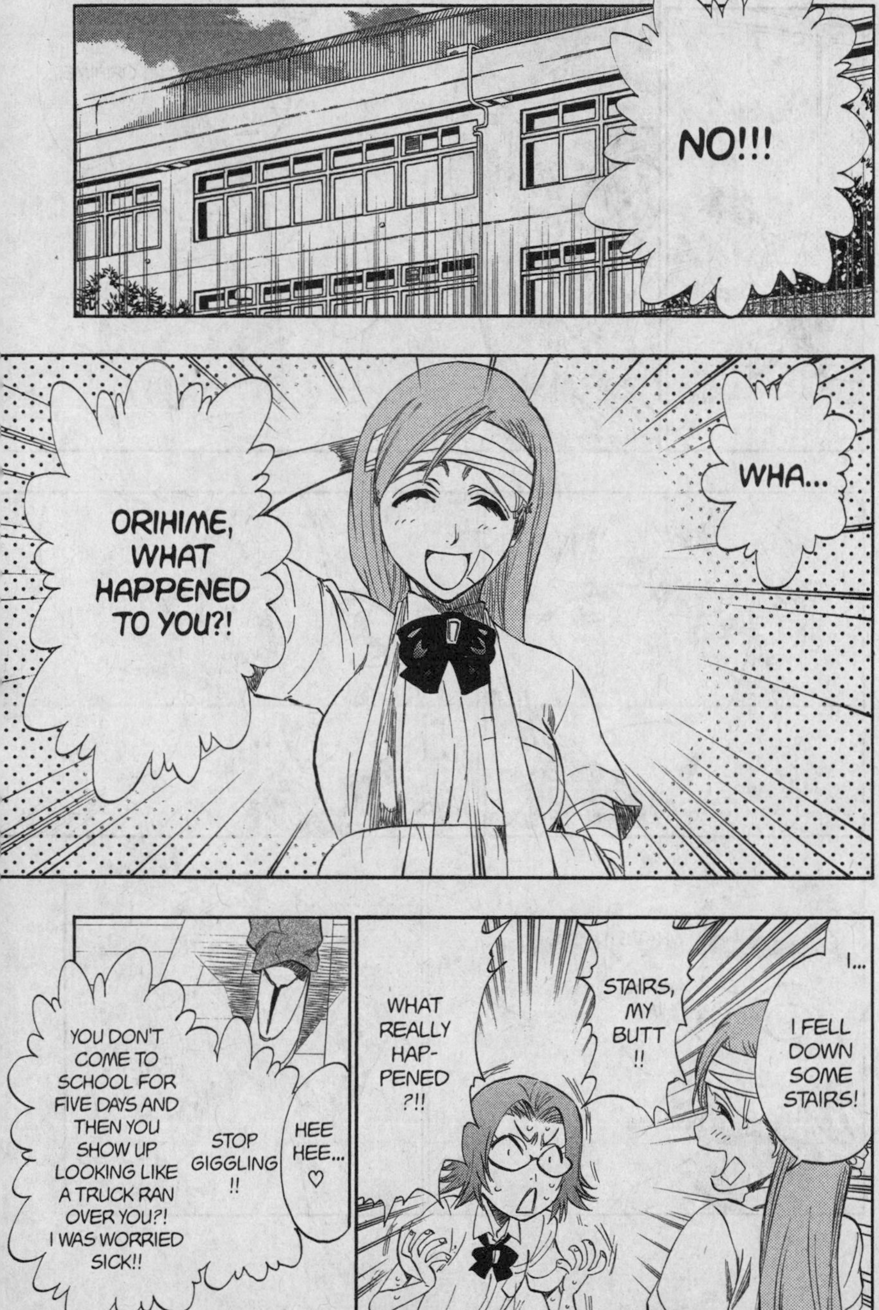
NO!!!
WHA...
ORIHIME, WHAT HAPPENED TO YOU?!
I...
I FELL DOWN SOME STAIRS!
STAIRS, MY BUTT!!
WHAT REALLY HAP-PENED?!!
HEE HEE... ♡
STOP GIGGLING!!
YOU DON'T COME TO SCHOOL FOR FIVE DAYS AND THEN YOU SHOW UP LOOKING LIKE A TRUCK RAN OVER YOU?! I WAS WORRIED SICK!!

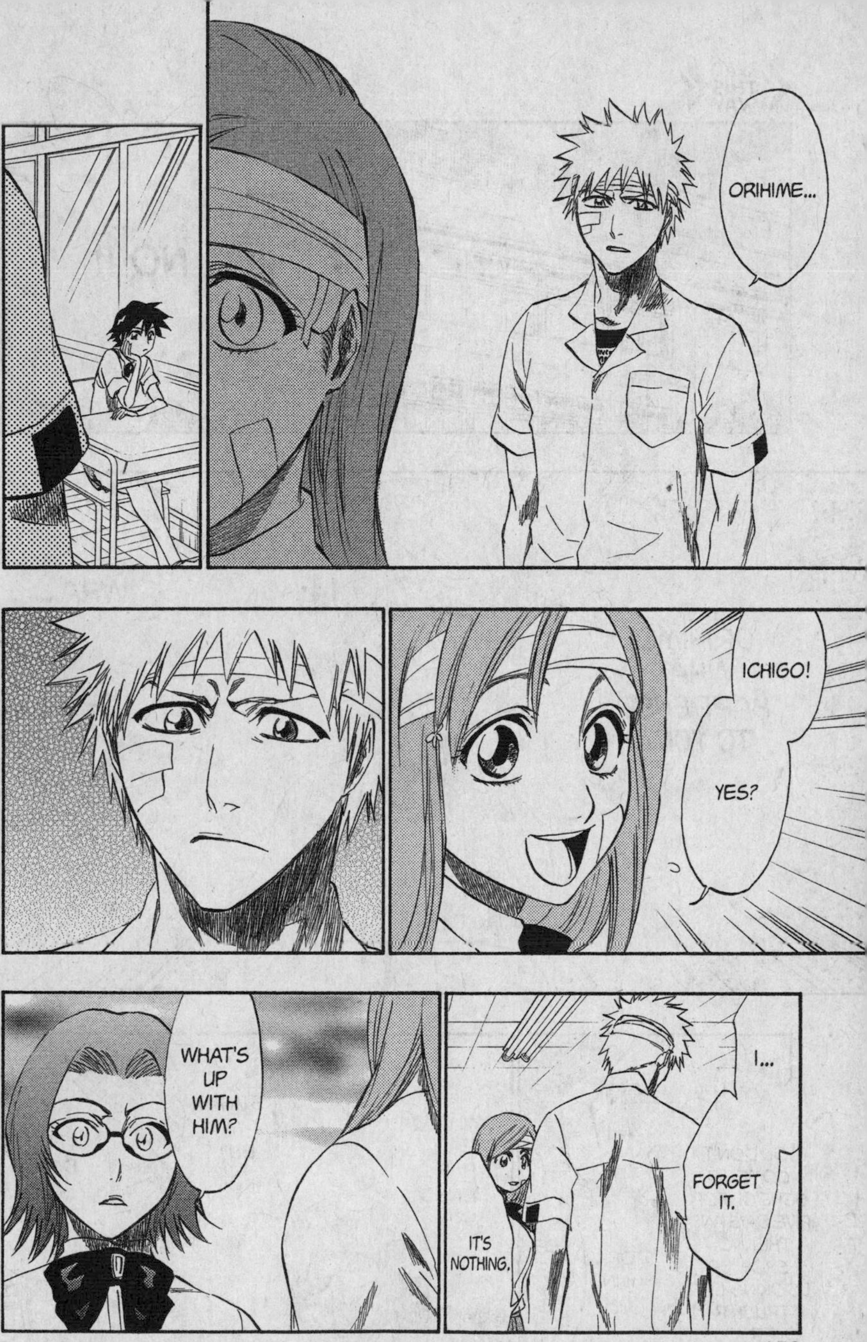
ORIHIME...
ICHIGO!
YES?
I...
FORGET IT.
IT'S NOTHING.
WHAT'S UP WITH HIM?

READ THIS WAY

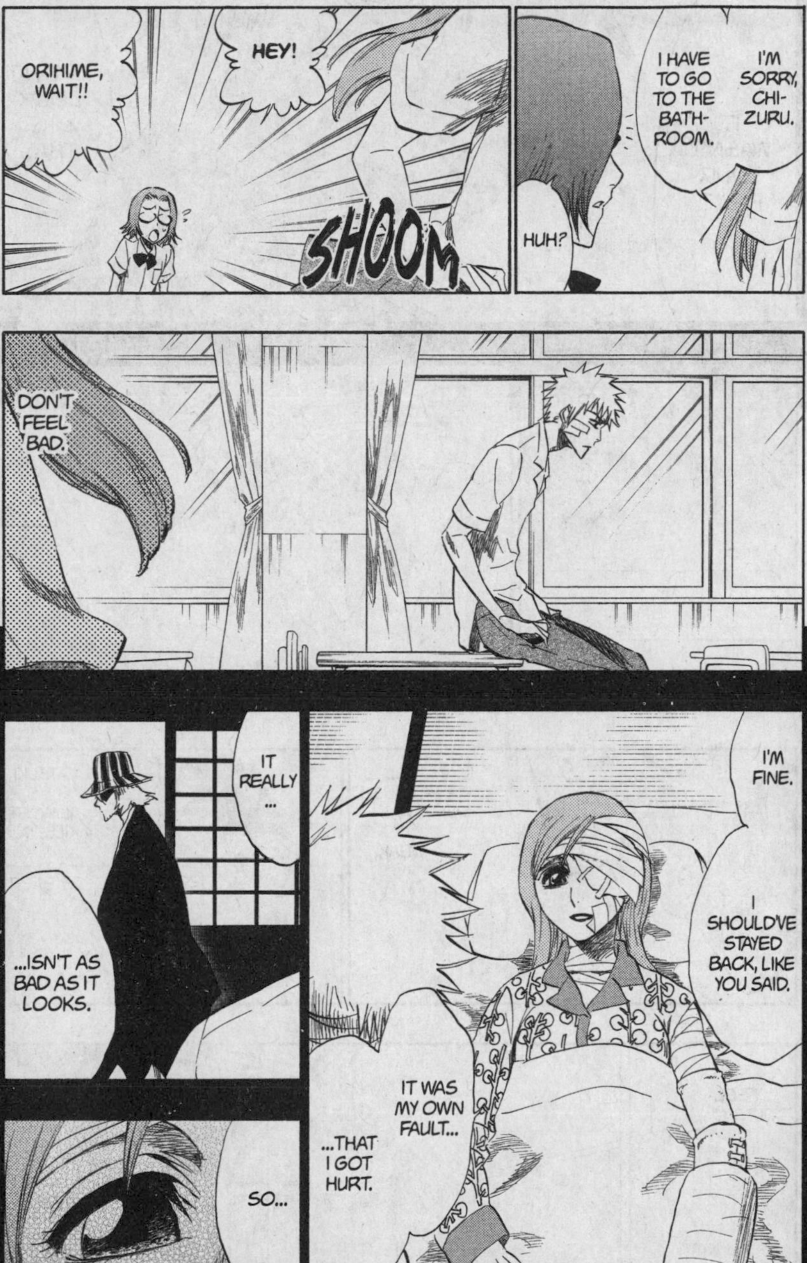
I'M SORRY, CHI-ZURU.
I HAVE TO GO TO THE BATH-ROOM.
HUH?
HEY!
ORIHIME, WAIT!!
SHOOM
DON'T FEEL BAD.
I'M FINE.
I SHOULD'VE STAYED BACK, LIKE YOU SAID.
IT WAS MY OWN FAULT...
...THAT I GOT HURT.
IT REALLY...
...ISN'T AS BAD AS IT LOOKS.
SO...

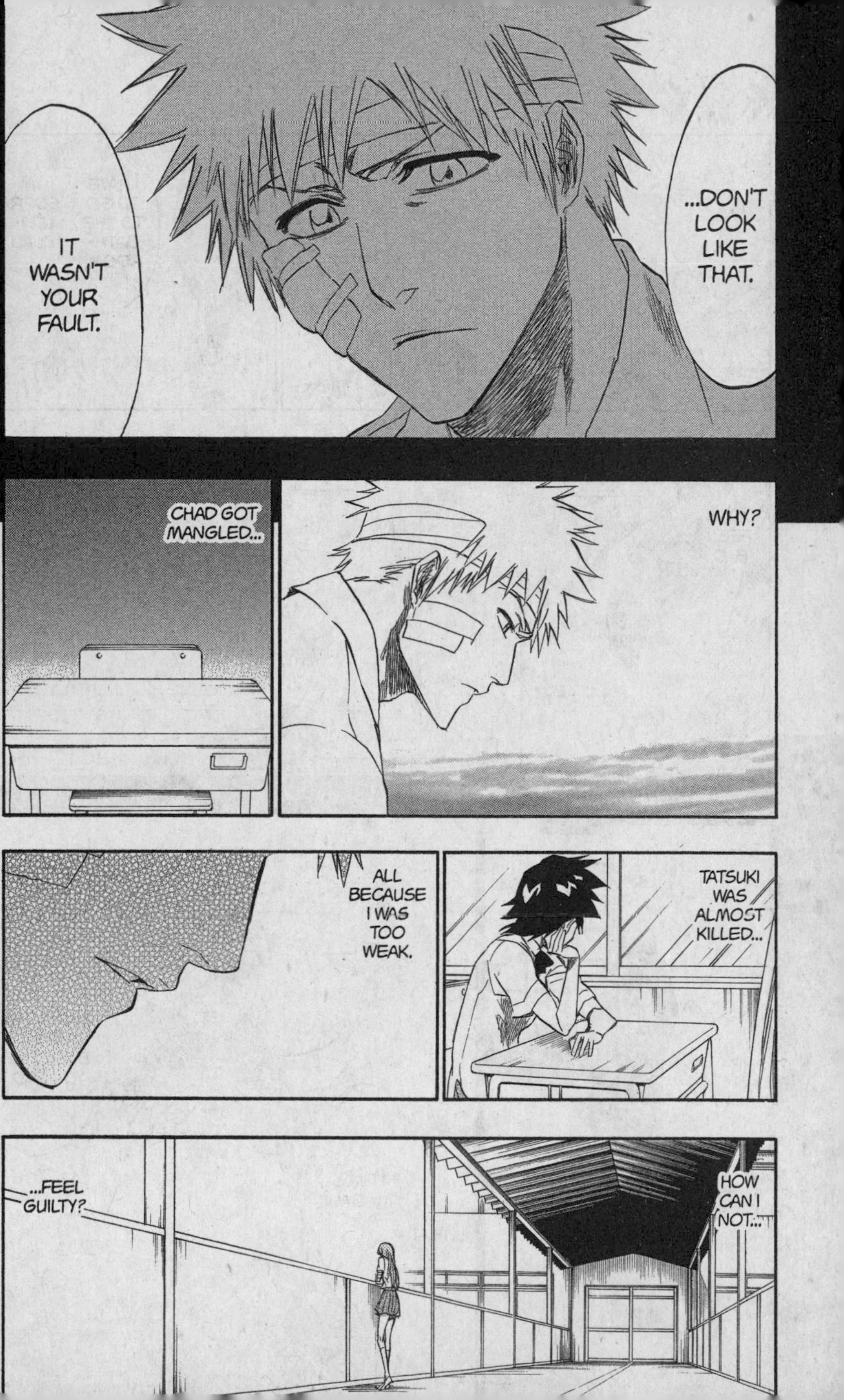
...DON'T LOOK LIKE THAT.
IT WASN'T YOUR FAULT.
WHY?
CHAD GOT MANGLED...
TATSUKI WAS ALMOST KILLED...
ALL BECAUSE I WAS TOO WEAK.
HOW CAN I NOT...
...FEEL GUILTY?

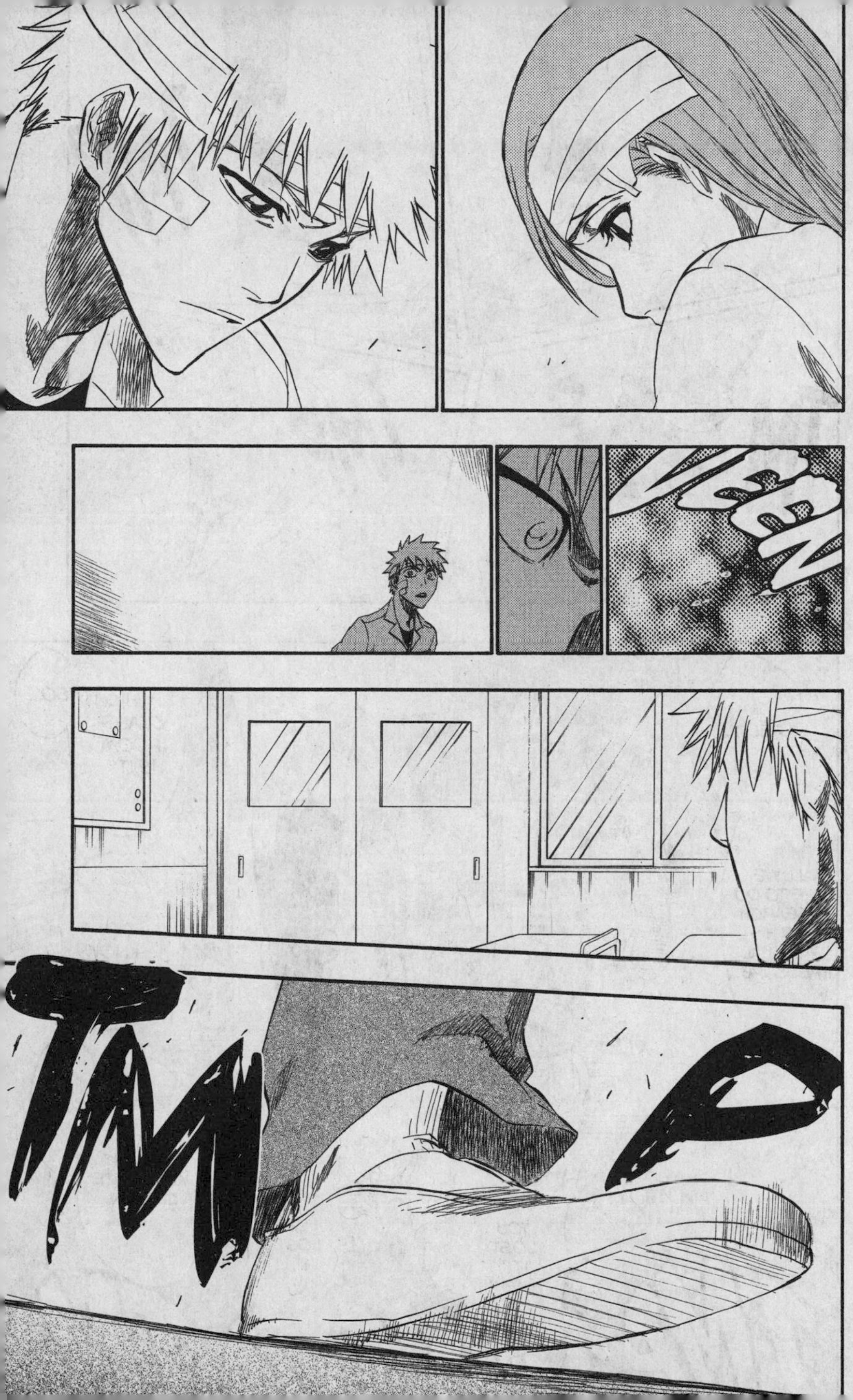
VEEN
TMP

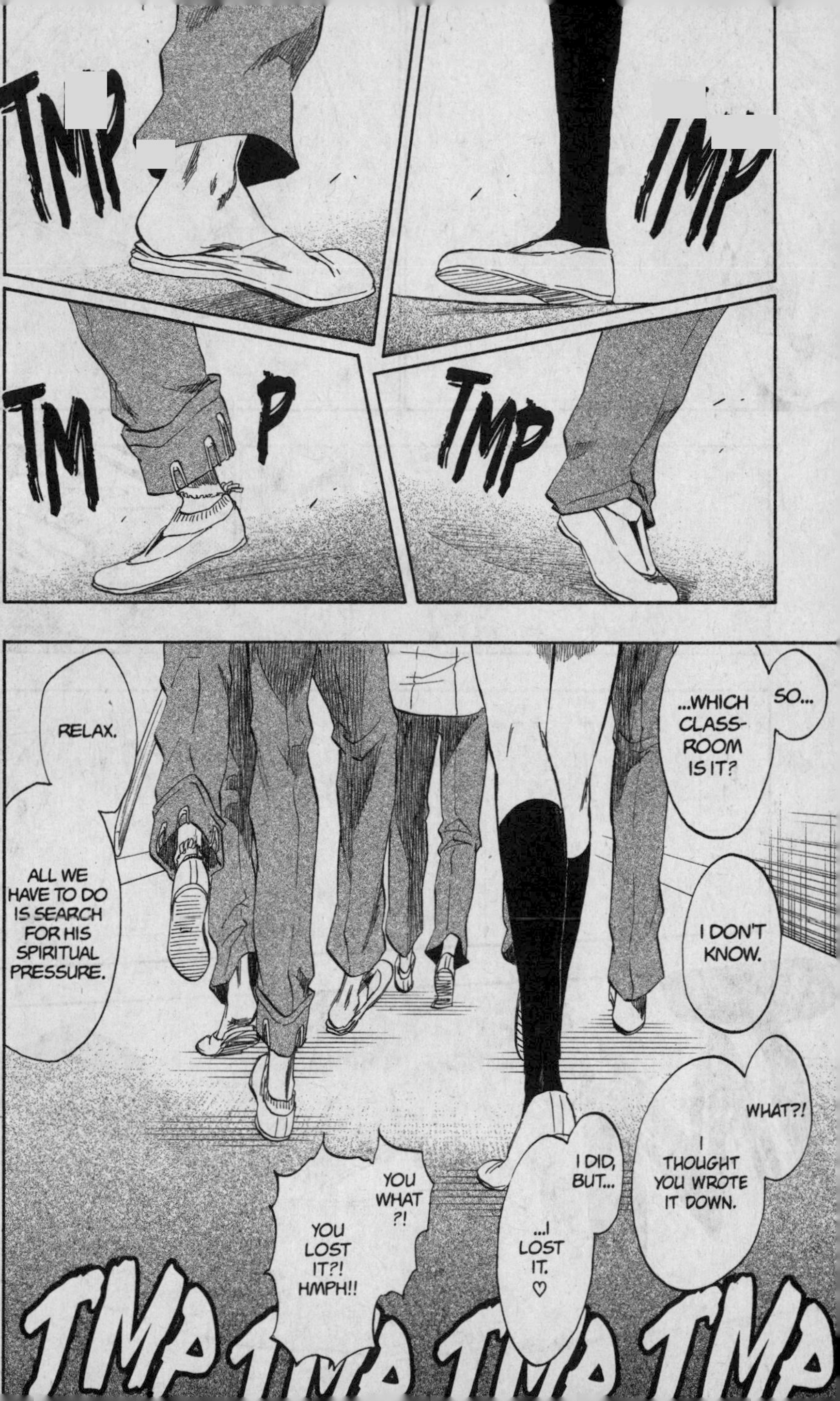
TMP
TMP
TMP
TM P
SO...
...WHICH CLASSROOM IS IT?
I DON'T KNOW.
WHAT?!
I THOUGHT YOU WROTE IT DOWN.
I DID, BUT...
...I LOST IT. ♥
YOU WHAT?!
YOU LOST IT?! HMPH!!
RELAX.
ALL WE HAVE TO DO IS SEARCH FOR HIS SPIRITUAL PRESSURE.
TMP TMP TMP TMP

READ THIS WAY

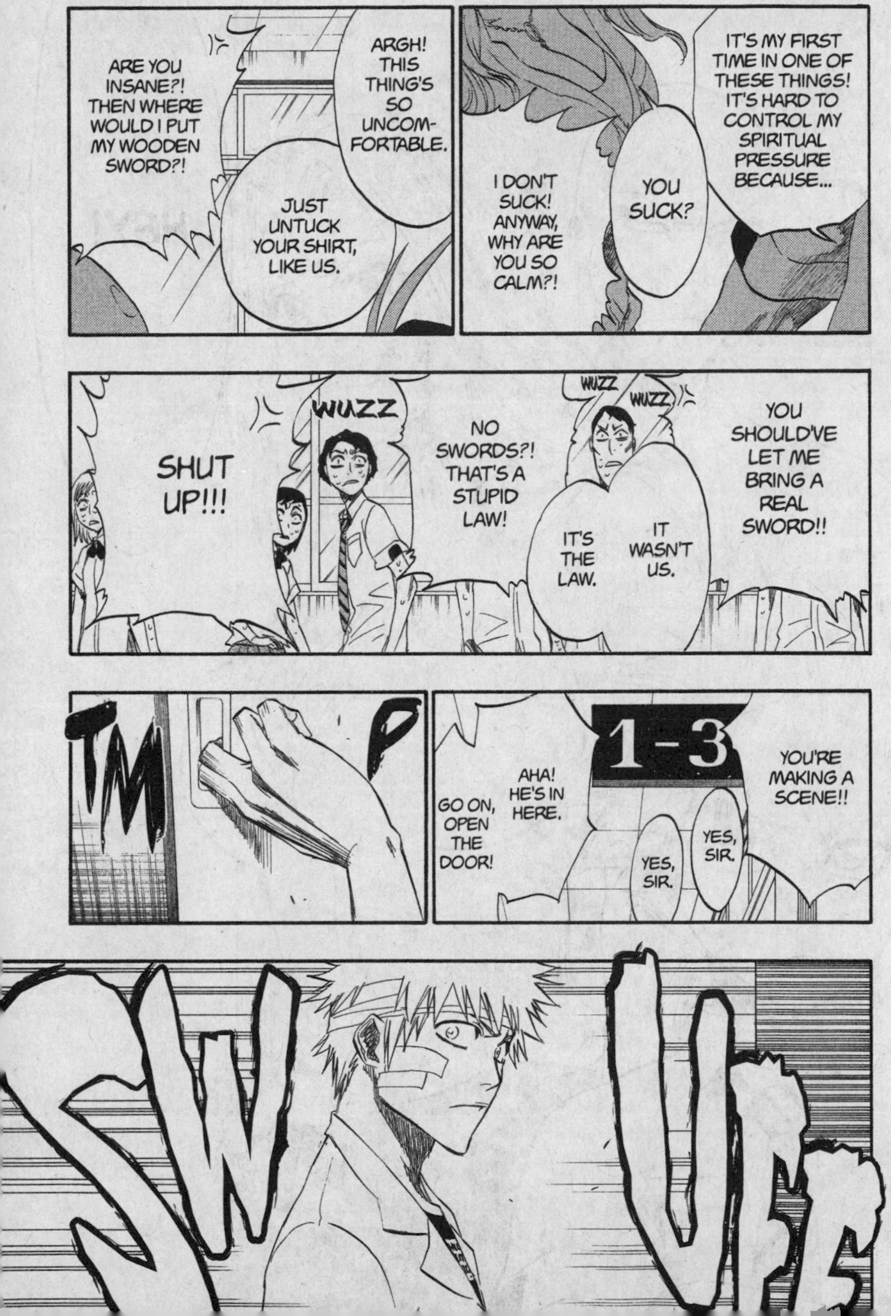

IT'S MY FIRST TIME IN ONE OF THESE THINGS! IT'S HARD TO CONTROL MY SPIRITUAL PRESSURE BECAUSE...
YOU SUCK?
I DON'T SUCK! ANYWAY, WHY ARE YOU SO CALM?!
ARGH! THIS THING'S SO UNCOMFORTABLE.
JUST UNTUCK YOUR SHIRT, LIKE US.
ARE YOU INSANE?! THEN WHERE WOULD I PUT MY WOODEN SWORD?!
YOU SHOULD'VE LET ME BRING A REAL SWORD!!
WUZZ
WUZZ
IT WASN'T US.
IT'S THE LAW.
NO SWORDS?! THAT'S A STUPID LAW!
WUZZ
SHUT UP!!!
YOU'RE MAKING A SCENE!!
YES, SIR.
YES, SIR.
1-3
AHA! HE'S IN HERE.
GO ON, OPEN THE DOOR!
TMP
SWUF

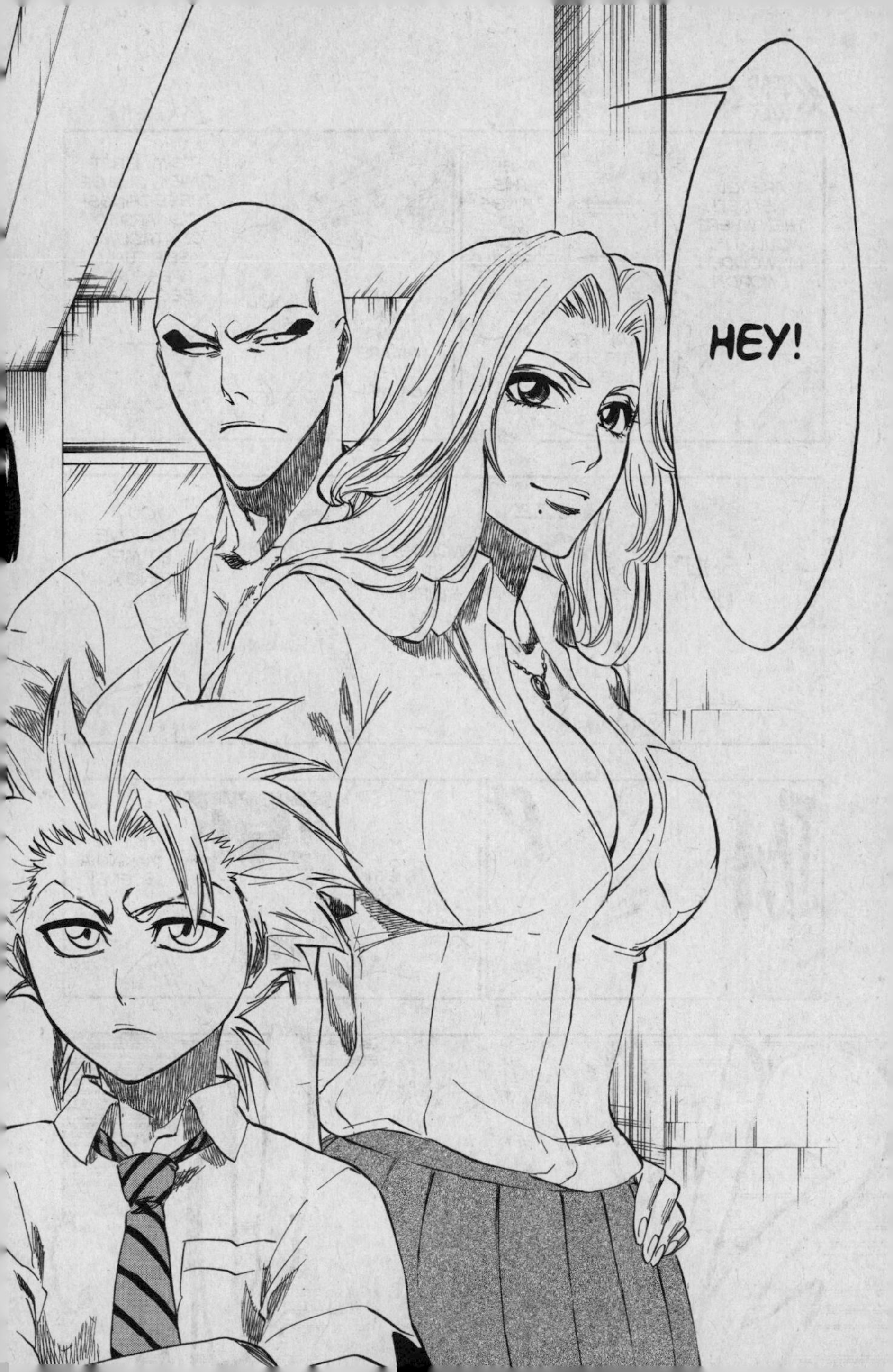
HEY!

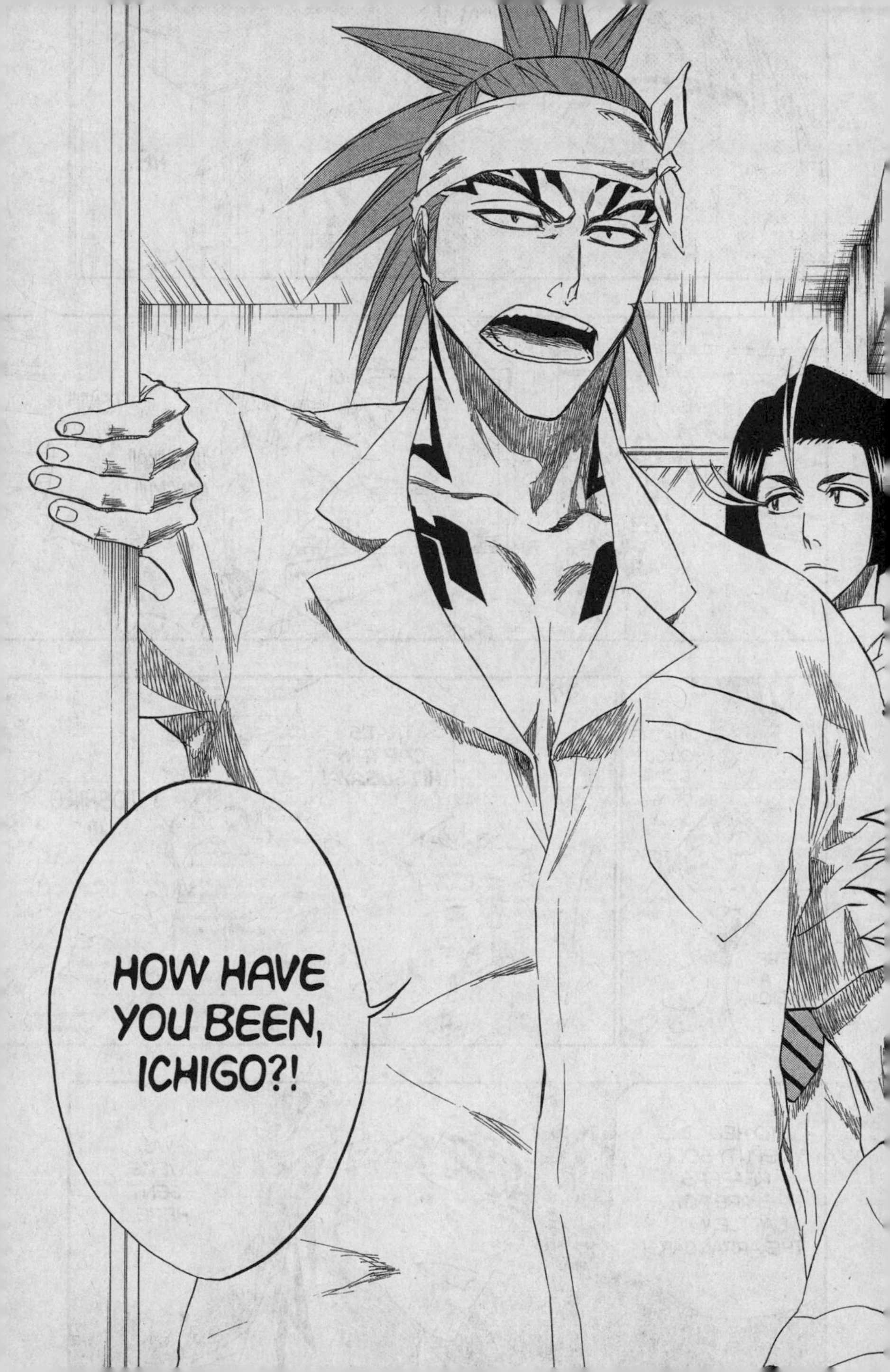
HOW HAVE YOU BEEN, ICHIGO?!

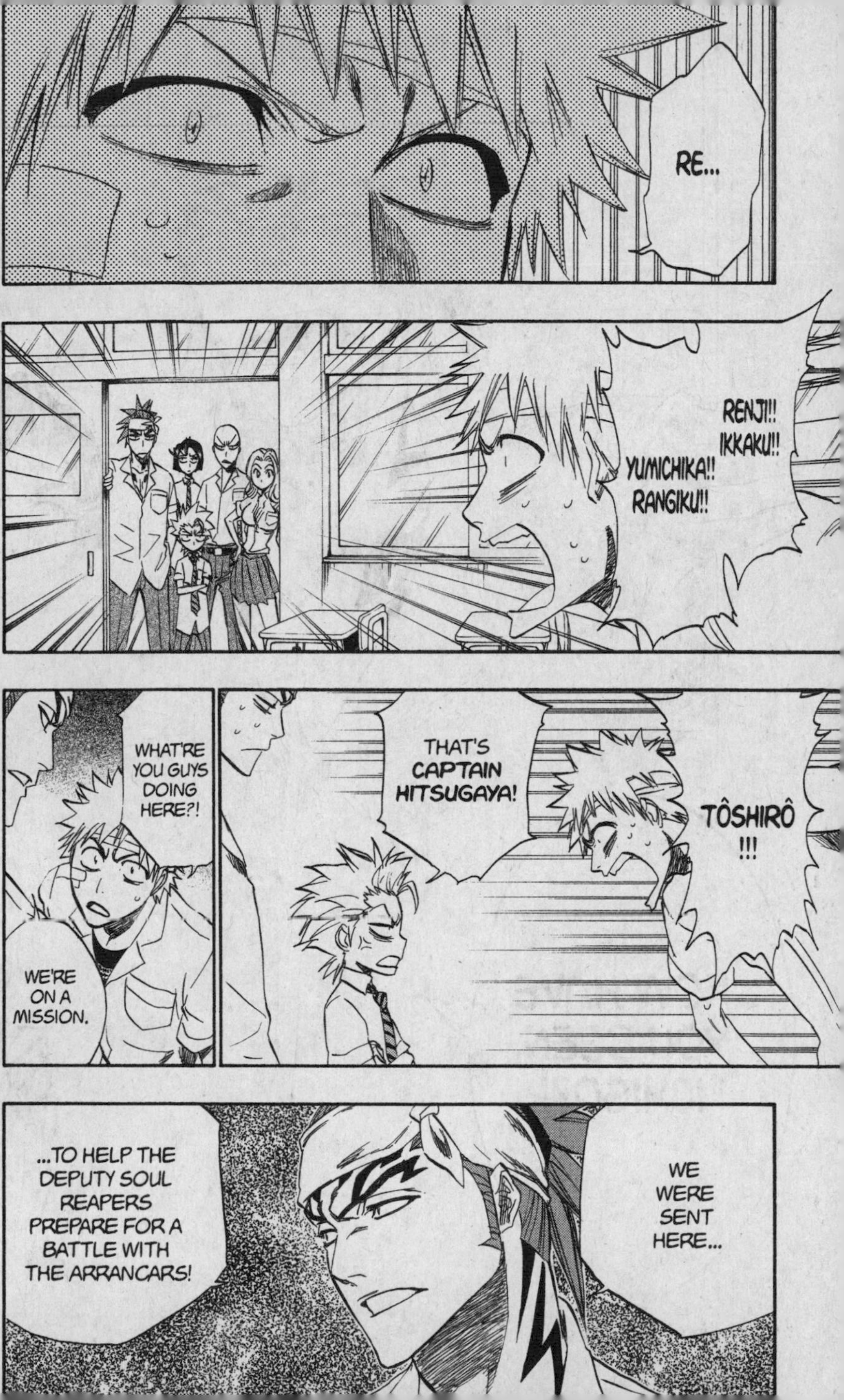
RE...
RENJI!! IKKAKU!!
YUMICHIKA!! RANGIKU!!
TÔSHIRÔ !!!
THAT'S CAPTAIN HITSUGAYA!
WHAT'RE YOU GUYS DOING HERE?!
WE'RE ON A MISSION.
WE WERE SENT HERE...
...TO HELP THE DEPUTY SOUL REAPERS PREPARE FOR A BATTLE WITH THE ARRANCARS!

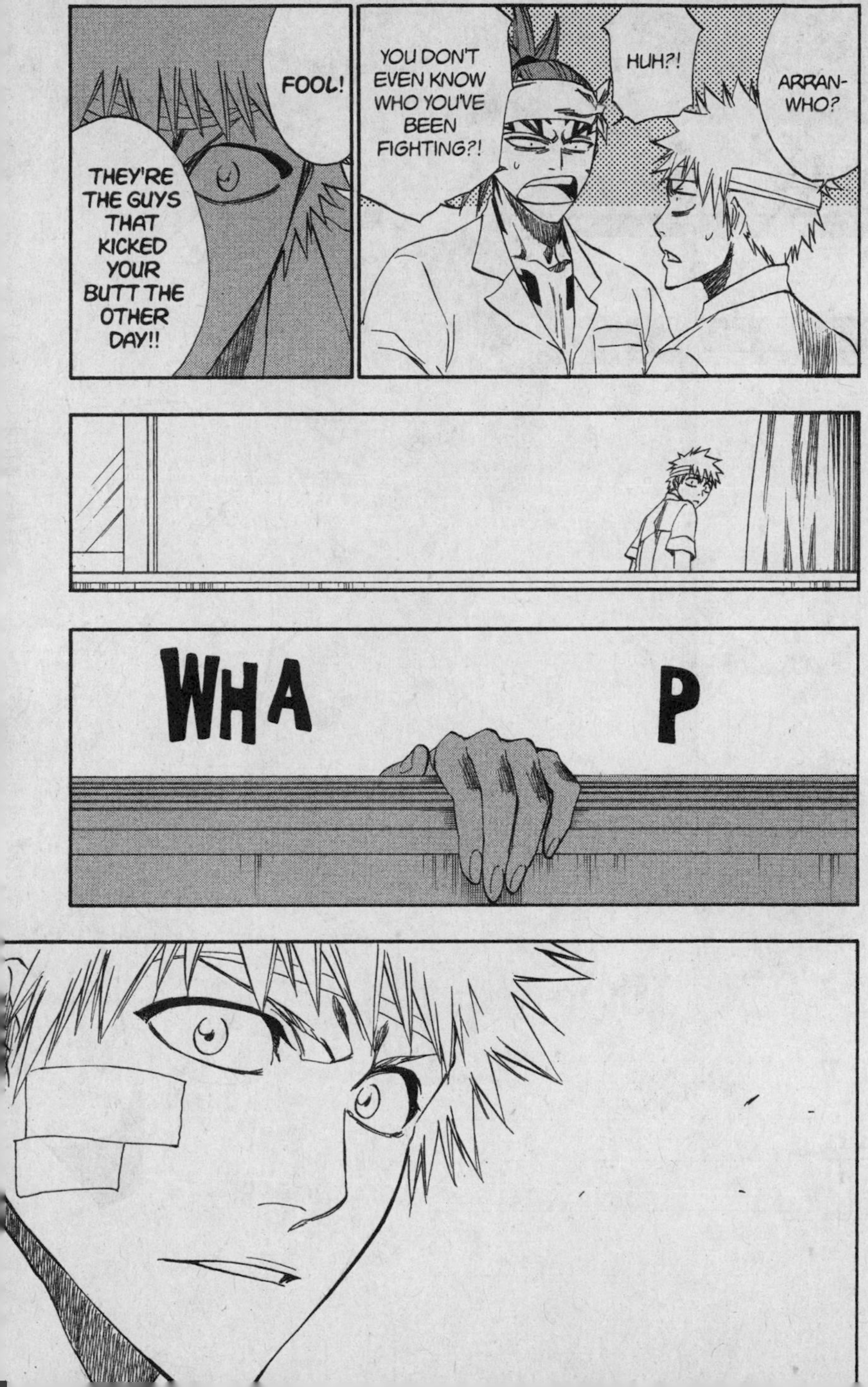
ARRAN-WHO?
HUH?!
YOU DON'T EVEN KNOW WHO YOU'VE BEEN FIGHTING?!
FOOL!
THEY'RE THE GUYS THAT KICKED YOUR BUTT THE OTHER DAY!!
WHAP

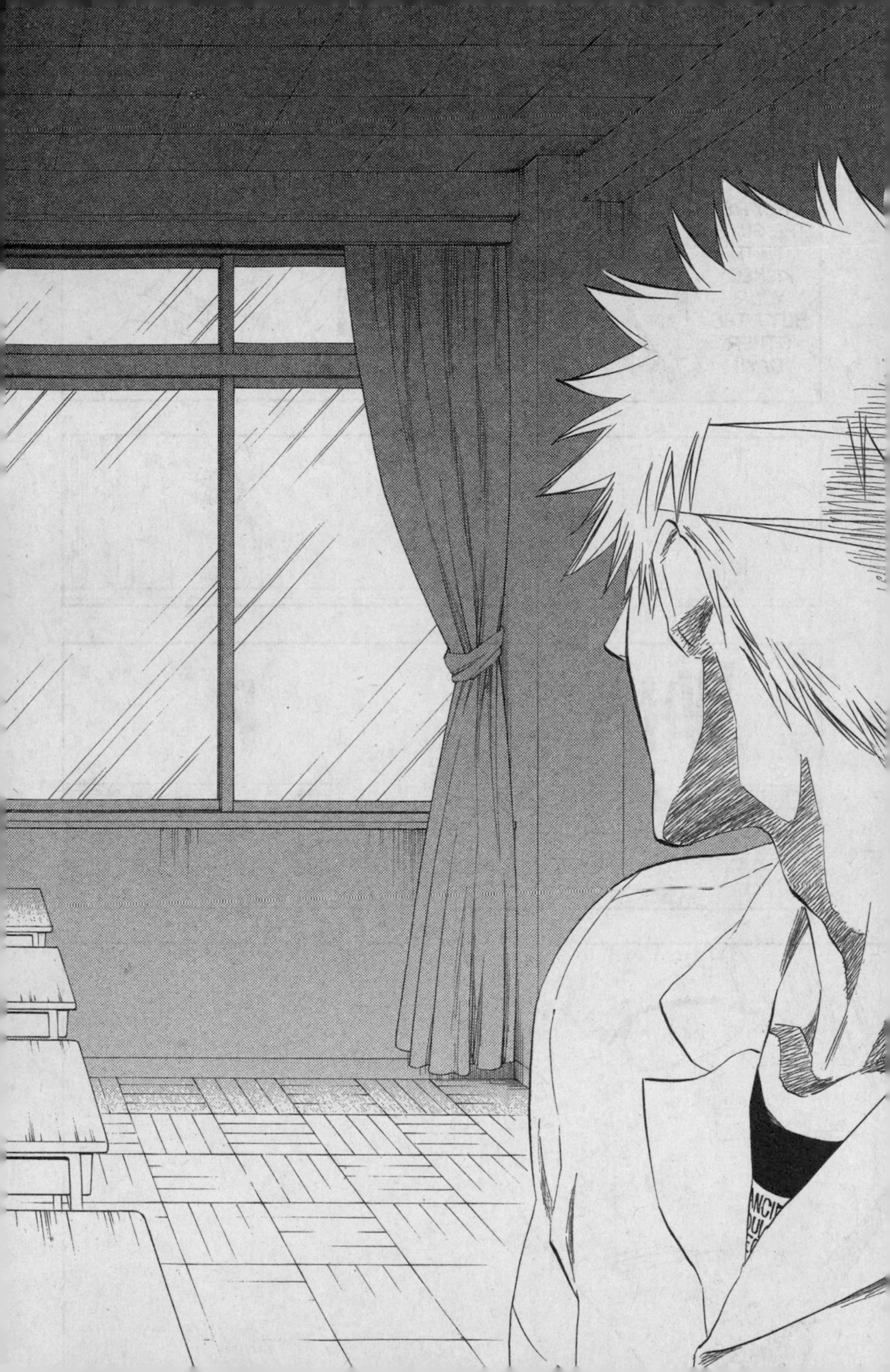

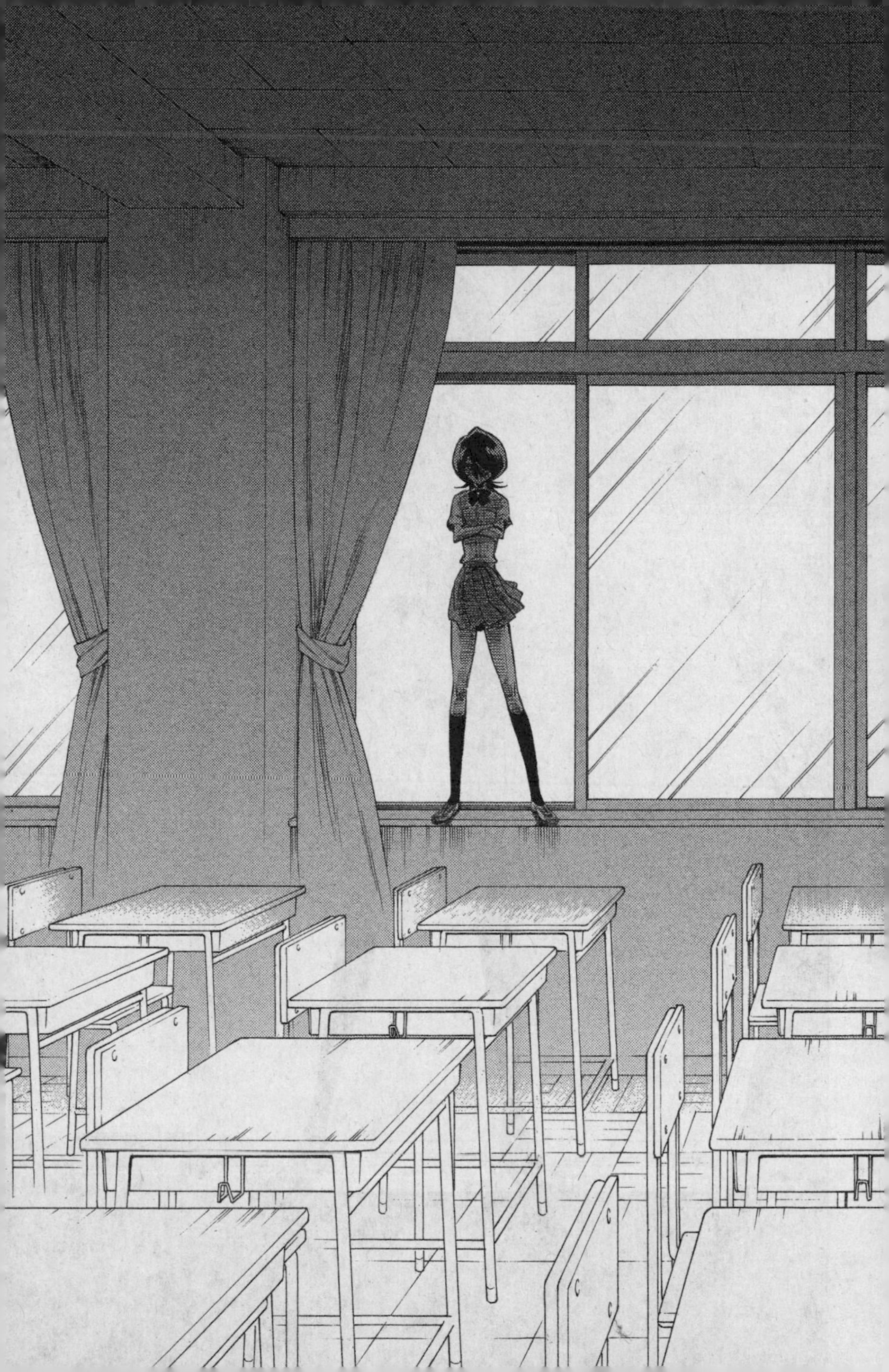

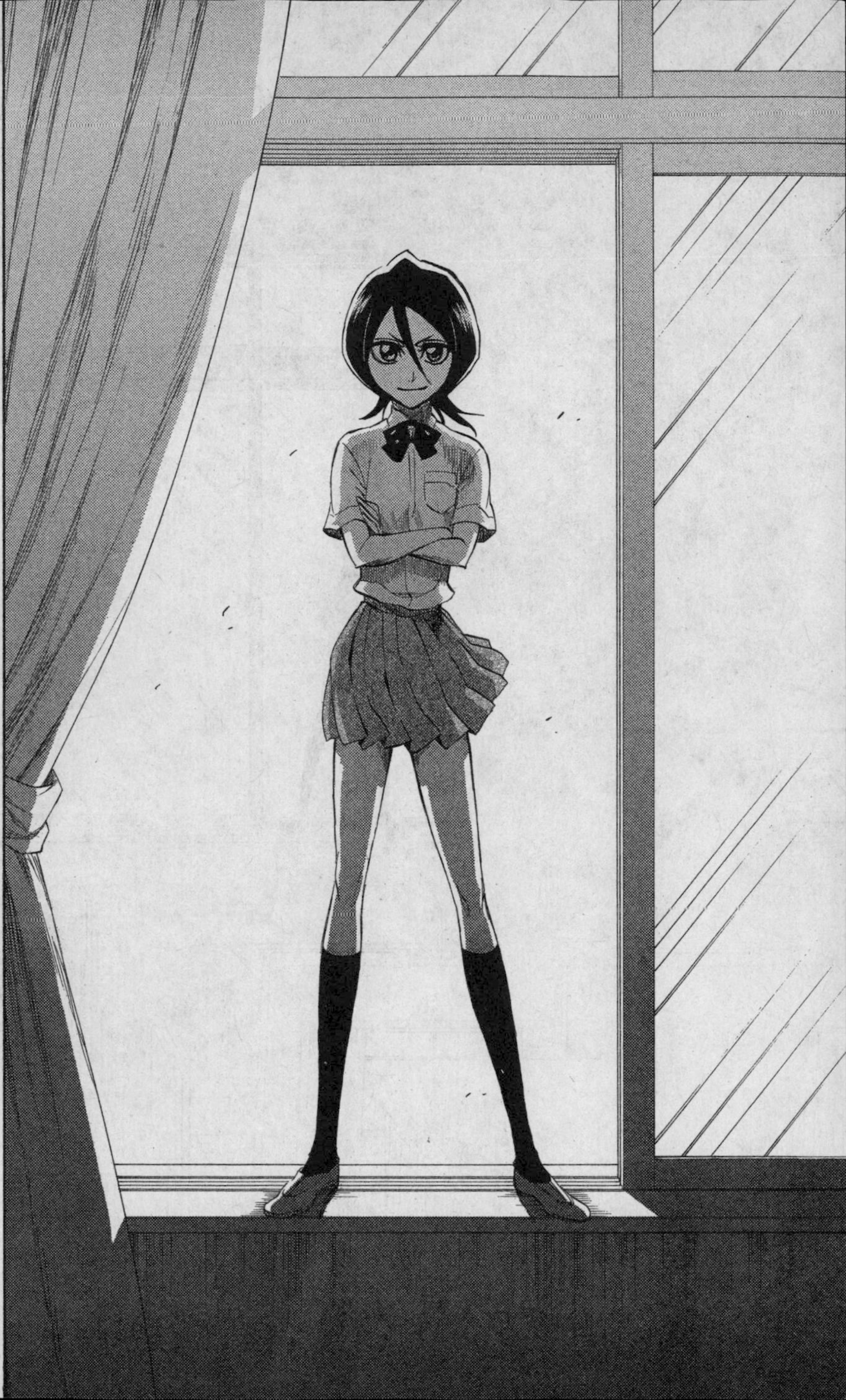

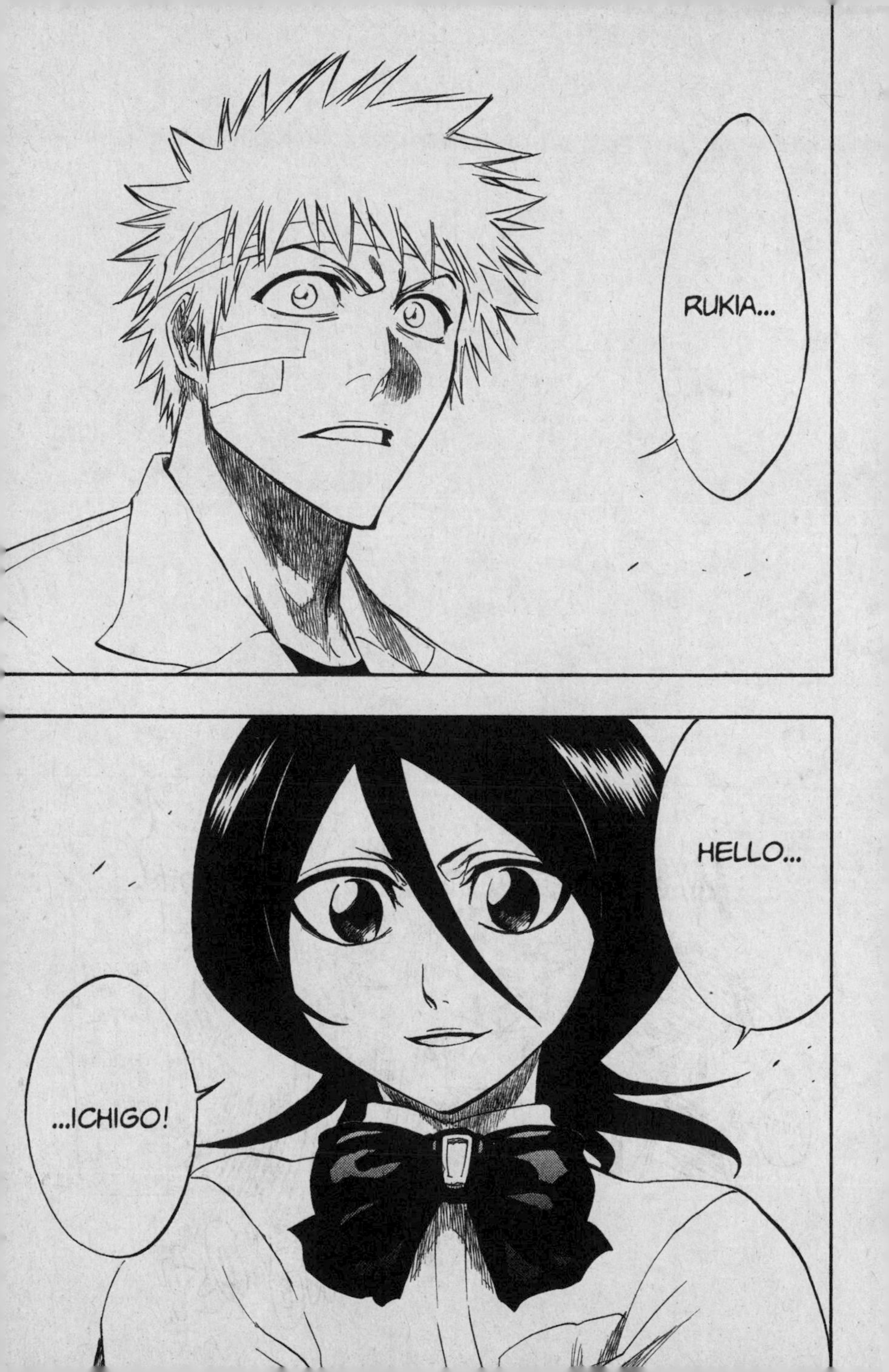
RUKIA...
HELLO...
...ICHIGO!

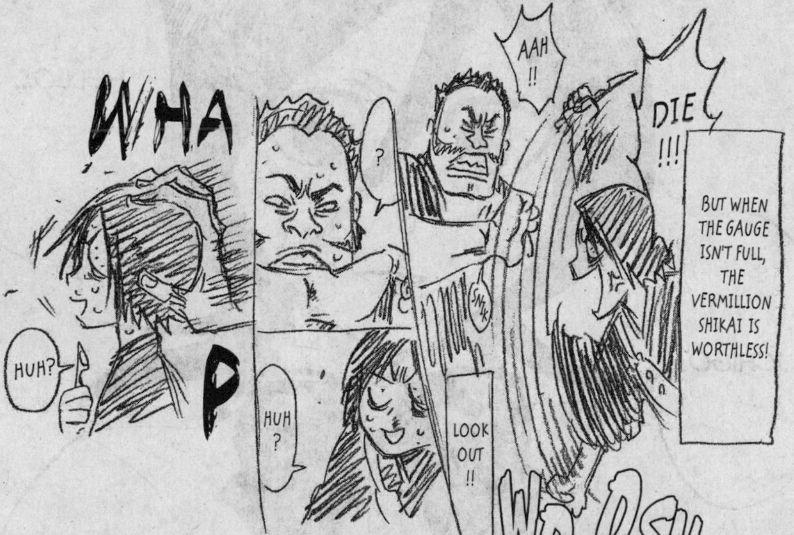
DIE!!!
BUT WHEN THE GAUGE ISN'T FULL, THE VERMILLION SHIKAI IS WORTHLESS!
WOOSH
AAH!!
LOOK OUT!!
?
HUH?
WHAP
HUH?

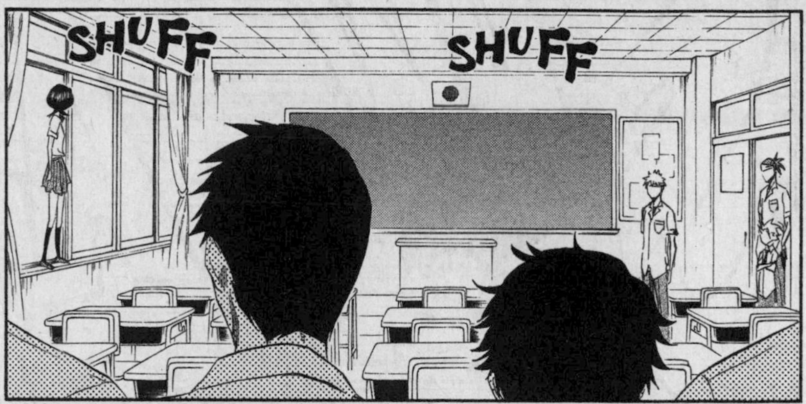
SHUFF
SHUFF

196. PUNCH DOWN THE STONE CIRCLE

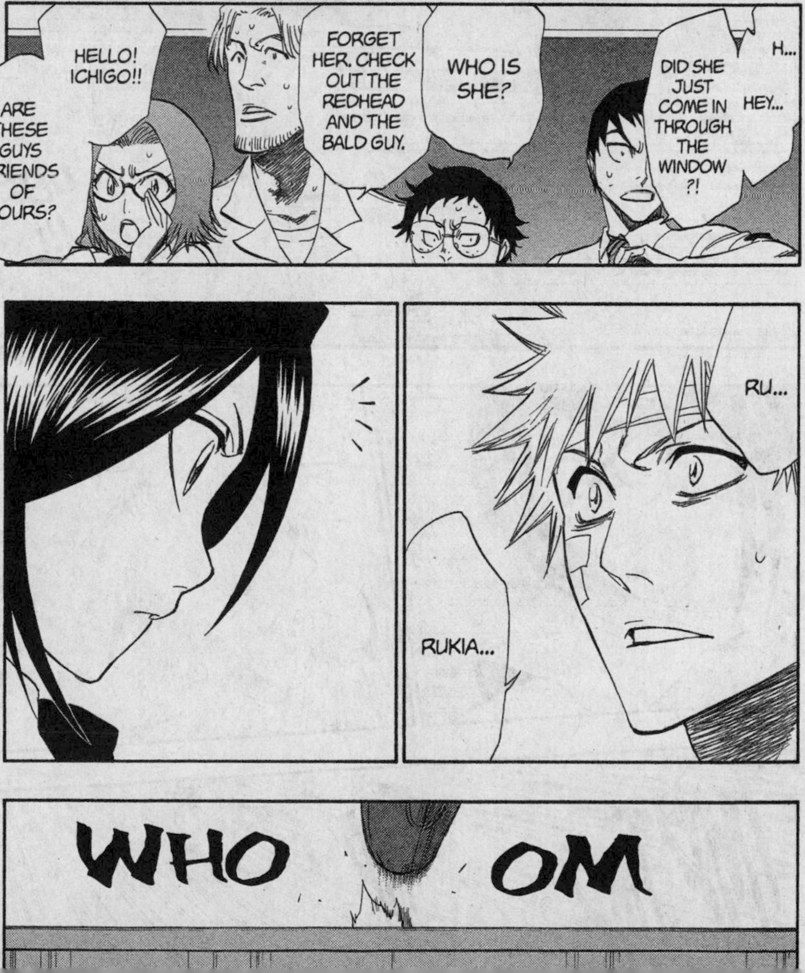
H... HEY...
DID SHE JUST COME IN THROUGH THE WINDOW?!
WHO IS SHE?
FORGET HER. CHECK OUT THE REDHEAD AND THE BALD GUY.
HELLO! ICHIGO!!
ARE THESE GUYS FRIENDS OF YOURS?
RU...
RUKIA...
WHO
OM

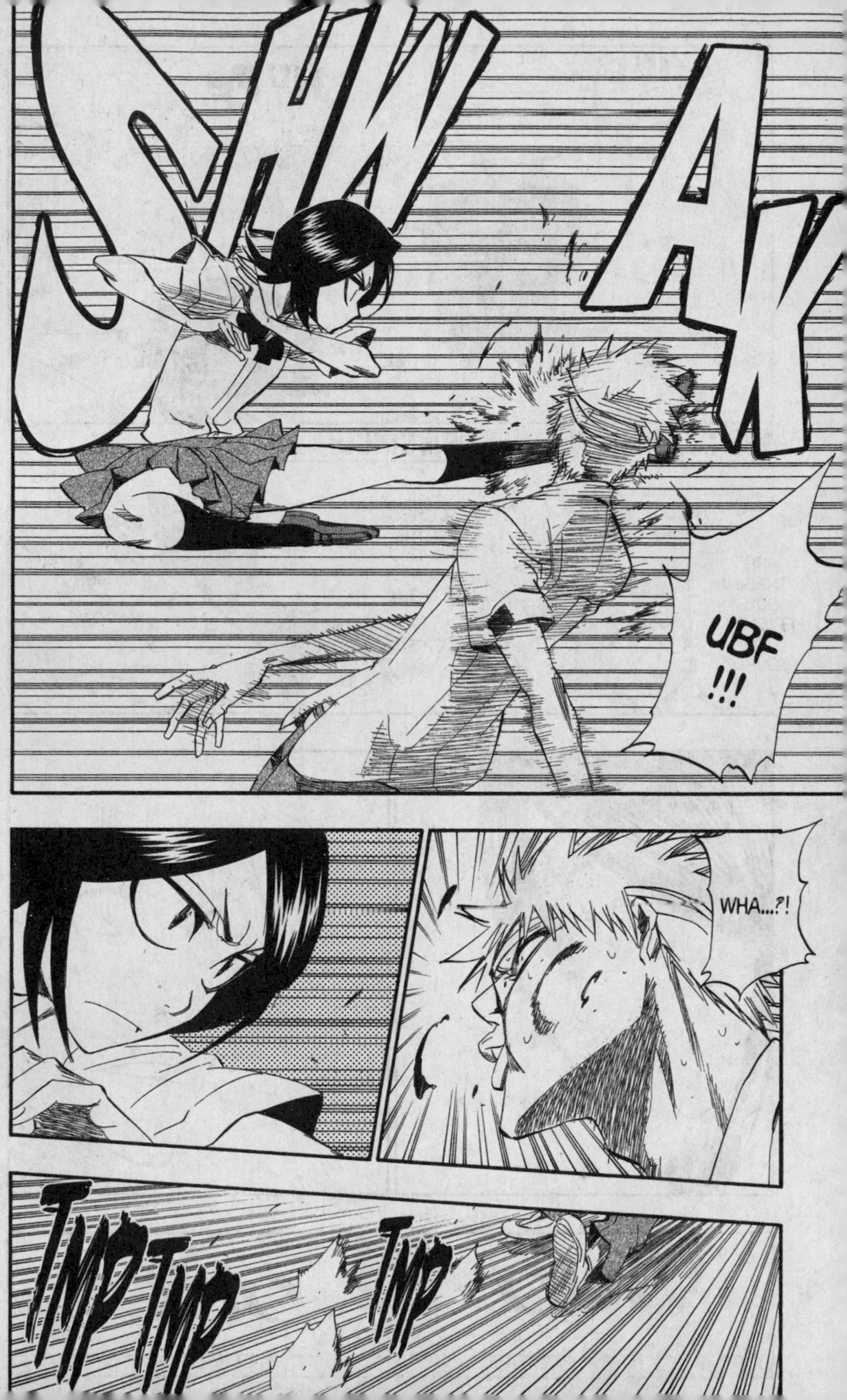
SCHWAK
UBF!!!
WHA...?!
TMP TMP TMP

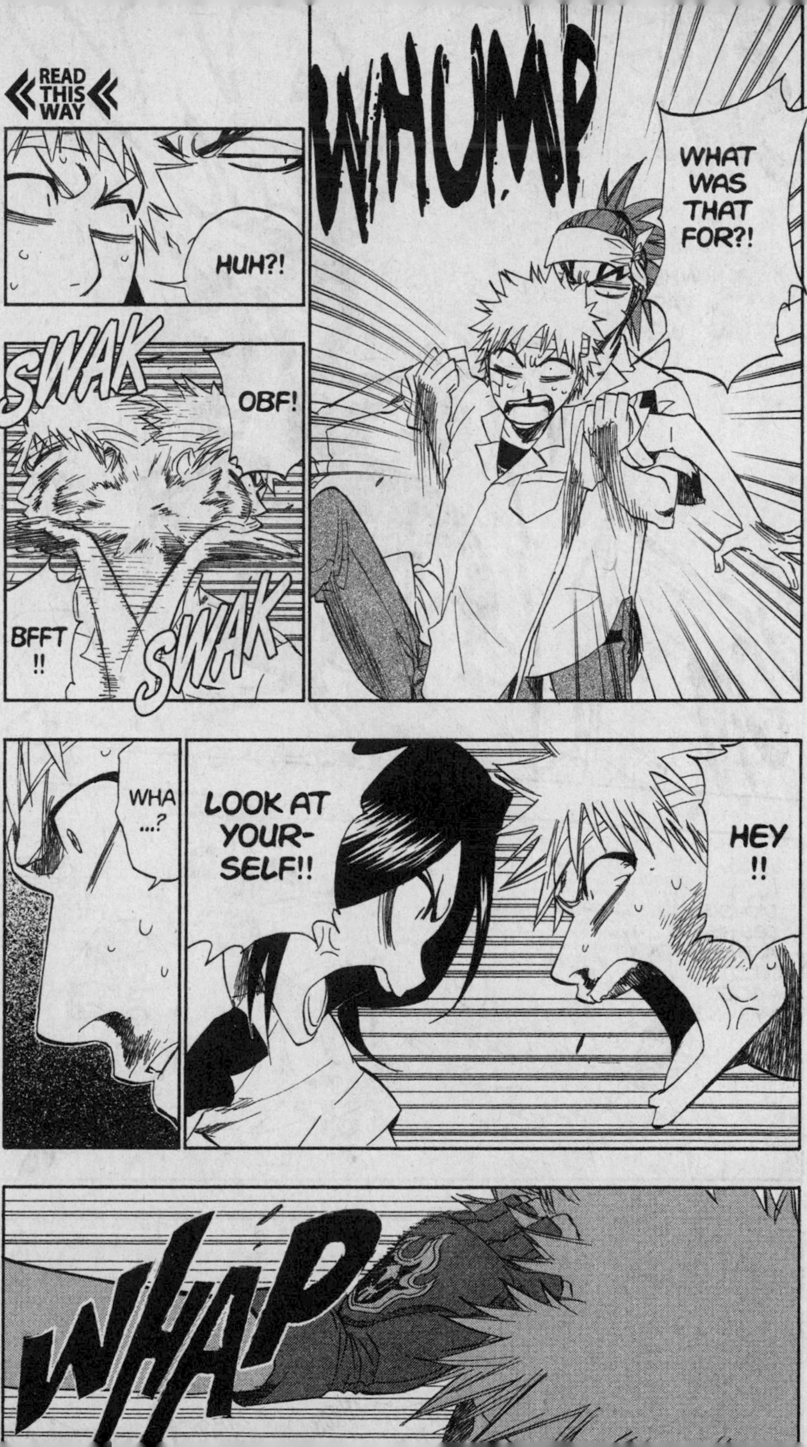
READ THIS WAY
WHUMP
WHAT WAS THAT FOR?!
HUH?!
SWAK
OBF!
BFFT!!
SWAK
HEY!!
LOOK AT YOURSELF!!
WHA...?
WHAP

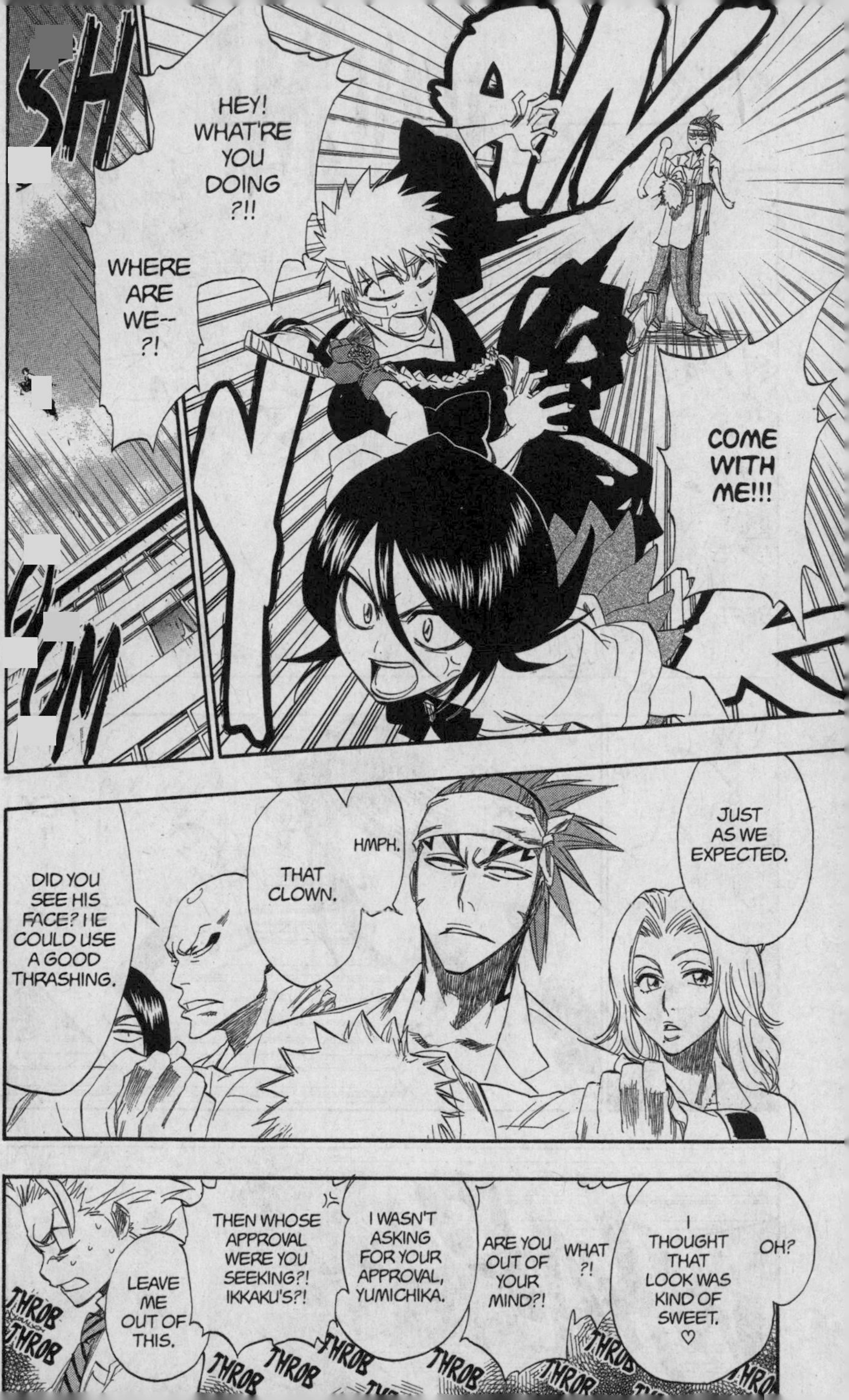
COME WITH ME!!!
HEY! WHAT'RE YOU DOING ?!!
WHERE ARE WE-- ?!
JUST AS WE EXPECTED.
HMPH.
THAT CLOWN.
DID YOU SEE HIS FACE? HE COULD USE A GOOD THRASHING.
OH?
I THOUGHT THAT LOOK WAS KIND OF SWEET. ♡
WHAT ?!
ARE YOU OUT OF YOUR MIND?!
I WASN'T ASKING FOR YOUR APPROVAL, YUMICHIKA.
THEN WHOSE APPROVAL WERE YOU SEEKING?! IKKAKU'S?!
LEAVE ME OUT OF THIS.
THROB THROB THROB THROB THROB THROB THROB THROB THROB

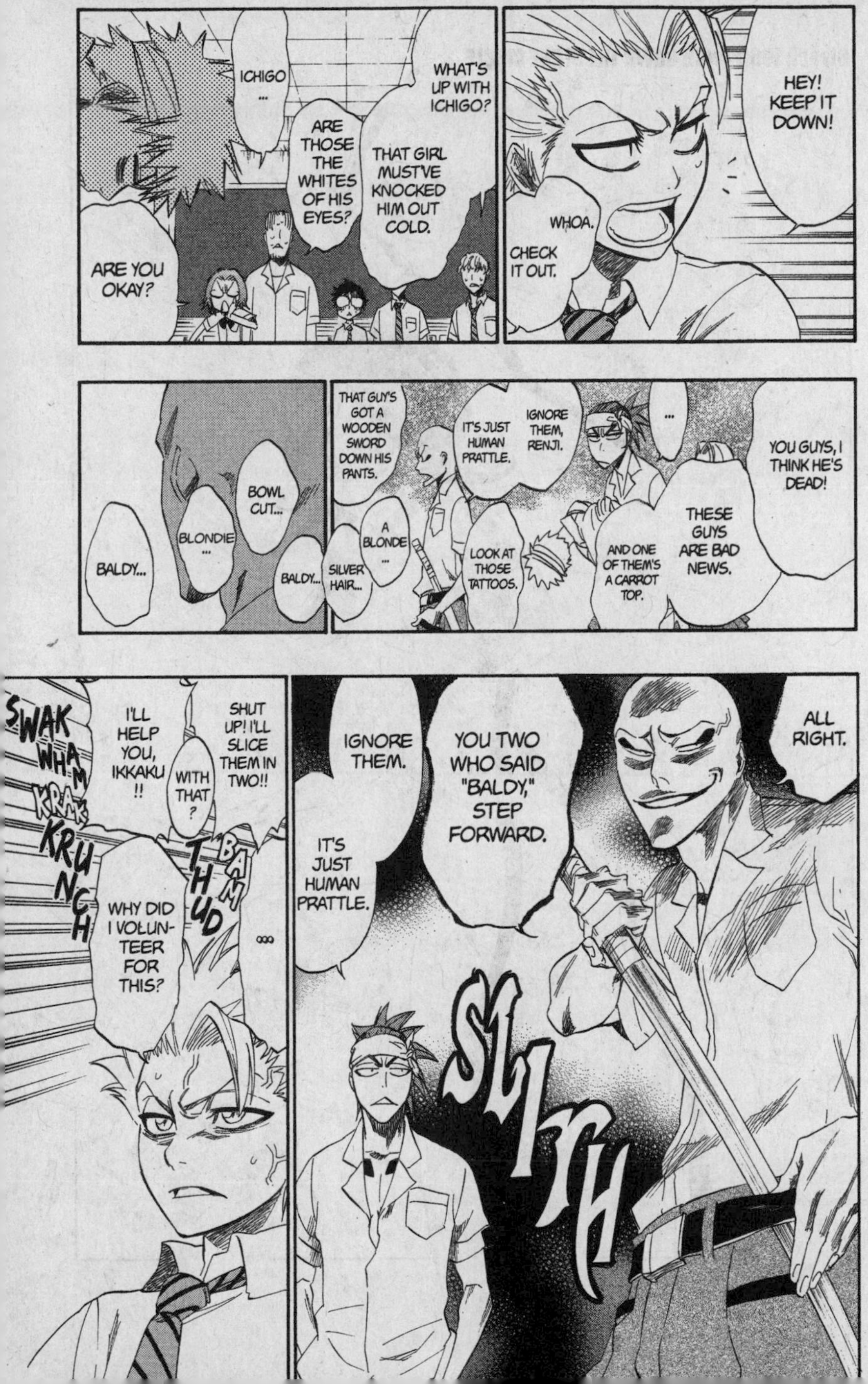
HEY! KEEP IT DOWN!
WHOA.
CHECK IT OUT.
WHAT'S UP WITH ICHIGO?
THAT GIRL MUST'VE KNOCKED HIM OUT COLD.
ARE THOSE THE WHITES OF HIS EYES?
ICHIGO ...
ARE YOU OKAY?
YOU GUYS, I THINK HE'S DEAD!
...
THESE GUYS ARE BAD NEWS.
IGNORE THEM, RENJI.
AND ONE OF THEM'S A CARROT TOP.
IT'S JUST HUMAN PRATTLE.
THAT GUY'S GOT A WOODEN SWORD DOWN HIS PANTS.
LOOK AT THOSE TATTOOS.
A BLONDE ...
SILVER HAIR...
BALDY...
BOWL CUT...
BLONDIE ...
BALDY...
ALL RIGHT.
YOU TWO WHO SAID "BALDY," STEP FORWARD.
IGNORE THEM.
IT'S JUST HUMAN PRATTLE.
SLRRH
SHUT UP! I'LL SLICE THEM IN TWO!!
I'LL HELP YOU, IKKAKU!!
WITH THAT?
SWAK WHAM KRAK KRUNCH
BAM THUD
...
WHY DID I VOLUNTEER FOR THIS?

Bleach 196. PUNCH DOWN THE STONE CIRCLE

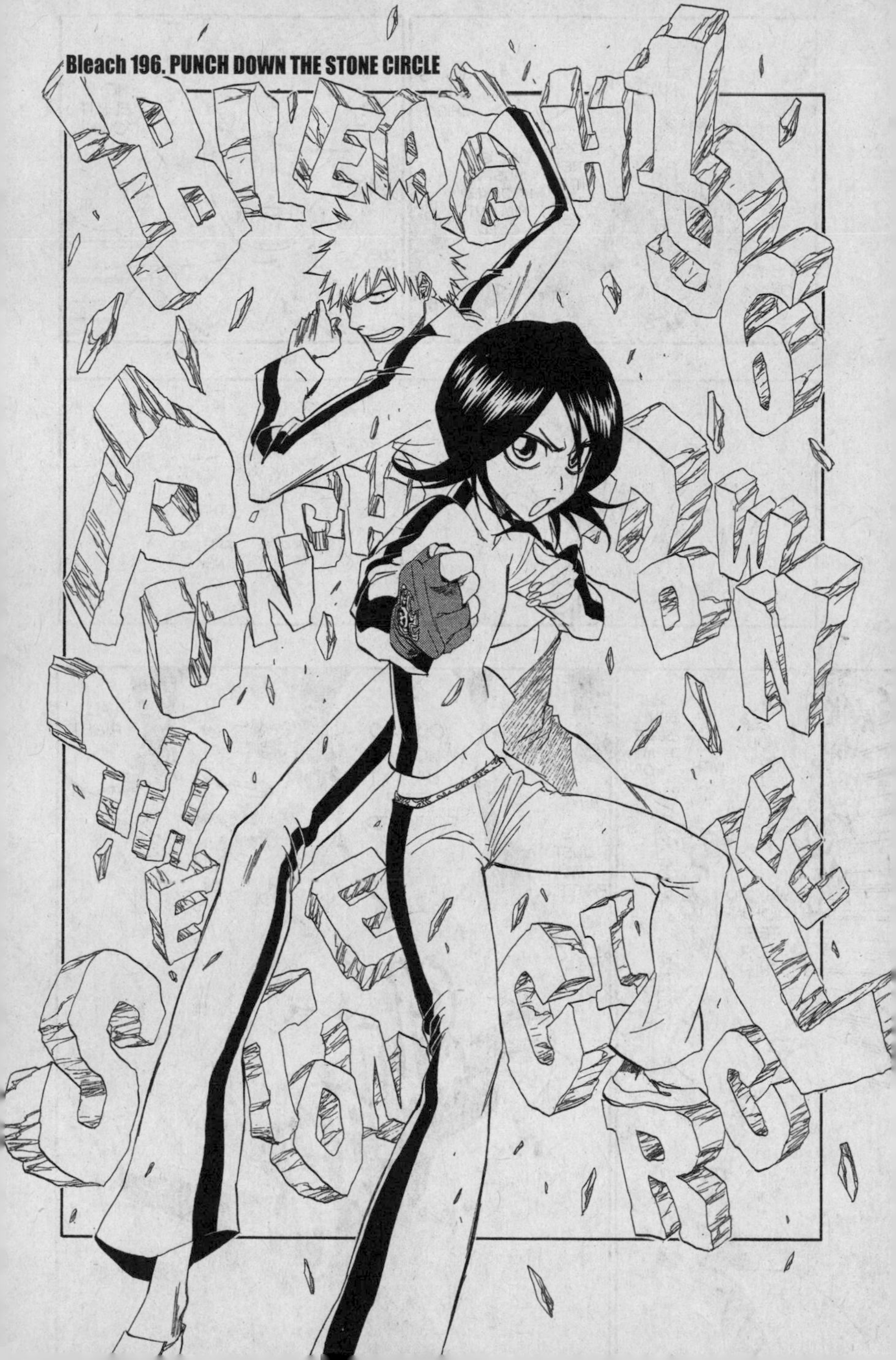
BLEACH 196
PUNCH DOWN
THE
STONE CIRCLE

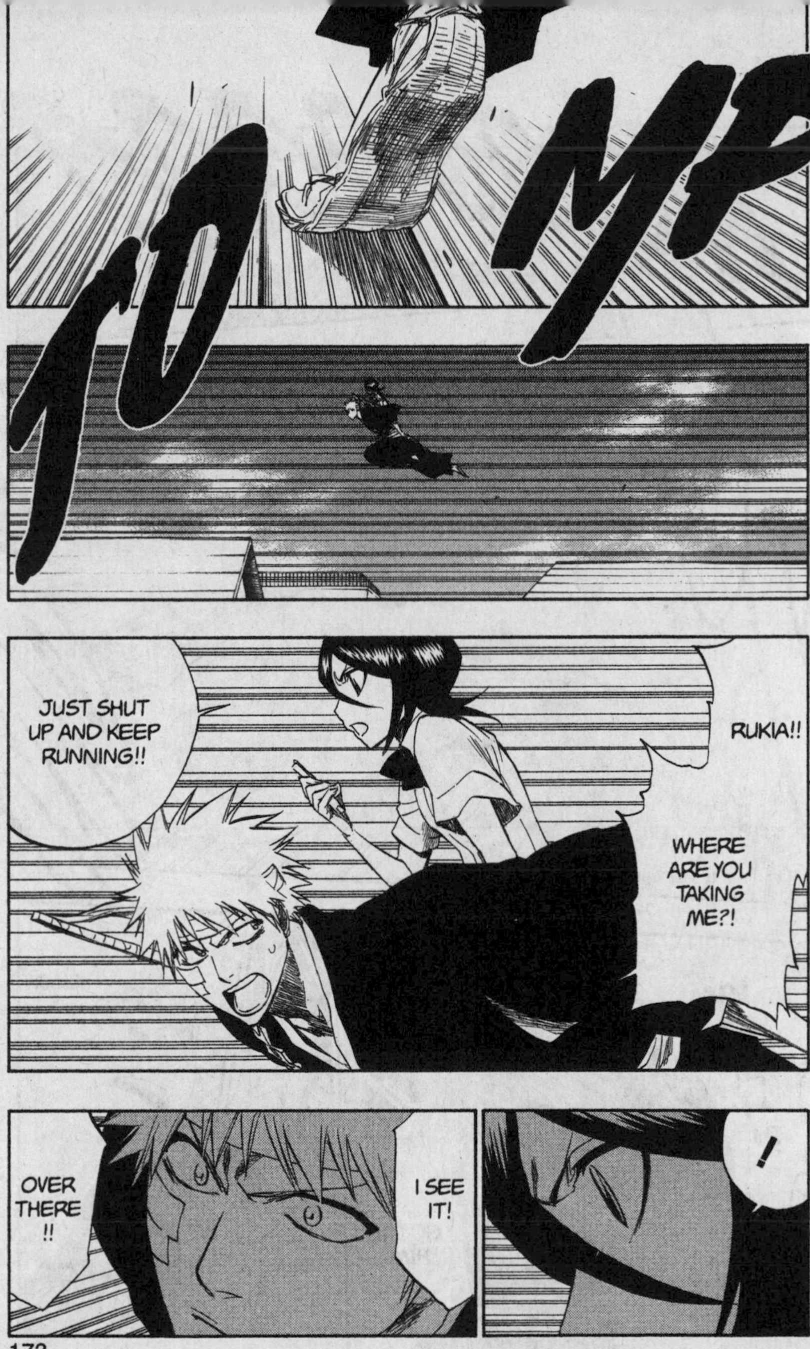
TOMP
RUKIA!!
WHERE ARE YOU TAKING ME?!
JUST SHUT UP AND KEEP RUNNING!!
!
I SEE IT!
OVER THERE !!

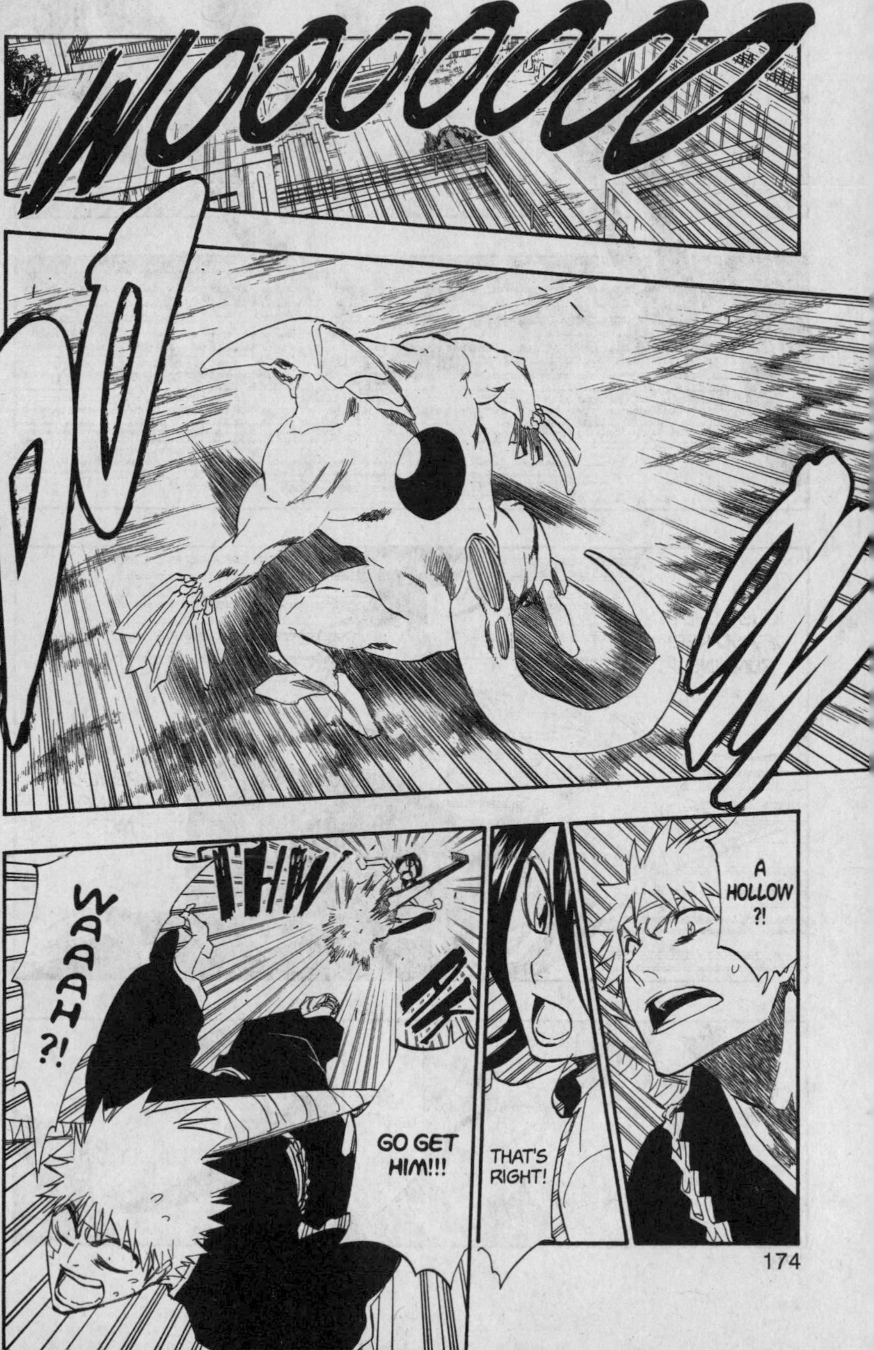
WOOOOOO
DOOM
A HOLLOW?!
THAT'S RIGHT!
THWAK
GO GET HIM!!!
WAAAH?!

READ THIS WAY

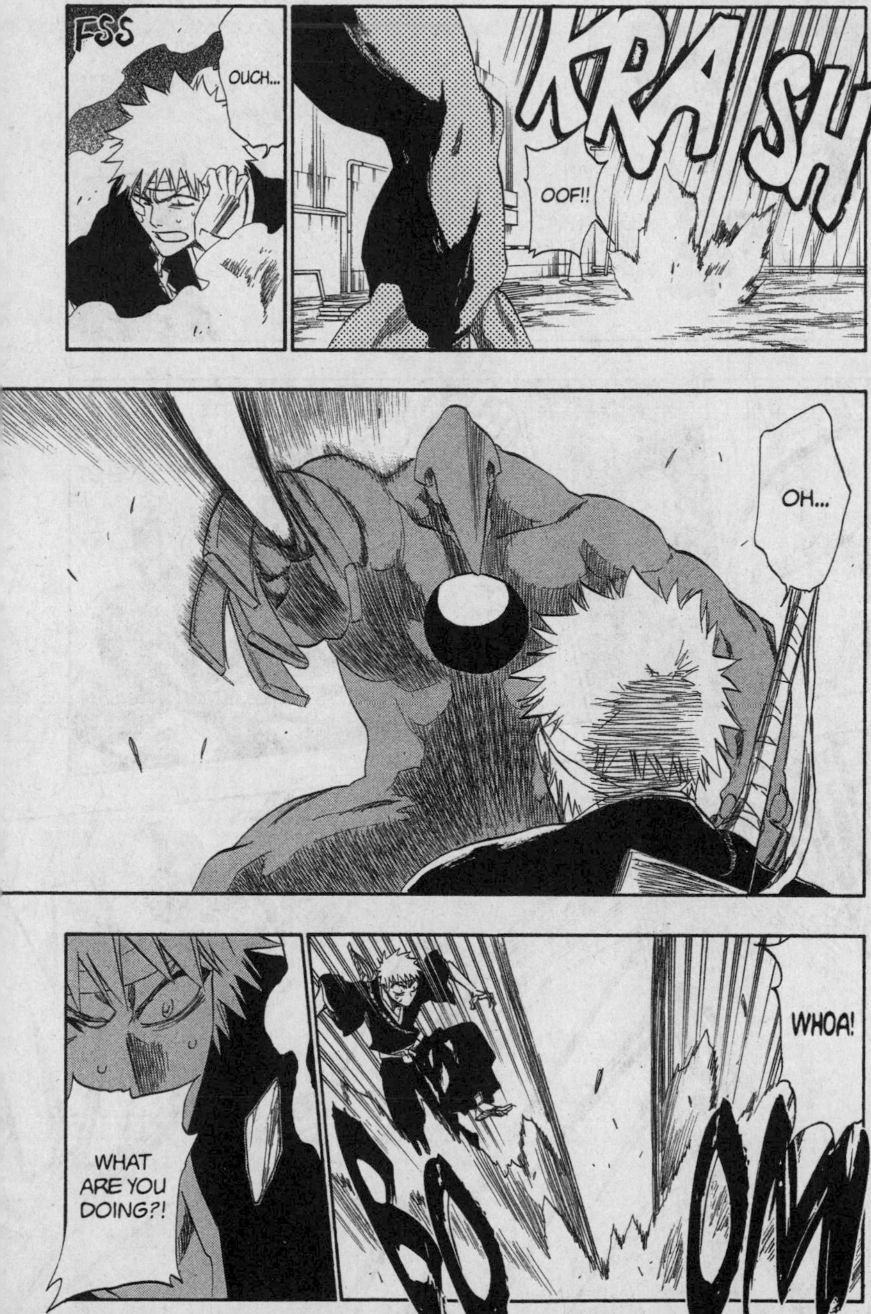
KRASH
OOF!!
FSS
OUCH...
OH...
WHOA!
BOOM
WHAT ARE YOU DOING?!

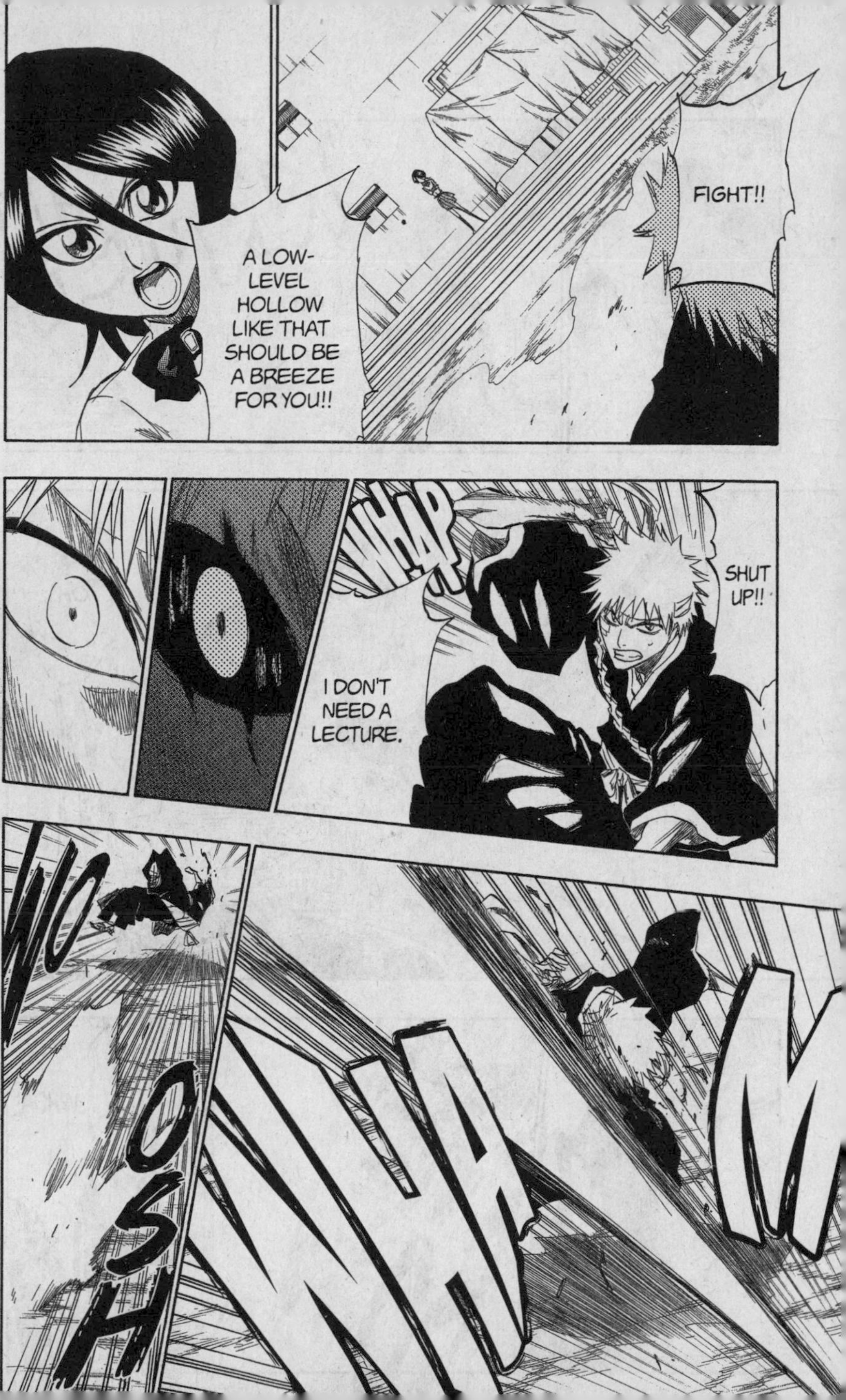
FIGHT!!
A LOW-LEVEL HOLLOW LIKE THAT SHOULD BE A BREEZE FOR YOU!!
WHAP
SHUT UP!!
I DON'T NEED A LECTURE.
WHAM
WHOOSH

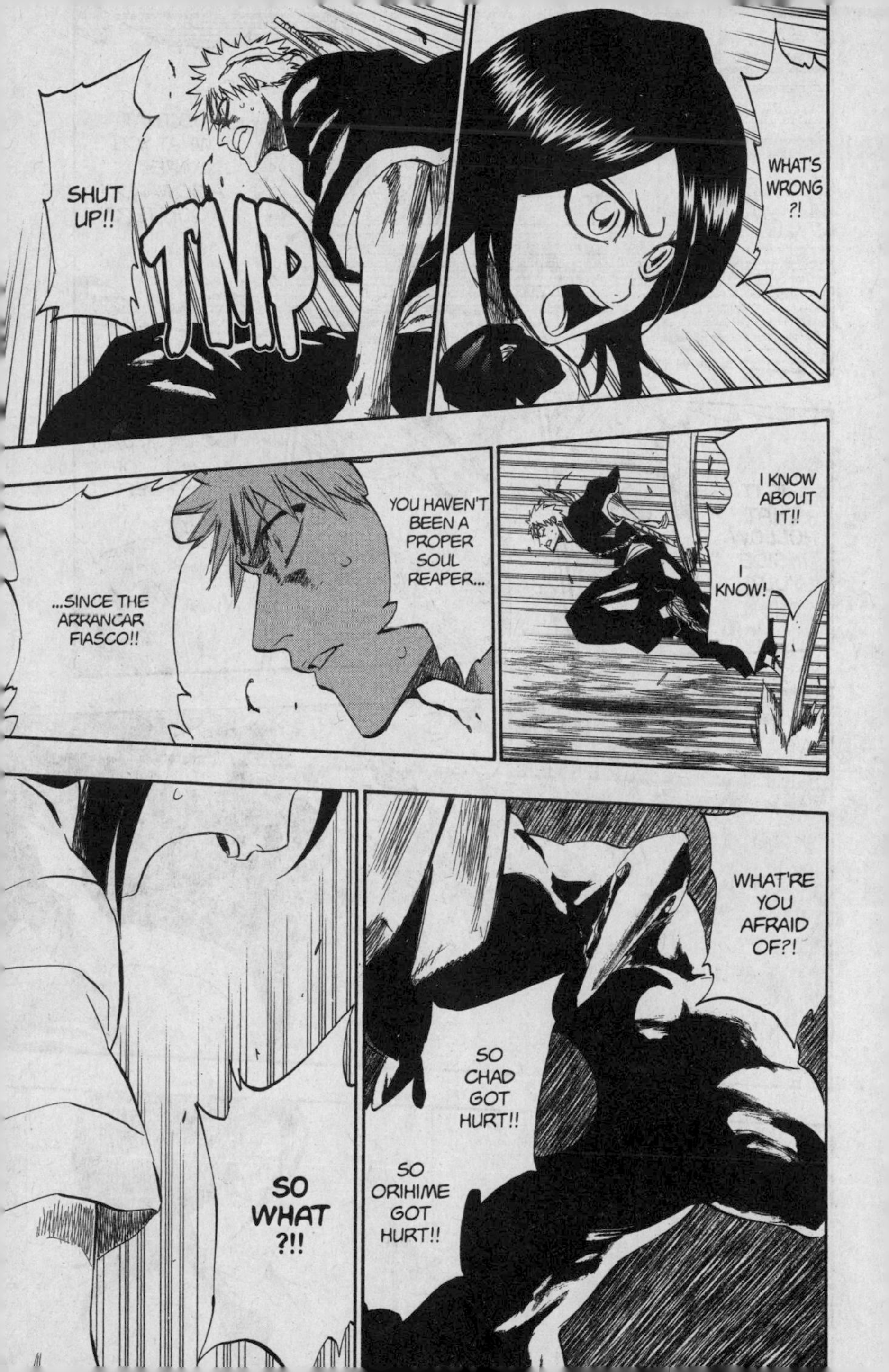
WHAT'S WRONG?!
SHUT UP!!
TMP
I KNOW ABOUT IT!!
I KNOW!
YOU HAVEN'T BEEN A PROPER SOUL REAPER...
...SINCE THE ARRANCAR FIASCO!!
WHAT'RE YOU AFRAID OF?!
SO CHAD GOT HURT!!
SO ORIHIME GOT HURT!!
SO WHAT?!!

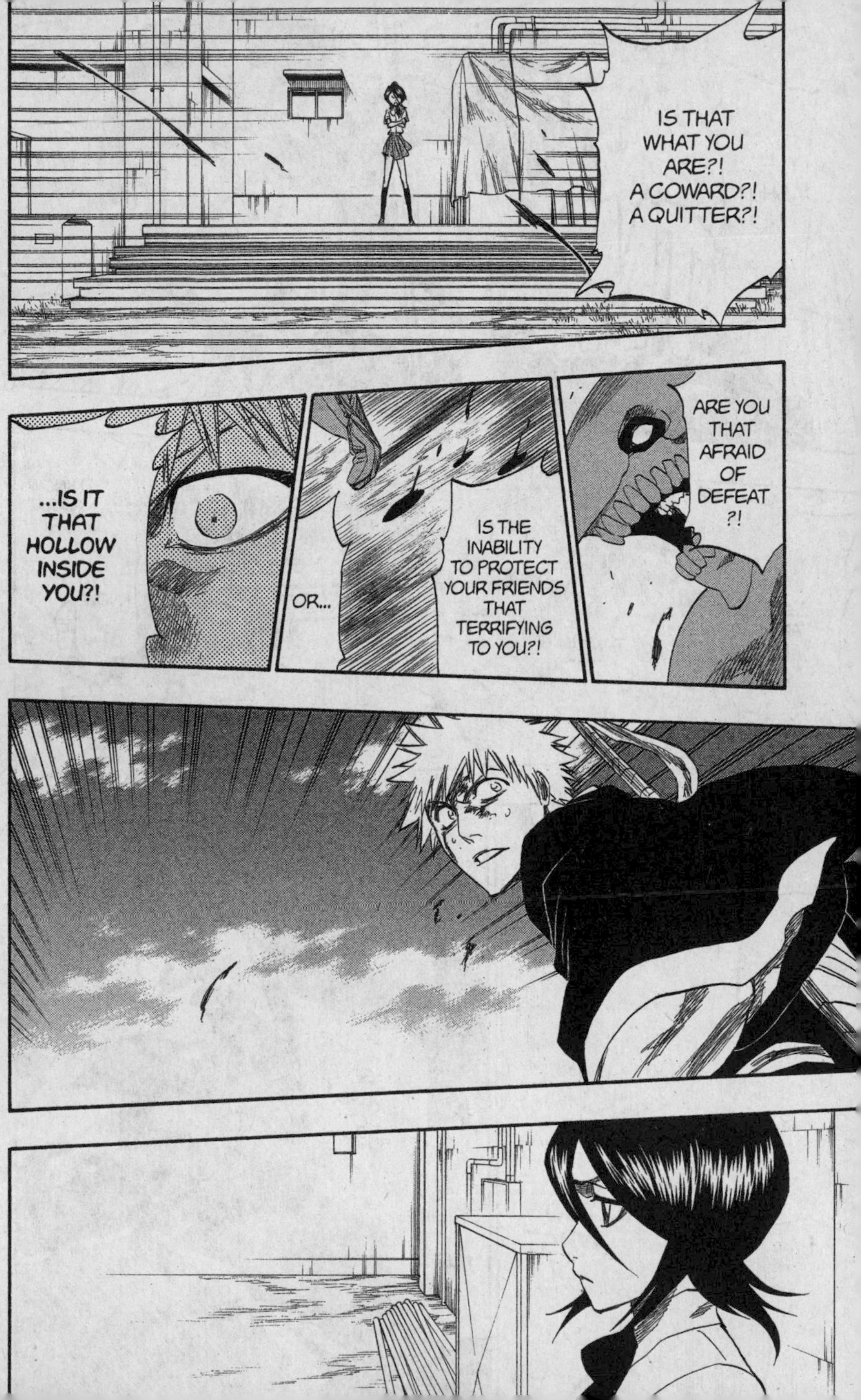
IS THAT WHAT YOU ARE?! A COWARD?! A QUITTER?!
ARE YOU THAT AFRAID OF DEFEAT ?!
IS THE INABILITY TO PROTECT YOUR FRIENDS THAT TERRIFYING TO YOU?!
OR...
...IS IT THAT HOLLOW INSIDE YOU?!

IF YOU'RE AFRAID TO LOSE, THEN GET STRONGER.

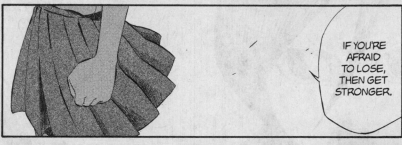

IF YOU WANT TO PROTECT THOSE YOU LOVE...

...THEN DO WHAT YOU HAVE TO DO TO PROTECT THEM.

IF THE HOLLOW INSIDE IS SO TERRIBLE...

...THEN GET STRONG ENOUGH TO CRUSH IT.

EVEN IF NO ONE IN THE WORLD BELIEVES IN YOU...

...STICK OUT YOUR CHEST AND SCREAM IN DEFIANCE!!

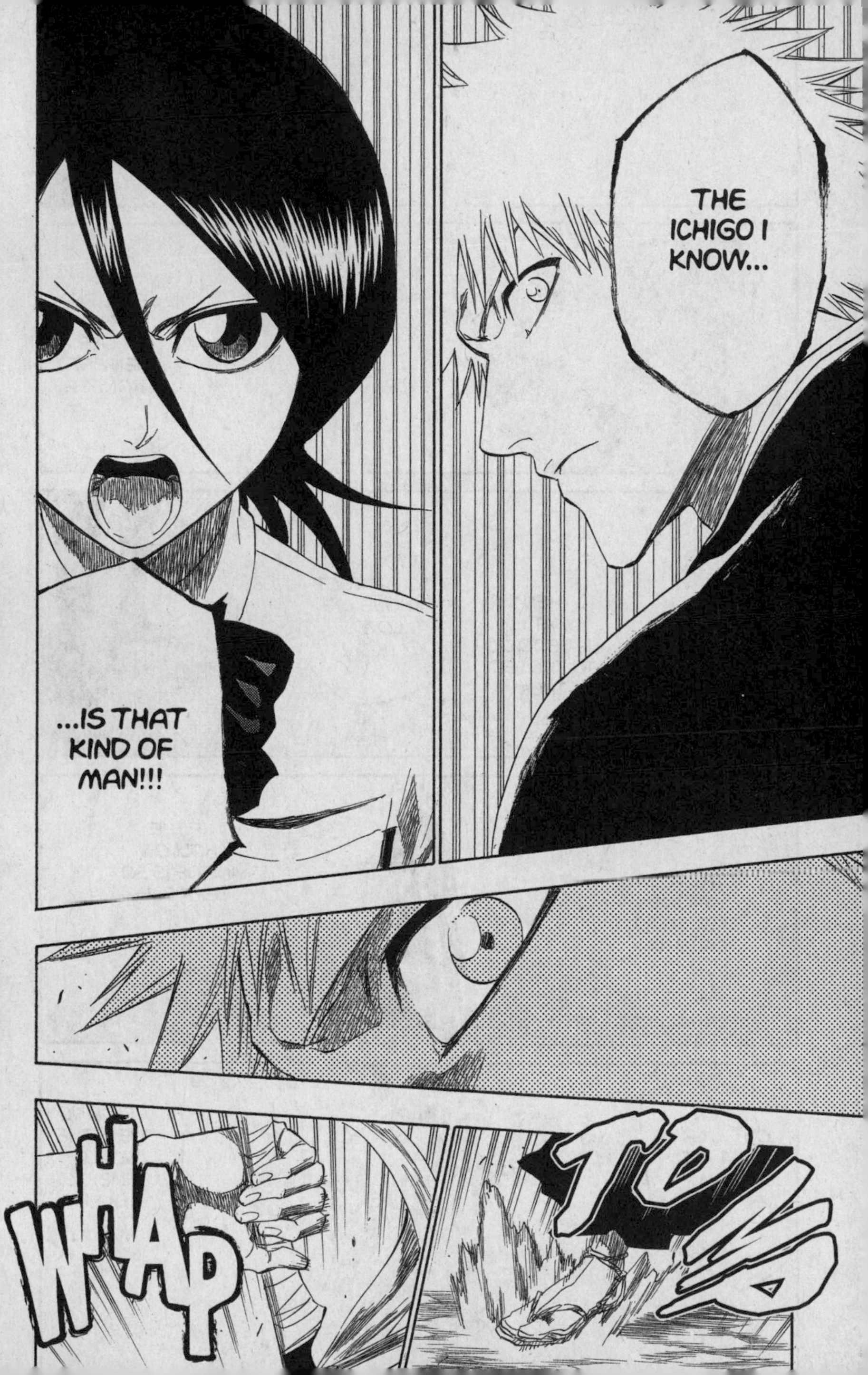
THE ICHIGO I KNOW...
...IS THAT KIND OF MAN!!!
TON
WHAP

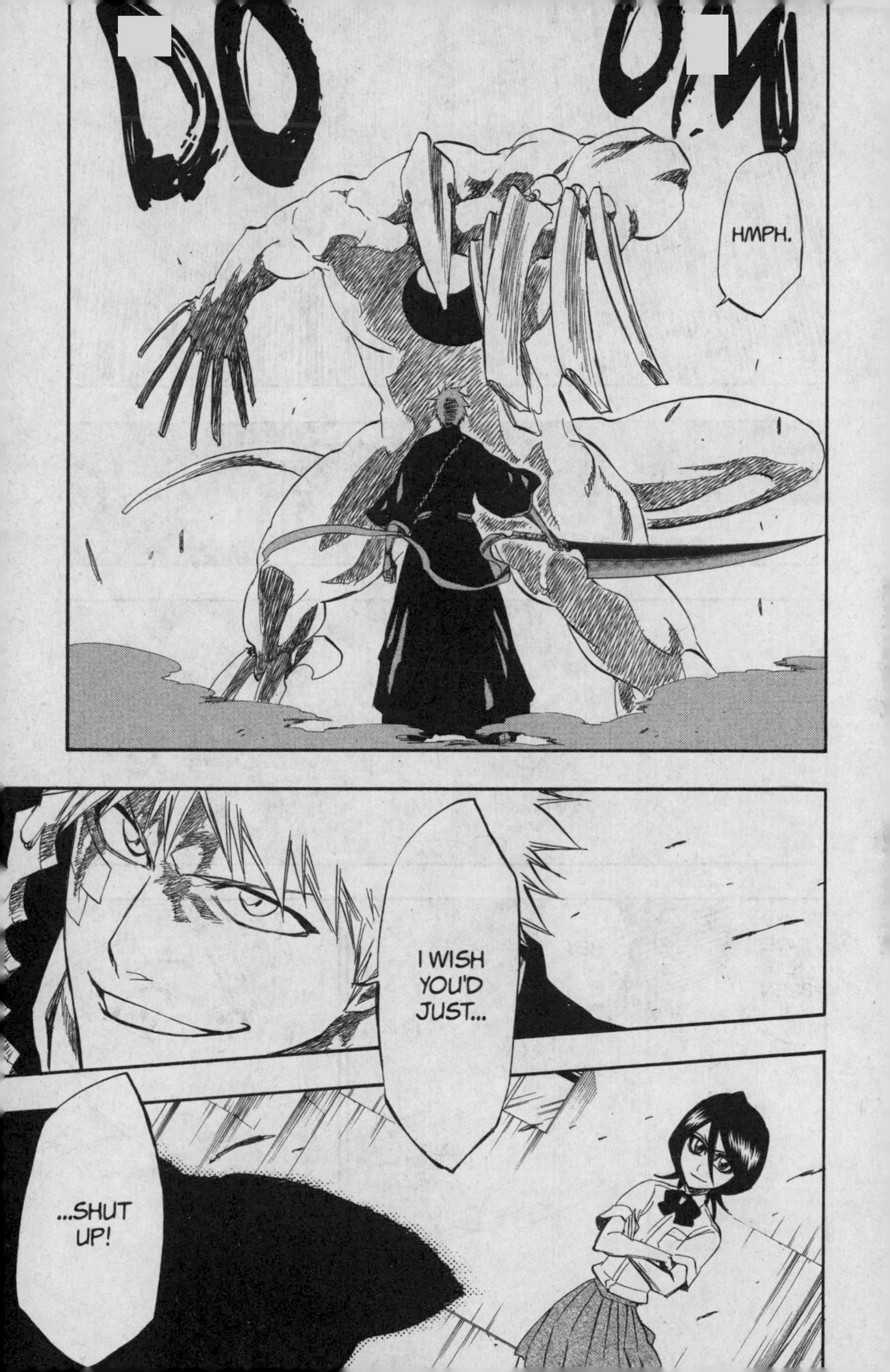
DO ON
HMPH.
I WISH YOU'D JUST...
...SHUT UP!

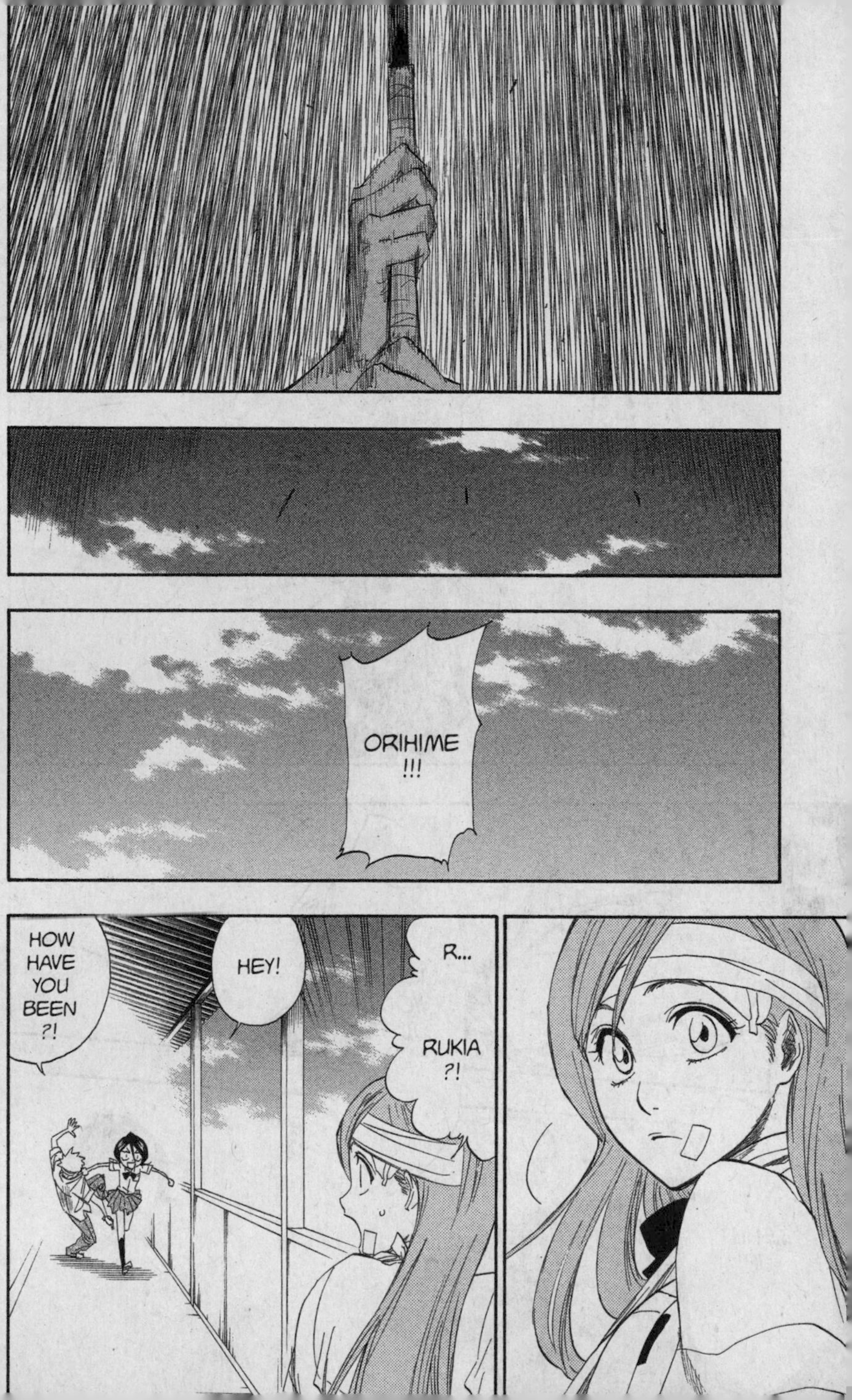
ORIHIME !!!
R...
RUKIA ?!
HEY!
HOW HAVE YOU BEEN ?!

READ THIS WAY

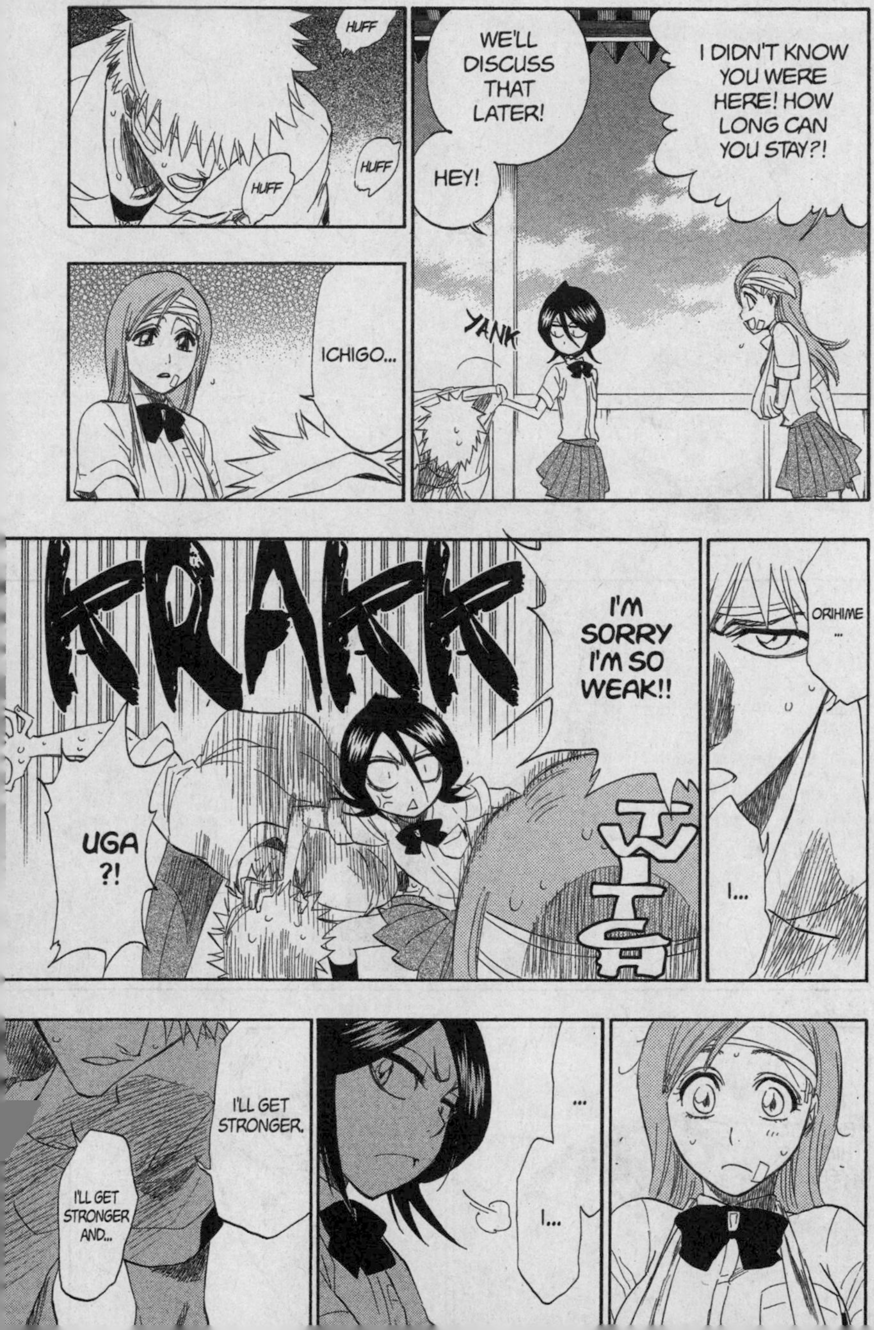
I DIDN'T KNOW YOU WERE HERE! HOW LONG CAN YOU STAY?!
WE'LL DISCUSS THAT LATER!
HEY!
YANK
HUFF
HUFF
HUFF
ICHIGO...
ORIHIME...
I...
I'M SORRY I'M SO WEAK!!
KRAKK
UGA ?!
...
I...
I'LL GET STRONGER.
I'LL GET STRONGER AND...

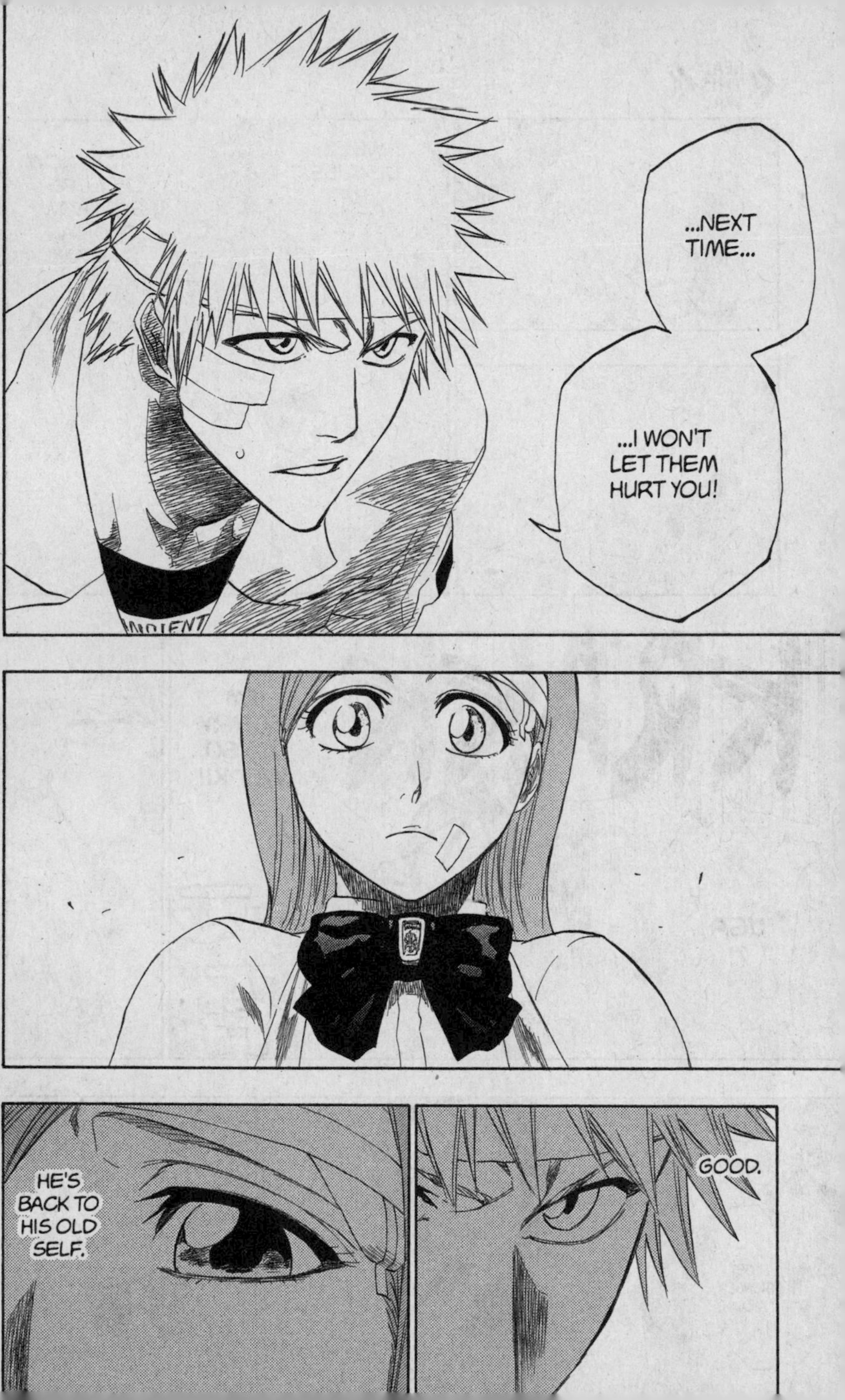
...NEXT TIME...
...I WON'T LET THEM HURT YOU!
GOOD.
HE'S BACK TO HIS OLD SELF.

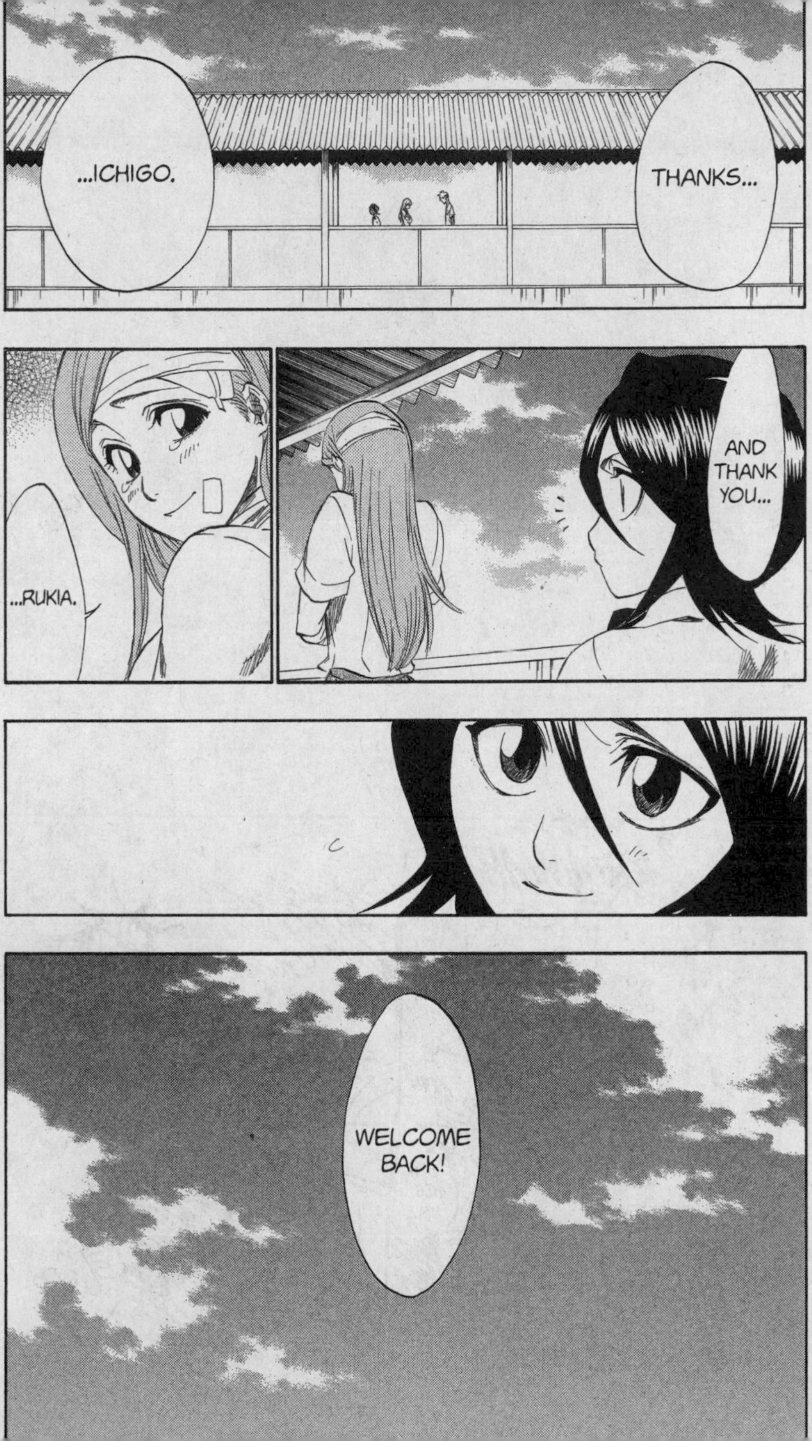
THANKS...
...ICHIGO.
AND THANK YOU...
...RUKIA.
WELCOME BACK!

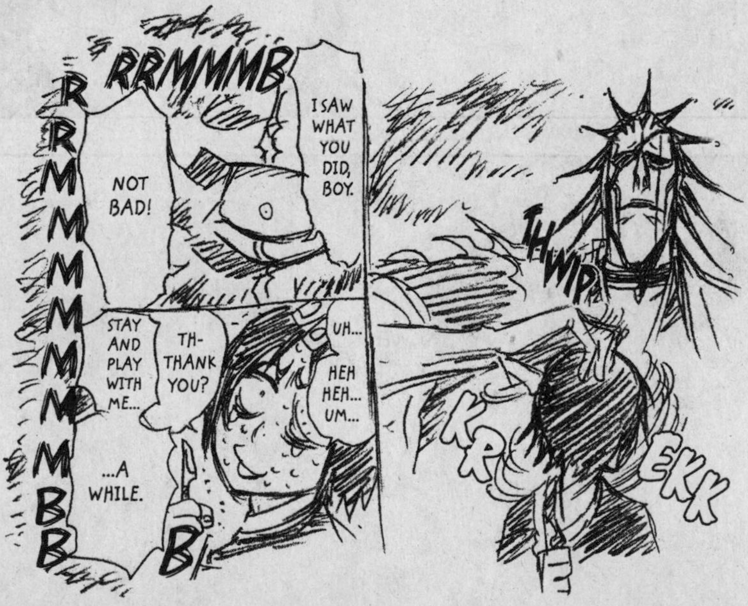
THWIP
KREKK
I SAW WHAT YOU DID, BOY.
RRMMMB
NOT BAD!
RRMMMMMMMBB
UH... HEH HEH... UM...
TH-THANK YOU?
STAY AND PLAY WITH ME...
...A WHILE.
B

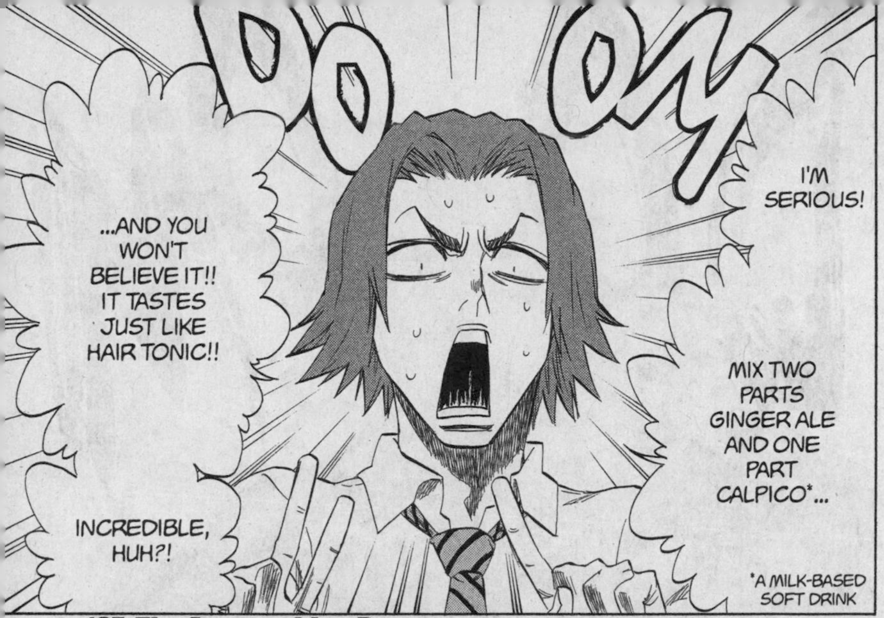
DO OY
I'M SERIOUS!
MIX TWO PARTS GINGER ALE AND ONE PART CALPICO*...
...AND YOU WON'T BELIEVE IT!! IT TASTES JUST LIKE HAIR TONIC!!
INCREDIBLE, HUH?!
*A MILK-BASED SOFT DRINK

197. The Approaching Danger

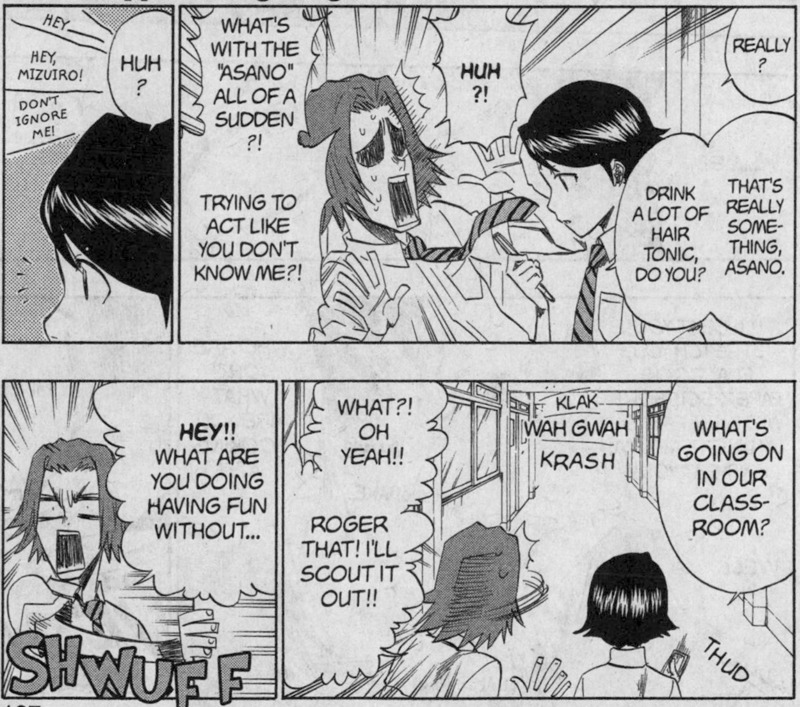
REALLY?
THAT'S REALLY SOME-THING, ASANO.
DRINK A LOT OF HAIR TONIC, DO YOU?
HUH?!
WHAT'S WITH THE "ASANO" ALL OF A SUDDEN?!
TRYING TO ACT LIKE YOU DON'T KNOW ME?!
HEY
HEY, MIZUIRO!
DON'T IGNORE ME!
HUH?
WHAT'S GOING ON IN OUR CLASS-ROOM?
KLAK
WAH GWAH
KRASH
WHAT?! OH YEAH!!
ROGER THAT! I'LL SCOUT IT OUT!!
THUD
HEY!! WHAT ARE YOU DOING HAVING FUN WITHOUT...
SHWUFF

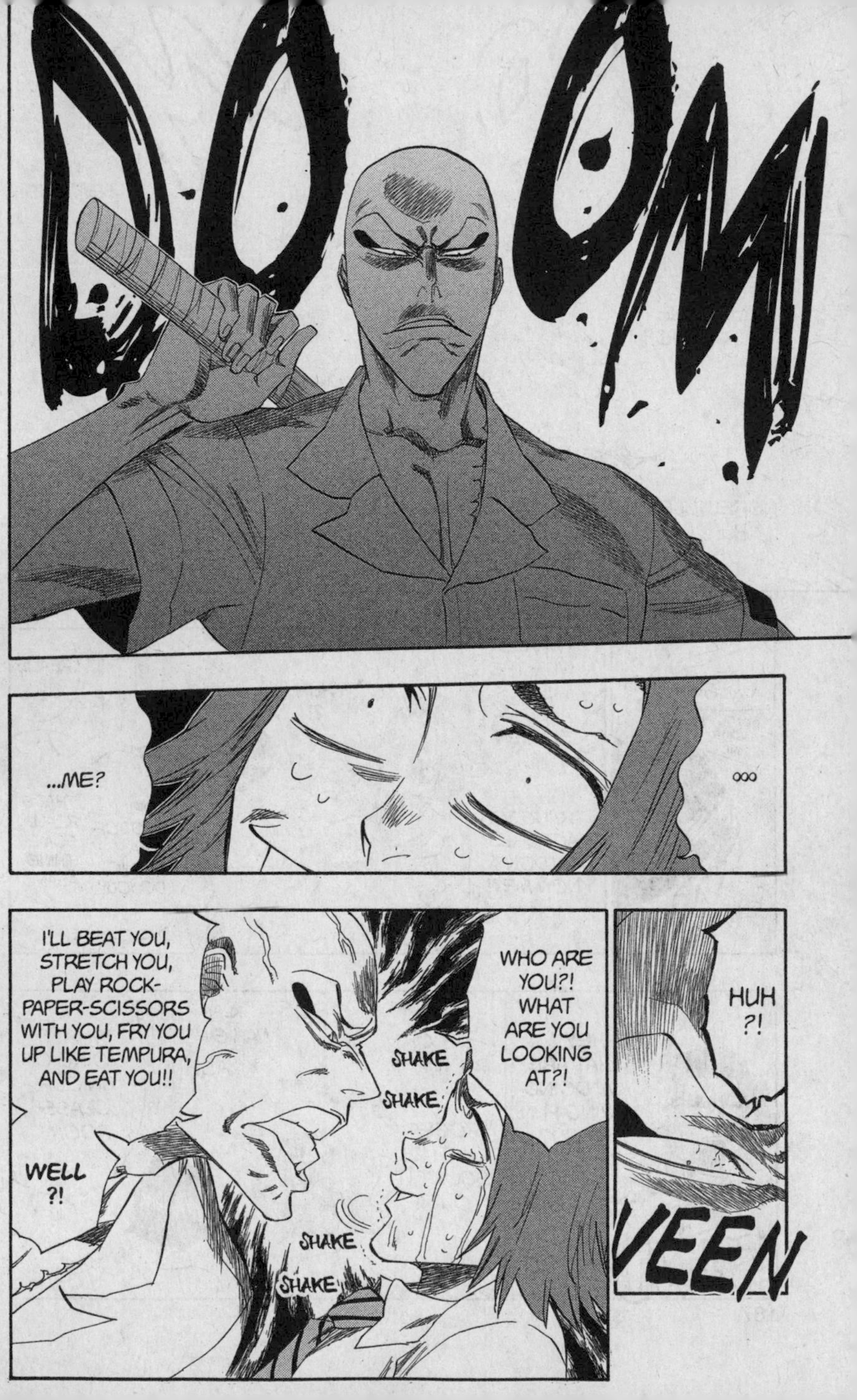
DOOM
...ME?
HUH ?!
VEEN
WHO ARE YOU?! WHAT ARE YOU LOOKING AT?!
SHAKE
SHAKE
I'LL BEAT YOU, STRETCH YOU, PLAY ROCK-PAPER-SCISSORS WITH YOU, FRY YOU UP LIKE TEMPURA, AND EAT YOU!!
WELL ?!
SHAKE
SHAKE

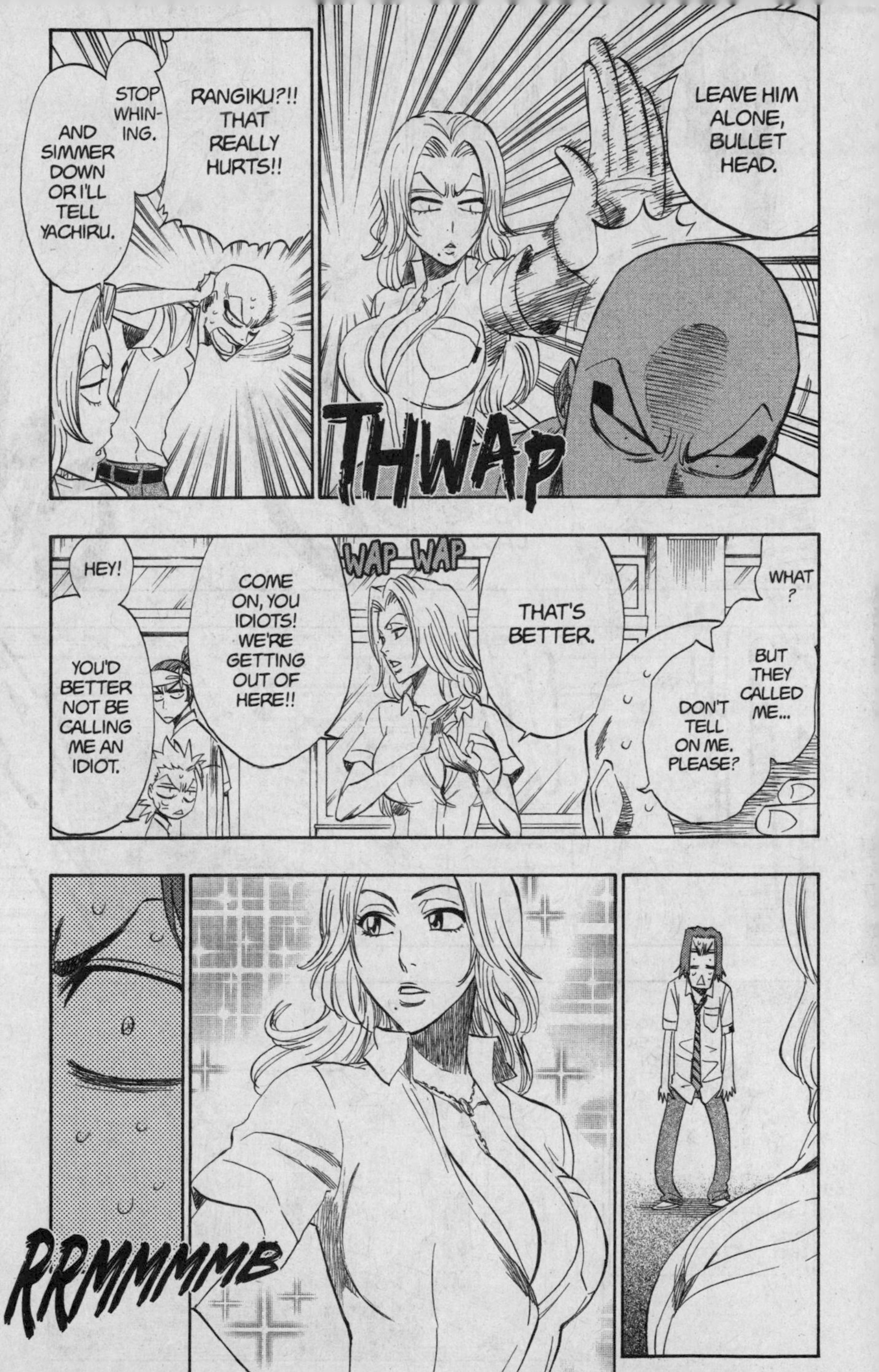
LEAVE HIM ALONE, BULLET HEAD.
THWAP
RANGIKU?!! THAT REALLY HURTS!!
STOP WHINING.
AND SIMMER DOWN OR I'LL TELL YACHIRU.
WHAT?
BUT THEY CALLED ME...
DON'T TELL ON ME. PLEASE?
THAT'S BETTER.
WAP WAP
COME ON, YOU IDIOTS! WE'RE GETTING OUT OF HERE!!
HEY!
YOU'D BETTER NOT BE CALLING ME AN IDIOT.
RRMMMMMB

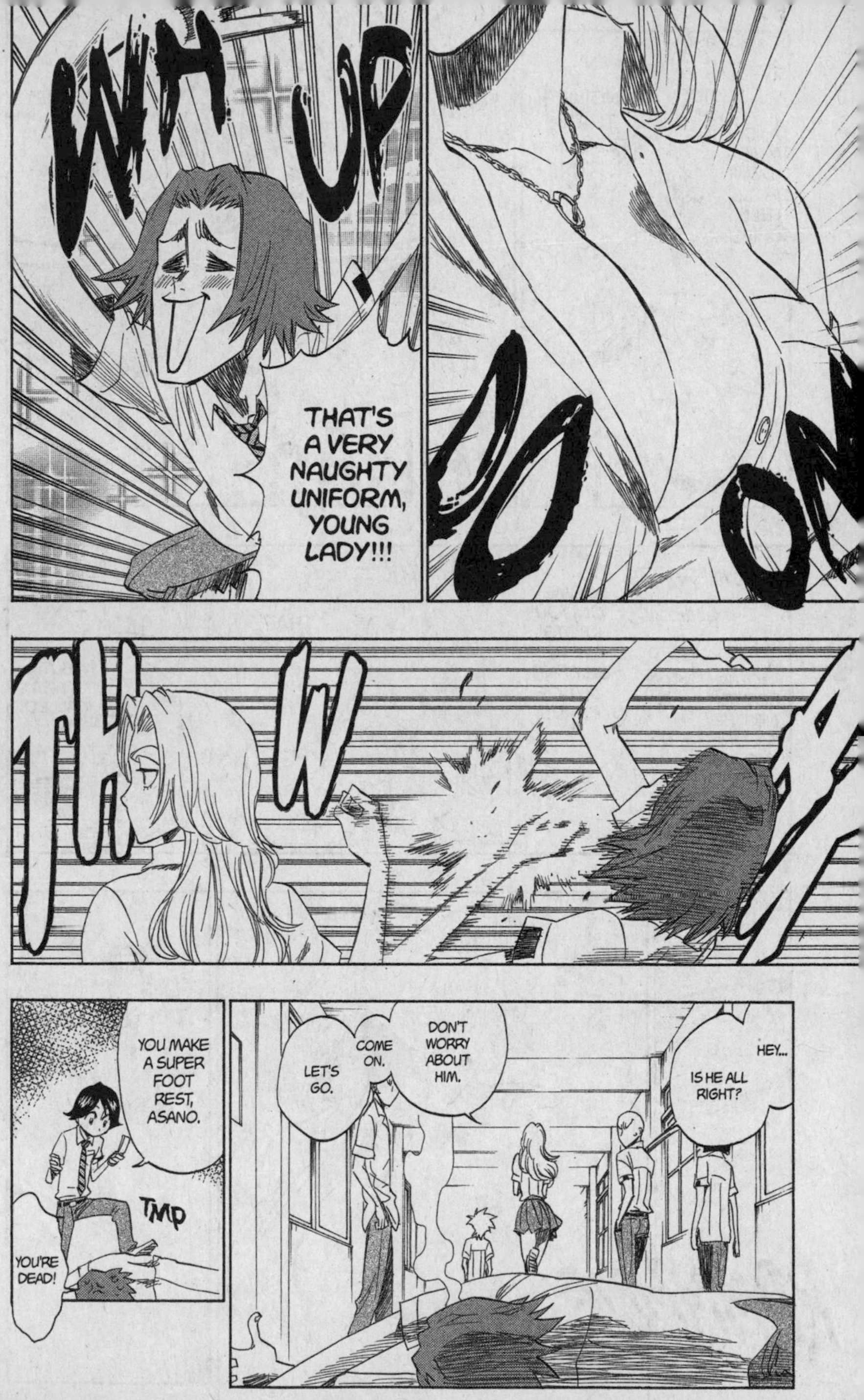
THAT'S A VERY NAUGHTY UNIFORM, YOUNG LADY!!!
HEY...
IS HE ALL RIGHT?
DON'T WORRY ABOUT HIM.
COME ON.
LET'S GO.
YOU MAKE A SUPER FOOT REST, ASANO.
TMP
YOU'RE DEAD!

Bleach 197. The Approaching Danger

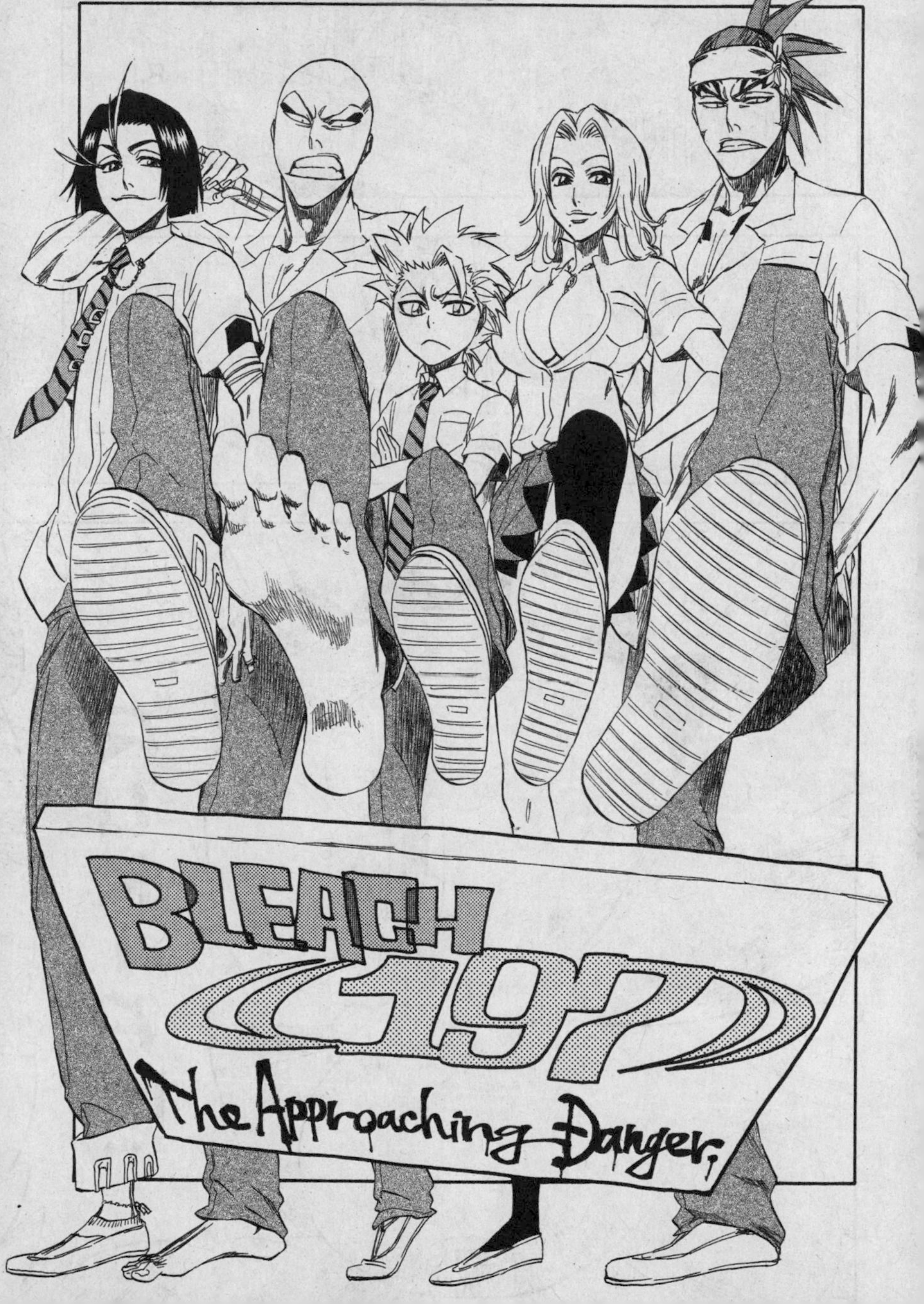
BLEACH
197
The Approaching Danger

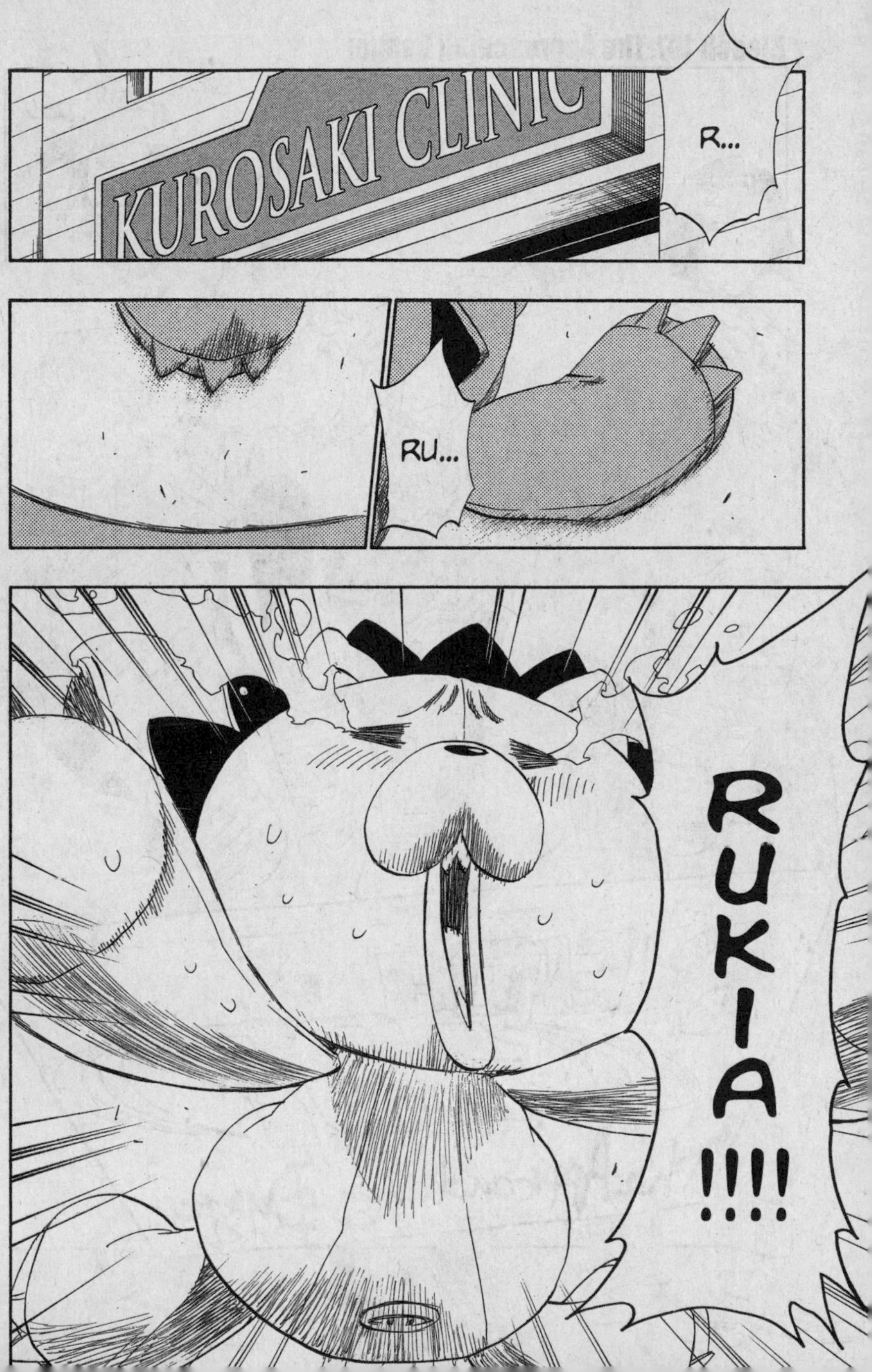
KUROSAKI CLINIC
R...
RU...
RUKIA!!!!

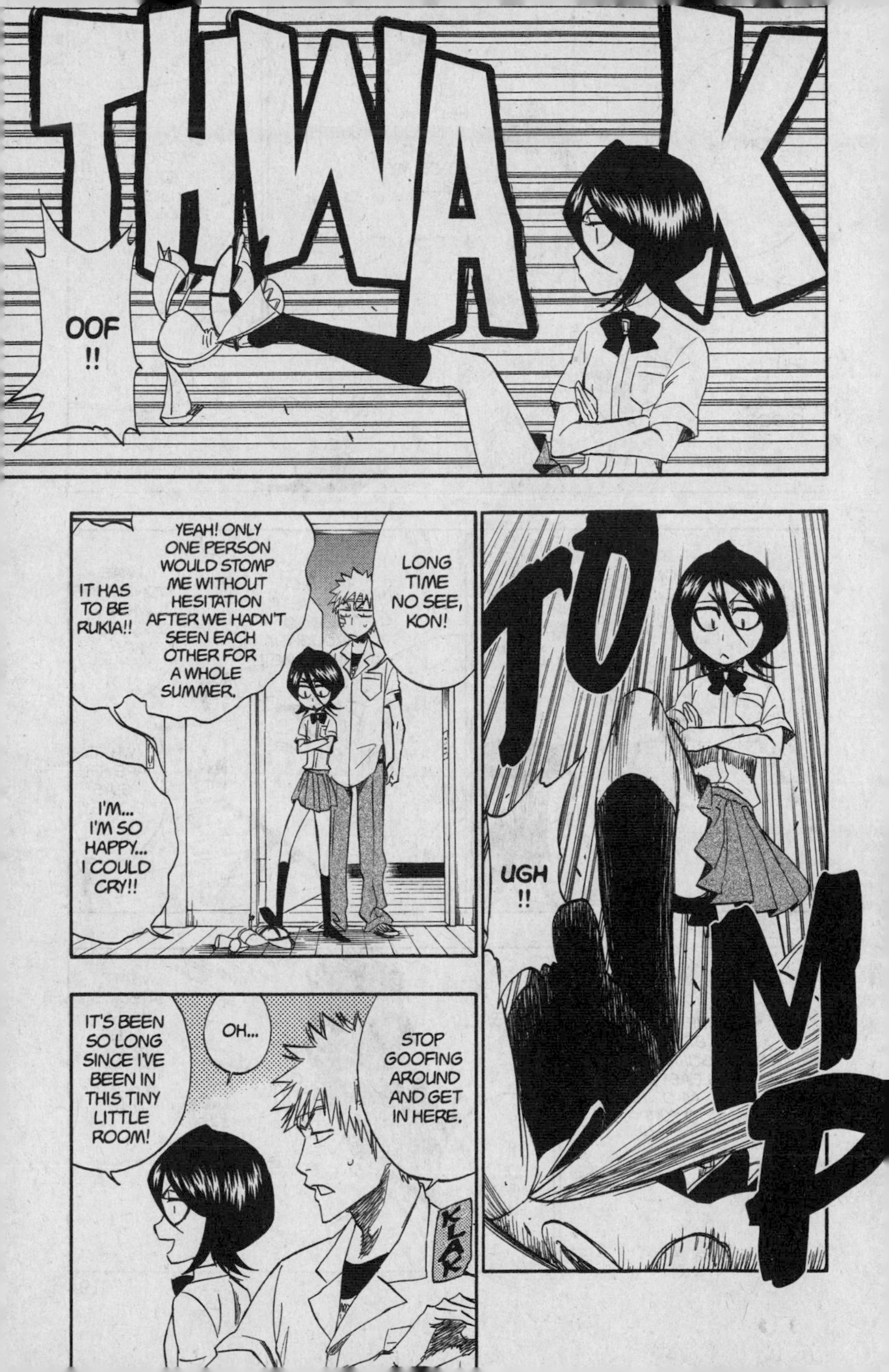
THWACK
OOF !!
TOMP
UGH !!
LONG TIME NO SEE, KON!
YEAH! ONLY ONE PERSON WOULD STOMP ME WITHOUT HESITATION AFTER WE HADN'T SEEN EACH OTHER FOR A WHOLE SUMMER.
IT HAS TO BE RUKIA!!
I'M... I'M SO HAPPY... I COULD CRY!!
STOP GOOFING AROUND AND GET IN HERE.
OH...
IT'S BEEN SO LONG SINCE I'VE BEEN IN THIS TINY LITTLE ROOM!
KLAK

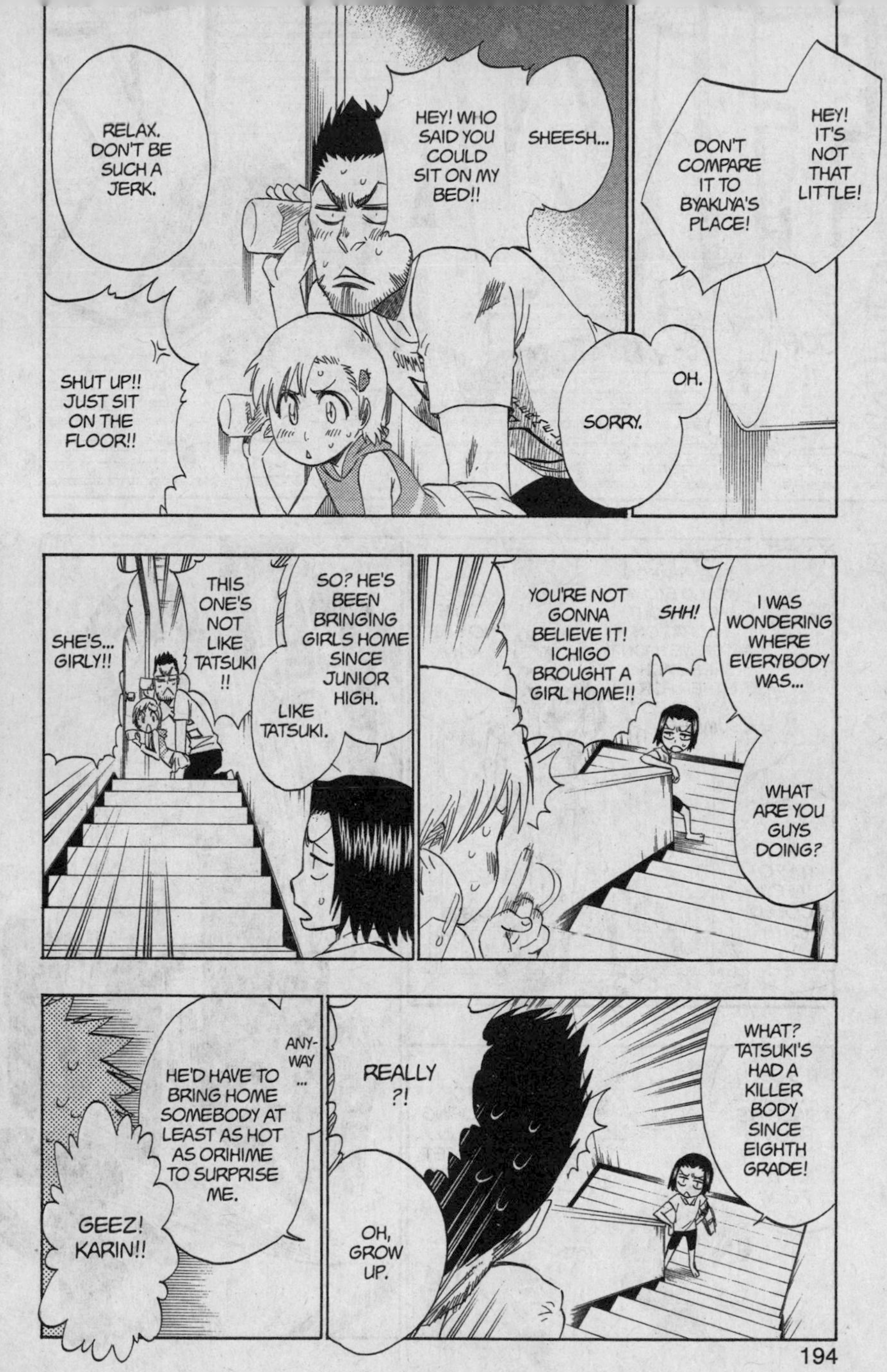
HEY! IT'S NOT THAT LITTLE!
DON'T COMPARE IT TO BYAKUYA'S PLACE!
OH.
SORRY.
SHEESH...
HEY! WHO SAID YOU COULD SIT ON MY BED!!
RELAX. DON'T BE SUCH A JERK.
SHUT UP!! JUST SIT ON THE FLOOR!!
I WAS WONDERING WHERE EVERYBODY WAS...
SHH!
YOU'RE NOT GONNA BELIEVE IT! ICHIGO BROUGHT A GIRL HOME!!
WHAT ARE YOU GUYS DOING?
SO? HE'S BEEN BRINGING GIRLS HOME SINCE JUNIOR HIGH.
LIKE TATSUKI.
THIS ONE'S NOT LIKE TATSUKI!!
SHE'S... GIRLY!!
WHAT? TATSUKI'S HAD A KILLER BODY SINCE EIGHTH GRADE!
REALLY?!
OH, GROW UP.
ANYWAY...
HE'D HAVE TO BRING HOME SOMEBODY AT LEAST AS HOT AS ORIHIME TO SURPRISE ME.
GEEZ! KARIN!!

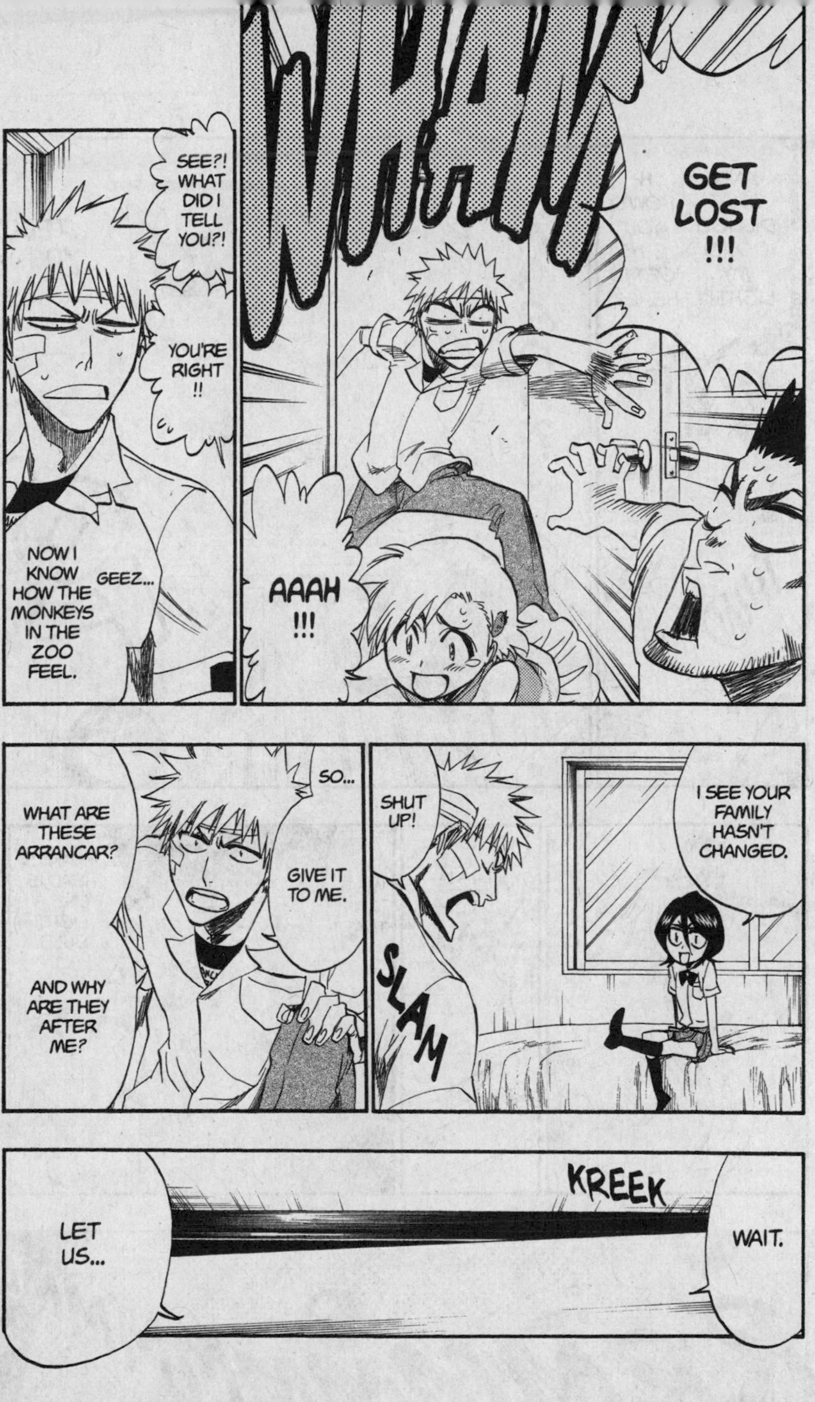
GET LOST !!!
AAAH !!!
SEE?! WHAT DID I TELL YOU?!
YOU'RE RIGHT !!
GEEZ...
NOW I KNOW HOW THE MONKEYS IN THE ZOO FEEL.
I SEE YOUR FAMILY HASN'T CHANGED.
SHUT UP!
SLAM
SO...
GIVE IT TO ME.
WHAT ARE THESE ARRANCAR?
AND WHY ARE THEY AFTER ME?
WAIT.
KREEK
LET US...

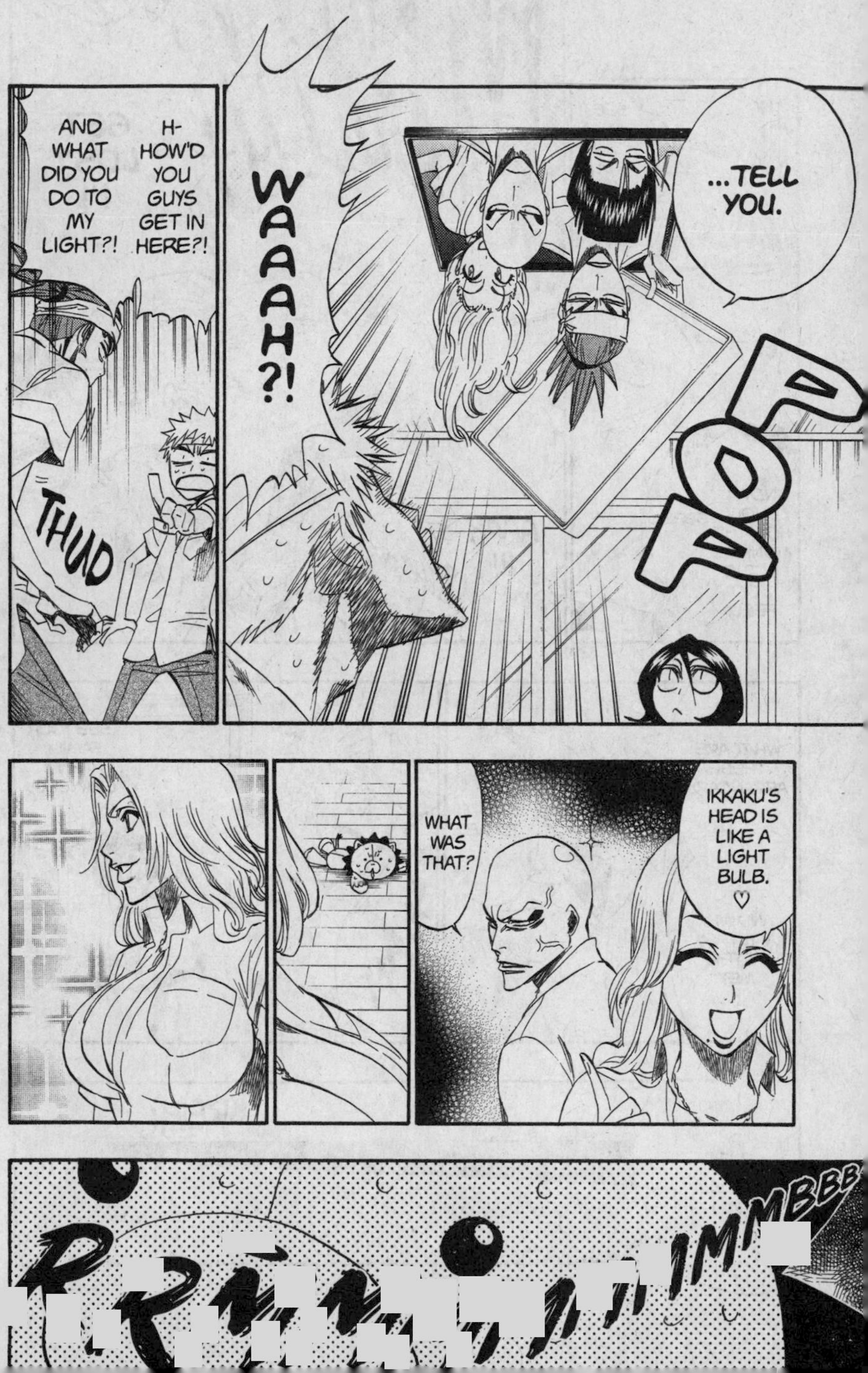
...TELL YOU.
POP
WAAAAH?!
H- HOW'D YOU GUYS GET IN HERE?!
AND WHAT DID YOU DO TO MY LIGHT?!
THUD
IKKAKU'S HEAD IS LIKE A LIGHT BULB. ♡
WHAT WAS THAT?

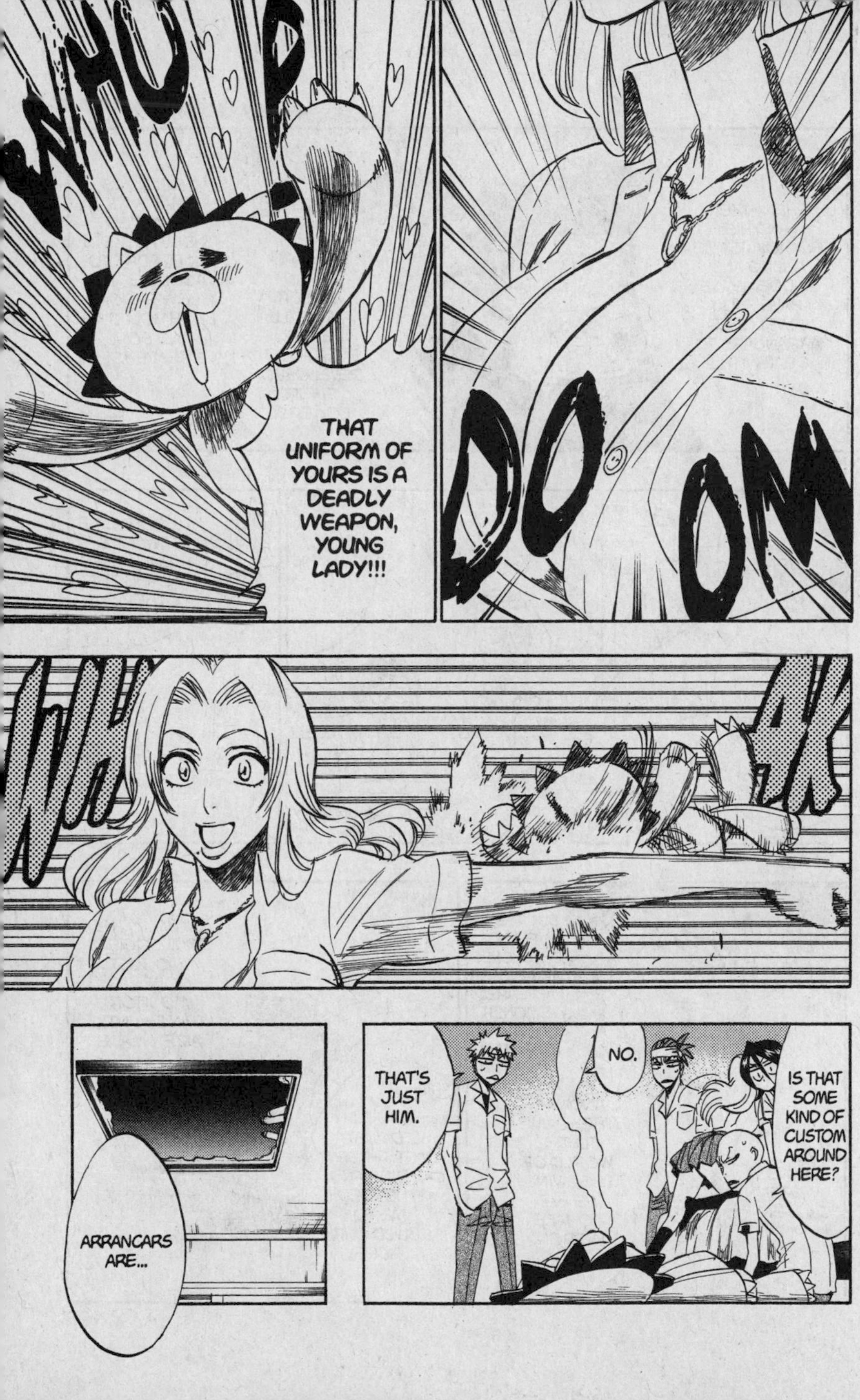
DOOM
WHUP
THAT UNIFORM OF YOURS IS A DEADLY WEAPON, YOUNG LADY!!!
WHAK
IS THAT SOME KIND OF CUSTOM AROUND HERE?
NO.
THAT'S JUST HIM.
ARRANCARS ARE...

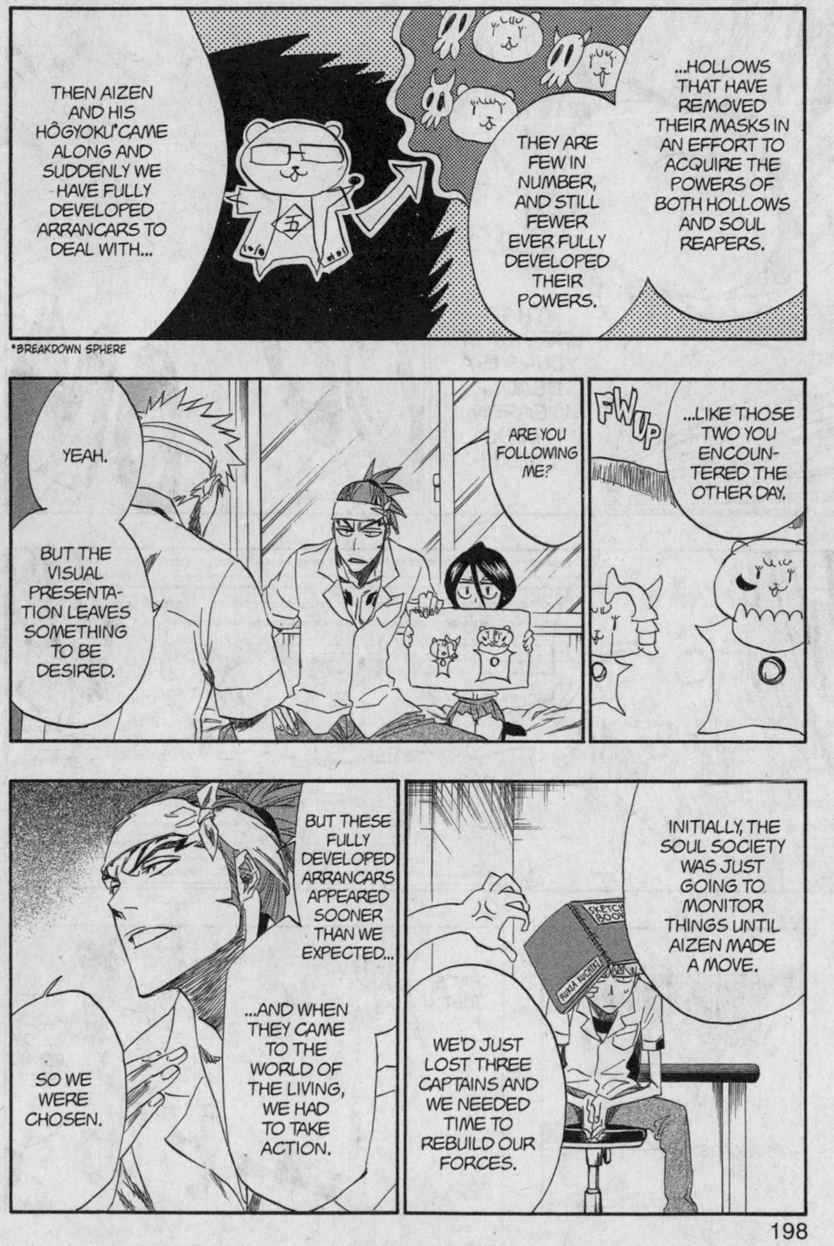
...HOLLOWS THAT HAVE REMOVED THEIR MASKS IN AN EFFORT TO ACQUIRE THE POWERS OF BOTH HOLLOWS AND SOUL REAPERS.
THEY ARE FEW IN NUMBER, AND STILL FEWER EVER FULLY DEVELOPED THEIR POWERS.
THEN AIZEN AND HIS HÔGYOKU* CAME ALONG AND SUDDENLY WE HAVE FULLY DEVELOPED ARRANCARS TO DEAL WITH...
FWUP
...LIKE THOSE TWO YOU ENCOUNTERED THE OTHER DAY.
ARE YOU FOLLOWING ME?
YEAH.
BUT THE VISUAL PRESENTATION LEAVES SOMETHING TO BE DESIRED.
INITIALLY, THE SOUL SOCIETY WAS JUST GOING TO MONITOR THINGS UNTIL AIZEN MADE A MOVE.
WE'D JUST LOST THREE CAPTAINS AND WE NEEDED TIME TO REBUILD OUR FORCES.
BUT THESE FULLY DEVELOPED ARRANCARS APPEARED SOONER THAN WE EXPECTED...
...AND WHEN THEY CAME TO THE WORLD OF THE LIVING, WE HAD TO TAKE ACTION.
SO WE WERE CHOSEN.

*BREAKDOWN SPHERE

READ THIS WAY

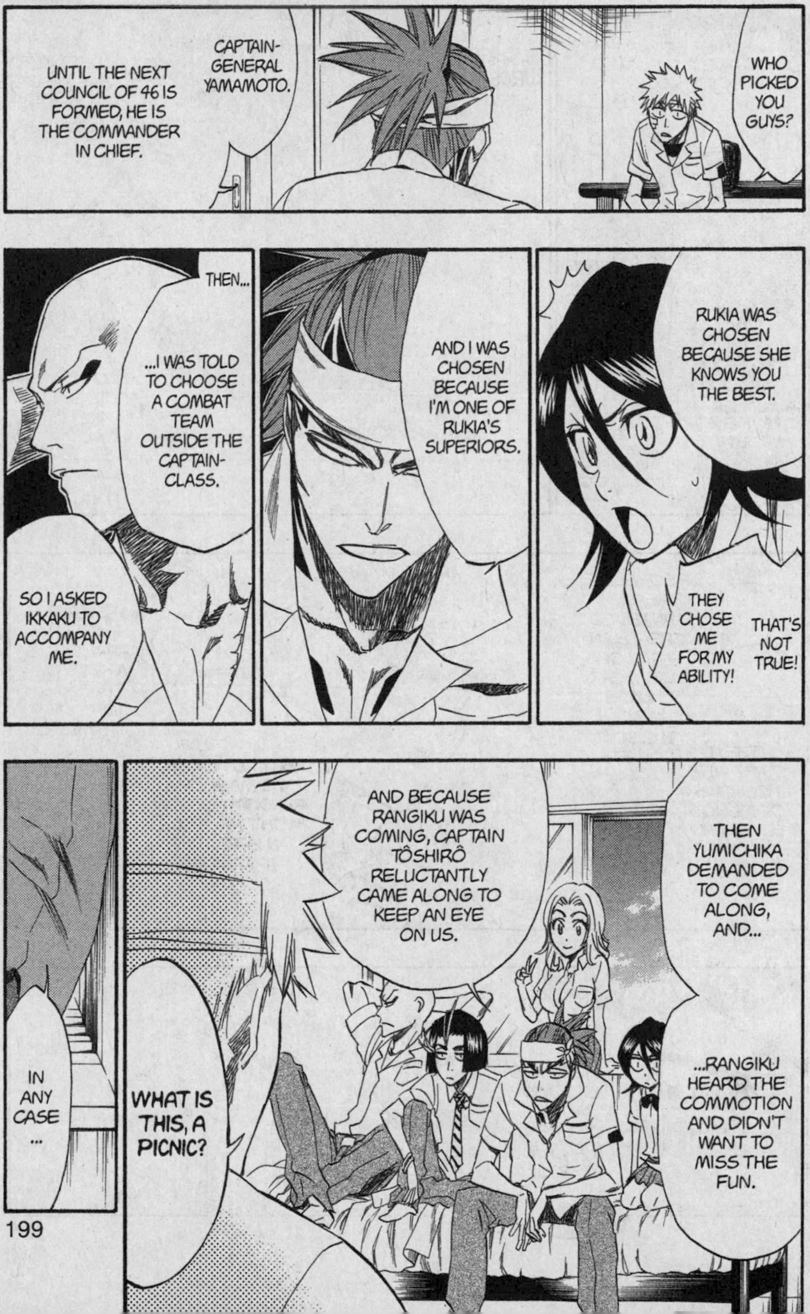
WHO PICKED YOU GUYS?
CAPTAIN-GENERAL YAMAMOTO.
UNTIL THE NEXT COUNCIL OF 46 IS FORMED, HE IS THE COMMANDER IN CHIEF.
RUKIA WAS CHOSEN BECAUSE SHE KNOWS YOU THE BEST.
THAT'S NOT TRUE!
THEY CHOSE ME FOR MY ABILITY!
AND I WAS CHOSEN BECAUSE I'M ONE OF RUKIA'S SUPERIORS.
THEN...
...I WAS TOLD TO CHOOSE A COMBAT TEAM OUTSIDE THE CAPTAIN-CLASS.
SO I ASKED IKKAKU TO ACCOMPANY ME.
THEN YUMICHIKA DEMANDED TO COME ALONG, AND...
AND BECAUSE RANGIKU WAS COMING, CAPTAIN TÔSHIRÔ RELUCTANTLY CAME ALONG TO KEEP AN EYE ON US.
...RANGIKU HEARD THE COMMOTION AND DIDN'T WANT TO MISS THE FUN.
WHAT IS THIS, A PICNIC?
IN ANY CASE ...

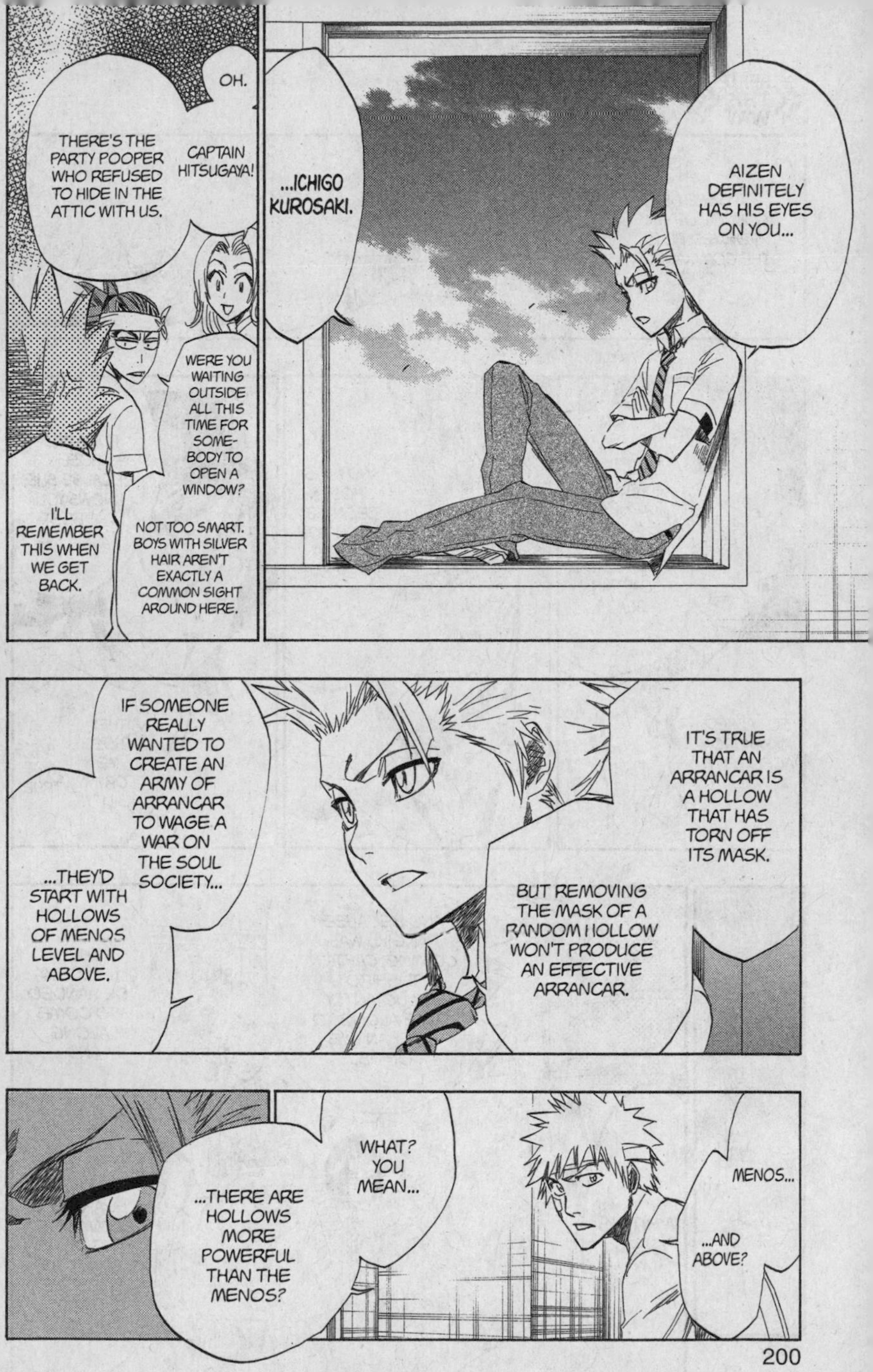
AIZEN DEFINITELY HAS HIS EYES ON YOU...
...ICHIGO KUROSAKI.
OH.
CAPTAIN HITSUGAYA!
THERE'S THE PARTY POOPER WHO REFUSED TO HIDE IN THE ATTIC WITH US.
WERE YOU WAITING OUTSIDE ALL THIS TIME FOR SOME-BODY TO OPEN A WINDOW?
NOT TOO SMART. BOYS WITH SILVER HAIR AREN'T EXACTLY A COMMON SIGHT AROUND HERE.
I'LL REMEMBER THIS WHEN WE GET BACK.
IT'S TRUE THAT AN ARRANCAR IS A HOLLOW THAT HAS TORN OFF ITS MASK.
BUT REMOVING THE MASK OF A RANDOM HOLLOW WON'T PRODUCE AN EFFECTIVE ARRANCAR.
IF SOMEONE REALLY WANTED TO CREATE AN ARMY OF ARRANCAR TO WAGE A WAR ON THE SOUL SOCIETY...
...THEY'D START WITH HOLLOWS OF MENOS LEVEL AND ABOVE.
MENOS...
...AND ABOVE?
WHAT? YOU MEAN...
...THERE ARE HOLLOWS MORE POWERFUL THAN THE MENOS?

READ THIS WAY

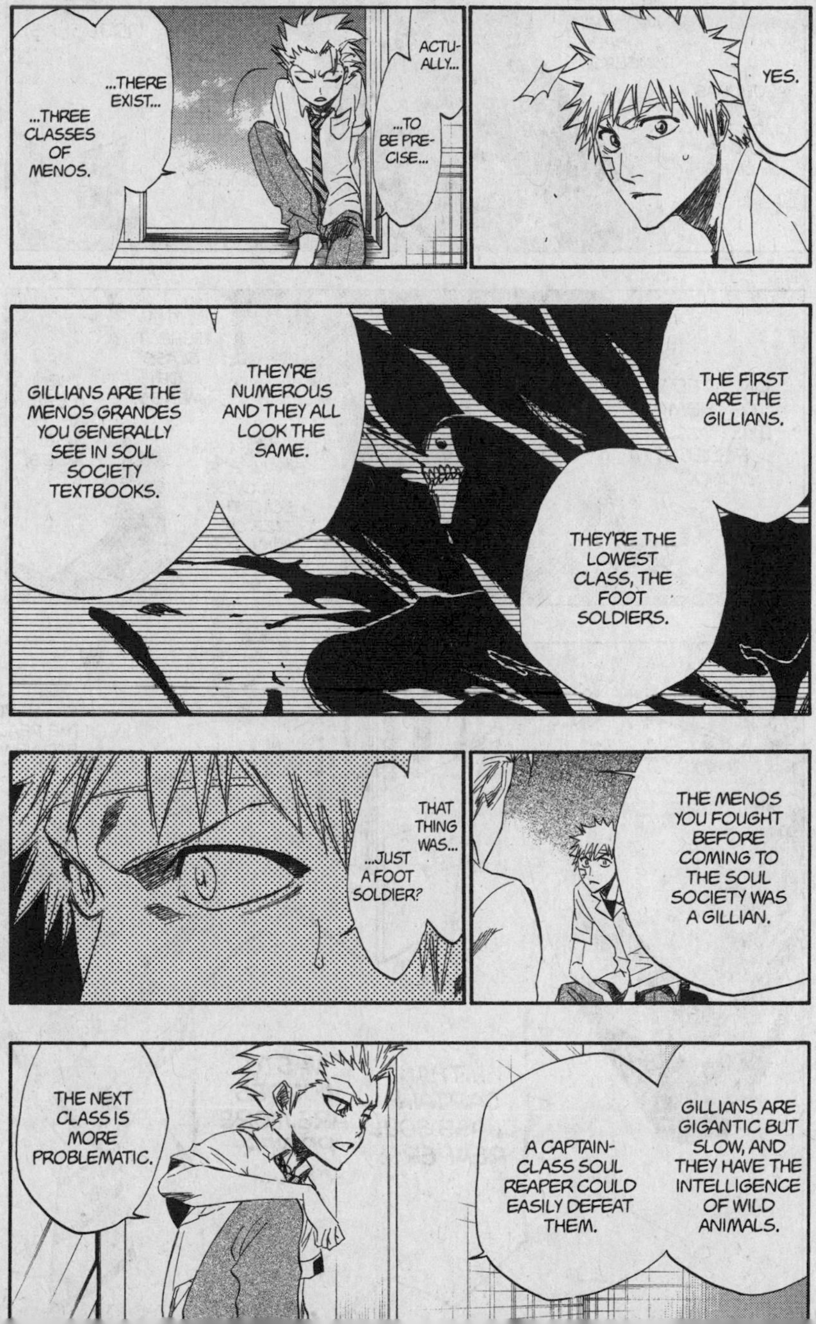
YES.
ACTUALLY...
...TO BE PRECISE...
...THERE EXIST...
...THREE CLASSES OF MENOS.
THE FIRST ARE THE GILLIANS.
THEY'RE THE LOWEST CLASS, THE FOOT SOLDIERS.
THEY'RE NUMEROUS AND THEY ALL LOOK THE SAME.
GILLIANS ARE THE MENOS GRANDES YOU GENERALLY SEE IN SOUL SOCIETY TEXTBOOKS.
THE MENOS YOU FOUGHT BEFORE COMING TO THE SOUL SOCIETY WAS A GILLIAN.
THAT THING WAS...
...JUST A FOOT SOLDIER?
GILLIANS ARE GIGANTIC BUT SLOW, AND THEY HAVE THE INTELLIGENCE OF WILD ANIMALS.
A CAPTAIN-CLASS SOUL REAPER COULD EASILY DEFEAT THEM.
THE NEXT CLASS IS MORE PROBLEMATIC.

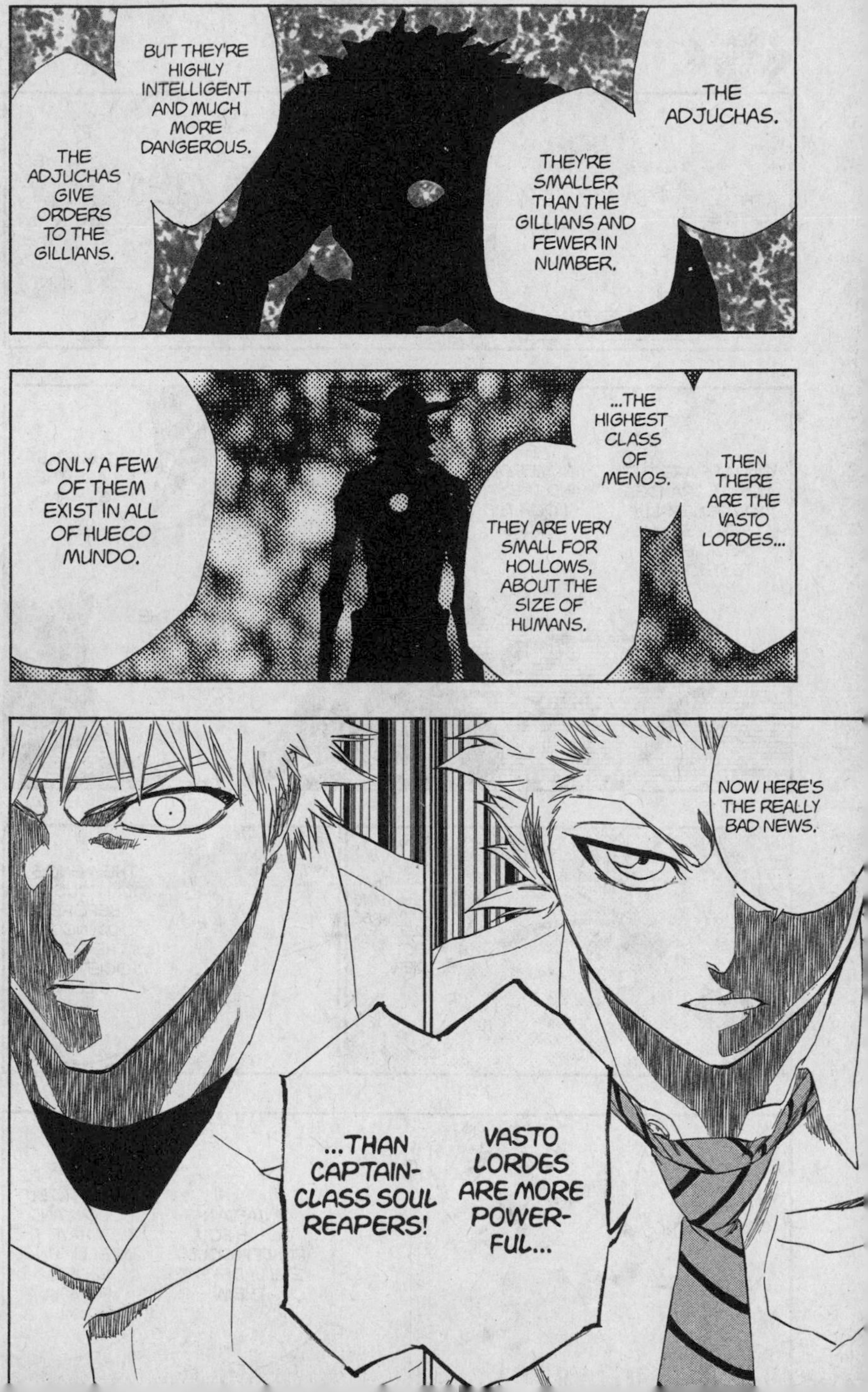
THE ADJUCHAS.
THEY'RE SMALLER THAN THE GILLIANS AND FEWER IN NUMBER.
BUT THEY'RE HIGHLY INTELLIGENT AND MUCH MORE DANGEROUS.
THE ADJUCHAS GIVE ORDERS TO THE GILLIANS.
THEN THERE ARE THE VASTO LORDES...
...THE HIGHEST CLASS OF MENOS.
THEY ARE VERY SMALL FOR HOLLOWS, ABOUT THE SIZE OF HUMANS.
ONLY A FEW OF THEM EXIST IN ALL OF HUECO MUNDO.
NOW HERE'S THE REALLY BAD NEWS.
VASTO LORDES ARE MORE POWER-FUL...
...THAN CAPTAIN-CLASS SOUL REAPERS!

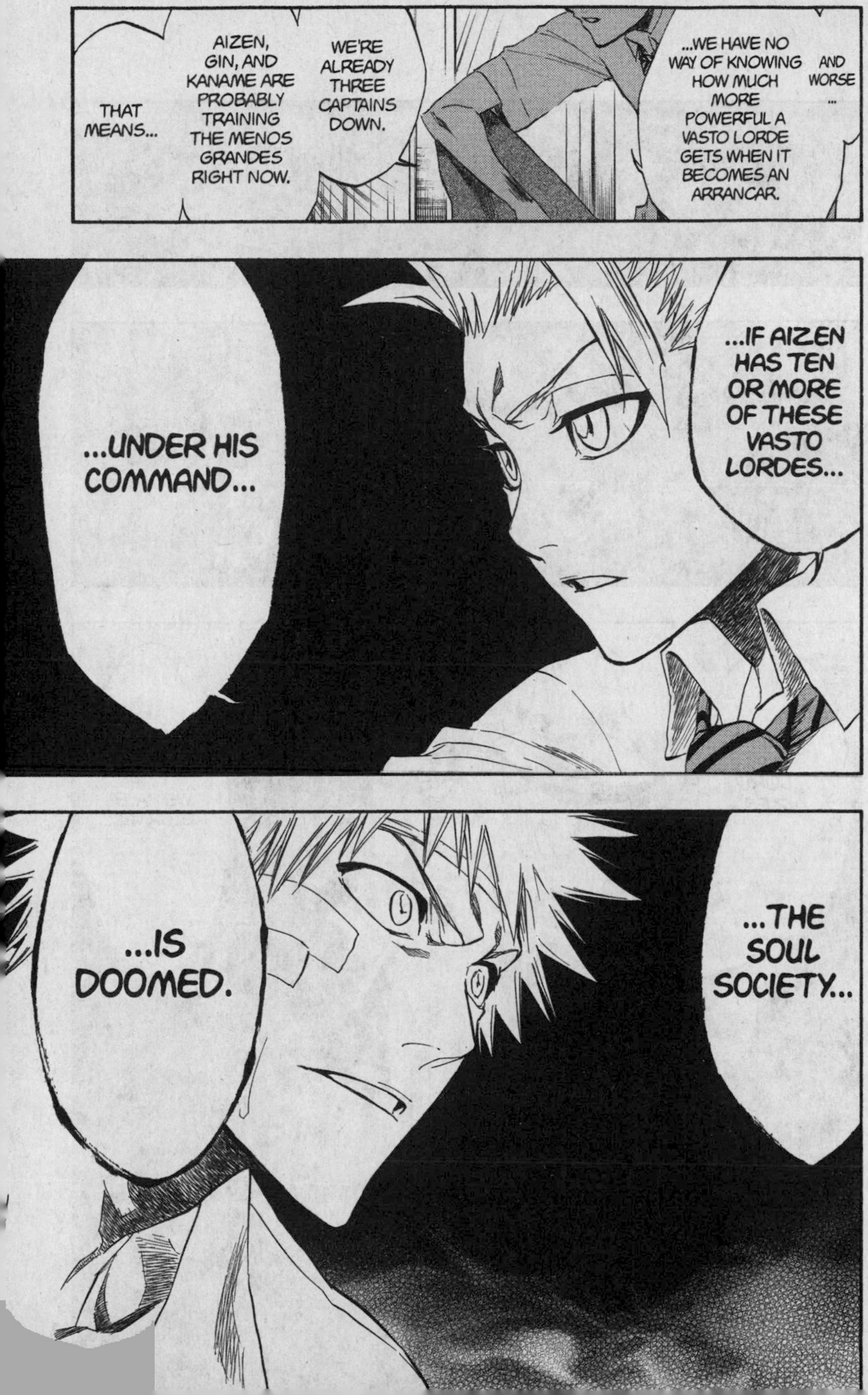
AND WORSE...
...WE HAVE NO WAY OF KNOWING HOW MUCH MORE POWERFUL A VASTO LORDE GETS WHEN IT BECOMES AN ARRANCAR.
WE'RE ALREADY THREE CAPTAINS DOWN.
AIZEN, GIN, AND KANAME ARE PROBABLY TRAINING THE MENOS GRANDES RIGHT NOW.
THAT MEANS...
...IF AIZEN HAS TEN OR MORE OF THESE VASTO LORDES...
...UNDER HIS COMMAND...
...THE SOUL SOCIETY...
...IS DOOMED.

KLAK.

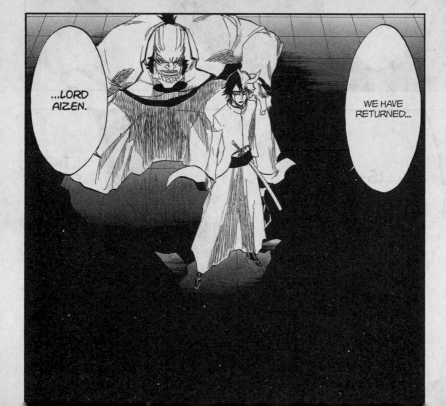

...LORD AIZEN.

WE HAVE RETURNED...

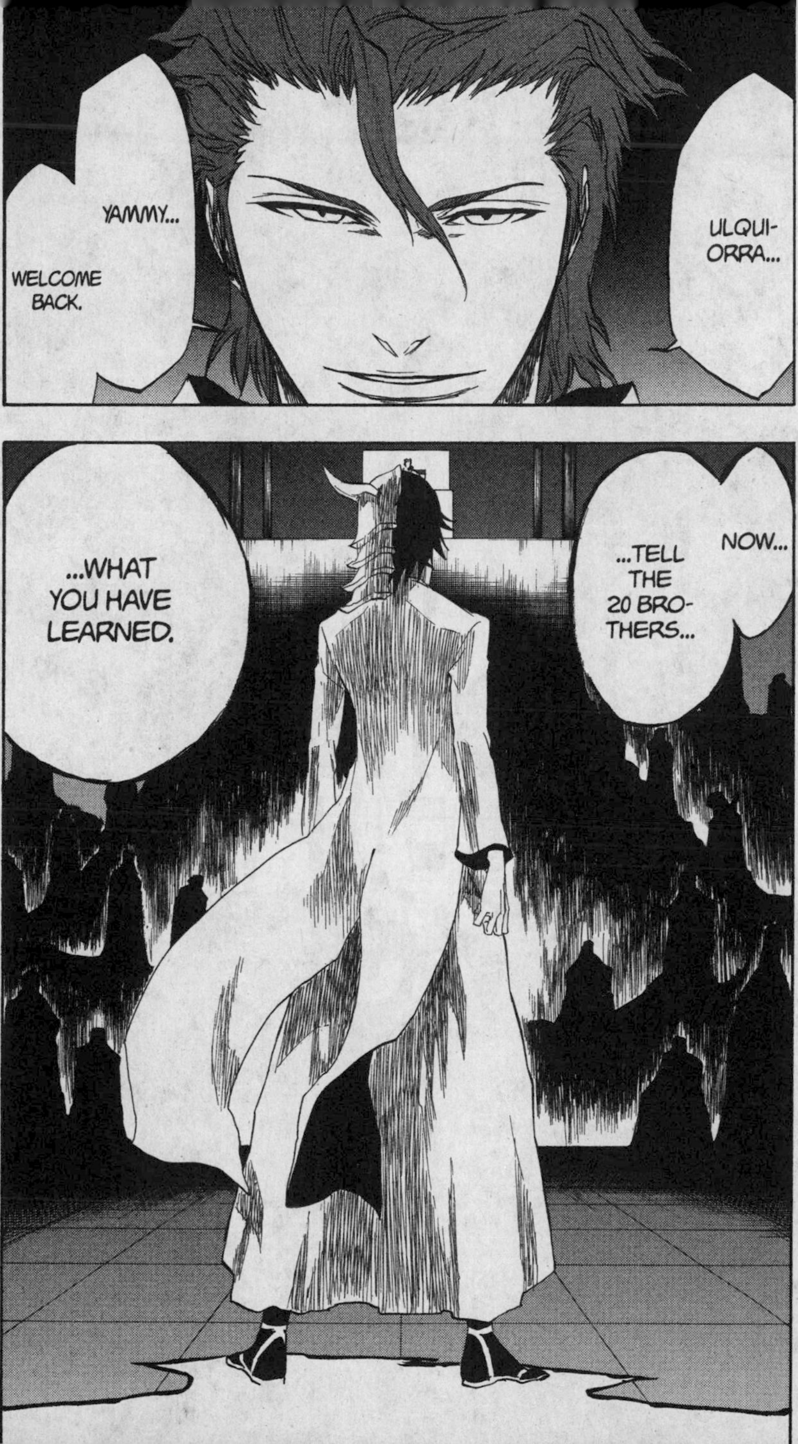
ULQUIORRA...
YAMMY...
WELCOME BACK.
NOW...
...TELL THE 20 BROTHERS...
...WHAT YOU HAVE LEARNED.

CONTI
NUED
IN
BLEACH
23

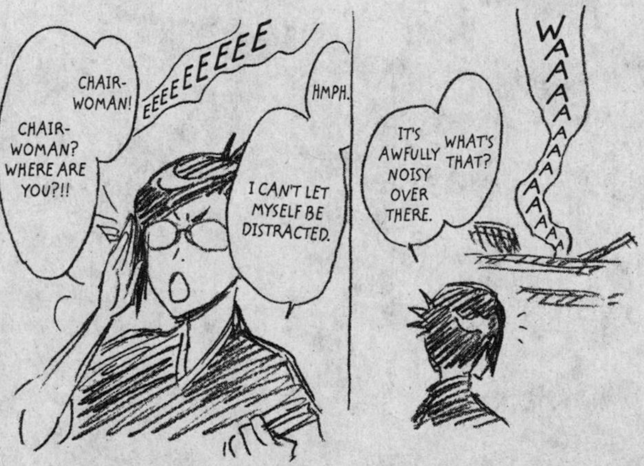
WAAAAAAAAAAAA
WHAT'S THAT?
IT'S AWFULLY NOISY OVER THERE.
HMPH.
I CAN'T LET MYSELF BE DISTRACTED.
EEEEEEEEE
CHAIR-WOMAN!
CHAIR-WOMAN? WHERE ARE YOU?!!

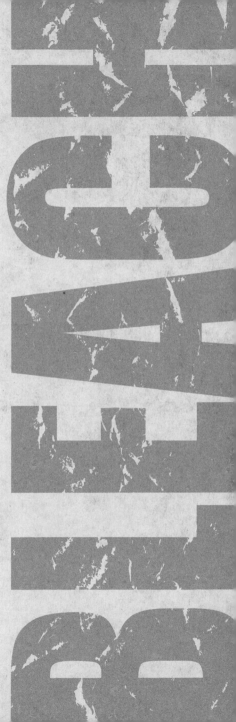

It's been four years since I've worked with my first editor, yet his is still the first name in my address book. I'm surprised just how little my social life has changed in the last four years. My resolution for this year is to make a new friend whose name will come before "Asada."

-Tite Kubo, 2006

We are the fish in front of the waterfall.
We are the insects inside the cage.

We are the ruins of the billows,
The skull on the crosier,
The force of the torrent and the whale that drinks it.

We are the five-horned bull.
We are the fire-breathing monster.
And the screaming children.

Oh, we are poisoned by the moonlight.

BLEACH23 ¡MALA SUERTE!

STARS AND

Orihime Inoue

Rukia Kuchiki

Ichigo Kurosaki

plot

When Ichigo Kurosaki meets Soul Reaper Rukia Kuchiki, his life is changed forever. Soon Ichigo is a Soul Reaper himself, cleansing lost souls called Hollows, and even traveling to the strange world of the Soul Society in order to rescue Rukia.

Now back in the world of the living, Ichigo has his hands full once more cleansing Hollows. But when Chad and Orihime are injured by Arrancars, the Soul Society sends a team to help fight this deadly new threat, and Rukia is with them. She wastes little time in giving the disheartened Ichigo a much-needed dose of tough love. And meanwhile, in another world, Aizen and his minions plan their next move.

BLEACH ALL

斑目一角

茶渡泰虎

Ikkaku Madarame

Chad Yasutora

Edorad

エドラド

STORIES

BLEACH23

¡MALA SUERTE!

Contents

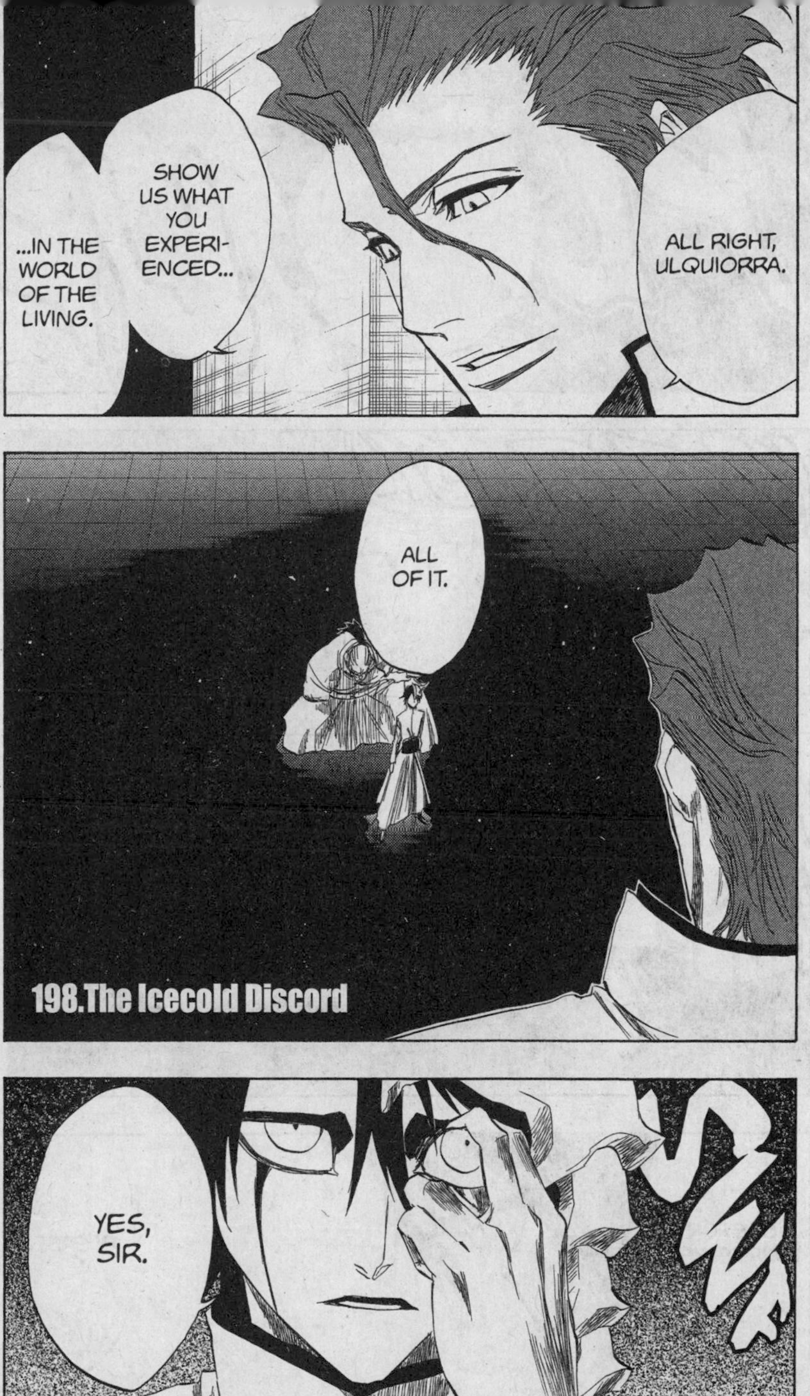
ALL RIGHT, ULQUIORRA.
SHOW US WHAT YOU EXPERIENCED...
...IN THE WORLD OF THE LIVING.
ALL OF IT.
198.The Icecold Discord
YES, SIR.

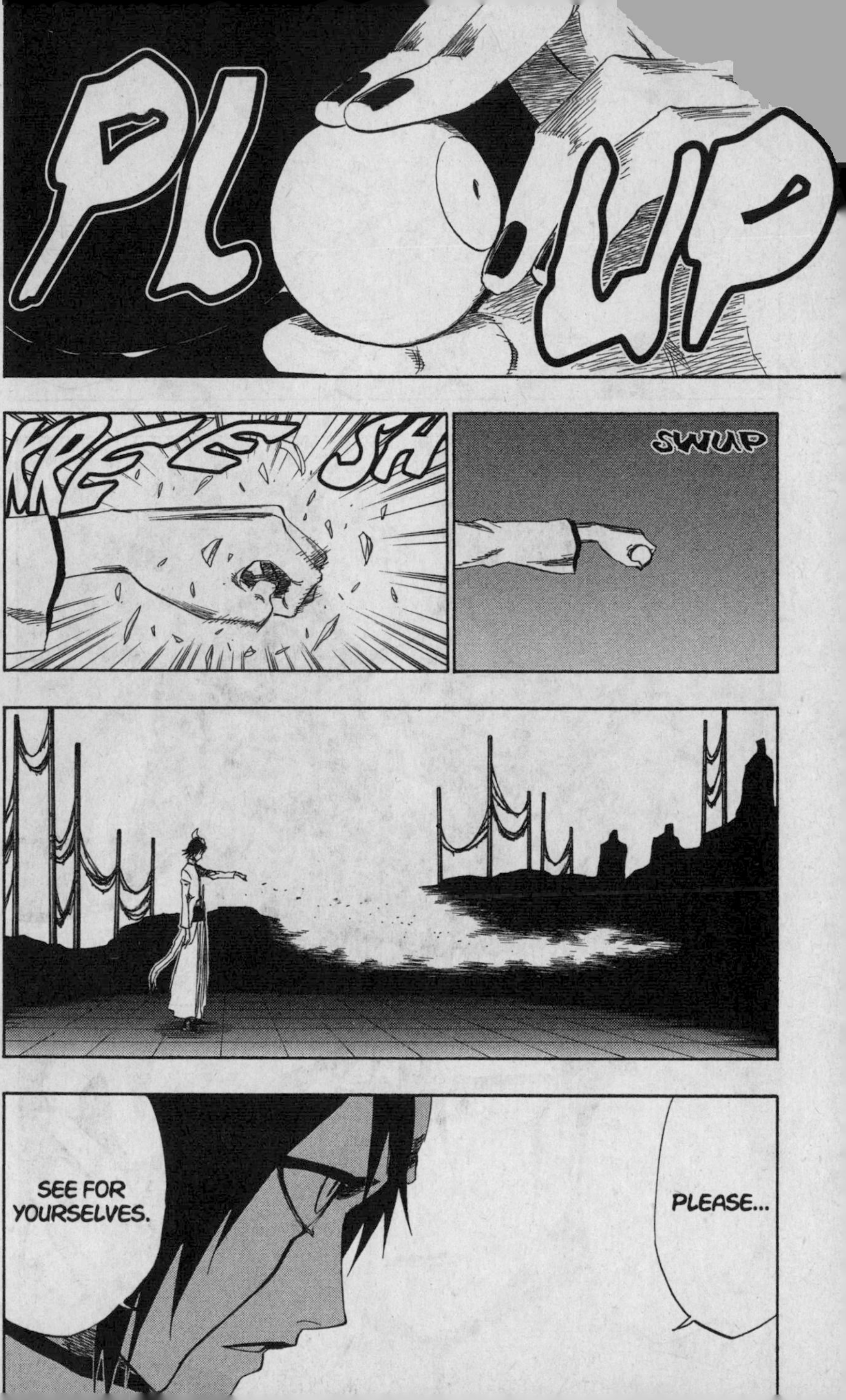
PLUP
SWUP
KREESH
PLEASE...
SEE FOR YOURSELVES.

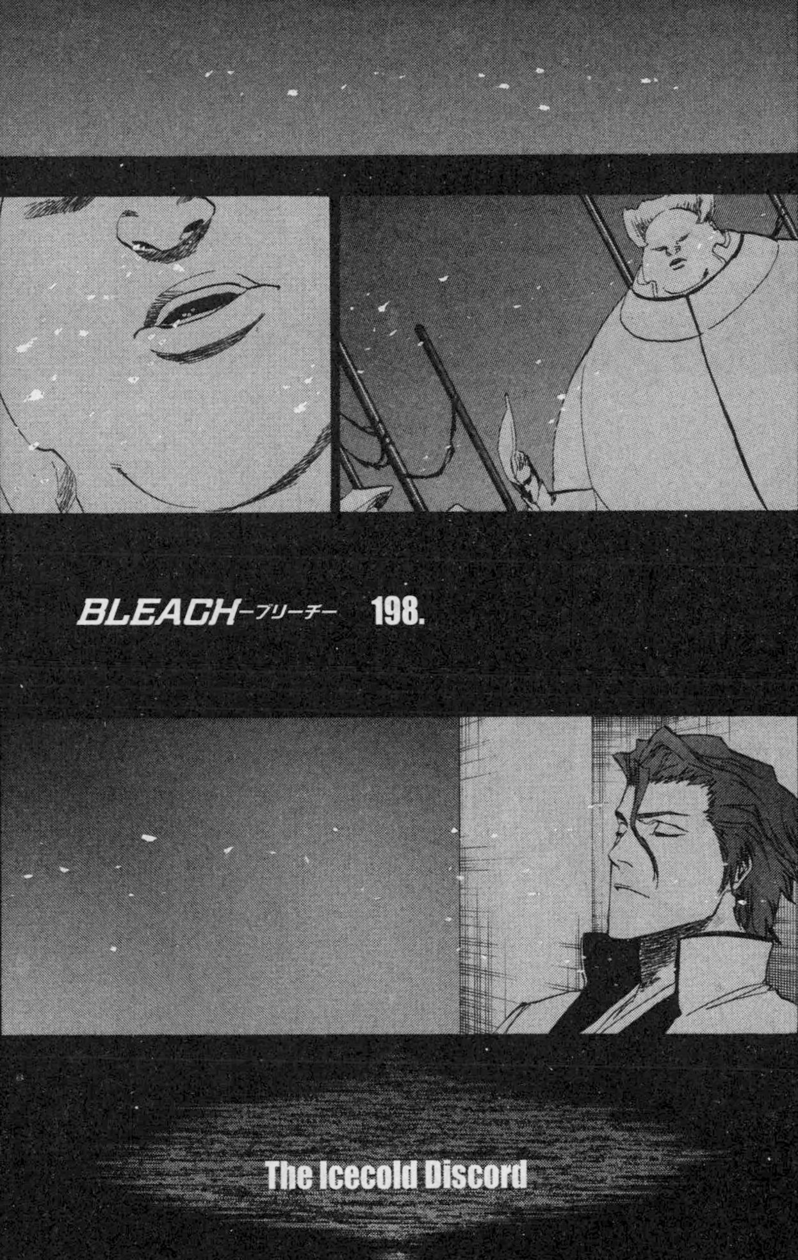
BLEACH-ブリーチ- 198.
The Icecold Discord

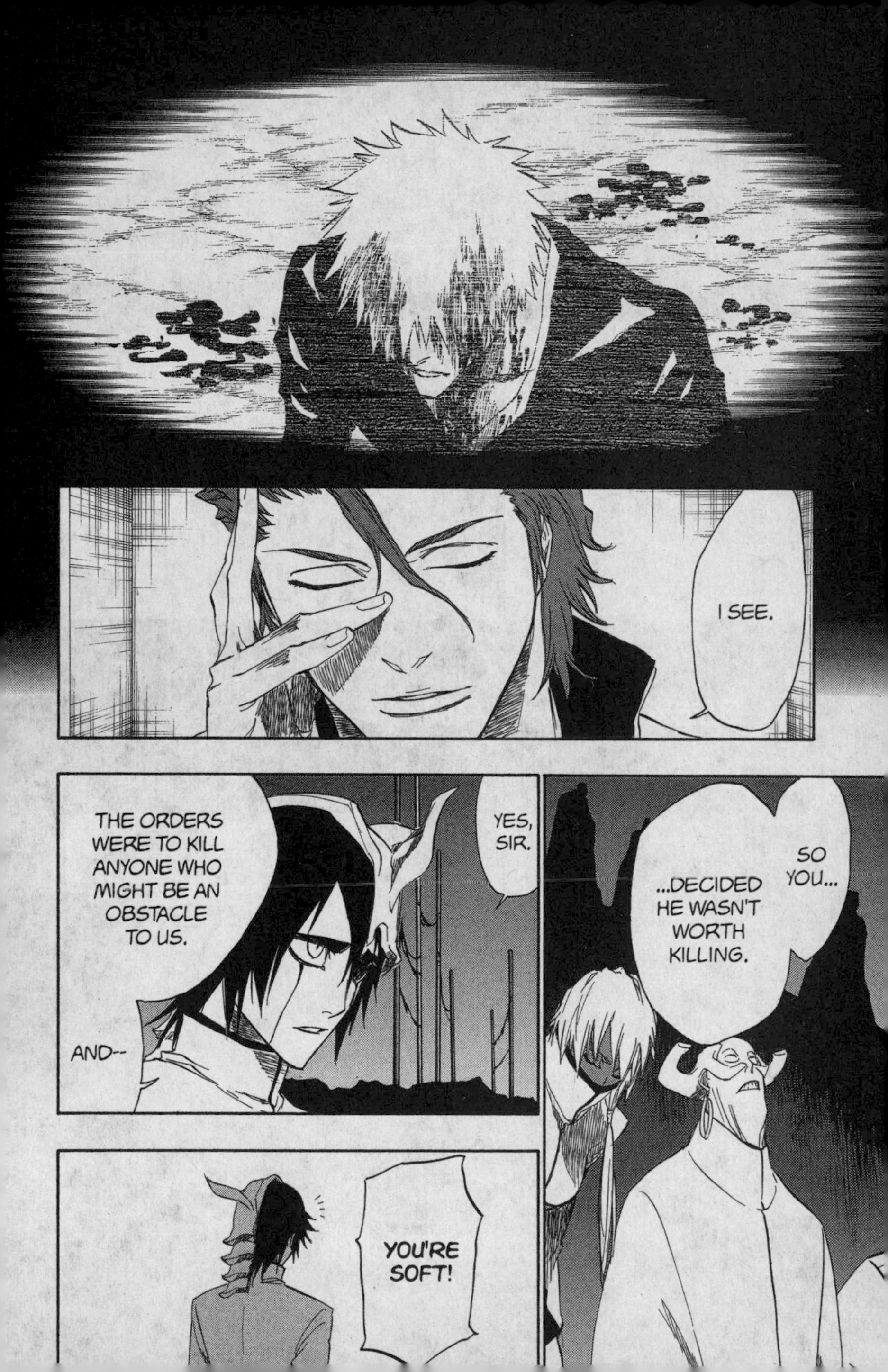
I SEE.
SO YOU...
...DECIDED HE WASN'T WORTH KILLING.
YES, SIR.
THE ORDERS WERE TO KILL ANYONE WHO MIGHT BE AN OBSTACLE TO US.
AND--
YOU'RE SOFT!

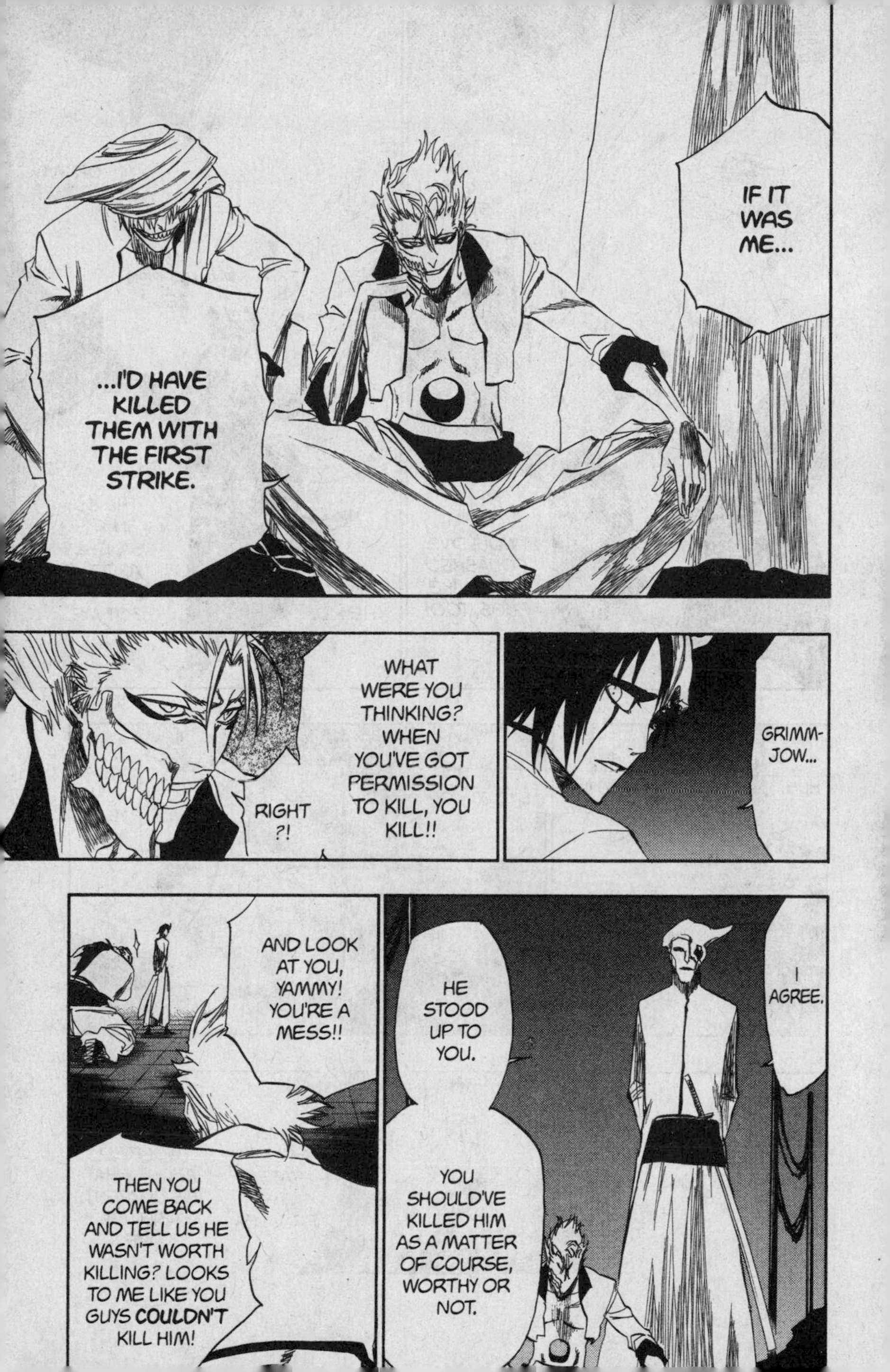
IF IT WAS ME...
...I'D HAVE KILLED THEM WITH THE FIRST STRIKE.
GRIMM-JOW...
WHAT WERE YOU THINKING? WHEN YOU'VE GOT PERMISSION TO KILL, YOU KILL!!
RIGHT ?!
I AGREE.
HE STOOD UP TO YOU.
YOU SHOULD'VE KILLED HIM AS A MATTER OF COURSE, WORTHY OR NOT.
AND LOOK AT YOU, YAMMY! YOU'RE A MESS!!
THEN YOU COME BACK AND TELL US HE WASN'T WORTH KILLING? LOOKS TO ME LIKE YOU GUYS **COULDN'T** KILL HIM!

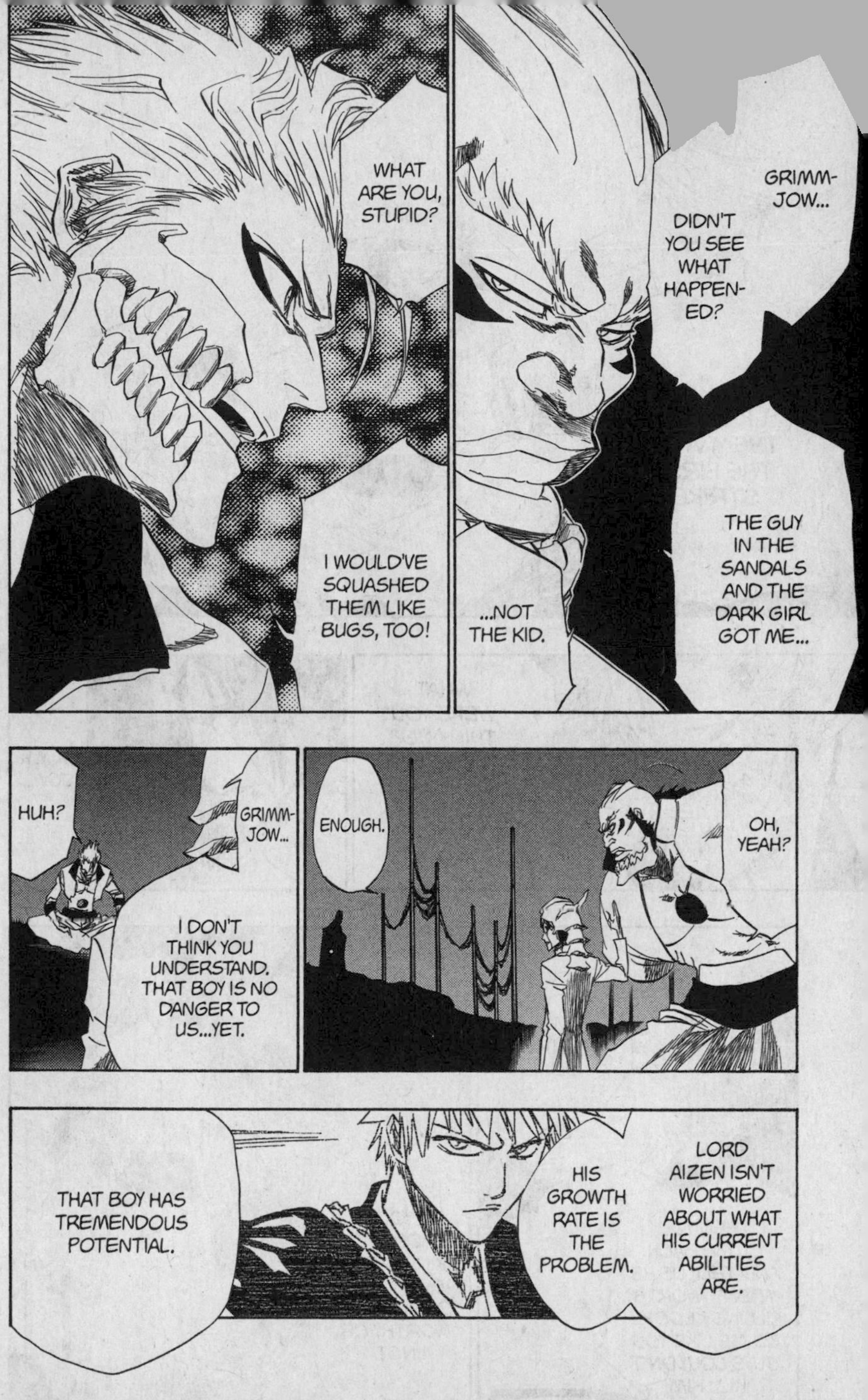
GRIMM-JOW...
DIDN'T YOU SEE WHAT HAPPEN-ED?
THE GUY IN THE SANDALS AND THE DARK GIRL GOT ME...
...NOT THE KID.
WHAT ARE YOU, STUPID?
I WOULD'VE SQUASHED THEM LIKE BUGS, TOO!
OH, YEAH?
ENOUGH.
GRIMM-JOW...
HUH?
I DON'T THINK YOU UNDERSTAND. THAT BOY IS NO DANGER TO US...YET.
LORD AIZEN ISN'T WORRIED ABOUT WHAT HIS CURRENT ABILITIES ARE.
HIS GROWTH RATE IS THE PROBLEM.
THAT BOY HAS TREMENDOUS POTENTIAL.

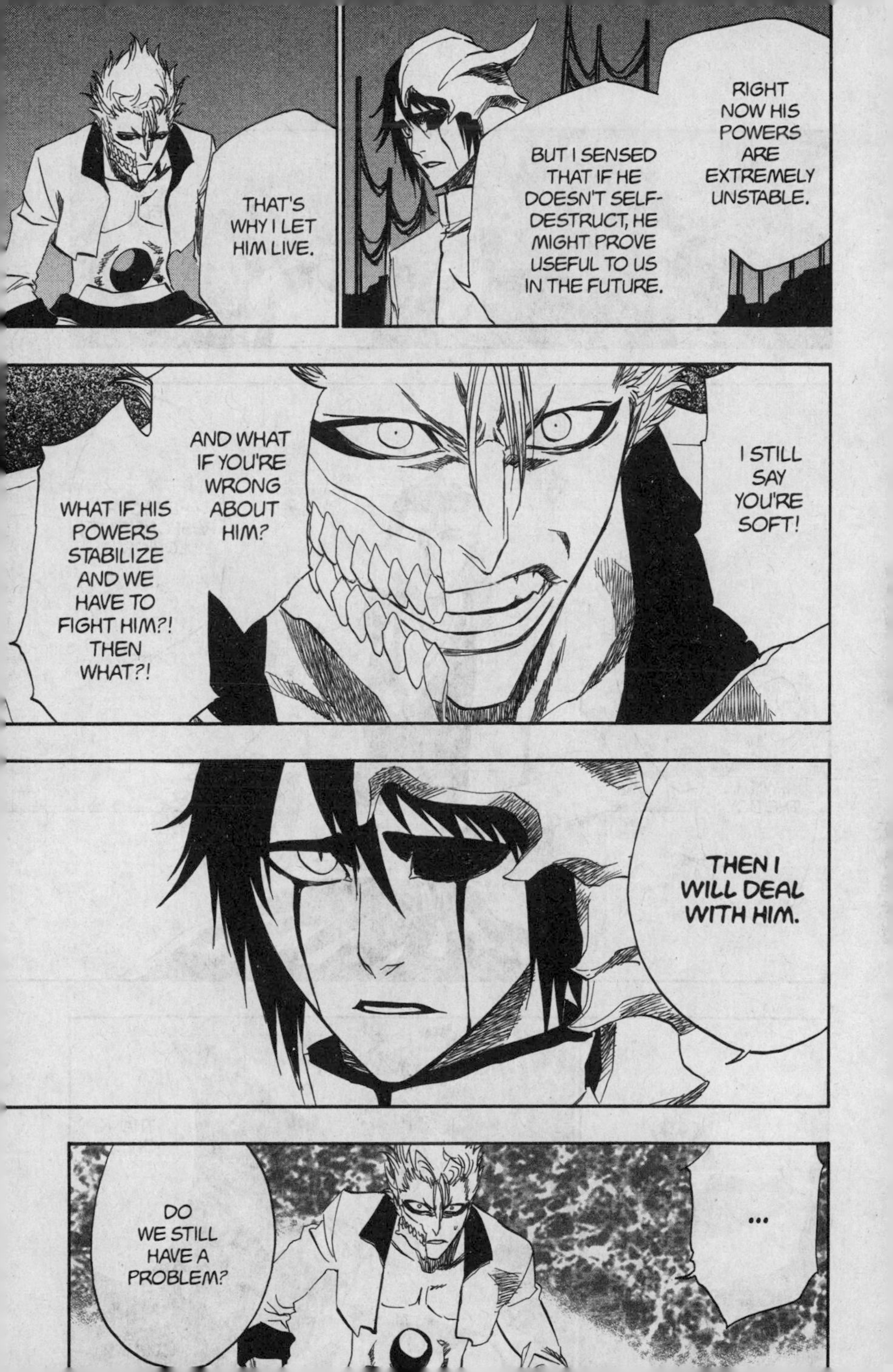
RIGHT NOW HIS POWERS ARE EXTREMELY UNSTABLE.
BUT I SENSED THAT IF HE DOESN'T SELF-DESTRUCT, HE MIGHT PROVE USEFUL TO US IN THE FUTURE.
THAT'S WHY I LET HIM LIVE.
I STILL SAY YOU'RE SOFT!
AND WHAT IF YOU'RE WRONG ABOUT HIM?
WHAT IF HIS POWERS STABILIZE AND WE HAVE TO FIGHT HIM?! THEN WHAT?!
THEN I WILL DEAL WITH HIM.
...
DO WE STILL HAVE A PROBLEM?

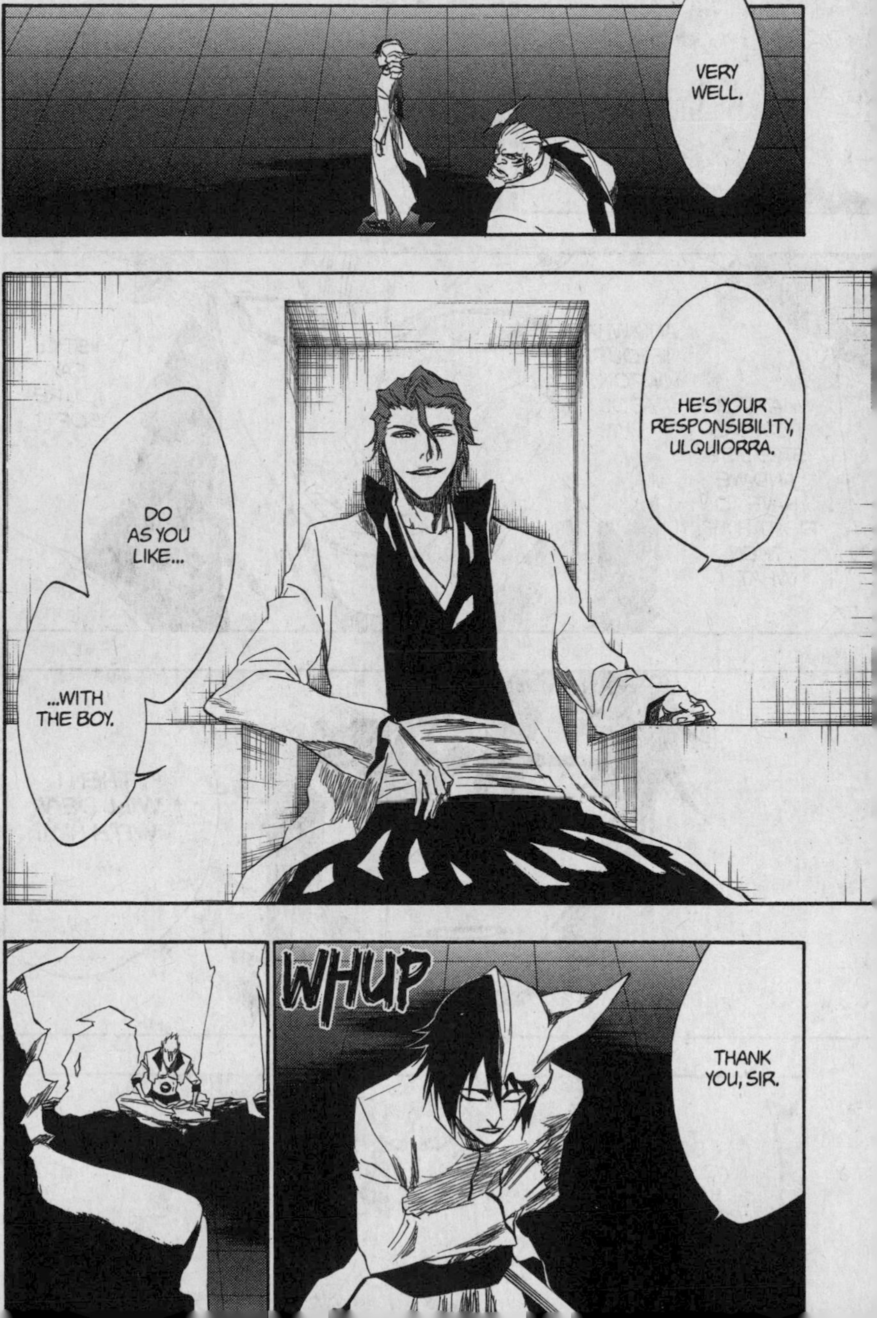
VERY WELL.
HE'S YOUR RESPONSIBILITY, ULQUIORRA.
DO AS YOU LIKE...
...WITH THE BOY.
WHUP
THANK YOU, SIR.

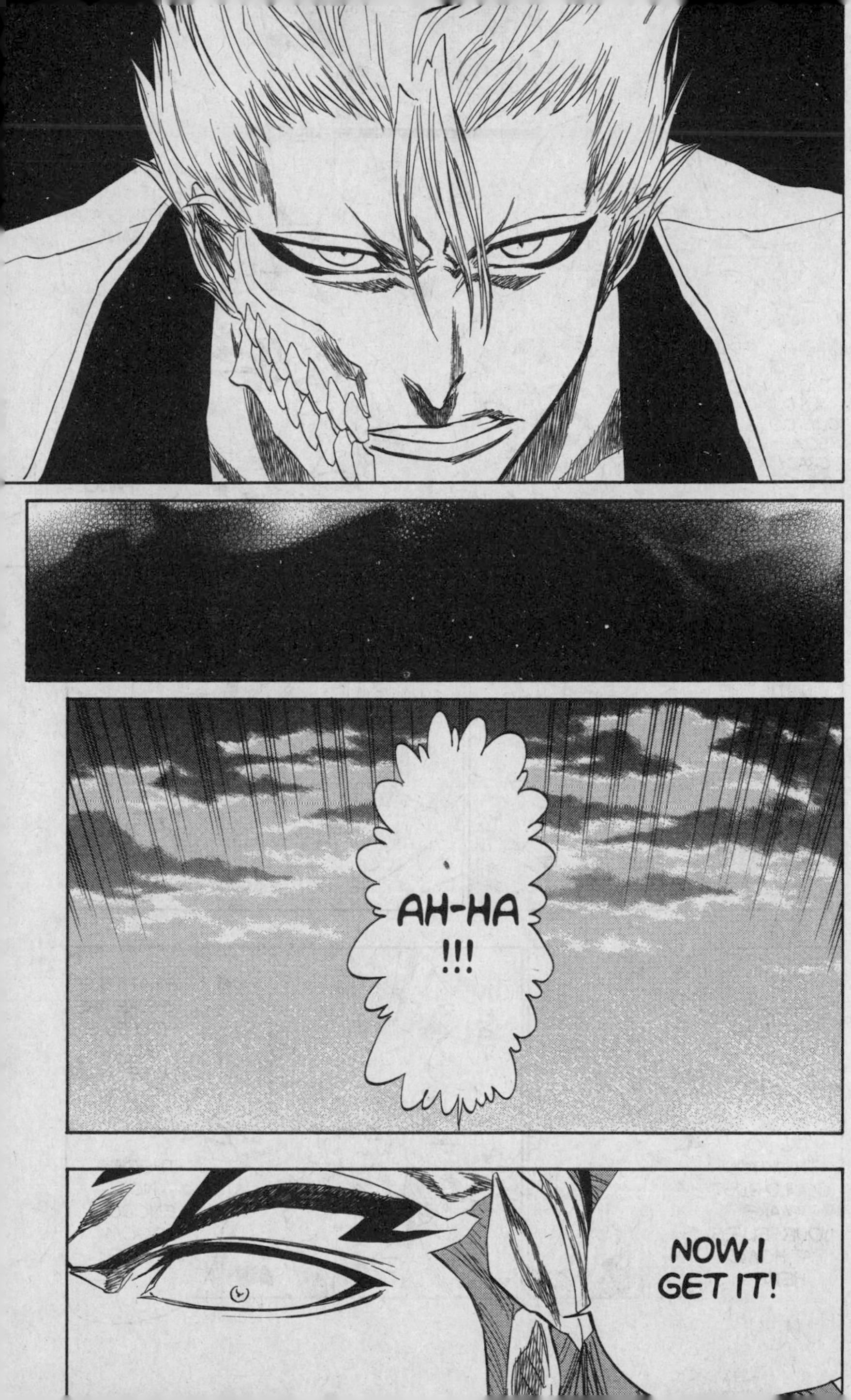
AH-HA !!!
NOW I GET IT!

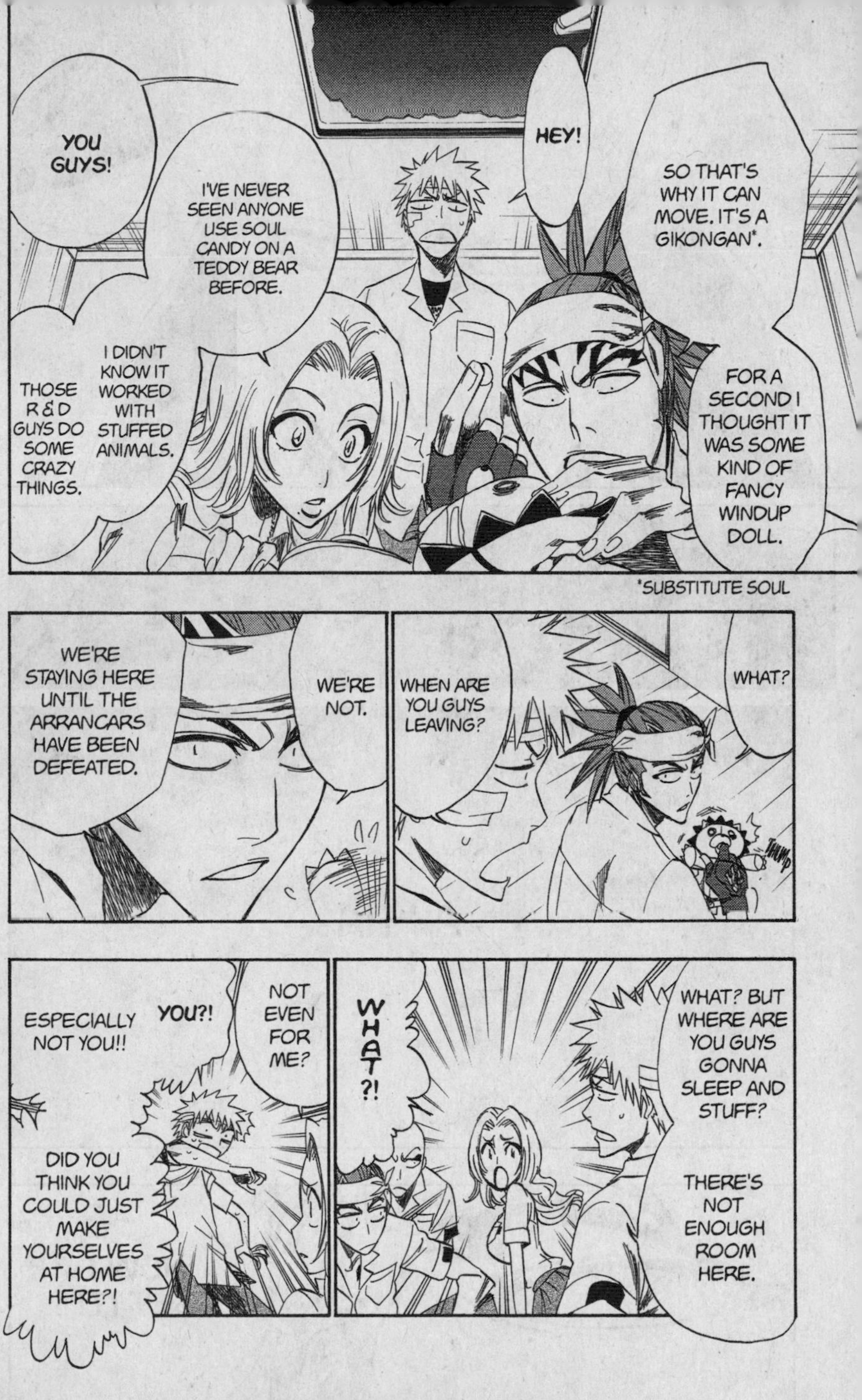
HEY!
SO THAT'S WHY IT CAN MOVE. IT'S A GIKONGAN*.
FOR A SECOND I THOUGHT IT WAS SOME KIND OF FANCY WINDUP DOLL.
YOU GUYS!
I'VE NEVER SEEN ANYONE USE SOUL CANDY ON A TEDDY BEAR BEFORE.
I DIDN'T KNOW IT WORKED WITH STUFFED ANIMALS.
THOSE R&D GUYS DO SOME CRAZY THINGS.
WHAT?
WHEN ARE YOU GUYS LEAVING?
THUMP
WE'RE NOT.
WE'RE STAYING HERE UNTIL THE ARRANCARS HAVE BEEN DEFEATED.
WHAT? BUT WHERE ARE YOU GUYS GONNA SLEEP AND STUFF?
THERE'S NOT ENOUGH ROOM HERE.
WHAT?!
NOT EVEN FOR ME?
YOU?!
ESPECIALLY NOT YOU!!
DID YOU THINK YOU COULD JUST MAKE YOURSELVES AT HOME HERE?!

*SUBSTITUTE SOUL

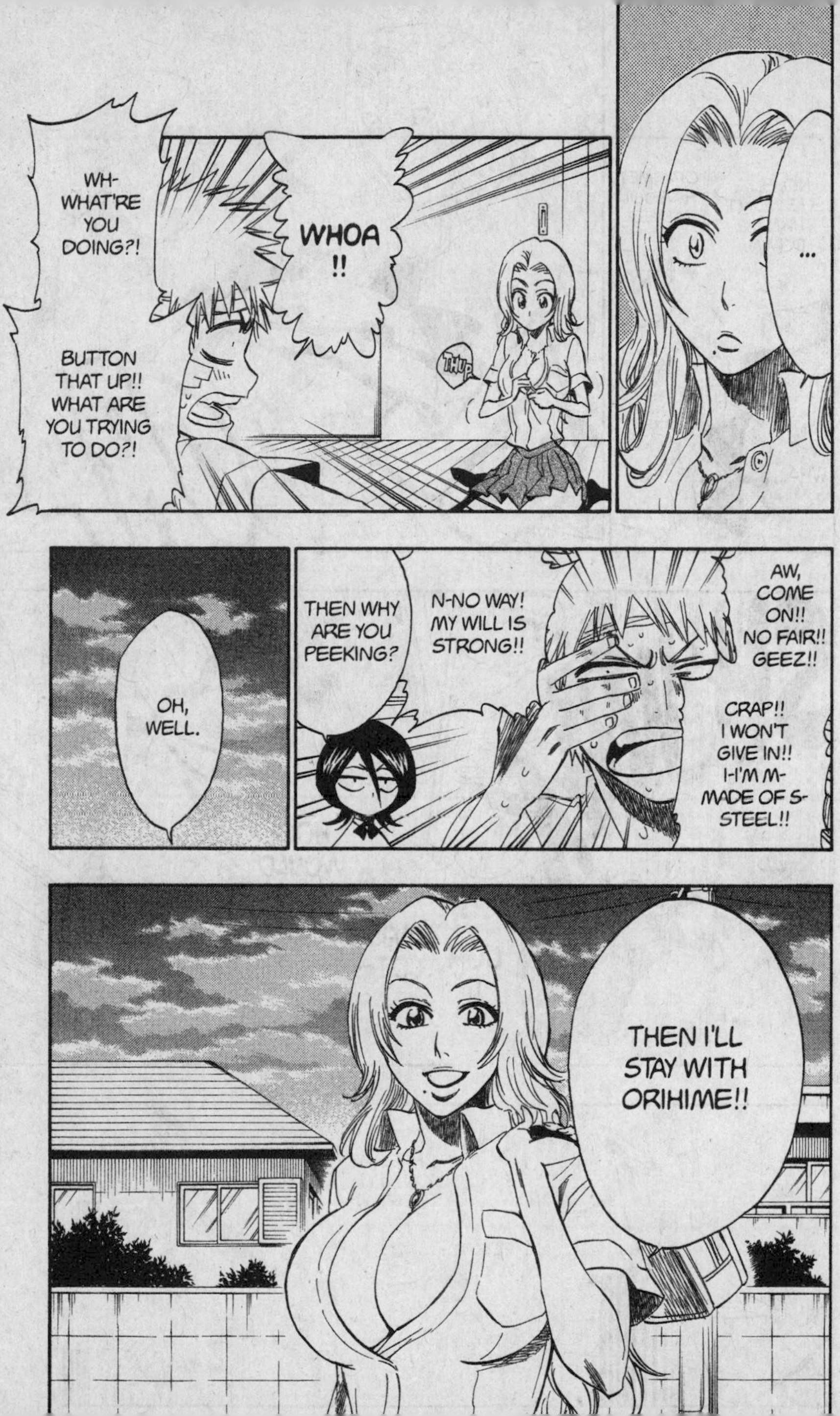
...
WHOA !!
WH- WHAT'RE YOU DOING?!
THUP
BUTTON THAT UP!! WHAT ARE YOU TRYING TO DO?!
AW, COME ON!! NO FAIR!! GEEZ!!
N-NO WAY! MY WILL IS STRONG!!
THEN WHY ARE YOU PEEKING?
CRAP!! I WON'T GIVE IN!! I-I'M M-MADE OF S-STEEL!!
OH, WELL.
THEN I'LL STAY WITH ORIHIME!!

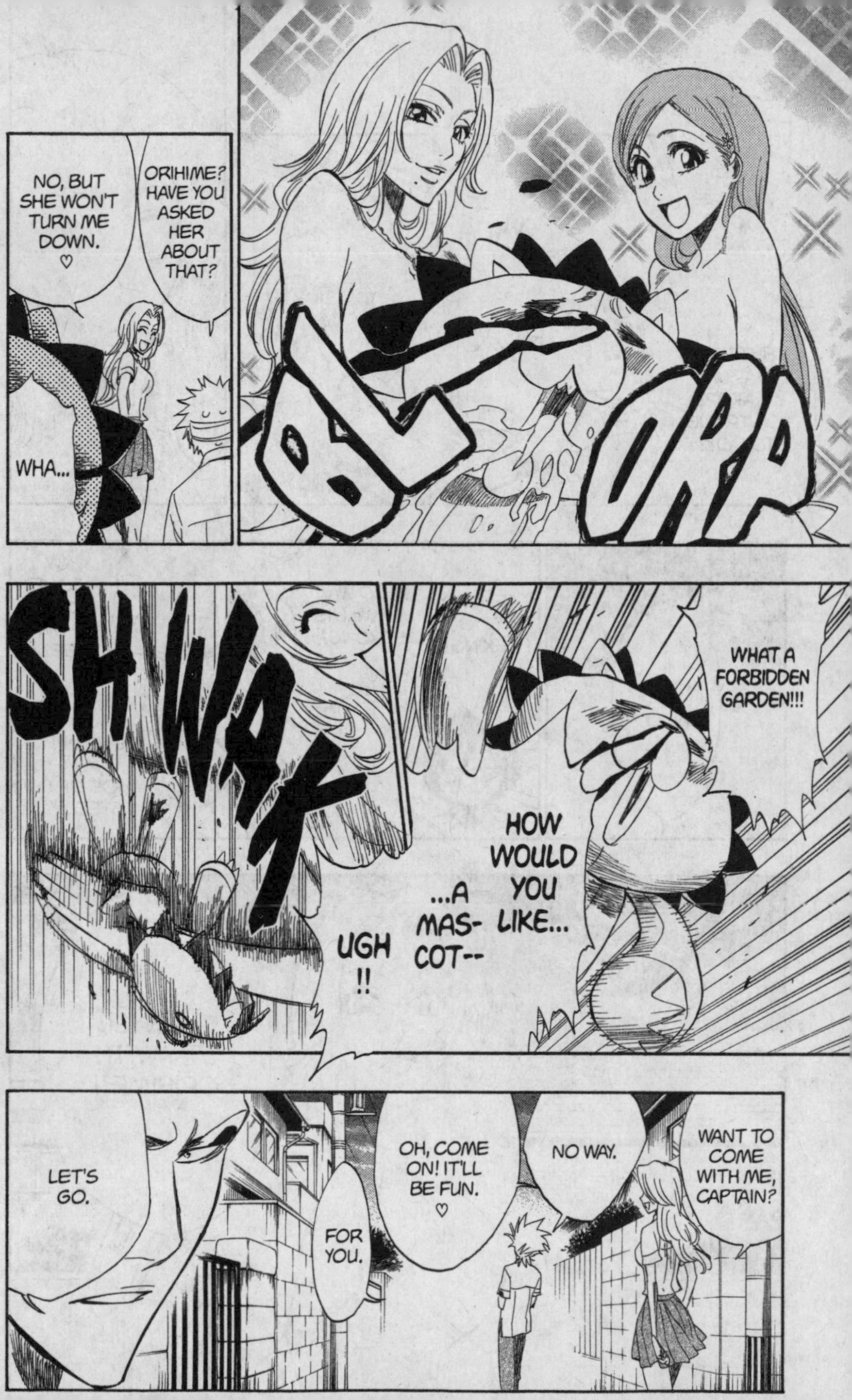
BLORP
ORIHIME? HAVE YOU ASKED HER ABOUT THAT?
NO, BUT SHE WON'T TURN ME DOWN. ♡
WHA...
WHAT A FORBIDDEN GARDEN!!!
HOW WOULD YOU LIKE...
...A MAS- COT--
SHWAK
UGH !!
WANT TO COME WITH ME, CAPTAIN?
NO WAY.
OH, COME ON! IT'LL BE FUN. ♡
FOR YOU.
LET'S GO.

READ THIS WAY

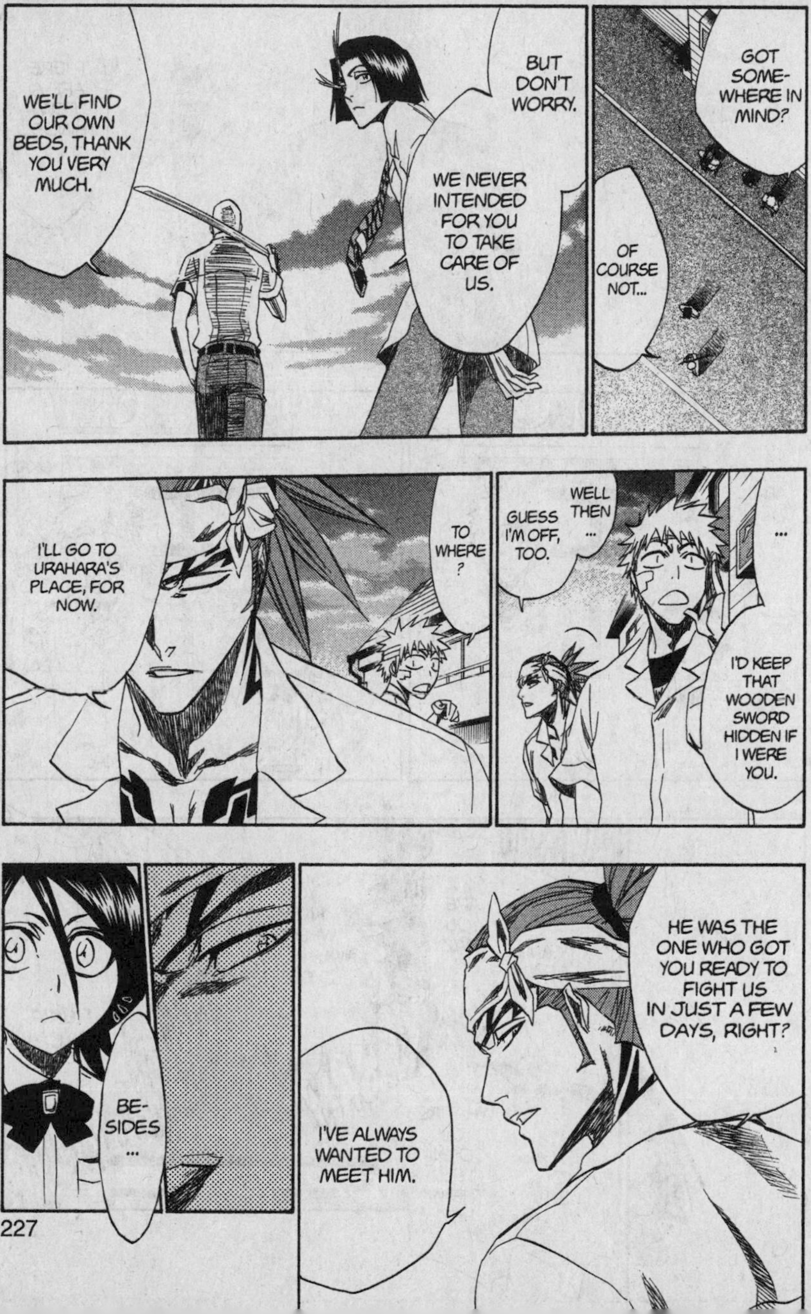
GOT SOME-WHERE IN MIND?
OF COURSE NOT...
BUT DON'T WORRY.
WE NEVER INTENDED FOR YOU TO TAKE CARE OF US.
WE'LL FIND OUR OWN BEDS, THANK YOU VERY MUCH.
...
WELL THEN ...
GUESS I'M OFF, TOO.
I'D KEEP THAT WOODEN SWORD HIDDEN IF I WERE YOU.
TO WHERE ?
I'LL GO TO URAHARA'S PLACE, FOR NOW.
HE WAS THE ONE WHO GOT YOU READY TO FIGHT US IN JUST A FEW DAYS, RIGHT?
I'VE ALWAYS WANTED TO MEET HIM.
BE-SIDES ...

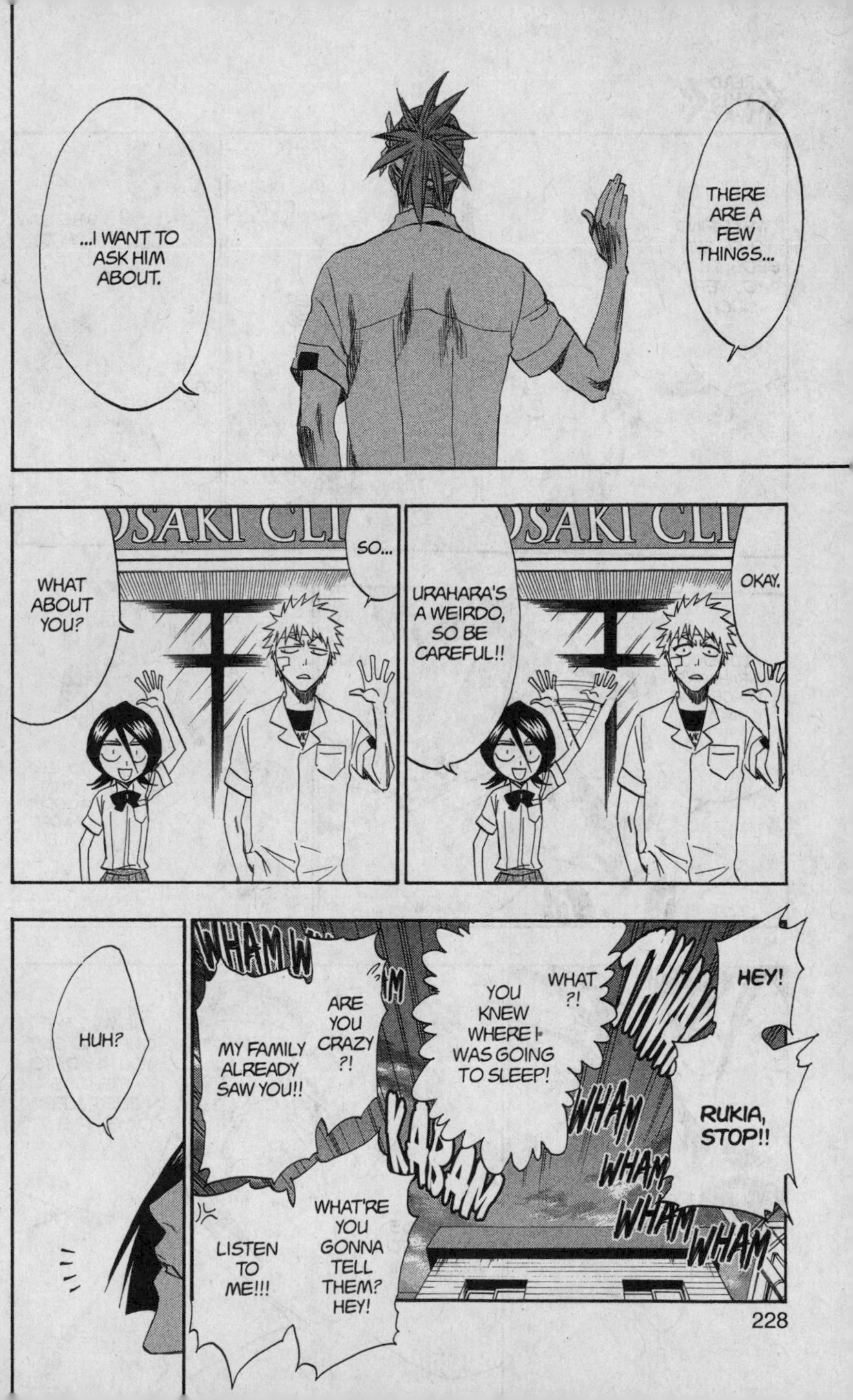
THERE ARE A FEW THINGS...
...I WANT TO ASK HIM ABOUT.
OKAY.
URAHARA'S A WEIRDO, SO BE CAREFUL!!
SO...
WHAT ABOUT YOU?
HEY!
WHAT ?!
YOU KNEW WHERE I WAS GOING TO SLEEP!
RUKIA, STOP!!
WHAM
WHAM
WHAM
WHAM
KABAM
ARE YOU CRAZY ?!
MY FAMILY ALREADY SAW YOU!!
WHAT'RE YOU GONNA TELL THEM? HEY!
LISTEN TO ME!!!
HUH?

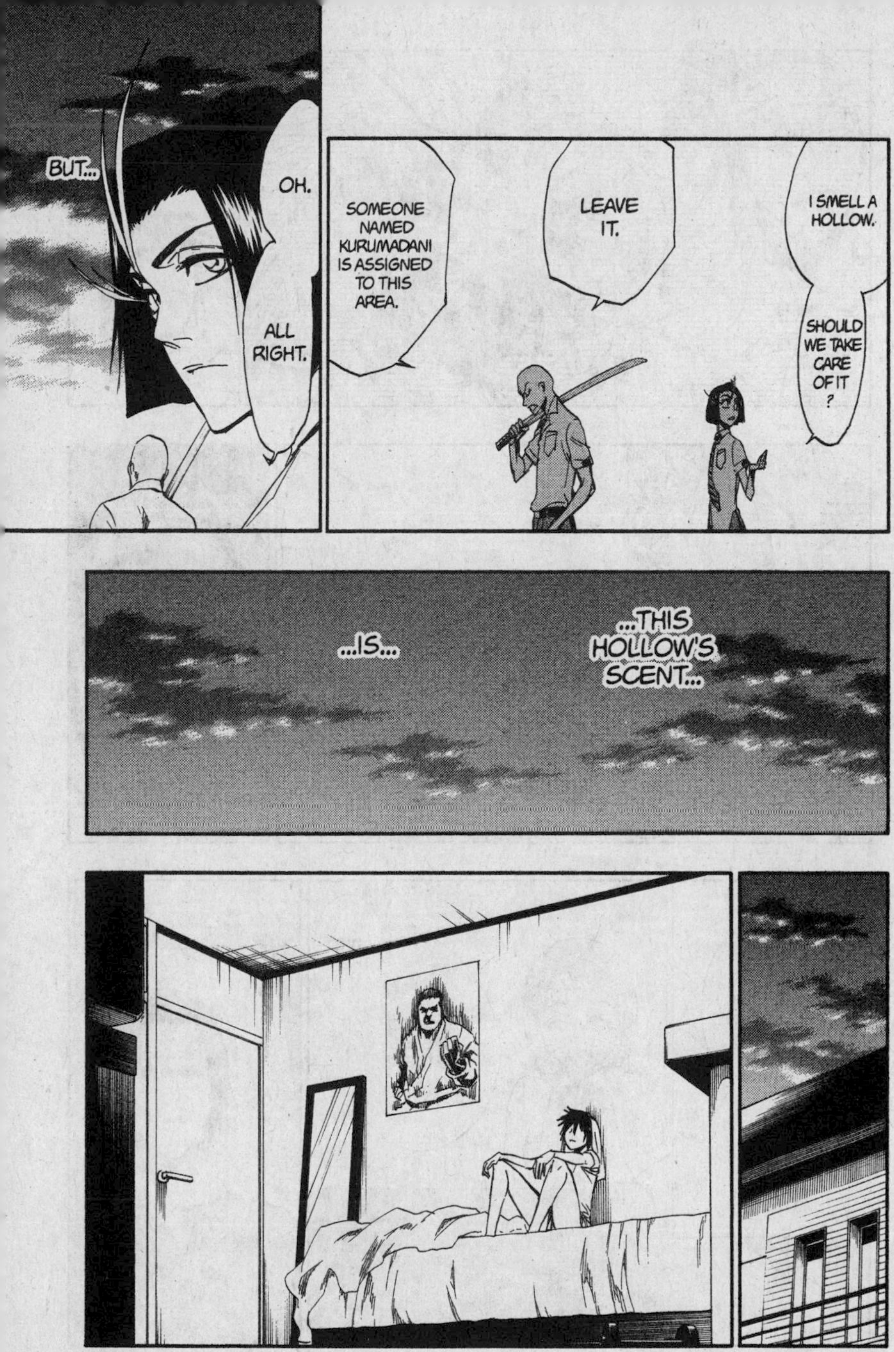
I SMELL A HOLLOW.
SHOULD WE TAKE CARE OF IT?
LEAVE IT.
SOMEONE NAMED KURUMADANI IS ASSIGNED TO THIS AREA.
OH.
ALL RIGHT.
BUT...
...THIS HOLLOW'S SCENT...
...IS...

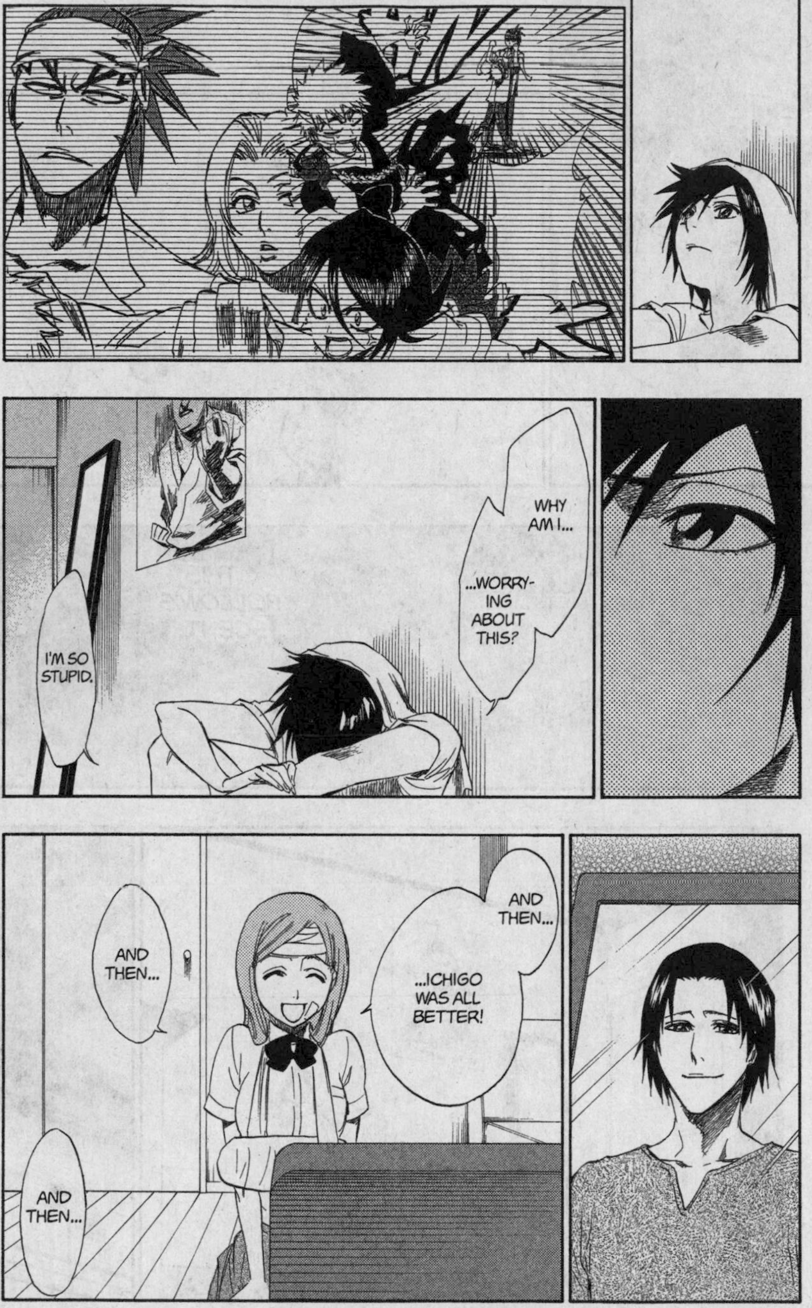
WHY AM I...
...WORRY-ING ABOUT THIS?
I'M SO STUPID.
AND THEN...
...ICHIGO WAS ALL BETTER!
AND THEN...
AND THEN...

RUKIA REALLY IS AMAZING.

BUT, WOW...

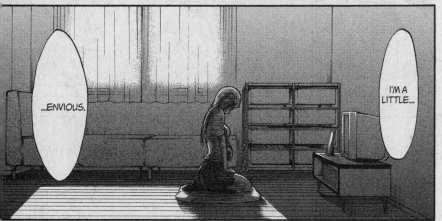

...ENVIOUS.

I'M A LITTLE...

RIGHT THEN, I KNEW IT!!

AND-- BOOM!

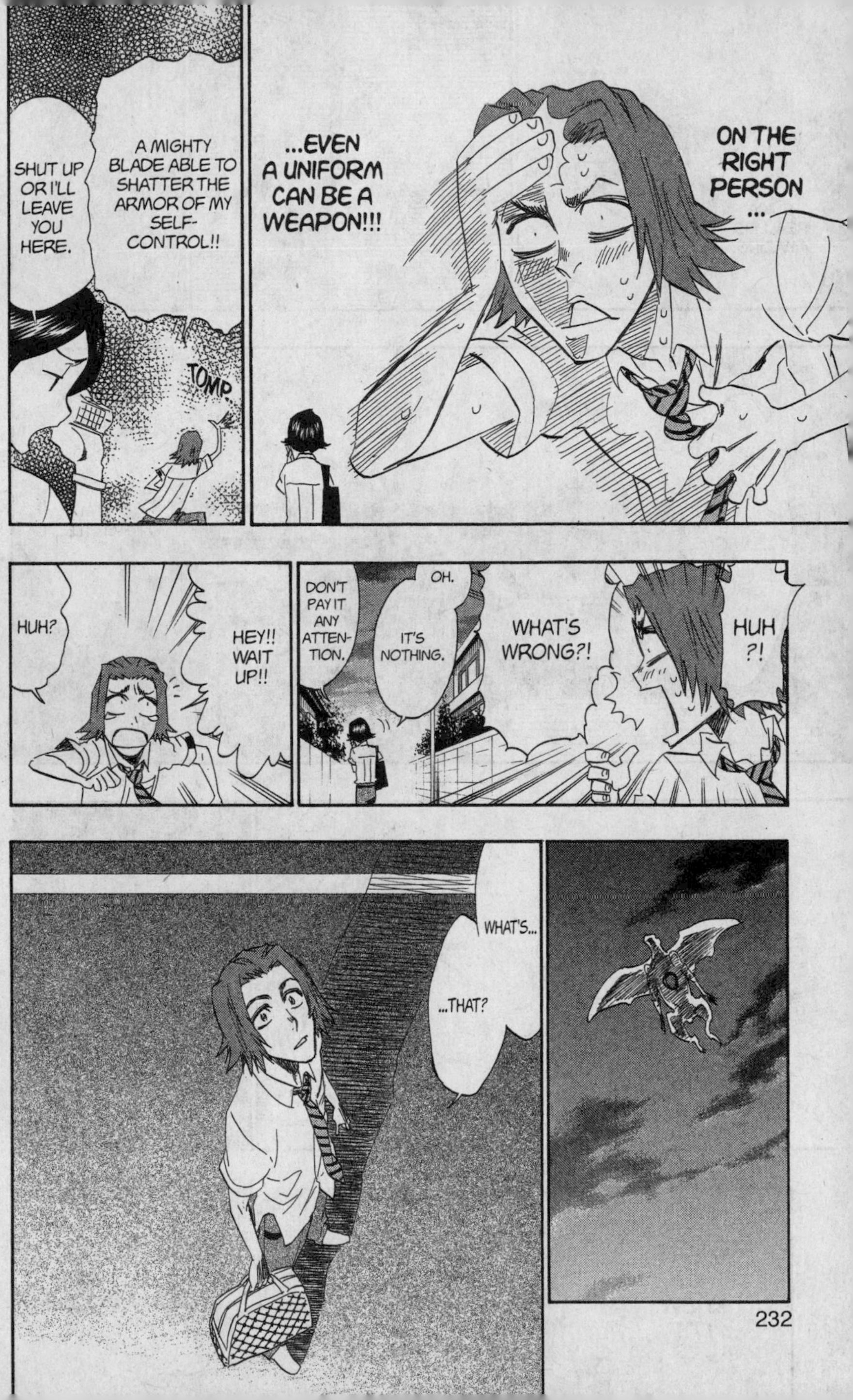
ON THE RIGHT PERSON...
...EVEN A UNIFORM CAN BE A WEAPON!!!
A MIGHTY BLADE ABLE TO SHATTER THE ARMOR OF MY SELF-CONTROL!!
SHUT UP OR I'LL LEAVE YOU HERE.
TOMP
HUH ?!
WHAT'S WRONG?!
OH.
IT'S NOTHING.
DON'T PAY IT ANY ATTENTION.
HEY!! WAIT UP!!
HUH?
WHAT'S...
...THAT?

READ THIS WAY

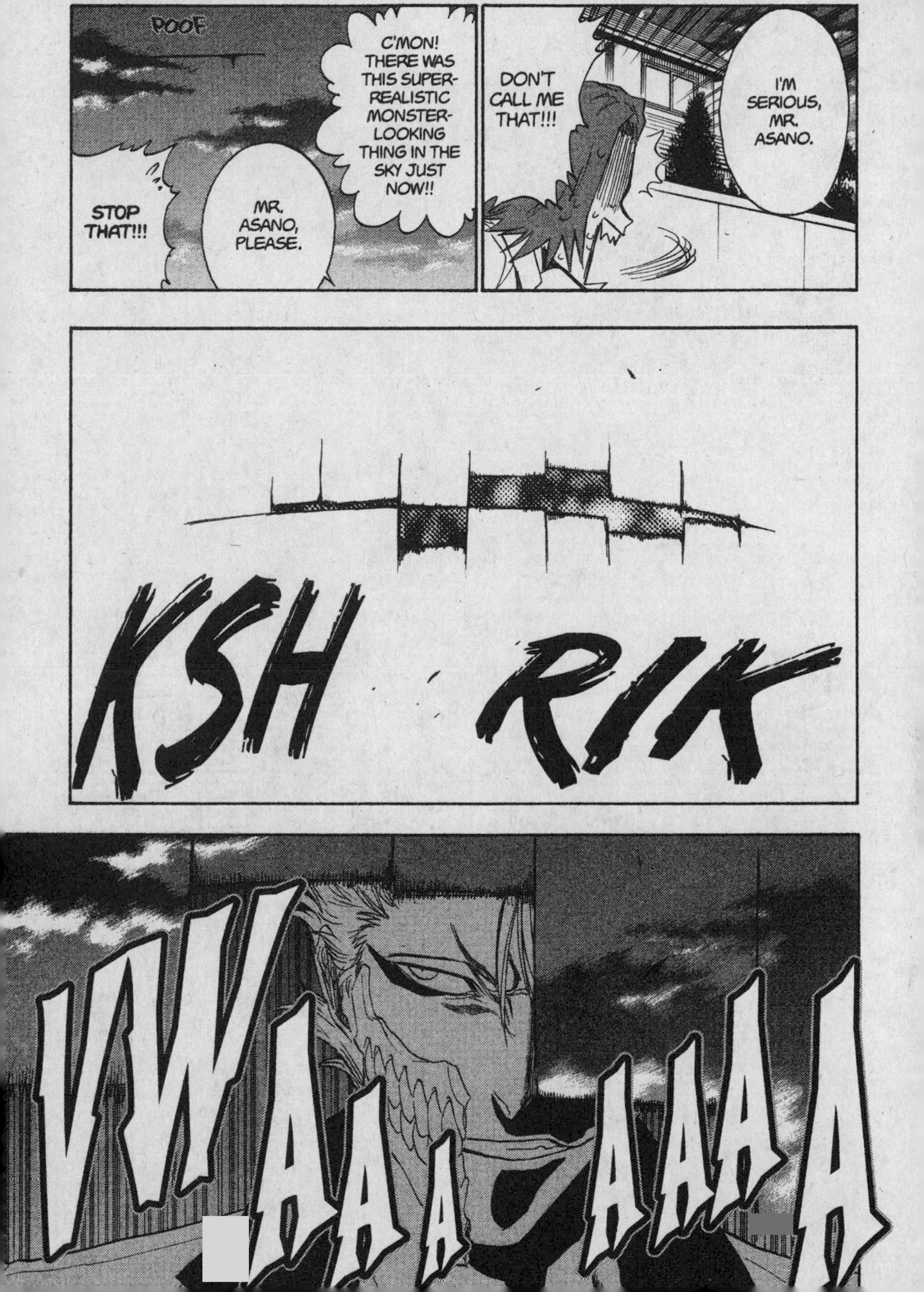
I'M SERIOUS, MR. ASANO.
DON'T CALL ME THAT!!!
C'MON! THERE WAS THIS SUPER-REALISTIC MONSTER-LOOKING THING IN THE SKY JUST NOW!!
POOF
MR. ASANO, PLEASE.
STOP THAT!!!
KSH RIK
VWAAAAAAA

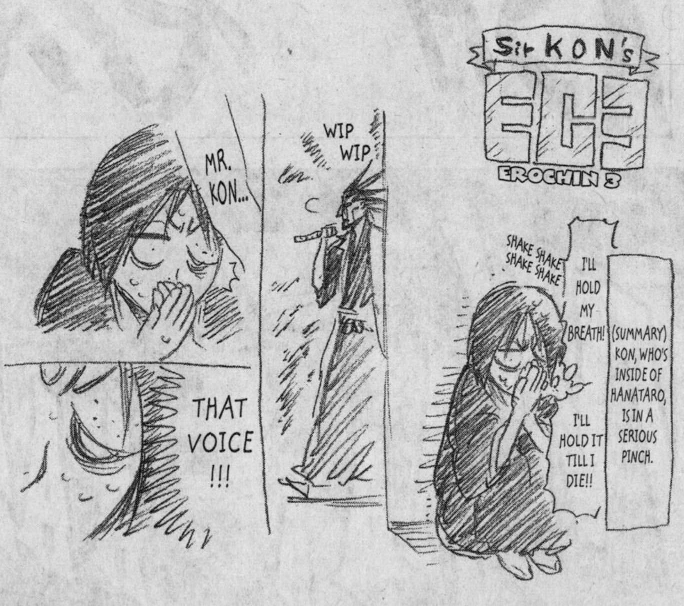
Sir KON's
EC3
EROCHIN 3
(SUMMARY) KON, WHO'S INSIDE OF HANATARO, IS IN A SERIOUS PINCH.
I'LL HOLD MY BREATH!
SHAKE SHAKE SHAKE SHAKE
I'LL HOLD IT TILL I DIE!!
WIP WIP
MR. KON...
THAT VOICE!!!

199. Ugly

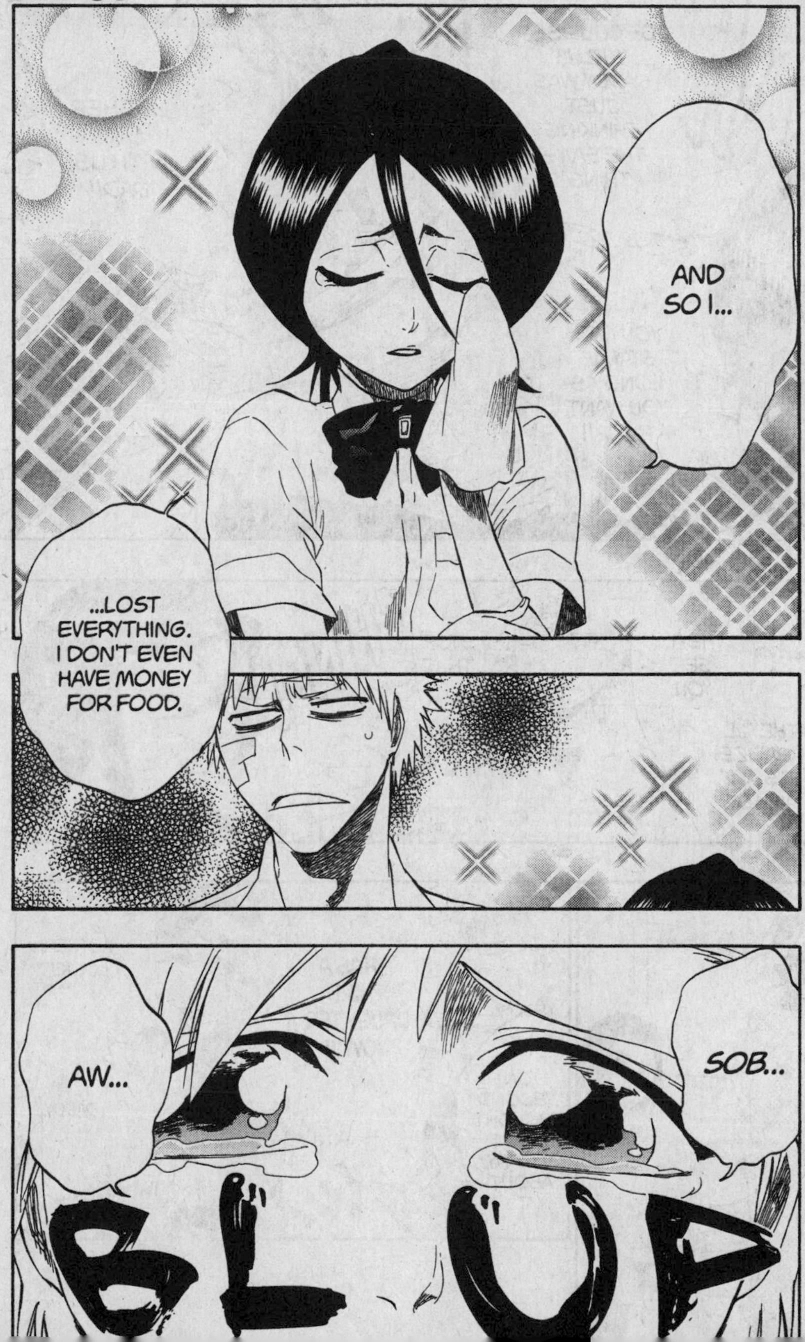
AND SO I...
...LOST EVERYTHING. I DON'T EVEN HAVE MONEY FOR FOOD.
SOB...
AW...
BLUP

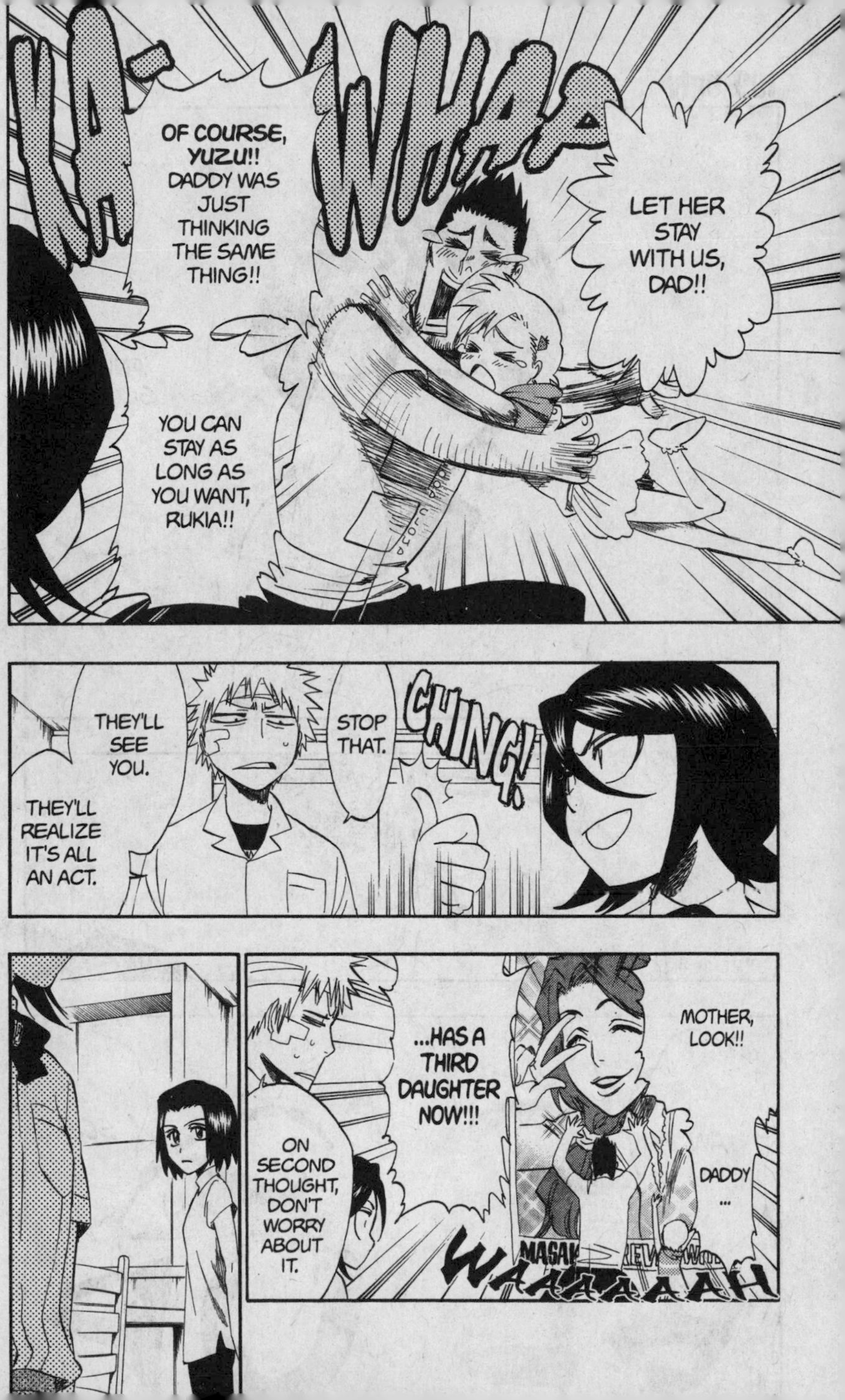
LET HER STAY WITH US, DAD!!
OF COURSE, YUZU!! DADDY WAS JUST THINKING THE SAME THING!!
YOU CAN STAY AS LONG AS YOU WANT, RUKIA!!
CHING!
STOP THAT.
THEY'LL SEE YOU.
THEY'LL REALIZE IT'S ALL AN ACT.
MOTHER, LOOK!!
DADDY ...
...HAS A THIRD DAUGHTER NOW!!!
WAAAAAAH
ON SECOND THOUGHT, DON'T WORRY ABOUT IT.

READ THIS WAY

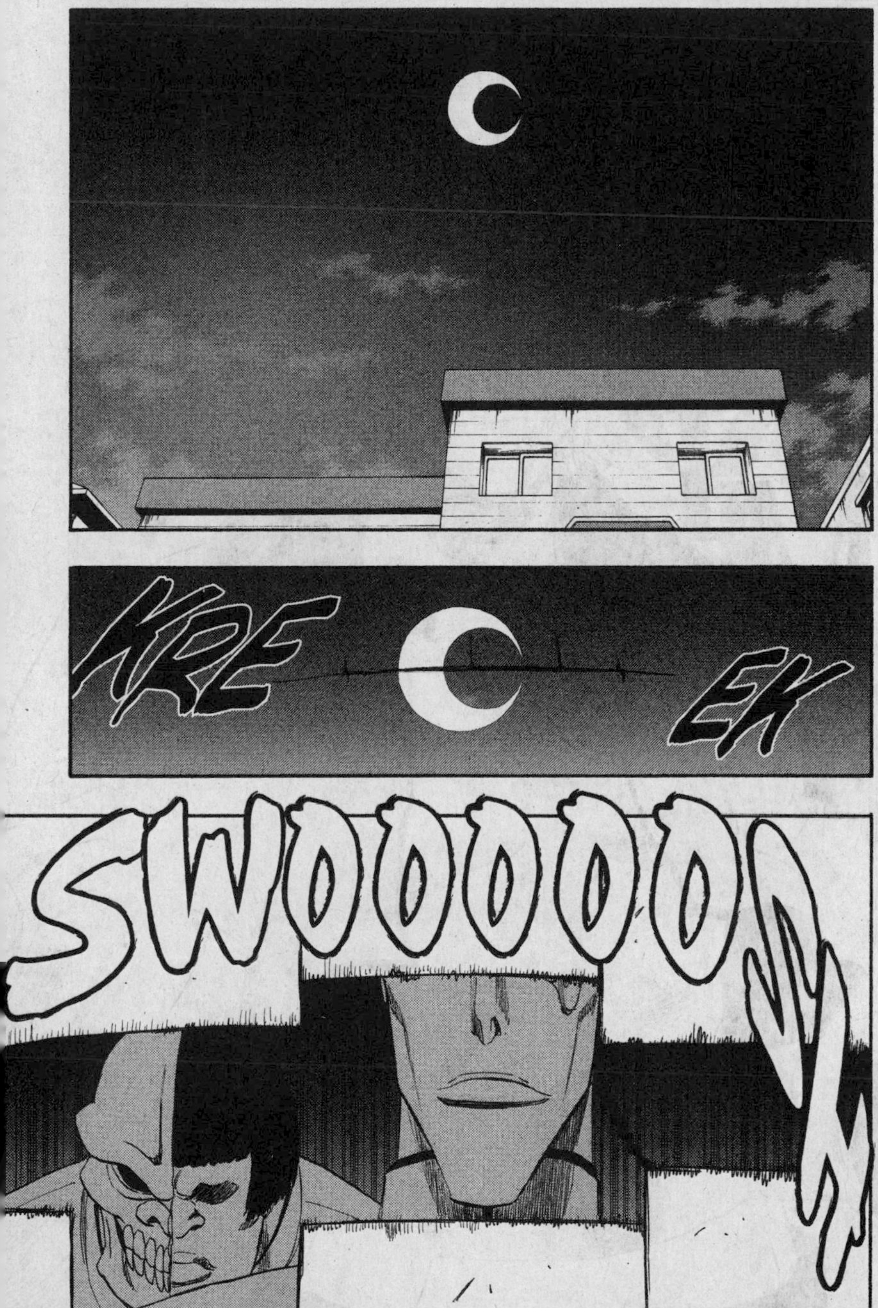
KRE EK
SWOOOOOSH

BLEACH-ブリーチ- 199. Ugly

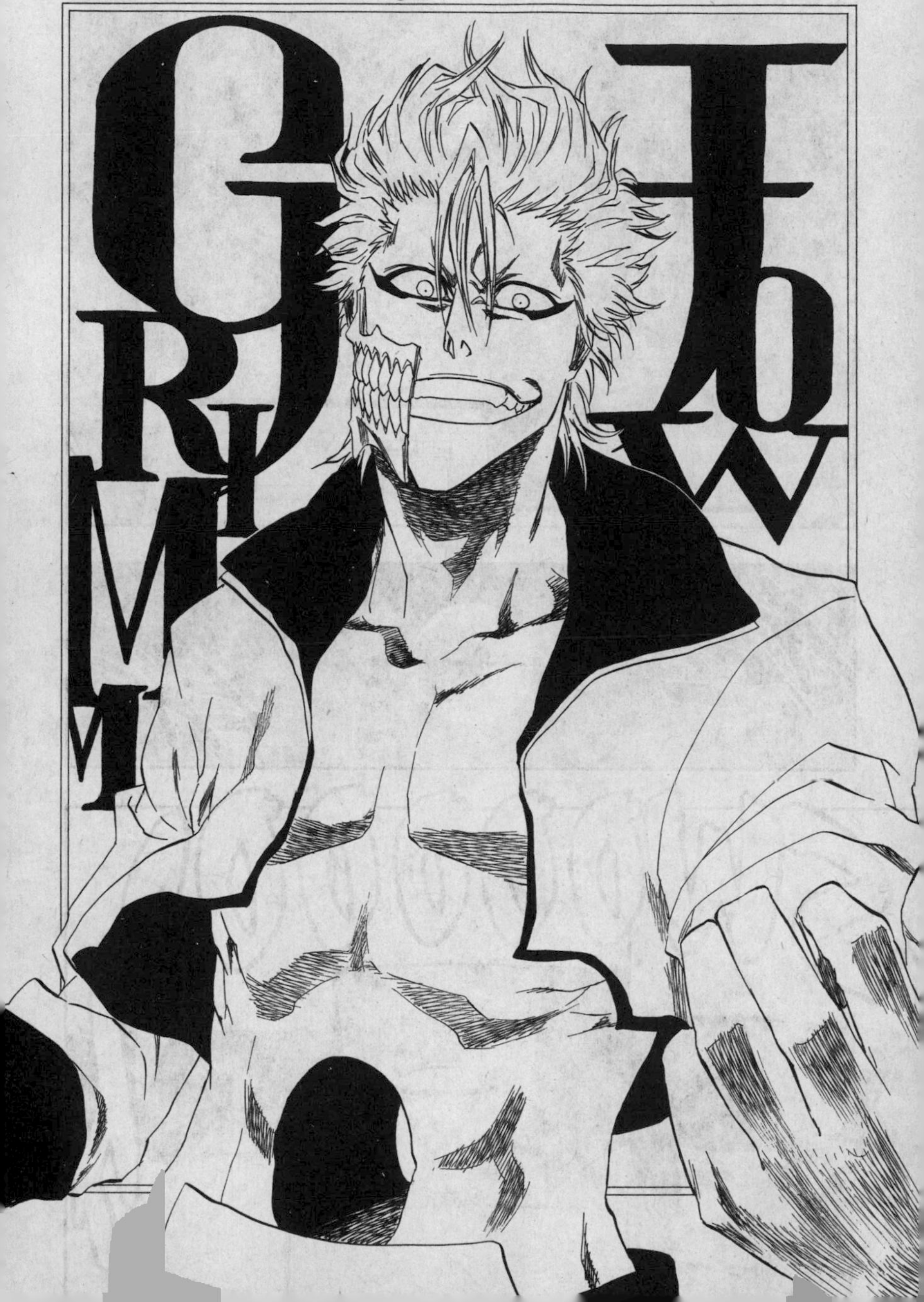
GRIMMJOW

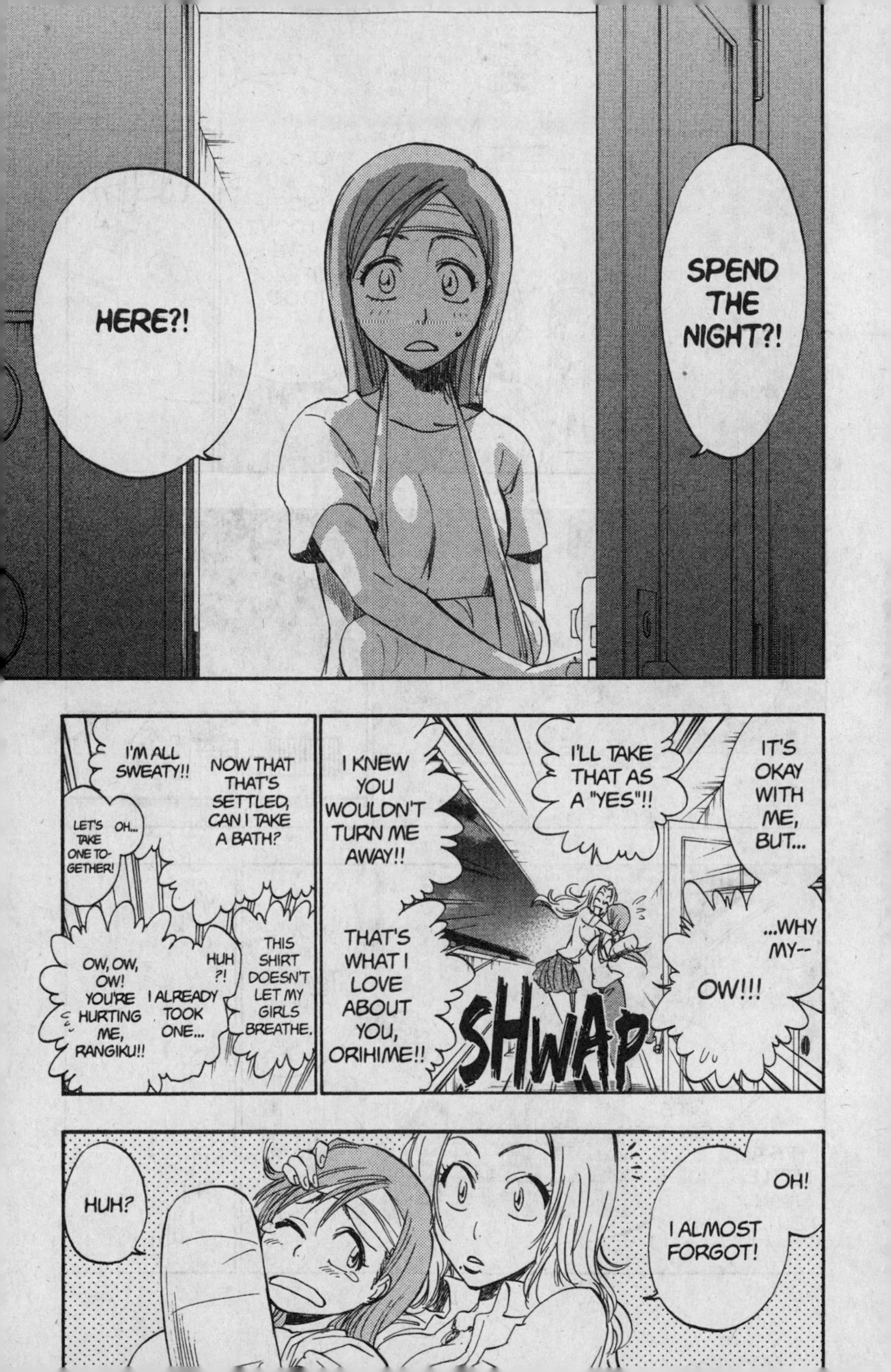
SPEND THE NIGHT?!
HERE?!
IT'S OKAY WITH ME, BUT...
I'LL TAKE THAT AS A "YES"!!
I KNEW YOU WOULDN'T TURN ME AWAY!!
...WHY MY--
OW!!!
SHWAP
THAT'S WHAT I LOVE ABOUT YOU, ORIHIME!!
NOW THAT THAT'S SETTLED, CAN I TAKE A BATH?
I'M ALL SWEATY!!
OH...
LET'S TAKE ONE TO-GETHER!
THIS SHIRT DOESN'T LET MY GIRLS BREATHE.
HUH ?!
I ALREADY TOOK ONE...
OW, OW, OW! YOU'RE HURTING ME, RANGIKU!!
OH!
I ALMOST FORGOT!
HUH?

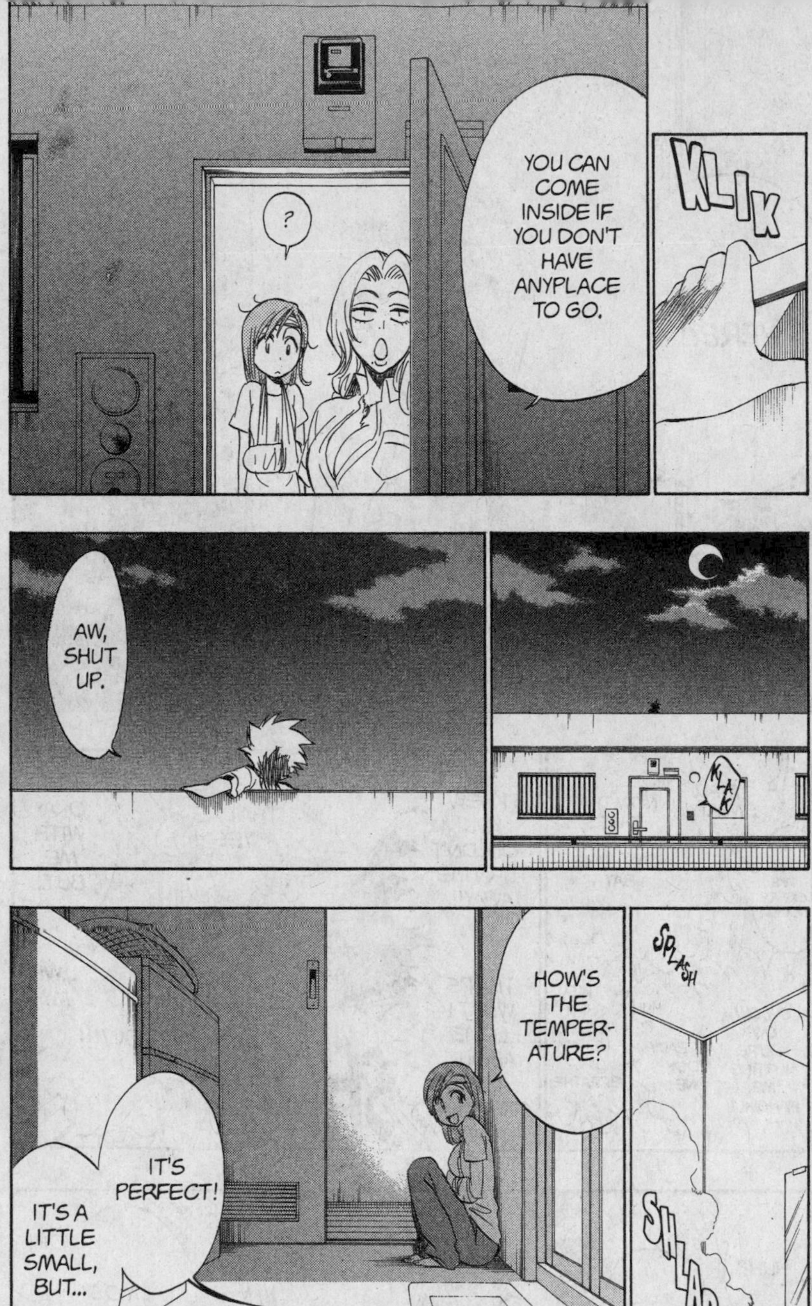
KLIK
YOU CAN COME INSIDE IF YOU DON'T HAVE ANYPLACE TO GO.
?
KLAK
AW, SHUT UP.
SPLASH
SHLAP
HOW'S THE TEMPER-ATURE?
IT'S PERFECT!
IT'S A LITTLE SMALL, BUT...

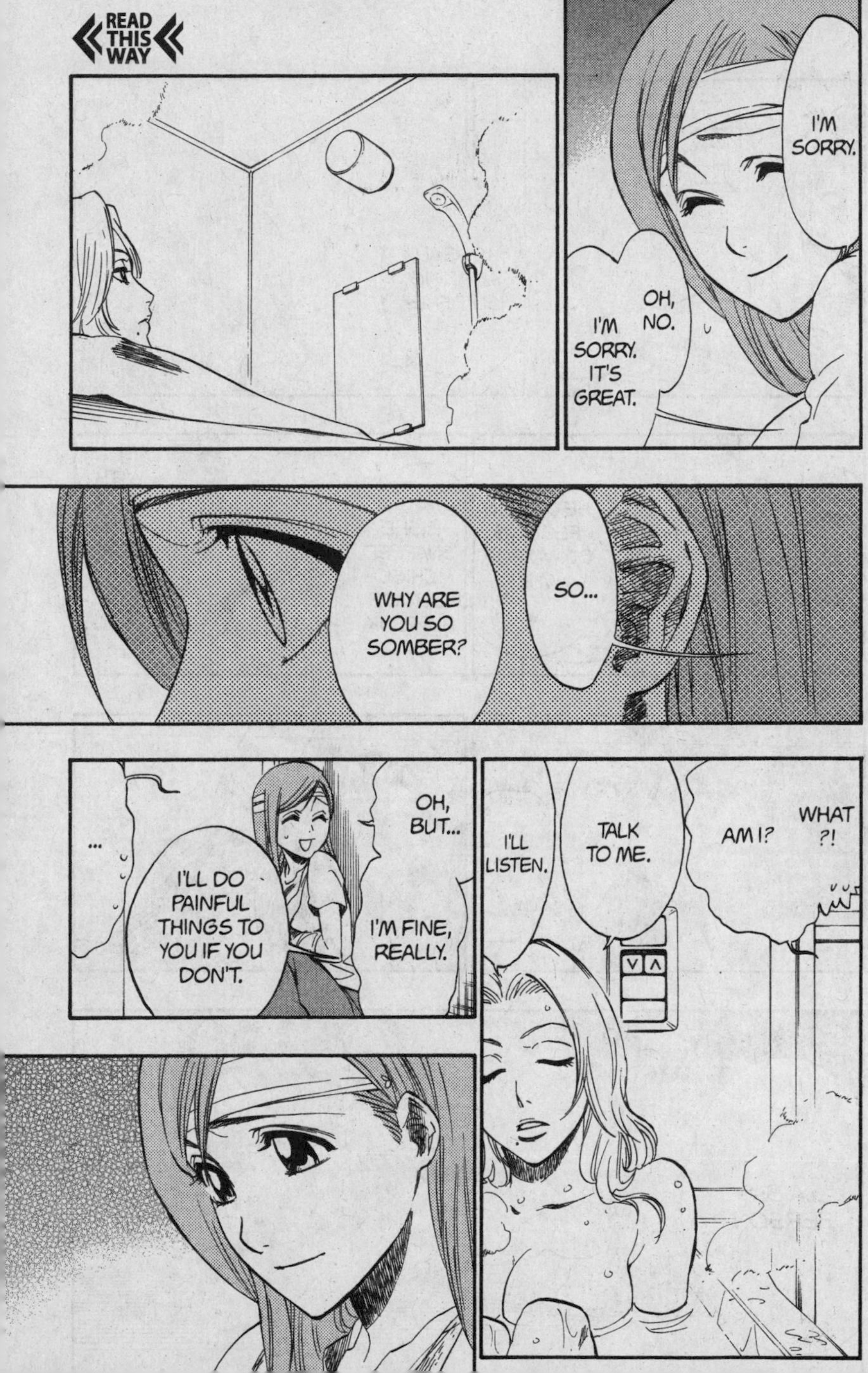

READ THIS WAY
I'M SORRY.
OH, NO.
I'M SORRY. IT'S GREAT.
SO...
WHY ARE YOU SO SOMBER?
WHAT ?!
AM I?
TALK TO ME.
I'LL LISTEN.
OH, BUT...
I'M FINE, REALLY.
...
I'LL DO PAINFUL THINGS TO YOU IF YOU DON'T.

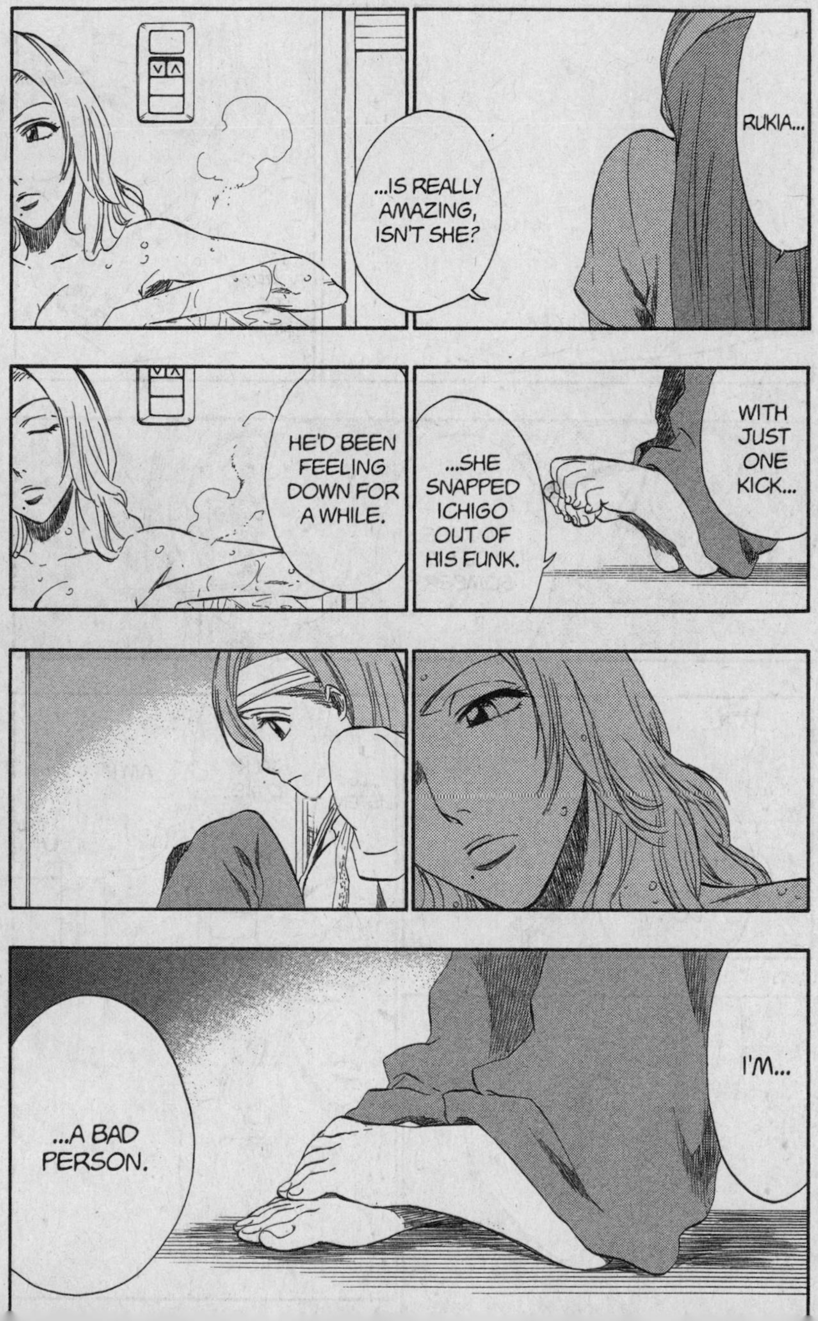
RUKIA...
...IS REALLY AMAZING, ISN'T SHE?
WITH JUST ONE KICK...
...SHE SNAPPED ICHIGO OUT OF HIS FUNK.
HE'D BEEN FEELING DOWN FOR A WHILE.
I'M...
...A BAD PERSON.

...I JUST WANTED ICHIGO...

I THOUGHT...

BUT NOW RUKIA'S BACK...

...TO BE HAPPY.

...AND SHE CHEERED UP ICHIGO.

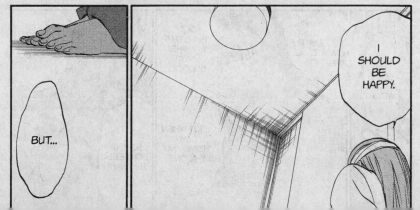

BUT...

I SHOULD BE HAPPY.

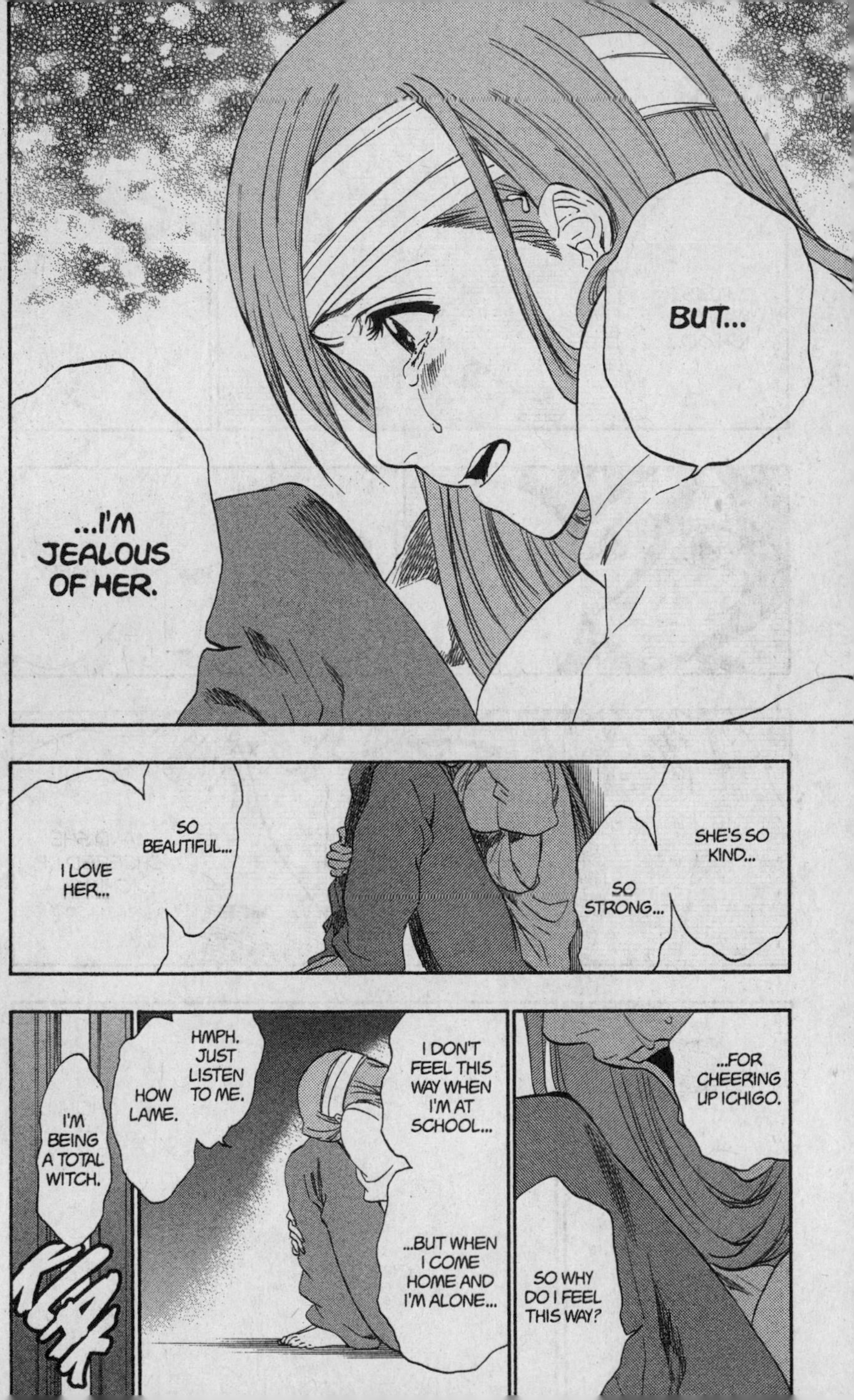
BUT...
...I'M JEALOUS OF HER.
SHE'S SO KIND...
SO STRONG...
SO BEAUTIFUL...
I LOVE HER...
...FOR CHEERING UP ICHIGO.
SO WHY DO I FEEL THIS WAY?
I DON'T FEEL THIS WAY WHEN I'M AT SCHOOL...
...BUT WHEN I COME HOME AND I'M ALONE...
HMPH. JUST LISTEN TO ME.
HOW LAME.
I'M BEING A TOTAL WITCH.
KLAK

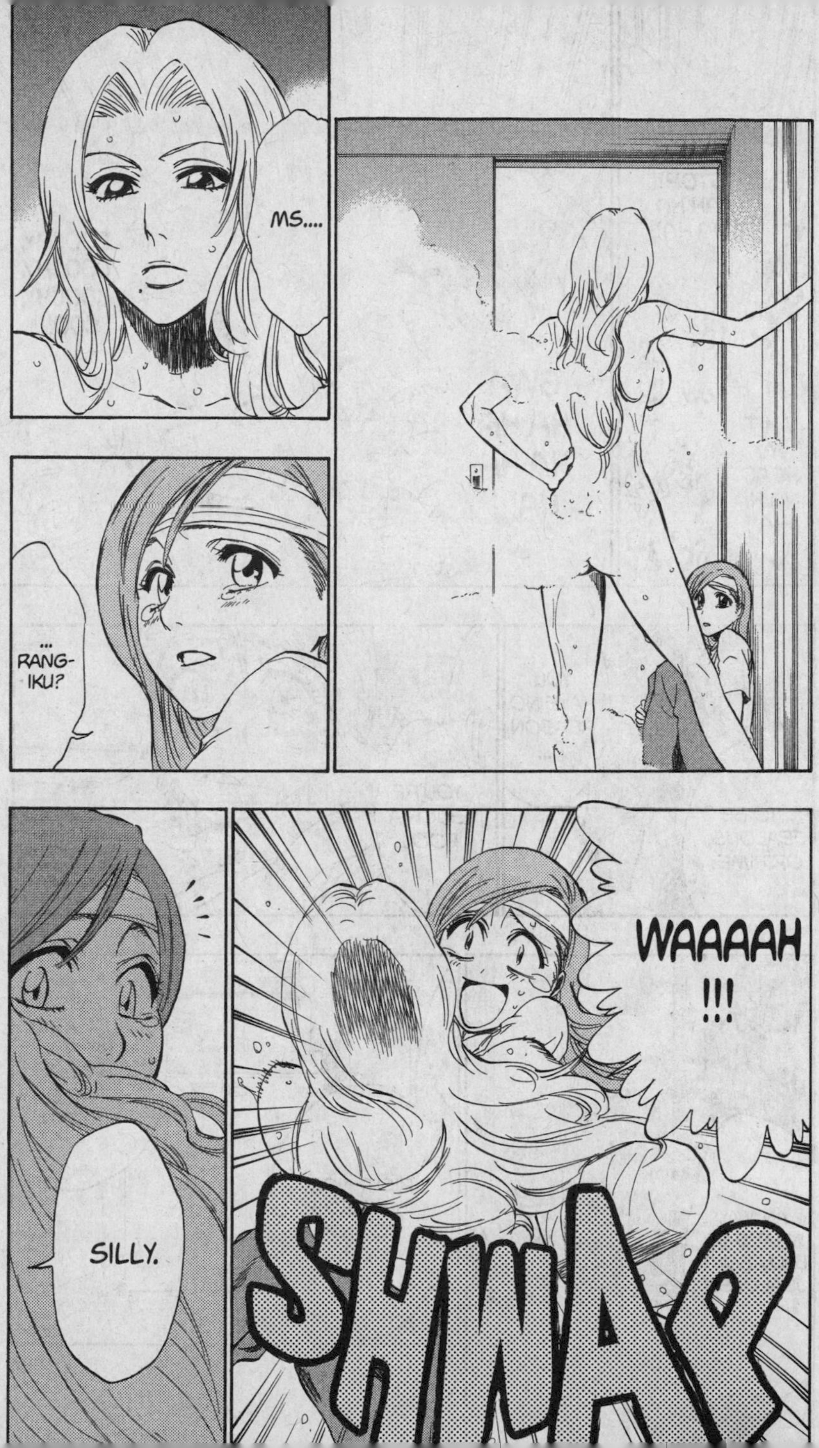

MS....
... RANG-IKU?
WAAAAH !!!
SHWAP
SILLY.

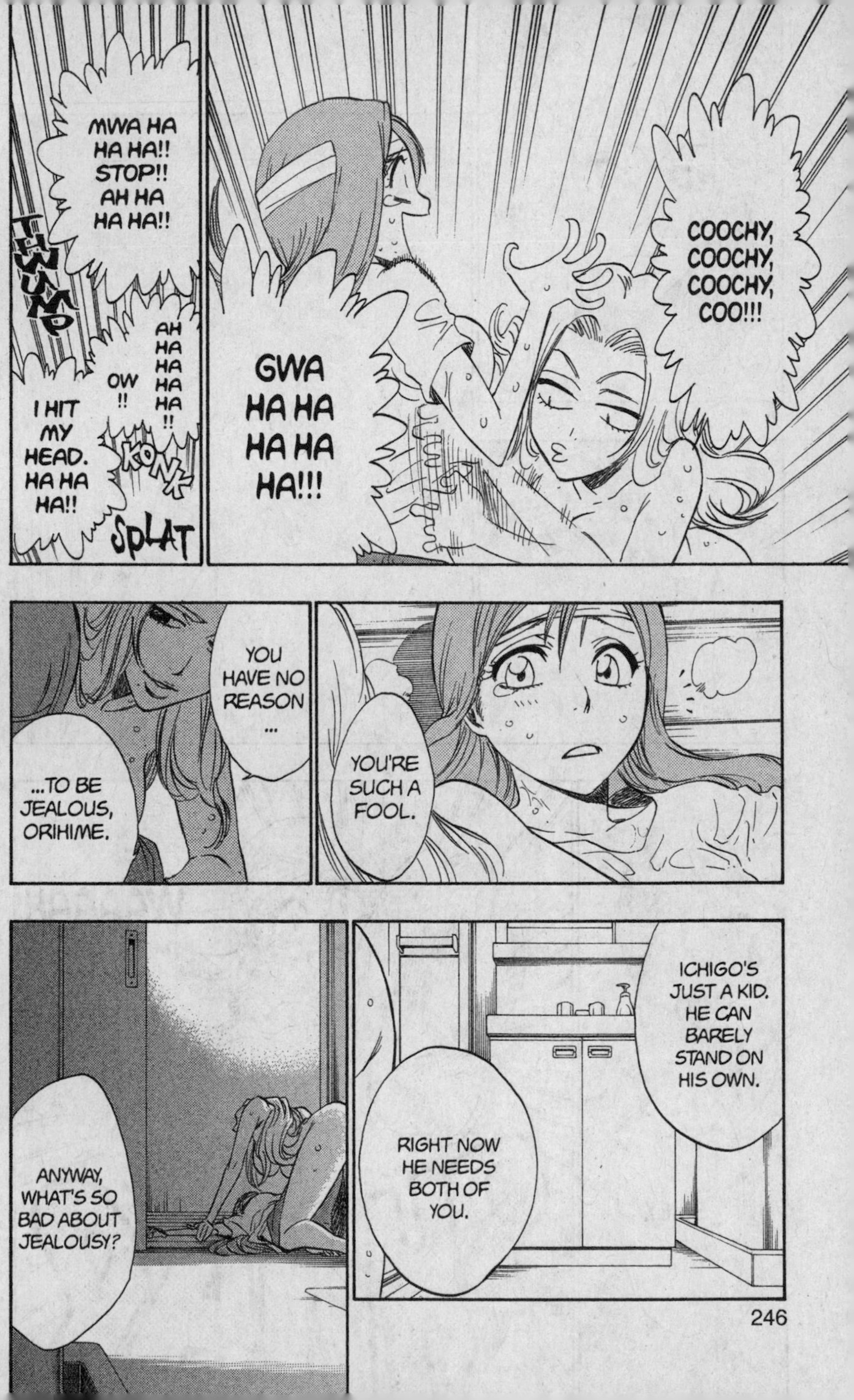
COOCHY, COOCHY, COOCHY, COO!!!
GWA HA HA HA HA HA!!!
MWA HA HA HA!! STOP!! AH HA HA HA!!
THWUMP
AH HA HA HA HA HA!!
OW!!
I HIT MY HEAD. HA HA HA!!
KONK
SPLAT
YOU'RE SUCH A FOOL.
YOU HAVE NO REASON...
...TO BE JEALOUS, ORIHIME.
ICHIGO'S JUST A KID. HE CAN BARELY STAND ON HIS OWN.
RIGHT NOW HE NEEDS BOTH OF YOU.
ANYWAY, WHAT'S SO BAD ABOUT JEALOUSY?

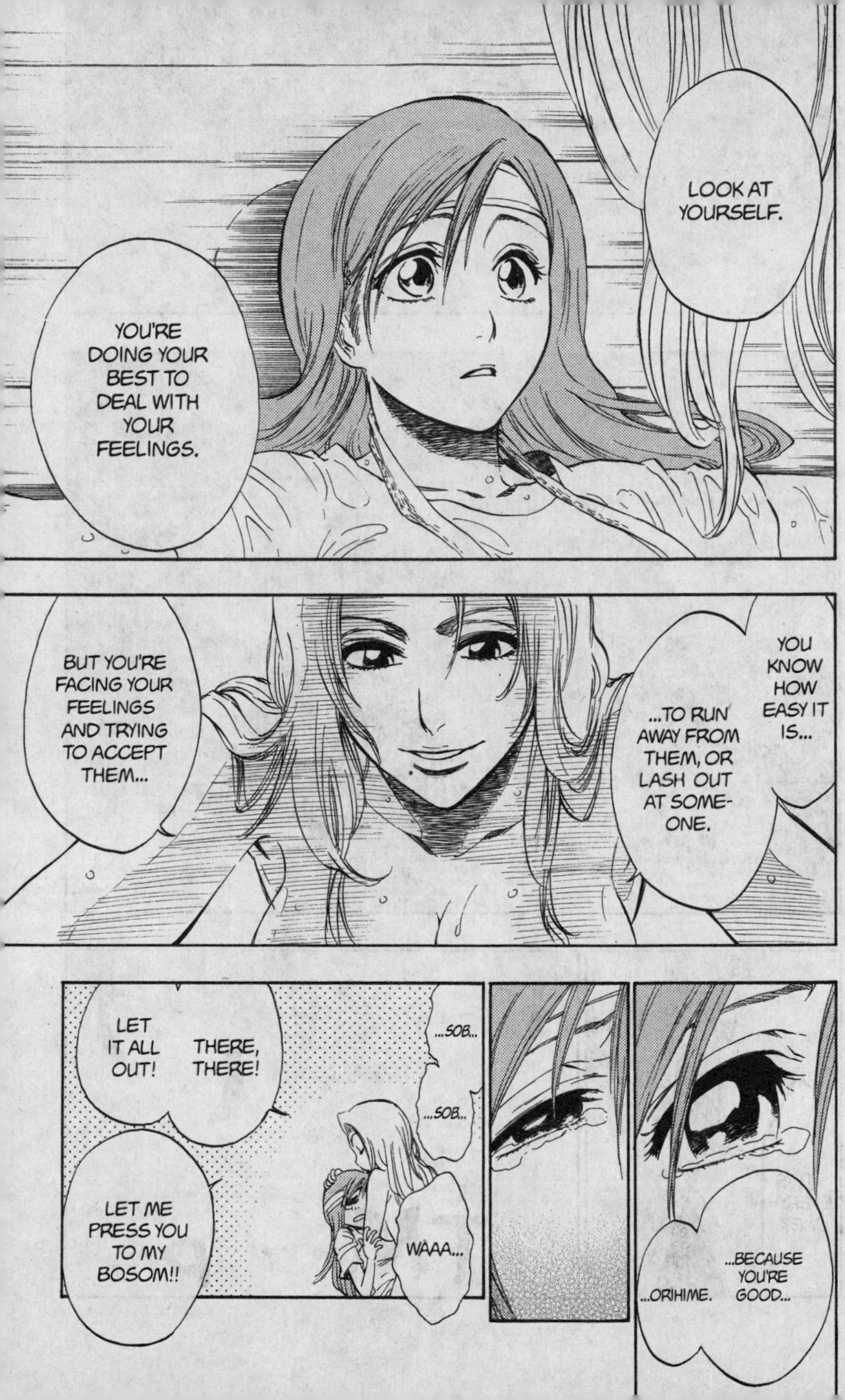
LOOK AT YOURSELF.
YOU'RE DOING YOUR BEST TO DEAL WITH YOUR FEELINGS.
YOU KNOW HOW EASY IT IS...
...TO RUN AWAY FROM THEM, OR LASH OUT AT SOME-ONE.
BUT YOU'RE FACING YOUR FEELINGS AND TRYING TO ACCEPT THEM...
...BECAUSE YOU'RE GOOD...
...ORIHIME.
...SOB...
...SOB...
THERE, THERE!
LET IT ALL OUT!
WAAA...
LET ME PRESS YOU TO MY BOSOM!!

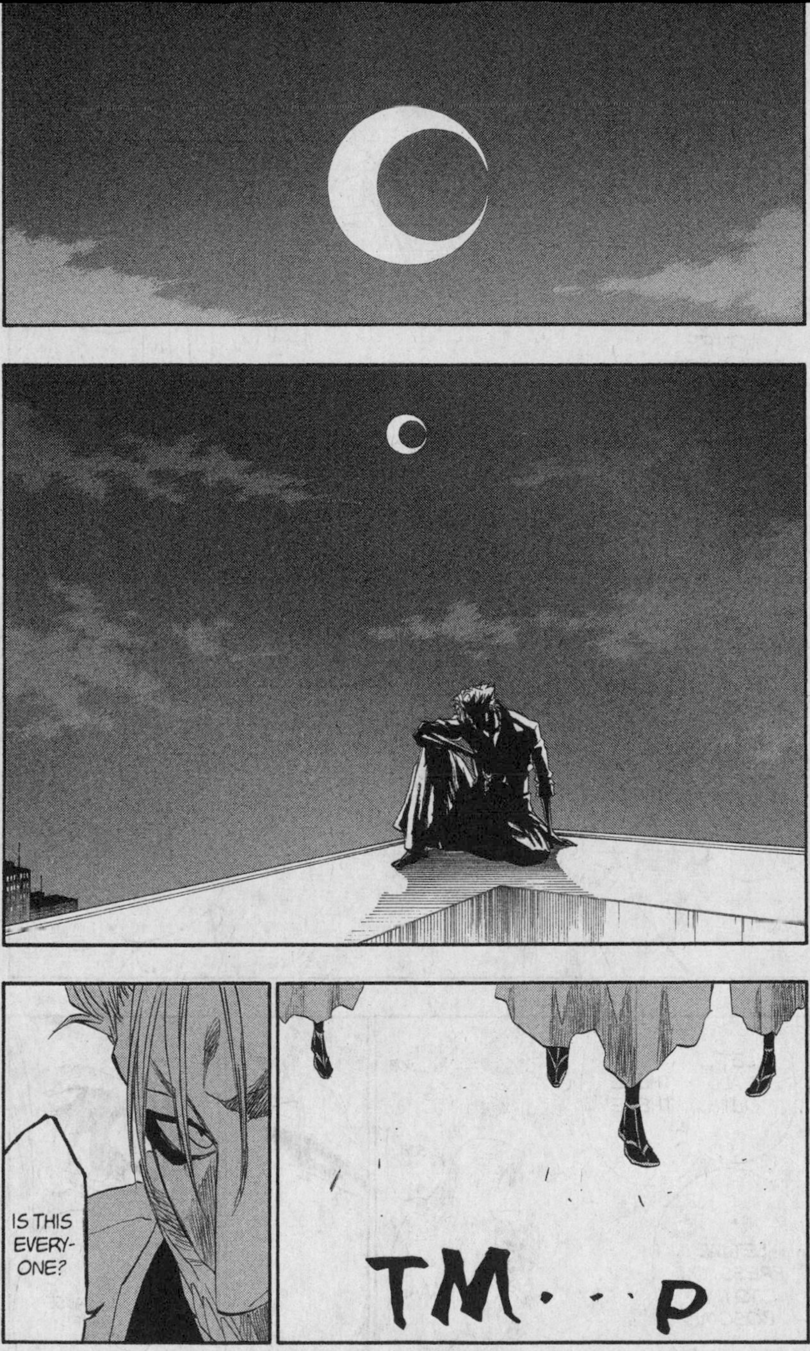
TM...P
IS THIS EVERY-ONE?

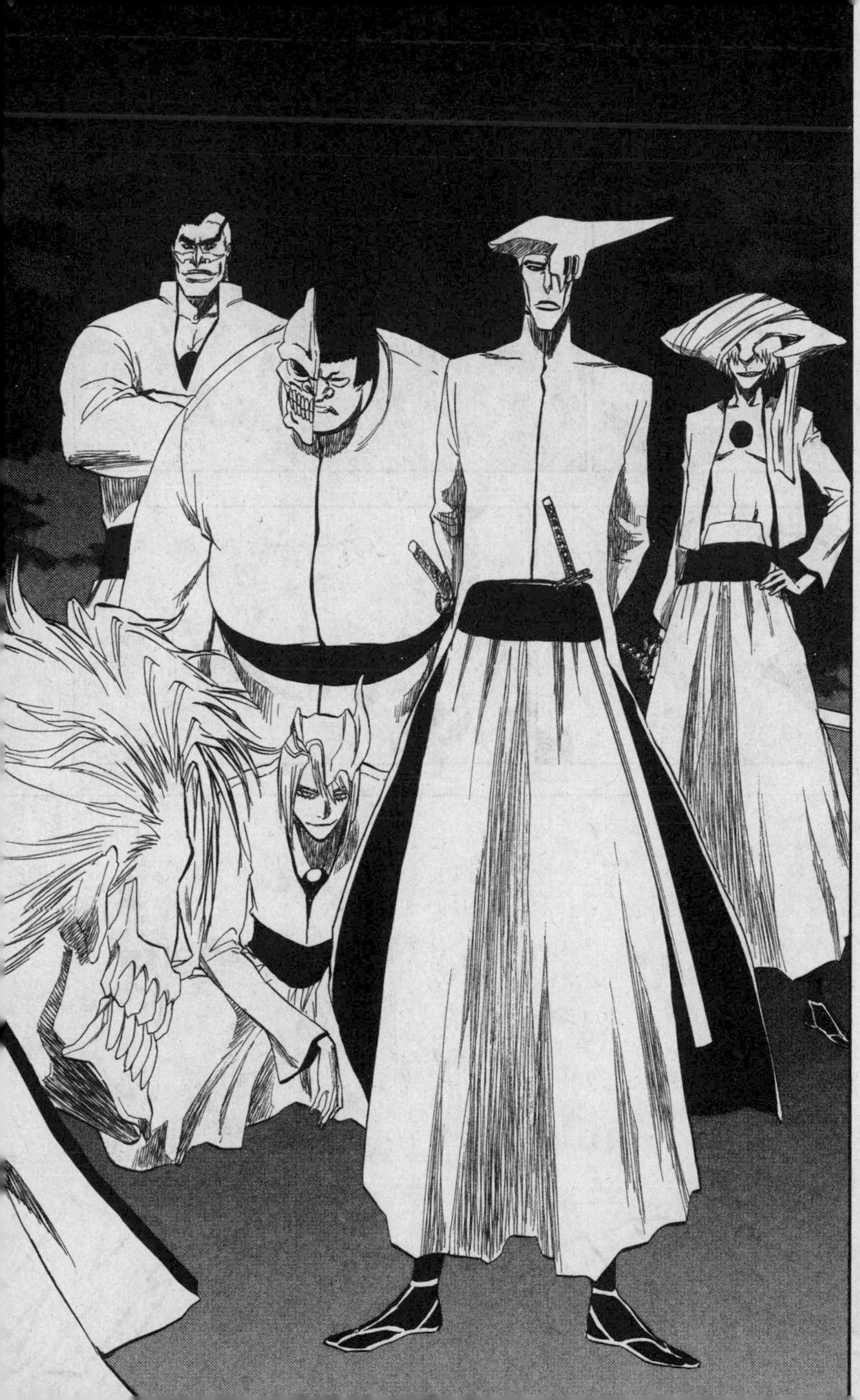

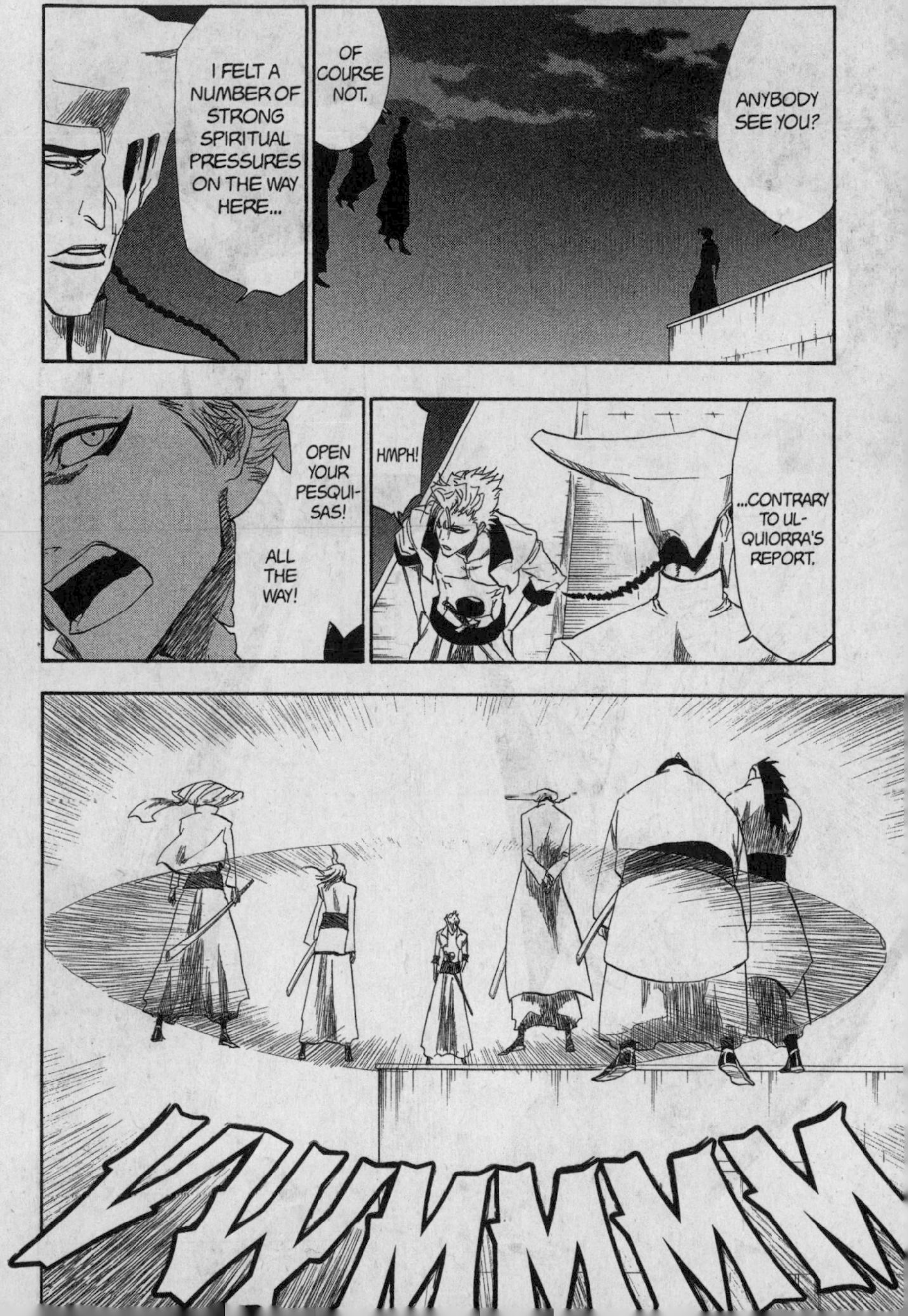
ANYBODY SEE YOU?
OF COURSE NOT.
I FELT A NUMBER OF STRONG SPIRITUAL PRESSURES ON THE WAY HERE...
...CONTRARY TO UL-QUIORRA'S REPORT.
HMPH!
OPEN YOUR PESQUI-SAS!
ALL THE WAY!
VUMMMM

READ THIS WAY

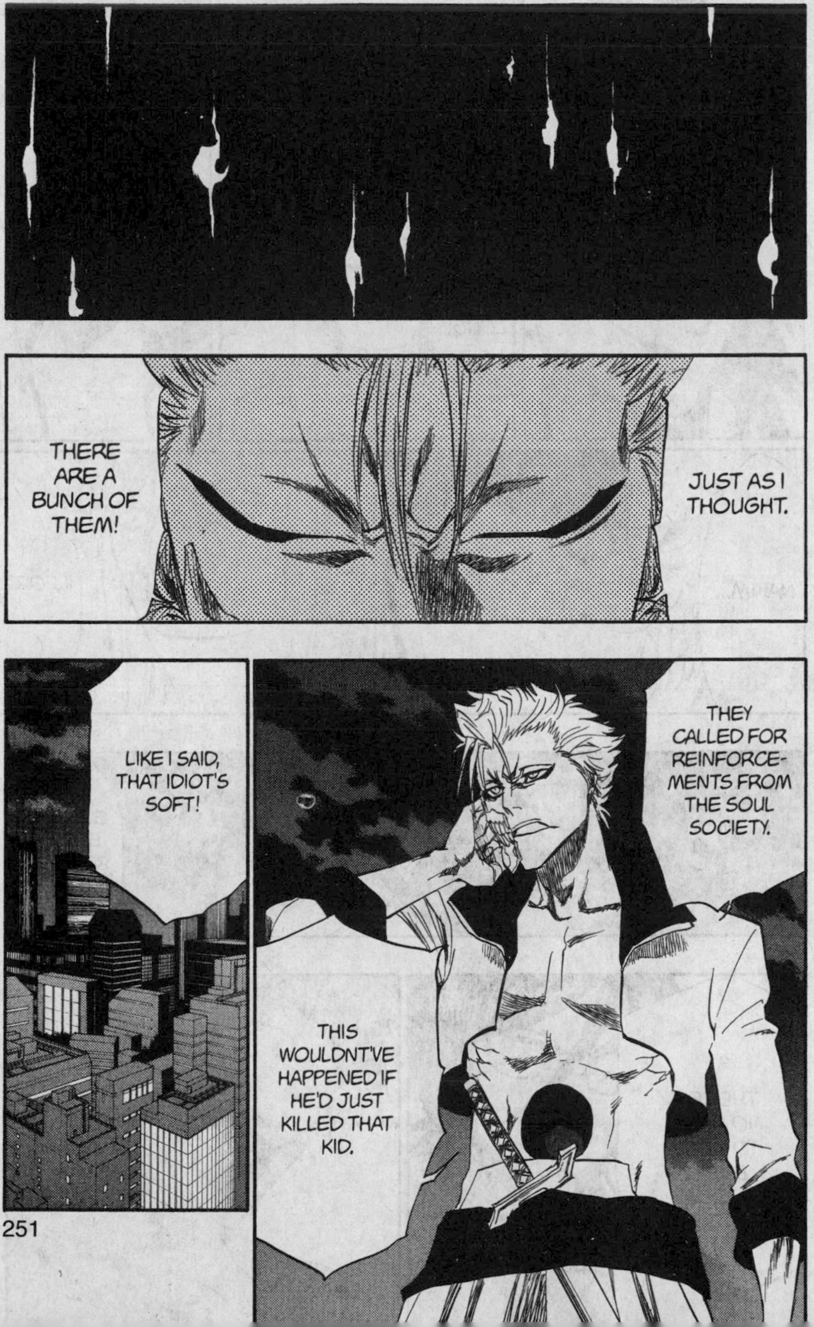
JUST AS I THOUGHT.
THERE ARE A BUNCH OF THEM!
THEY CALLED FOR REINFORCE-MENTS FROM THE SOUL SOCIETY.
THIS WOULDNT'VE HAPPENED IF HE'D JUST KILLED THAT KID.
LIKE I SAID, THAT IDIOT'S SOFT!

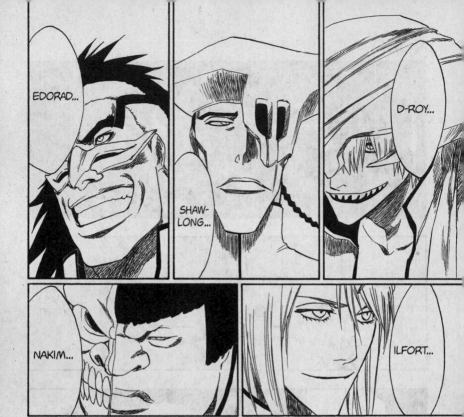

EDORAD...

SHAW-
LONG...

D-ROY...

NAKIM...

ILFORT...

EVERY-
BODY
READY?

THERE'S
NO NEED
TO HOLD
BACK.

READ THIS WAY

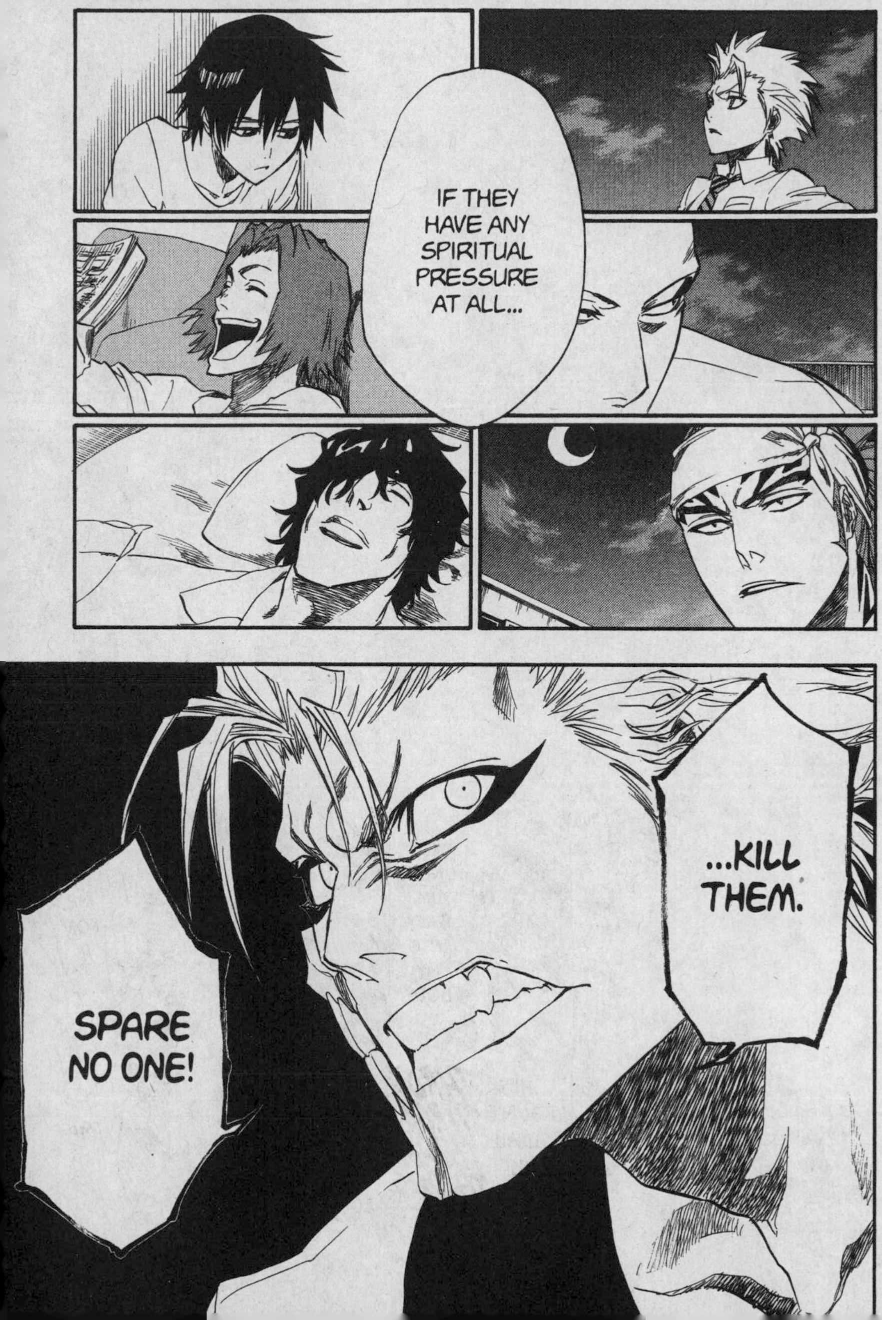
IF THEY HAVE ANY SPIRITUAL PRESSURE AT ALL...
...KILL THEM.
SPARE NO ONE!

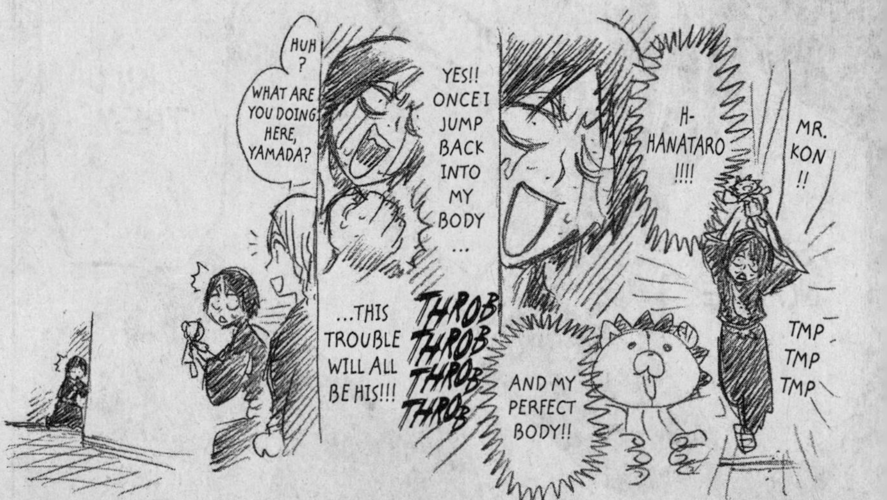
MR. KON!!
H-HANATARO!!!!
TMP TMP TMP
AND MY PERFECT BODY!!
YES!! ONCE I JUMP BACK INTO MY BODY...
THROB THROB THROB THROB
...THIS TROUBLE WILL ALL BE HIS!!!
HUH? WHAT ARE YOU DOING HERE, YAMADA?

200. Night of Sledgehammer

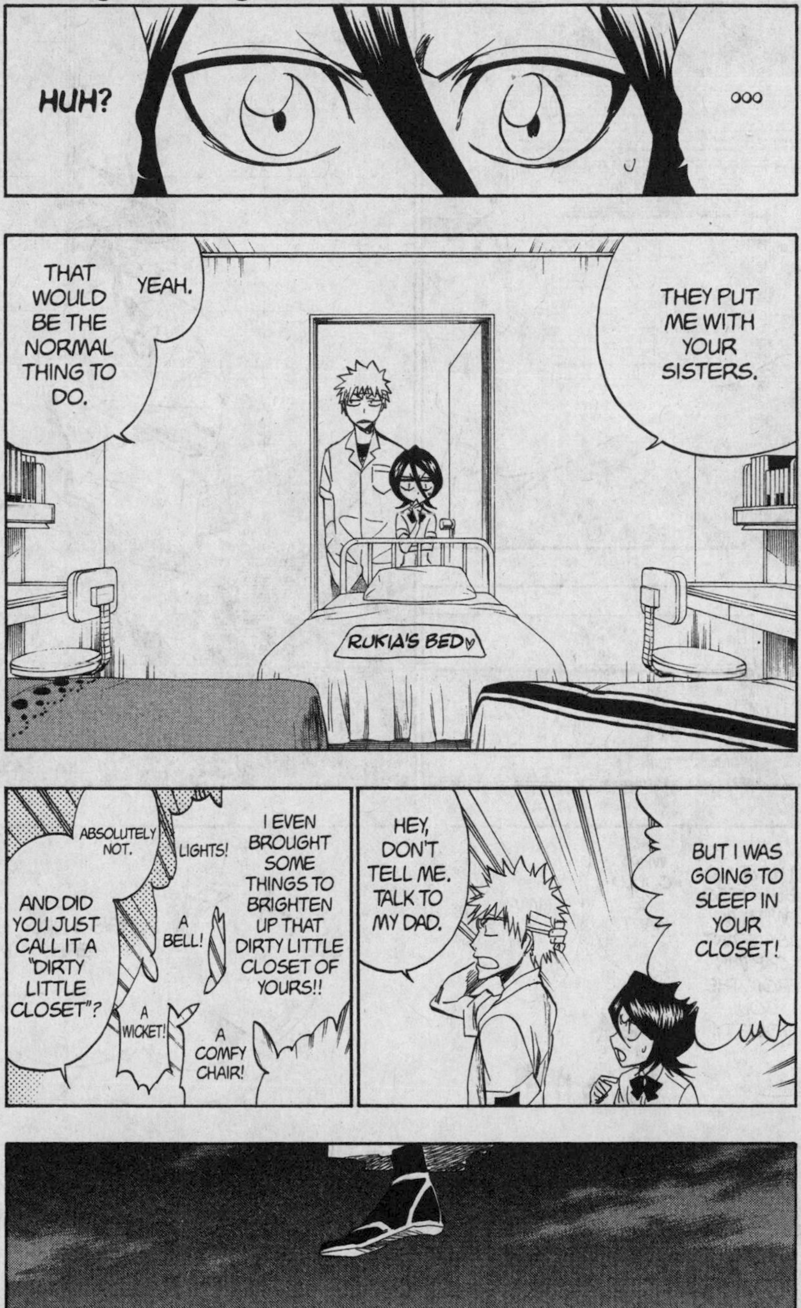
ooo
HUH?
THEY PUT ME WITH YOUR SISTERS.
YEAH.
THAT WOULD BE THE NORMAL THING TO DO.
RUKIA'S BED♥
BUT I WAS GOING TO SLEEP IN YOUR CLOSET!
HEY, DON'T TELL ME. TALK TO MY DAD.
I EVEN BROUGHT SOME THINGS TO BRIGHTEN UP THAT DIRTY LITTLE CLOSET OF YOURS!!
LIGHTS!
A BELL!
A WICKET!
A COMFY CHAIR!
ABSOLUTELY NOT.
AND DID YOU JUST CALL IT A "DIRTY LITTLE CLOSET"?

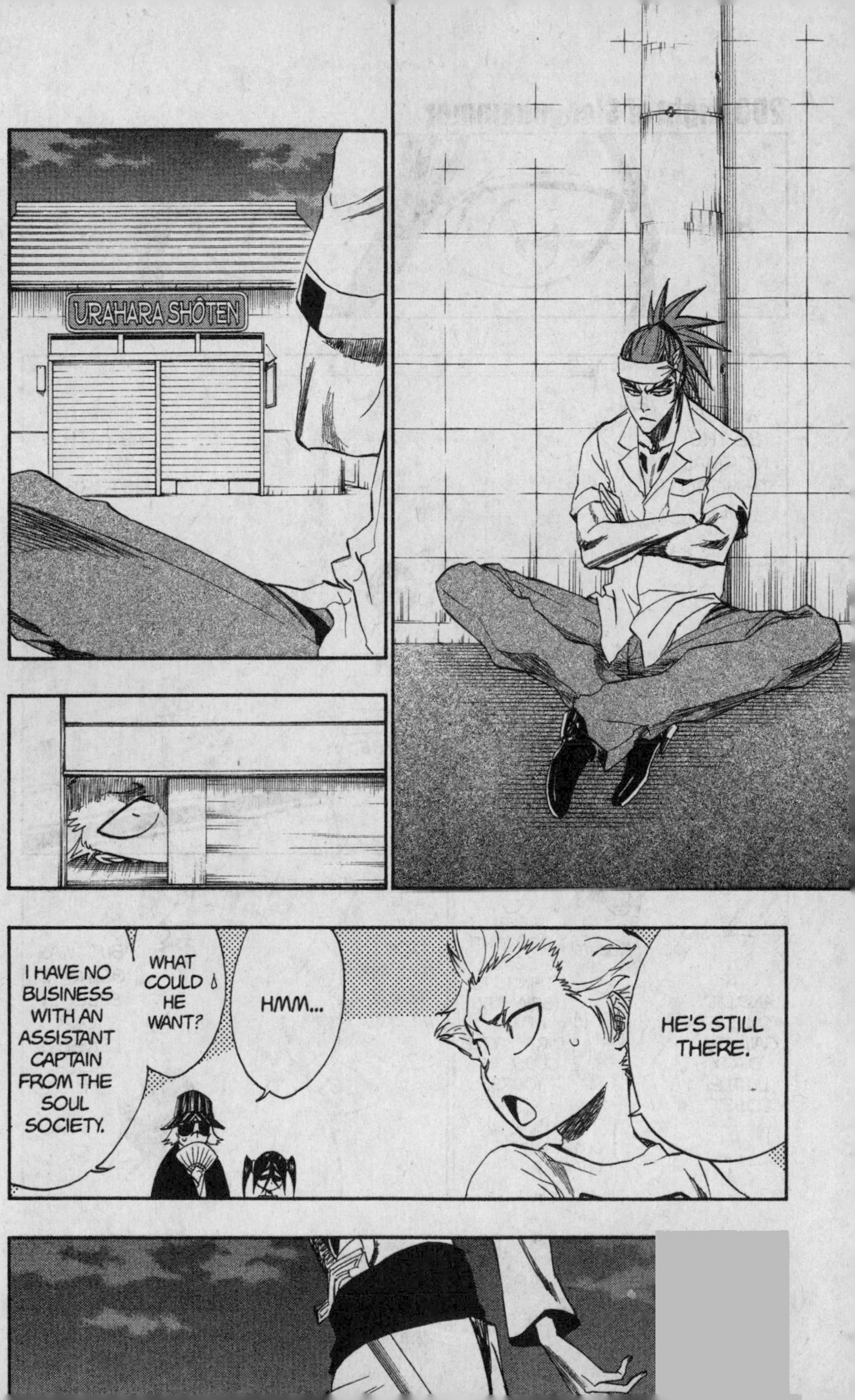
URAHARA SHÔTEN
HE'S STILL THERE.
HMM...
WHAT COULD HE WANT?
I HAVE NO BUSINESS WITH AN ASSISTANT CAPTAIN FROM THE SOUL SOCIETY.

READ THIS WAY

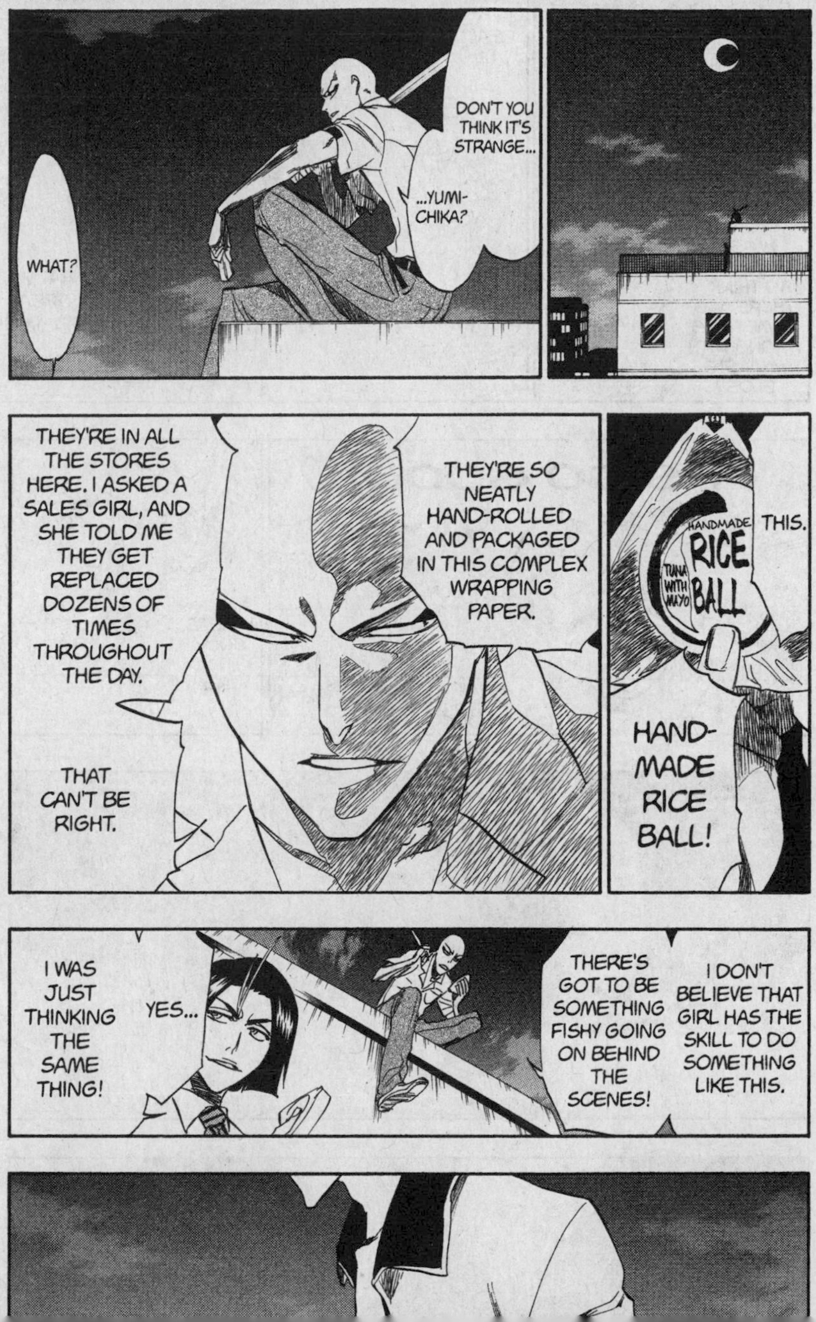
DON'T YOU THINK IT'S STRANGE...
...YUMI-CHIKA?
WHAT?
THIS.
HANDMADE RICE BALL TUNA WITH MAYO
HAND-MADE RICE BALL!
THEY'RE SO NEATLY HAND-ROLLED AND PACKAGED IN THIS COMPLEX WRAPPING PAPER.
THEY'RE IN ALL THE STORES HERE. I ASKED A SALES GIRL, AND SHE TOLD ME THEY GET REPLACED DOZENS OF TIMES THROUGHOUT THE DAY.
THAT CAN'T BE RIGHT.
I DON'T BELIEVE THAT GIRL HAS THE SKILL TO DO SOMETHING LIKE THIS.
THERE'S GOT TO BE SOMETHING FISHY GOING ON BEHIND THE SCENES!
YES...
I WAS JUST THINKING THE SAME THING!

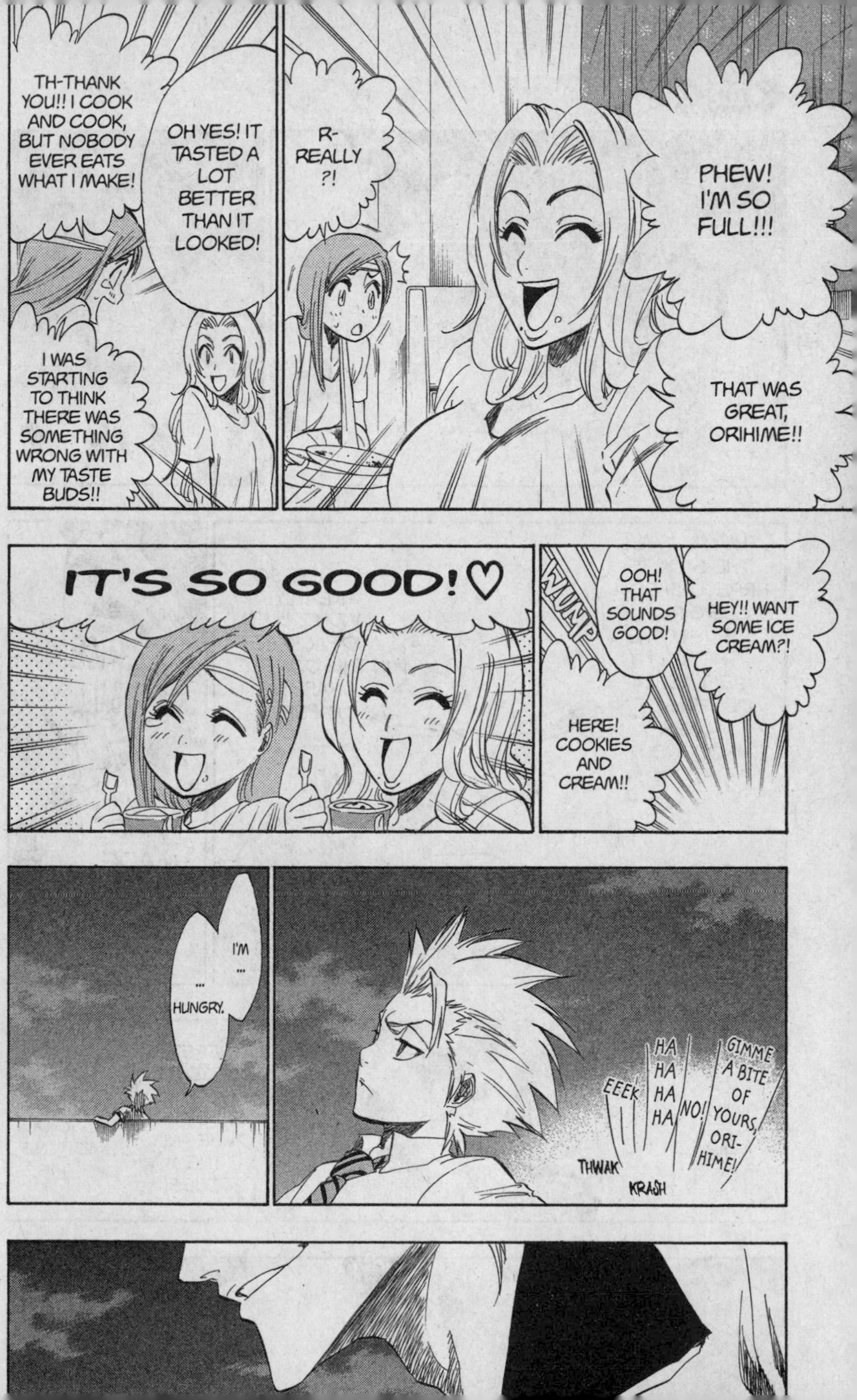
PHEW! I'M SO FULL!!!
THAT WAS GREAT, ORIHIME!!
R-REALLY?!
OH YES! IT TASTED A LOT BETTER THAN IT LOOKED!
TH-THANK YOU!! I COOK AND COOK, BUT NOBODY EVER EATS WHAT I MAKE!
I WAS STARTING TO THINK THERE WAS SOMETHING WRONG WITH MY TASTE BUDS!!
HEY!! WANT SOME ICE CREAM?!
OOH! THAT SOUNDS GOOD!
WUMP
HERE! COOKIES AND CREAM!!
IT'S SO GOOD! ♡
GIMME A BITE OF YOURS, ORI-HIME!
NO!
HA HA HA HA
EEEK
THWAK
KRASH
I'M ...
... HUNGRY.

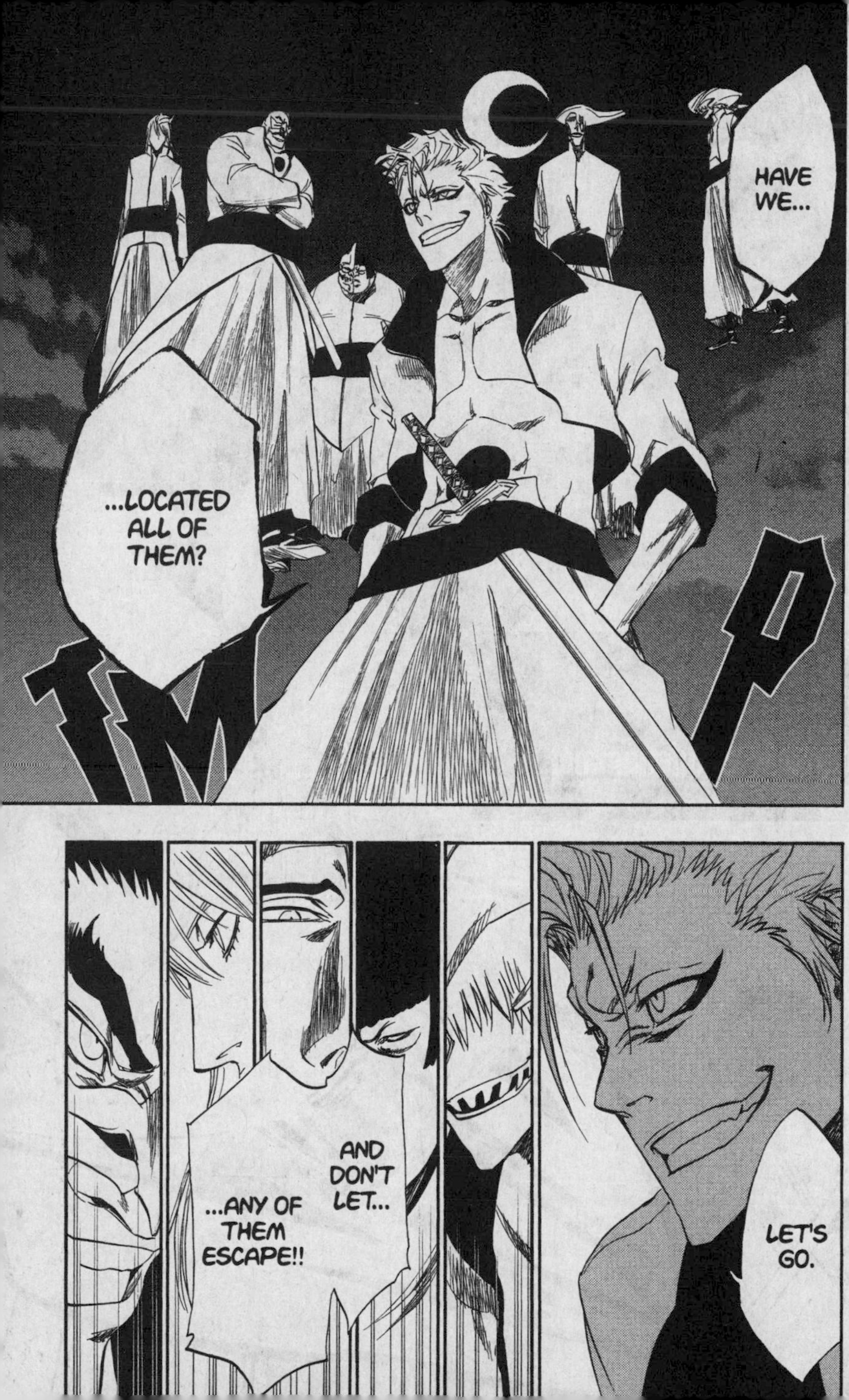
HAVE WE...
...LOCATED ALL OF THEM?
TMP
LET'S GO.
AND DON'T LET...
...ANY OF THEM ESCAPE!!

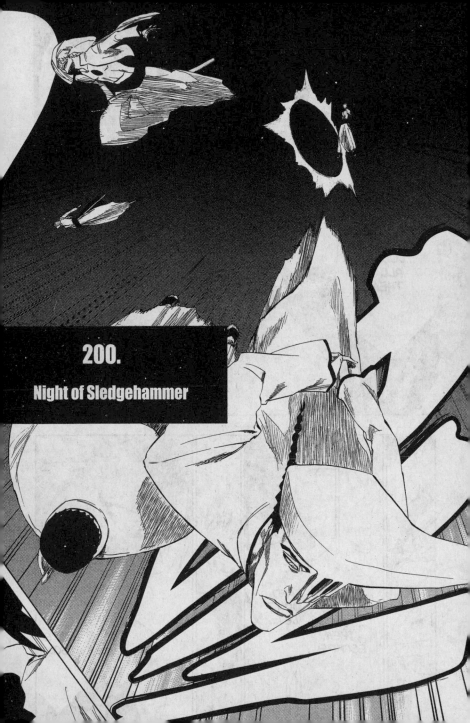

200.

Night of Sledgehammer

BLEACH
-ブリーチ-

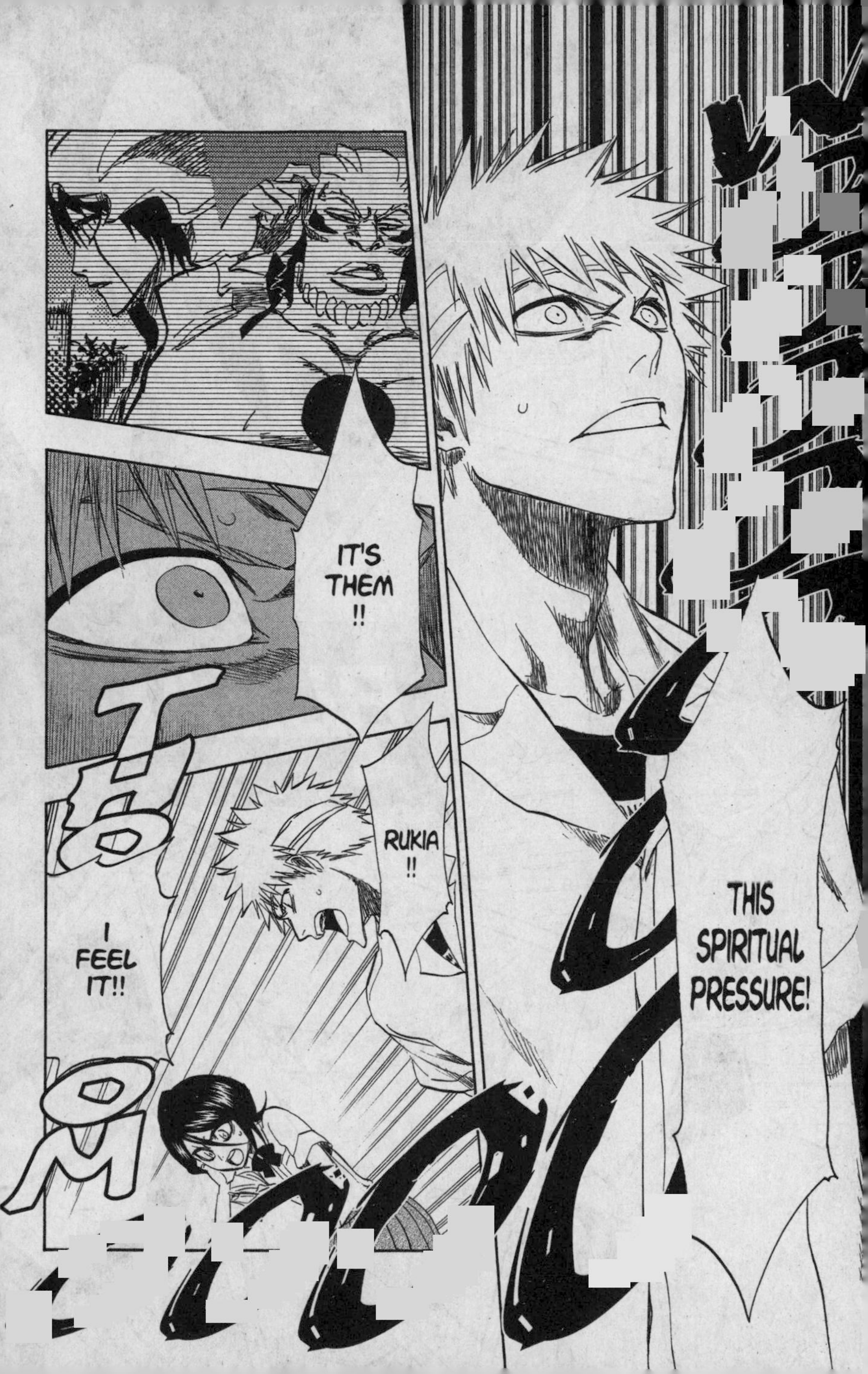
THIS SPIRITUAL PRESSURE!
IT'S THEM!!
RUKIA!!
I FEEL IT!!

READ THIS WAY

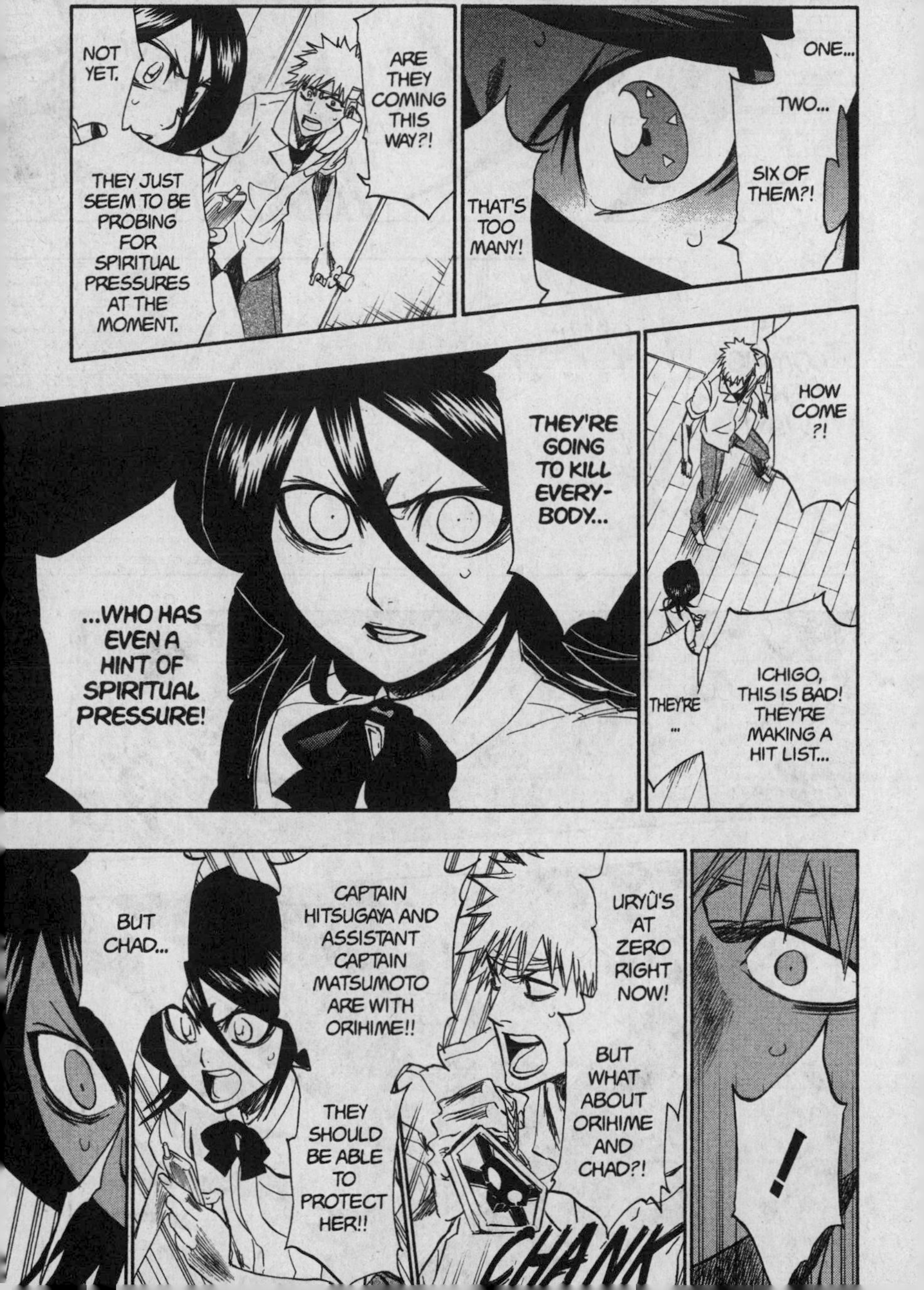

ONE...
TWO...
SIX OF THEM?!
THAT'S TOO MANY!
ARE THEY COMING THIS WAY?!
NOT YET.
THEY JUST SEEM TO BE PROBING FOR SPIRITUAL PRESSURES AT THE MOMENT.
HOW COME?!
ICHIGO, THIS IS BAD! THEY'RE MAKING A HIT LIST...
THEY'RE...
THEY'RE GOING TO KILL EVERYBODY...
...WHO HAS EVEN A HINT OF SPIRITUAL PRESSURE!
!
URYÛ'S AT ZERO RIGHT NOW!
BUT WHAT ABOUT ORIHIME AND CHAD?!
CAPTAIN HITSUGAYA AND ASSISTANT CAPTAIN MATSUMOTO ARE WITH ORIHIME!!
THEY SHOULD BE ABLE TO PROTECT HER!!
BUT CHAD...
CHANK

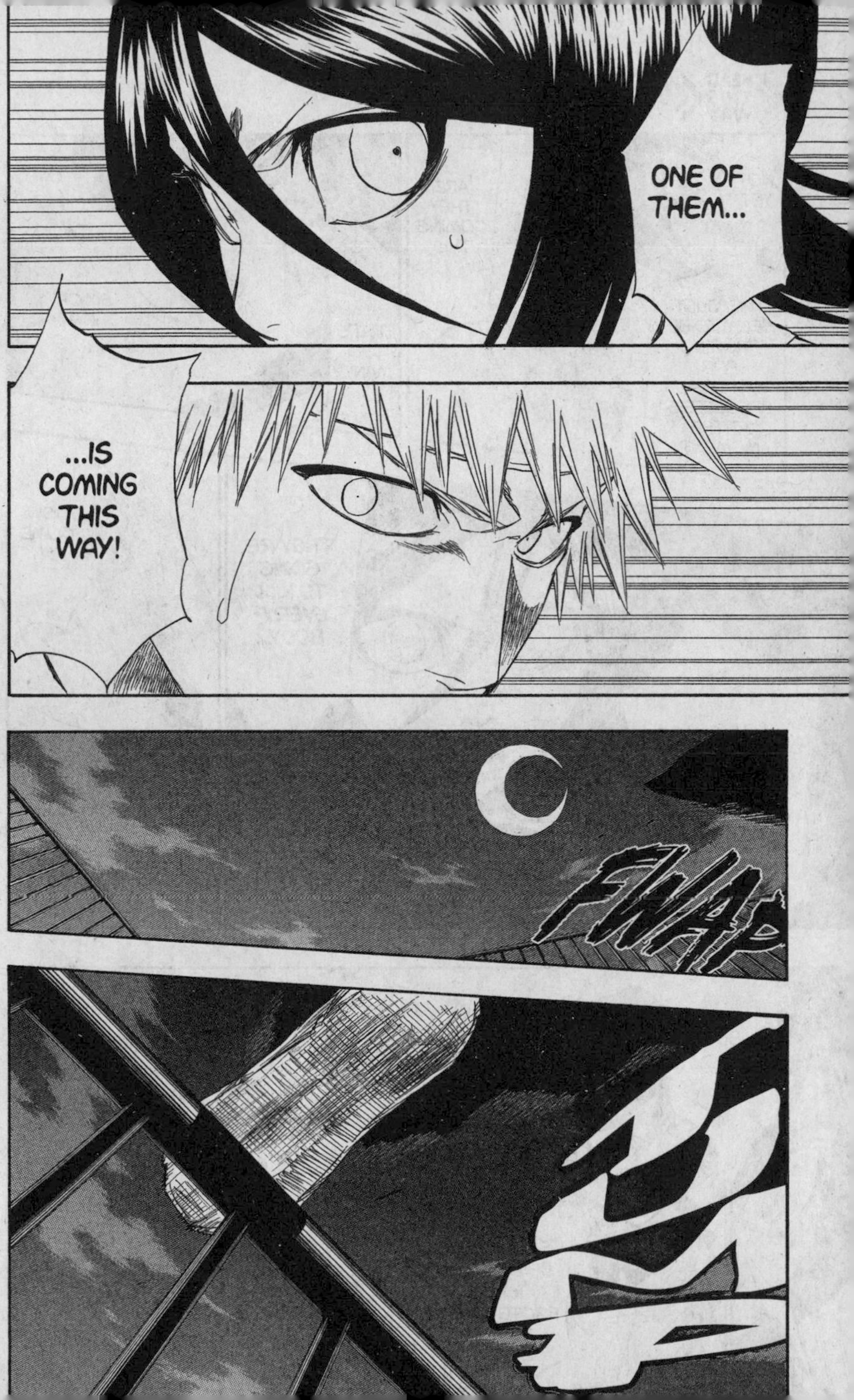
ONE OF THEM...
...IS COMING THIS WAY!
FWAP

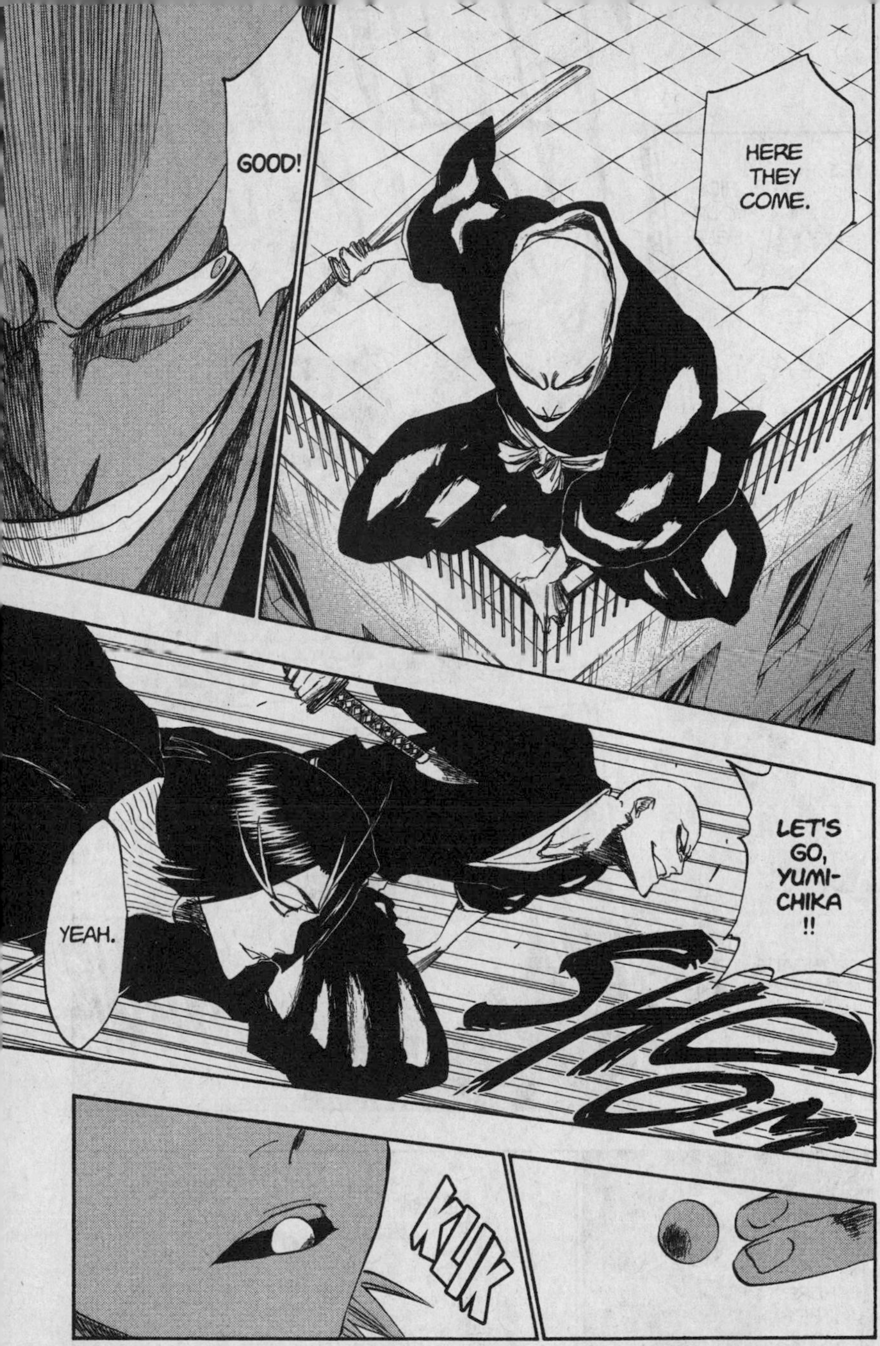
HERE THEY COME.
GOOD!
LET'S GO, YUMI-CHIKA!!
YEAH.
SHOOM
KLIK

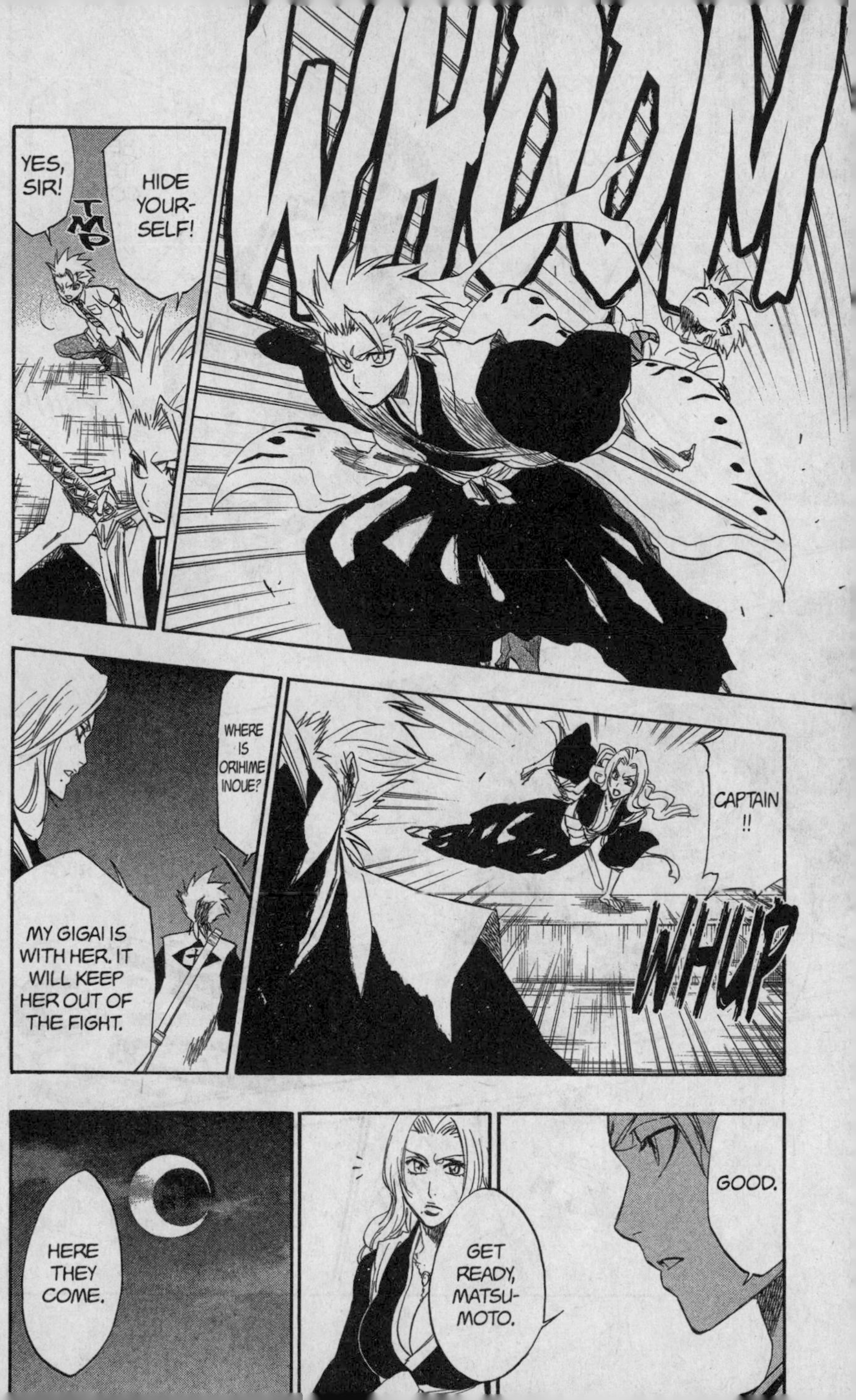
WHOOM
HIDE YOUR-SELF!
YES, SIR!
TMP
CAPTAIN!!
WHUP
WHERE IS ORIHIME INOUE?
MY GIGAI IS WITH HER. IT WILL KEEP HER OUT OF THE FIGHT.
GOOD.
GET READY, MATSU-MOTO.
HERE THEY COME.

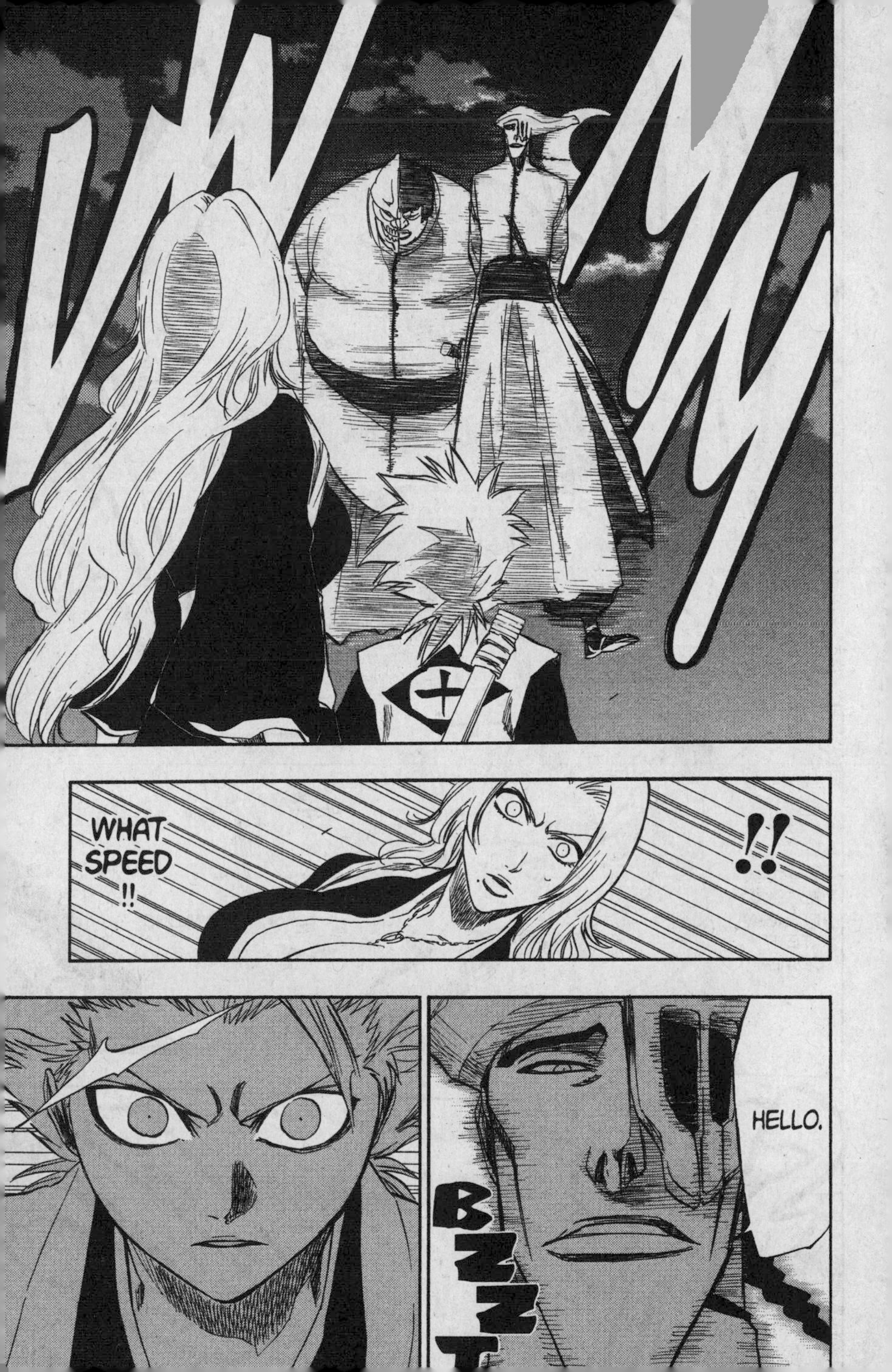

WHAT SPEED !!
!!
HELLO.
BZZT

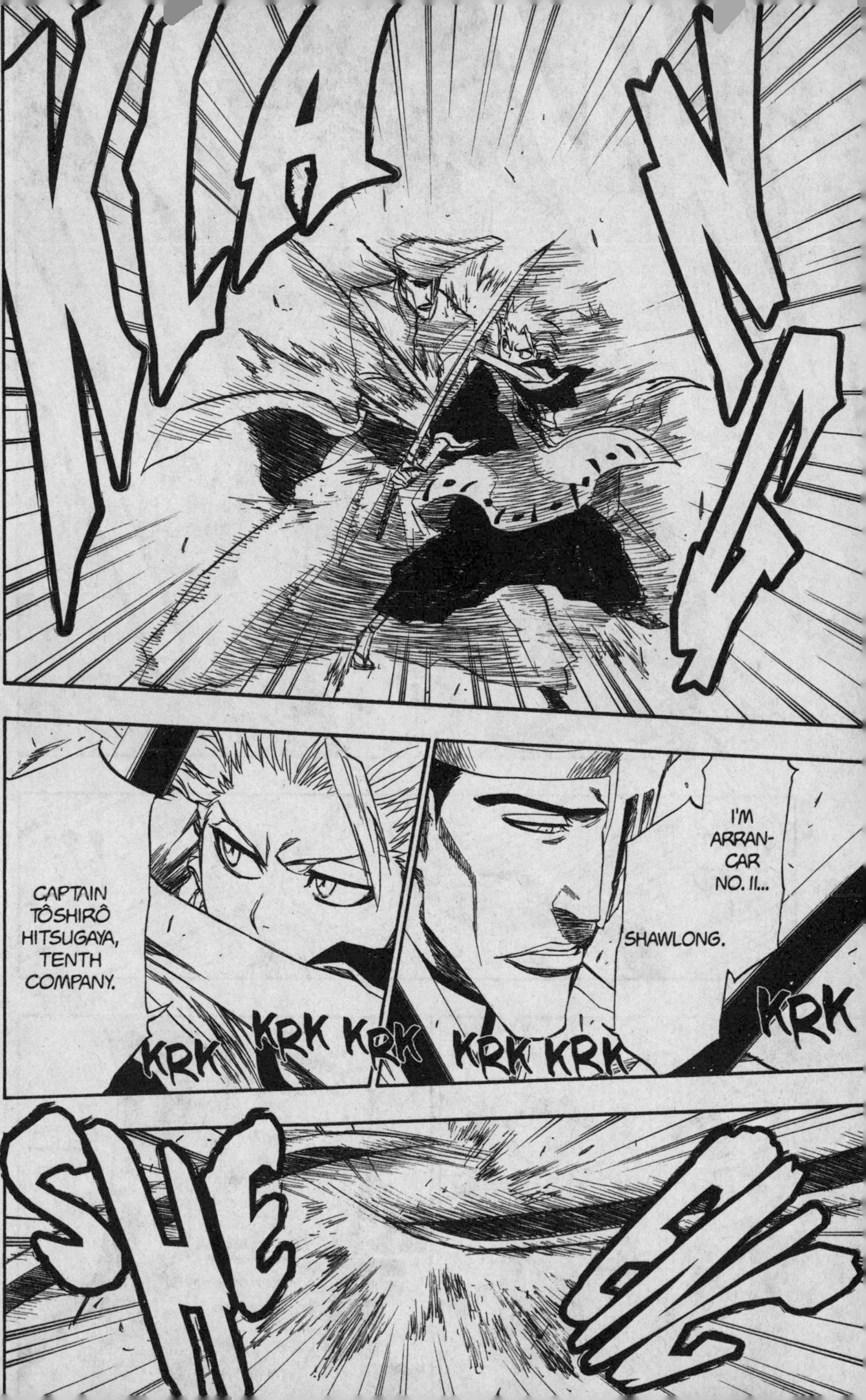
I'M ARRAN-CAR NO. 11...
SHAWLONG.
CAPTAIN TÔSHIRÔ HITSUGAYA, TENTH COMPANY.
KRK
KRK KRK
KRK KRK KRK KRK

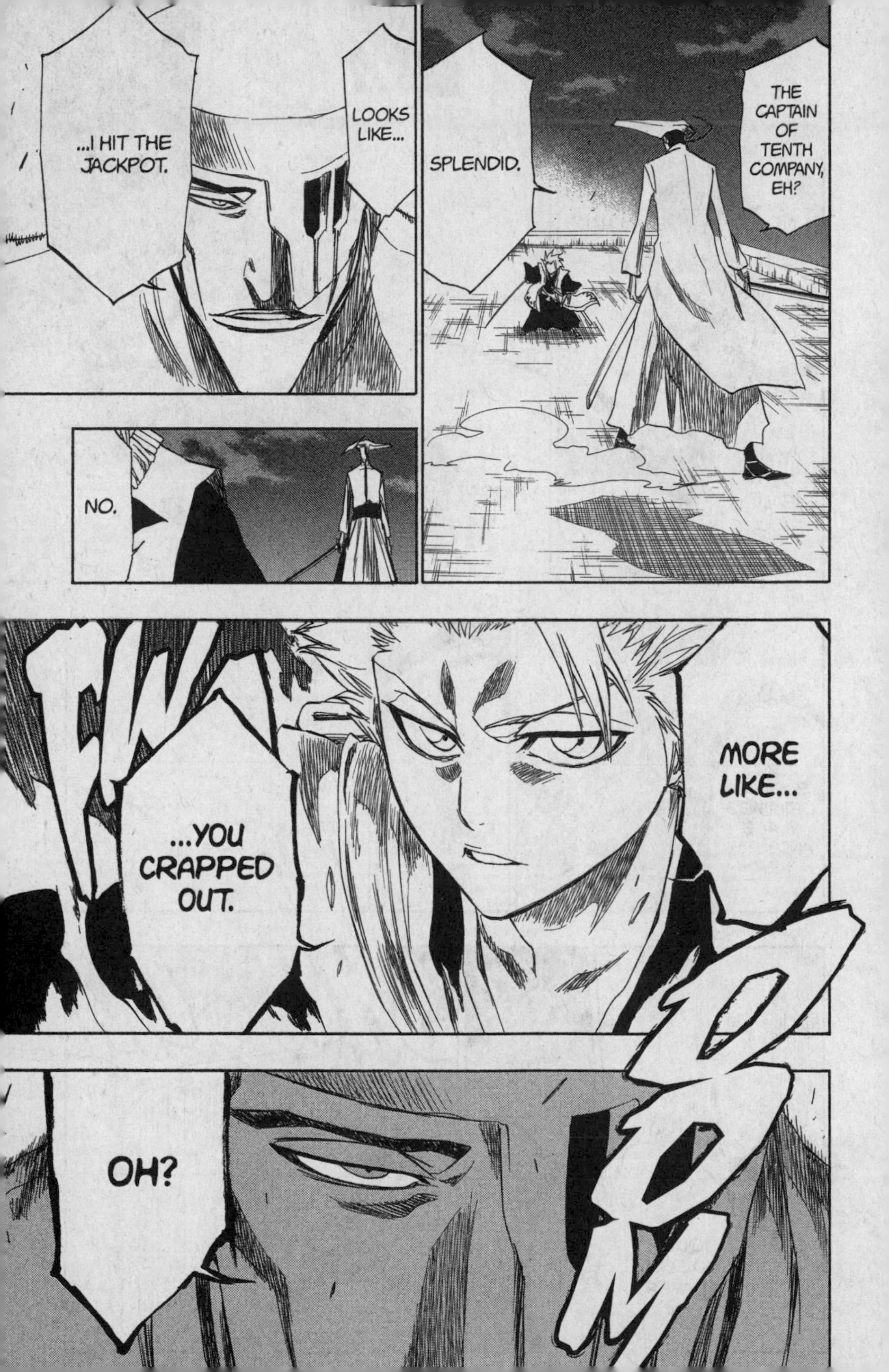
THE CAPTAIN OF TENTH COMPANY, EH?
SPLENDID.
LOOKS LIKE...
...I HIT THE JACKPOT.
NO.
MORE LIKE...
...YOU CRAPPED OUT.
OH?

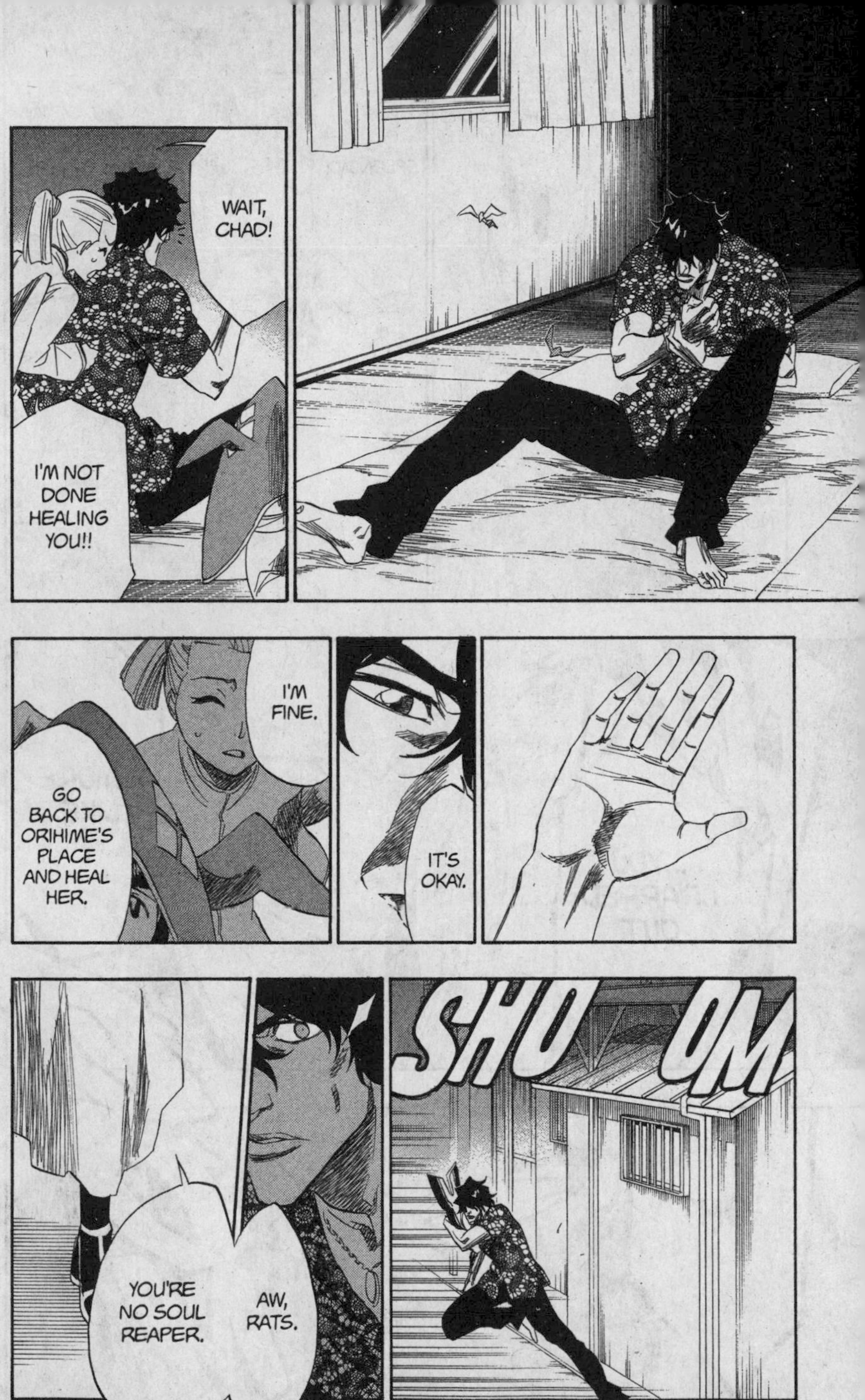
WAIT, CHAD!
I'M NOT DONE HEALING YOU!!
I'M FINE.
IT'S OKAY.
GO BACK TO ORIHIME'S PLACE AND HEAL HER.
SHO OM
AW, RATS.
YOU'RE NO SOUL REAPER.

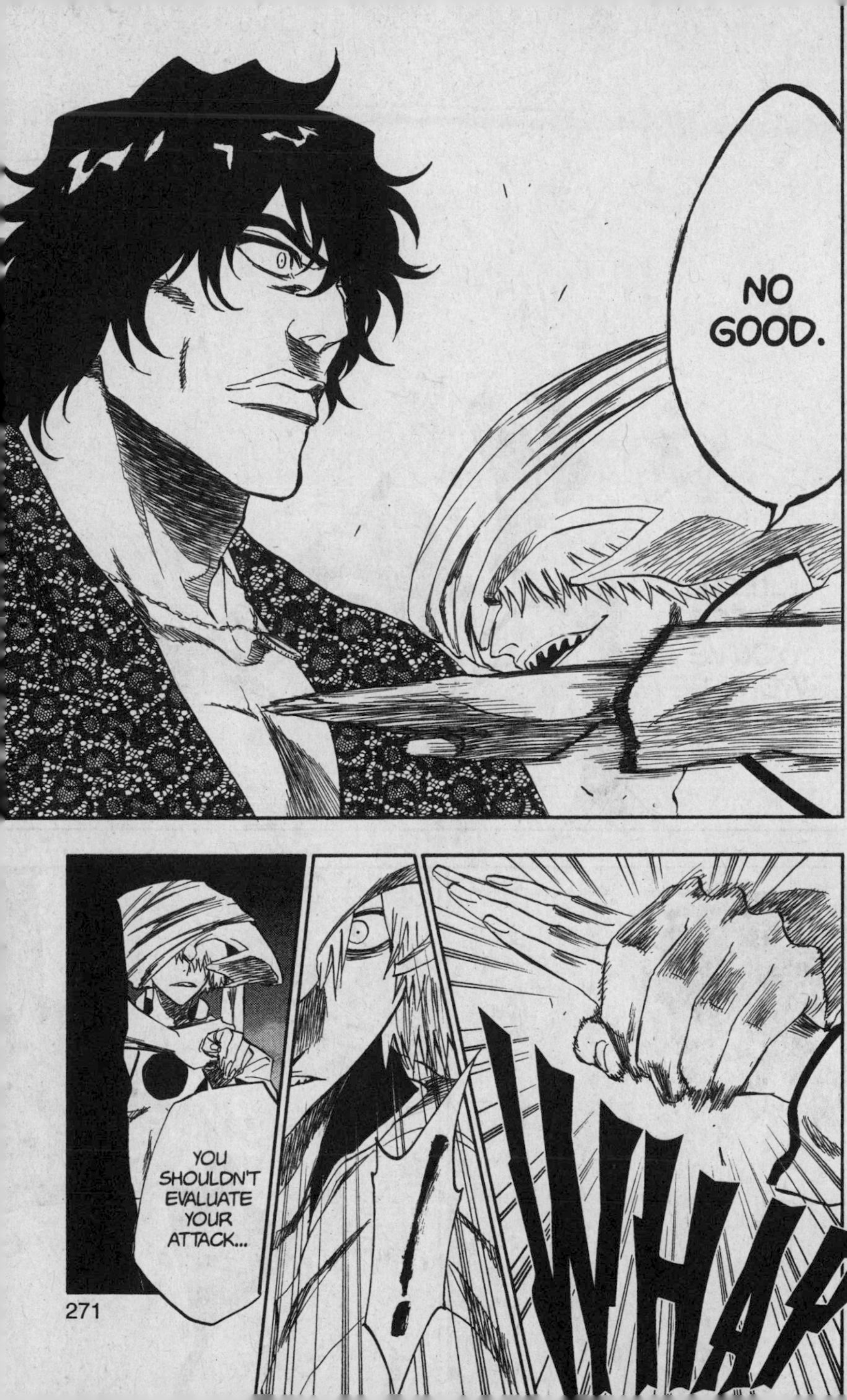
NO GOOD.
WHAP
!
YOU SHOULDN'T EVALUATE YOUR ATTACK...

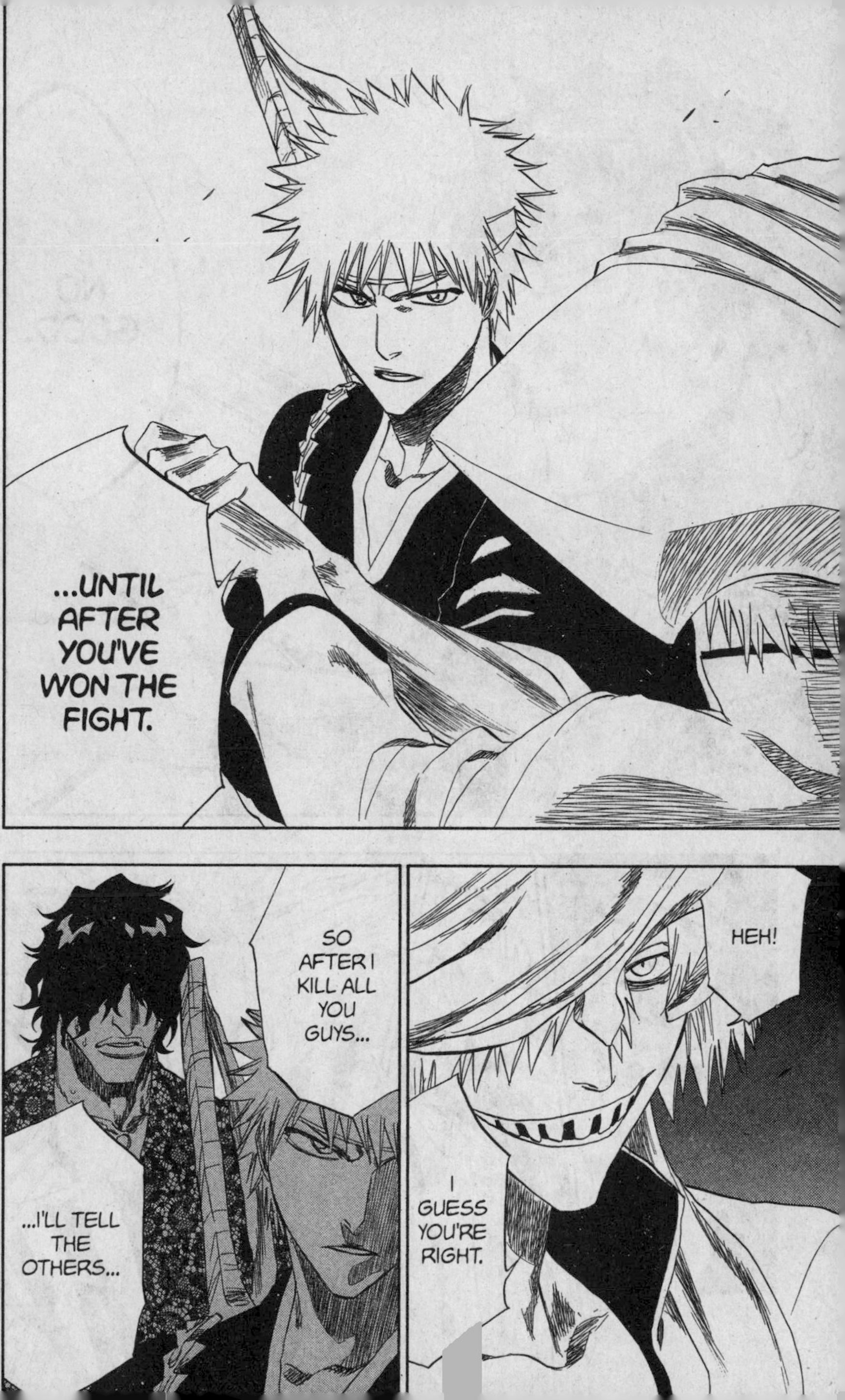
...UNTIL AFTER YOU'VE WON THE FIGHT.
HEH!
I GUESS YOU'RE RIGHT.
SO AFTER I KILL ALL YOU GUYS...
...I'LL TELL THE OTHERS...

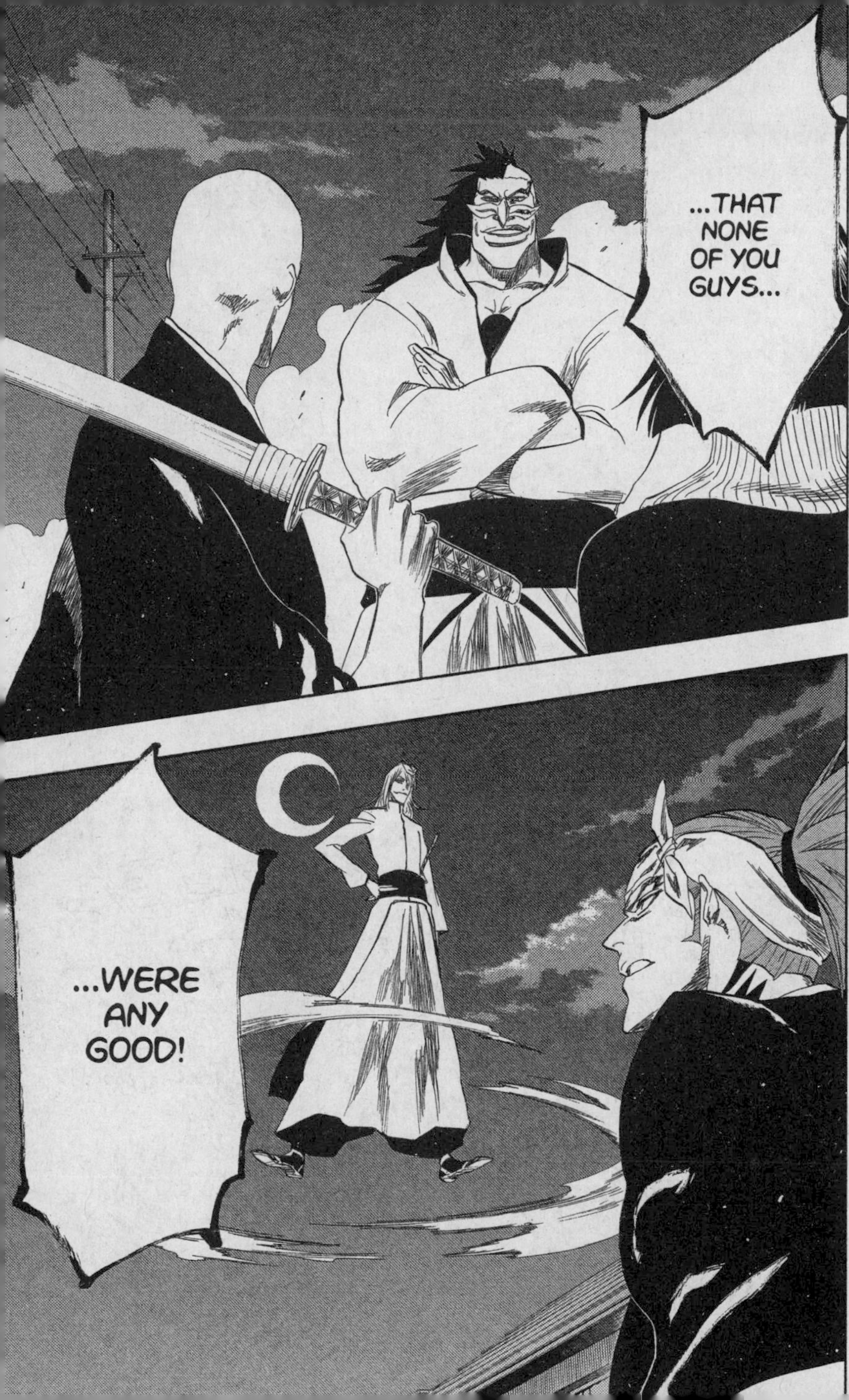
...THAT NONE OF YOU GUYS...
...WERE ANY GOOD!

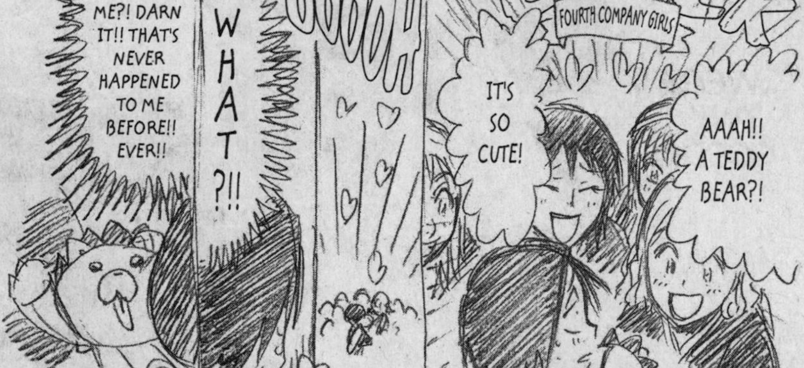
EEEEK
FOURTH COMPANY GIRLS
AAAH!! A TEDDY BEAR?!
IT'S SO CUTE!
OOOOH
WHAT?!!
THEY LIKE ME?! DARN IT!! THAT'S NEVER HAPPENED TO ME BEFORE!! EVER!!
SWUFF

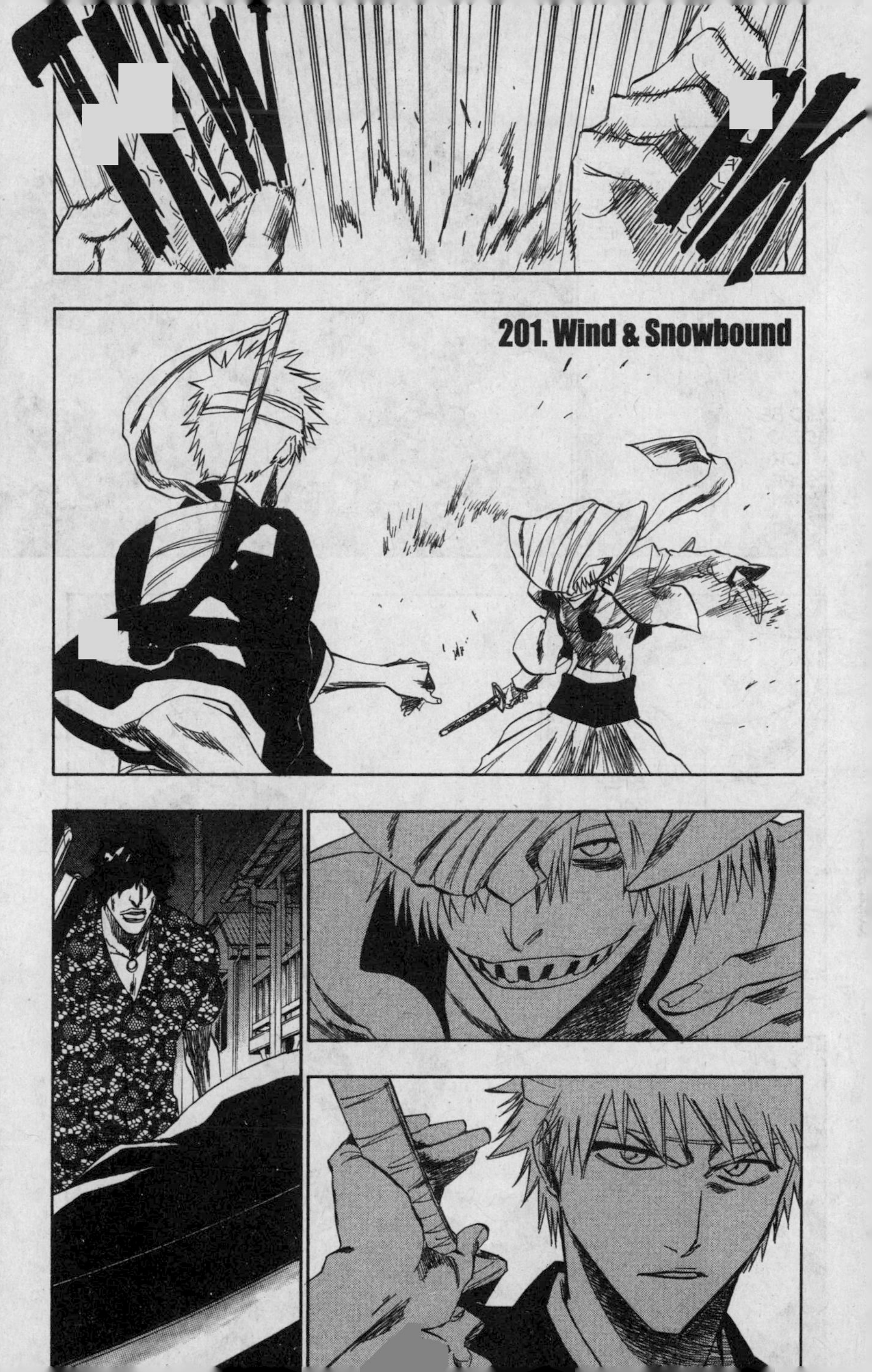
201. Wind & Snowbound

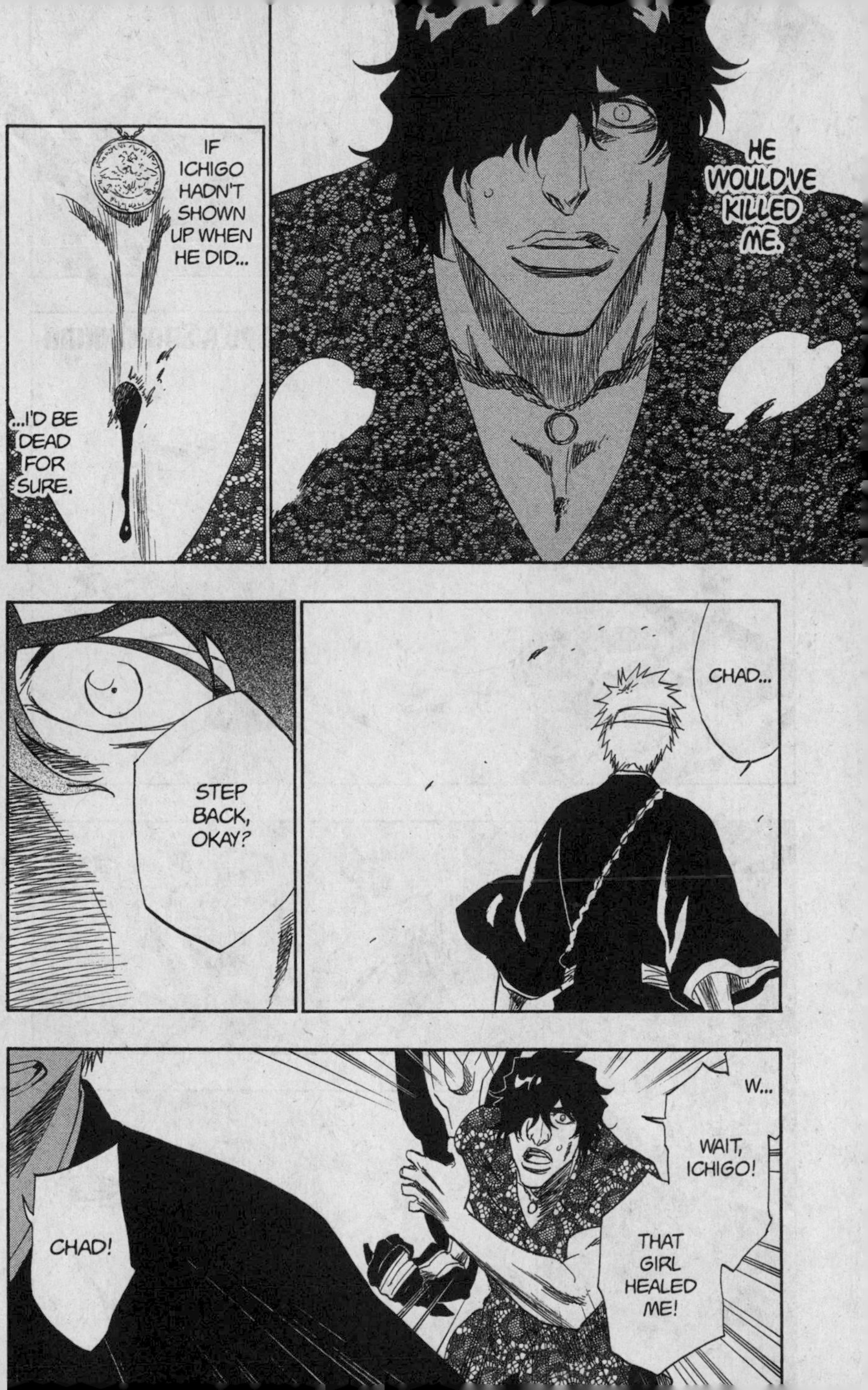
HE WOULD'VE KILLED ME.
IF ICHIGO HADN'T SHOWN UP WHEN HE DID...
...I'D BE DEAD FOR SURE.
CHAD...
STEP BACK, OKAY?
W...
WAIT, ICHIGO!
THAT GIRL HEALED ME!
CHAD!

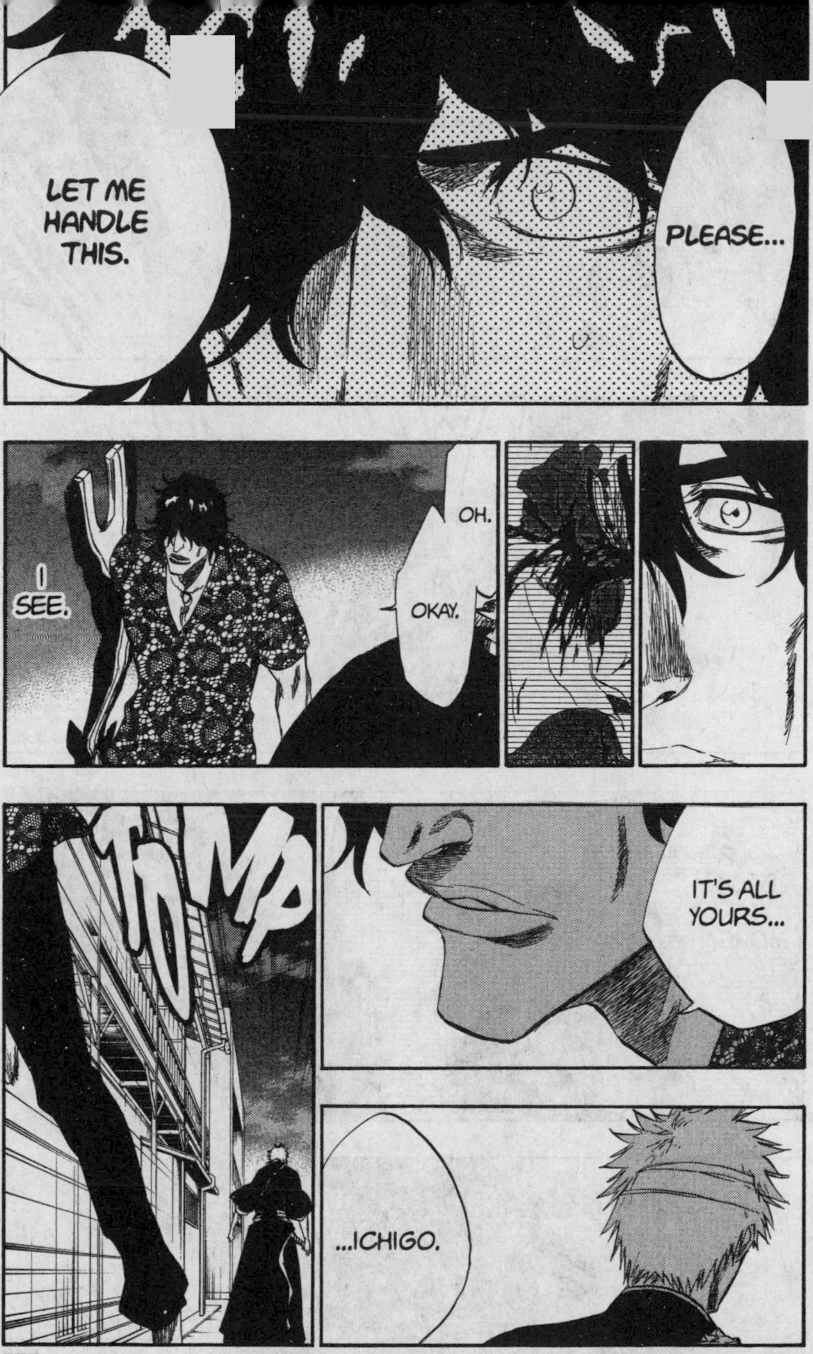
PLEASE...
LET ME HANDLE THIS.
OH.
OKAY.
I SEE.
IT'S ALL YOURS...
...ICHIGO.
TOMP

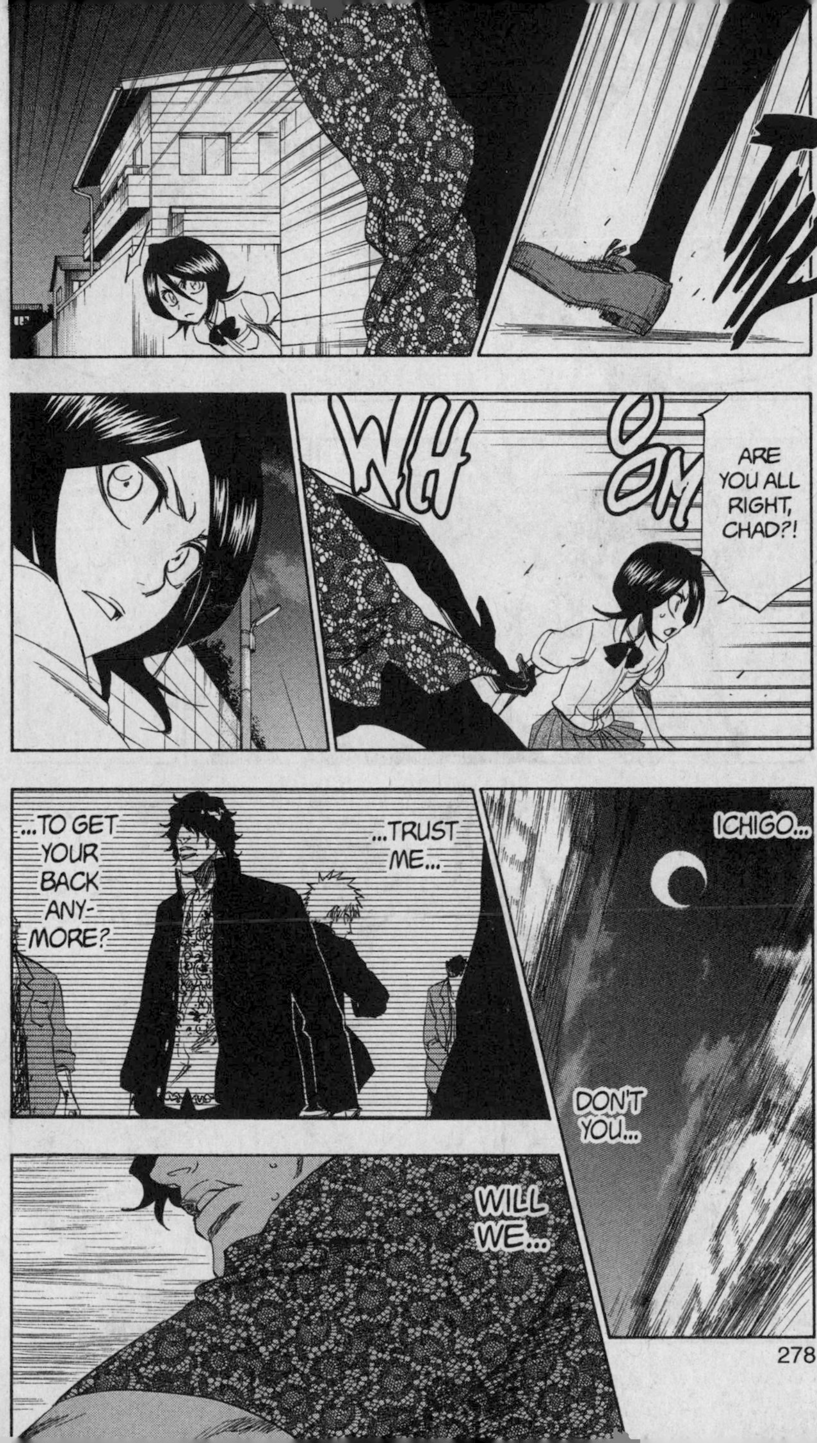
TMP
WHOOM
ARE YOU ALL RIGHT, CHAD?!
ICHIGO...
DON'T YOU...
...TRUST ME...
...TO GET YOUR BACK ANY-MORE?
WILL WE...

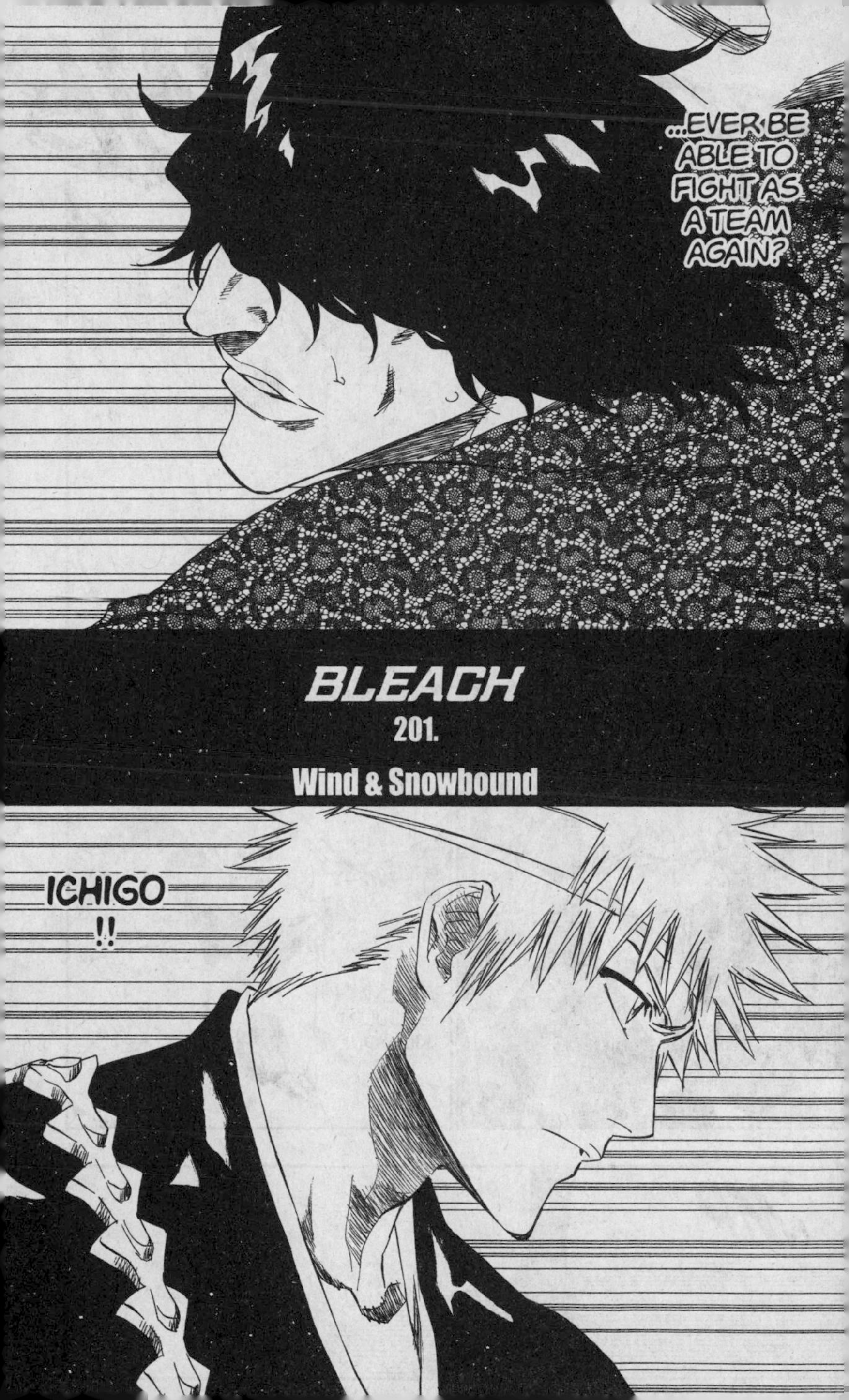
...EVER BE ABLE TO FIGHT AS A TEAM AGAIN?
BLEACH
201.
Wind & Snowbound
ICHIGO !!

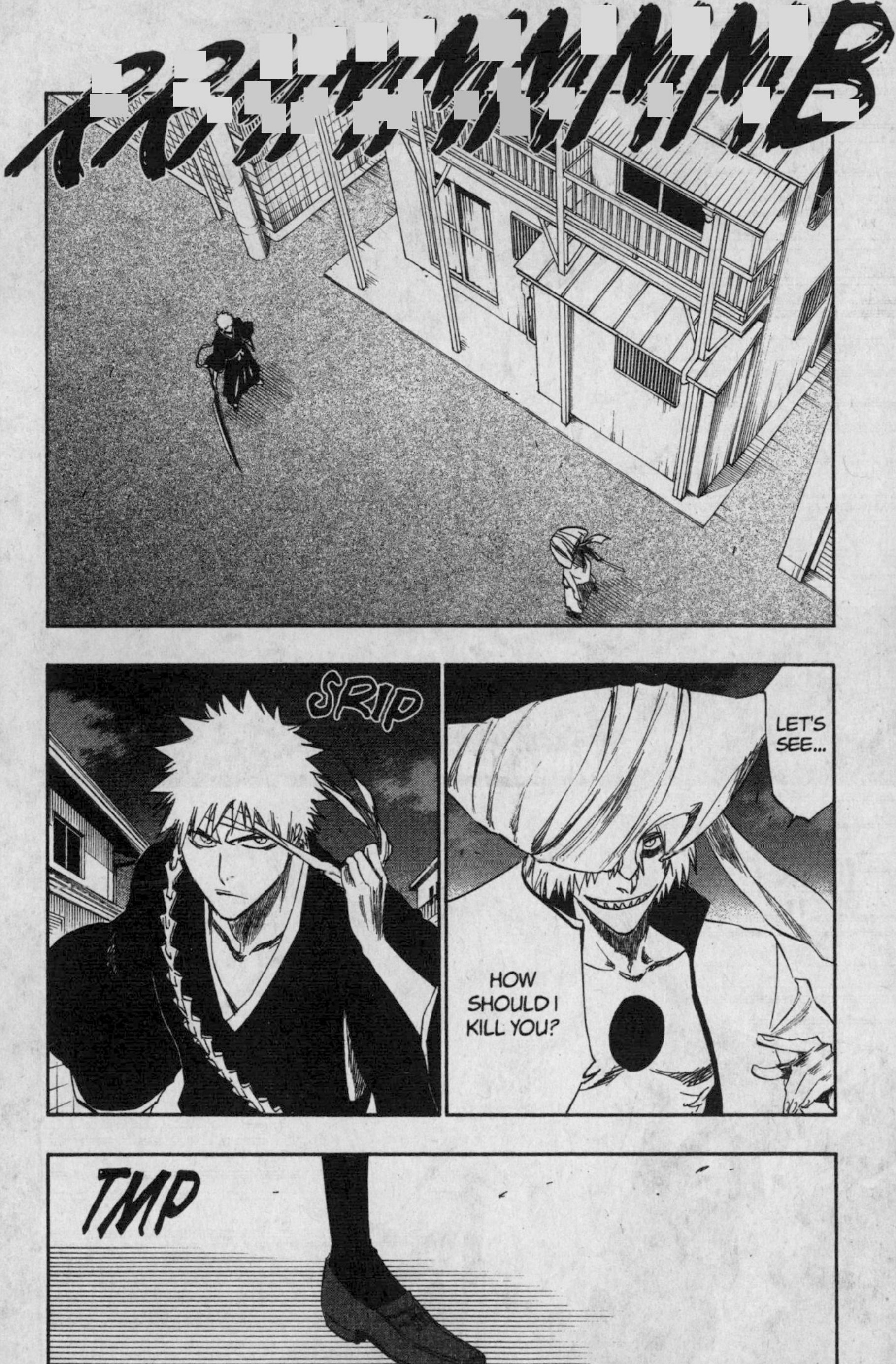
LET'S SEE...
HOW SHOULD I KILL YOU?
SRIP
TMP

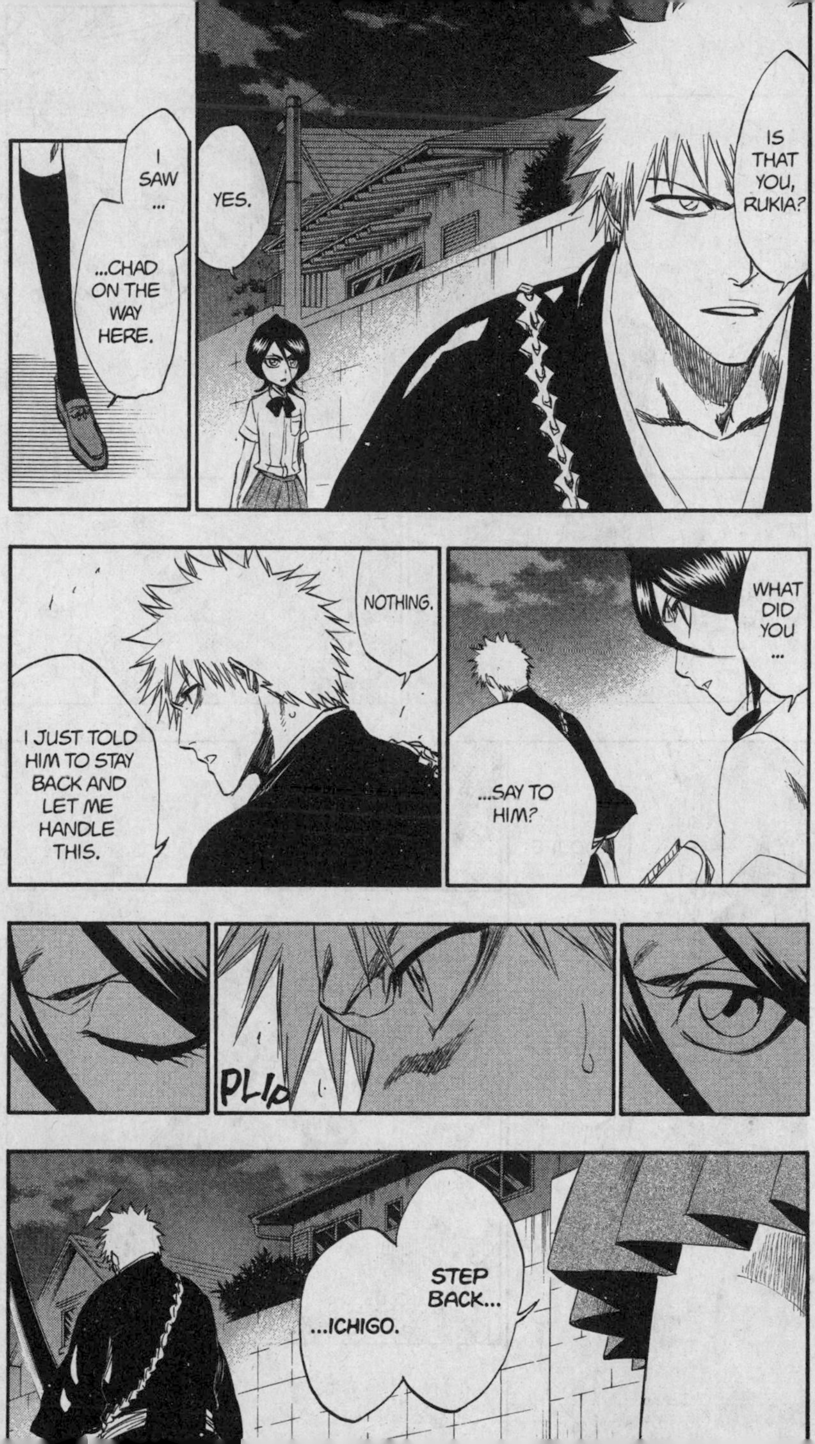
IS THAT YOU, RUKIA?
YES.
I SAW ...
...CHAD ON THE WAY HERE.
WHAT DID YOU ...
...SAY TO HIM?
NOTHING.
I JUST TOLD HIM TO STAY BACK AND LET ME HANDLE THIS.
PLIP
STEP BACK...
...ICHIGO.

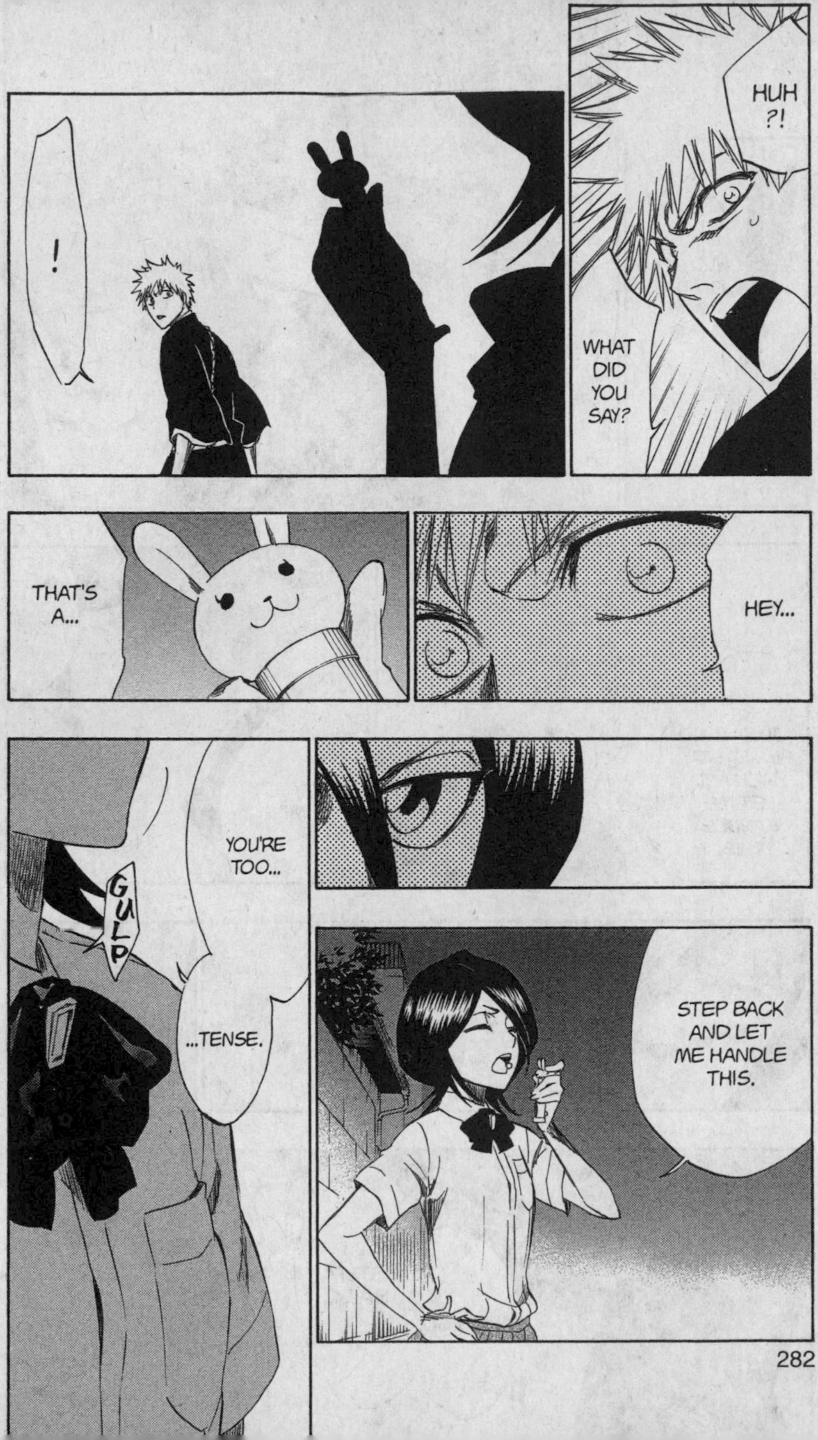
HUH ?!
WHAT DID YOU SAY?
!
HEY...
THAT'S A...
STEP BACK AND LET ME HANDLE THIS.
YOU'RE TOO...
GULP
...TENSE.

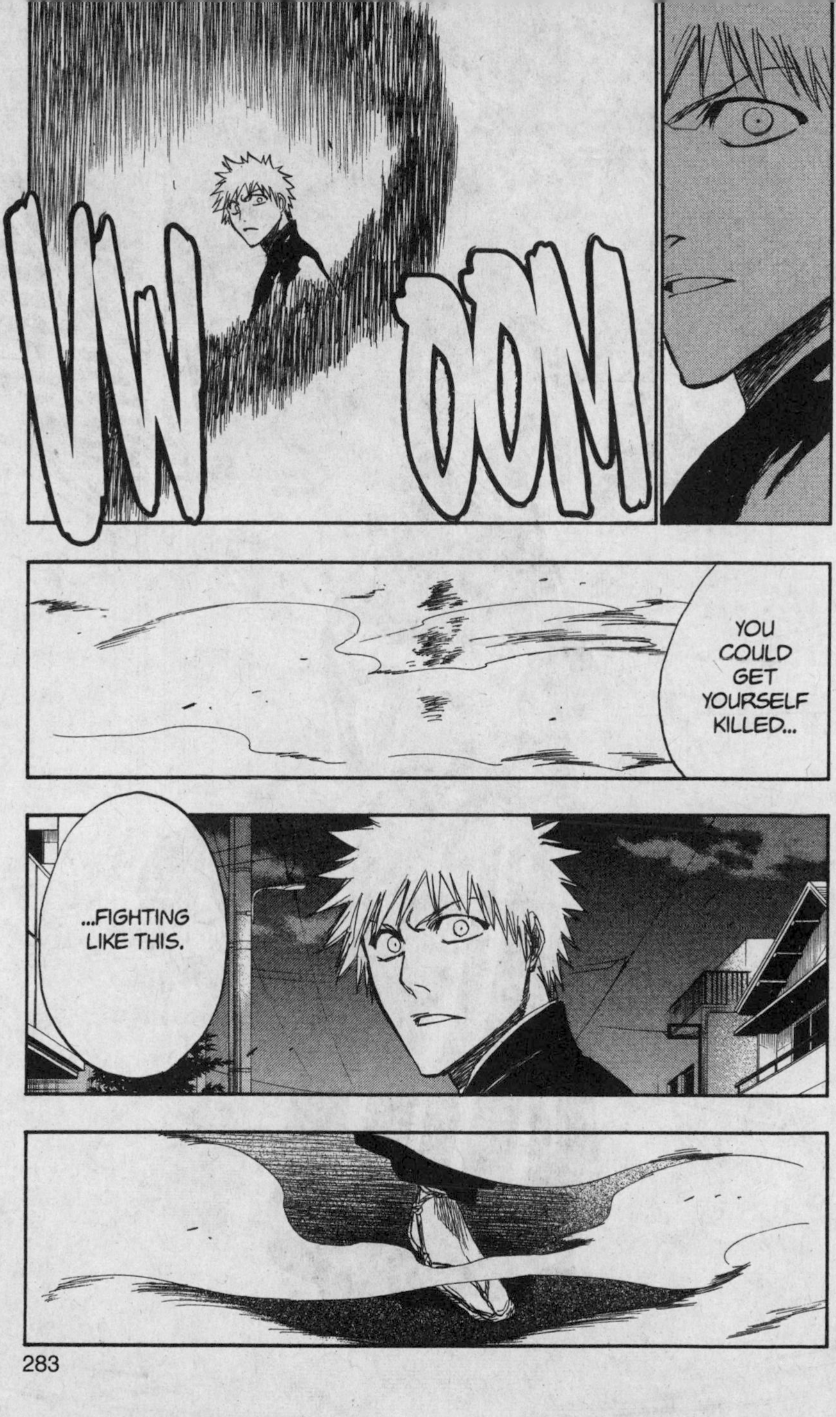
VWOOM
YOU COULD GET YOURSELF KILLED...
...FIGHTING LIKE THIS.

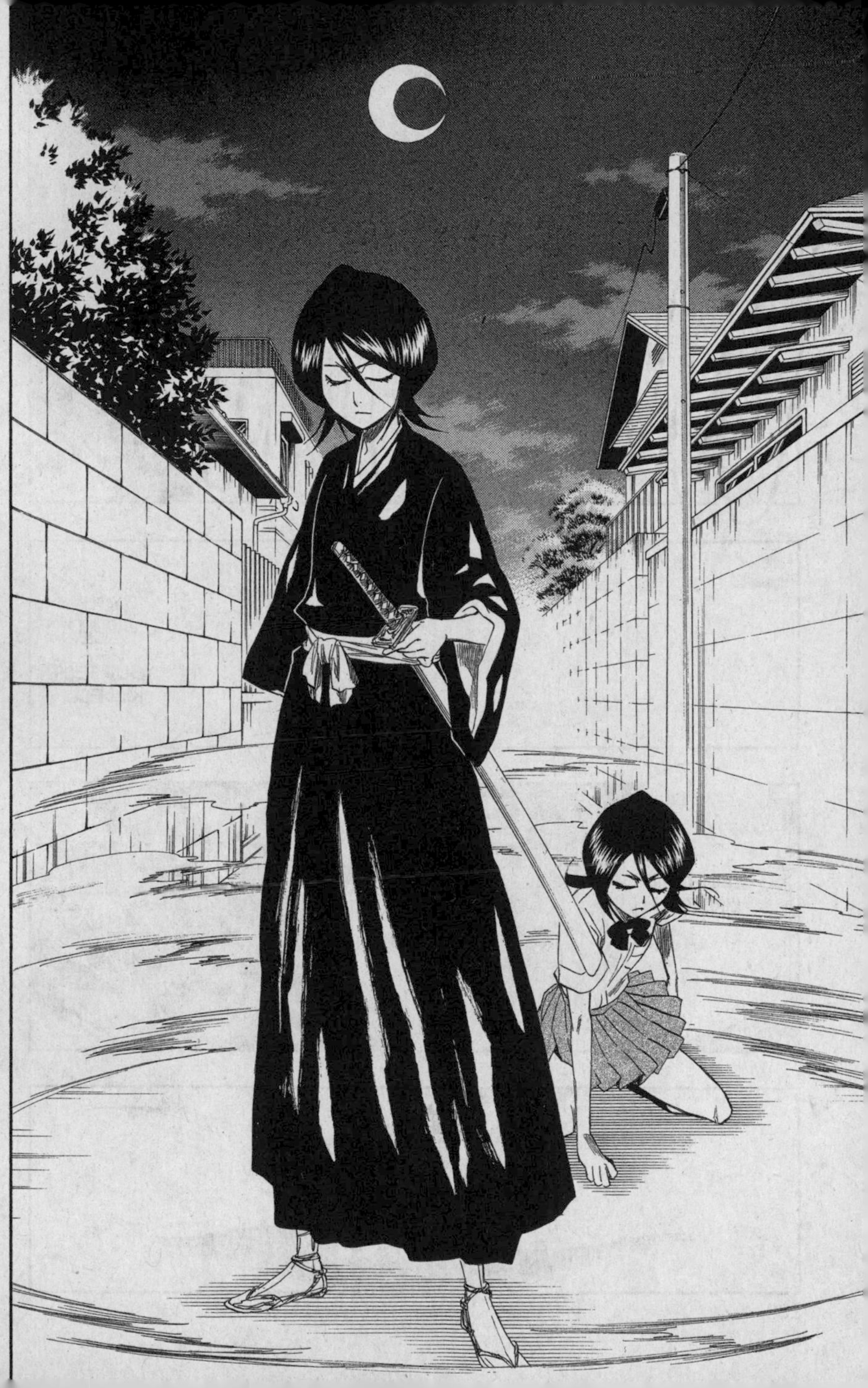

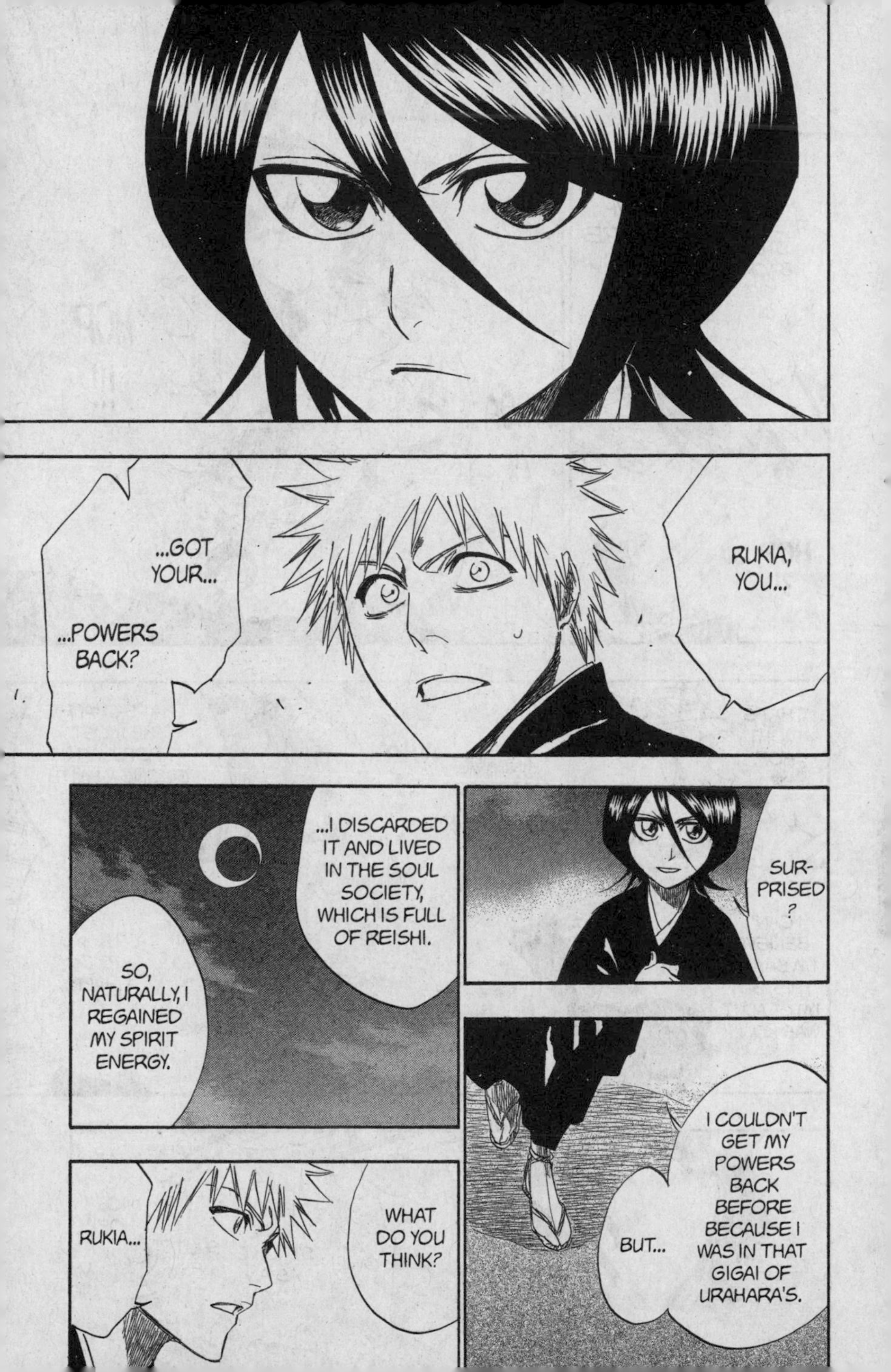
RUKIA, YOU...
...GOT YOUR...
...POWERS BACK?
SUR-PRISED?
I COULDN'T GET MY POWERS BACK BEFORE BECAUSE I WAS IN THAT GIGAI OF URAHARA'S.
BUT...
...I DISCARDED IT AND LIVED IN THE SOUL SOCIETY, WHICH IS FULL OF REISHI.
SO, NATURALLY, I REGAINED MY SPIRIT ENERGY.
WHAT DO YOU THINK?
RUKIA...

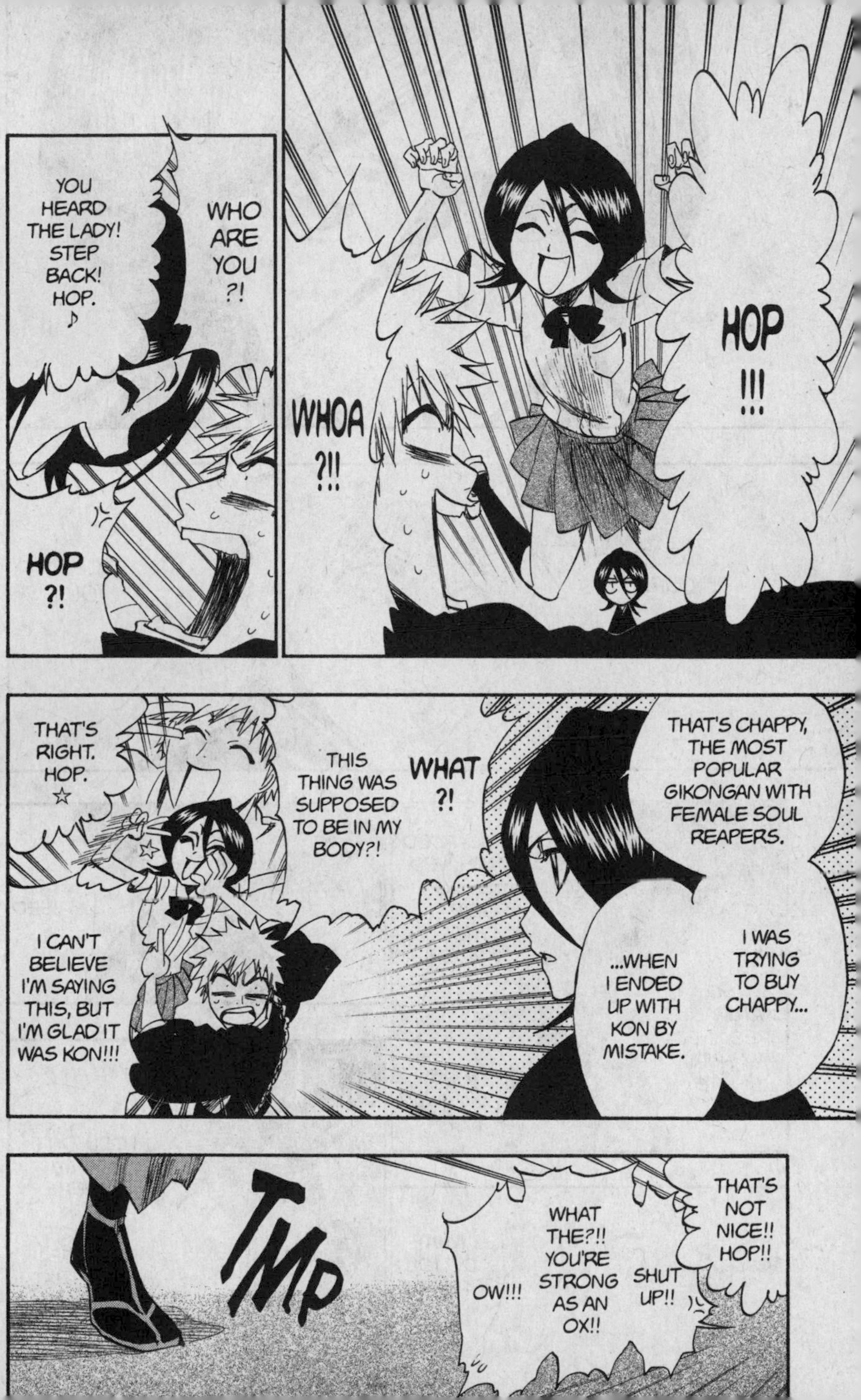
HOP !!!
WHOA ?!!
WHO ARE YOU ?!
YOU HEARD THE LADY! STEP BACK! HOP. ♪
HOP ?!
THAT'S CHAPPY, THE MOST POPULAR GIKONGAN WITH FEMALE SOUL REAPERS.
I WAS TRYING TO BUY CHAPPY...
...WHEN I ENDED UP WITH KON BY MISTAKE.
WHAT ?!
THIS THING WAS SUPPOSED TO BE IN MY BODY?!
THAT'S RIGHT. HOP. ☆
I CAN'T BELIEVE I'M SAYING THIS, BUT I'M GLAD IT WAS KON!!!
THAT'S NOT NICE!! HOP!!
SHUT UP!!
WHAT THE?!! YOU'RE STRONG AS AN OX!!
OW!!!
TMP

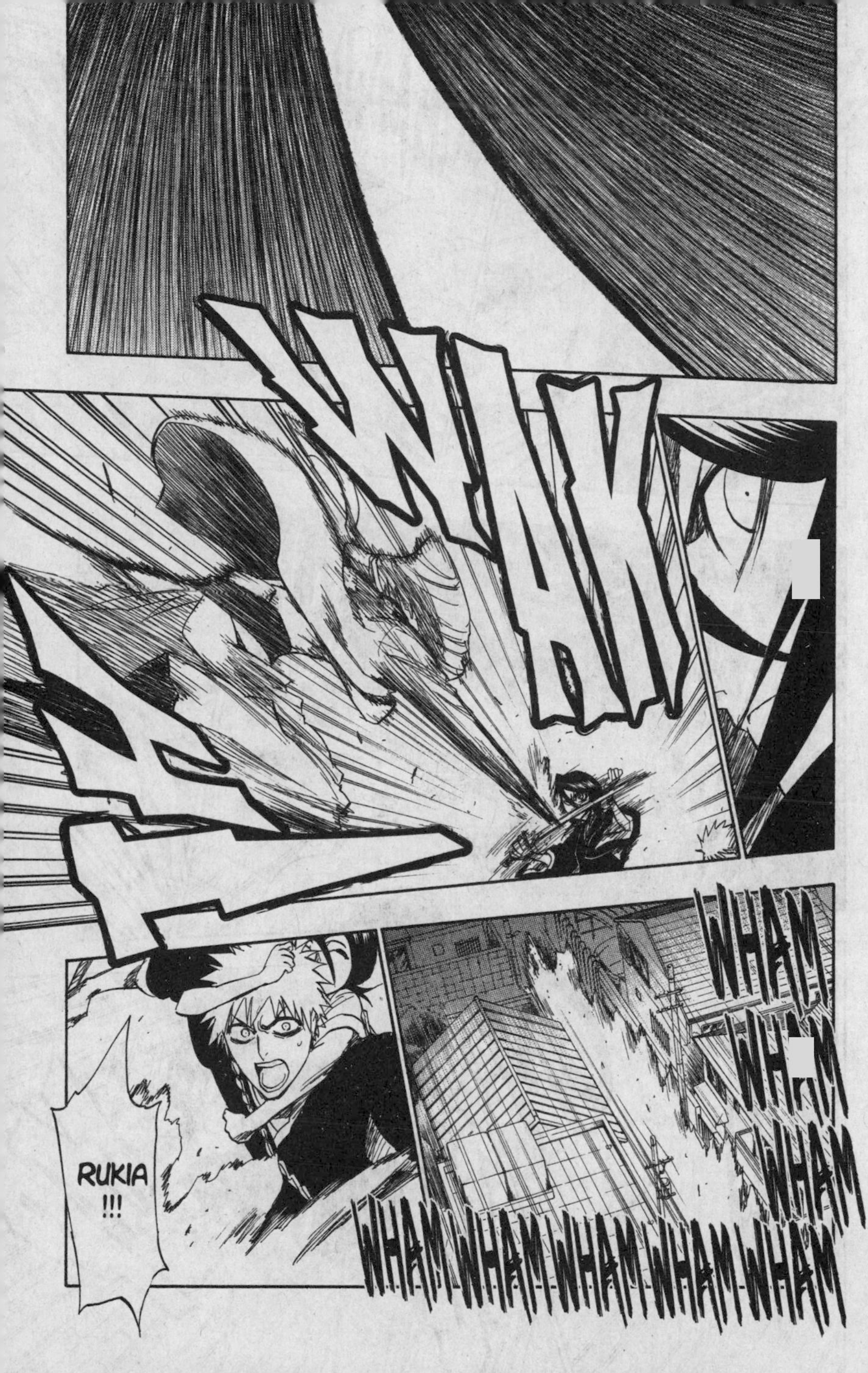
WHAK
WHAM
WHAM
WHAM
WHAM WHAM WHAM WHAM WHAM
RUKIA !!!

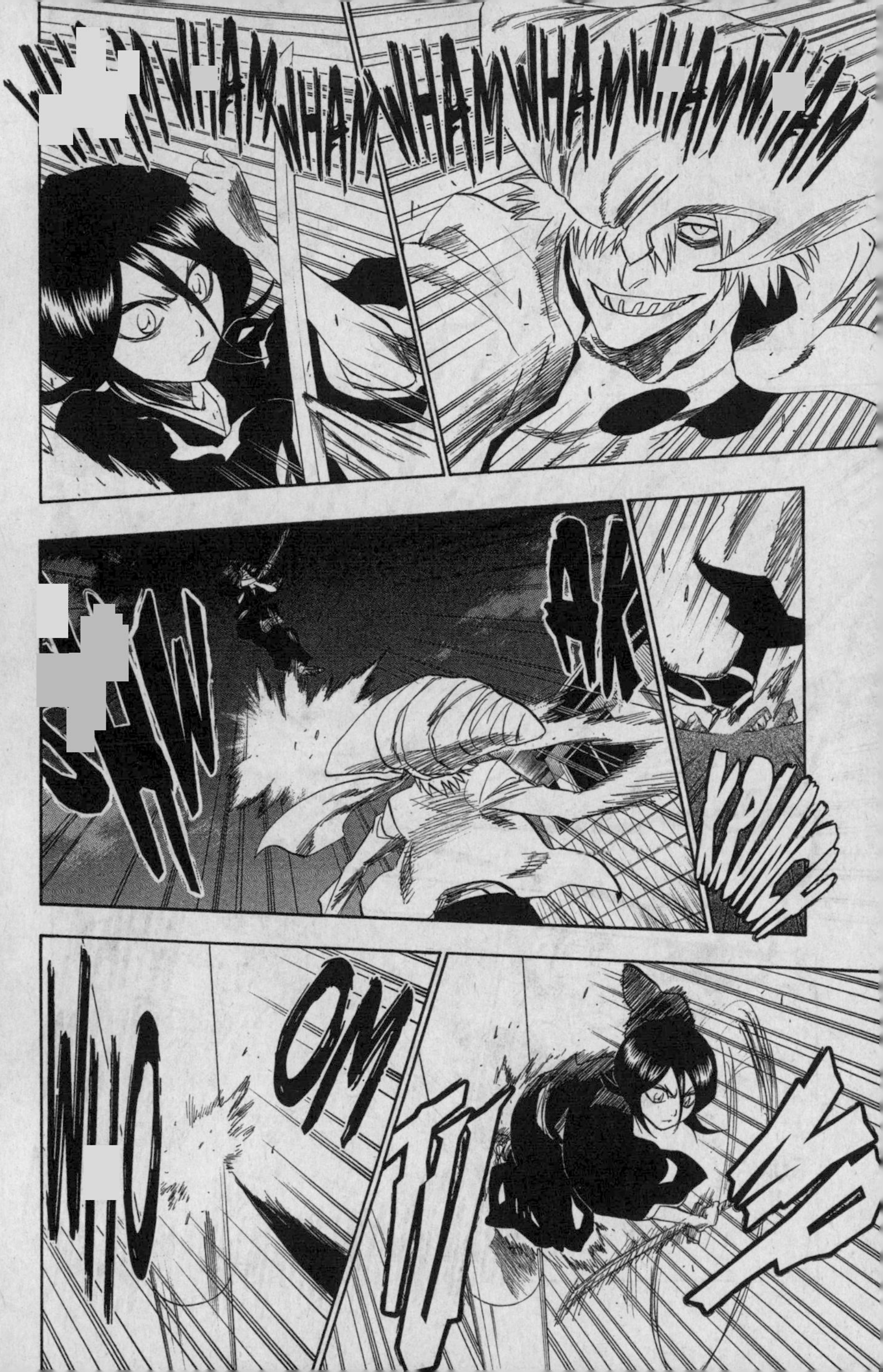
WHAM
WHAM
WHAM
WHAM

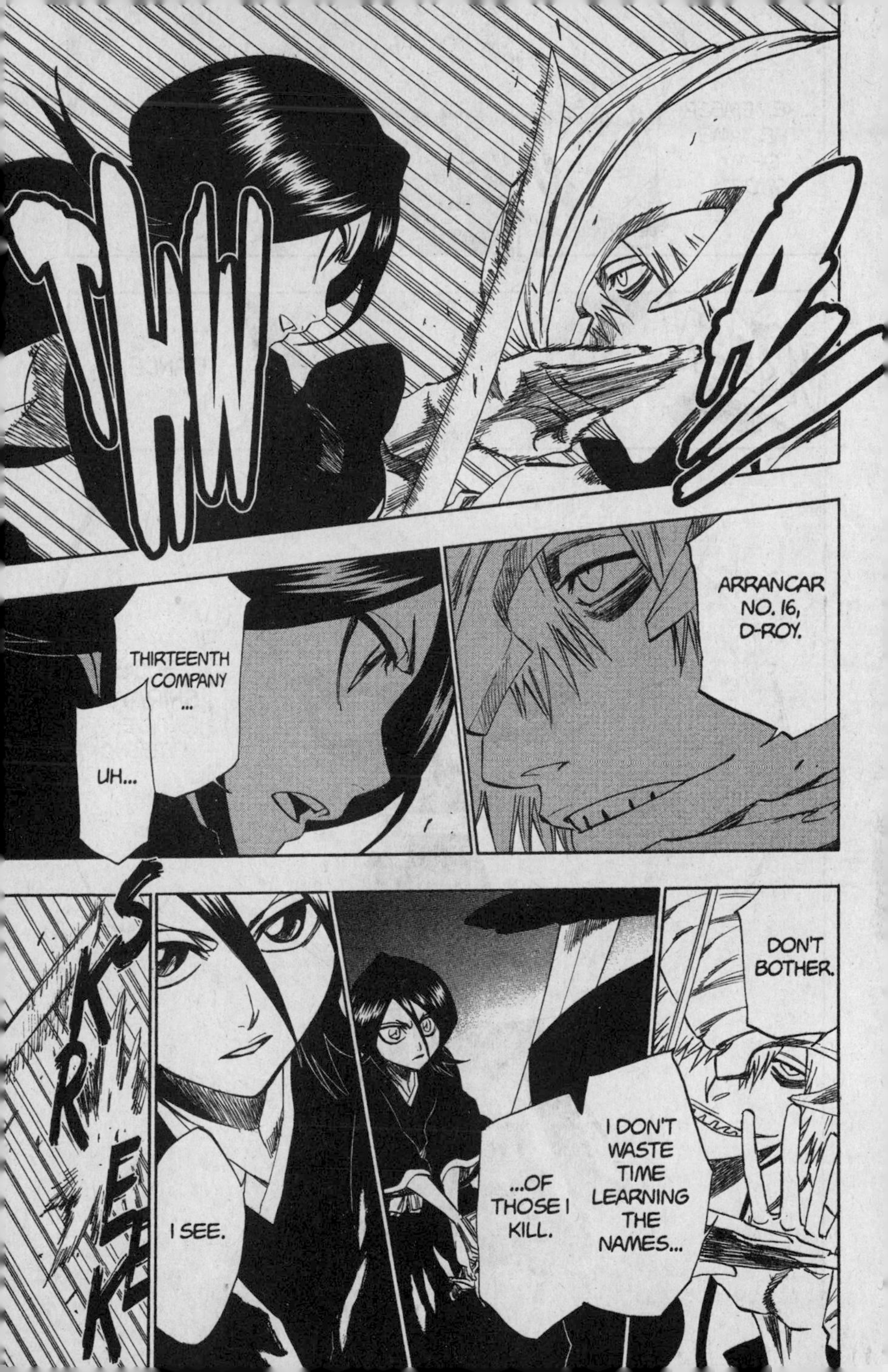
THW
ARRANCAR NO. 16, D-ROY.
THIRTEENTH COMPANY ...
UH...
DON'T BOTHER.
I DON'T WASTE TIME LEARNING THE NAMES...
...OF THOSE I KILL.
I SEE.
SKREEK

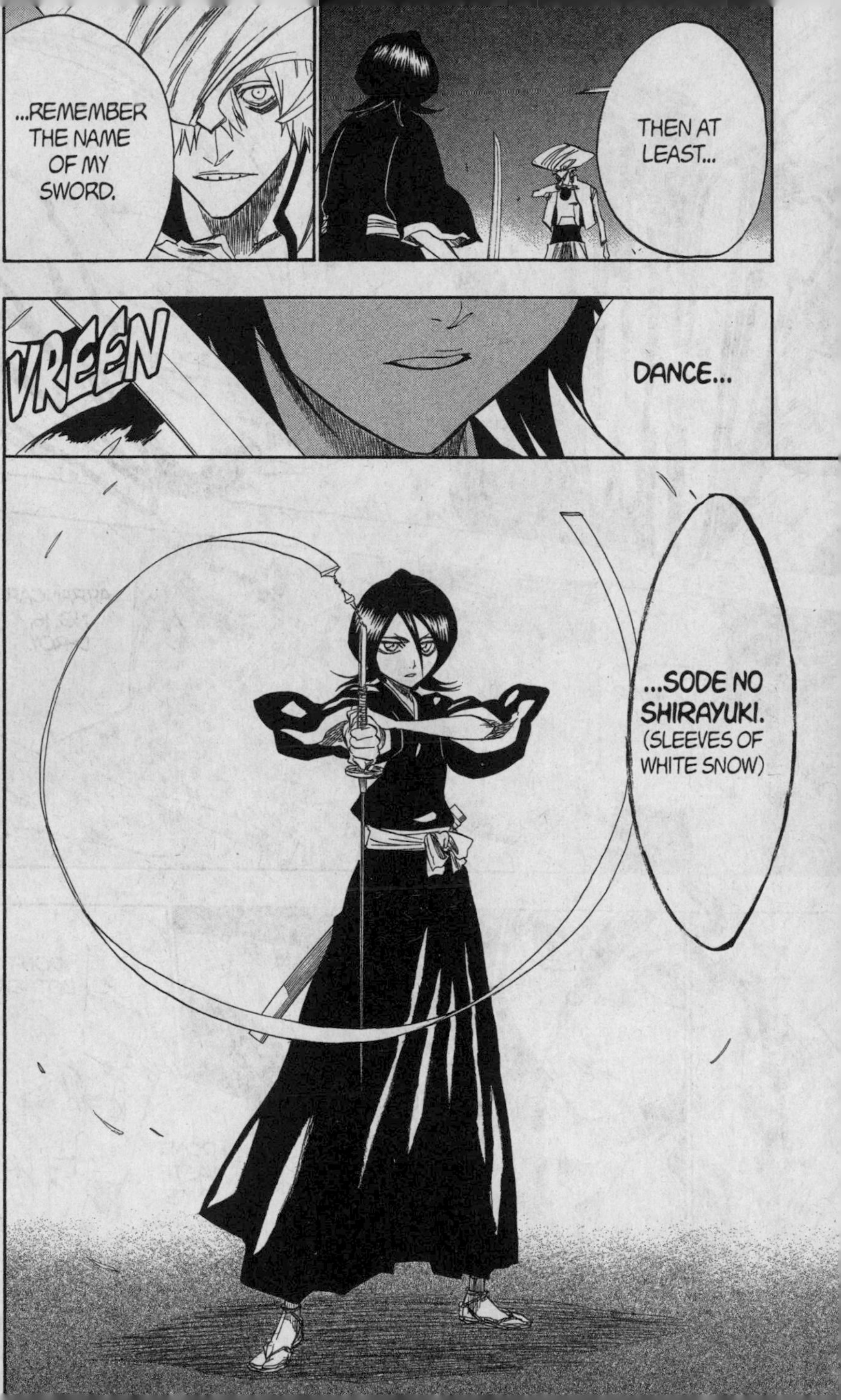
THEN AT LEAST...
...REMEMBER THE NAME OF MY SWORD.
DANCE...
VREEN
...SODE NO SHIRAYUKI.
(SLEEVES OF WHITE SNOW)

...ZANPAKU-TÔ!

A WHITE...

FWUP

DANCE NUMBER ONE...

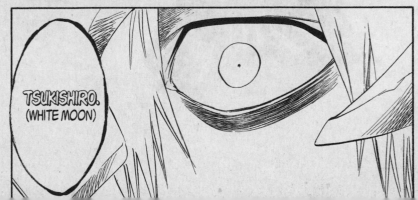

TSUKISHIRO. (WHITE MOON)

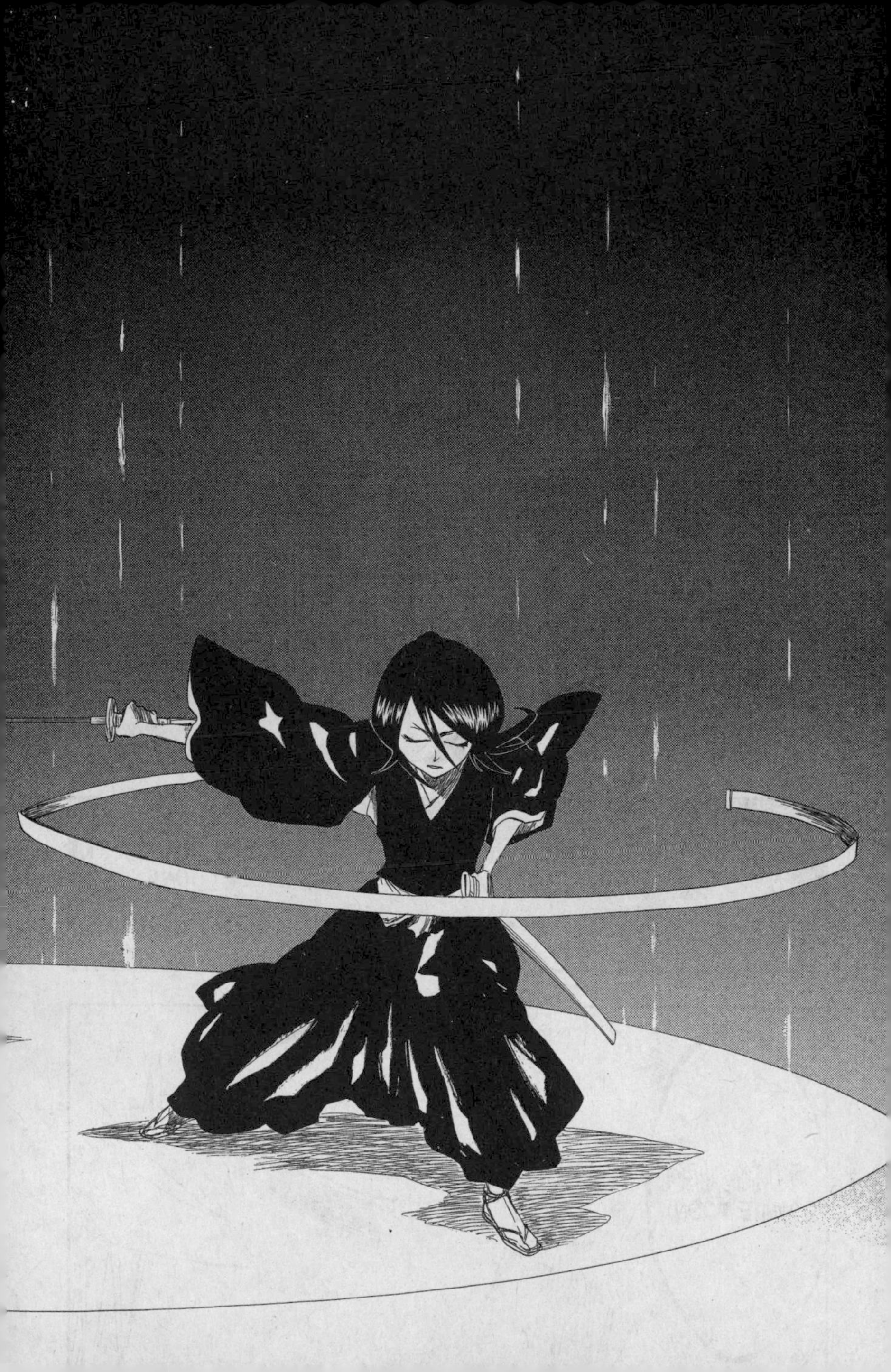

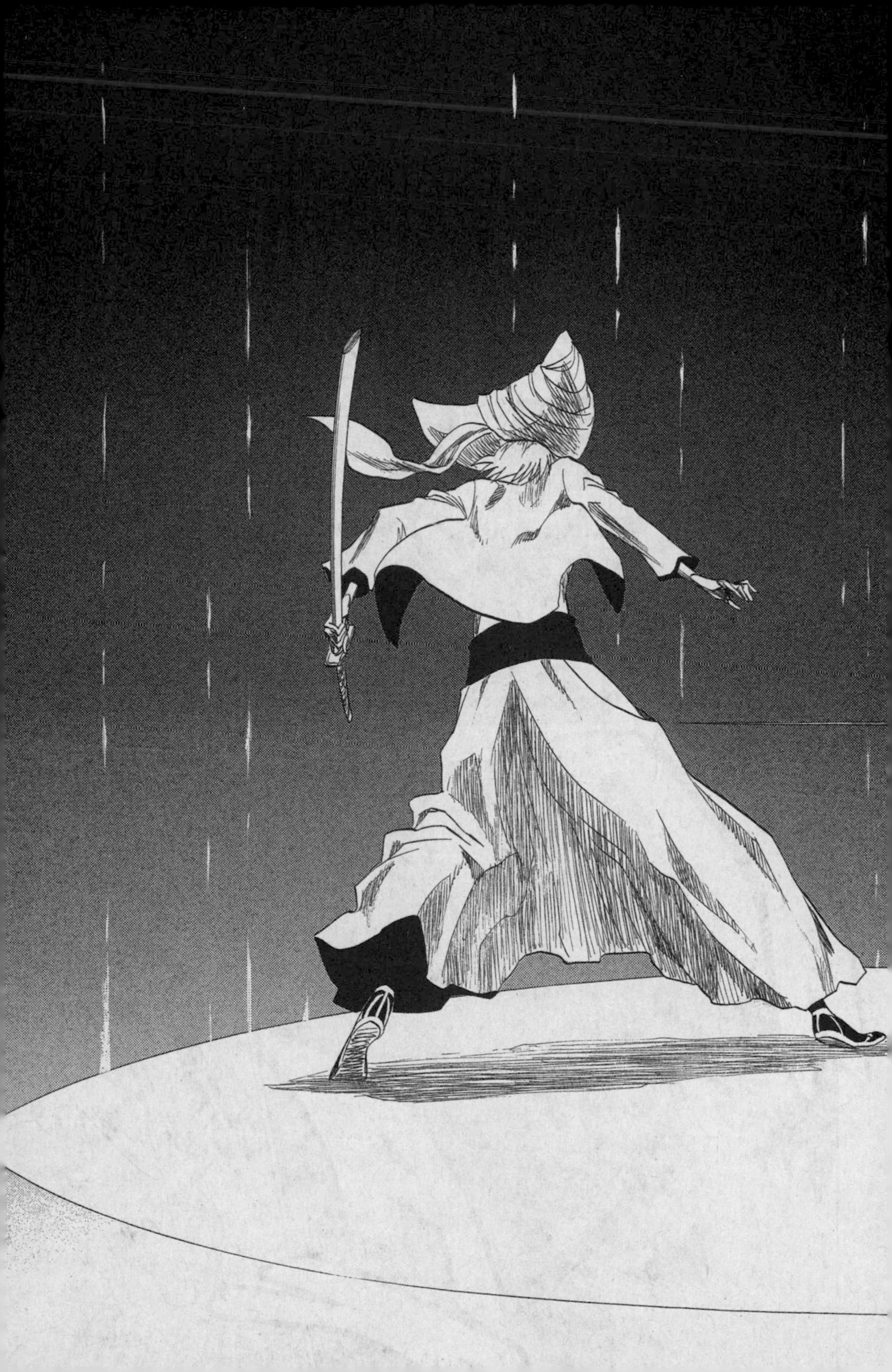

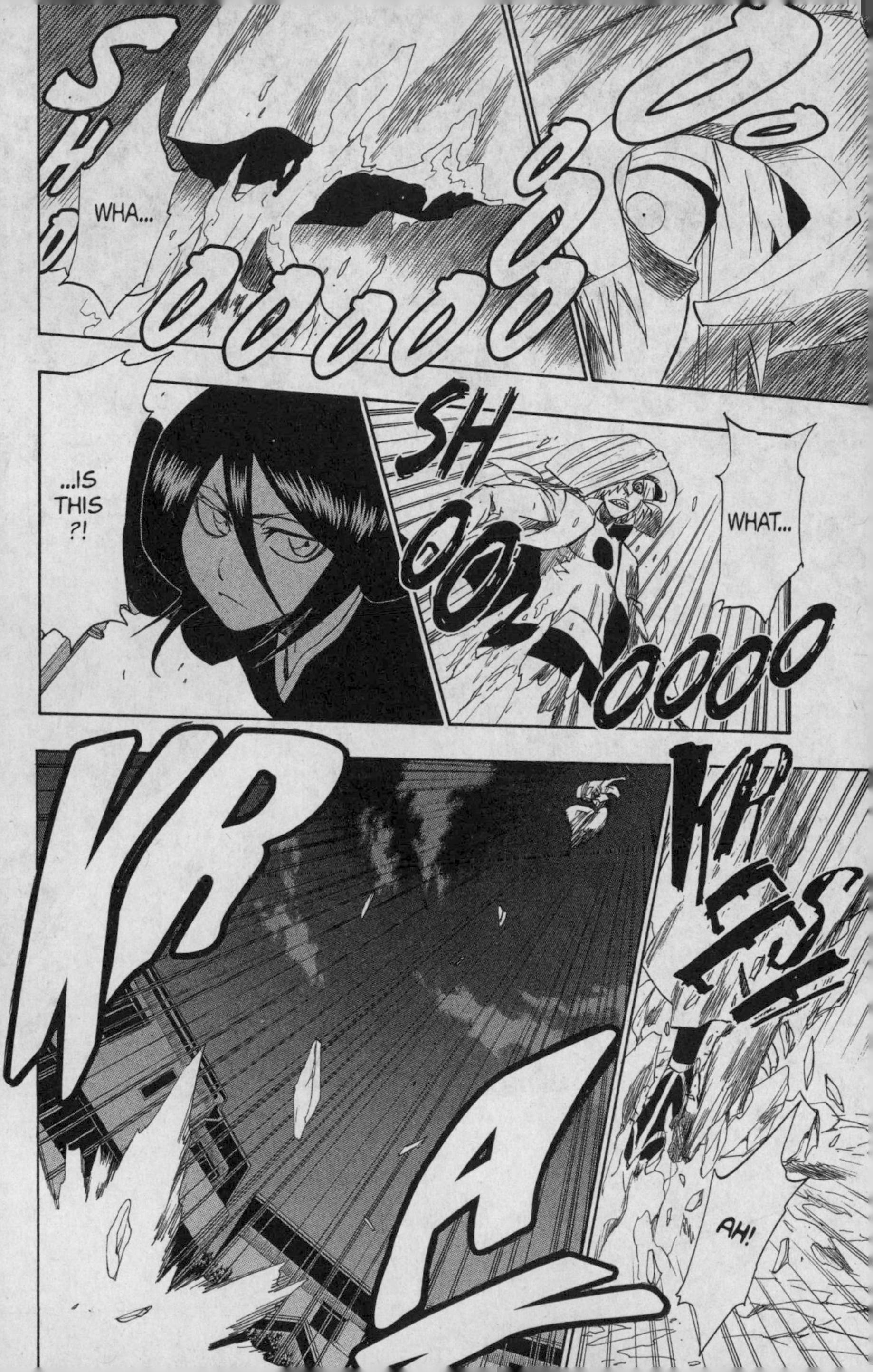
WHA...
WHAT...
...IS THIS ?!
AH!

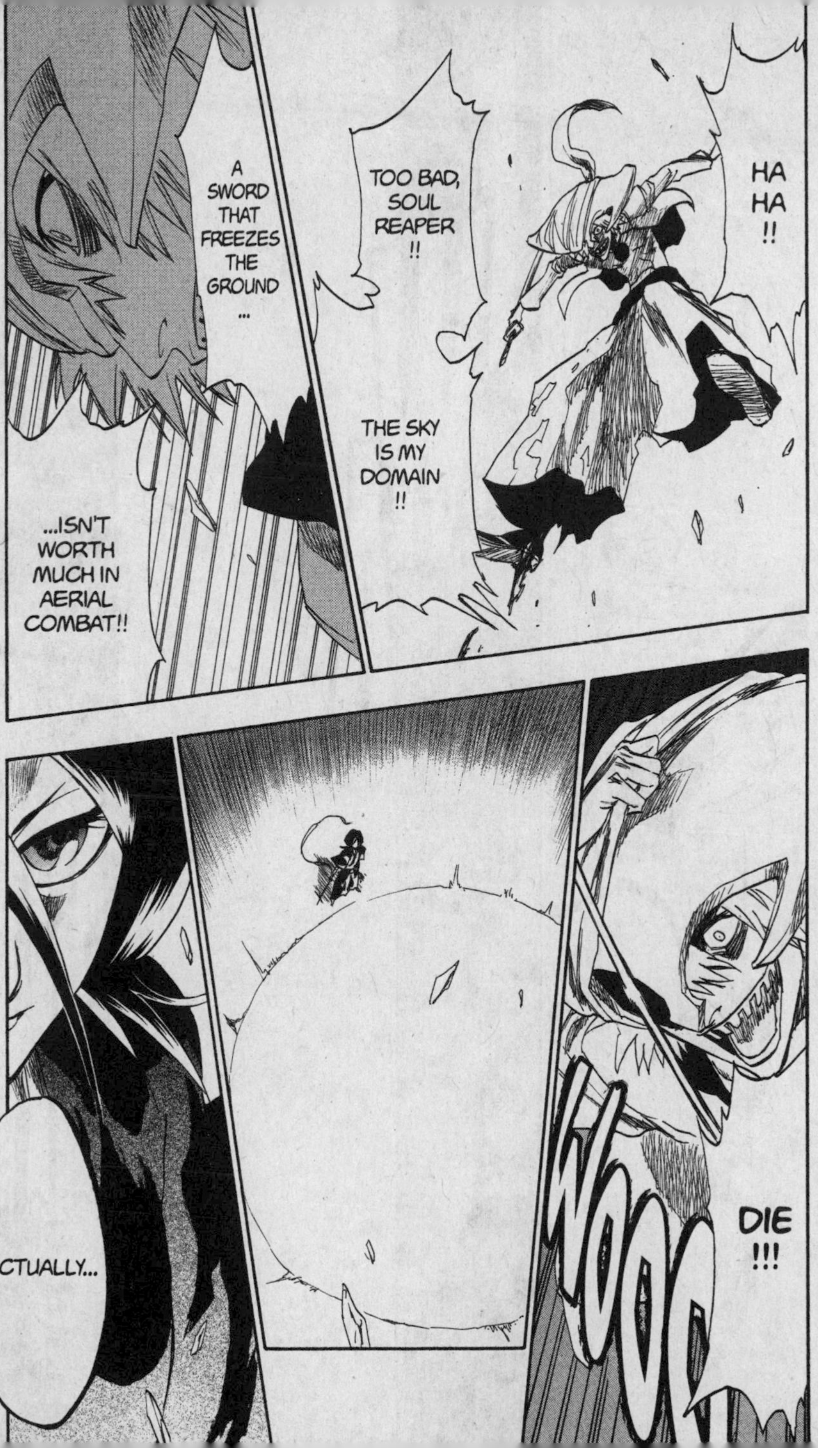
HA HA !!
TOO BAD, SOUL REAPER !!
THE SKY IS MY DOMAIN !!
A SWORD THAT FREEZES THE GROUND ...
...ISN'T WORTH MUCH IN AERIAL COMBAT!!
DIE !!!
ACTUALLY...

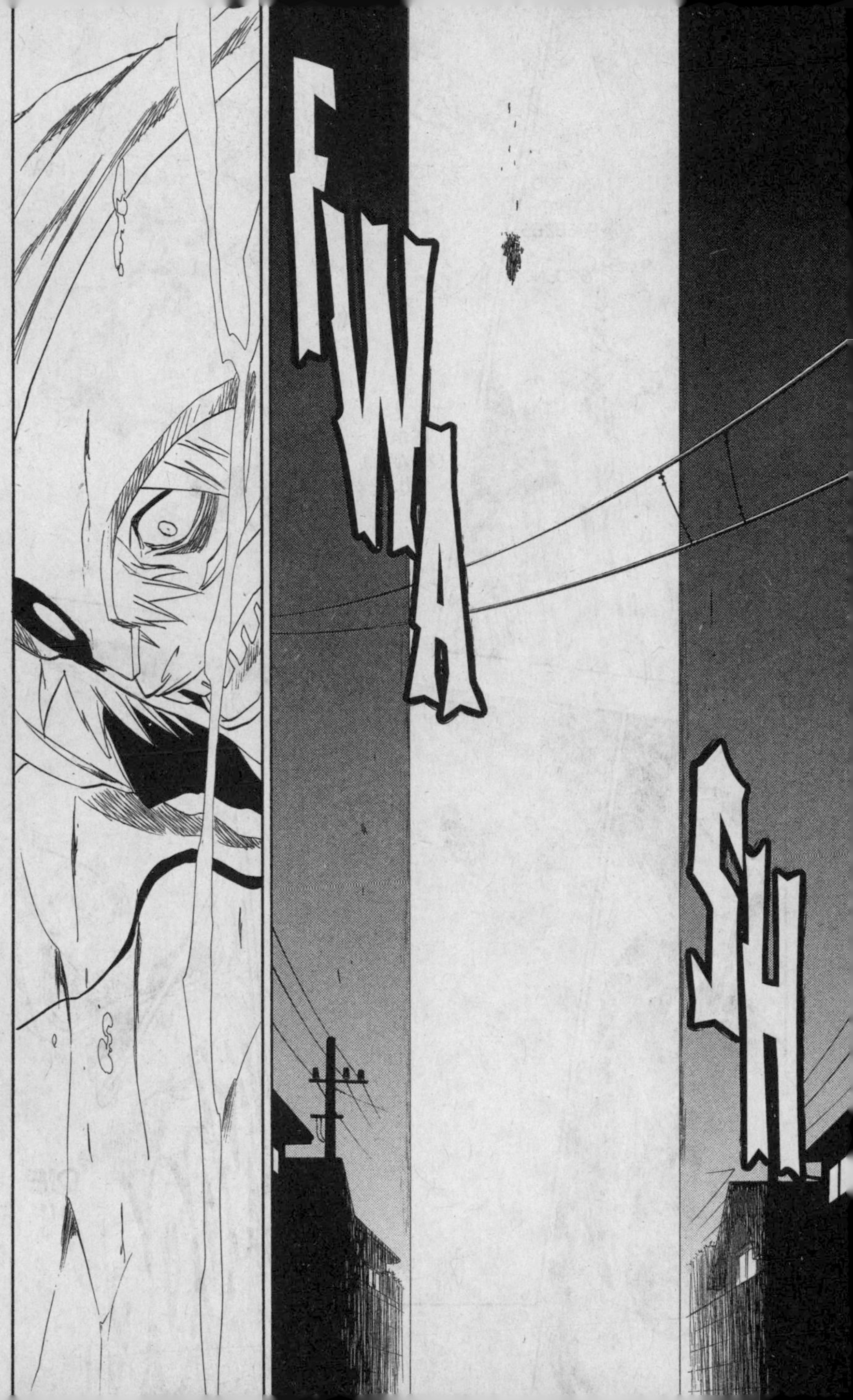
SH
FWA

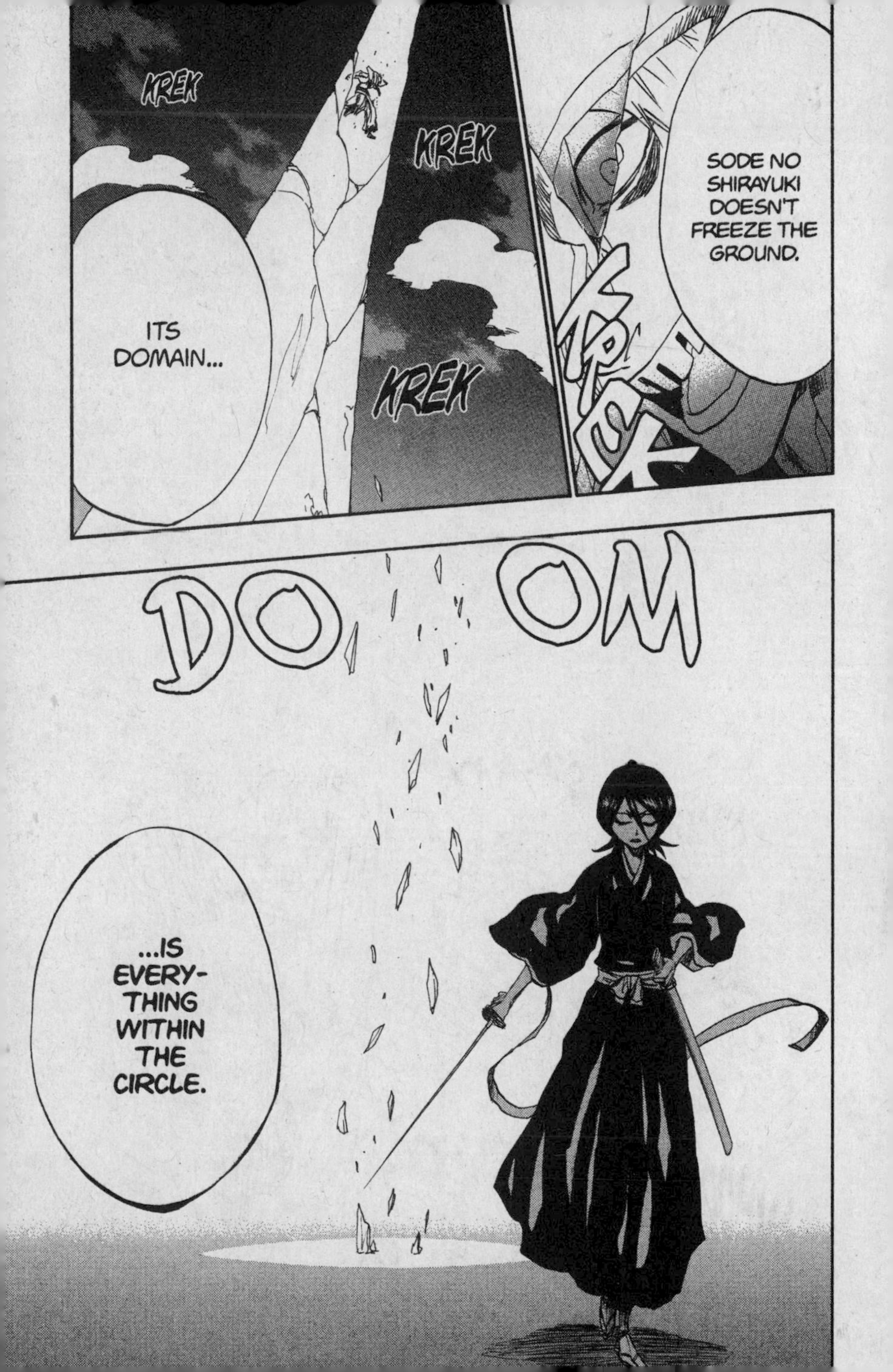
SODE NO SHIRAYUKI DOESN'T FREEZE THE GROUND.
KREK
KREK
KREK
ITS DOMAIN...
DOOM
...IS EVERY-THING WITHIN THE CIRCLE.

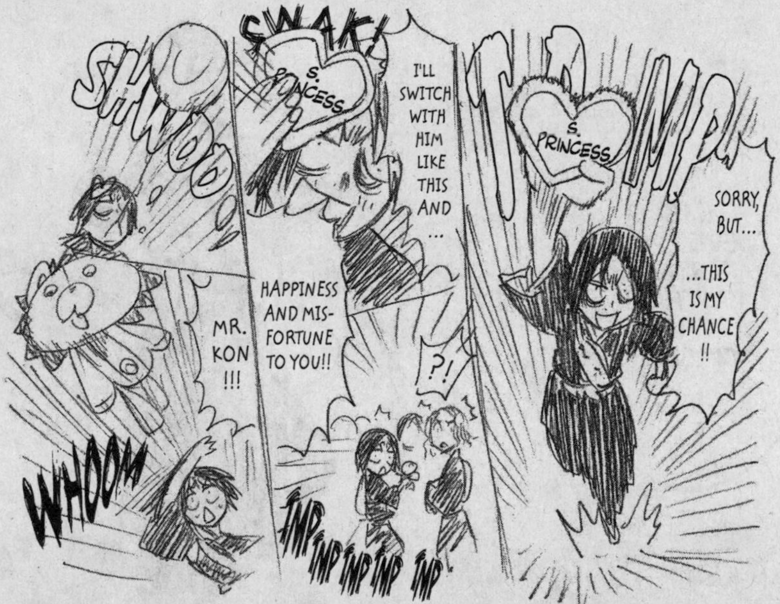
TOMP!
S. PRINCESS
SORRY, BUT...
...THIS IS MY CHANCE!!
SWAK!
S. PRINCESS
I'LL SWITCH WITH HIM LIKE THIS AND...
HAPPINESS AND MIS-FORTUNE TO YOU!!
?!
TMP TMP TMP TMP TMP
SHWOO
MR. KON!!!
WHOOM

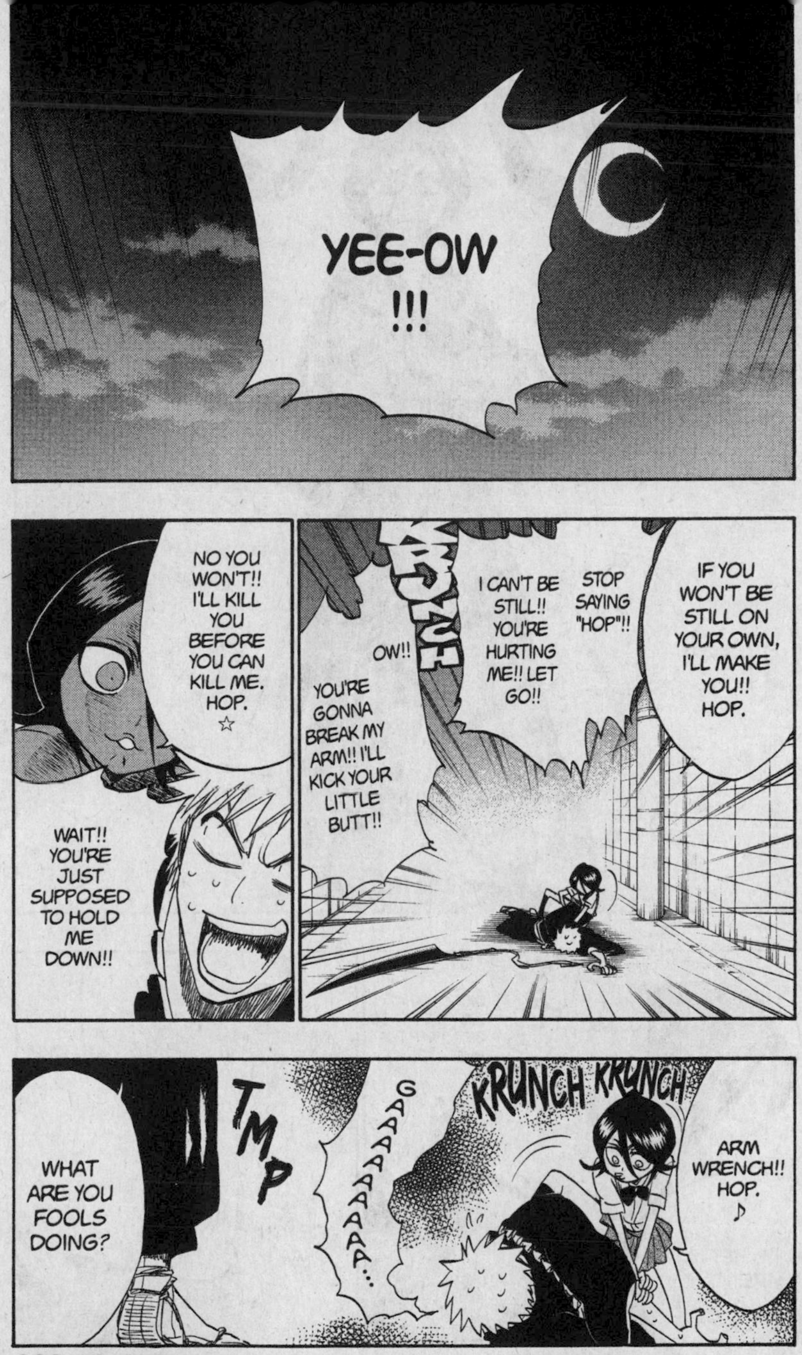
YEE-OW !!!
IF YOU WON'T BE STILL ON YOUR OWN, I'LL MAKE YOU!! HOP.
STOP SAYING "HOP"!!
I CAN'T BE STILL!! YOU'RE HURTING ME!! LET GO!!
KRUNCH
OW!!
YOU'RE GONNA BREAK MY ARM!! I'LL KICK YOUR LITTLE BUTT!!
NO YOU WON'T!! I'LL KILL YOU BEFORE YOU CAN KILL ME. HOP. ☆
WAIT!! YOU'RE JUST SUPPOSED TO HOLD ME DOWN!!
ARM WRENCH!! HOP. ♪
KRUNCH KRUNCH
GAAAAAAAAA...
TMP
WHAT ARE YOU FOOLS DOING?

202. ¡Mala Suerte!

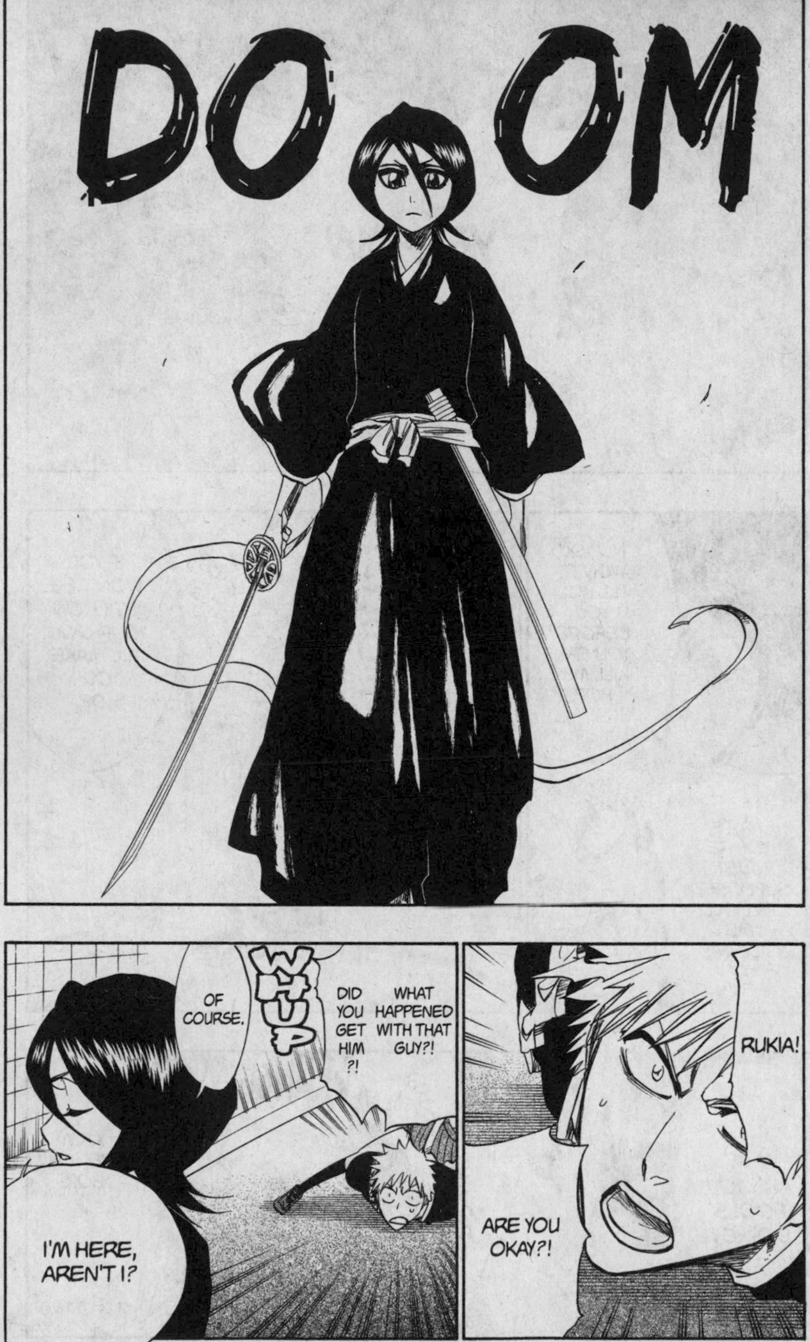
DOOOM
RUKIA!
ARE YOU OKAY?!
WHAT HAPPENED WITH THAT GUY?!
DID YOU GET HIM?!
WHUP
OF COURSE.
I'M HERE, AREN'T I?

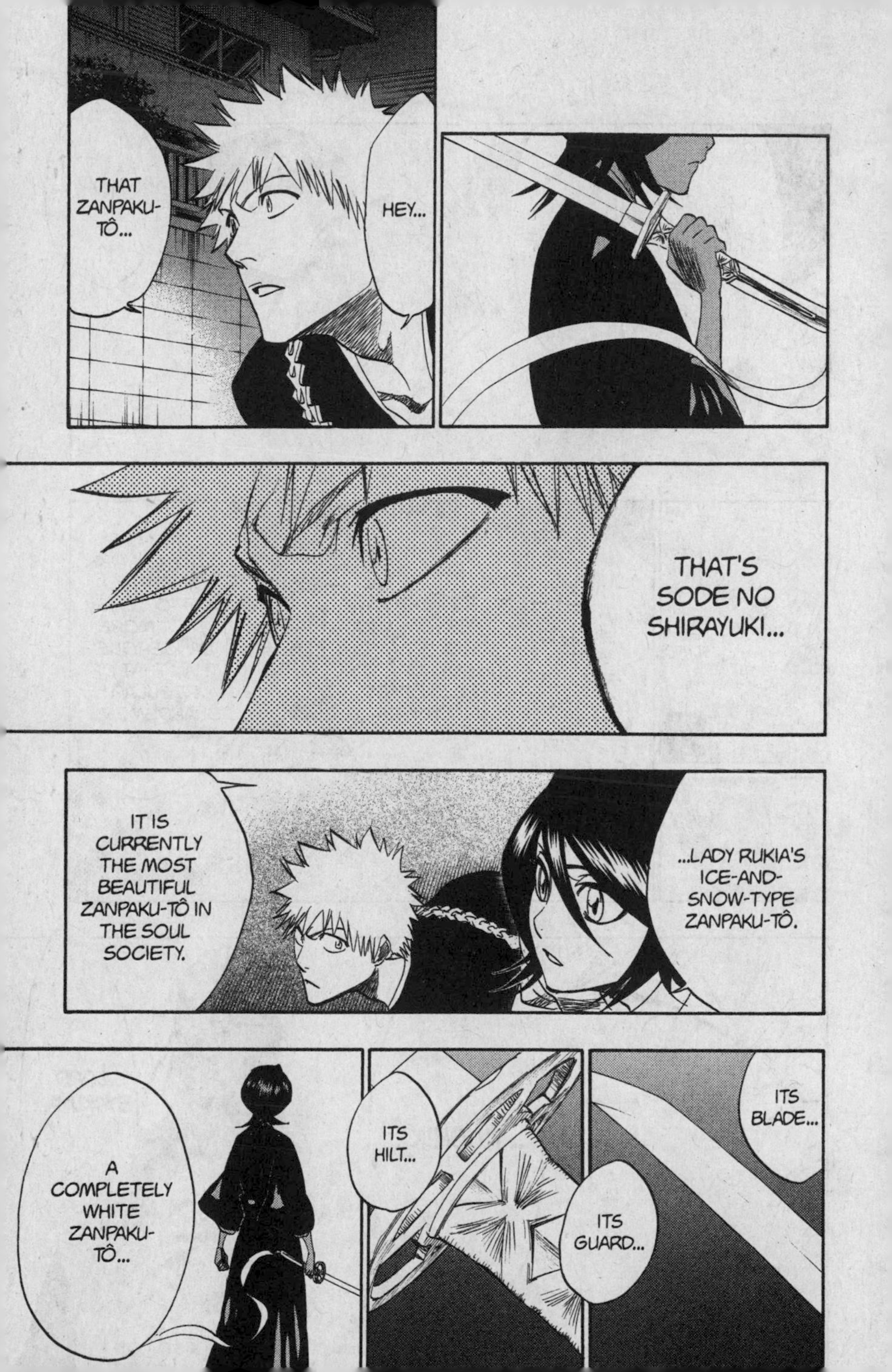
HEY...
THAT ZANPAKU-TÔ...
THAT'S SODE NO SHIRAYUKI...
...LADY RUKIA'S ICE-AND-SNOW-TYPE ZANPAKU-TÔ.
IT IS CURRENTLY THE MOST BEAUTIFUL ZANPAKU-TÔ IN THE SOUL SOCIETY.
ITS BLADE...
ITS GUARD...
ITS HILT...
A COMPLETELY WHITE ZANPAKU-TÔ...

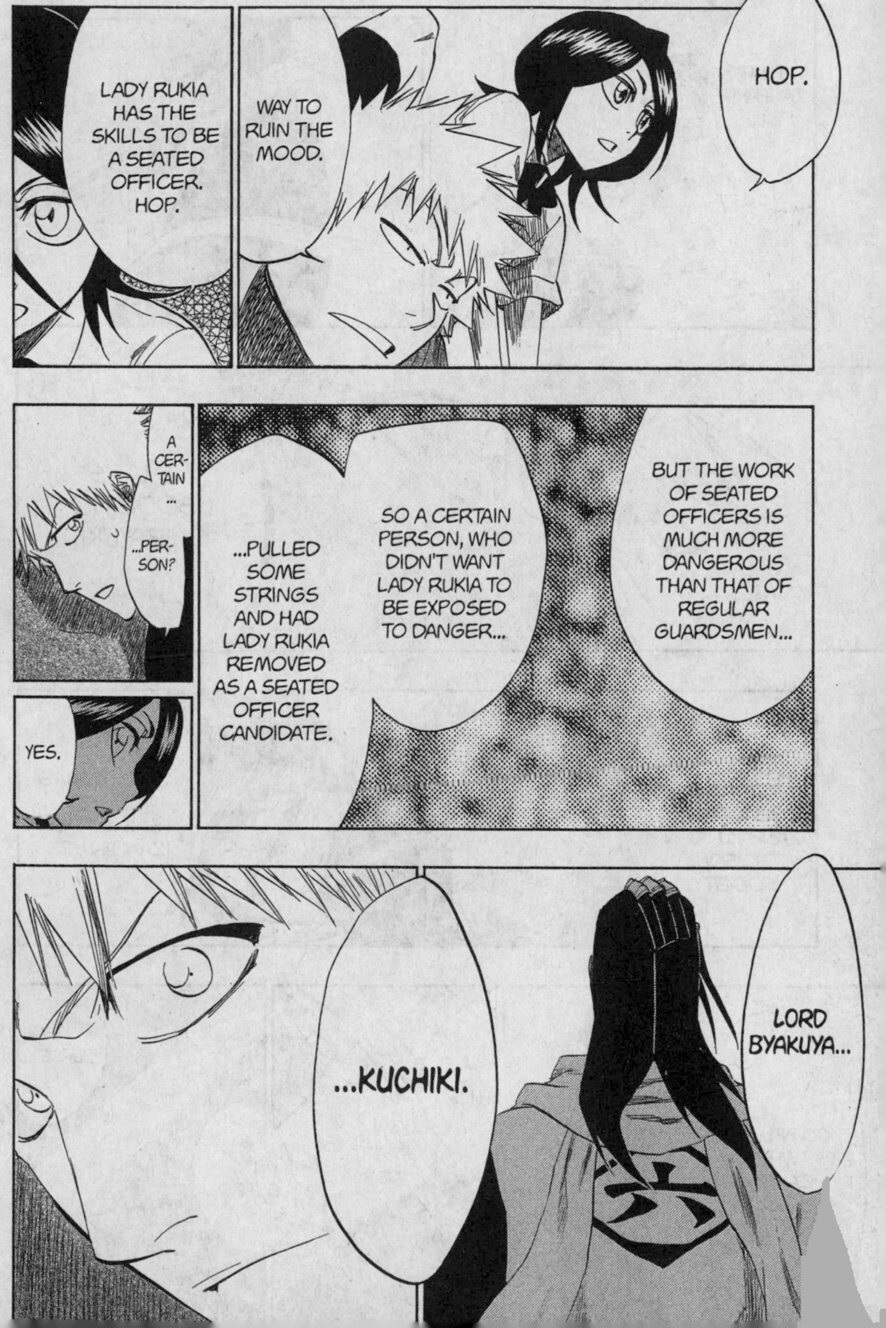
HOP.
WAY TO RUIN THE MOOD.
LADY RUKIA HAS THE SKILLS TO BE A SEATED OFFICER. HOP.
BUT THE WORK OF SEATED OFFICERS IS MUCH MORE DANGEROUS THAN THAT OF REGULAR GUARDSMEN...
SO A CERTAIN PERSON, WHO DIDN'T WANT LADY RUKIA TO BE EXPOSED TO DANGER...
...PULLED SOME STRINGS AND HAD LADY RUKIA REMOVED AS A SEATED OFFICER CANDIDATE.
A CER-TAIN...
...PER-SON?
YES.
LORD BYAKUYA...
...KUCHIKI.

READ THIS WAY

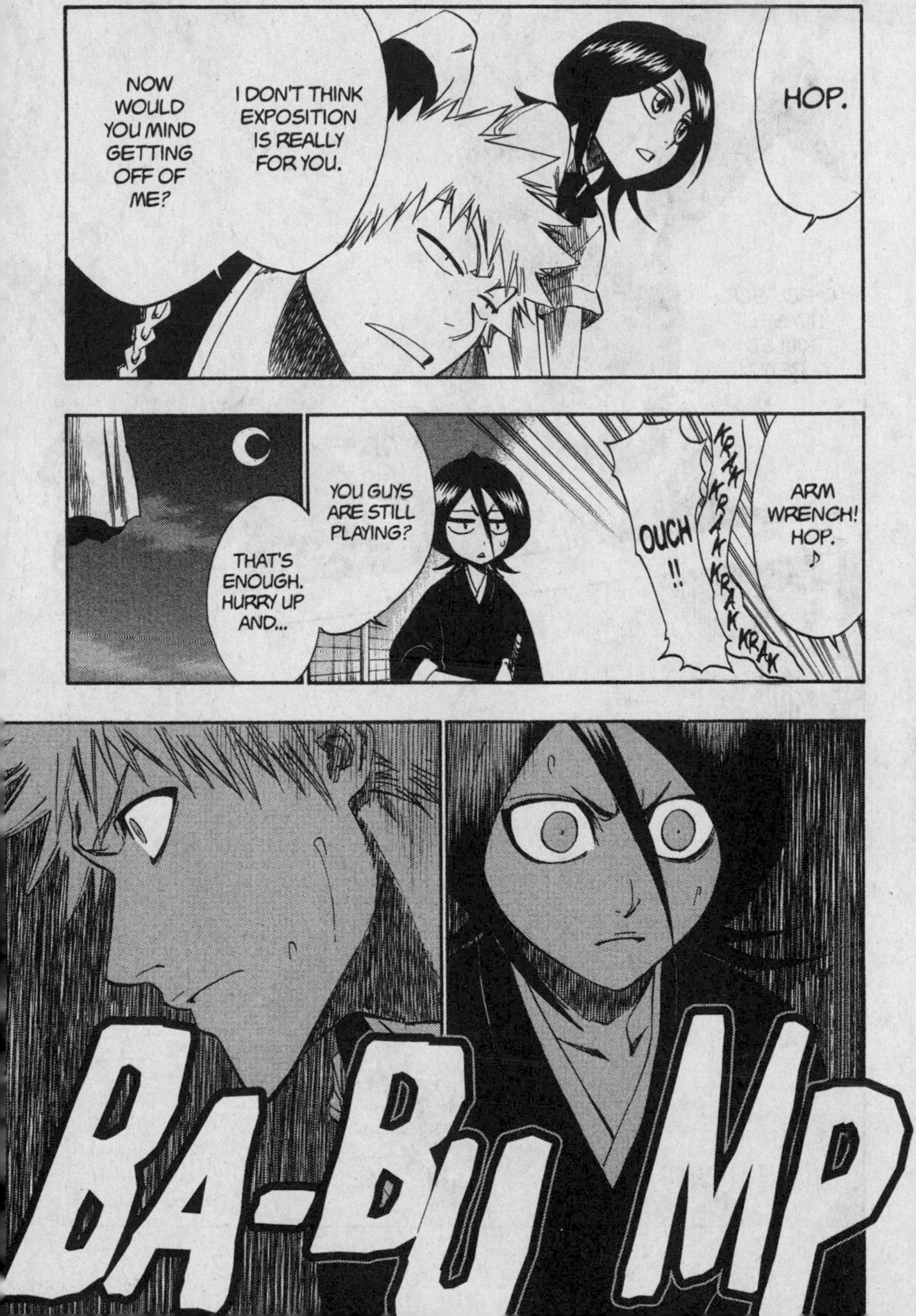
HOP.
I DON'T THINK EXPOSITION IS REALLY FOR YOU.
NOW WOULD YOU MIND GETTING OFF OF ME?
ARM WRENCH! HOP. ♪
KRAK KRAK KRAK KRAK KRAK KRAK
OUCH!!
YOU GUYS ARE STILL PLAYING?
THAT'S ENOUGH. HURRY UP AND...
BA-BUMP

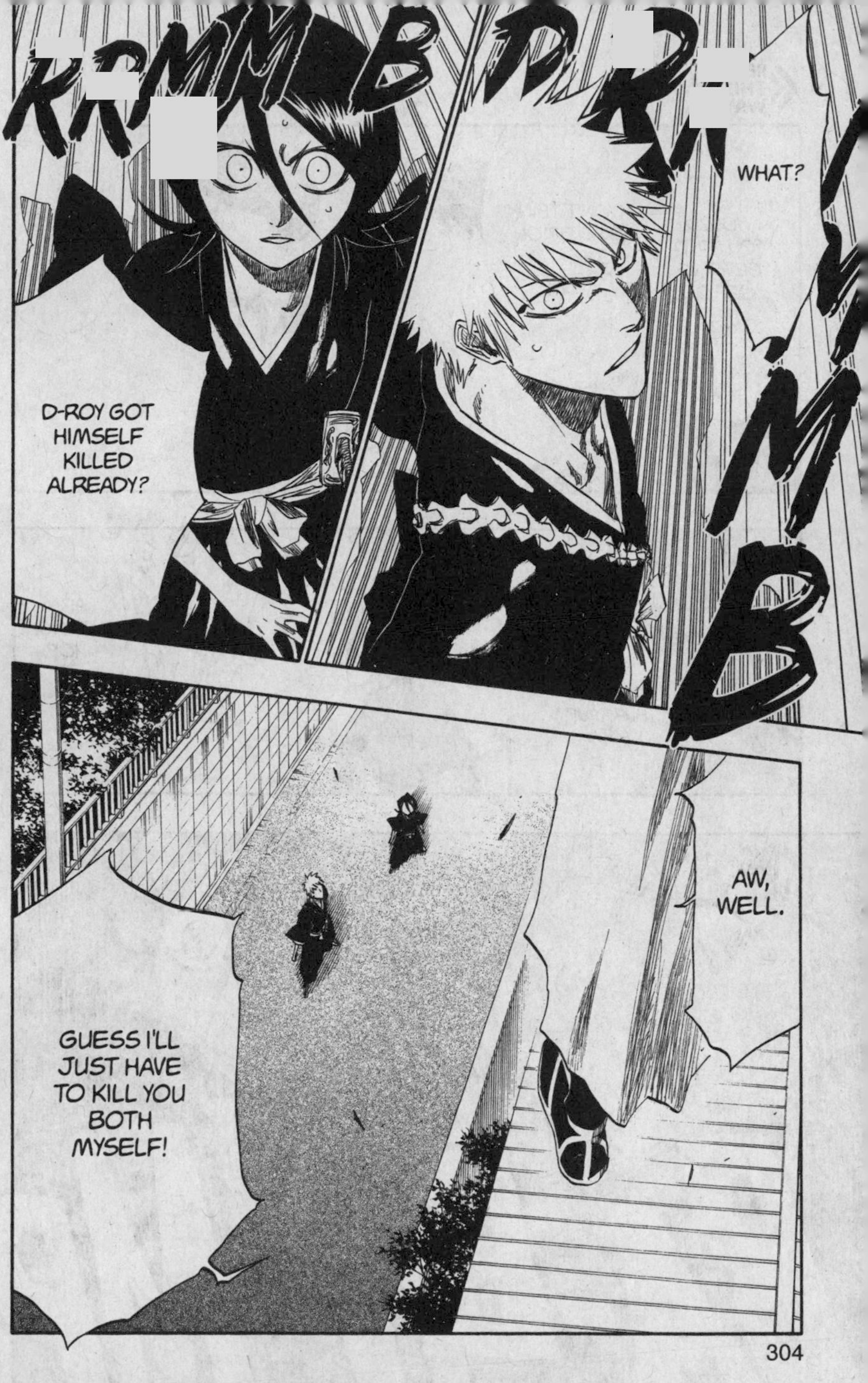
WHAT?
D-ROY GOT HIMSELF KILLED ALREADY?
AW, WELL.
GUESS I'LL JUST HAVE TO KILL YOU BOTH MYSELF!

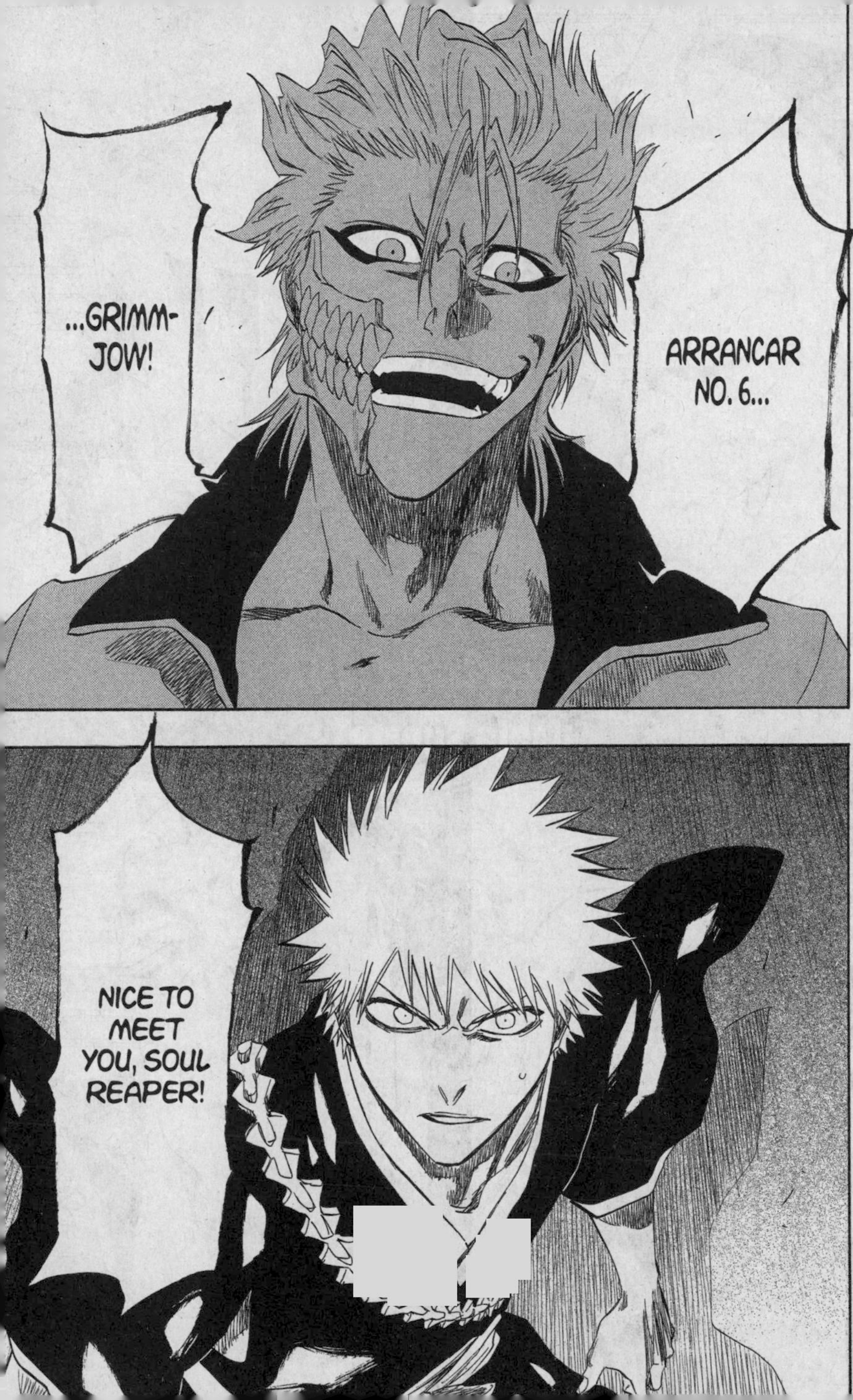
ARRANCAR NO. 6...
...GRIMM-JOW!
NICE TO MEET YOU, SOUL REAPER!

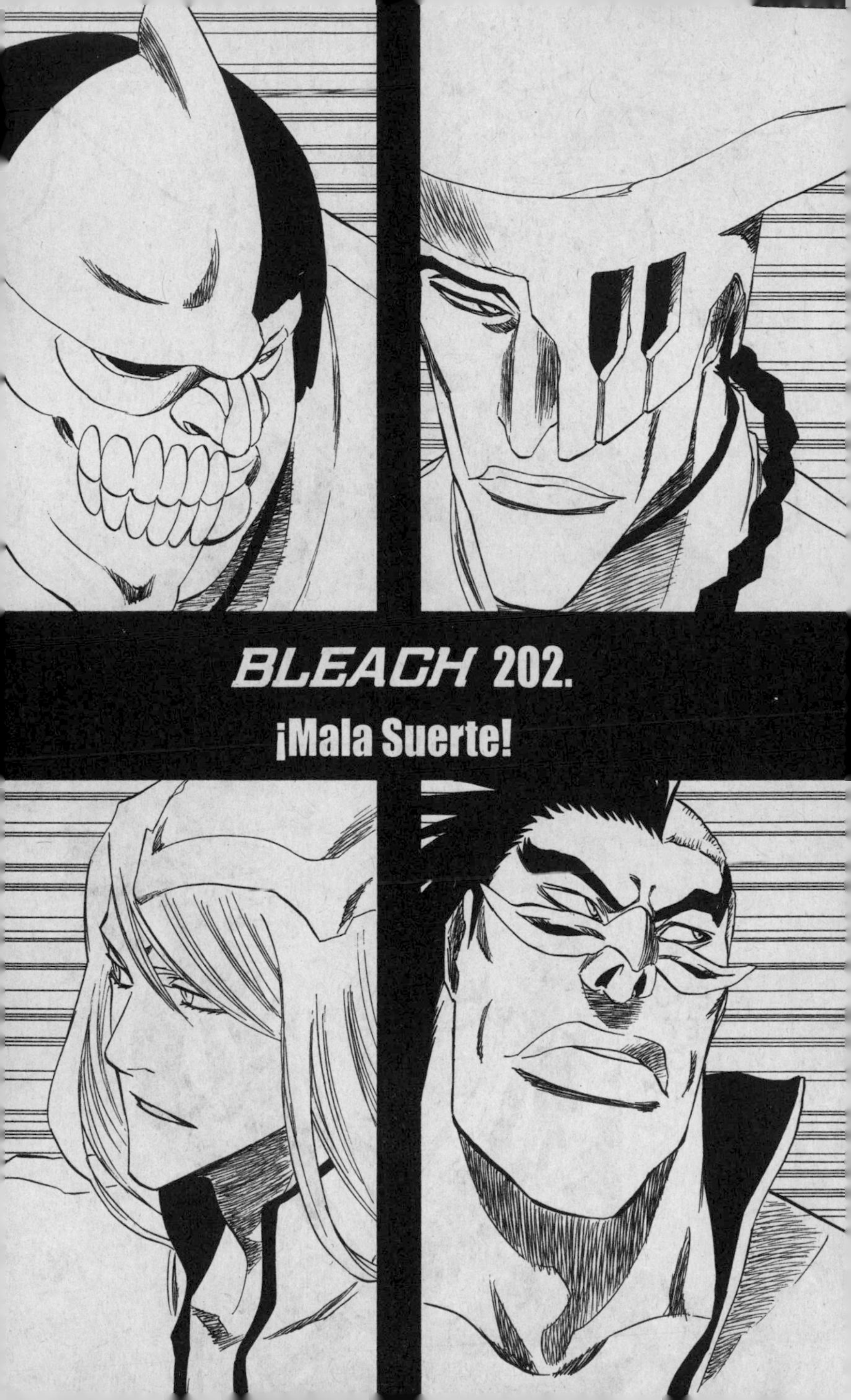
BLEACH 202.
¡Mala Suerte!

READ THIS WAY

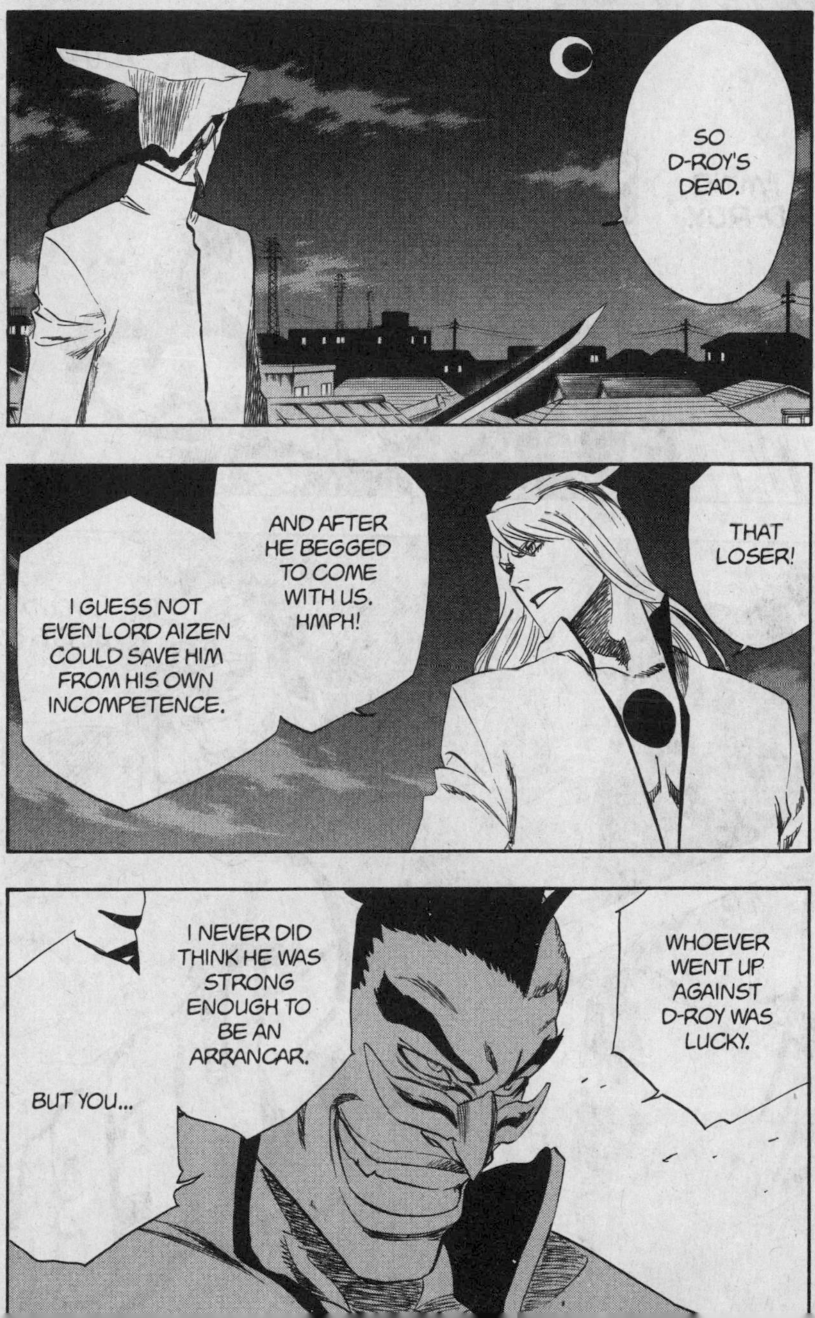
SO D-ROY'S DEAD.
THAT LOSER!
AND AFTER HE BEGGED TO COME WITH US. HMPH!
I GUESS NOT EVEN LORD AIZEN COULD SAVE HIM FROM HIS OWN INCOMPETENCE.
WHOEVER WENT UP AGAINST D-ROY WAS LUCKY.
I NEVER DID THINK HE WAS STRONG ENOUGH TO BE AN ARRANCAR.
BUT YOU...

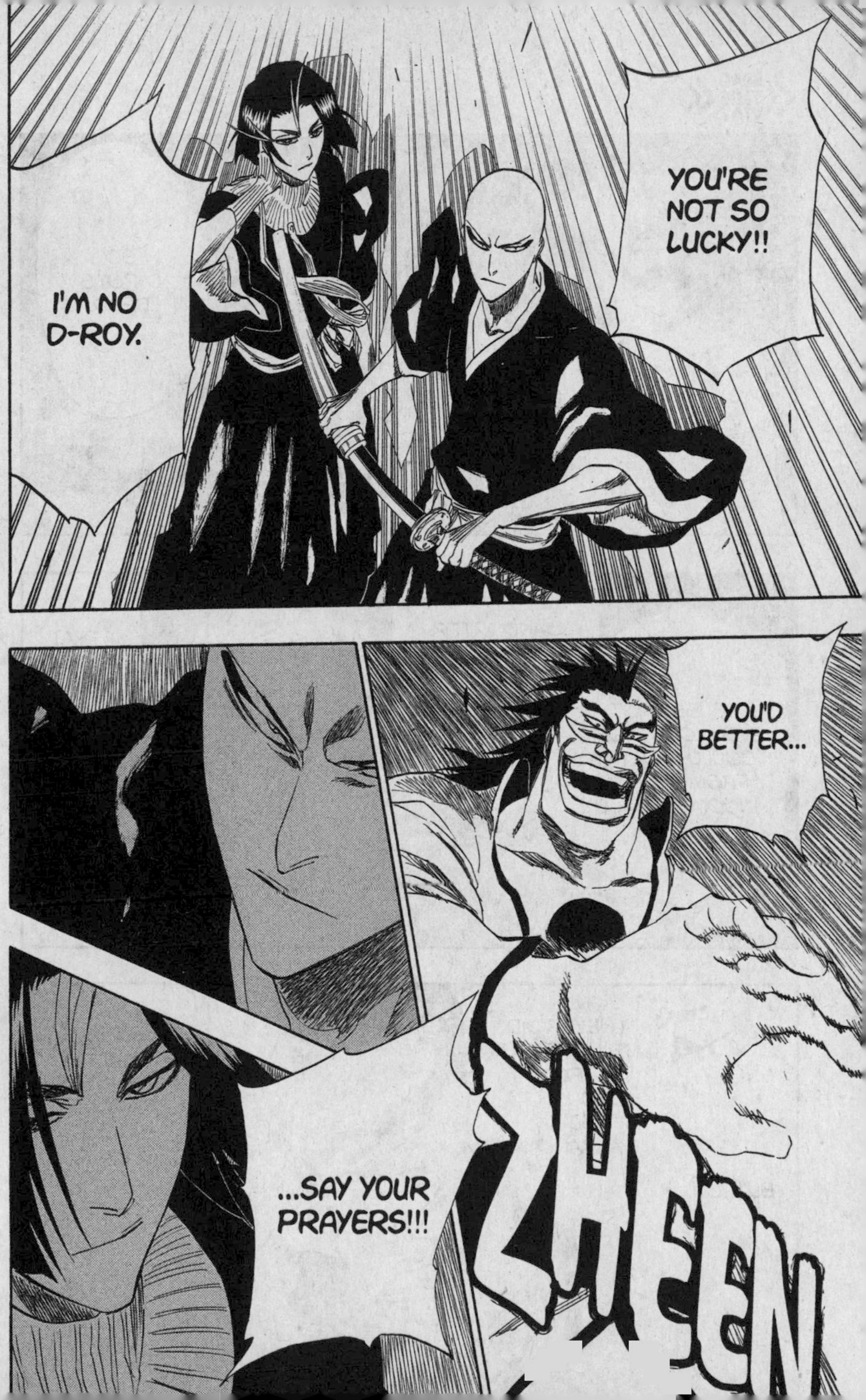
YOU'RE NOT SO LUCKY!!
I'M NO D-ROY.
YOU'D BETTER...
...SAY YOUR PRAYERS!!!

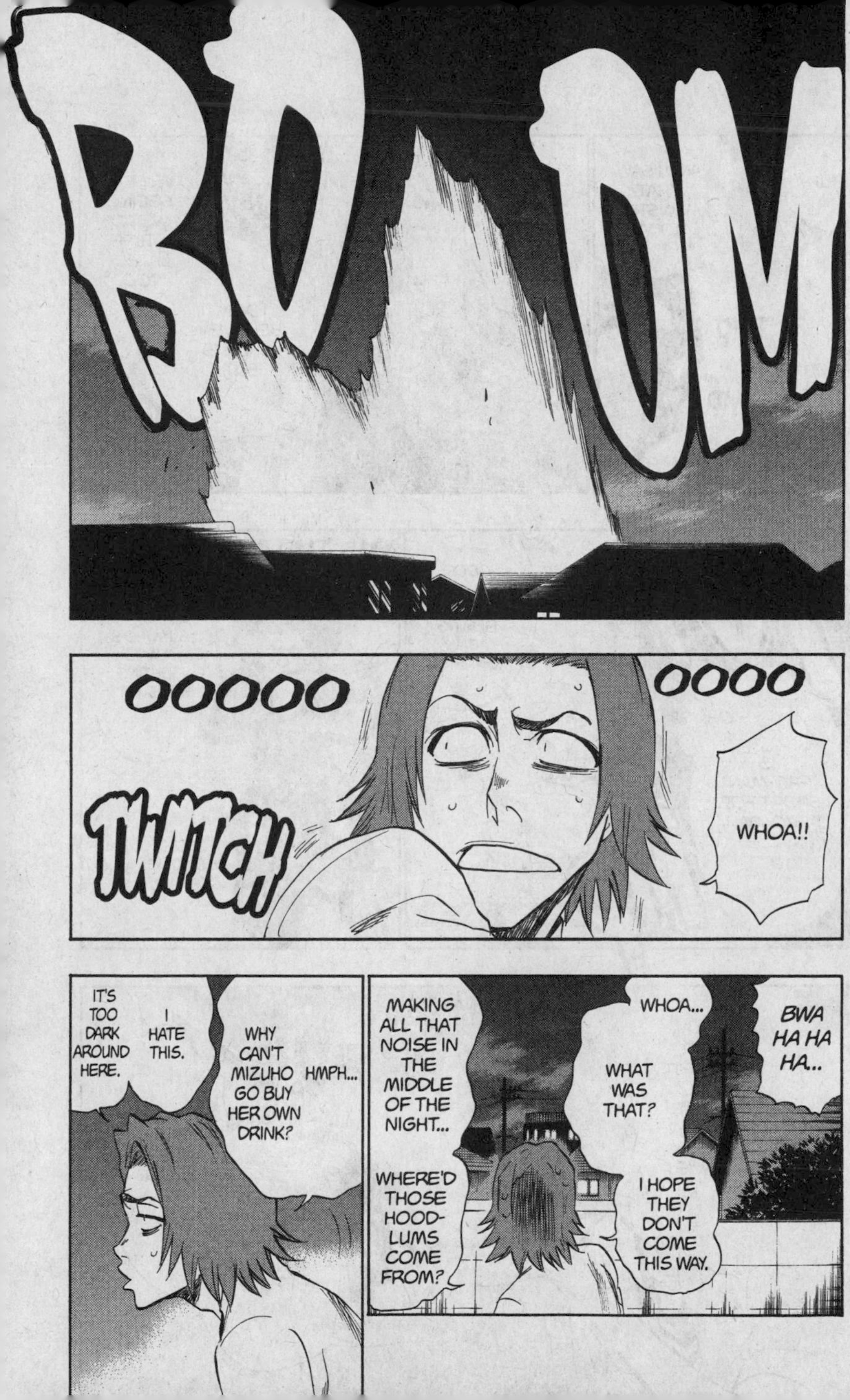
BOOM
OOOO
WHOA!!
OOOOO
TWITCH
BWA HA HA HA...
WHOA...
WHAT WAS THAT?
I HOPE THEY DON'T COME THIS WAY.
MAKING ALL THAT NOISE IN THE MIDDLE OF THE NIGHT...
WHERE'D THOSE HOODLUMS COME FROM?
HMPH...
WHY CAN'T MIZUHO GO BUY HER OWN DRINK?
I HATE THIS.
IT'S TOO DARK AROUND HERE.

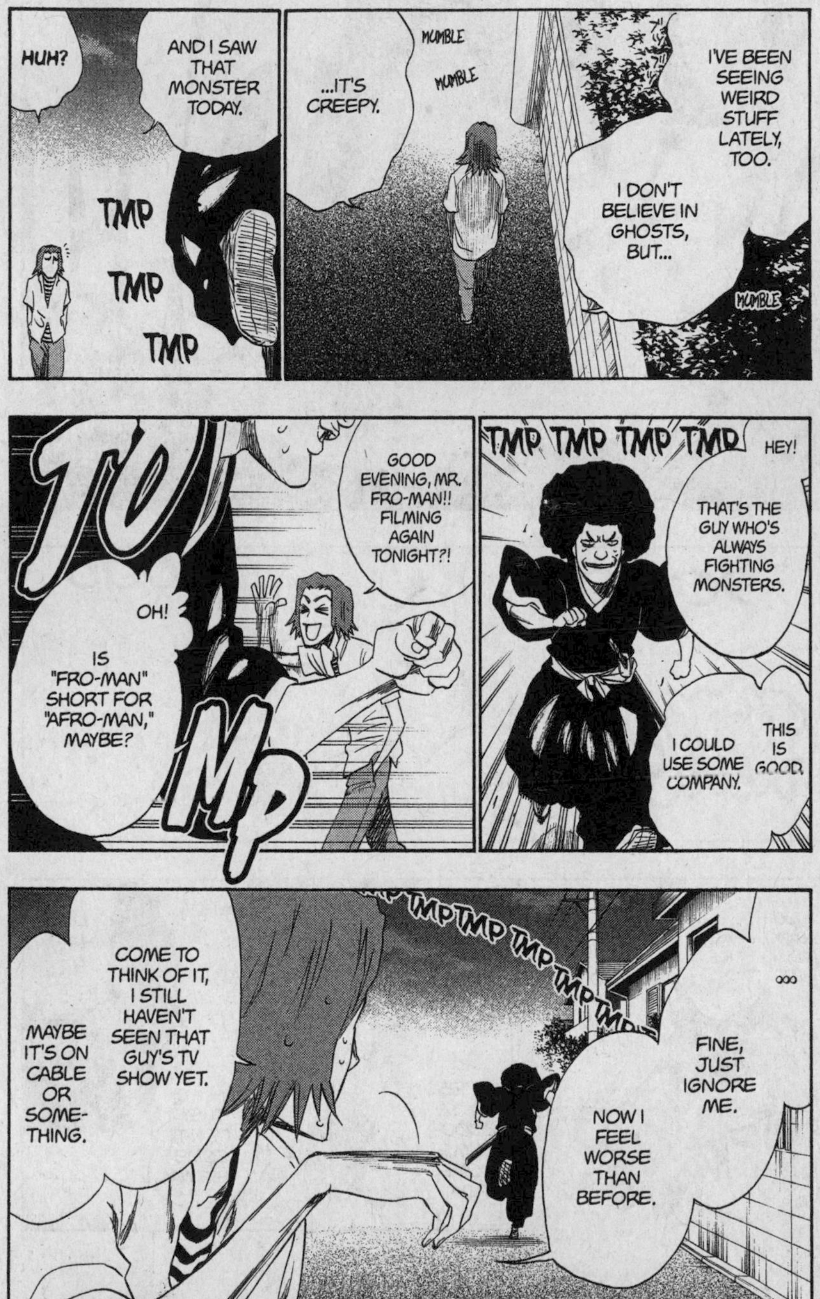
I'VE BEEN SEEING WEIRD STUFF LATELY, TOO.
MUMBLE
I DON'T BELIEVE IN GHOSTS, BUT...
MUMBLE
MUMBLE
...IT'S CREEPY.
AND I SAW THAT MONSTER TODAY.
HUH?
TMP
TMP
TMP
TMP TMP TMP TMP
HEY!
THAT'S THE GUY WHO'S ALWAYS FIGHTING MONSTERS.
THIS IS GOOD.
I COULD USE SOME COMPANY.
GOOD EVENING, MR. FRO-MAN!! FILMING AGAIN TONIGHT?!
TOMP
OH!
IS "FRO-MAN" SHORT FOR "AFRO-MAN," MAYBE?
...
FINE, JUST IGNORE ME.
NOW I FEEL WORSE THAN BEFORE.
TMP TMP TMP TMP TMP TMP
COME TO THINK OF IT, I STILL HAVEN'T SEEN THAT GUY'S TV SHOW YET.
MAYBE IT'S ON CABLE OR SOME-THING.

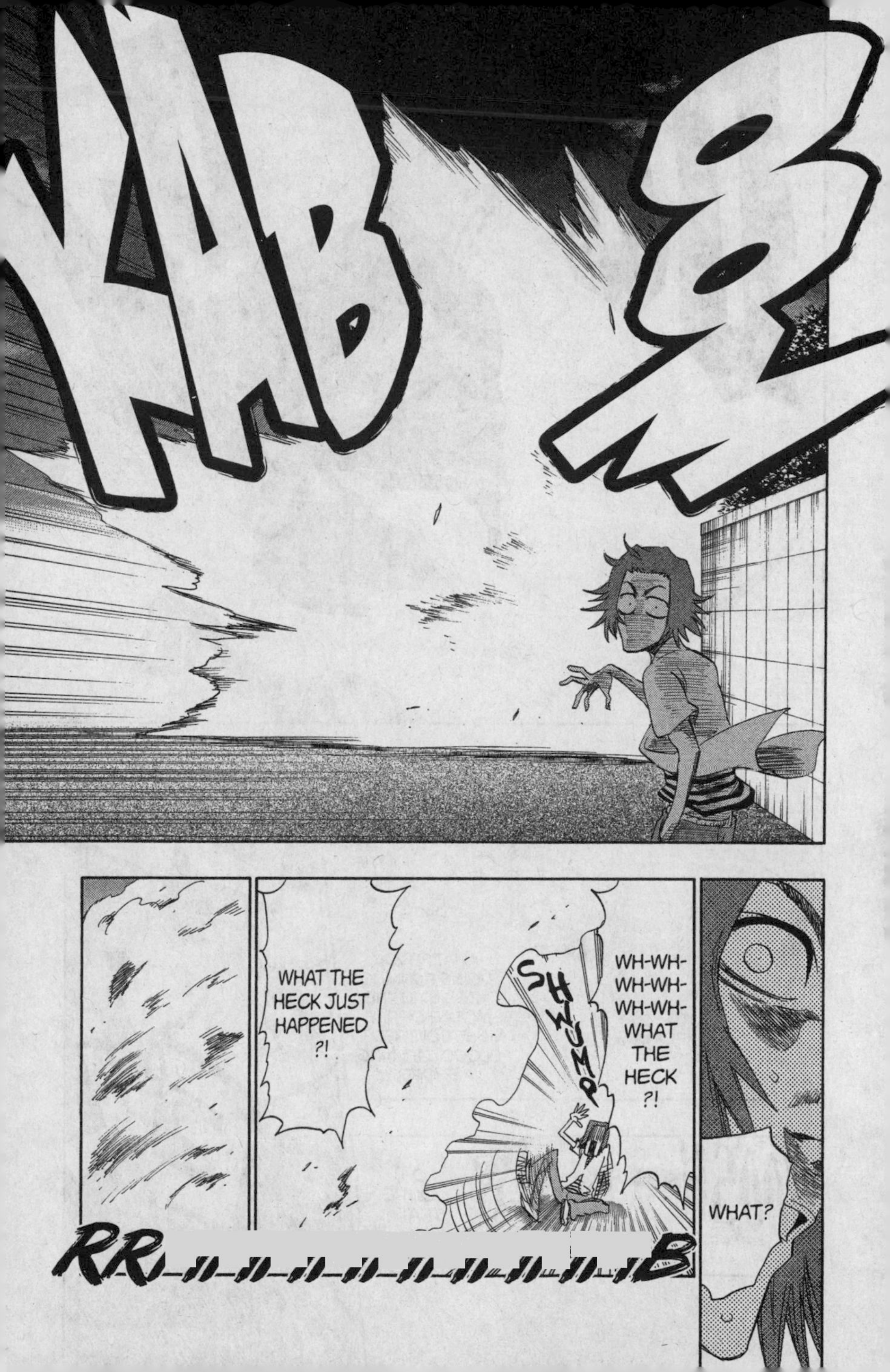
WHAT?
WH-WH-WH-WH-WH-WH-WHAT THE HECK ?!
SHWUMP
WHAT THE HECK JUST HAPPENED ?!

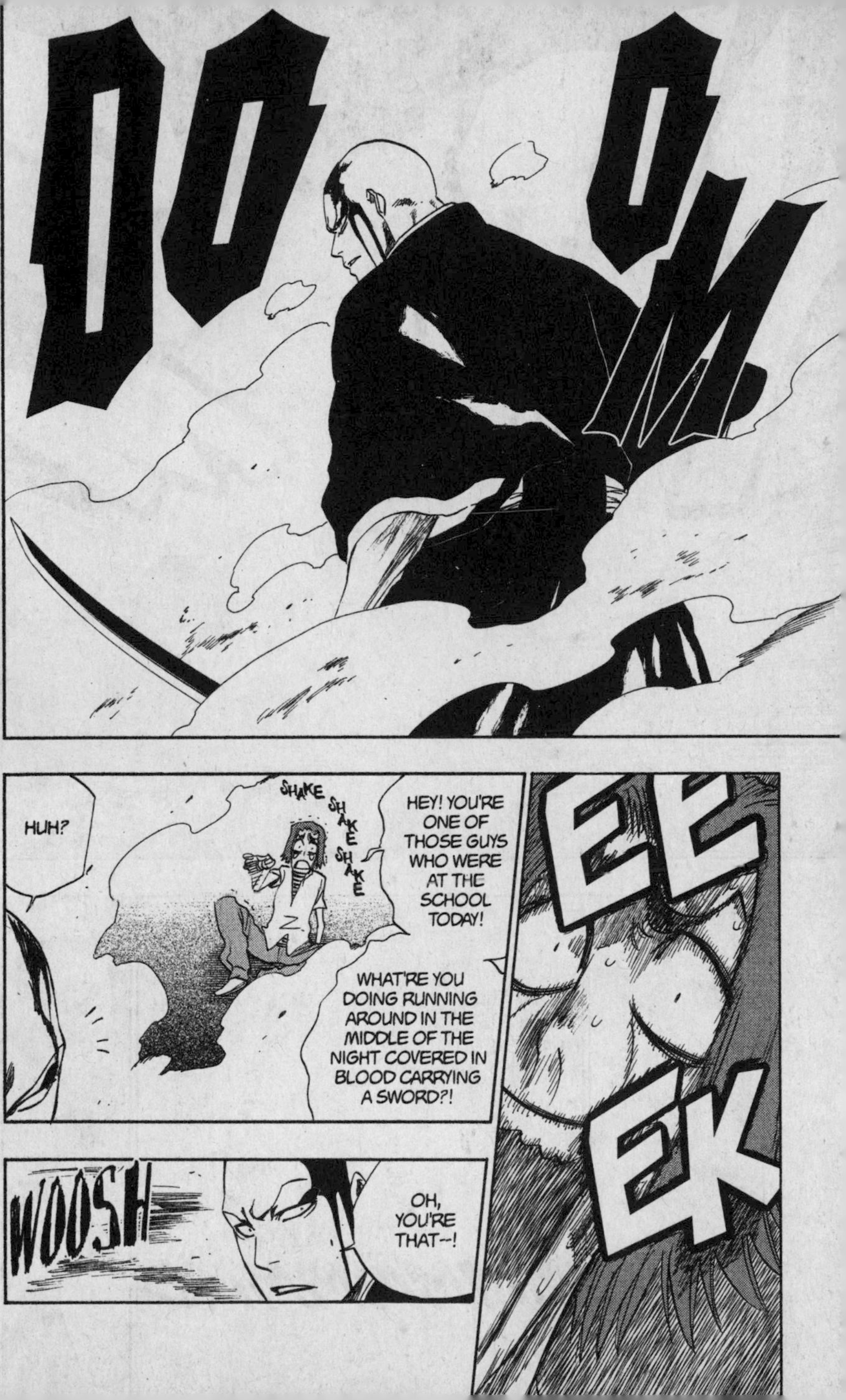
DOOOM
EEEK
SHAKE SHAKE SHAKE SHAKE
HEY! YOU'RE ONE OF THOSE GUYS WHO WERE AT THE SCHOOL TODAY!
WHAT'RE YOU DOING RUNNING AROUND IN THE MIDDLE OF THE NIGHT COVERED IN BLOOD CARRYING A SWORD?!
HUH?
WOOSH
OH, YOU'RE THAT--!

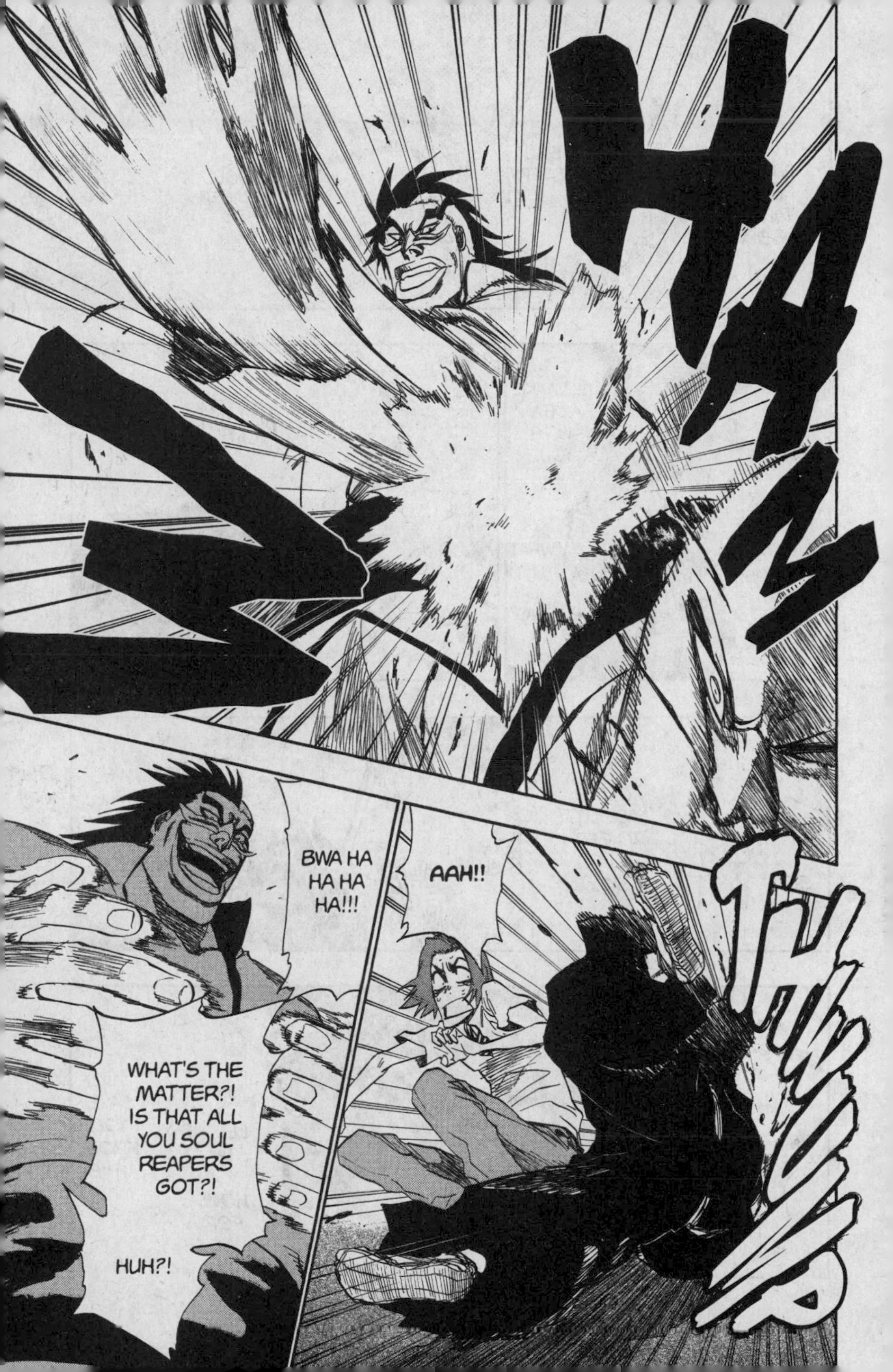
WHAM
THWUMP
AAH!!
BWA HA HA HA HA!!!
WHAT'S THE MATTER?! IS THAT ALL YOU SOUL REAPERS GOT?!
HUH?!

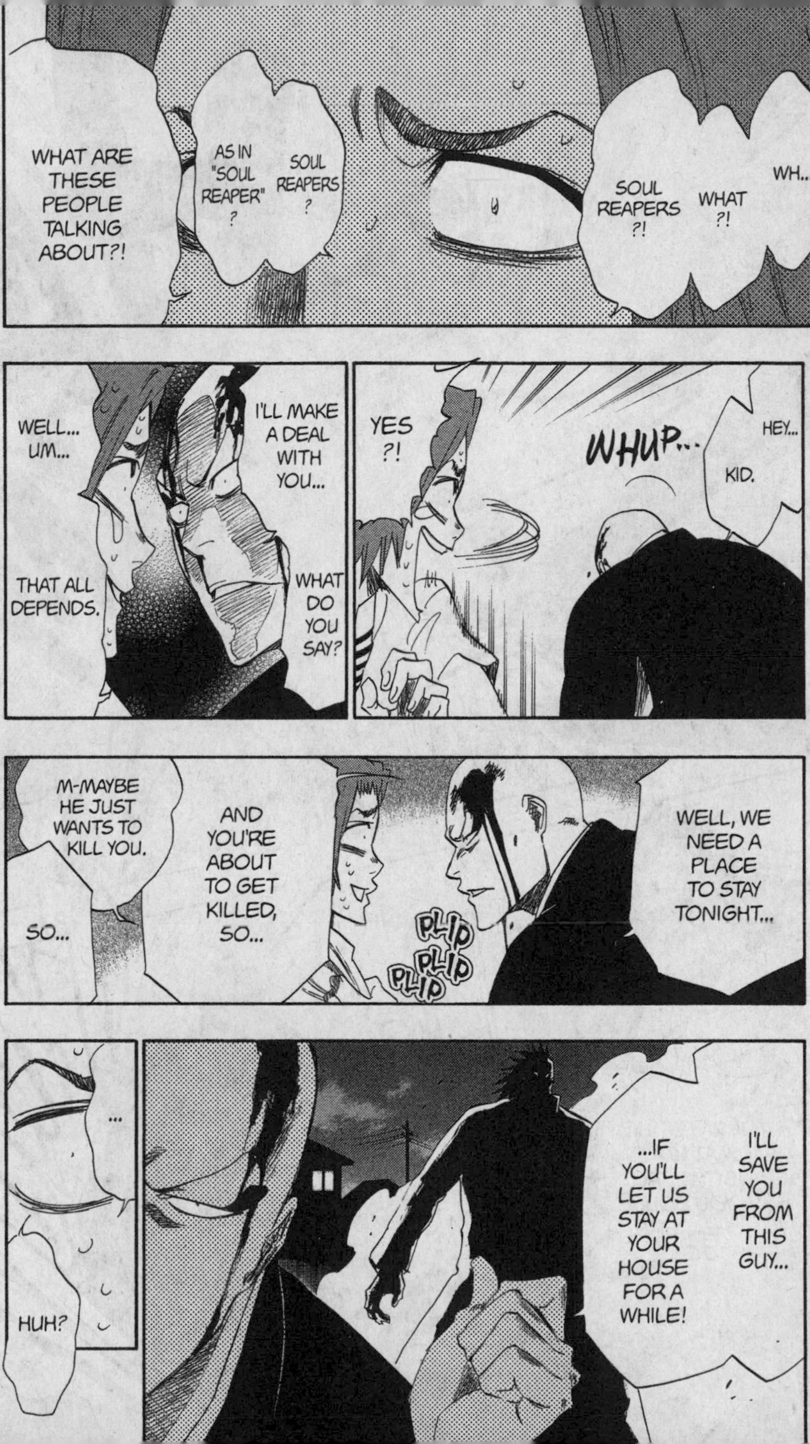
WH...
WHAT ?!
SOUL REAPERS ?!
SOUL REAPERS ?
AS IN "SOUL REAPER" ?
WHAT ARE THESE PEOPLE TALKING ABOUT?!
HEY... KID.
WHUP...
YES ?!
I'LL MAKE A DEAL WITH YOU...
WHAT DO YOU SAY?
WELL... UM...
THAT ALL DEPENDS.
WELL, WE NEED A PLACE TO STAY TONIGHT...
PLIP PLIP PLIP
AND YOU'RE ABOUT TO GET KILLED, SO...
M-MAYBE HE JUST WANTS TO KILL YOU.
SO...
I'LL SAVE YOU FROM THIS GUY...
...IF YOU'LL LET US STAY AT YOUR HOUSE FOR A WHILE!
...
HUH?

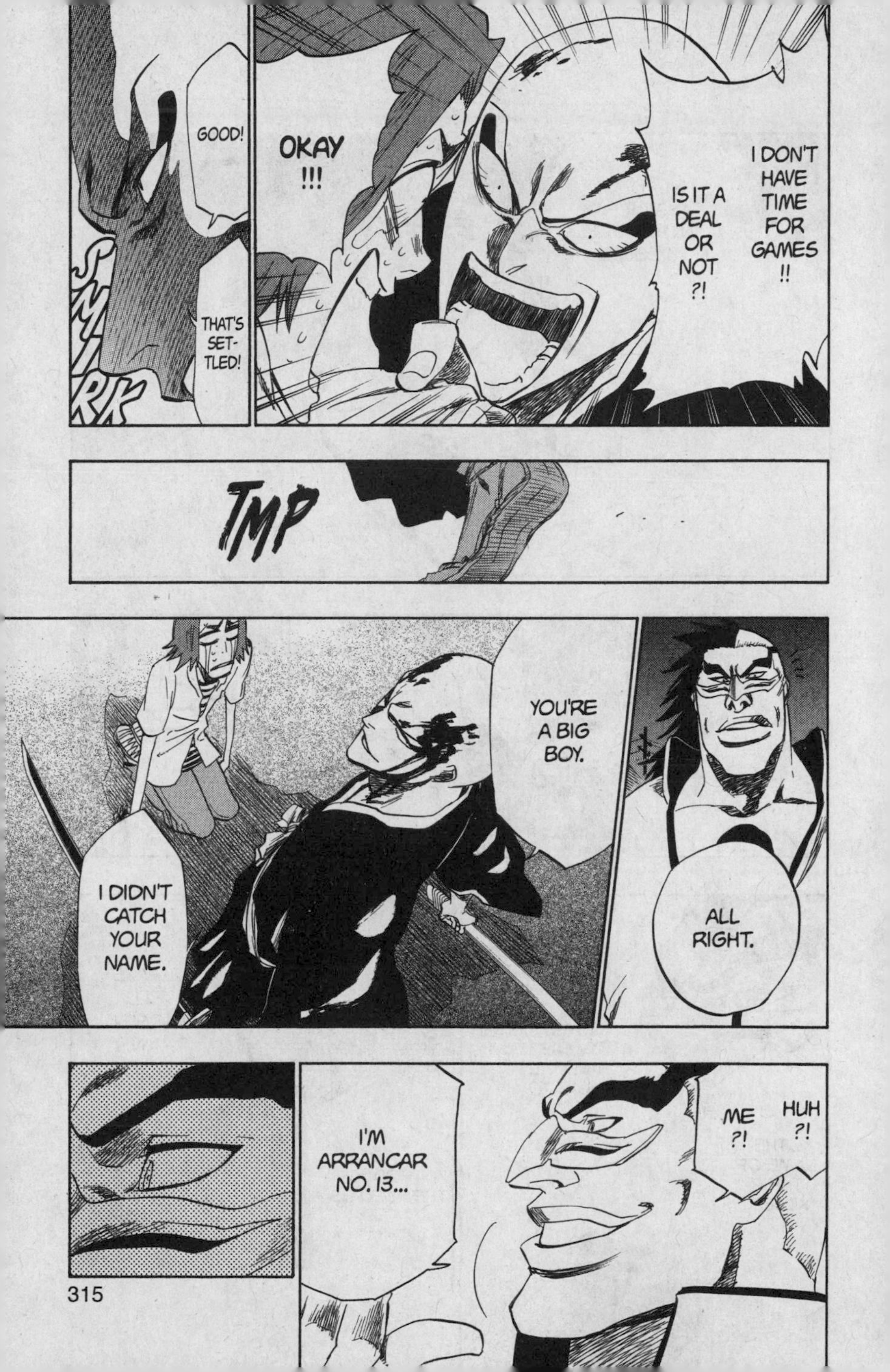
I DON'T HAVE TIME FOR GAMES!!
IS IT A DEAL OR NOT?!
OKAY!!!
GOOD!
THAT'S SETTLED!
SMIRK
TMP
ALL RIGHT.
YOU'RE A BIG BOY.
I DIDN'T CATCH YOUR NAME.
HUH?!
ME?!
I'M ARRANCAR NO. 13...

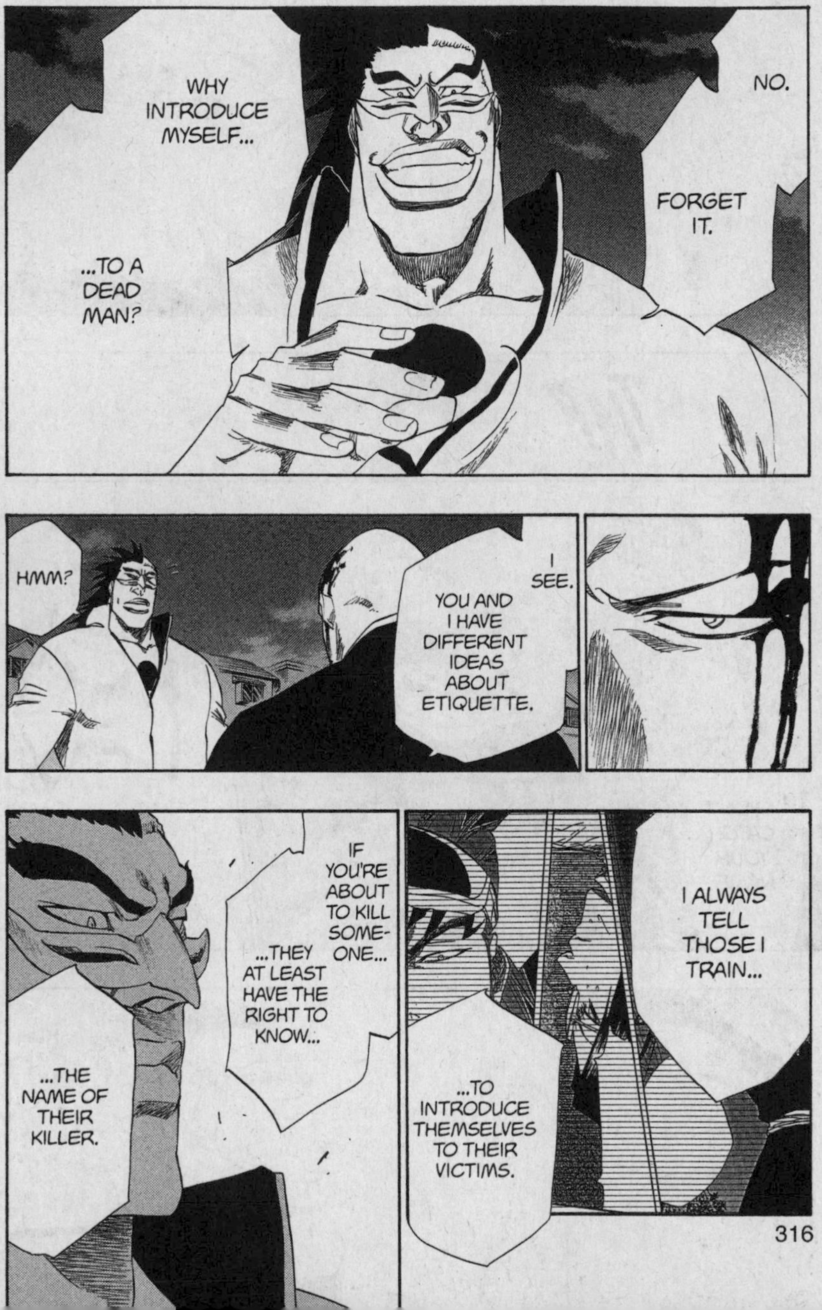
NO.
FORGET IT.
WHY INTRODUCE MYSELF...
...TO A DEAD MAN?
I SEE.
YOU AND I HAVE DIFFERENT IDEAS ABOUT ETIQUETTE.
HMM?
I ALWAYS TELL THOSE I TRAIN...
...TO INTRODUCE THEMSELVES TO THEIR VICTIMS.
IF YOU'RE ABOUT TO KILL SOME-ONE...
...THEY AT LEAST HAVE THE RIGHT TO KNOW...
...THE NAME OF THEIR KILLER.

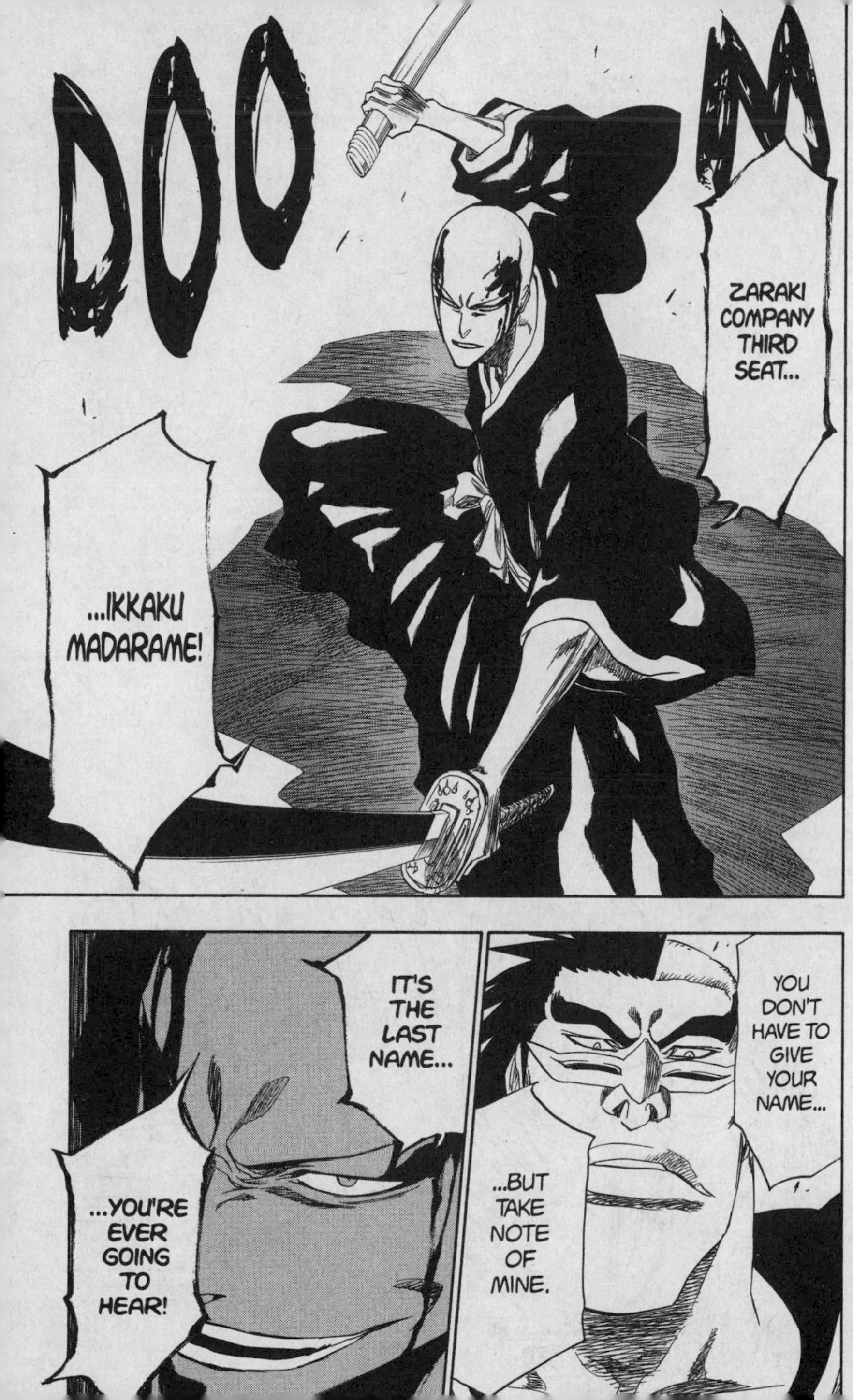
DOOOM
ZARAKI COMPANY THIRD SEAT...
...IKKAKU MADARAME!
YOU DON'T HAVE TO GIVE YOUR NAME...
...BUT TAKE NOTE OF MINE.
IT'S THE LAST NAME...
...YOU'RE EVER GOING TO HEAR!

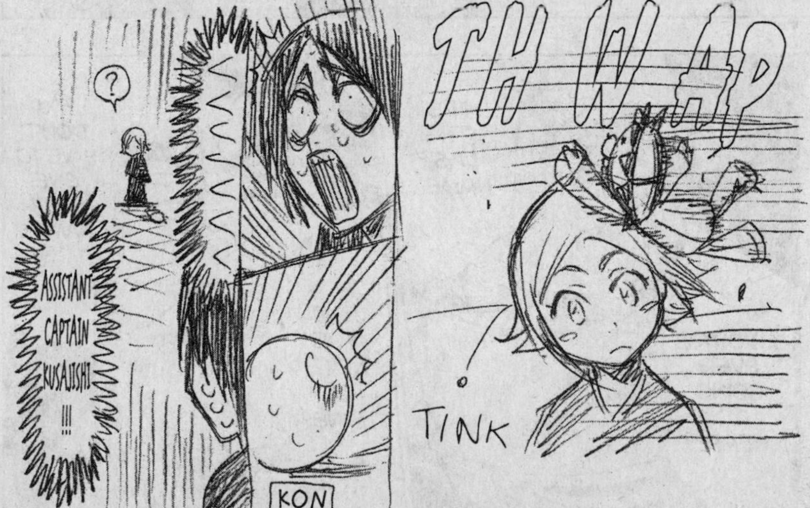
THWAP
TINK
KON
?
ASSISTANT CAPTAIN KUSAJISHI!!!

203. ¡Mala Suerte! 2 [El Monstruo]

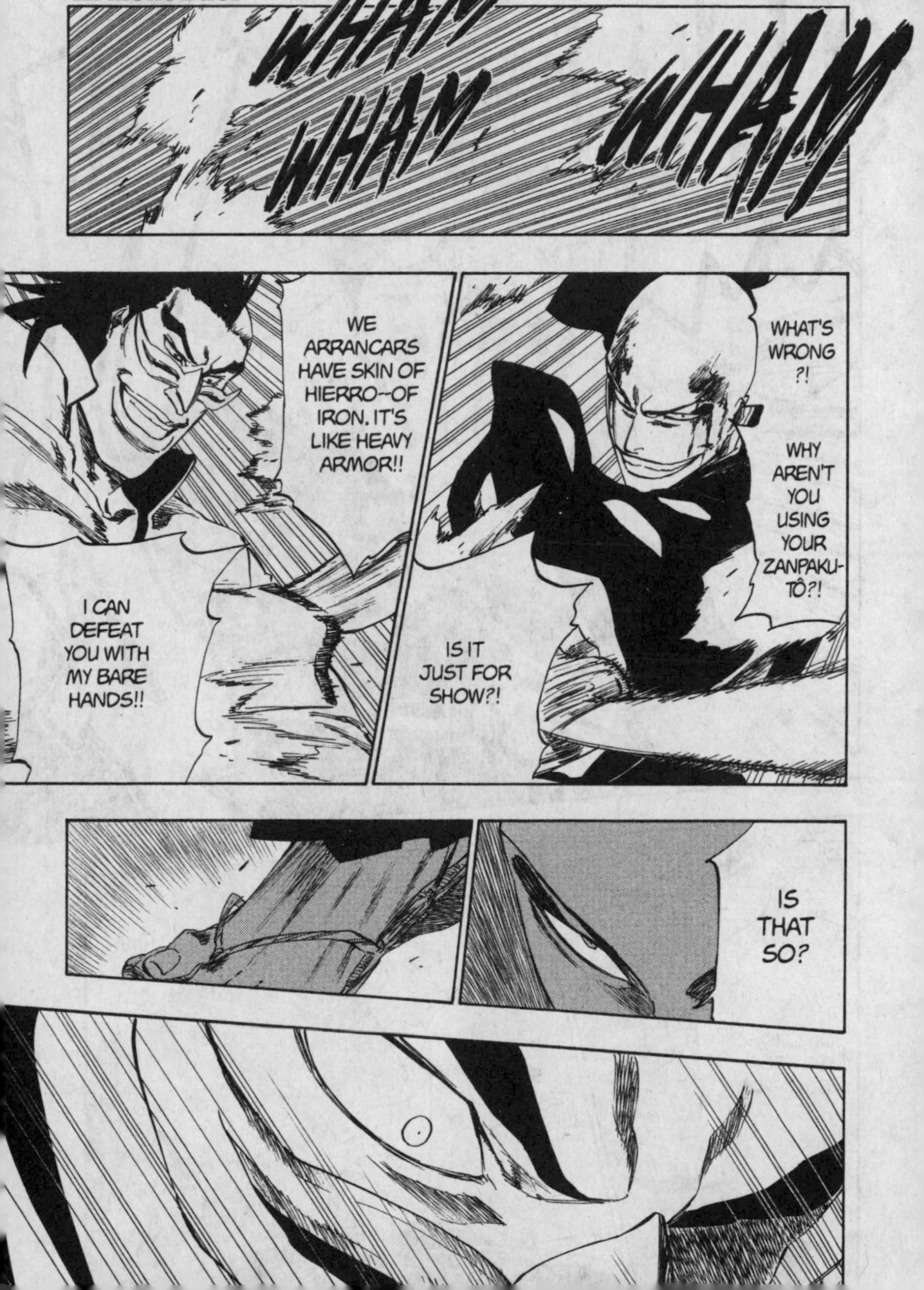
WHAM
WHAM
WHAM
WHAM
WHAT'S WRONG?!
WHY AREN'T YOU USING YOUR ZANPAKU-TÔ?!
IS IT JUST FOR SHOW?!
WE ARRANCARS HAVE SKIN OF HIERRO--OF IRON. IT'S LIKE HEAVY ARMOR!!
I CAN DEFEAT YOU WITH MY BARE HANDS!!
IS THAT SO?

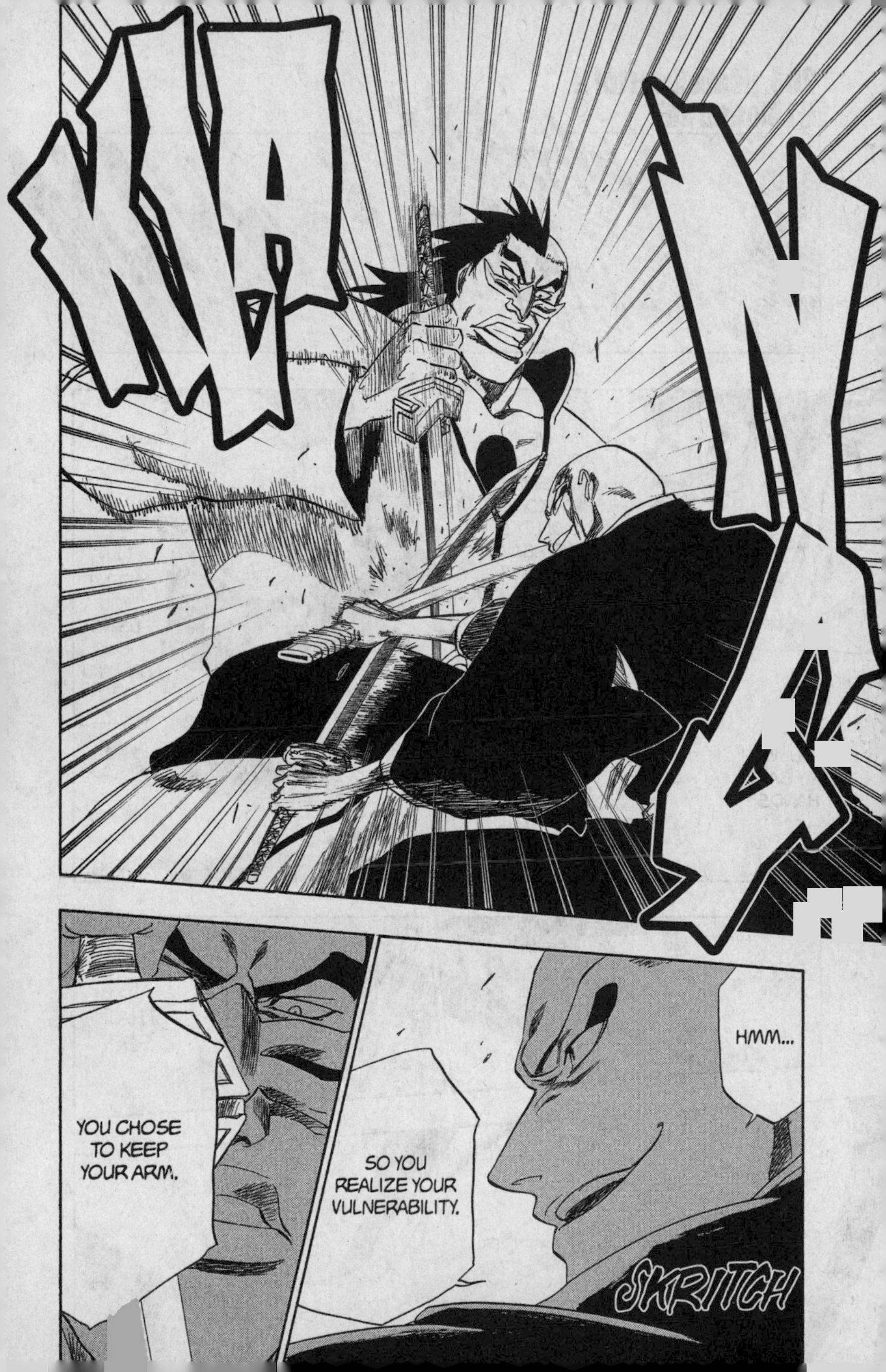
HMM...
SO YOU REALIZE YOUR VULNERABILITY.
SKRITCH
YOU CHOSE TO KEEP YOUR ARM.

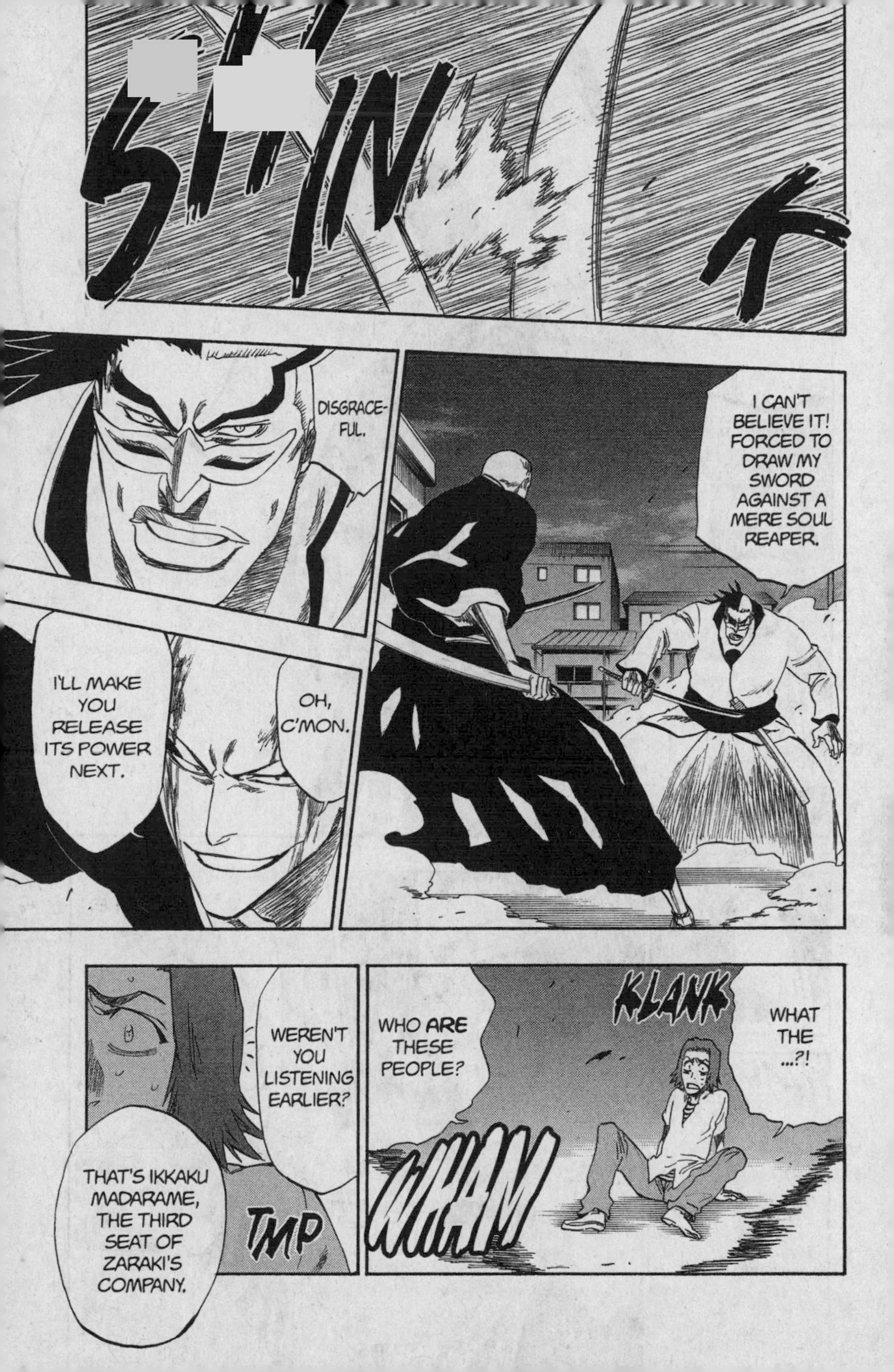
I CAN'T BELIEVE IT! FORCED TO DRAW MY SWORD AGAINST A MERE SOUL REAPER.
DISGRACE-FUL.
OH, C'MON.
I'LL MAKE YOU RELEASE ITS POWER NEXT.
KLANK
WHAT THE ...?!
WHO ARE THESE PEOPLE?
WHAM
WEREN'T YOU LISTENING EARLIER?
THAT'S IKKAKU MADARAME, THE THIRD SEAT OF ZARAKI'S COMPANY.
TMP

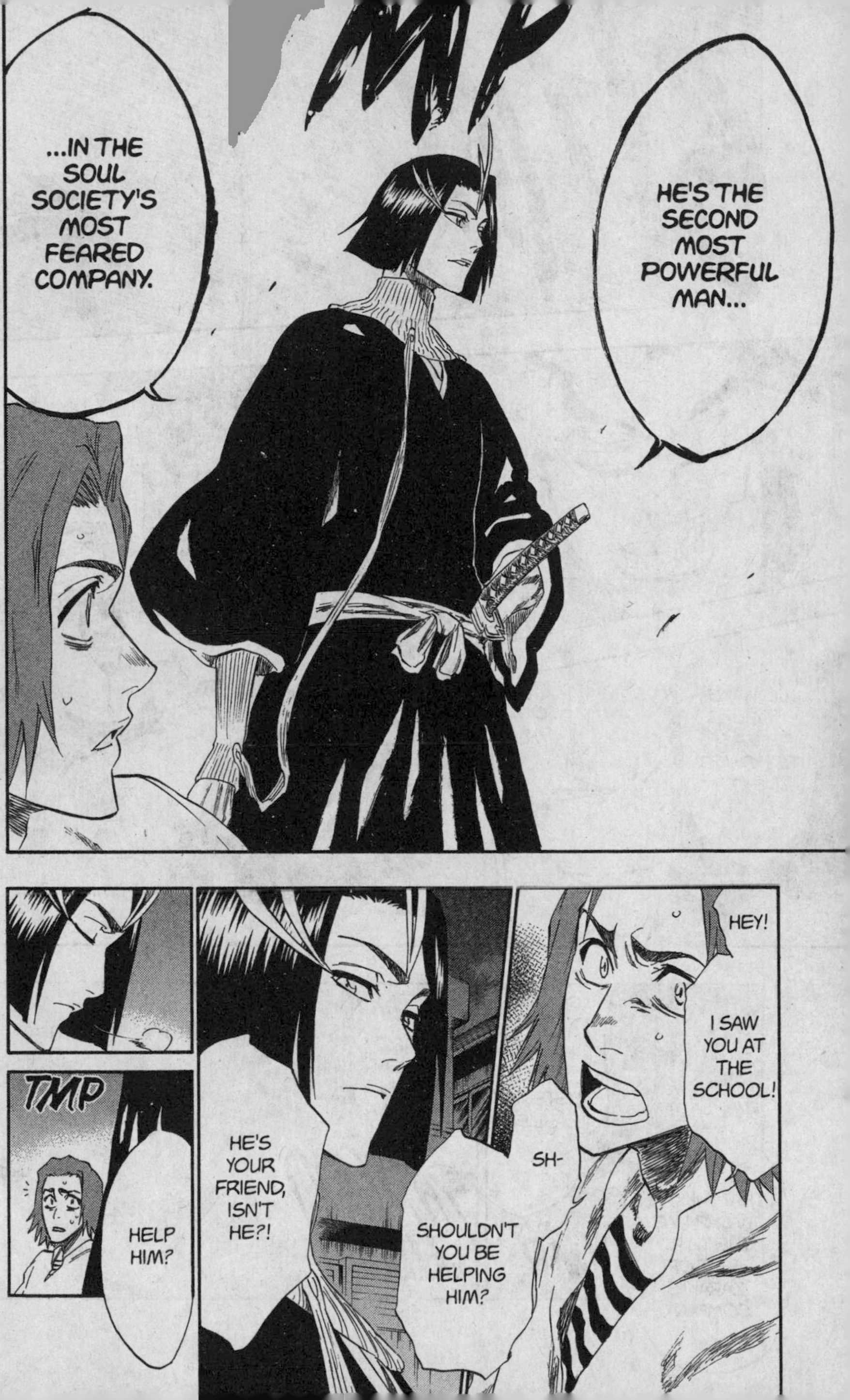
MP
HE'S THE SECOND MOST POWERFUL MAN...
...IN THE SOUL SOCIETY'S MOST FEARED COMPANY.
HEY!
I SAW YOU AT THE SCHOOL!
SH-
SHOULDN'T YOU BE HELPING HIM?
HE'S YOUR FRIEND, ISN'T HE?!
TMP
HELP HIM?

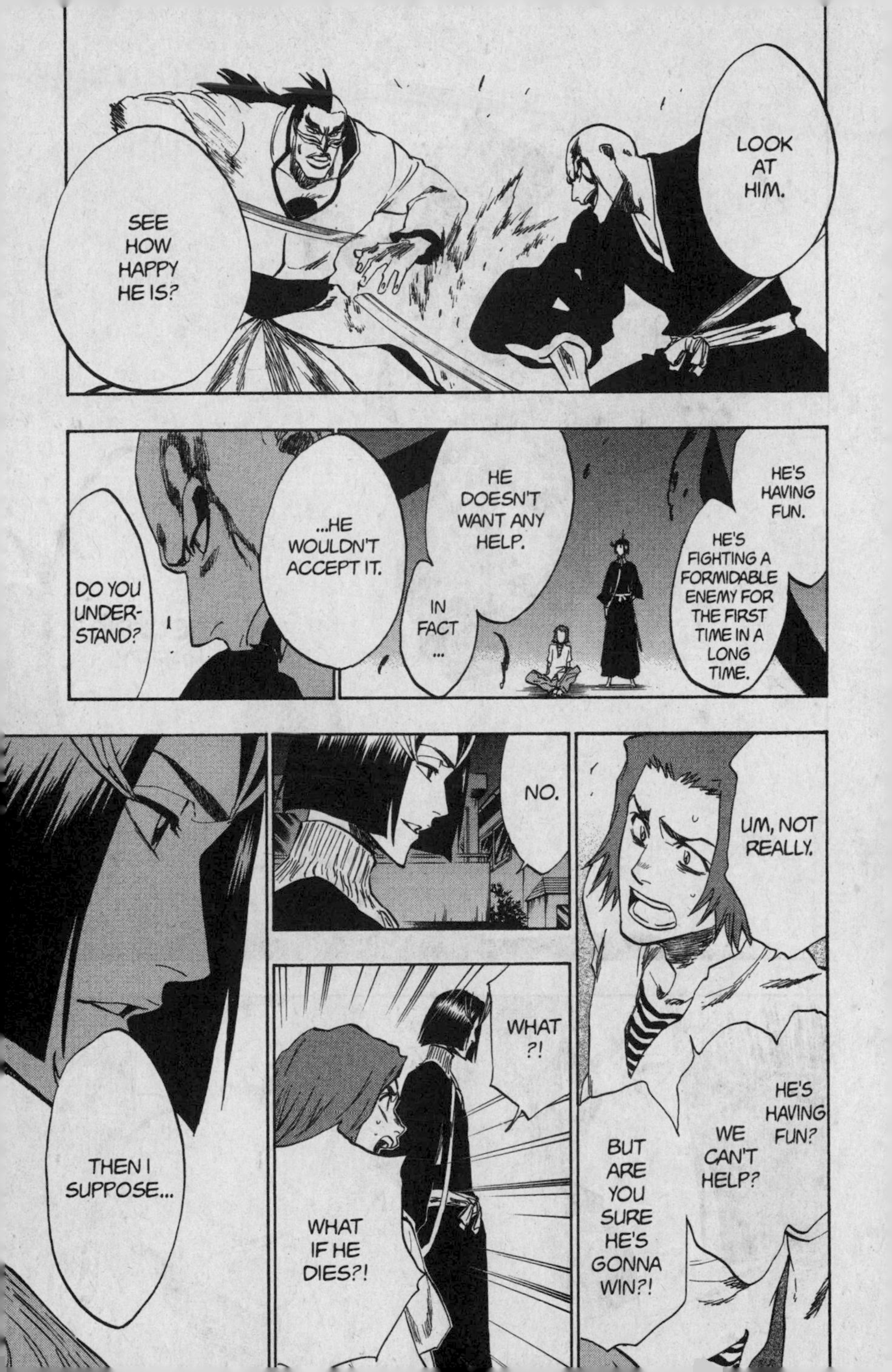
LOOK AT HIM.
SEE HOW HAPPY HE IS?
HE'S HAVING FUN.
HE'S FIGHTING A FORMIDABLE ENEMY FOR THE FIRST TIME IN A LONG TIME.
HE DOESN'T WANT ANY HELP.
IN FACT ...
...HE WOULDN'T ACCEPT IT.
DO YOU UNDER-STAND?
UM, NOT REALLY.
HE'S HAVING FUN?
WE CAN'T HELP?
BUT ARE YOU SURE HE'S GONNA WIN?!
NO.
WHAT ?!
WHAT IF HE DIES?!
THEN I SUPPOSE...

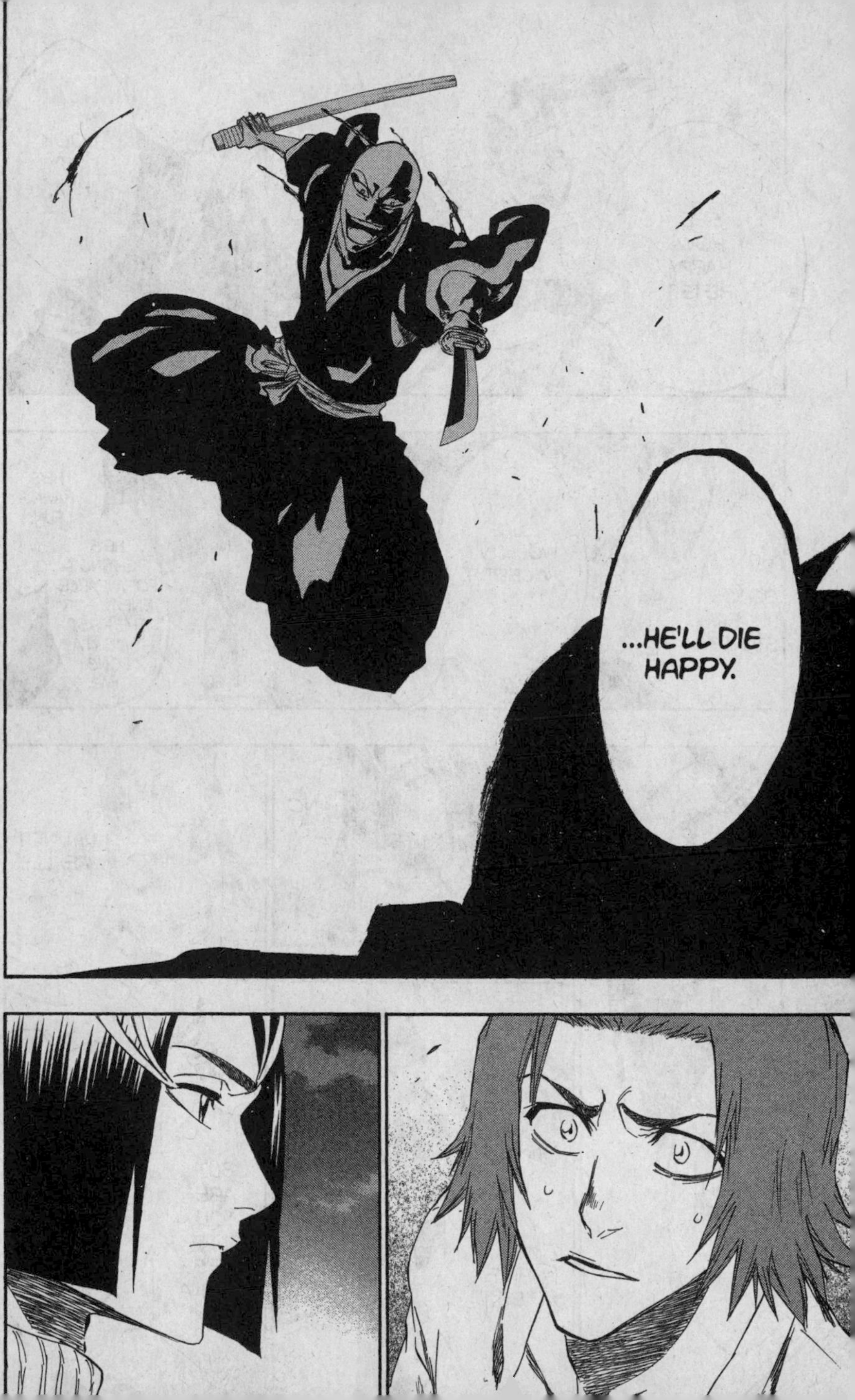
...HE'LL DIE HAPPY.

Bleach 203. ¡Mala Suerte! 2 [El Monstruo]

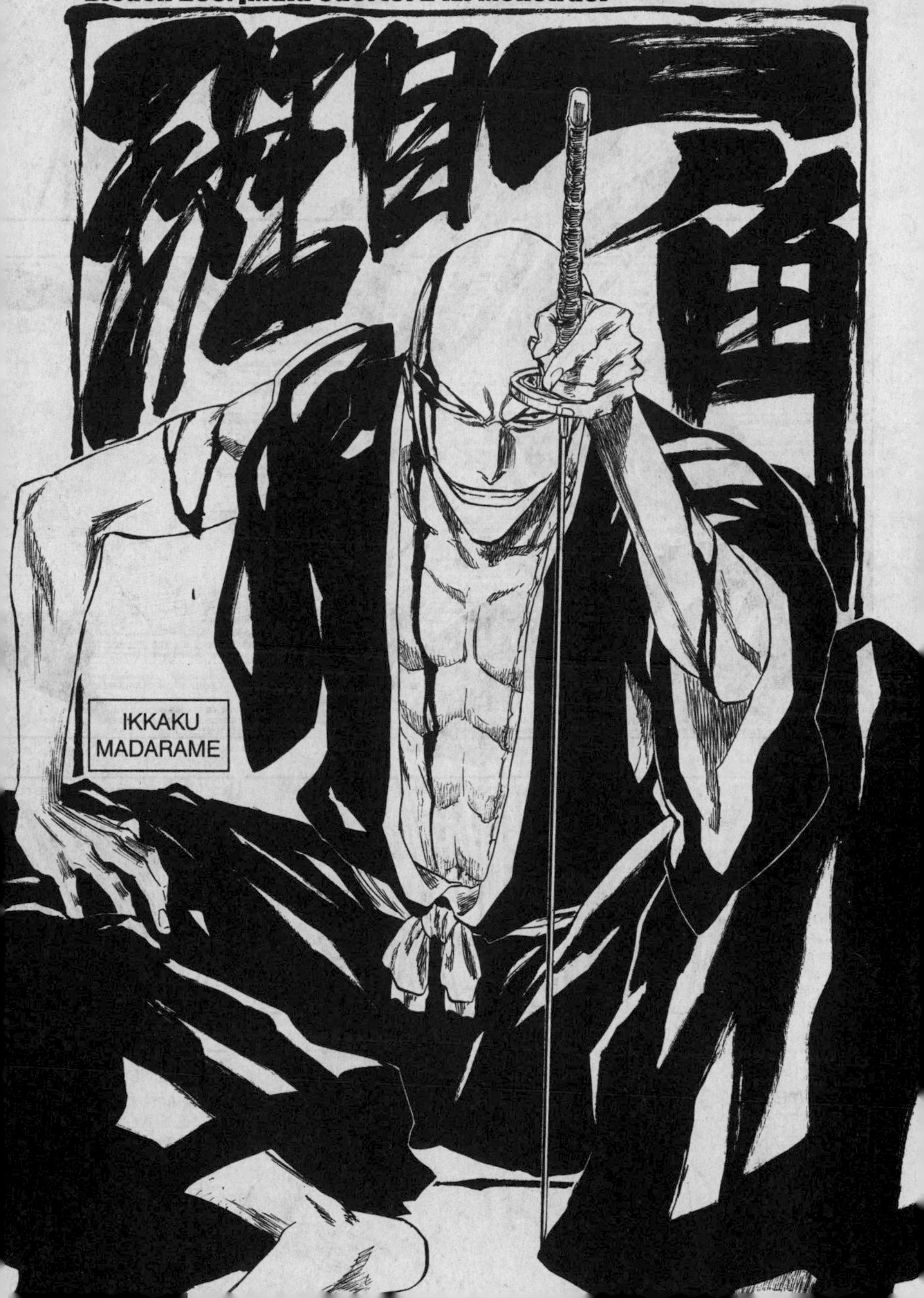
IKKAKU
MADARAME

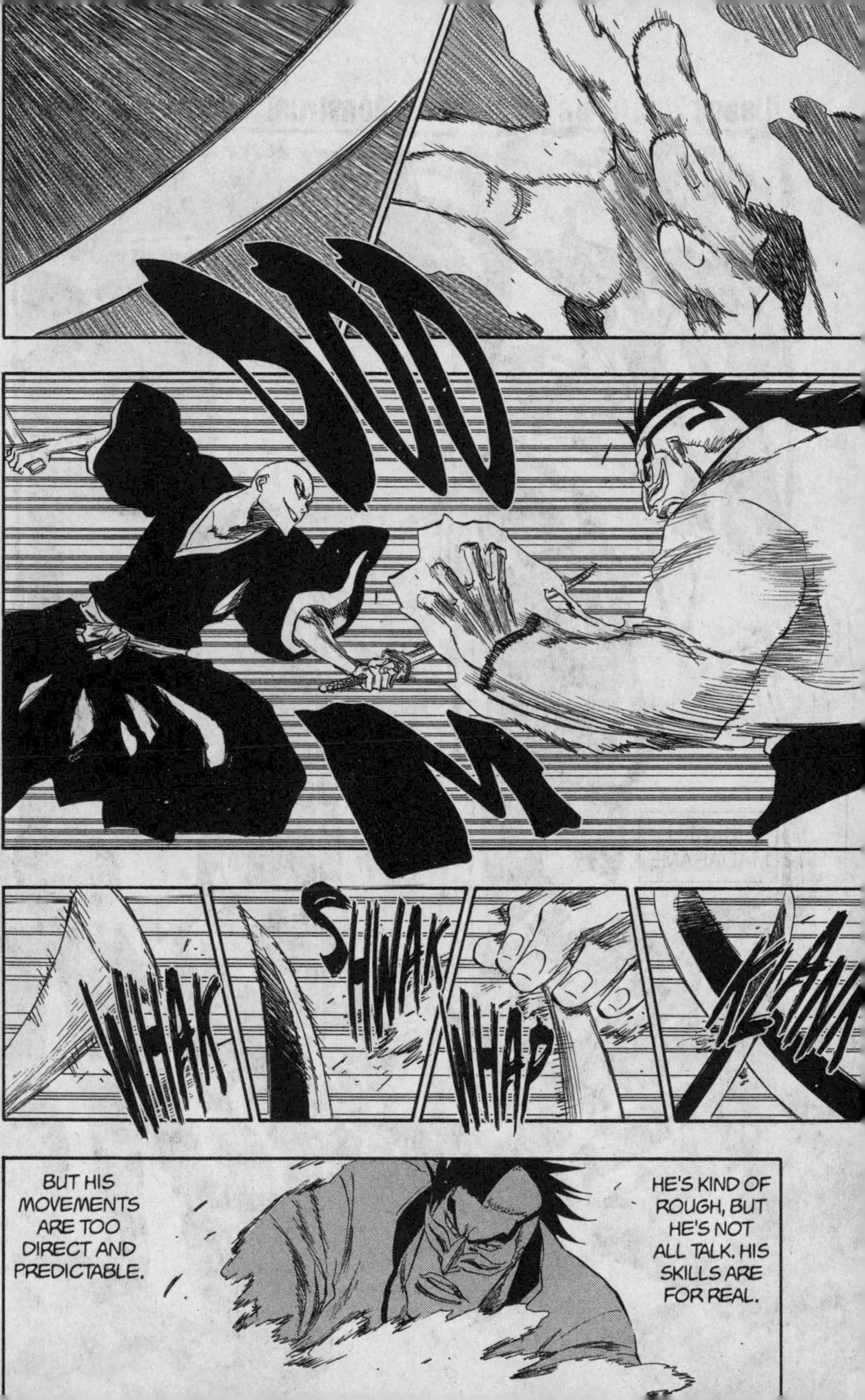
DOOM
WHAP
SHWAK
WHAK
HE'S KIND OF ROUGH, BUT HE'S NOT ALL TALK. HIS SKILLS ARE FOR REAL.
BUT HIS MOVEMENTS ARE TOO DIRECT AND PREDICTABLE.

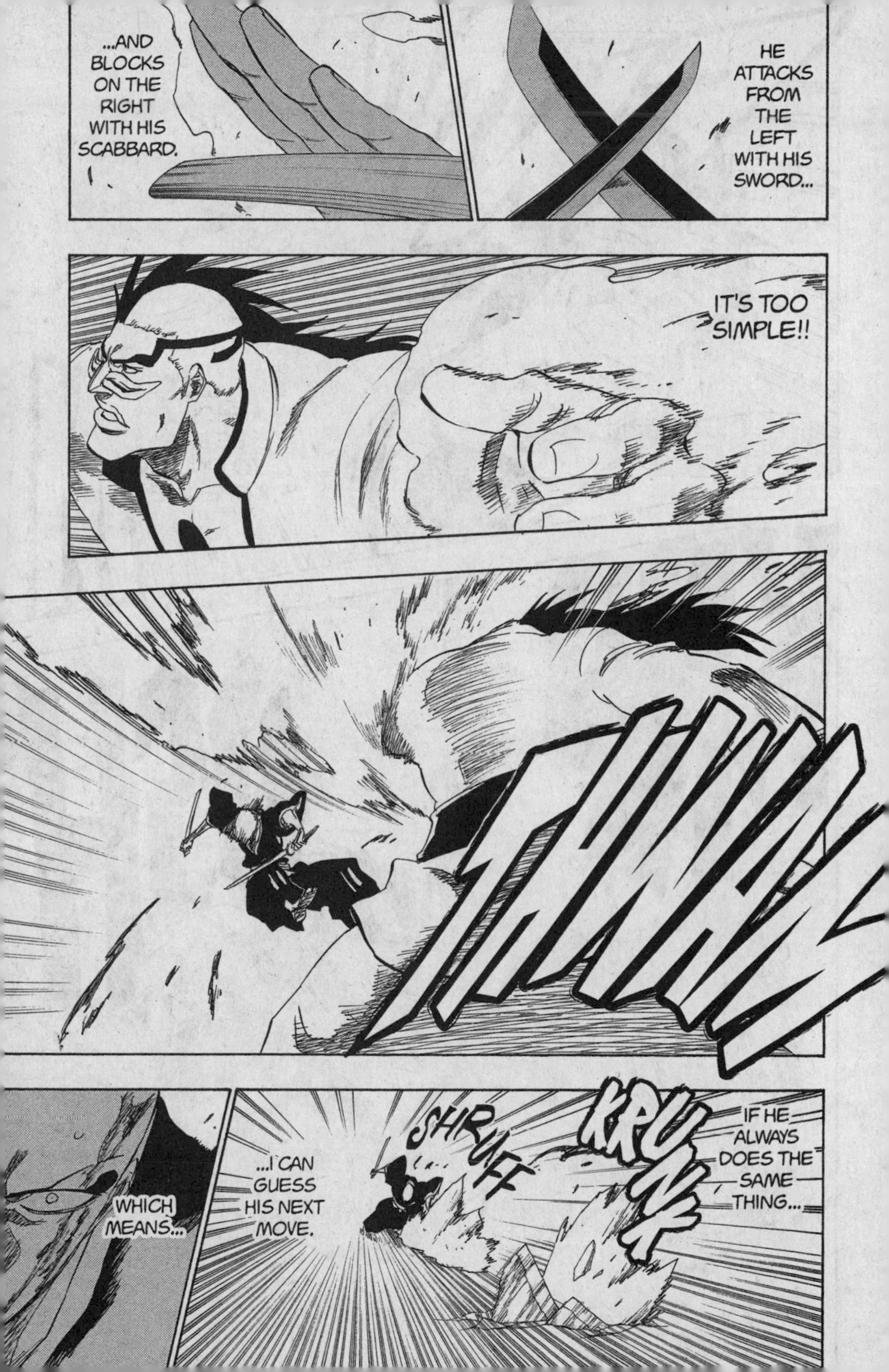
HE ATTACKS FROM THE LEFT WITH HIS SWORD...
...AND BLOCKS ON THE RIGHT WITH HIS SCABBARD.
IT'S TOO SIMPLE!!
THWAK
IF HE ALWAYS DOES THE SAME THING...
KRUNK
SHRUFF
...I CAN GUESS HIS NEXT MOVE.
WHICH MEANS...

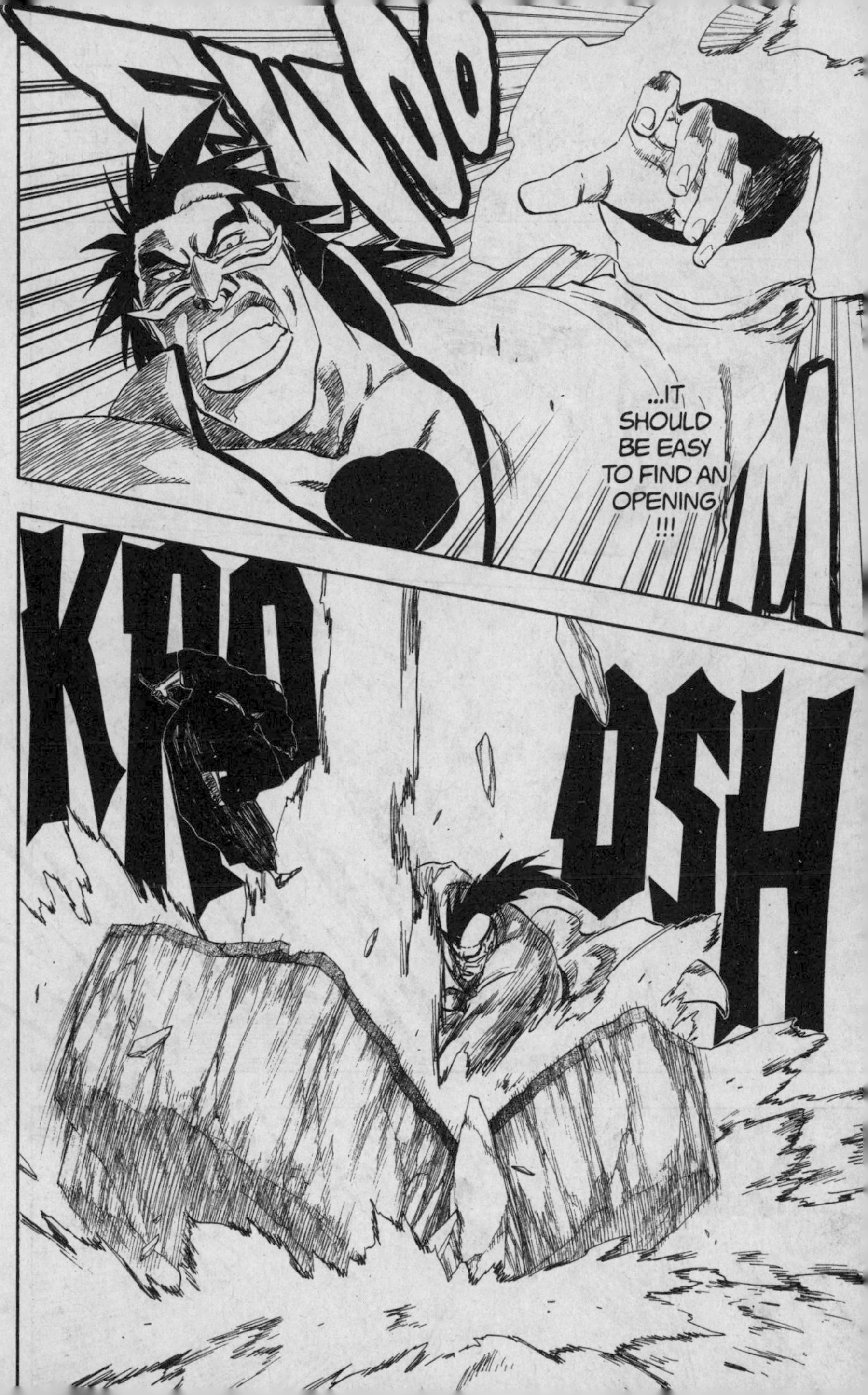
...IT SHOULD BE EASY TO FIND AN OPENING!!!

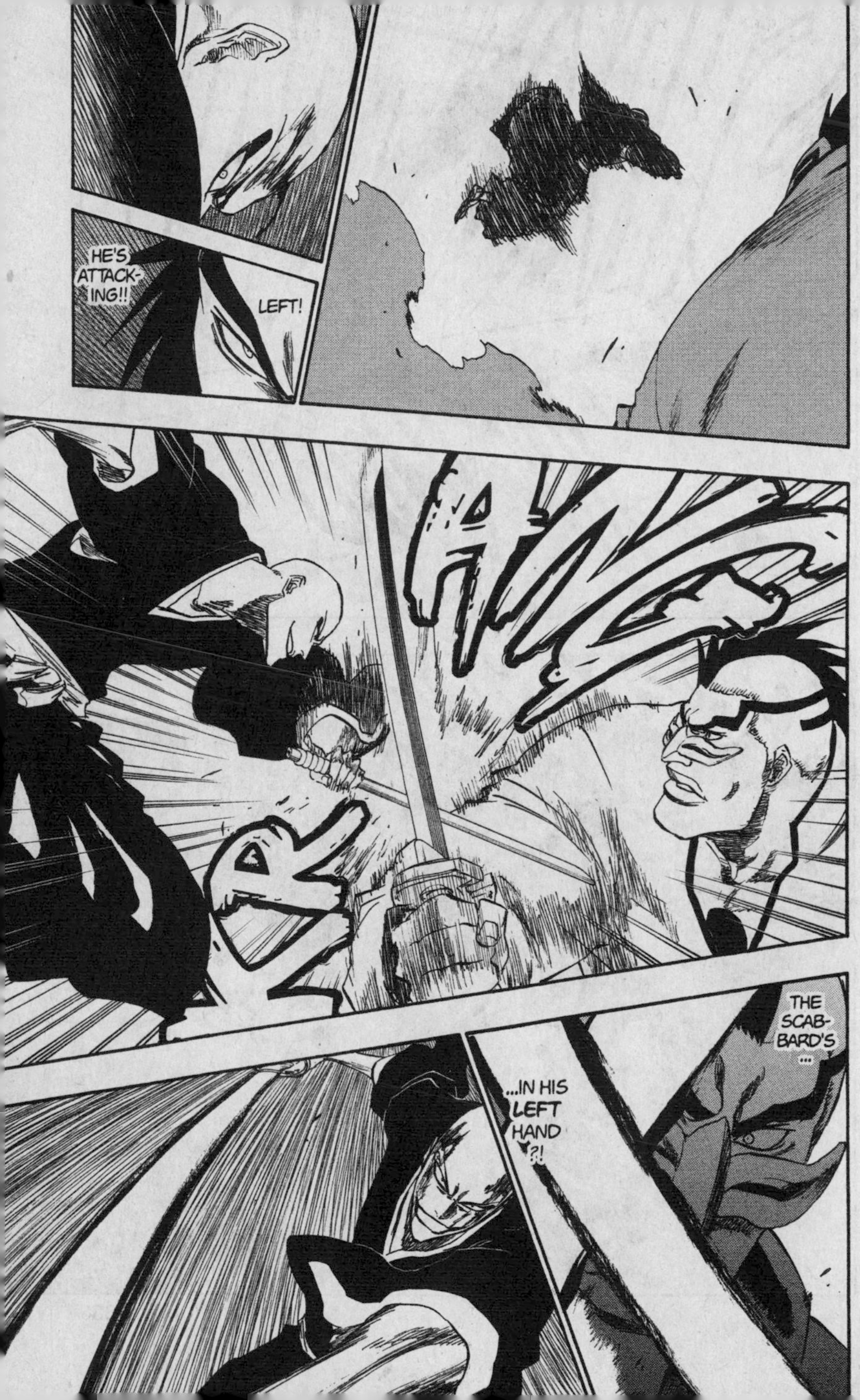
HE'S ATTACK-ING!!
LEFT!
THE SCAB-BARD'S ...
...IN HIS LEFT HAND ?!

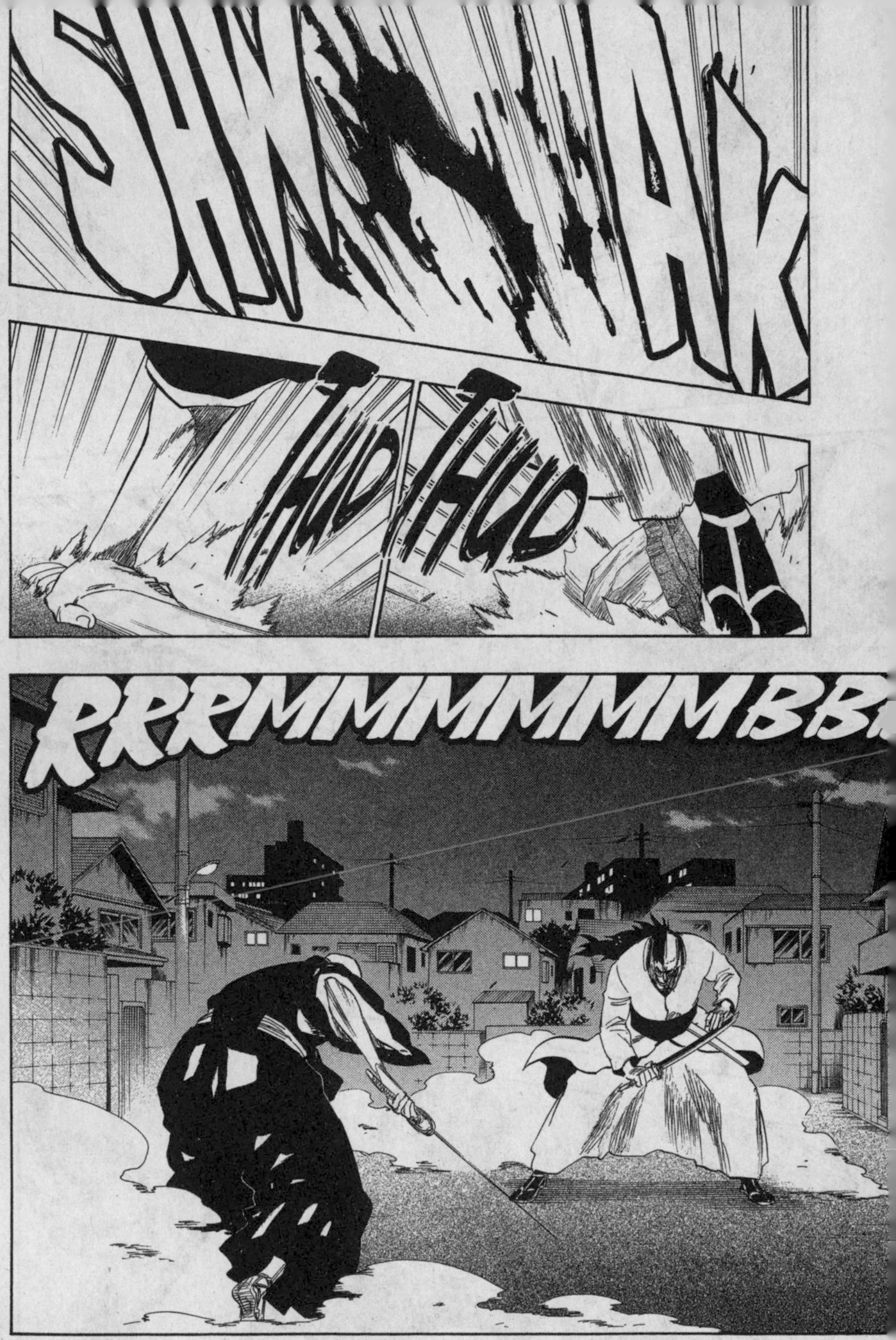
THUD
THUD
RRRMMMMMMMMBB

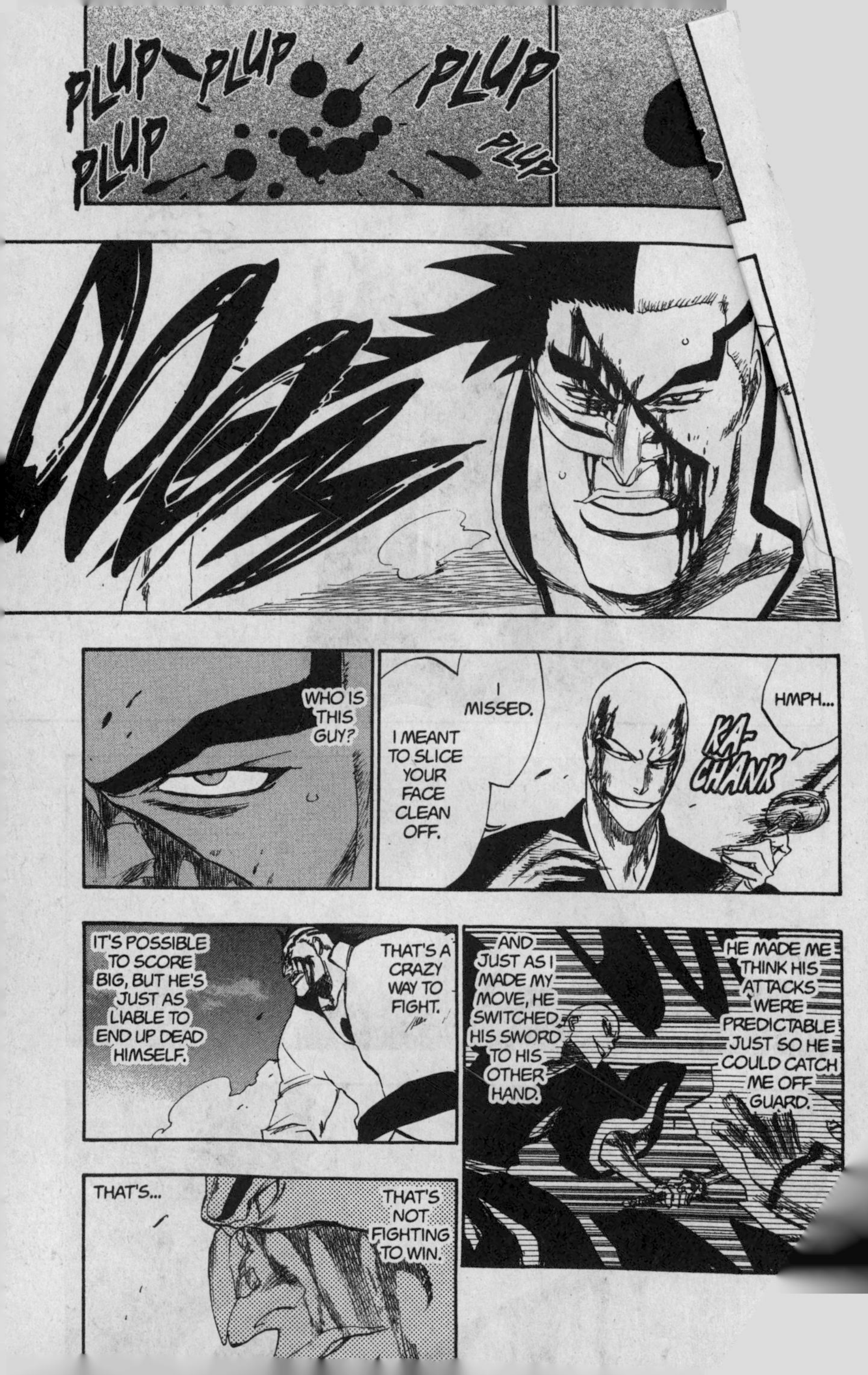
PLUP
PLUP
PLUP
PLUP
PLUP
HMPH...
KA-CHANK
I MISSED.
I MEANT TO SLICE YOUR FACE CLEAN OFF.
WHO IS THIS GUY?
HE MADE ME THINK HIS ATTACKS WERE PREDICTABLE JUST SO HE COULD CATCH ME OFF GUARD.
AND JUST AS I MADE MY MOVE, HE SWITCHED HIS SWORD TO HIS OTHER HAND.
THAT'S A CRAZY WAY TO FIGHT.
IT'S POSSIBLE TO SCORE BIG, BUT HE'S JUST AS LIABLE TO END UP DEAD HIMSELF.
THAT'S...
THAT'S NOT FIGHTING TO WIN.

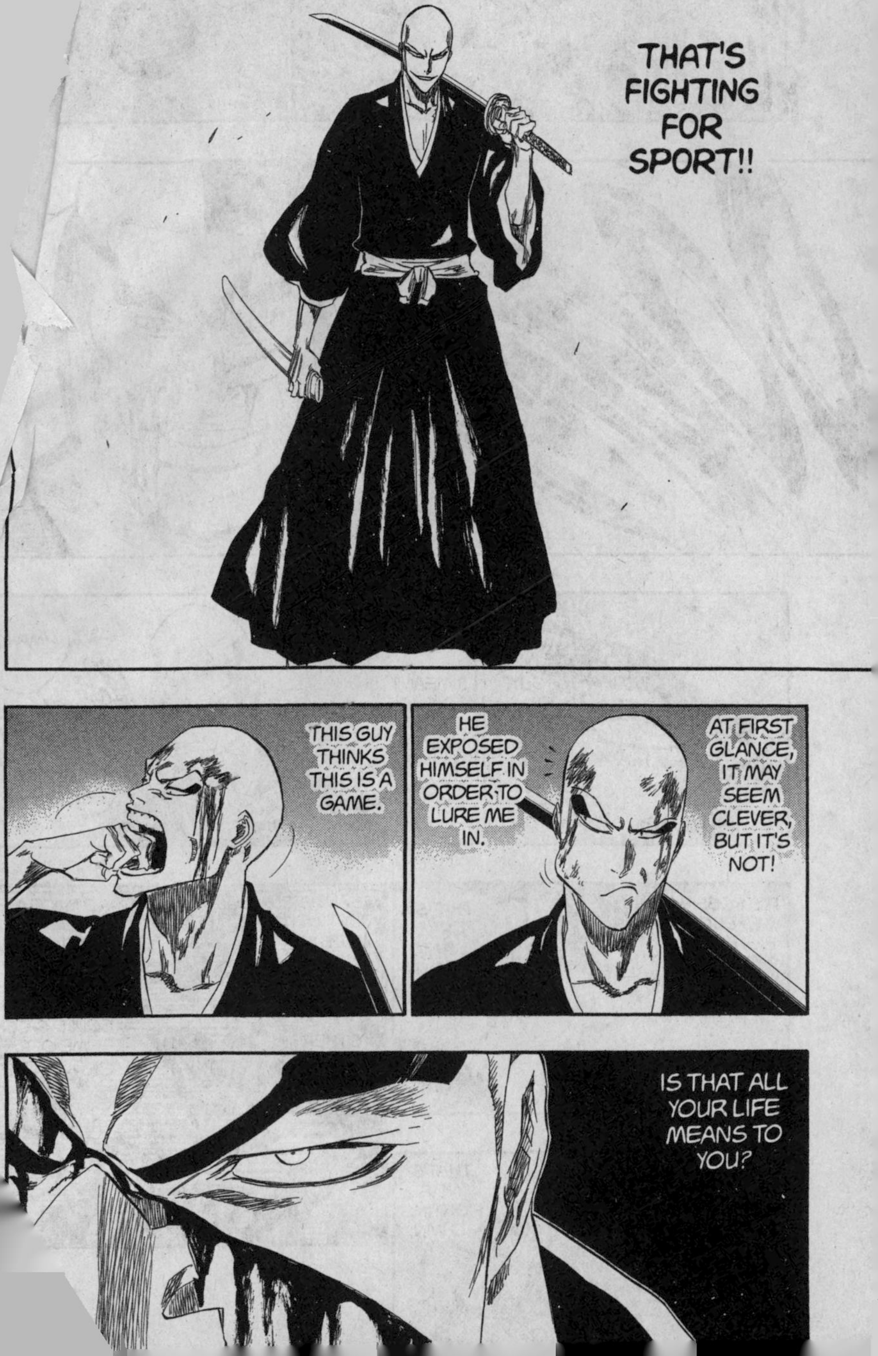
THAT'S FIGHTING FOR SPORT!!
AT FIRST GLANCE, IT MAY SEEM CLEVER, BUT IT'S NOT!
HE EXPOSED HIMSELF IN ORDER TO LURE ME IN.
THIS GUY THINKS THIS IS A GAME.
IS THAT ALL YOUR LIFE MEANS TO YOU?

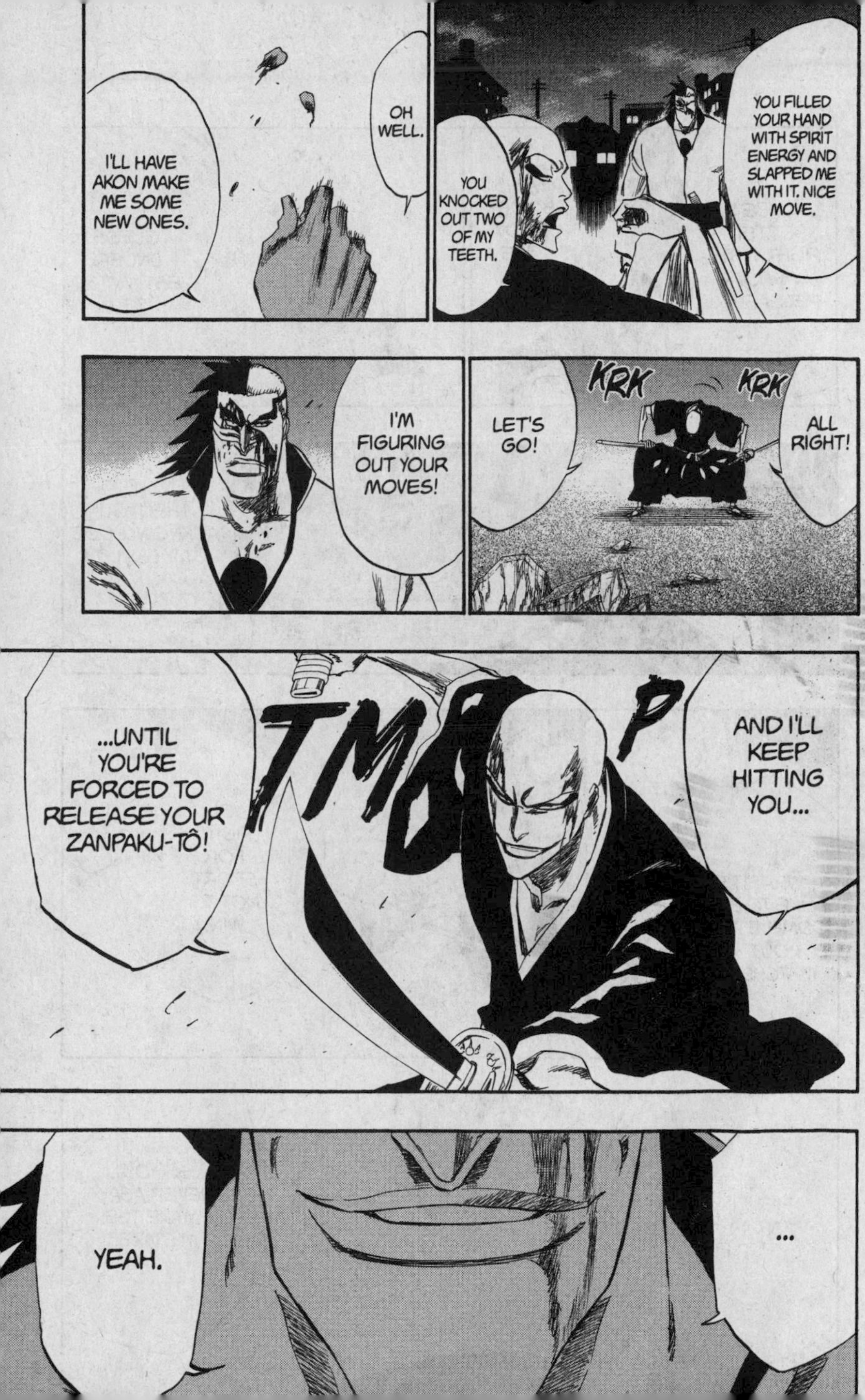
YOU FILLED YOUR HAND WITH SPIRIT ENERGY AND SLAPPED ME WITH IT. NICE MOVE.
YOU KNOCKED OUT TWO OF MY TEETH.
OH WELL.
I'LL HAVE AKON MAKE ME SOME NEW ONES.
KRK
ALL RIGHT!
KRK
LET'S GO!
I'M FIGURING OUT YOUR MOVES!
AND I'LL KEEP HITTING YOU...
TMP
...UNTIL YOU'RE FORCED TO RELEASE YOUR ZANPAKU-TÔ!
...
YEAH.

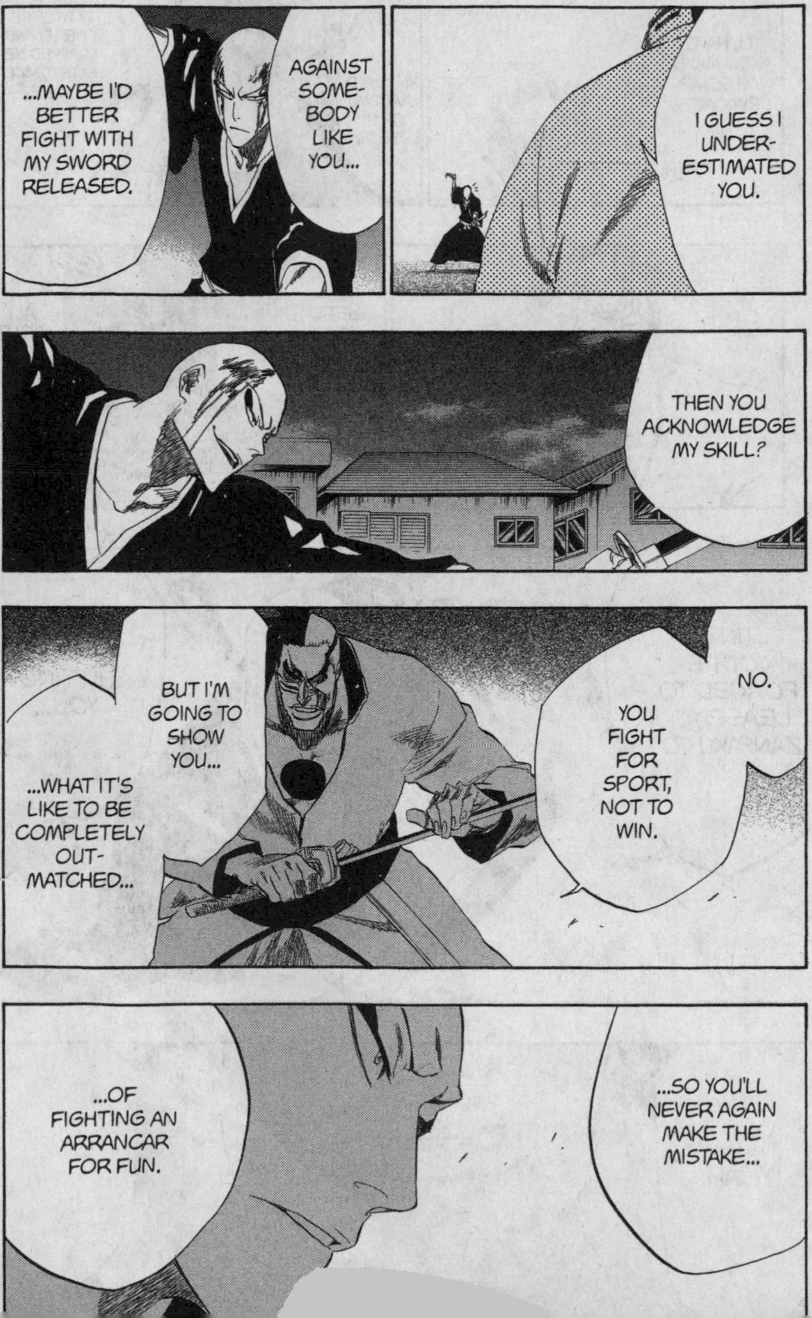
I GUESS I UNDER-ESTIMATED YOU.
AGAINST SOME-BODY LIKE YOU...
...MAYBE I'D BETTER FIGHT WITH MY SWORD RELEASED.
THEN YOU ACKNOWLEDGE MY SKILL?
NO.
YOU FIGHT FOR SPORT, NOT TO WIN.
BUT I'M GOING TO SHOW YOU...
...WHAT IT'S LIKE TO BE COMPLETELY OUT-MATCHED...
...SO YOU'LL NEVER AGAIN MAKE THE MISTAKE...
...OF FIGHTING AN ARRANCAR FOR FUN.

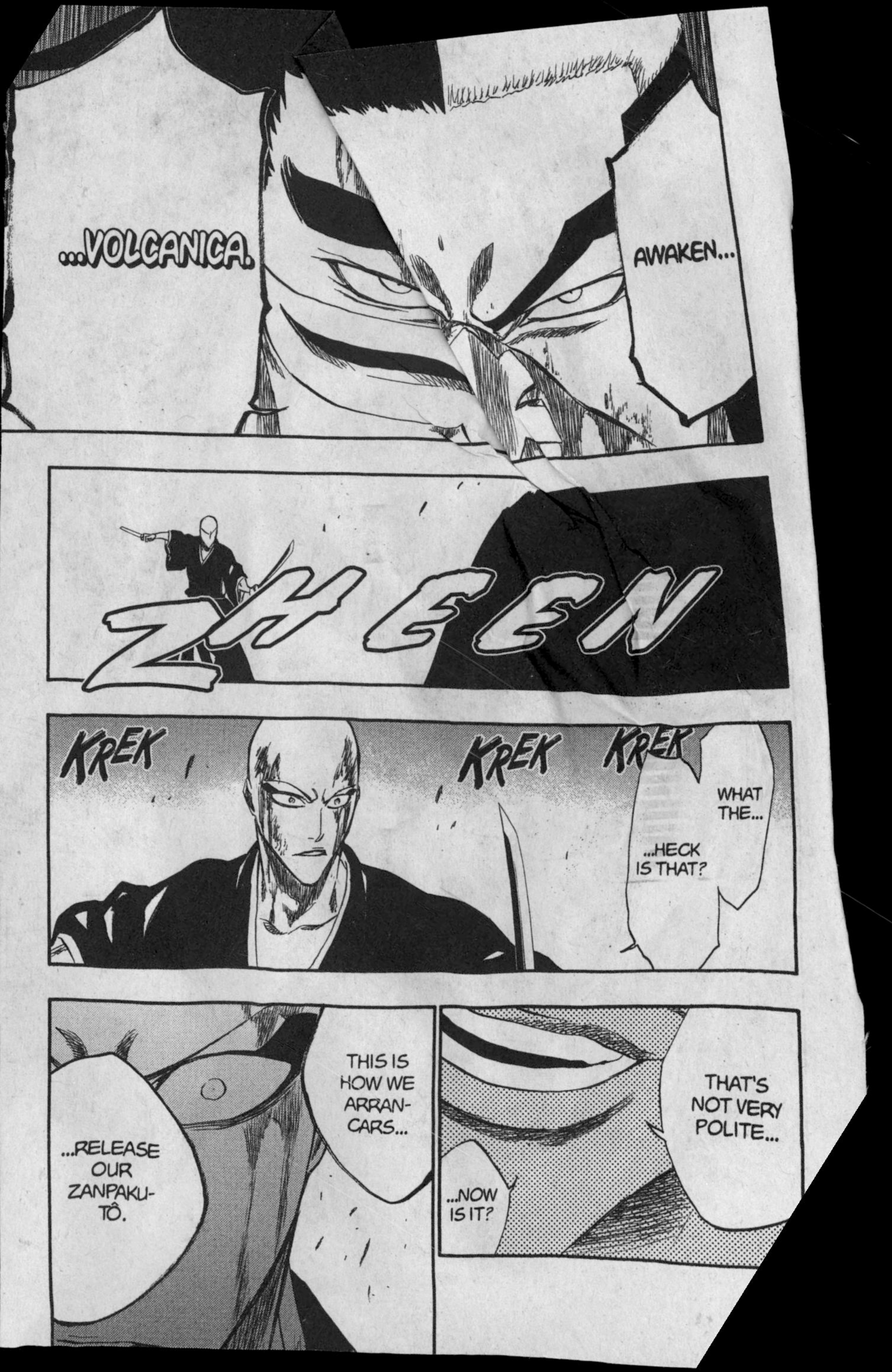
AWAKEN...
...VOLCANICA.
ZHEEN
KREK
KREK
KREK
WHAT THE...
...HECK IS THAT?
THAT'S NOT VERY POLITE...
...NOW IS IT?
THIS IS HOW WE ARRAN-CARS...
...RELEASE OUR ZANPAKU-TÔ.

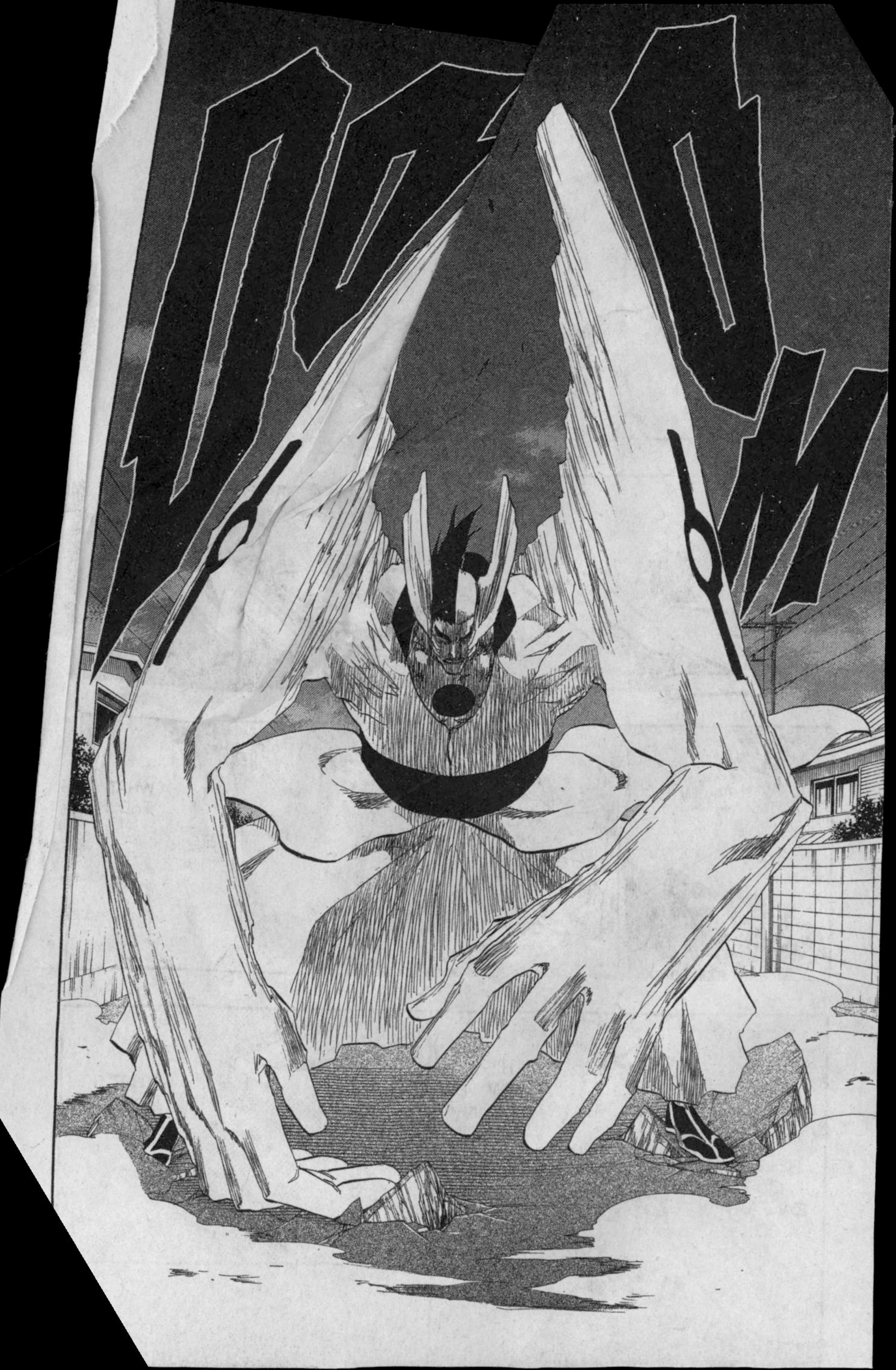

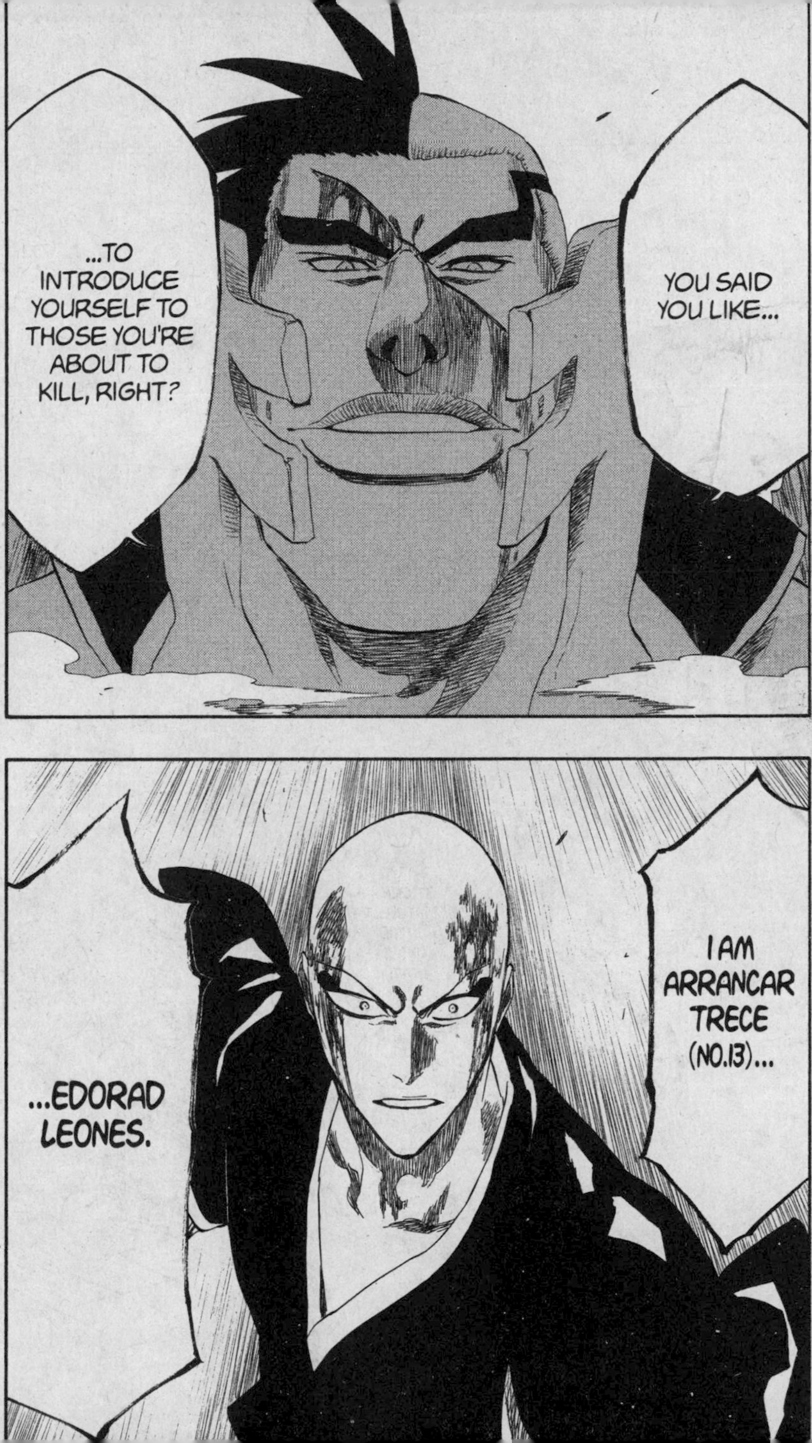
YOU SAID YOU LIKE...
...TO INTRODUCE YOURSELF TO THOSE YOU'RE ABOUT TO KILL, RIGHT?
I AM ARRANCAR TRECE (NO.13)...
...EDORAD LEONES.

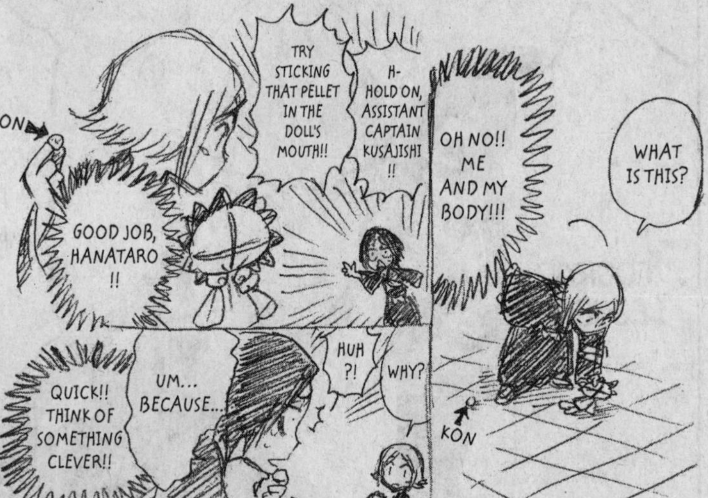
WHAT IS THIS?
OH NO!! ME AND MY BODY!!!
KON
H-HOLD ON, ASSISTANT CAPTAIN KUSAJISHI!!
TRY STICKING THAT PELLET IN THE DOLL'S MOUTH!!
KON
GOOD JOB, HANATARO!!
WHY?
HUH?!
UM... BECAUSE...
QUICK!! THINK OF SOMETHING CLEVER!!

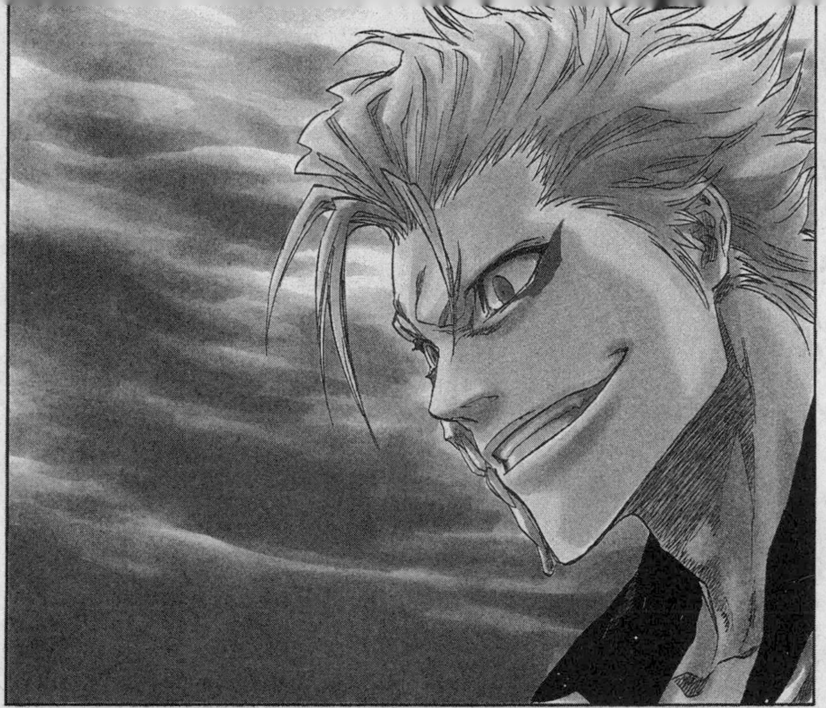

204. ¡Mala Suerte! 3 [Monstruo Sangrienta]

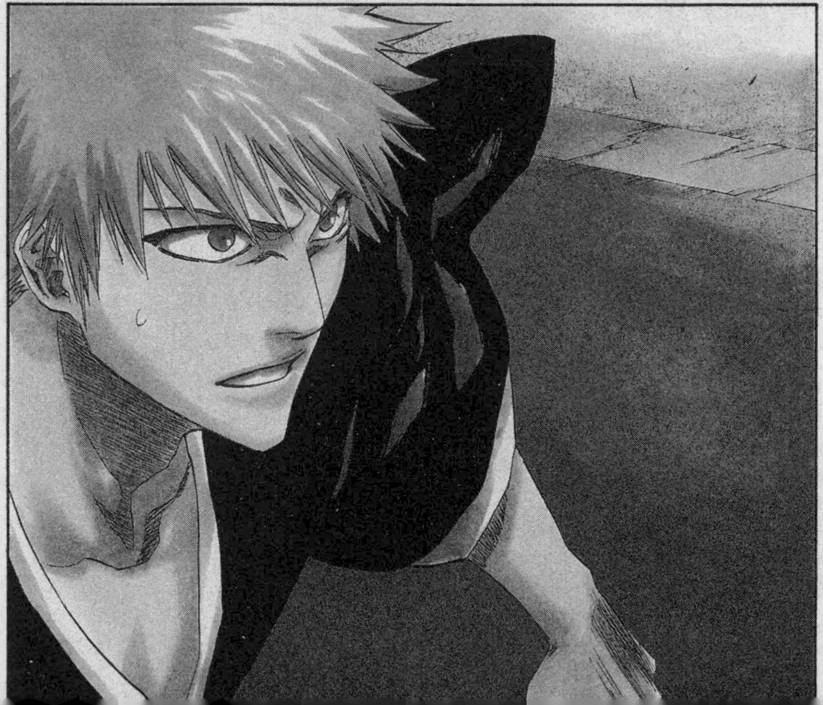

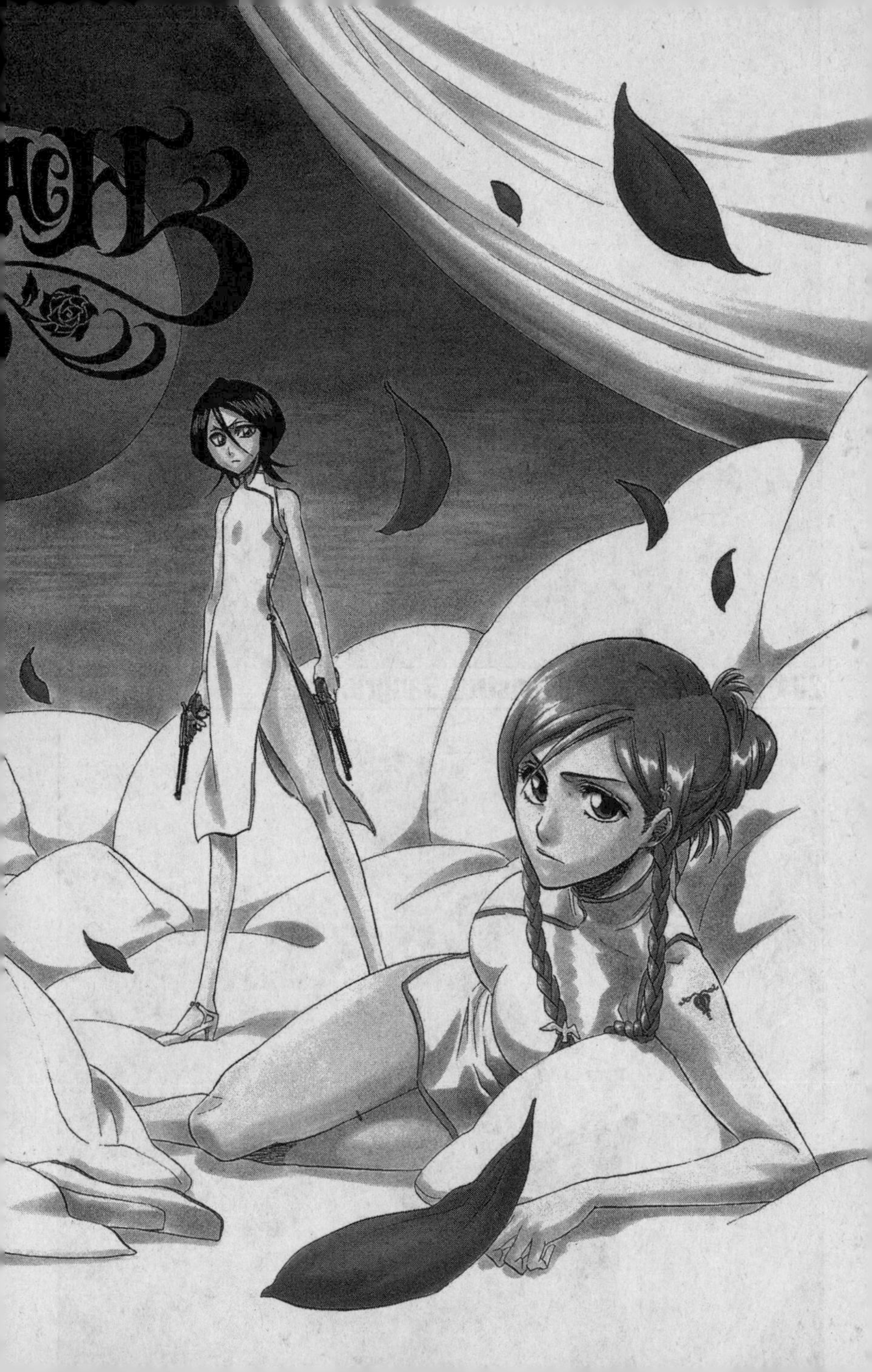

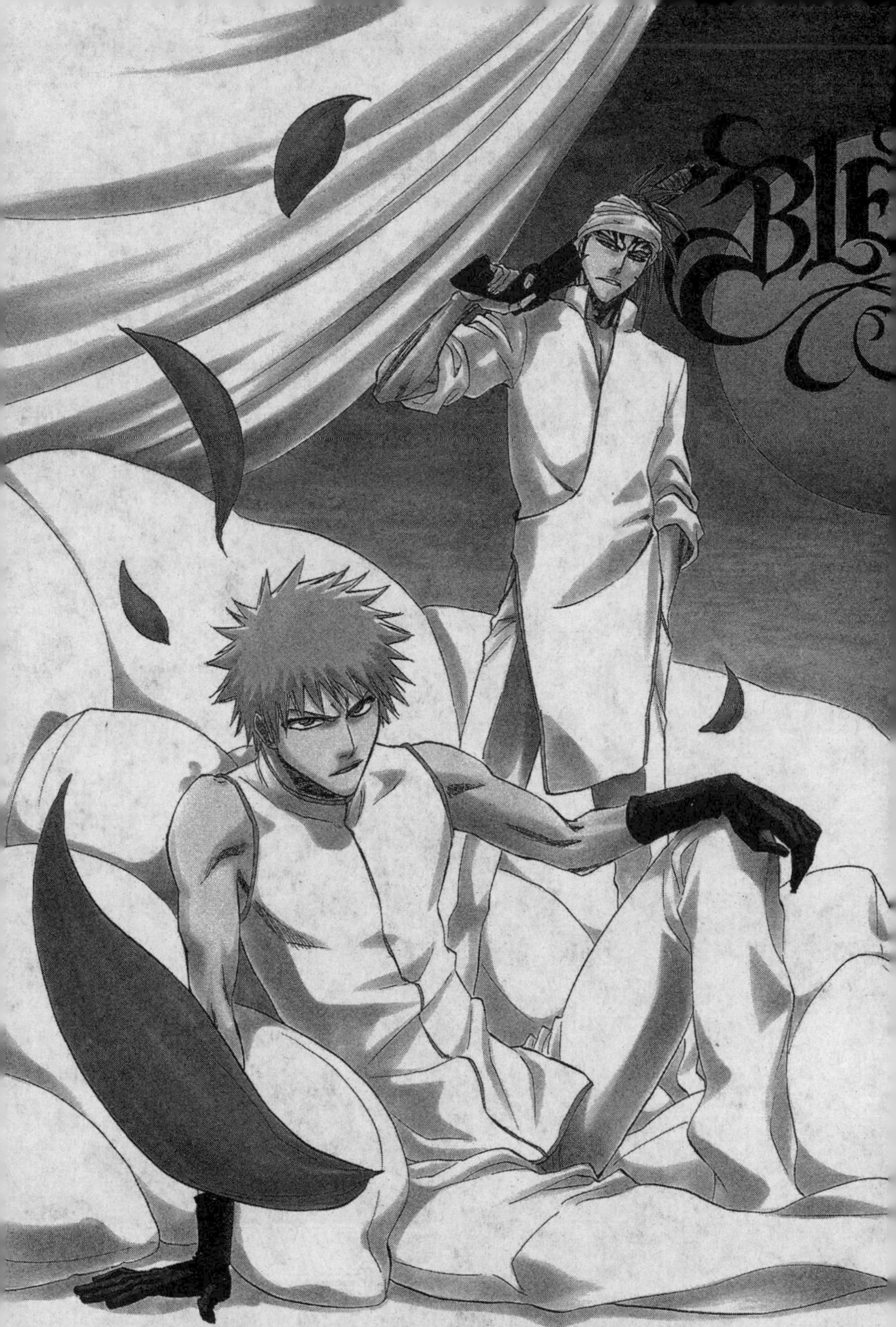

204. ¡Mala Suerte! 3 [Monstruo Sangrienta]

BLEACH
ブリーチ

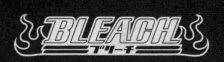

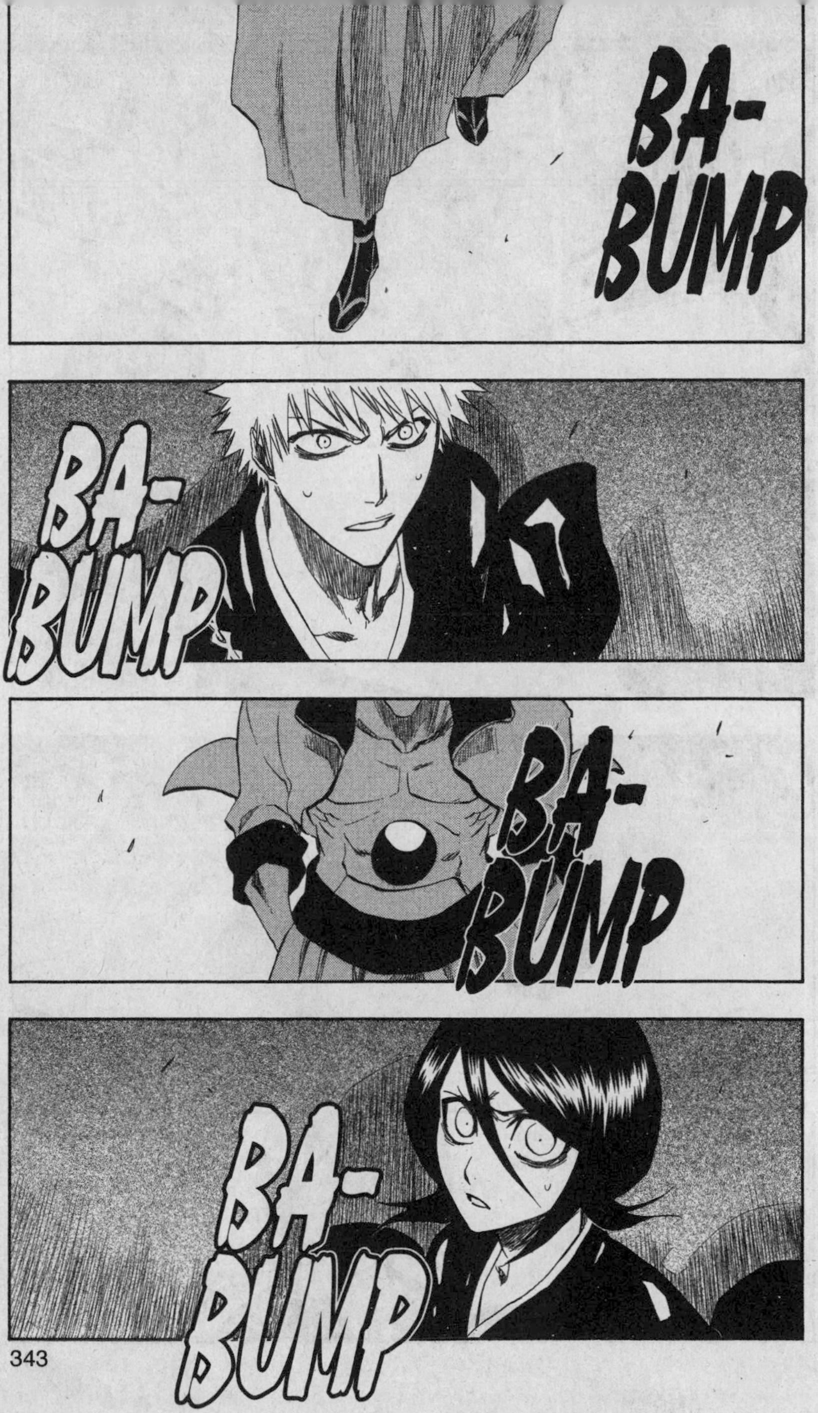
BA-BUMP
BA-BUMP
BA-BUMP
BA-BUMP

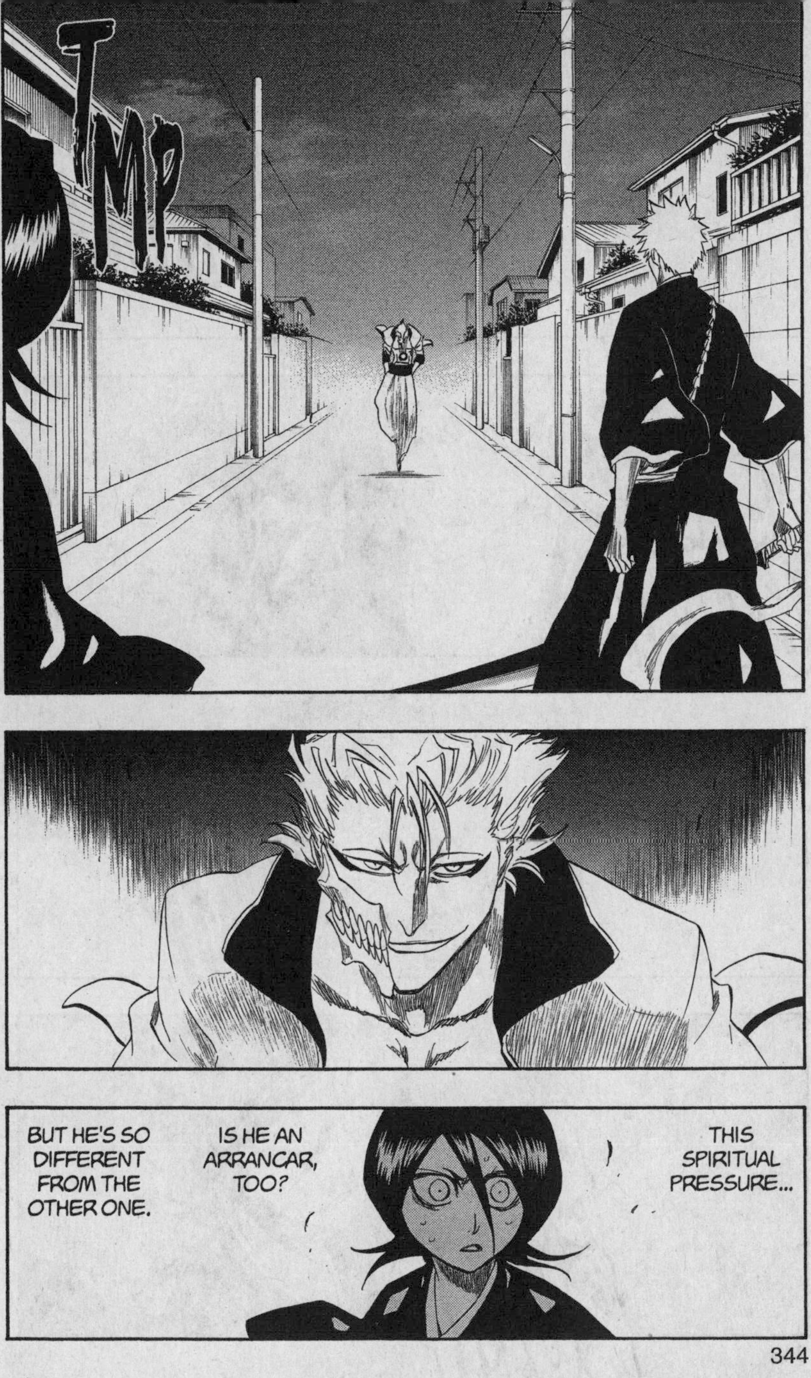
TMP
THIS SPIRITUAL PRESSURE...
IS HE AN ARRANCAR, TOO?
BUT HE'S SO DIFFERENT FROM THE OTHER ONE.

READ THIS WAY

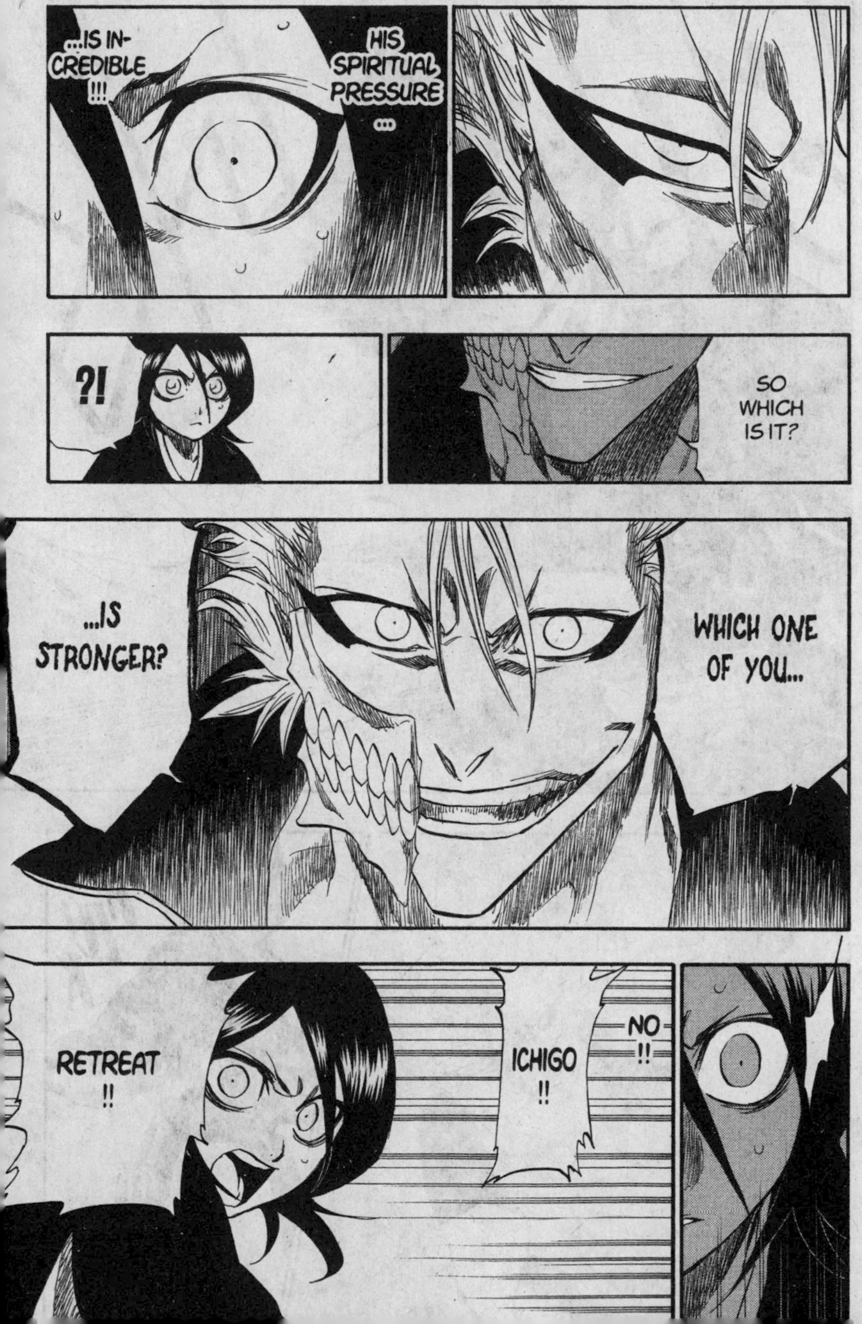
HIS SPIRITUAL PRESSURE ...
...IS IN-CREDIBLE !!!
SO WHICH IS IT?
?!
WHICH ONE OF YOU...
...IS STRONGER?
NO !!
ICHIGO !!
RETREAT !!

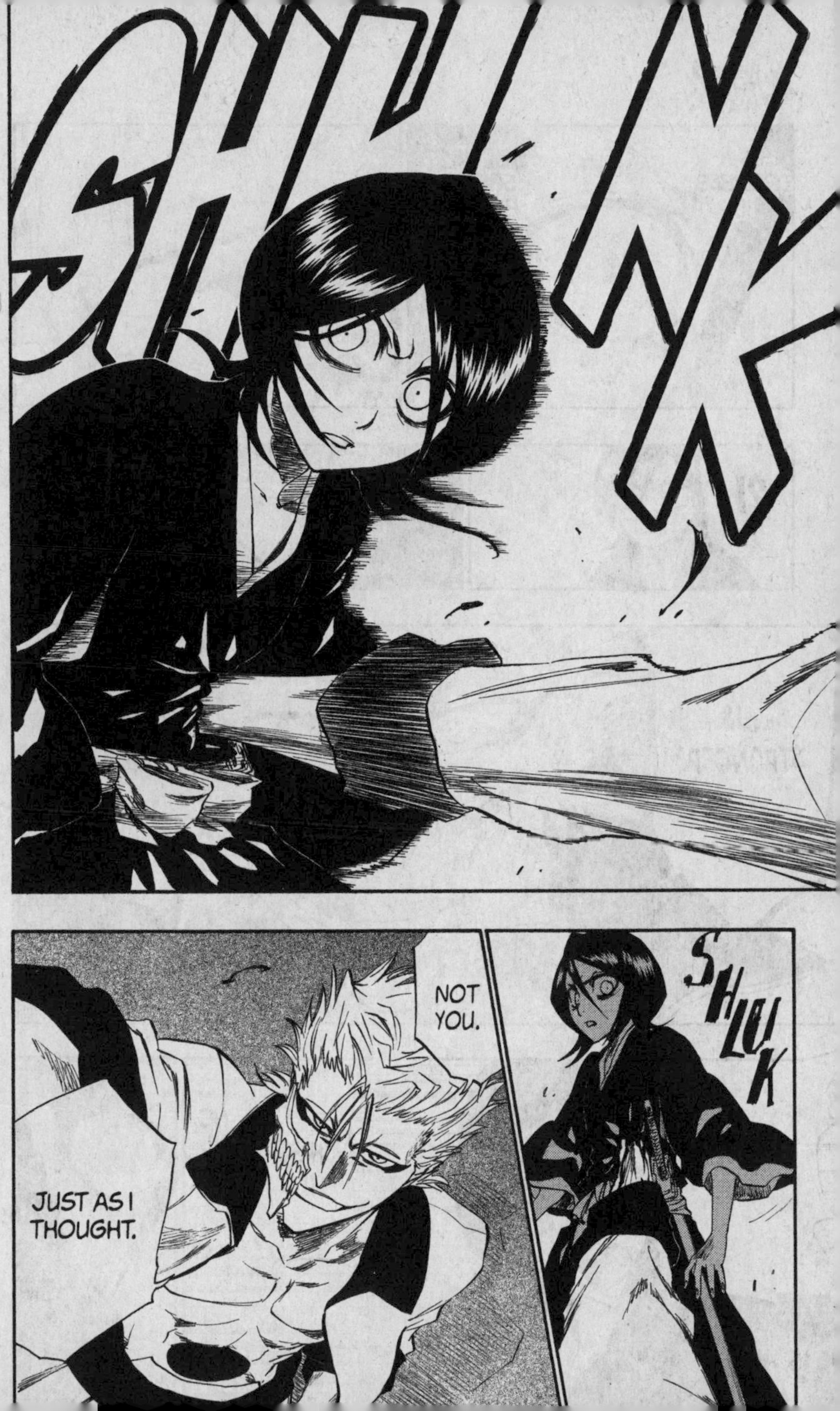
SHLUK
NOT YOU.
JUST AS I THOUGHT.

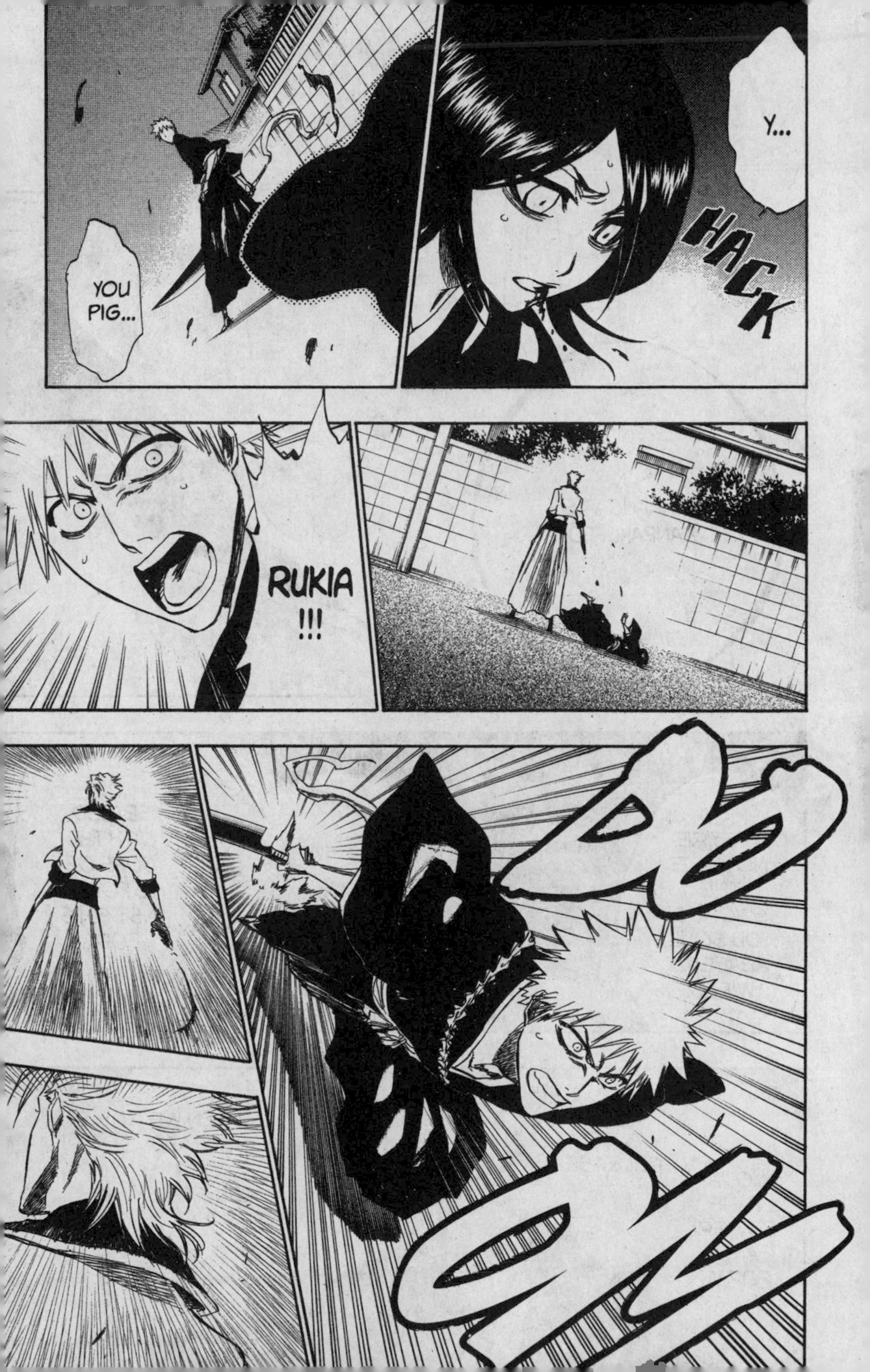
Y...
HACK
YOU PIG...
RUKIA !!!

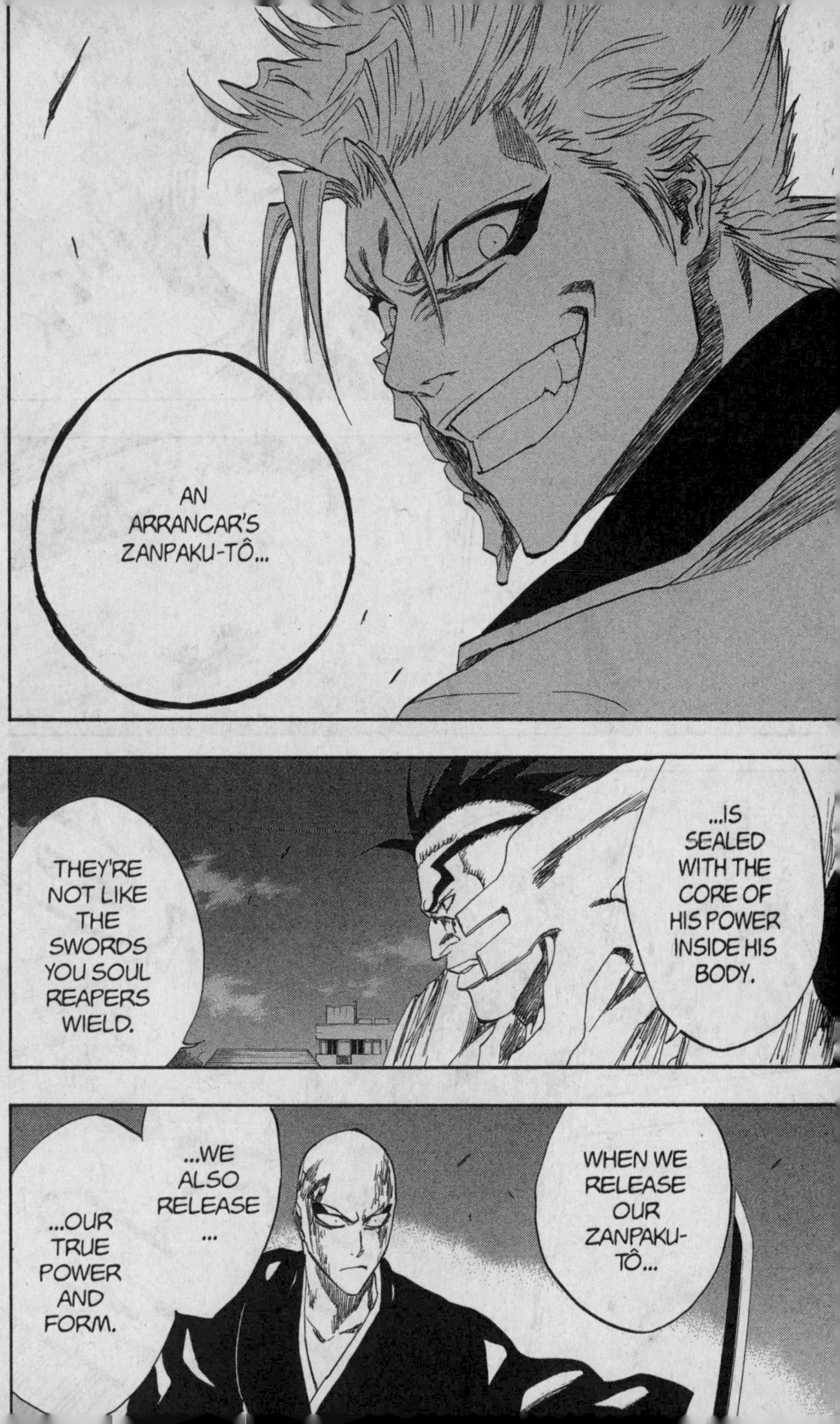
AN ARRANCAR'S ZANPAKU-TÔ...
...IS SEALED WITH THE CORE OF HIS POWER INSIDE HIS BODY.
THEY'RE NOT LIKE THE SWORDS YOU SOUL REAPERS WIELD.
WHEN WE RELEASE OUR ZANPAKU-TÔ...
...WE ALSO RELEASE ...
...OUR TRUE POWER AND FORM.

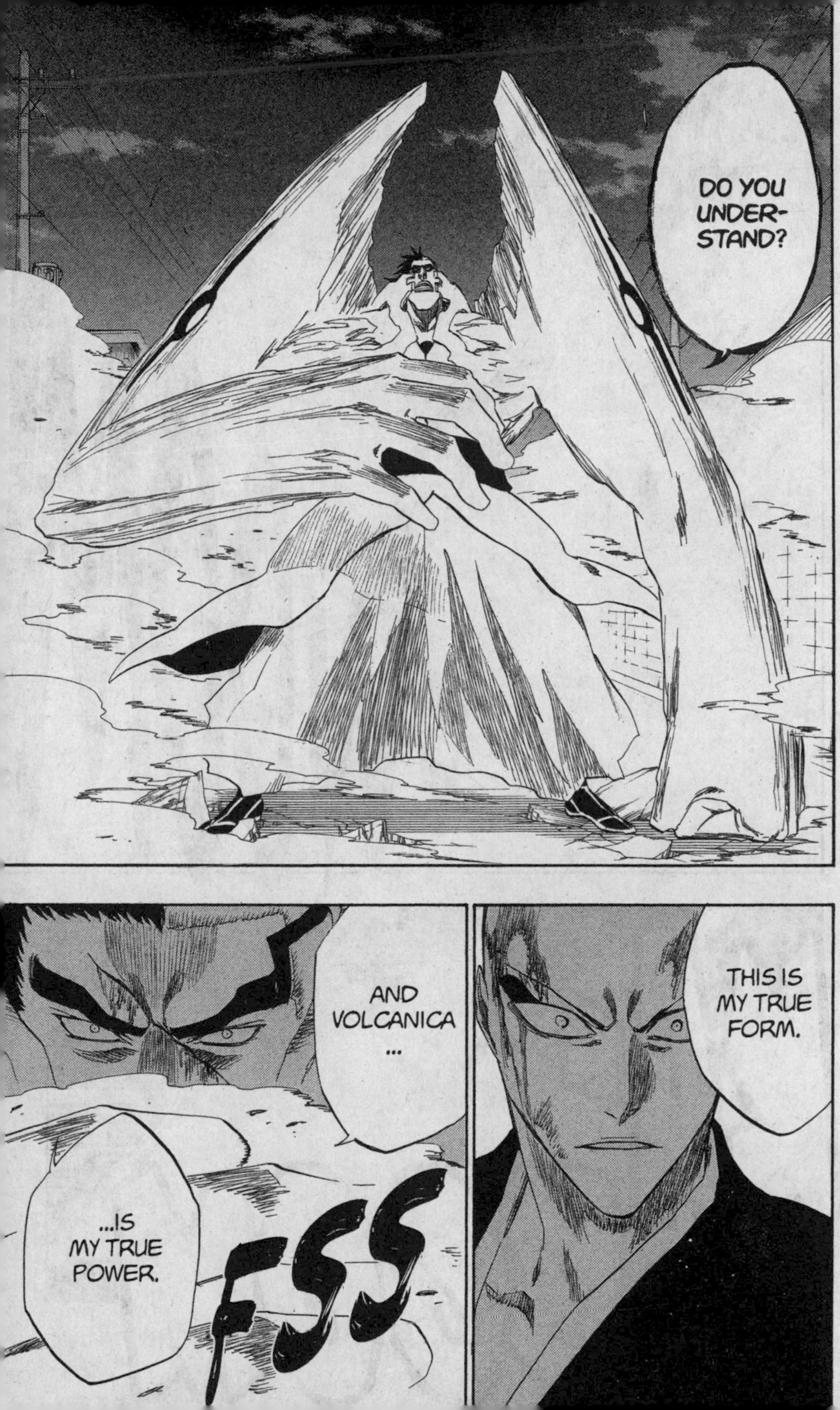
DO YOU UNDER-STAND?
THIS IS MY TRUE FORM.
AND VOLCANICA ...
...IS MY TRUE POWER.
FSS

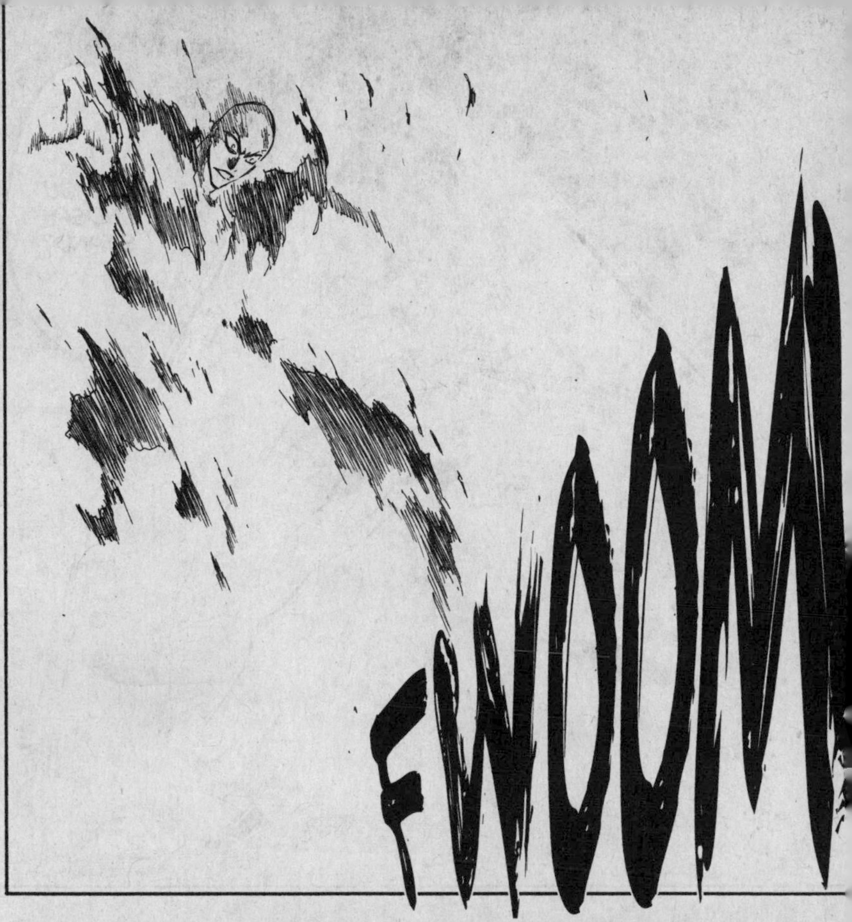
FWOOM

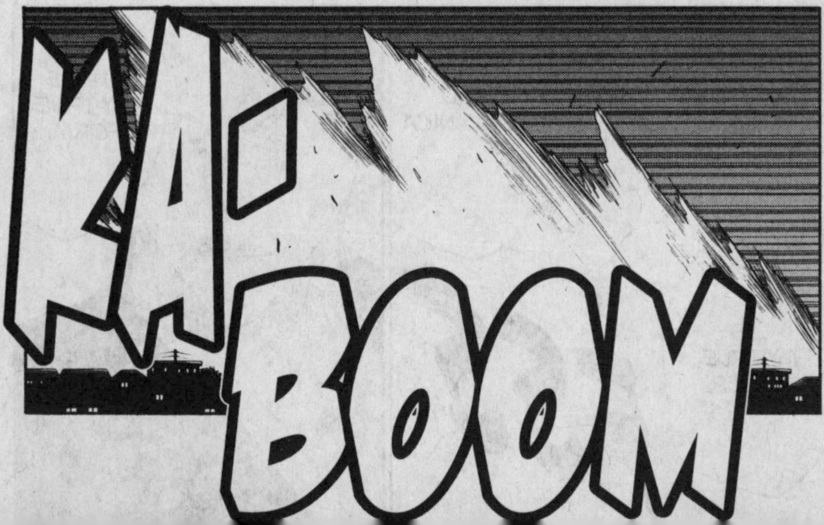
KA-BOOM

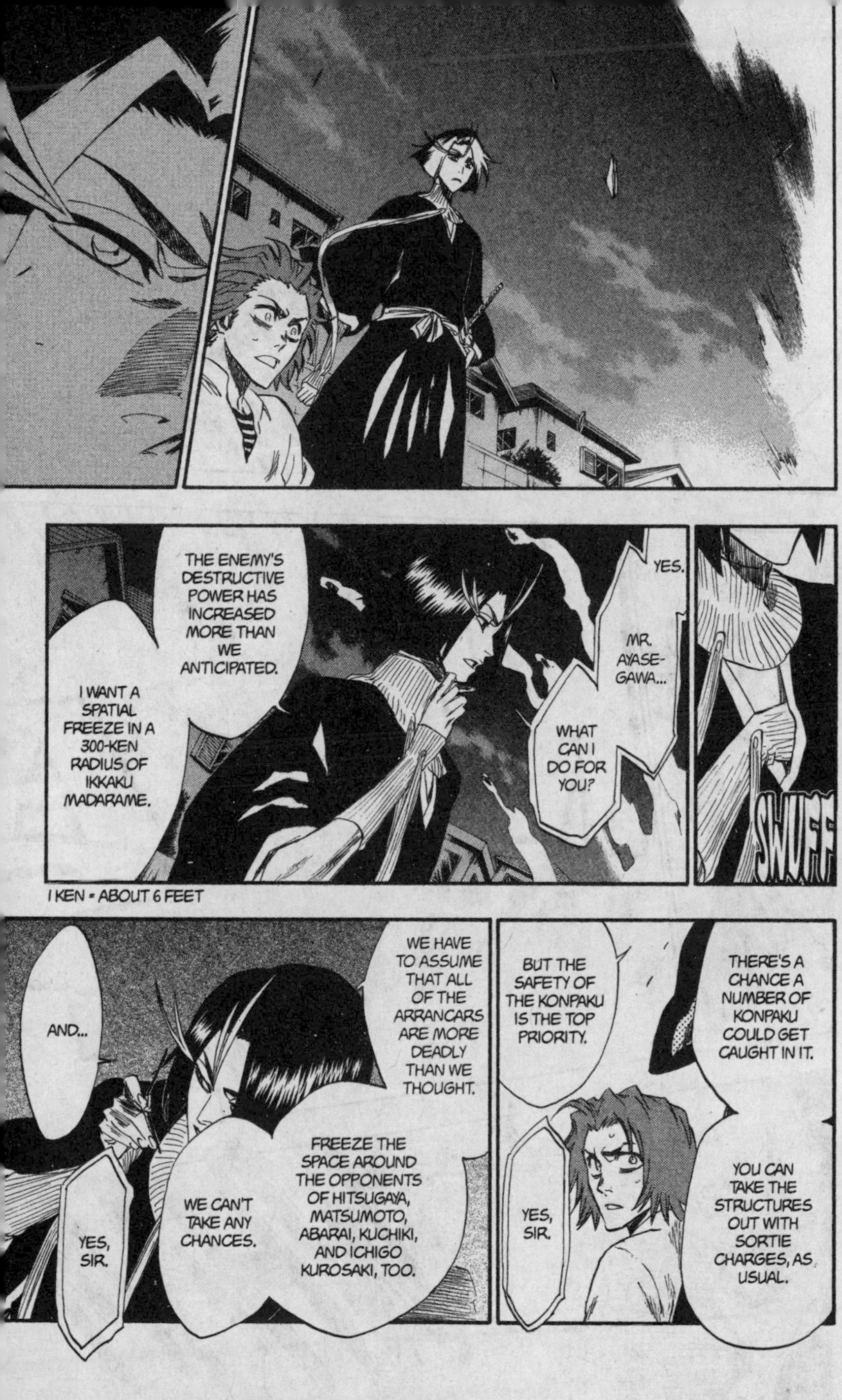
SWUFF
YES.
MR. AYASE-GAWA...
WHAT CAN I DO FOR YOU?
THE ENEMY'S DESTRUCTIVE POWER HAS INCREASED MORE THAN WE ANTICIPATED.
I WANT A SPATIAL FREEZE IN A 300-KEN RADIUS OF IKKAKU MADARAME.
THERE'S A CHANCE A NUMBER OF KONPAKU COULD GET CAUGHT IN IT.
BUT THE SAFETY OF THE KONPAKU IS THE TOP PRIORITY.
YOU CAN TAKE THE STRUCTURES OUT WITH SORTIE CHARGES, AS USUAL.
YES, SIR.
WE HAVE TO ASSUME THAT ALL OF THE ARRANCARS ARE MORE DEADLY THAN WE THOUGHT.
AND...
FREEZE THE SPACE AROUND THE OPPONENTS OF HITSUGAYA, MATSUMOTO, ABARAI, KUCHIKI, AND ICHIGO KUROSAKI, TOO.
WE CAN'T TAKE ANY CHANCES.
YES, SIR.

1 KEN = ABOUT 6 FEET

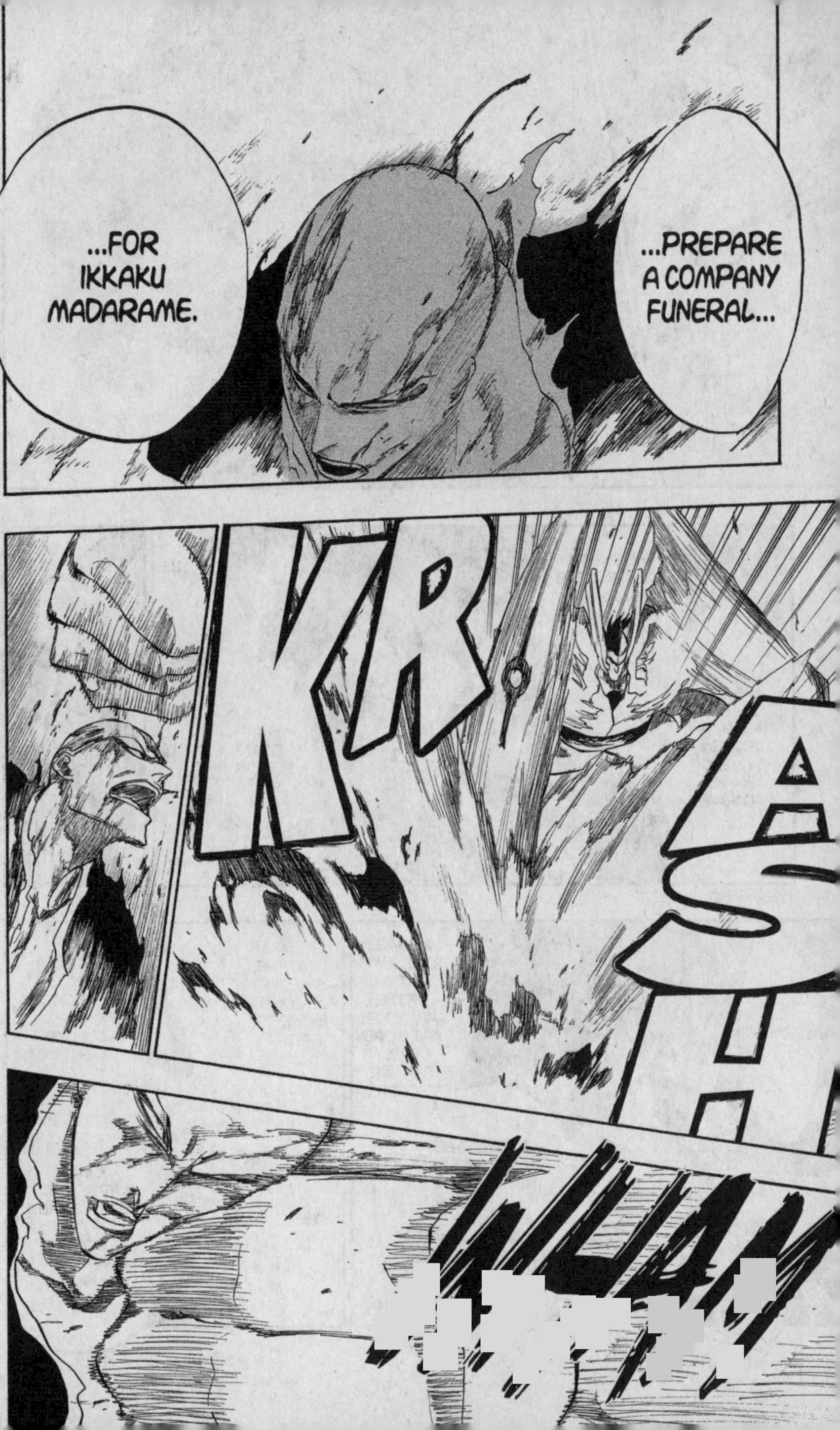
...PREPARE A COMPANY FUNERAL...
...FOR IKKAKU MADARAME.
KRASH

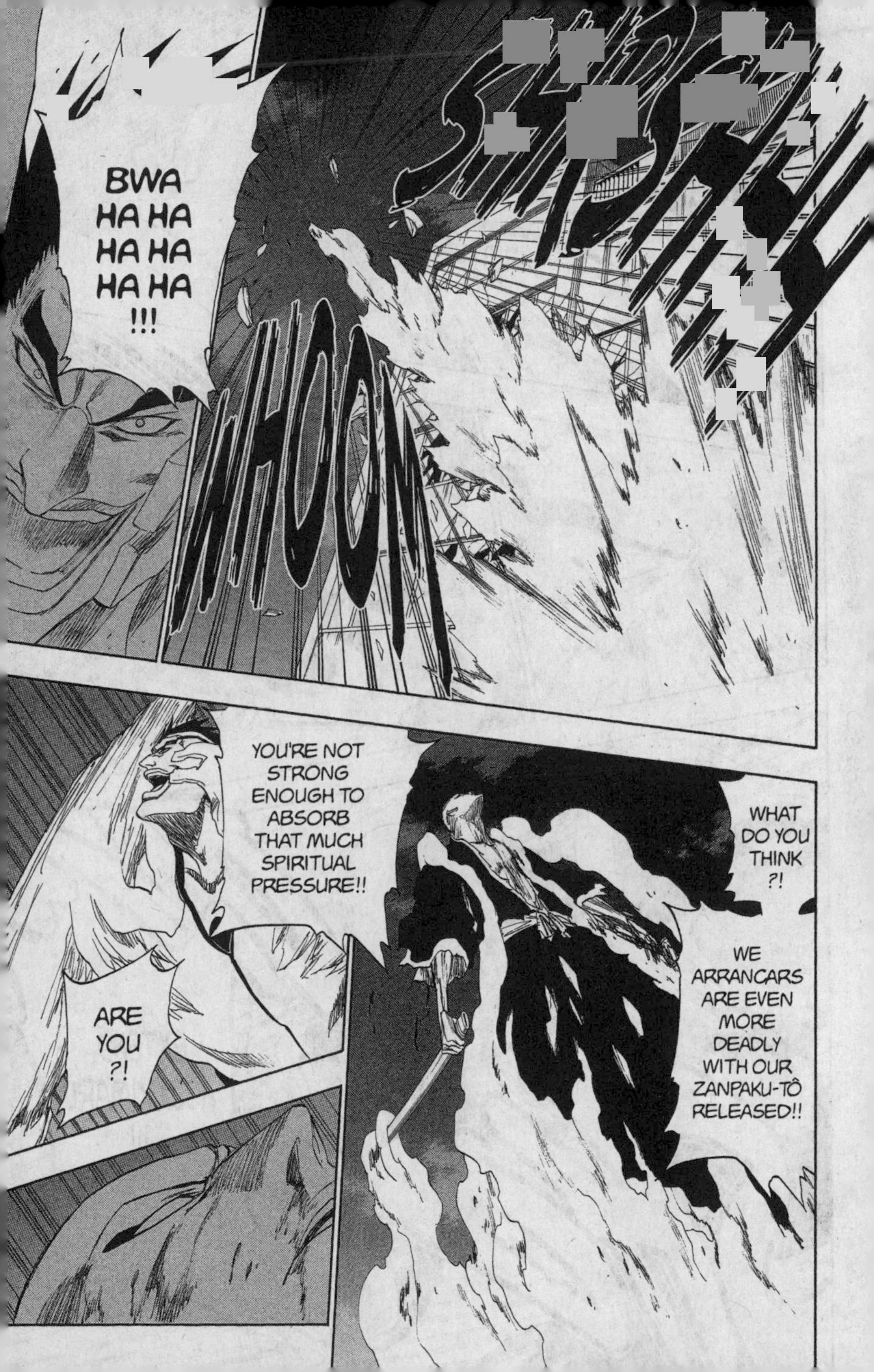
WHOOM
BWA HA HA HA HA HA HA !!!
WHAT DO YOU THINK ?!
WE ARRANCARS ARE EVEN MORE DEADLY WITH OUR ZANPAKU-TÔ RELEASED!!
YOU'RE NOT STRONG ENOUGH TO ABSORB THAT MUCH SPIRITUAL PRESSURE!!
ARE YOU ?!

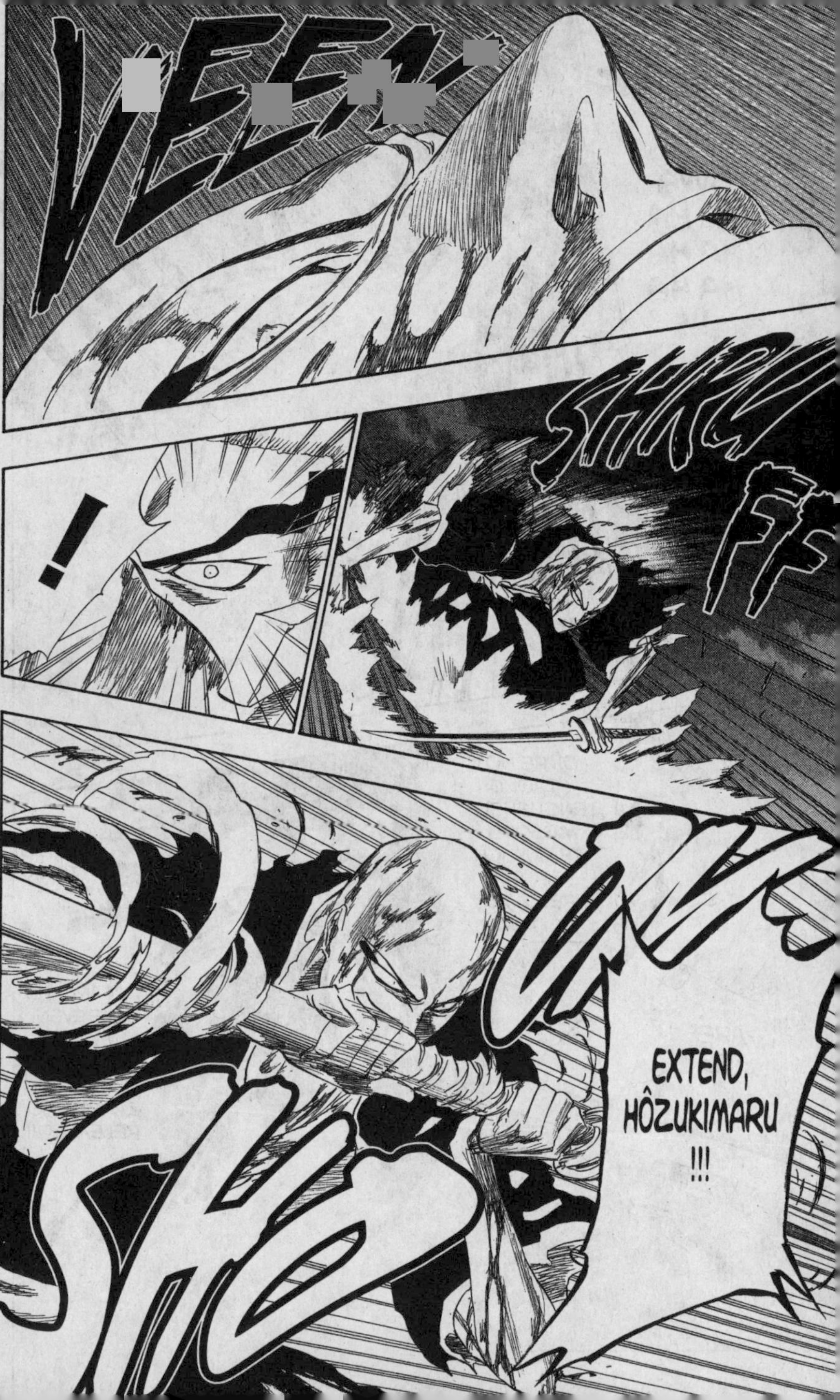
!
EXTEND, HÔZUKIMARU !!!

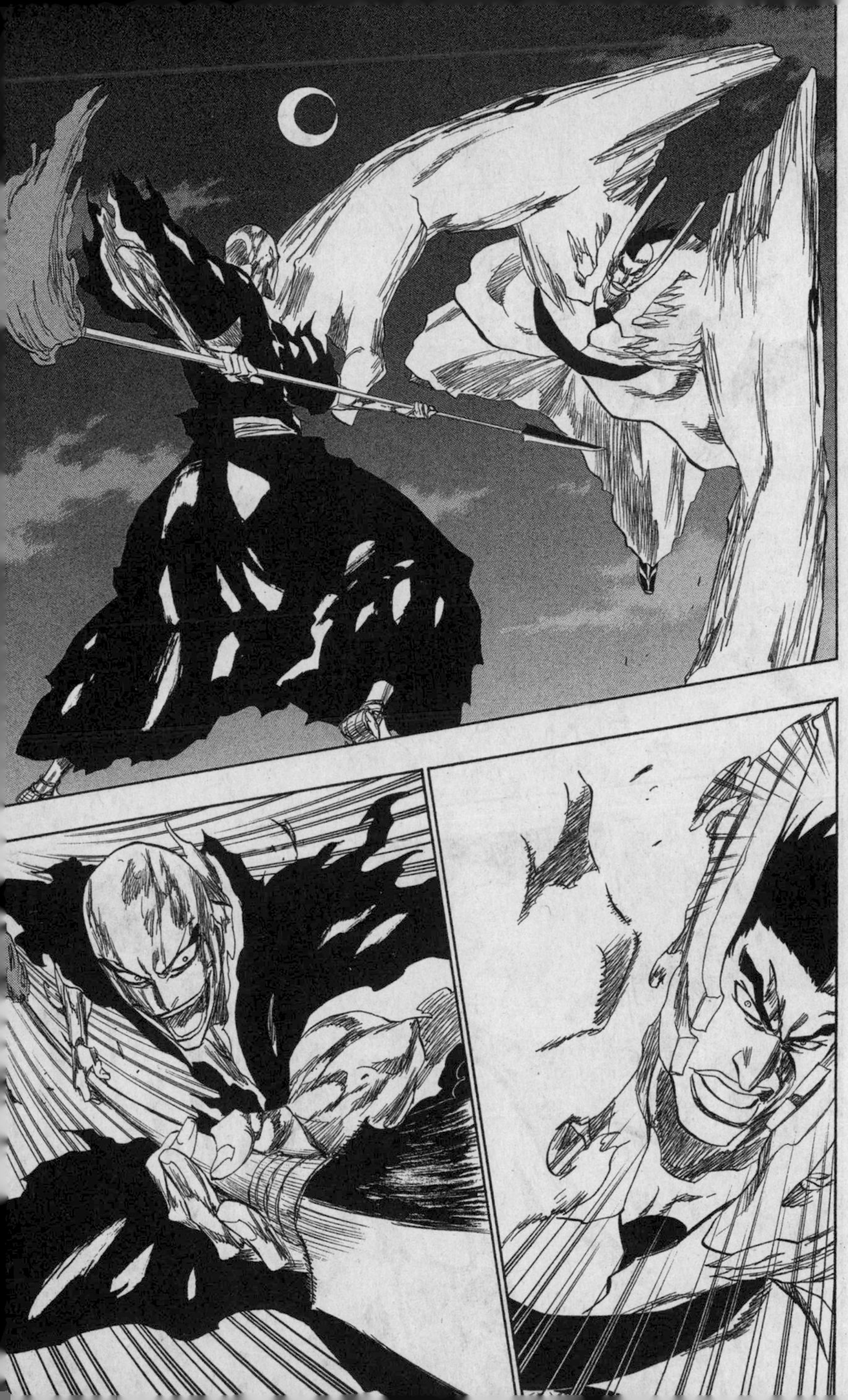

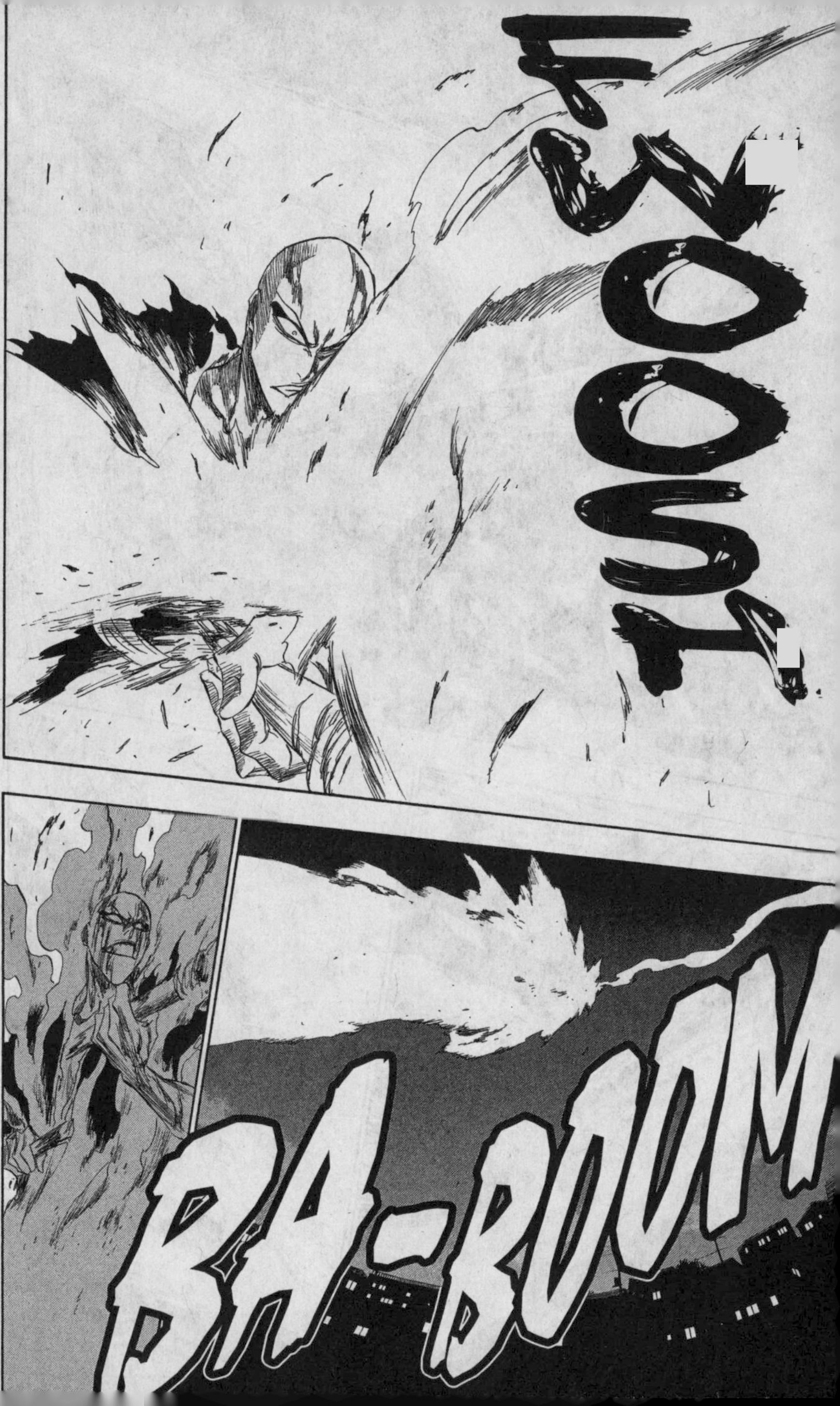
FWOOSH
BA-BOOM

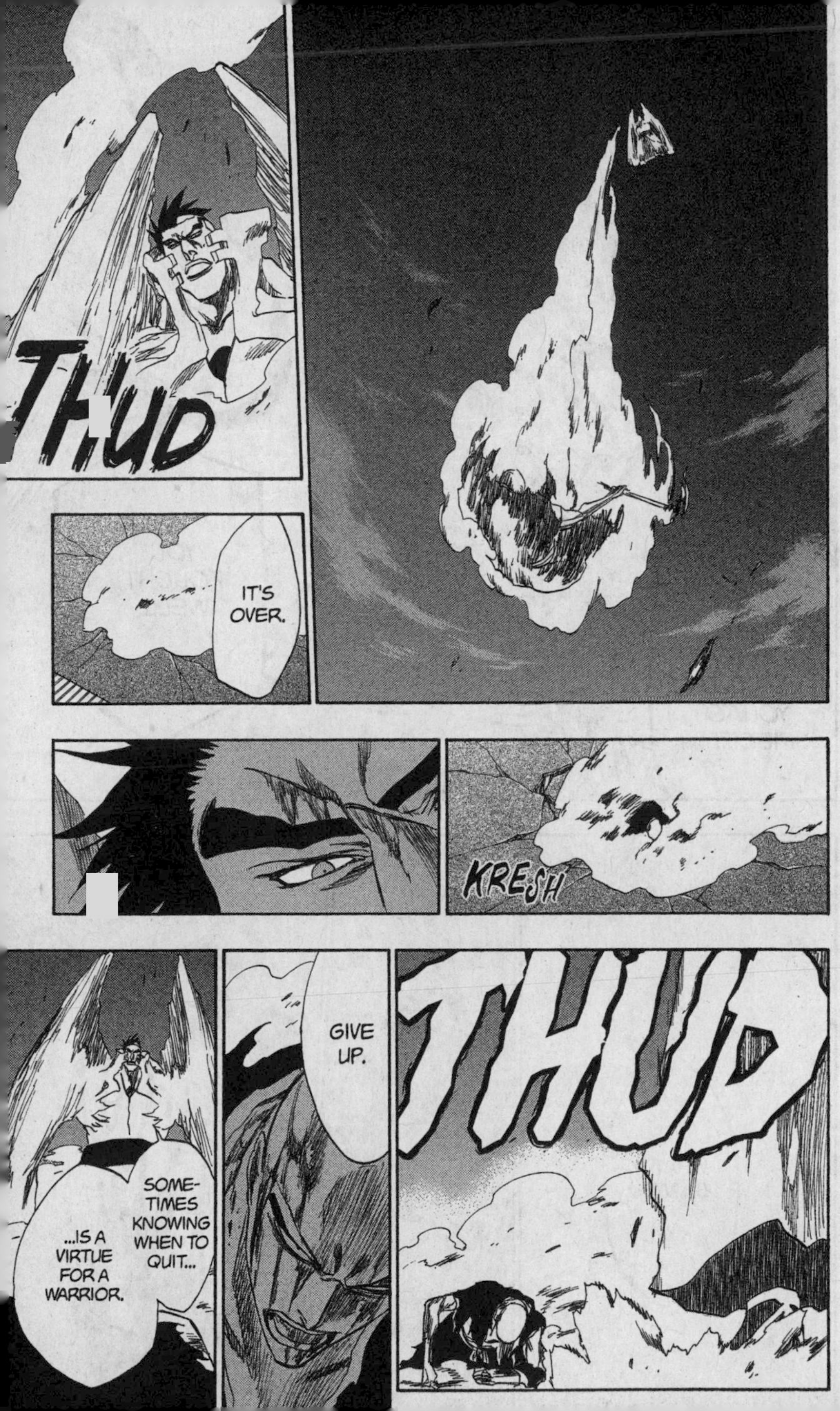
THUD
IT'S OVER.
KRESH
THUD
GIVE UP.
SOME-TIMES KNOWING WHEN TO QUIT...
...IS A VIRTUE FOR A WARRIOR.

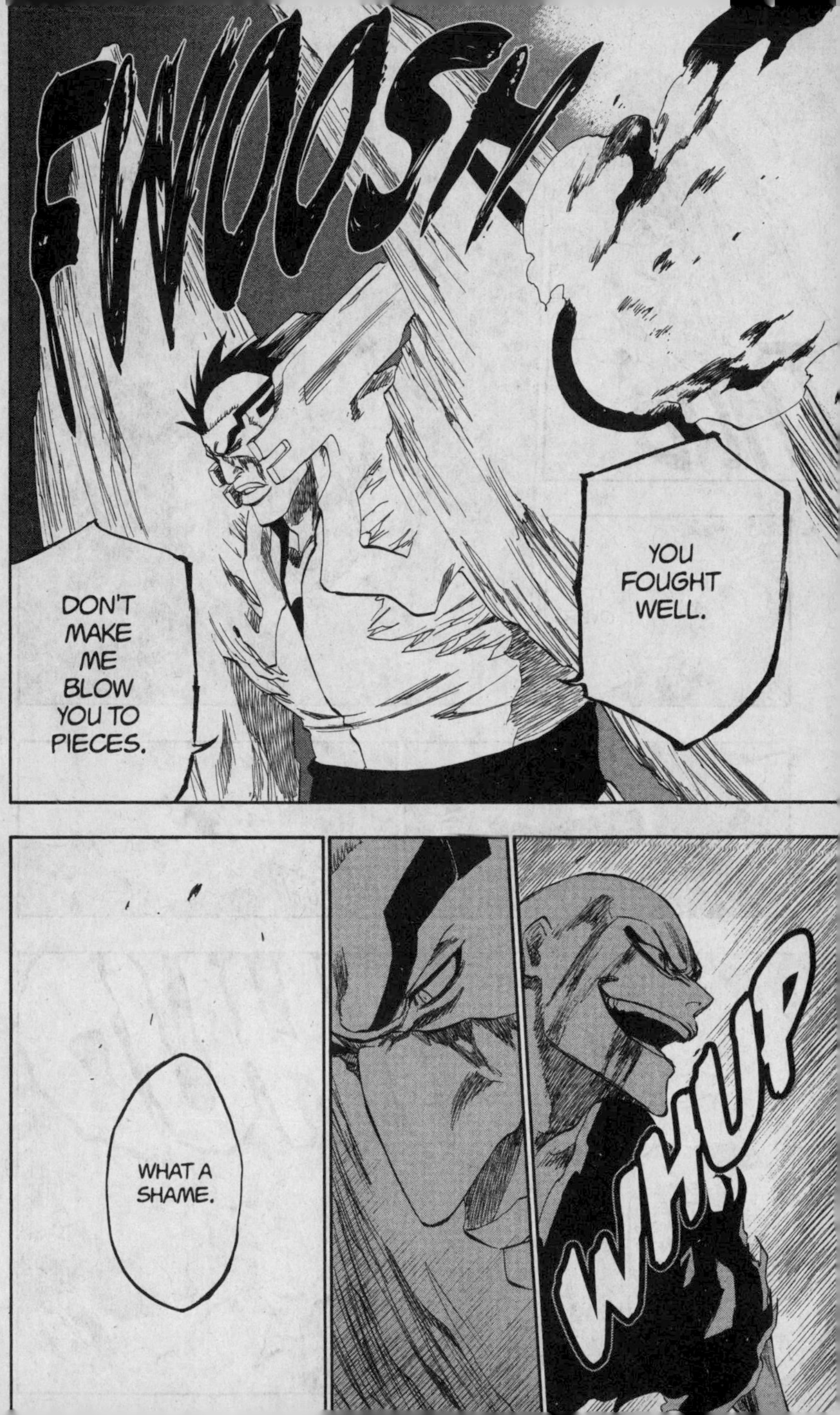
FWOOSH
YOU FOUGHT WELL.
DON'T MAKE ME BLOW YOU TO PIECES.
WHUP
WHAT A SHAME.

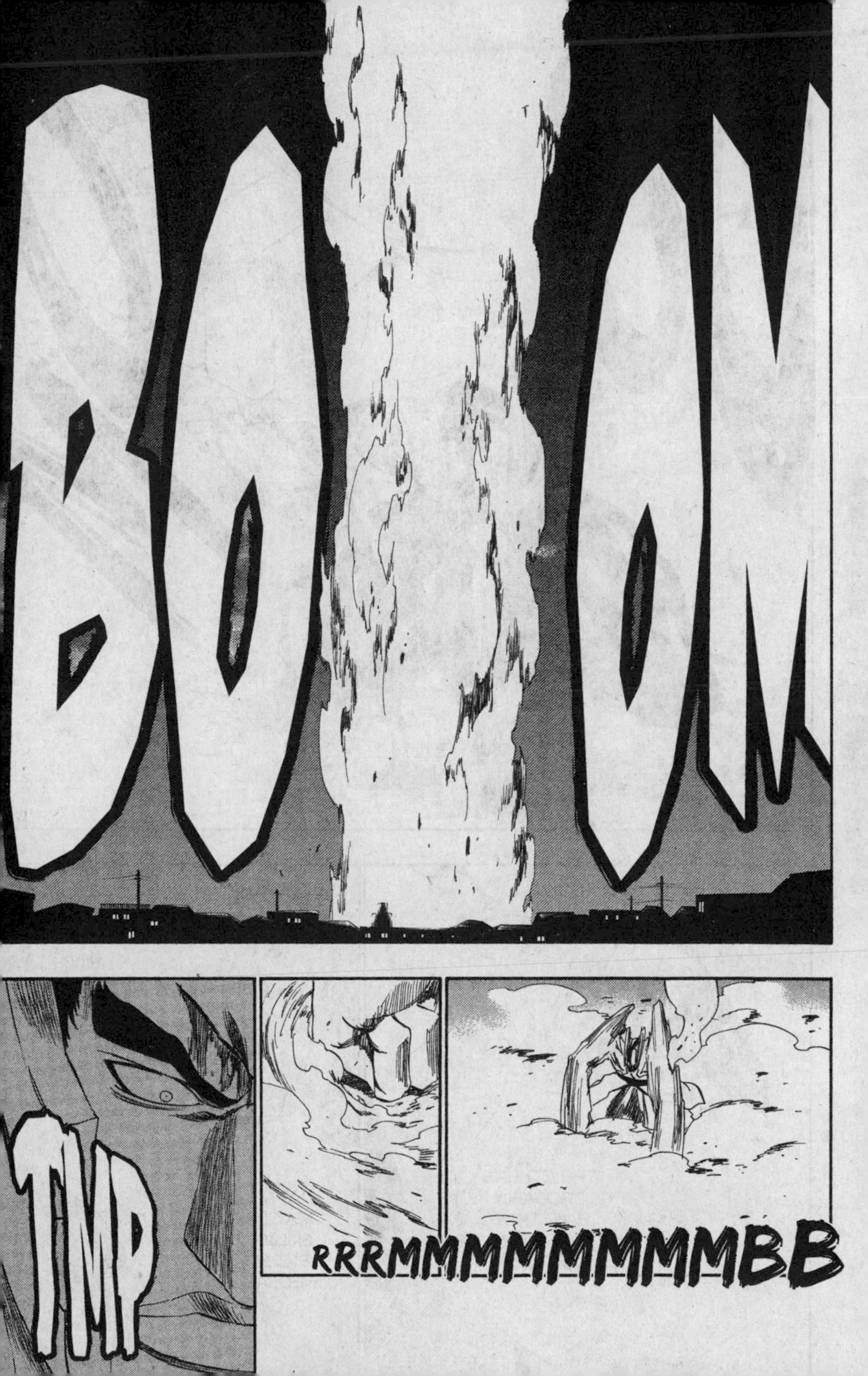
BOOM
RRRMMMMMMMMBB
TMP

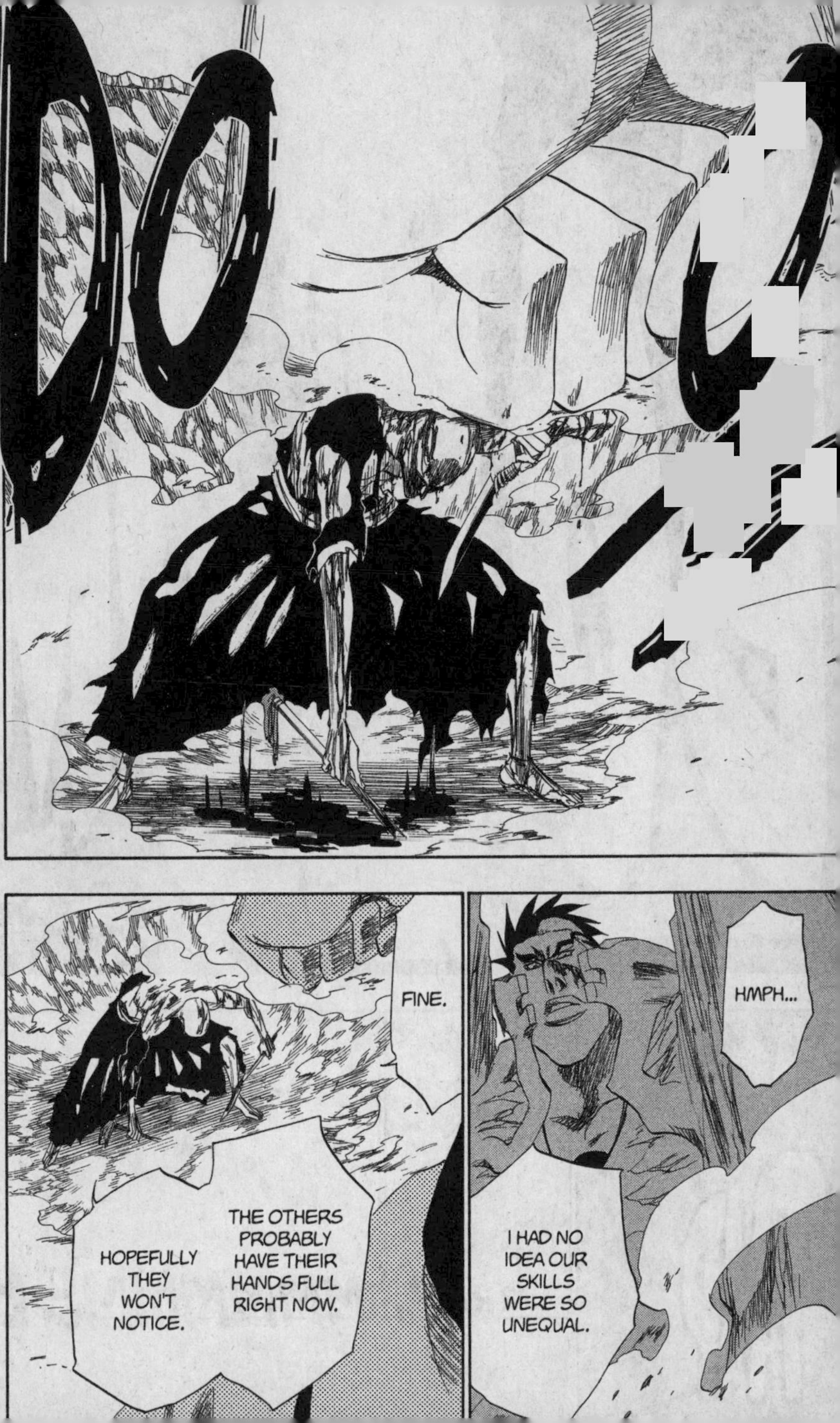
DODO
HMPH...
I HAD NO IDEA OUR SKILLS WERE SO UNEQUAL.
FINE.
THE OTHERS PROBABLY HAVE THEIR HANDS FULL RIGHT NOW.
HOPEFULLY THEY WON'T NOTICE.

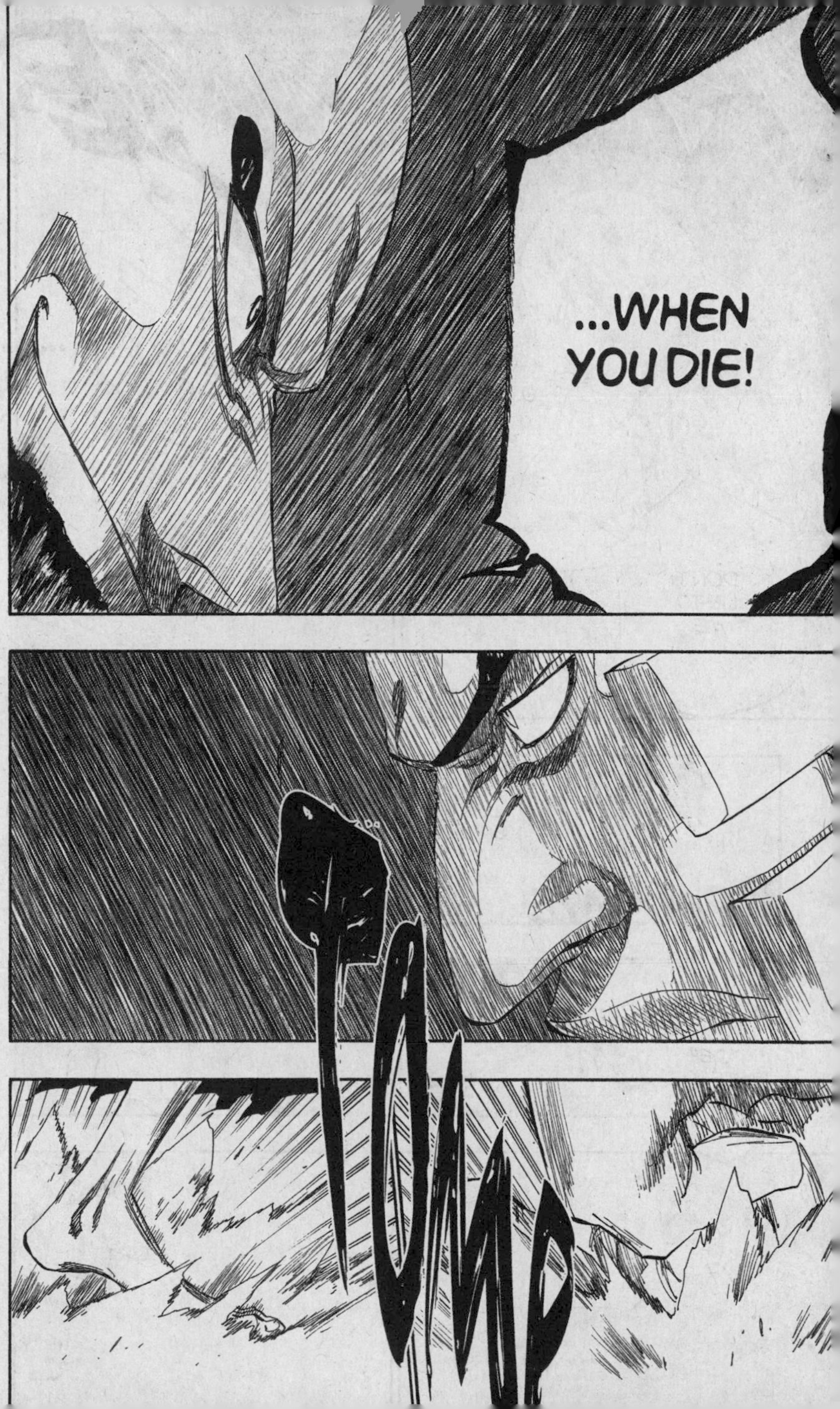
...WHEN
YOU DIE!
TOMP

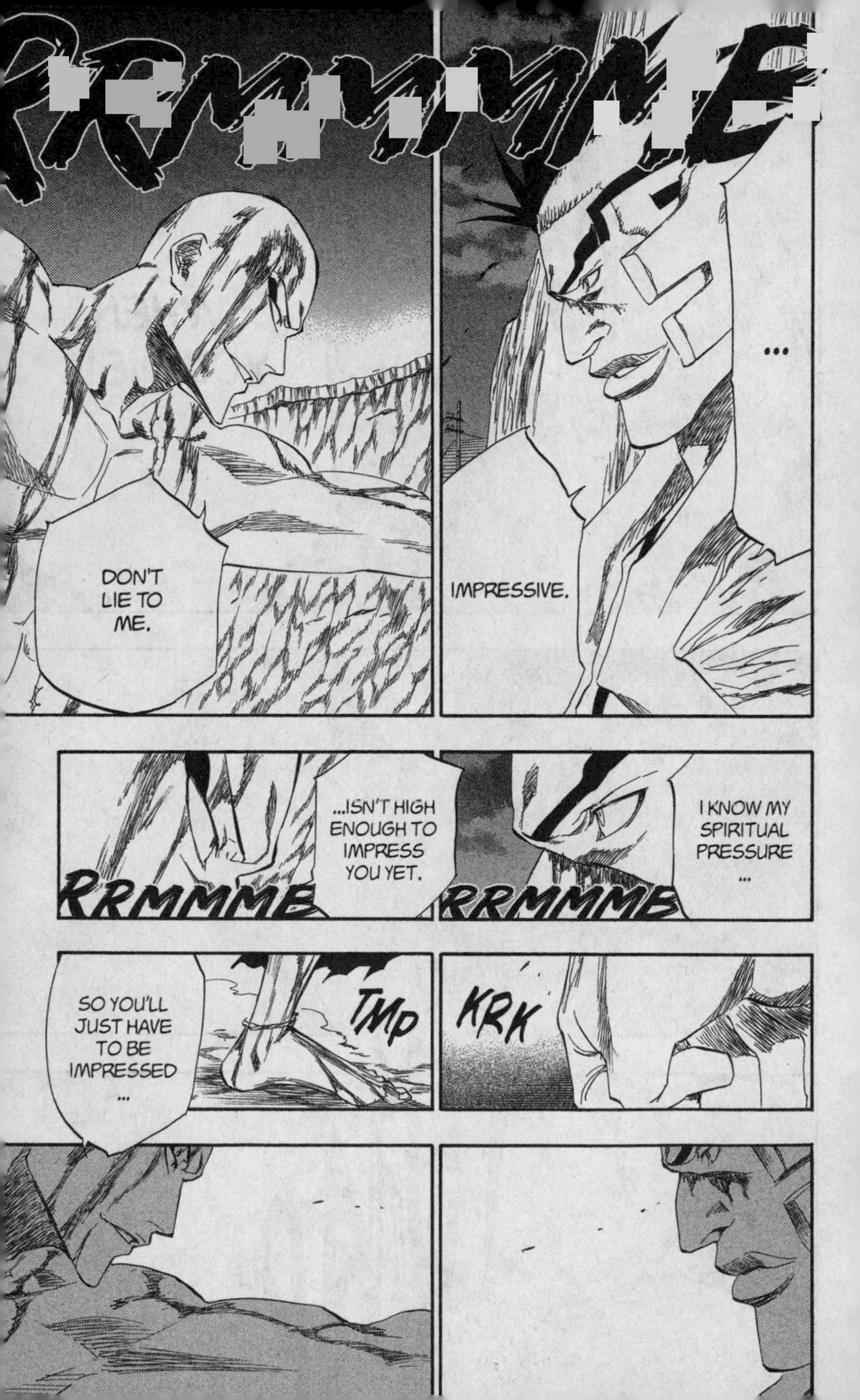
...
IMPRESSIVE.
DON'T LIE TO ME.
I KNOW MY SPIRITUAL PRESSURE ...
RRMMMMB
...ISN'T HIGH ENOUGH TO IMPRESS YOU YET.
RRMMMB
KRK
TMP
SO YOU'LL JUST HAVE TO BE IMPRESSED ...

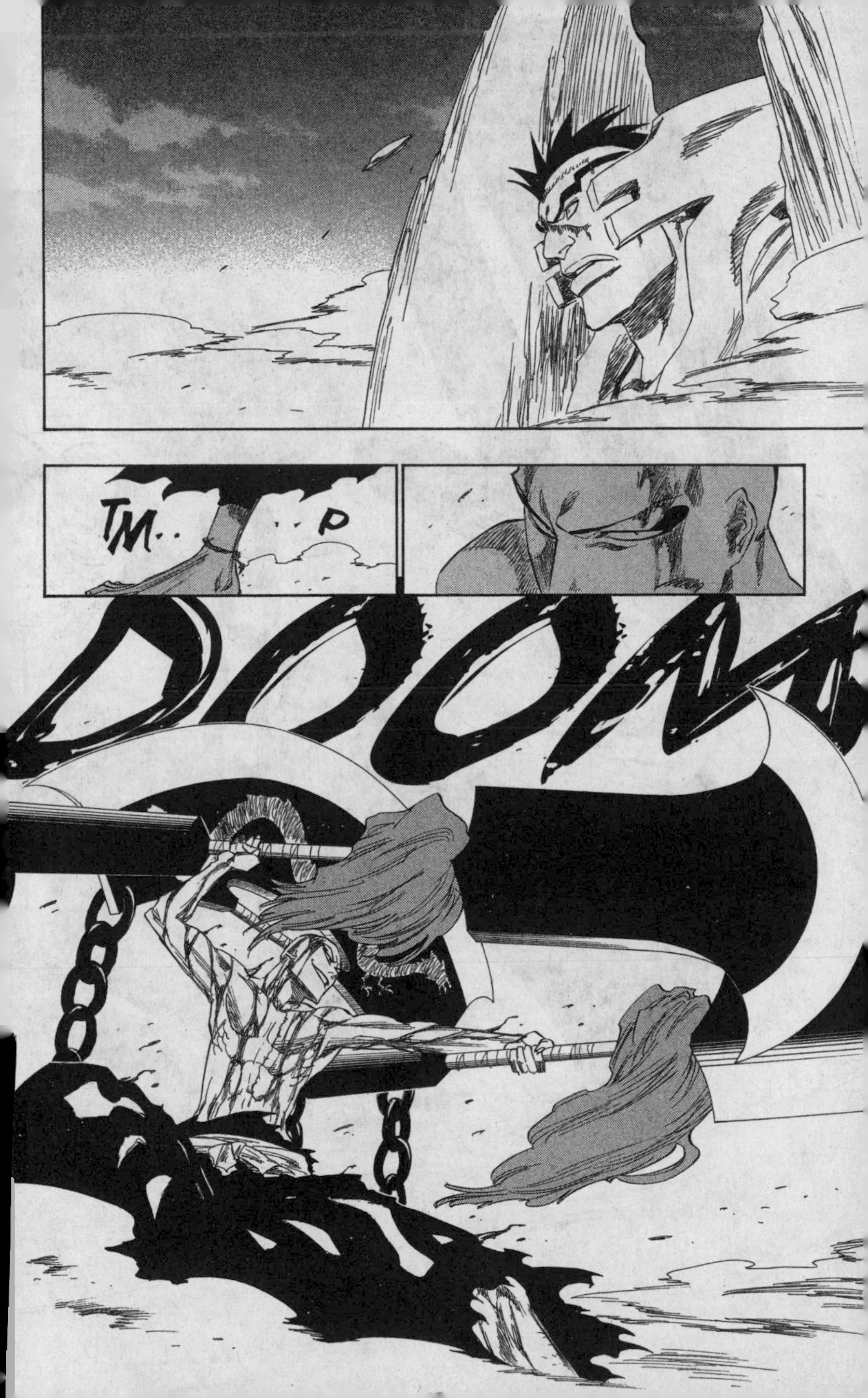
TM... ...P
DOOM

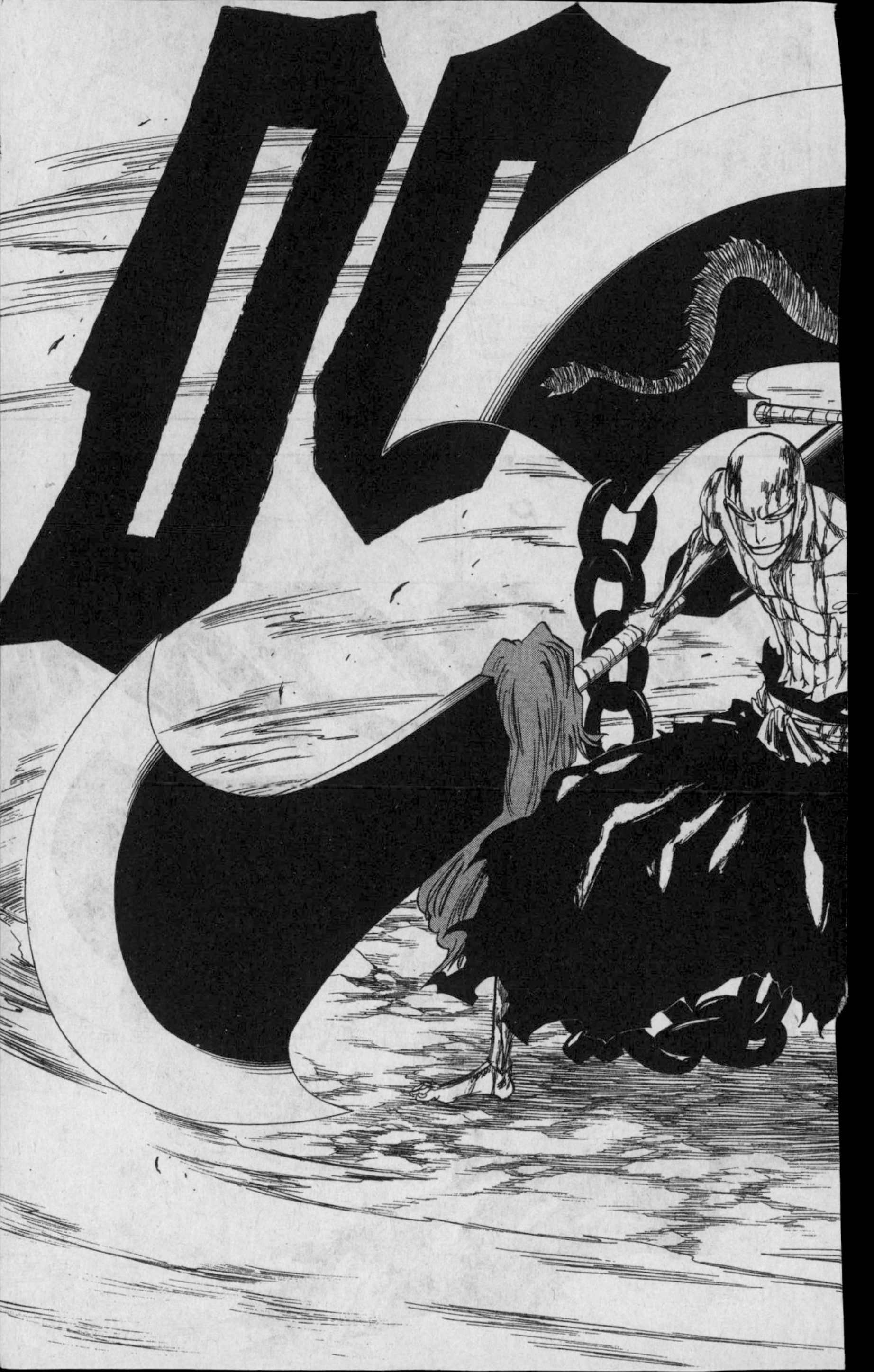

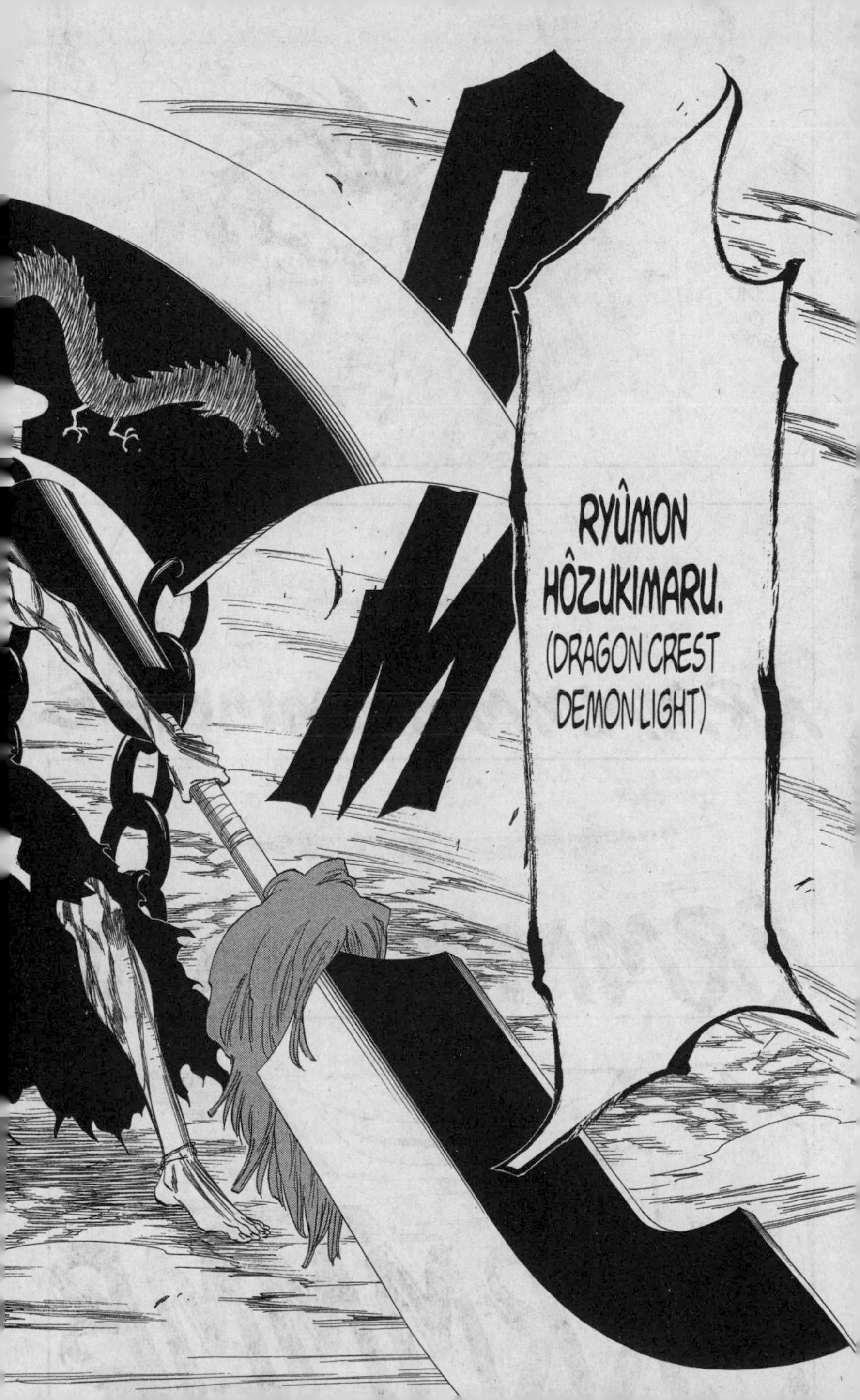
RYÛMON HÔZUKIMARU.
(DRAGON CREST DEMON LIGHT)

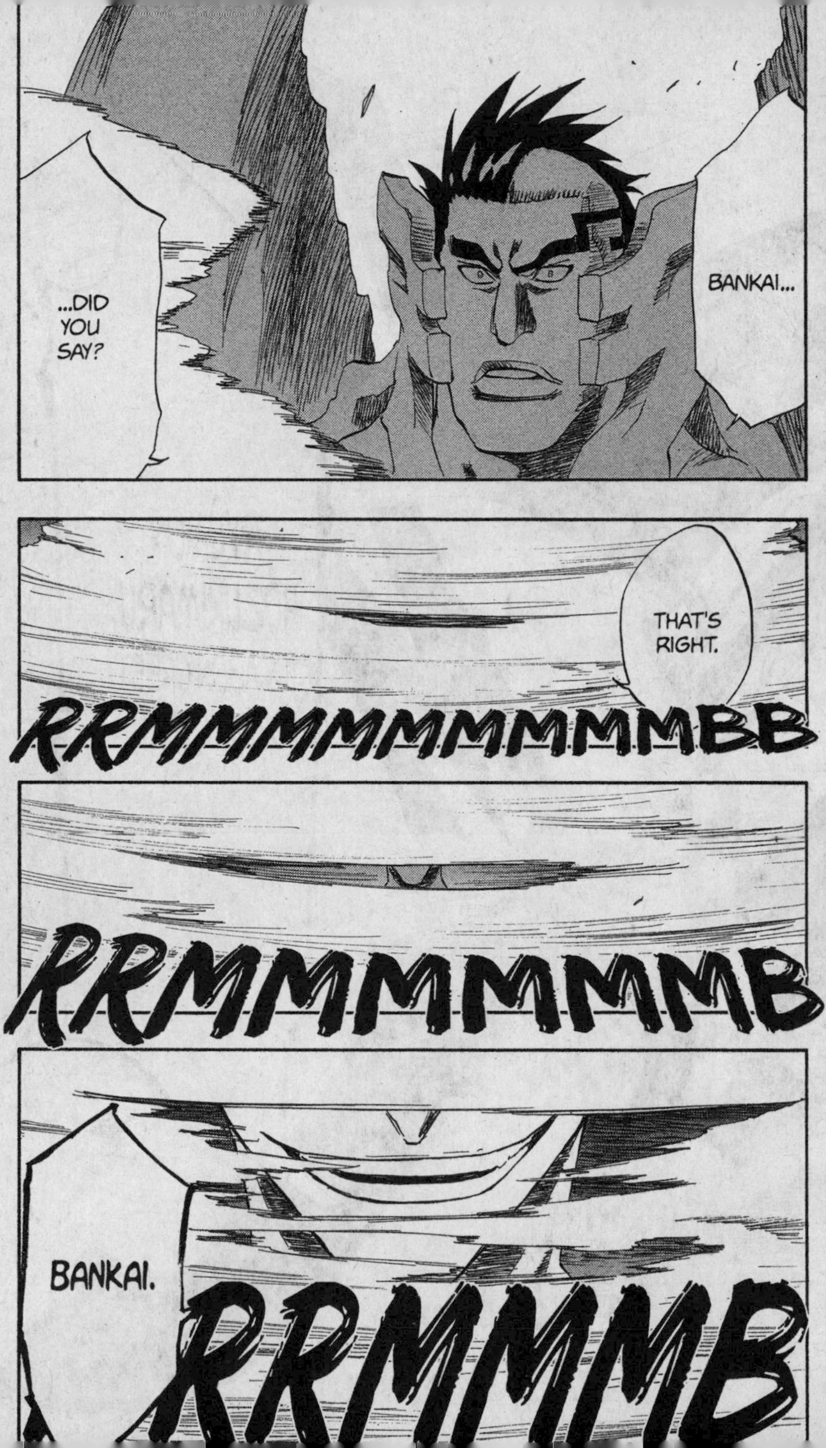
BANKAI...
...DID YOU SAY?
THAT'S RIGHT.
RRMMMMMMMMMBB
RRMMMMMMB
BANKAI.
RRMMMB

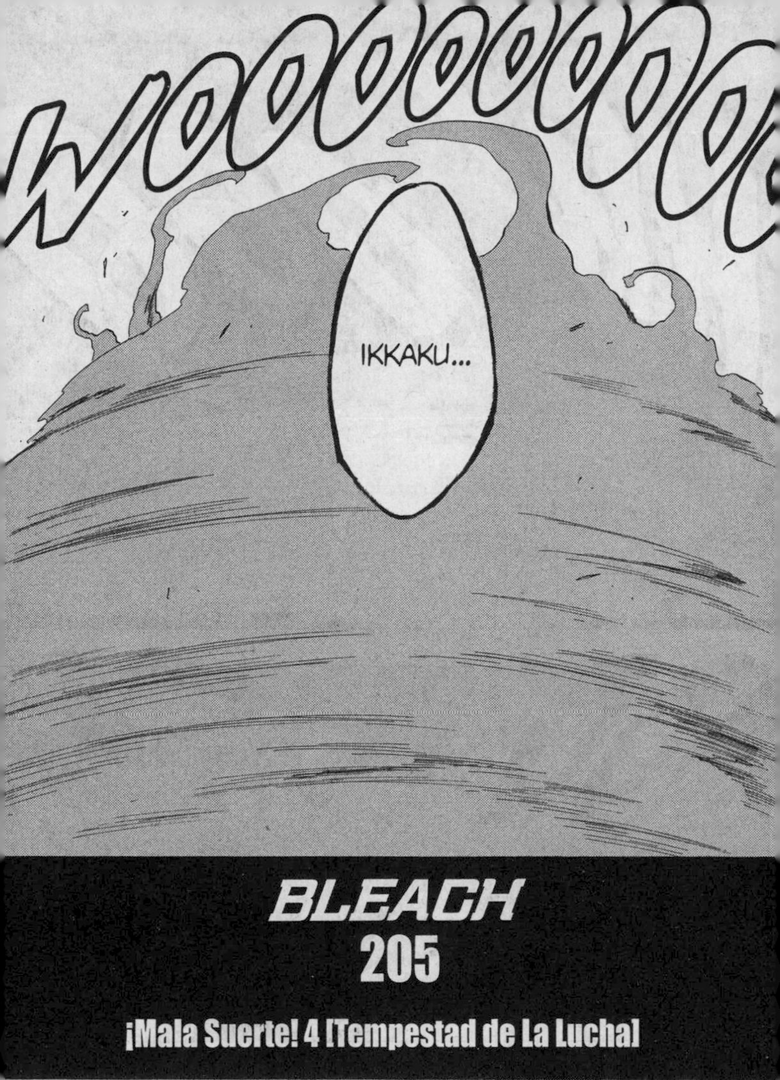
IKKAKU...

BLEACH
205
¡Mala Suerte! 4 [Tempestad de La Lucha]

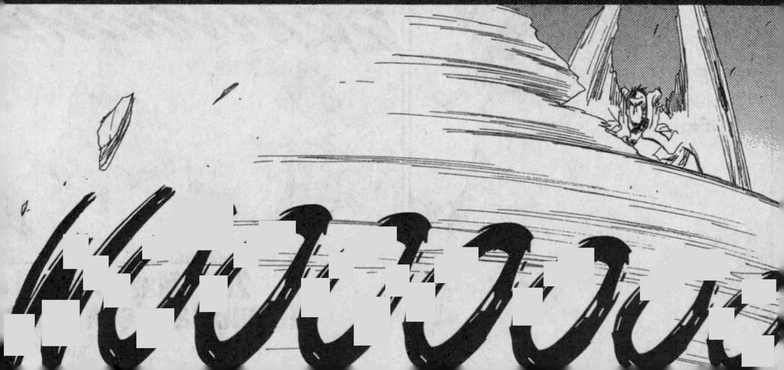

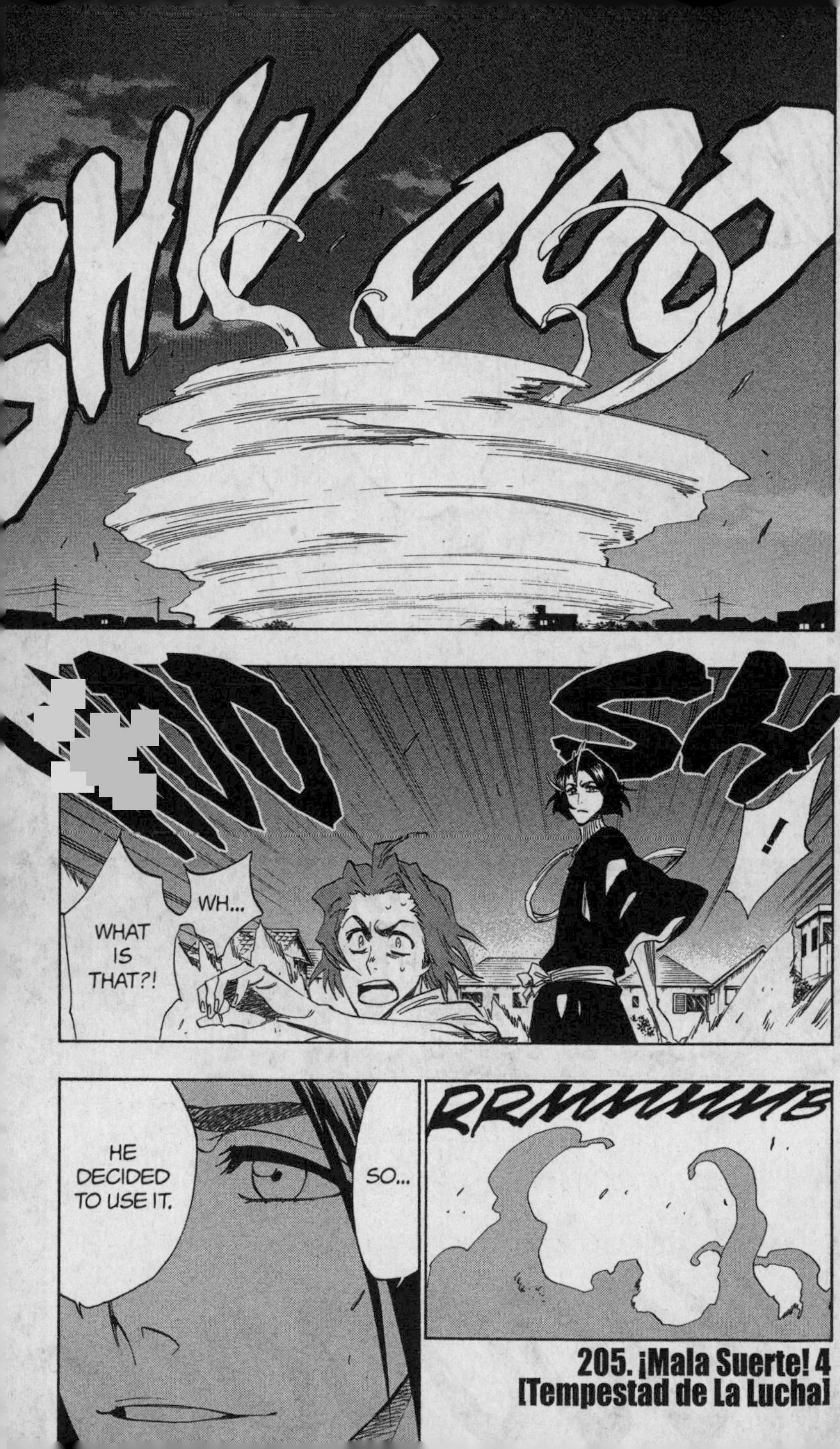
WH...
WHAT IS THAT?!
!
SO...
HE DECIDED TO USE IT.

205. ¡Mala Suerte! 4
[Tempestad de La Lucha]

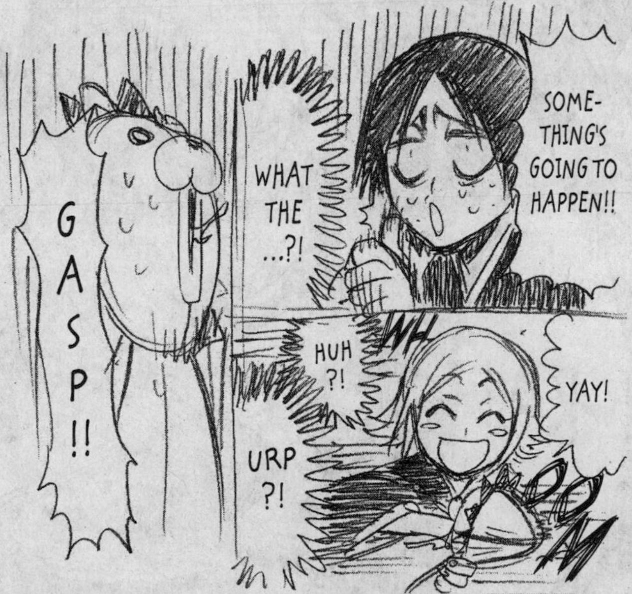
SOME-THING'S GOING TO HAPPEN!!
WHAT THE...?!
YAY!
BOOM
WH
HUH?!
URP?!
GASP!!

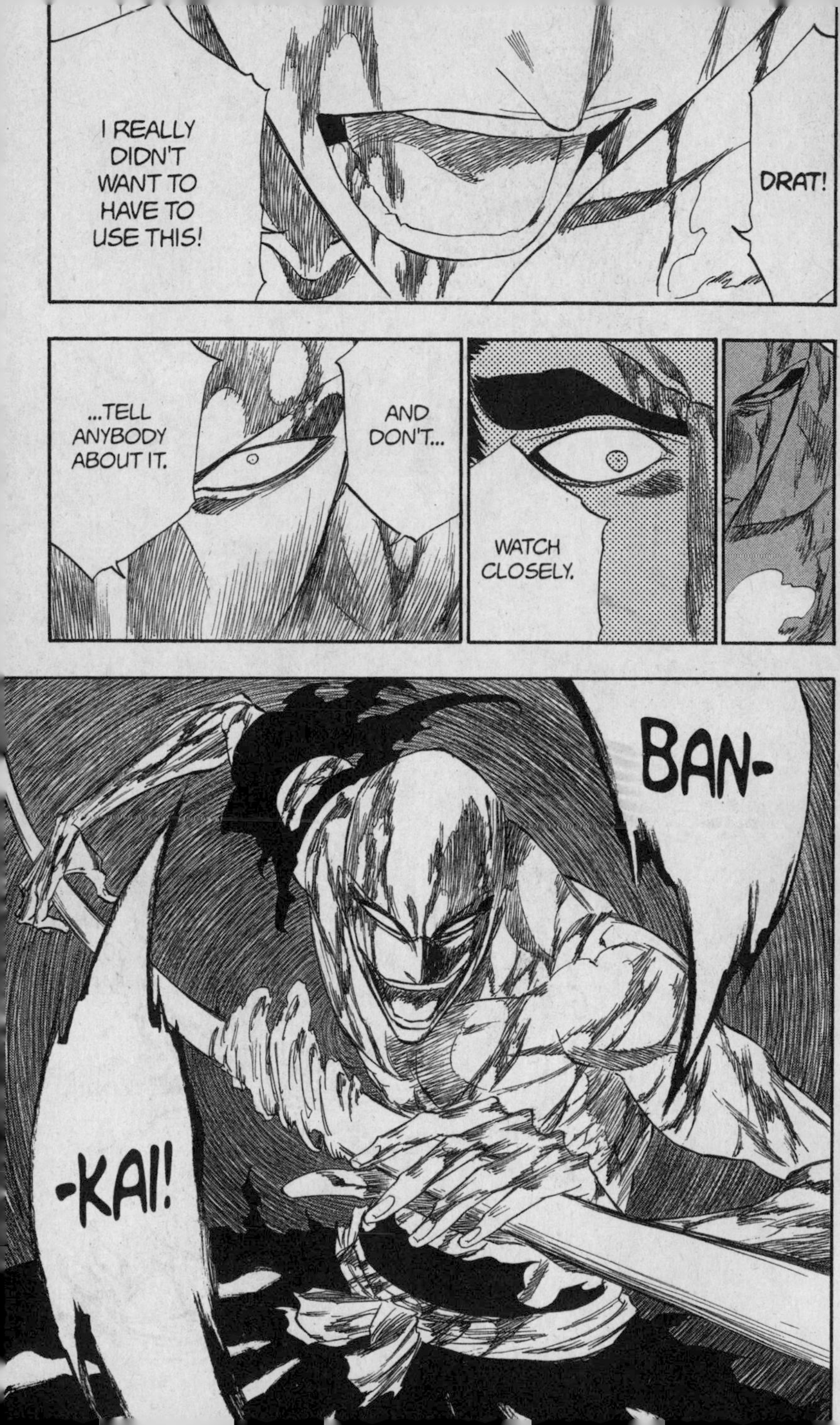
DRAT!
I REALLY DIDN'T WANT TO HAVE TO USE THIS!
WATCH CLOSELY.
AND DON'T...
...TELL ANYBODY ABOUT IT.
BAN-
-KAI!

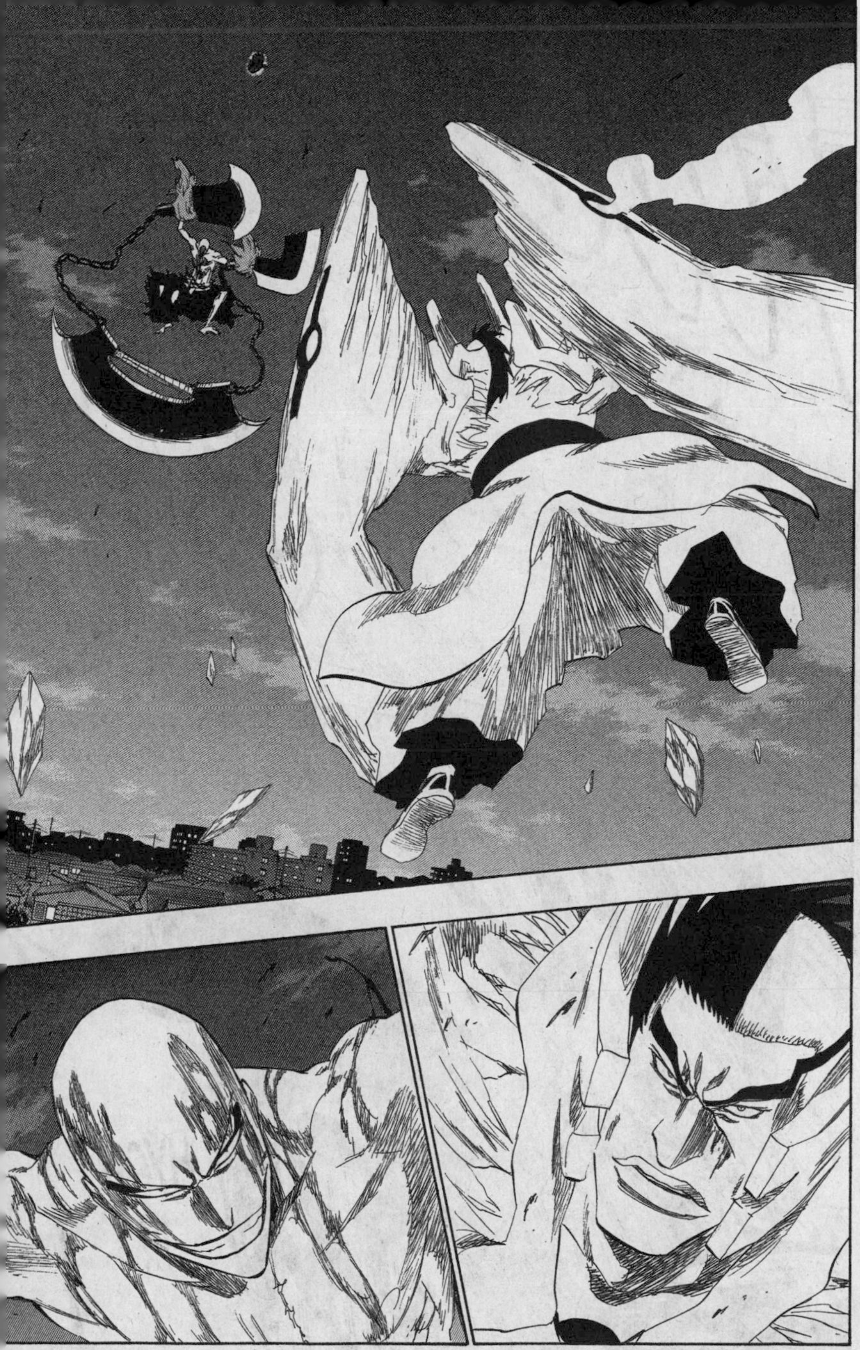

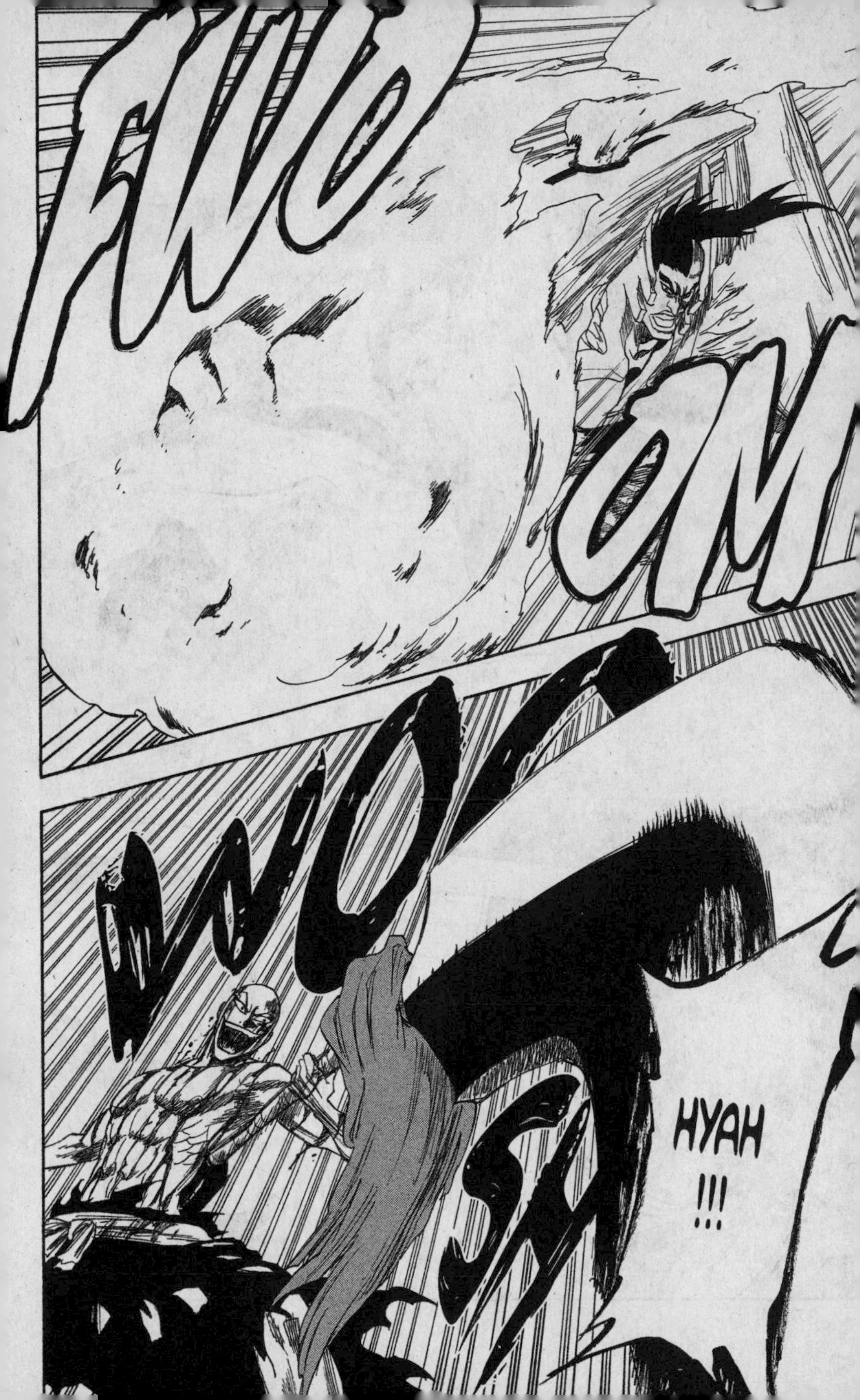
HYAH !!!

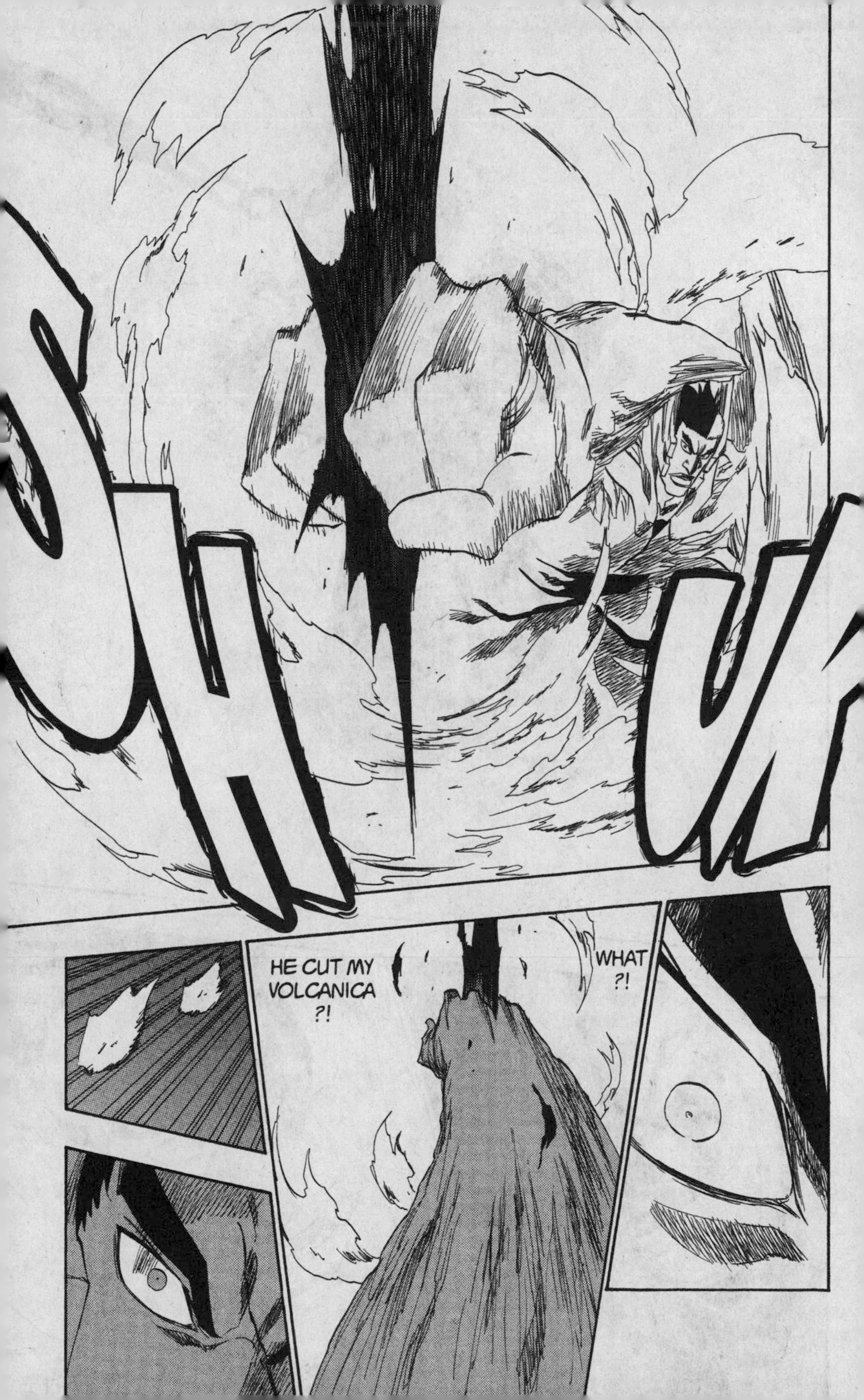
WHAT ?!
HE CUT MY VOLCANICA ?!

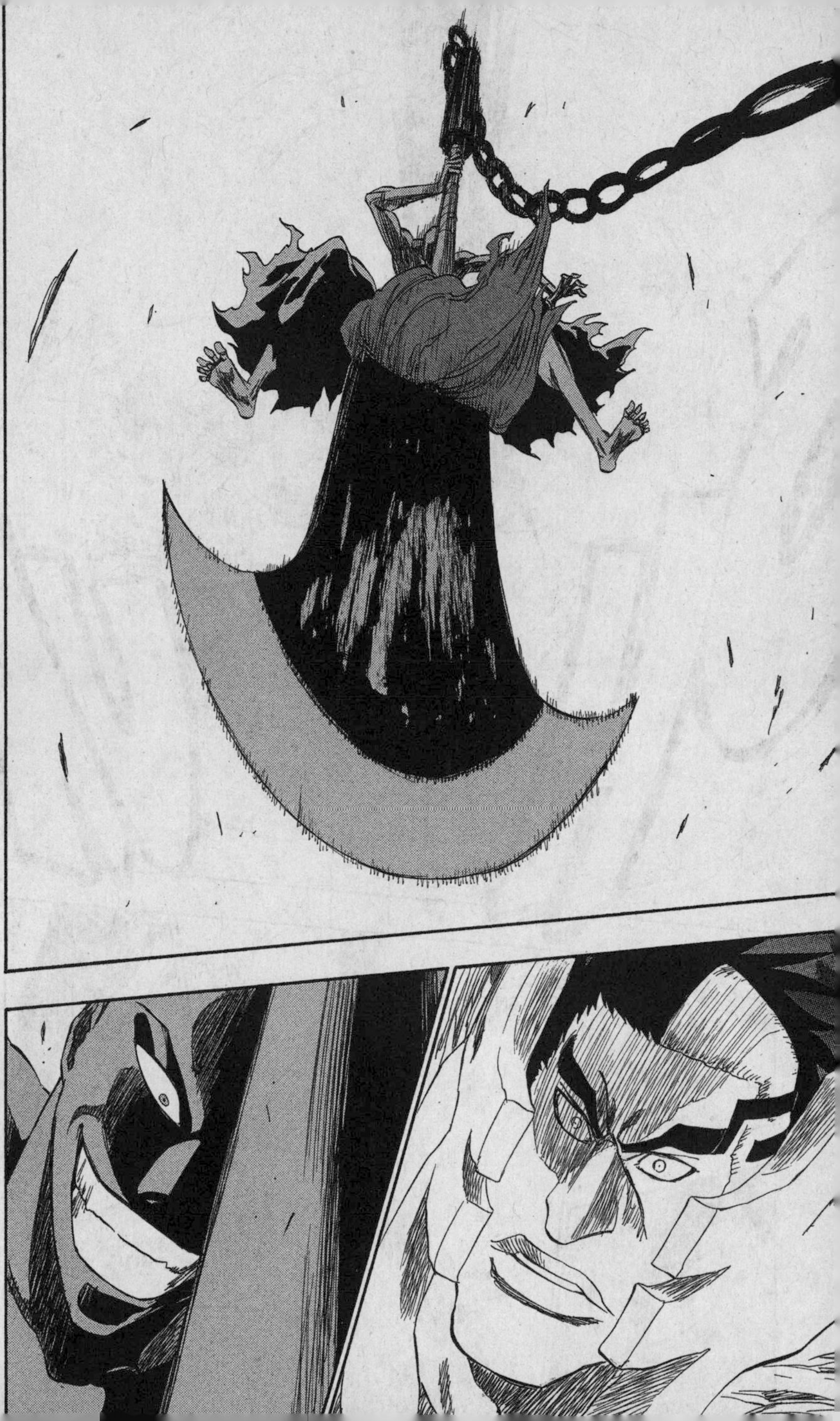

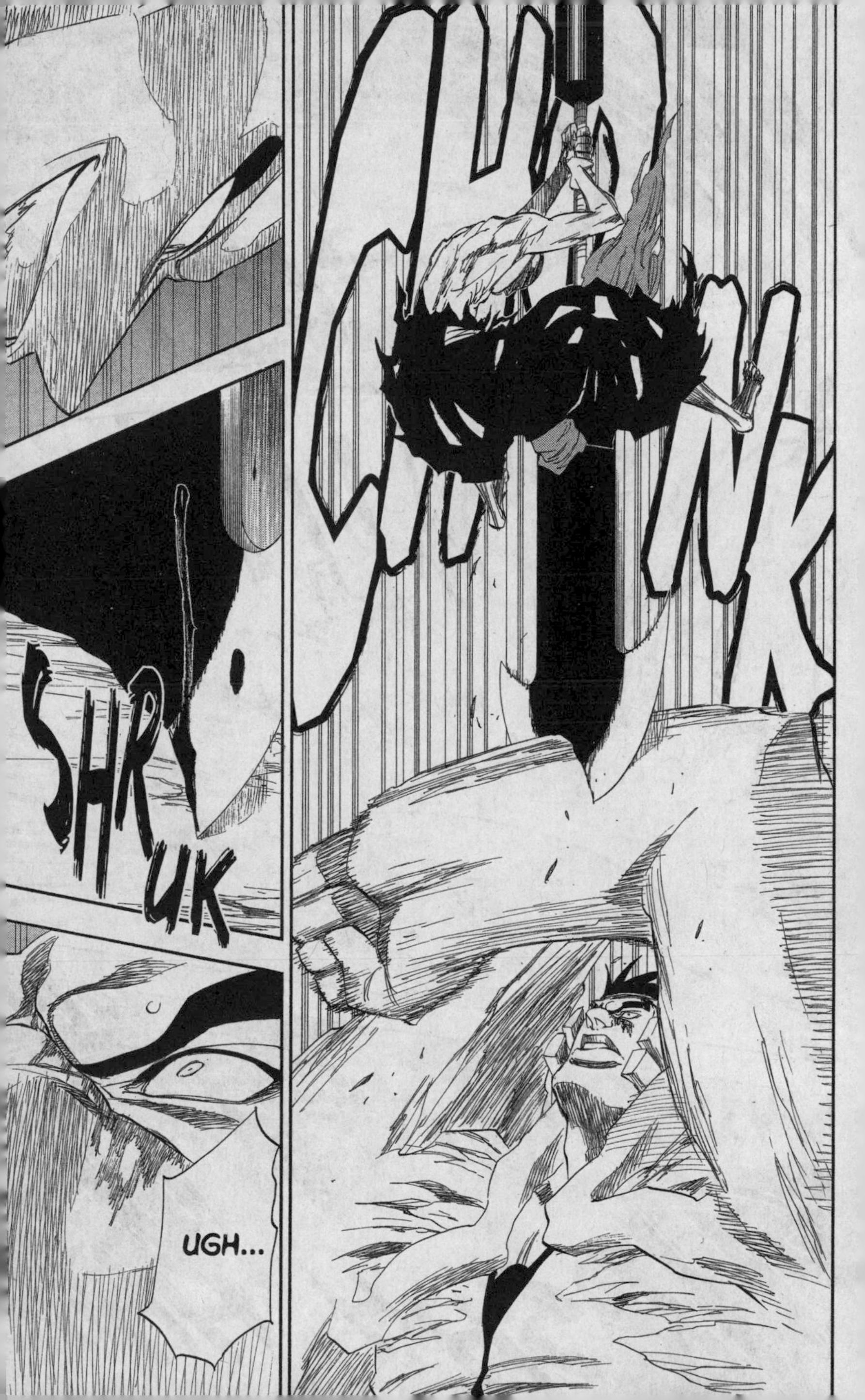
CHUNK
SHRUK
UGH...

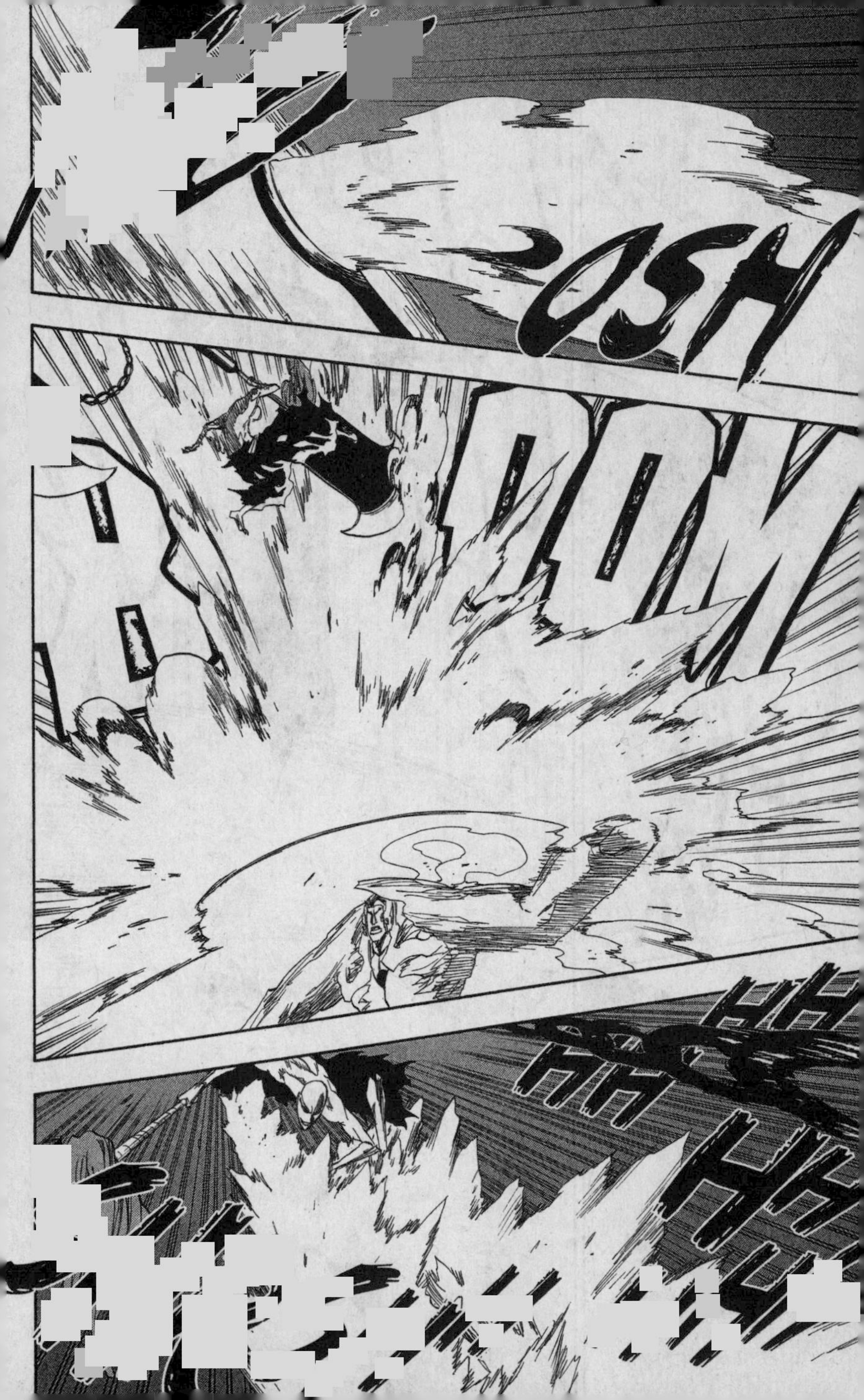
OSH
DOM

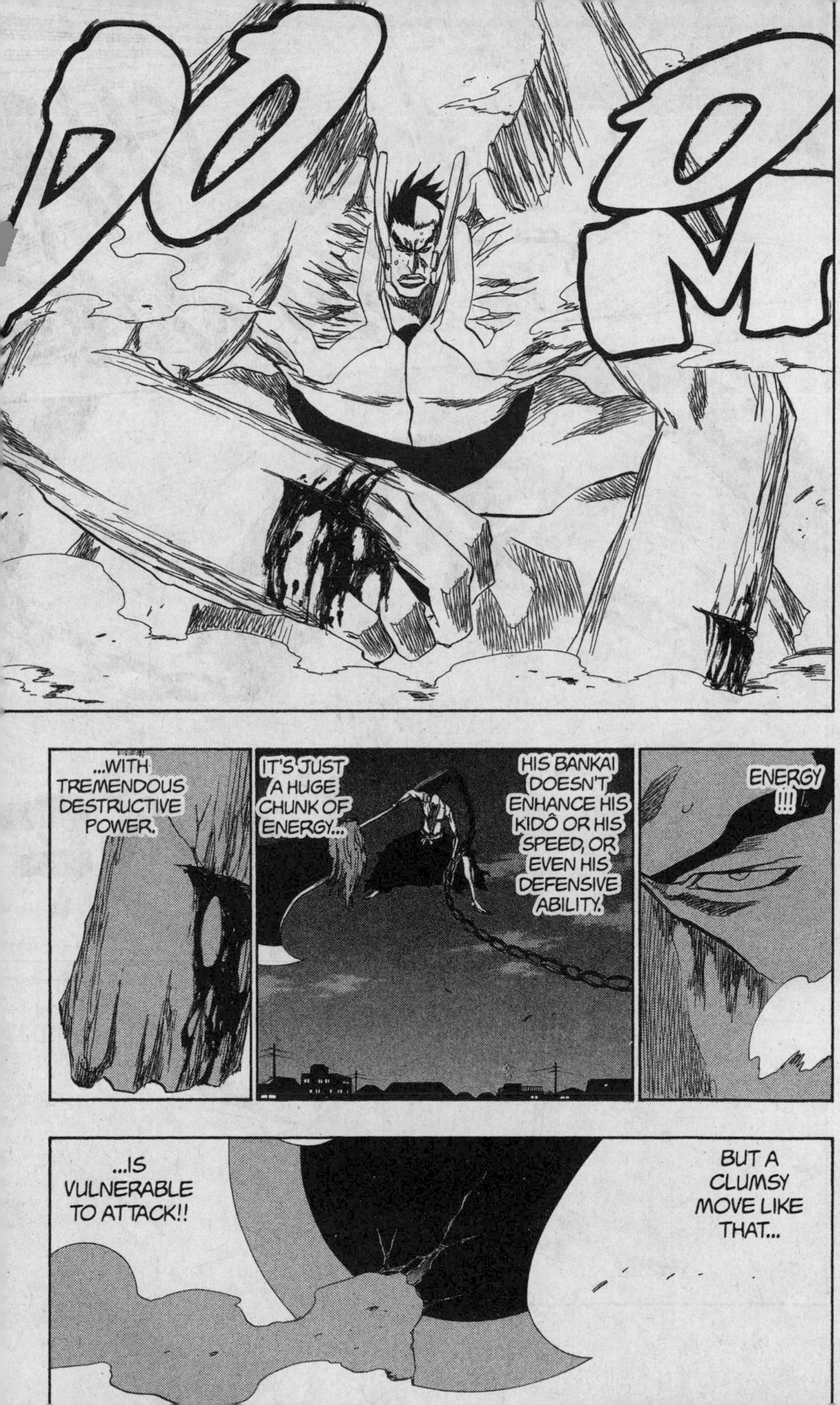
DOOM
ENERGY !!!
HIS BANKAI DOESN'T ENHANCE HIS KIDÔ OR HIS SPEED, OR EVEN HIS DEFENSIVE ABILITY.
IT'S JUST A HUGE CHUNK OF ENERGY...
...WITH TREMENDOUS DESTRUCTIVE POWER.
BUT A CLUMSY MOVE LIKE THAT...
...IS VULNERABLE TO ATTACK!!

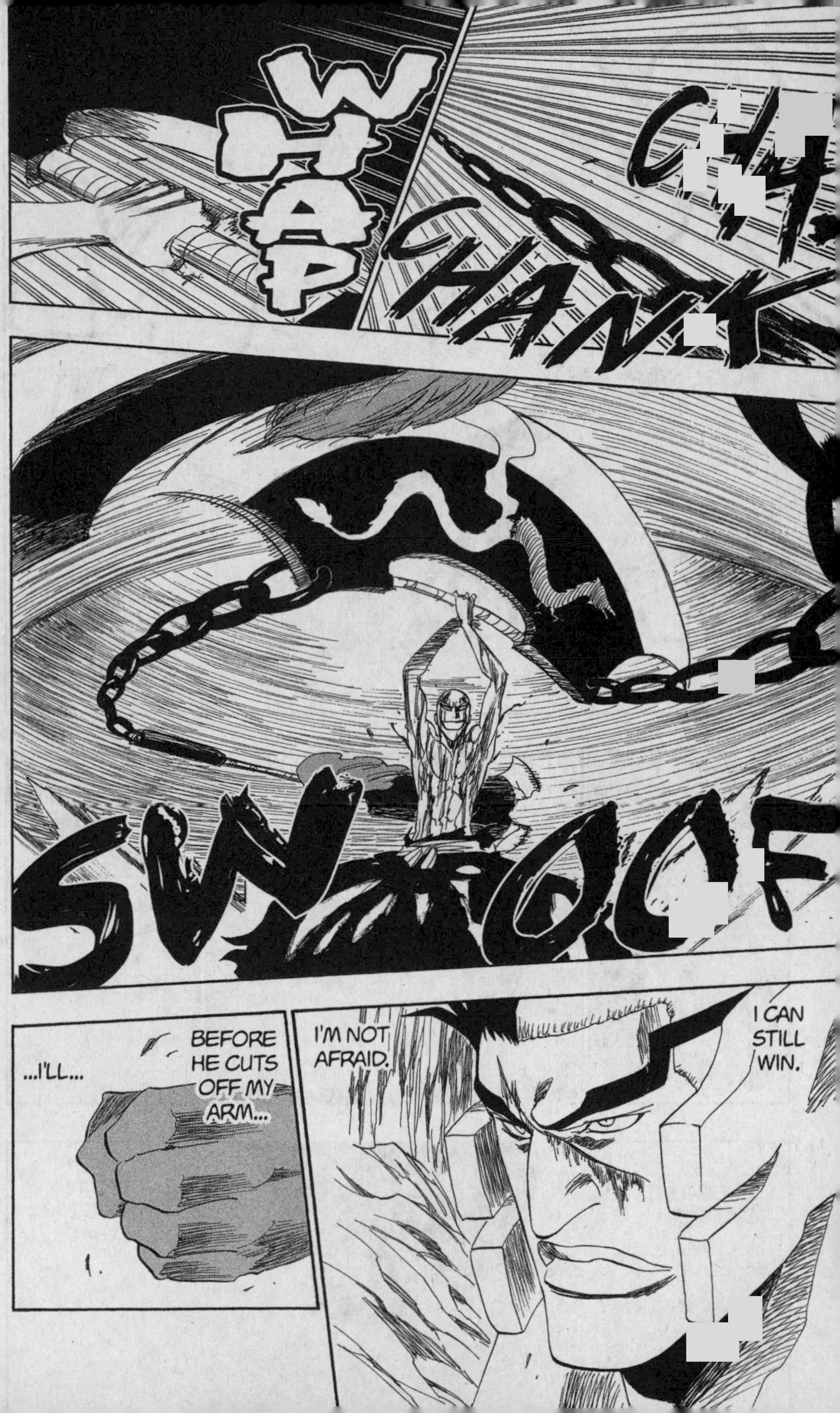
CHANK
WHAP
SWOOF
I CAN STILL WIN.
I'M NOT AFRAID.
BEFORE HE CUTS OFF MY ARM...
...I'LL...

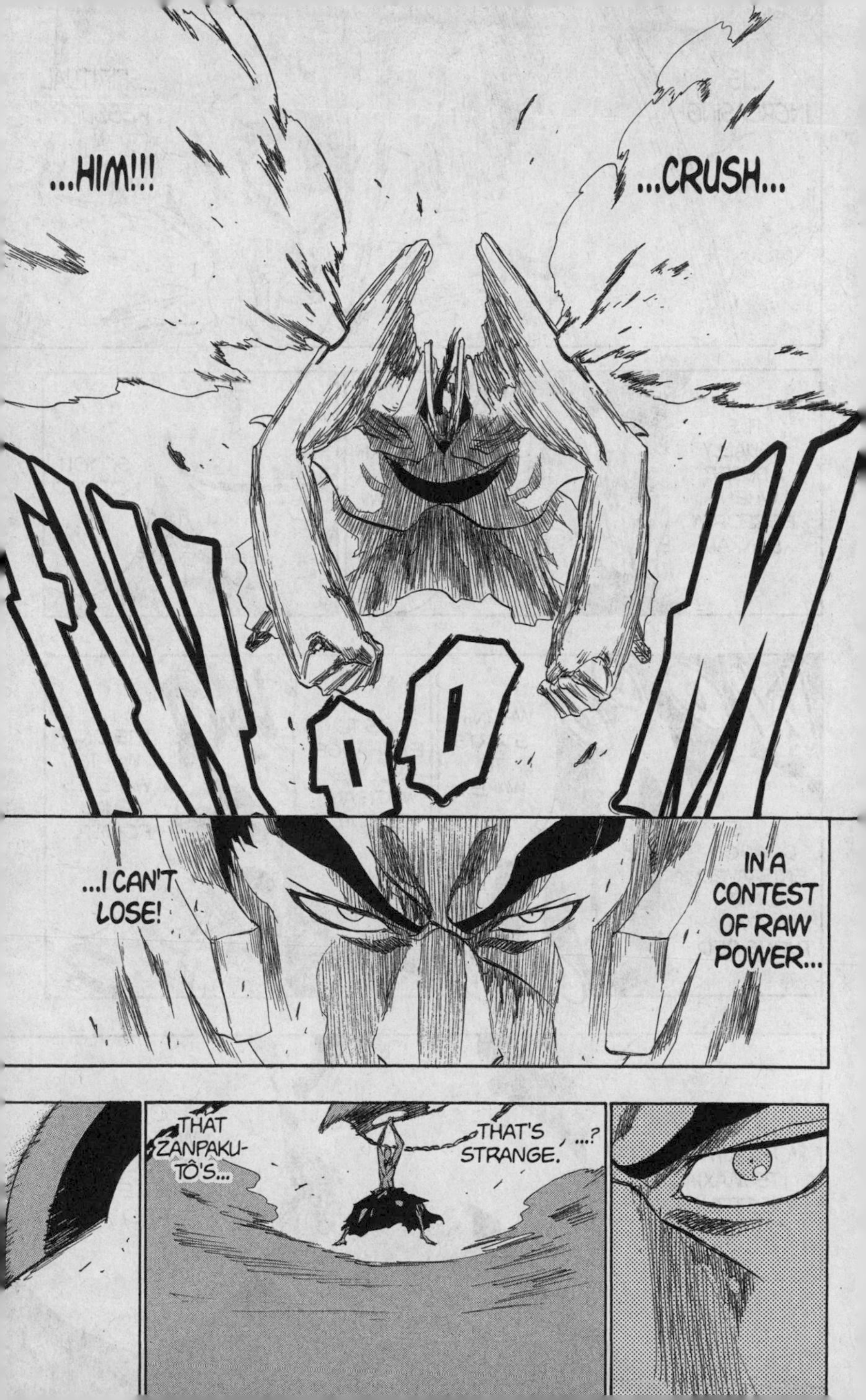
...CRUSH...
...HIM!!!
IN A CONTEST OF RAW POWER...
...I CAN'T LOSE!
...?
THAT'S STRANGE.
THAT ZANPAKU-TÔ'S...

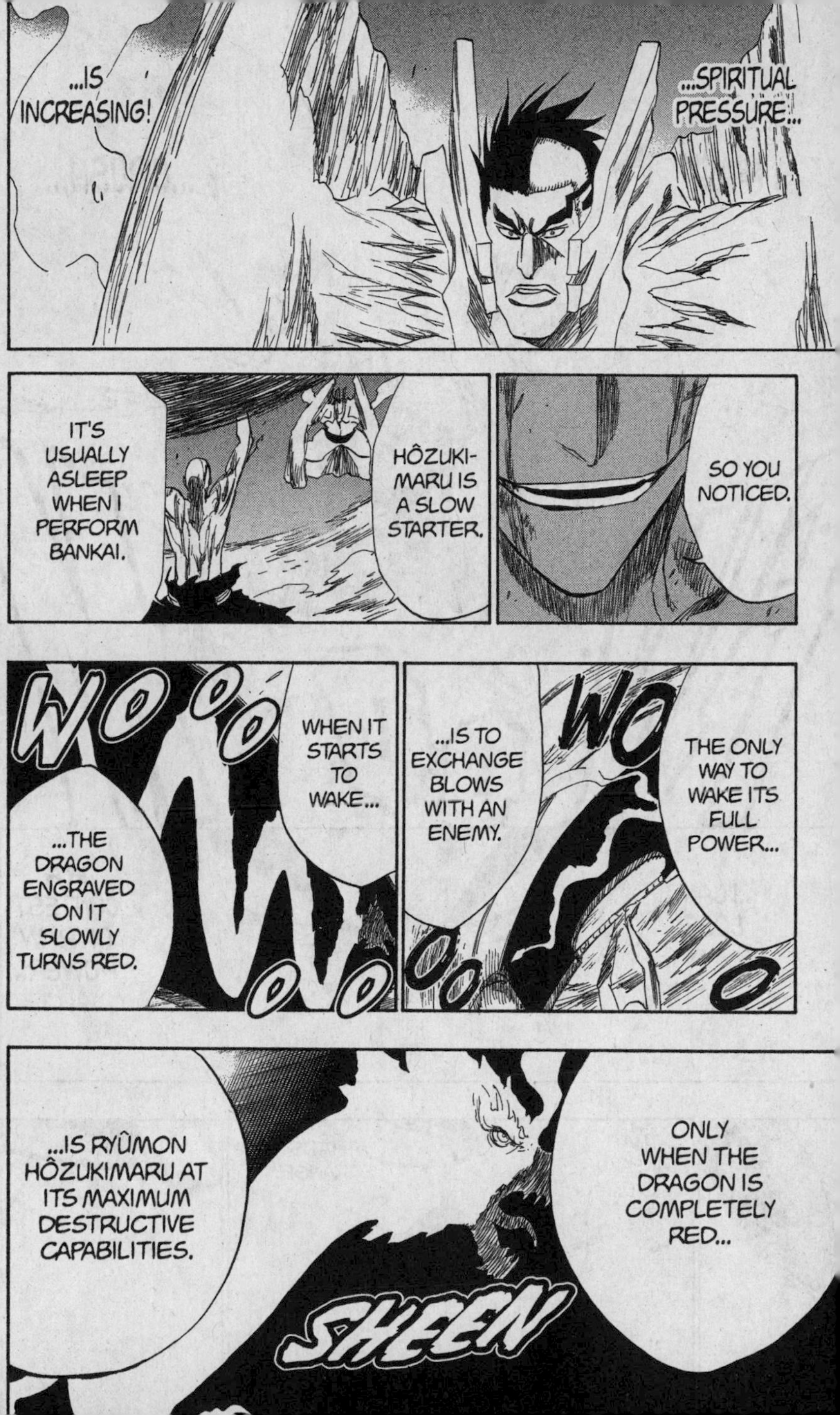
...SPIRITUAL PRESSURE...
...IS INCREASING!
SO YOU NOTICED.
HÔZUKI-MARU IS A SLOW STARTER.
IT'S USUALLY ASLEEP WHEN I PERFORM BANKAI.
WOOOO
THE ONLY WAY TO WAKE ITS FULL POWER...
...IS TO EXCHANGE BLOWS WITH AN ENEMY.
WHEN IT STARTS TO WAKE...
WOOOOOO
...THE DRAGON ENGRAVED ON IT SLOWLY TURNS RED.
ONLY WHEN THE DRAGON IS COMPLETELY RED...
...IS RYÛMON HÔZUKIMARU AT ITS MAXIMUM DESTRUCTIVE CAPABILITIES.
SHEEN

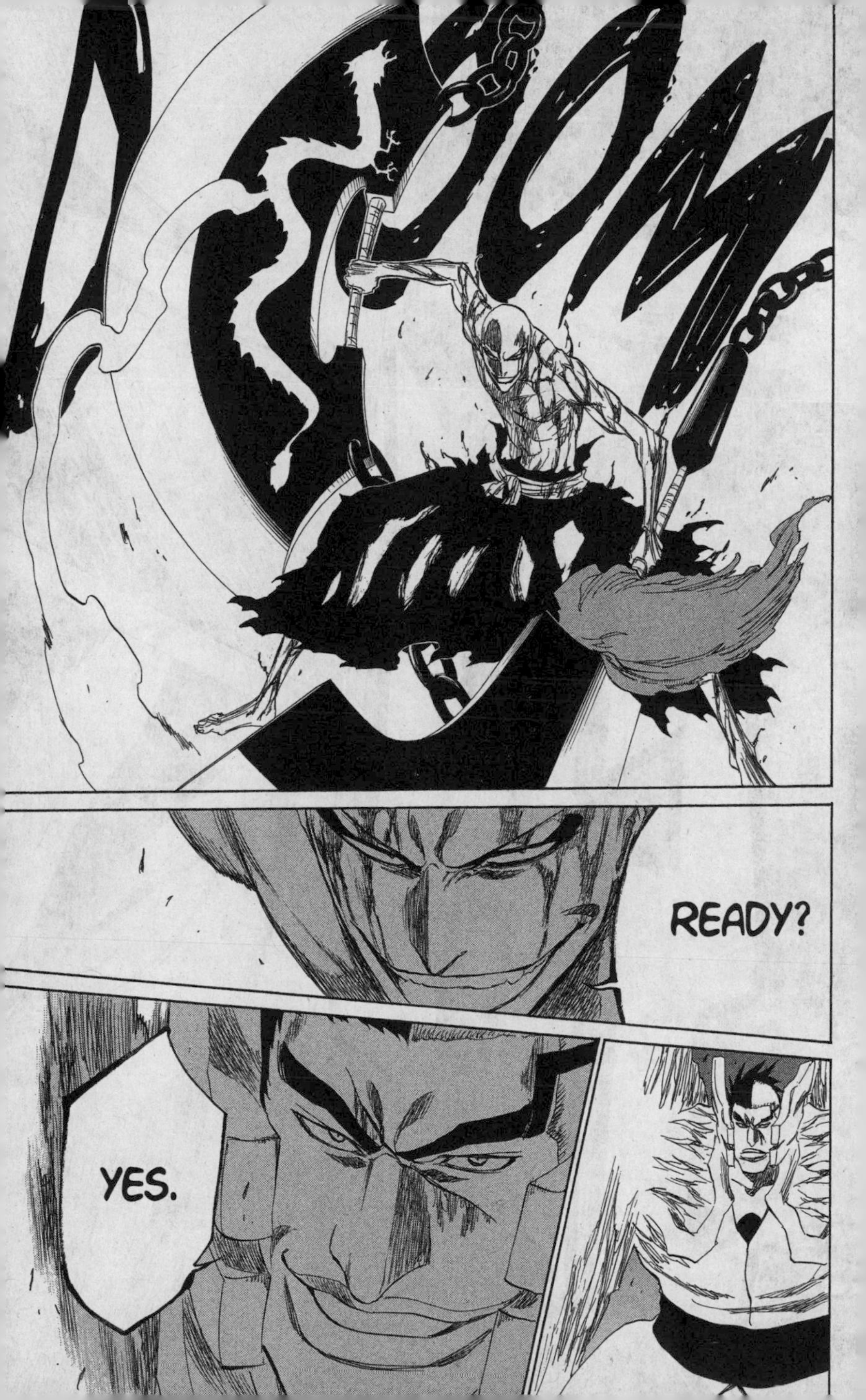
DOOM
READY?
YES.

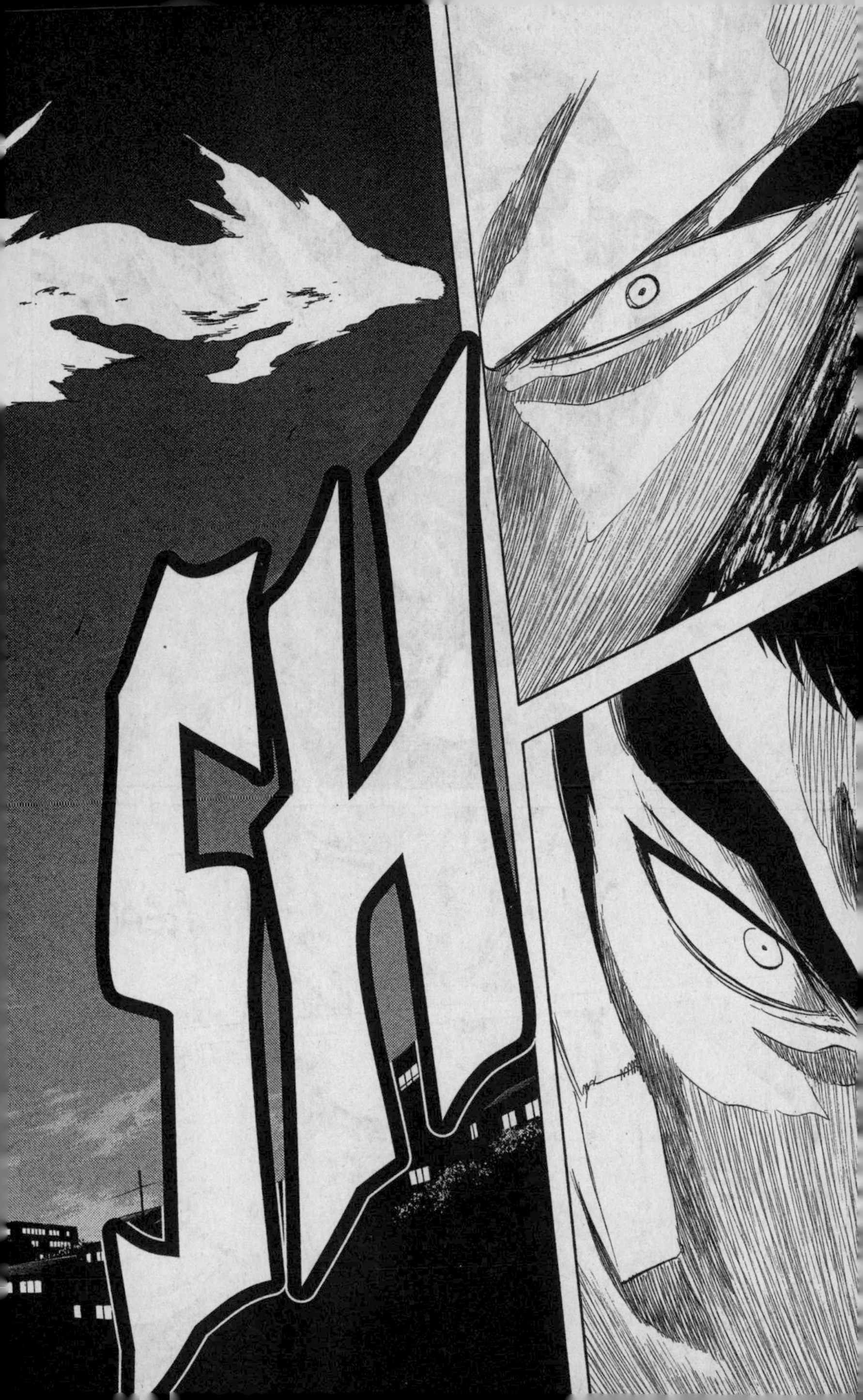

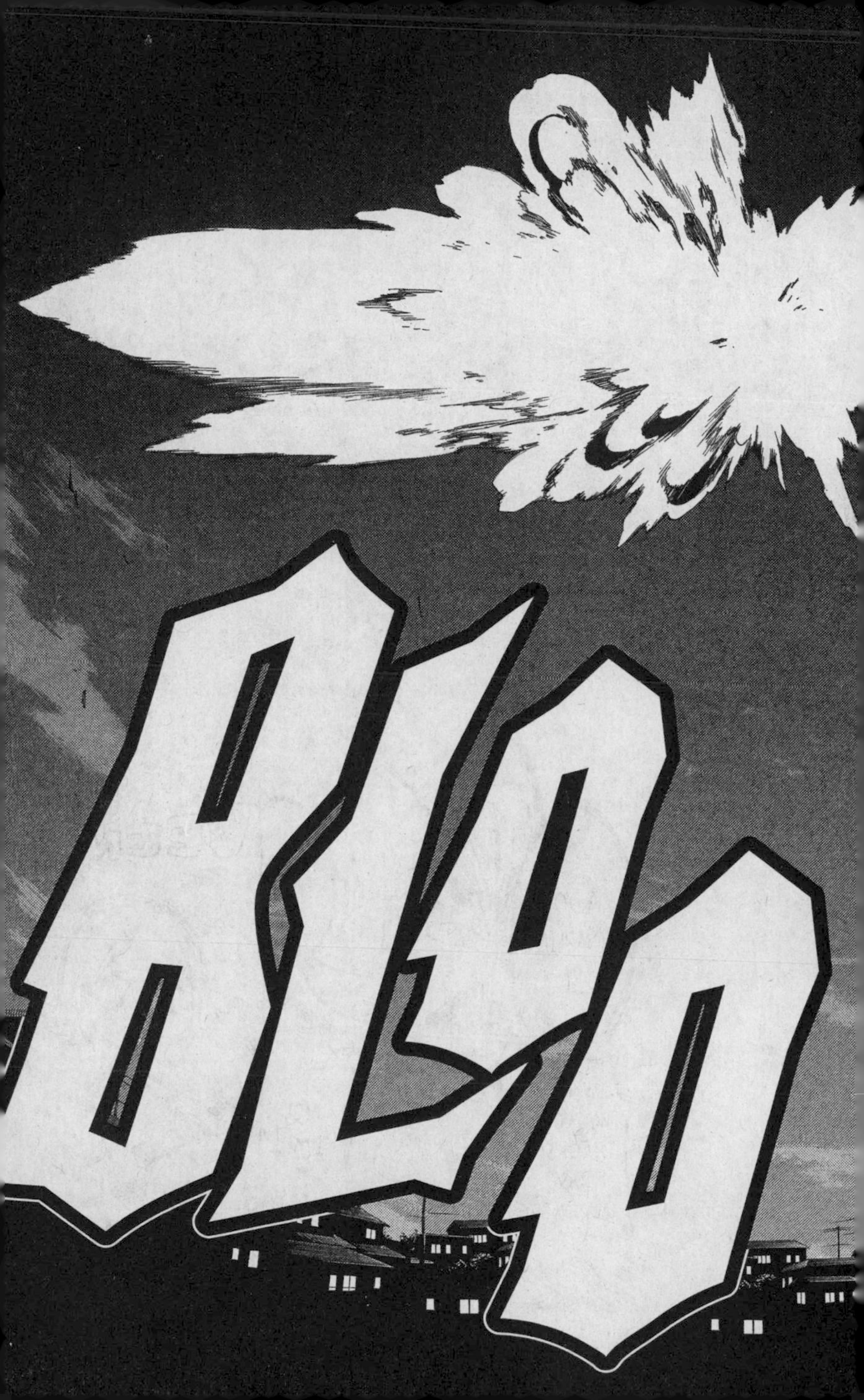

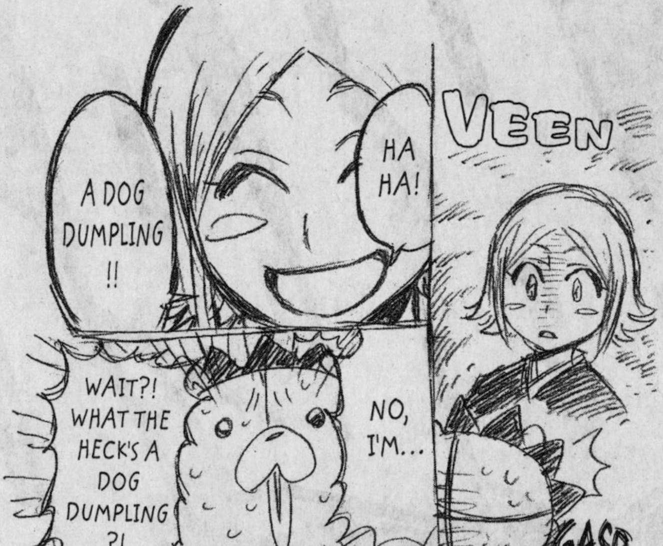
VEEN
GASP
HA HA!
A DOG DUMPLING !!
NO, I'M...
WAIT?! WHAT THE HECK'S A DOG DUMPLING ?!

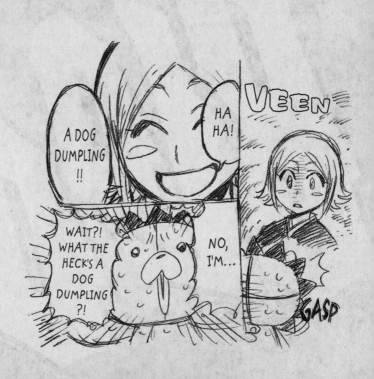

It spins.

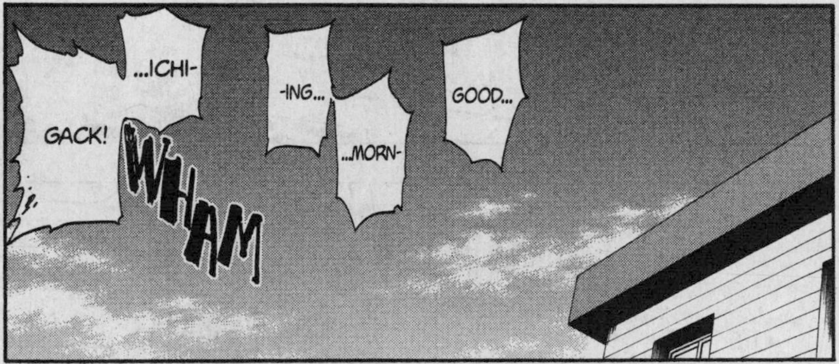
GOOD...
...MORN-
-ING...
...ICHI-
WHAM
GACK!

BLEACH *0* *side-A*

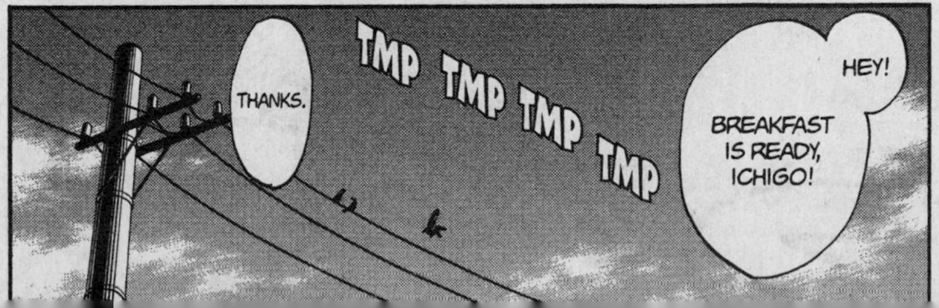
HEY!
BREAKFAST IS READY, ICHIGO!
TMP TMP TMP TMP
THANKS.

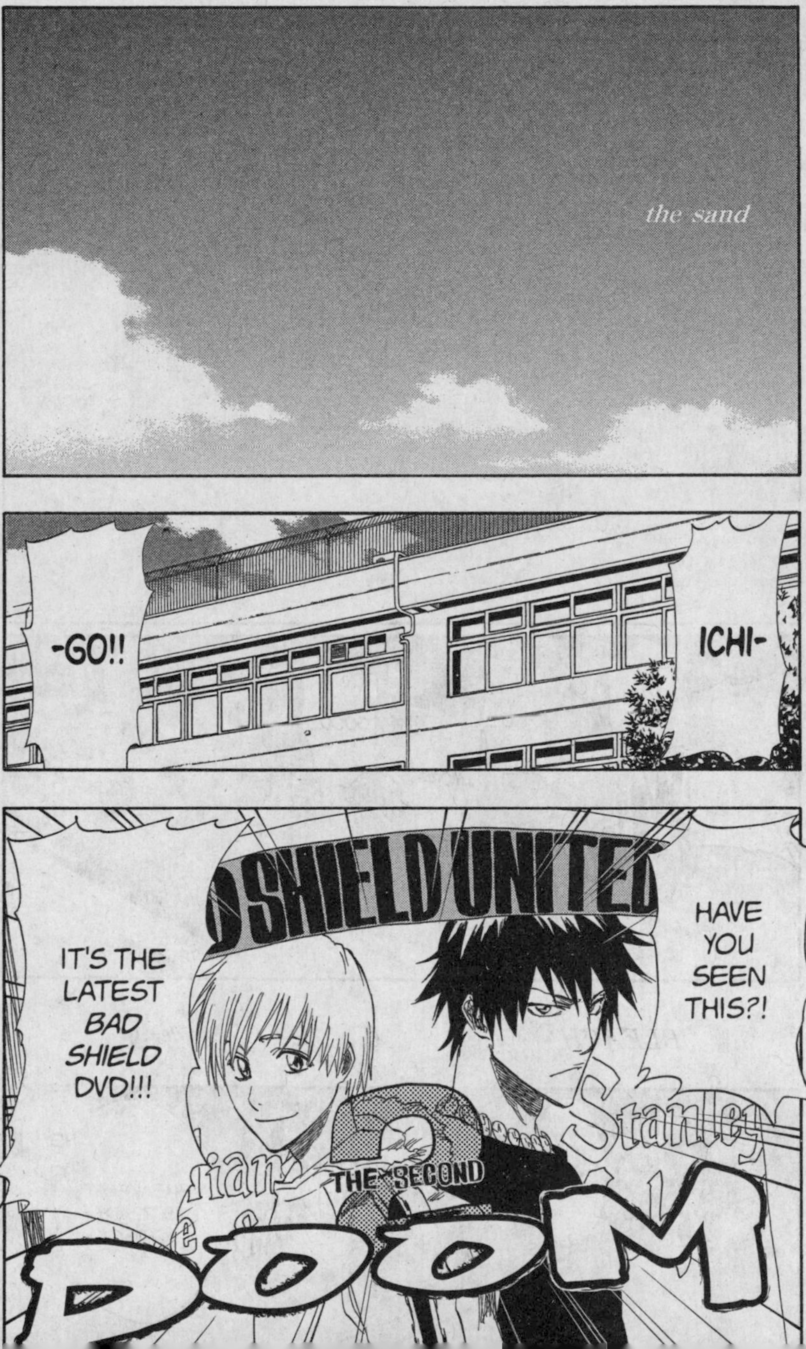
the sand
ICHI-
-GO!!
HAVE YOU SEEN THIS?!
IT'S THE LATEST BAD SHIELD DVD!!!
SHIELD UNITE
Stanley
THE SECOND
DOOM

READ THIS WAY

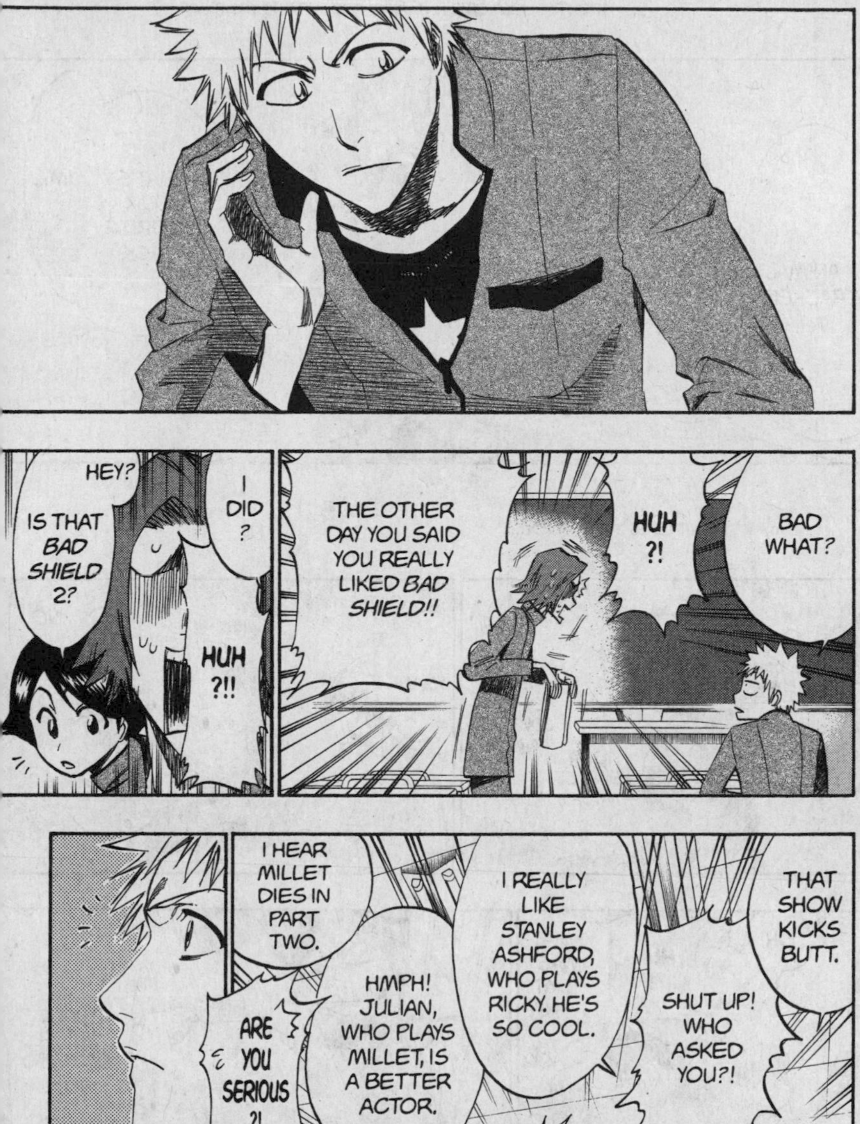
BAD WHAT?
HUH ?!
THE OTHER DAY YOU SAID YOU REALLY LIKED *BAD SHIELD*!!
I DID ?
HEY?
IS THAT *BAD SHIELD* 2?
HUH ?!!
THAT SHOW KICKS BUTT.
I REALLY LIKE STANLEY ASHFORD, WHO PLAYS RICKY. HE'S SO COOL.
I HEAR MILLET DIES IN PART TWO.
SHUT UP! WHO ASKED YOU?!
HMPH! JULIAN, WHO PLAYS MILLET, IS A BETTER ACTOR.
ARE YOU SERIOUS ?!

The world changes.

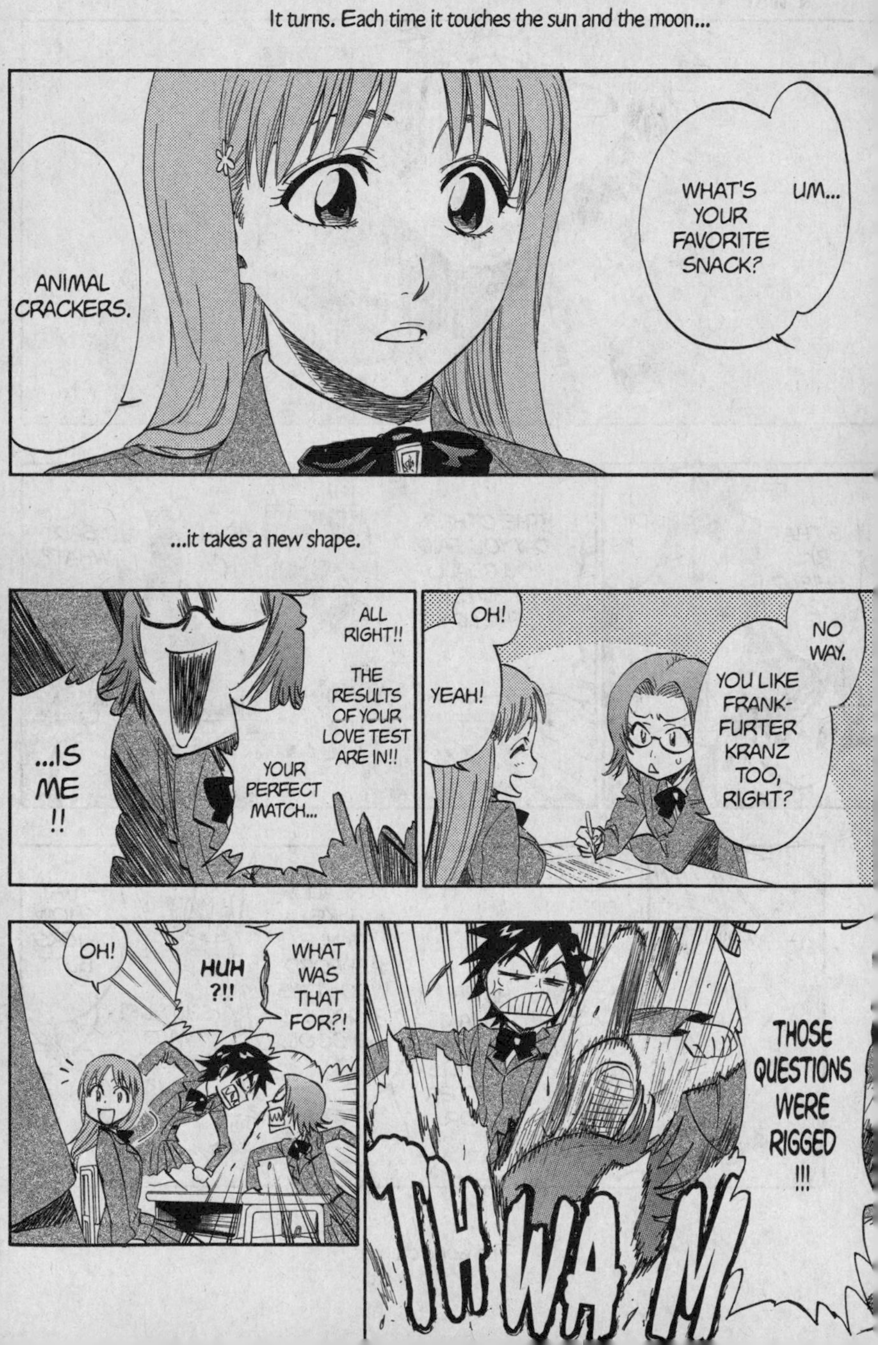
It turns. Each time it touches the sun and the moon...
UM...
WHAT'S YOUR FAVORITE SNACK?
ANIMAL CRACKERS.
...it takes a new shape.
NO WAY.
YOU LIKE FRANK-FURTER KRANZ TOO, RIGHT?
OH!
YEAH!
ALL RIGHT!!
THE RESULTS OF YOUR LOVE TEST ARE IN!!
YOUR PERFECT MATCH...
...IS ME !!
THOSE QUESTIONS WERE RIGGED !!!
THWAM
WHAT WAS THAT FOR?!
HUH ?!!
OH!

READ THIS WAY

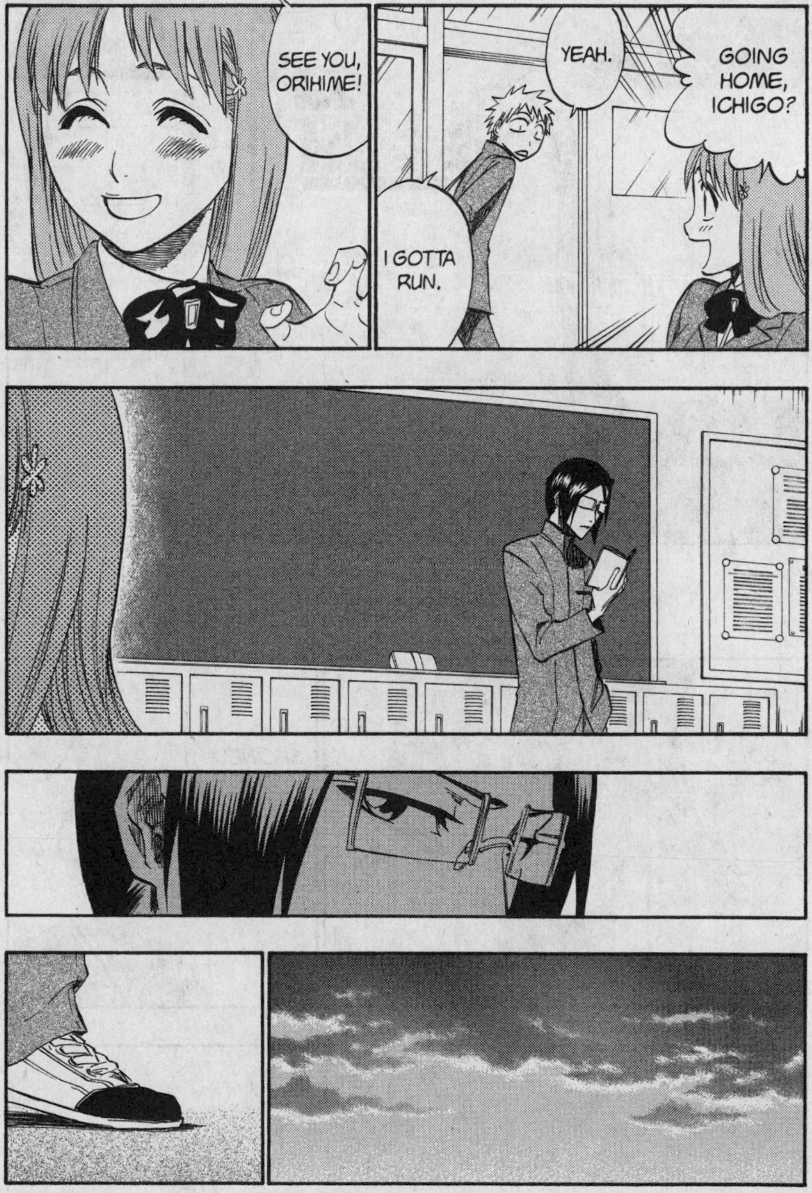

GOING HOME, ICHIGO?
YEAH.
I GOTTA RUN.
SEE YOU, ORIHIME!

The one thing that does not change...

...is my powerlessness.

THE BOY'S GONE.

I'M SORRY.

YOU SHOWED UP.

SO...

YEAH.

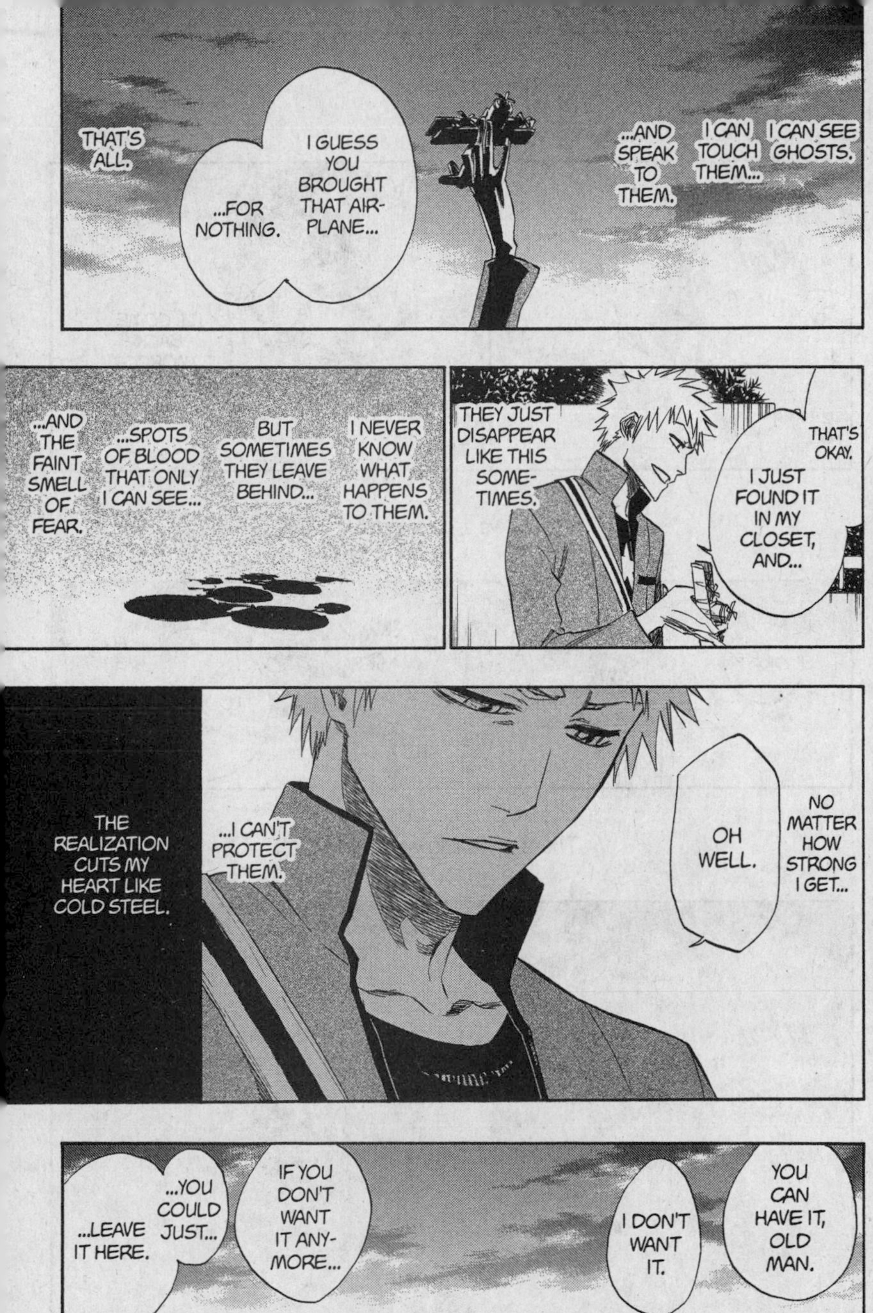
I CAN SEE GHOSTS.
I CAN TOUCH THEM...
...AND SPEAK TO THEM.
I GUESS YOU BROUGHT THAT AIRPLANE...
...FOR NOTHING.
THAT'S ALL.
THAT'S OKAY.
I JUST FOUND IT IN MY CLOSET, AND...
THEY JUST DISAPPEAR LIKE THIS SOMETIMES.
I NEVER KNOW WHAT HAPPENS TO THEM.
BUT SOMETIMES THEY LEAVE BEHIND...
...SPOTS OF BLOOD THAT ONLY I CAN SEE...
...AND THE FAINT SMELL OF FEAR.
NO MATTER HOW STRONG I GET...
OH WELL.
...I CAN'T PROTECT THEM.
THE REALIZATION CUTS MY HEART LIKE COLD STEEL.
YOU CAN HAVE IT, OLD MAN.
I DON'T WANT IT.
IF YOU DON'T WANT IT ANYMORE...
...YOU COULD JUST...
...LEAVE IT HERE.

It's turning.

If fate is a millstone...

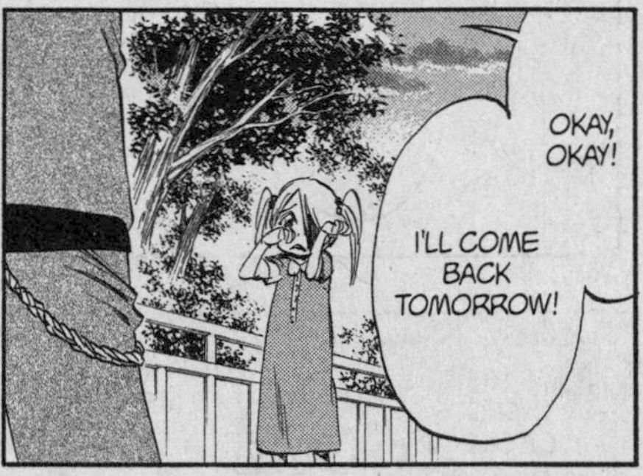
OKAY, OKAY!
I'LL COME BACK TOMORROW!

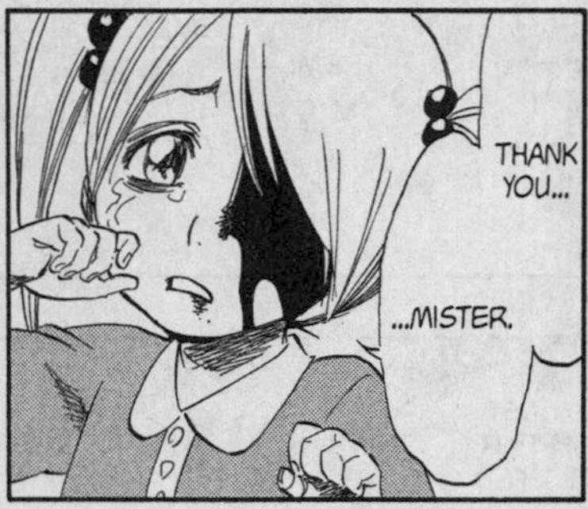
THANK YOU...
...MISTER.

...then we are the grist.

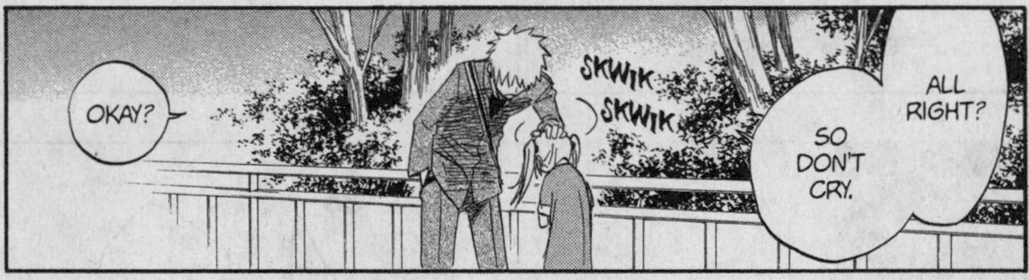
ALL RIGHT?
SO DON'T CRY.
SKWIK SKWIK
OKAY?

There is nothing we can do.

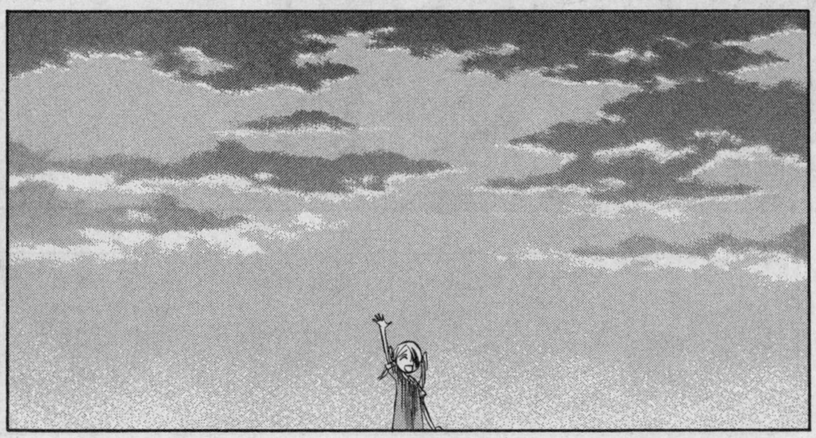

So I wish for strength.

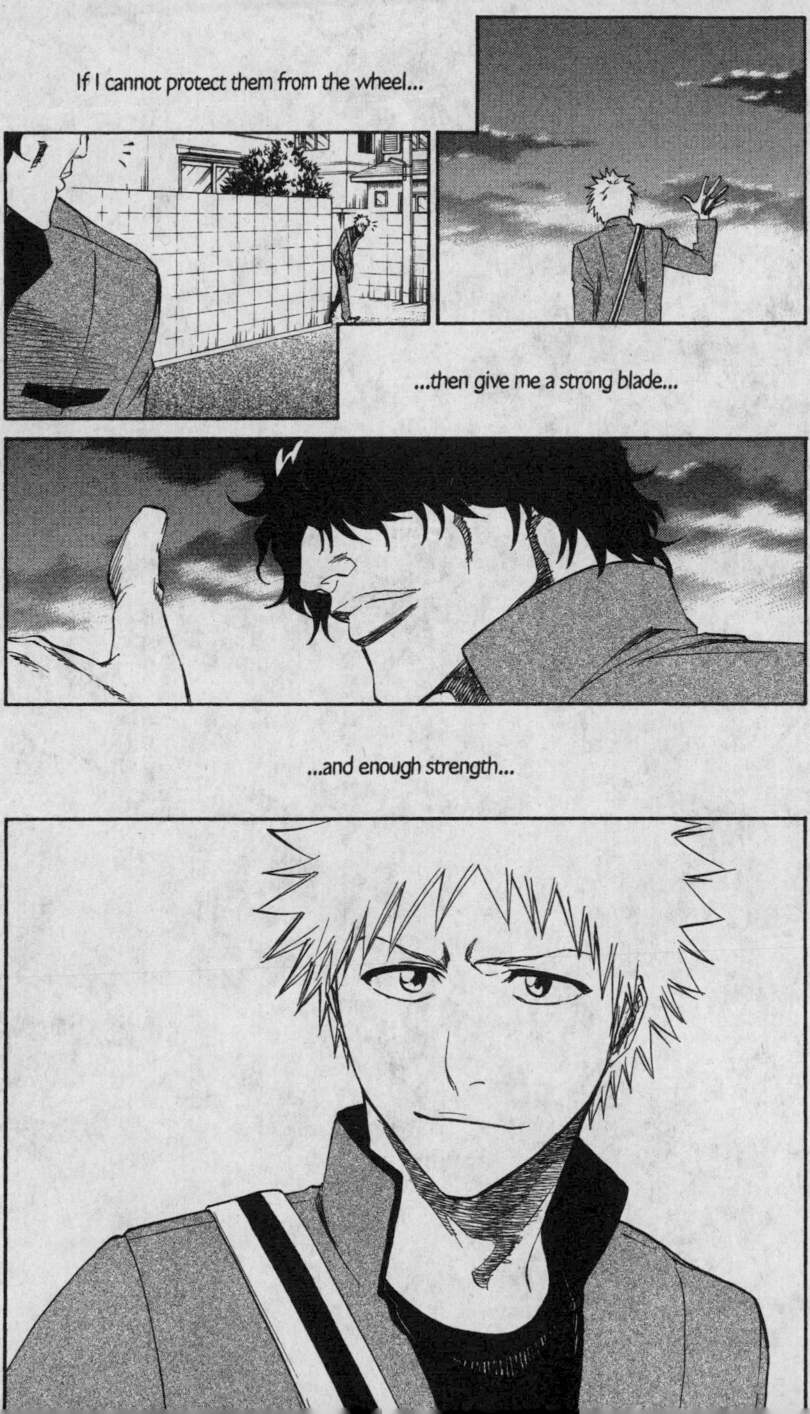
If I cannot protect them from the wheel...
...then give me a strong blade...
...and enough strength...

...TO
SHATTER
FATE.

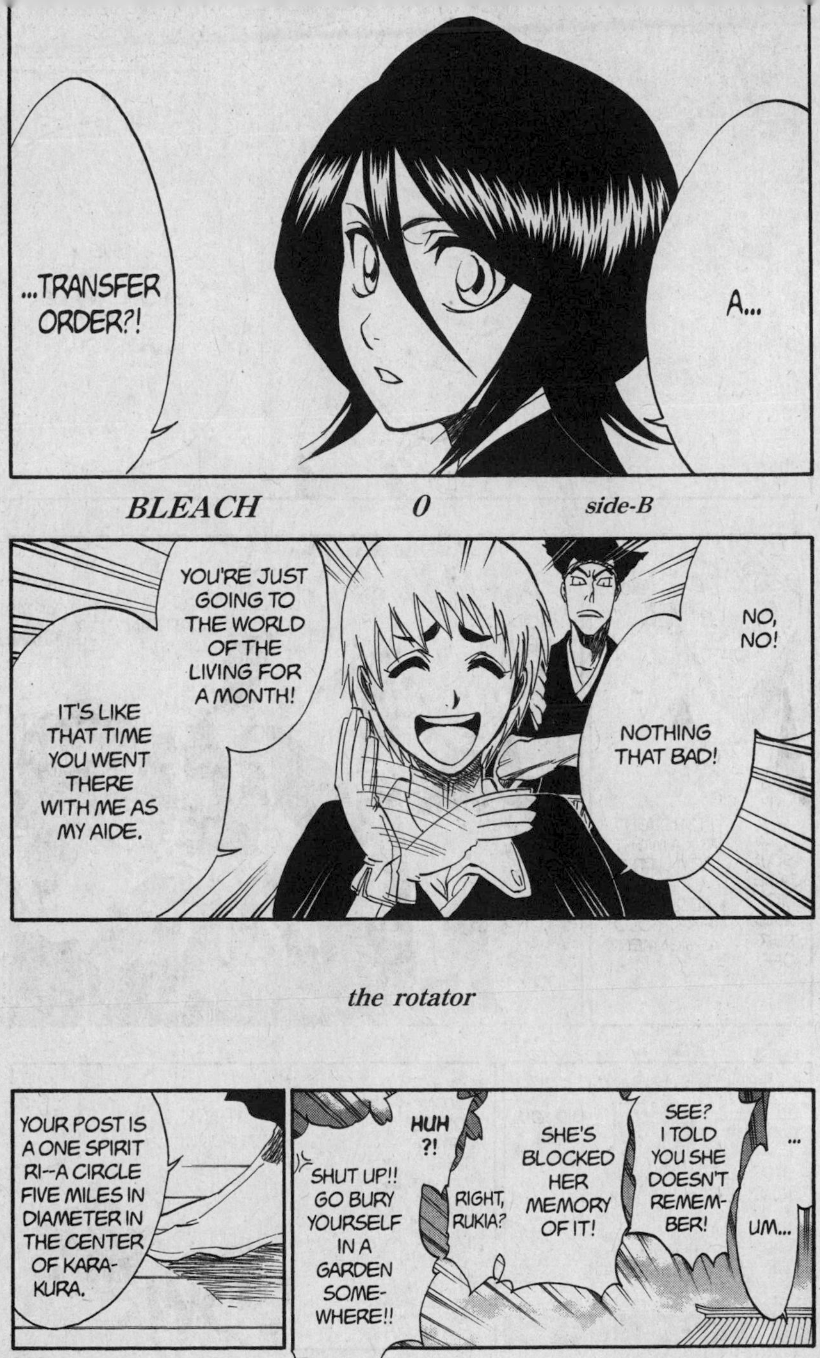
A...
...TRANSFER ORDER?!
BLEACH 0 side-B
NO, NO! NOTHING THAT BAD!
YOU'RE JUST GOING TO THE WORLD OF THE LIVING FOR A MONTH!
IT'S LIKE THAT TIME YOU WENT THERE WITH ME AS MY AIDE.
the rotator
...
UM...
SEE? I TOLD YOU SHE DOESN'T REMEMBER!
SHE'S BLOCKED HER MEMORY OF IT!
HUH?!
RIGHT, RUKIA?
SHUT UP!! GO BURY YOURSELF IN A GARDEN SOMEWHERE!!
YOUR POST IS A ONE SPIRIT RI--A CIRCLE FIVE MILES IN DIAMETER IN THE CENTER OF KARAKURA.

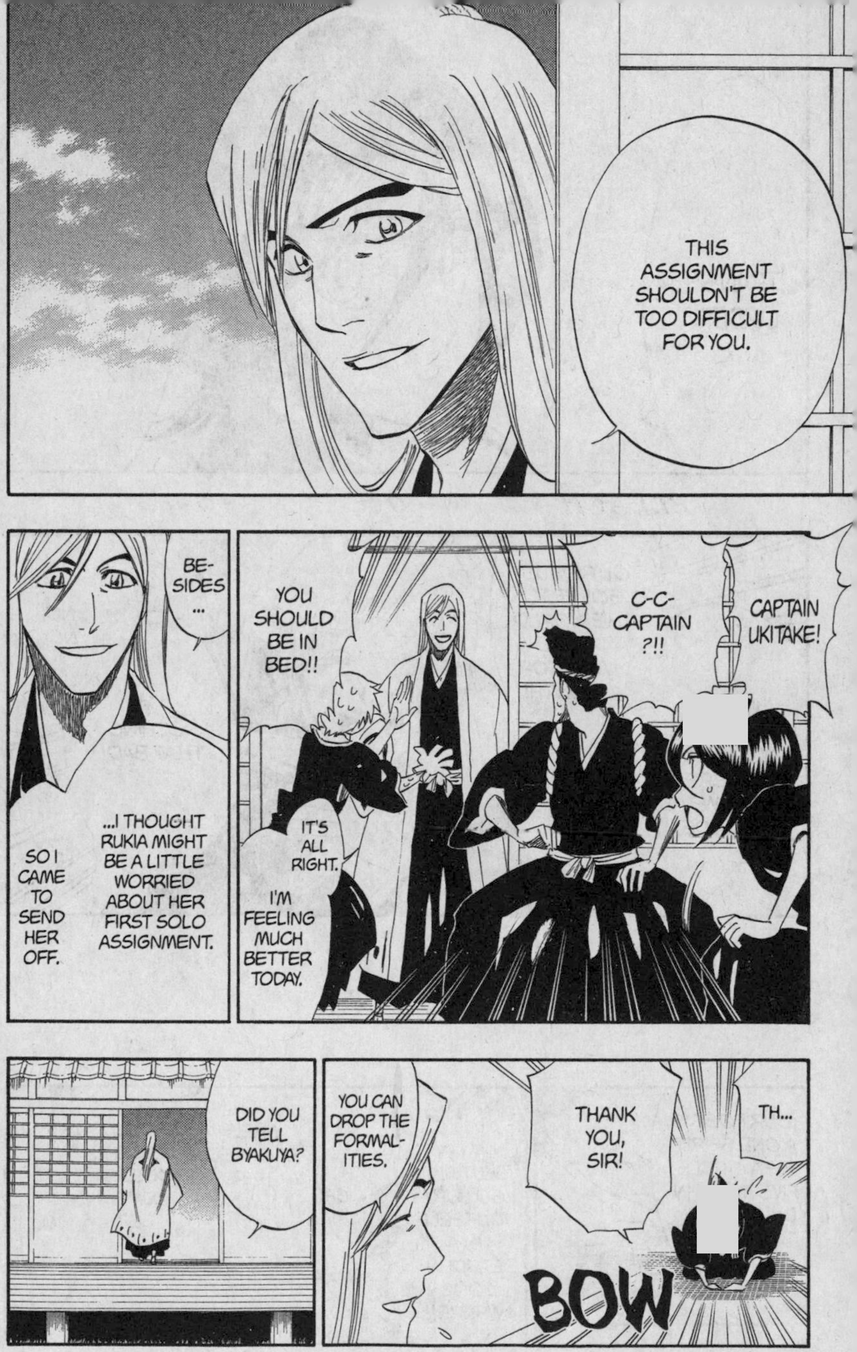
THIS ASSIGNMENT SHOULDN'T BE TOO DIFFICULT FOR YOU.
CAPTAIN UKITAKE!
C-C-CAPTAIN ?!!
YOU SHOULD BE IN BED!!
IT'S ALL RIGHT.
I'M FEELING MUCH BETTER TODAY.
BE-SIDES...
...I THOUGHT RUKIA MIGHT BE A LITTLE WORRIED ABOUT HER FIRST SOLO ASSIGNMENT.
SO I CAME TO SEND HER OFF.
TH...
THANK YOU, SIR!
BOW
YOU CAN DROP THE FORMAL-ITIES.
DID YOU TELL BYAKUYA?

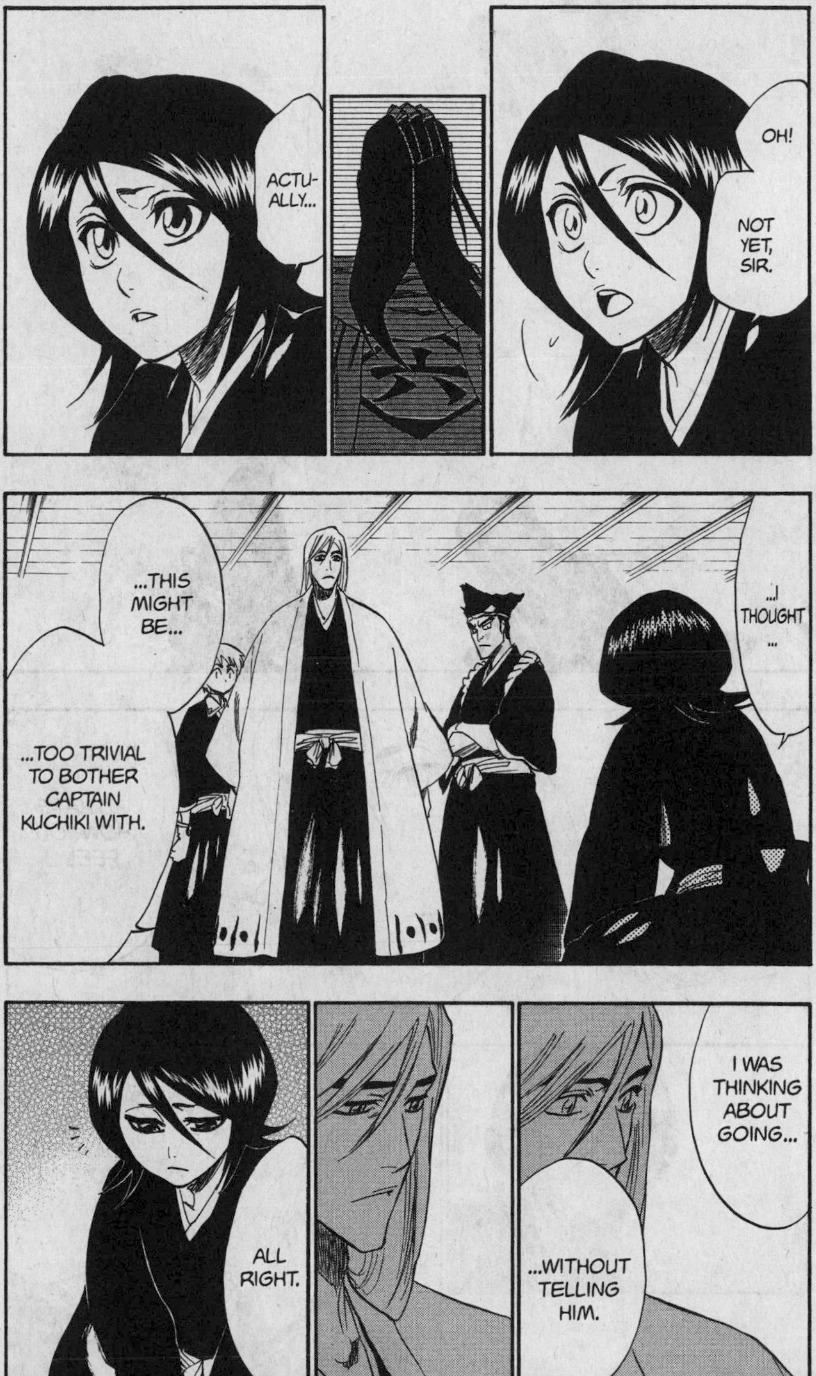
OH!
NOT YET, SIR.
ACTU-ALLY...
...I THOUGHT...
...THIS MIGHT BE...
...TOO TRIVIAL TO BOTHER CAPTAIN KUCHIKI WITH.
I WAS THINKING ABOUT GOING...
...WITHOUT TELLING HIM.
ALL RIGHT.

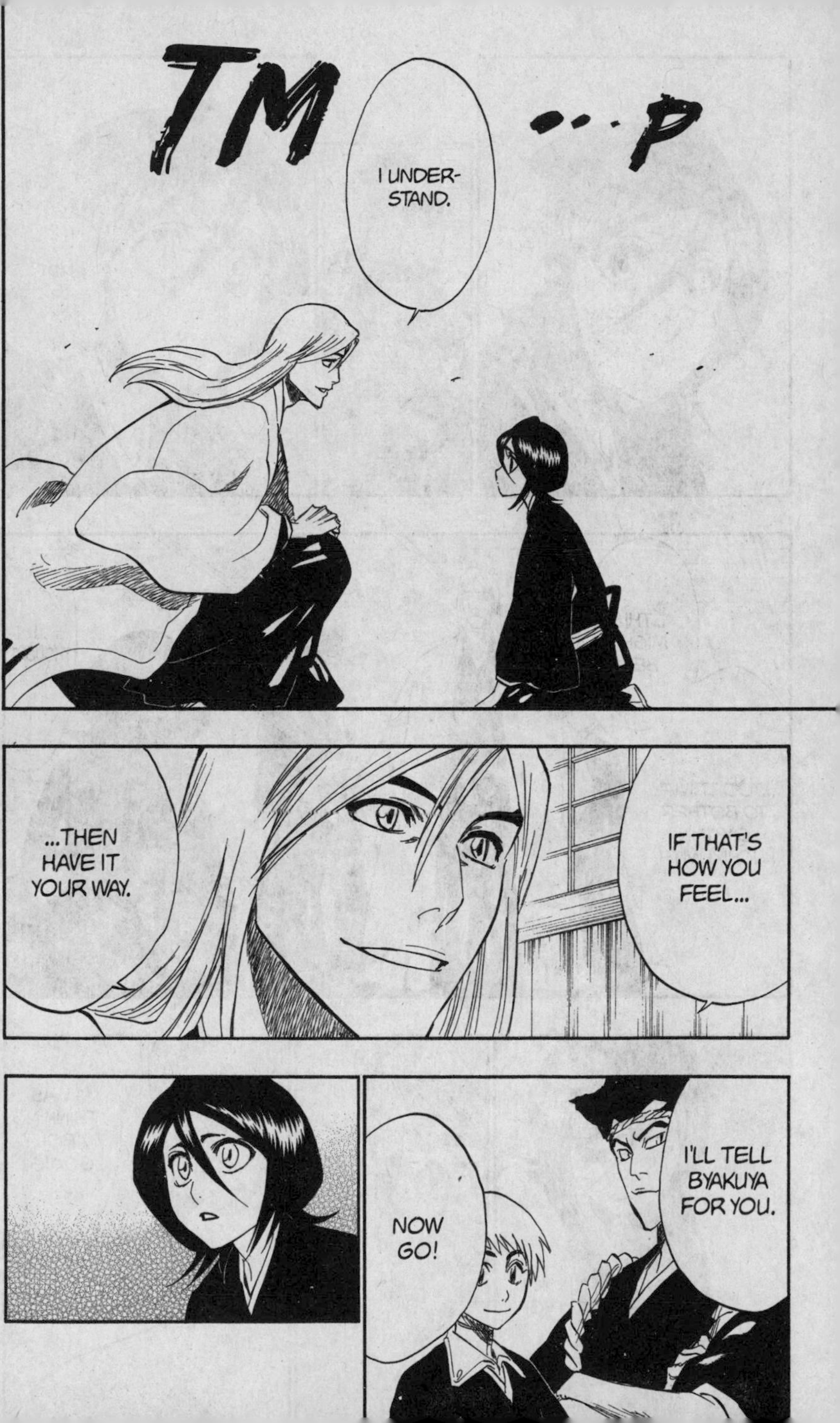
TM...P
I UNDERSTAND.
IF THAT'S HOW YOU FEEL...
...THEN HAVE IT YOUR WAY.
I'LL TELL BYAKUYA FOR YOU.
NOW GO!

READ THIS WAY

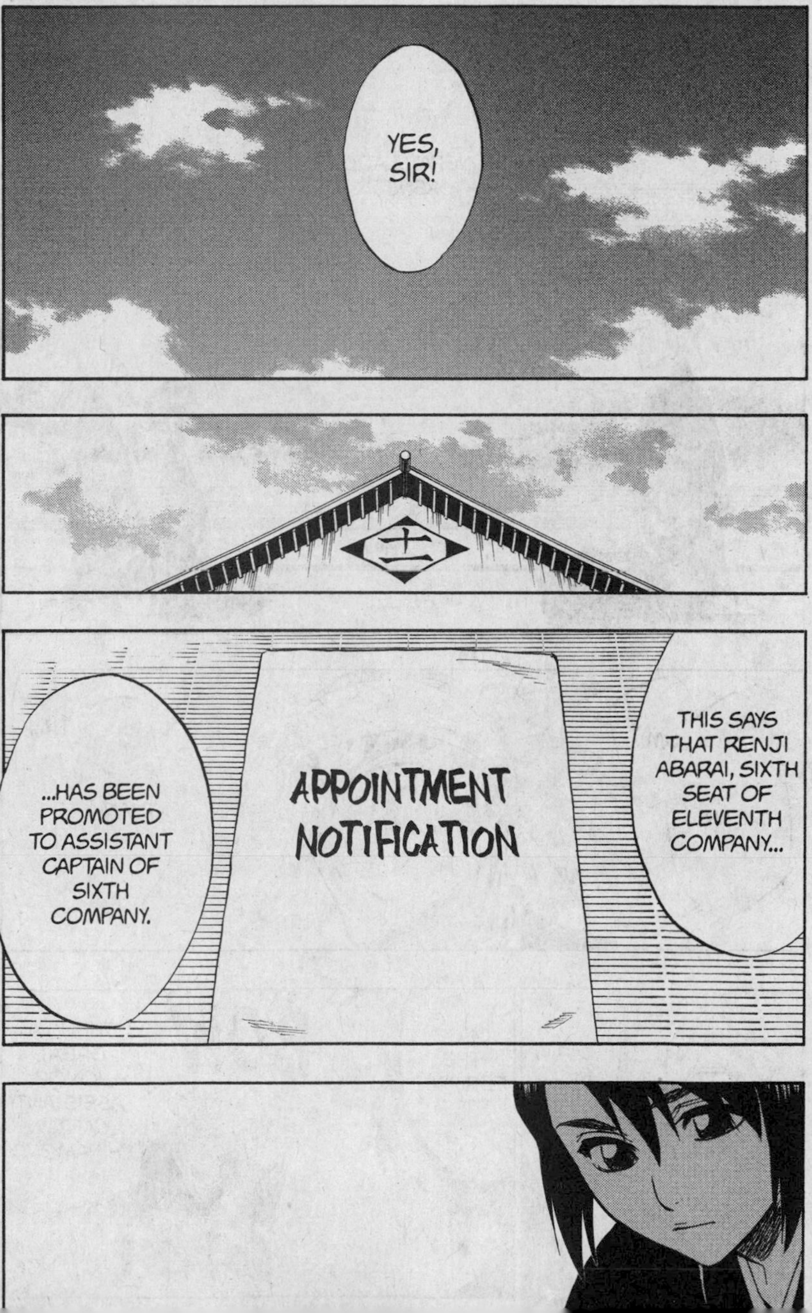
YES, SIR!
THIS SAYS THAT RENJI ABARAI, SIXTH SEAT OF ELEVENTH COMPANY...
APPOINTMENT NOTIFICATION
...HAS BEEN PROMOTED TO ASSISTANT CAPTAIN OF SIXTH COMPANY.

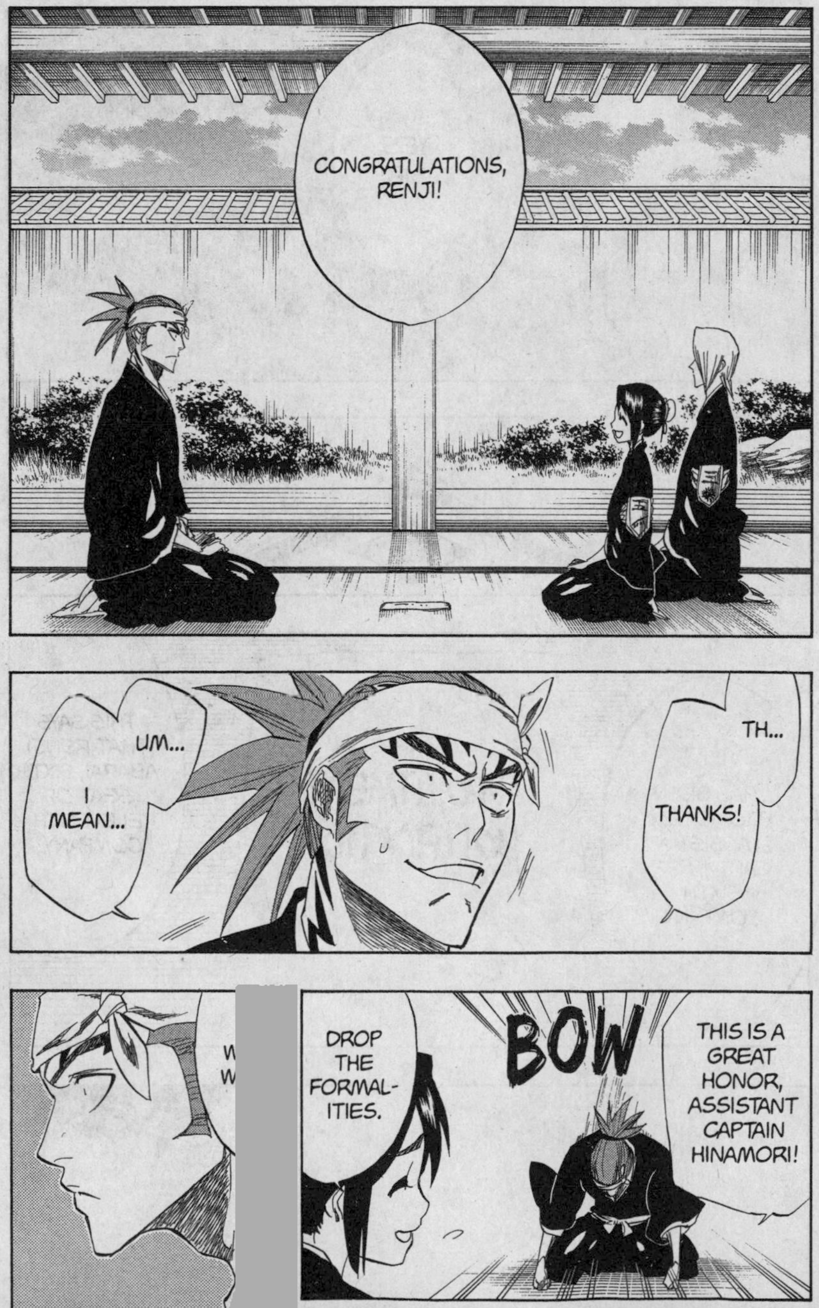
CONGRATULATIONS, RENJI!
TH...
THANKS!
UM...
I MEAN...
THIS IS A GREAT HONOR, ASSISTANT CAPTAIN HINAMORI!
BOW
DROP THE FORMAL-ITIES.

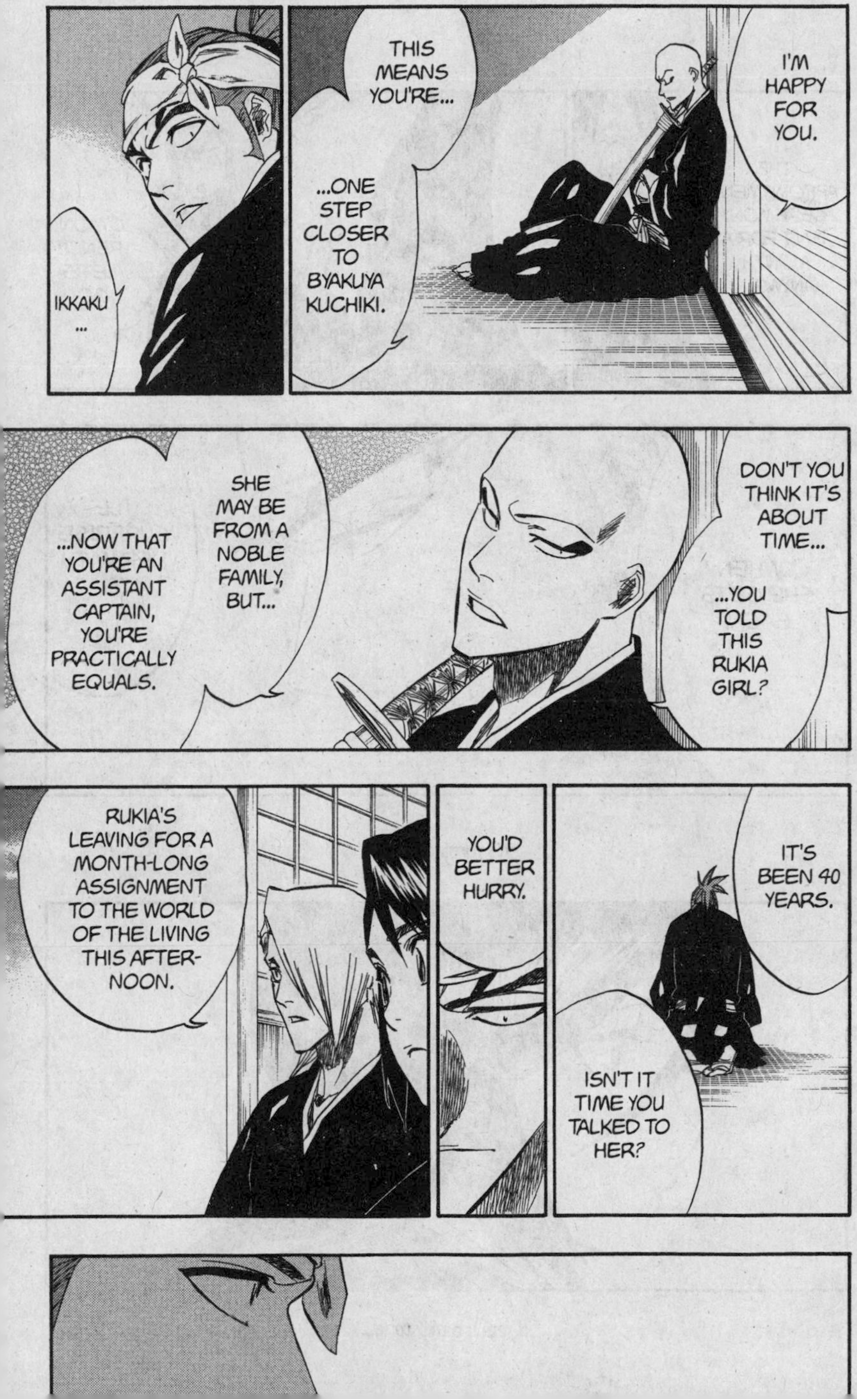
I'M HAPPY FOR YOU.
THIS MEANS YOU'RE...
...ONE STEP CLOSER TO BYAKUYA KUCHIKI.
IKKAKU ...
DON'T YOU THINK IT'S ABOUT TIME...
...YOU TOLD THIS RUKIA GIRL?
SHE MAY BE FROM A NOBLE FAMILY, BUT...
...NOW THAT YOU'RE AN ASSISTANT CAPTAIN, YOU'RE PRACTICALLY EQUALS.
IT'S BEEN 40 YEARS.
ISN'T IT TIME YOU TALKED TO HER?
YOU'D BETTER HURRY.
RUKIA'S LEAVING FOR A MONTH-LONG ASSIGNMENT TO THE WORLD OF THE LIVING THIS AFTER-NOON.

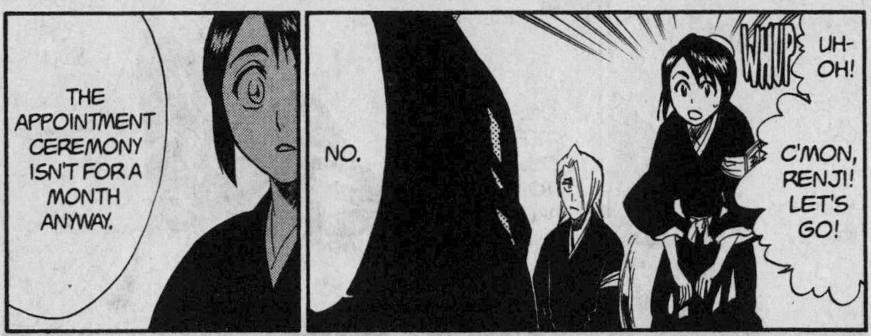
WHUP
UH-OH!
C'MON, RENJI! LET'S GO!
NO.
THE APPOINTMENT CEREMONY ISN'T FOR A MONTH ANYWAY.

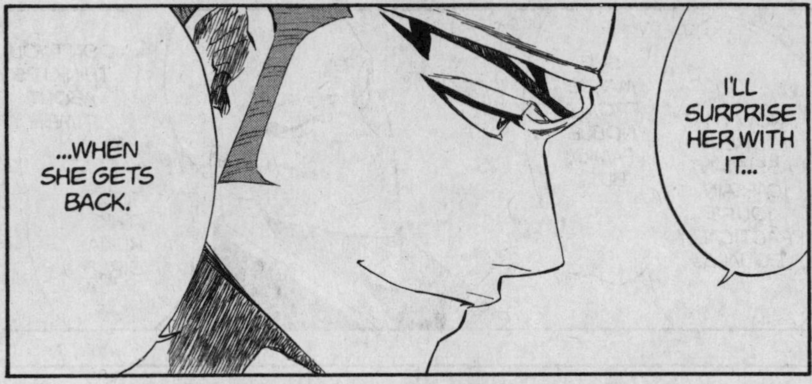
I'LL SURPRISE HER WITH IT...
...WHEN SHE GETS BACK.

It's turning.

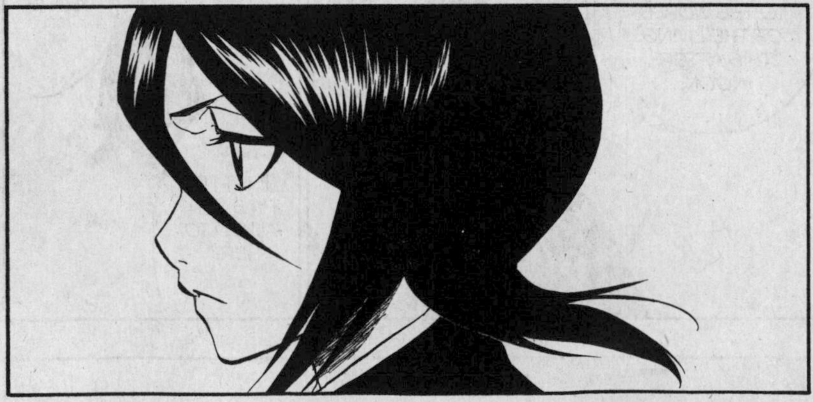

If fate is a millstone...

...we are the ones that make it turn.

We believe that the crushing wheel...

...is guided by an infallible power.

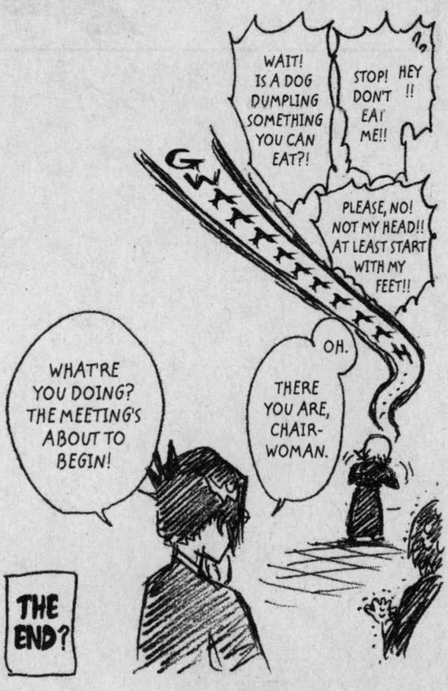
HEY !!
STOP! DON'T EAT ME!!
WAIT! IS A DOG DUMPLING SOMETHING YOU CAN EAT?!
PLEASE, NO! NOT MY HEAD!! AT LEAST START WITH MY FEET!!
OH.
THERE YOU ARE, CHAIR-WOMAN.
WHAT'RE YOU DOING? THE MEETING'S ABOUT TO BEGIN!
THE END?

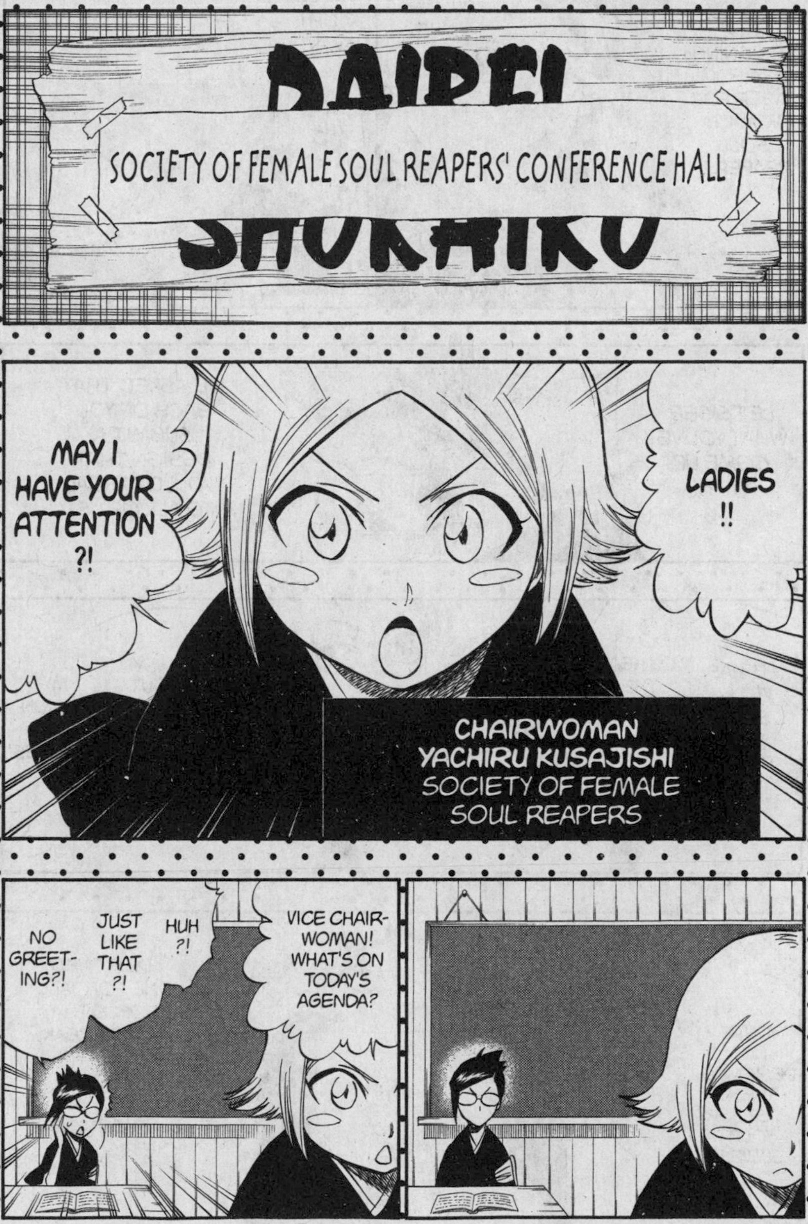
SOCIETY OF FEMALE SOUL REAPERS' CONFERENCE HALL
LADIES !!
MAY I HAVE YOUR ATTENTION ?!
CHAIRWOMAN YACHIRU KUSAJISHI
SOCIETY OF FEMALE SOUL REAPERS
VICE CHAIR-WOMAN! WHAT'S ON TODAY'S AGENDA?
HUH ?!
JUST LIKE THAT ?!
NO GREET-ING?!

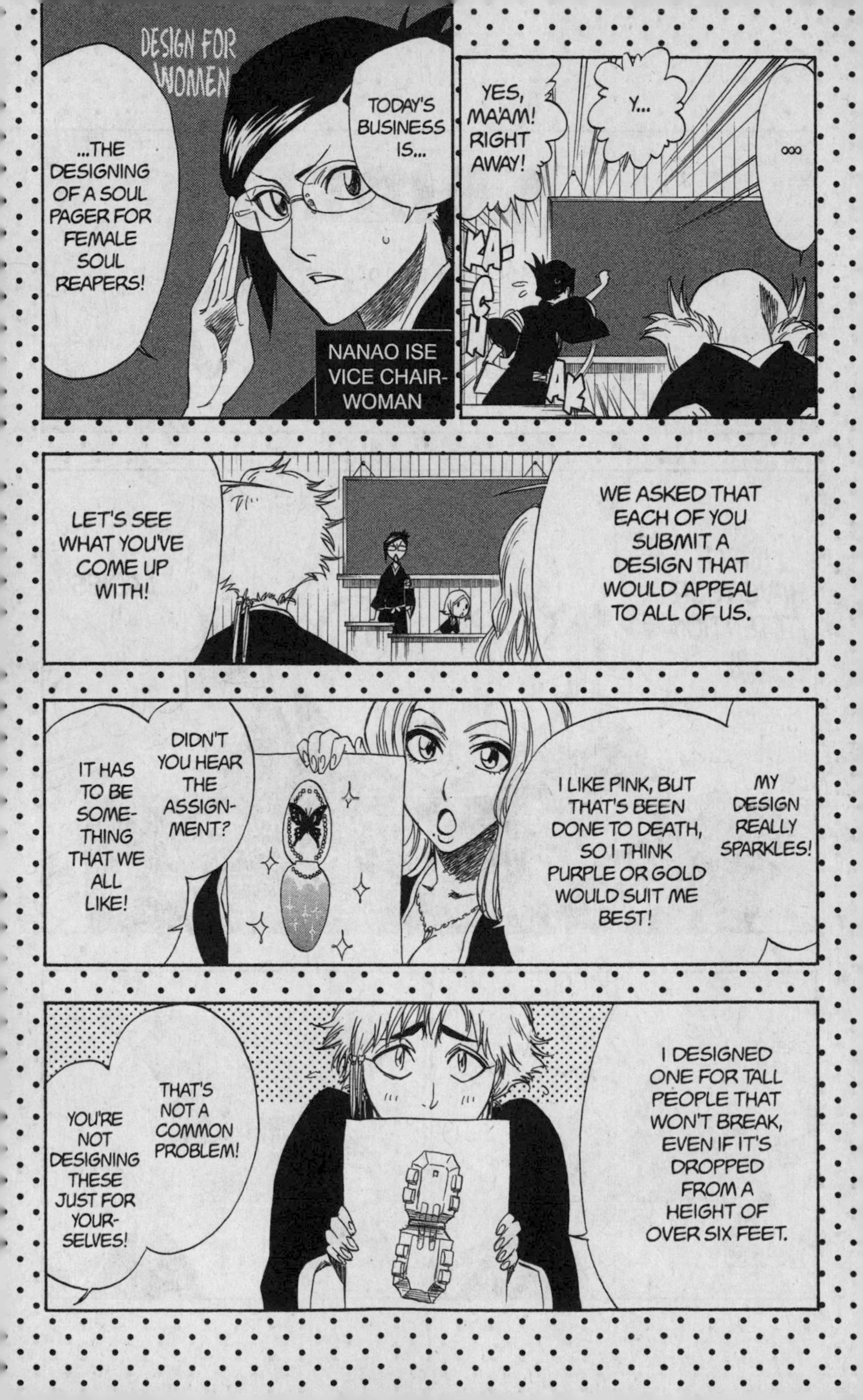
...
Y...
YES, MA'AM! RIGHT AWAY!
DESIGN FOR WOMEN
TODAY'S BUSINESS IS...
...THE DESIGNING OF A SOUL PAGER FOR FEMALE SOUL REAPERS!
NANAO ISE VICE CHAIR-WOMAN
WE ASKED THAT EACH OF YOU SUBMIT A DESIGN THAT WOULD APPEAL TO ALL OF US.
LET'S SEE WHAT YOU'VE COME UP WITH!
MY DESIGN REALLY SPARKLES!
I LIKE PINK, BUT THAT'S BEEN DONE TO DEATH, SO I THINK PURPLE OR GOLD WOULD SUIT ME BEST!
DIDN'T YOU HEAR THE ASSIGN-MENT?
IT HAS TO BE SOME-THING THAT WE ALL LIKE!
I DESIGNED ONE FOR TALL PEOPLE THAT WON'T BREAK, EVEN IF IT'S DROPPED FROM A HEIGHT OF OVER SIX FEET.
THAT'S NOT A COMMON PROBLEM!
YOU'RE NOT DESIGNING THESE JUST FOR YOUR-SELVES!

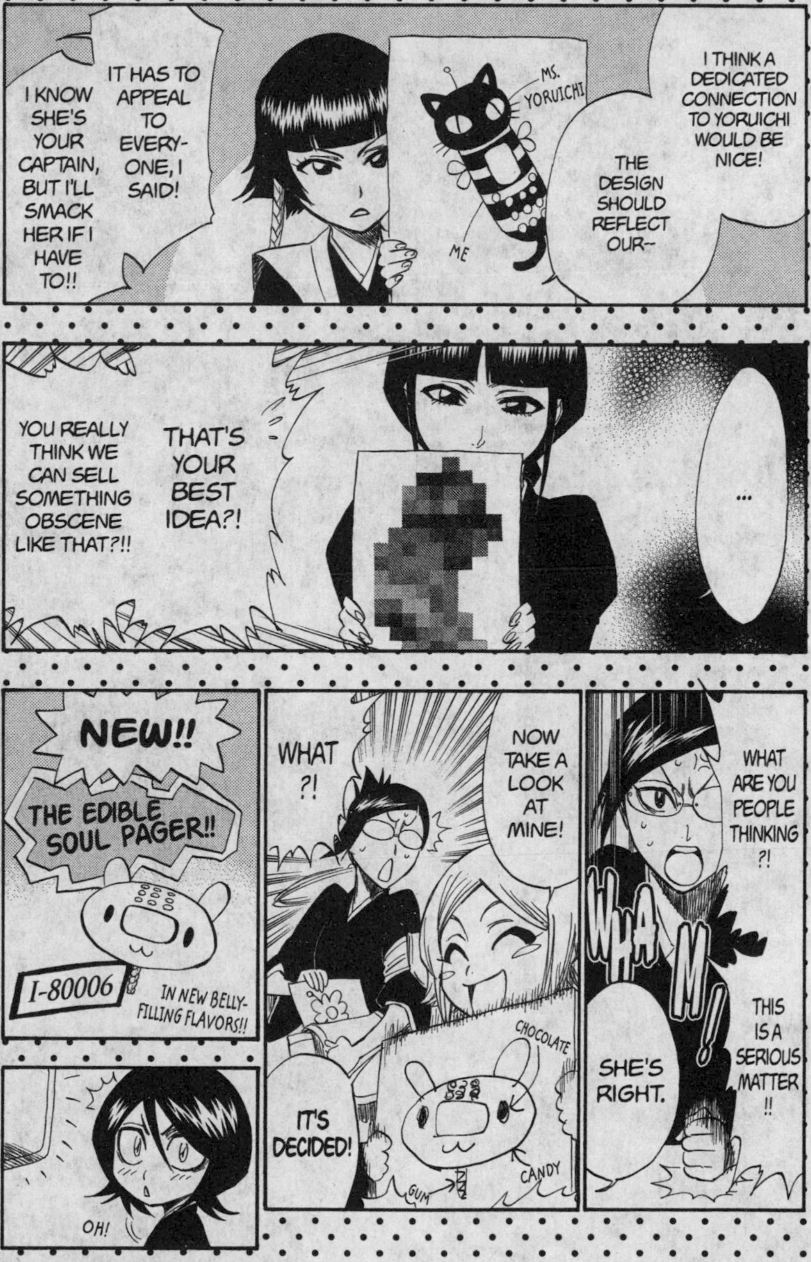
I THINK A DEDICATED CONNECTION TO YORUICHI WOULD BE NICE!
THE DESIGN SHOULD REFLECT OUR--
MS. YORUICHI
ME
IT HAS TO APPEAL TO EVERY-ONE, I SAID!
I KNOW SHE'S YOUR CAPTAIN, BUT I'LL SMACK HER IF I HAVE TO!!
...
THAT'S YOUR BEST IDEA?!
YOU REALLY THINK WE CAN SELL SOMETHING OBSCENE LIKE THAT?!!
WHAT ARE YOU PEOPLE THINKING?!
WHAM!
THIS IS A SERIOUS MATTER!!
SHE'S RIGHT.
NOW TAKE A LOOK AT MINE!
WHAT?!
CHOCOLATE
CANDY
GUM
IT'S DECIDED!
NEW!!
THE EDIBLE SOUL PAGER!!
I-80006
IN NEW BELLY-FILLING FLAVORS!!
OH!

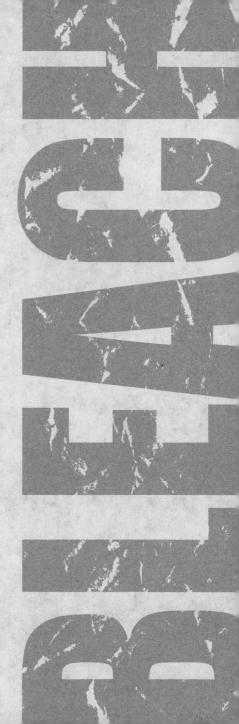

There's a feature in the *Bleach* PSP video game that lets you increase the trust between you and your partner character. I decided to build trust with Rangiku, but I soon found that I have no idea what she's thinking. It's scary how often she gets mad at me when I answer one of her questions. And I created her!

-Tite Kubo, 2006

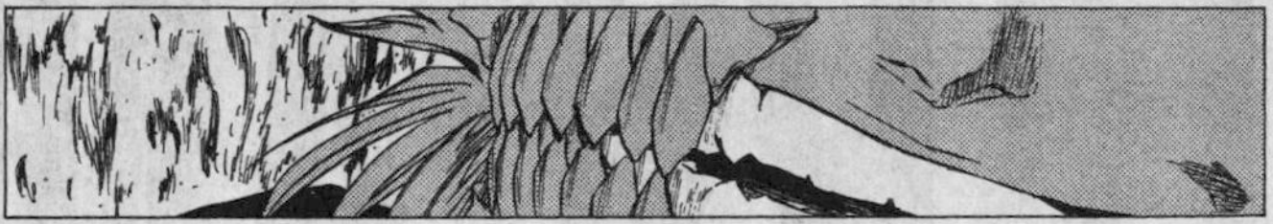

Break down, every single one of you.

BLEACH 24
IMMANENT GOD BLUES

Shonen Jump Manga

STARS AND

Tôshiro Hitsugaya

Renji Abarai

Ichigo Kurosaki

plot

When Ichigo Kurosaki meets Soul Reaper Rukia Kuchiki his life is changed forever. Soon Ichigo is a Soul Reaper himself, cleansing lost souls called Hollows.

Ichigo and his friends travel to the Soul Society to rescue Rukia, and uncover a sinister plot orchestrated by Sôsuke Aizen. Aizen and his cohorts are forced to flee, but they are far from neutralized. When deadly Arrancars begin to appear in the world of the living, Rukia and a team of Soul Reapers are sent to stop them. But they soon find themselves fighting for their lives against powerful enemies who will stop at nothing to achieve their terrible ends.

BLEACH ALL

 グリムジョー
Grimmjow

 松本乱菊
Rangiku
Matsumoto

Shawlong
 シャウロン

STORIES

BLEACH 24

IMMANENT GOD BLUES

Contents

206. ¡Mala Suerte! 5 [LUCKY]

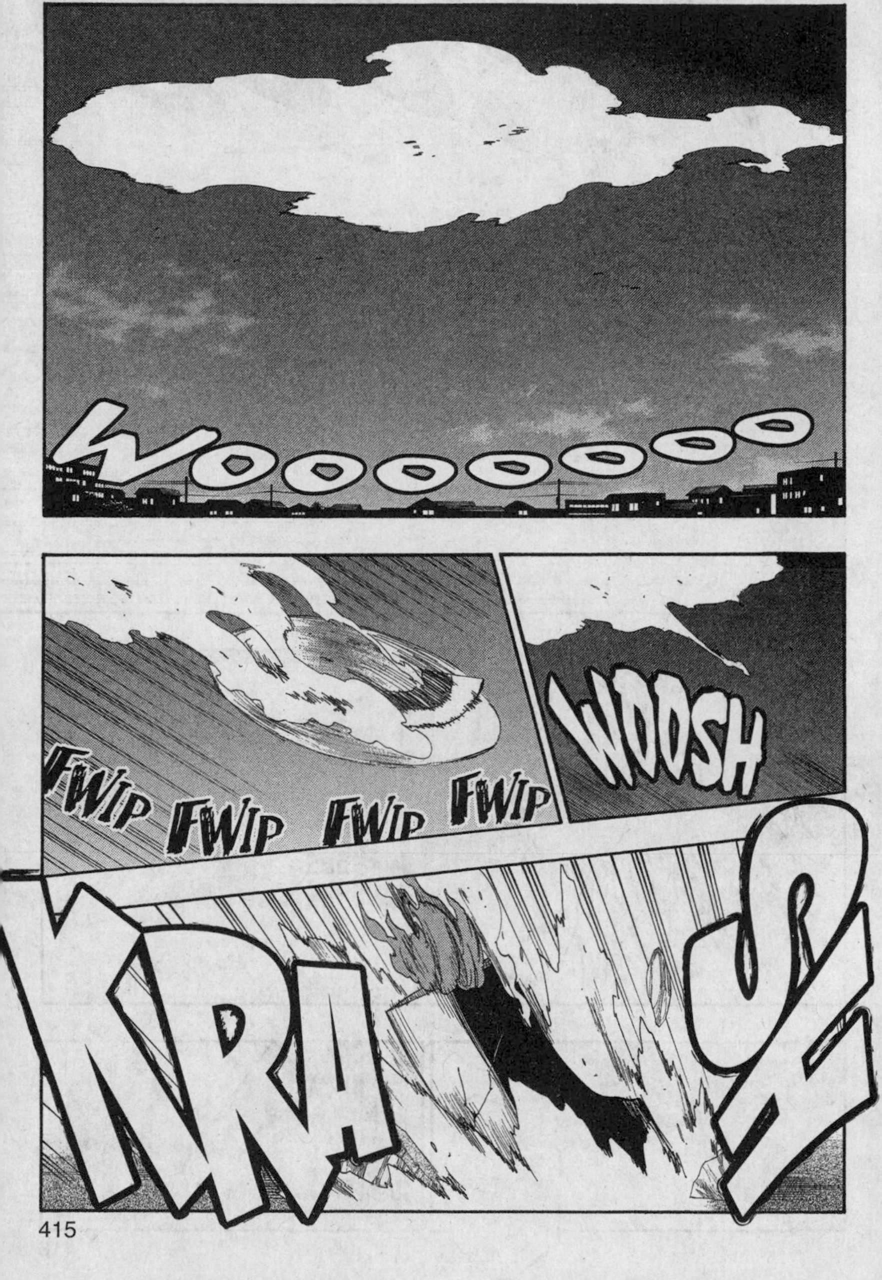
WOOOOOOO
WOOSH
FWIP FWIP FWIP FWIP
KRA
SH

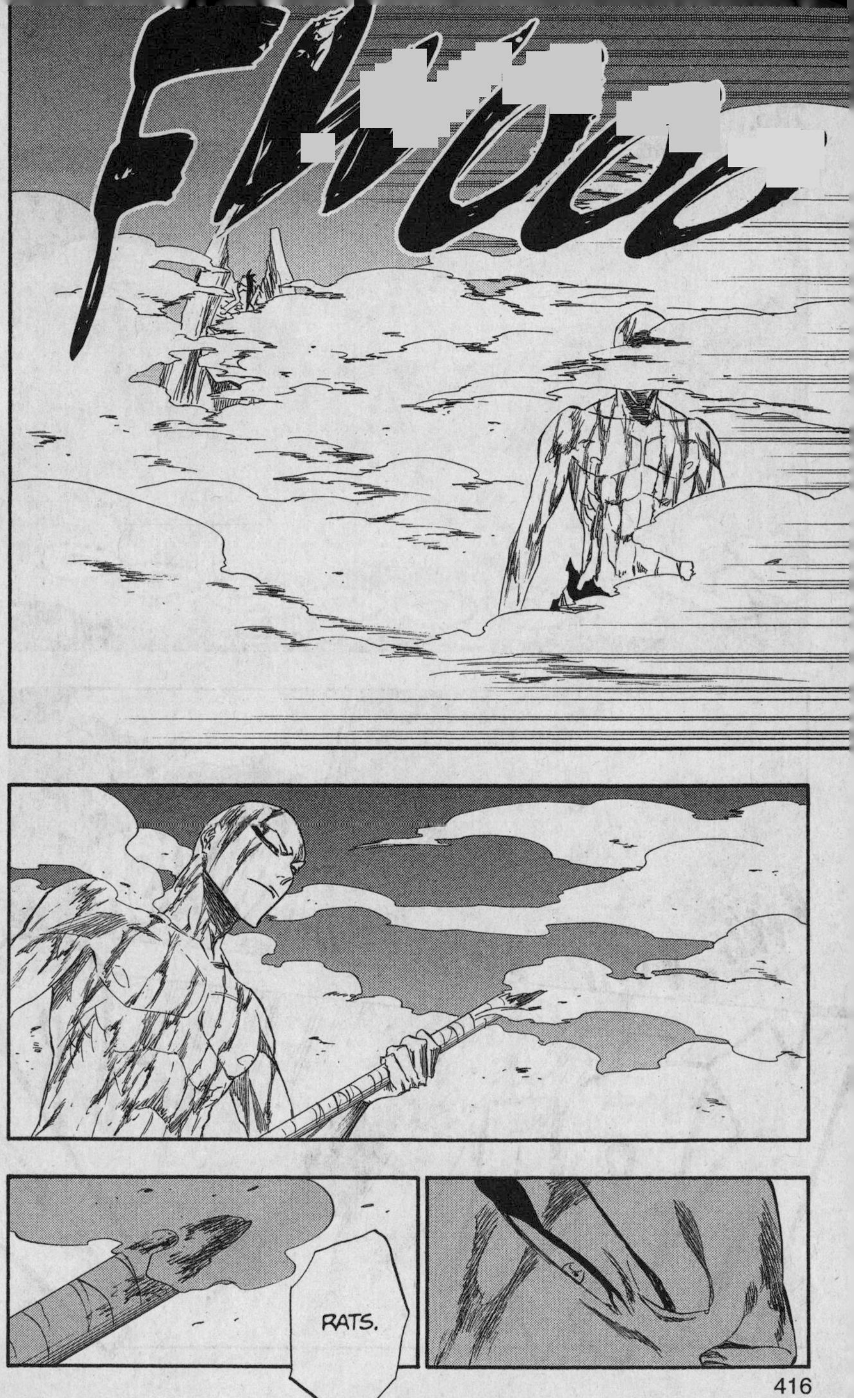
RATS.

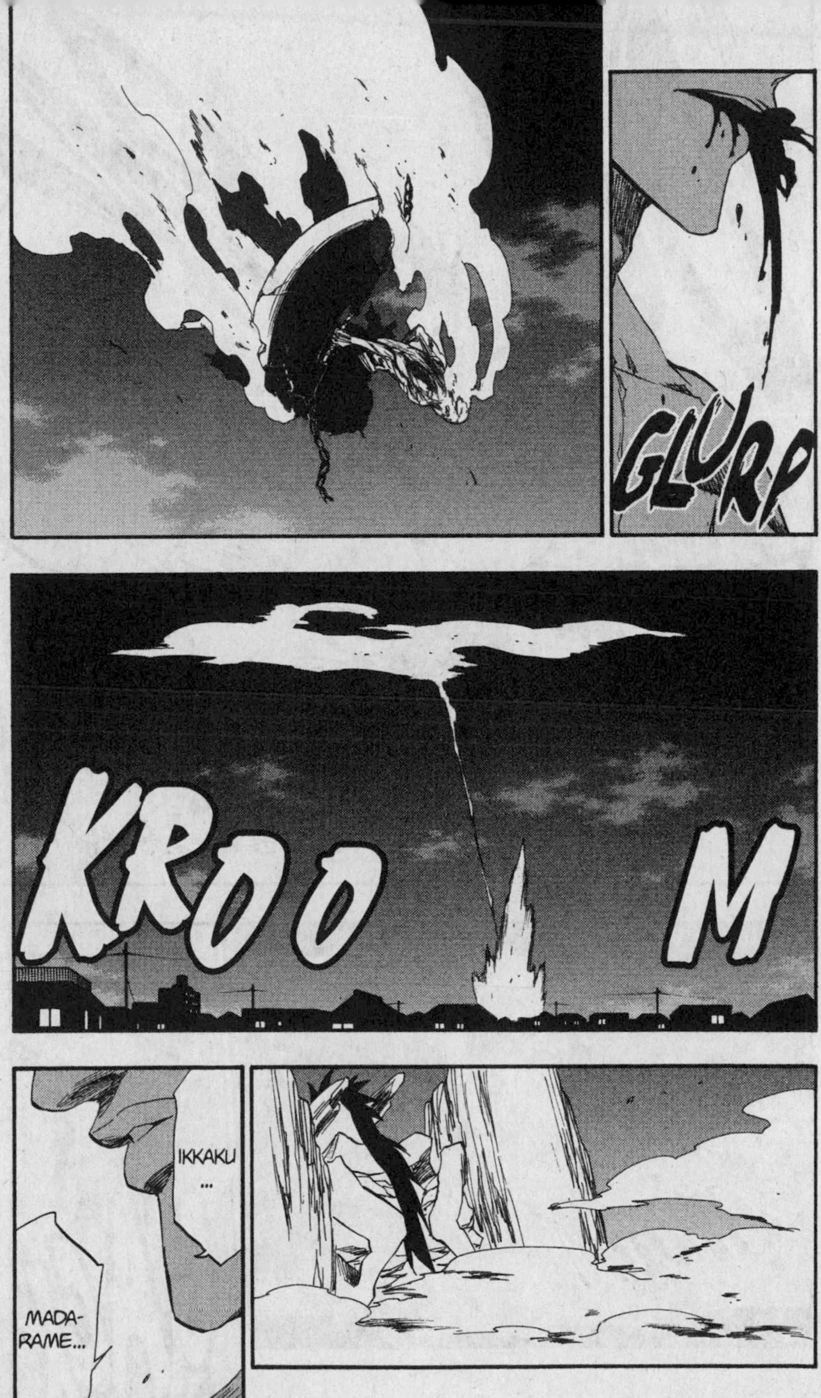
GLURP
KROOM
IKKAKU
...
MADA-
RAME...

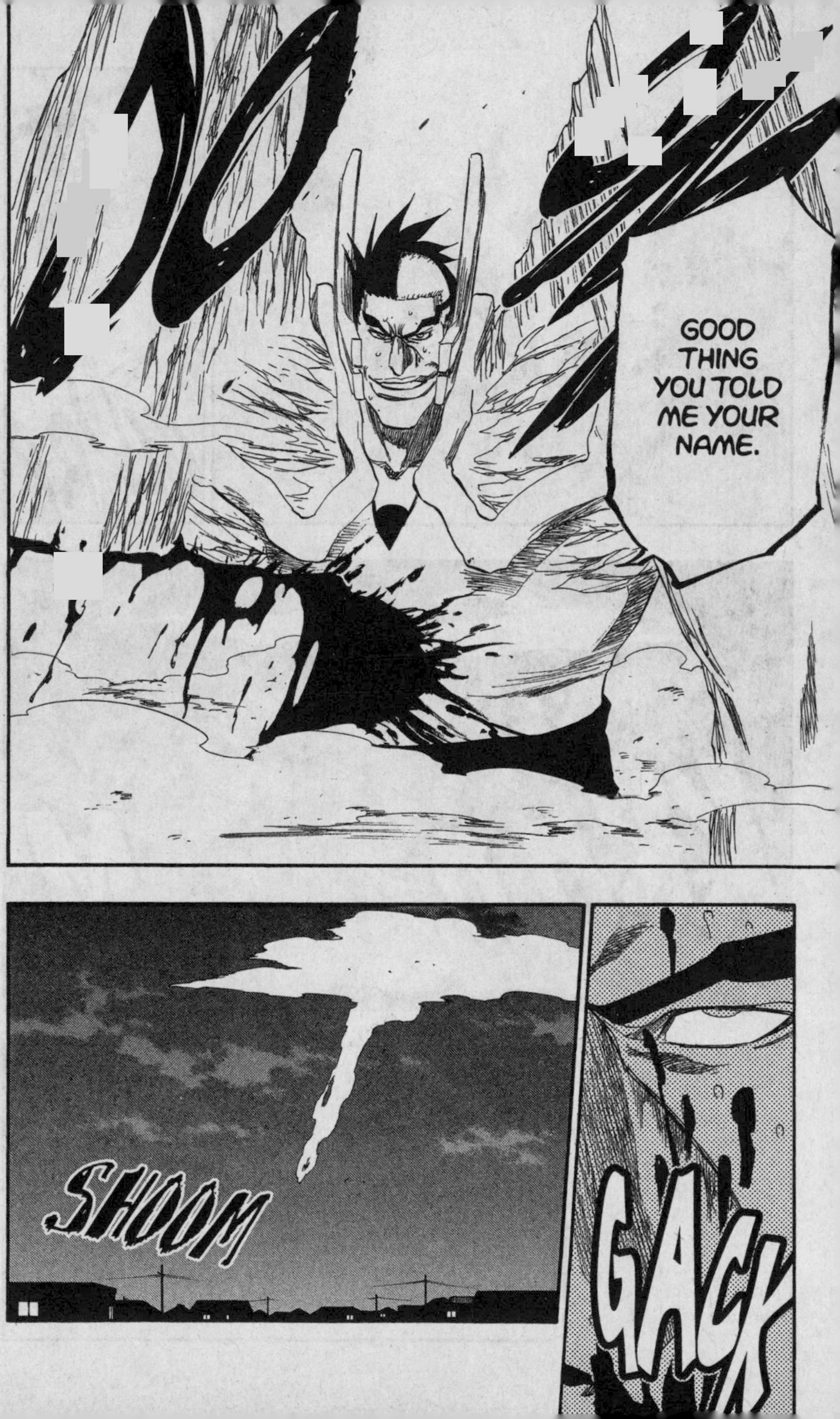
GOOD THING YOU TOLD ME YOUR NAME.
GACK
SHOOM

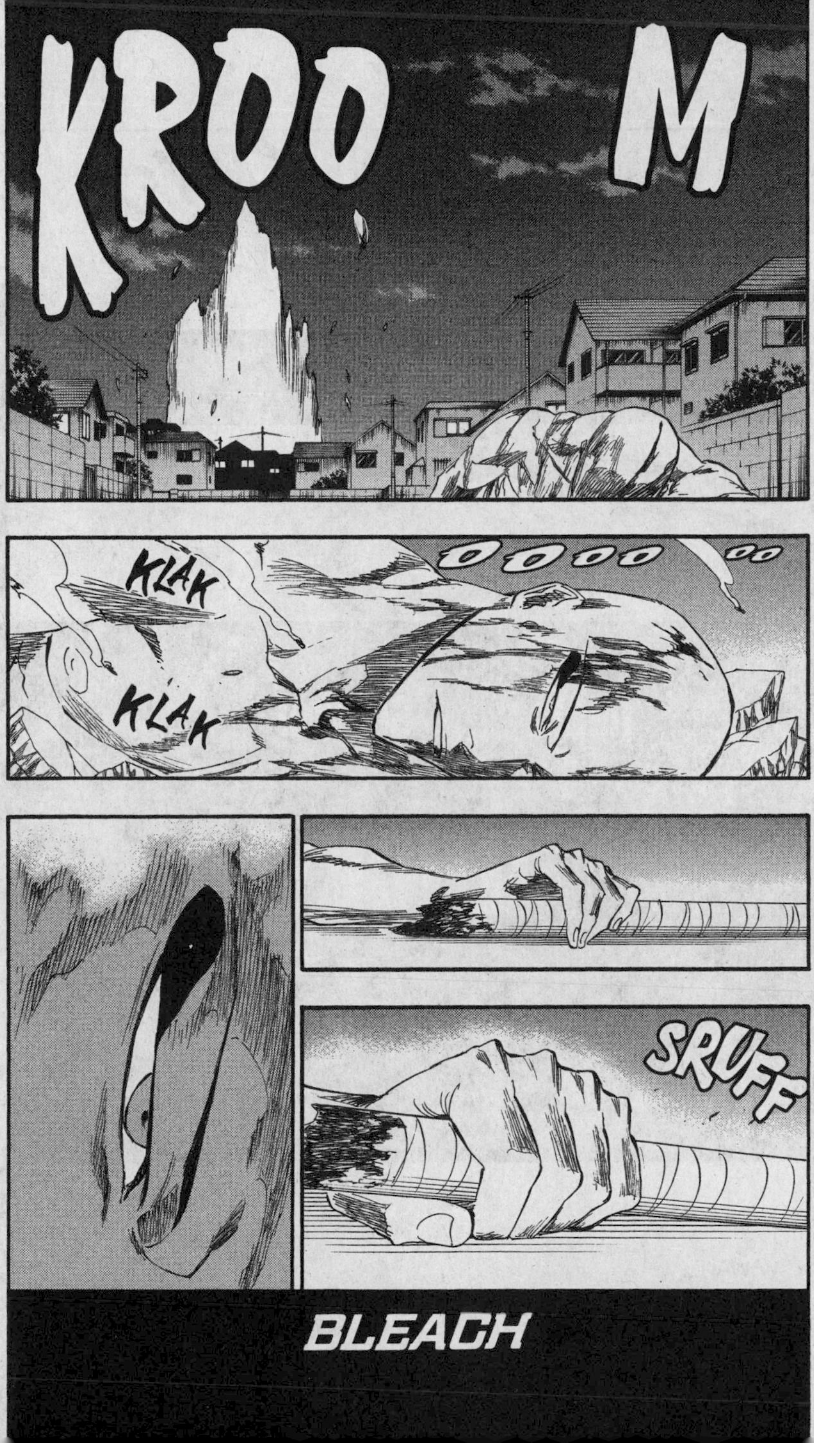
KROOM
OOOO..
KLAK
KLAK
SRUFF

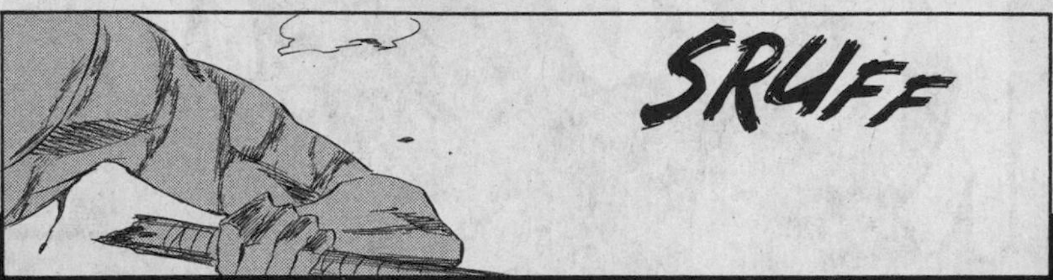
SRUFF

206.

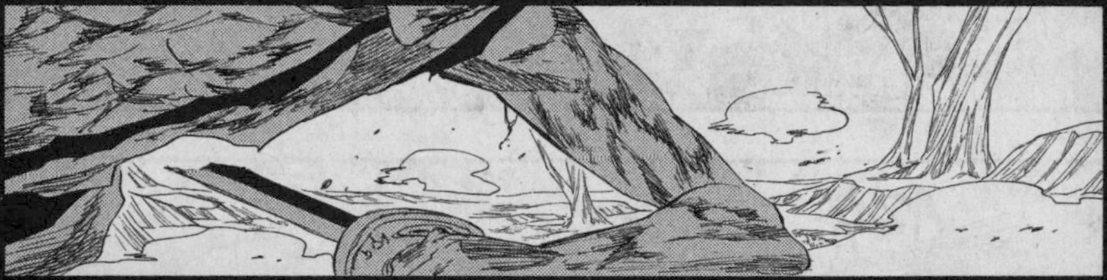

¡Mala Suerte! 5

[LUCKY]

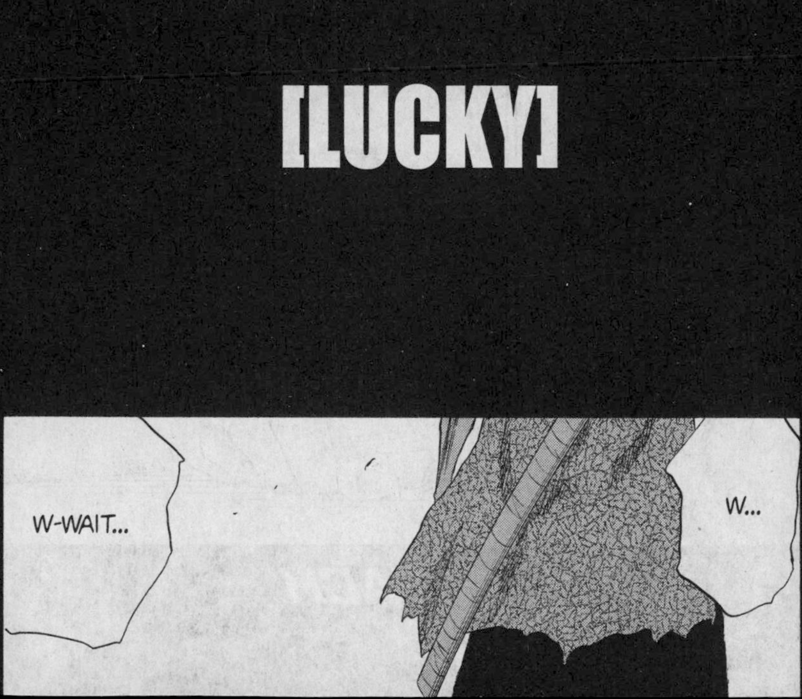
W...
W-WAIT...

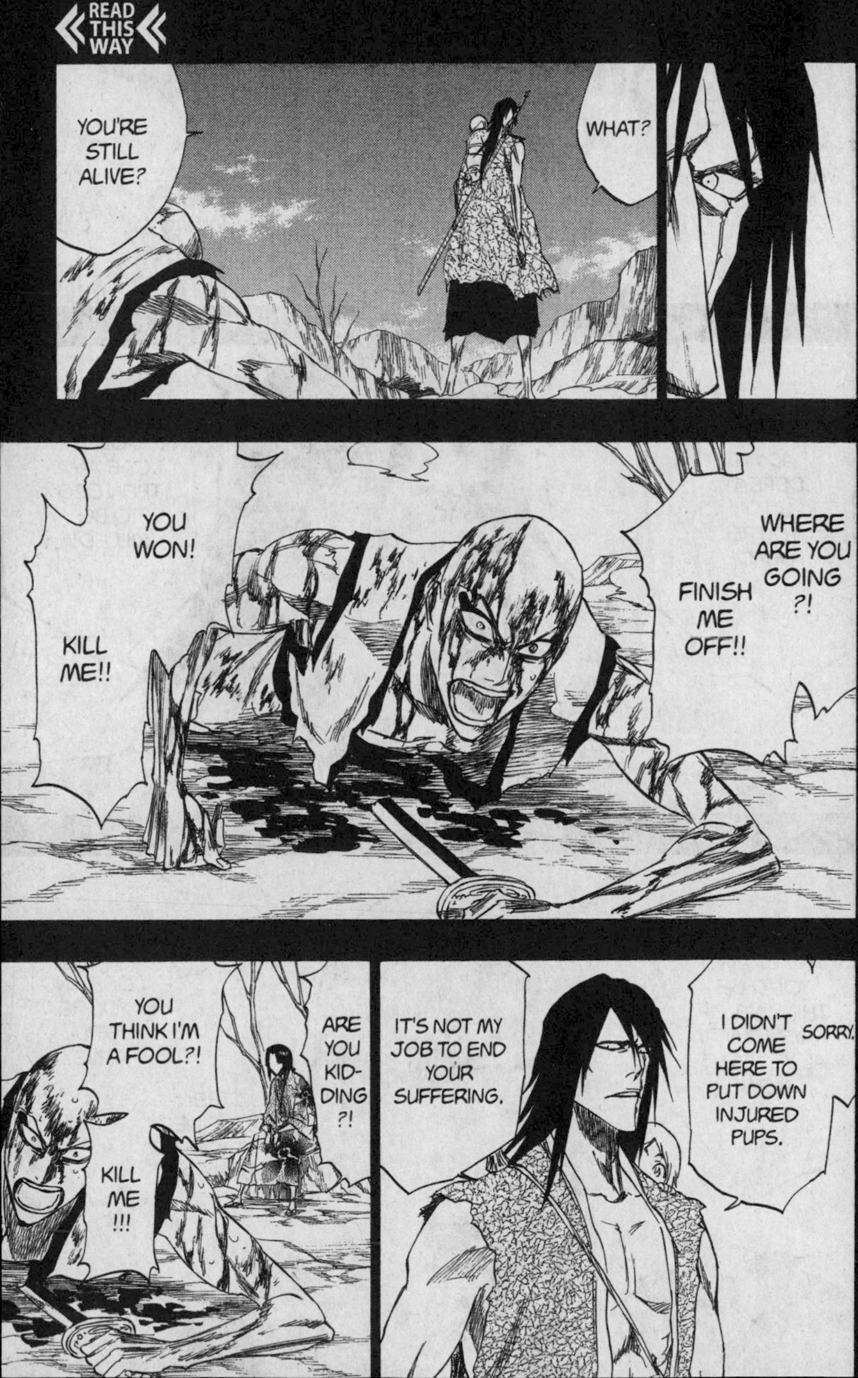
READ THIS WAY
WHAT?
YOU'RE STILL ALIVE?
WHERE ARE YOU GOING ?!
FINISH ME OFF!!
YOU WON!
KILL ME!!
SORRY.
I DIDN'T COME HERE TO PUT DOWN INJURED PUPS.
IT'S NOT MY JOB TO END YOUR SUFFERING.
ARE YOU KID-DING ?!
YOU THINK I'M A FOOL?!
KILL ME !!!

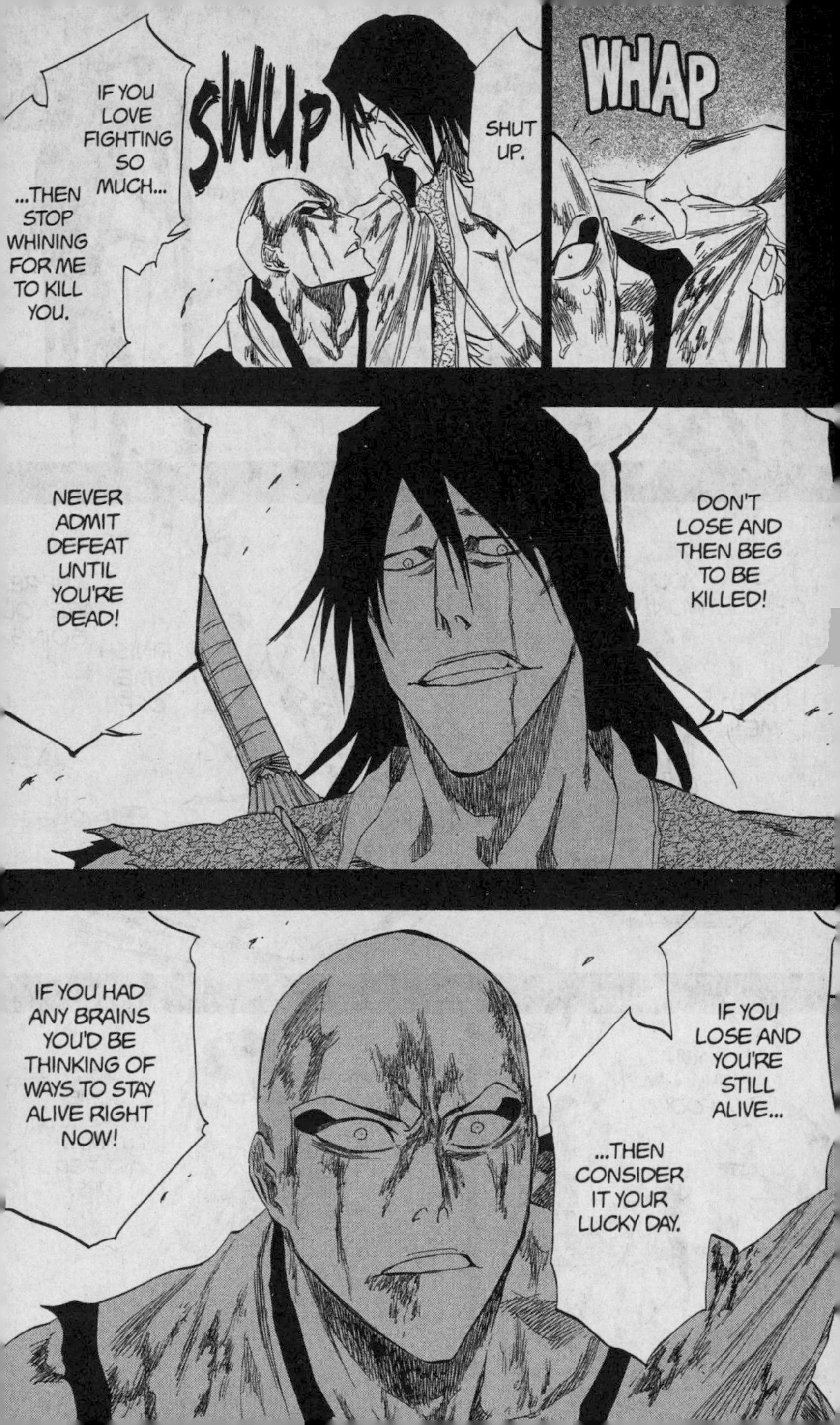
WHAP
SHUT UP.
SWUP
IF YOU LOVE FIGHTING SO MUCH...
...THEN STOP WHINING FOR ME TO KILL YOU.
DON'T LOSE AND THEN BEG TO BE KILLED!
NEVER ADMIT DEFEAT UNTIL YOU'RE DEAD!
IF YOU LOSE AND YOU'RE STILL ALIVE...
...THEN CONSIDER IT YOUR LUCKY DAY.
IF YOU HAD ANY BRAINS YOU'D BE THINKING OF WAYS TO STAY ALIVE RIGHT NOW!

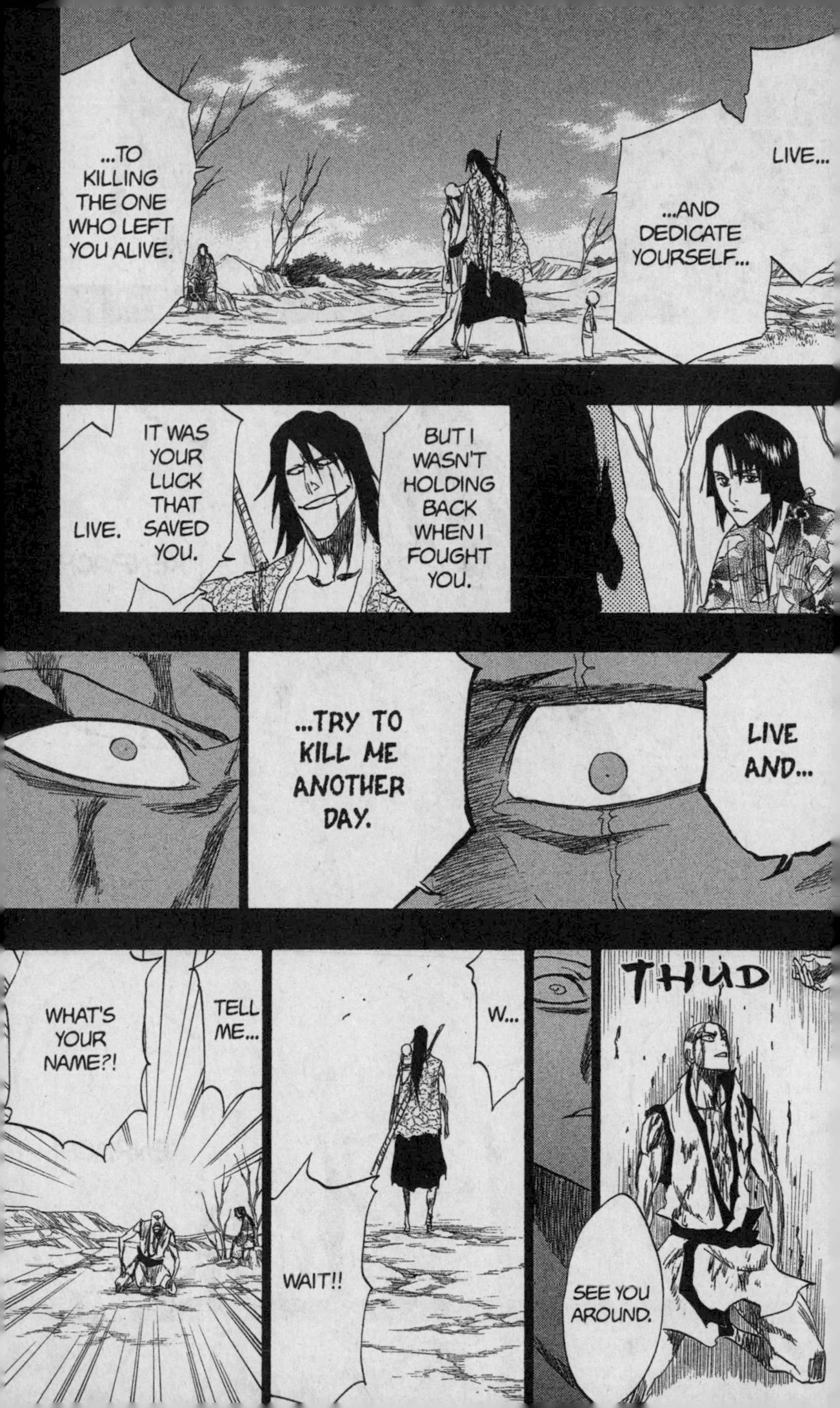
LIVE...
...AND DEDICATE YOURSELF...
...TO KILLING THE ONE WHO LEFT YOU ALIVE.
BUT I WASN'T HOLDING BACK WHEN I FOUGHT YOU.
IT WAS YOUR LUCK THAT SAVED YOU.
LIVE.
LIVE AND...
...TRY TO KILL ME ANOTHER DAY.
THUD
SEE YOU AROUND.
W...
WAIT!!
TELL ME...
WHAT'S YOUR NAME?!

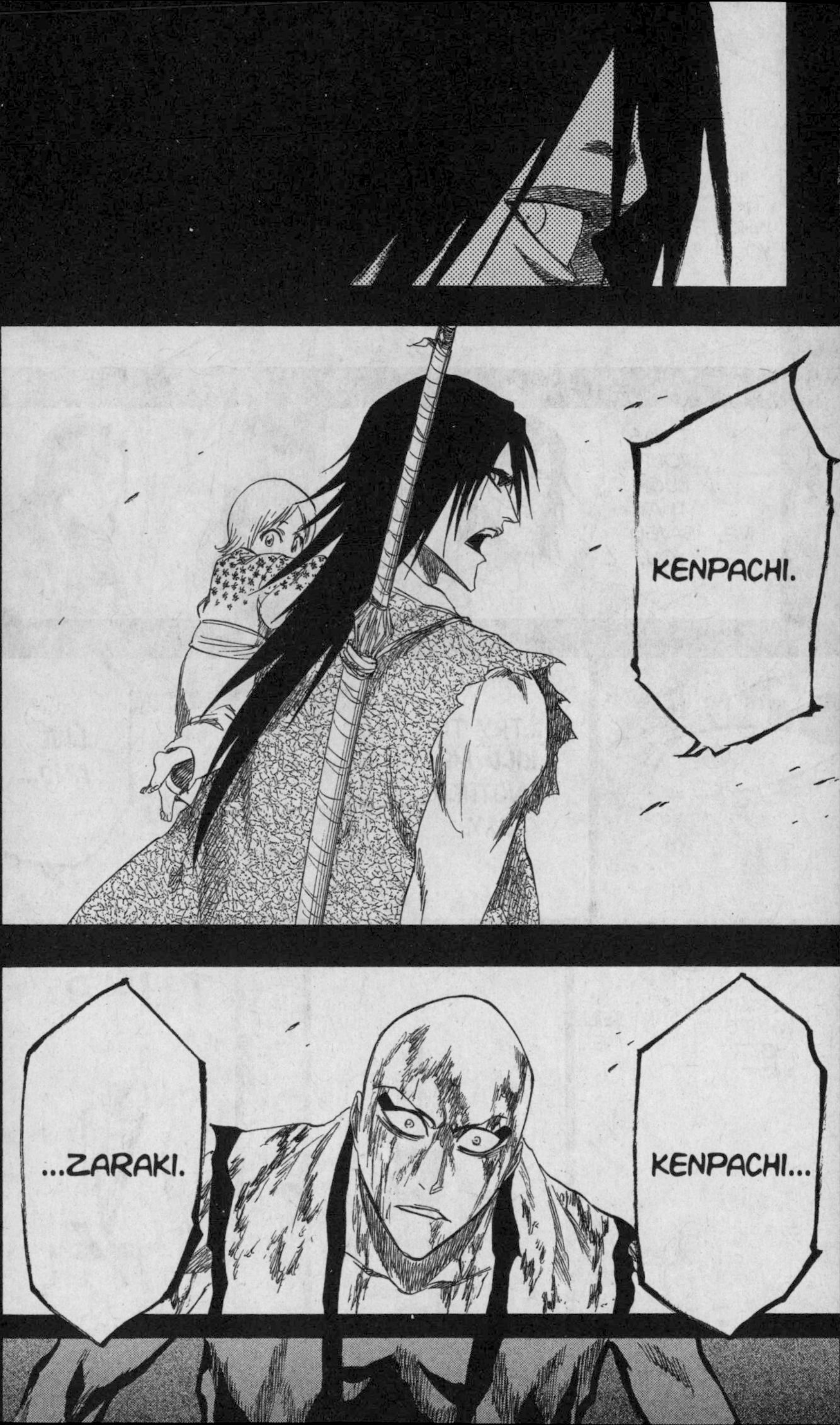
KENPACHI.
KENPACHI...
...ZARAKI.

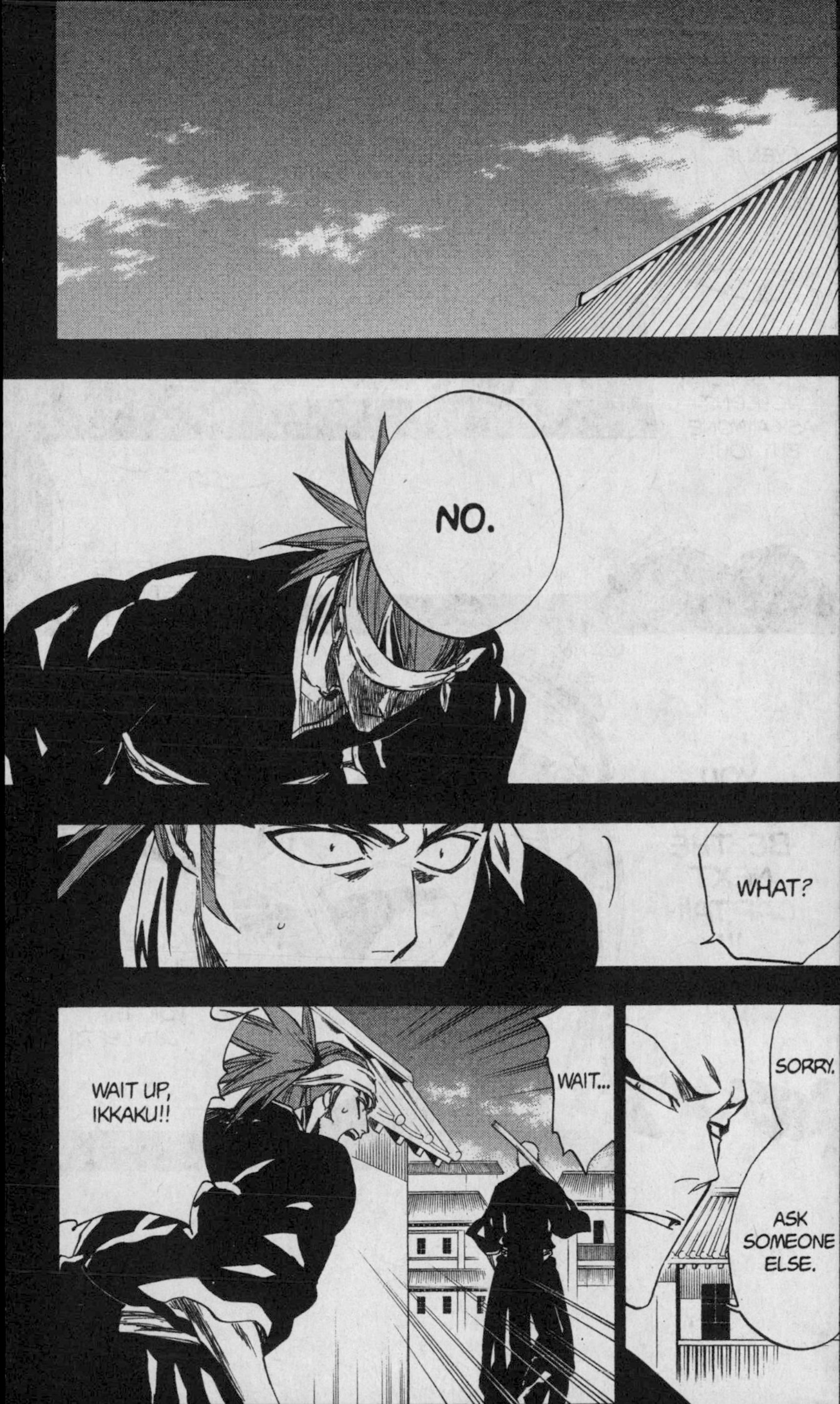
NO.
WHAT?
SORRY.
ASK SOMEONE ELSE.
WAIT...
WAIT UP, IKKAKU!!

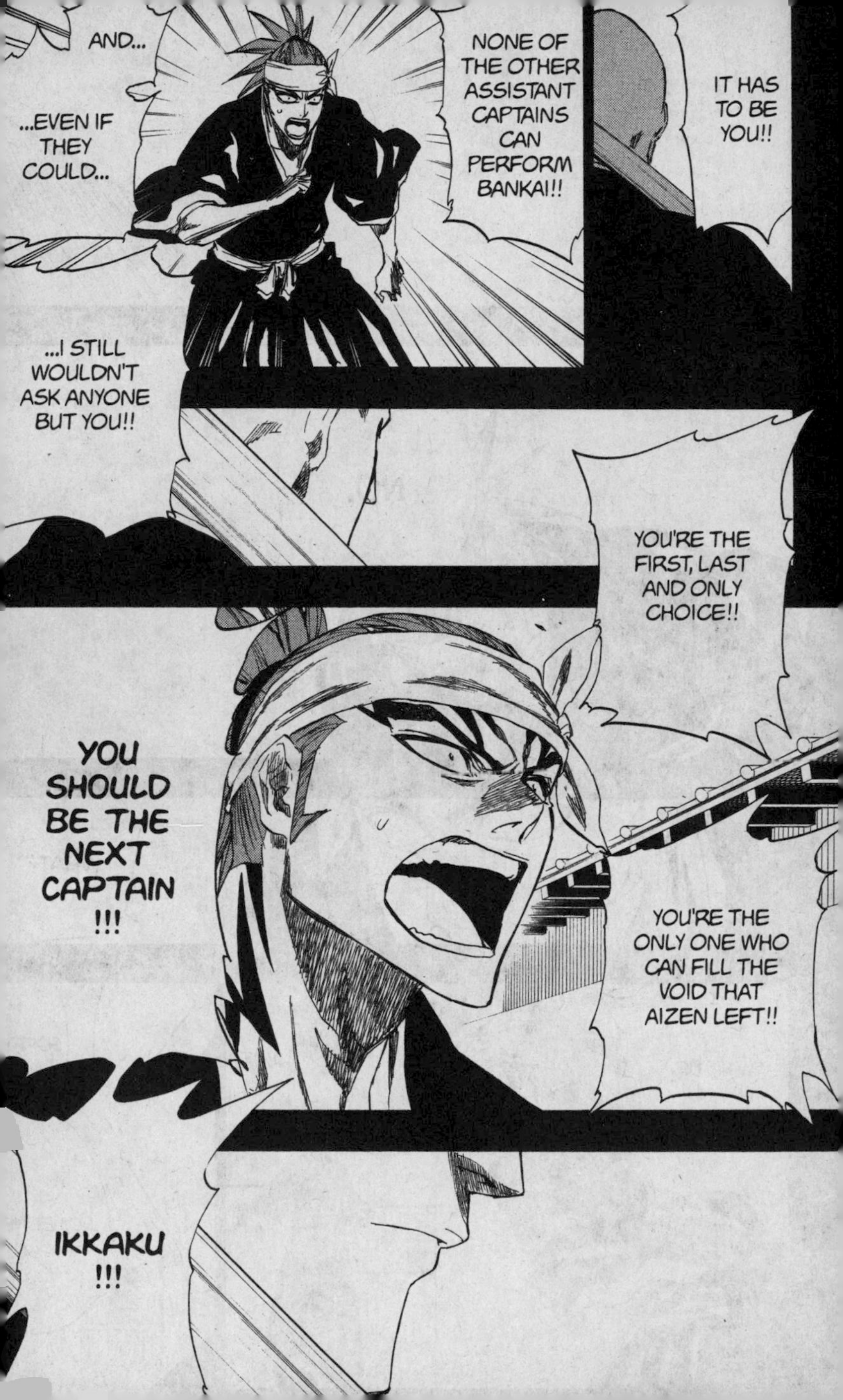
IT HAS TO BE YOU!!
NONE OF THE OTHER ASSISTANT CAPTAINS CAN PERFORM BANKAI!!
AND...
...EVEN IF THEY COULD...
...I STILL WOULDN'T ASK ANYONE BUT YOU!!
YOU'RE THE FIRST, LAST AND ONLY CHOICE!!
YOU'RE THE ONLY ONE WHO CAN FILL THE VOID THAT AIZEN LEFT!!
YOU SHOULD BE THE NEXT CAPTAIN !!!
IKKAKU !!!

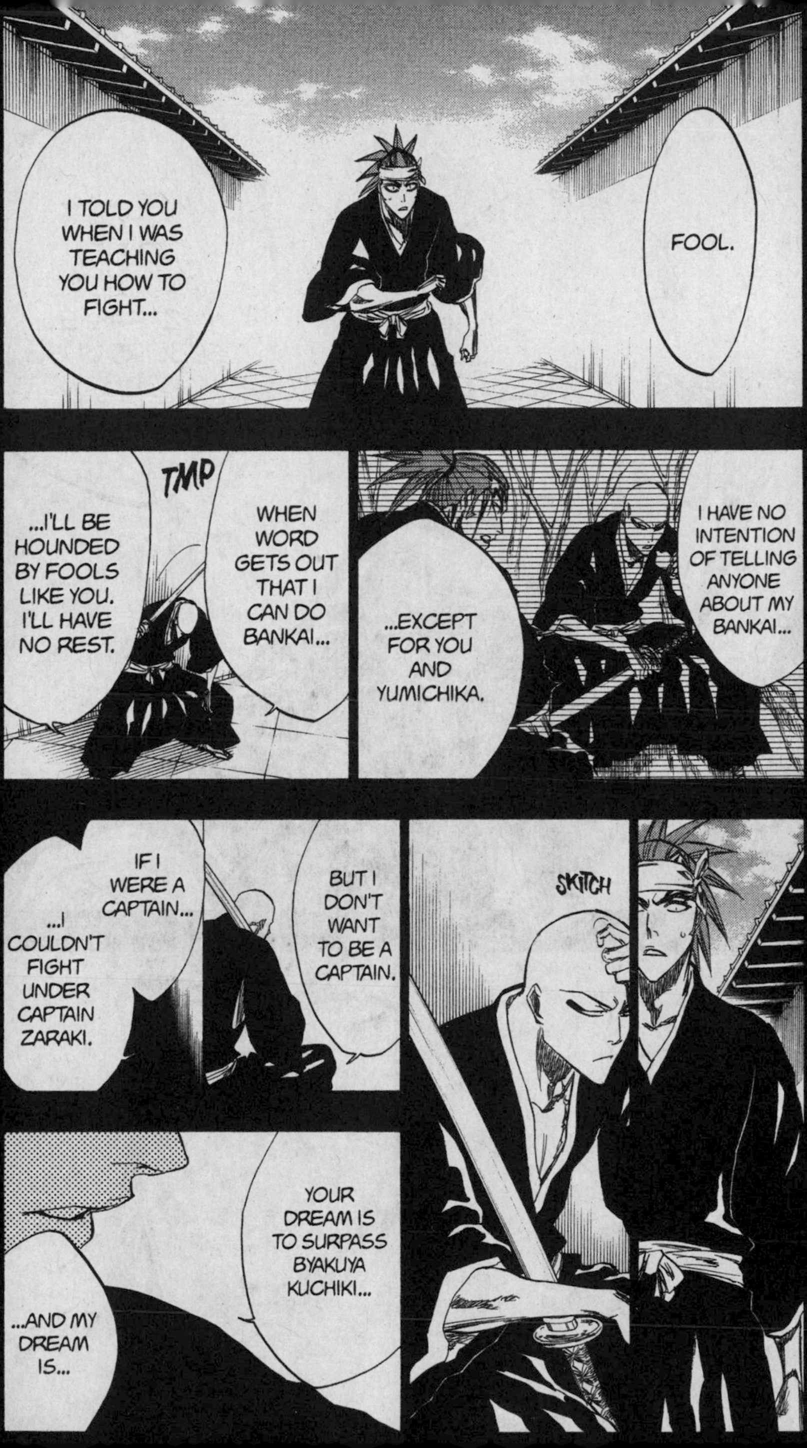
FOOL.
I TOLD YOU WHEN I WAS TEACHING YOU HOW TO FIGHT...
I HAVE NO INTENTION OF TELLING ANYONE ABOUT MY BANKAI...
...EXCEPT FOR YOU AND YUMICHIKA.
TMP
WHEN WORD GETS OUT THAT I CAN DO BANKAI...
...I'LL BE HOUNDED BY FOOLS LIKE YOU. I'LL HAVE NO REST.
SKITCH
BUT I DON'T WANT TO BE A CAPTAIN.
IF I WERE A CAPTAIN...
...I COULDN'T FIGHT UNDER CAPTAIN ZARAKI.
YOUR DREAM IS TO SURPASS BYAKUYA KUCHIKI...
...AND MY DREAM IS...

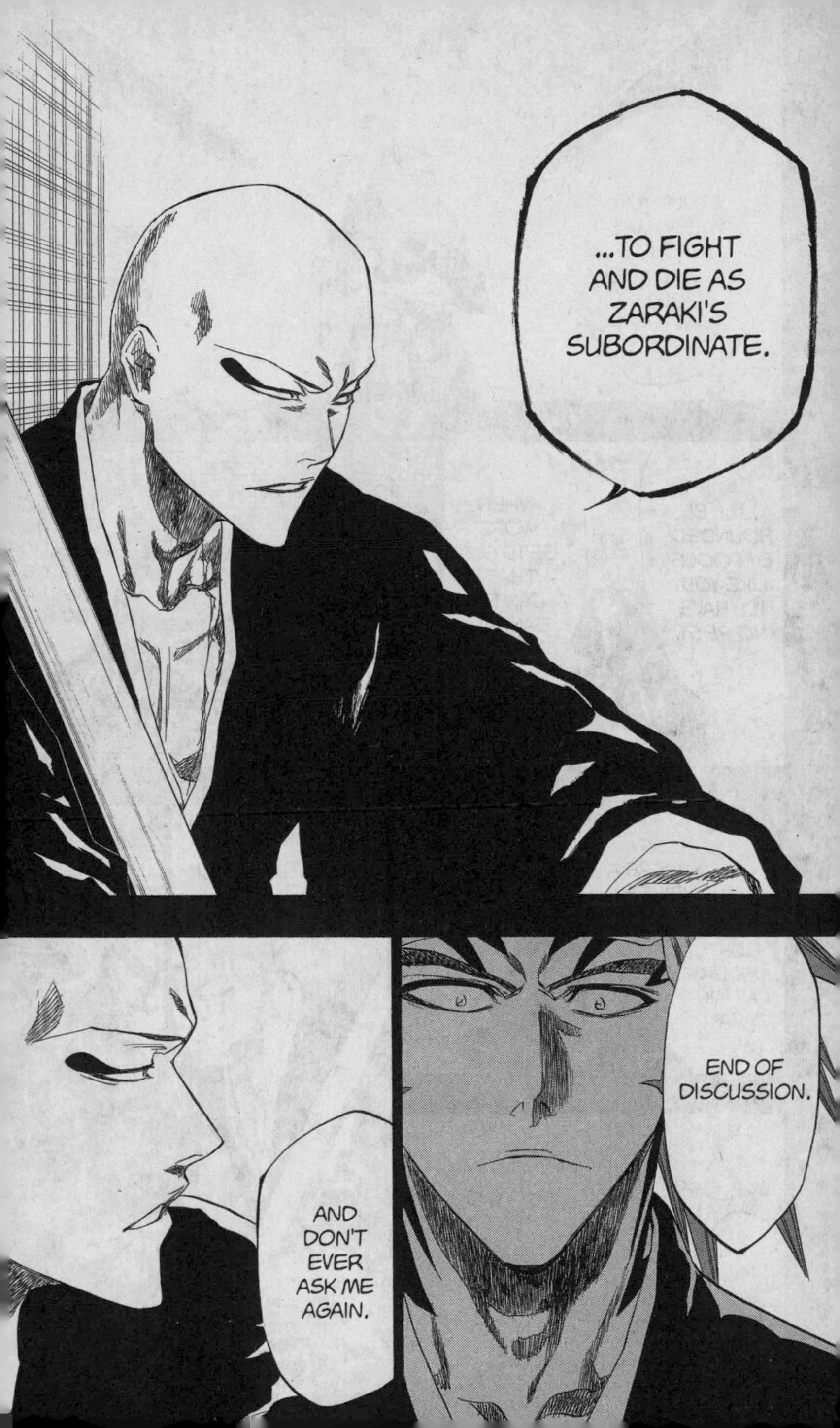
...TO FIGHT AND DIE AS ZARAKI'S SUBORDINATE.
END OF DISCUSSION.
AND DON'T EVER ASK ME AGAIN.

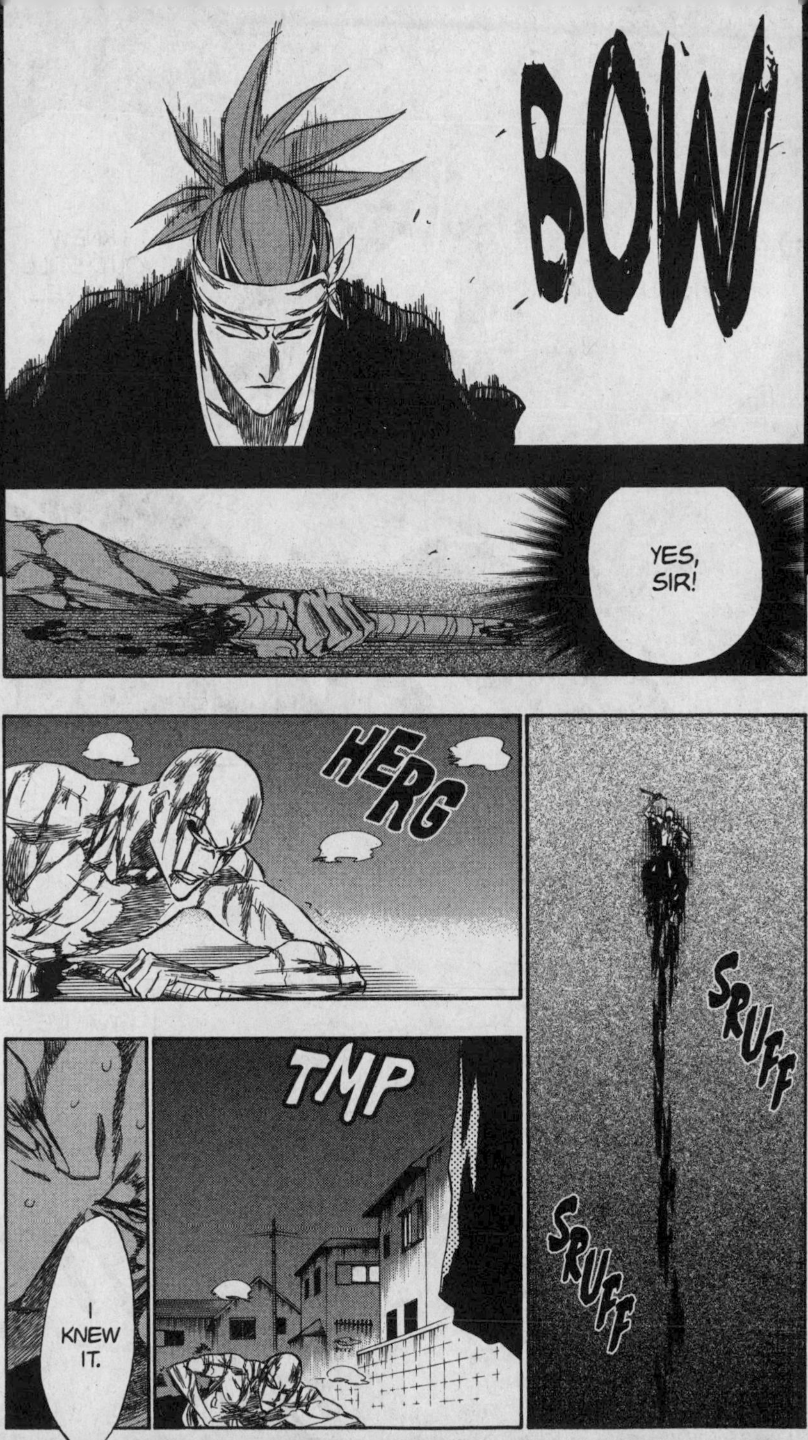
BOW
YES, SIR!
SRUFF
SRUFF
HERG
TMP
I KNEW IT.

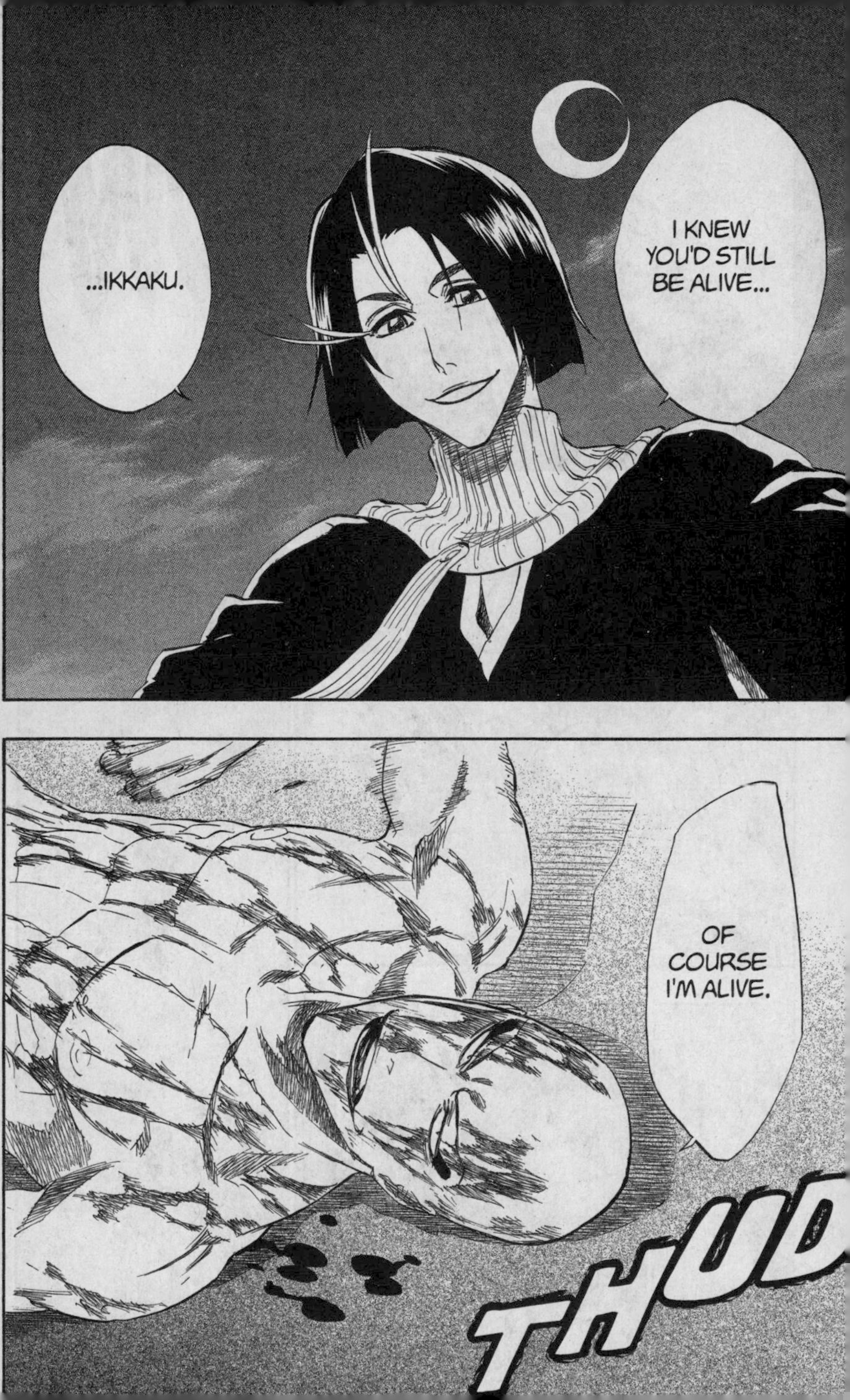
I KNEW YOU'D STILL BE ALIVE...
...IKKAKU.
OF COURSE I'M ALIVE.
THUD

READ THIS WAY

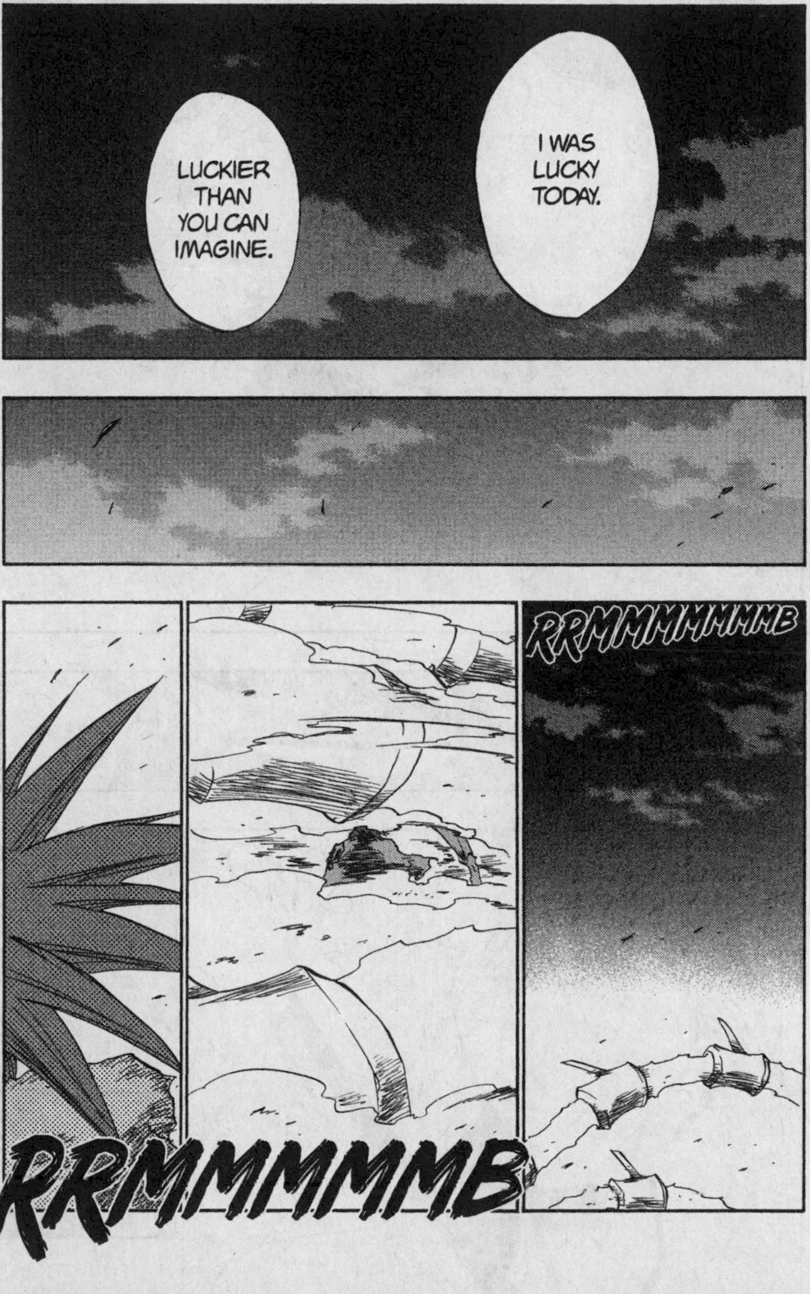

I WAS LUCKY TODAY.
LUCKIER THAN YOU CAN IMAGINE.
RRMMMMMMMB
RRMMMMMMB

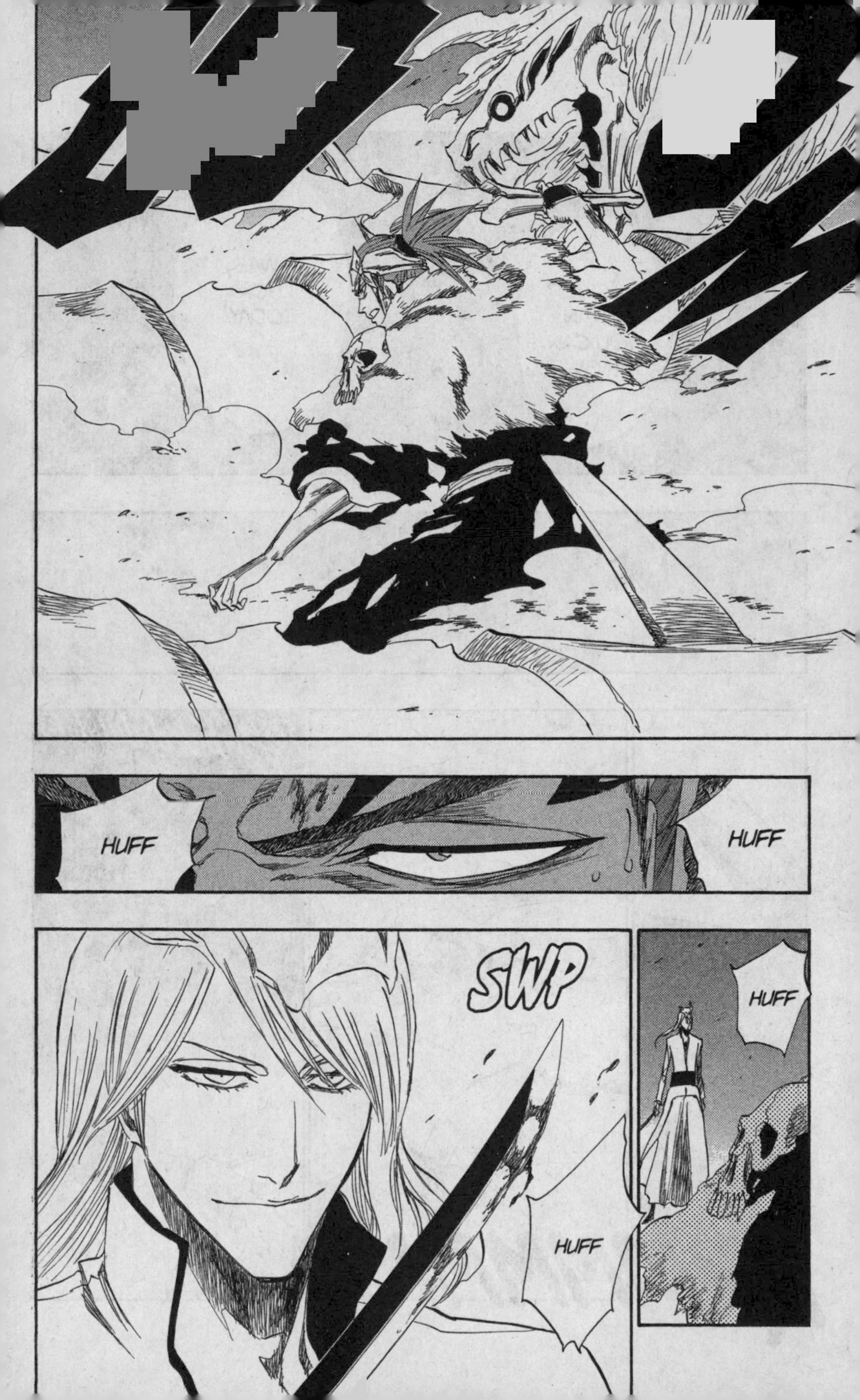
HUFF
HUFF
HUFF
SWP
HUFF

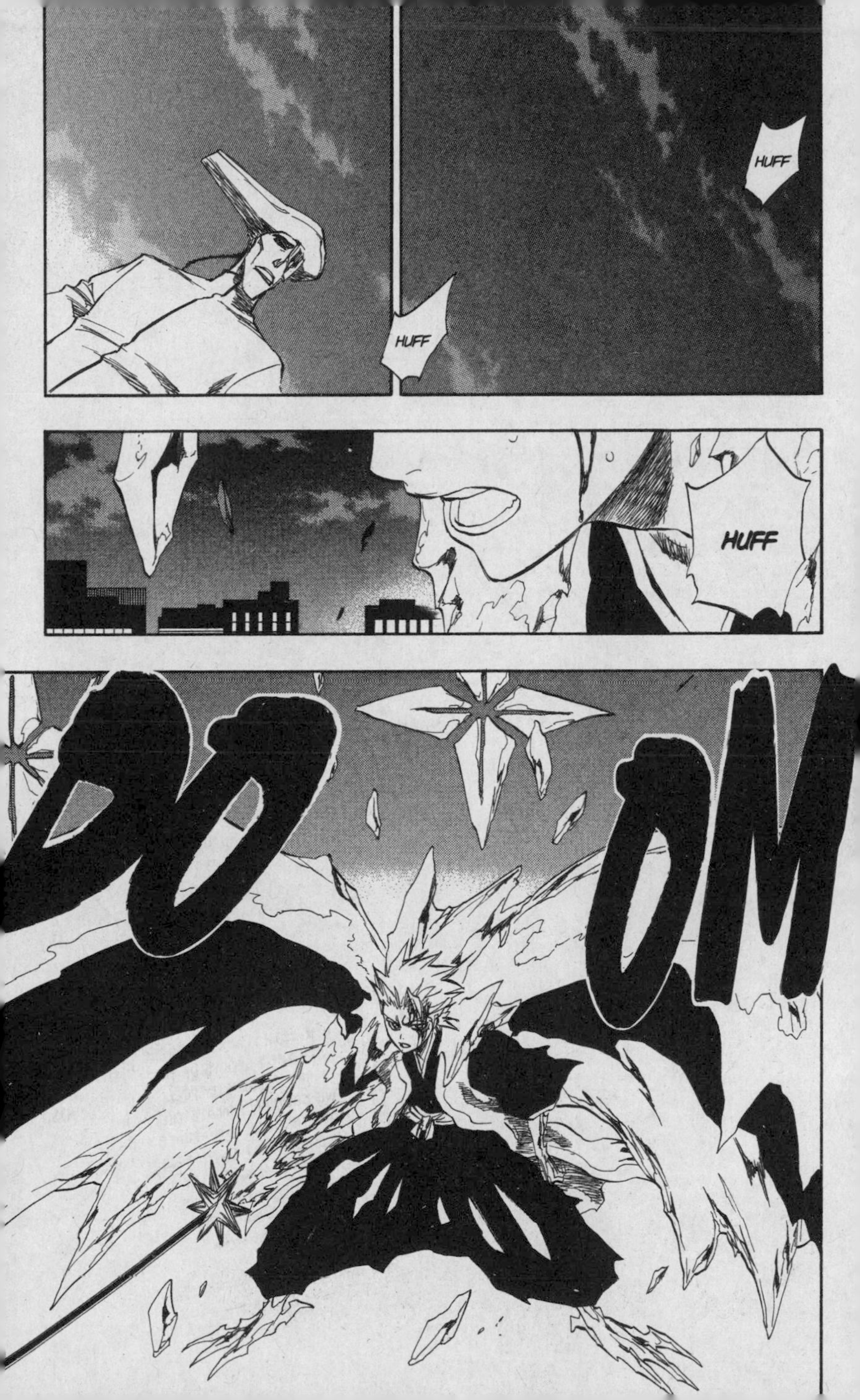
HUFF
HUFF
HUFF
BOOM

TAKE A LOOK AT THIS.
11TH-20TH PLACE FINISHERS WITH THE RESULTS OF THE THIRD POPULARITY POLL, WE CORDIALLY INVITE THE 11TH-THROUGH 20TH-PLACE FINISHERS TO A SNOW BALL TOURNAMENT ON THE SEVENTEENTH OF THIS MONTH. ALL WHO ATTEND SHOULD BRING
TEN TOTAL.

207. Mode: Genocide

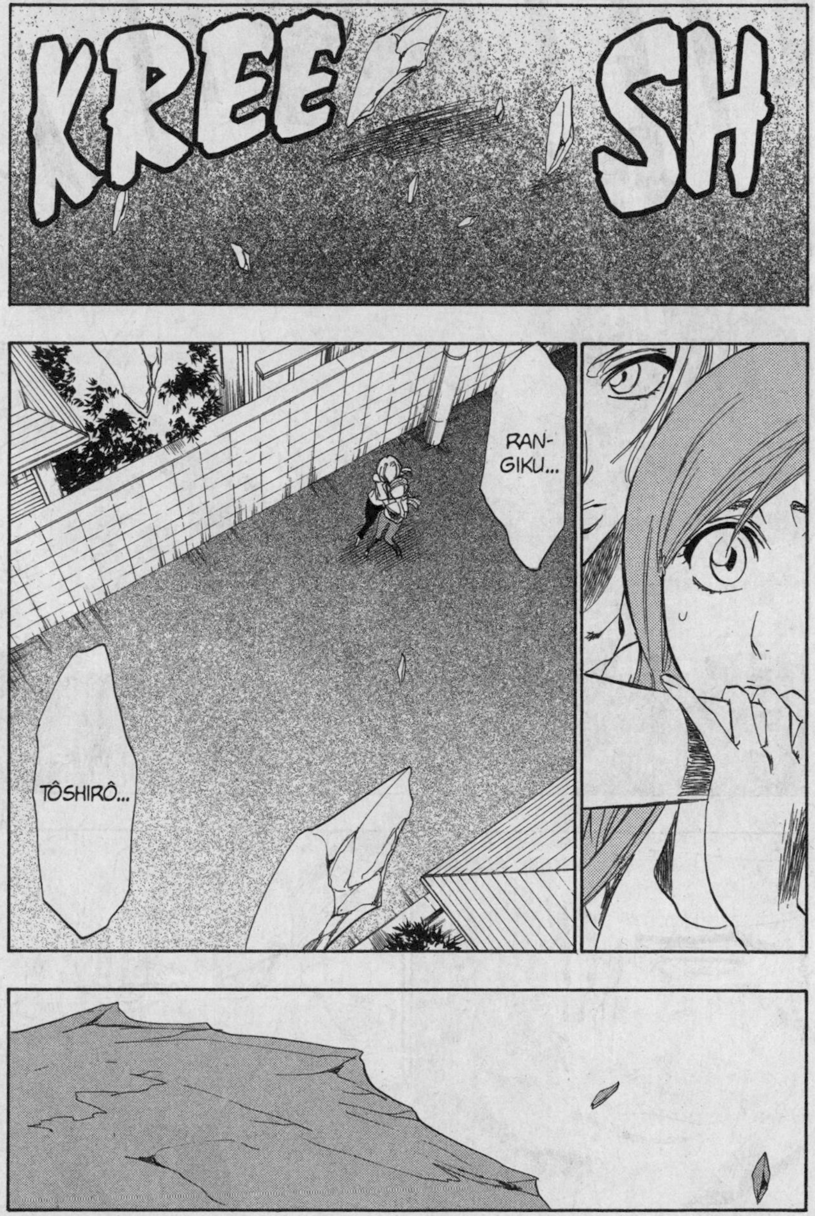
KREE SH
RAN-GIKU...
TÔSHIRÔ...

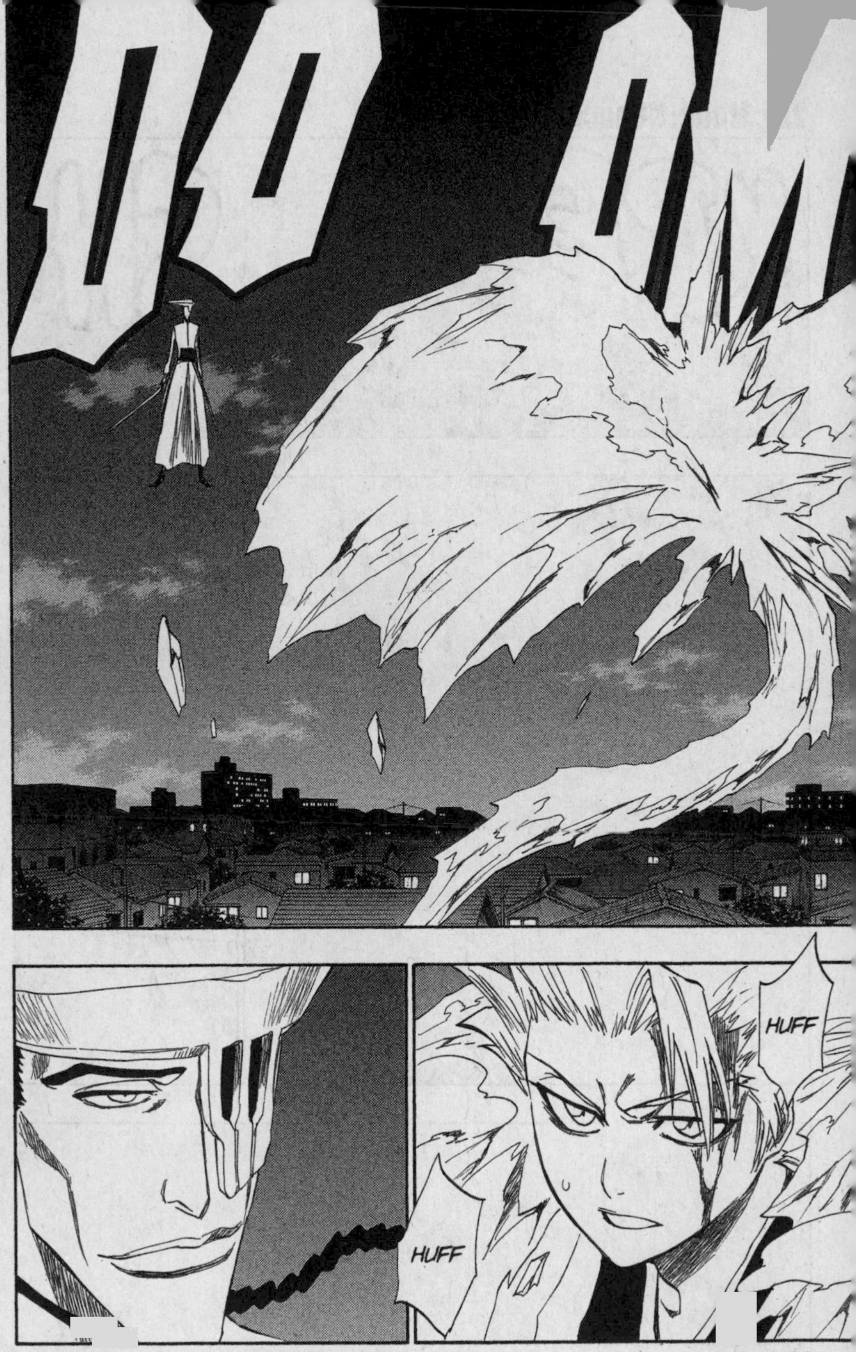
DO OM
HUFF
HUFF

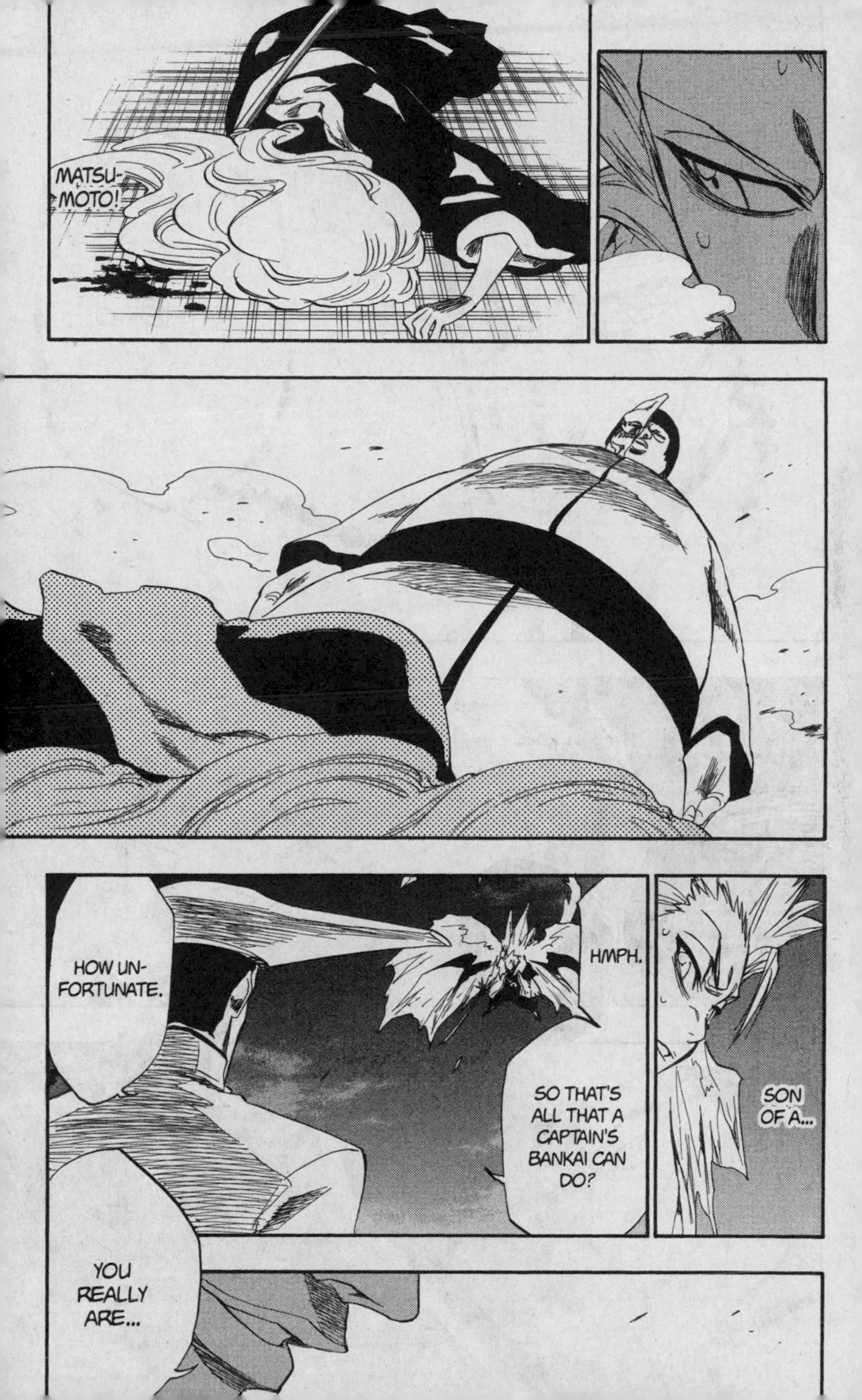
MATSU-MOTO!
SON OF A...
HMPH.
HOW UN-FORTUNATE.
SO THAT'S ALL THAT A CAPTAIN'S BANKAI CAN DO?
YOU REALLY ARE...

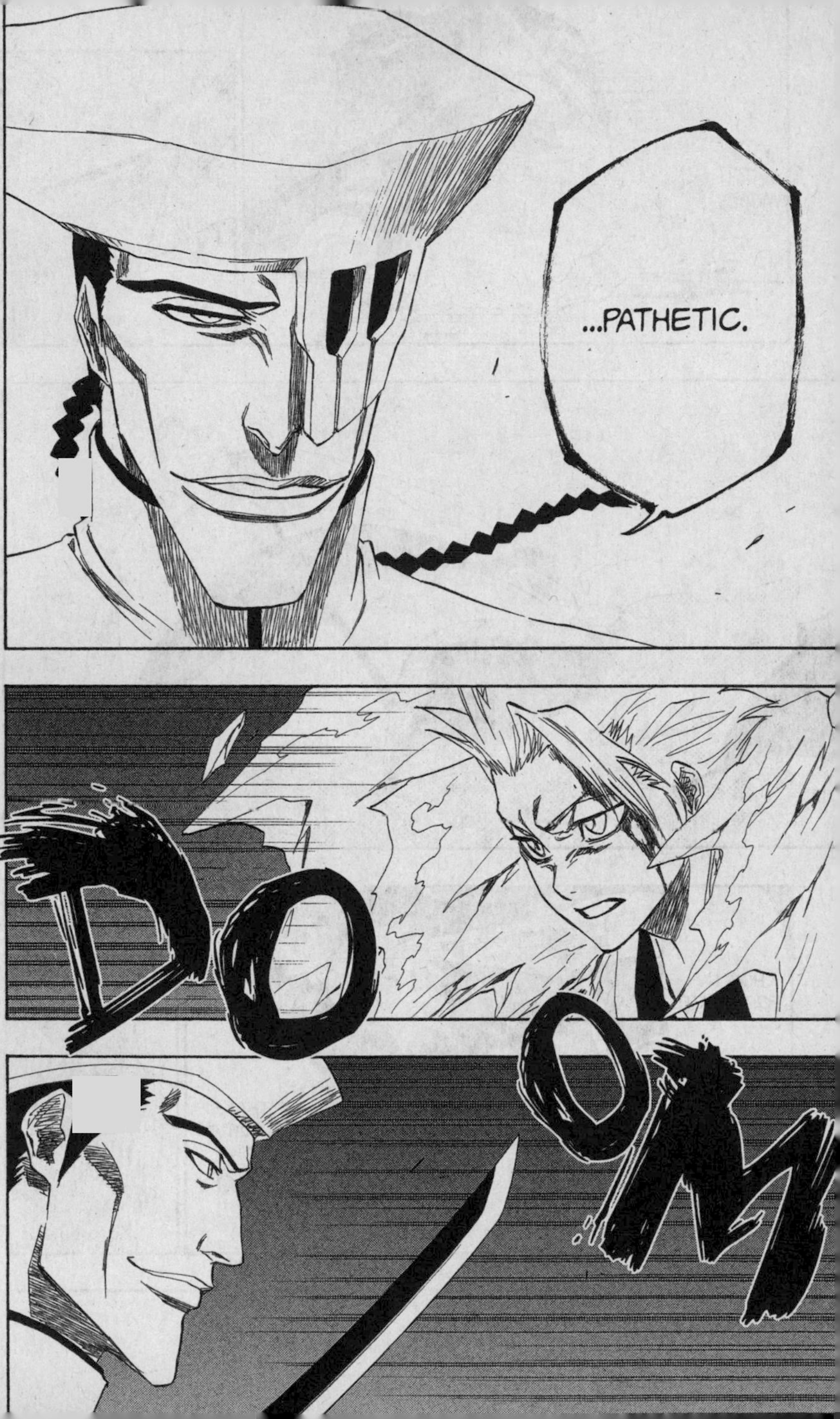
...PATHETIC.
DOOOM

BLEACH 207. Mode: Genocide

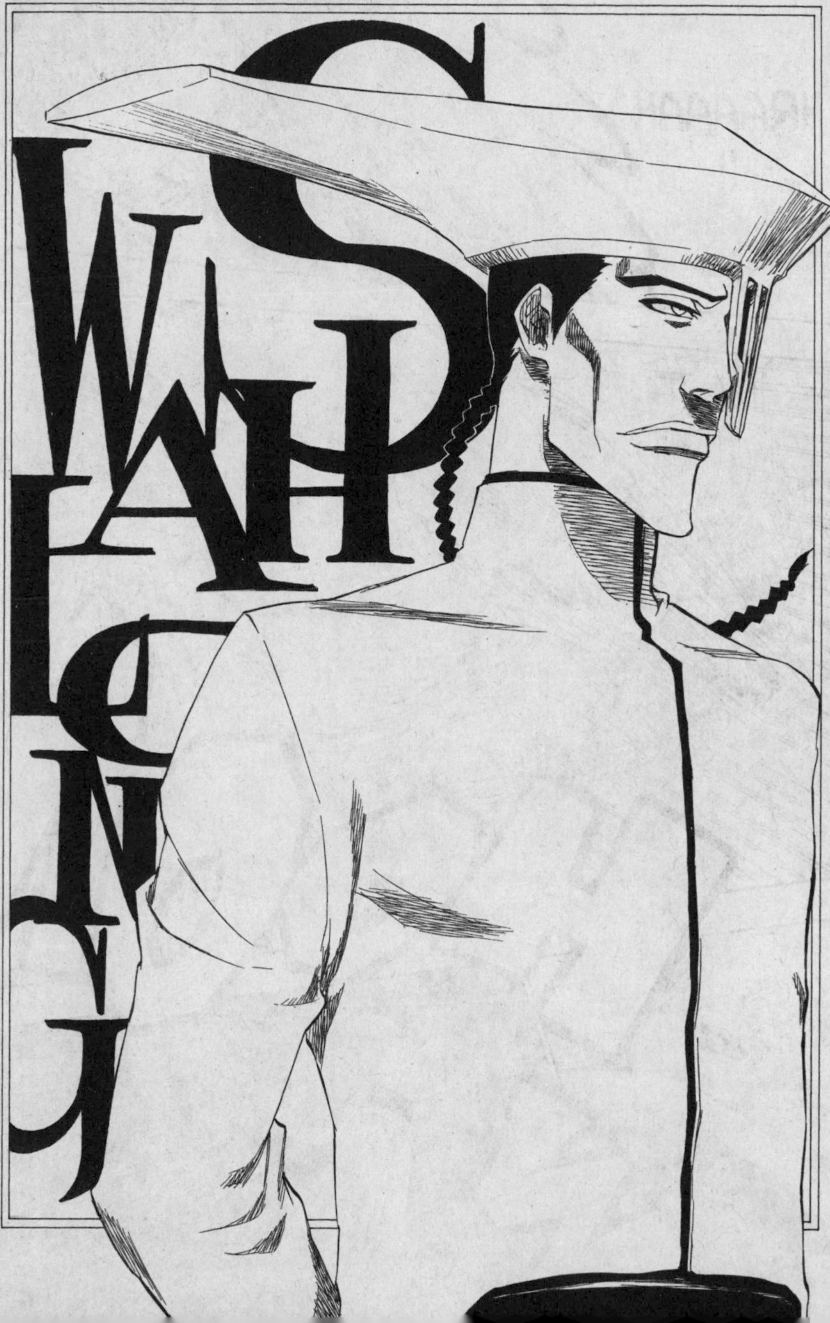

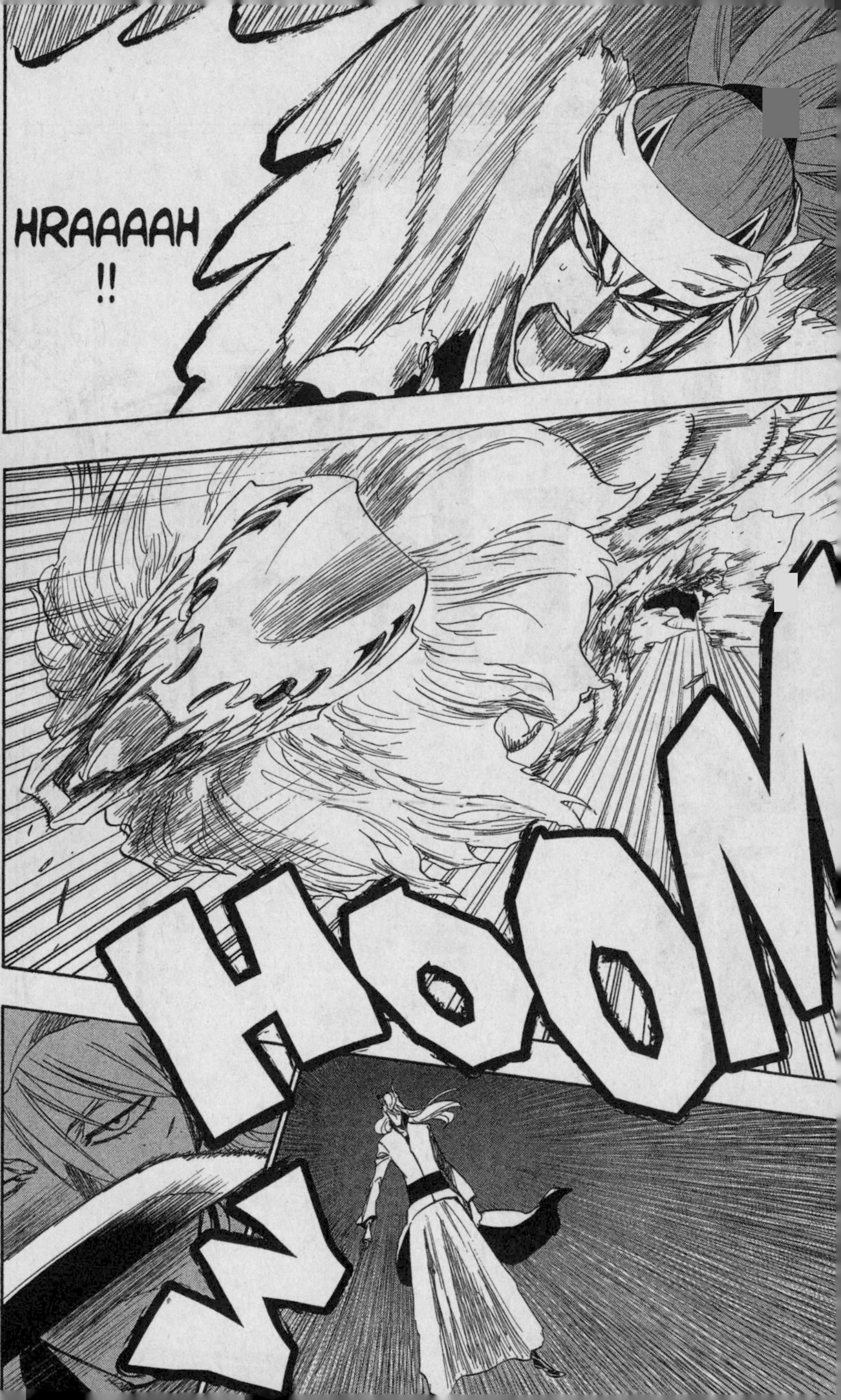
HRAAAAH
!!
WHOOM

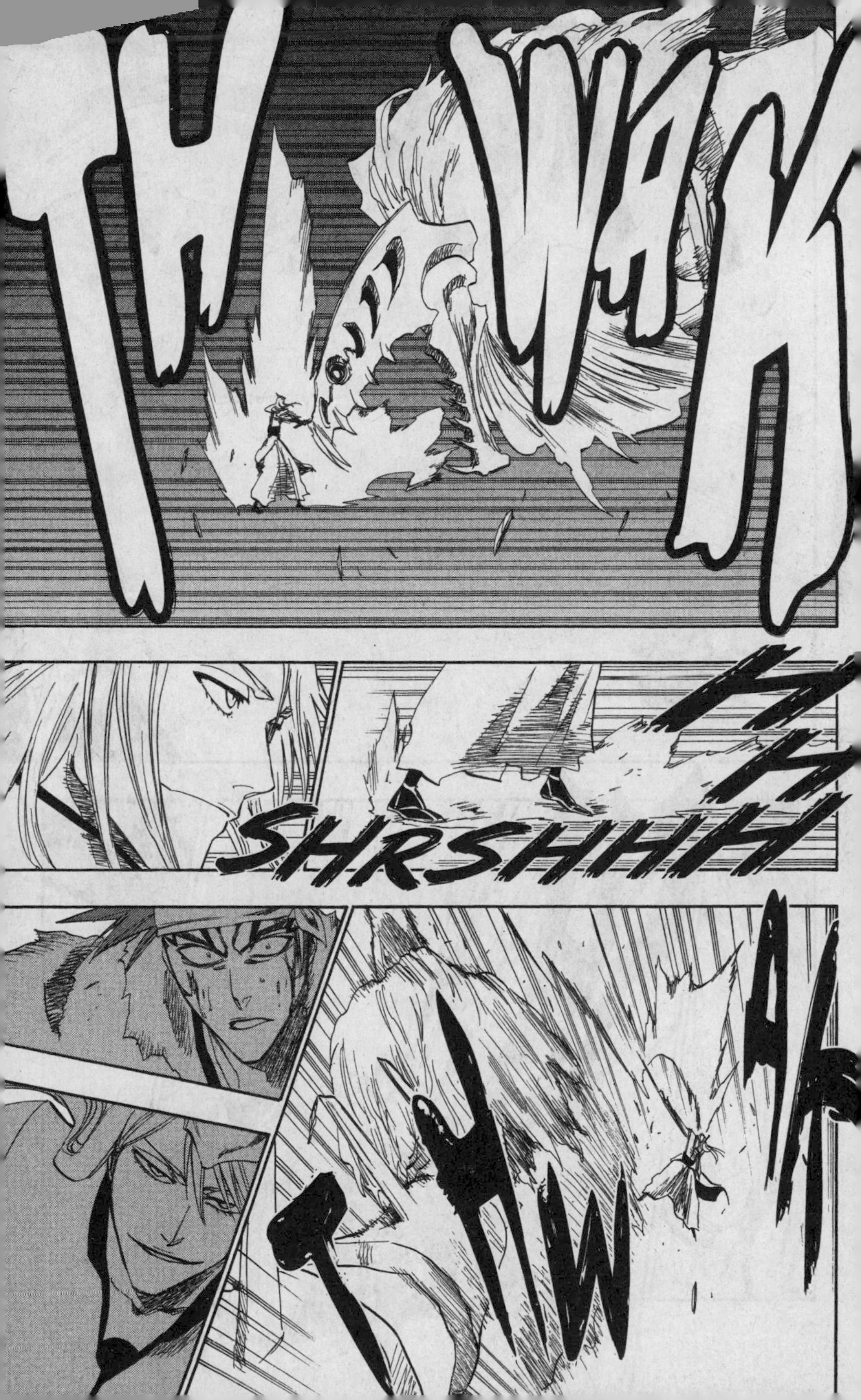
THWAK
SHRSHHH
THWA

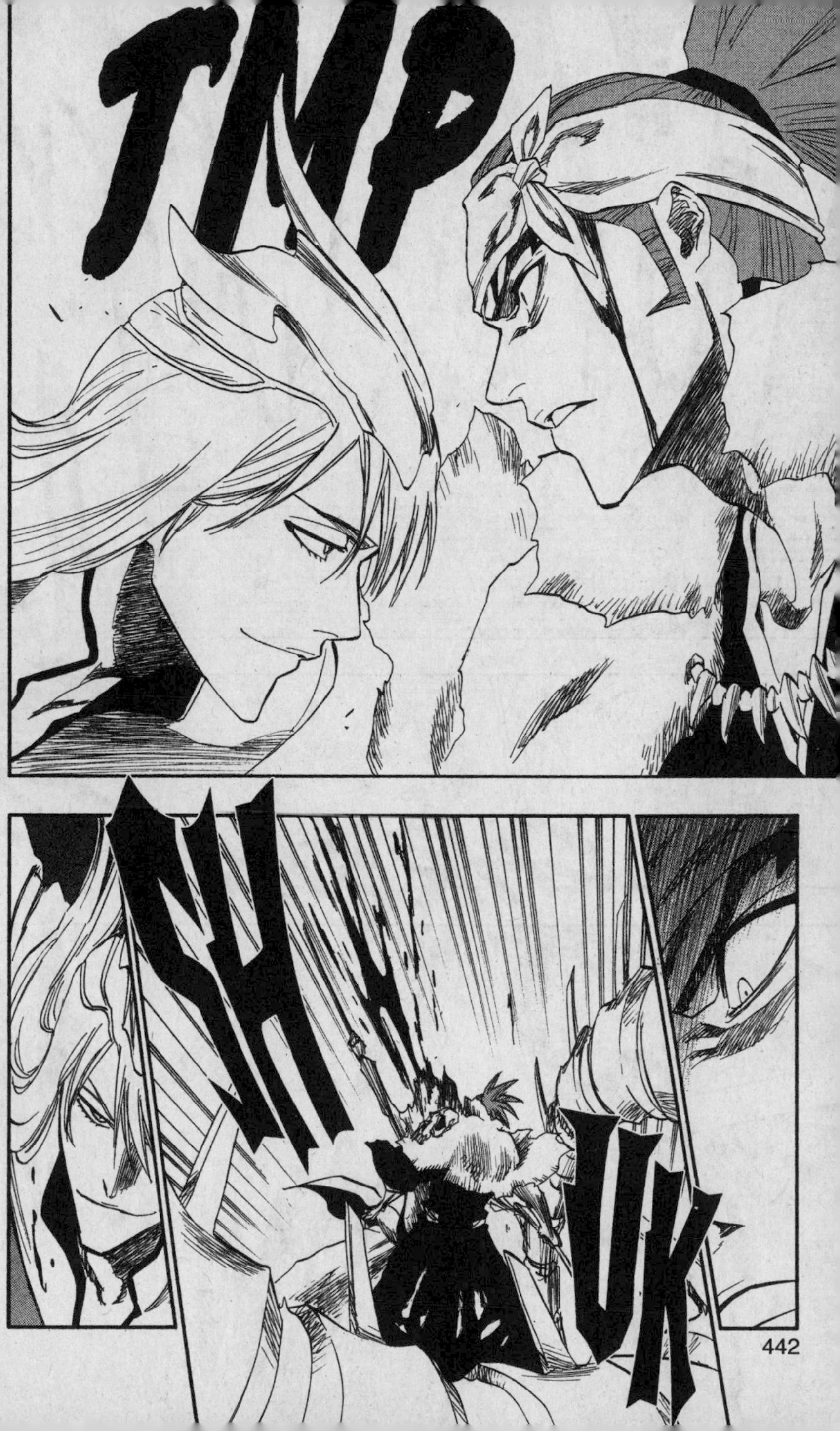
TMP
SH
UK

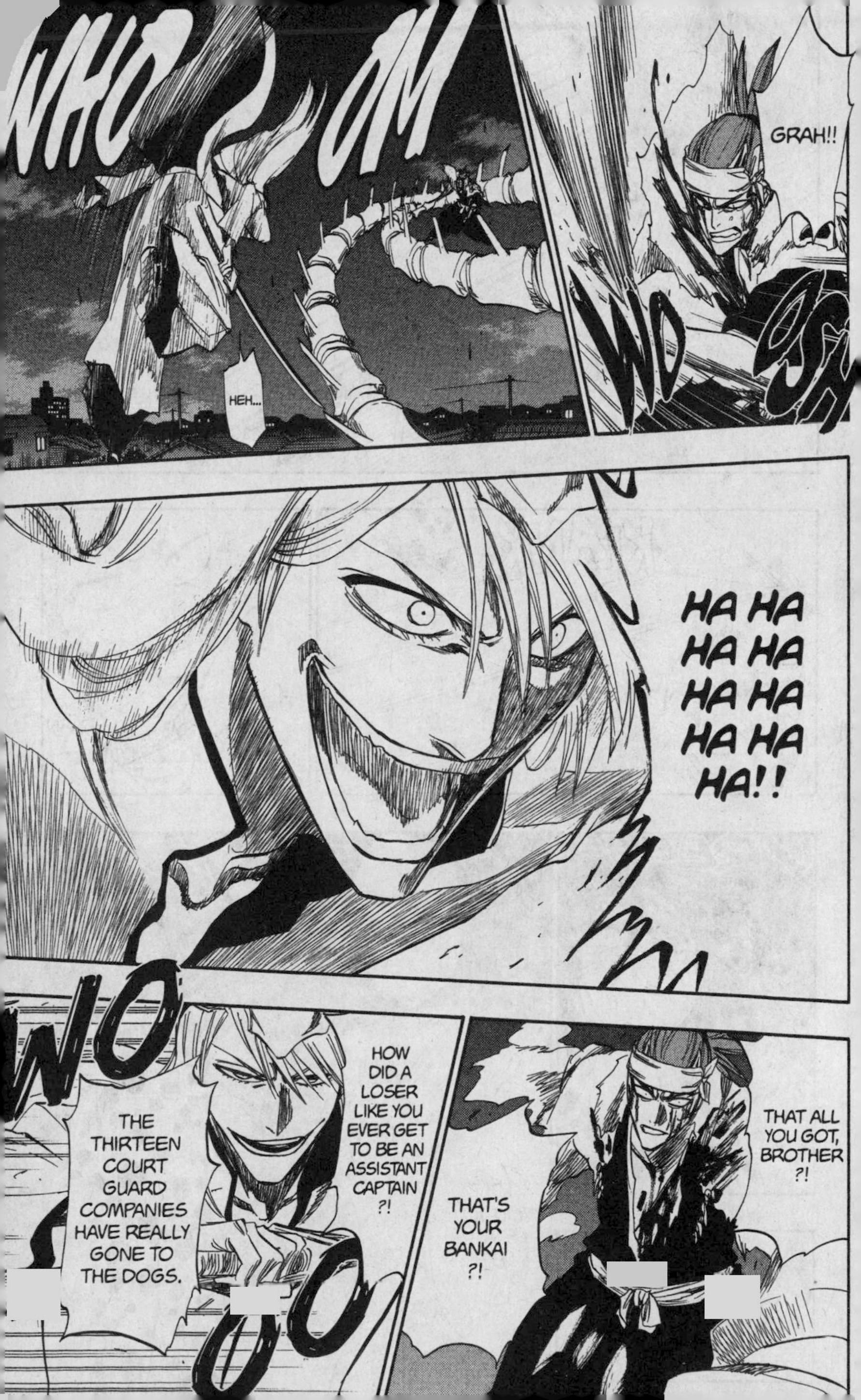
GRAH!!
WO OSH
WHO OM
HEH...
HA HA HA HA HA HA HA HA HA!!
THAT ALL YOU GOT, BROTHER?!
THAT'S YOUR BANKAI?!
HOW DID A LOSER LIKE YOU EVER GET TO BE AN ASSISTANT CAPTAIN?!
THE THIRTEEN COURT GUARD COMPANIES HAVE REALLY GONE TO THE DOGS.
WO OO

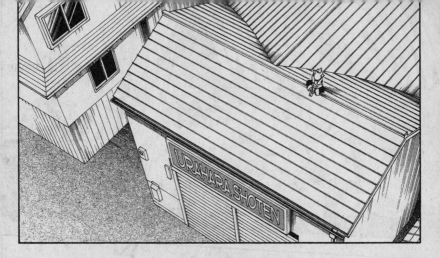

KLANK

THEY'RE LOSING.

DARN...

VREEEE

URURU?

TMP

I TOLD YOU TO STAY IN BED.

UH-OH!

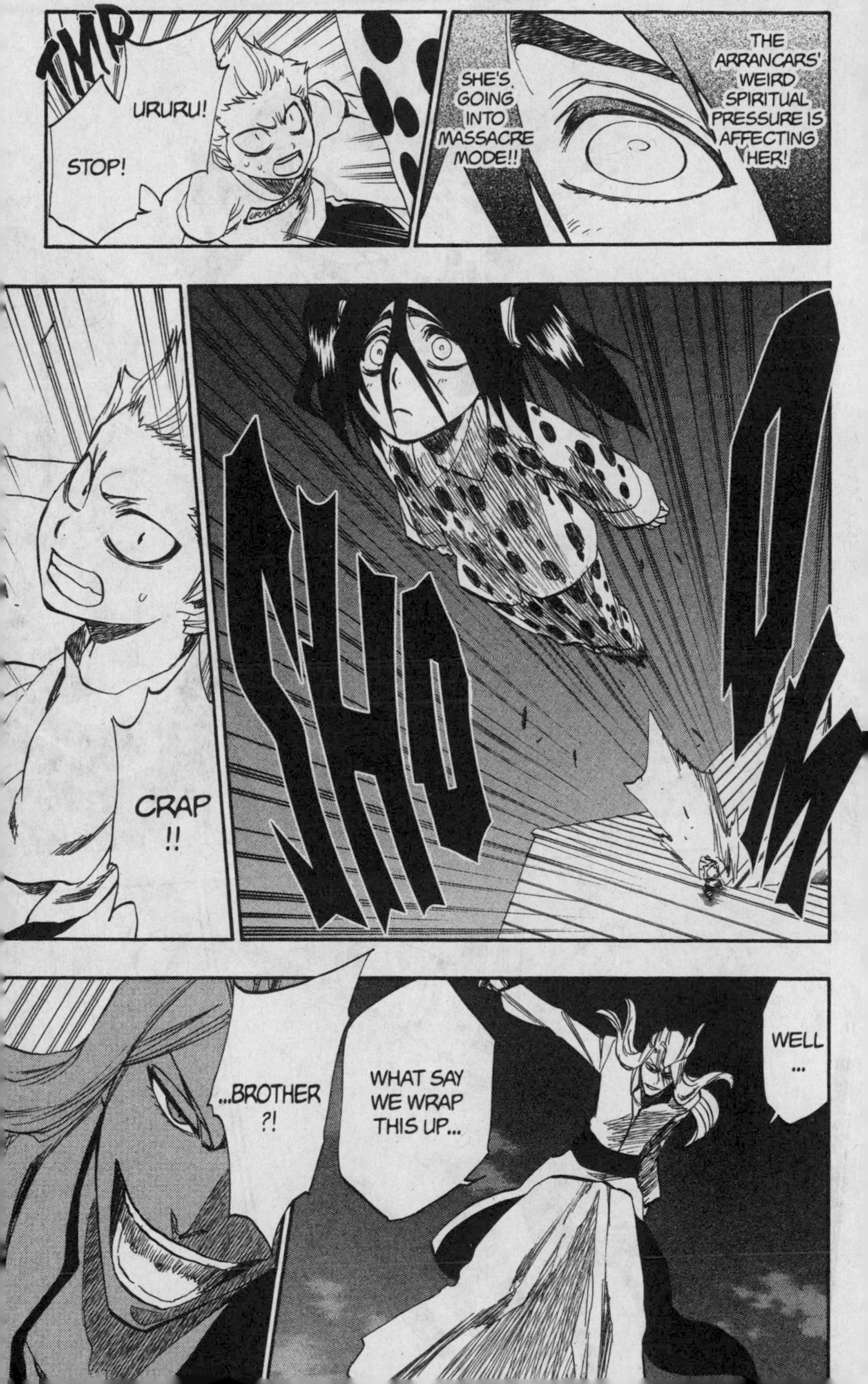

THE ARRANCARS' WEIRD SPIRITUAL PRESSURE IS AFFECTING HER!
SHE'S GOING INTO MASSACRE MODE!!
TMP
URURU!
STOP!
SHOOM
CRAP!!
WELL...
WHAT SAY WE WRAP THIS UP...
...BROTHER?!

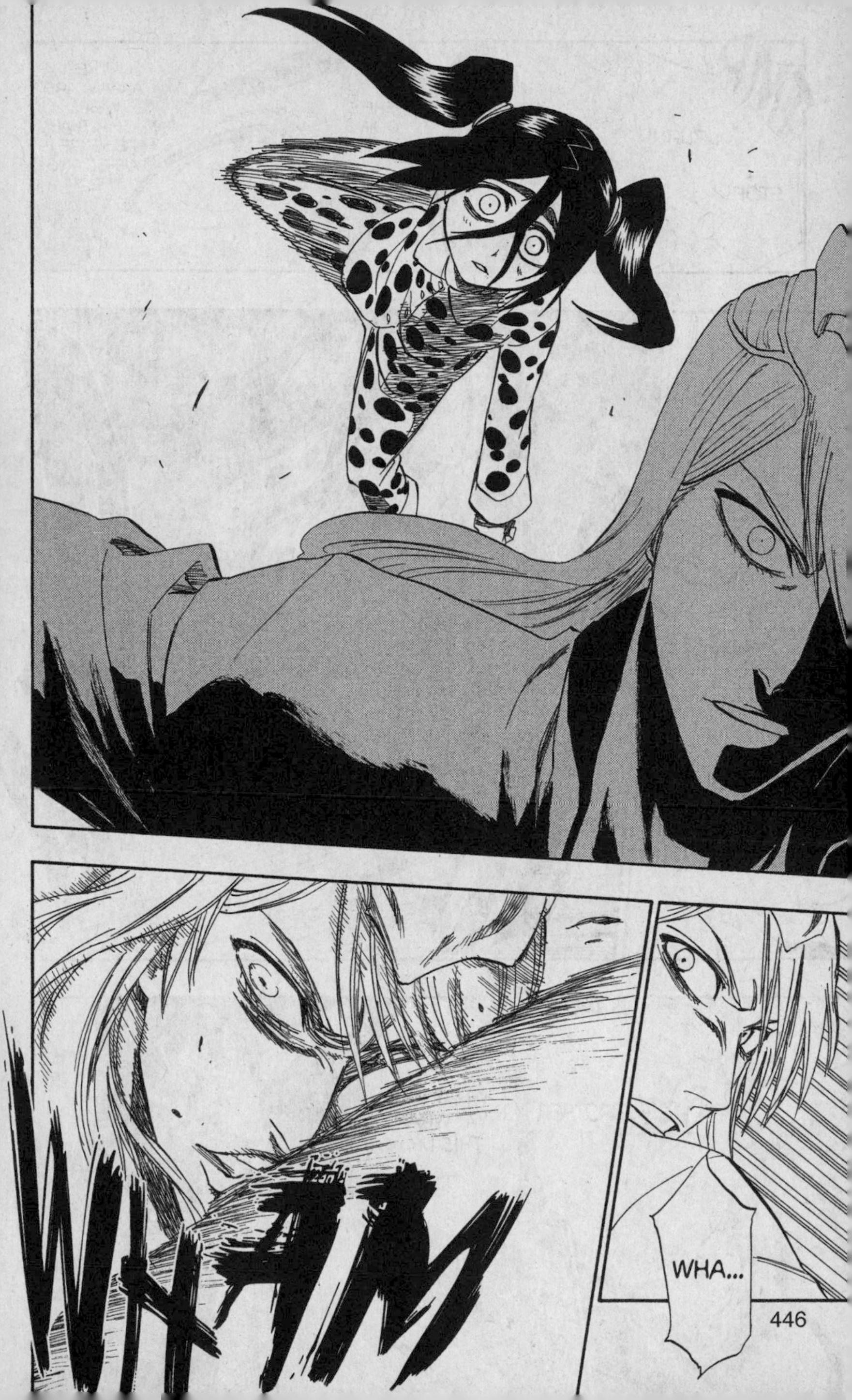
WHA...
WHAM

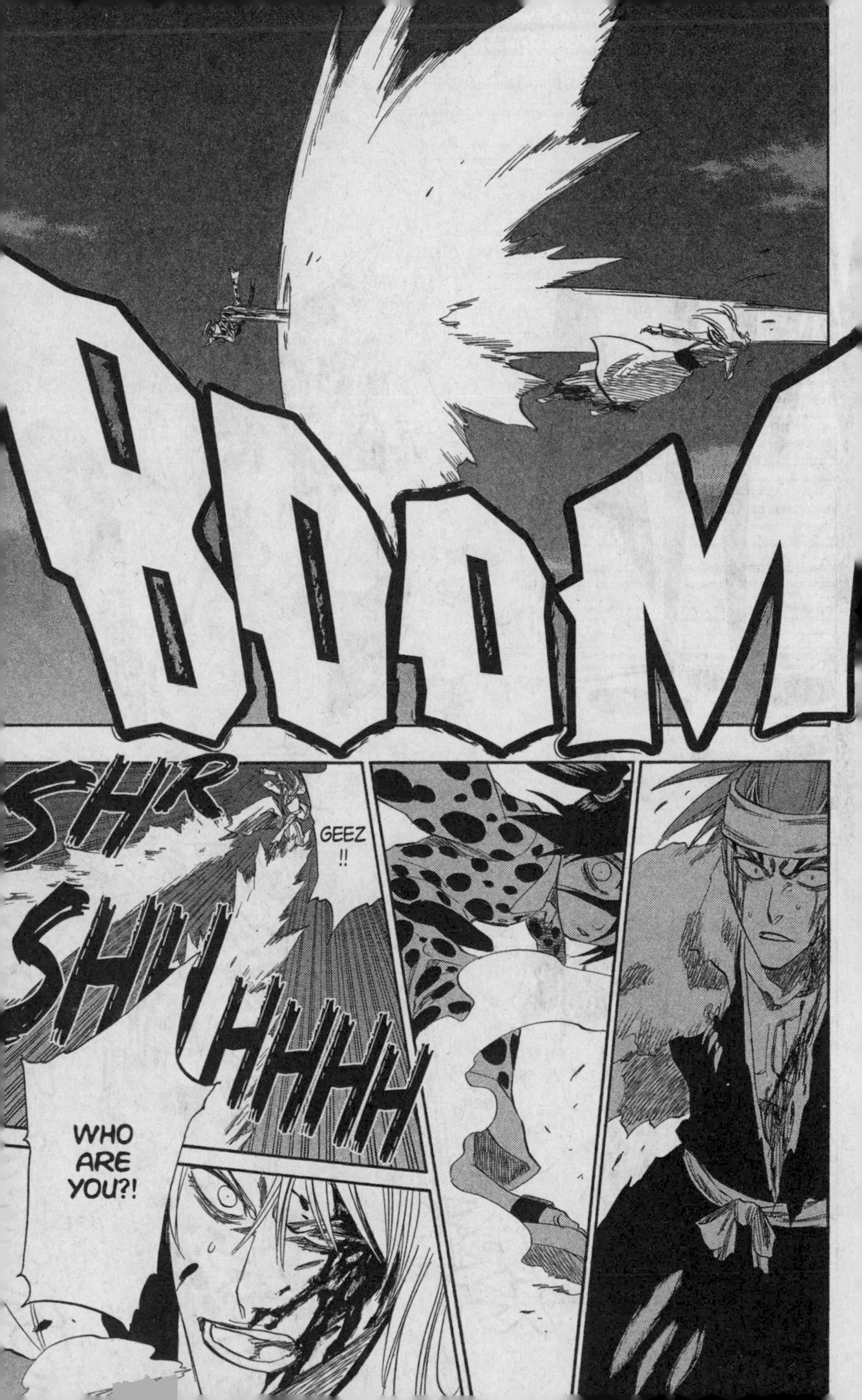
BOOM
GEEZ !!
SHR
SHHHHHH
WHO ARE YOU?!

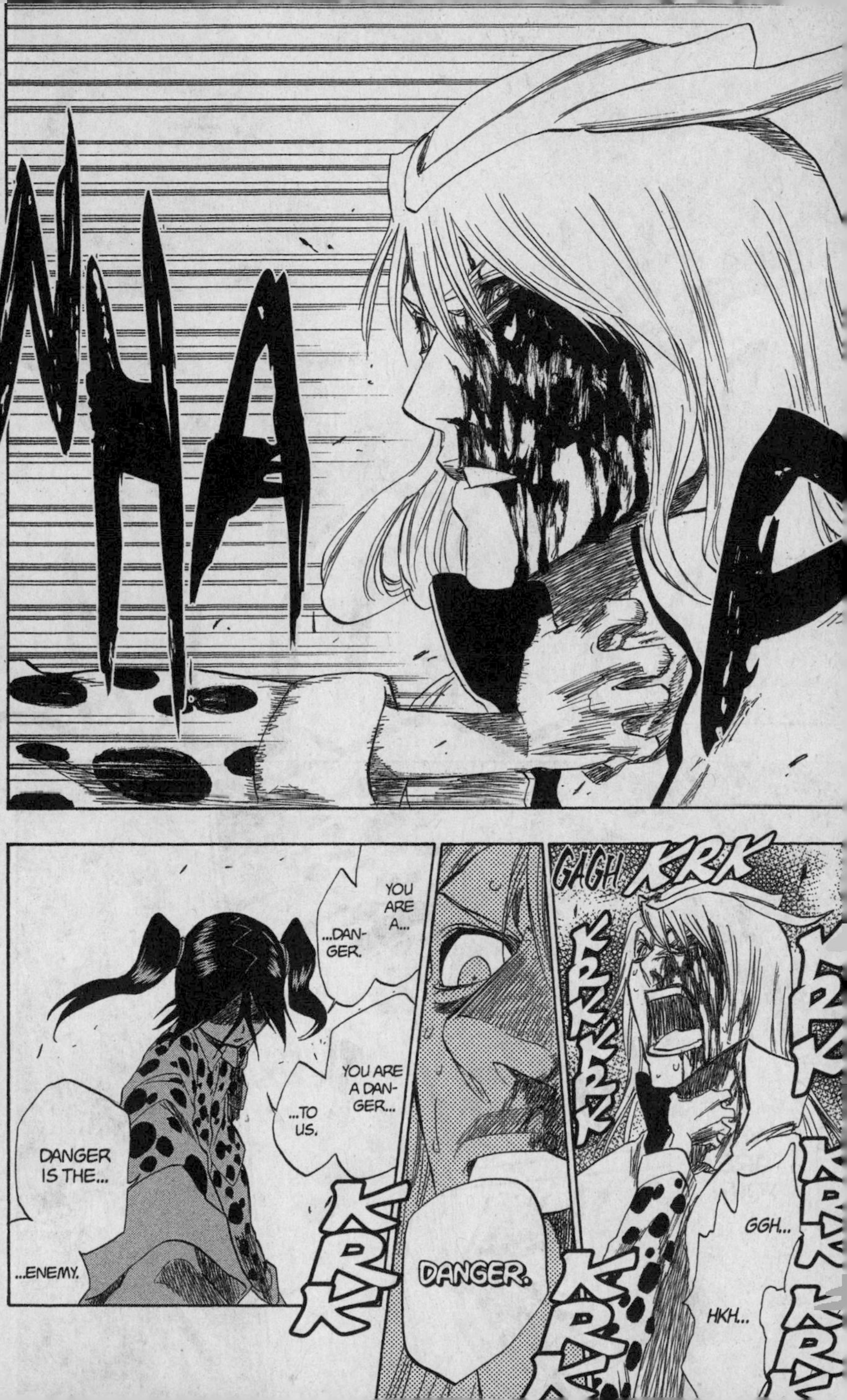
WHAP
GAGH KRK
KRKKRK
KRK
GGH...
HKH...
DANGER.
KRK
YOU ARE A...
...DAN-GER.
YOU ARE A DAN-GER...
...TO US.
DANGER IS THE...
...ENEMY.

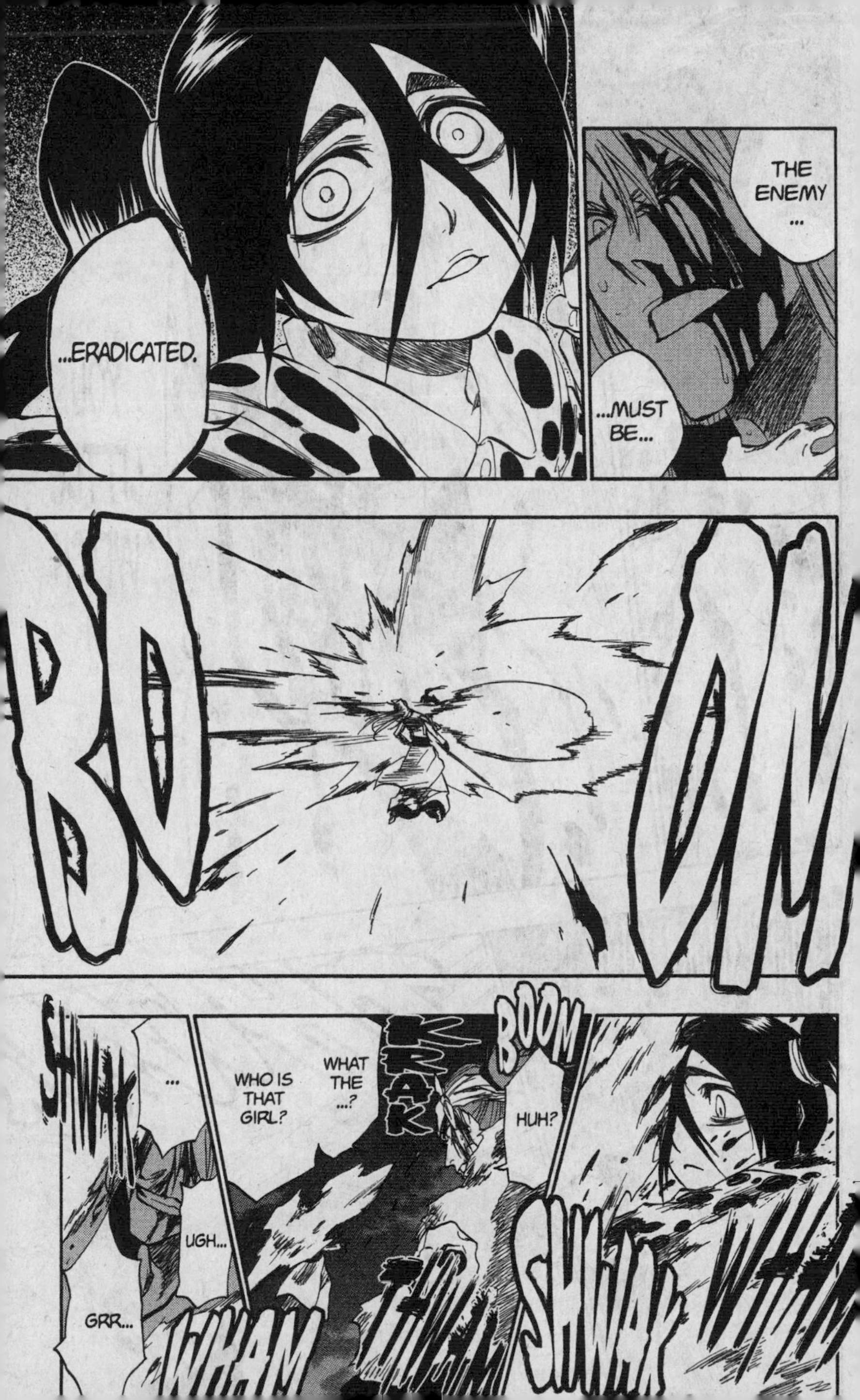
THE ENEMY ...
...MUST BE...
...ERADICATED.
BOOM
HUH?
SHWAK
BOOM
KRAK
WHAT THE ...?
WHO IS THAT GIRL?
UGH...
WHAM
SHWAK
...
GRR...

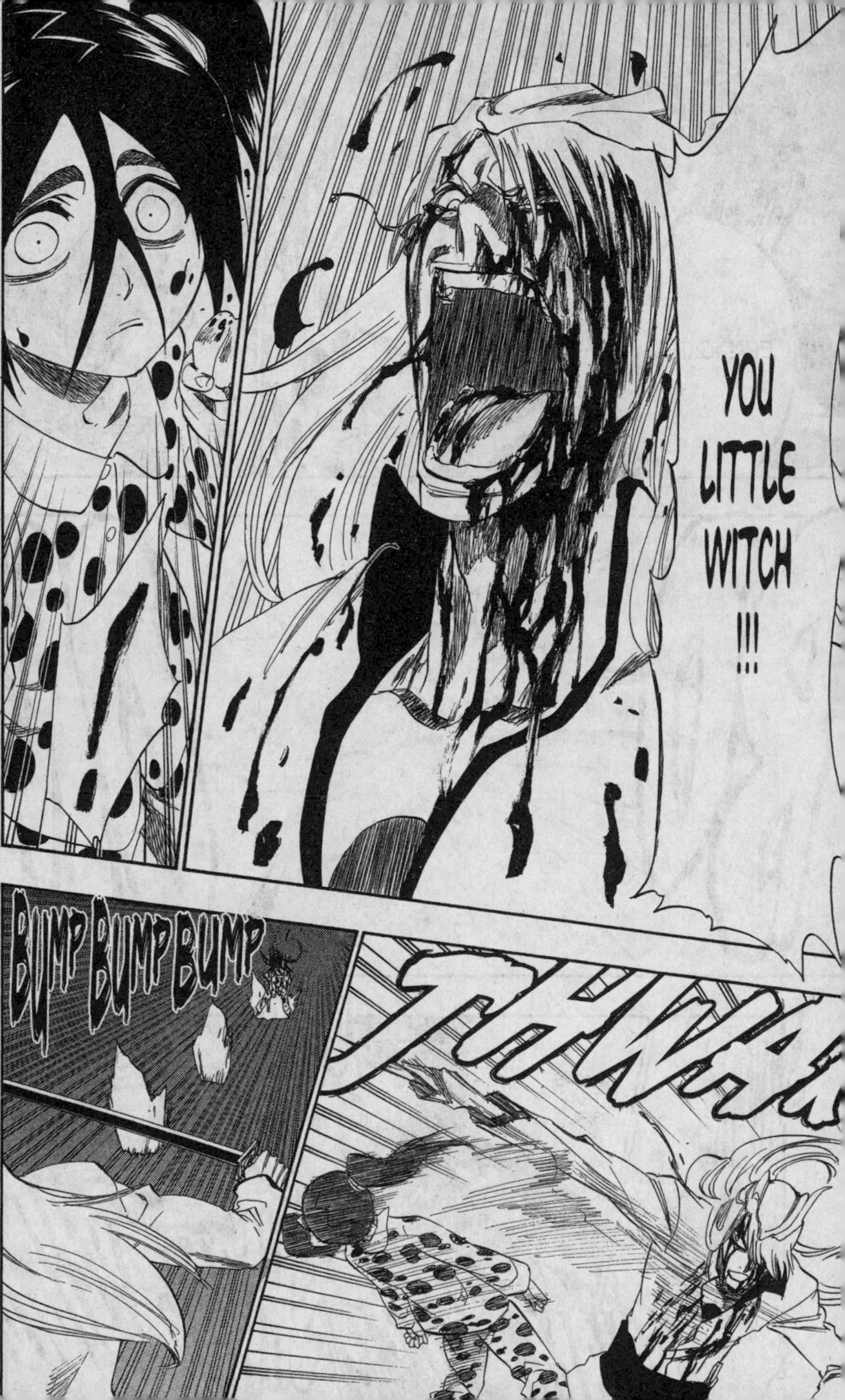
YOU LITTLE WITCH!!!
THWAK
BUMP BUMP BUMP

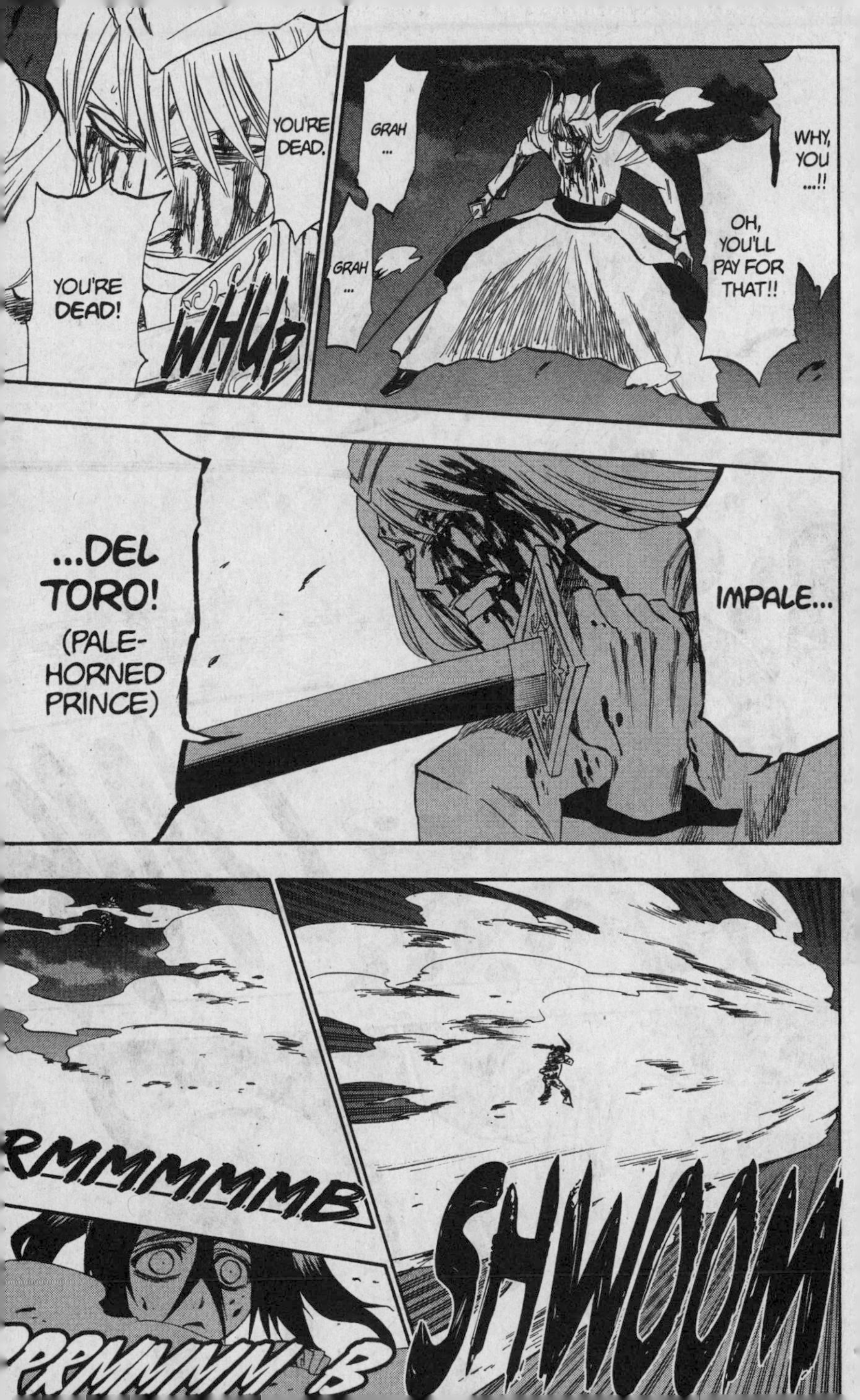
WHY, YOU ...!!
OH, YOU'LL PAY FOR THAT!!
GRAH ...
GRAH ...
YOU'RE DEAD.
YOU'RE DEAD!
WHUP
IMPALE...
...DEL TORO!
(PALE-HORNED PRINCE)
SHWOOM
RMMMMMMB

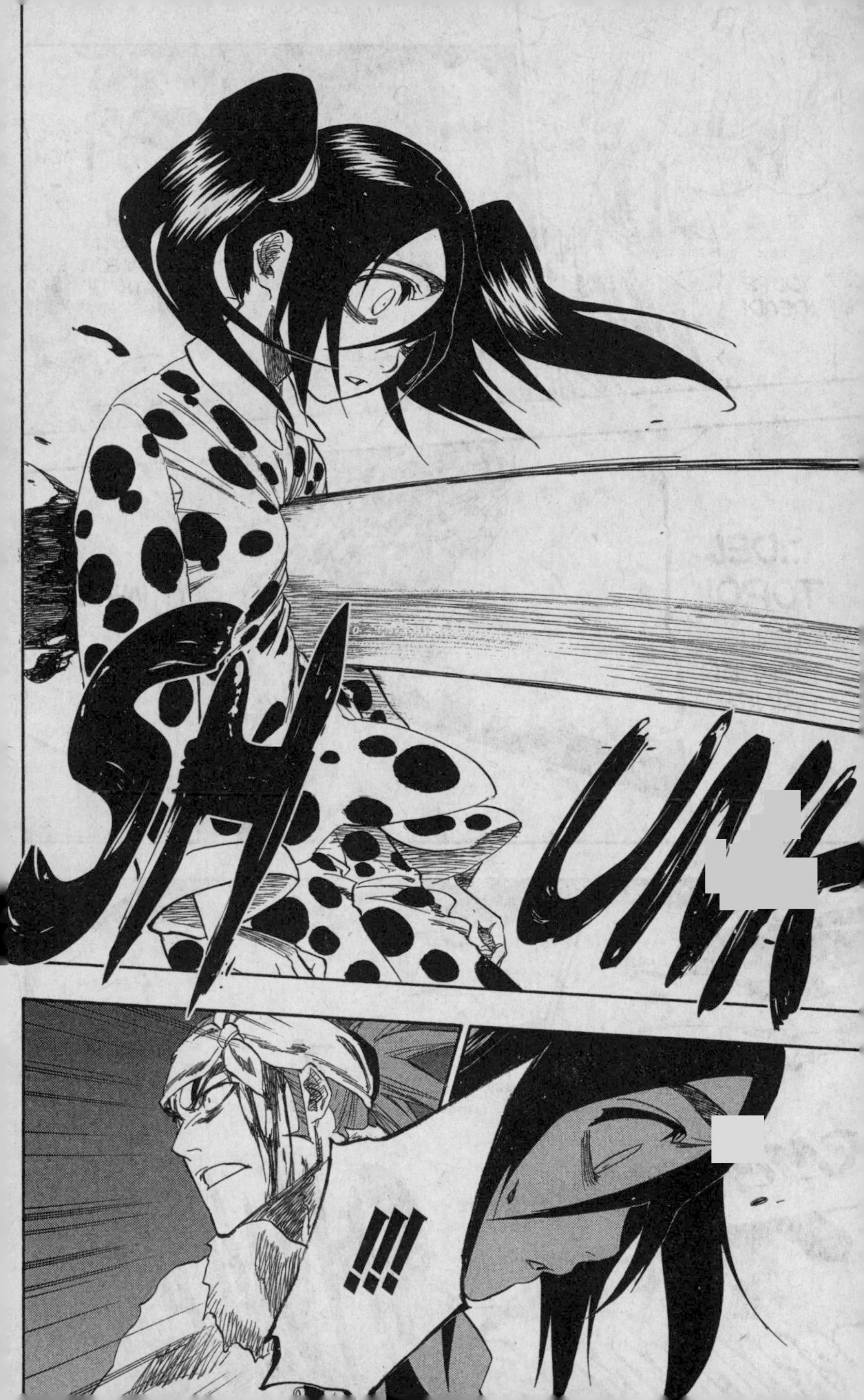
SHUN
!!!

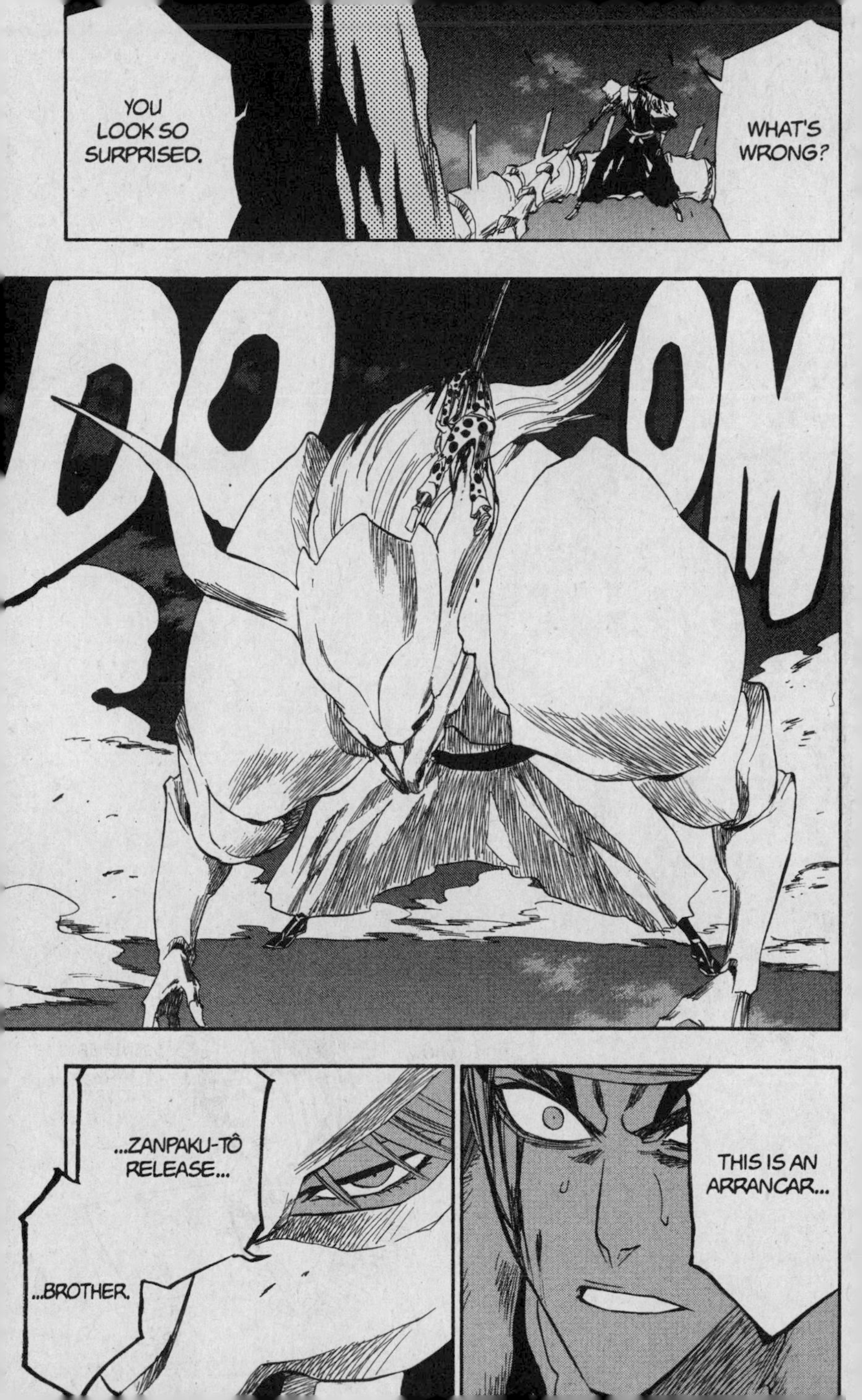
WHAT'S WRONG?
YOU LOOK SO SURPRISED.
DOOM
THIS IS AN ARRANCAR...
...ZANPAKU-TÔ RELEASE...
...BROTHER.

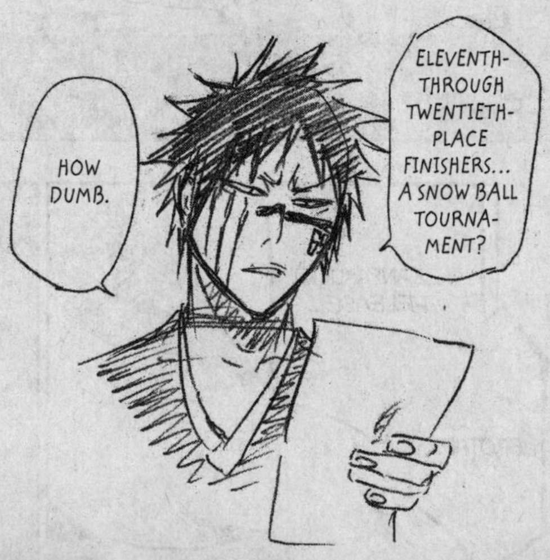
ELEVENTH-THROUGH TWENTIETH-PLACE FINISHERS... A SNOW BALL TOURNAMENT?
HOW DUMB.

208. The Scissors

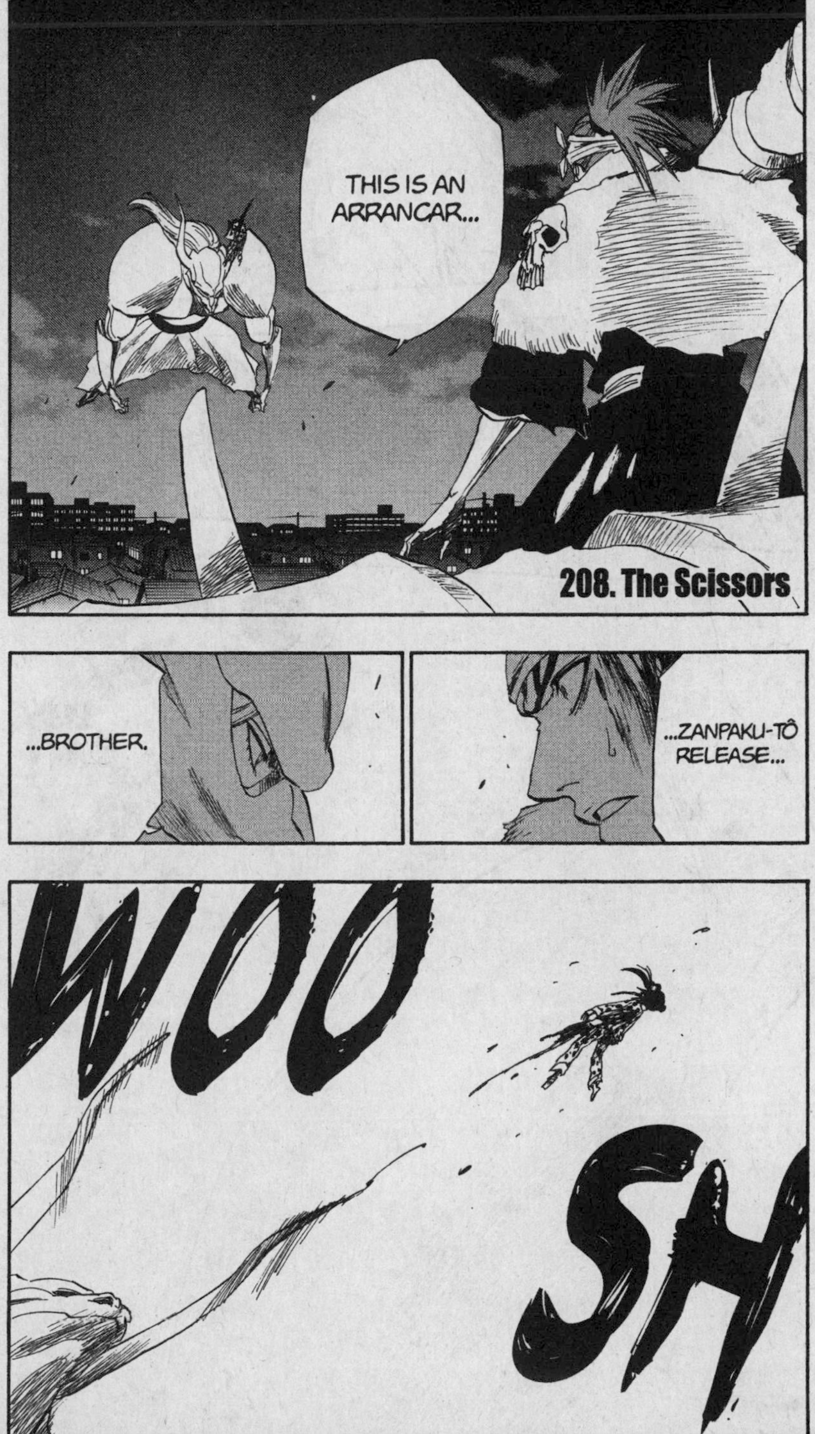
THIS IS AN ARRANCAR...
...ZANPAKU-TÔ RELEASE...
...BROTHER.
WOOSH

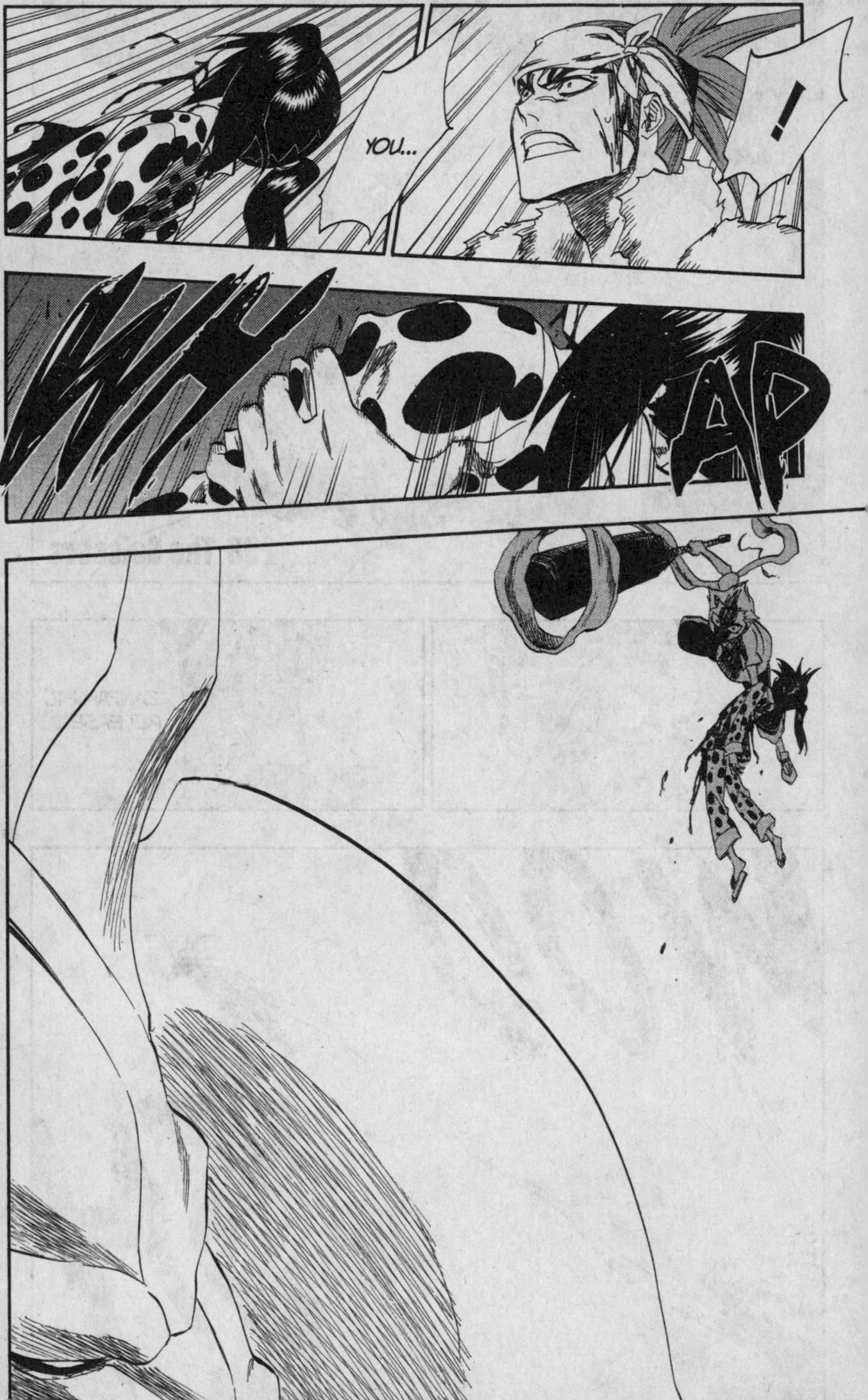
!
YOU...
WHAP

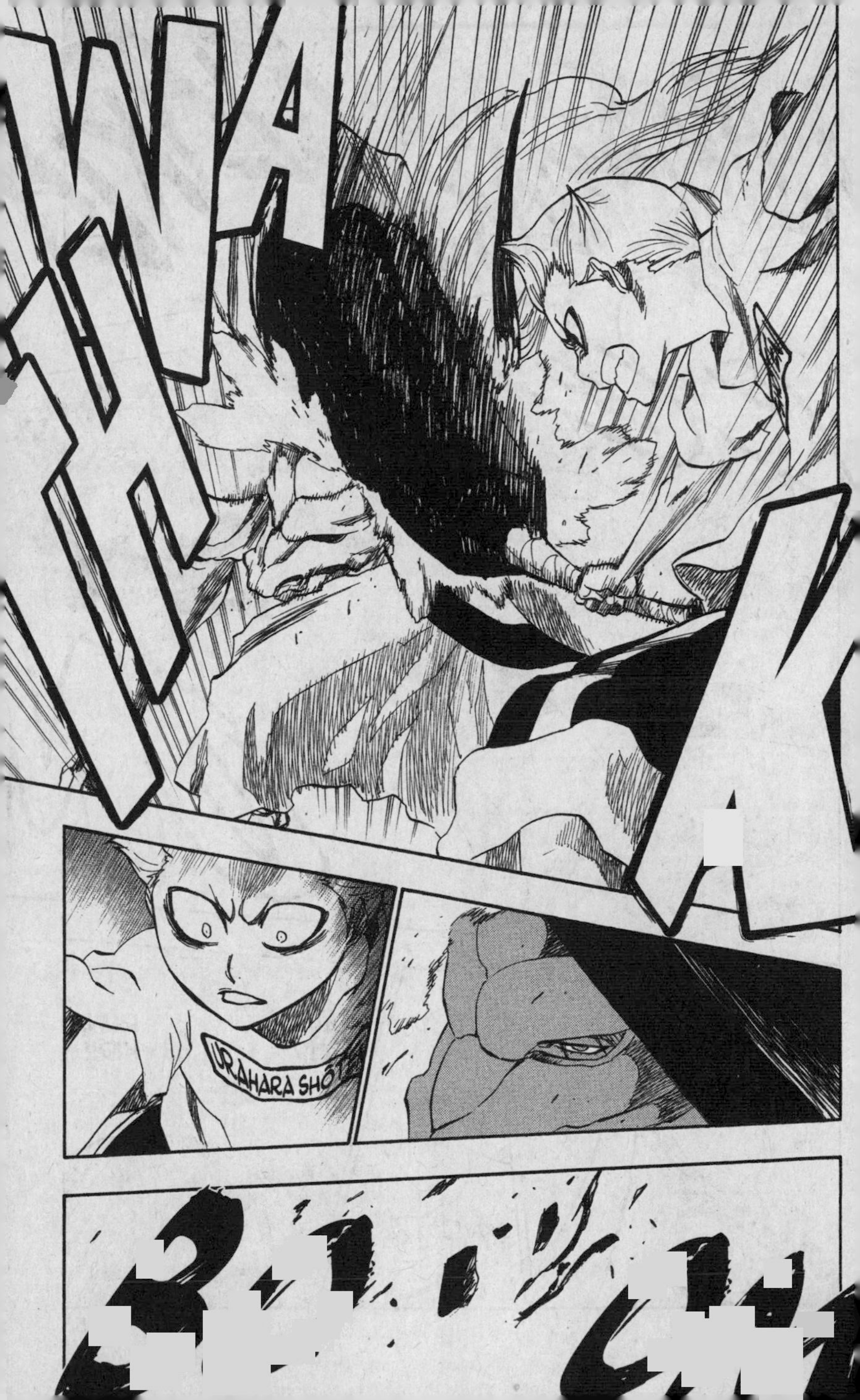
URAHARA SHŌT

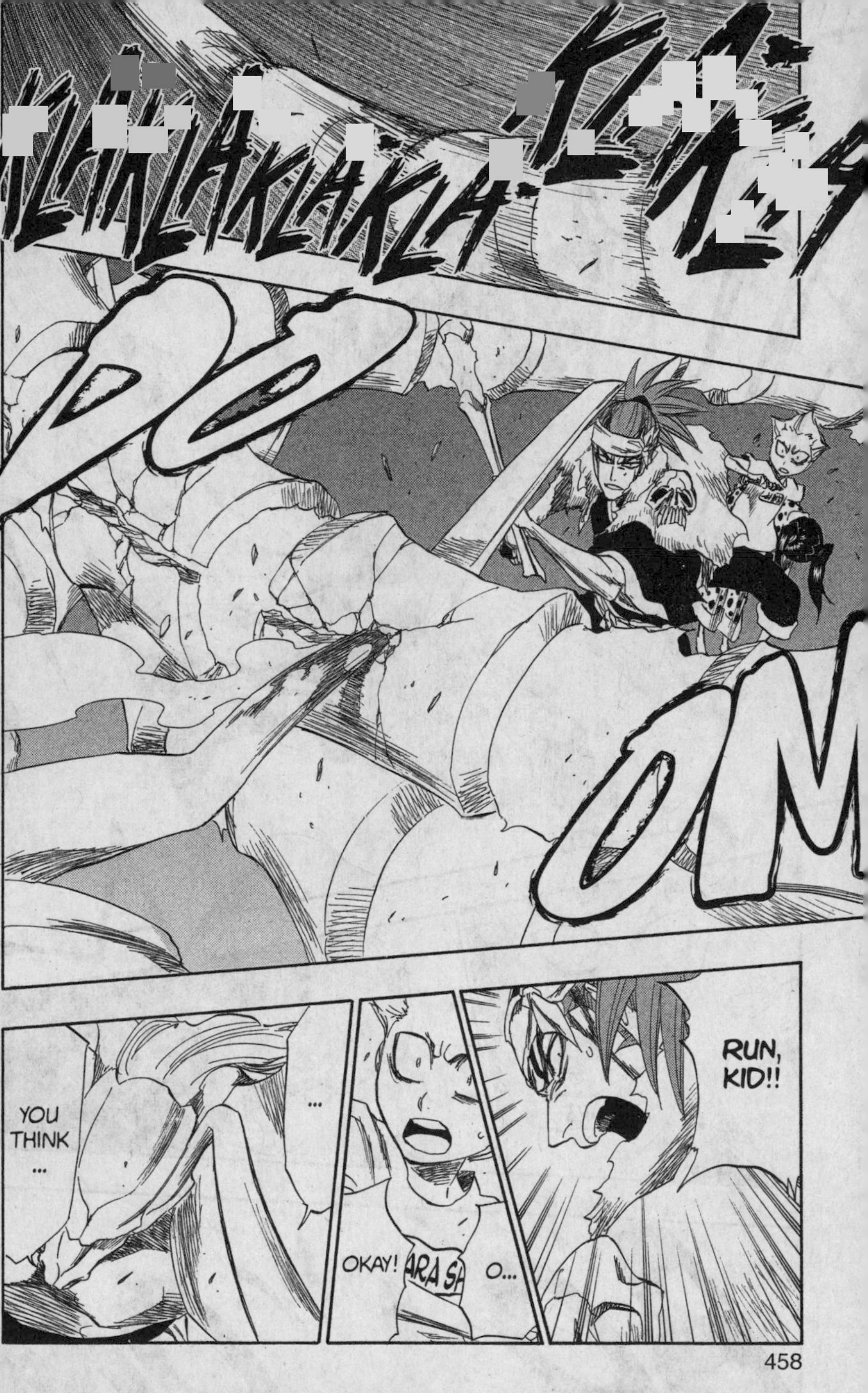
KLAKLAKLAKLA
DO
OM
RUN, KID!!
O...
OKAY!
...
YOU THINK ...

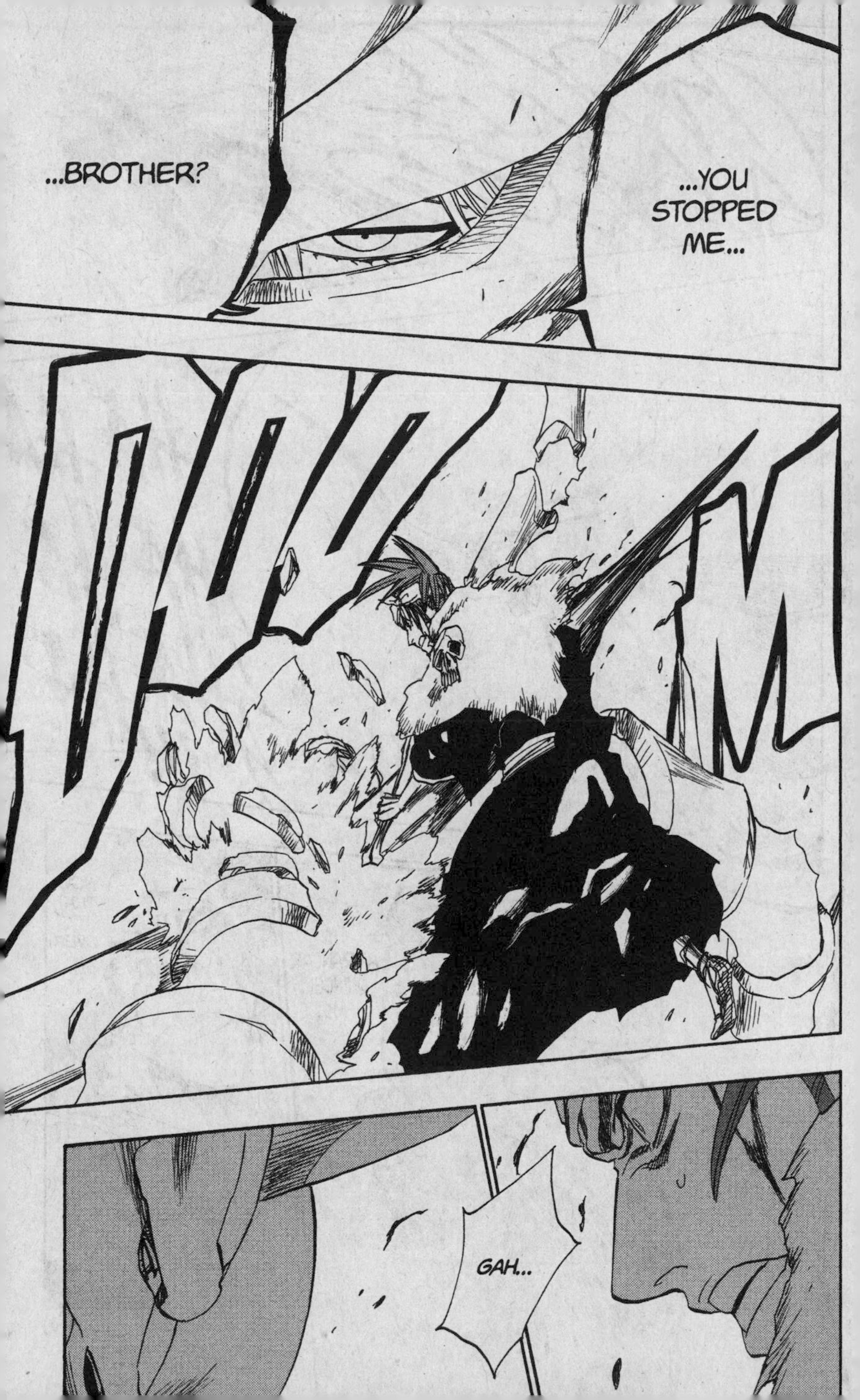
...YOU STOPPED ME...
...BROTHER?
GAH...

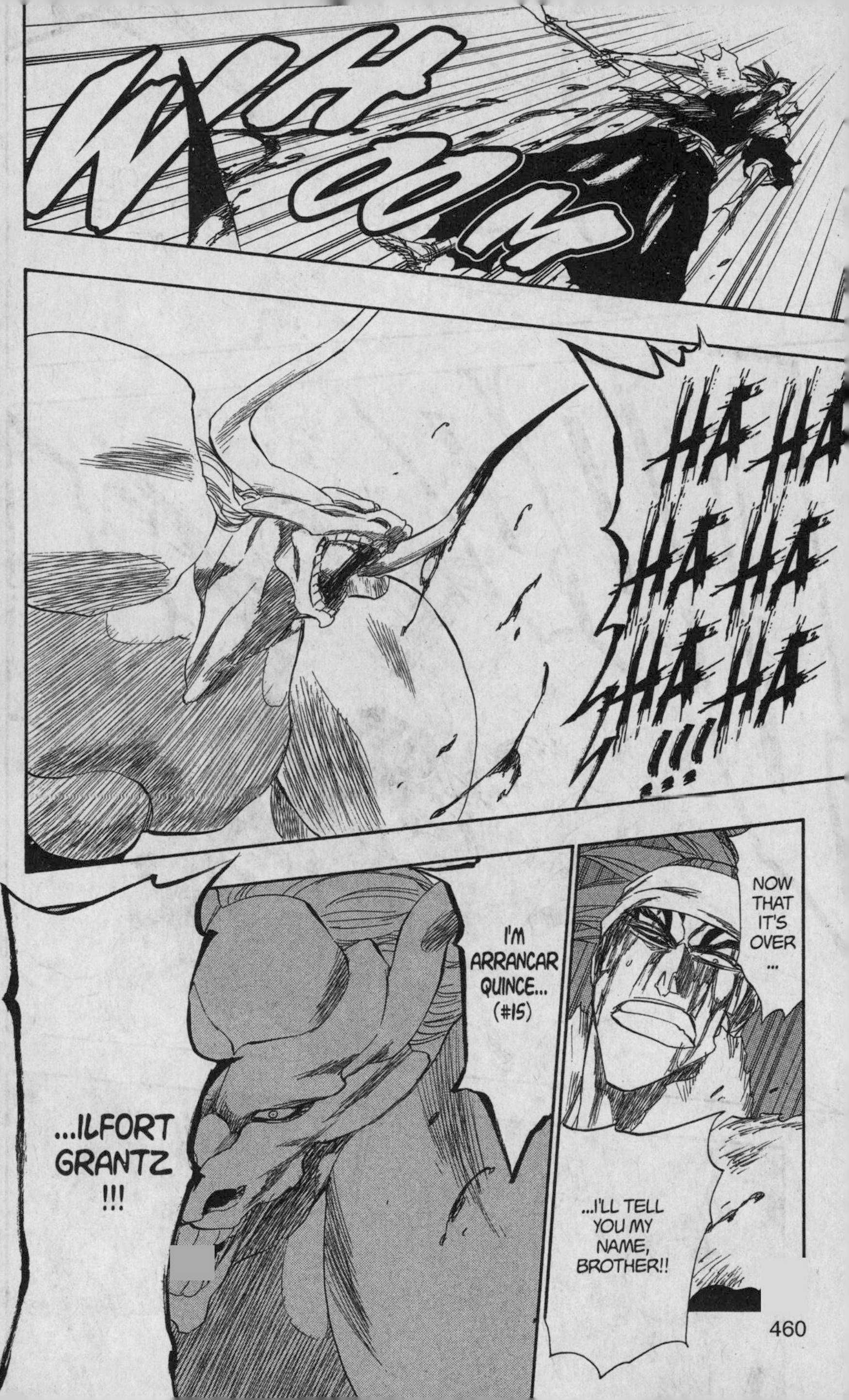
WHOOM
HA HA HA HA HA HA!!!
NOW THAT IT'S OVER...
...I'LL TELL YOU MY NAME, BROTHER!!
I'M ARRANCAR QUINCE... (#15)
...ILFORT GRANTZ!!!

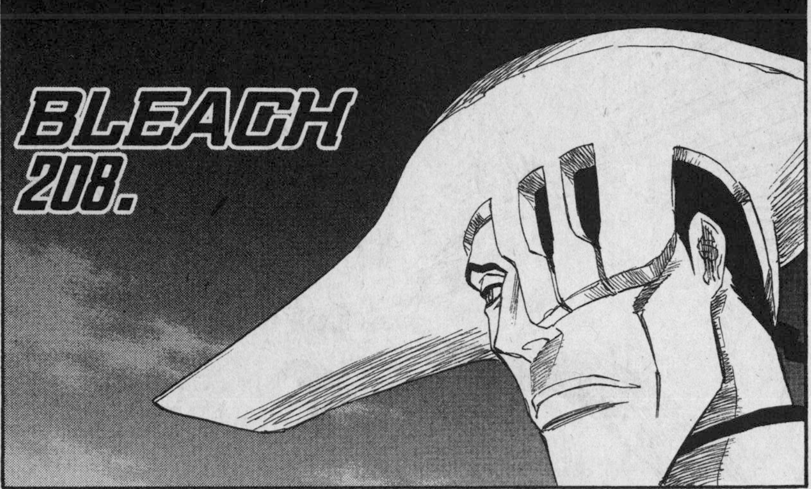
BLEACH
208.

The Scissors

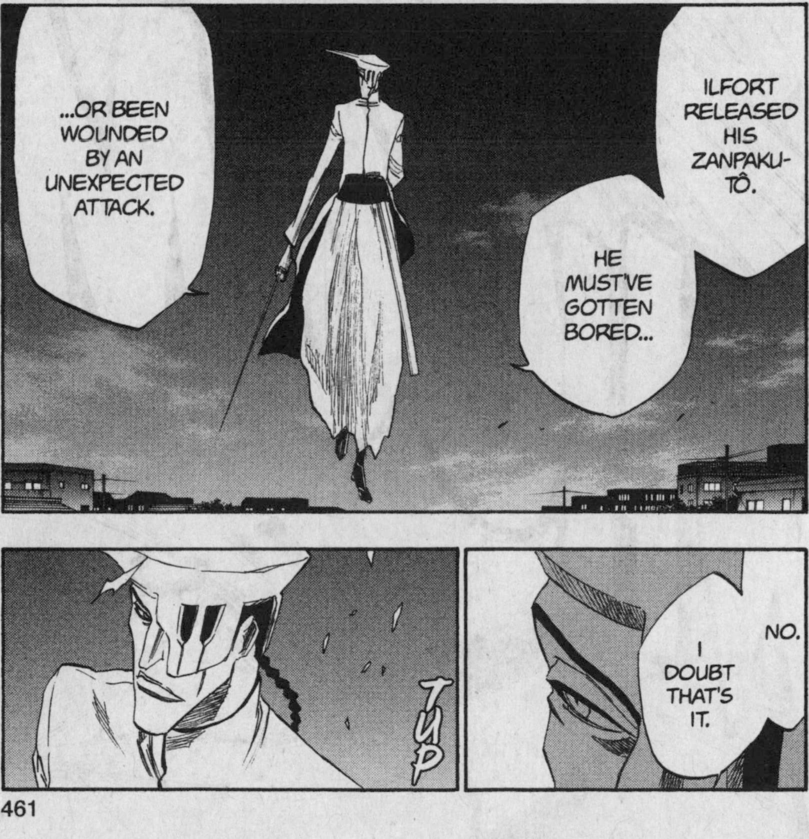
ILFORT RELEASED HIS ZANPAKU-TÔ.
HE MUST'VE GOTTEN BORED...
...OR BEEN WOUNDED BY AN UNEXPECTED ATTACK.
NO.
I DOUBT THAT'S IT.
TUP

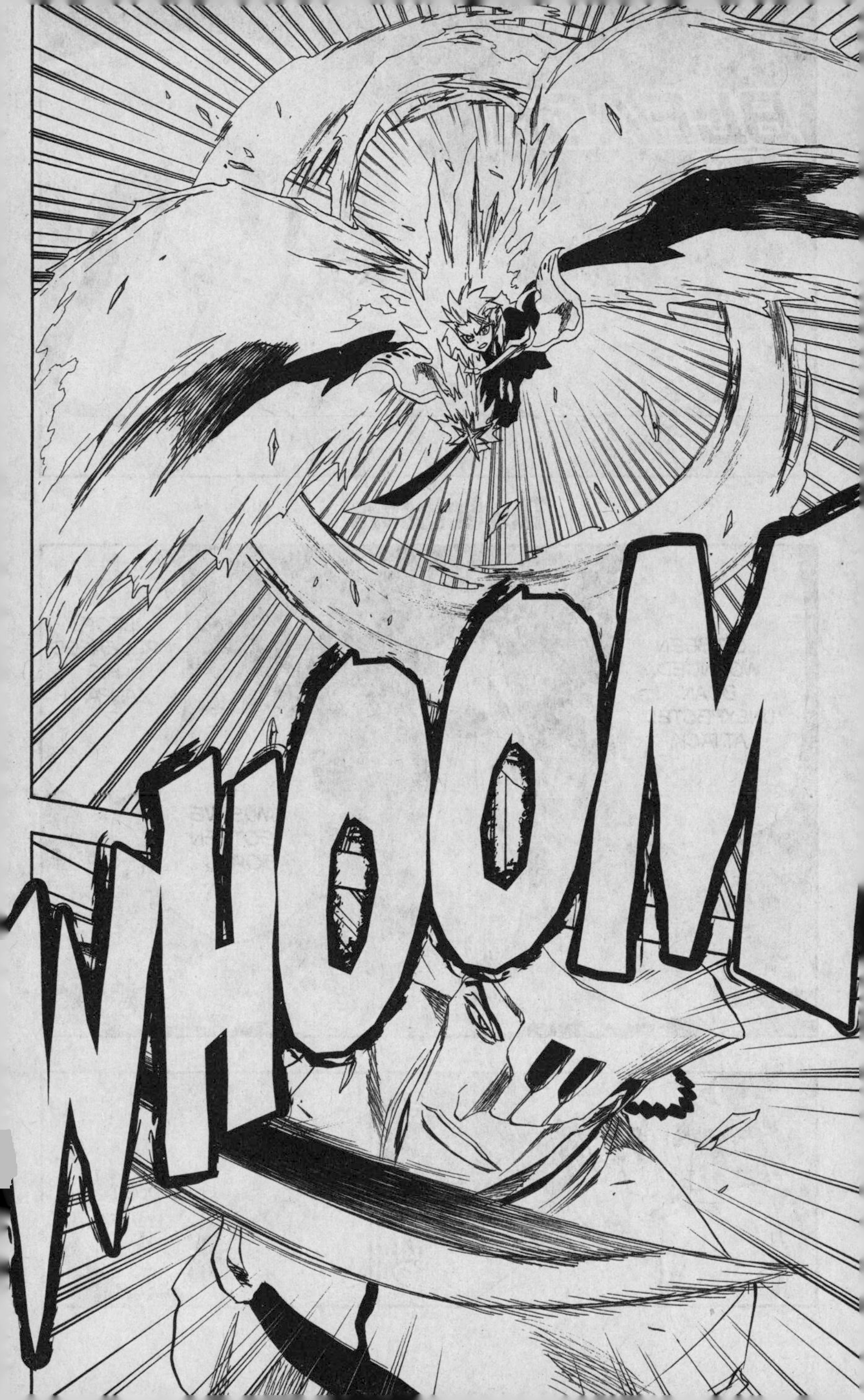
WHOOM!!

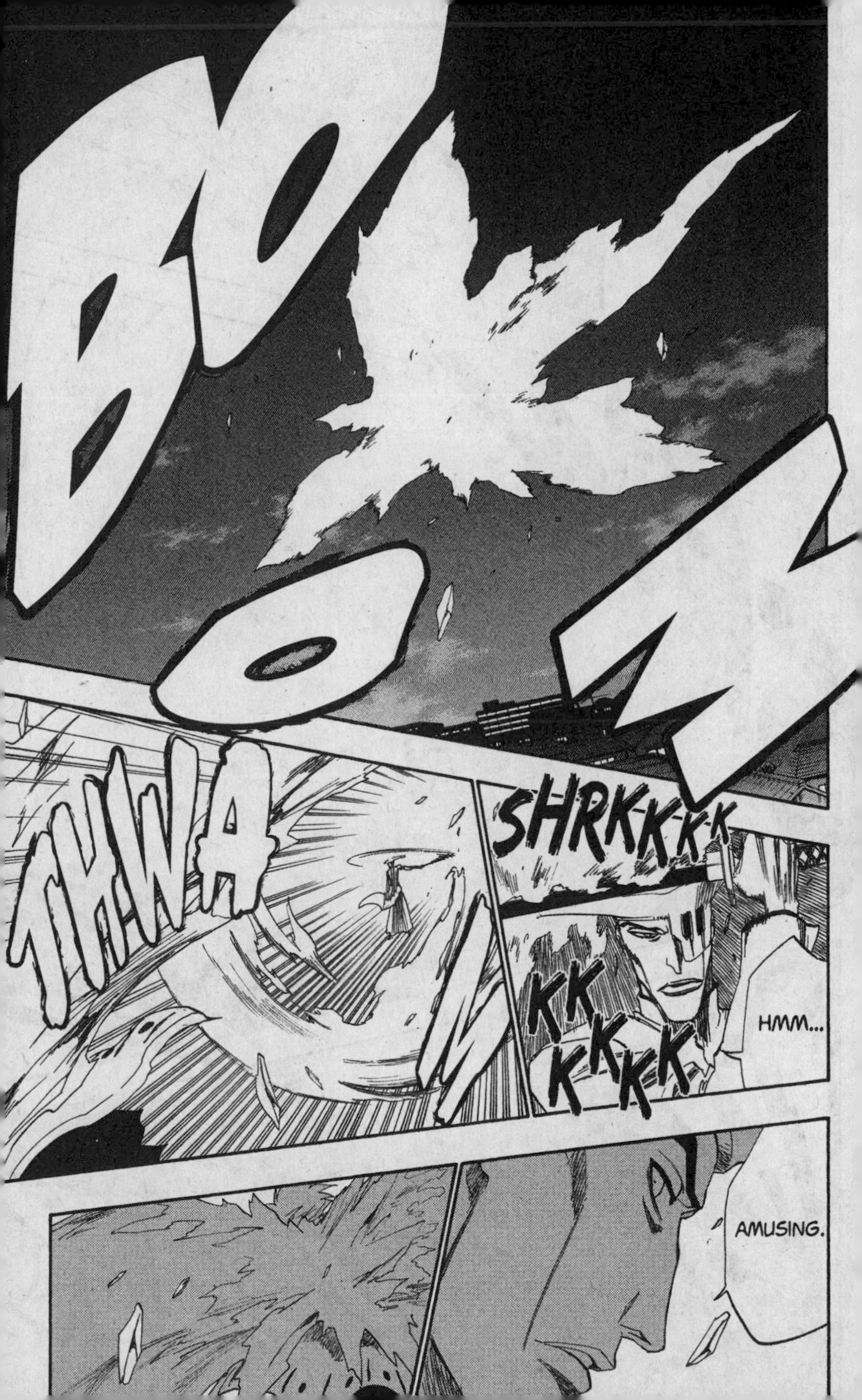
BOOM
SHRKKKK
KK
KKKK
HMM...
THWA
AMUSING.

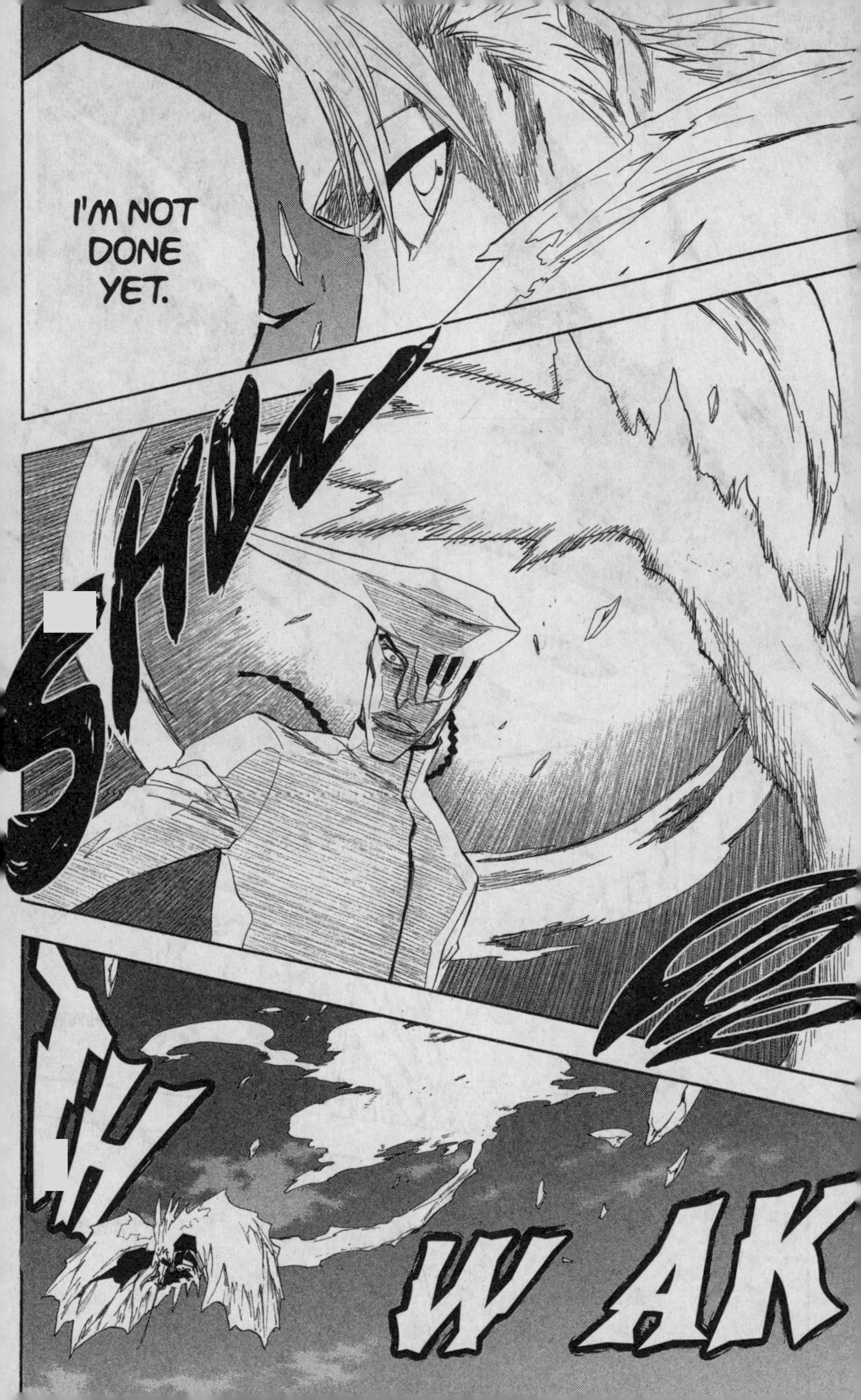
I'M NOT DONE YET.

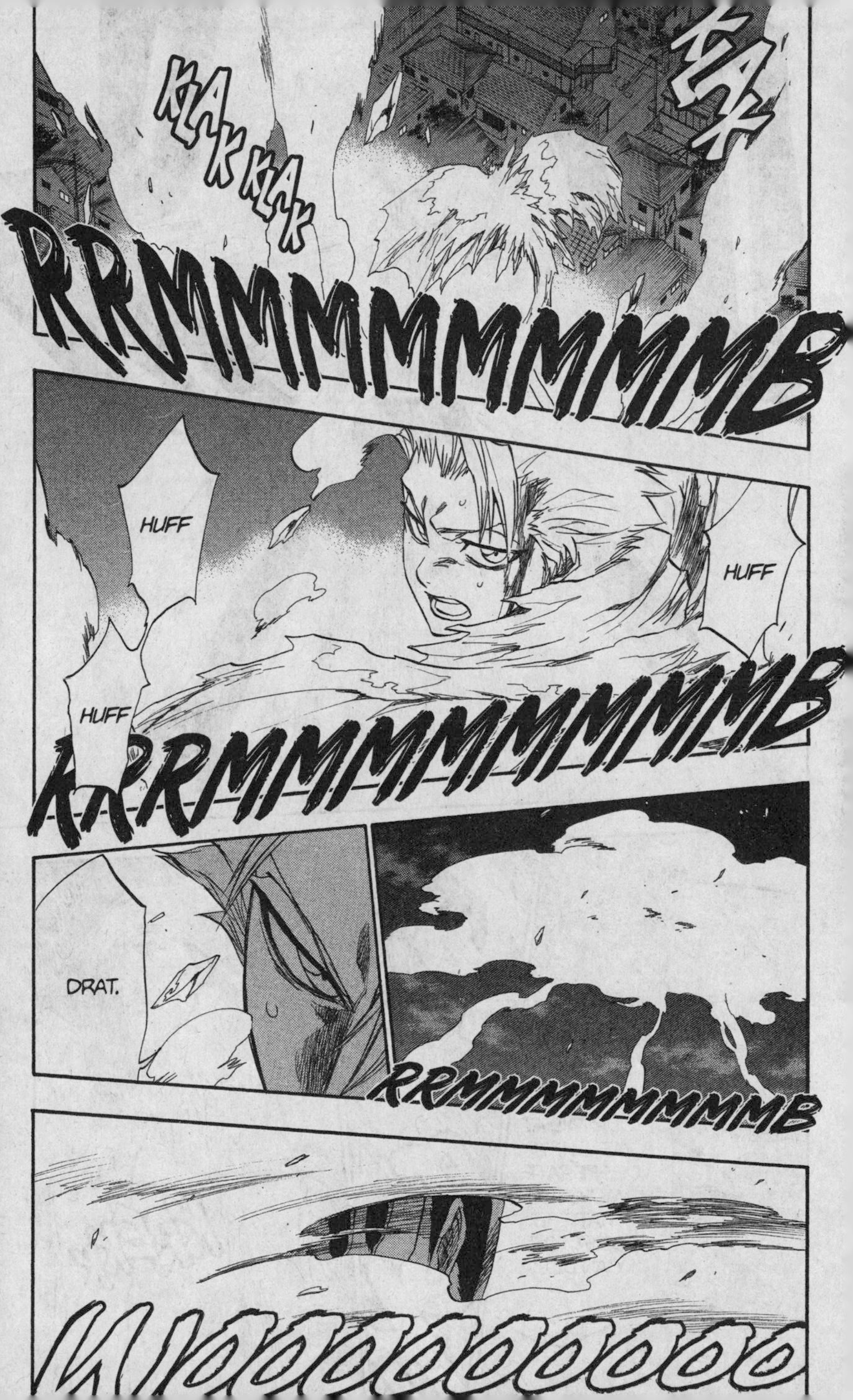
KLAK
KLAK KLAK
RRMMMMMMMMMMB
HUFF
HUFF
HUFF
RRRMMMMMMMMMB
RRMMMMMMMMMMB
DRAT.
WOOOOOOOOOOO

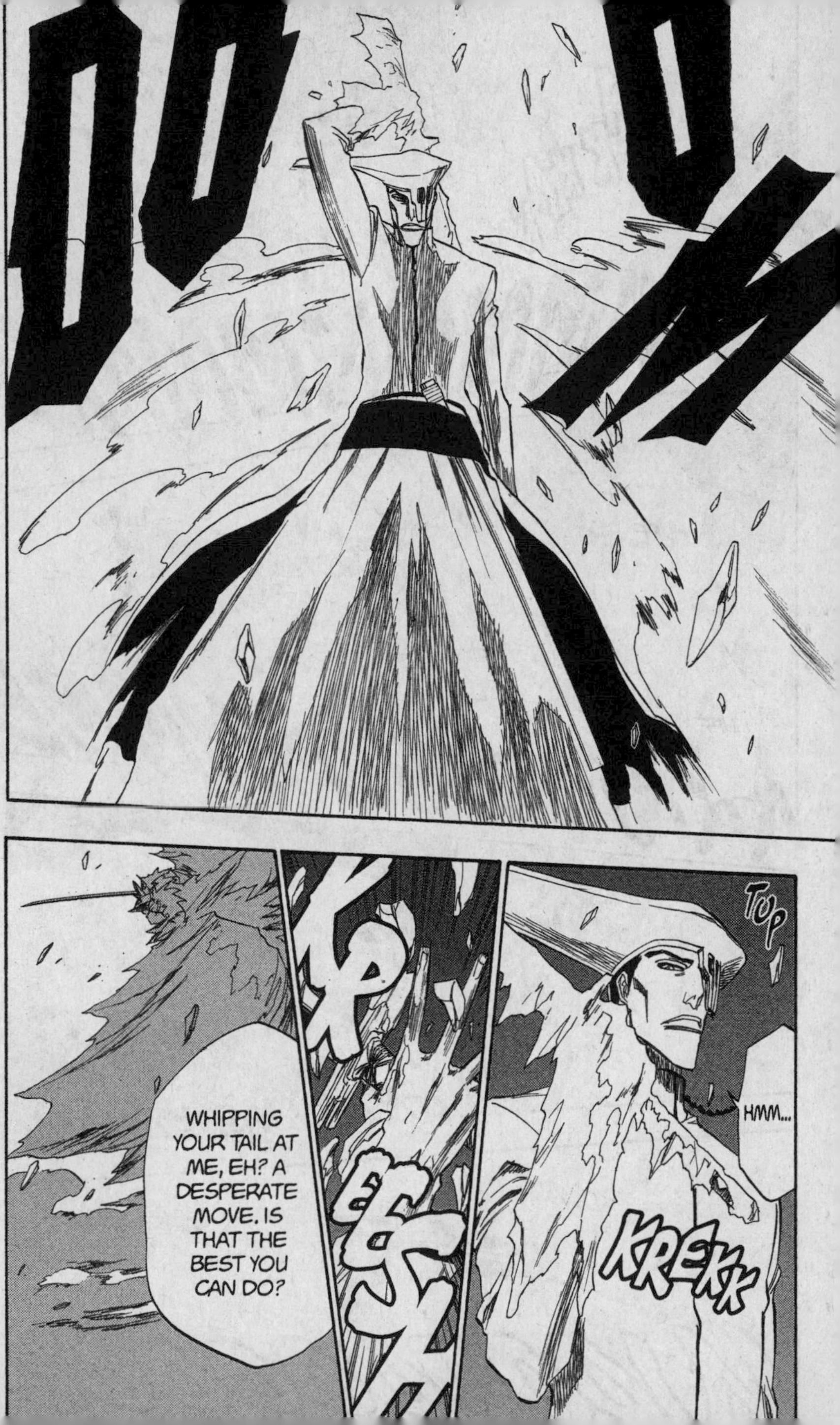
DOOM
TUP
HMM...
KREKK
WHIPPING YOUR TAIL AT ME, EH? A DESPERATE MOVE. IS THAT THE BEST YOU CAN DO?

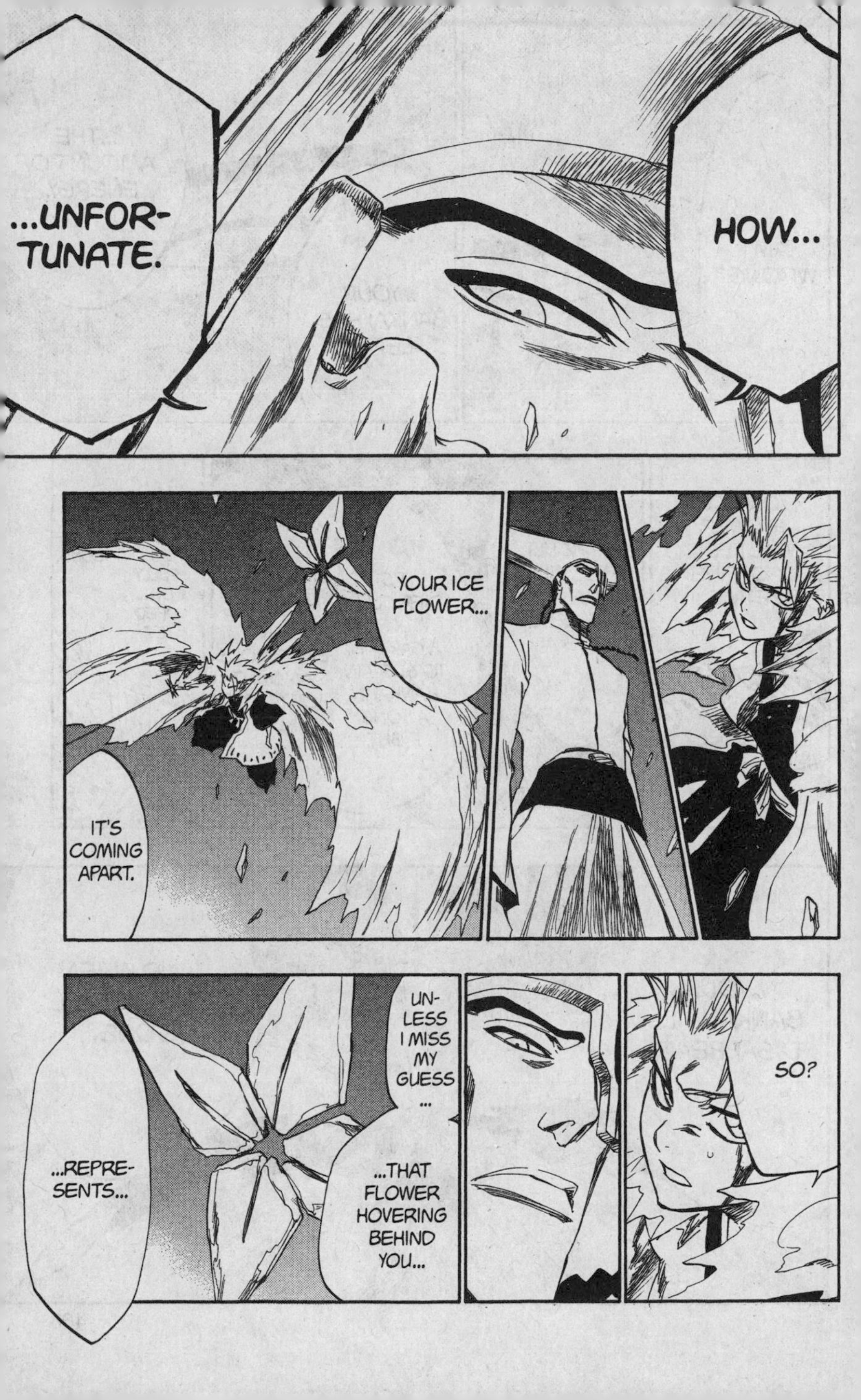
HOW...
...UNFOR-TUNATE.
YOUR ICE FLOWER...
IT'S COMING APART.
SO?
UN-LESS I MISS MY GUESS...
...THAT FLOWER HOVERING BEHIND YOU...
...REPRE-SENTS...

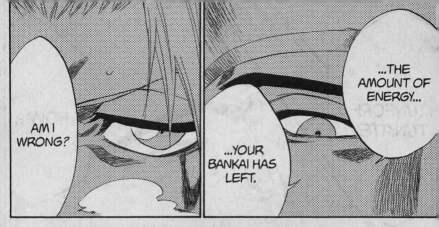

...THE AMOUNT OF ENERGY...
...YOUR BANKAI HAS LEFT.
AM I WRONG?
YOU'RE YOUNG.
YOUR BANKAI PROBABLY ISN'T FULLY DEVEL-OPED YET.
BANKAI REQUIRES AN ENORMOUS AMOUNT OF SPIRIT ENERGY.
IT'S DIFFICULT EVEN FOR A CAPTAIN TO SUSTAIN BANKAI IN A LONG FIGHT.
MORE DIFFICULT STILL WITH AN IMPERFECT BANKAI.
YOUR ICE FLOWER WILL KEEP DROPPING PETALS.
AND WHEN THEY'RE ALL GONE...
...YOUR BANKAI WILL DISAPPEAR.

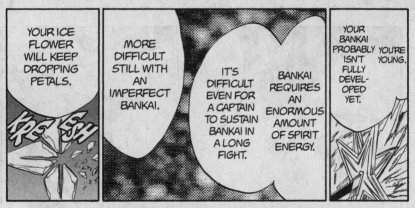

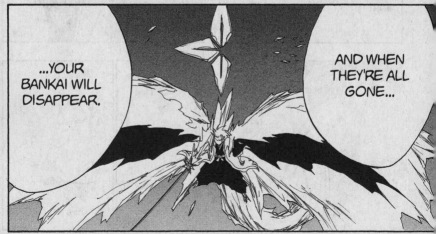

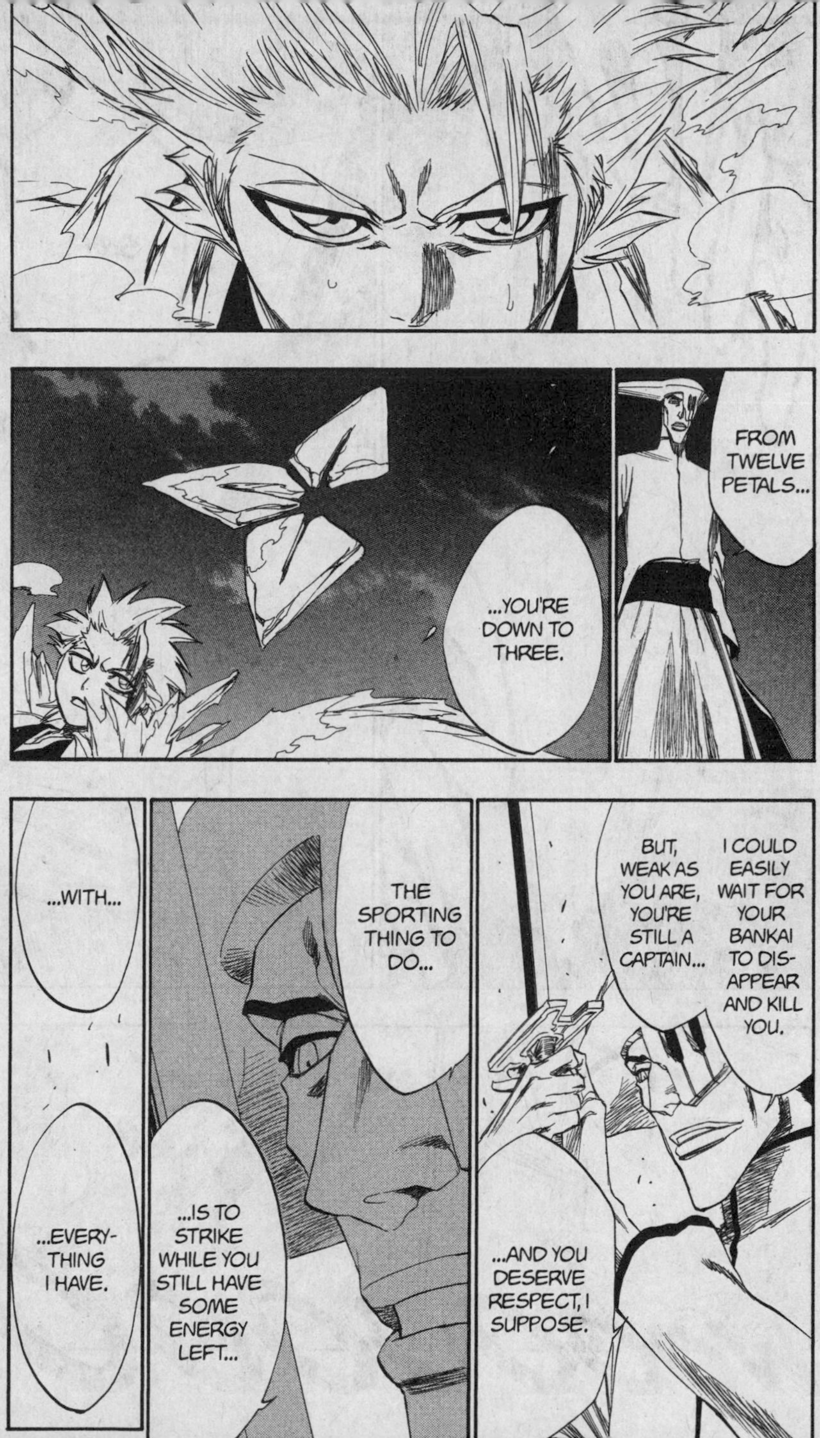
FROM TWELVE PETALS...
...YOU'RE DOWN TO THREE.
I COULD EASILY WAIT FOR YOUR BANKAI TO DIS-APPEAR AND KILL YOU.
BUT, WEAK AS YOU ARE, YOU'RE STILL A CAPTAIN...
...AND YOU DESERVE RESPECT, I SUPPOSE.
THE SPORTING THING TO DO...
...IS TO STRIKE WHILE YOU STILL HAVE SOME ENERGY LEFT...
...WITH...
...EVERY-THING I HAVE.

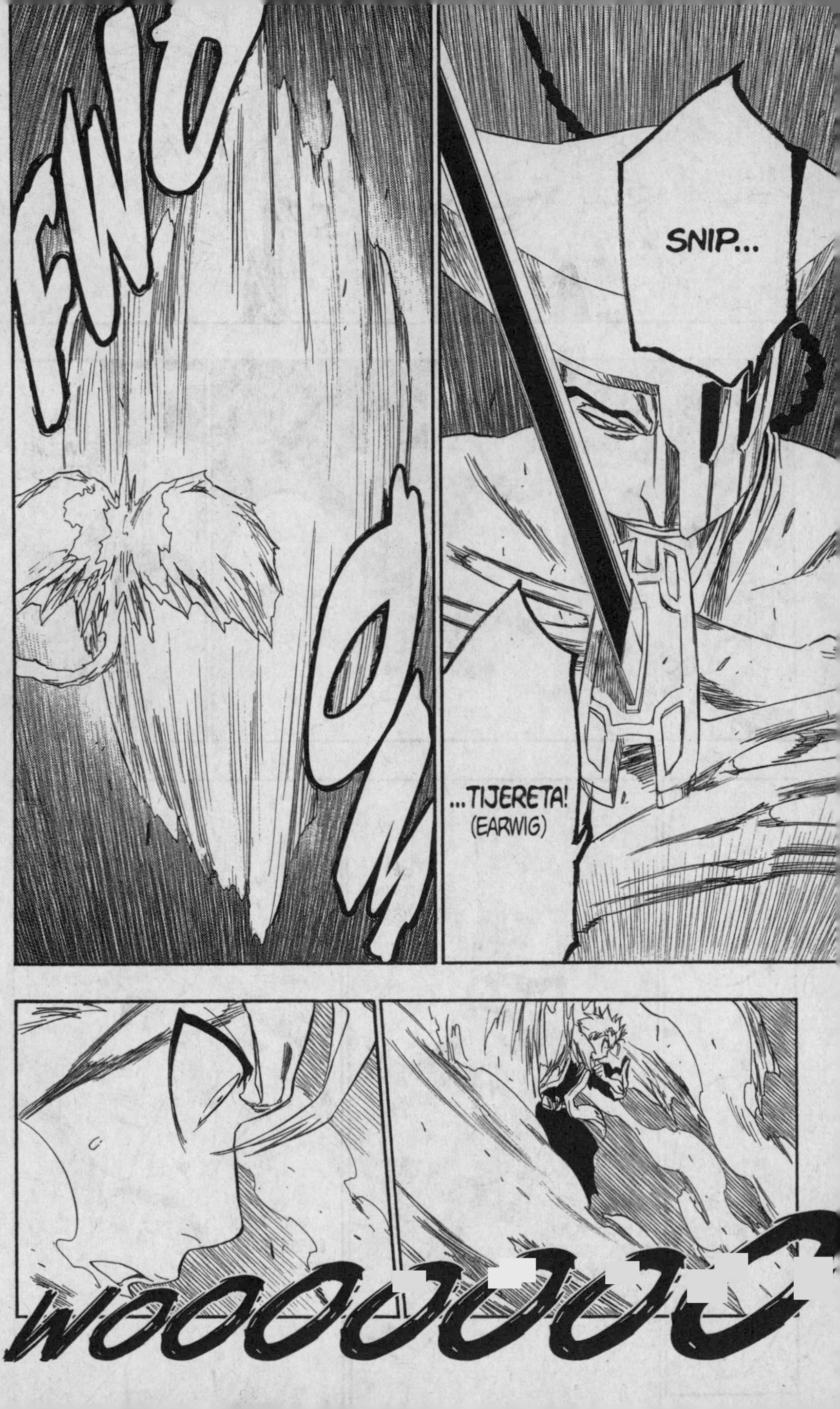
SNIP...
...TIJERETA!
(EARWIG)

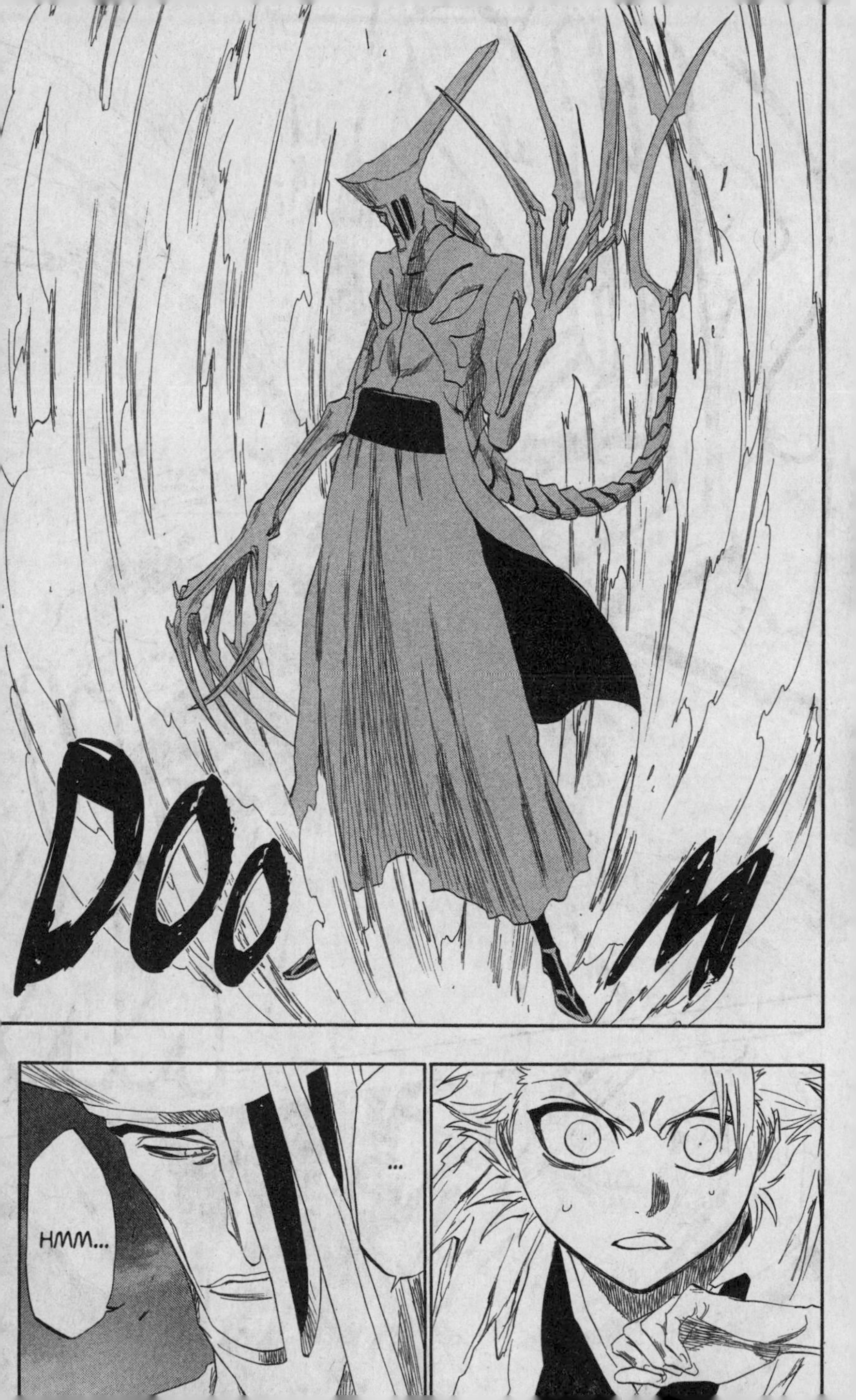
DOOOM
...
HMM...

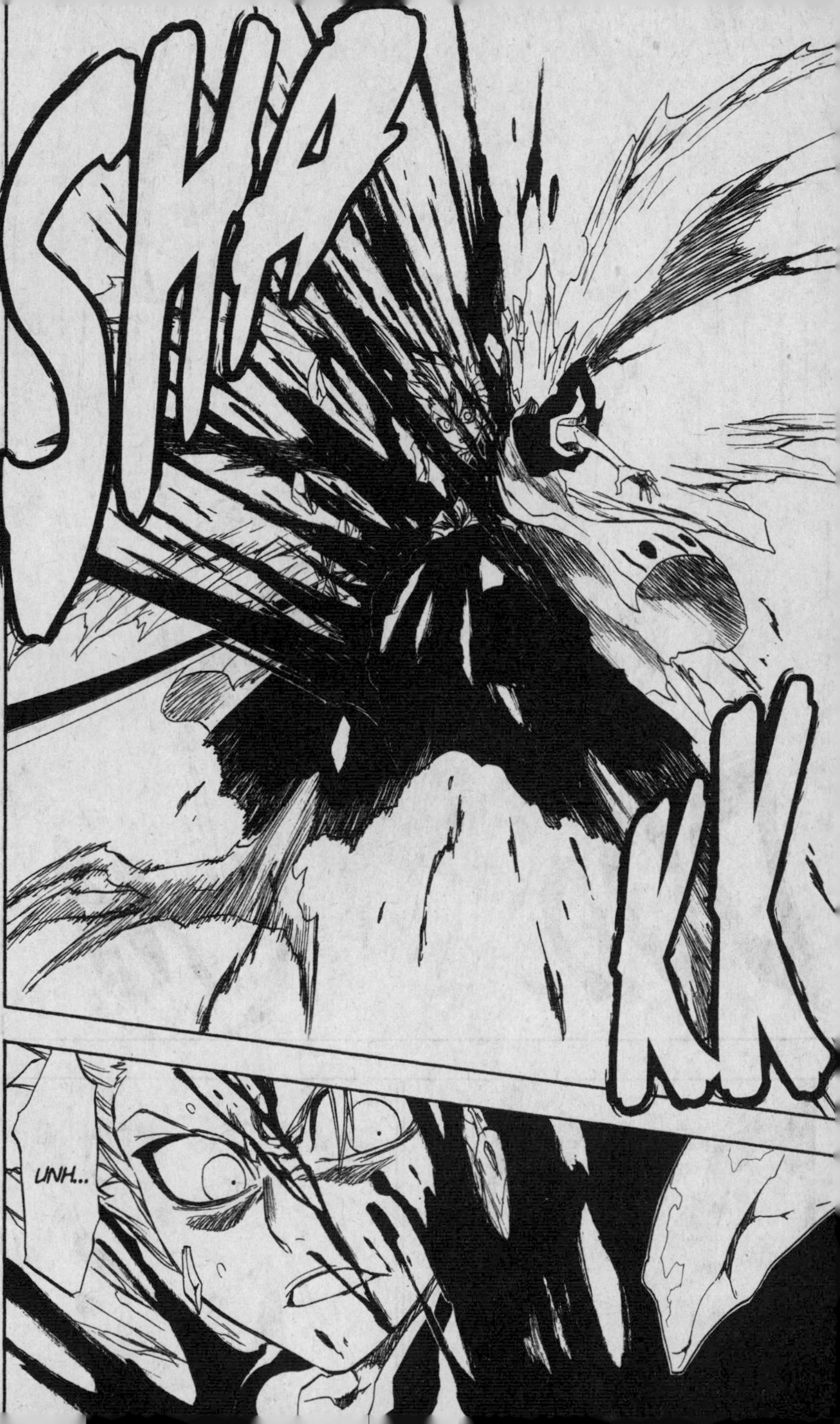
SHA
KK
UNH...

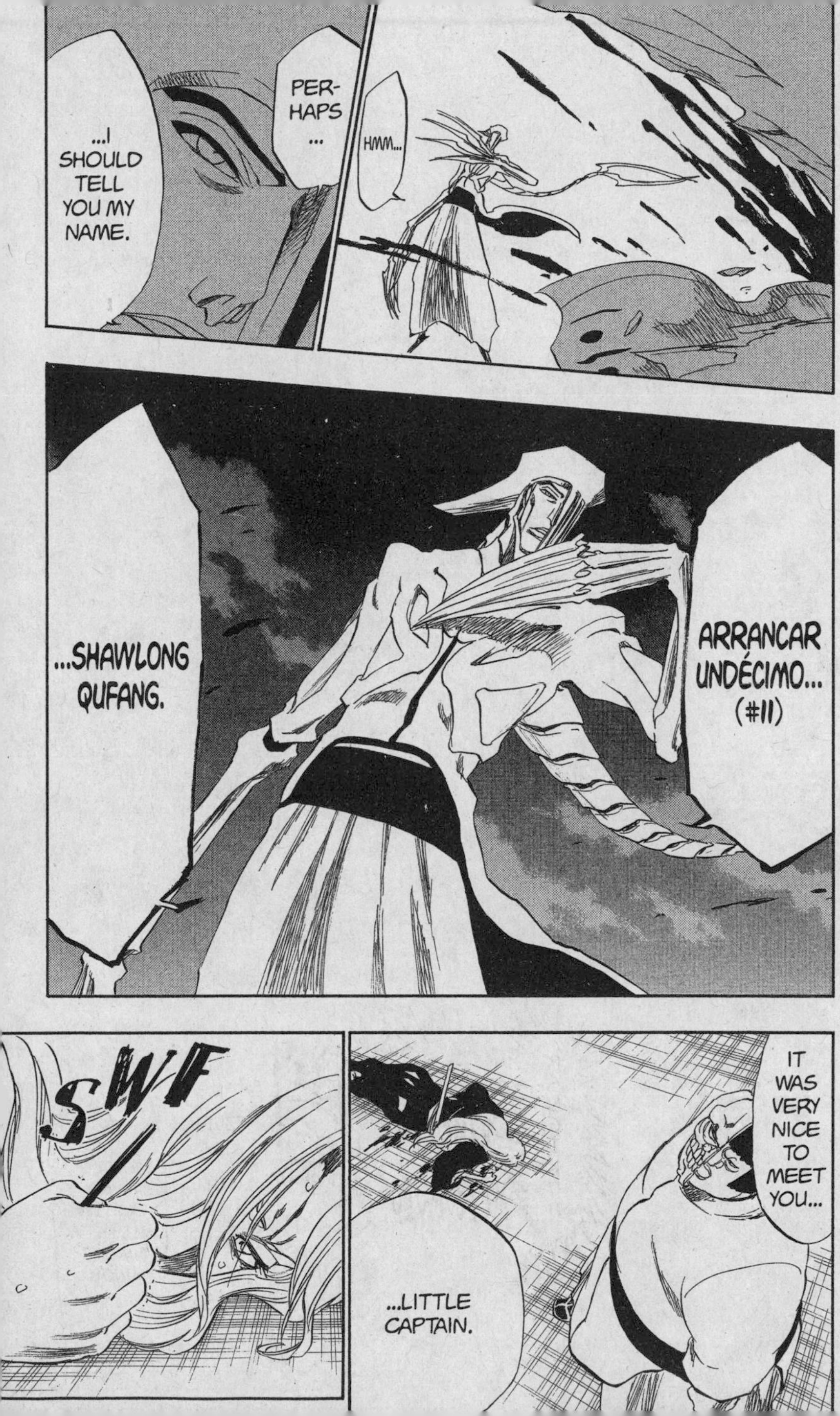
HMM...
PER-HAPS...
...I SHOULD TELL YOU MY NAME.
ARRANCAR UNDÉCIMO... (#11)
...SHAWLONG QUFANG.
IT WAS VERY NICE TO MEET YOU...
...LITTLE CAPTAIN.
SWF

HMM...
NOT A VERY EXCITING LIST. JUST A BUNCH OF MINOR...
IZURU KIRA
URYÛ ISHIDA
MOMO HINAMORI
SOI FON
WHAT?
R...
RANGIKU MATSUMOTO
RANGIKU!!

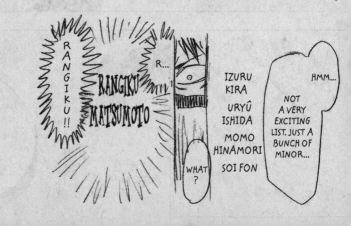

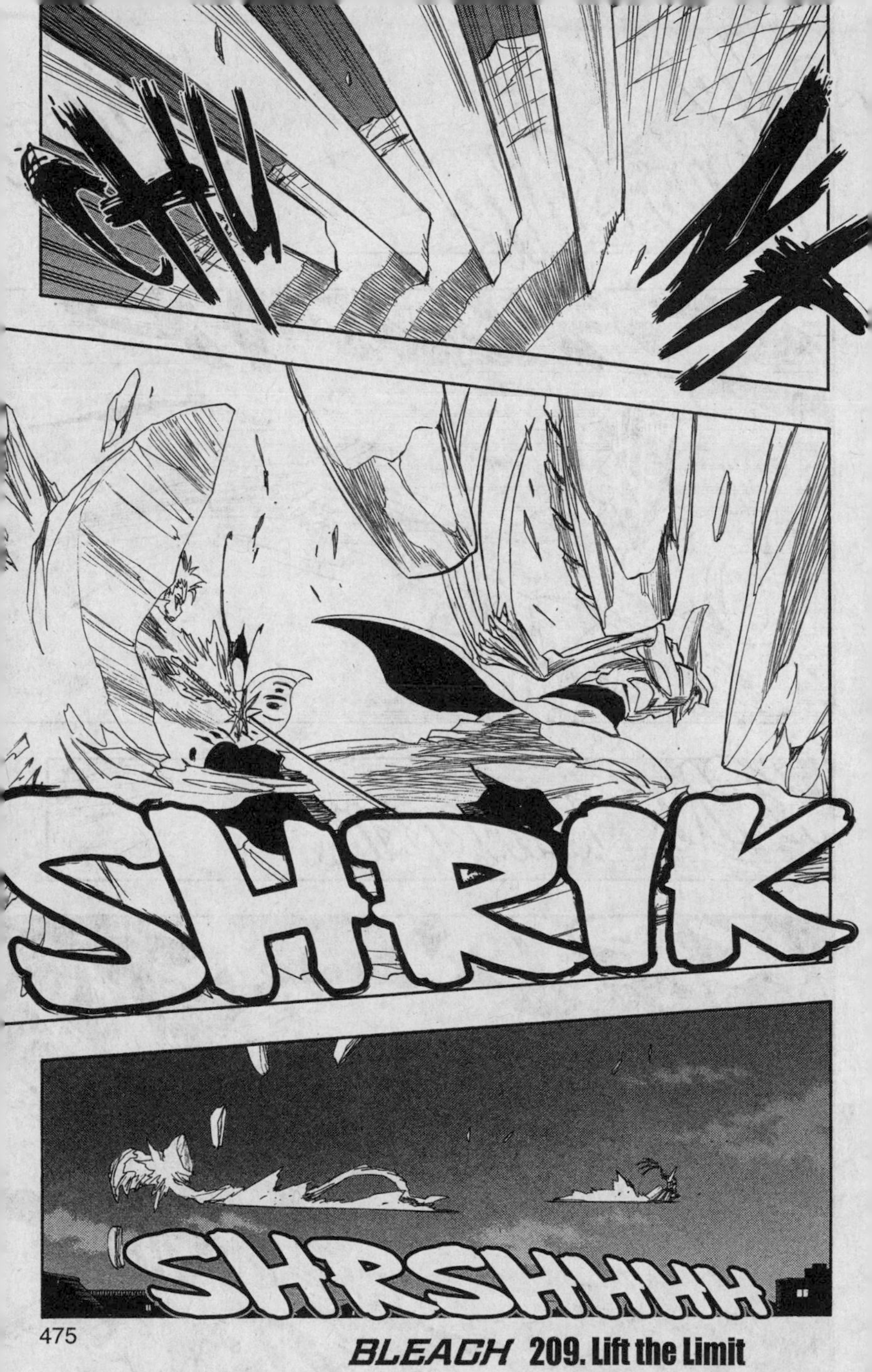
CHUNK
SHRIK
SHRSHHHH

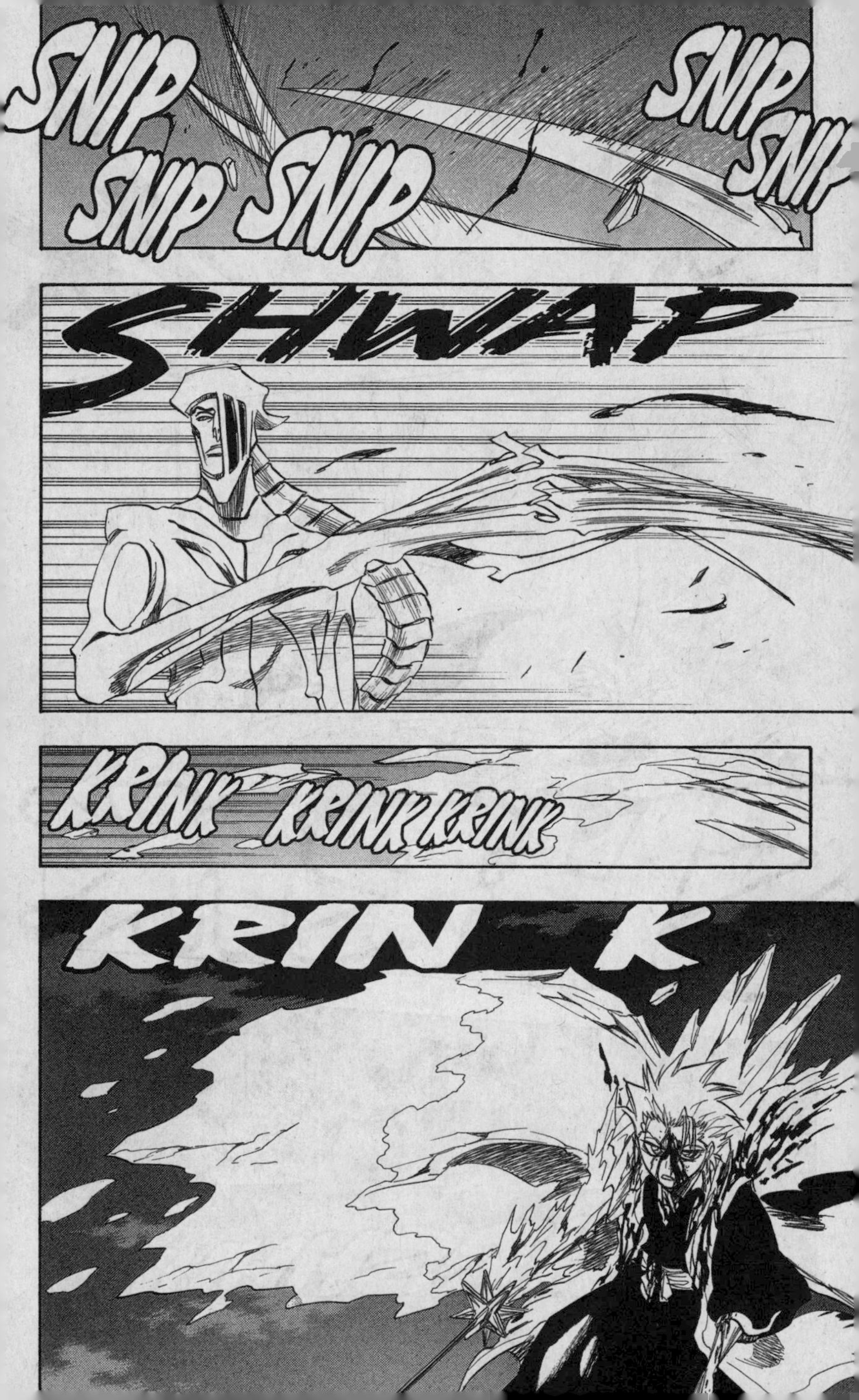

SNIP
SNI
SNIP
SNIP
SNIP
SHWAP
KRINK KRINK
KRINK
KRIN K

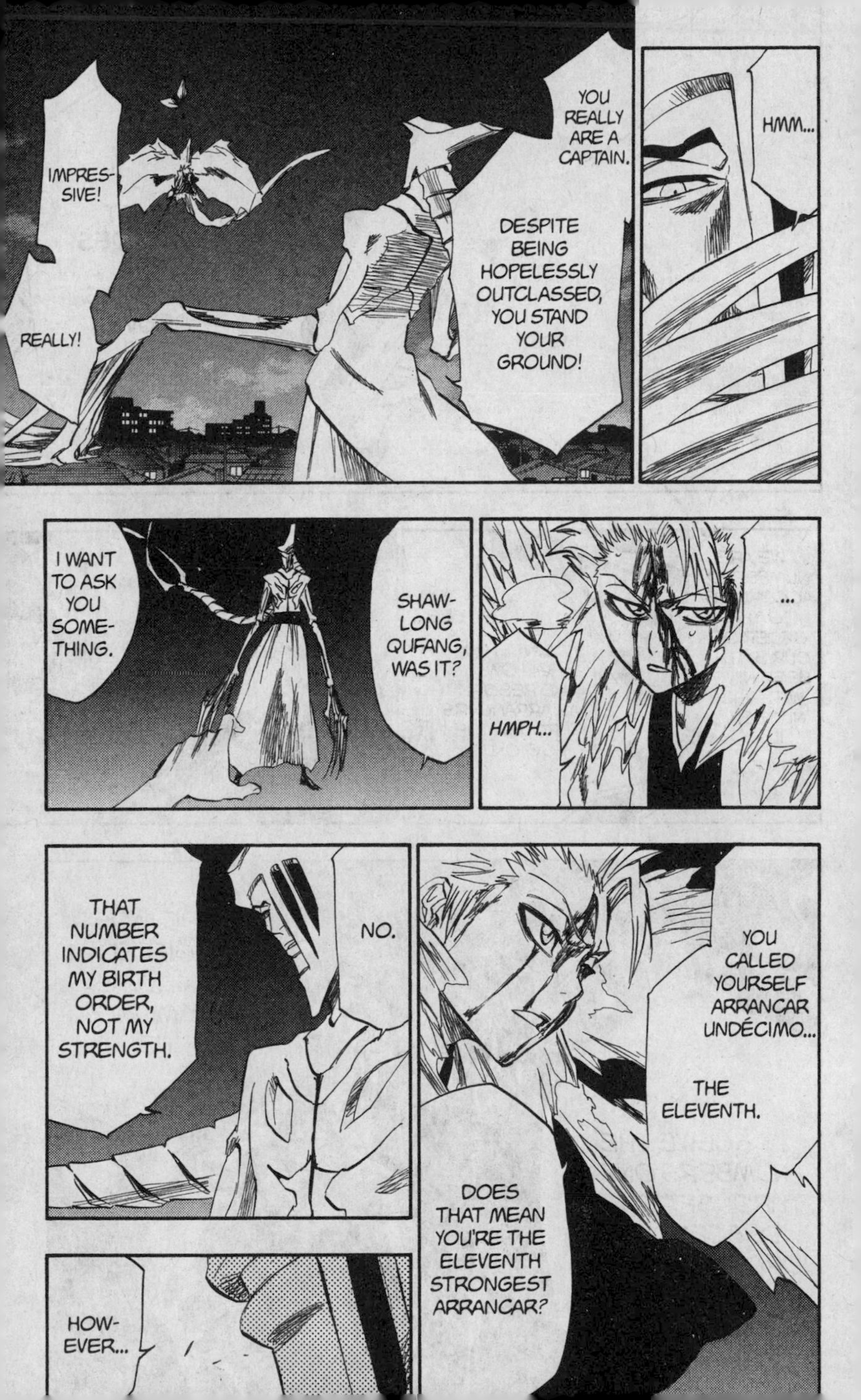
HMM...
YOU REALLY ARE A CAPTAIN.
DESPITE BEING HOPELESSLY OUTCLASSED, YOU STAND YOUR GROUND!
IMPRESSIVE!
REALLY!
...
HMPH...
SHAWLONG QUFANG, WAS IT?
I WANT TO ASK YOU SOMETHING.
YOU CALLED YOURSELF ARRANCAR UNDÉCIMO...
THE ELEVENTH.
DOES THAT MEAN YOU'RE THE ELEVENTH STRONGEST ARRANCAR?
NO.
THAT NUMBER INDICATES MY BIRTH ORDER, NOT MY STRENGTH.
HOWEVER...

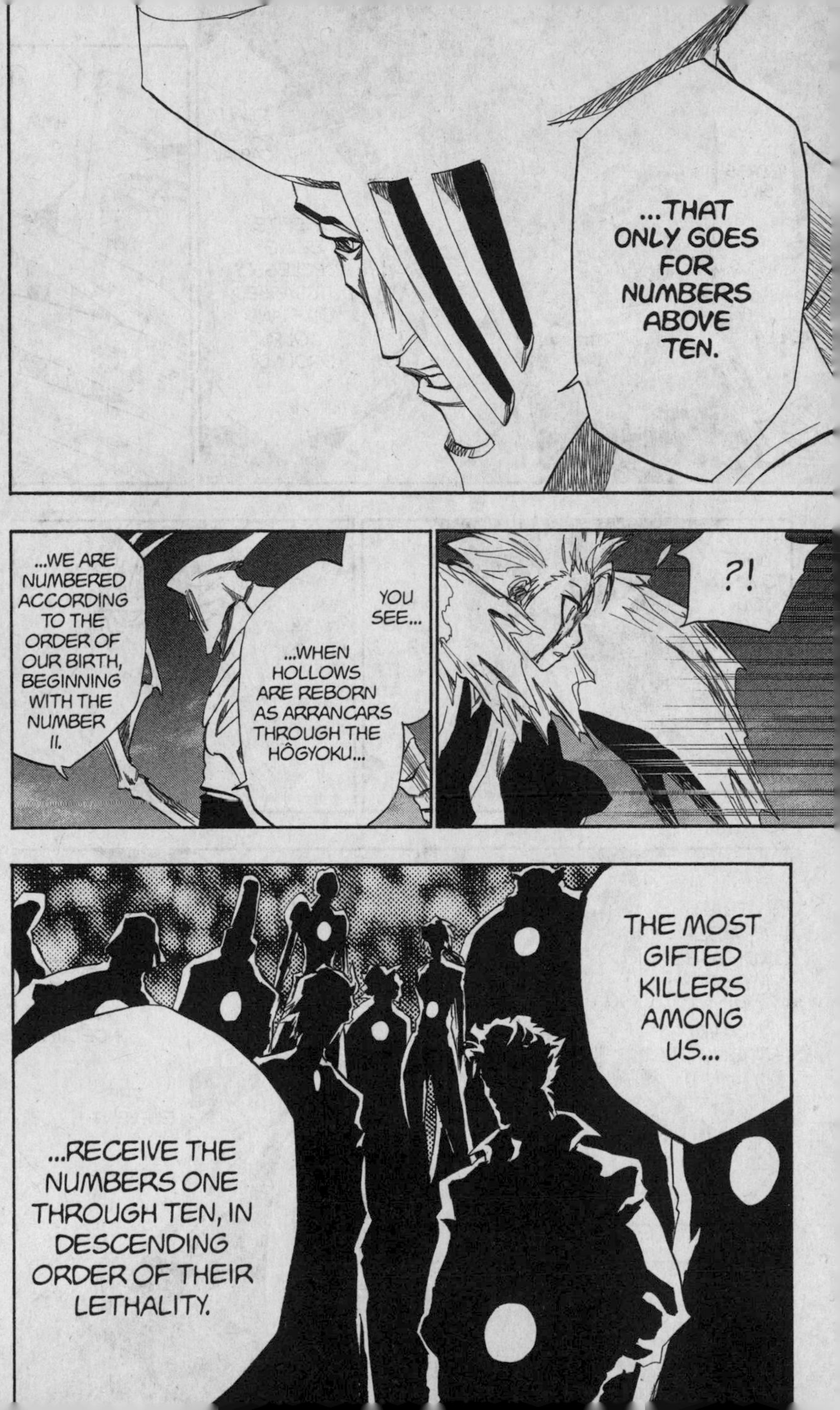
...THAT ONLY GOES FOR NUMBERS ABOVE TEN.
?!
YOU SEE...
...WHEN HOLLOWS ARE REBORN AS ARRANCARS THROUGH THE HÔGYOKU...
...WE ARE NUMBERED ACCORDING TO THE ORDER OF OUR BIRTH, BEGINNING WITH THE NUMBER 11.
THE MOST GIFTED KILLERS AMONG US...
...RECEIVE THE NUMBERS ONE THROUGH TEN, IN DESCENDING ORDER OF THEIR LETHALITY.

READ THIS WAY

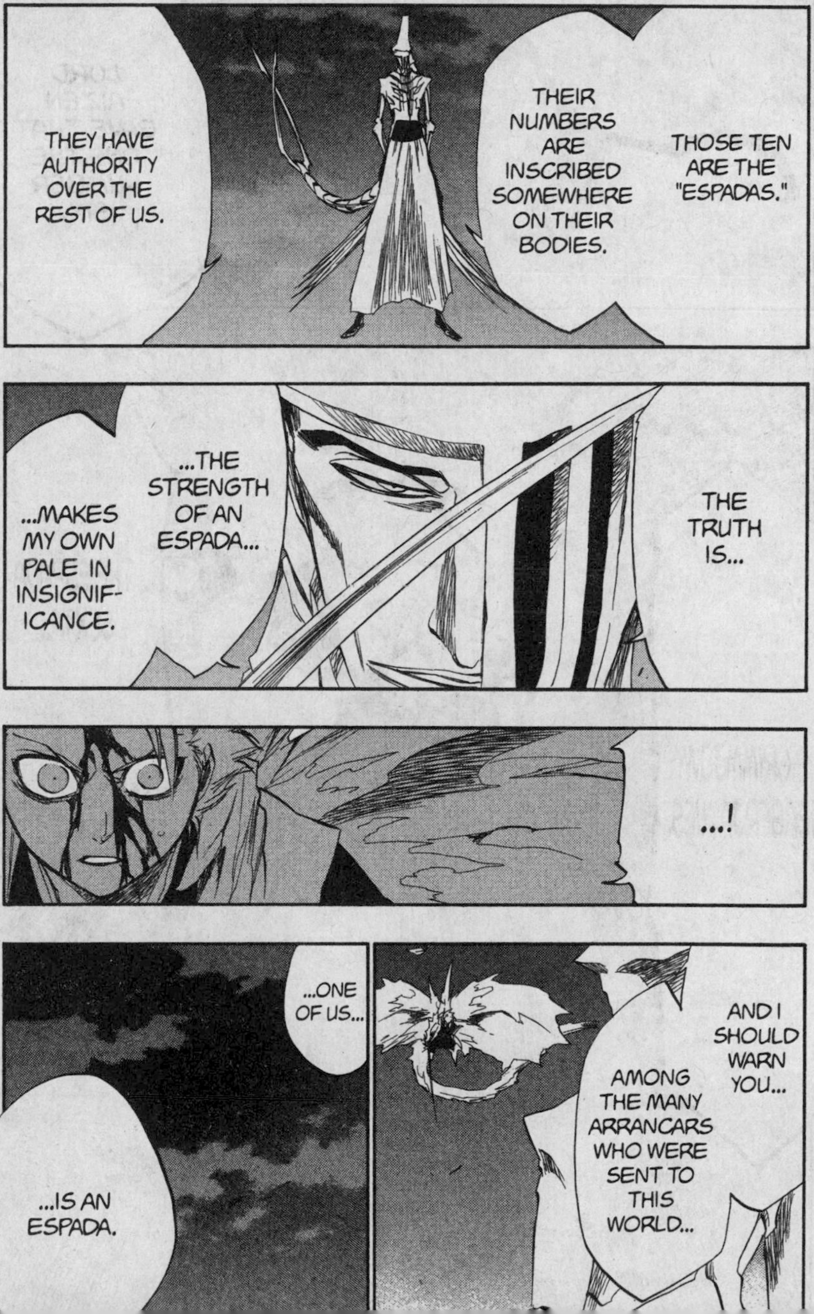
THOSE TEN ARE THE "ESPADAS."
THEIR NUMBERS ARE INSCRIBED SOMEWHERE ON THEIR BODIES.
THEY HAVE AUTHORITY OVER THE REST OF US.
THE TRUTH IS...
...THE STRENGTH OF AN ESPADA...
...MAKES MY OWN PALE IN INSIGNIF-ICANCE.
...!
AND I SHOULD WARN YOU...
AMONG THE MANY ARRANCARS WHO WERE SENT TO THIS WORLD...
...ONE OF US...
...IS AN ESPADA.

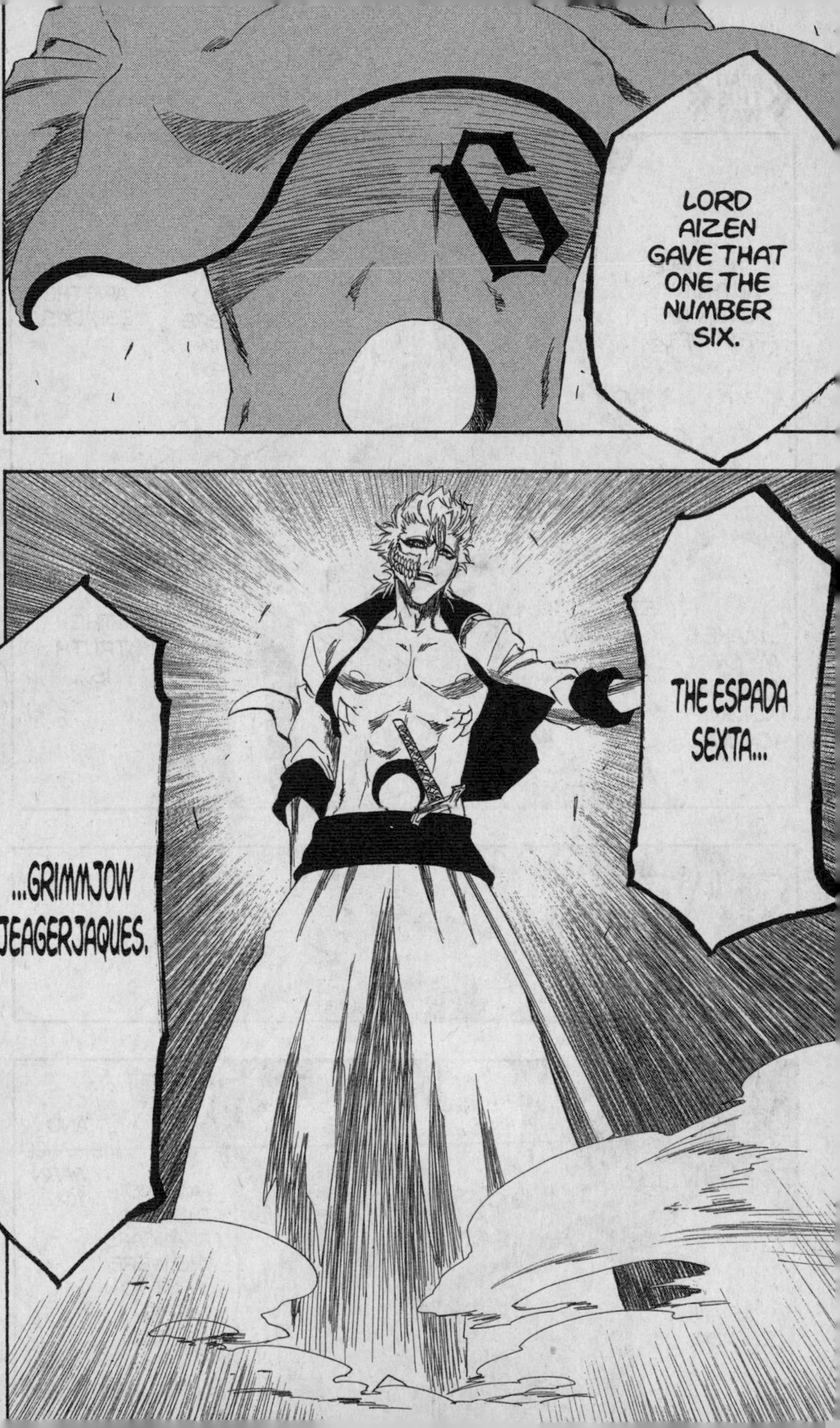
LORD AIZEN GAVE THAT ONE THE NUMBER SIX.
THE ESPADA SEXTA...
...GRIMMJOW JEAGERJAQUES.

READ THIS WAY

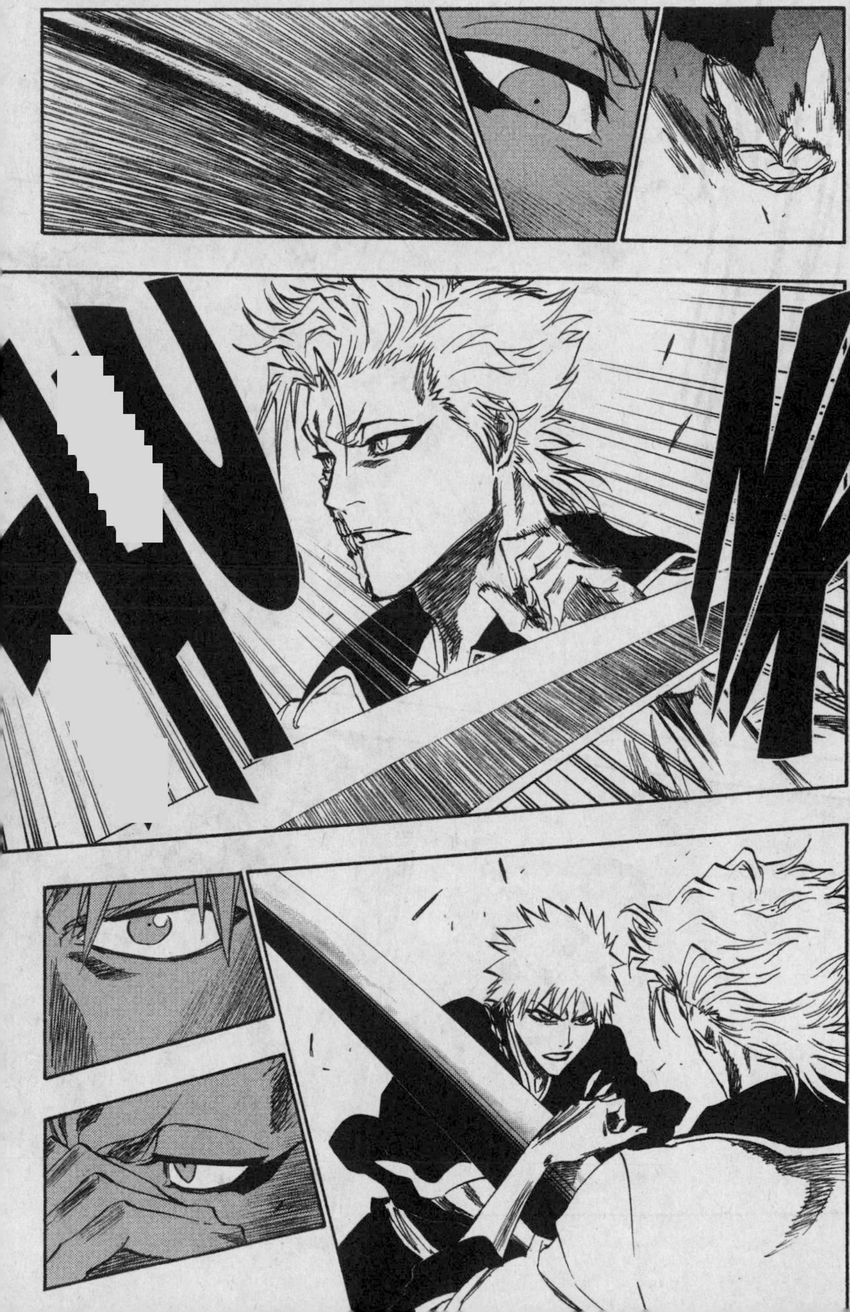

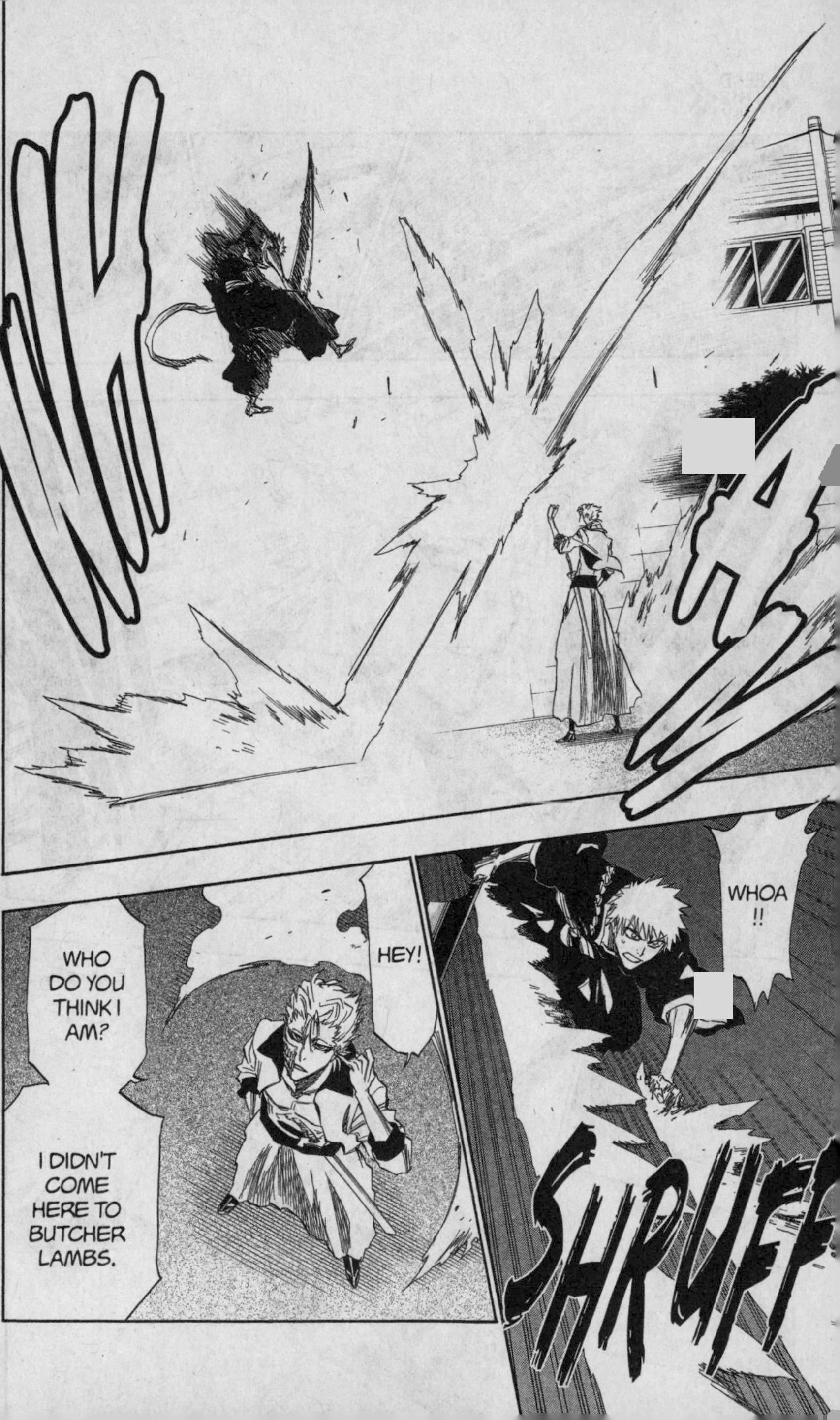
WHOA!!
HEY!
WHO DO YOU THINK I AM?
I DIDN'T COME HERE TO BUTCHER LAMBS.

READ THIS WAY

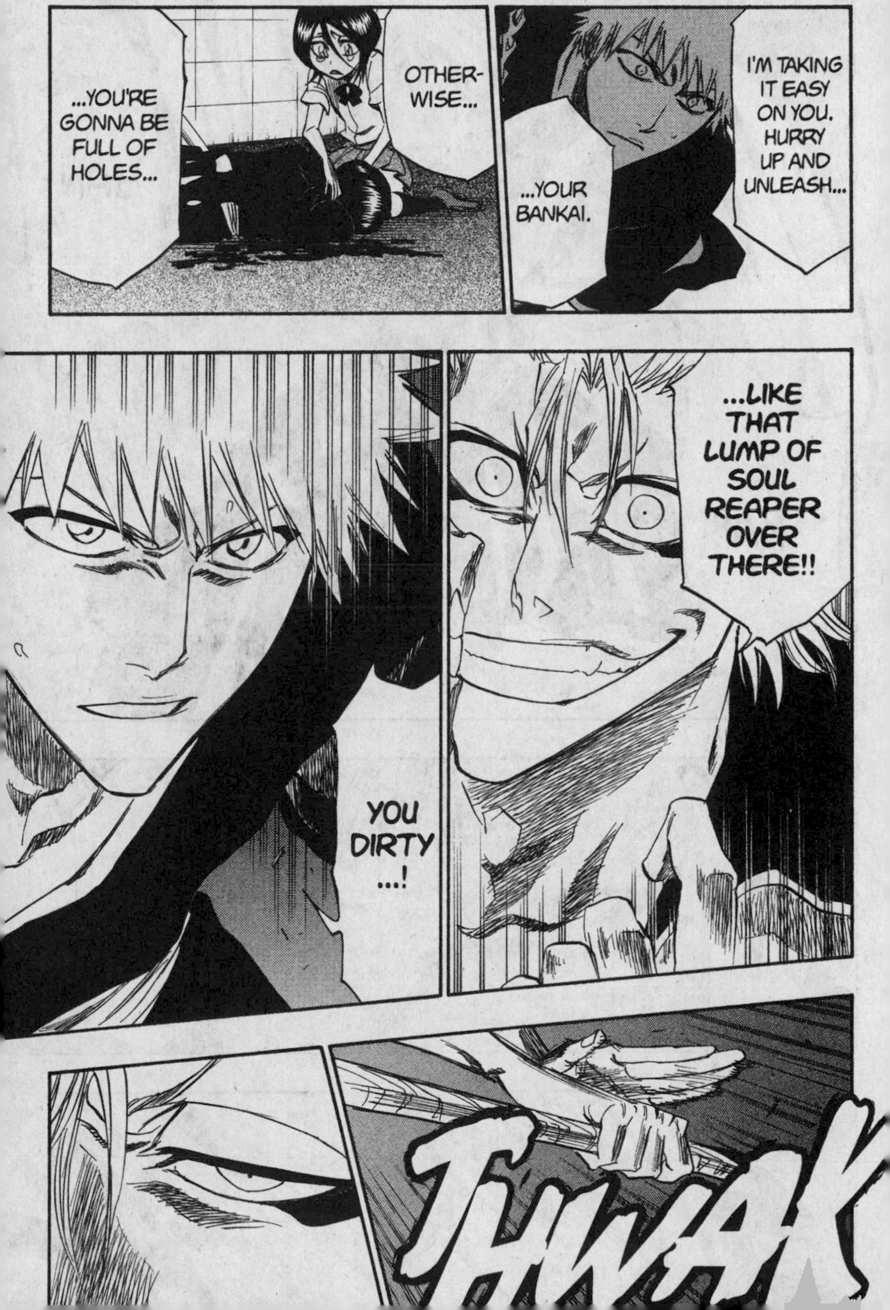
I'M TAKING IT EASY ON YOU. HURRY UP AND UNLEASH...
...YOUR BANKAI.
OTHER-WISE...
...YOU'RE GONNA BE FULL OF HOLES...
...LIKE THAT LUMP OF SOUL REAPER OVER THERE!!
YOU DIRTY ...!
THWAK

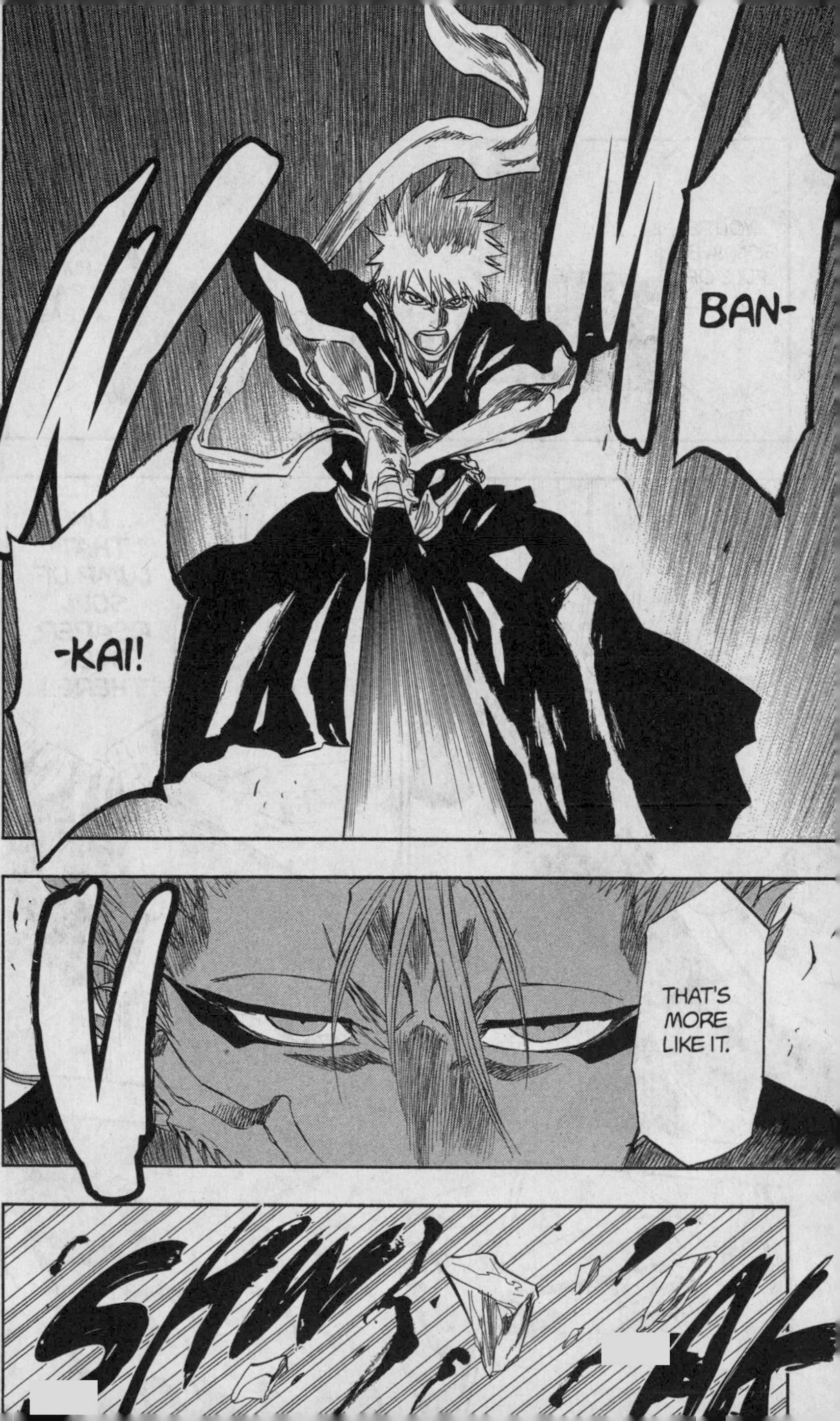
BAN-
-KAI!
THAT'S MORE LIKE IT.

READ THIS WAY

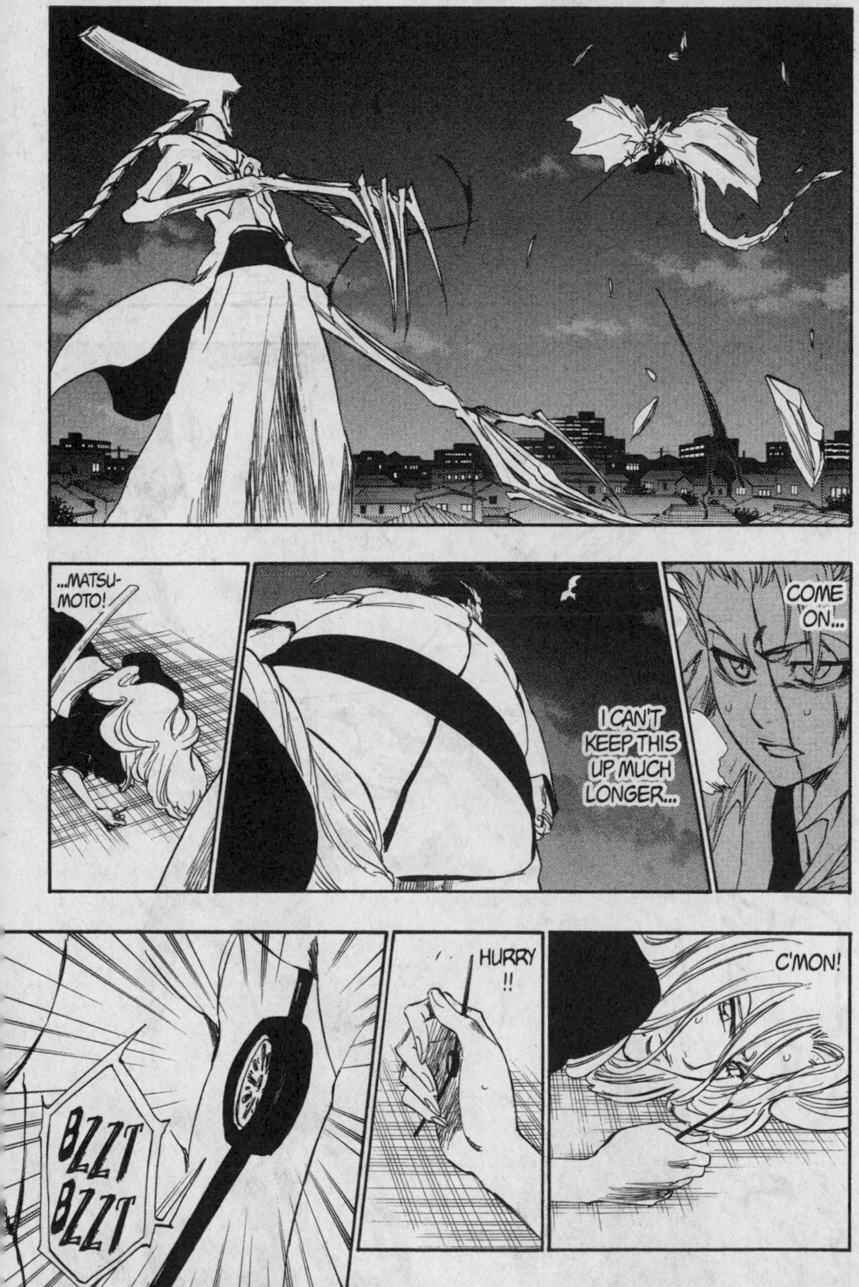
COME ON...
I CAN'T KEEP THIS UP MUCH LONGER...
...MATSU-MOTO!
C'MON!
HURRY!!
BZZT BZZT

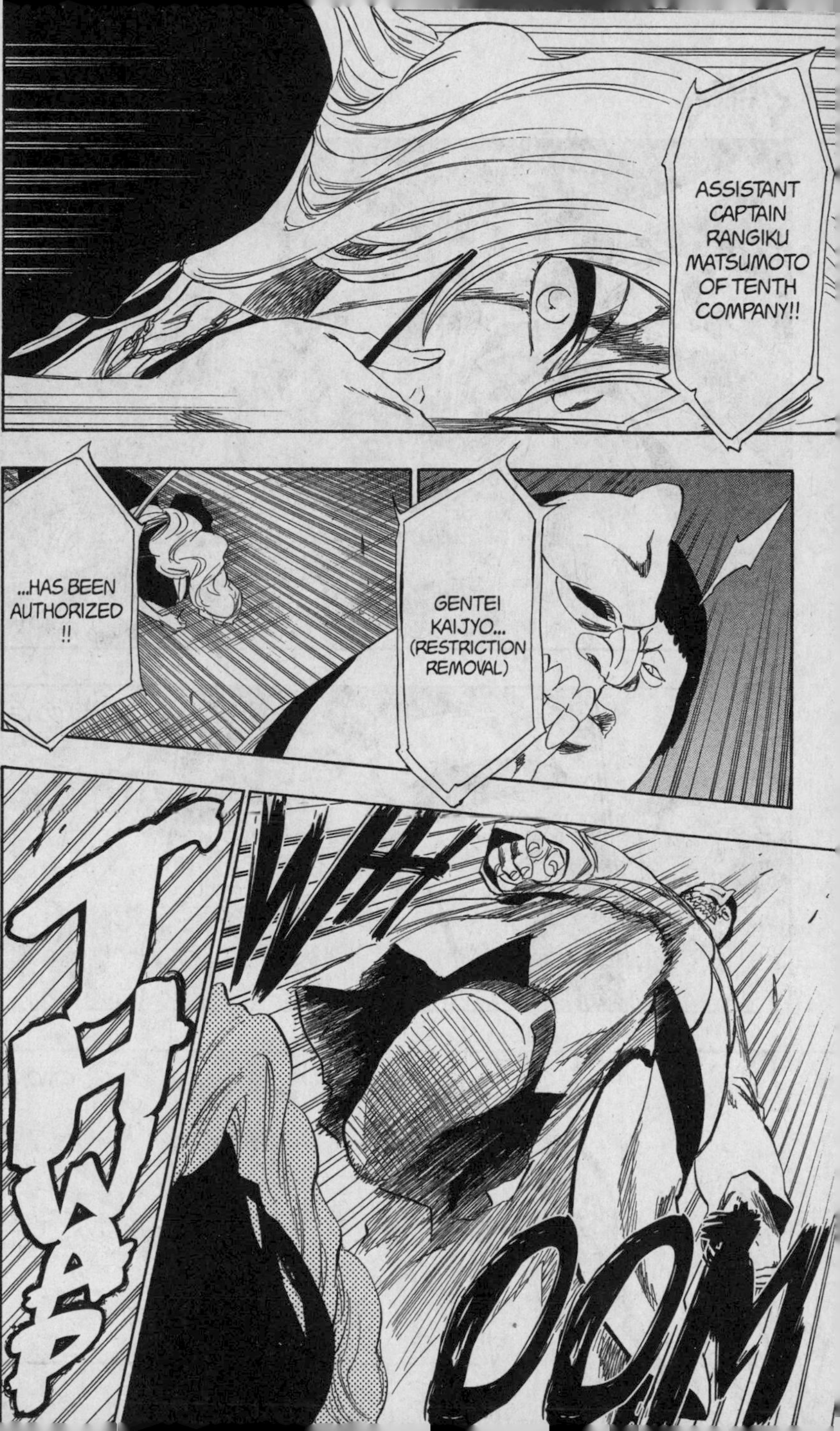
ASSISTANT CAPTAIN RANGIKU MATSUMOTO OF TENTH COMPANY!!
GENTEI KAIJYO... (RESTRICTION REMOVAL)
...HAS BEEN AUTHORIZED !!
WHOOM
THWAP

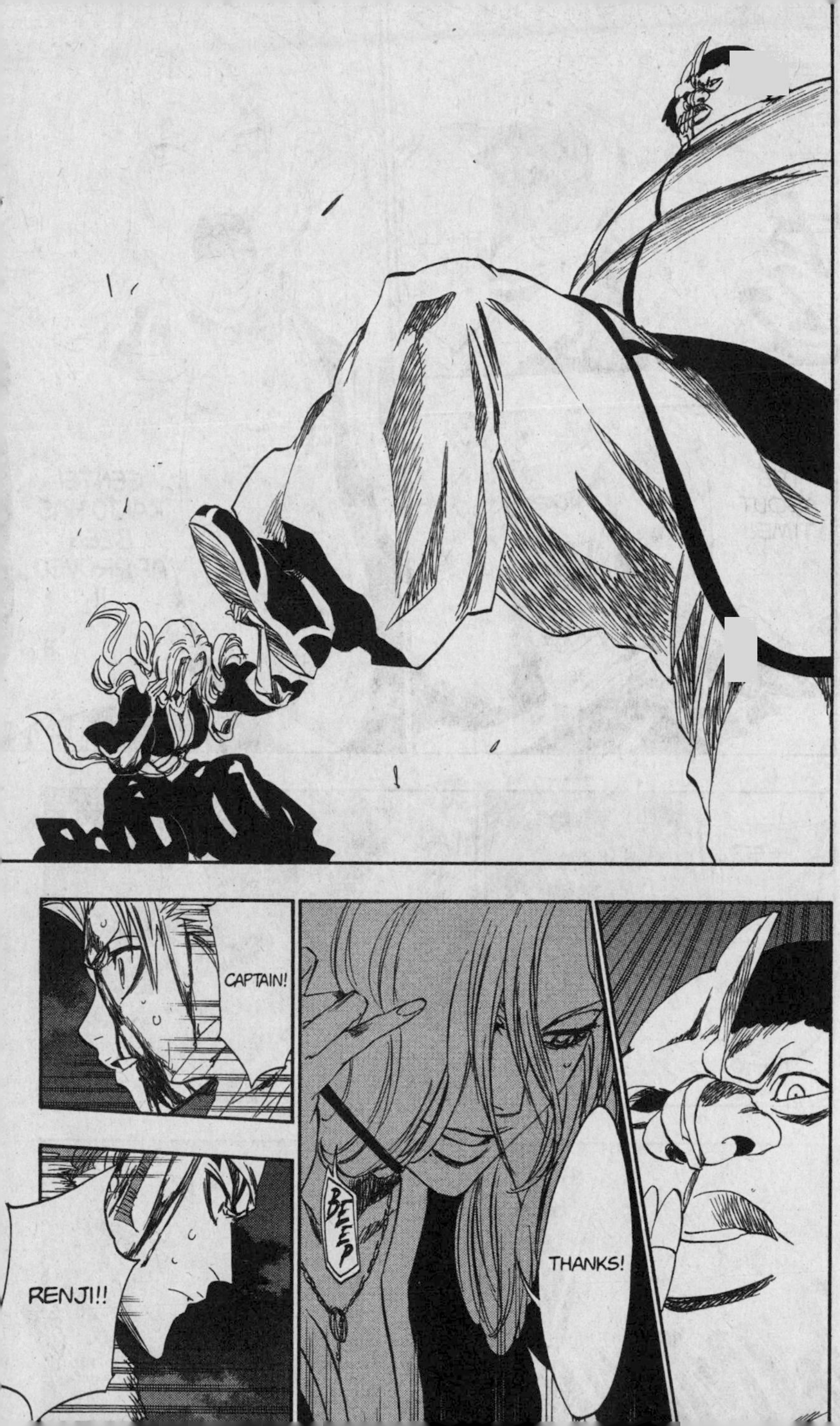
BEEP
THANKS!
CAPTAIN!
RENJI!!

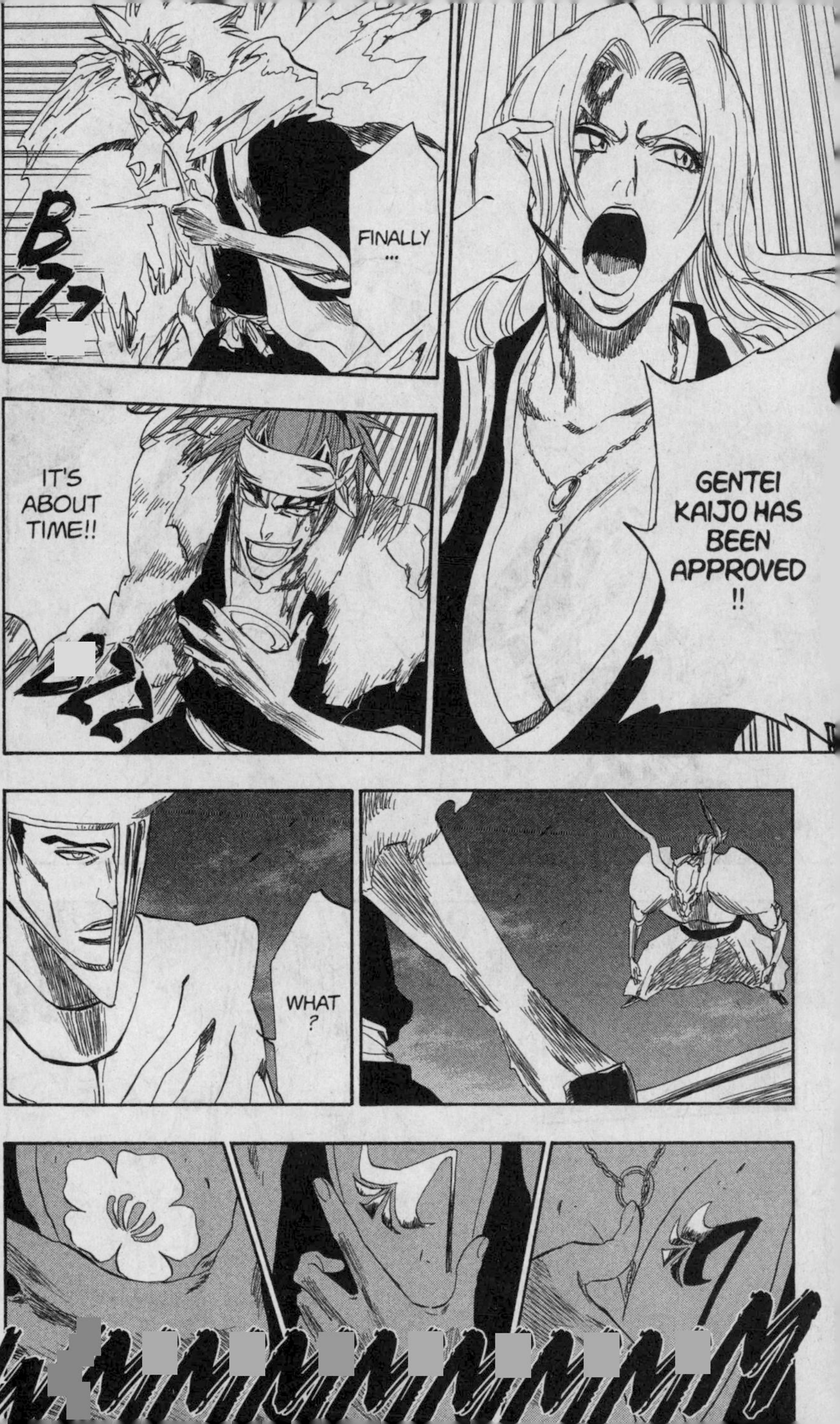
GENTEI KAIJO HAS BEEN APPROVED!!
FINALLY...
IT'S ABOUT TIME!!
WHAT?

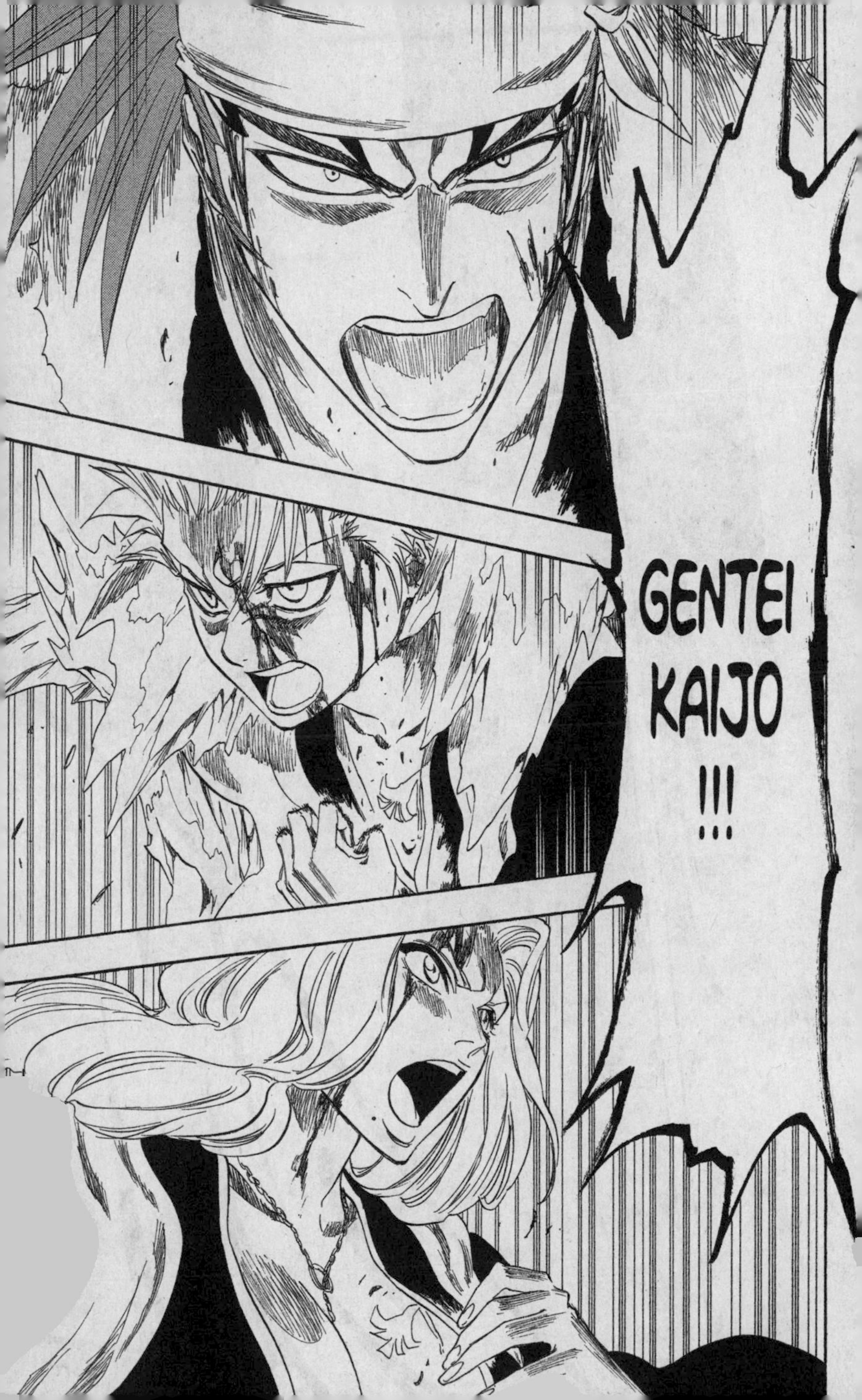
GENTEI KAIJO !!!

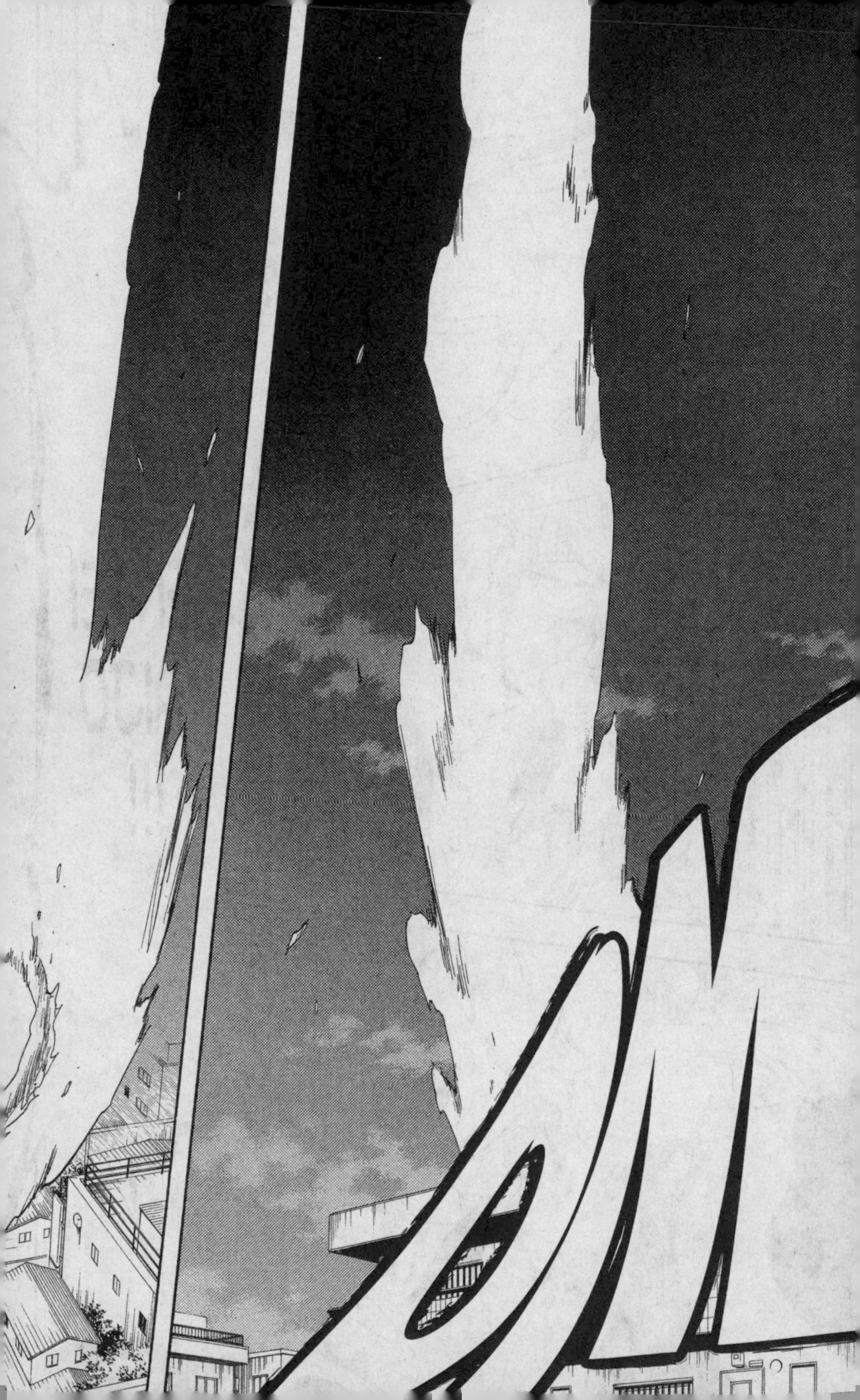

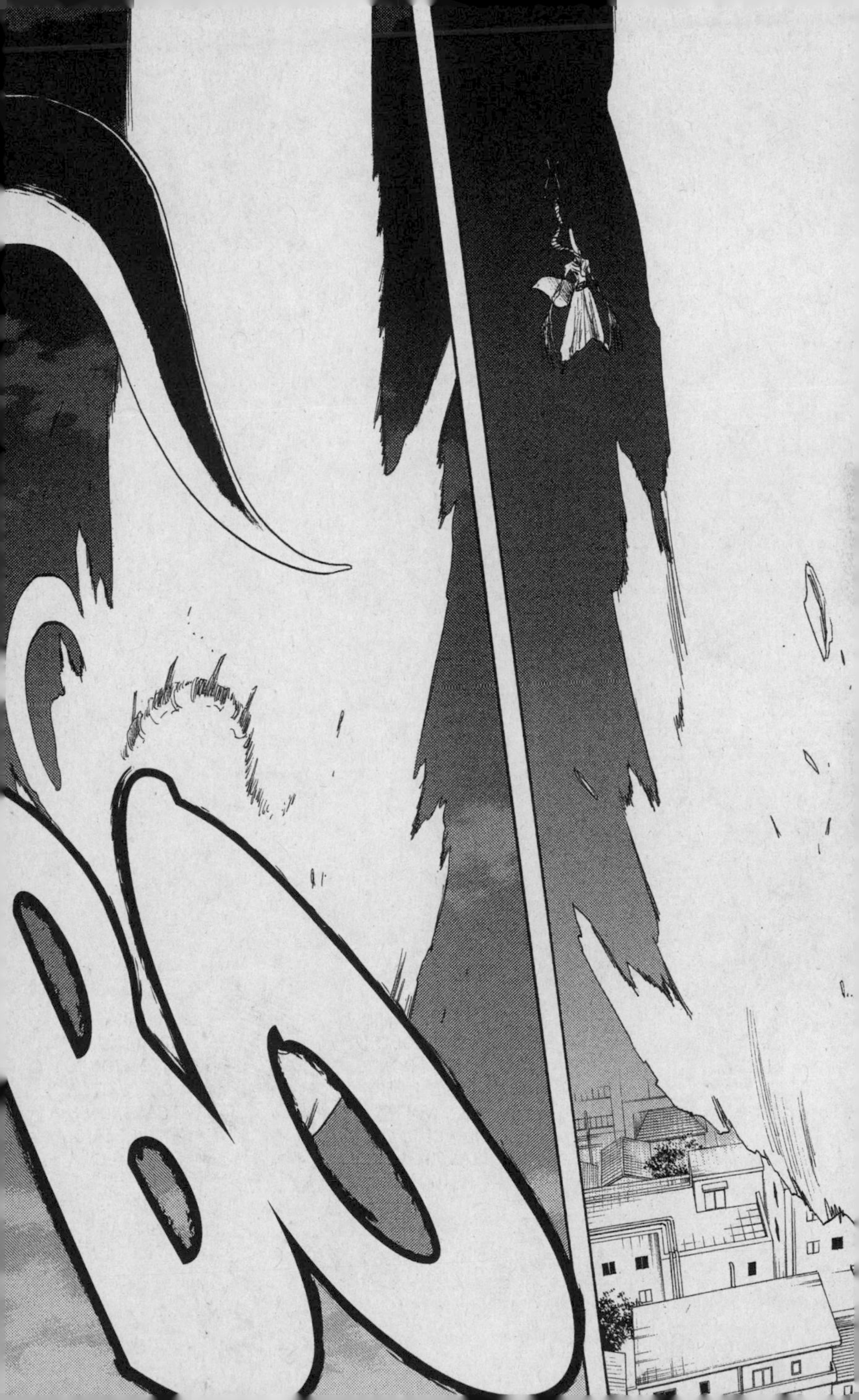

THIS IS MY
CHANCE TO SHOW
HOW COOL IT IS
THAT I DON'T
APPEAR VERY
MUCH. NO! IT'S MY
CHANCE TO SHOW
RANGIKU WHO I
REALLY AM!!!

THIS IS MY
CHANCE TO CALL
ATTENTION TO MY
OBSCURITY. NO!
I CAN SHOW THAT
THE REASON
I'M SUCH A
CIPHER IS
THAT I DON'T
APPEAR VERY
MUCH. NO!

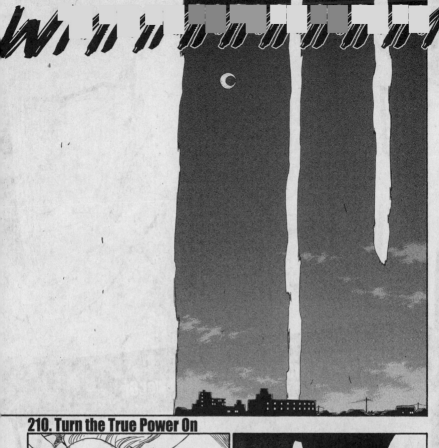

210. Turn the True Power On

WHAT...

...IS THAT?

GENTEI...

...KAIJYO?

BLEACH 210. Turn the True Power On

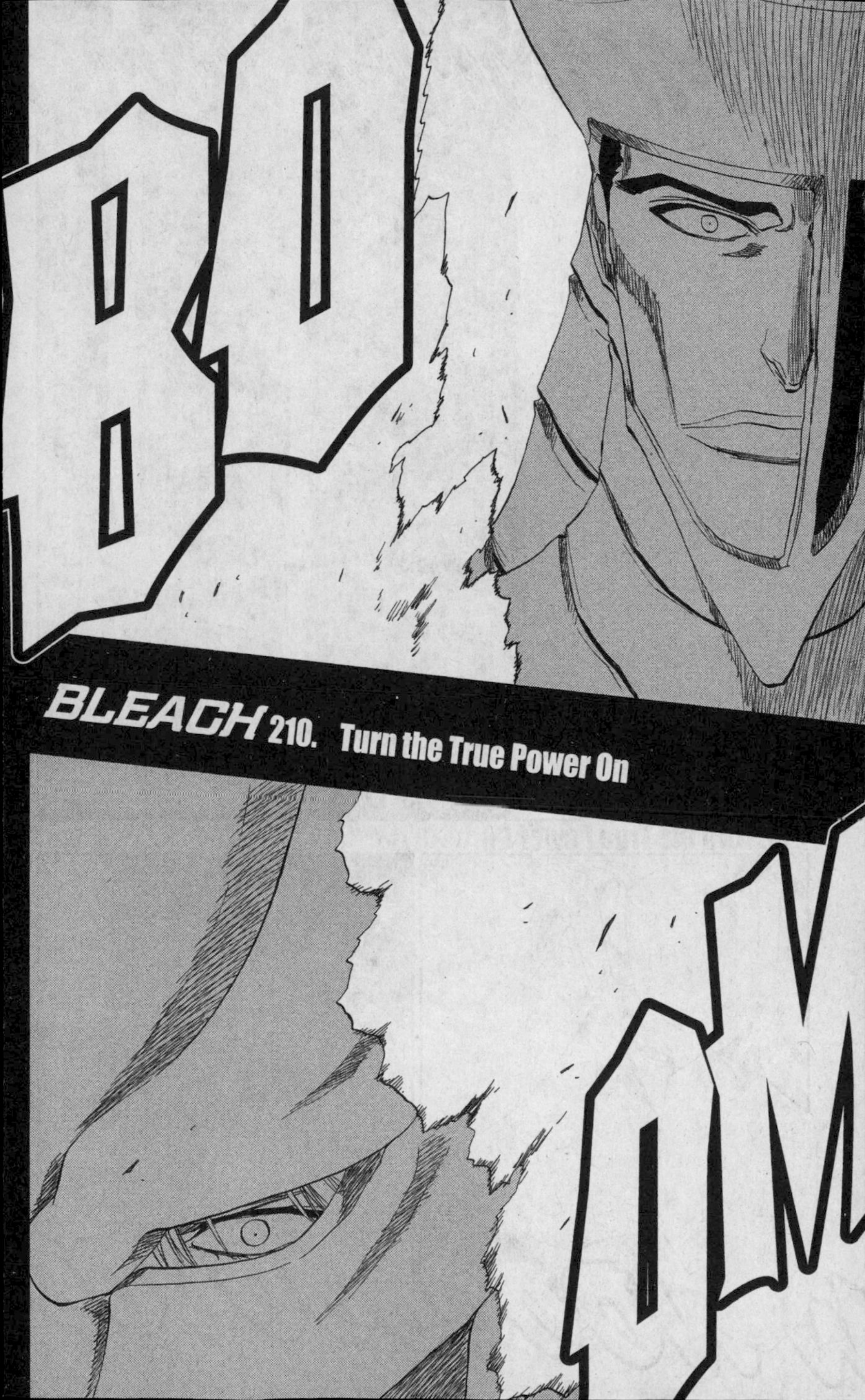
BO
OM

READ THIS WAY

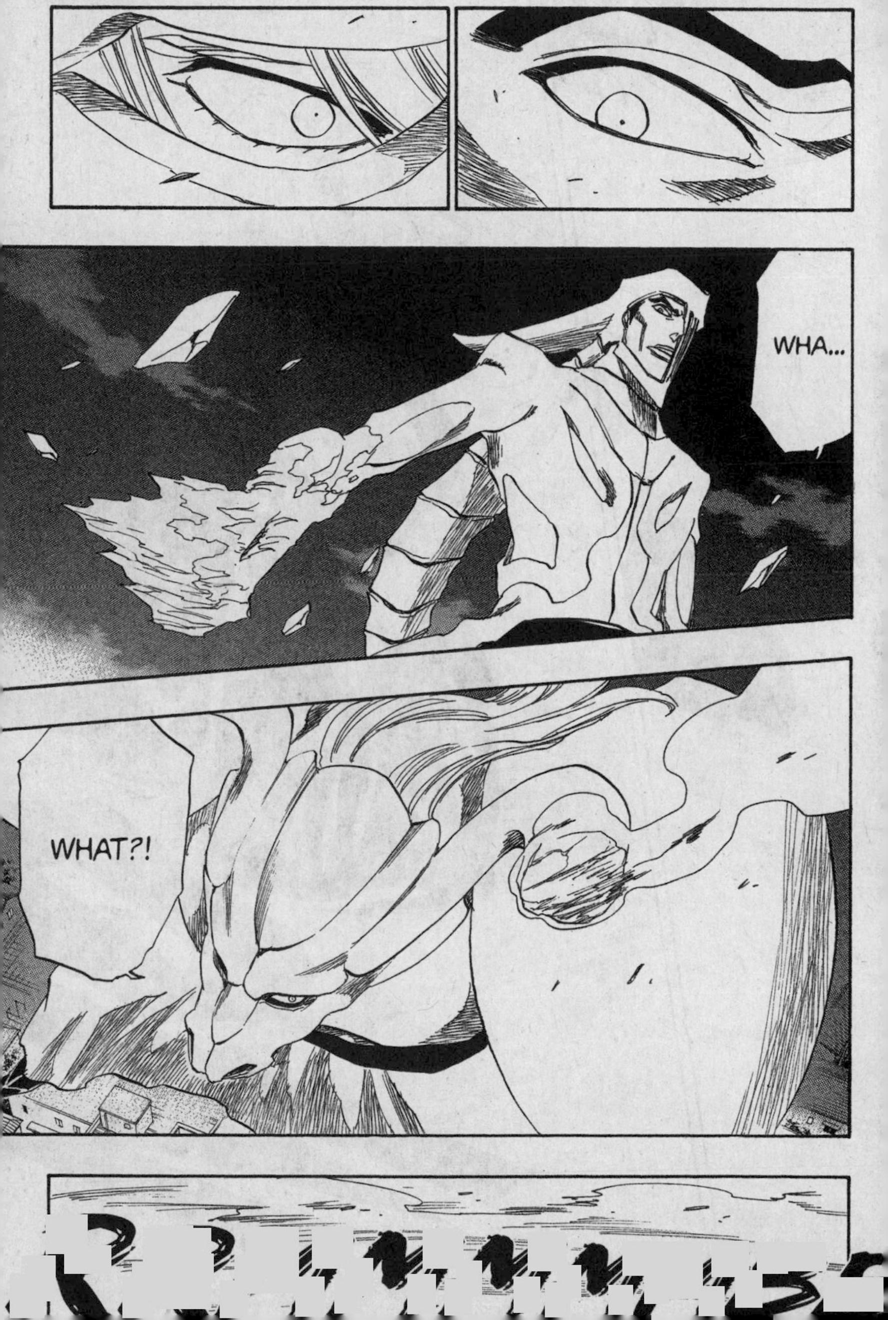
WHA...
WHAT?!

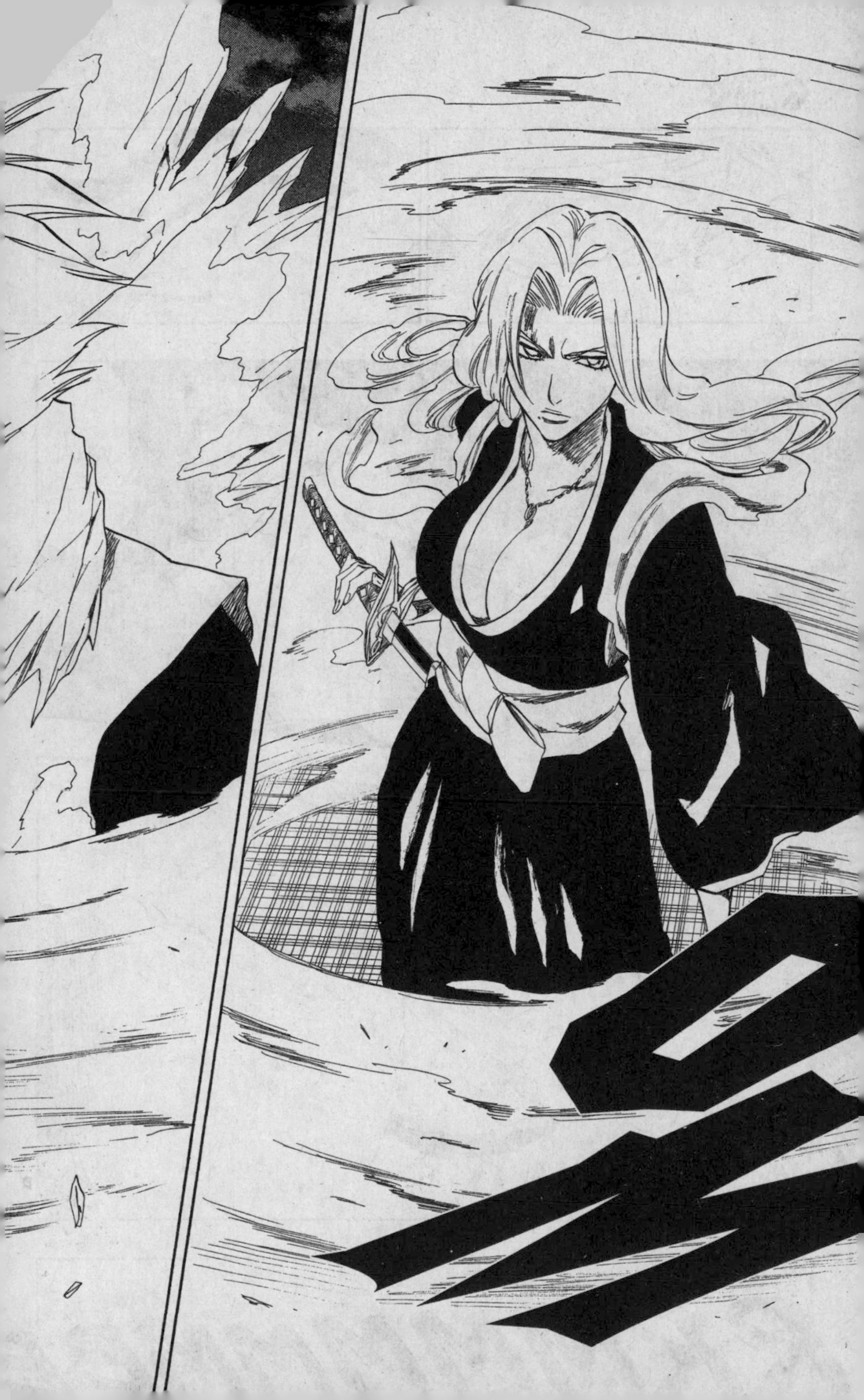

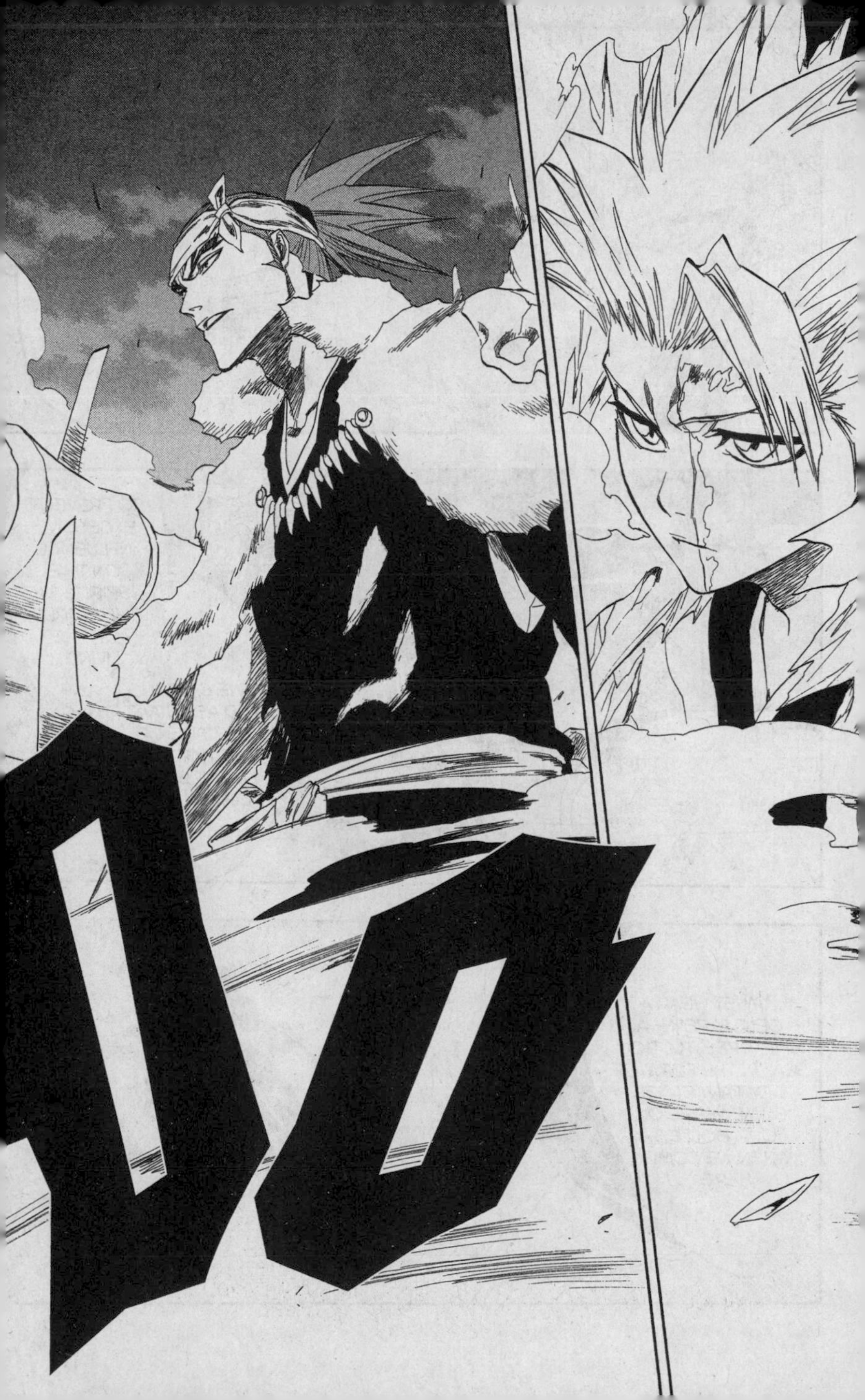
DO

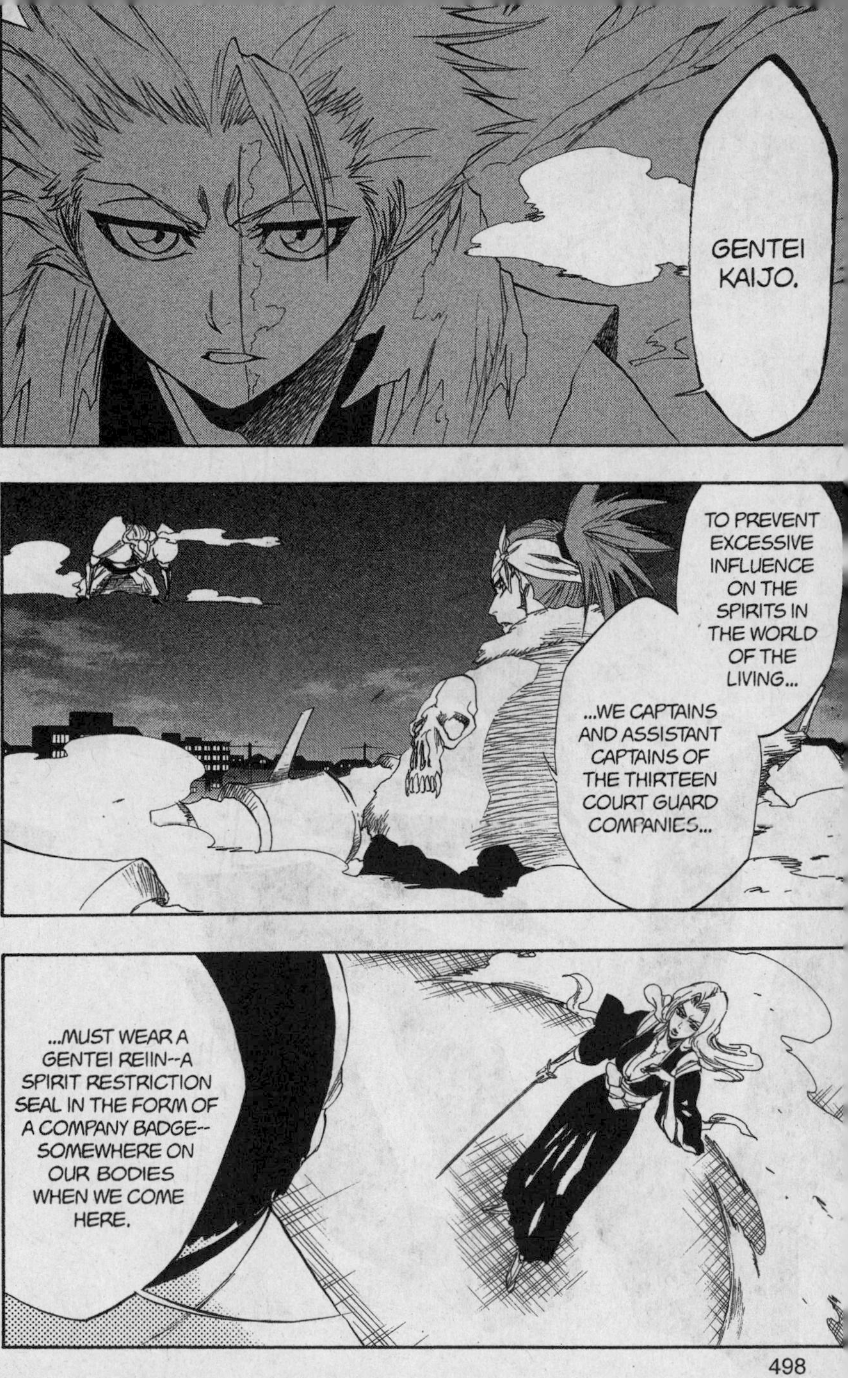
GENTEI KAIJO.
TO PREVENT EXCESSIVE INFLUENCE ON THE SPIRITS IN THE WORLD OF THE LIVING...
...WE CAPTAINS AND ASSISTANT CAPTAINS OF THE THIRTEEN COURT GUARD COMPANIES...
...MUST WEAR A GENTEI REIIN--A SPIRIT RESTRICTION SEAL IN THE FORM OF A COMPANY BADGE--SOMEWHERE ON OUR BODIES WHEN WE COME HERE.

READ THIS WAY

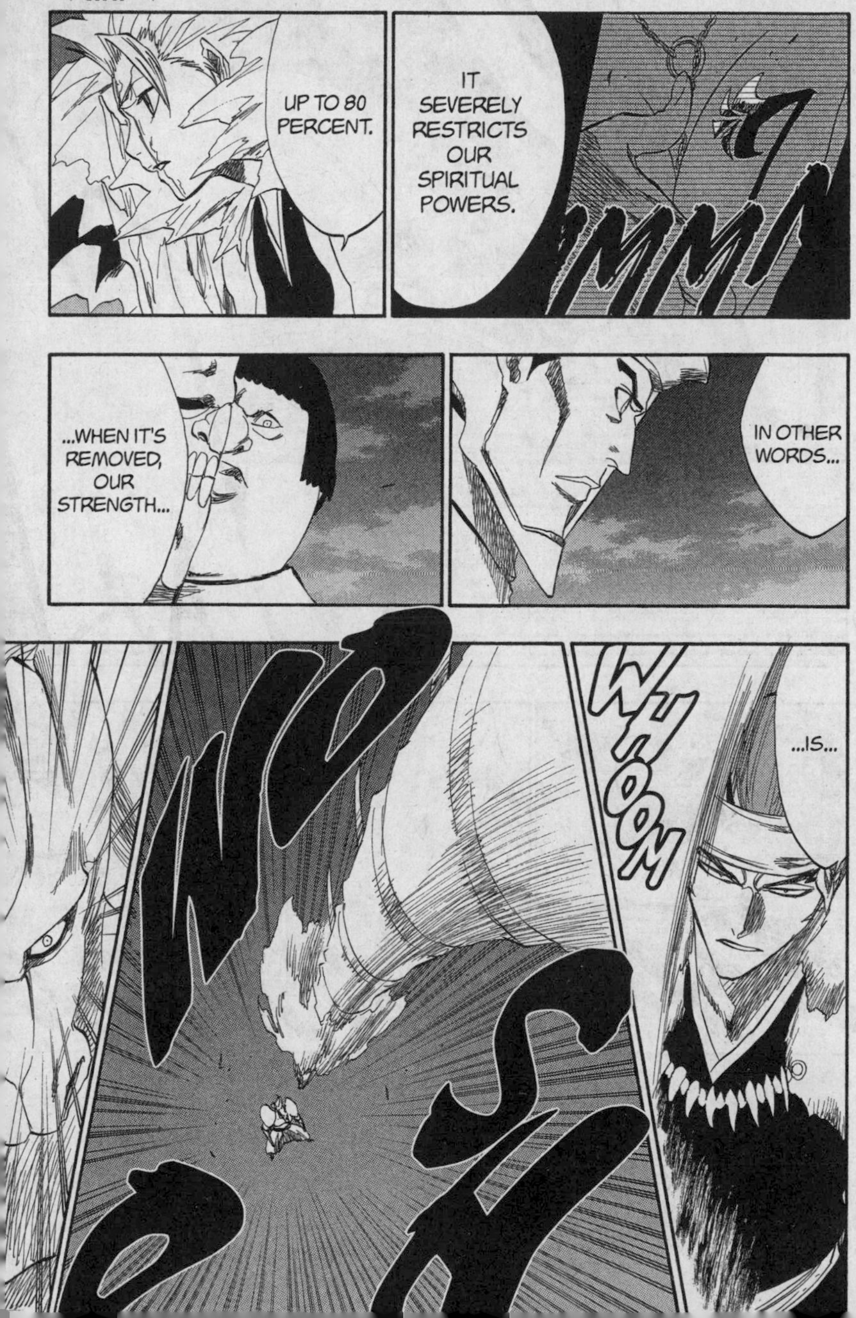
IT SEVERELY RESTRICTS OUR SPIRITUAL POWERS.
UP TO 80 PERCENT.
IN OTHER WORDS...
...WHEN IT'S REMOVED, OUR STRENGTH...
WHOOM
...IS...

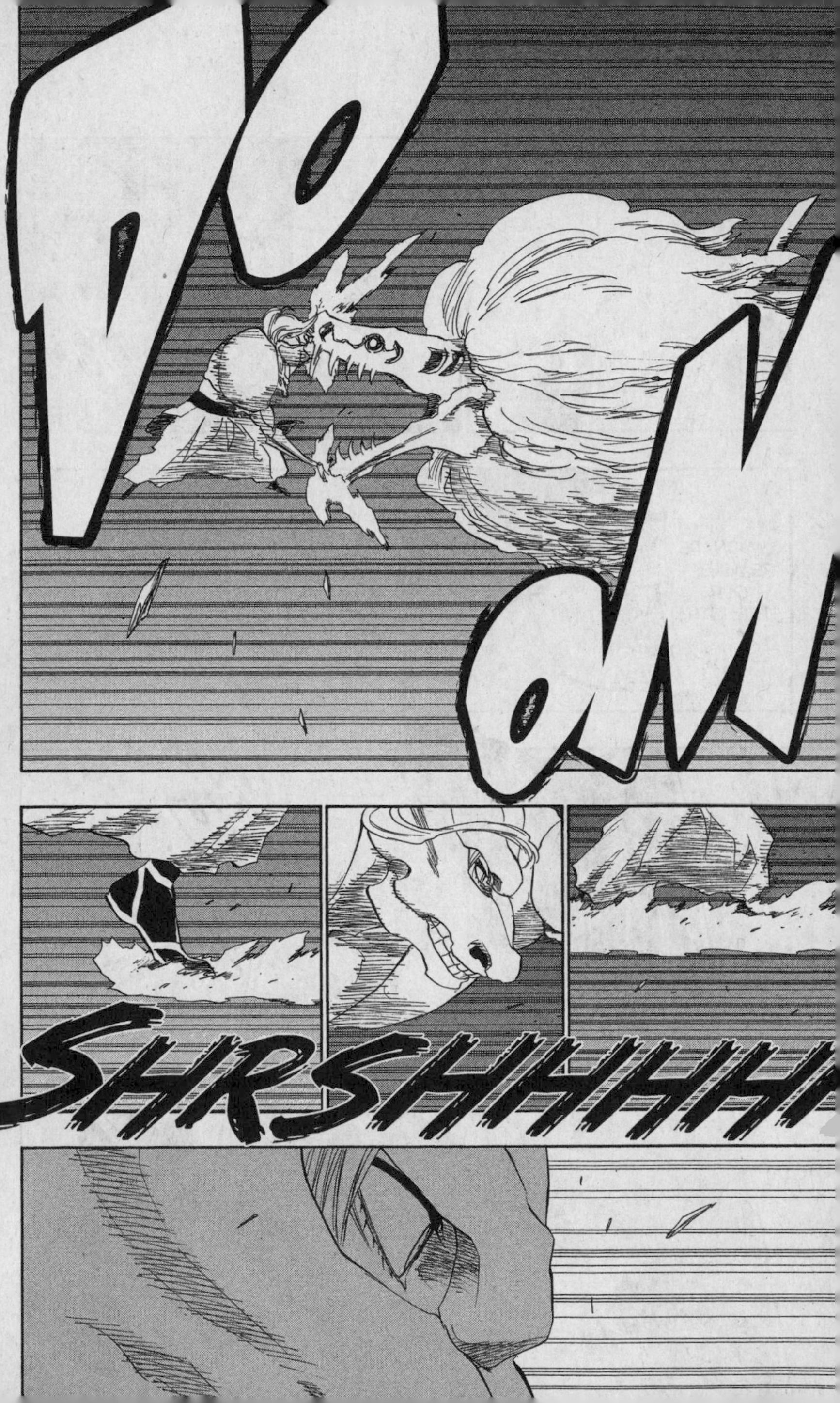
DOOM
SHRSHHHH

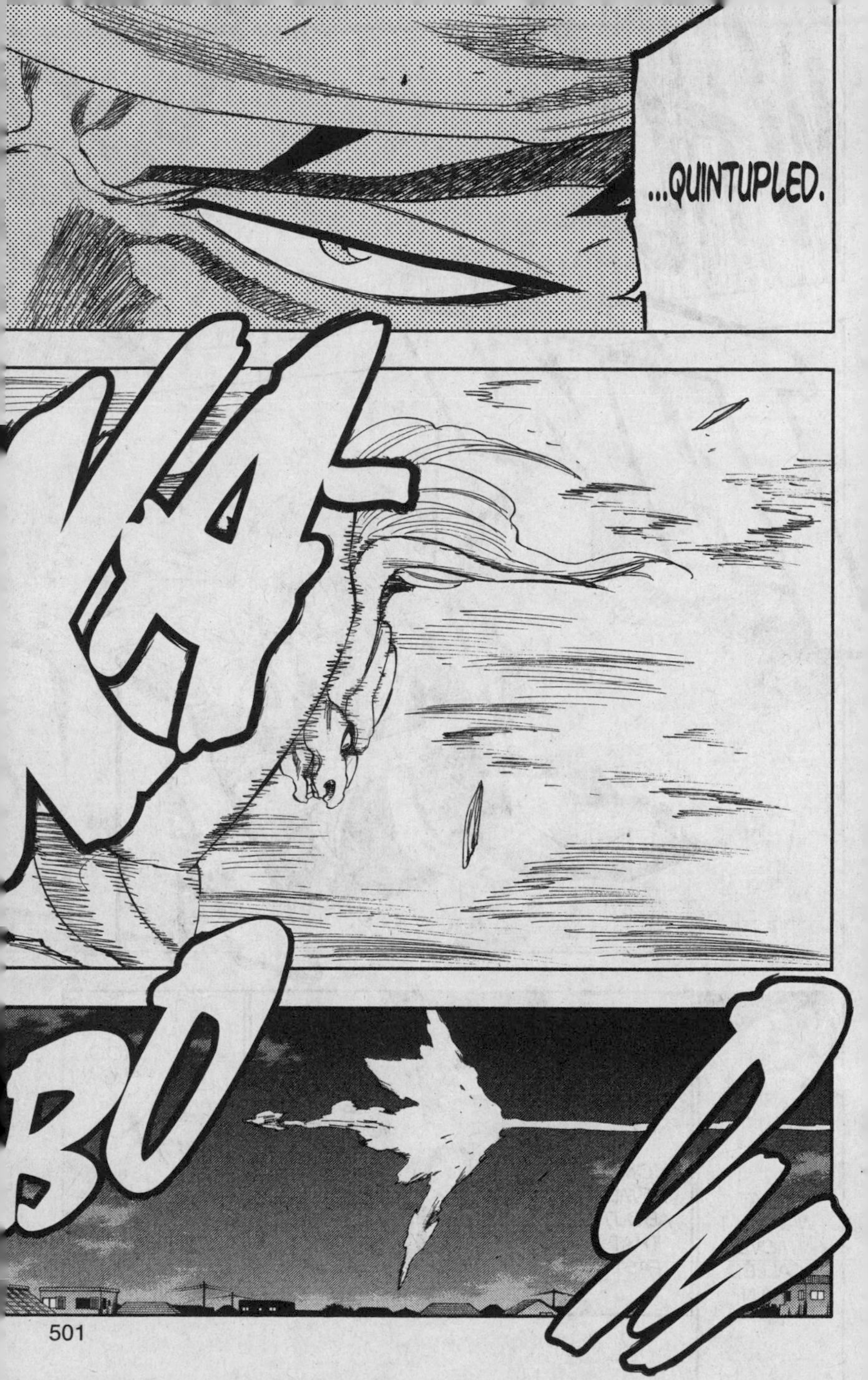
...QUINTUPLED.
VSH
BOOM

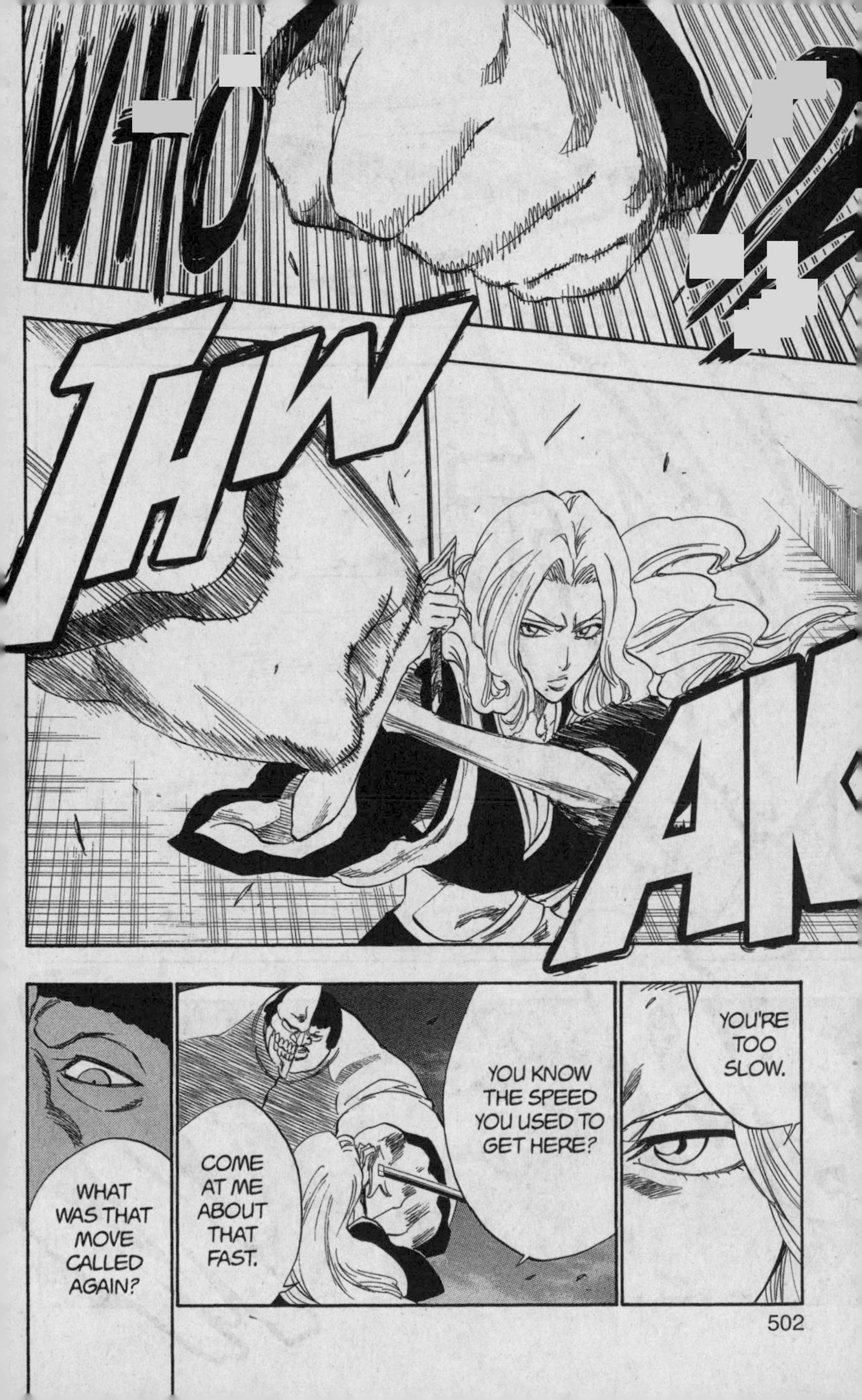

WHO
THW
AK
YOU'RE TOO SLOW.
YOU KNOW THE SPEED YOU USED TO GET HERE?
COME AT ME ABOUT THAT FAST.
WHAT WAS THAT MOVE CALLED AGAIN?

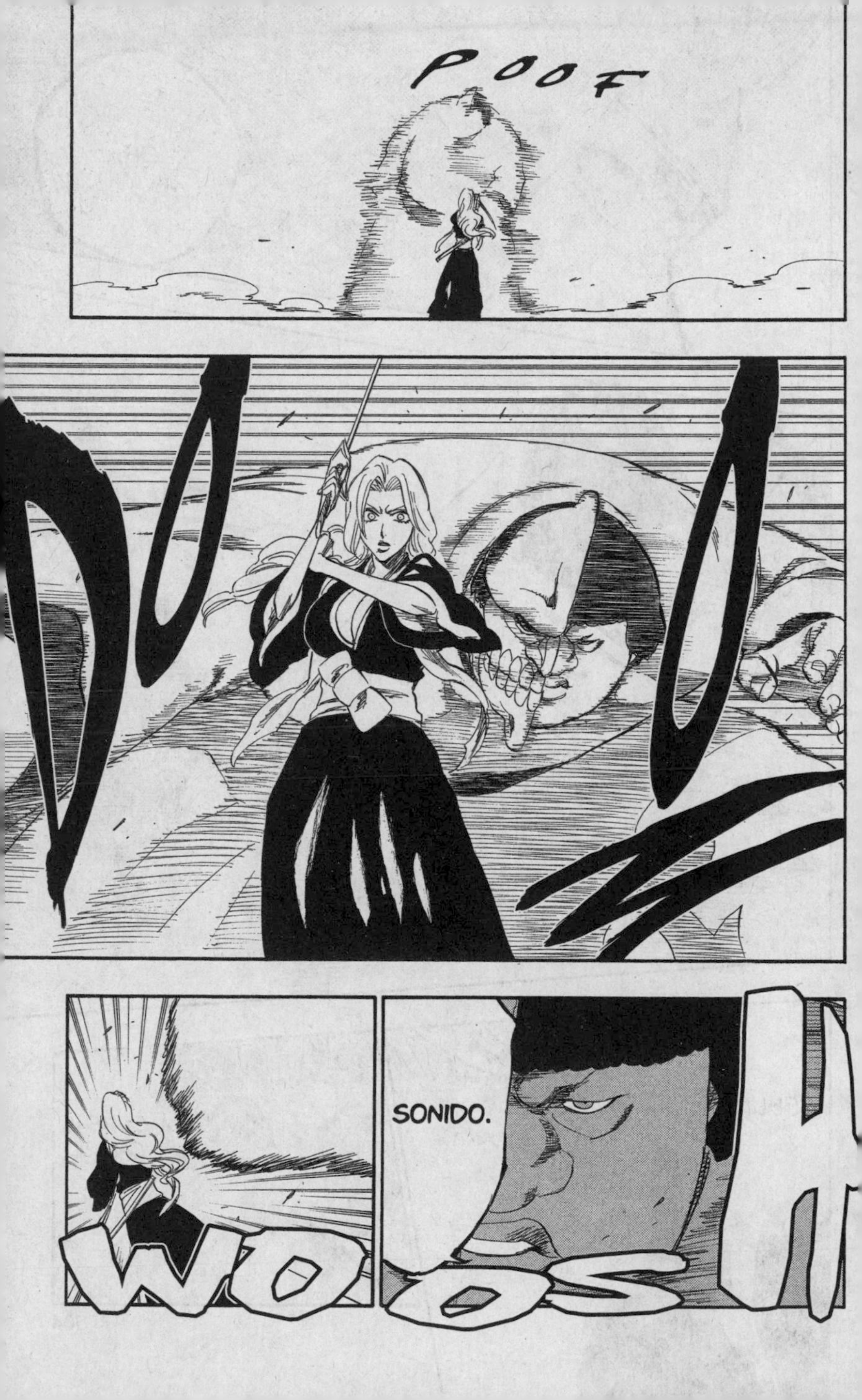
POOF
SONIDO.
WOOSH

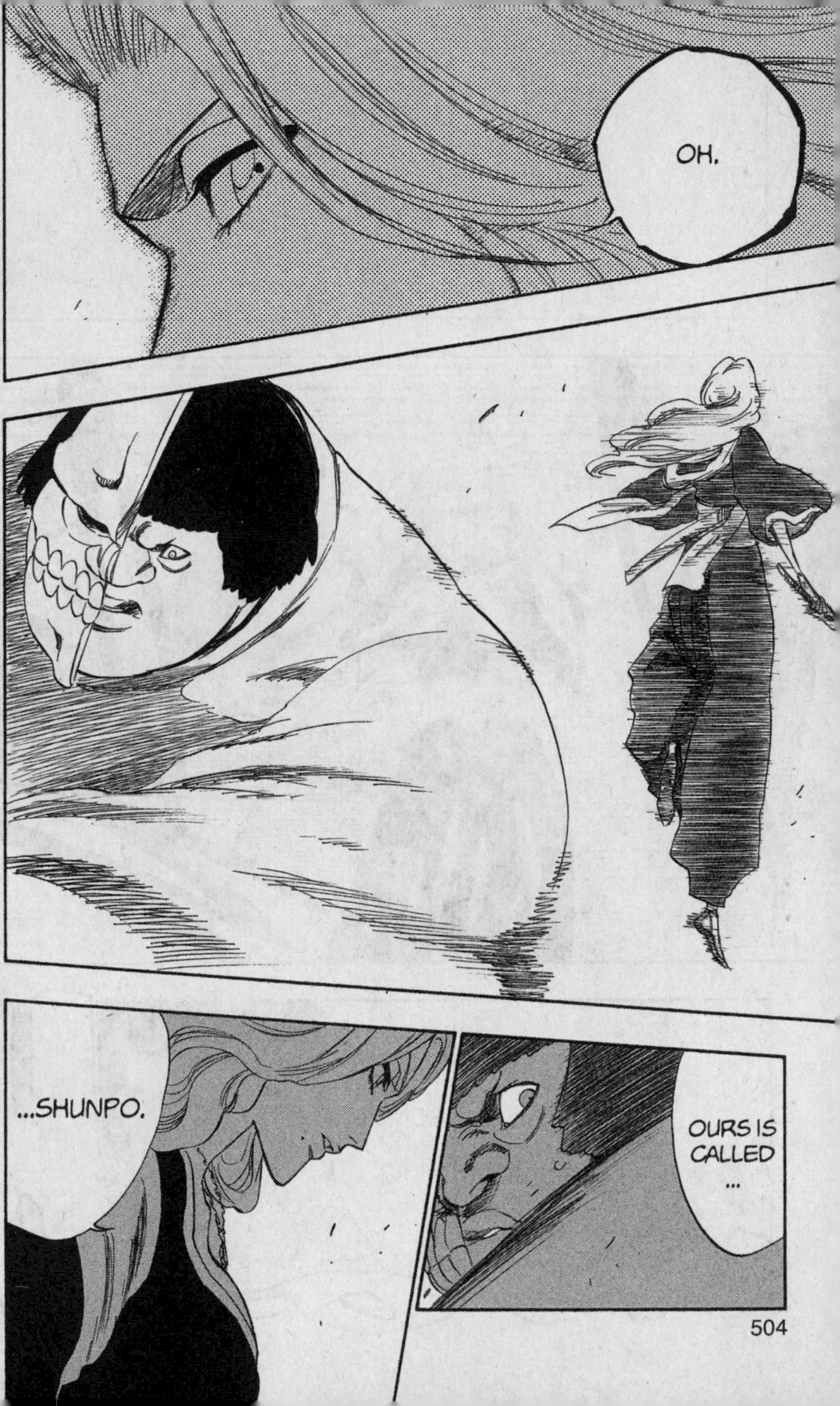
OH.
OURS IS CALLED ...
...SHUNPO.

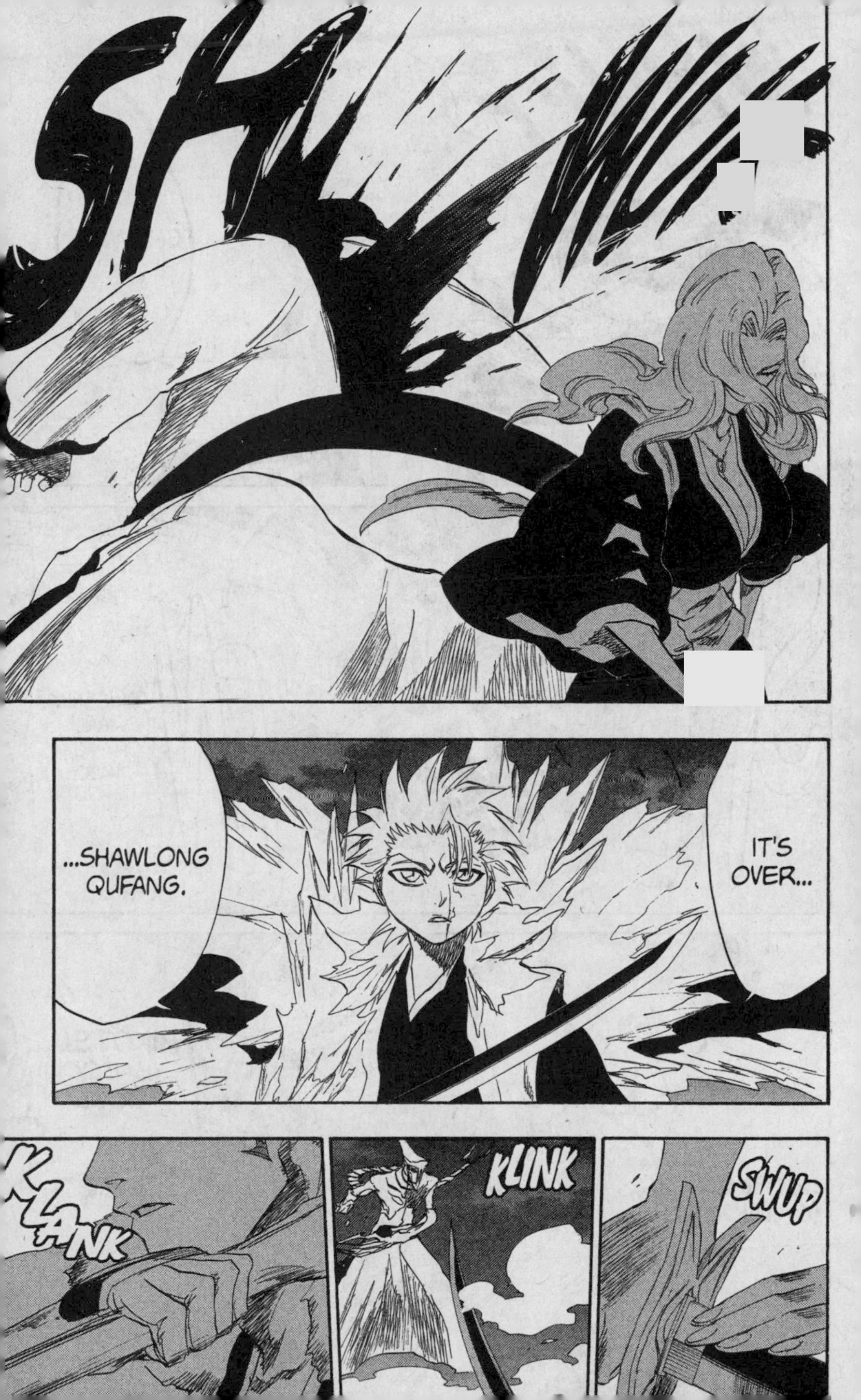
IT'S OVER...
...SHAWLONG QUFANG.
SWUP
KLINK
KLANK

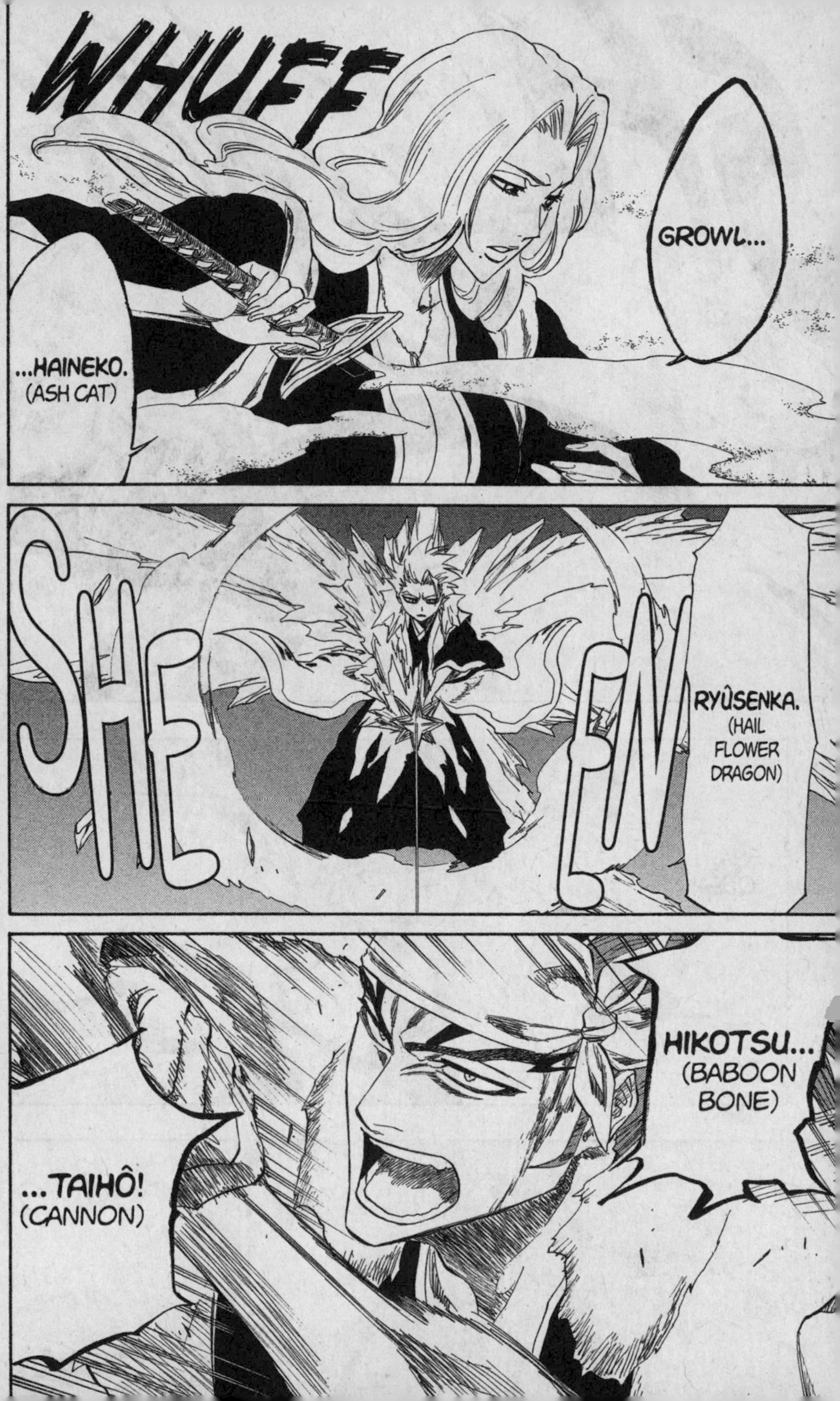

GROWL...
WHUFF
...HAINEKO.
(ASH CAT)
RYÛSENKA.
(HAIL FLOWER DRAGON)
SHEEN
HIKOTSU...
(BABOON BONE)
...TAIHÔ!
(CANNON)

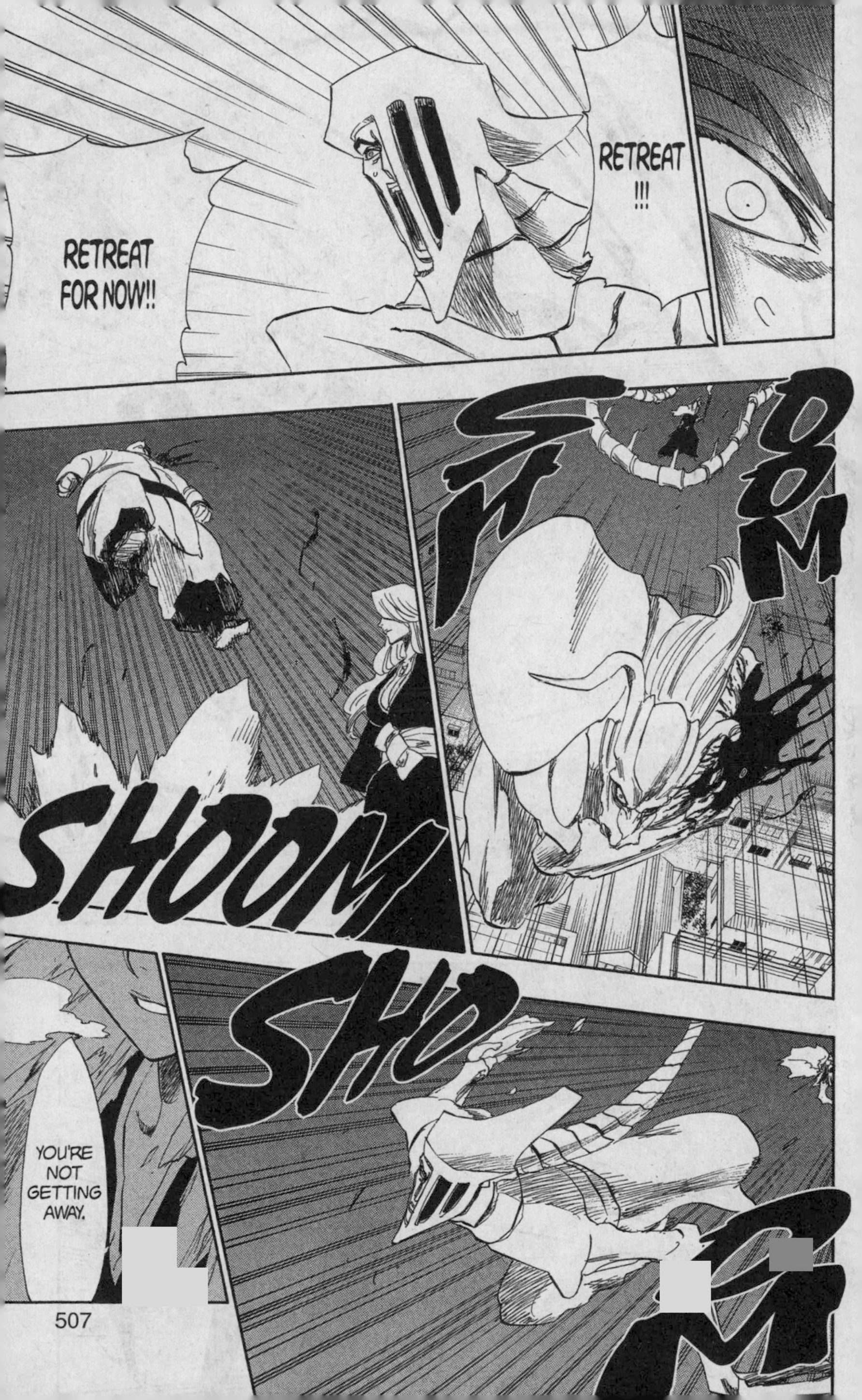
RETREAT !!!
RETREAT FOR NOW!!
BOOM
SH
SHOOM
SHO
YOU'RE NOT GETTING AWAY.

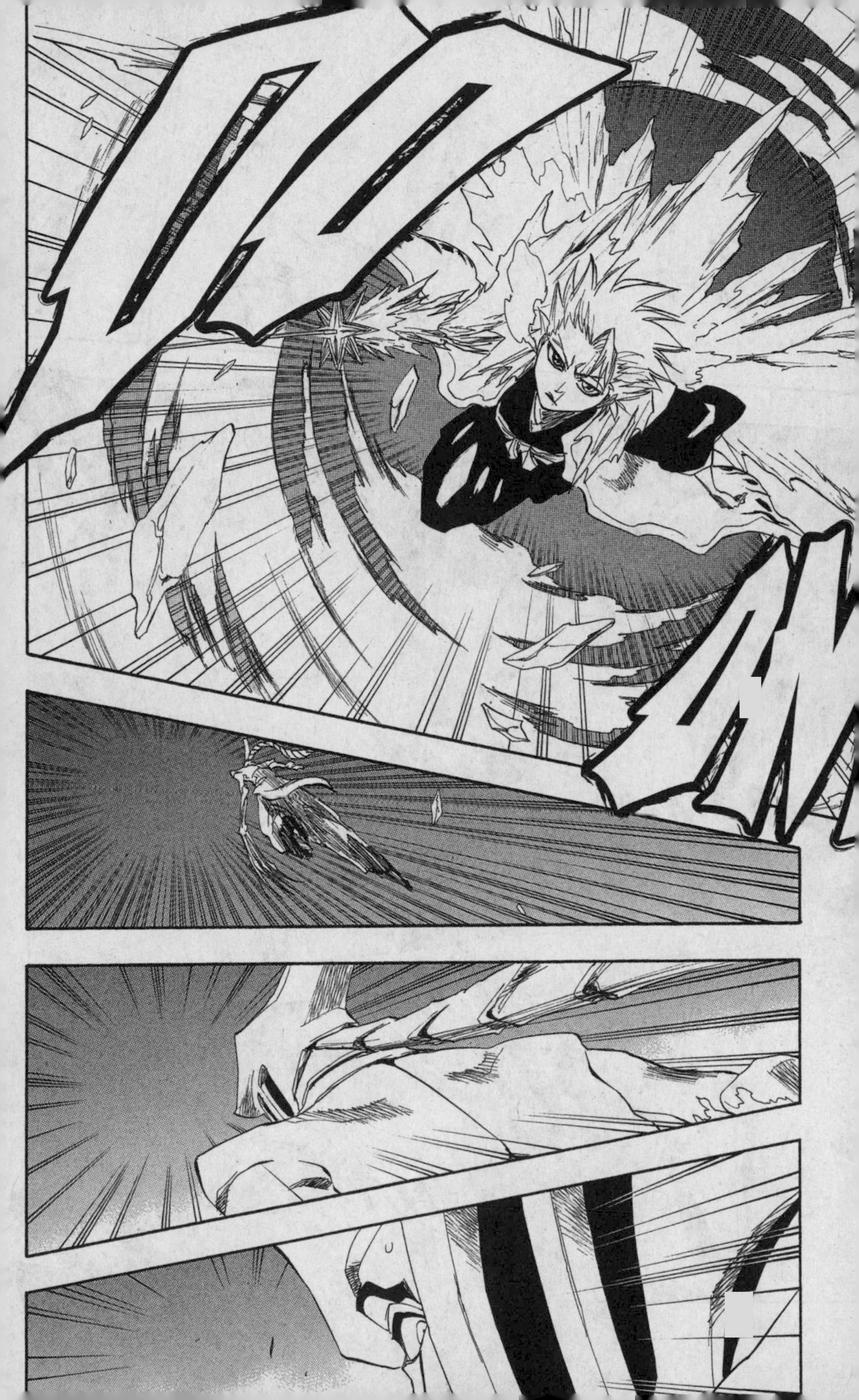

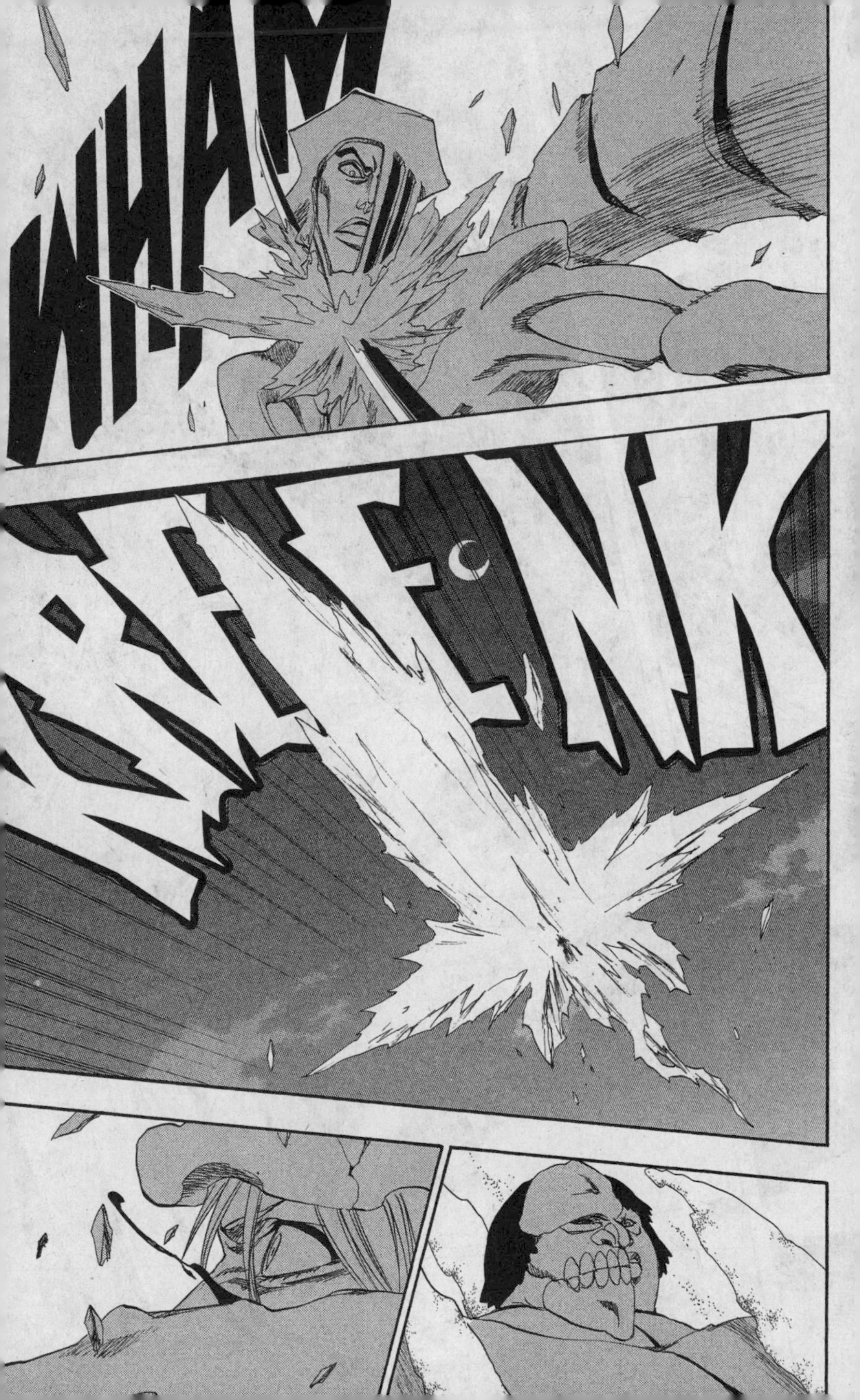
WHAM

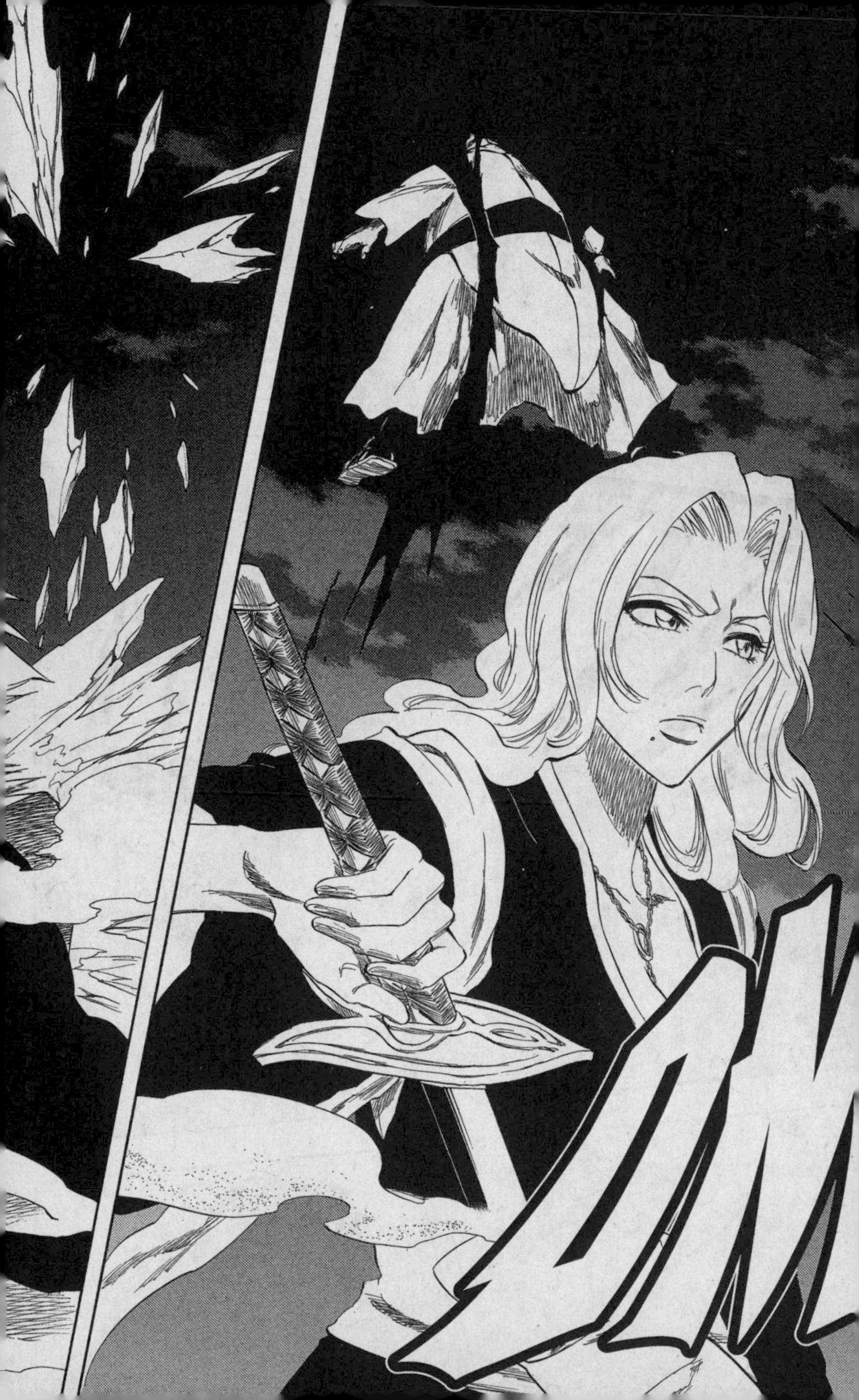

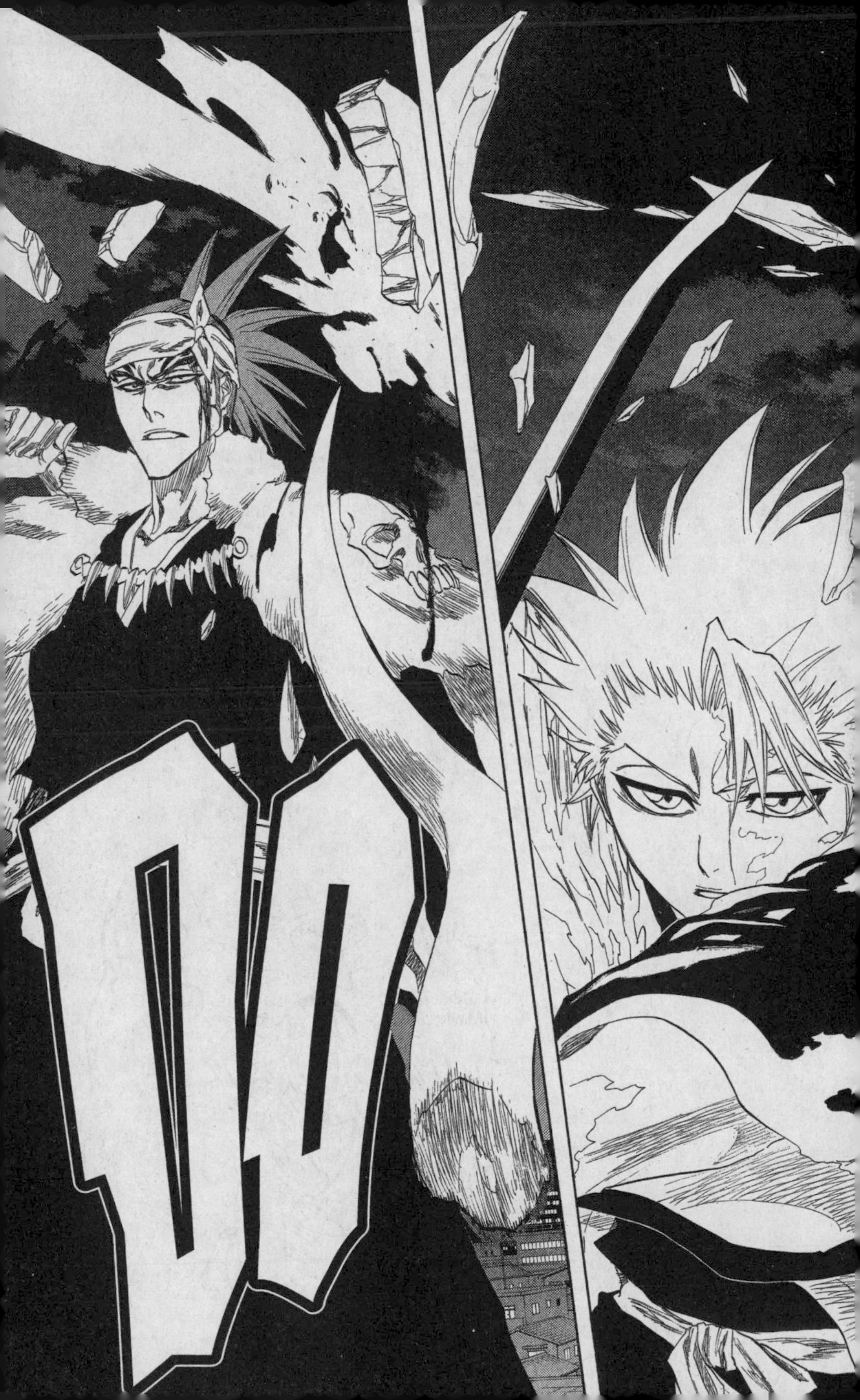
DO

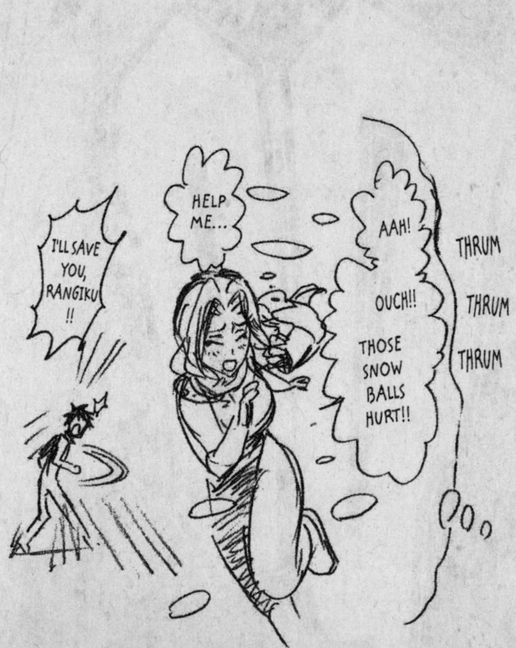
THRUM
THRUM
THRUM
AAH!
OUCH!!
THOSE SNOW BALLS HURT!!
HELP ME...
I'LL SAVE YOU, RANGIKU!!

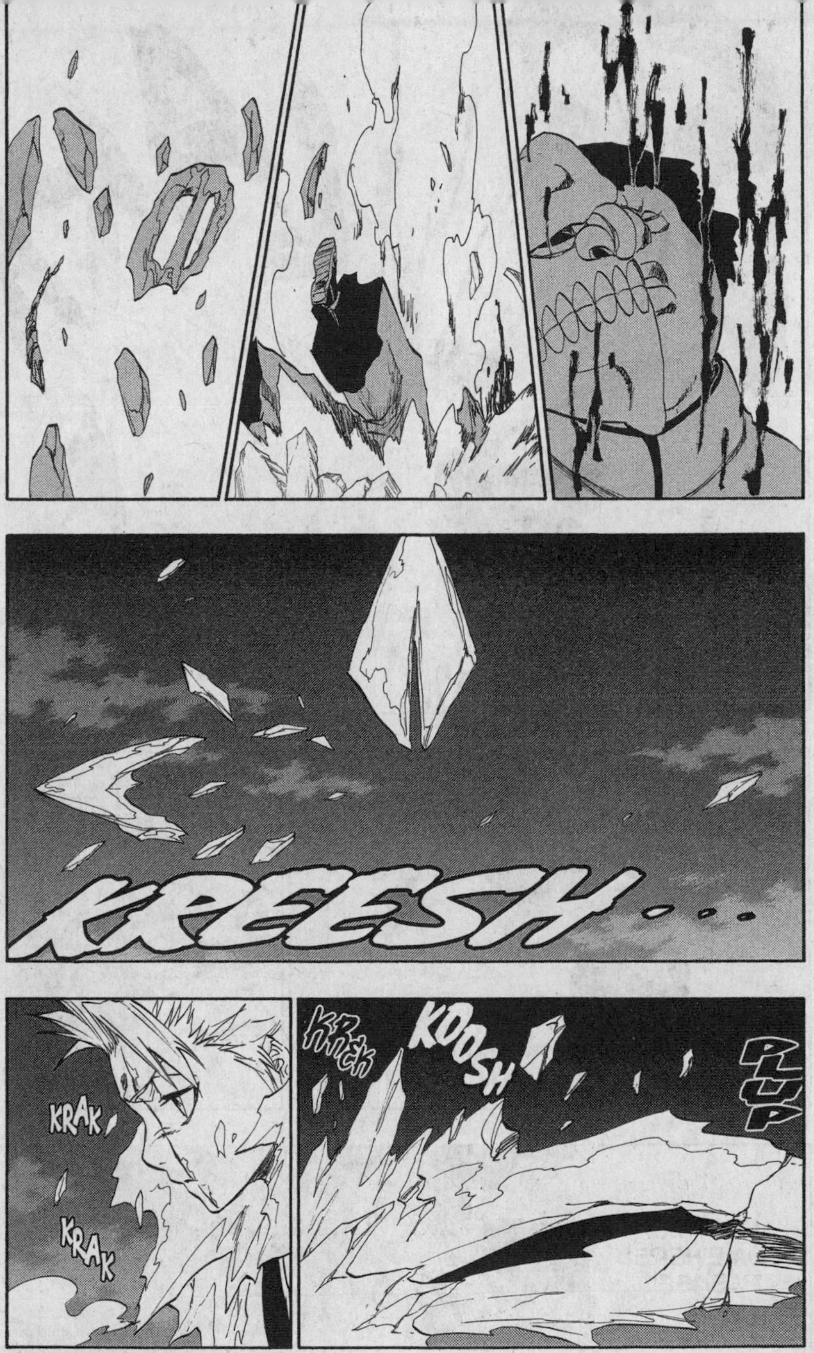
KREESH...
PLUP
KOOSH
KRAK
KRAK

211. Stroke of Sanity

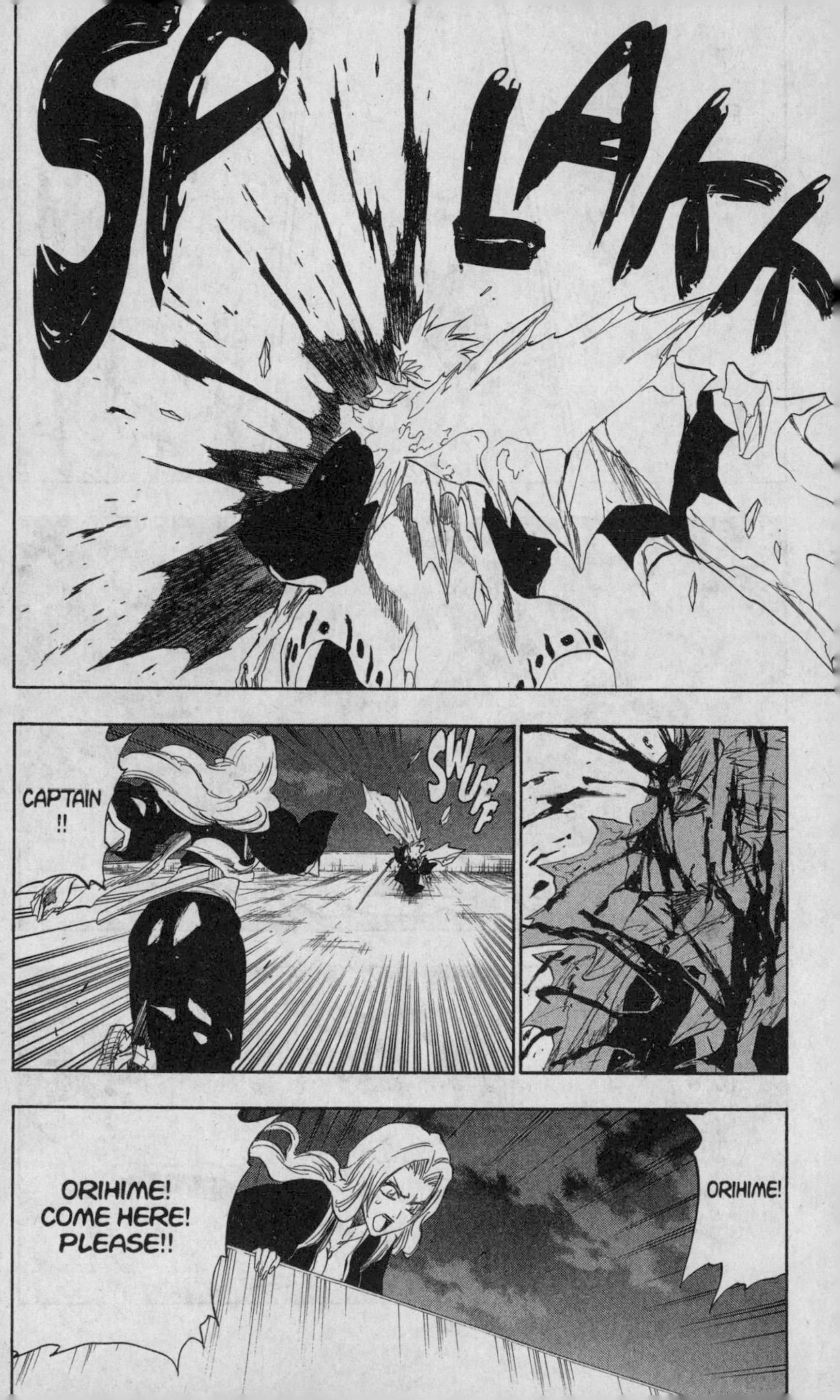
SPLAKK
SWUFF
CAPTAIN !!
ORIHIME!
ORIHIME! COME HERE! PLEASE!!

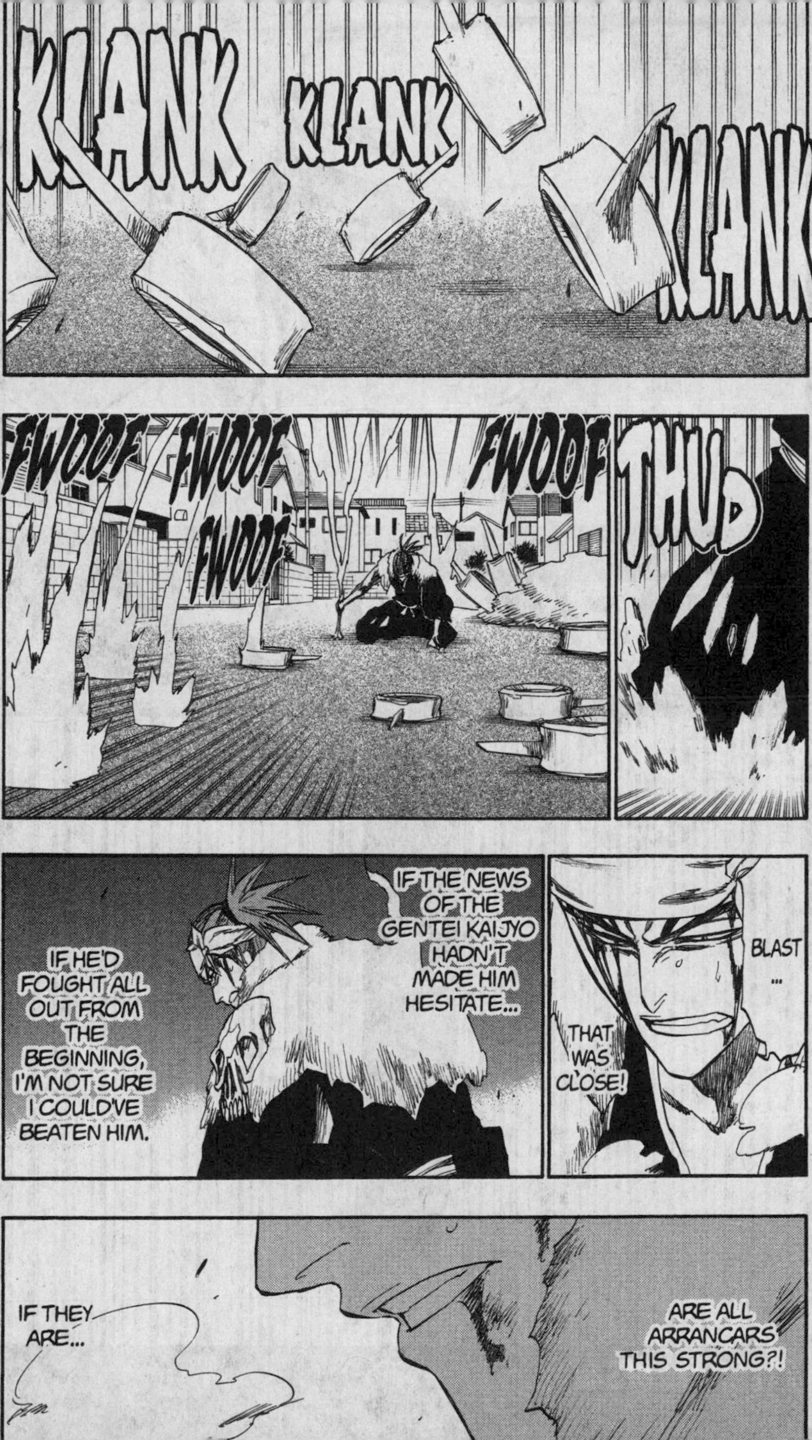
KLANK
KLANK
KLANK
THUD
FWOOF
FWOOF
FWOOF
FWOOF
BLAST...
THAT WAS CLOSE!
IF THE NEWS OF THE GENTEI KAIJYO HADN'T MADE HIM HESITATE...
IF HE'D FOUGHT ALL OUT FROM THE BEGINNING, I'M NOT SURE I COULD'VE BEATEN HIM.
ARE ALL ARRANCARS THIS STRONG?!
IF THEY ARE...

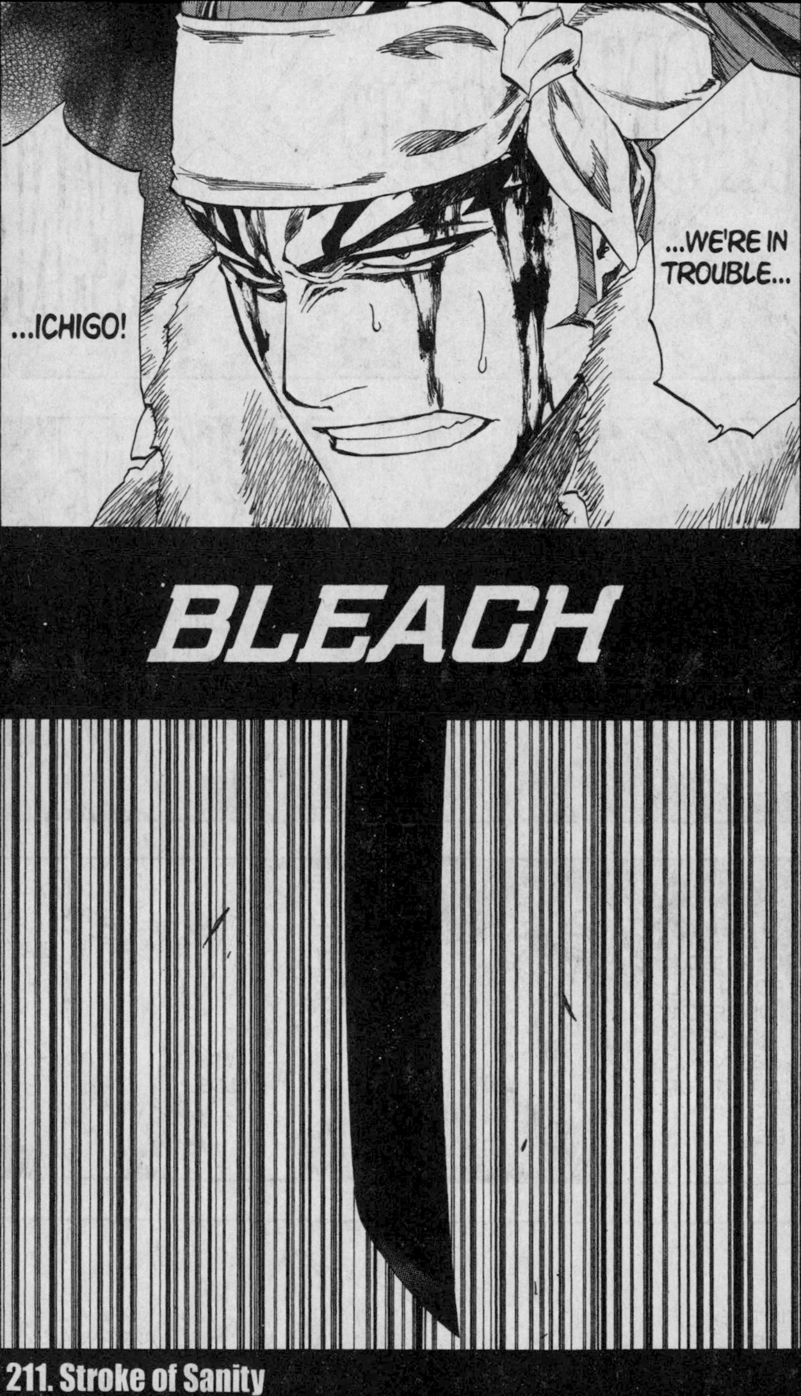
...WE'RE IN TROUBLE...
...ICHIGO!
BLEACH
211. Stroke of Sanity

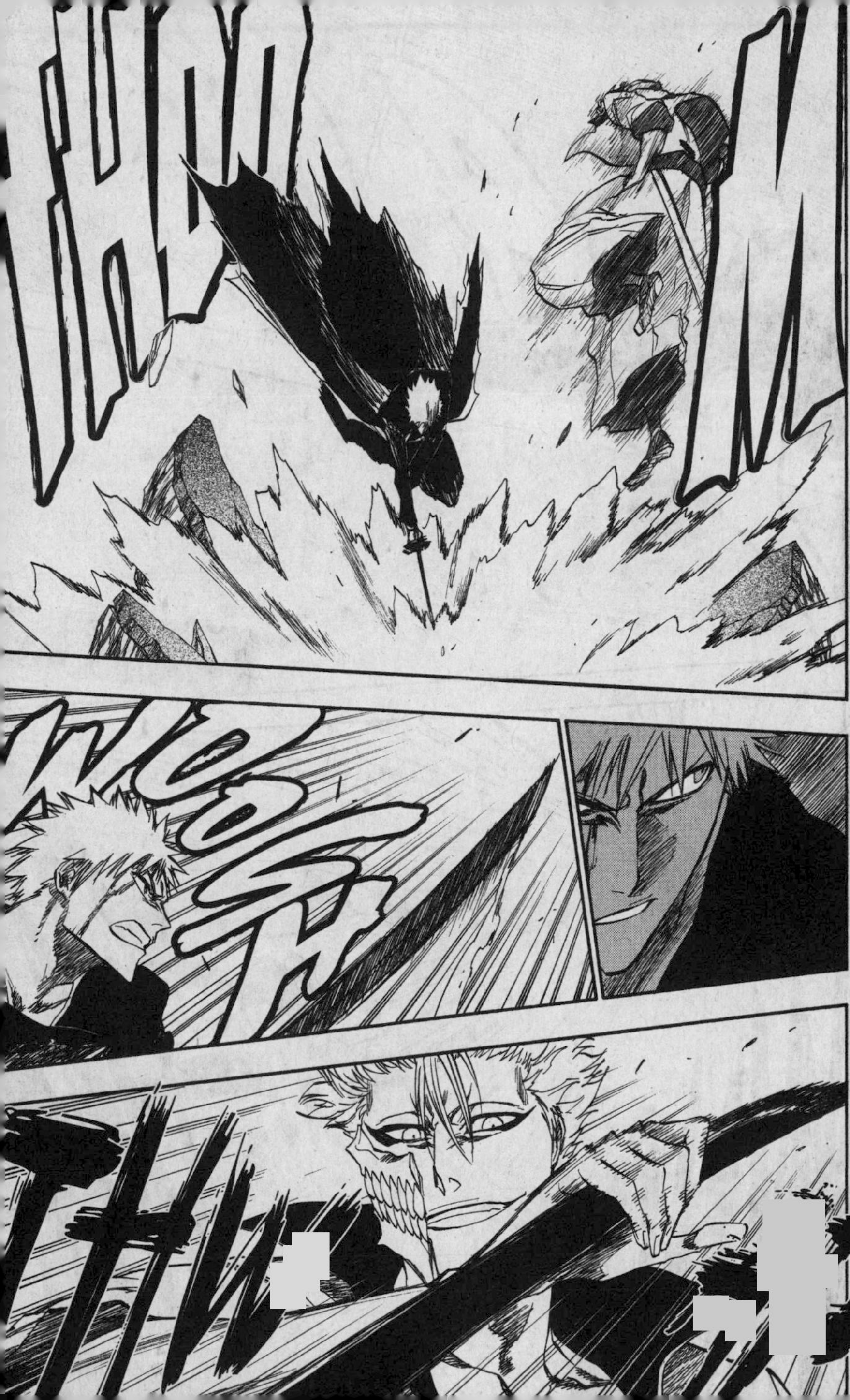

WHOOSH

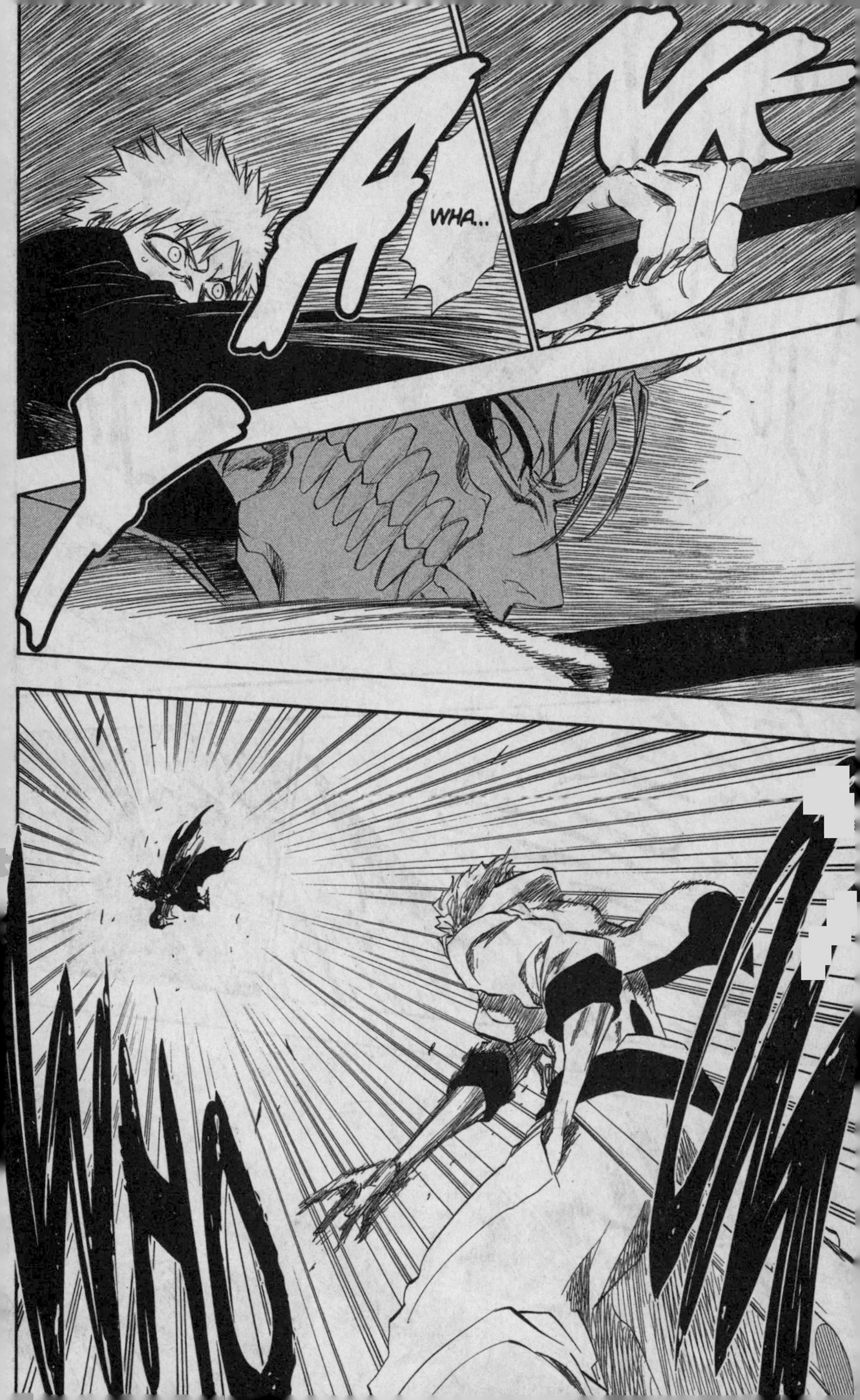
YANK
WHA...

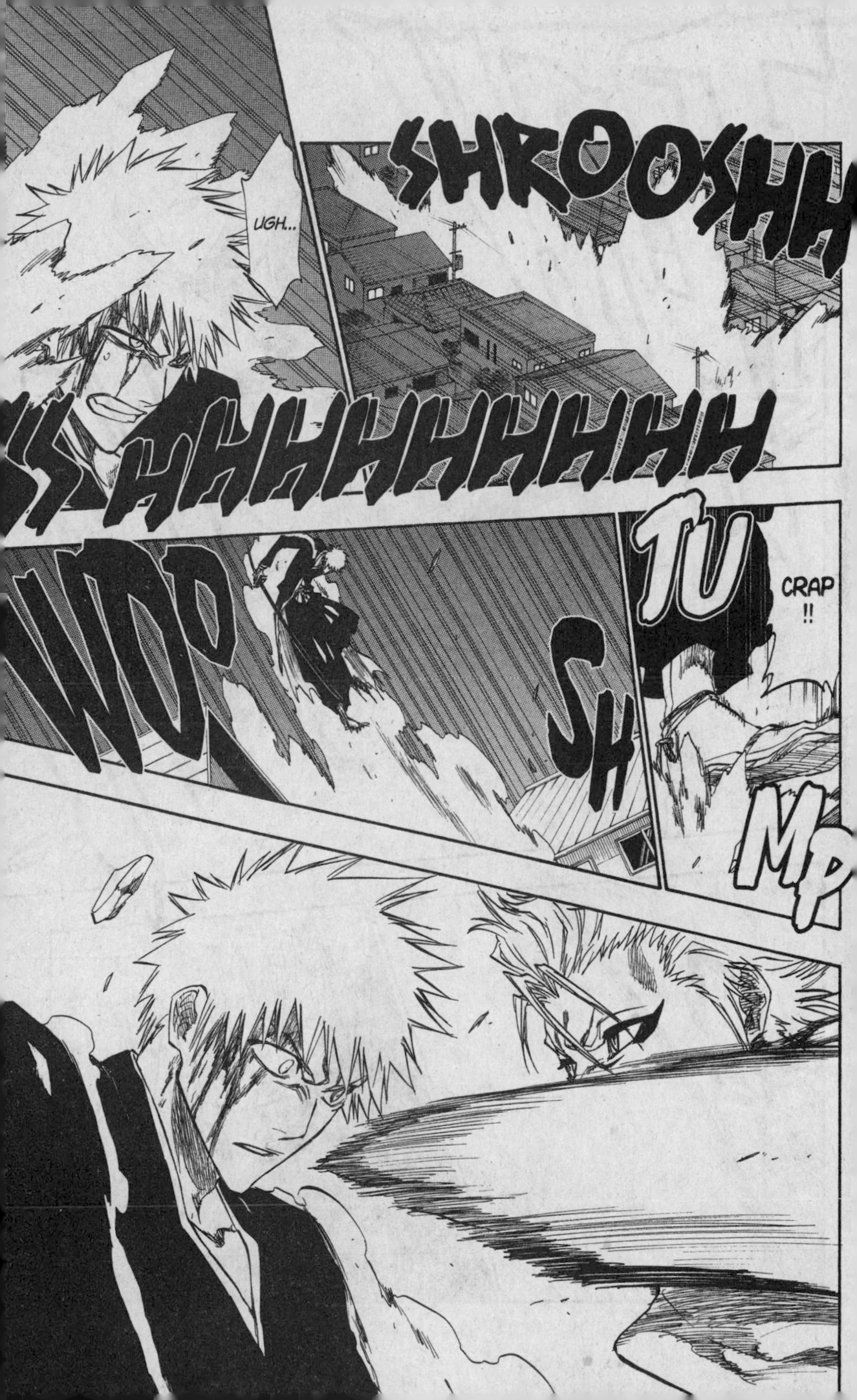
SHROOSHH
UGH...
SHHHHHHHHHHHHH
TU
CRAP !!
MP
SH
WOO

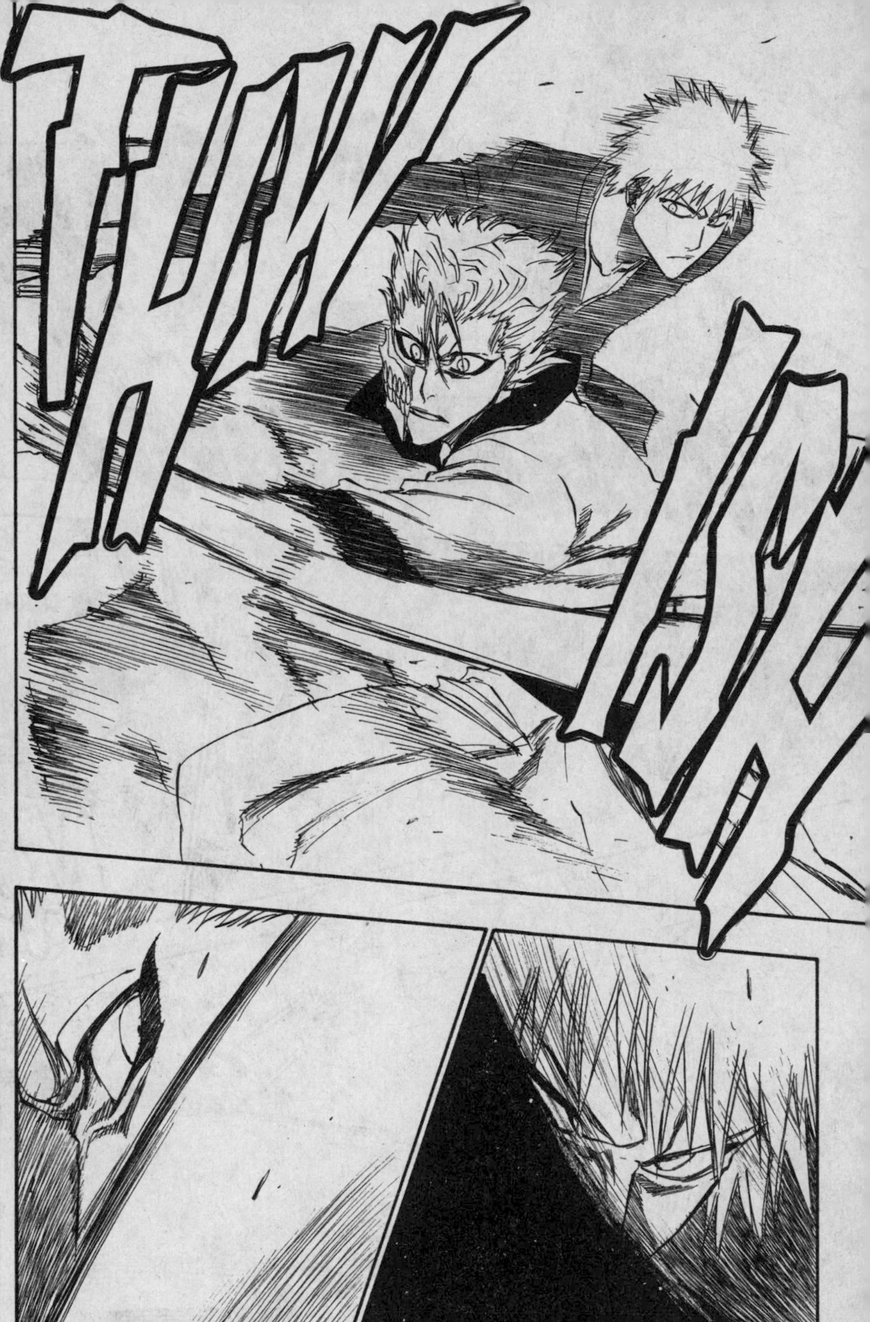

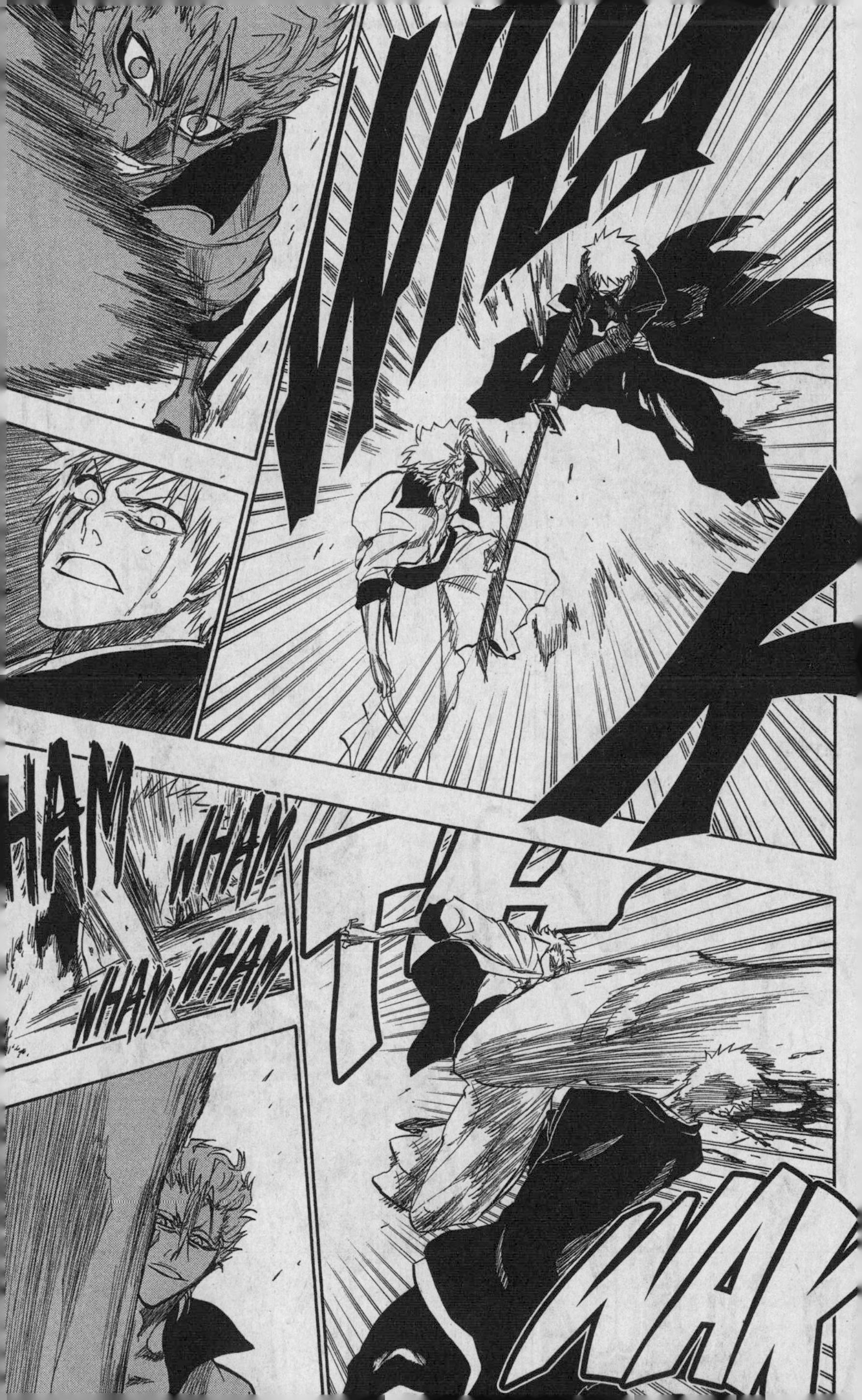
WHAK
WHAM WHAM
WHAM WHAM
WAK

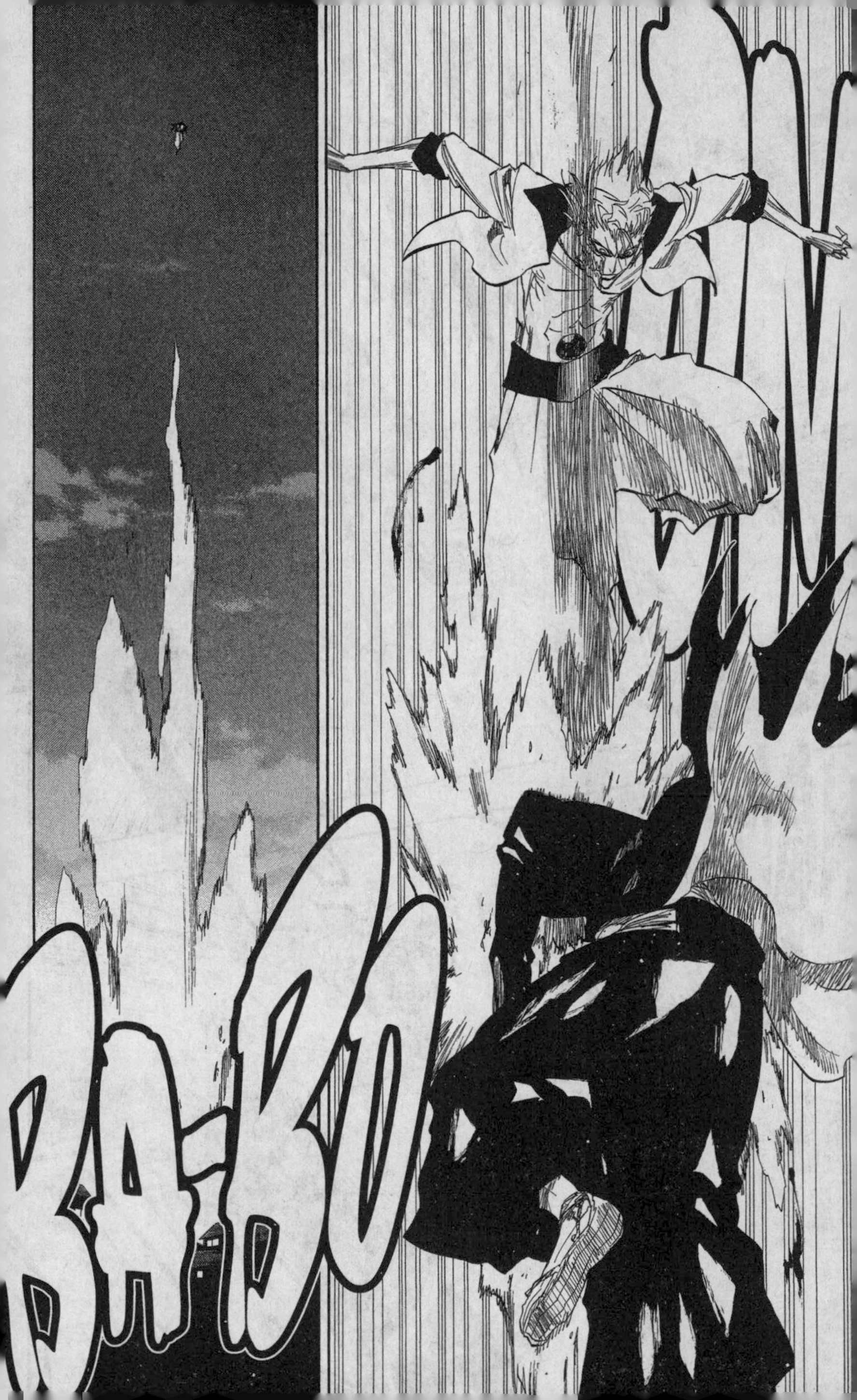
BA-BO

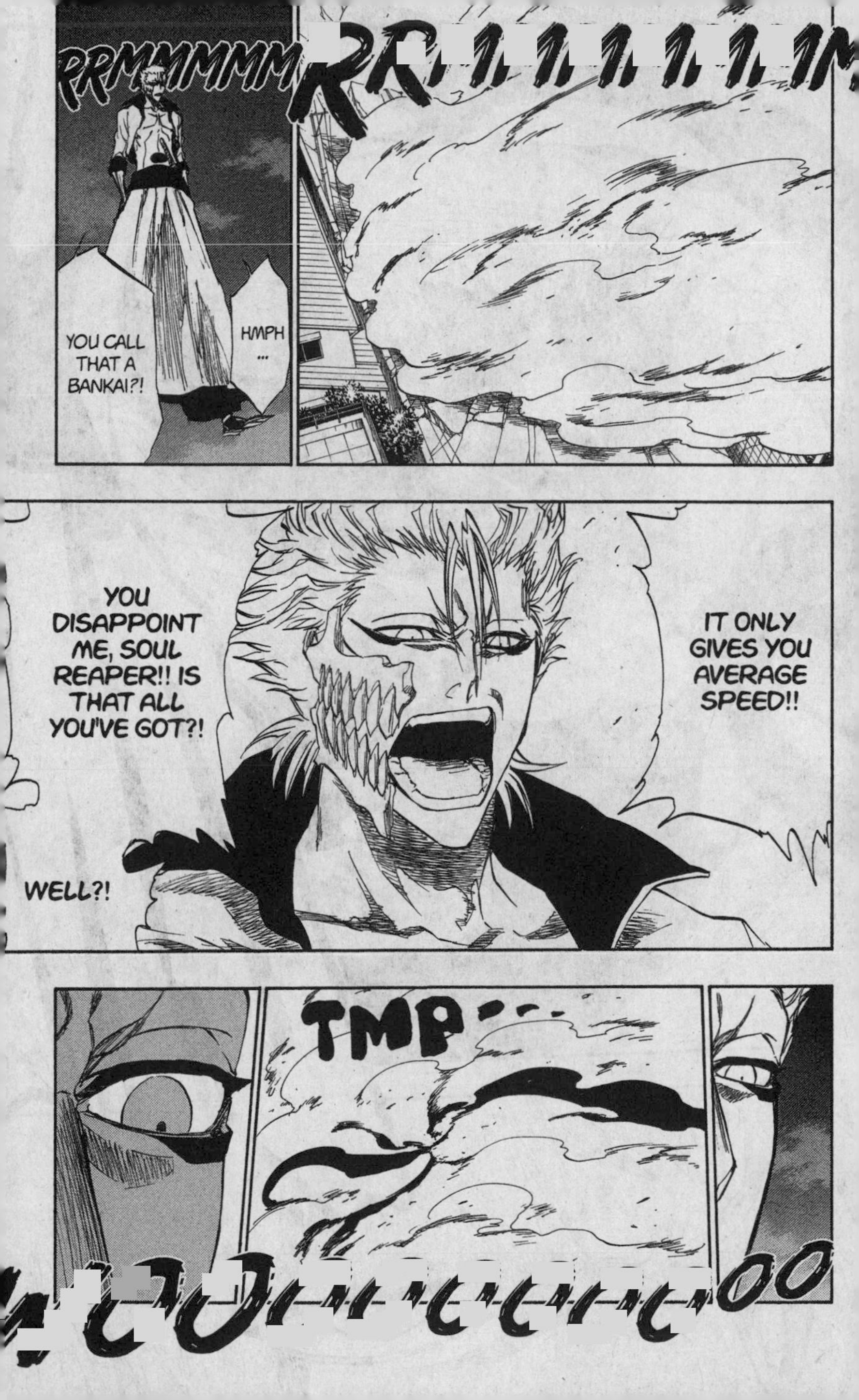
RRMMMMMM
HMPH ...
YOU CALL THAT A BANKAI?!
IT ONLY GIVES YOU AVERAGE SPEED!!
YOU DISAPPOINT ME, SOUL REAPER!! IS THAT ALL YOU'VE GOT?!
WELL?!
TMP...

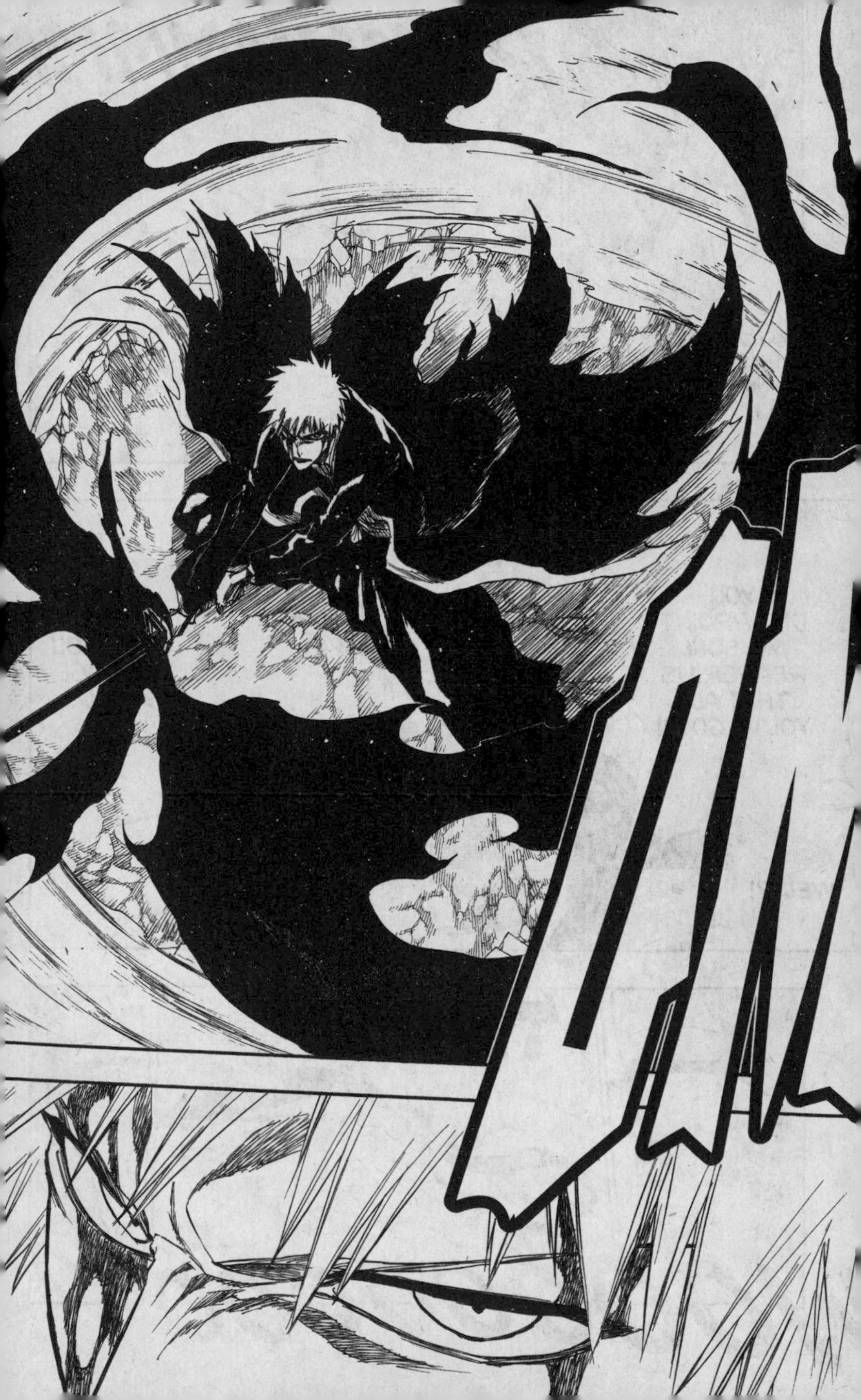

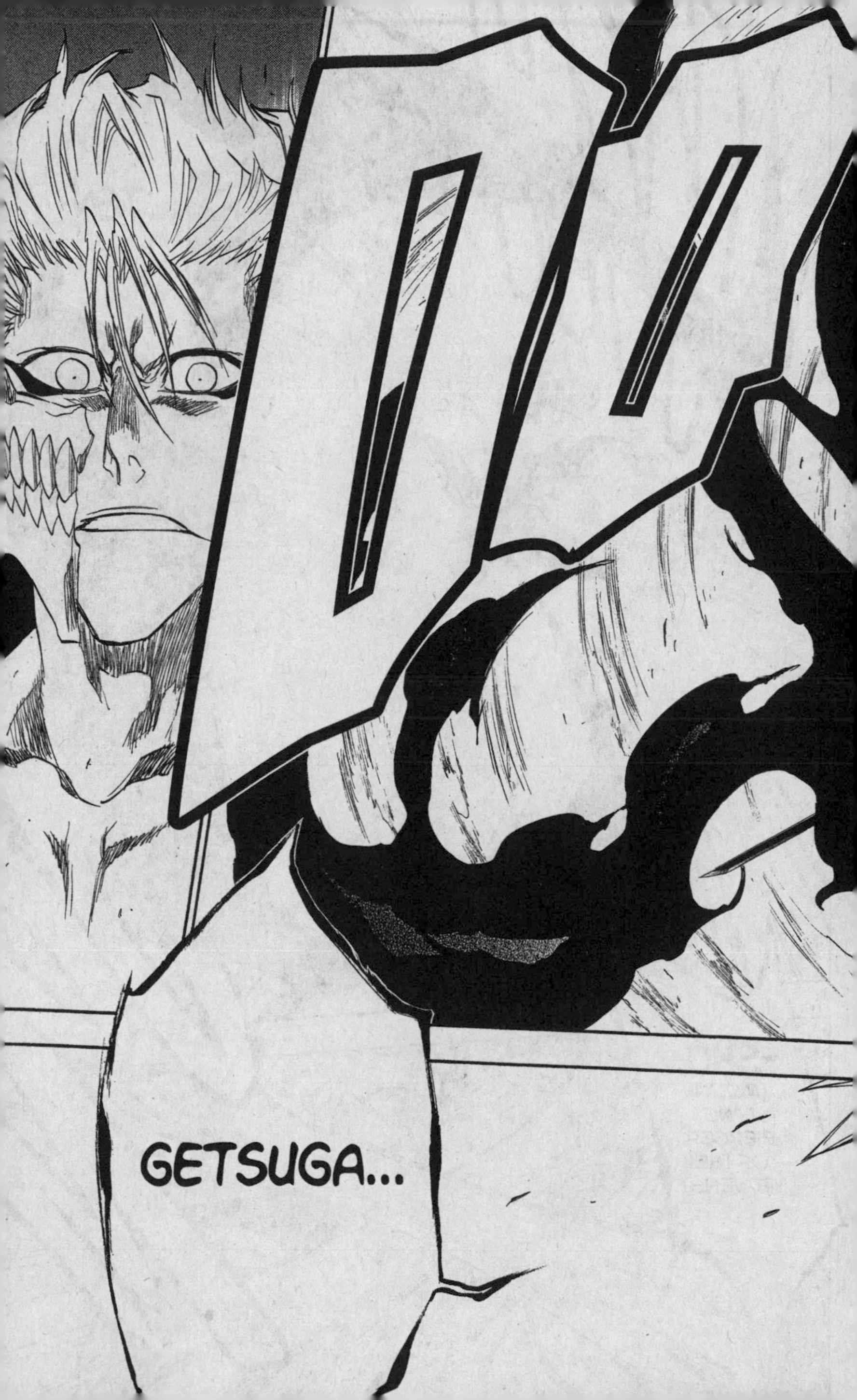
GETSUGA...

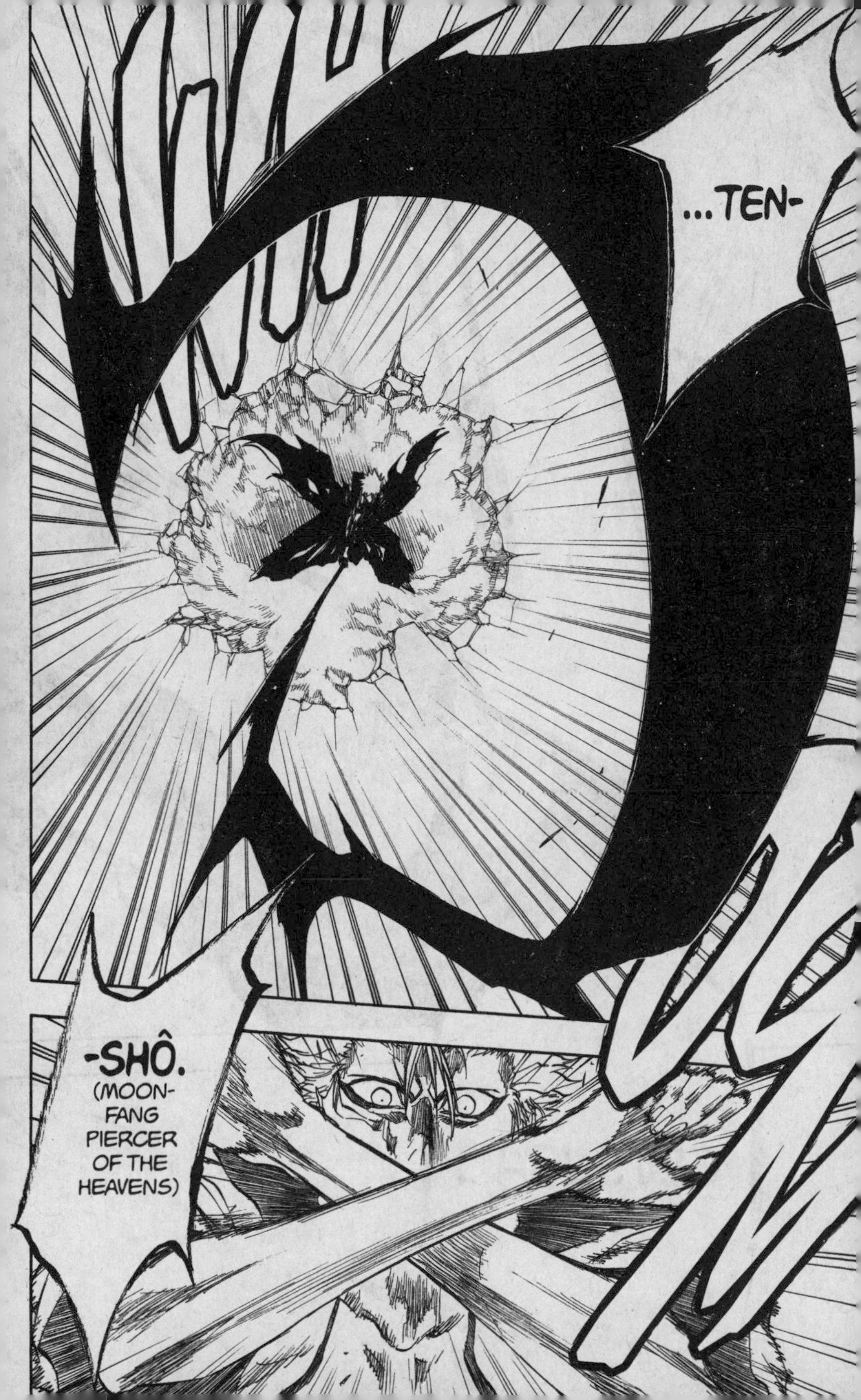
...TEN-
-SHÔ.
(MOON-
FANG
PIERCER
OF THE
HEAVENS)

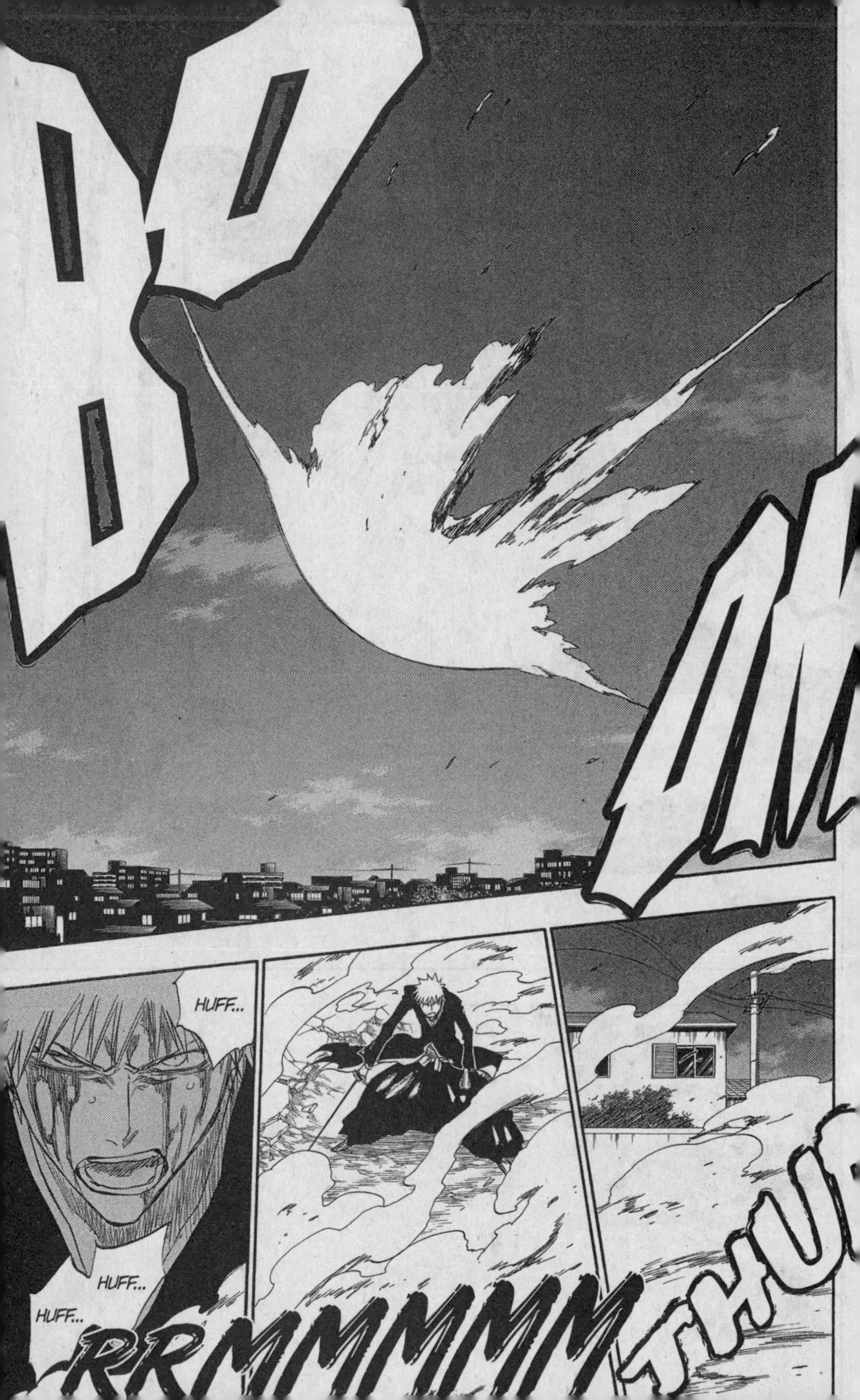
HUFF...
HUFF...
HUFF...
RRMMMMMM

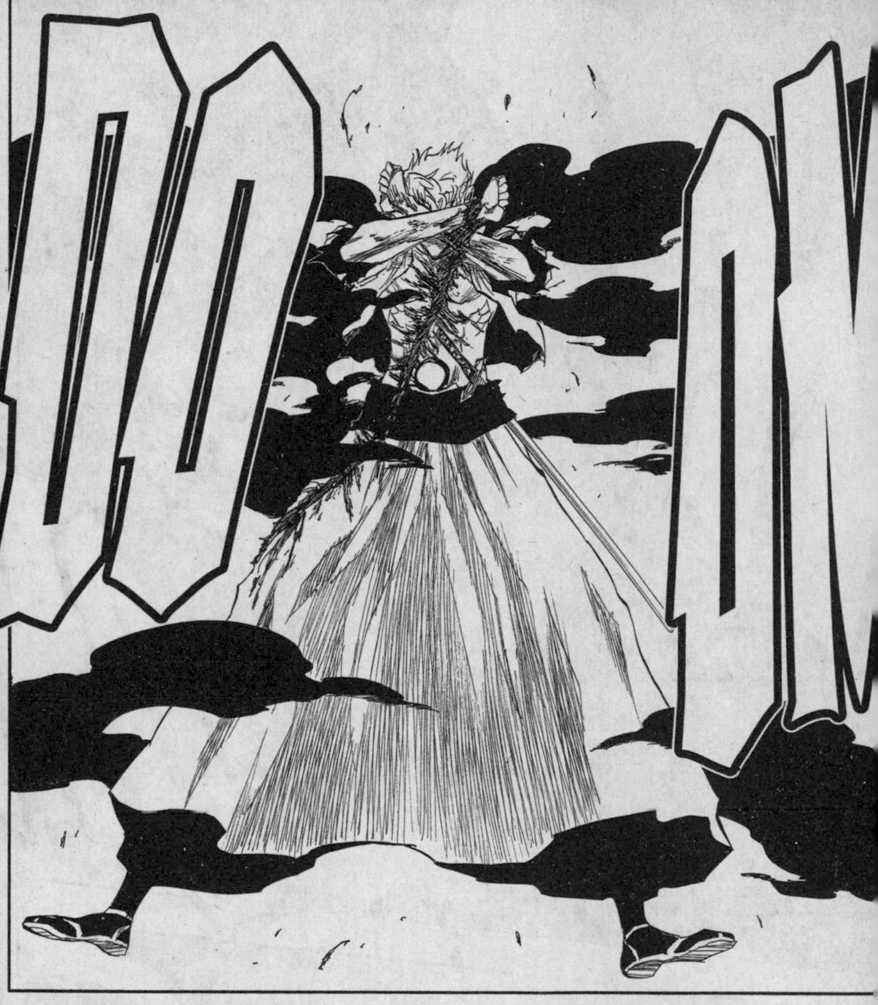
DOOM
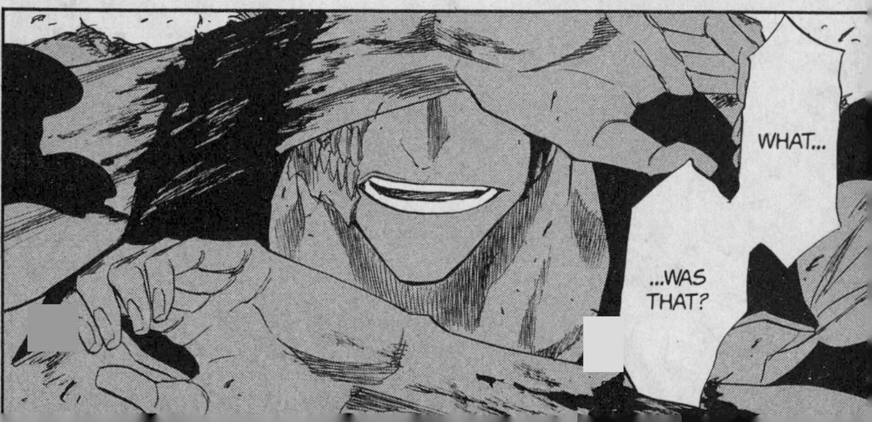
WHAT...
...WAS THAT?

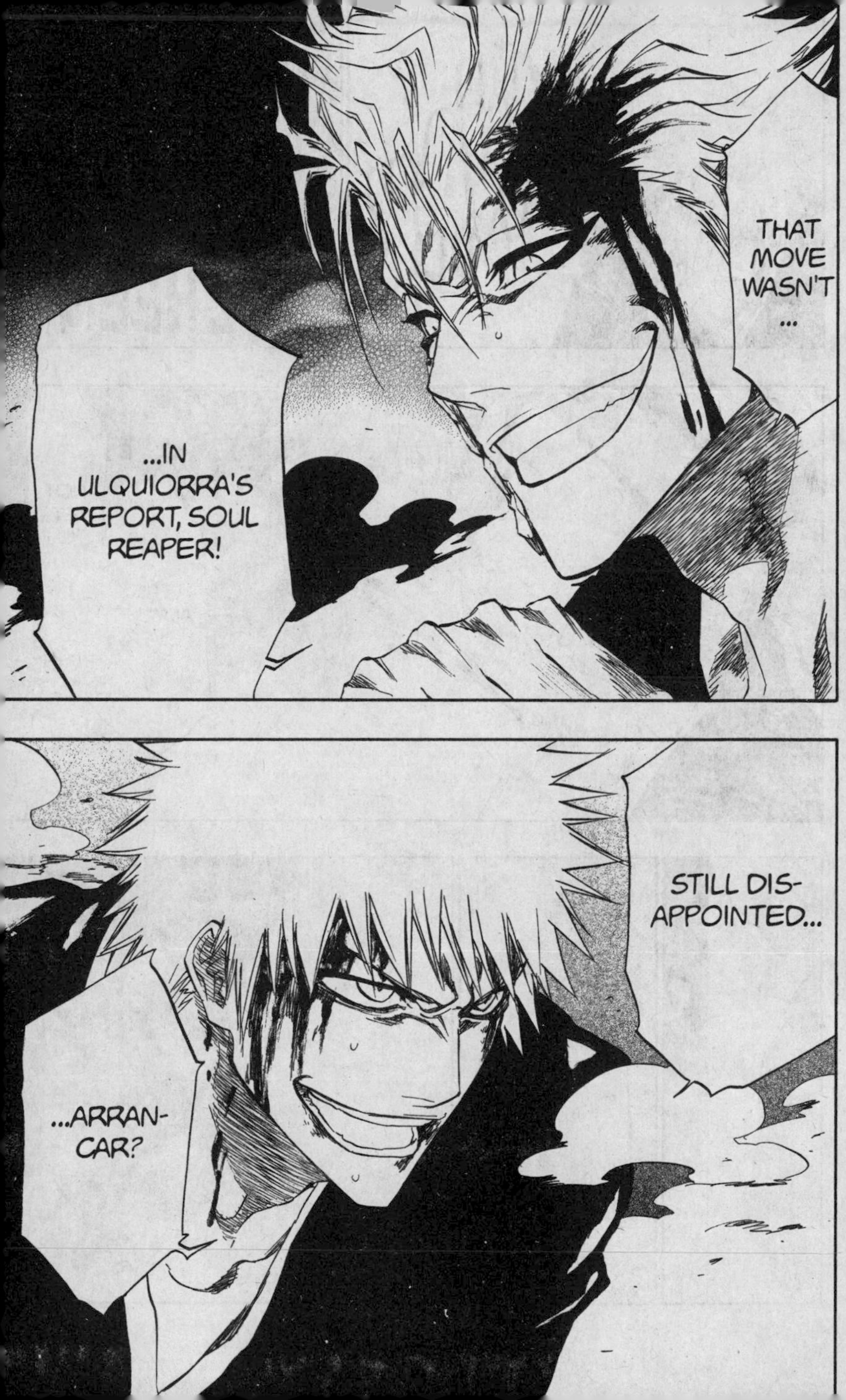
THAT MOVE WASN'T ...
...IN ULQUIORRA'S REPORT, SOUL REAPER!
STILL DIS-APPOINTED...
...ARRAN-CAR?

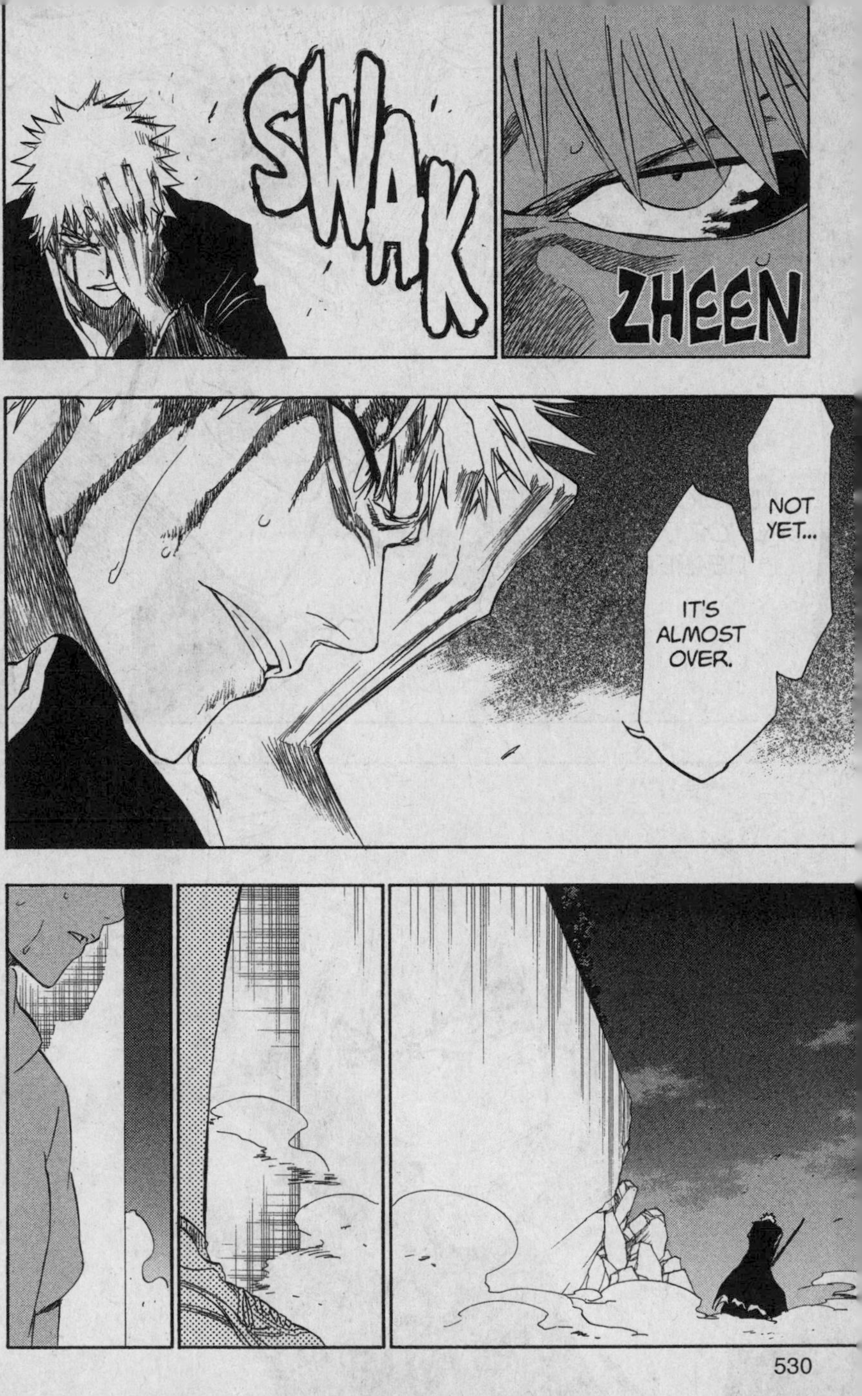
ZHEEN
SWAK
NOT YET...
IT'S ALMOST OVER.

KREEK

ICHIGO...

KREKKKKKK

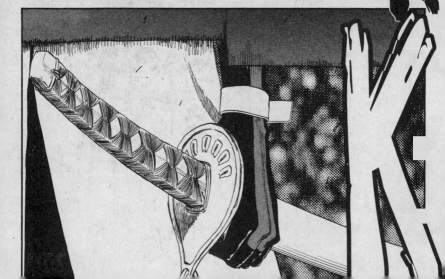

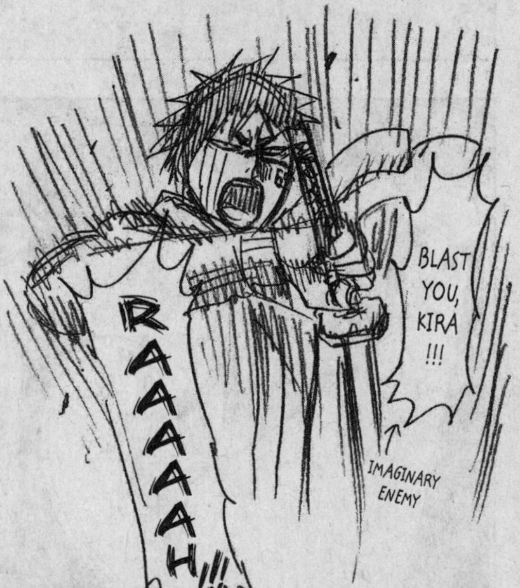
BLAST YOU, KIRA !!!
RAAAAAH!!!
IMAGINARY ENEMY

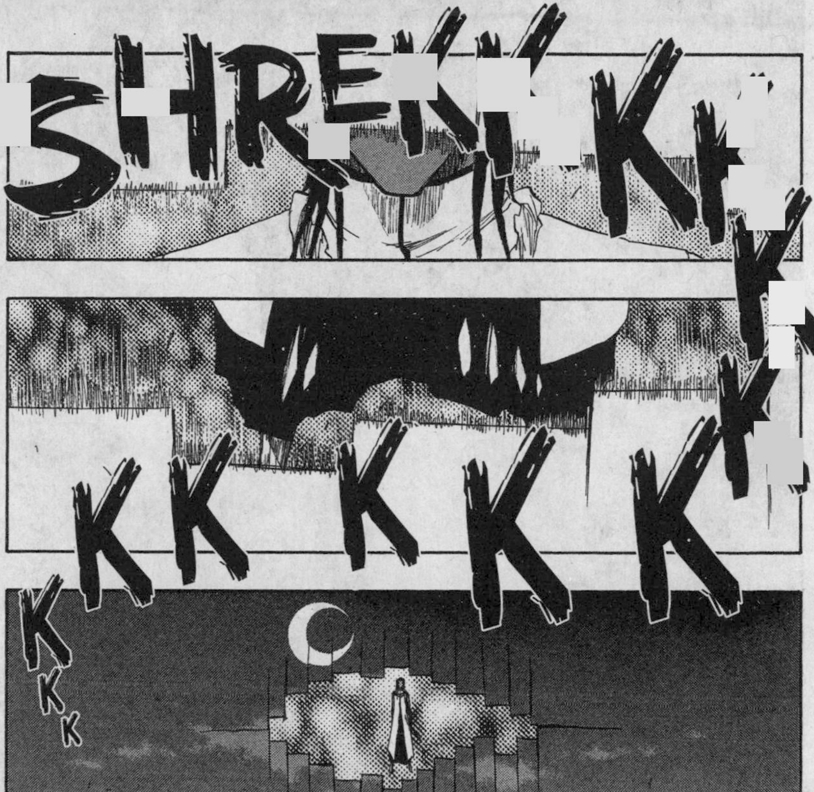
SHRE
KKKKK
KKK

212. You Don't Hear My Name Anymore

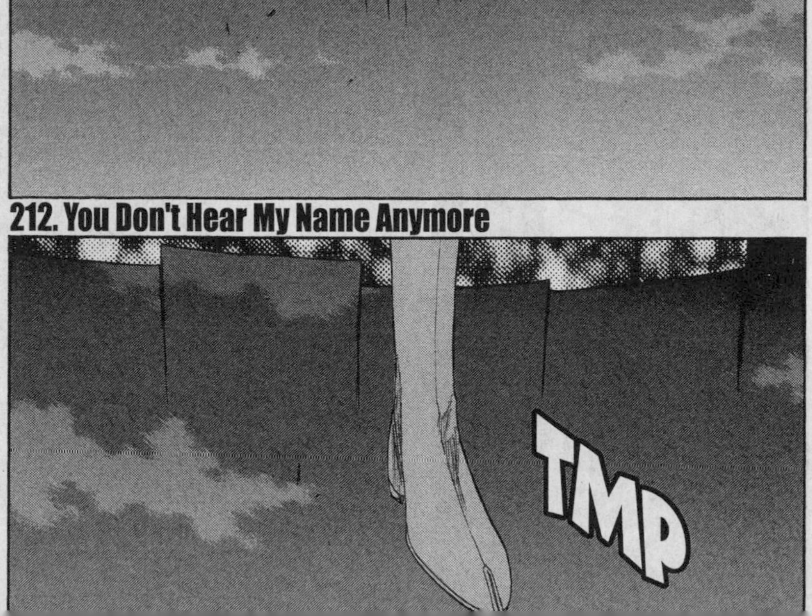
TMP

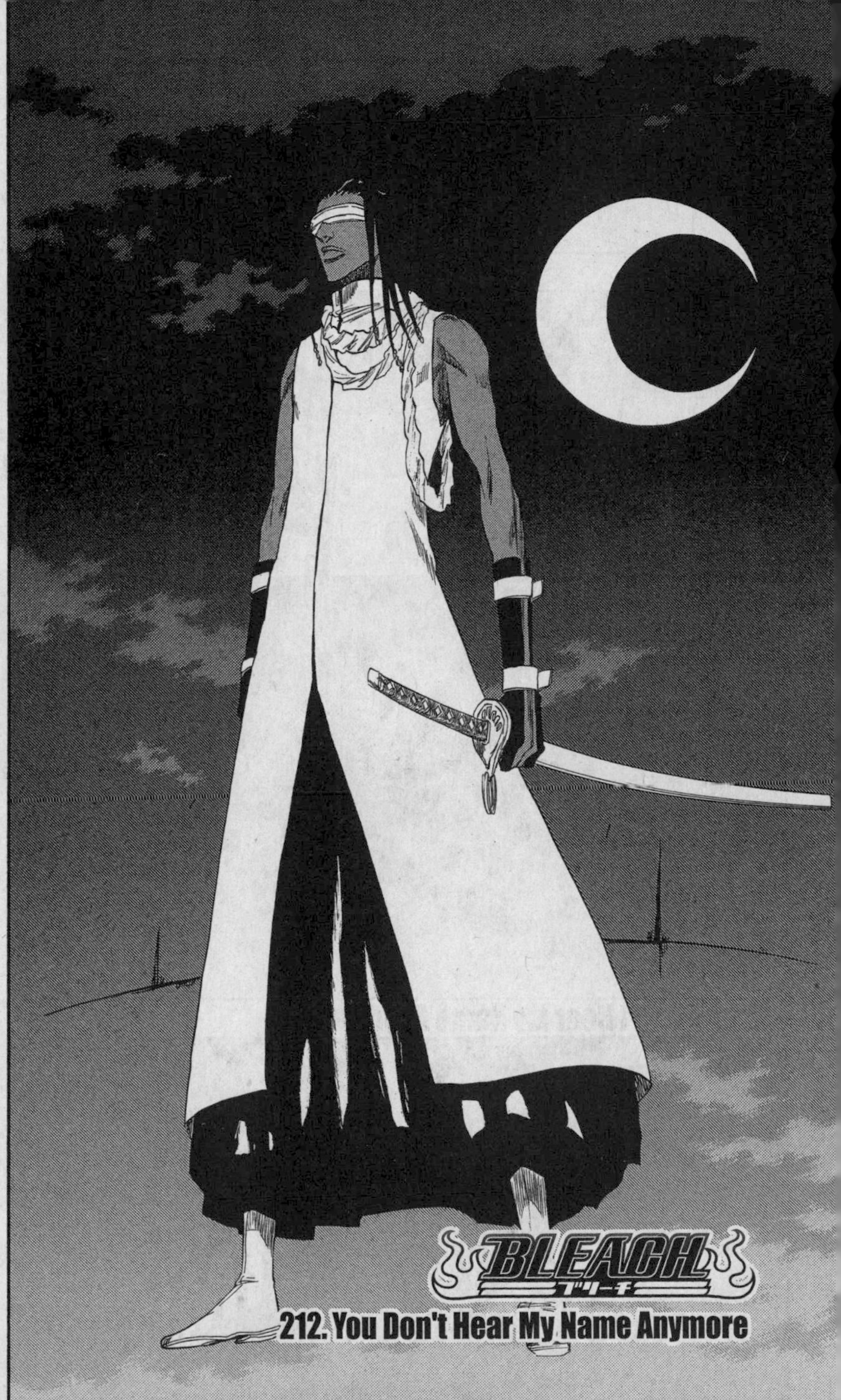
BLEACH
ブリーチ
212. You Don't Hear My Name Anymore

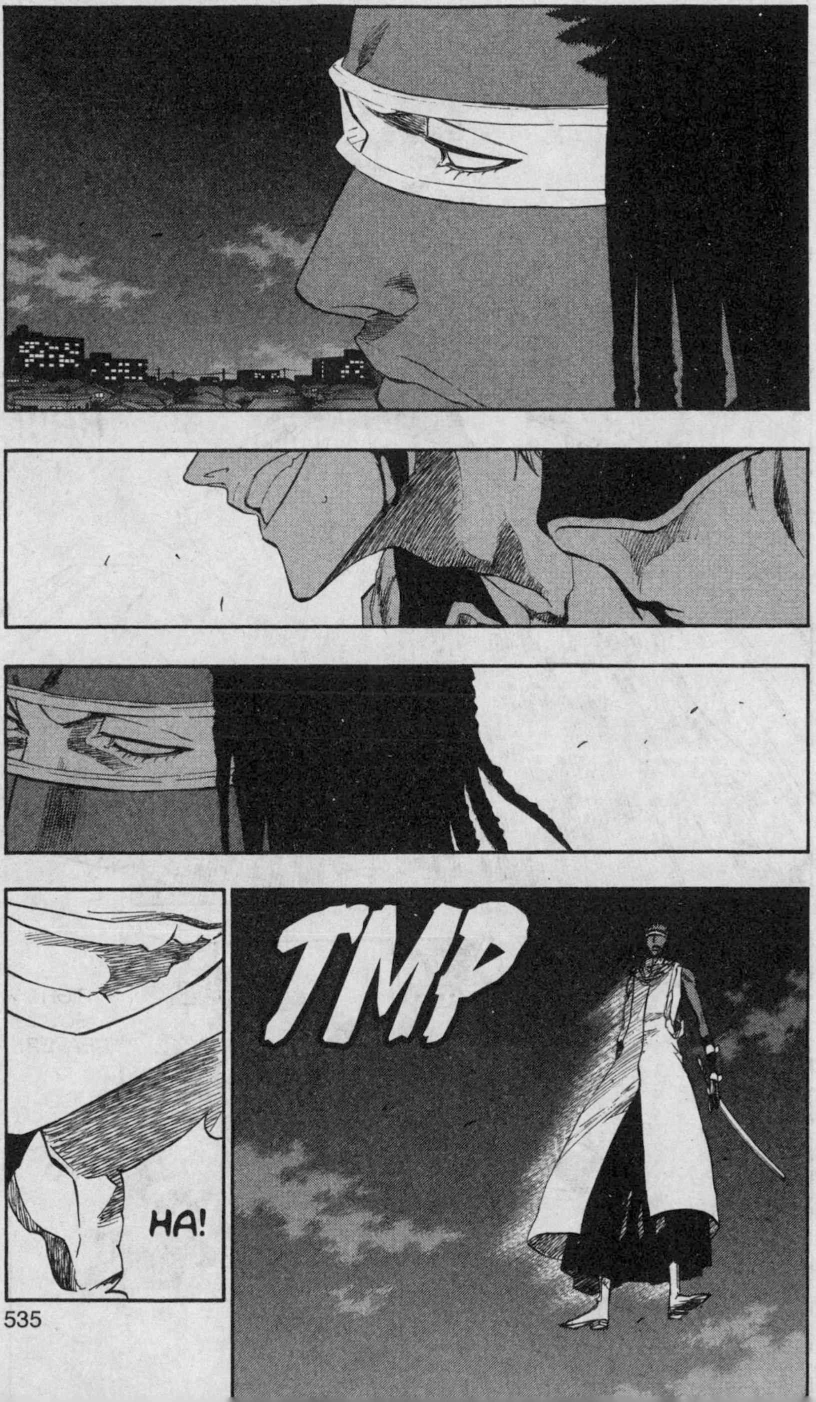
TMP
HA!

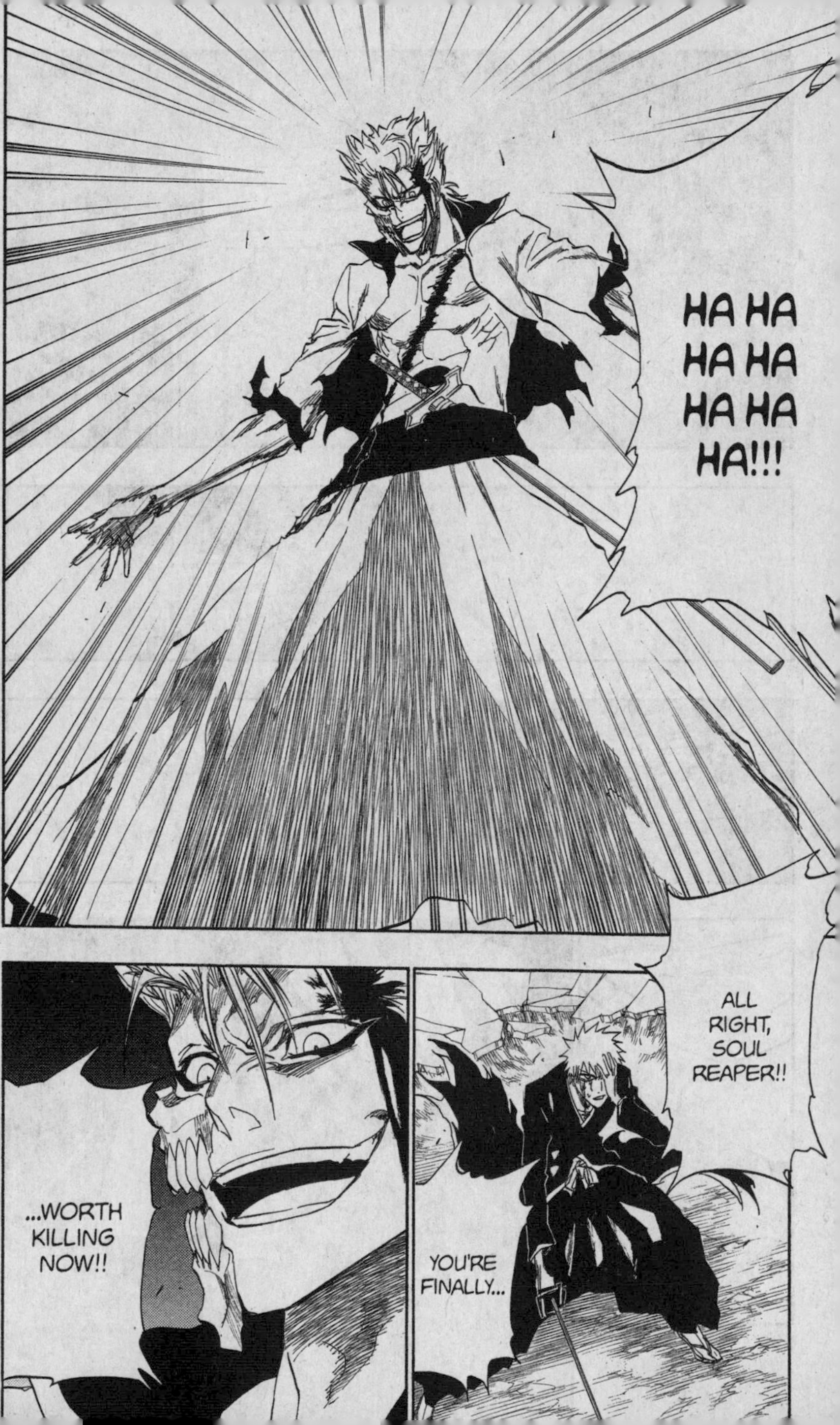

HA HA HA HA HA HA HA!!!
ALL RIGHT, SOUL REAPER!!
YOU'RE FINALLY...
...WORTH KILLING NOW!!

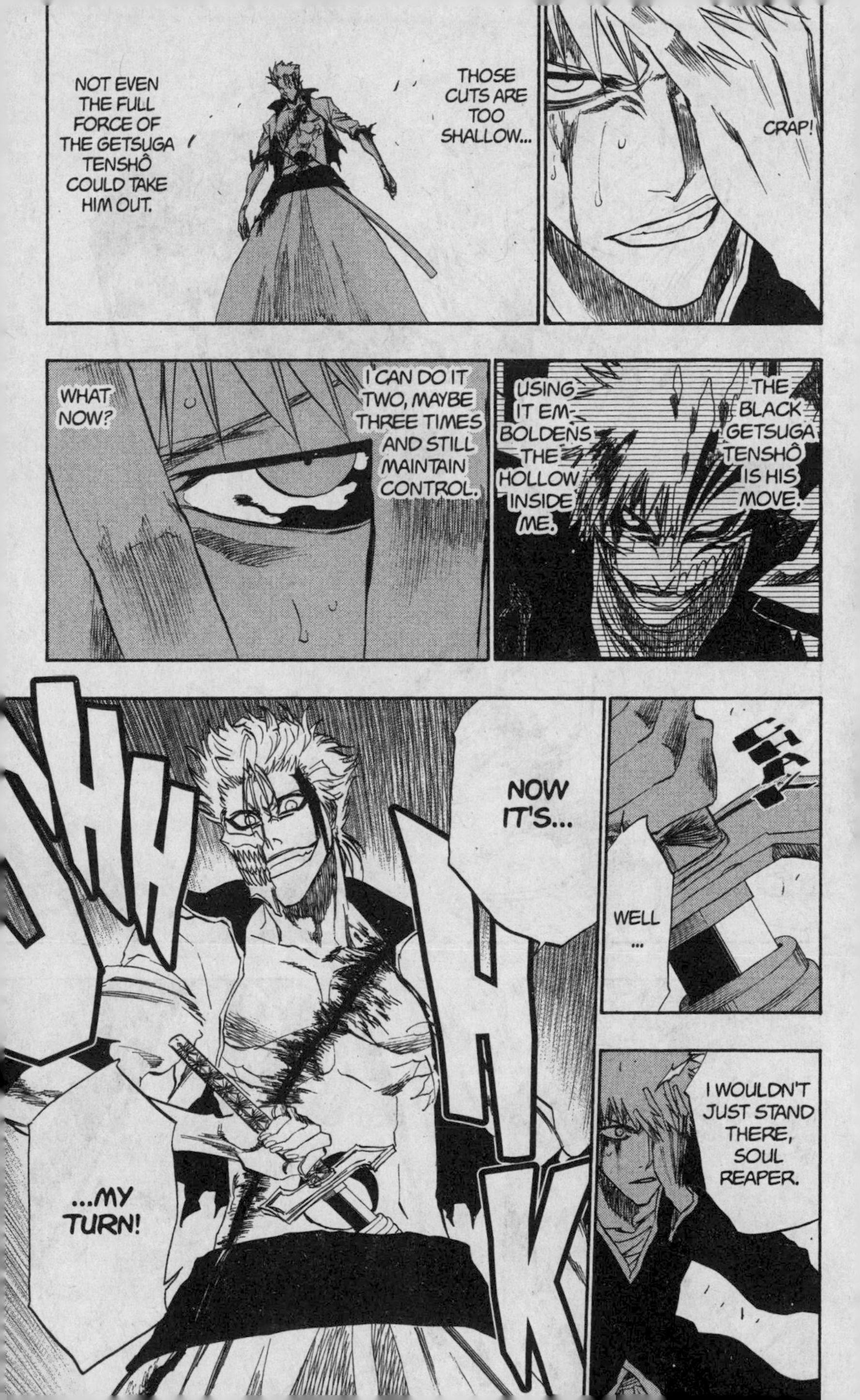
CRAP!
THOSE CUTS ARE TOO SHALLOW...
NOT EVEN THE FULL FORCE OF THE GETSUGA TENSHÔ COULD TAKE HIM OUT.
THE BLACK GETSUGA TENSHÔ IS HIS MOVE.
USING IT EMBOLDENS THE HOLLOW INSIDE ME.
I CAN DO IT TWO, MAYBE THREE TIMES AND STILL MAINTAIN CONTROL.
WHAT NOW?
WELL ...
I WOULDN'T JUST STAND THERE, SOUL REAPER.
NOW IT'S...
...MY TURN!

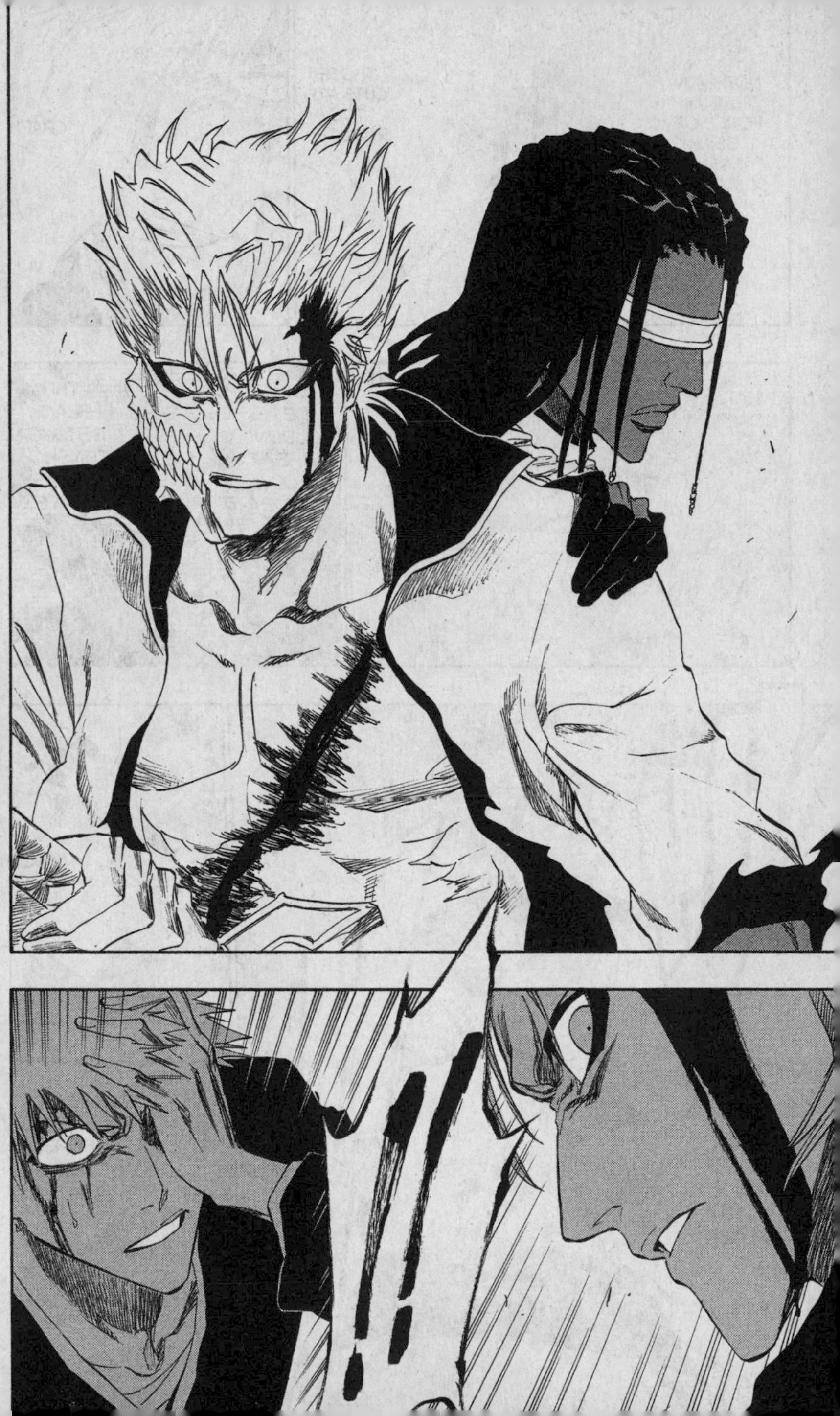

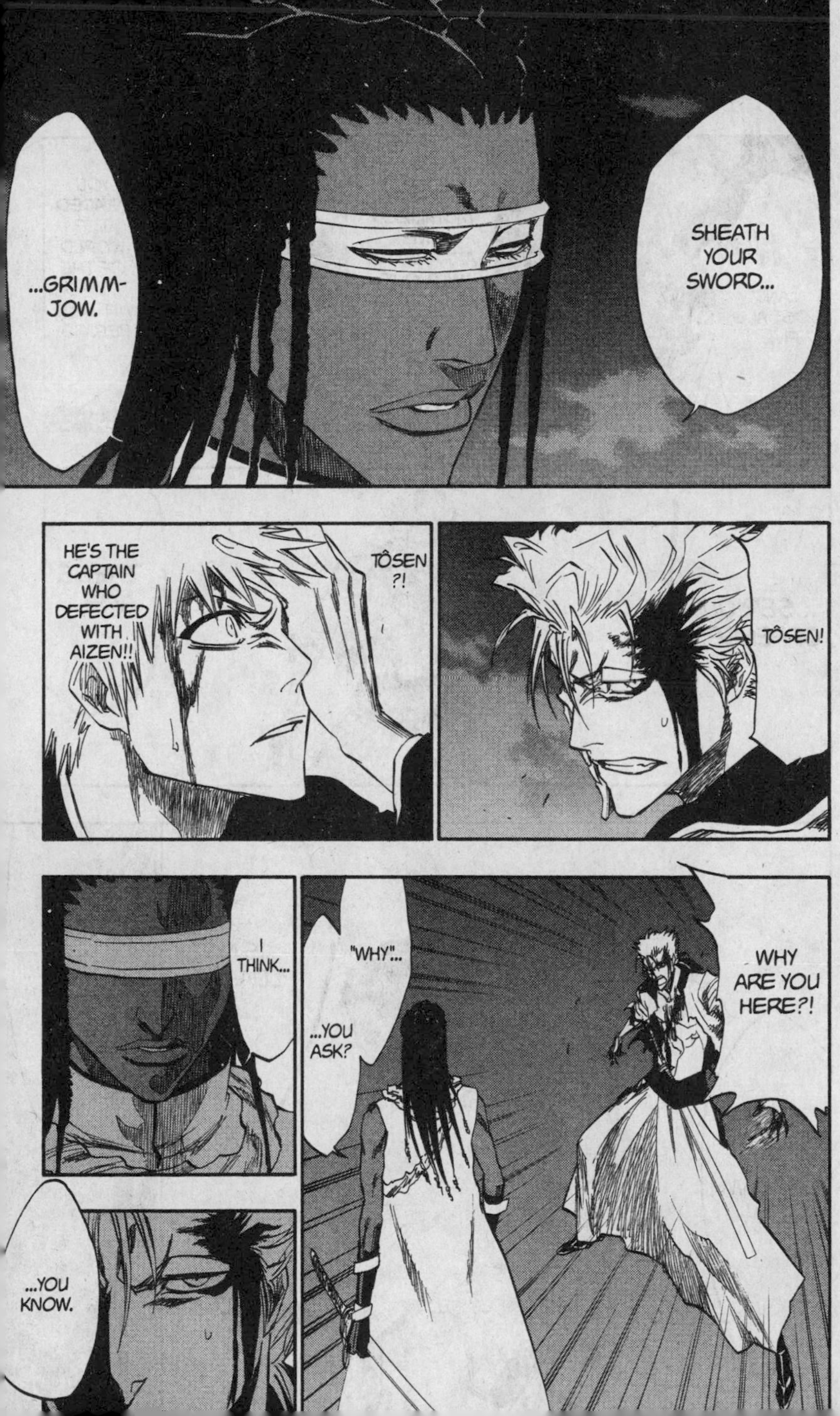
SHEATH YOUR SWORD...
...GRIMM-JOW.
TÔSEN!
TÔSEN?!
HE'S THE CAPTAIN WHO DEFECTED WITH AIZEN!!
WHY ARE YOU HERE?!
"WHY"...
...YOU ASK?
I THINK...
...YOU KNOW.

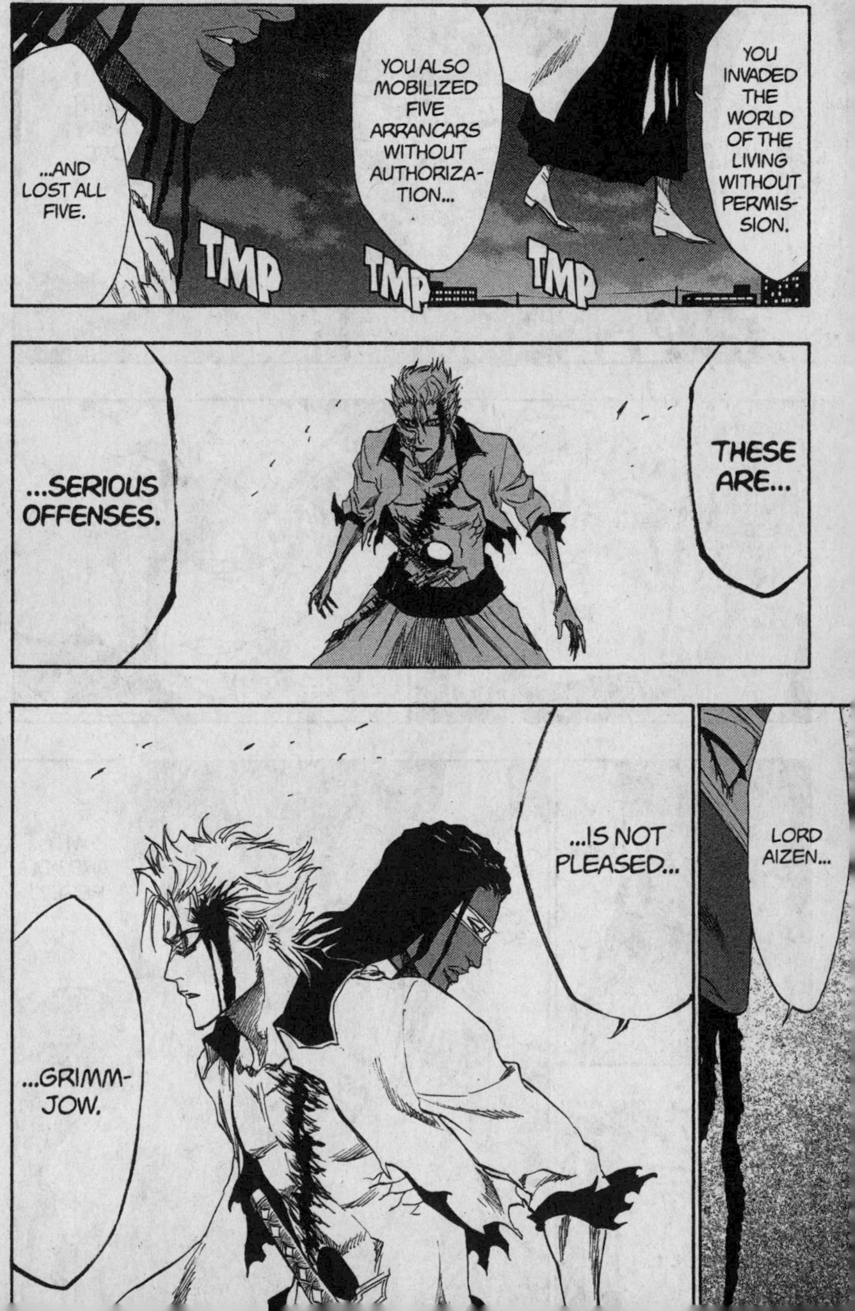
YOU INVADED THE WORLD OF THE LIVING WITHOUT PERMIS-SION.
TMP
YOU ALSO MOBILIZED FIVE ARRANCARS WITHOUT AUTHORIZA-TION...
TMP
TMP
...AND LOST ALL FIVE.
THESE ARE...
...SERIOUS OFFENSES.
LORD AIZEN...
...IS NOT PLEASED...
...GRIMM-JOW.

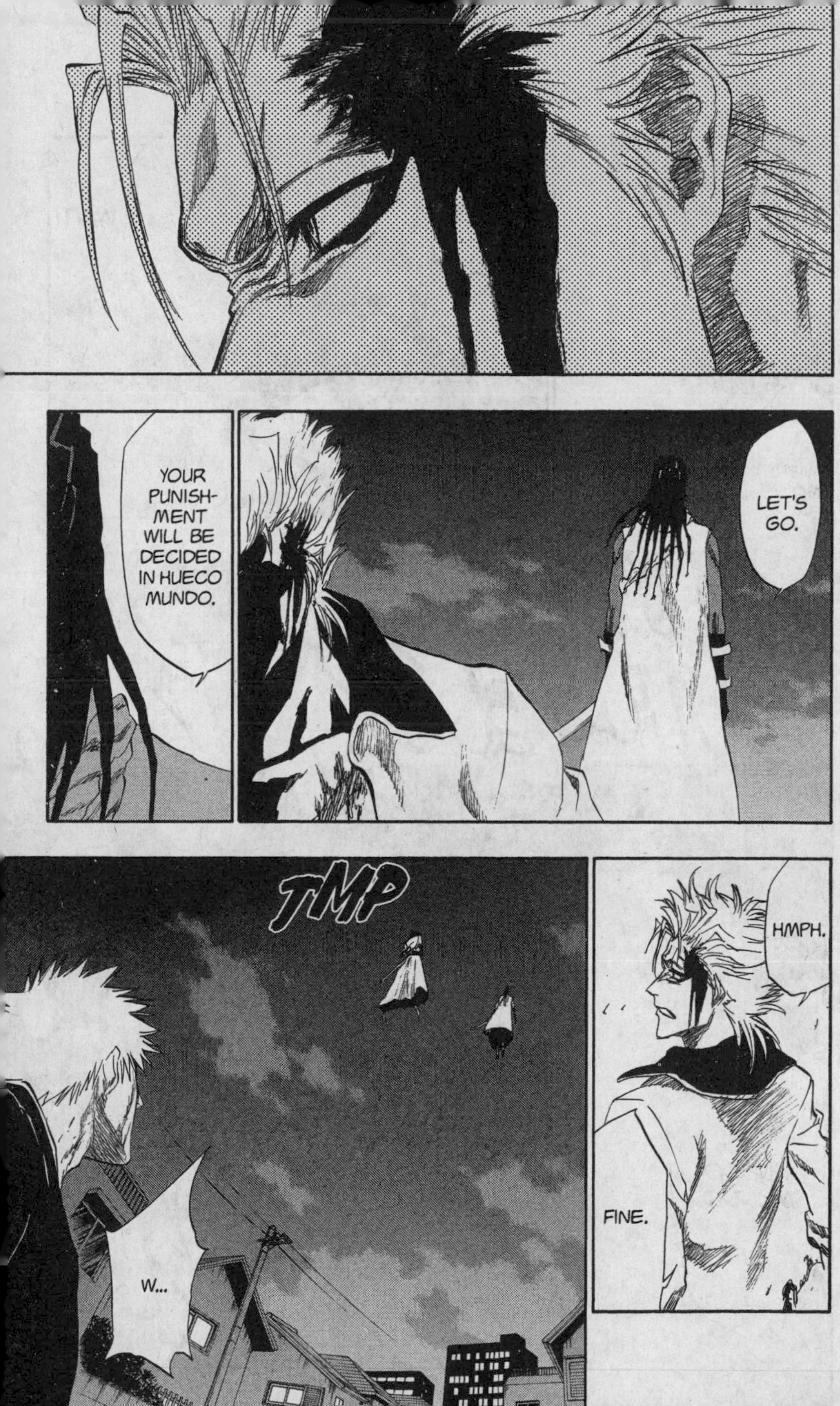
LET'S GO.
YOUR PUNISHMENT WILL BE DECIDED IN HUECO MUNDO.
HMPH.
FINE.
TMP
W...

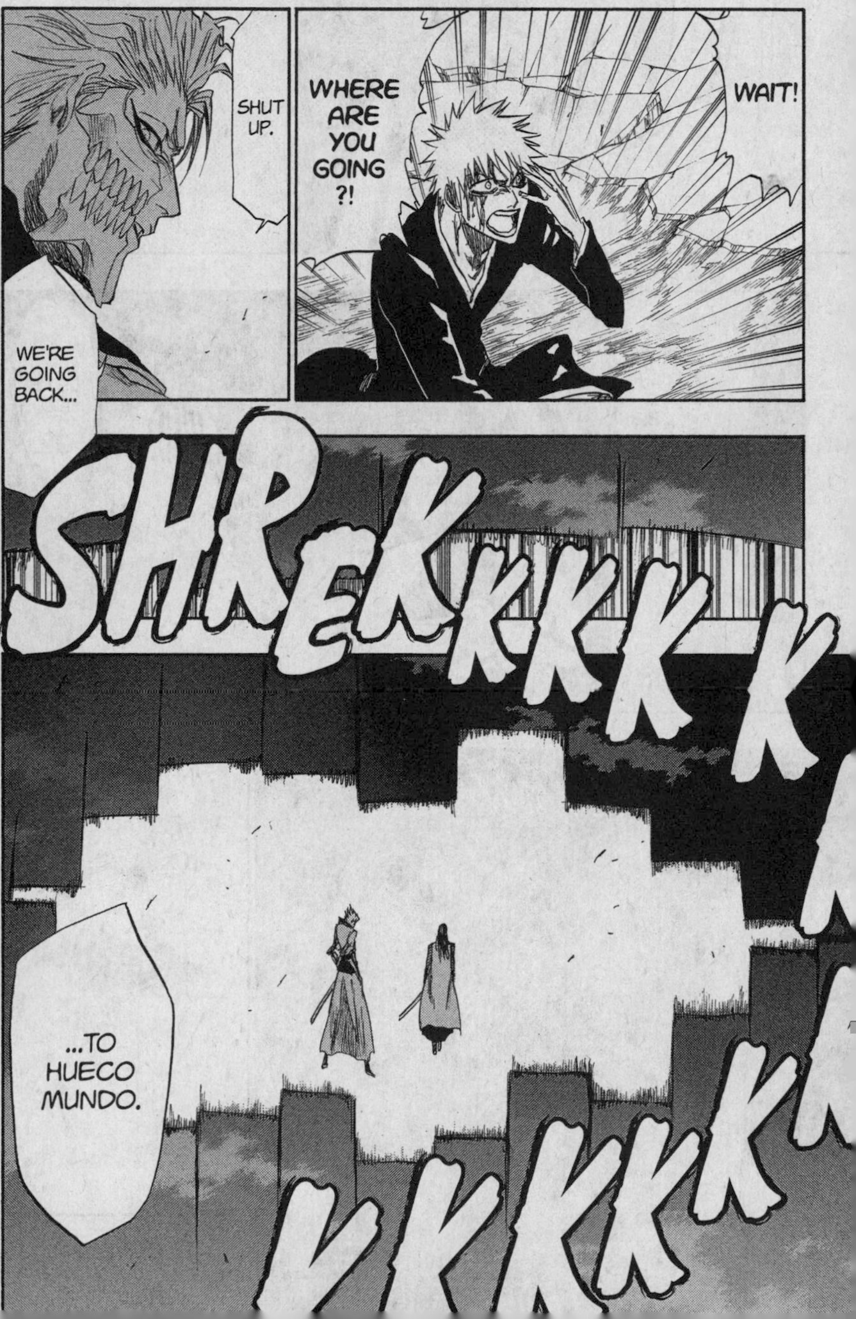
WAIT!
WHERE ARE YOU GOING ?!
SHUT UP.
WE'RE GOING BACK...
SHREKKKKK
...TO HUECO MUNDO.
KKKKK

READ THIS WAY

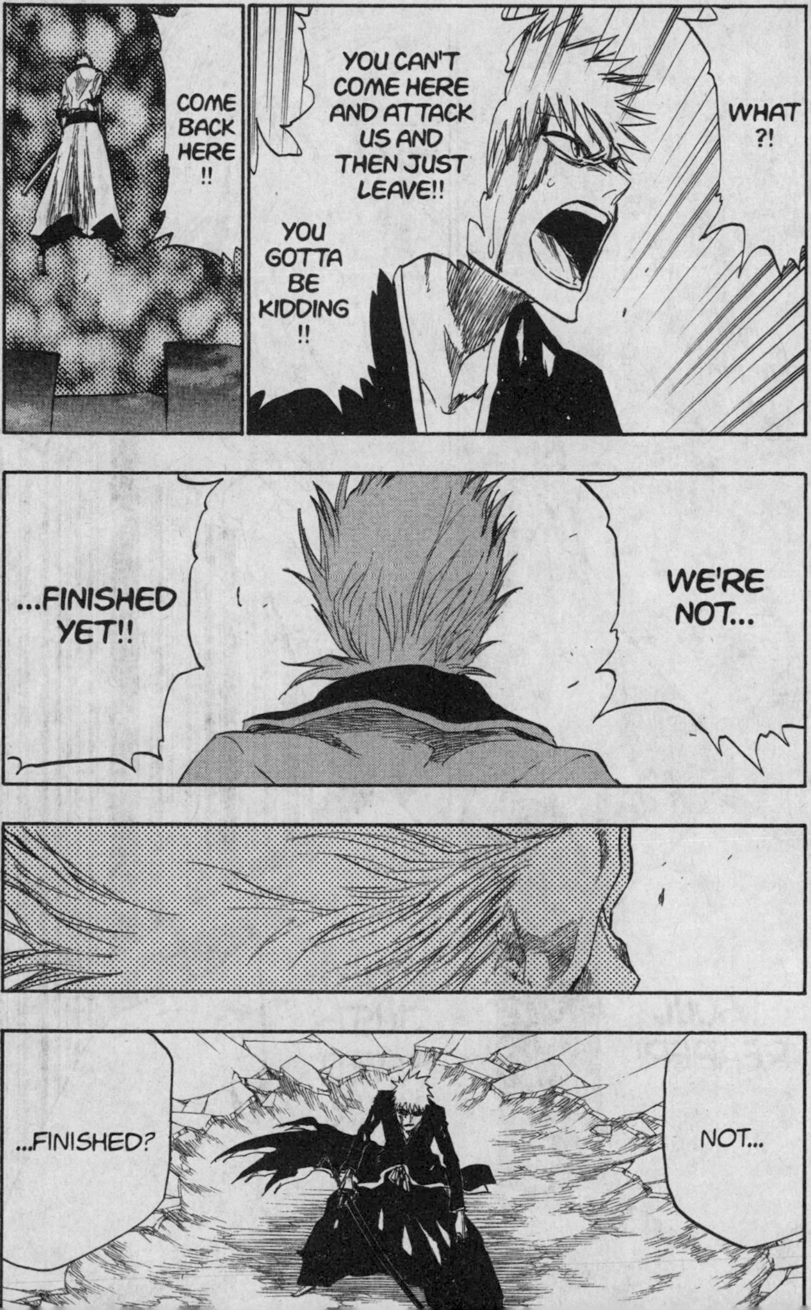

WHAT?!
YOU CAN'T COME HERE AND ATTACK US AND THEN JUST LEAVE!!
YOU GOTTA BE KIDDING!!
COME BACK HERE!!
WE'RE NOT...
...FINISHED YET!!
NOT...
...FINISHED?

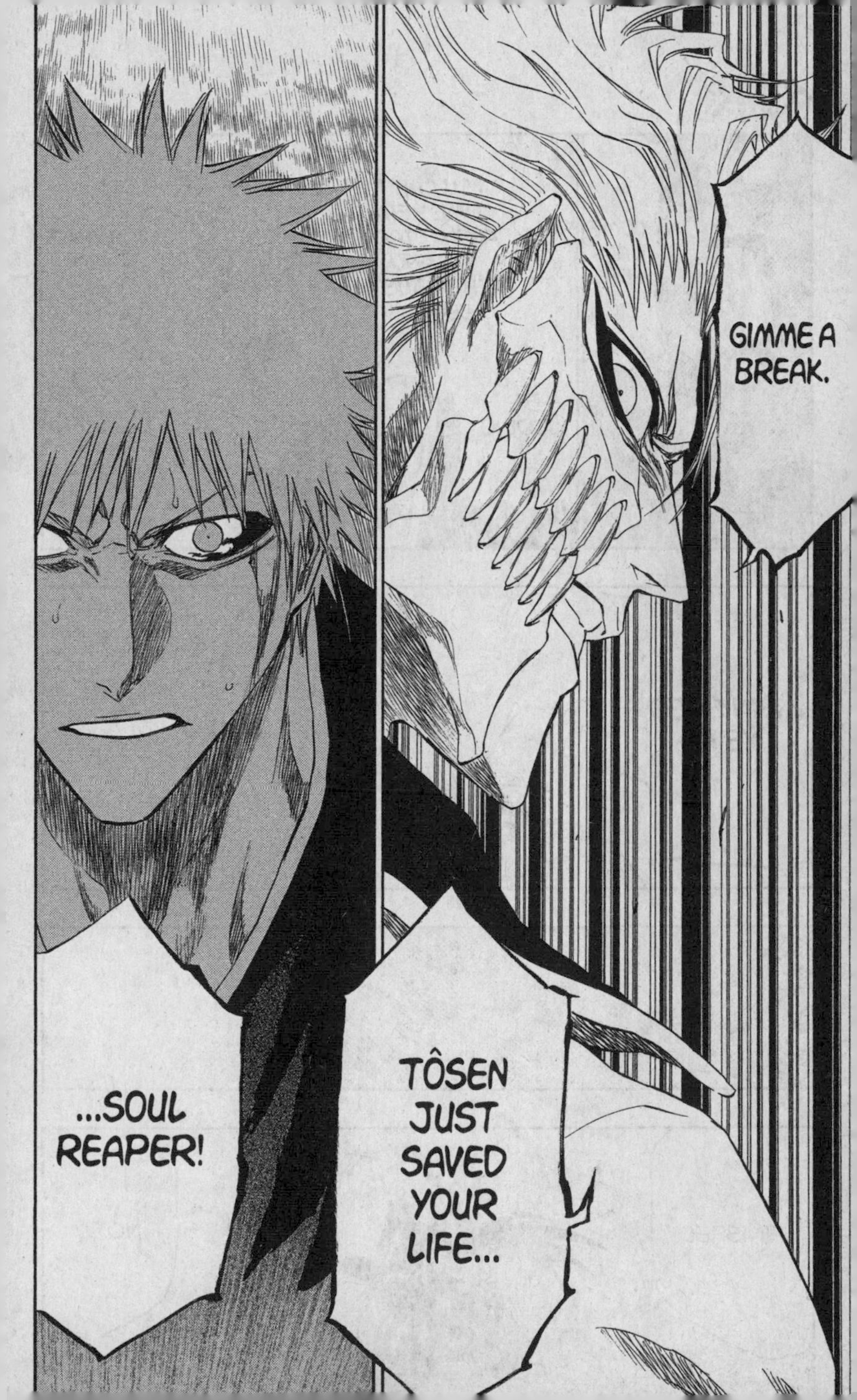
GIMME A BREAK.
TÔSEN JUST SAVED YOUR LIFE...
...SOUL REAPER!

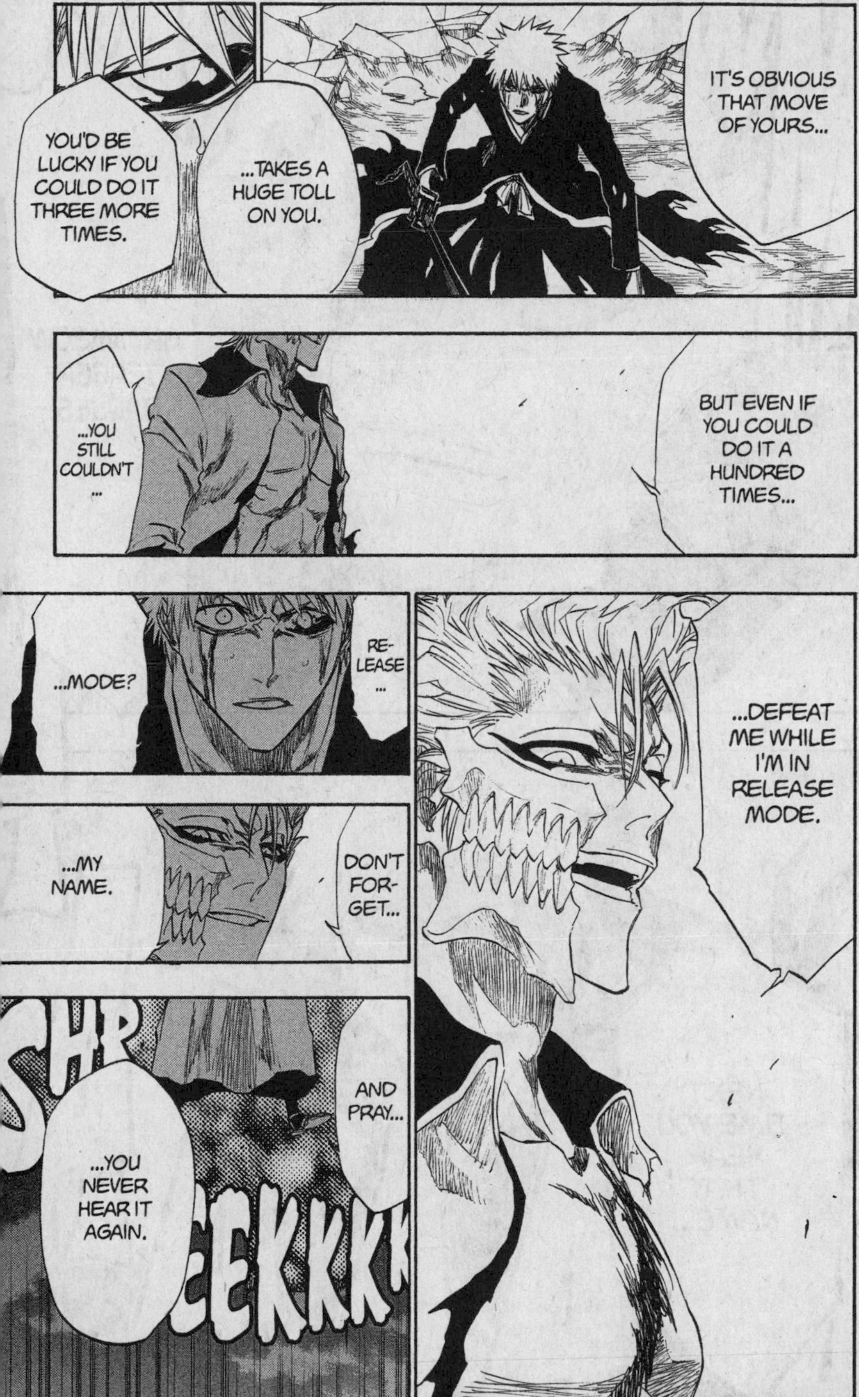
IT'S OBVIOUS THAT MOVE OF YOURS...
...TAKES A HUGE TOLL ON YOU.
YOU'D BE LUCKY IF YOU COULD DO IT THREE MORE TIMES.
BUT EVEN IF YOU COULD DO IT A HUNDRED TIMES...
...YOU STILL COULDN'T ...
...DEFEAT ME WHILE I'M IN RELEASE MODE.
RE-LEASE ...
...MODE?
DON'T FOR-GET...
...MY NAME.
AND PRAY...
...YOU NEVER HEAR IT AGAIN.
SHR
EKKKK

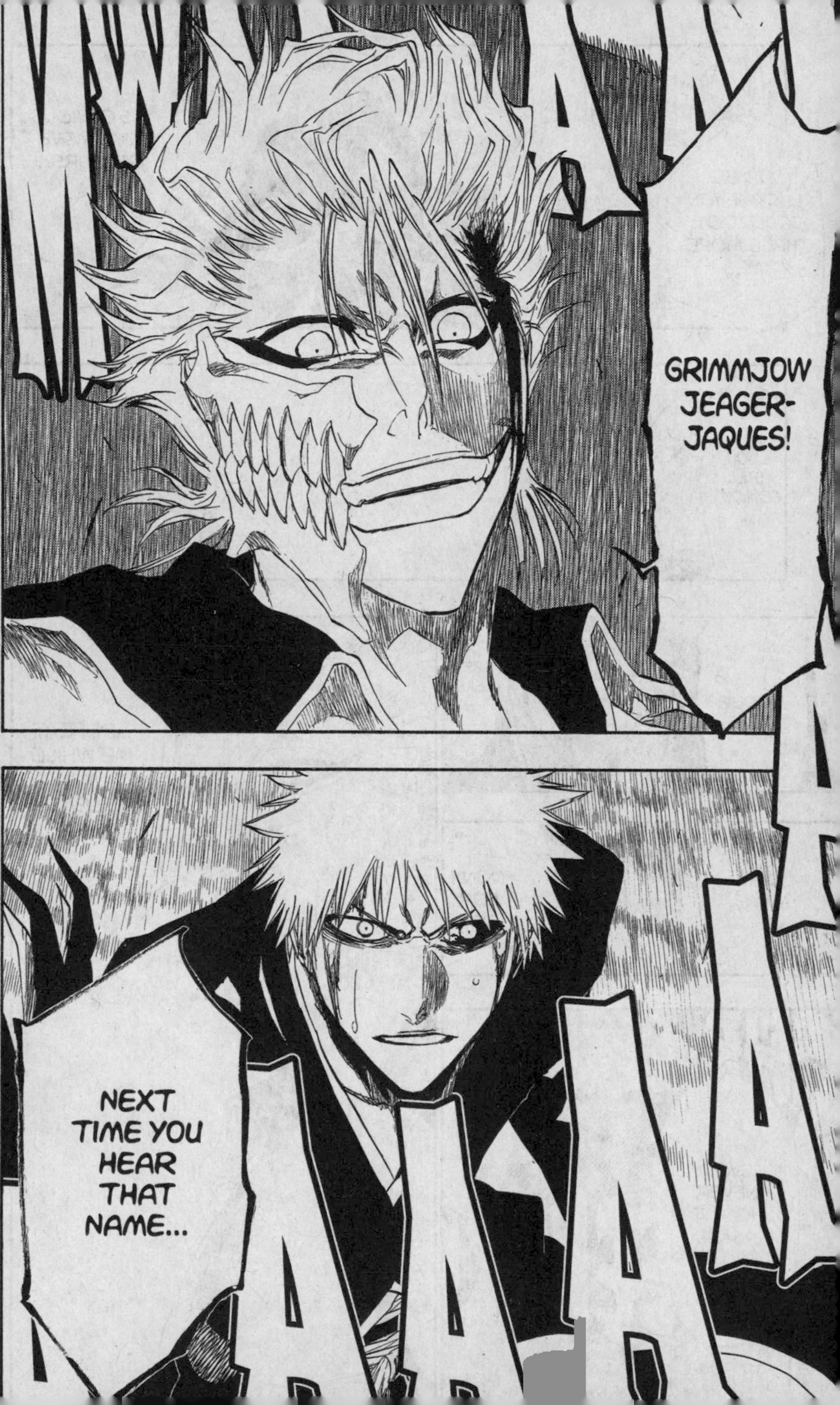
GRIMMJOW JEAGER-JAQUES!
NEXT TIME YOU HEAR THAT NAME...

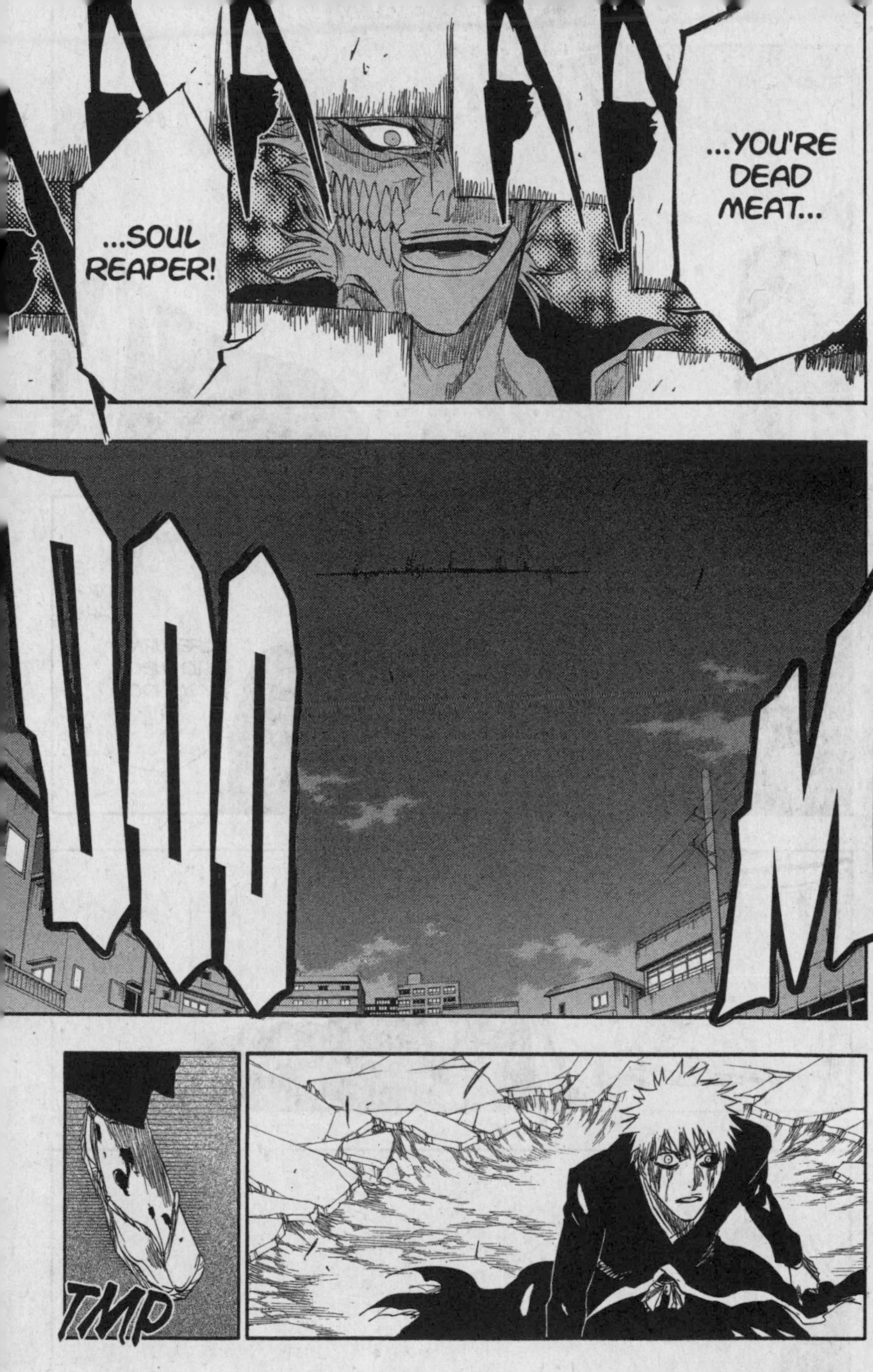
...YOU'RE DEAD MEAT...
...SOUL REAPER!
TMP

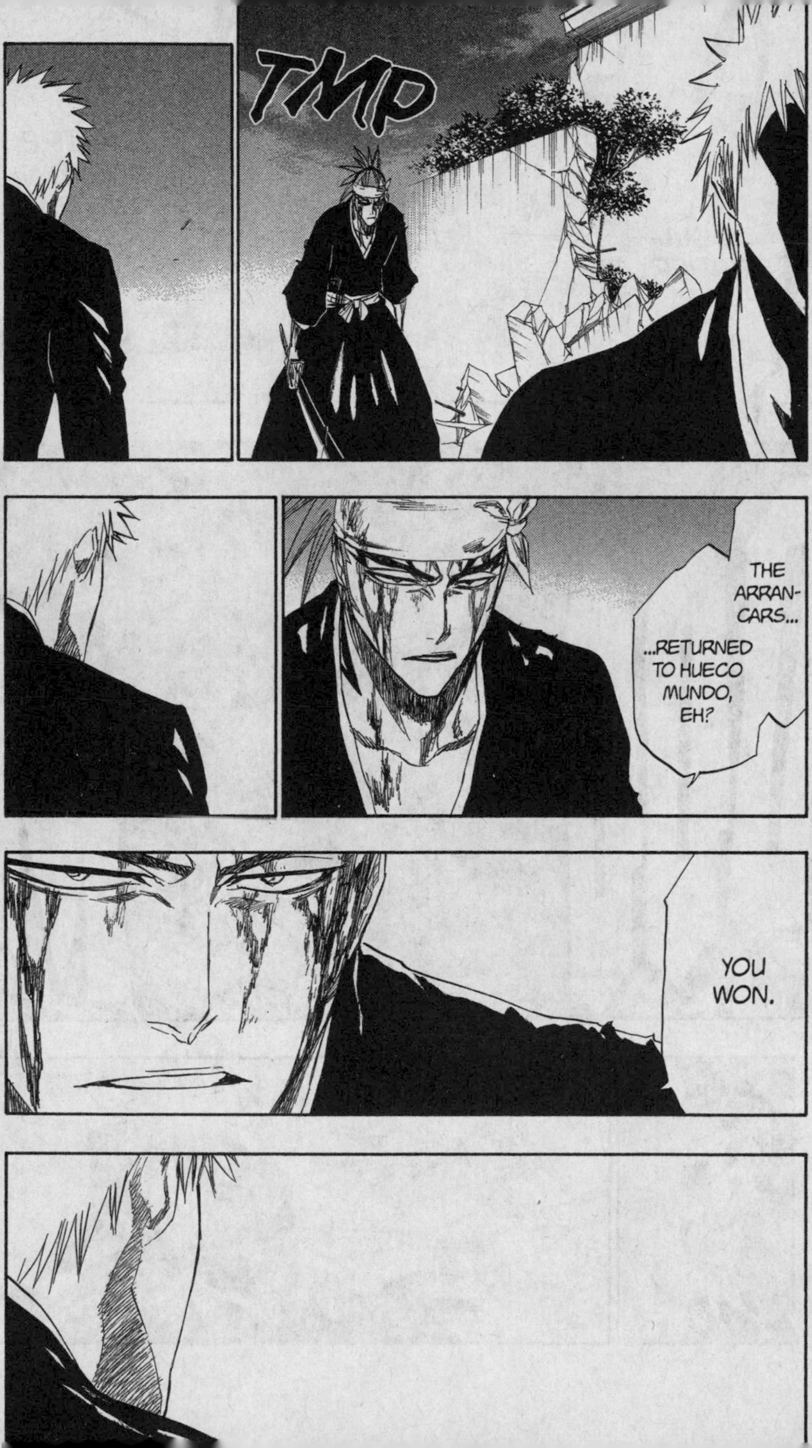
TMP
THE ARRAN-CARS...
...RETURNED TO HUECO MUNDO, EH?
YOU WON.

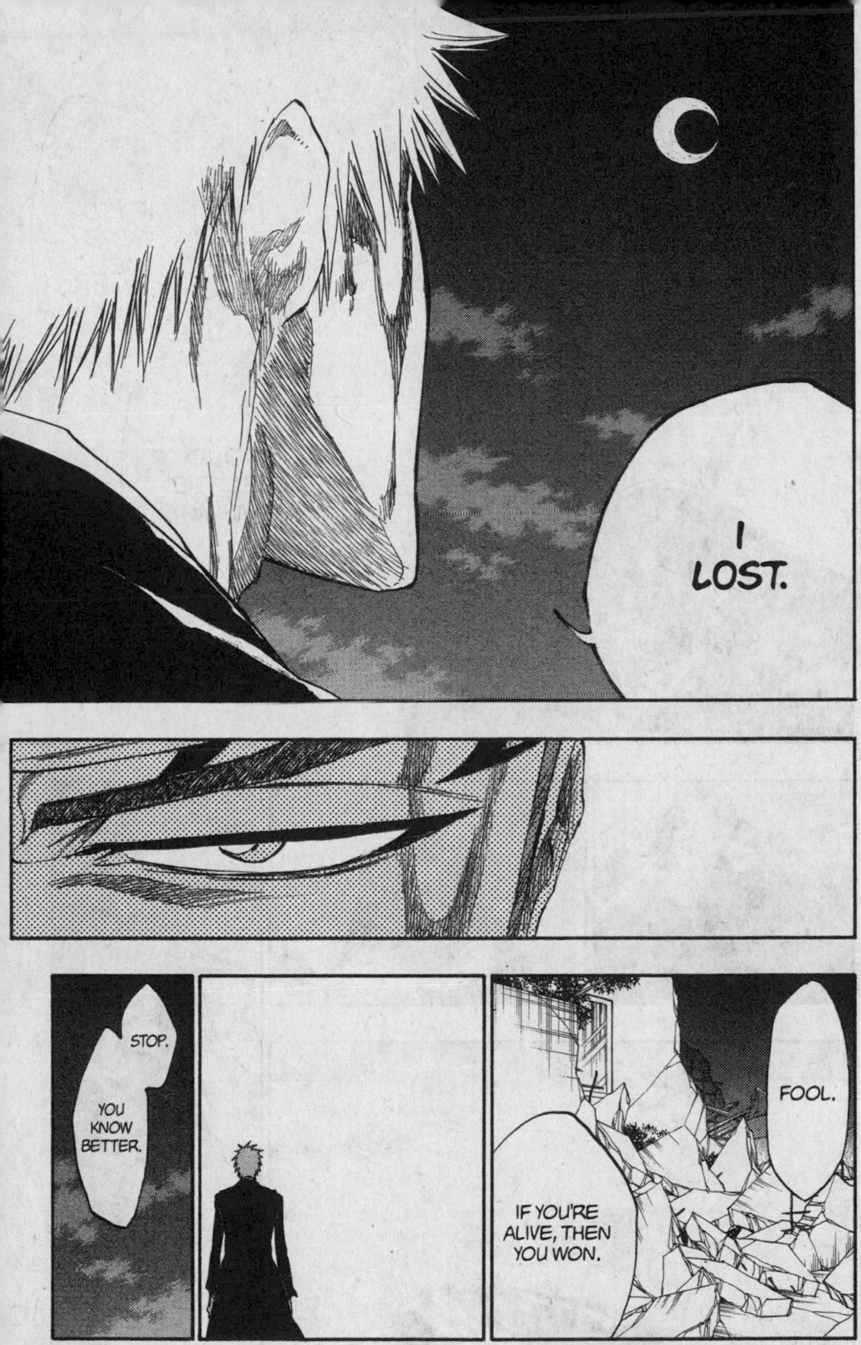
I LOST.
FOOL.
IF YOU'RE ALIVE, THEN YOU WON.
STOP.
YOU KNOW BETTER.

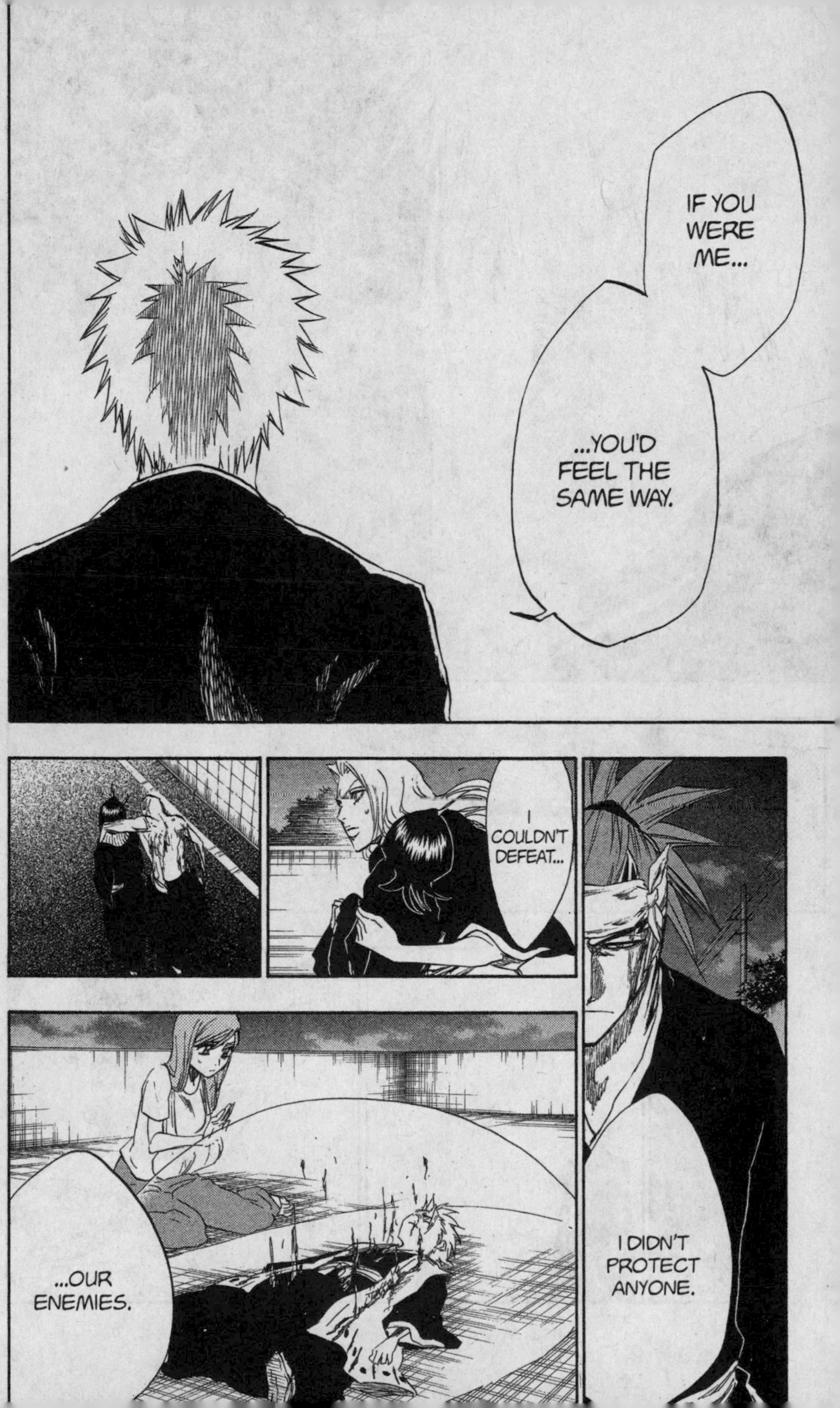
IF YOU WERE ME...
...YOU'D FEEL THE SAME WAY.
I DIDN'T PROTECT ANYONE.
I COULDN'T DEFEAT...
...OUR ENEMIES.

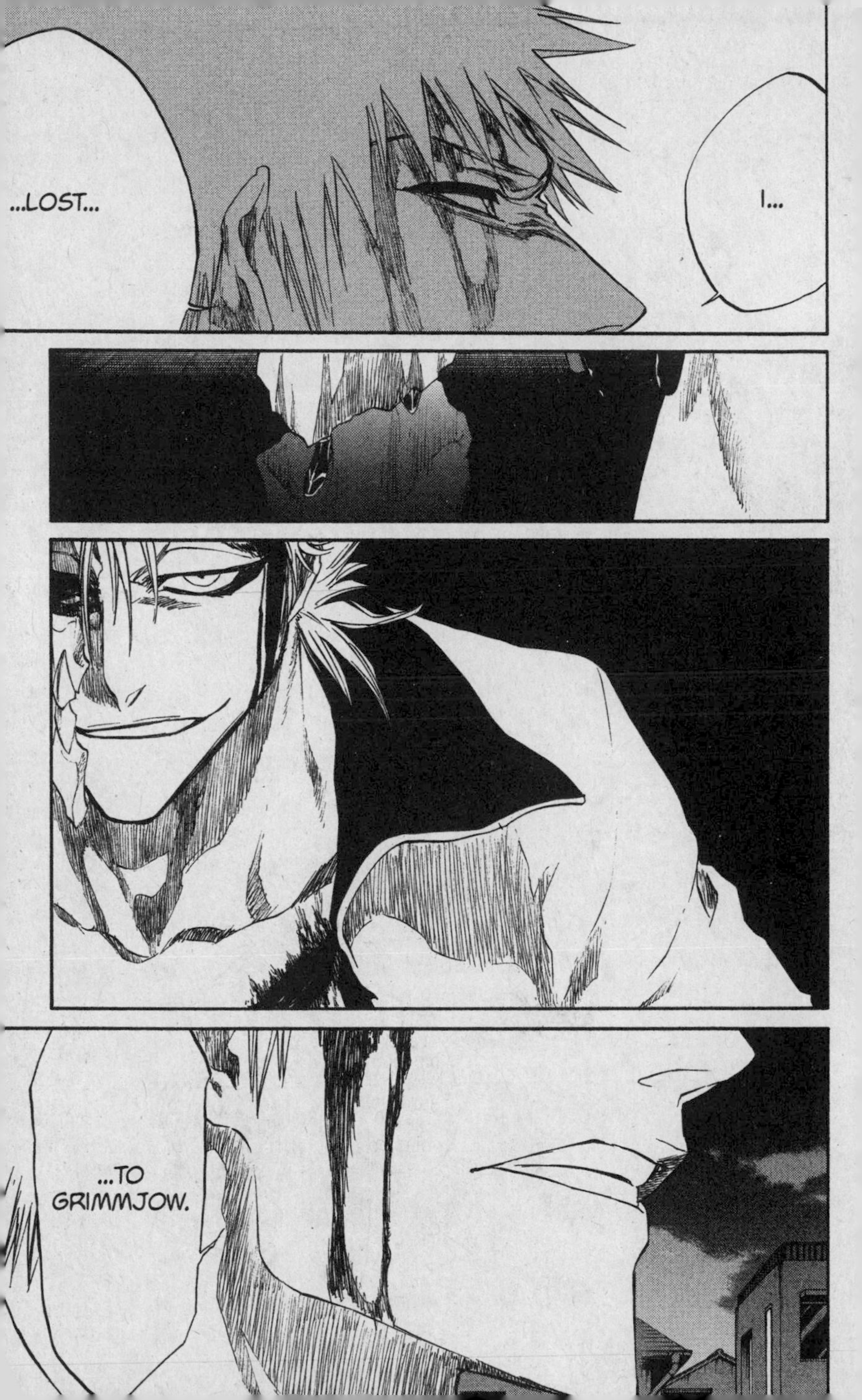
I...
...LOST...
...TO GRIMMJOW.

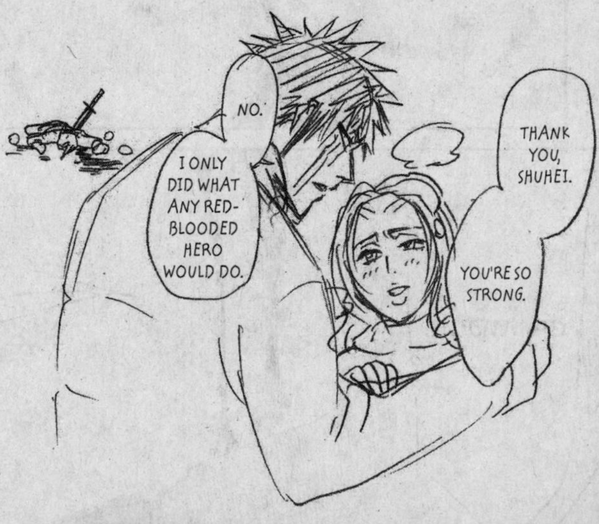
THANK YOU, SHUHEI.
YOU'RE SO STRONG.
NO.
I ONLY DID WHAT ANY RED-BLOODED HERO WOULD DO.

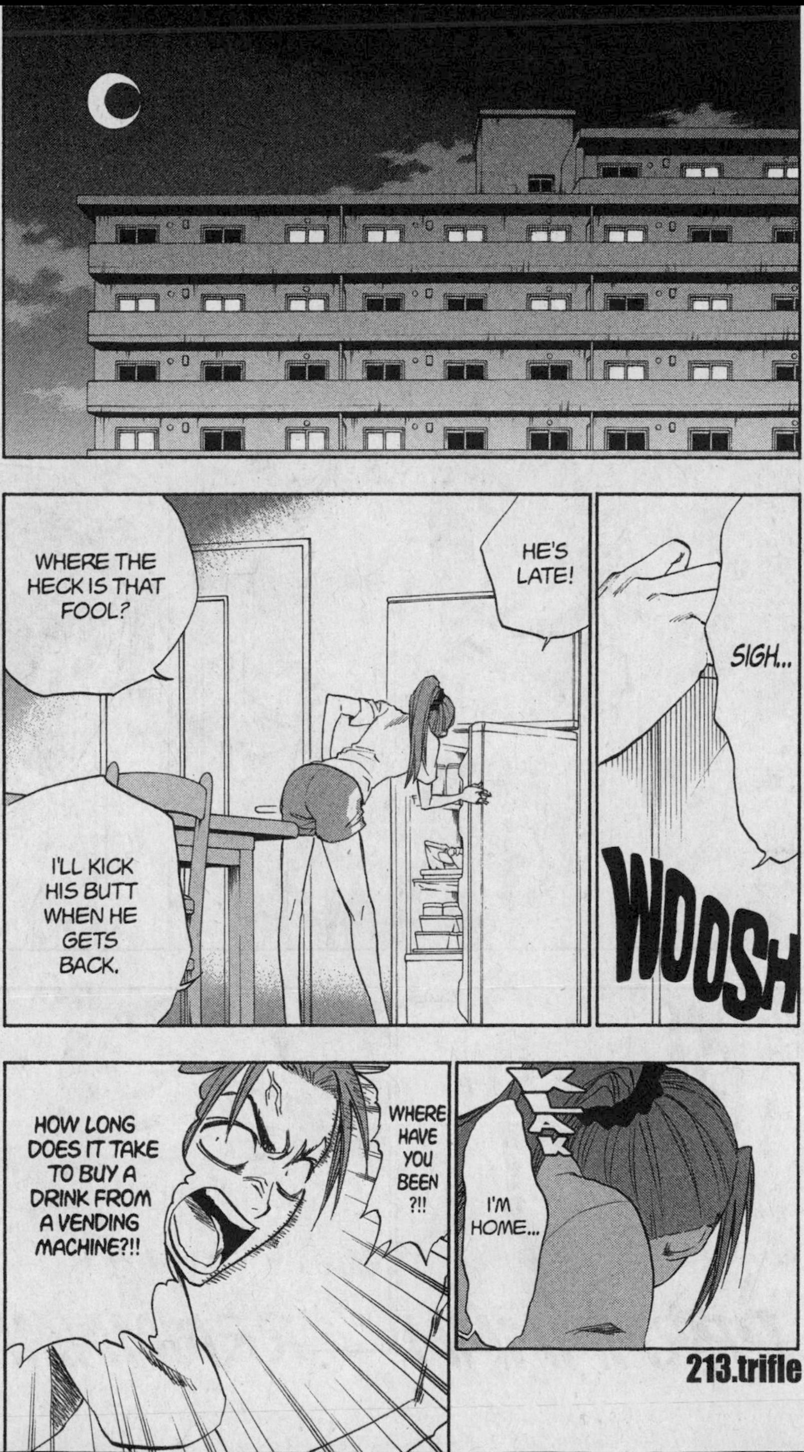
SIGH...
WOOSH
HE'S LATE!
WHERE THE HECK IS THAT FOOL?
I'LL KICK HIS BUTT WHEN HE GETS BACK.
KLAK
I'M HOME...
WHERE HAVE YOU BEEN ?!!
HOW LONG DOES IT TAKE TO BUY A DRINK FROM A VENDING MACHINE?!!

213.trifle

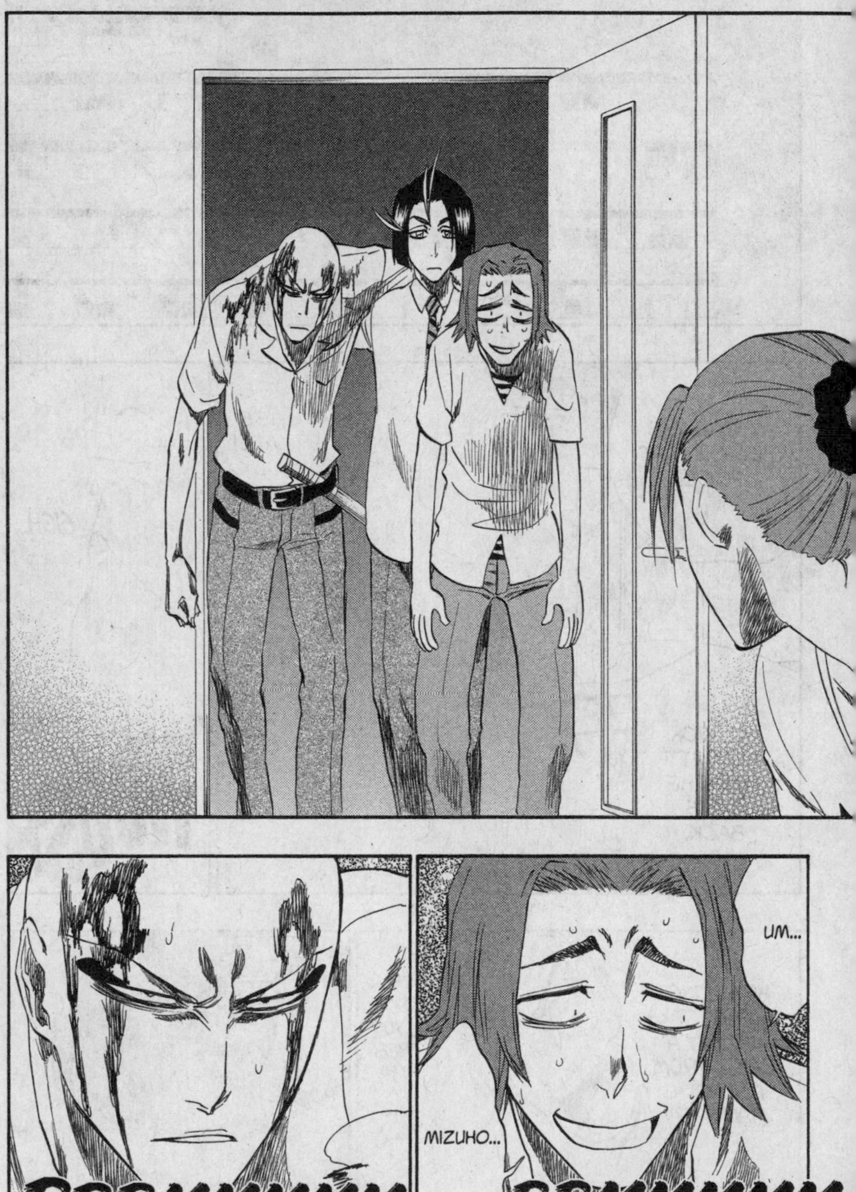
UM...
MIZUHO...
RRMMMMMM
RRRMMMMMM

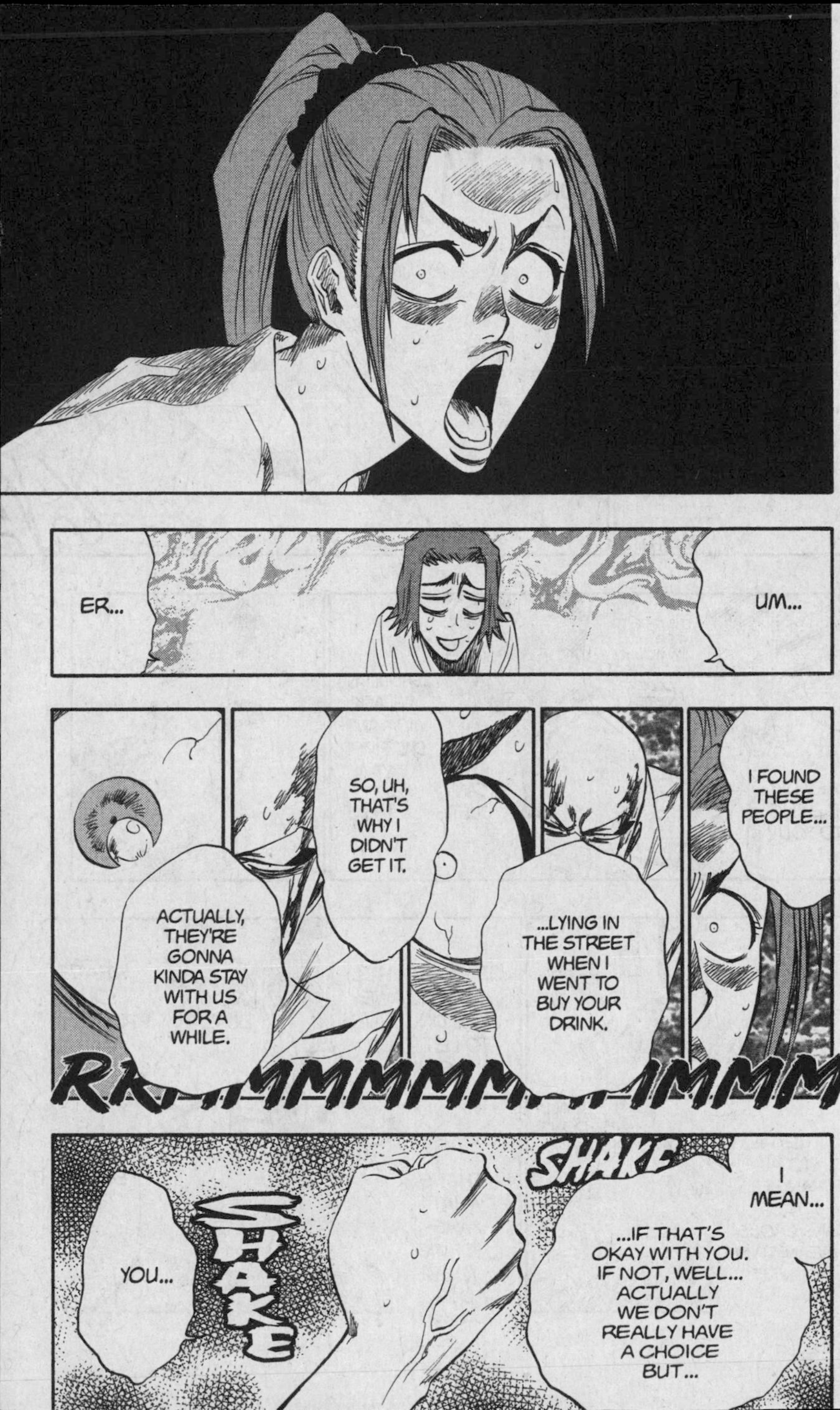
UM...
ER...
I FOUND THESE PEOPLE...
...LYING IN THE STREET WHEN I WENT TO BUY YOUR DRINK.
SO, UH, THAT'S WHY I DIDN'T GET IT.
ACTUALLY, THEY'RE GONNA KINDA STAY WITH US FOR A WHILE.
I MEAN...
...IF THAT'S OKAY WITH YOU. IF NOT, WELL... ACTUALLY WE DON'T REALLY HAVE A CHOICE BUT...
SHAKE
SHAKE
YOU...

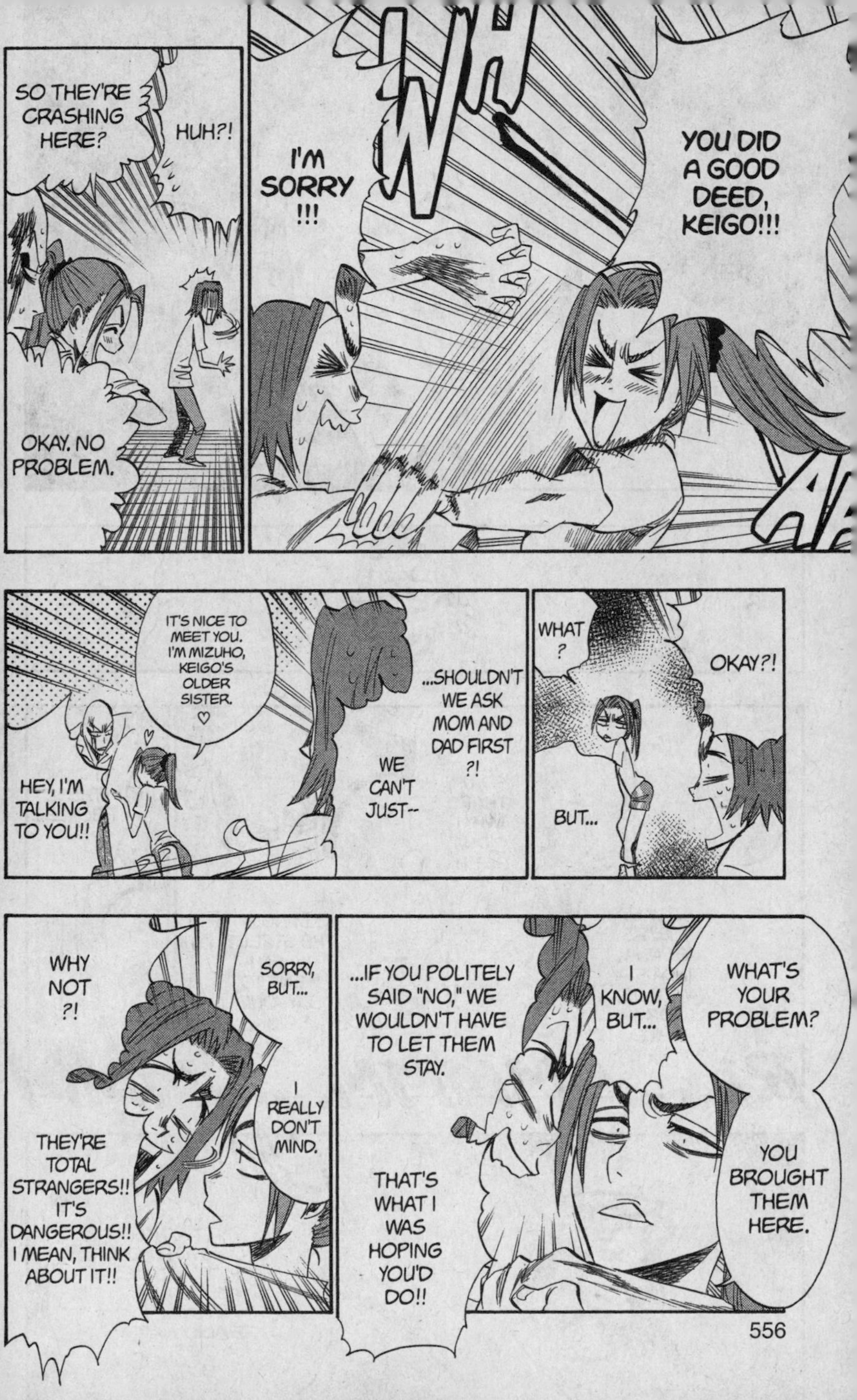
YOU DID A GOOD DEED, KEIGO!!!
I'M SORRY!!!
SO THEY'RE CRASHING HERE?
HUH?!
OKAY. NO PROBLEM.
OKAY?!
WHAT?
BUT...
WE CAN'T JUST--
...SHOULDN'T WE ASK MOM AND DAD FIRST?!
IT'S NICE TO MEET YOU. I'M MIZUHO, KEIGO'S OLDER SISTER. ♡
HEY, I'M TALKING TO YOU!!
WHAT'S YOUR PROBLEM?
YOU BROUGHT THEM HERE.
I KNOW, BUT...
...IF YOU POLITELY SAID "NO," WE WOULDN'T HAVE TO LET THEM STAY.
THAT'S WHAT I WAS HOPING YOU'D DO!!
SORRY, BUT...
I REALLY DON'T MIND.
WHY NOT?!
THEY'RE TOTAL STRANGERS!! IT'S DANGEROUS!! I MEAN, THINK ABOUT IT!!

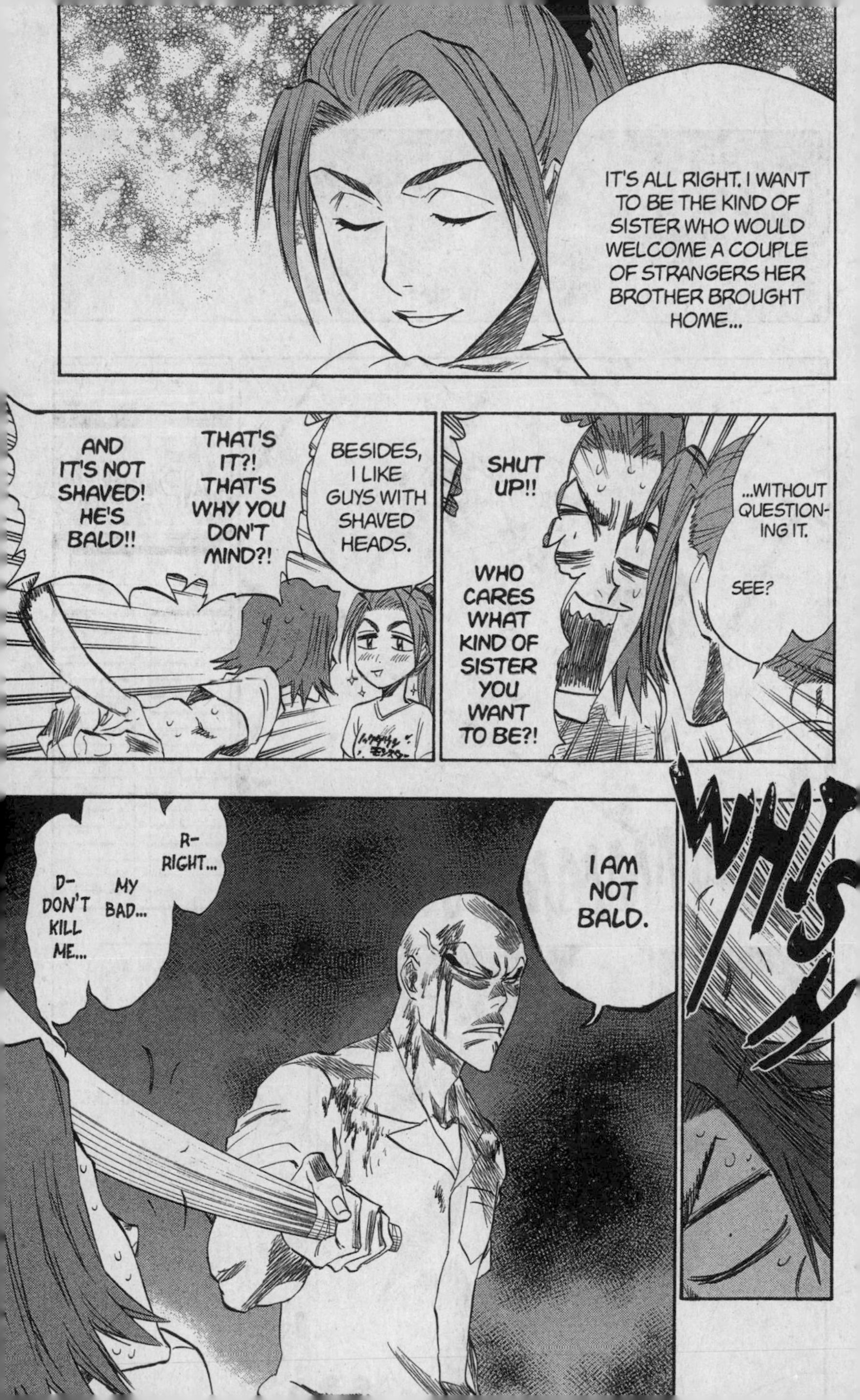
IT'S ALL RIGHT. I WANT TO BE THE KIND OF SISTER WHO WOULD WELCOME A COUPLE OF STRANGERS HER BROTHER BROUGHT HOME...
...WITHOUT QUESTIONING IT.
SEE?
SHUT UP!!
WHO CARES WHAT KIND OF SISTER YOU WANT TO BE?!
BESIDES, I LIKE GUYS WITH SHAVED HEADS.
THAT'S IT?! THAT'S WHY YOU DON'T MIND?!
AND IT'S NOT SHAVED! HE'S BALD!!
WHISH
I AM NOT BALD.
R-RIGHT...
MY BAD...
D-DON'T KILL ME...

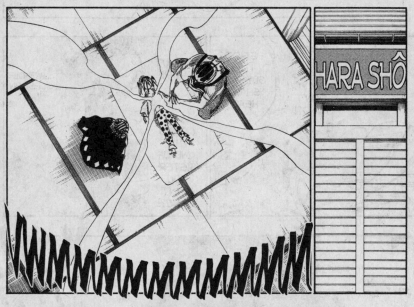

HARA SHÔ

...URURU.

IT'S ALL RIGHT...

KISUKE...

KI...

KISUKE...

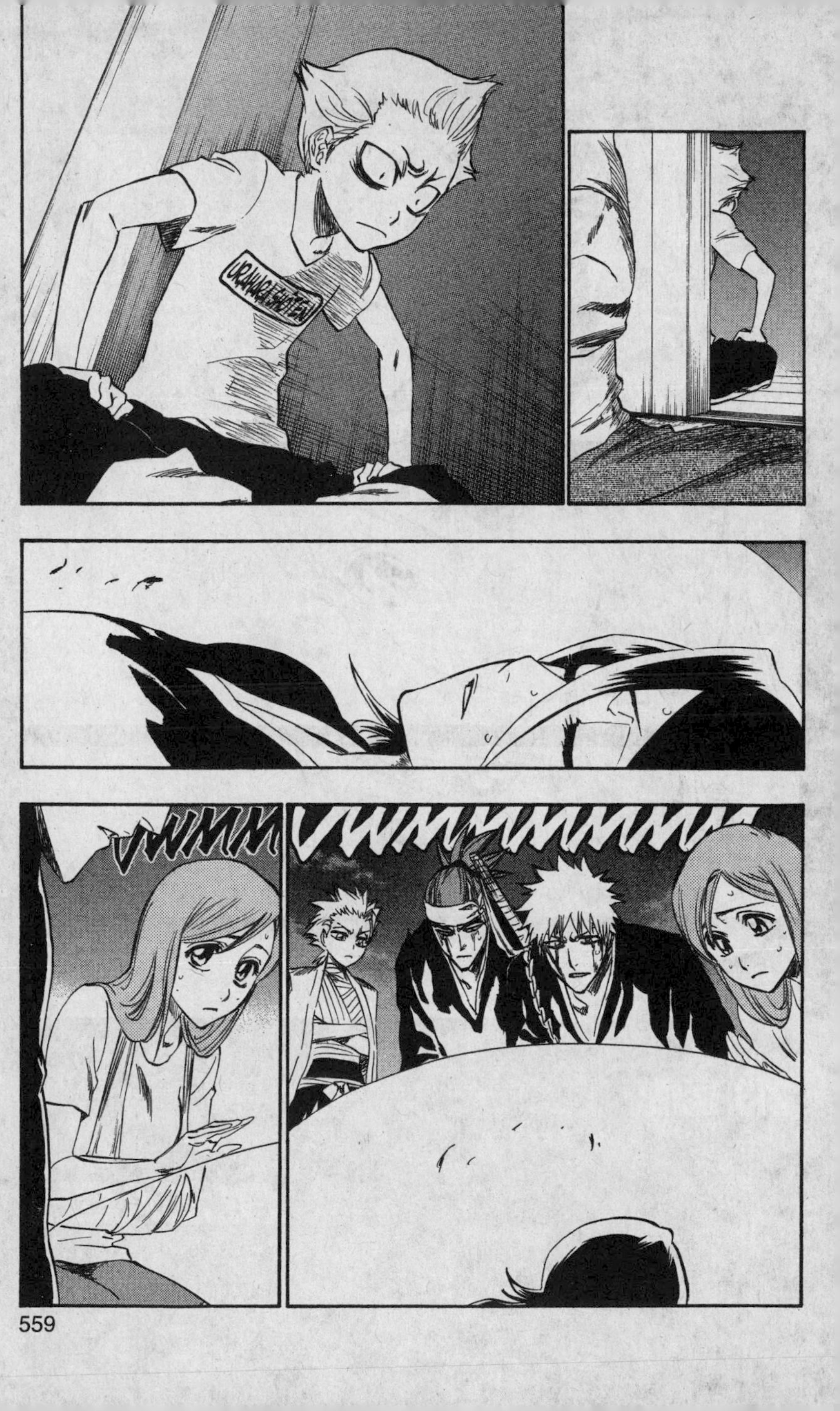
URAHARA SHOTEN
VVMMMMMMMM
VWMM

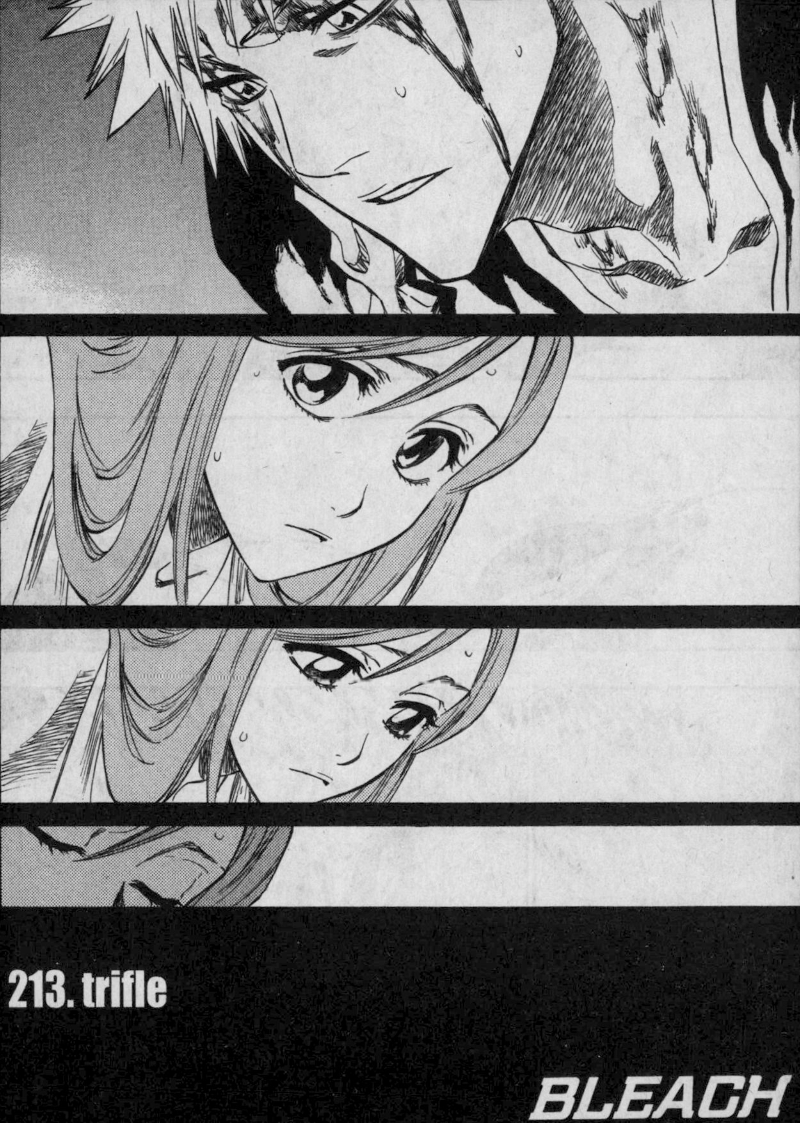

213. trifle

BLEACH

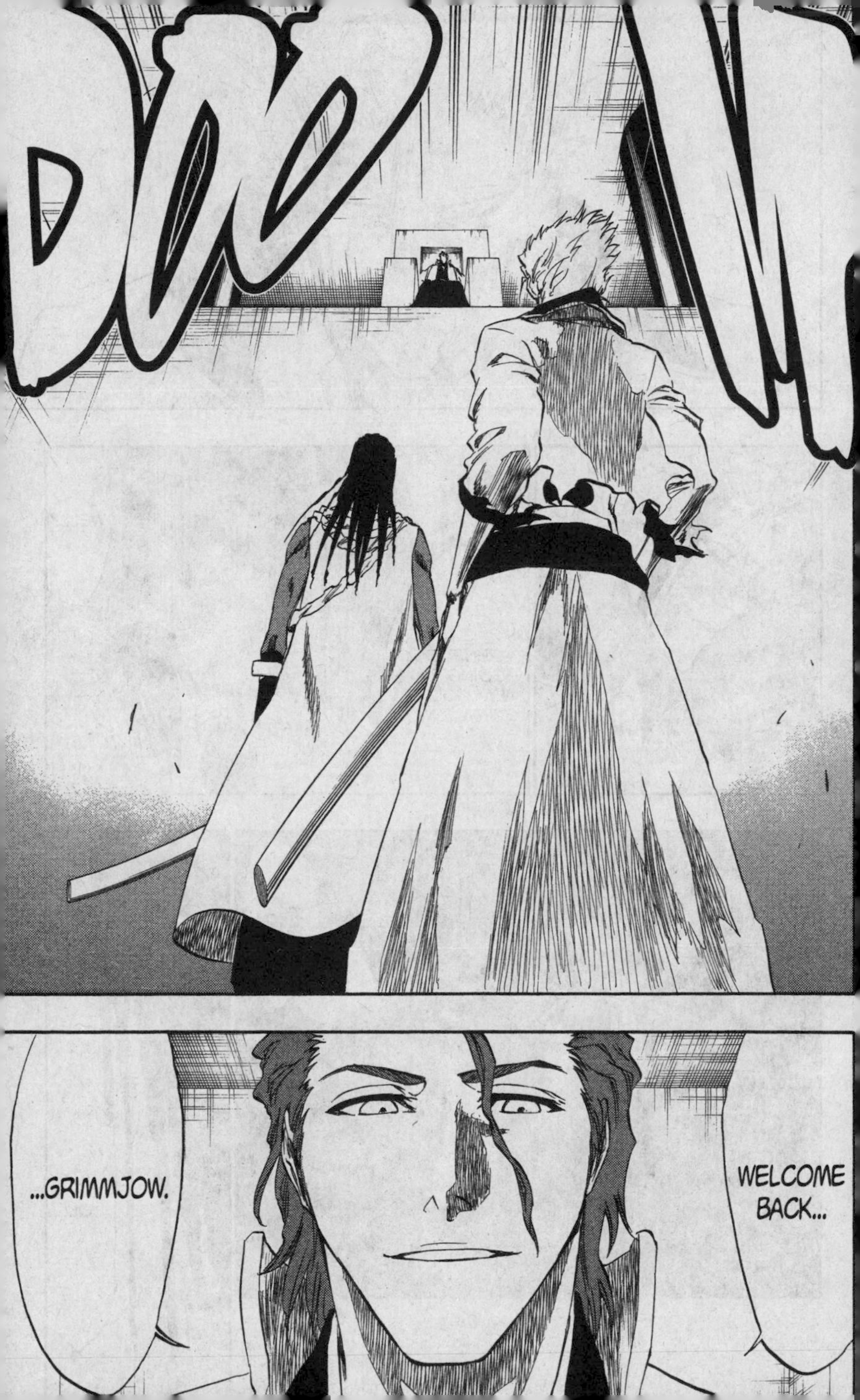
WELCOME BACK...
...GRIMMJOW.

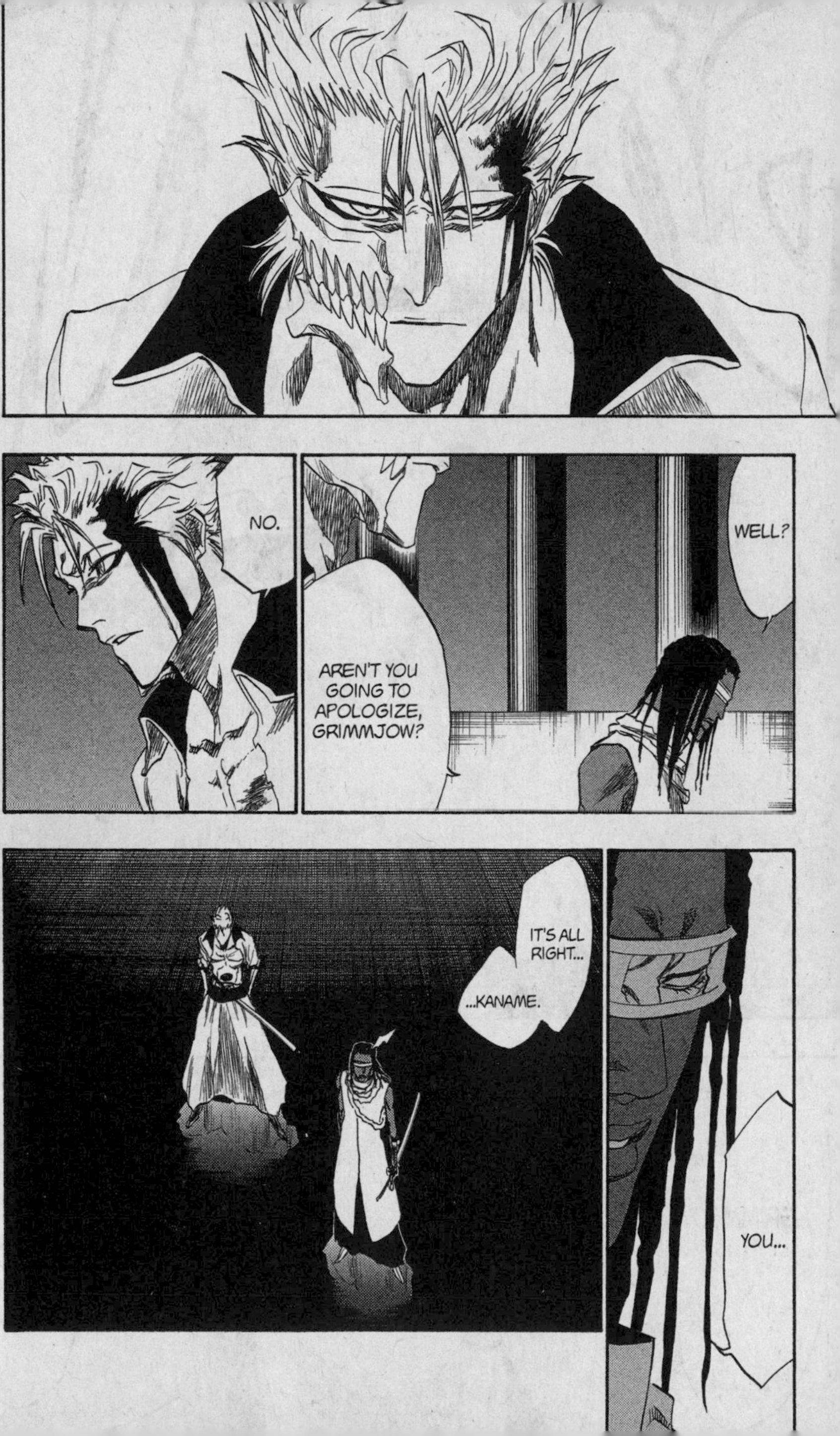
WELL?
AREN'T YOU GOING TO APOLOGIZE, GRIMMJOW?
NO.
YOU...
IT'S ALL RIGHT...
...KANAME.

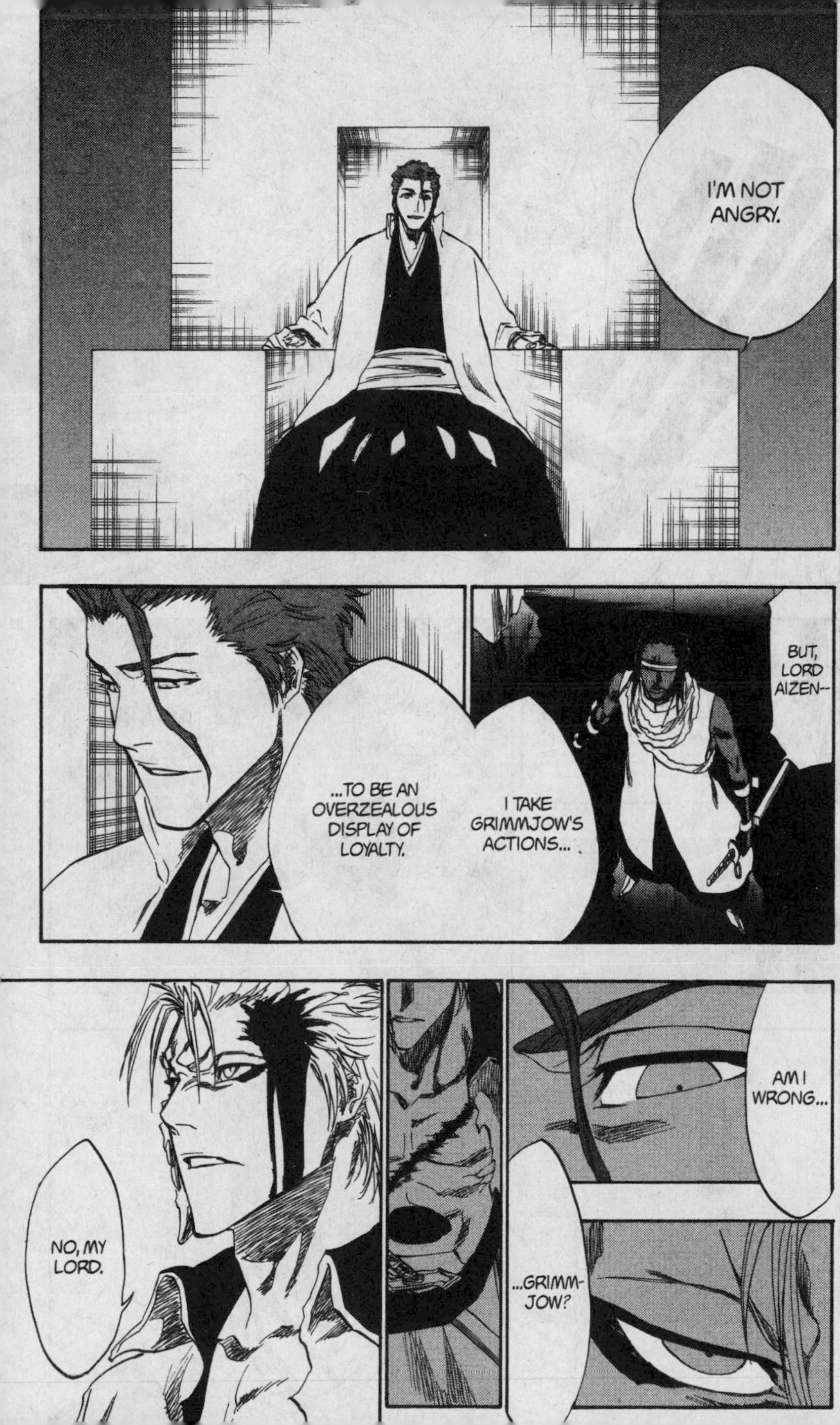
I'M NOT ANGRY.
BUT, LORD AIZEN--
I TAKE GRIMMJOW'S ACTIONS...
...TO BE AN OVERZEALOUS DISPLAY OF LOYALTY.
AM I WRONG...
...GRIMM-JOW?
NO, MY LORD.

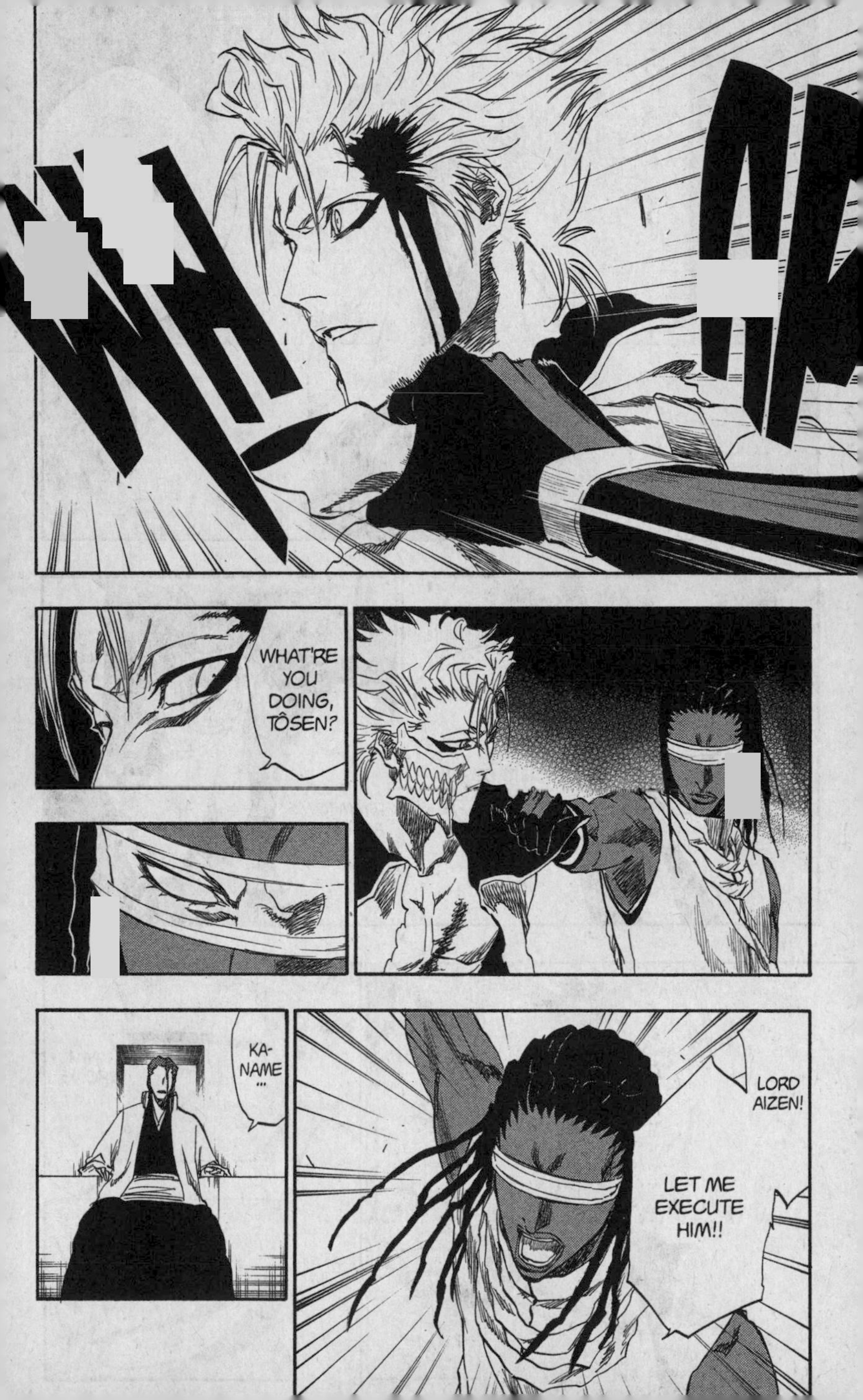
WHA
AK
WHAT'RE YOU DOING, TÔSEN?
LORD AIZEN!
LET ME EXECUTE HIM!!
KA-NAME...

READ THIS WAY

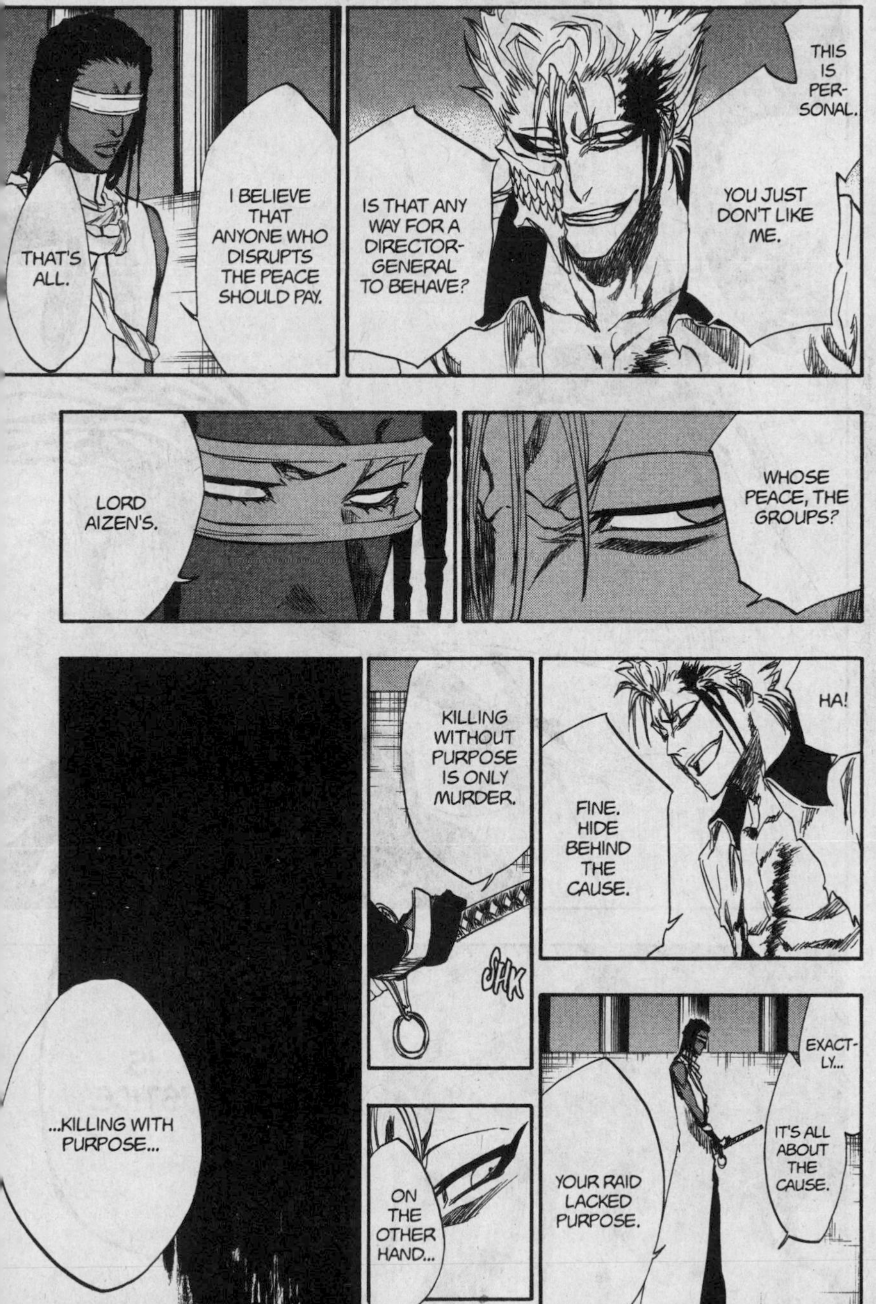
THIS IS PER-SONAL.
YOU JUST DON'T LIKE ME.
IS THAT ANY WAY FOR A DIRECTOR-GENERAL TO BEHAVE?
I BELIEVE THAT ANYONE WHO DISRUPTS THE PEACE SHOULD PAY.
THAT'S ALL.
WHOSE PEACE, THE GROUPS?
LORD AIZEN'S.
HA!
FINE. HIDE BEHIND THE CAUSE.
KILLING WITHOUT PURPOSE IS ONLY MURDER.
SHK
EXACT-LY...
IT'S ALL ABOUT THE CAUSE.
YOUR RAID LACKED PURPOSE.
ON THE OTHER HAND...
...KILLING WITH PURPOSE...

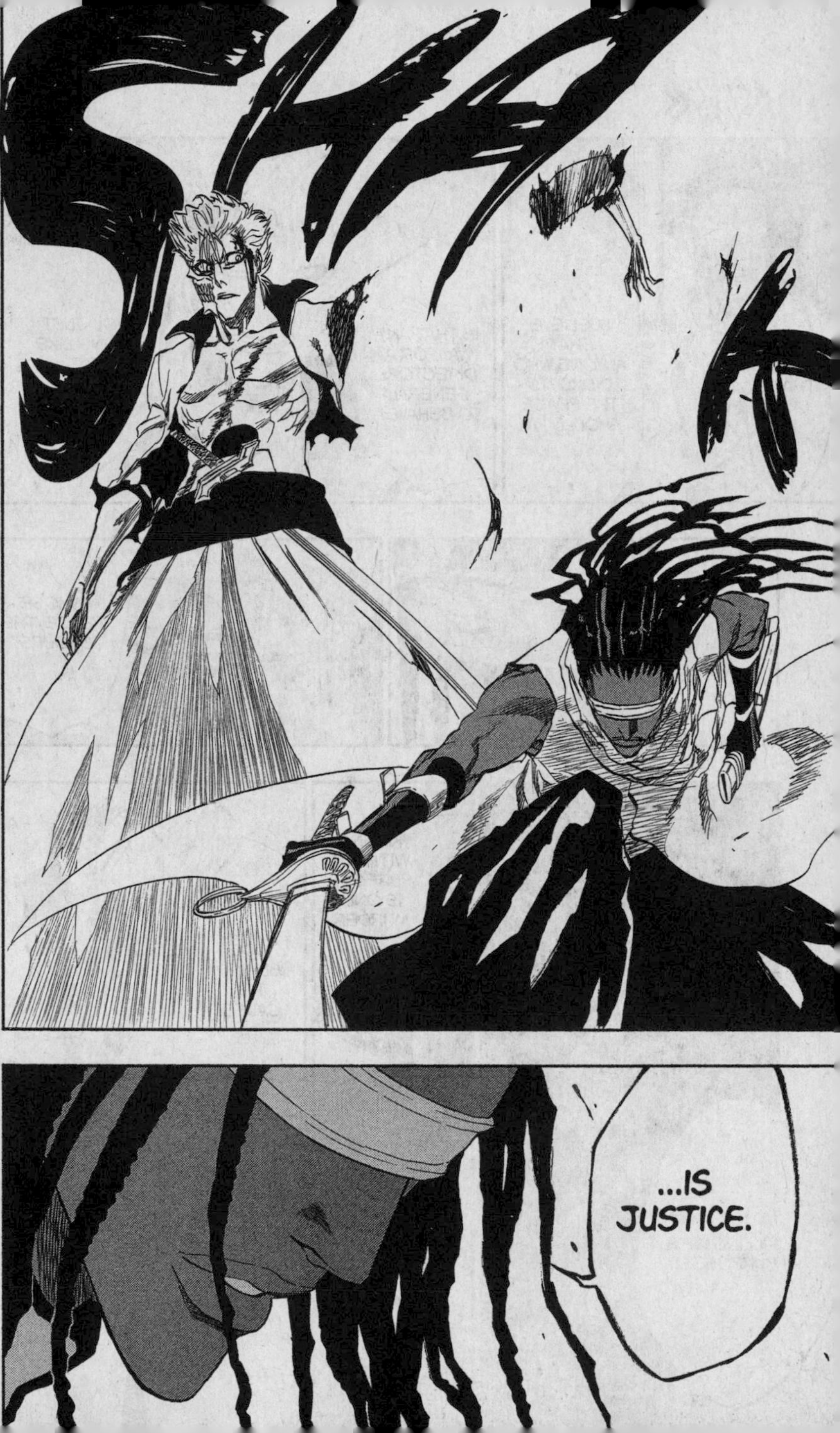
...IS JUSTICE.

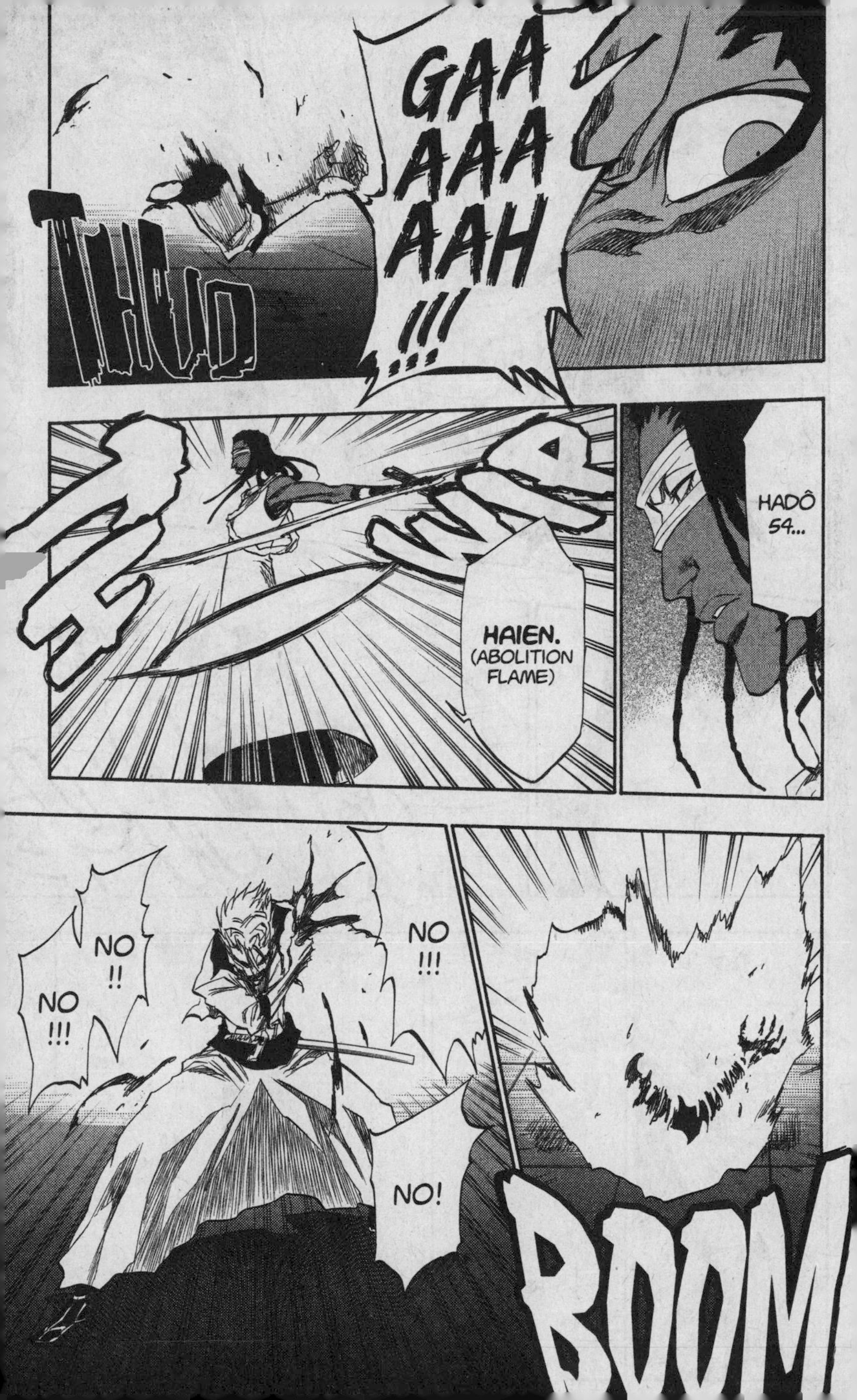
GAAAAAAAH!!!
THUD
HADÔ 54...
HAIEN. (ABOLITION FLAME)
BOOM
NO!!!
NO!!
NO!!!
NO!

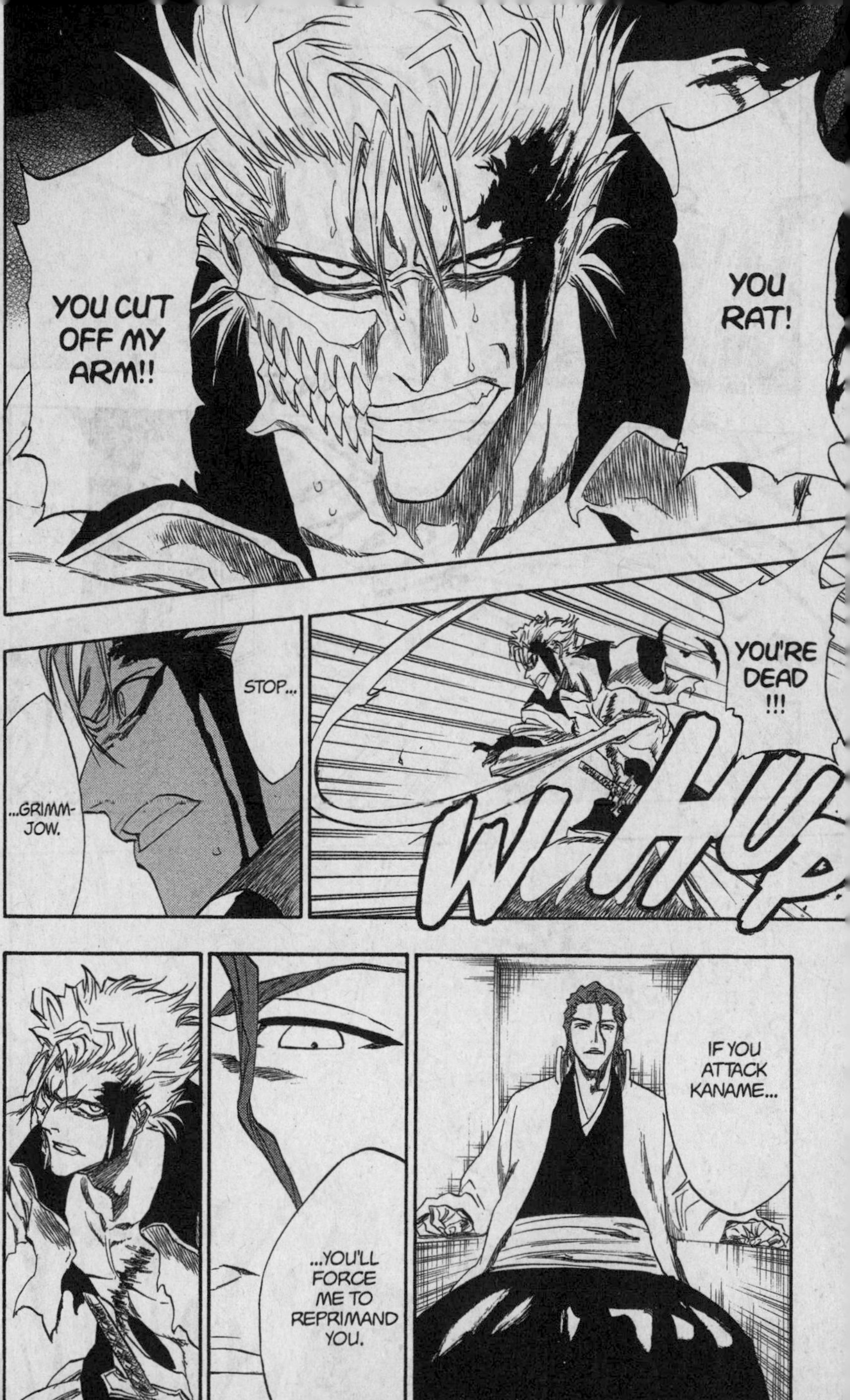
YOU RAT!
YOU CUT OFF MY ARM!!
YOU'RE DEAD!!!
WHUP
STOP...
...GRIMM-JOW.
IF YOU ATTACK KANAME...
...YOU'LL FORCE ME TO REPRIMAND YOU.

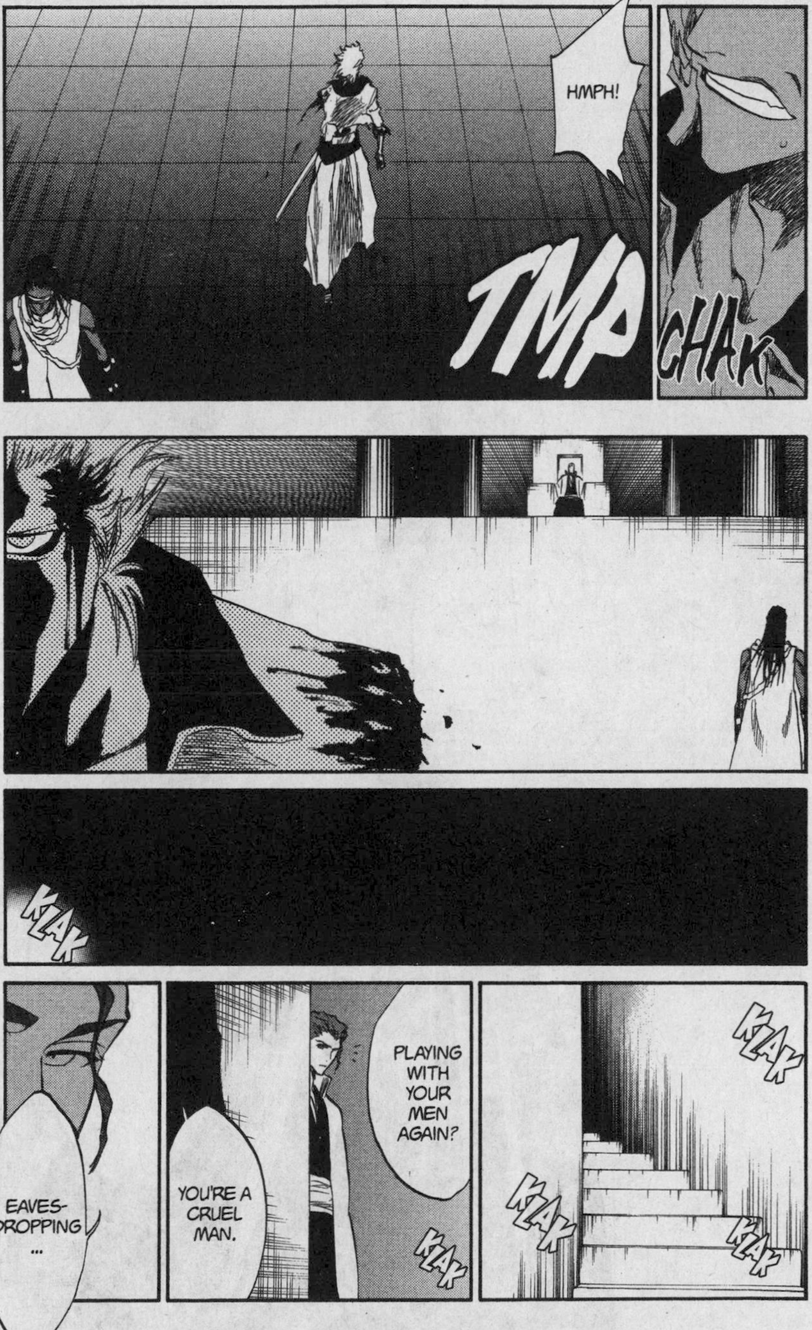
HMPH!
CHAK
TMP
KLAK
KLAK
KLAK
KLAK
PLAYING WITH YOUR MEN AGAIN?
YOU'RE A CRUEL MAN.
KLAK
EAVES-DROPPING ...

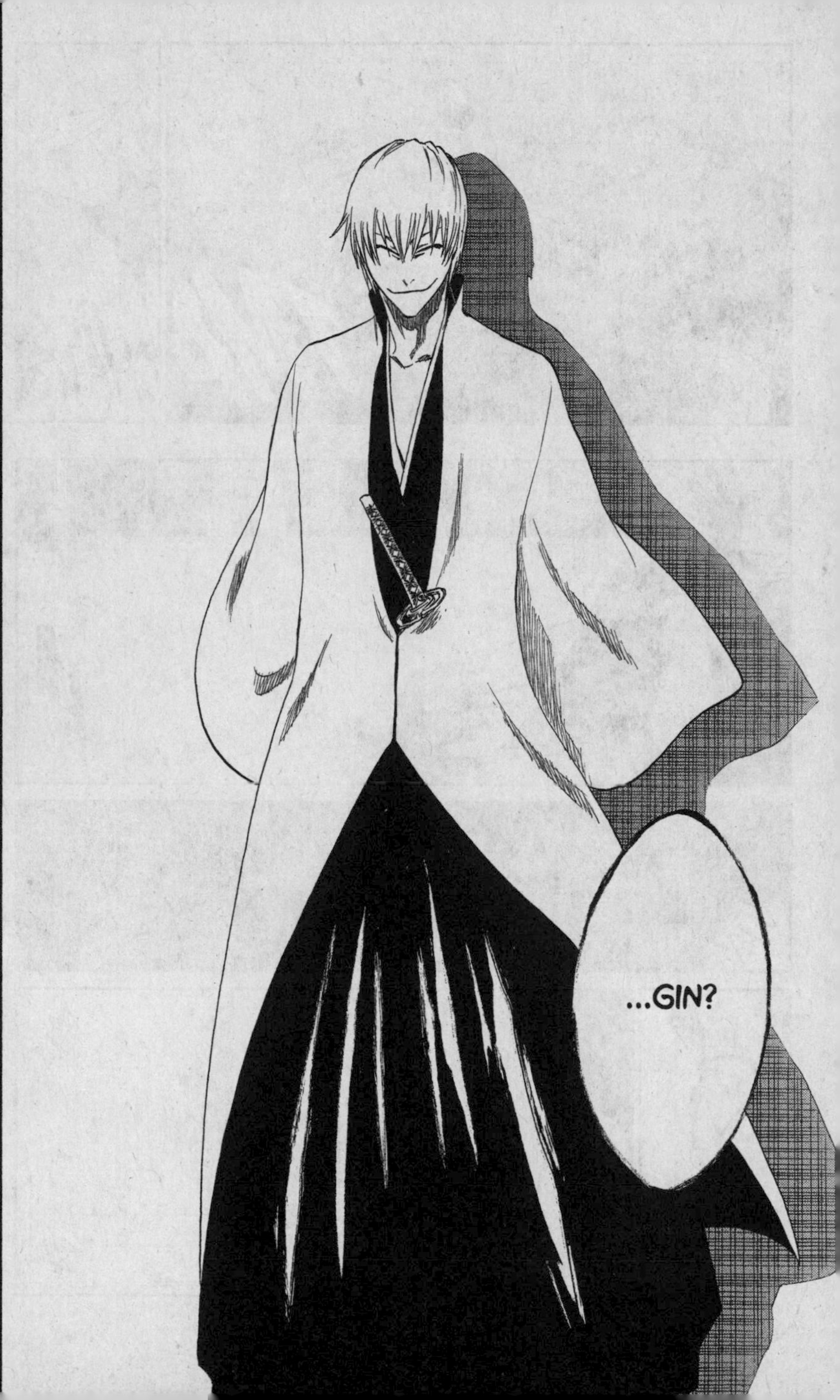
...GIN?

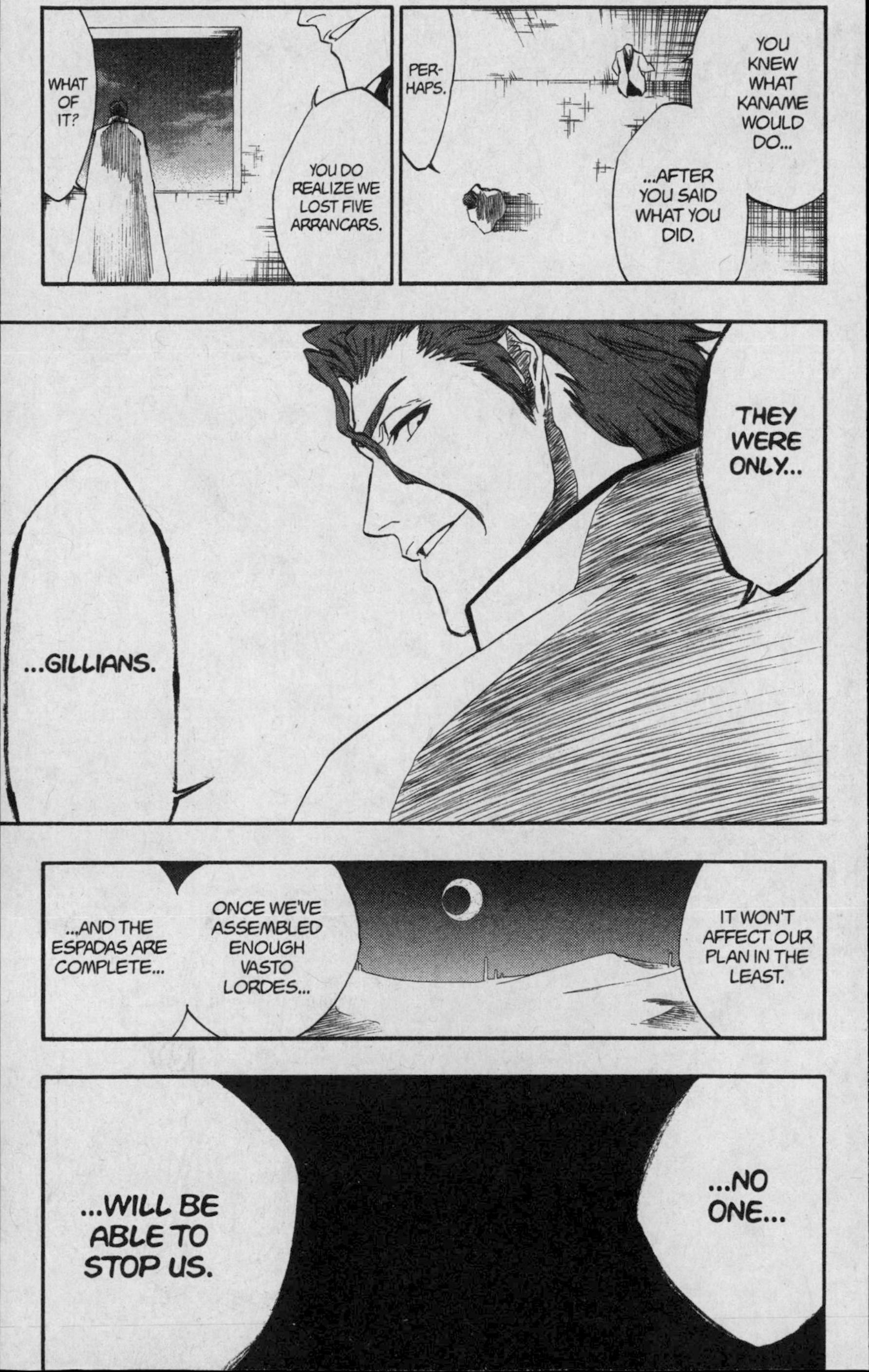
YOU KNEW WHAT KANAME WOULD DO...
...AFTER YOU SAID WHAT YOU DID.
PER-HAPS.
YOU DO REALIZE WE LOST FIVE ARRANCARS.
WHAT OF IT?
THEY WERE ONLY...
...GILLIANS.
IT WON'T AFFECT OUR PLAN IN THE LEAST.
ONCE WE'VE ASSEMBLED ENOUGH VASTO LORDES...
...AND THE ESPADAS ARE COMPLETE...
...NO ONE...
...WILL BE ABLE TO STOP US.

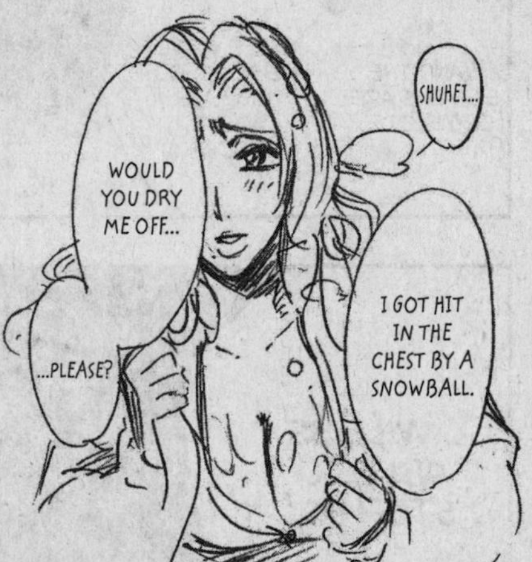
SHUHEI...
I GOT HIT IN THE CHEST BY A SNOWBALL.
WOULD YOU DRY ME OFF...
...PLEASE?

214. Immanent God Blues

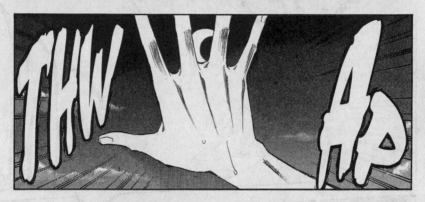

...HAS STOPPED.

THAT VIBRATING SPIRITUAL PRESSURE...

HAS THE ENEMY...

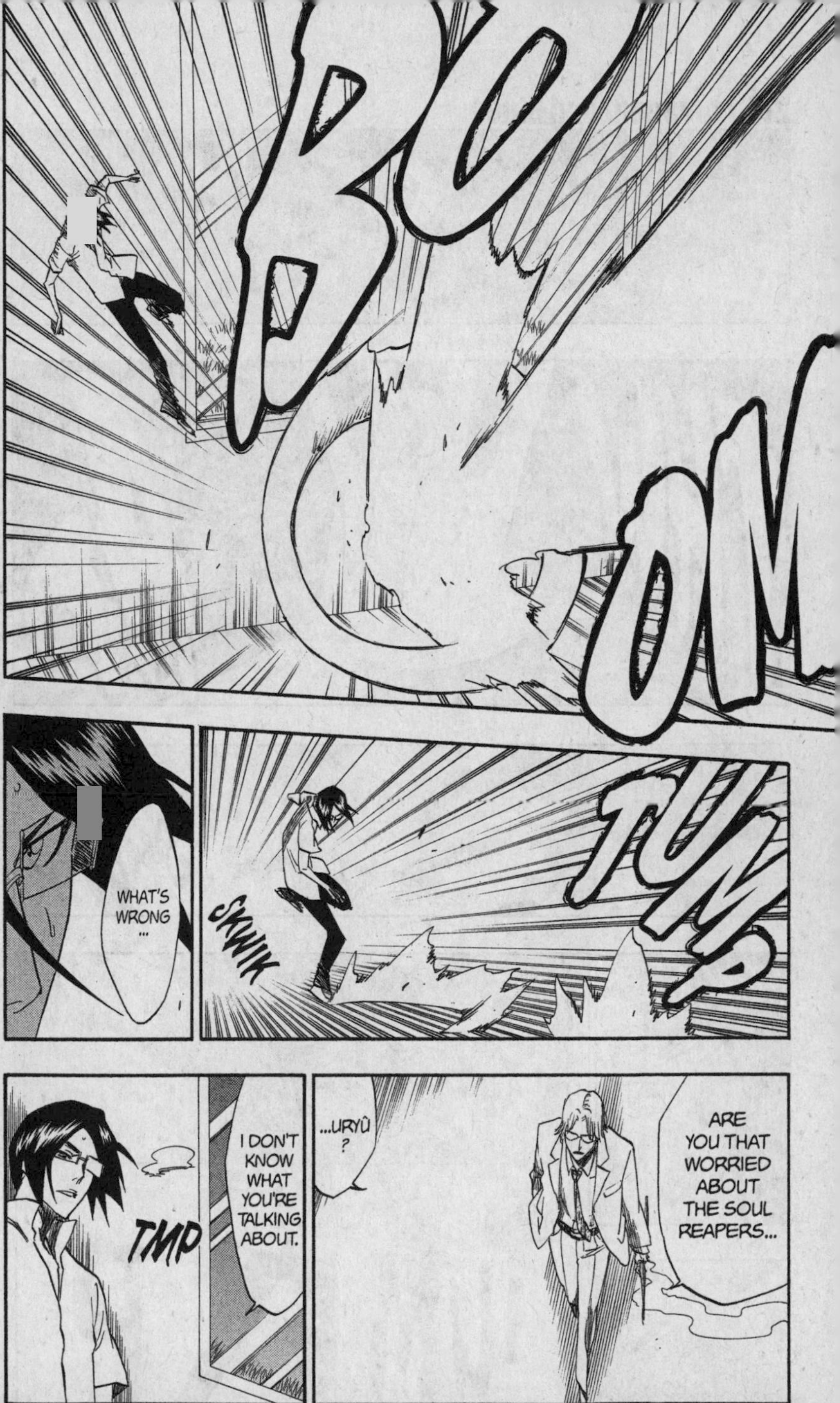
BOOM
TUMP
SKWIK
WHAT'S WRONG ...
ARE YOU THAT WORRIED ABOUT THE SOUL REAPERS...
...URYÛ ?
I DON'T KNOW WHAT YOU'RE TALKING ABOUT.
TMP

READ THIS WAY

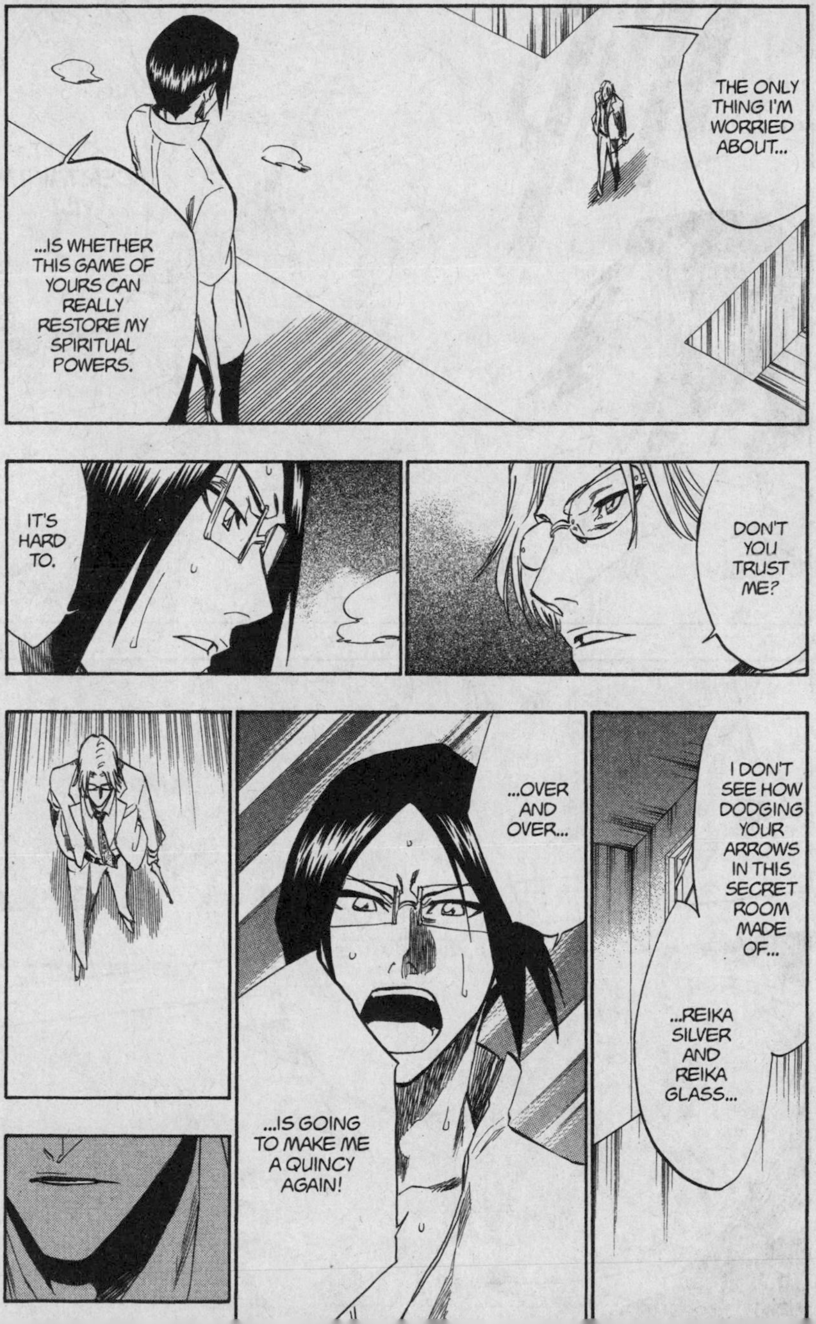
THE ONLY THING I'M WORRIED ABOUT...
...IS WHETHER THIS GAME OF YOURS CAN REALLY RESTORE MY SPIRITUAL POWERS.
DON'T YOU TRUST ME?
IT'S HARD TO.
I DON'T SEE HOW DODGING YOUR ARROWS IN THIS SECRET ROOM MADE OF...
...REIKA SILVER AND REIKA GLASS...
...OVER AND OVER...
...IS GOING TO MAKE ME A QUINCY AGAIN!

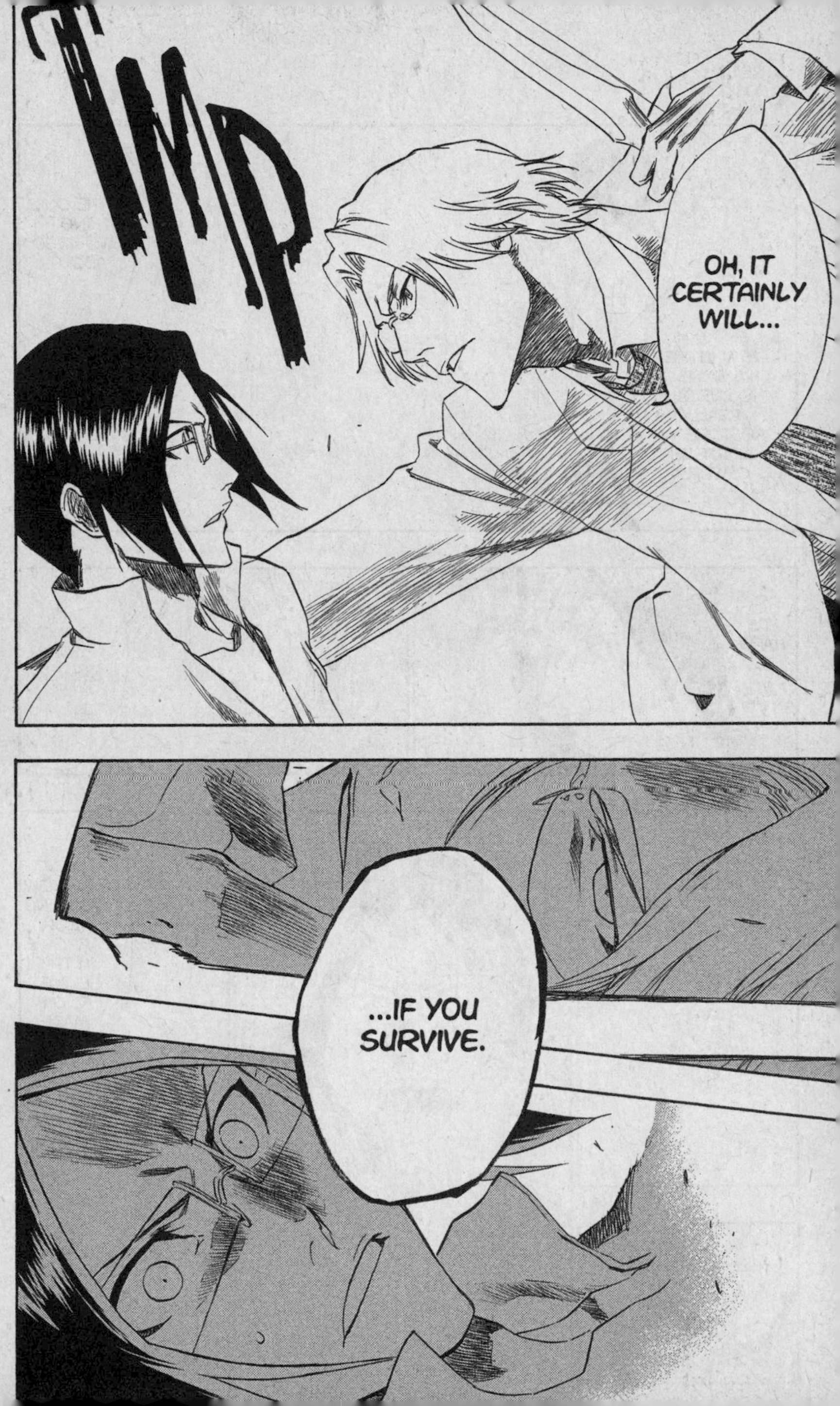
TMP
OH, IT CERTAINLY WILL...
...IF YOU SURVIVE.

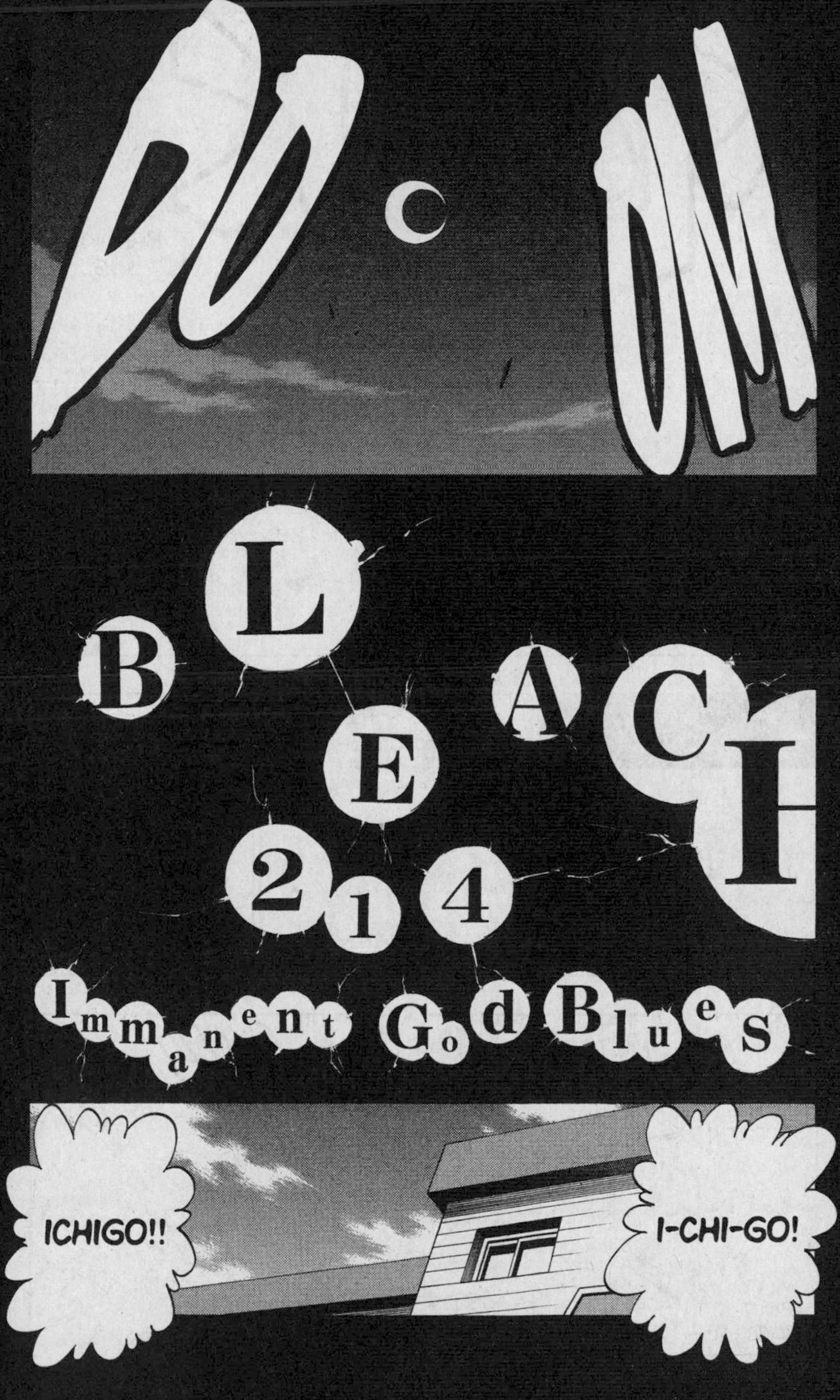
DOOM
BLEACH
214
Immanent God Blues
I-CHI-GO!
ICHIGO!!

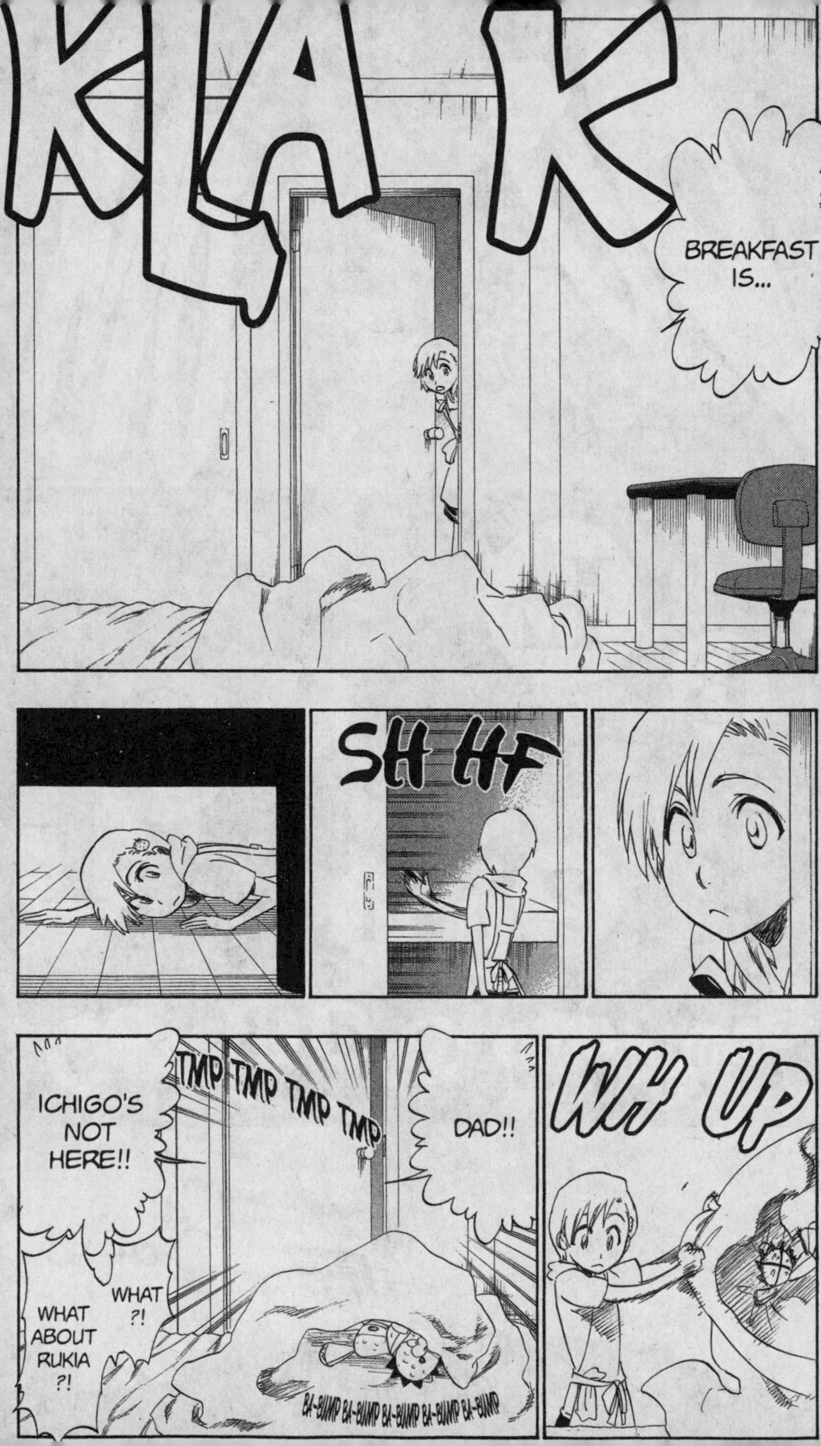
KLAK
BREAKFAST IS...
SHHF
WHUP
DAD!!
TMP TMP TMP TMP
ICHIGO'S NOT HERE!!
WHAT ?!
WHAT ABOUT RUKIA ?!
BA-BUMP BA-BUMP BA-BUMP BA-BUMP BA-BUMP

READ THIS WAY

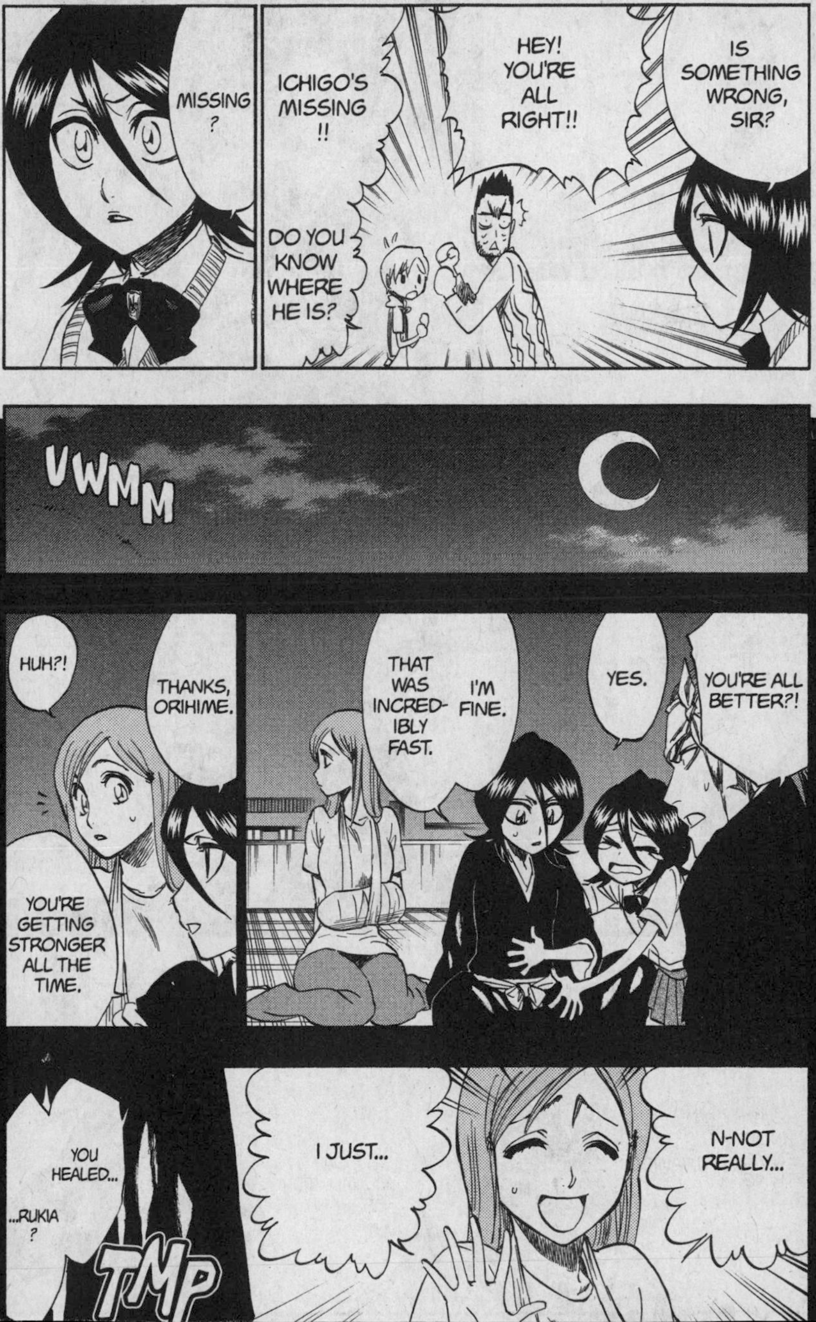
IS SOMETHING WRONG, SIR?
HEY! YOU'RE ALL RIGHT!!
ICHIGO'S MISSING !!
DO YOU KNOW WHERE HE IS?
MISSING ?
VWMM
YOU'RE ALL BETTER?!
YES.
I'M FINE.
THAT WAS INCRED-IBLY FAST.
THANKS, ORIHIME.
HUH?!
YOU'RE GETTING STRONGER ALL THE TIME.
N-NOT REALLY...
I JUST...
YOU HEALED...
...RUKIA ?
TMP

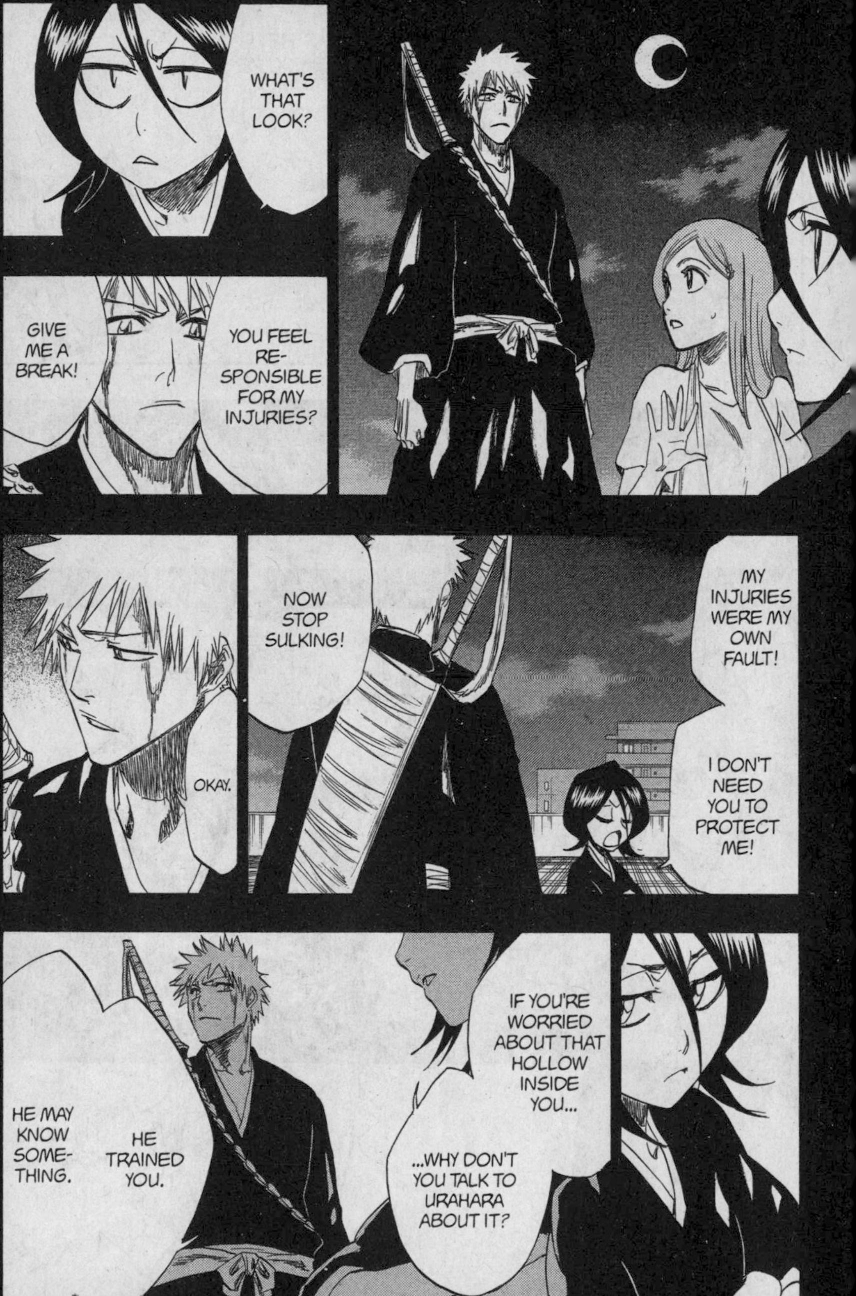
WHAT'S THAT LOOK?
YOU FEEL RE-SPONSIBLE FOR MY INJURIES?
GIVE ME A BREAK!
MY INJURIES WERE MY OWN FAULT!
I DON'T NEED YOU TO PROTECT ME!
NOW STOP SULKING!
OKAY.
IF YOU'RE WORRIED ABOUT THAT HOLLOW INSIDE YOU...
...WHY DON'T YOU TALK TO URAHARA ABOUT IT?
HE TRAINED YOU.
HE MAY KNOW SOME-THING.

READ THIS WAY

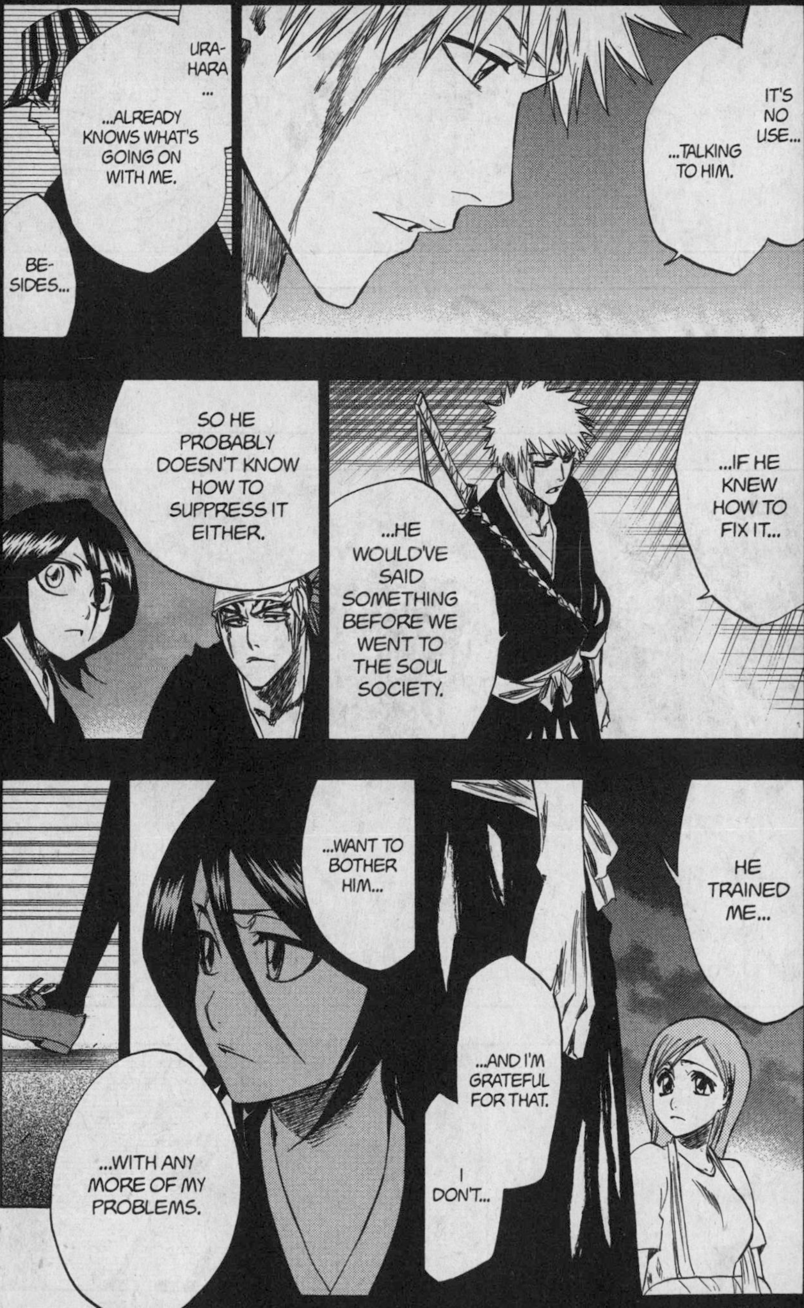
IT'S NO USE...
...TALKING TO HIM.
URA-HARA ...
...ALREADY KNOWS WHAT'S GOING ON WITH ME.
BE-SIDES...
...IF HE KNEW HOW TO FIX IT...
...HE WOULD'VE SAID SOMETHING BEFORE WE WENT TO THE SOUL SOCIETY.
SO HE PROBABLY DOESN'T KNOW HOW TO SUPPRESS IT EITHER.
HE TRAINED ME...
...AND I'M GRATEFUL FOR THAT.
I DON'T...
...WANT TO BOTHER HIM...
...WITH ANY MORE OF MY PROBLEMS.

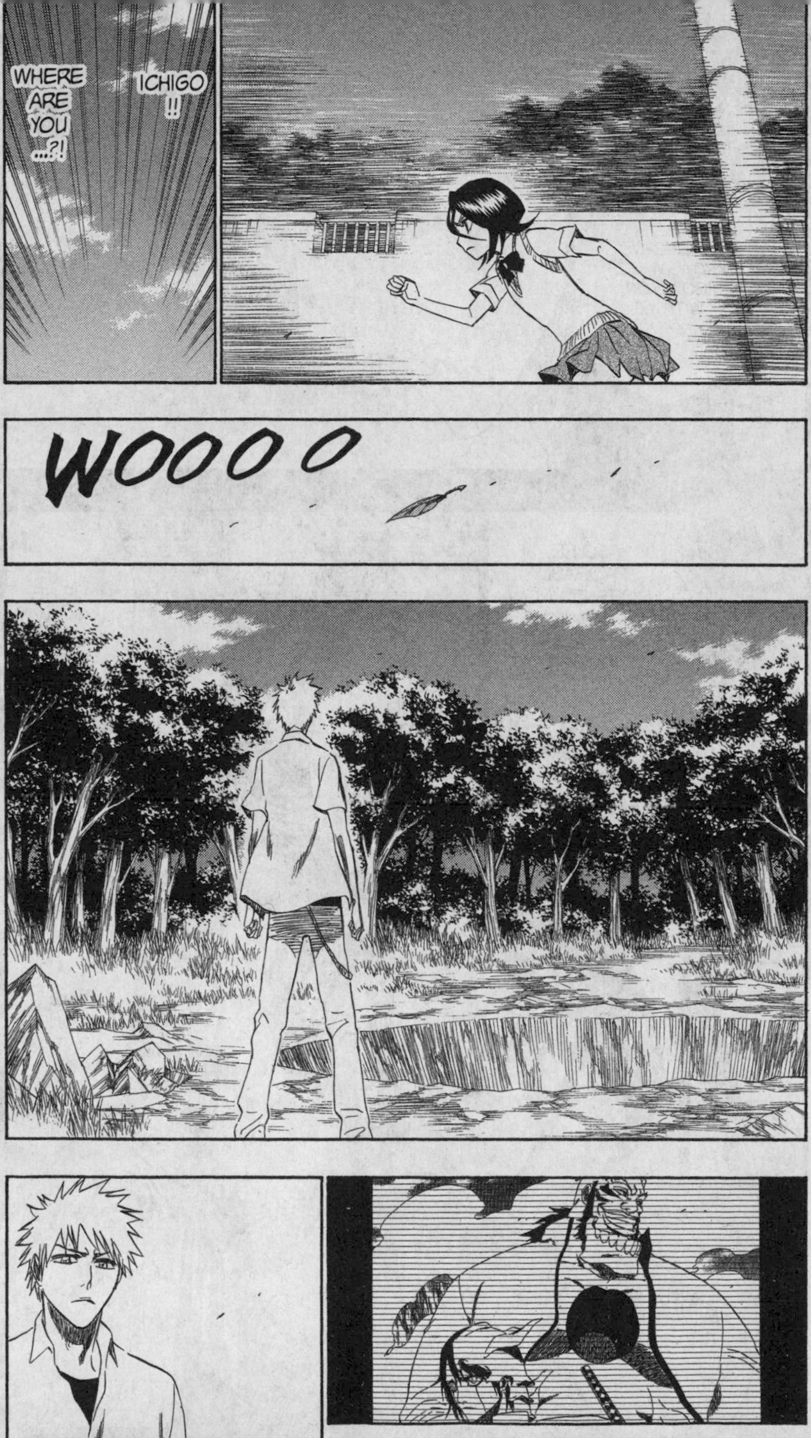
ICHIGO !!
WHERE ARE YOU ...?!
WOOOO

READ THIS WAY

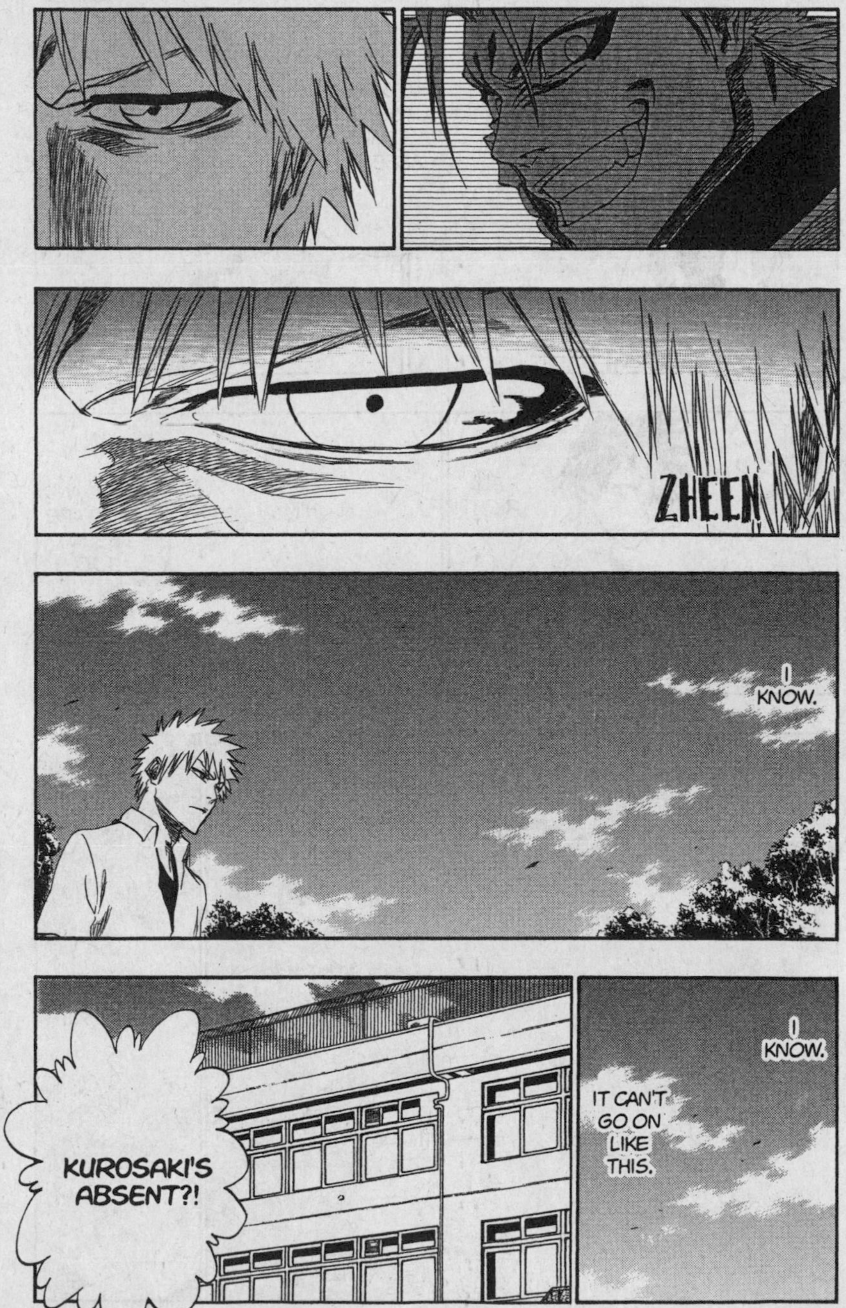
ZHEEN
I KNOW.
I KNOW.
IT CAN'T GO ON LIKE THIS.
KUROSAKI'S ABSENT?!

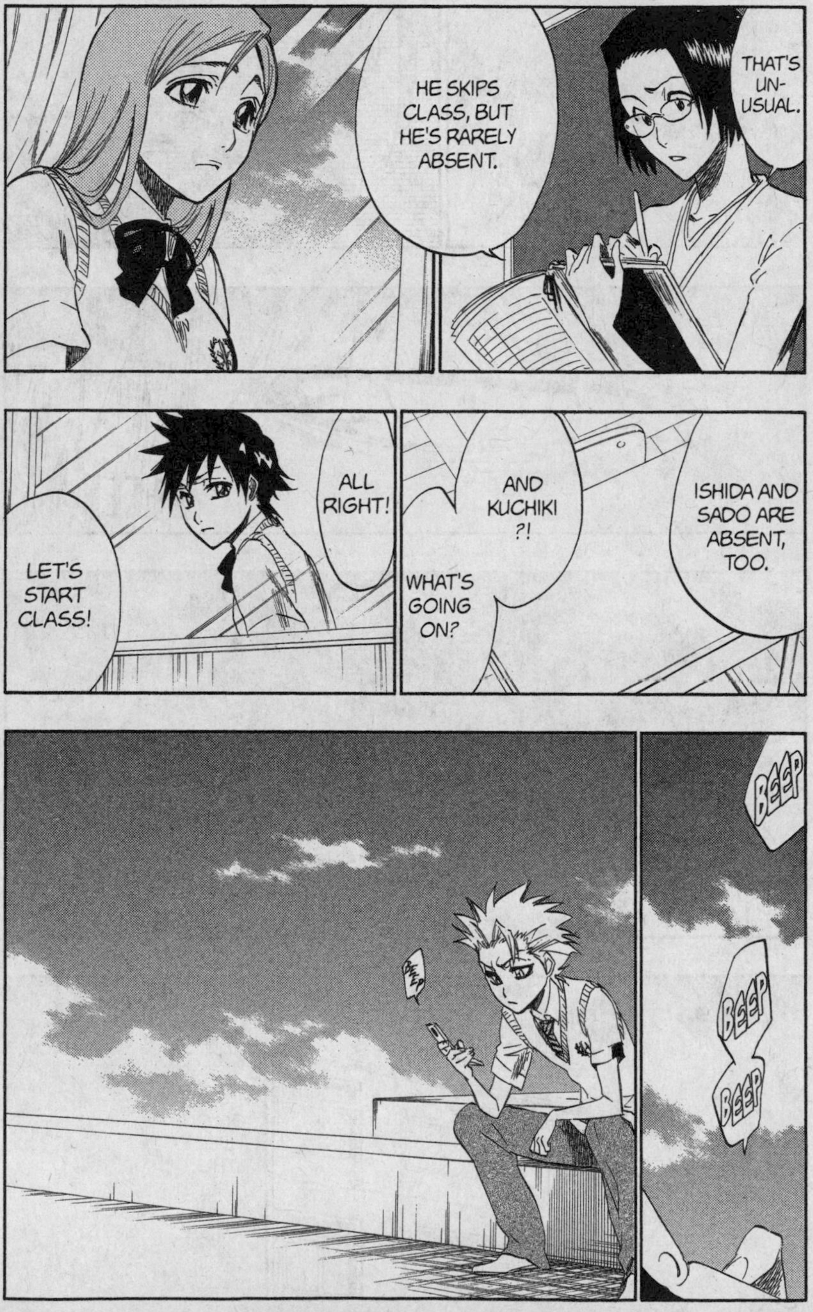
THAT'S UN-USUAL.
HE SKIPS CLASS, BUT HE'S RARELY ABSENT.
ISHIDA AND SADO ARE ABSENT, TOO.
AND KUCHIKI ?!
WHAT'S GOING ON?
ALL RIGHT!
LET'S START CLASS!
BEEP
BEEP
BEEP

READ THIS WAY

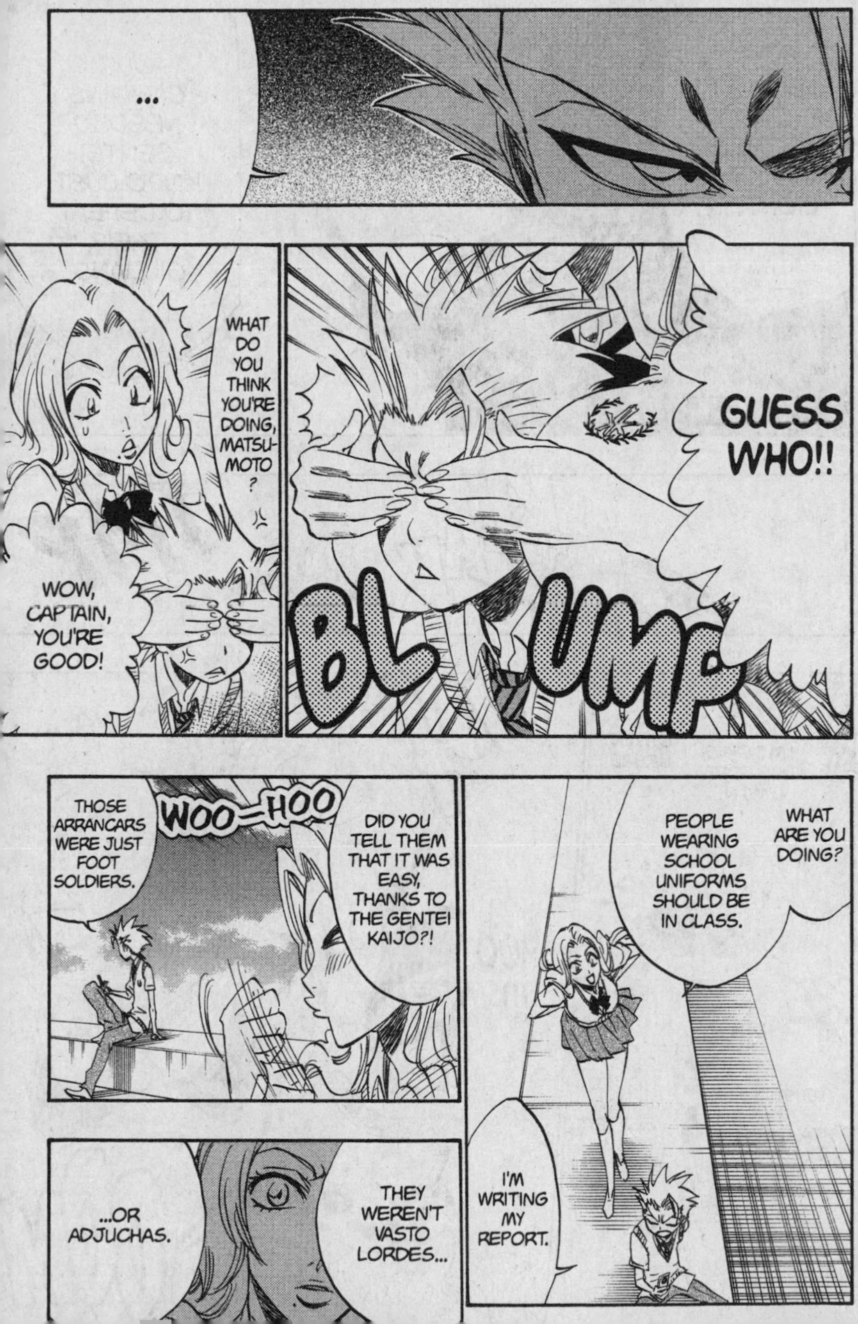
...
GUESS WHO!!
BLUMP
WHAT DO YOU THINK YOU'RE DOING, MATSUMOTO?
WOW, CAPTAIN, YOU'RE GOOD!
WHAT ARE YOU DOING?
PEOPLE WEARING SCHOOL UNIFORMS SHOULD BE IN CLASS.
I'M WRITING MY REPORT.
DID YOU TELL THEM THAT IT WAS EASY, THANKS TO THE GENTEI KAIJO?!
WOO-HOO
THOSE ARRANCARS WERE JUST FOOT SOLDIERS.
THEY WEREN'T VASTO LORDES...
...OR ADJUCHAS.

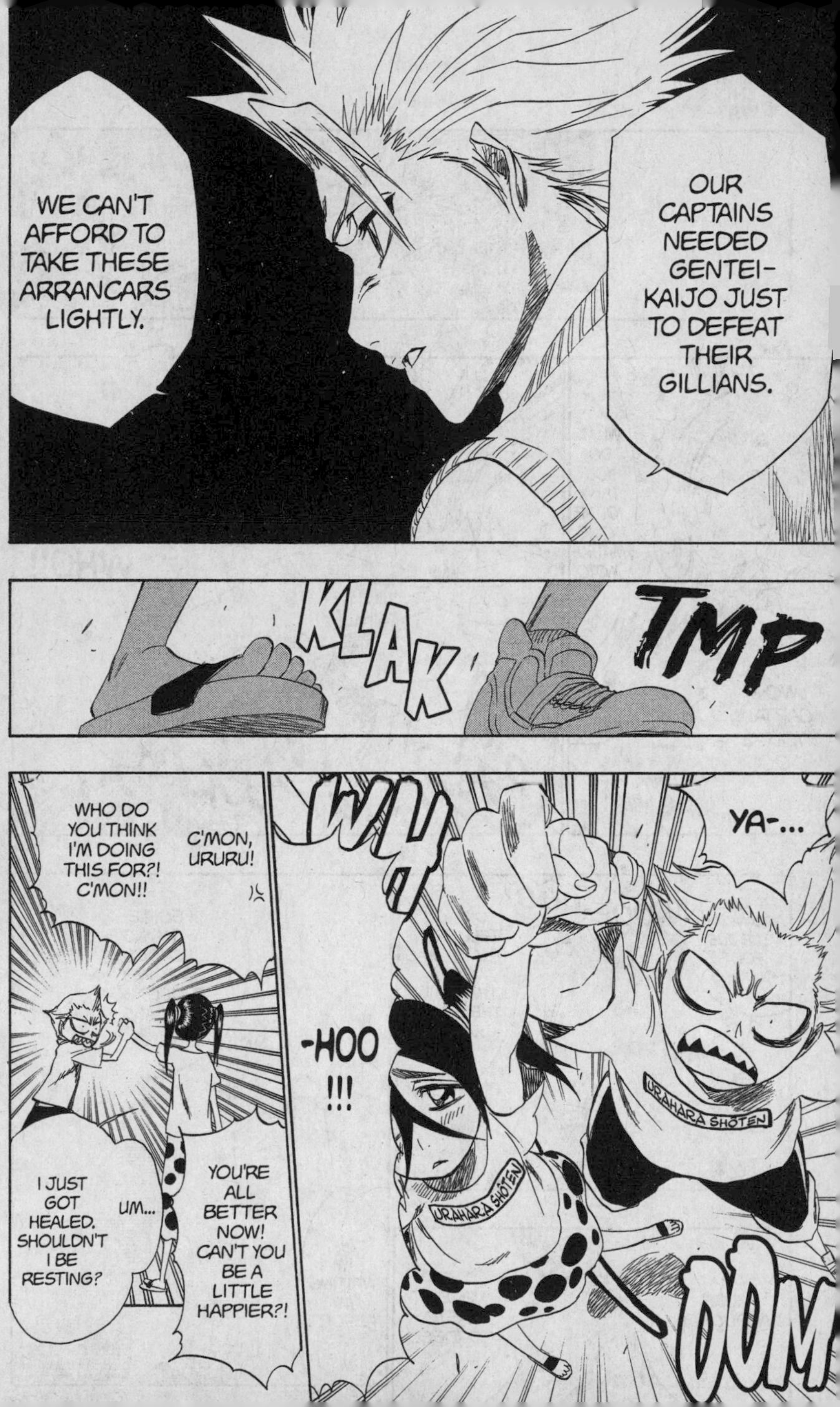
OUR CAPTAINS NEEDED GENTEI-KAIJO JUST TO DEFEAT THEIR GILLIANS.
WE CAN'T AFFORD TO TAKE THESE ARRANCARS LIGHTLY.
TMP
KLAK
YA-...
WH
-HOO!!!
URAHARA SHŌTEN
URAHARA SHŌTEN
DOOM
C'MON, URURU!
WHO DO YOU THINK I'M DOING THIS FOR?! C'MON!!
YOU'RE ALL BETTER NOW! CAN'T YOU BE A LITTLE HAPPIER?!
UM...
I JUST GOT HEALED. SHOULDN'T I BE RESTING?

READ THIS WAY

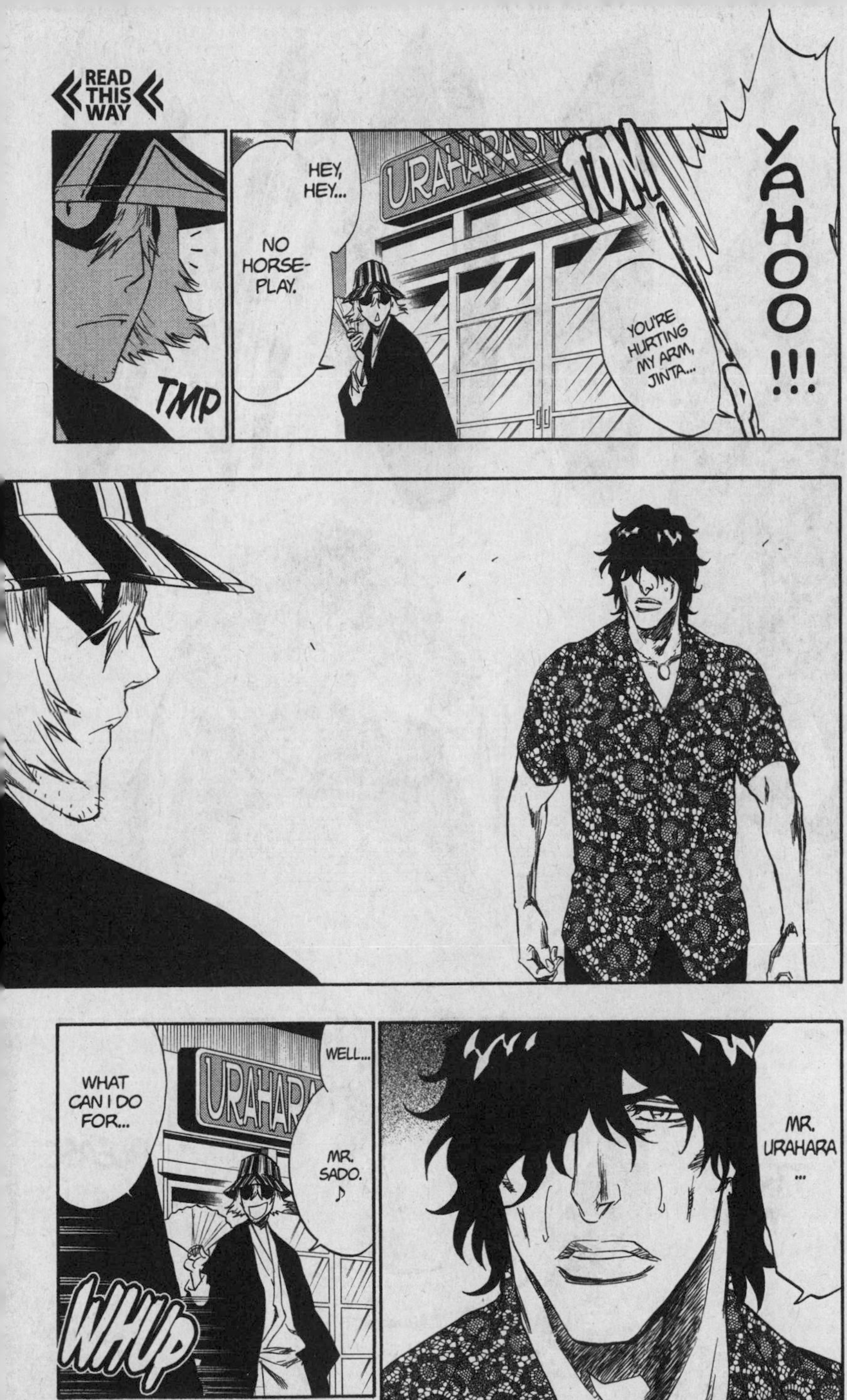
YAHOO!!!
YOU'RE HURTING MY ARM, JINTA...
TOM
HEY, HEY...
NO HORSE-PLAY.
TMP
MR. URAHARA ...
WELL...
WHAT CAN I DO FOR...
MR. SADO. ♪
WHUP

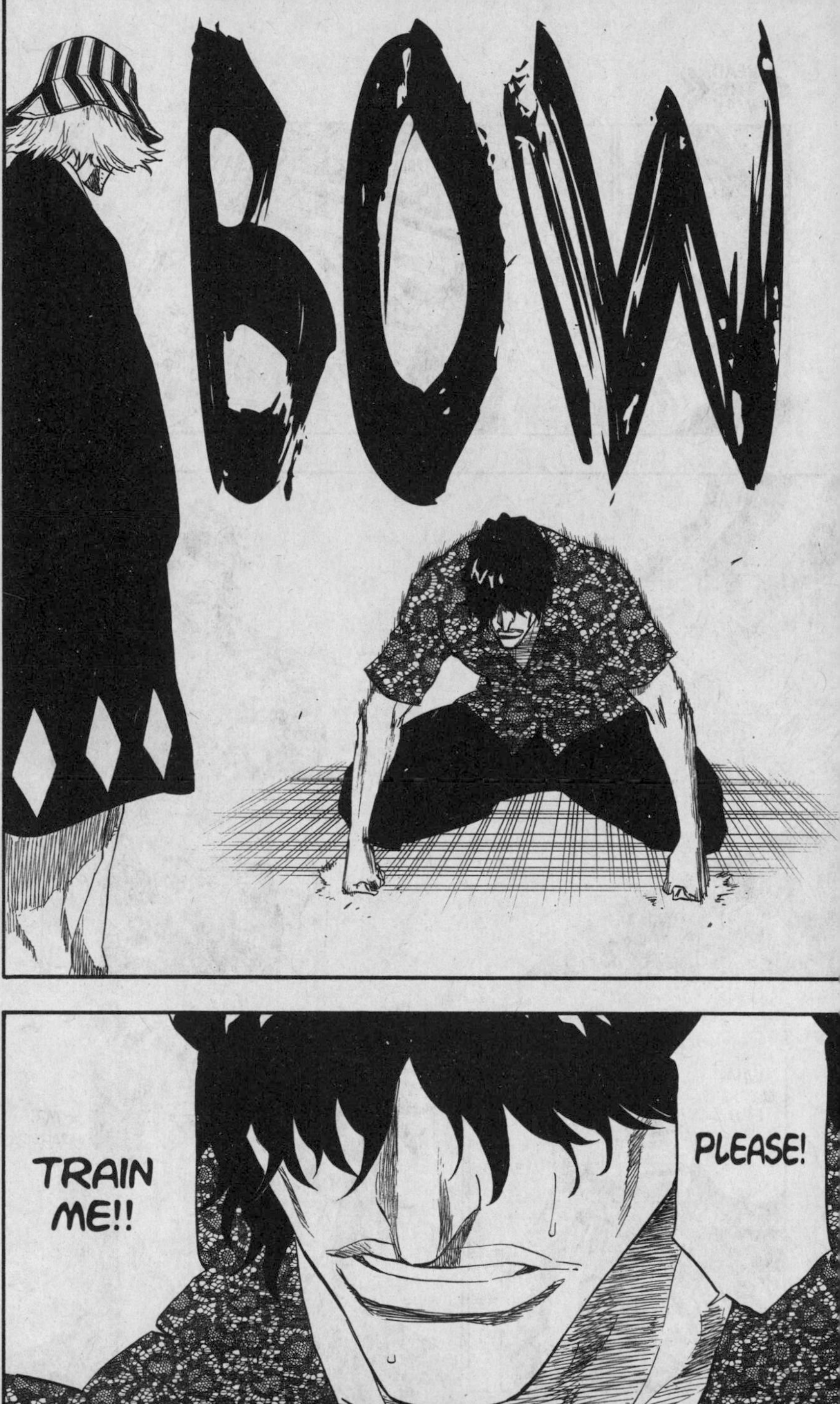
BOW
PLEASE!
TRAIN ME!!

READ THIS WAY

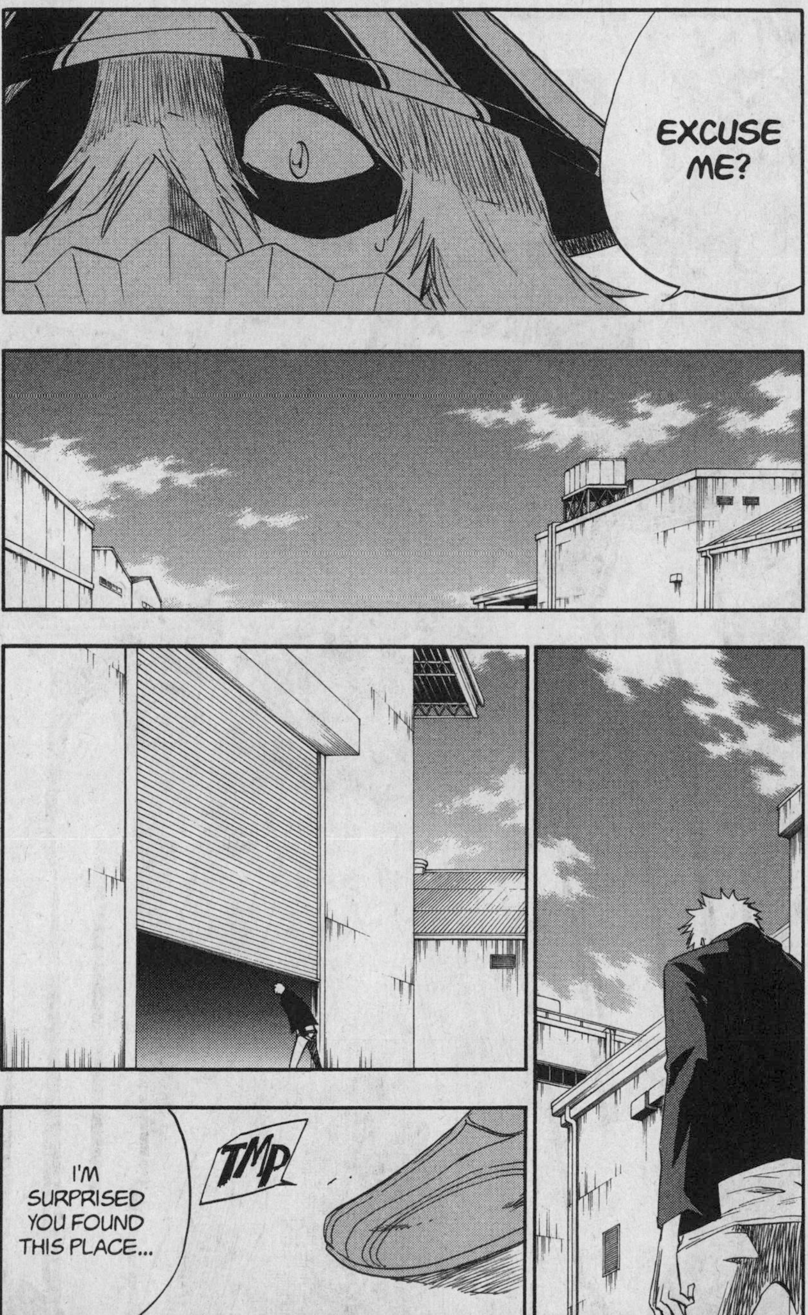
EXCUSE ME?
TMP
I'M SURPRISED YOU FOUND THIS PLACE...

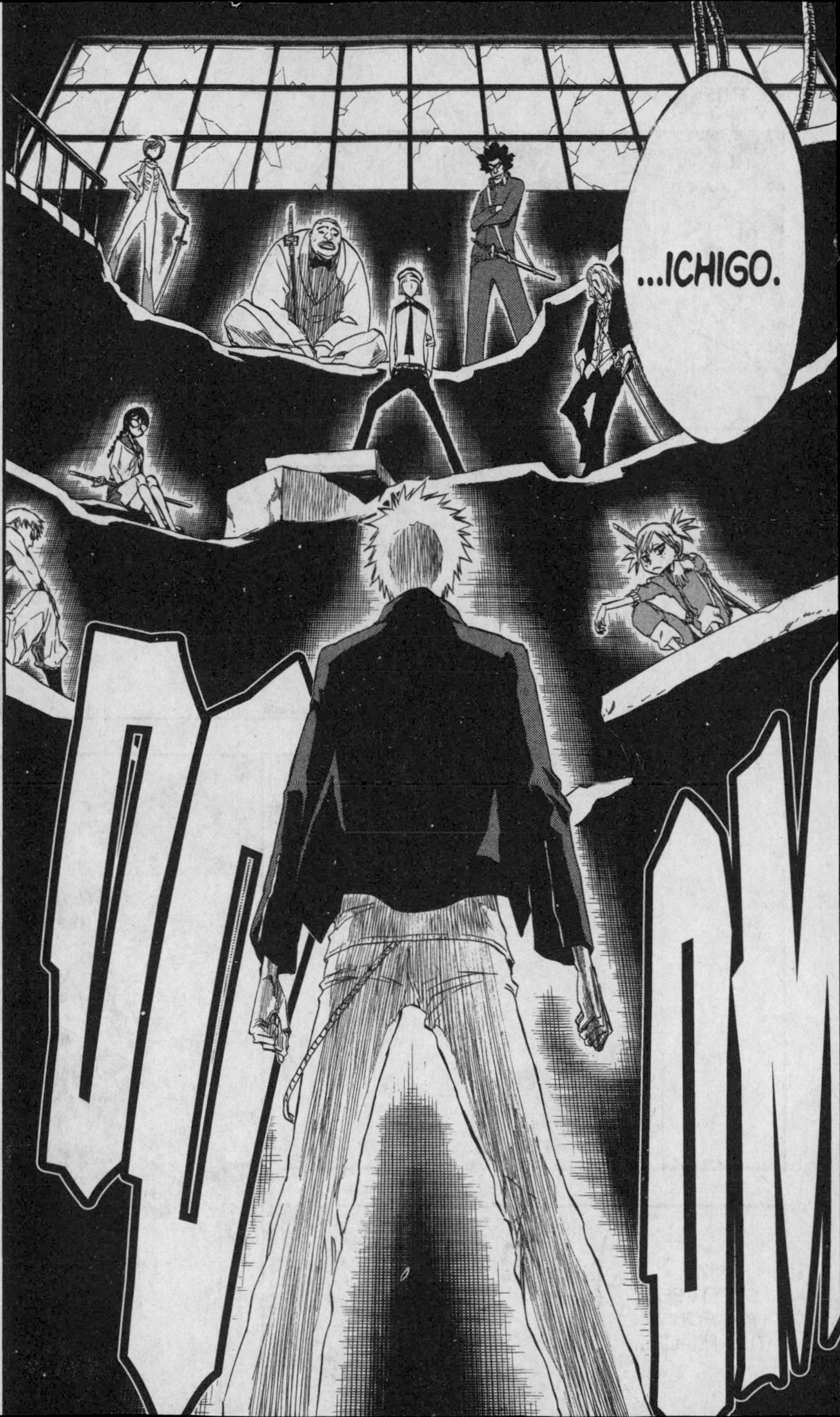
...ICHIGO.

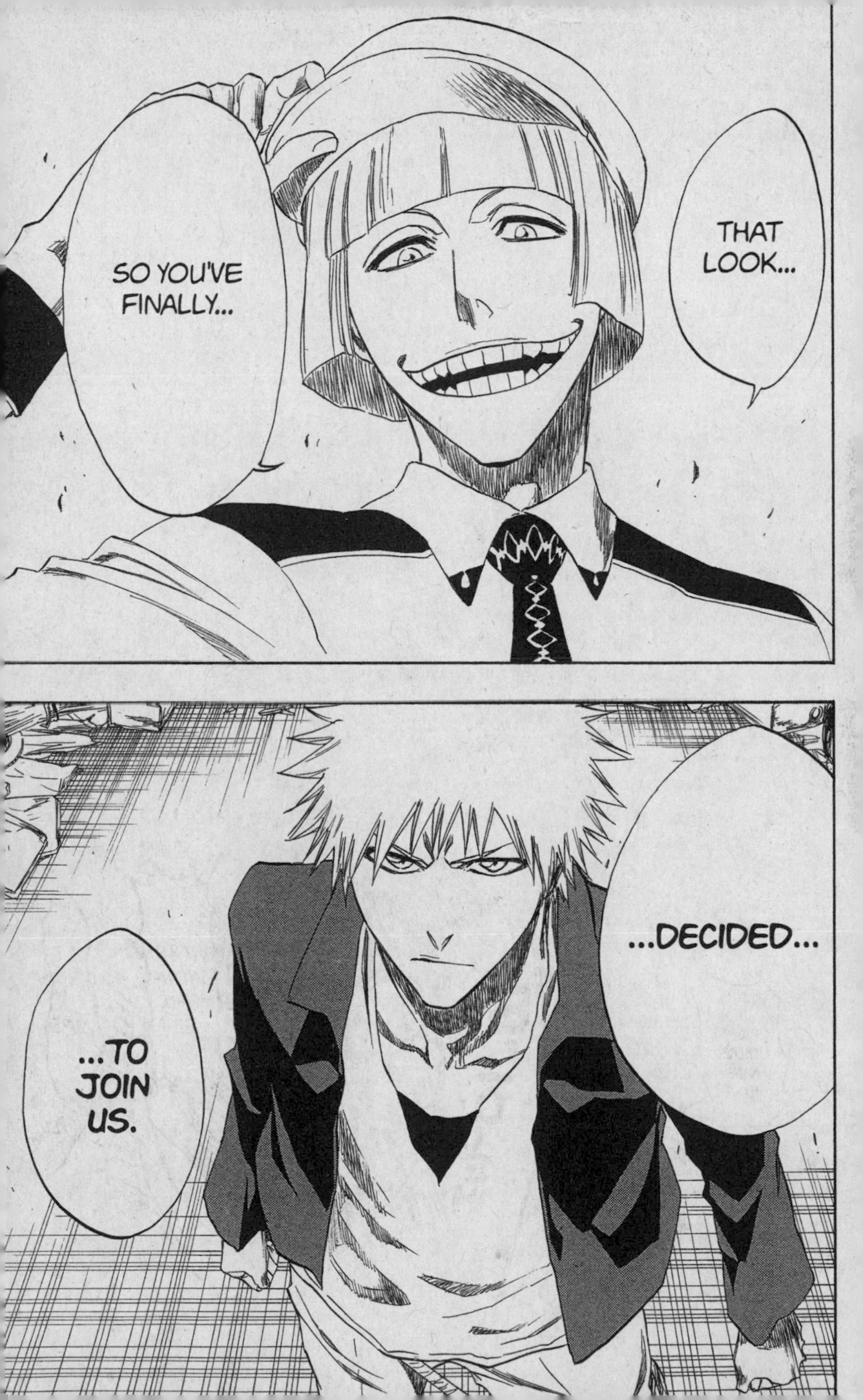
THAT LOOK...
SO YOU'VE FINALLY...
...DECIDED...
...TO JOIN US.

HUH? SURE!!
PLURT
DARN SNOW-BALL!!!
BLOOSH
I'D... BE GLAD TO!!
BE RIGHT THERE, RAN-GIKU!!

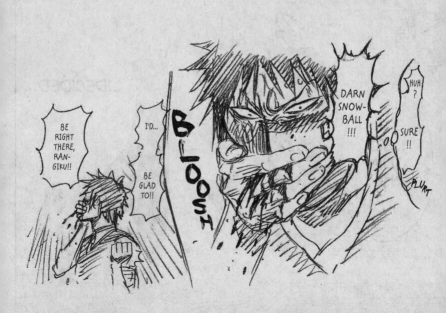

BLEACH POPULARITY POLL 3

DETAILED RESULTS!!

THE COMPLETE LIST

OVER 75,000 VOTES! THE THIRD CHARACTER POPULARITY POLL RESULTS!!

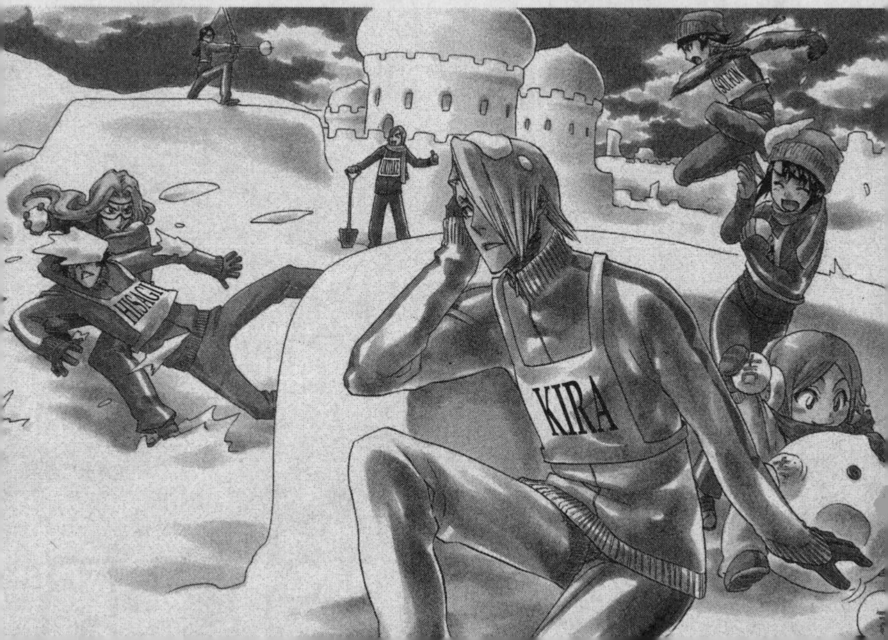
HISAGI
KIRA

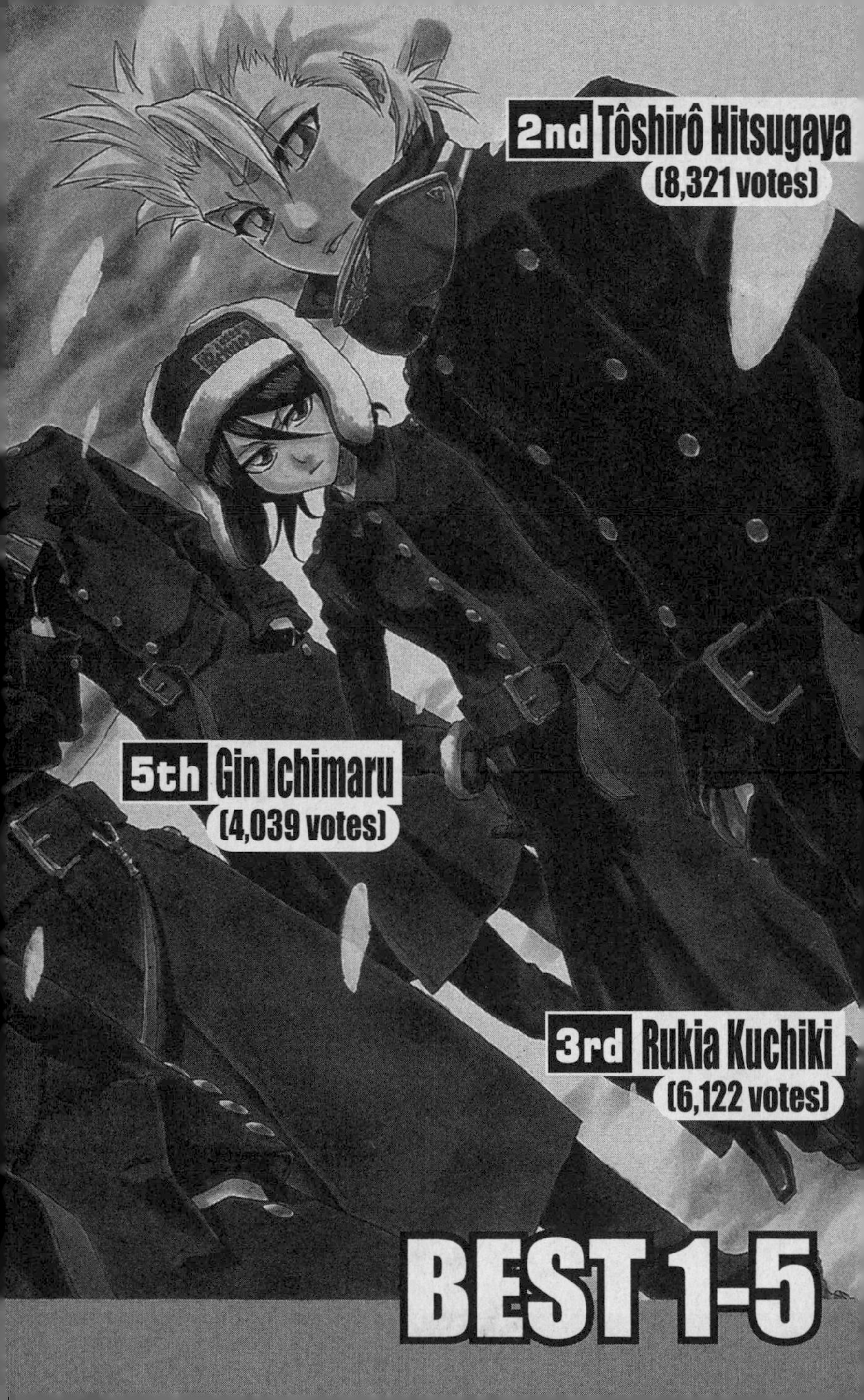
2nd Tôshirô Hitsugaya
(8,321 votes)
5th Gin Ichimaru
(4,039 votes)
3rd Rukia Kuchiki
(6,122 votes)
BEST 1-5

BLEACH POPULARITY POLL 3

DETAILED RESULTS!!

THE COMPLETE LIST

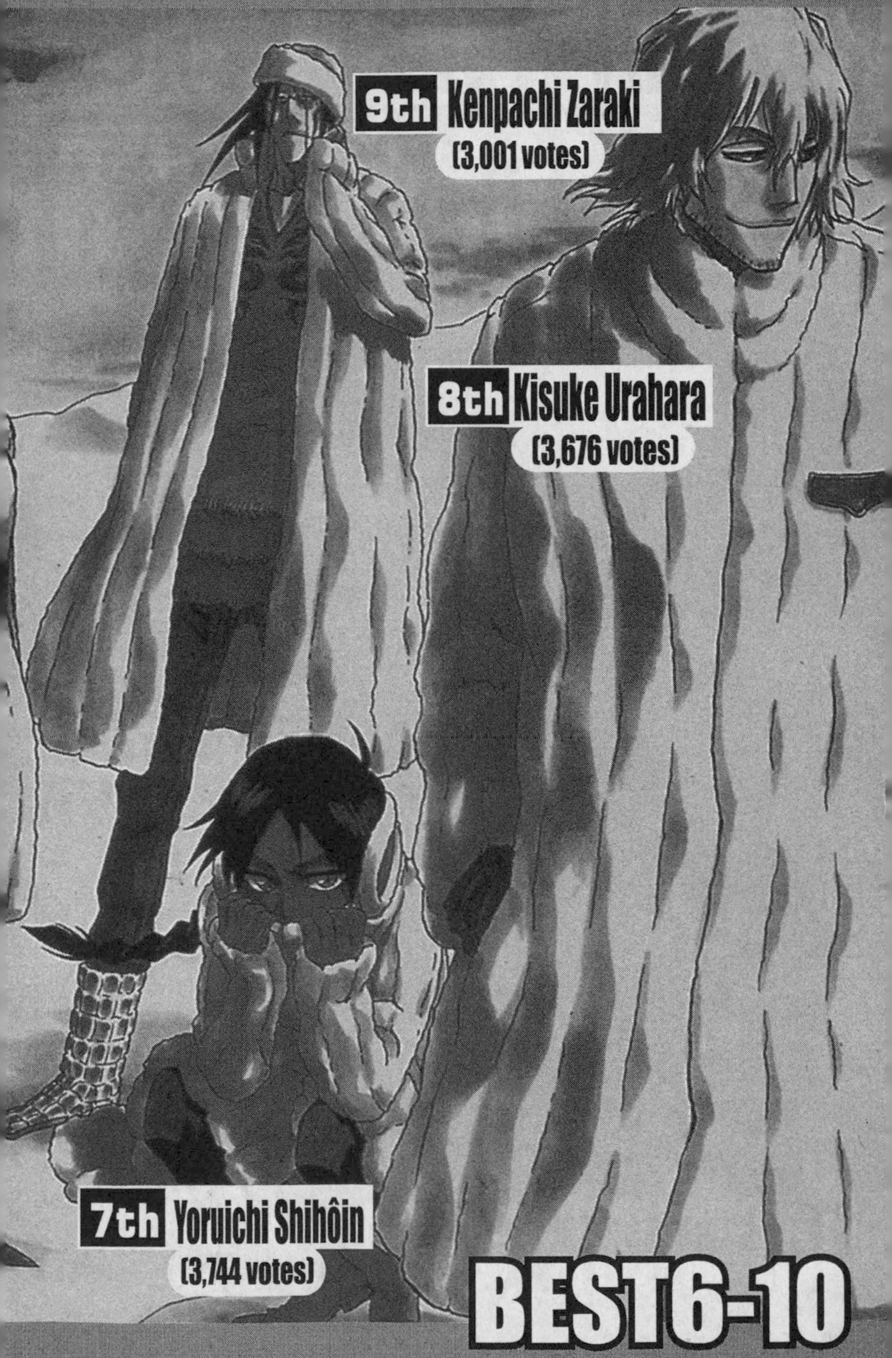
9th Kenpachi Zaraki
(3,001 votes)
8th Kisuke Urahara
(3,676 votes)
7th Yoruichi Shihôin
(3,744 votes)
BEST6-10

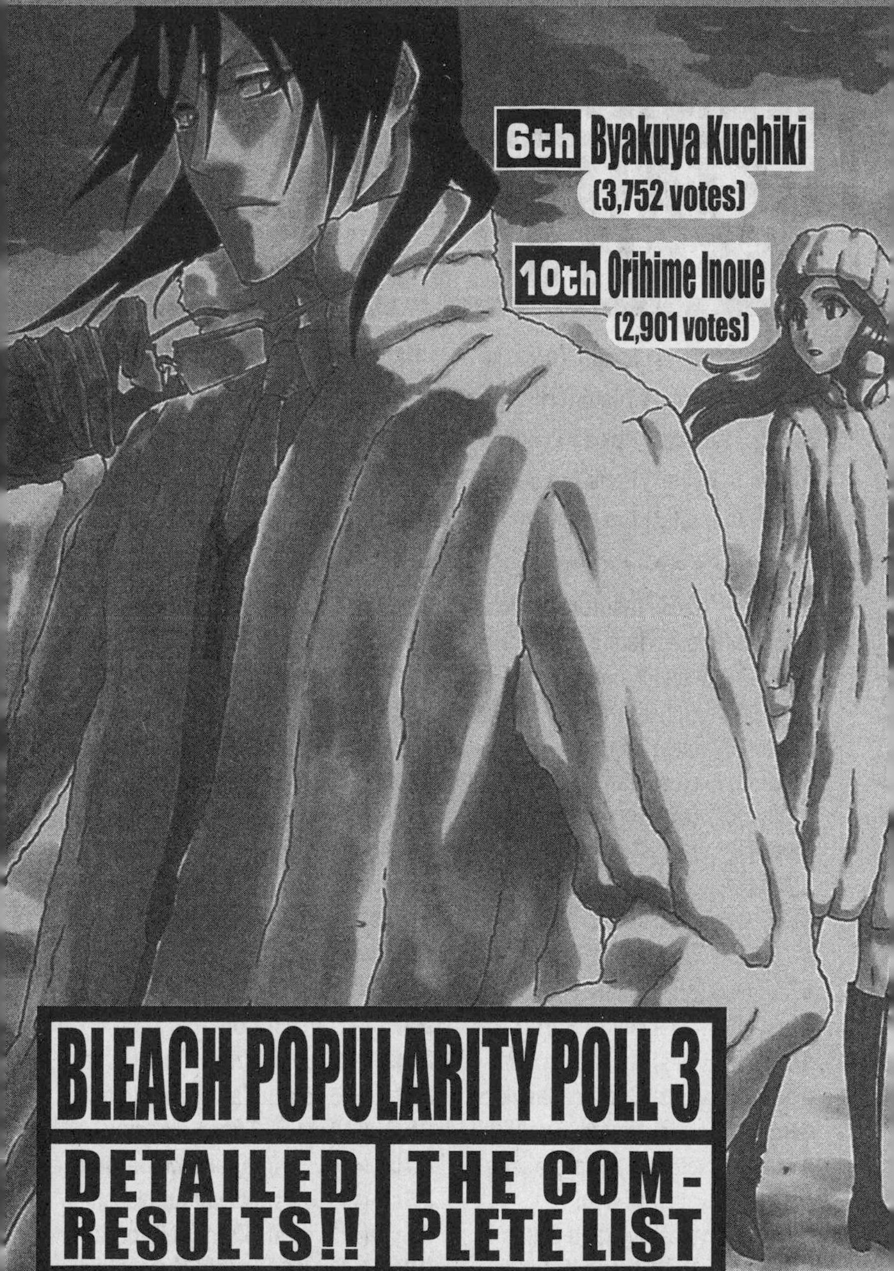
6th Byakuya Kuchiki
(3,752 votes)
10th Orihime Inoue
(2,901 votes)
BLEACH POPULARITY POLL 3
DETAILED RESULTS!!
THE COM-PLETE LIST

BLEACH POPULARITY POLL 3

DETAILED RESULTS!! THE COMPLETE LIST

1st (8,370 votes) Ichigo Kurosaki
2nd (8,321 votes) Tôshirô Hitsugaya
3rd (6,122 votes) Rukia Kuchiki
4th (4,517 votes) Renji Abarai
5th (4,039 votes) Gin Ichimaru
6th (3,752 votes) Byakuya Kuchiki
7th (3,744 votes) Yoruichi Shihôin
8th (3,676 votes) Kisuke Urahara
9th (3,001 votes) Kenpachi Zaraki
10th (2,901 votes) Orihime Inoue

11th (2,873 votes) Izuru Kira
12th (2,735 votes) Momo Hinamori
13th (2,317 votes) Shûhei Hisagi
14th (2,298 votes) Jûshiro Ukitake
15th (1,742 votes) Uryû Ishida
16th (1,628 votes) Soi Fon
17th (1,377 votes) Rangiku Matsumoto
18th (1,266 votes) Sôsuke Aizen
19th (1,244 votes) Yachiru Kusajishi
20th (737 votes) Ulquiorra
21st (641 votes) Yumichika Ayasegawa
22nd (609 votes) Nanao Ise
23rd (601 votes) Kon
24th (566 votes) Ururu Tsumugiya
25th (545 votes) Hanatarô Yamada
26th (519 votes) Tôsen Kaname
27th (456 votes) Ikkaku Madarame
28th (448 votes) Mayuri Kurotsuchi
29th (445 votes) Shunsui Kyoraku
30th (440 votes) Isshin Kurosaki
31st (370 votes) Yasutora Sado
32nd (346 votes) Isane Kotetsu
33rd (316 votes) Kaien Shiba
Akon
35th (258 votes) Zangetsu
36th (217 votes) Ganju Shiba
37th (202 votes) Nemu Kurotsuchi
38th (181 votes) Retsu Unohana
39th (175 votes) Sajin Komamura
40th (174 votes) Tatsuki Arisawa
41st (171 votes) Keigo Asano
42nd (155 votes) Shinji Hirako
43rd (151 votes) Hiyori Sarugaki
44th (145 votes) Ryûken Ishida
45th (142 votes) Chojiro Sasakibe
46th (137 votes) Hisana Kuchiki
47th (137 votes) Aizen's glasses
48th (129 votes) Rikichi
49th (109 votes) Kûkaku Shiba
50th (88 votes) Kiyone Kotetsu

BEST 1-146

Horiuchi/Kenseikan/Pupples/The 12th Company member who was tricked by Kurotsuchi/Uryû's glasses/Kenpachi's Zanpaku-tô/The leaf Shunsui has in his mouth/Enraku/The cover with Kenpachi covered in blood that got nixed/Rukia's Zanpaku-tô/Isshin's charm/The button on Kon's belly/Reiichi Ohshima/Michiru's broken doll/Monshirochô/Yumichika's wig/Acidwire/Elwood

146th (1 vote) Sora Inoue/Chappy/Shunshun Rikka/Koganehiko/Mareyo Ohmaeda/Suzumebachi/Zangetsu's sunglasses/Gillian/Senzai-kyu/The Champs-Élysées/Melon & Cookie/Kurôemon Tsujishiro/Lord Baron/Ugendô/Matatabi?!/Tessai Deathcatch/Madame Akiyama/Mod Konpaku/Kurosaki Clinic/The Karakura High School guidebook/Kenpachi's eye patch/Comedian guidebook 2001/Konpaku in pain during Konsô/Asano's head cracking game/Kisuke's hat/Chain of Fate/Ginosuke/Chinamidama/Rangiku's memo with lips on it/Rukia's letter/ Hômonka/Shihôin Family Crest/Suzumushi/Tsuki Tsuki Dance/Hojiku-zai/Wasabi and Honey Taiyaki-style Ramen/Tokkuri Monaka from Kuriya/Kurotsuchi's detonation button/Dai-Kukaku-Wan/Marriane's older sister/Francois/The Hollow that could either be a cow or pig/Toshirin/Yama-chan/Assistant Captain Hirayama/Fujio/Onodera/Hitomi Victoria Odagiri/Gengoro Ohunabara/Hotarukazura/Lily/Kidô-shu/Numb Chandelier/Frozen Snow/Komamura's Tetsugasa/Shinji's Hollow mask/Tessai's Jûtai Glasses/Iba's sunglasses/The god who made Keigo stupid

★ Others: Around 100 votes for characters (can they be called that?) that couldn't fit due to lack of space.

51st (84 votes) Yuzu Kurosaki
52nd (72 votes) Karin Kurosaki
53rd (71 votes) Tite Kubo
54th (56 votes) Rin Tsubokura
55th (42 votes) Tetsuzaemon Iba
56th (40 votes) Hollowfied Ichigo
57th (37 votes) Genryûsai Shigekuni Yamamoto
58th (35 votes) Mizuiro Kojima
59th (21 votes) Don Kanonji
60th (19 votes) Harunobu Ogidô
61st (17 votes) Yasochika Iemura
62nd (16 votes) Chizuru Honshô
63rd (15 votes) Kizô Aramaki/Menos Grande
65th (14 votes) Minazuki
66th (13 votes) Marechiyo Ohmaeda/Zabimaru
68th (12 votes) Jinta Hanakari/Wabisuke/Editor Nakano
71st (11 votes) Tetsuo Momohara/Bulbous G
73rd (10 votes) Tessai Tsukabishi/Yammy
75th (9 votes) Kôkichiro Takezoe/Jidanbô/Benihime
78th (8 votes) Masaki Kurosaki/Tsubaki/Hyôrinmaru
81st (7 votes) Maremi Ohmaeda/Pictures Rukia drew/Kanisawa/Deputy Badge
85th (6 votes) Michiru Ogawa/Hiyosu/Hanataro's Energy Drink/Isshin's T-shirt/Yuichi Shibata
90th (5 votes) Misato Ochi/Ryo Kunieda/Bonnie/Kokujotengen Myoô/Hexapodus/The shark Kûkaku caught/Hitsugaya's grandmother/Shrieker
98th (4 votes) Miyako Shiba/Midoriko Tôno/Shunô/Kiko-oh/Kagekiyo Kira/bandana Soul Reaper in chapter 99/The training wheels on Yachiru's Zanpaku-tô/Renji's loincloth
106th (3 votes) Tatsuhusa Enjôji/Mahana Natsui/Tensa Zangetsu/Shizuka Kira/Jennifer/Ishida's fitting room/Zabimaru that became a woman in its fantasy/Oil rice cracker/Denrei Shinki/Tobiume/The bell in Kenpachi's hair/Edible Denrei Shinki
118th (2 votes) Kaiwan/Ayame/Yokochin/Bostov/Hell Butterfly/Fishbone D/Gamma Akutabi/Shiroganehiko/Heita Tôjôin/Tomohiro Conrad Odagiri/Hironari

Next Volume Preview

Ichigo's only hope for facing down Aizen and the new menace of the Arrancars is to master his inner Hollow. But can he win a battle where the enemy is **himself**?!

BLEACH 3-in-1 Edition Volume 9 on sale September 2014!

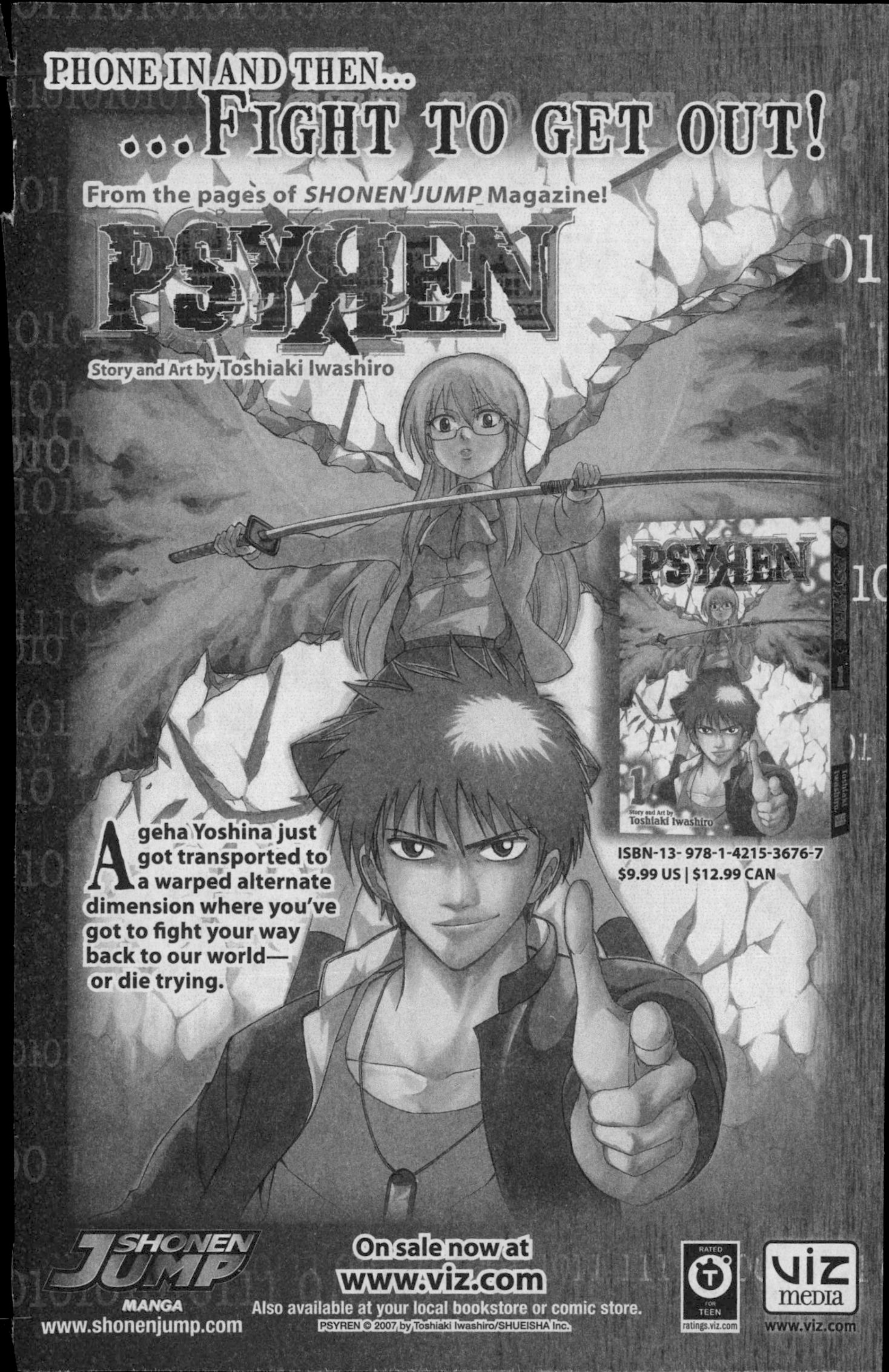
PHONE IN AND THEN...
...FIGHT TO GET OUT!
From the pages of SHONEN JUMP Magazine!
PSYREN
Story and Art by Toshiaki Iwashiro
PSYREN
1
Story and Art by Toshiaki Iwashiro
ISBN-13- 978-1-4215-3676-7
$9.99 US | $12.99 CAN
Ageha Yoshina just got transported to a warped alternate dimension where you've got to fight your way back to our world—or die trying.
SHONEN JUMP MANGA
www.shonenjump.com
On sale now at
www.viz.com
Also available at your local bookstore or comic store.
PSYREN © 2007 by Toshiaki Iwashiro/SHUEISHA Inc.
RATED T FOR TEEN
ratings.viz.com
viz media
www.viz.com

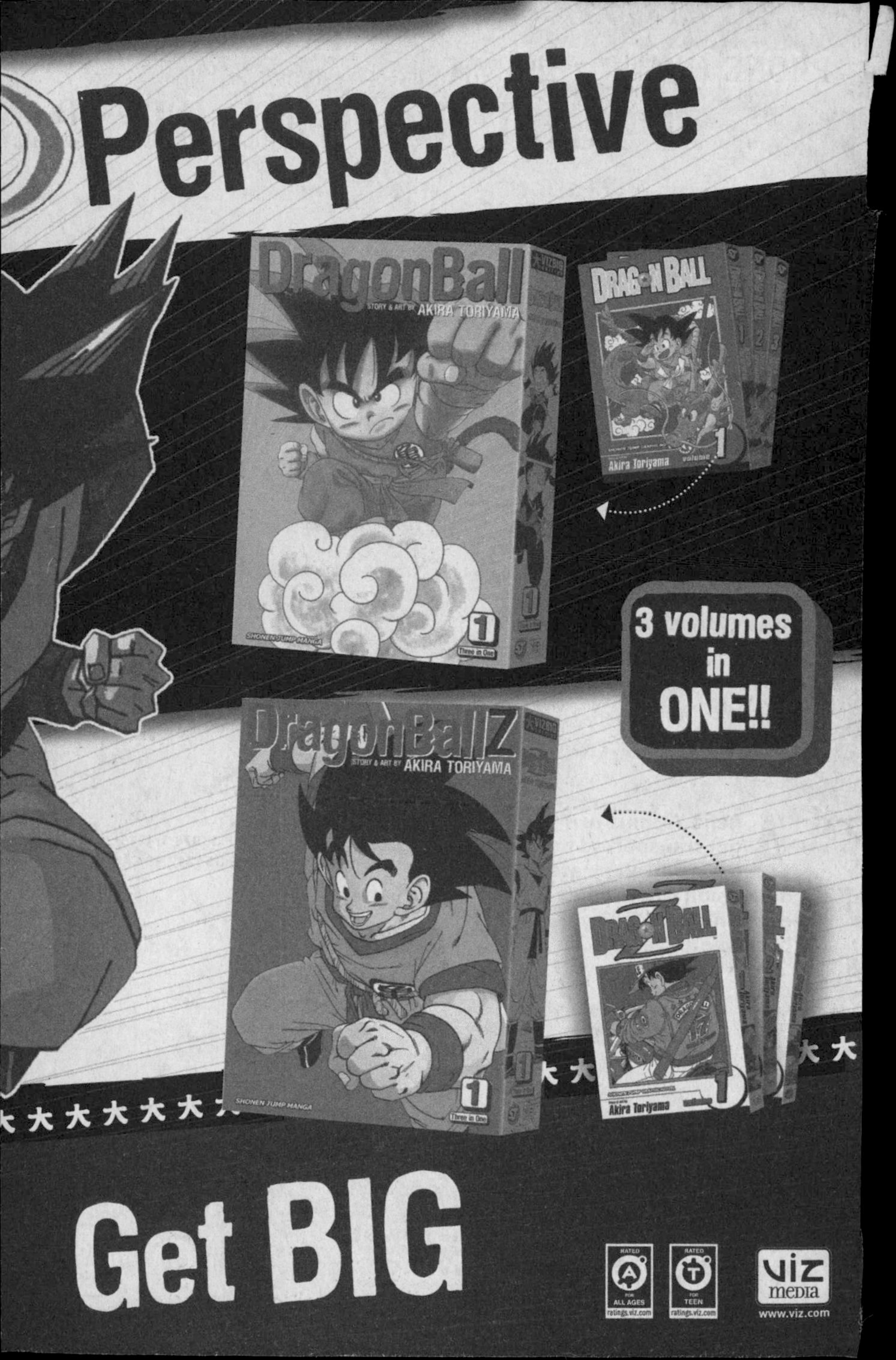
Perspective
DragonBall
STORY & ART BY AKIRA TORIYAMA
SHONEN JUMP MANGA
1
Three in One
DRAGON BALL
Akira Toriyama
volume 1
3 volumes
in
ONE!!
DragonBallZ
STORY & ART BY AKIRA TORIYAMA
SHONEN JUMP MANGA
1
Three in One
DRAGON BALL Z
Akira Toriyama
volume 1
Get BIG
RATED A FOR ALL AGES ratings.viz.com
RATED T FOR TEEN ratings.viz.com
VIZ media
www.viz.com

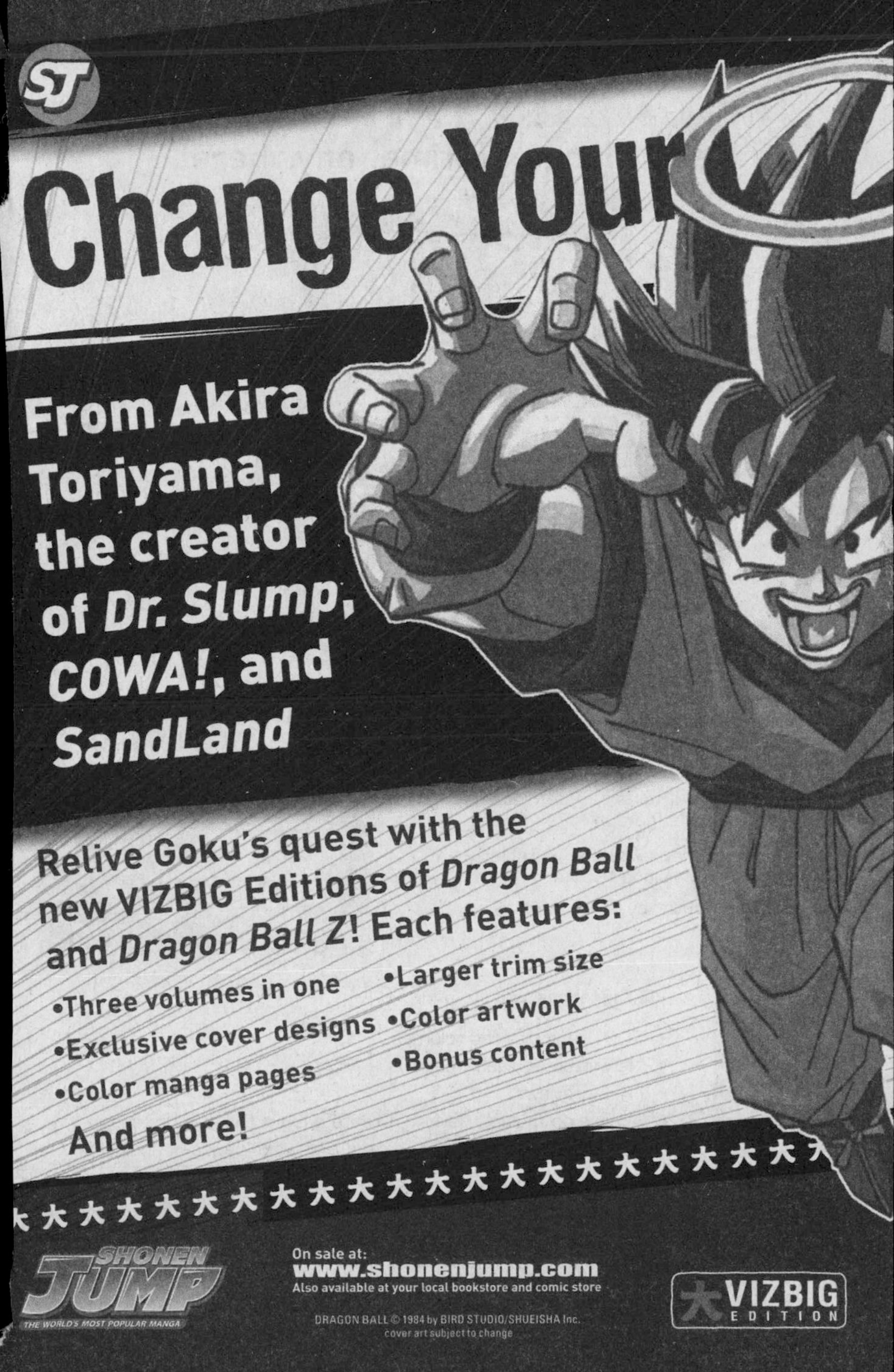
SJ
Change Your
From Akira Toriyama, the creator of Dr. Slump, COWA!, and SandLand
Relive Goku's quest with the new VIZBIG Editions of Dragon Ball and Dragon Ball Z! Each features:
•Three volumes in one
•Exclusive cover designs
•Color manga pages
•Larger trim size
•Color artwork
•Bonus content
And more!
SHONEN JUMP
THE WORLD'S MOST POPULAR MANGA
On sale at:
www.shonenjump.com
Also available at your local bookstore and comic store
DRAGON BALL © 1984 by BIRD STUDIO/SHUEISHA Inc.
cover art subject to change
大 VIZBIG EDITION

VIZMANGA

Read manga anytime, anywhere!

From our newest hit series to the classics you know and love, the best manga in the world is now available digitally. Buy a volume* of digital manga for your:

- iOS device (**iPad**®, **iPhone**®, **iPod**® touch) through the **VIZ Manga** app

- Android-powered device (**phone or tablet**) with a browser by visiting **VIZManga.com**

- **Mac or PC computer** by visiting **VIZManga.com**

VIZ Digital has loads to offer:

- 500+ ready-to-read volumes
- New volumes each week
- FREE previews
- Access on multiple devices! Create a log-in through the app so you buy a book once, and read it on your device of choice!*

To learn more, visit www.viz.com/apps

* Some series may not be available for multiple devices.
  Check the app on your device to find out what's available.

RATED
T
FOR OLDER
TEEN
ratings.viz.com

viz.com/apps

...g in
...ction!!

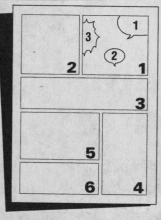

Whoops! Guess what? You're starting at the wrong end of the comic!

...It's true! In keeping with the original Japanese format, **Bleach** is meant to be read from right to left, starting in the upper-right corner.

Unlike English, which is read from left to right, Japanese is read from right to left, meaning that action, sound effects and word-balloon order are completely reversed... something which can make readers unfamiliar with Japanese feel pretty backwards themselves. For this reason, manga or Japanese comics published in the U.S. in English have sometimes been published "flopped"—that is, printed in exact reverse order, as though seen from the other side of a mirror.

By flopping pages, U.S. publishers can avoid confusing readers, but the compromise is not without its downside. For one thing, a character in a flopped manga series who once wore in the original Japanese version a T-shirt emblazoned with "M A Y" (as in "the merry month of") now wears one which reads "Y A M"! Additionally, many manga creators in Japan are themselves unhappy with the process, as some feel the mirror-imaging of their art skews their original intentions.

We are proud to bring you Tite Kubo's **Bleach** in the original unflopped format. For now, though, turn to the other side of the book and let the adventure begin...!

—Editor